Under the editorship of Leonard Carmichael

Elliott McGinnies
C. B. Ferster

Houghton Mifflin Company · Boston
New York · Atlanta · Geneva, Illinois · Dallas · Palo Alto

The Reinforcement of Social Behavior

For Bessie, Michelle, and Lisa

and for Elyce, William, Andrea, Samuel, and Warren

Printed in the U.S.A.

Library of Congress Card Number 74–129284

ISBN: 0–395–04867–2

Editor's Foreword

One can defend the thesis that an original and carefully prepared book of readings is not only a valuable pedagogical aid for students but also a genuine contribution to scientific psychology. Dr. Elliott M. McGinnies and Dr. C. B. Ferster, who conceived and developed this volume, are well-known modern scientific psychologists. Each has written many research papers on the role of reinforcement in determining human behavior. On the basis of their intimate and extensive knowledge of this relatively new field, these two scholarly scientists evaluated about four hundred articles before they selected the 73 papers that are reproducd here. Both scientific significance and clarity of presentation were considered in their final choices. The editors have also added greatly to the value of the book by writing insightful and instructive critical notes to introduce the selected readings.

The psychological profession thus surely owes a debt of gratitude to both editors of this book. It is a useful tool that will save hundreds of hours of library search time for all who wish to know the scientific facts about how reinforcement changes the behavior of human beings in that most complex of ecological settings, modern social life.

Leonard Carmichael

Acknowledgments

Our greatest debt, of course, is to the authors and publishers who granted us permission to reprint their works in this volume. In the several instances where we felt obliged to condense an article to increase its intelligibility to students, the authors were understanding and cooperative. A great deal of secretarial work is involved in preparing a manuscript of this nature, and we were ably assisted by Eunice Burton, who handled the permissions requests and did scores of other necessary tasks. Duangduen Lekhyananda helped us to track down articles and contributed in a variety of other ways to the project. Leonard Carmichael and Robert Rooney were sources of continuous support and encouragement. Finally, we thank Diane Faissler for her unusually competent and imaginative editing of the manuscript.

The American University

Elliott McGinnies

C. B. Ferster

Introduction

Reinforcement concepts have been with us at least since 1898, when Thorndike published his book, *Animal Intelligence.* Although Thorndike's early formulations, as well as his revisions during the early 1900s, came under vigorous and prolonged attack from other theorists, notably those favoring either *field* or *cognitive* interpretations of behavior, they have left an indelible imprint upon much of our current psychological thinking and usage. "Many of our educational, social, and legal practices," as Postman (1962) has pointed out, "are based on the assumption that rewards and punishments are effective and reliable tools for the modification of behavior" (p. 331). During the past decade, we have witnessed a burgeoning of research dealing with reinforcement variables in social behavior and the appearance of a number of volumes bringing together those materials that seem relevant to behavior control and modification (Staats, 1964; Krasner and Ullmann, 1965; Honig, 1966; Ulrich, Stachnik, and Mabry, 1966; Verhave, 1966; Bijou and Baer, 1967; Catania, 1968).

Somewhat paradoxically, the same period has seen an accelerated interest in cognition, or the higher mental processes, and several collections of selected journal articles and original pieces have appeared in elaboration of this systematic viewpoint (Harvey, 1963; Harper, Anderson, Christensen, and Hunka, 1964; Anderson and Ausubel, 1965; Tomkins and Izard, 1965; Feldman, 1966; Abelson, Aronson, McGuire, Newcomb, Rosenberg, and Tannenbaum, 1968). Alternative predictions and interpretations have been offered by cognitive and S–R theorists in such diverse areas of psychological interest as maze learning by rats and persuasibility in humans. The observed behavioral changes have been explained in terms of incentives and reinforcers, as well as a rebalancing of cognitive elements. It is our view that a great deal of research in social psychology has relied excessively on such concepts as motivation, volition, information processing, consistency, and the like. Although there is undoubtedly some heuristic value in speculating about intervening processes such as these in behavior, an emphasis on unobservables tends to divert one's attention from what seems to us to be a central problem of psychology; namely, identifying those potentially manipulable environmental events of which all behavior is ultimately a function.

The sheer complexity of the social environment makes heavy demands upon reinforcement theory, which has been derived largely from experiments performed on the lower animals under carefully controlled laboratory conditions. It is understandably tempting to abandon the relatively simplistic statements of causality that are likely to be generated from a reinforcement approach and to search instead for understanding at the more abstract levels of cognitive functioning. But the fact remains that the behavior of a man is functionally related to stimuli from his past and present environment, and no comprehensive account of a performance will be attained until this relationship is understood. The key to such an understanding appears to some psychologists to lie in those stimulus events that (a) prompt the performance and (b) are a consequence of the performance. This, in its most elementary form, is the fundamental assumption made by reinforcement theorists.

In this volume we have put together a selection of writings that have to do with derivations from reinforcement theory in social settings. To arrive at this compendium, we screened over four hundred original research papers and theoretical essays. Our criteria for including an article in this volume were, first, that it possess scientific merit and, second, that it be comprehensible to its intended readers—intelligent undergraduates. To achieve brevity, we have abridged some of the papers as seemed appropriate. In every instance, we looked for a linkage of reinforcement concepts with some form of social interaction. This particular requirement led us to omit from consideration a great number of experiments whose results could be reinterpreted in terms of controlling and reinforcing stimuli. To attempt such a restatement of findings would have led us into virtually the entire literature of social psychology, and this was not our intent. What we hope to have accomplished is an underscoring of the research possibilities in social psychology based on functional behaviorism. We have rejected mentalism as a base of operation and have presented for the student's critical appraisal a number of theoretical and empirical accounts that lend themselves to a systematic analysis—via the concepts of functional behaviorism.

References

Abelson, R., Aronson, E., McGuire, W., Newcomb, T., Rosenberg, M., and Tannenbaum, P. (Eds.) *Theories of cognitive consistency: A sourcebook.* New York: Rand McNally, 1968.

Anderson, R. C., and Ausubel, D. P. (Eds.) *Readings in the psychology of cognition.* New York: Holt, Rinehart and Winston, 1965.

Bijou, S. W., and Baer, D. M. (Eds.) *Child development: Readings in experimental analysis.* New York: Appleton-Century-Crofts, 1967.

Catania, A. C. (Ed.) *Contemporary research in operant behavior.* Glenview, Ill.: Scott, Foresman, 1968.

Feldman, S. (Ed.) *Cognitive consistency.* New York: Academic Press, 1966.

Harper, J. C., Anderson, C. C., Christensen, C. M., and Hunka, S. M. (Eds.) *The cognitive processes: Readings.* Englewood Cliffs, N.J.: Prentice-Hall, 1964.

Harvey, O. J. (Ed.) *Motivation and social interaction: Cognitive determinants.* New York: Ronald Press, 1963.

Honig, W. K. (Ed.) *Operant behavior: Areas of research and application.* New York: Appleton-Century-Crofts, 1966.

Hull, C. L. *Principles of behavior.* New York: Appleton-Century-Crofts, 1943.

Krasner, L., and Ullmann, L. P. (Eds.) *Research in behavior modification.* New York: Holt, Rinehart and Winston, 1965.

Postman, L. Rewards and punishments in human learning. Ch. 6 in L. Postman (Ed.), *Psychology in the making.* New York: Alfred A. Knopf, 1962.

Staats, A. W. (Ed.) *Human learning: Studies extending conditioning principles to complex behavior.* New York: Holt, Rinehart and Winston, 1964.

Tomkins, S. S., and Izard, C. E. (Eds.) *Affect, cognition and personality: Empirical studies.* New York: Springer, 1965.

Ulrich, R., Stachnik, T., and Mabry, J. (Eds.) *Control of human behavior.* Glenview, Ill.: Scott, Foresman, 1966.

Verhave, T. (Ed.) *The experimental analysis of behavior.* New York: Appleton-Century-Crofts, 1966.

Contents

Theory and General Issues

1

Since 1950, reinforcement theorists, beginning with Miller and Dollard and Mowrer, have increasingly turned their attention to complex social phenomena. Principles of reinforcement currently are being applied to social and clinical problems under the rubrics of behavior modification, operant conditioning, functional analysis of behavior, and the behavioral approach. The increased use of reinforcement principles in psychotherapy, education, animal learning, and physiological psychology has been paralleled in social psychology, where experimenters are beginning to penetrate social processes using the methods and standards of natural science.

Our first task in this book of readings is to describe reinforcement theory and show in some very general ways how this language and concept of human nature may be used in trying to understand the social behavior of man. The articles which follow will analyze some of the ways in which the behaviors of group members are reinforced. The introductory selections are necessarily general because they are intended to provide a framework for observing and recording social behavior rather than to answer questions about the details and facts of social interaction. It is hoped that these articles guide the reader when he observes social phenomena and help him to highlight the significant dimensions from a kaleidoscopic array of facts. All of the articles emphasize an objective, natural-science language and a functional analysis of behavior processes. We believe that such a language and framework is, in the long run, the best route toward understanding the complexities of social life. The individual experiments which are reprinted will give the reader first-hand experience in applying these terms and concepts to specific situations and problems. The theoretical framework is a tool rather than a goal to be achieved, and if it perhaps raises more issues than it resolves, that does not make it any less valid.

Our emphasis will be on the data of social psychology rather than on the development of theory. Theory is useful because it helps one to see, organize, and find facts. However, our starting point must be the fundamental events of social behavior. Traditionally, experimental psychologists have ignored many issues dealt with by psychologists operating from different biases and frameworks, usually because both the language and approach have been mentalistic. Historically, experimental psychologists have been loath to deal with attitudes, feelings, beliefs, values, and social motives. Experiments in social psychology frequently have been carried out with questionnaires or opinion surveys rather than by the direct measurement of behavior that is the usual custom of the classic experimentalist.

While we believe that a factual behavioral language is in the long run the best way to describe social phenomena, it is not always possible to make such an analysis.

Sometimes we do not understand the phenomenon well enough; sometimes we fail to observe important elements of the phenomenon; and sometimes our theory needs additional strength it does not have. While we prefer a language dealing with observable events—behavior and environment—we cannot ignore certain facts because they are in the wrong language or because they do not fit our theory or descriptive framework. We shall distinguish between a way of talking about something and the thing we are talking about. We shall assume that the host of writers in social psychology, whatever language they use to describe and explain what they see, are attempting to find order and reason in significant phenomena that they have observed. The purpose of a functional analysis of behavior is to find the actual behavioral events that so far have been described indirectly or summarized by mentalistic, cognitive, or other nonbehavioral approaches. Hence, our purpose will be to guide the reader toward using a functional analysis that will help him to understand the experiments and problems which follow.

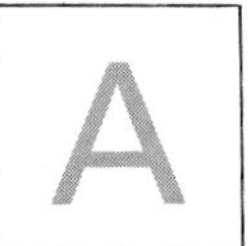

The Component Processes of Social Behavior

In this first article, *Skinner* provides a theory for social psychology. He formulates the basic behavior processes which he believes are the constituents of social situations. Skinner's article is best viewed as a guide to undertaking a behavioral analysis of social environments and social interactions. But the chapter does not concern itself directly with social psychology; rather it is about social psychology. Skinner himself states, "There are, of course, many facts—concerning governments, wars, migrations, economic conditions, cultural practices, and so on—which would never present themselves for study if people did not gather together and behave in groups. . . ." Certainly these facts could never come from the component behavior processes that lay behind them. The behavioral framework that Skinner presents is included here to help the student identify the basic constituent processes in complex social phenomena. He first presents an event from common experience and then analyzes the component behaviors and their functional relation to the environment. This systematic framework enables us to identify the relevant, important variables so that the large number of events and observations can be organized into a meaningful pattern. In his chapter, Skinner alludes to many topics in social psychology, such as leadership, cooperation, imitation, communication, attitude, conflict, and the socialization process. But he does not observe the content of actual events, nor does he describe the actual conduct that occurs in these various kinds of social activities. Rather, he gives us a system for viewing each of these kinds of conduct which will help us to sort the relevant from the irrelevant facts and to describe complex occurrences in simple, behavioral terms.

1 Social Behavior

B. F. SKINNER

Social behavior may be defined as the behavior of two or more people with respect to one another or in concert with respect to a common environment. It is often argued that this is different from individual behavior and that there are "social situations" and "social forces" which cannot be described in the language of natural science. A special discipline called "social science" is said to be required because of this apparent break in the continuity of nature. There are, of course, many facts—concerning governments, wars, migrations, economic conditions, cultural practices, and so on—which would never present themselves for study if people did not gather together and behave in groups, but whether the basic data are fundamentally different is still a question. We are interested here in the methods of the natural sciences as we see them at work in physics, chemistry, and biology, and as we have so far applied them in the field of behavior. How far will they carry us in the study of the behavior of groups?

Many generalizations at the level of the group need not refer to behavior at all. There is an old law in economics, called Gresham's Law, which states that bad money drives good money out of circulation. If we can agree as to what money is, whether it is good or bad, and when it is in circulation, we can express this general principle without making specific reference to the use of money by individuals. Similar generalizations are found in sociology, cultural anthropology, linguistics, and history. But a "social law" must be generated by the behavior of individuals. It is always an individual who behaves, and he behaves with the same body and according to the same processes as in a nonsocial situation. If an individual possessing two pieces of money, one good and one bad, tends to spend the bad and save the good—a tendency which may be explained in terms of reinforcing contingencies—and if this is true of a large number of people, the phenomenon described by Gresham's Law arises. The individual behavior explains the group phenomenon. Many economists feel the need for some such explanation of all economic law, although there are others who would accept the higher level of description as valid in its own right.

We are concerned here simply with the extent to which an analysis of the behavior of the individual which has received substantial validation under the favorable conditions of a natural science may contribute to the understanding of social phenomena. To apply our analysis to the phenomena of the group is an excellent way to test its adequacy, and if we are able to account for the behavior of people in groups without using any new term or presupposing any new process or principle, we shall have revealed a promising simplicity in the data. This does not mean that the social sciences will then inevitably state their generalizations in terms of individual behavior, since another level of description may also be valid and may well be more convenient.

The Social Environment

Social behavior arises because one organism is important to another as part of its environment. A first step, therefore, is an analysis of the social environment and of any special features it may possess.

Social Reinforcement. Many reinforcements require the presence of other people. In some of these, as in certain forms of sexual and pugilistic behavior, the other person participates merely as an object. We cannot describe the reinforcement without referring to another organism. But social reinforcement is usually a matter of personal mediation. When a mother feeds her child, the food, as a primary reinforcer, is not social, but the mother's behavior in presenting it is. The difference is slight—as one may see by comparing breast-feeding with bottle-feeding. Verbal behavior always involves social reinforcement and derives its characteristic properties from this fact. The response, "A glass of water, please," has no effect upon the mechanical environment, but in an appropriate verbal environment it may lead to primary reinforcement. In the field of social behavior special emphasis is laid upon reinforcement with attention, approval, affection, and submission. These important generalized reinforcers are social because the process of generalization usually requires the mediation of another organism. Negative reinforcement—particularly as a form of punishment—is most often administered by others in the form of unconditioned aversive stimulation or of disapproval, contempt, ridicule, insult, and so on.

Behavior reinforced through the mediation of other people will differ in many ways from behavior rein-

Reprinted with permission of The Macmillan Company from *Science and Human Behavior* (Chapter XIX), by B. F. Skinner.

forced by the mechanical environment. Social reinforcement varies from moment to moment, depending upon the condition of the reinforcing agent. Different responses may therefore achieve the same effect, and one response may achieve different effects, depending upon the occasion. As a result, social behavior is more extensive than comparable behavior in a non-social environment. It is also more flexible, in the sense that the organism may shift more readily from one response to another when its behavior is not effective.

Since the reinforcing organism often may not respond appropriately, reinforcement is likely to be intermittent. The result will depend upon the schedule. An occasional success may fit the pattern of *variable-interval* reinforcement, and the behavior will show a stable intermediate strength. We might express this by saying that we respond to people with less confidence than we respond to the inanimate environment but are not so quickly convinced that the reinforcing mechanism is "out of order." The persistent behavior which we call teasing is generated by a *variable-ratio* schedule, which arises from the fact that the reinforcer responds only when a request has been repeated until it becomes aversive—when it acquires nuisance value.

The contingency established by a social reinforcing system may slowly change. In teasing, for example, the mean ratio of unreinforced to reinforced responses may rise. The child who has gained attention with three requests on the average may later find it necessary to make five, then seven, and so on. The change corresponds to an increasing tolerance for aversive stimulation in the reinforcing person. Contingencies of positive reinforcement may also drift in the same direction. When a reinforcing person becomes harder and harder to please, the reinforcement is made contingent upon more extensive or highly differentiated behavior. By beginning with reasonable specifications and gradually increasing the requirements, very demanding contingencies may be made effective which would be quite powerless without this history. The result is often a sort of human bondage. The process is easily demonstrated in animal experimentation where extremely energetic, persistent, or complicated responses which would otherwise be quite impossible may be established through a gradual change in contingencies. A special case arises in the use of piecework pay. As production increases, and with it the wages received, the piecework scale may be changed so that more work is required per unit of reinforcement. The eventual result may be a much higher rate of production at only a slight increase in pay—a condition of reinforcement which could not have become effective except through some such gradual approach.

We have already noted another peculiarity of social reinforcement: the reinforcing system is seldom independent of the behavior reinforced. This is exemplified by the indulgent but ambitious parent who withholds reinforcement when his child is behaving energetically, either to demonstrate the child's ability or to make the most efficient use of available reinforcers, but who reinforces an early response when the child begins to show extinction. This is a sort of combined ratio-and-interval reinforcement. Educational reinforcements are in general of this sort. They are basically governed by ratio schedules, but they are not unaffected by the level of the behavior reinforced. As in piecework pay, more and more may be demanded for each reinforcement as performance improves, but remedial steps may be needed.

Schedules of reinforcement which adjust to the rate of the behavior reinforced do not often occur in inorganic nature. The reinforcing agent which modifies the contingency in terms of the behavior must be sensitive and complex. But a reinforcing system which is affected in this way may contain inherent defects which lead to unstable behavior. This may explain why the reinforcing contingencies of society cause undesirable behavior more often than those apparently comparable contingencies in inanimate nature.

The Social Stimulus. Another person is often an important source of stimulation. Since some properties of such stimuli appear to defy physical description, it has been tempting to assume that a special process of intuition or empathy is involved when we react to them. What, for example, are the physical dimensions of a smile? In everyday life we identify smiles with considerable accuracy and speed, but the scientist would find it a difficult task. He would have to select some identifying response in the individual under investigation—perhaps the verbal response, "That is a smile"—and then investigate all the facial expressions which evoked it. These expressions would be physical patterns and presumably susceptible to geometric analysis, but the number of different patterns to be tested would be very great. Moreover, there would be borderline instances where the stimulus control was defective or varied from moment to moment.

That the final identification of the stimulus pattern called a smile would be much more complicated and time-consuming than the identification of a smile in daily life does not mean that scientific observation neglects some important approach available to the layman. The difference is that the scientist must identify a stimulus with respect to the behavior of someone else. He cannot trust his own personal reaction. In studying an objective pattern as simple and as common to everyone as "triangle," the scientist may safely use his own identification of the pattern. But such a pattern as "smile" is another matter. A social stimulus, like any other stimulus, becomes important in controlling behavior because of the contingencies into which it enters. The facial expressions which we group together and call "smiles" are important because they are the occasions upon which certain kinds of social behavior receive certain kinds of reinforcement. Any unity in the stimulus class follows from these contingencies. But these are determined by the culture and by a particular history. Even in the behavior of a single individual there may be several groups of patterns all of which come to be called smiles if they all stand in the same relation to reinforcing contingencies. The scientist may appeal to his own culture or history only when it resembles that of the subject he is studying. Even then he may be wrong, just as the layman's quick practical reaction may be wrong, especially when he attempts to identify a smile in a different culture.

This issue is far reaching because it applies to many descriptive terms, such as "friendly" and "aggressive," without which many students of social behavior would feel lost. The nonscientist working within his own culture may satisfactorily describe the behavior of others with expressions of this sort. Certain patterns of behavior have become important to him because of the reinforcements based upon them: he judges behavior to be friendly or unfriendly by its social consequences. But his frequent success does not mean that there are objective aspects of behavior which are as independent of the behavior of the observer as are such geometrical forms as squares, circles, and triangles. He is observing an objective event—the behavior of an organism; there is no question here of physical status, but only of the significance of classificatory terms. The geometrical properties of "friendliness" or "aggressiveness" depend upon the culture, change with the culture, and vary with the individual's experience within a single culture.

Some social stimuli are also frequently set apart because a very slight physical event appears to have an extremely powerful effect. But this is true of many nonsocial stimuli as well; to one who has been injured in a fire a faint smell of smoke may be a stimulus of tremendous power. Social stimuli are important because the social reinforcers with which they are correlated are important. An example of the surprising power of an apparently trivial event is the common experience of "catching someone's eye." Under certain circumstances the change in behavior which follows may be considerable, and this has led to the belief that some nonphysical "understanding" passes from one person to another. But the reinforcing contingencies offer an alternative explanation. Our behavior may be very different in the presence or absence of a particular person. When we simply see such a person in a crowd, our available repertoire immediately changes. If, in addition, we catch his eye, we fall under the control of an even more restrictive stimulus—he is not only present, he is watching us. The same effect might arise without catching his eye if we saw him looking at us in a mirror. When we catch his eye, we also know that he knows that we are looking at him. A much narrower repertoire of behavior is under the control of this specific stimulus: if we are to behave in a way which he censures, it will now be not only in opposition to his wishes but brazen. It may also be important that "we know that he knows that we know that he is looking at us" and so on. In catching someone's eye, in short, a social stimulus suddenly arises which is important because of the reinforcements which depend upon it. The importance will vary with the occasion. We may catch someone's eye in a flirtation, under amusing circumstances, at a moment of common guilt, and so on—with an appropriate degree of control in each case. The importance of the event is seen in the use we make of the behavior of "looking someone in the eye" as a test of other variables responsible for such characteristics of behavior as honesty, brazenness, embarrassment, or guilt.

Social stimuli are important to those to whom social reinforcement is important. The salesman, the courtier, the entertainer, the seducer, the child striving for the favor of his parents, the "climber" advancing from one social level to another, the politically ambitious—all are likely to be affected by subtle properties of human behavior, associated with favor or disapproval, which are overlooked by many people. It is significant that the novelist, as a specialist in the description of human behavior, often shows an early history in which social reinforcement has been especially important.

The social stimulus which is least likely to vary from culture to culture is that which controls imitative behavior. The ultimate consequences of imitative behavior may be peculiar to the culture, but the correspondence between the behavior of the imitator and that of the imitatee is relatively independent of it. Imitative behavior is not entirely free of style or convention, but the special features of the imitative repertoire characteristic of a group are slight. When a sizable repertoire has once been developed, imitation may be so skillful, so easy, so "instinctive," that we are likely to attribute it to some such special mode of interpersonal contact as empathy. It is easy to point to a history of reinforcement, however, which generates behavior of this sort.

The Social Episode

We may analyze a social episode by considering one organism at a time. Among the variables to be considered are those generated by a second organism. We then consider the behavior of the second organism, assuming the first as a source of variables. By putting the analyses together we reconstruct the episode. The account is complete if it embraces all the variables needed to account for the behavior of the individuals. Consider, for example, the interaction between predator and prey called "stalking." We may limit ourselves to that behavior of the predator which reduces the distance between itself and its prey and that behavior of the prey which increases the distance. A reduction in the distance is positively reinforcing to the predator and negatively reinforcing to the prey; an increase is negatively reinforcing to the predator and positively reinforcing to the prey. If the predator is stimulated by the prey, but not vice versa, then the predator simply reduces the distance between itself and the prey as rapidly as possible. If the prey is stimulated by the predator, however, it will respond by increasing the distance. This need not be open flight, but simply any movement sufficient to keep the distance above a critical value. In the behavior called stalking the predator reduces the distance as rapidly as possible without stimulating the prey to increase it. When the distance has become short enough, the predator may break into open pursuit, and the prey into open flight. A different sort of interaction follows.

A similar formulation may be applied where "distance" is not so simple as in movement in space. In conversation, for example, one speaker may approach a topic from which another moves away uneasily. The first may be said to stalk the second if he approaches the topic in such a way as to avoid stimulating the second to escape. We eliminate the figure of speech in "approaching a topic" by analyzing the reinforcing and aversive properties of verbal stimuli.

Another example of a social episode is leading and following. This generally arises when two or more individuals are reinforced by a single external system which requires their combined action—for example, when two men pull on a rope which cannot be moved by either one alone. The behavior of one is similar to that of the other, and the interaction may be slight. If the timing is important, however, one man will pace the other. The first sets a rhythmic pattern relatively independent of the second; the second times his behavior by that of the first. The first may facilitate this by amplifying the stimuli which affect the second—as by saying, "All together now, one, two, three, *pull!*" Collateral behavior with a marked temporal pattern—for example, a sea chanty—may reduce the importance of the leader but will not eliminate it.

The nature of leading and following is clear when the two kinds of behavior differ considerably and the contingency of reinforcement is complex. A division of labor is usually then required. The leader is primarily under the control of external variables, while the follower is under the control of the leader. A simple example is ballroom dancing. The reinforcing consequences—both positive and negative—depend upon a double contingency: (1) the dancers must execute certain sequences of steps in certain directions with respect to the available space and (2) the behavior of one must be timed to correspond with that of the other. This double contingency is usually divided between the dancers. The leader sets the pattern and responds to the available space; the follower is controlled by the movements of the leader and responds appropriately to satisfy the second contingency.

It is easy to set up cooperative situations with two or more experimental organisms and to observe the emergence of leading and following. In a demonstration experiment two pigeons are placed in adjacent cages separated by a glass plate. Side by side near the glass are two vertical columns of three buttons each, one column being available to each pigeon. The apparatus is set to reinforce both pigeons with food but only when they peck corresponding buttons simultaneously. Only one pair of buttons is effective at any one time. The situation calls for a rather complicated cooperation. The pigeons must explore the three pairs to discover which is effective, and they must strike both buttons in each pair at the same time. These contingencies must be divided. One bird —the leader—explores the buttons, striking them in some characteristic order or more or less at random. The other bird—the follower—strikes the button opposite whichever button is being struck by the leader. The behavior of the follower is controlled almost exclusively by the behavior of the leader, whose behavior in turn is controlled by the apparatus which randomizes the reinforcements among the three pairs of buttons. Two followers or two leaders placed together can solve the problem only accidentally. The function of leader may shift from one bird to another over a period of time, and a temporary condition may arise in which both are followers. The behavior then resembles that of two people who, meeting under circumstances where the convention of passing on the right is not strongly observed, oscillate from side to side before passing.

Between such an experiment and the relation of leader to follower in politics, for example, there is more than a simple analogy. Most cultures produce some people whose behavior is mainly controlled by the exigencies of a given situation. The same cultures also produce people whose behavior is controlled mainly by the behavior of others. Some such division of the contingencies in any cooperative venture seems to be required. The leader is not wholly independent of the follower, however, for his behavior requires the support of corresponding behavior on the part of others, and to the extent that cooperation is necessary, the leader is, in fact, led by his followers.

Verbal Episodes. Verbal behavior supplies many examples in which one person is said to have an effect upon another beyond the scope of the physical sciences. Words are said to "symbolize" or "express" ideas or meanings, which are then "communicated" to the listener. An alternative formulation would require too much space here, but a single example may suggest how this sort of social behavior may be brought within range of a natural science. Consider a simple episode in which *A* asks *B* for a cigarette and gets one. To account for the occurrence and maintenance of this behavior we have to show that *A* provides adequate stimuli and reinforcement for *B* and vice versa. *A*'s response, "Give me a cigarette," would be quite ineffective in a purely mechanical environment. It has been conditioned by a verbal community which occasionally reinforces it in a particular way. *A* has long since formed a discrimination by virtue of which the response is not emitted in the absence of a member of that community. He has also probably formed more subtle discriminations in which he is more likely to respond in the presence of an "easy touch." *B* has either reinforced this response in the past or resembles someone who has. The first interchange between the two is in the direction of *B* to *A: B* is a discriminative stimulus in the presence of which *A* emits the verbal response. The second interchange is in the direction *A* to *B:* the response generates auditory stimuli acting upon *B*. If *B* is already disposed to give a cigarette to *A*—for example, if *B* is "anxious to please *A*" or "in love with *A*," the auditory pattern is a discriminative stimulus for the response of giving a cigarette. *B* does not offer cigarettes indiscriminately; he waits for a response from *A* as an occasion upon which a cigarette will be accepted. *A*'s acceptance depends upon a condition of deprivation in which the receipt of a cigarette is reinforcing. This is also the condition in which *A* emits the response, "Give me a cigarette," and the contingency which comes to control *B*'s behavior is thus established. The third interchange is *A*'s receipt of the cigarette from *B*. This is the reinforcement of *A*'s original response and completes our account of it. If *B* is reinforced simply by evidence of the effect of the cigarette upon *A*, we may consider *B*'s account closed also. But such behavior is more likely to remain a stable part of the culture if these evidences are made conspicuous. If *A* not only accepts the cigarette but also says, "Thank you," a fourth interchange takes place: the auditory stimulus is a conditioned reinforcer to *B*, and *A* produces it just because it is. *B* may in turn increase the likelihood of future "Thank you's" on the part of *A* by saying, "Not at all."

When *B*'s behavior in responding to *A*'s verbal response is already strong, we call *A*'s response a "request." If *B*'s behavior requires other conditions, we have to reclassify *A*'s response. If "Give me a cigarette" is not only the occasion for a particular response but also a conditioned aversive stimulus from which *B* can escape only by complying, then *A*'s response is a "demand." In this case, *B*'s behavior is reinforced by a reduction in the threat generated by *A*'s demand, and *A*'s "Thank you" is mainly effective as a conspicuous indication that the threat has been reduced.

Even such a brief episode is surprisingly complex, but the four or five interchanges between *A* and *B* can all be specified in physical terms and can scarcely be ignored if we are to take such an analysis seriously. That the complete episode occupies only a few seconds does not excuse us from the responsibility of identifying and observing all its features.

Unstable Interaction. Although many of these interlocking social systems are stable, others show a progressive change. A trivial example is the behavior of a group of people who enter an unfamiliar room containing a sign which reads, "Silence, please." Such a verbal stimulus is generally effective only in combination with the behavior of other members of the group. If many people are talking noisily, the sign may have little or no effect. But let us assume that our group enters silently. After a moment two members least under the control of the sign begin to whisper. This slightly alters the situation for other members so that they also begin to whisper. This alters the situation for the two who are least under the control of the sign, and they then begin to speak in a low voice. This further changes the situation for the others, who also begin to speak in low voices. Eventually the conversation may be quite noisy. This is a simple "autocatalytic" process arising from a repeated interchange between the members of the group.

Another example is a practice common on sailing ships in the eighteenth century. Sailors would amuse themselves by tying several boys or younger men in a ring to a mast by their left hands, their right hands remaining free. Each boy was given a stick or whip and told to strike the boy in front of him whenever he felt himself being struck by the boy behind. The game was begun by striking one boy lightly. This boy then struck the boy ahead of him, who in turn struck the boy next ahead, and so on. Even though it was clearly in the interest of the group that all blows be gentle, the inevitable result was a furious lashing. The unstable elements in this interlocking system are easy to identify. We cannot assume that each boy gave precisely the kind of blow he received because this is not an easy comparison to make. It is probable that he underestimated the strength of the blows he gave. The slightest tendency to give a little harder than he received would produce the ultimate effect. Moreover, repeated blows probably generate an emotional disposition in which one naturally strikes harder. A comparable instability is seen when two individuals engage in a casual conversation which leads to a vituperative quarrel. The aggressive effect of a remark is likely to be underestimated by the man who makes it, and repeated effects generate further aggression. The principle is particularly dangerous when the conversation consists of an exchange of notes between governments.

Supporting Variables in the Social Episode

Although the interchange between two or more individuals whose behavior is interlocked in a social system must be explained in its entirety, certain variables may remain obscure. For example, we often observe merely that one person is predisposed to act with respect to another in certain ways. The mother caring for her child is a familiar case in point. The social emotions are by definition observed simply as predispositions to act in ways which may be positively or negatively reinforcing to others. Such terms as "favor" and "friendship" refer to tendencies to administer positive reinforcement, and love might be analyzed as the mutual tendency of two individuals to reinforce each other, where the reinforcement may or may not be sexual.

Sometimes a reciprocal interchange explains the behavior in terms of reinforcement. Each individual has something to offer by way of reinforcing the other, and once established, the interchange sustains itself. We may detect mutual reinforcement in the case of mother and child. Instead of tendencies to behave in certain ways, they may illustrate tendencies to be reinforced by certain social stimuli. Aside from this, the group may manipulate special variables to generate tendencies to behave in ways which result in the reinforcement of others. The group may reinforce the individual for telling the truth, helping others, returning favors, and reinforcing others in turn for doing the same. The Golden Rule is a generalized statement of the behavior thus supported by the group. Many important interlocking systems of social behavior could not be maintained without such conventional practices. This is an important point in explaining the success of the cultural practices characteristic of a group.

To the extent that prior reinforcement by the group determines the suitability of the behavior of the individual for an interlocking system, the system itself is not wholly self-sustaining. The instability is demonstrated when an individual who is not adequately controlled by the culture gains a temporary personal advantage by exploiting the system. He lies, refuses to return a favor, or breaks a promise, but this exploitation of the system eventually leads to its deterioration. The boy in the fable cries, "Wolf!" because certain patterns of social behavior have been established by the community and he finds the resulting behavior of his neighbors amusing. The aggressive door-to-door salesman imposes upon the good manners of the housewife to hold her attention in the same way. In each case the system eventually breaks down: the neighbors no longer respond to the cry of "Wolf!" and the housewife slams the door.

The behavior of two individuals may be related in a social episode, not primarily through an interchange between them, but through common external variables. The classic example is competition. Two individuals come into competition when the behavior of one can be reinforced only at the cost of the reinforcement of the other. Social behavior as here defined is not necessarily involved. Catching a rabbit before it runs away is not very different from catching it before someone else does. In the latter case, a social interchange may occur as a by-product if one individual attacks the other. Cooperation, in which the reinforcement of two or more individuals depends upon the behavior of both or all of them, is obviously not the opposite of competition, for it appears to require an interlocking system.

The Group as a Behaving Unit

It is common to speak of families, clans, nations, races, and other groups as if they were individuals. Such concepts as "the group mind," "the instinct of the herd," and "national character" have been invented to support this practice. It is always an individual who behaves, however. The problem presented by the larger group is to explain why many individuals behave *together*. Why does a boy join a gang? Why does a man join a club or fall in with a lynching mob? We may answer questions of this sort by examining the variables generated by the group which encourage the behavior of joining and conforming. We cannot do this simply by saying that two individuals will behave together cooperatively if it is "in their common interest to do so." We must point to specific variables affecting the behavior of each of them. From a practical point of view, as in setting up cooperative behavior in the pigeon demonstration just described, an analysis of the relevant variables is also essential. The particular contingencies controlling the behavior of the cooperators must be carefully maintained.

Some progress toward explaining participation in a group is made by the analysis of imitation. In general, behaving as others behave is likely to be reinforcing. Stopping to look in a store window which has already attracted a crowd is more likely to be reinforced than stopping to look in store windows which have not attracted crowds. Using words which have already been used by others, rather than strange terms, is more likely to be reinforced positively or to be free of aversive consequences. Situations of this sort multiplied a thousandfold generate and sustain an enormous tendency to behave as others are behaving.

To this principle we must add another of perhaps greater importance. If it is always the individual who behaves, it is nevertheless the group which has the more powerful effect. By joining a group the individual increases his power to achieve reinforcement. The man who pulls on a rope is reinforced by the movement of the rope regardless of the fact that others may need to be pulling at the same time. The man attired in full uniform, parading smartly down the street, is reinforced by the acclaim of the crowd even though it would not be forthcoming if he were marching alone. The coward in the lynching mob is reinforced when his victim writhes in terror as he shouts at him—regardless of the fact that a hundred others are, and must be, shouting at him also. The reinforcing consequences generated by the group easily exceed the sums of the consequences which could be achieved by the members acting separately. The total reinforcing effect is enormously increased.

The interchanges within a group and the heightened effect of the group upon the environment may be studied within the framework of a natural science. They need to be explored further before we accept the proposition that there are social units, forces, and laws which require scientific methods of a fundamentally different sort.

In *Ferster's* article, the component behavior processes that go into social interaction are taken up in a little more detail so that the reader can see how these principles are applied in specific kinds of human interactions. In contrast to Skinner's article, which focused on the broad dimensions of social behavior, this article emphasizes specific processes and the way they operate in the natural environment—both individually and socially. The approach is similar to Skinner's, because it is basically an elaboration of his theoretical framework. It also continues the major thrust of Skinner's article by focusing on the dimensions of complex behavior to which one would pay attention in analyzing complex natural situations or devising experiments about them.

2 *Reinforcement and Punishment in the Control of Human Behavior by Social Agencies*

C. B. FERSTER

The Nature of the Social Agency

Most of the behavior of organisms exists because of its effect on the environment (operant reinforcement). The paradigm is: An event following a given instance of behavior subsequently increases the frequency of occurrence of that behavior. The verbal response "good morning" is maintained because it produces a reply from most audiences. In the absence of a reply, the response would disappear. Not all events have this property, and those that do are called reinforcements. Most human behavior is social because it has its effect on other organisms, which in turn arrange the reinforcements; this is in contrast to the physical environment, which reinforces directly. The same reinforcement paradigm may be extended to larger groups of people, such as social institutions and agencies; less well-defined groups involved in

From *Psychiatric Research Reports,* December 1958, pp. 101–118. Reprinted by permission of the American Psychiatric Association. [Portions of the original have been omitted or changed slightly, with the permission of the publisher.]

social practices, codes of conduct, etc.; small groups, such as the milieu in a certain factory, or neighborhood "gang" of children. These social practices ultimately refer to a set of reinforcements and punishments which the people who constitute the social agency or social practice apply to the behavior of an individual. The social situation is unique only in so far as other organisms mediate the reinforcements, punishments, or other important environmental effects.

A fundamental psychological analysis must deal with the behavior of the individual, and the functional dimensions of social behavior appear only when they are expressed in terms of the consequences that the members of a group of people arrange for an individual. Social approval, for example, refers to a high disposition to supply favorable consequences to a wide range of specific behaviors of the individual; and conversely, a low disposition to arrange punishments. Similarly, an individual with "social prestige" is one whose repertoire is reinforcing to members of a group and will maintain the behavior of listening, reading, seeking close contact, and supplying reinforcements designed to maximize further performances.

Other social institutions such as law, government, religious agencies, and the family arrange very specific consequences which are somewhat easier to specify. The law and government, for example, have effects on the individual, largely by punishing specified forms of behavior by fines and incarceration. The religious agencies have some of their effects on the behaviors of the individual by similar processes. The punishments of hell and the rewards of heaven, as well as the more usual contingencies involved in the approval and disapproval by the membership of the religious agency, are used to maintain or suppress various behaviors.

The Large Order of Magnitude of Social Control

The importance of social behavior in human affairs is heightened by the fact that the most human reinforcements are mediated by another individual. Many of the reinforcements deriving their effect from groups of people have a larger order of magnitude of effect than reinforcements supplied only by a single individual or the physical environment. The heightened control by social reinforcement comes about because:

1. Some reinforcements are possible only when a performance is carried out in connection with other individuals. The appeal of the parade and uniform comes primarily from the prestige which the individual can share only by being a member of a group which in turn is important to the community. The process referred to here is similar to *identification* in dynamic psychology. Other examples in which the individual can have an effect in the community only when he behaves in concert with other individuals include the "gang," the revival meeting, and the cooperative action of three men lifting an object too heavy for any one of them.

2. Large numbers of individuals can potentially arrange reinforcements and punishments contingent on the behavior of the individual. The potential of an audience in rewarding or punishing depends in turn on the relevance of the reinforcements and punishments for the behavioral repertoire of the individual. The larger the number of individuals who can potentially reward, punish, or discontinue reinforcing behavior, the greater the effect is likely to be. Also, as the social agency involves more persons, there is less chance that an individual can avoid the punishment by escaping to another social group or to another environment for the reinforcements to maintain his existing repertoire. The control on the speaker by a relevant and effective audience illustrates this property of social reinforcements. When the audience has only a few members, the speaker may react to punishment or nonreinforcement by turning to other audiences. As the size of the audience increases, however, the effect of the contingencies they arrange on the behavior of the speaker becomes more and more inevitable. The control achieved in brainwashing illustrates the large order of magnitude of effect from controlling all of the audiences affecting an individual. Similarly, a group practice or a set of cultural mores has a large order of magnitude of control because the larger number of individuals who will arrange the reinforcements and punishments which constitute the social practice make this almost inevitable.

Deficient Behavioral Repertoires

Many unhappy individuals may be characterized as having repertoires whose performances are not producing the reinforcements of the world: because too much behavior is being punished; because nearly all of the individual's behavior is maintained by avoiding aversive consequences rather than producing positive effects; or a combination of all of these. A potential reinforcing environment exists for every individual, however, if he will only emit the required performances on the proper occasions. One has merely to paint the picture, write the symphony, produce the machine, tell the funny story, give affection artfully, and the world will respond in kind with prestige, money, social response, and love. Conversely, a repertoire which will make contact with the reinforcements of the world will be subsequently maintained because of the effect of the reinforcement on the performance. The problem is social because most of the reinforcements are mediated by other individuals.

A deficient behavioral repertoire may arise because:

1. *Inadequate reinforcement history.* Under this category belong individuals who are not making contact with important parts of their environment simply because their history did not include a set of experiences (educational) which could develop these performances during the normal maturation of the individual. Especially in the area of everyday social contacts, considerable skill is necessary for producing social reinforcements, and the absence of this skill either results in an individual without a social repertoire or one who achieves effects on his social environment by indirect means, as, for example, using aversive stimulation to gain attention. It is possible that this latter behavior would disappear if the individual had a repertoire which was effective in producing positive reinforcements. The existence of weak, positively reinforced repertoires, particularly in the field of ordinary social contacts, could result in "unsocial behavior" designed to affect the behavior of others by generating aversive conditions which are strong enough to produce avoidance, escape, and punishment. The reinforcing effect of these "antisocial" reactions might be large only in respect to the weak, positively reinforced repertoire.

2. *Schedule of reinforcement.* The schedule of reinforcement of a given performance might also produce a weakened disposition to engage in this performance so that the normal reinforcements do not occur. This kind of absence of behavior would be produced particularly in situations where large amounts of work are required for reinforcements, as, for example, in the case of the writer, housewife, student, or salesman, where reinforcement depends on a fixed amount of work. The individual's repertoire contains the required performances, but the existing schedule of reinforcement is such as to weaken the repertoire and thereby prevent its occurrence even though the correct form of the behavior would be available if the schedules of reinforcement were more optimal.

3. *Punishment may distort a performance which otherwise would be reinforced.* The absence of adequate repertoires in the individual could result from the distortion of the form of the behavior so that the performance does not have its customary effect. Excessive punishment may also generate avoidance behavior which is strong enough to be prepotent over the currently positively reinforced repertoires of the individual.

Remedying a Deficient Repertoire

The basic principles governing the development and maintenance of behavior are relevant to the task of generating new performances in an individual whose existing repertoire is not making contact with the reinforcements potentially available to him. The same principles are also relevant to the problem of generating adequate repertoires which will escape punishment.

Some of the reasons for a currently inadequate behavioral repertoire may be found in the history of the organism, perhaps even in early infancy. In many cases, however, the behavioral history of an individual is inaccessible. To the extent, however, that a current environment exists which can potentially maintain performances in all of the important segments in the individual's life by positive reinforcement, the history of the individual is relevant only in so far as it is useful in assessing the current repertoire of the individual. A functional program of therapy relying on the manipulatable factors in the person's environment may have important therapeutic effects, without reference to speculative accounts of the person's history, the current verbal reports of his feelings, and attitudes. Little more is to be desired if a person is content with his lot, works productively in a job, achieves affection and respect from his fellows, has an adequately sexual and home life, enjoys food and drink in moderation, and has diversions and adequate social relations.

The Processes by Which Social Agencies Affect the Behavior of the Individual

The major processes of behavior provide the technology for generating and eliminating behavior in the individual and are basic to the analysis of social effects. In the final analysis, the agency can have an effect on the individual only by arranging some environmental event contingent on the behavior of the individual. The social situation differs from the nonsocial one by the mediation of another organism in the delivery of the reward, punishment, or other consequence. It must be assumed, in the absence of contrary evidence, that the processes and laws operating in social situations are the same ones which are the bases for all behavioral processes.

Reinforcement. Reinforcement is the most important process by which behavior is generated and maintained. Most of an organism's behavior exists because of the effect on the environment, perhaps with the exception of the psychotic whose repertoire reflects the absence of behavior maintained with positive reinforcement. Reinforcement differs from the colloquial reward in its specificity; it is the immediate environmental consequences of a specific performance. The major effect of reinforcement needs to be distinguished from the classical or Pavlovian-type conditioning where the conditioned response is some elicited reflex, usually autonomic. The increase in the frequency of occurrence of the performance that is reinforced is the property of reinforcement that permits the tremendous variety and subtlety that occurs in the field of "voluntary" behavior as opposed to reflex and autonomic behavior.

Most reinforcements of everyday life are social rather than involving immediately important biological conditions. These social-maintaining-events operate as reinforcements because they are in a chain of events leading ultimately to a more basic consequence. Money provides an example of a conditioned reinforcer—*par excellence*—which derives its effect because its possession is a condition under which other performances will produce basic environmental effects. The important social consequences of money occur because the reinforcing properties of money nearly always depend immediately or ultimately upon the behavior of other individuals. Similarly, a smile can reinforce behavior because an individual who is smiling is more likely to supply subsequent reinforcements than one who is not.

As with money, many reinforcements in human behavior can be effective in the absence of any specific deprivation, unlike most reinforcements demonstrated in animal experiments. These "generalized" reinforcements maintain much of human behavior, and have large order of magnitudes of effect because their reinforcing power comes from a variety of reinforcements and deprivations and does not depend upon a current level of deprivation. This is especially true of nearly all reinforcements mediated by other organisms, because the mediation by another organism, in general, permits the application of a wider range of reinforcements. Other examples of generalized reinforcers include paying attention, affection, saying "right" or "correct," smiling, etc. These are important reinforcements because they are the usual conditions under which another organism will reinforce a behavior of an individual.

The Development of Complex Forms of Behavior: "Shaping." A major corollary of reinforcement is a procedure by which a reinforcing agency can produce progressively complex forms of behavior by small increments from a preceding simpler form. A commonly used animal-demonstration experiment illustrates the process. If we wish to teach a pigeon to peck at a small disc on the wall of his chamber, we first establish a reinforcer by presenting grain to the bird whenever the grain hopper is illuminated. The bird soon comes to approach the hopper only when it is illuminated, and it is then possible to use the lighted hopper as a reinforcement. The bird faces in the direction of the small disc, is reinforced, and the effect is an immediate increase in the tendency to face the disc. Reinforcement is then withheld until the bird nods slightly in the direction of the disc, and the reinforcement of this slightly more complex form increases its frequency. When the bird is nodding in the direction of the disc, the variation in the magnitude of the nod is noted and the reinforcement is shifted in the direction of those nods bringing the bird's head closer to the disc. By continuing the process, the pigeon can soon be made to strike the disc.

The same process occurs in the development of human behavior, particularly in the formative years. The process by which complex forms are generated is relevant to the therapy situation whenever a patient is lacking parts of the complex repertoire necessary to achieve reinforcement from the complicated social environment. Simply telling a patient what kind of performance is necessary for reinforcement will seldom generate the required complex performance. The situation is analogous to that of the golfer who would like to drive the ball 250 yards. The necessary performance must be acquired in small steps, beginning with an existing repertoire and approximating the final performance with intermediate, temporary reinforcements.

An effective procedure in shaping someone's behavior would be to start with a performance already in his repertoire and expose him to selected portions of his environment designed to generate the new, more complex form. One might select an environment in which a reinforcing agent is operating which will reinforce with a high degree of probability a variation in the person's performance in the direction of the desired, more complicated form. For example, consider the hypothetical case of an individual who has never acquired the performances necessary for facile enough social contact. A first step in this hypothetical case might be to send him to a college campus one morning and have him say "Good morning" to several people he passes. The environment of the campus is chosen to almost guarantee the reinforcement of this response. This kind of exercise would also illustrate to the individual that it is possible to command a verbal response from an audience. In a similar vein, the complexity of the verbal repertoire of the individual could be increased further. Commands, such as "Could you please tell me the time," also produce almost inevitable responses in most situations; and if the rate of development of the new behavior from the preceding forms which the person is emitting successfully is made small enough, there would be no difficulty from nonreinforcement because of inaudible remarks, mumbling, or other distortion of the behavior which would prevent the reinforcement.

Intermittent Reinforcement. Social reinforcements are intermittent because the reinforcements mediated by another organism are less reliable than those produced by the physical environment. This arises because the social reinforcement depends upon behavioral processes in the reinforcer which are not always under good control by the reinforcee. For example, if one is asked to look outside and report whether it is raining, many factors in the repertoire of the listener could interfere with the successful completion of the report: the listener is afraid of height, some more urgent audience catches the attention of the listener, the listener happens not to be attentive at the moment the request is made, the listener's eyeglasses are off at the moment, etc. In contrast, the effects of most behavior on the physical environment are almost inevitable.

The nature of the intermittency has a great influence on the disposition to engage in a given behavior. It is possible to produce an almost complete cessation of some behavior which the individual has emitted literally thousands of times by alteration of the schedule of reinforcement. Similarly, identical frequencies of reinforcement on different reinforcement schedules produce widely differing dispositions to engage in the behavior.

The history by which the individual is exposed to many schedules is also of great importance. Certain schedules of reinforcement will sustain behavior normally if approached in gradual steps but will produce complete cessation (abulia) if the individual is exposed to the final schedule at once. In the most prevalent schedule of reinforcement found in human affairs (ratio reinforcement), the reinforcement occurs as a function of a certain number of instances of a performance. One of the major properties of this schedule of reinforcement is a decline in the disposition to emit the behavior when the amount of work for reinforcement becomes too large. This lessened disposition occurs particularly as inability to begin work just after a reinforcement. The disinclination of the novelist to begin a new novel just after completing one is a pure example of this effect. There is some suggestion that there are inductive effects among the various repertoires of the individual.

An optimal schedule of reinforcement in one area will help sustain a performance under a less optimal schedule of reinforcement in another area; and, conversely, reinforcement on nonoptimal schedules of reinforcement may have the opposite effect of weakening a repertoire whose reinforcement schedule is more optimal. These "ratio" or piecework schedules of reinforcement are contrasted with another major schedule class where the reinforcement of a response becomes more likely with passage of time since the previous reinforcement. These schedules are less prevalent in human affairs than ratio schedules and tend to produce a level of performance more appropriate to the frequency of reinforcement regardless of the history of the individual. Examples of this latter class of schedules of reinforcement include looking in the mailbox when the mail delivery occurs somewhat unpredictably (variable-interval reinforcement), and looking into the pot on the stove as the water is being boiled.

Optimum parameters of a schedule of reinforcement may also result in very large amounts of behavior and a strong disposition to engage in the reinforced behavior. The behavior of the gambler is an excellent example where an explicit program of reinforcement (technically classified variable-ratio) generates a strong disposition to gamble, even though the individual operates at a loss over a longer period of time. Here the heightened disposition to gamble arising from the optimal variable-ratio schedule of reinforcements (even the loser wins frequently) overrides the over-all low net reinforcement.

It is possible that the general condition of an individual whose behavior is weak because of too much behavior emitted with too little reinforcement resembles conditions arising from aversive control. This may be especially true when the "strained" repertoire is supplemented by aversive conditions such as threats which can be avoided only by emitting more of the "strained" behavior. For example, the factory worker on a piecework pay schedule may be threatened, lose his job, or be fined when he stops working even though his rate of pay is proportional to the amount of work he does. Secondary factors may also influence the way in which a given repertoire is maintained on a schedule of reinforcement. Physical exhaustion, poor health, and inductive effects from other repertoires may produce strain under a schedule of reinforcement which under other conditions might have been satisfactory.

Early exposure to intermittent reinforcement. Many behavioral repertoires are weak because of an accidental history which supplied an inadequate reinforcement at any early stage. This could come about especially when punishment produces forms of behavior which go unreinforced because they are distorted. An optimal schedule of reinforcement of a repertoire is essential at an early stage of development if a strong disposition to engage in the performance is to be maintained later under less optimal schedules. The genesis of avid gamblers illustrates the importance of the schedule of reinforcement during the initial acquisition of the repertoire. Professional gamblers, for example, will arrange a high frequency of reinforcement for the beginner in order to provide conditions under which the beginner will continue to gamble later when the schedule of reinforcement is less adequate. Similarly, at least a part of the difference between the person who continues to gamble and those who fail to continue after a brief exposure lies in the initial "luck." The fisherman is on the same schedule of reinforcement as the gambler, and the result is the same. The avid interest of the fishing devotee is extreme compared with others and probably represents the result of an optimal schedule of reinforcement during the initial fishing experiences.

The community maximizes the frequency of reinforcement during the educational phase of an individual by providing reinforcements for rough approximations to the ultimately effective forms. For example, a young child emitting the response "wawer" is likely to be reinforced by a glass of water, while the same response at a later stage of development will be unreinforced, or even punished. Thus, in the early stages of development of the repertoire a higher frequency of reinforcement is more easily achieved than later, when the community demands a more differentiated and closely specified form of behavior and environmental control. Whether newly developing behavior will persist depends upon whether the initial frequency and manner of reinforcement will sustain the performance as it comes under the control of the relevant stimuli, as the form of the behavior becomes more and more differentiated, and as the audience selectively reinforces more effective forms. Whenever a repertoire becomes weakened because of accidental nonreinforcement during the early development of the repertoire, it becomes more difficult to reinstate the repertoire because the form of the behavior must now be more exact and under more precise environmental control than during the early stages of development.

Compare, for example, the successful and the unsuccessful adult in their sexual-social relations with the opposite sex. Very highly differentiated behavior under close stimulus control is required. Once an individual matures beyond a given age without developing the performances in respect to the opposite sex which will be reinforced, it becomes more difficult to acquire effective performances. The situation is comparable to the difficulties of the algebra student who tries to learn factoring without being facile in algebraic multiplication and division.

Superstitious Reinforcement. A reinforcing event will increase the disposition to engage in the behavior reinforced even though the reinforcement is spurious or accidental. As in the case of the gambler, the chance history of reinforcement is important in determining whether accidental or spurious reinforcements will sustain the behavior. Once there is some tendency to emit the behavior as the result of some accidental reinforcements, the resulting tendency to continue behaving increases the likelihood that the behavior will be in progress subsequently when another reinforcement occurs. These superstitious performances are most likely to occur under high motivation, as for example the gambler addressing the dice "come seven" or the "posturing" of the bowler. These spurious reinforcements are probably even more effective in the field of aversive control. If the aversively maintained behavior is conditioned strongly enough, the behavior may never extinguish because the avoidance behavior prevents the occurrence of the conditioned aversive stimuli which now would no longer be followed by the aversive event.

Stimulus Control of Behavior. The reinforcement or punishment of a verbal or nonverbal response depends upon the nature of the audience. Not all performances of an individual are reinforced on all occasions, and the situation characteristically present when a given kind of behavior is reinforced comes to control the likelihood that the performance will occur. Nearly all of the behavior of the normal adult comes under very close stimulus control of the various audiences to which he is exposed. Details of speech as subtle as vocabulary and intonation change with different audiences. The thematic material of a conversation varies widely depending upon the audience, from shop talk to a co-worker to the "baby-talk" maximally effective in producing a reaction from an infant. Poor development of stimulus control will result in a lower net frequency of reinforcement. The nonreinforcement of behavior that occurs during the development of stimulus control is tantamount to intermittent reinforcement until the stimulus control develops. To the extent that performances are reinforced only on specific occasions and by particular audiences, a failure of stimulus control results in an increase in the proportion of an individual's behavior which goes unreinforced.

The normal maturation of an individual into childhood and adulthood illustrates the interrelation between intermittent reinforcement and stimulus control. We reinforce almost any form of behavior in infants and very young children so long as there is a remote resemblance to the required performance. As the child grows older, however, the reinforcement is continually shifted in the direction of forms which approximate the normal cultural practices. Many members of the community will reinforce the behavior of the young child even though it has little importance for the listener. As the child develops through school age, however, the audience becomes more selective, and now properly differentiated forms of behavior will go unreinforced if they are not reinforcing for the listener. Hence, a further possibility of nonreinforcement arises whenever a performance is inappropriate for a given audience. The better an individual's performances are controlled by the environment, therefore, the more optimal will be the schedule of positive reinforcement. Inadequate stimulus and audience control of behavior could be one of the conditions under which an inadequate repertoire develops because of performances occurring where they will not be reinforced and not occurring when they will be reinforced.

Just as accidental reinforcements may generate forms of behavior which are superstitious in the sense that the behavior is not a necessary condition for the occurrence of the reinforcement, it is possible for irrelevant aspects of a situation to acquire stimulus control of a performance. Every occasion on which a reinforcement occurs has multiple dimensions, and the aspects which come to control are somewhat undetermined until there are differential consequences in terms of the various elements. For example, an individual has a history in which many of the people who have given good advice have worn double-breasted suits, bow ties, and spoken with a cosmopolitan accent. There will, therefore, be a heightened disposition to follow advice from persons exhibiting these characteristics until enough individuals have been encountered who shared some of these properties but have given bad advice. In a similar manner, an audience resembling a parent may increase the likelihood of occurrence of performances previously reinforced by a parent, even though that audience is not a potential reinforcer. This kind of inadequate stimulus control may simply be an accident of the historical conditions under which past reinforcements have occurred in situations which have multiple dimensions, some of which are irrelevant. More adequate stimulus control can develop only by exposure to the irrelevant aspect of the situation and the corresponding nonreinforcement. General motivational factors may also heighten the control by irrelevant aspects of a situation or audience. The man lost on the desert without water is more likely to mistake irrelevant stimuli for water.

It should be possible to sharpen the stimulus control of behavior by alternately exposing the individual to situations containing the various elements separately and allowing the resulting reinforcement and nonreinforcement to strengthen the tendency to emit the performance on the relevant occasions and weaken the disposition to emit the behavior when the irrelevant aspects are present.

Aversive Control. In social situations most control by aversive stimuli involves the removal or discontinuation of positive reinforcement rather than some kind of primary aversive stimulation. The usual social punishments are (1) *disapproval:* a state of affairs where the reinforcer is not likely to continue reinforcements for specific performances; (2) *fines:* a loss of money or privilege which effectively reduces the amount of various kinds of behavior that can be reinforced; (3) *criticism:* an indication of specific performances which will not be reinforced or which will bring about nonreinforcement in other spheres, and (4) *incarceration:* the extreme case, where large portions of the repertoire of the individual can no longer produce their characteristic reinforcement.

While the discontinuation of positive reinforcement can be used as a punishment, it is important to distinguish between the effect of nonreinforcement *per se* and its use as a punishment. As noted earlier, the nonreinforcement of a performance on one occasion and its consistent reinforcement on a second occasion is the main process by which environmental control of behavior takes place. The decline of frequency of occurrence of a performance as a function of nonreinforcement has very different properties from punishment by the discontinuation of reinforcement. In the latter case, the punishment is carried out by presenting a stimulus which is already correlated with a low probability of response because of previous nonreinforcement. Its aversive effect probably derives from the over-all importance in the repertoire of the individual of the behavior being blocked. The simple discontinuation of positive reinforcement shares some of the properties of an aversive stimulus, particularly during the transient phase while the frequency of the nonreinforced performance is still falling. Once the stimulus control is established, however, the resulting low disposition to engage in the eliminated behavior allows concurrent repertoires to take over. The salient feature of punishment is that an aversive stimulus is applied to some performance which is maintained by a positive reinforcement; thus the original source of strength of the performance is still present and the performance can reappear in some strength when the punishment is discontinued. This is to be contrasted with simple extinction or nonreinforcement where the maintaining event for the behavior is discontinued and the performance no longer occurs simply because it no longer has its characteristic effect on the environment.

A second major effect of an aversive stimulus is the disruption of substantial segments of the repertoire of the individual by the situation characteristically preceding the aversive event. The pre-aversive situation (anxiety) has an emotional effect in the sense that it produces a state of affairs where there is a disruption of parts of the individual's repertoire not directly related to the aversive event. For example, the student just before the crucial examination, the patient in the dentist's waiting room, the child just before the parent discovers the broken ashtray, and the soldier just before the battle will all show considerable disruption of the normal repertoire; marked changes in the frequency of occurrence of all of the performances which might normally occur under these situations without the aversive event.

The third function of the aversive stimulus is in maintaining behavior which terminates or postpones (escapes or avoids) the aversive event. Examples of these kinds of reinforcements in a normal repertoire include opening or closing a window to alter an extreme temperature, buying fuel in advance of cold weather, or making an apology to reduce the threat of punishment.

The clinical effects of excessive punishment have been fairly widely recognized and analyzed, and much of current therapy is analyzed as eliminating the aversive effects of situations which no longer are associated with punishment.

The disruptive effects of aversive control will interfere with the development of the precise forms of behavior being generated by positive reinforcement. This would be particularly true in the area of social contact, such as sexual behavior, where punishment is widely applied, and where complex and precise forms of behavior are required. A practical program would be designed to develop forms of behavior which would avoid punishment as well as maximize reinforcement. Situations which would disrupt positively maintained repertoires because of a history of punishment would have to be approached in small steps so that the strength of the positively maintained behavior is large in respect to the disruptive effect and the aversive history.

Another corollary of aversive control is its prepotency over positively reinforced behavior. The use of aversive control generates immediate escape and avoidance behavior, and the wide use of punishment and aversive stimulation as a technique of control probably stems from the immediate effects which this kind of stimulation achieves as opposed to the slower development of behavior by a positive reinforcement. When an aversive condition is set up in order to generate some performance which must ultimately be maintained by positive reinforcement (for example, nagging), the control often backfires when the individual terminates the nagging by counter aversive control rather than emitting the performance which will reinforce the "nagger" and terminate the nagging. It is possible that some psychiatric patients have repertoires almost entirely composed of immediate reactions to threats and punishments which are entirely prepotent over reinforced repertoires. To the extent that this is true, the development of strong positively reinforced repertoires would provide an avenue of therapy.

References

Ferster, C. B., and Skinner, B. F. *Schedules of reinforcement.* New York: Appleton-Century-Crofts, 1957.

Hull, C. L. *Principles of behavior.* New York: Appleton-Century-Crofts, 1953.

Lindsley, O. R. Operant conditioning methods applied to research in chronic schizophrenia. *Psychiatric Research Reports,* 1956, *5,* 118–139.

Meyer, V. The treatment of two phobic patients on the basis of learning principles. *Journal of Abnormal and Social Psychology,* 1953, *55,* 261–266.

Miller, N. E., and Dollard, J. *Personality and psychotherapy.* New York: McGraw-Hill, 1950.

Mowrer, O. H. A stimulus-response analysis of anxiety and its role as a reinforcing agent. *Psychological Review,* 1939, *46,* 553–566.

Skinner, B. F. *Science and human behavior.* New York: Macmillan, 1953.

B A Functional Analysis of Social Behavior

Bijou and Baer describe in still more detail the processes by which the newborn infant begins to develop into a social individual. The article is included here in the chapter on theory and conceptual issues because it illustrates our concern with the basic processes and methods of analysis and description rather than with an actual account of a child's social repertoire. Bijou and Baer echo Skinner's injunction that the behavior processes of individual organisms are the components of social behavior, and in this selection they painstakingly analyze all of the component factors which go into the early socialization of the child. We see here in microcosm a model for a behavioral approach to complex social processes. Bijou and Baer assume that the reader understands the basic behavior processes by which performances are created, maintained, and brought into relation with the environment. The repertoire of the newborn infant provides an opportunity to analyze the specific stimuli and events which are the constituents of the infant's early socialization. The actual terms which go into the analysis are the moment-to-moment changes in the child's environment, such as changing the diaper, a touch to the child's skin, receiving food, a smile, or the mother holding her child. These are the events and forms of conduct which are referred to when we pose problems about affection, relationship to the mother, perception of the mother, perception of self-identity, or attitude formation.

3 *Socialization—The Development of Behavior to Social Stimuli*

S. W. BIJOU
D. M. BAER

The skill of an infant in manipulating his physical world with reinforcing consequences is a steadily but slowly developing one. Consequently, in the early stages of development, the reinforcers necessary for life must be arranged for him by the person who performs the usual mothering functions—feeding, bathing, changing, and the like. In doing so, she also provides social stimuli. The principles describing the development of behavior to these social stimuli are not different from those describing his development to physical and organismic stimuli. However, social stimuli are distinctive enough to merit separate discussion, as are the consequences of this development for the infant's future behavior (Gewirtz, 1961).

Development of the Discriminative Function of Mother for Reinforcing Events

A newborn baby is a thoroughly helpless creature. Without consistent care, he certainly will not survive. All of the frequent and consistent care he requires must be provided by others. In our culture (as in many) it is usually the mother who does most of this; the father does some, too, and other relatives, like grandparents and older siblings, may take a hand. We shall refer to the person providing the care as the "mother," whoever the person may be on any specific occasion.

The essential function of the mother is to provide positive reinforcers to the infant and remove negative ones. This is not the ordinary description a mother gives of her duties, but it is a technical one—a functional and fairly comprehensive specification of her behavior as a mother. Thus, she feeds her infant six to eight times a day at first, frequently ensures that his skin temperature is neither too hot nor too cold, holds him to her and strokes him, rescues him from any situation which she thinks is hurting him, adds toys to his crib, moves him and the objects in his world about, and puts him to bed for rest and sleep.

In doing these things and many others, the mother herself will, as a stimulus object, become discriminated as a "time" and a place for either the addition of positive reinforcers to the baby's environment or the subtraction of negative reinforcers from it. Thus she is discriminative, as a stimulus, for the two reinforcement procedures which strengthen operant behavior. Thereby, she acquires a positive reinforcing function and lays the foundation for the further social development of her infant.

The mother is discriminative for some reinforcement procedures by necessity, and for others by accident or through common cultural practice. To illustrate this, we consider a number of reinforcers separately, noting the discriminative role of the mother for each.

Food and Water. The mother feeds the infant several times a day, every day for many months. If she is breast-feeding the child, then she is a stimulus that appears just before the receipt of milk (and sucking stimulation, too) and one that remains throughout the nursing period. If she is bottle-feeding him, she accompanies the initial presentation of the bottle, and the insertion of the nipple into the infant's mouth. Typically, she holds both infant and bottle throughout the feeding, thus remaining discriminative for milk throughout the ingestion process. Occasionally, she may prop up infant and bottle and leave for a time; even so, she has been discriminative for the first milk's presentation.

Even as the infant develops increasing competence to feed himself, the mother still retains much of her discriminative function for reinforcement derived from feeding. She typically prepares the food and places it before the infant or hands it to him. Indeed, long into his later life, when he is capable of preparing it for himself, she continues to engage in the cultural practice of feeding him.

Taste Stimuli. The nearly universal behavior of giving candy to children may be singled out (somewhat arbitrarily) from the other feeding behaviors of the mother. Candy certainly is a food, but it often is given to children when they are fairly satiated with other foods, and presumably is consumed primarily for its taste. Cookies and fruit juices are also instances of distinctive tastes given to children by mothers. Thus the mother is discriminative for taste reinforcement too. However, the infant encounters some tastes without the help of the mother, since he sucks on nearly every object which can be fitted into his mouth. Some of these objects will have a taste that may be reinforcing. Some of these will be positive reinforcers, but some will be negative. Tastes of objects given by the mother, however, are almost always positive ones (except when she must give the child evil-tasting medicines).

Skin Temperature. The infant's internal temperature is self-regulating. His skin temperature, however, depends on the temperature of his surroundings and the kinds and numbers of layers of clothing and blankets covering his body. For the regulation of external temperature change, he must at first depend upon his mother. By removing layers of clothing when he is hot, and adding them when he is cold, she marks an occasion of removal of a negative reinforcer and return of a positive one. Later, as part of the baby's increase in motor skills, he learns to dress and undress himself and adjust his own blankets, whereupon the mother loses much of her discriminative function from this source. Until then, however, her role is definitely discriminative.

Rest and Sleep. The very young infant typically rests and sleeps most of his day. Many infants can drop off to sleep anywhere and anytime, and the sight of an infant sleeping in a grocery cart, stroller, car seat, on a store counter, or in the aisle is not uncommon. Thus no help from the mother is consistently needed to mark occasions of rest and sleep reinforcement. However, cultural practices may give the mother a role in the infant's rest and sleep routines that would make her discriminative for rest and sleep. It is common in our society for a baby (or older child) to be "put to bed." This practice may consist of a change of clothes (usually into sleeping garments), placing the child in his crib, covering him with blankets, and sometimes, singing a lullaby; alternatively, it may consist of rocking and perhaps singing until the baby is asleep or shows signs of drowsiness. Through this feature of child-rearing practice the mother gratuitously acquires a discriminative function for rest and sleep reinforcers.

Tactual Stimulation. It is a common practice in our society for mothers to hold their infants. For one thing, this is often the only way to transport them; moreover, it sometimes quiets them; and, thirdly, it is often reinforcing to the mother. Another common practice of mothers in our society is to pet and stroke their infants, to kiss them, to tap them on the "tummy," and to ruffle their hair (however sparse). These customs, too, seem to provide some reinforcement for the mother, possibly because of the tactual stimulation provided by the baby and his responses to such stimulation. At any rate, such practices provide tactual stimulation to the baby. If this type of tactual stimulation is reinforcing, and it seems to be in most instances, then the mother is discriminative for it. However, it is a discriminative function she shares with a variety of other stimuli, such as the baby's blanket, his clothes, his Teddy Bear, the cat, etc. In other words, the mother may be a significant source of tactual reinforcement, but she is by no means the only source, especially as the baby grows older.

Opportunity to Breathe. The infant does his own breathing, of course. On infrequent occasions breathing may prove difficult for him, as when he has croup or asthma, or has managed to get his nose and mouth thoroughly covered by something he cannot remove by his own actions. On the occasions of internal obstructions brought about by physiological disturbances, mother may rescue him, perhaps by taking him into a warm, moist place (the bathroom with a hot shower running, seems a favorite prescription); or possibly by holding him upright, a position in which congested respiratory passages drain better. When breathing has been obstructed accidentally by such things as pillows or clinging sheets of plastic, it is necessary for the mother to remove them since the baby cannot. Thus there are scattered times when the mother takes on a discriminative role for the opportunity for the infant to breathe better. These occurrences are quite rare, but when they do occur they may be urgent (highly aversive) from the infant's point of view. Thus it is worthwhile to note these kinds of contributions to the mother's discriminative role.

Negative Reinforcers. Despite meticulous care, negative reinforcers manage to act upon the infant from time to time. He may, for example, roll upon hard toys, pinch himself between mattress and crib bars, bang his head into the headboard, be exposed to hot, bright sunlight, have gastric pains, cut a tooth, and be manhandled by an older sibling or a house pet. From some of these accidents, the mother must rescue him, thereby functioning as a stimulus discriminative for the removal of negative reinforcers. She can, for example, roll him off the hard object, free him from the clutches of the mattress and crib, move him into the shade, "burp" him, massage his gums, and drive off the older sibling or pet.

In many situations she can do little about removing negative reinforcers, since they have had their full impact before she can get into effective action. Yet even in these instances, she often plays something of a discriminative role by virtue of the nature of the course of a hurt. When an infant experiences a negative reinforcer, he usually cries. This respondent signal of distress often attracts the mother, who, seeing that he has been hurt but that it is all over, nevertheless picks him up and comforts him. In so doing, she marks an occasion of the waning of the stimulus which hurt him. Speaking loosely, he is just starting to feel better and there he is in mother's arms. How is he to know it wasn't mother who actually reduced the intensity of the hurt?

Stimulus Change. If stimulus change is reinforcing to an infant, then at least some stimulus change is provided by the mother. She picks him up and moves him from one place to another; she places new toys in his view; she speaks and sings to him; and she plays games with him, such as peek-a-boo, patty-cake, and making faces. Thus, her appearance on the scene frequently is discriminative for rather wide-spread stimulus changes. Indeed, the younger the infant, the less accomplished he is in arranging his environment to produce changes; hence long hours in his crib constitute a considerable deprivation of stimulus change, and the greater is his dependence upon the mother to make something happen. As the baby grows older, however, many more responses which produce such changes become available to him, and hence the mother will constitute a smaller source of stimulus change in his total environment. Thus mother's initial discriminative status for much of this kind of reinforcement will diminish during the course of development.

Control of Environment. If it is reinforcing to an infant to control his environment, then it should be true that in the early days of development this control is highly imperfect. In such instances, an ally could provide the aid necessary to turn failure into success. The mother often is such an ally, helping the baby to pick up and hold objects, pushing things so that they are within his reach, propping up objects so that they will stand, etc. In so doing, she is discriminative for the baby's exercising greater control of his environment than he could effect in her absence. To the extent that this happens, it adds to the discriminative status of the mother.

Development of the Discriminative Functions of Mother for Aversive Events

The preceding discussion has concentrated on the actions of the mother which make her discriminative for the addition of positive reinforcers and the removal of negative ones. Obviously, there will be occasions when she will have the reverse discriminative role: she will take away positive reinforcers and add negative reinforcers. For example, she may remove tasty substances from the baby's mouth on the grounds that they are not edible; she may take away entertaining objects because they are sharp or economically valuable; or she may wake up the baby because she must give him medicine or take him with her on an errand. Through clumsiness, she may occasionally bump or drop the baby; she may deliver him to doctors who must stick him with needles; she may force nasty-tasting medicines upon him; or she may scrub him with more vigor than is necessary. In all of these examples and many similar ones, the mother develops and adds to her acquired negative reinforcing function, not her acquired positive reinforcing function.

We may refer to the operation or act of taking away positive reinforcers and adding negative reinforcers as "punishment by loss" and "punishment by hurt." These terms, borrowed from everyday language, are only loose descriptions of the interactions involved. It would be more accurate to say that under the circumstances described the mother develops a discriminative function for aversive stimulation. (This phrase also carries fewer unintended meanings.) The mere presence of the mother during these acts of aversive stimulation makes it likely that some stimulus aspect of her behavior will develop conditioned aversive functions. If it can be demonstrated that the behavior which accomplishes the removal of that aspect of mother is strengthened, then we may say that she has acquired negative reinforcing functions.

In general, of course, aversive occurrences are fewer than those in which the mother adds positive and subtracts negative reinforcers. In balancing the two sets of circumstances, then, the acquired reinforcing function of the mother is usually positive. How strongly positive she is depends upon the proportion of times she is discriminative for the addition of positive and the subtraction of negative reinforcers relative to the proportion of the subtraction of positive and the addition of negative reinforcers. Her overall reinforcement strength also depends on the value of the positive and negative reinforcers involved, the baby's relevant deprivation states, the schedules of reinforcement involved, and so on. Thus, depending upon how the mother performs her functions, her net strength as an acquired positive reinforcer is determined.

It is conceivable that the mother could be more discriminative for the removal of positive reinforcers and the presentation of negative ones than the opposite. In that case, her overall acquired reinforcing function would be negative. This is certainly possible with older children. In the case of infants, however, it may well be that the actual survival of the infant requires that the mother has been discriminative for the presentation of positive reinforcers and the removal of negative ones more often and more intensively than for the removal of positive reinforcers and the addition of negative ones, at least during the first year or so. Thus, for all infants who survive their first months of development, we may assume that their mothers have acquired at least some reinforcing function.

The Stimulus Components of the Mother

The functional characterization of the mother presented thus far is that of a discriminative social stimulus. Having outlined what she is discriminative for, it is now appropriate to identify more precisely the stimuli involved.

The equation of a person to a stimulus is of course an oversimplification. There are innumerable ways of characterizing the stimuli which make up a human being. Many of these, however, will have little or no functional value for the behavior of other people, especially of their children. For example, we might describe a mother by the number of calories of heat she radiated per hour. This is certainly one of her stimulus characteristics, but it is of little significance to her baby unless the mother provides a source of heat for the baby in an otherwise cold environment. Similarly, a mother could be characterized by the number of hairs on her head. Her baby may respond to the color of her hair and the shape of its arrangement on her head, but he is not responsive to the number of discrete hairs.

The characteristics of a mother which are important stimuli for her baby clearly are those which are involved in her discriminative functions. In effect, they are the stimuli, in all their variety, which allow the mother to be discriminated from the rest of the house and the objects in it and from other people who are not caretakers, at least to some degree. To a great extent, these are visual stimuli; but auditory, tactual, and olfactory stimulus elements also play a part. The mother has the usual shape of *homo sapiens* plus her own individual biological differences. The shape is seen by the baby in a variety of wrappings and positions, some more often than others.

The baby's initial discriminations may be no more elegant than that reinforcement often follows the appearance of a certain shape wrapped in gray bending over him. The shape has a distinctive top, a face crowned with hair. The hair is of fairly constant color (ordinarily), but is seen in a variety of arrangements about the face. The face has certain constant elements consisting of its basic lines, the shape of the nose, and so on. The variations on the patterns of the face are considerable, however, ranging from broad smiles to stormy frowns. Some of these arrangements, such as smiles, may be more discriminative for positive reinforcement than others, such as frowns. The shape has a voice which occasionally makes noise, and the frequencies and tenor of this noise are fairly consistent. It does, however, include coos, gurgles, shouts, and happy, angry, and placid tones. The happy sounds may be more reliable cues for positive reinforcers than the angry ones (which, in time, often will be clearly discriminative for negative reinforcers). The specific patterns of sound making up the mother's language will initially have little discriminative value for the infant. Later they will acquire this function, and after about five years of age these sounds will control a highly complex assortment of discriminated operants.

The mother also has a number of surfaces providing tactual stimulation which the infant might experience. These stimuli are provided by her skin (especially her hands), the clothes she wears, and her hair. The touch of the mother's hands may be discriminative for subsequent reinforcement. The feel of the mother's face sometimes might be modified by a layer of cosmetics or of perspiration. The feel of her clothes obviously will be a frequently changeable stimulus.

The mother also might provide a number of odors. Some of these are eminently associated with her appearance; some are added from time to time by perfumes, cosmetics, mouthwashes and toothpastes, smoking, and the like. It is unlikely that any of the latter are particularly discriminative for any reinforcing consequences for the infant (except, possibly, that a highly perfumed and made-up mother is likely to leave soon and be replaced by another person [babysitter]. The nature of this sequence of events is hardly systematic in its effects. It depends upon the types of care given by the mother and the substitute mother).

These are at least some of the stimuli, then, which contribute to the baby's recognition of the mother. They allow him to discriminate her from other parts of his environment which also have shapes, make sounds, and provide tactual and olfactory stimulation. But because so many stimuli from mother vary within wide limits, it is necessary to consider her not as a fixed class of stimuli, but rather as a continuously changing array of stimuli from many classes. The classes of stimuli from which the mother's samples of stimuli are drawn are, of course, shared by other people. Thus the positions of the mother's body relative to the baby are duplicated by many other bodies from time to time, and clothes on the mother are much like those of others who come and go. Perhaps no one else has quite the mother's nose, but the general shape and location of her nose relative to her eyes and mouth, and the variations of facial contours arranged by smiles, frowns, and the like, are like the facial expressions of others. The mother's voice may have a characteristic tenor and style of inflection, but the voices of many persons produce similar frequencies and inflections, and share much of the same language, idioms, and exclamations. Other individuals will feel much like the mother to the baby and, on occasion, will also provide similar odors.

In effect, the mother is a changing sample of stimuli, some of which are unique to her, but many of which are shared by other people. Thus stimuli from a mother which become discriminative for reinforcement may overlap with stimuli from other people, and the baby's behaviors which have become strengthened to mother's stimulation may be evoked by others who present the same or similar stimuli. Consequently, there are natural bases for both *discrimination* of the mother from all other people and for *generalization* from the mother to others. Thus, the baby can unfailingly pick out his parents when necessary; yet, just as he smiles at them, makes noises, waves, claps, and does other "tricks" for them, so he may do the same for others, even without previous direct experience with them.

As the mother becomes a social reinforcer for the baby, other people acquire a generalized reinforcing value (to the extent that they, as samples of stimuli, are like the mother). This process may be the basic learning operation which gives the child a social character and allows the figurative label of man as a "social animal." That is, man is an organism whose mother, in being discriminative for reinforcement, is sufficiently changeable as a stimulus complex to be much like other people he meets later in his life; he will respond to them at least in part as he has responded to his mother. (It is often said that the child learns about society "through the eyes of his mother.") Basically, the mother has been discriminative for the presentation of positive and for the removal of negative reinforcers; therefore the child's mother, and, by generalization, others similar to her, will acquire the stimulus property of a positive acquired reinforcer, i.e., a social reinforcer.

It is now essential to analyze in more specific terms the stimuli of the mother which are discriminative for behaviors leading to reinforcement. So far, discussion has centered on stimuli which make it apparent that the mother is distinct from other parts of the baby's environment. But the mother provides cues which are a part of the reinforcement procedures she performs; she provides more detailed stimuli: her *proximity* or nearness, her *attention*, and her *affection* or warmth. These stimulus components of the mother are of special significance for the future development of the baby and child.

Proximity of the Mother to the Baby. The majority of reinforcement operations the mother performs are administered in close physical relationship to the baby. Mother cannot feed the baby, adjust his temperature, rescue him from hurtful objects, hold him, or prepare him for sleep at a distance. Such caretaking functions require handling of the baby while providing reinforcers, and thus the mother, to reinforce, must be near the baby—within reaching distance, at least. As a consequence, mother at a distance is hardly discriminative for reinforcement, but mother nearby is discriminative.

The stimulus dimensions involved in reacting to objects at different distances away, or distance perception, have long been an interesting problem in visual perception and discrimination. For an adult, the cues reacted to in discriminating distance include at least: (1) the angle of convergence the eyeballs assume in fixating an object at various distances, (2) the disparity or differences in images falling on the two retinas, (3) the texture, brightness, and parallel line characteristics, and (4) the interposition of other objects between the viewer and the object (Gibson, 1950). An infant may not use all of these cues in discriminating distances; indeed, some of them may be learned during his early days in the child-rearing situations under discussion. In these situations, the mother in close proximity to the baby is more discriminative for reinforcement than the mother at a distance, and it follows that any stimuli marking these differences in distance will themselves become functional for the baby. If mother is close, reinforcement follows, sometimes after a short delay: if mother is far, reinforcement follows only after a long delay or not at all.

The nearness of the mother is one of the basic social discriminative stimuli. Closeness-to-the-mother thereby takes on positive reinforcing power, and behaviors of the baby producing proximity of the mother will be strengthened, while behaviors losing this proximity will be weakened. For the young baby who does not move about, certain responses often will produce the essential proximity of a mother. These include crying and fussing, calling "Mommy," or any responses with objects that make noise of the sort that will attract a curious parent. Certain facial expressions of a "cute" sort often will attract a distant adult, as may other tricks which mothers interpret as especially charming or advanced, such as playing patty-cake.

For the baby who moves about, creeping, crawling, toddling, walking, or running are some of the responses that can produce the proximity of the mother and maintain it as the mother moves about. Tagging along after the mother is clearly one of the most prominent behaviors of young children, and may be viewed as a set of discriminated operants maintained by the proximity functioning as a positive reinforcer. The contribution of this basic social reinforcer to increasing skill and speed in locomotor behaviors may be great; it has often been clinically described (frequently in terms of the baby's need for security) but has not as yet been experimentally analyzed. However, Gewirtz (1945) has made an analysis of the role of proximity in stimulating a number of social responses such as attention-seeking.

Proximity should be a less distinctive stimulus for babies reared in small living quarters than for those living in large houses. Where the environment is quite small, as in a cramped one-room apartment, the mother is rarely far from the baby. Thus the difference between a distant mother and a near one is minimal: the mother when she is giving reinforcers is hardly much nearer than when she is not. When the baby and mother live in a large room, however, the nonreinforcing mother may be much farther away than when she is reinforcing, and the distance dimension is much more prominent. In a house with many rooms, the nonreinforcing mother may frequently be out of the child's sight, and the role of proximity as a distinctive cue for reinforcement is maximized.

Casual observation shows that many young crawlers and toddlers spend a considerable proportion of their waking day near the mother. Even when a special room has been equipped with attractive toys for the baby, the mother may find that these play objects are displaced to the vicinity of her feet as she stands washing dishes at the kitchen sink and that, in effect, her baby's recreation room is whatever room she is in at the time. Although proximity seems to be a rather simple pattern of stimuli, it is a potent social reinforcer for babies and young children.

Proximity may not remain potent. It may even reverse its function from being discriminative for positive stimulation to being discriminative for aversive stimulation under special circumstances. If, for example, a mother should become very punitive, giving more negative than positive reinforcers, her proximity becomes a discriminative stimulus for aversive stimulation or punishment. Proximity thereby acquires a negative reinforcing function which may override and displace its previously acquired positive function. The child may avoid her nearness. To put it simply, he cannot be spanked from a distance.

Paying Attention to the Baby. Just as the mother must be near in order to reinforce, she must also be attentive to present positive and remove negative reinforcers with any degree of effectiveness. It is difficult to imagine her feeding her baby, adjusting his clothes or blankets, or rescuing him from harm without paying some attention to him in the process. Her attention is another aspect of her behavior which, as a social stimulus, is discriminative for reinforcement for her baby. Like her proximity, her attention is a constellation of stimuli which will become increasingly established as a social reinforcer for her baby.

The physical components of attention are complex. One of the prominent features of attentive behavior involves *looking at the object or person* attended to. The attentive mother will often be a person whose face is pointed at the baby, the eyes aimed directly at him in a distance angle of convergence. Frequently, the mother's entire body will *turn toward the baby,* if she was oriented elsewhere just previously. This motion, too, will be a part of the act of attending. There may be characteristic *vocal stimuli,* such as "Hi, baby" or "What's wrong, baby?" *Facial changes* include the raising of eybrows in the fashion characteristic of adult interrogation. If the mother had previously been occupied with something else, there may be a sudden *cessation of other activity* as her attention is captured by the baby. These and similar stimuli are generated by the responses mother makes as she attends on various reinforcement occasions.

The stimuli she displays in paying attention are discriminative for the reinforcement procedures she practices, and will become discriminated by her baby. The variability in style of attending by various mothers will correspond to the various kinds of attention which will prove reinforcing to their children later in life. Thus some children may be more reinforced by a quiet audience and others may be more reinforced by highly talkative company. The differences in the kind of effective reinforcer may be due to mothers who attended quietly with the former group and noisily with the latter.

It should be pointed out that these differences may also be due to a more recent reinforcement history. For example, a baby may have had a quiet mother and thus be more reinforced by quiet attention than by noisy. However, later in school, he may find that when the teacher talks or reads to him, it is generally a positive state of affairs, but that when he talks (recites) to the quietly attentive teacher, he often receives correction and disapproval (and perhaps ridicule from unsympathetic classmates). These school experiences might well reverse his previous rank order of responsiveness to these two forms of attention.

In babies and young children the behaviors which are strengthened by attention are similar to those strengthened by proximity of a positive social reinforcer. Any behaviors on the part of the baby which are delightful, *or* irritating, or otherwise significant to the mother will attract her attention, and the behaviors involved in her paying attention to the baby are strengthened. Note that some of the baby's most effective behaviors in getting the mother's attention are crying, fussing, and fretting. These responses produce stimuli which constitute negative reinforcers to the mother. The mother, in an effort to terminate this type of behavior (and thereby escape from the negative reinforcers these sights and sounds constitute), will attend to the baby, seeking the stimulus or condition responsible for it. To the extent that such fussing involves operant behaviors (and this could be considerable), these behaviors are strengthened by her attention.

Situations involving slight frustrations for the baby (which initially elicit crying as a respondent process) become thus discriminative for the operant responses as a part of crying and fussing, since on such occasions these operants are frequently reinforced with the mother's attending behaviors. One possible result: fussing, as a discriminated operant, becomes a prevalent form of behavior of the baby. This type of outcome is distasteful to most mothers, yet it occurs frequently, for the mother becomes involved in a detrimental contingency. Since the baby's crying is a negative reinforcer for her, she attends to the baby and is immediately reinforced by the stopping of the crying. By so doing, she makes it more likely that *operant crying* will occur again on the next occasion of slight frustration for the baby. As *operant* crying grows in strength, the range of occasions on which it occurs increases correspondingly. If it is reinforced with mother's attention in these new situations, too, then it becomes generalized further to a greater variety of situations, and a disadvantageous cycle results, the outcome being a baby who cries in almost any situation.

For the mother, this situation may be a distressing state of affairs, yet she will in all probability continue to attend to such annoying behaviors, since she is reinforced for doing so by the temporary cessations of the baby's fussing behaviors. Simple extinction of crying (not attending) may serve to disrupt the cycle. Note, however, that the mother's behavior of attending to fussing must be inhibited at the same time. Note, too, that it would be desirable for the mother to be alert to reinforce at the same time the kinds of behaviors she would prefer to strengthen, such as asking or calling. Note, finally, that it would be highly inappropriate and even detrimental for the mother to cease attending to all of her baby's crying, since on some occasions it would represent responses (respondents) to genuinely harmful circumstances (aversive) from which she must rescue her baby.

This example illustrates a critical characteristic of mother's behavior in giving attention to her children.

"Bad" behavior is consistently attended to, in many instances more consistently than "good" behavior. To the extent that her attention functions as a positive reinforcer, any behaviors on the part of the baby, bad as well as good, that produce attention will be strengthened. If bad behaviors are more consistently attended to, they may well strengthen faster than the good ones. This simple formula suggests that a child's behavior may become increasingly and systematically more distasteful to his mother. That this frequently does *not* happen suggests the operation of other processes in addition to the one described here. However, that this frequently *does* happen suggests that the principle is a powerful one, and sometimes does operate more consistently than others which would produce a happier outcome.

Affection Toward the Baby. Some mothers are prompted to display affection by the reinforcing occasions involved in child rearing practices. On such occasions their affection takes the form of smiles, kisses, hugs, and pats, special crooning tones of voice, loving words, nuzzling, hair-ruffling, tickling, and similar behaviors associated with delighted and effusive parents. Other mothers are, by contrast, inclined to provide affection most reliably only when they are in the midst of an affectionate display generated by conditions not directly associated with child caring activities. In either situation there is a correlation between such stimuli and reinforcement which is sufficient to give the affectionate stimuli discriminative status. As with attention, the variability in individual mothers' styles of being affectionate will correspond to the kinds of affection which will prove maximally reinforcing for their children later. Thus, some children may be more responsive to smiles than to extravagant displays of hugging, kissing, and fondling; others may be more reinforced by an affectionate word or phrase; still others may be most susceptible to a pat on the head, and so on.

Few experimental studies have been conducted to provide specific information on affectionate stimuli, the range of their physical properties, the probable time of their initial effectiveness, etc. One study by Brackbill on smiling (1958) is described because it is instructive for further research in this area.

Brackbill's study of smiling in four-month-old infants was generated by her interest in the response in relation to its presumed social nature and its early role in social learning. The infants chosen were old enough to remain awake throughout the experimental sessions, young enough not to respond discriminatively to "mother" versus "others," placid enough not to cry too often during sessions and to lie on their backs for at least five minutes without struggling, and responsive enough to show an operant level of at least two smiles within a five-minute session. Brackbill does not give a verbal description of smiling, but reports that prior to the main study, she and another judge observed some 970 occasions of smiling or nonsmiling in infants, and agreed in 97.5% of their judgments.

Two limiting factors should be kept in mind in reviewing this study. First, smiling (like vocalization) is a lingering response in infants, which adds to the difficulty in perceiving changes in its rate. Second, limitations were imposed by the length of time it took to offer the social reinforcement given as a consequence of smiling: "Five seconds were required for picking S up; 30 seconds for reinforcement; five seconds for putting S down; and five seconds for recording. Therefore, no more than six responses could occur and be reinforced during any five-minute interval."

Despite these less than ideal conditions, the experimental conditions, which consisted of (1) an operant level period, (2) a conditioning period (of either continuous or intermittent reinforcement), and (3) an extinction period, produced differences in smiling frequencies. The operant level was taken as the rate observed through at least eight separate five-minute intervals, during which the investigator stood motionless over the infant (who lay on his back in his crib), and maintained an expressionless face at about 15 inches from the infant's face. During conditioning sessions (consisting of 10 to 12 five-minute intervals), the investigator reinforced smiling by smiling at, picking up, and cuddling the infant, using continuous reinforcement with one group and working steadily from continuous to variable ratios of 1, 2, 3, and 4 with another group. (These behaviors typify the activities of many affectionate mothers.) Extinction was similar to the operant level condition, and was observed over 15 or more five-minute intervals.

The rate of smiling during the conditioning period was reliably higher than the rate during the operant level. During extinction, the intermittently reinforced group extinguished less rapidly; both groups fell below their previous operant level rate of smiling, and both displayed "protest" behavior to the unsmiling investigator, crying or turning away from her.

All subjects were studied immediately after nursing and following a nap. The mother in each case phoned Brackbill when her infant awoke, and Brackbill arrived at the infant's home to work with a freshly diapered infant just satiated with food. The mother cooperated to the extent of engaging in minimal contact with the infant prior to each experimental session. The study took place in the infant's own home and crib.

Returning to the general concept of affection, it seems that affection is a much more variable stimulus constellation than is either proximity or attention. It is variable to the point of being entirely absent in some mothers. It is clear that in order for a mother to reinforce, she must be both near and attentive, but she need not be affectionate. Some mothers are not characteristically affectionate, and their children should be quite unresponsive to affection. However, they may be well reinforced by both the proximity and attention of adults. The literature of clinical child psychology is rich in descriptions of children who are "social," in that they are extremely sensitive to having an audience, but "psychopathic," in that the respect or affection of that audience is entirely without value to them. Such a child might well have a history in which displays of affection were never discriminative for other reinforcers.

For children with mothers who have made their affection discriminative to the baby for the other reinforcers in caretaking activities, affection operates as a positive reinforcer. It serves as an important stimulus in the developing behavior of these children because it is not ordinarily used to strengthen bad behavior (as attention and proximity often are). The mother may not be able to avoid attending to the baby's undesirable behavior, bringing herself in close proximity to him, but she is unlikely to meet it with affection. In fact, she is much more likely to cease all displays of affection on occasions that displease her. Because the withdrawal or loss of a positive reinforcer acts to weaken any preceding operant behavior, bad behaviors may be weakened more by the mother's withdrawal of affection than they are strengthened through her attention.

The ease of giving affection for good behavior, and the natural tendency not to present it and to withdraw it when confronted with bad behavior, set up situations which strengthen selectively those behaviors which please the mother, rather than those which displease her. This line of reasoning suggests that children who are maximally responsive to affection as a positive reinforcer are more readily influenced by the mother's goals for them than are children more responsive to her attention than to her affection.

References

Brackbill, Yvonne. Extinction of the smiling response in infants as a function of reinforcement schedule. *Child Development,* 1958, *29,* 115–124.

Gewirtz, J. L. Three determinants of attention-seeking in young children. *Monographs of the Society for Research in Child Development,* 1954, *19,* No. 2.

Gewirtz, J. L. A learning analysis of the effects of normal stimulation, privation and deprivation on the acquisition of social motivation and attachment. In B. M. Moss (Ed.), *Determinants of infant behavior.* New York: Wiley, 1961.

Gibson, J. J. *The perception of the visual world.* Boston: Houghton Mifflin, 1950.

In the final article of this chapter, *Skinner* argues that man's culture, which is a product of his own behavior, is as much subject to empirical analysis, experimentation, and practical change as any other natural phenomenon. He goes on to plead that the knowledge of human behavior gained both from the experimental laboratory and from a natural-science conception of human nature is an effective tool for studying, redesigning, and implementing changes in our basic cultural institutions. He further argues that a natural-science approach emphasizing the functional properties of the behavior of individuals is the most useful way to proceed with the task. We can see in this article some of the ways in which broad issues of cultural practices and human institutions are analyzed from a behavioral point of view. Skinner argues for the use of an experimental approach to behavior as the basic conceptual and descriptive tool in analyzing government as well as religious, economic, educational, and therapeutic institutions. He assumes that cultural institutions are products of individual behavior—natural events in a natural world which can best be understood by objective principles of behavior. It follows, then, that man can apply his technical knowledge about human behavior to the design of the very institutions which have shaped his conduct in the same way that he has applied natural, physical, and biological principles to shape and mold the physical environment in which he lives.

4 | *The Design of Cultures*

B. F. SKINNER

Anyone who undertakes to improve cultural practices by applying a scientific analysis of human behavior is likely to be told that improvement involves a value judgment beyond the pale of his science and that he is exemplifying objectionable values by proposing to meddle in human affairs and infringe on human freedoms. Scientists themselves often accept this standard contention of Western philosophy, even though it implies that there is a kind of wisdom which is mysteriously denied to them and even though the behavioral scientists among them would be hard pressed to give an empirical account of such wisdom or to discover its sources.

The proposition gains unwarranted strength from the fact that it appears to champion the natural against the artificial. Man is a product of nature, the argument runs, but societies are contrived by men. Man is the measure of all things, and our plans for him—our customs and institutions—will succeed only if they allow for his nature. To this it might be answered that man is more than an immutable product of biological processes; he is a psychological entity, and as such also largely man-made. His cause may be as contrived as society's and possibly as weak. He is, nevertheless, an individual, and his defenders are individuals, too, who may borrow zeal in his defense from their own role in the great conflict between the one and the many. To side with the individual against the state, to take a specific example, is reassuringly to defend one's own, even though it might be answered that mankind has won its battles only because individual men have lost theirs.

These are merely answers in kind, which can no doubt be met with plausible rejoinders. The disputing of values is not only possible, it is interminable. To escape from it we must get outside the system. We can do this by developing an empirical account of the behavior of both protagonists. All objections to cultural design, like design itself, are forms of human behavior and may be studied as such. It is possible that a plausible account of the design of cultures will allay our traditional anxieties and prepare the way for the effective use of man's intelligence in the construction of his own future.

It is reasonable to hope that a scientific analysis will someday satisfactorily explain how cultural practices arise and are transmitted and how they affect those who engage in them, possibly to further the survival of the practices themselves or at least to contribute to their successors. Such an analysis will embrace the fact that men talk about their cultures and sometimes change them. Changing a culture is itself a cultural practice, and we must know as much as possible about it if we are to question it intelligently. Under what circumstances do men redesign—or, to use a discredited term, reform—their way of life? What is the nature of their behavior in doing so? Is the deliberate manipulation of a culture a threat to the very essence of man or, at the other extreme, an unfathomed source of strength for the culture which encourages it?

We need not go into the details of a scientific account of behavior to see how it bears on this issue. Its contribution must, however, be distinguished from any help to be drawn from historical analogy or the extrapolation of historical trends or cycles, as well as from interpretations based on sociological principles or structures. Such an account must make contact with biology, on the one hand, but serve in an interpretation of social phenomena, on the other. If it is to yield a satisfactory analysis of the design and implementation of social practices, it must be free of a particular defect. Evolutionary theory, especially in its appeal to the notion of survival, suffered for a long time from circularity. It was not satisfying to argue that forms of life which had survived must therefore have had survival value and had survived because of it. A similar weakness is inherent in psychologies based on adjustment or adaptation. It is not satisfying to argue that a man adapts to a new environment because of his intelligence and emotional stability if these are then defined in terms of capacities to adapt. It is true that organisms usually develop in directions which maximize, phylogenetically, the survival of the species and, ontogenetically, the adjustment of the individual; but the mechanisms responsible for both kinds of change need to be explained without recourse to the selective effect of their consequences.

In biology this is now being done. Genetics clarifies and supports evolutionary theory with new kinds of facts, and in doing so eliminates the circularity in the

---

Reprinted by permission from *Daedalus,* Journal of the American Academy of Arts and Sciences, Boston, Massachusetts, 1961, Volume 90, Number 3, pp. 534–546.

concept of survival. A comparable step in the study of human behavior is to analyze the mechanisms of human action apart from their contribution to personal and cultural adjustment. It is not enough to point out that a given form of behavior is advantageous to the individual or that a cultural practice strengthens the group. We must explain the origin and the perpetuation of both behavior and practice.

A scientific analysis which satisfies these conditions confines itself to individual organisms rather than statistical constructs or interacting groups of organisms, even in the study of social behavior. Its basic datum is the probability of the occurrence of the observable events we call behavior (or of inferred events having the same dimensions). The probability of behavior is accounted for by appeal to the genetic endowment of the organism and its past and present environments, described wholly in the language of physics and biology. The laboratory techniques of such an analysis, and their technological applications, emphasize the prediction and control of behavior via the manipulation of variables. Validation is found primarily in the success with which the subject matter can be controlled.

An example of how such an analysis differs from its predecessors is conveniently at hand. An important group of variables which modify behavior have to do with the consequences of action. "Rewards" and "punishments" are variables of this sort, though rather inadequately identified by those terms. We are interested in the fact (apart from any theory which explains it) that by arranging certain consequences—that is, by making certain kinds of events *contingent upon behavior*—we achieve a high degree of experimental control.[1] Our present understanding of the so-called "contingencies of reinforcement" is undoubtedly incomplete, but it nevertheless permits us to construct new forms of behavior, to bring behavior under the control of new aspects of the environment, and to maintain it under such control for long periods of time—and all of this often with surprising ease. Extrapolation to less rigorously controlled samples of behavior outside the laboratory has already led to promising technological developments.

But the importance of the principle is embarrassing. Almost any instance of human behavior involves contingencies of reinforcement, and those who have been alerted to their significance by laboratory studies often seem fanatical in pointing them out. Yet behavior *is* important mainly because of its consequences. We may more readily accept this fact if we recall the ubiquity of the concept of purpose. The experimental study of reinforcing contingencies is nothing more than a nonteleological analysis of the *directed effects* of behavior, of relations which have traditionally been described as purpose. By manipulating contingencies of reinforcement in ways which conform to standard practices in the physical sciences, we study and use them without appealing to final causes.

We can put this reinterpretation of purpose to immediate use, for it bears on a confusion between the phylogenetic and the ontogenetic development of behavior which has clouded our thinking about the origin and growth of cultures. Contingencies of reinforcement are similar to what we might call contingencies of survival. Inherited patterns of behavior must have been selected by their contributions to survival in ways which are not unlike those in which the behavior of the individual is selected or shaped by its reinforcing consequences. Both processes exemplify adaptation or adjustment, but very different mechanisms must be involved.

The evolution of inherited forms of behavior is as plausible as the evolution of any function of the organism when the environment can be regarded as reasonably stable. The internal environment satisfies this requirement, and a genetic endowment of behavior related to the internal economy—say, peristalsis or sneezing—is usually accepted without question. The external environment is much less stable from generation to generation, but some kinds of responses to it are also plausibly explained by evolutionary selection. The genetic mechanisms are presumably similar to those which account for other functions. But environments change, and any process which permits an organism to modify its behavior is then important. The structures which permit modification must have evolved when organisms were being selected by their survival in novel environments.

Although the mechanisms which permit modification of behavior are inherited, learned behavior does not emerge from, and is not an extension of, the unlearned behavior of the individual. The organism does not simply refine or extend a genetic behavioral endowment to make it more effective or more inclusive. Instead, it develops collateral behavior, which must be distinguished from an inherited response system even when both serve similar functions. It is important to remember this when considering social behavior. In spite of certain intriguing analogies,

[1] To a hungry organism food is a reinforcement. An experimenter "makes food contingent on a response" by connecting the response with the operation of a food magazine. For example, if the response is pressing a lever, the lever may be made to close a switch which operates a magazine electrically. The receipt of food is said to reinforce pressing the lever.

it is not likely that the social institutions of man are founded on or that they emerged from the instinctive patterns of animal societies. They are the achievements of individuals, modifying their behavior as inherited mechanisms permit. The coordinated activities of the anthill or beehive operate on very different principles from those of a family, a large company, or a great city. The two kinds of social behavior must have developed through different processes, and they are maintained in force for different reasons.

To take a specific example, verbal behavior is not a refinement upon instinctive cries of alarm, distress, and so on, even though the reinforcing contingencies in the one case are analogous to the conditions of survival in the other. Both may be said to serve similar adaptive functions, but the mechanisms involved in acquiring verbal behavior clearly set it apart from instinctive responses. The innate vocal endowment of an organism is indeed particularly refractory to modification, most if not all verbal responses being modifications of a nonspecific behavioral endowment.

In general, the evolution of man has emphasized modifiability rather than the transmission of specific forms of behavior. Inherited verbal or other social responses are fragmentary and trivial. By far the greater part of behavior develops in the individual through processes of conditioning, given a normal biological endowment. Man becomes a social creature only because other men are important parts of his environment. The behavior of a child born into a flourishing society is shaped and maintained by variables, most of which are arranged by other people. These social variables compose the "culture" in which the child lives, and they shape his behavior in conformity with that culture, usually in such a way that he in turn tends to perpetuate it. The behavioral processes present no special problems. Nevertheless, a satisfactory account calls for some explanation of how a social environment can have arisen from nonsocial precursors. This may seem to raise the hoary question of the origin of society, but we have no need to reconstruct an actual historical event or even a speculative beginning, such as a social compact from which conclusions about the nature of society can be drawn. We have only to show that a social environment could have emerged from nonsocial conditions. As in explaining the origin of life, we cannot discover an actual historical event but must be satisfied with a demonstration that certain structures with their associated functions could have arisen under plausible conditions.

The emergence of a given form of social behavior from nonsocial antecedents is exemplified by imitation. Inherited imitative behavior is hard to demonstrate. The parrot may possibly owe its distinction only to an inherited capacity to be reinforced by the production of imitative sounds. In any case, an inherited repertoire of imitative behavior in man is insignificant, compared with the product of certain powerful contingencies of reinforcement which establish and maintain behaving-as-others-behave. For example, if organism *A* sees organism *B* running in obvious alarm, *A* will probably avoid aversive consequences by running in the same direction. Or, if *A* sees *B* picking and eating ripe berries, *A* will probably be reinforced for approaching the same berry patch. Thousands of instances of this sort compose a general contingency providing for the reinforcement of doing-as-others-do. In this sense, behavior exemplifying imitation is acquired, yet it is practically inevitable whenever two or more organisms live in contact with one another. The essential conditions are not in themselves social.

Most social behavior, however, arises from social antecedents. Transmission is more important than social invention. Unlike the origin of cultural practices, their transmission need not be a matter for speculation, since the process can be observed. Deliberate transmission (that is, transmission achieved because of practices which have been reinforced by their consequences) is not needed. For example, some practices are perpetuated as the members of a group are severally replaced. If *A* has already developed specific controlling behavior with respect to *B*, depending partly upon incidental characteristics of *B*'s behavior, he may impose the same control on a new individual, *C*, who might not himself have generated just the same practices in *A*. A mother who has shaped the vocal responses of her first baby into a primitive verbal repertoire may bring already established contingencies to bear on a second child. A leader who has acquired aversive controlling practices in his interactions with a submissive follower may take by storm a second follower even though, without this preparation, the leader-follower relation might have been reversed in the second case. Overlapping group membership is, of course, only one factor contributing to manners, customs, folkways, and other abiding features of a social environment.

These simple examples are offered not as solutions to important problems but to illustrate an approach to the analysis of social behavior and to the design of a culture. A special kind of social behavior emerges when *A* responds in a definite way *because of the effect on the behavior of B*. We must consider the importance of *B* to *A* as well as of *A* to *B*. For example, when *A* sees *B* looking into a store window, he is likely to be reinforced if he looks too, as in the example of the berry patch. But if his looking is important to *B*, or to a third person who controls *B*, a change may take place in *B*'s behavior. *B* may look into the window in order to induce *A* to do the same. The carnival shill plays on the behavior of prospective customers in this way. *B*'s behavior is no longer controlled by what is seen in the window but (directly or indirectly) by the effect of that behavior on *A*. (The original contingencies for *A* break down: the window may not now be "worth looking into.") Action taken by *A* because of its effect on the behavior of *B* may be called "personal control." An important subdivision is verbal behavior, the properties of which derive from the fact that reinforcements are mediated by other organisms. (Skinner, 1957). Another subdivision is cultural design.

In analyzing any social episode from this point of view a complete account must be given of the behaviors of both parties as they contribute to the origin and maintenance of the behavior of each other. For example, in analyzing a verbal episode, we must account for both speaker and listener. This is seldom done in the case of nonverbal personal control. In noticing how the master controls the slave or the employer the worker, we commonly overlook reciprocal effects and, by considering action in one direction only, are led to regard control as exploitation, or at least the gaining of a onesided advantage; but the control is actually mutual. The slave controls the master as completely as the master the slave, in the sense that the techniques of punishment employed by the master have been selected by the slave's behavior in submitting to them. This does not mean that the notion of exploitation is meaningless or that we may not appropriately ask, *Cui bono?* In doing so, however, we go beyond the account of the social episode itself and consider certain long-term effects which are clearly related to the question of value judgments. A comparable consideration arises in the analysis of any behavior which alters a cultural practice.

We may not be satisfied with an explanation of the behavior of two parties in a social interaction. The slaves in a quarry cutting stone for a pyramid work to escape punishment or death, and the rising pyramid is sufficiently reinforcing to the reigning pharaoh to induce him to devote part of his wealth to maintaining the forces which punish or kill. An employer pays sufficient wages to induce men to work for him, and the products of their labor reimburse him, let us say, with a great deal to spare. These are on-going social systems, but in thus analyzing them we may not have taken everything into account. The system may be altered by outsiders in whom sympathy with, or fear of, the lot of the slave or exploited worker may be generated. More important, perhaps, is the possibility that the system may not actually be in equilibrium. It may breed changes which lead to its destruction. Control through punishment may lead to increasing viciousness, with an eventual loss of the support of those needed to maintain it; and the increasing poverty of the worker and the resulting increase in the economic power of the employer may also lead to countercontrolling action.

A culture which raises the question of collateral or deferred effects is most likely to discover and adopt practices which will survive or, as conditions change, will lead to modifications which in turn will survive. This is an important step in cultural design, but it is not easily taken. Long-term consequences are usually not obvious, and there is little inducement to pay any attention to them. We may admire a man who submits to aversive stimulation for the sake of later reinforcement or who eschews immediate reinforcement to avoid later punishment, but the contingencies which lead him to be "reasonable" in this sense (our admiration is part of them) are by no means overpowering. It has taken civilized societies a long time to invent the verbal devices—the precepts of morals and ethics—which successfully promote such an outcome. Ultimate advantages seem to be particularly easy to overlook in the control of behavior, where a quick though slight advantage may have undue weight. Thus, although we boast that the birch rod has been abandoned, most school children are still under aversive control—not because punishment is more effective in the long run, but because it yields immediate results. It is easier for the teacher to control the student by threatening punishment than by using positive reinforcement with its deferred, though more powerful, effects.

A culture which has become sensitive to the long-term consequences of its measures is usually supported by a literature or philosophy which includes a set of statements expressing the relations between measures and consequences. To the cultural designer, these statements function as prescriptions for effective action; to the members of the group, they are important variables furthering effective self-management. (To both, and to the neutral observer, they are sometimes said to "justify" a measure, but this may mean nothing more than strengthening the measure by classifying it with certain kinds of events characteristically called "good" or "right.") Thus, a government may induce its citizens to submit to the hardship and tragedy of war by picturing a future in which the world is made safe for democracy or free of Communism, or to a program of austerity by pointing to economic changes which will eventually lead to an abundance of good things for all. In so doing, it strengthens certain behavior on the part of its citizens which is essential to its purposes, and the resulting gain in power reinforces the government's own concern for deferred effects and its efforts to formulate them.

The scientific study of behavior underlines the collateral effects of controlling practices and reveals unstable features of a given interaction which may lead to long-deferred consequences. It may dictate effective remedial or preventive measures. It does not do this, however, by taking the scientist out of the causal stream. The scientist also is the product of a genetic endowment and an environmental history. He also is controlled by the culture or cultures to which he belongs. Doing-something-about-human-behavior is a kind of social action, and its products and by-products must be understood accordingly.

A reciprocal relationship between the knower and the known, common to all the sciences, is important here. A laboratory for the study of behavior contains many devices for controlling the environment and for recording and analyzing the behavior of organisms. With the help of these devices and their associated techniques, we change the behavior of an organism in various ways, with considerable precision. *But note that the organism changes our behavior in quite as precise a fashion.* Our apparatus was designed by the organism we study, for it was the organism which led us to choose a particular manipulandum, particular categories of stimulation, particular modes of reinforcement, and so on, and to record particular aspects of its behavior. Measures which were successful were for that reason reinforcing and have been retained, while others have been, as we say, extinguished. The verbal behavior with which we analyze our data has been shaped in a similar way: order and consistency emerged to reinforce certain practices which were adopted, while other practices suffered extinction and were abandoned. (All scientific techniques, as well as scientific knowledge itself, are generated in this way. A cyclotron is "designed" by the particles it is to control, and a theory is written by the particles it is to explain, as the behavior of these particles shapes the nonverbal and verbal behavior of the scientist.)

A similarly reciprocal effect is involved in social action, especially in cultural design. Governmental, religious, economic, educational, and therapeutic institutions have been analyzed in many ways—for example, as systems which exalt such entities as sovereignty, virtue, utility, wisdom, and health. There is a considerable advantage in considering these institutions simply as behavioral technologies. Each one uses an identifiable set of techniques for the control of human behavior, distinguished by the variables manipulated. The discovery and invention of such techniques and their later abandonment or continued use—in short, their evolution—are, or should be, a part of the history of technology. The issues they raise, particularly with respect to the behavior of the discoverer or inventor, are characteristic of technology in general.

Both physical and behavioral technologies have shown progress or improvement in the sense that new practices have been discovered or invented and tested and that some of them have survived because their effects were reinforcing. Men have found better ways, not only to dye a cloth or build a bridge, but to govern, teach, and employ. The conditions under which all such practices originate range from sheer accident to the extremely complex behaviors called thinking. (Skinner, 1953). The conditions under which they are tested and selected are equally diverse. Certain immediate personal advantages may well have been the only important variables in the behavior of the primitive inventors of both physical and cultural devices. But the elaboration of moral and ethical practices has reduced the importance of personal aggrandizement. The honorific reinforcements with which society encourages action for the common weal, as well as the sanctions it applies to selfish behavior, generate a relatively disinterested creativity. Even in the field of personal control, improvements may be proposed, not for immediate exploitation, but—as by religious leaders, benevolent rulers, political philosophers, and educators—for "the good of all."

Only an analysis of moral and ethical practices will clarify the behavior of the cultural designer at this stage. He has faced a special difficulty in the fact that it is easier to demonstrate the right way to build a bridge than the right way to treat one's fellowmen (the difference reducing to the immediacy and clarity of the results). The cultural inventor, even though relatively disinterested, has found it necessary to appeal for support to secular or divine authorities, supposedly inviolable philosophical premises, and even to military persuasion. Nothing of the sort has been needed for the greater part of physical technology. The wheel was not propagated by the sword or by promises of salvation—it made its own way. Cultural practices have survived or fallen only in part because of their effect on the strength of the group, and those which have survived are usually burdened with unnecessary impedimenta. By association, the current designer is handicapped by the fact that men look behind any cultural invention for irrelevant, ingenuous, or threatening forces.

There is another step in physical technology, however, which must have a parallel in cultural design. The practical application of scientific knowledge shows a new kind of disinterestedness. The scientist is usually concerned with the control of nature apart from his personal aggrandizement. He is perhaps not wholly "pure," but he seeks control mainly for its own sake or for the sake of furthering other scientific activity. There are practical as well as ethical reasons for this: as technology becomes more complex, for example, the scientist himself is less and less able to pursue the practical implications of his work. There is very little personal reimbursement for the most profitable ideas of modern science. As a result, a new idea may yield immediate technological improvements without bringing the scientist under suspicion of plotting a personal coup. But social technology has not yet reached this stage. A disinterested consideration of cultural practices from which suggestions for improvement may emerge is still often regarded as impossible. This is the price we pay for the fact that men (1) have so often improved their control of other men for purposes of exploitation, (2) have had to bolster their social practices with spurious justifications and (3) have so seldom shared the attitudes of the basic scientist.

Most people would subscribe to the proposition that there is no value judgment involved in deciding how to build an atomic bomb, but would reject the proposition that there is none involved in deciding to build one. The most significant difference here may be that the scientific practices which guide the designer of the bomb are clear, while those which guide the designer of the culture which builds a bomb are not. We cannot predict the success or failure of a cultural invention with the same accuracy as we do that of a physical invention. It is for this reason that we are said to resort to value judgments in the second case. What we resort to is guessing. It is only in this sense that value judgments take up where science leaves off. When we can design small social interactions and, possibly, whole cultures with the confidence we bring to physical technology, the question of value will not be raised.

So far, men have designed their cultures largely by guesswork, including some very lucky hits; but we are not far from a stage of knowledge in which this can be changed. The change does not require that we be able to describe some distant state of mankind toward which we are moving or "deciding" to move. Early physical technology could not have foreseen the modern world, though it led to it. Progress and improvement are local changes. We better ourselves and our world as we go.

We change our cultural practices because it is in our nature as men to be reinforced in certain ways. This is not an infallible guide. It could, indeed, lead to fatal mistakes. For example, we have developed sanitation and medical science to escape from aversive events associated with illness and death, yet a new virus could conceivably arise to wipe out everyone except those to whom chronic illness and filth had granted immunity. On the present evidence, our decision in favor of sanitation and medicine seems to make for survival, but in the light of unforeseeable developments we may in time look back upon it as having had no survival value.

From time to time, men have sought to reassure themselves about the future by characterizing progress as the working out of some such principle as the general will, universal or collective reason, or the greatest good. Such a principle, if valid, would seem to guarantee an inevitable, if devious, improvement in the human condition. No such principle is clearly supported by a scientific analysis of human behavior. Yet the nature of man tells us something. Just as an ultimate genetic effect cannot be reached if immediate effects are not beneficial, so we must look only to the immediate consequences of behavior for modifications in a cultural pattern. Nevertheless, cultural inventions have created current conditions which have at least a probabilistic connection with future consequences. It is easy to say that men work for pleasure and to avoid pain, as the hedonists would have it. These are, indeed, powerful principles; but in affecting the day-to-day behavior of men, they have led to the construction of cultural devices which extend the range of both pleasure and pain almost beyond recognition. It is the same man, biologically speaking, who acts selfishly or for the good of the group, and it is the same man who, as a disinterested scientist, will make human behavior vastly more effective through cultural invention.

References

SKINNER, B. F. *Science and human behavior.* New York: Macmillan, 1953.

SKINNER, B. F. *Verbal behavior.* New York: Appleton-Century-Crofts, 1957.

The Social Reinforcement Process

2

One aspect of human behavior that sets it off from the behavior of lower forms is its relatively greater plasticity. Even among animals, of course, we can observe that the environment produces wider behavioral changes with some performances and some species than with others. For example, there are fewer ways in which a pigeon can peck at a key than there are ways a rat can press a lever. This is due in part to the nature of the manipulandum—the key or disc which the bird pecks at versus a lever—and in part to the structures of the two organisms. The key moves in only one direction in response to a peck, while the lever may move in any of several directions, depending upon how it is hinged. The pigeon must manipulate the key with its beak, whereas the rat can use any of its four feet as well as its teeth to move the lever. In fact, we arrange our experimental equipment with a view to the physical capabilities of the animal subject. Primates, for example, may be presented with problems that can be solved only when they manipulate appropriate toggle switches, something that neither a pigeon nor a rat is equipped by nature to do. Humans, due primarily to their more highly developed nervous systems, are capable of incomparably more complex behaviors than we can observe in other species.

Among humans, as well as animals, a great variety of topographically different responses may produce essentially the same effect on the environment. There are many ways of throwing a ball, of swimming, of writing, or of speaking. As long as the ball reaches its target, or the swimmer makes progress in the water, or the written material secures a reader, or the speaker is attended to by a listener, it matters little that some of the performances were highly idiosyncratic. Joe Kapp's passes may wobble more than Joe Namath's, but if they reach the intended receiver, the net effect is scarcely less. A manuscript typed with two fingers may evoke as much reader interest as one produced by the "touch" system. In short, the consequences of a performance, rather than its form, determine its future rate. Very often a response that is grossly inept and inefficient comes to be repeated simply because it is positively reinforced. A rat that is initially rewarded with food when it hangs from the top of the cage and kicks the lever with its feet may continue to operate the food magazine in this manner indefinitely. Similarly, a human who has developed an awkward tennis stroke or an unusual speech mannerism may persist in these behaviors so long as they produce reinforcing consequences from the environment. Many superstitions continue for similar reasons.

Some responses, like the patellar (knee-jerk) reflex, are regular and predictable; they follow an immediately preceding stimulus. Others, like those that occur in word association, are not controlled in such a simple fashion. The patellar reflex is *elicited* by a light blow to the patellar tendon, whereas a verbal association is said to be *prompted* by the stimulus word. Nevertheless, word associations may be highly predictable—as in the case of associating "white" to "black." In other cases complex responses may become more predictable when we learn how to unravel some of the complexities. Operant behavior is usually less predictable than reflex behavior because the prompting stimulus may not be identifiable. Even when the stimulus can be identified, the correlated performance may not occur. For example, a food-deprived rat may press a lever to produce food, but there is no stimulus before the fact that will elicit the performance; one can only provide a lever and wait for the inherent (or operant) frequency of performance which might move it.

Virtually all social behavior is of the operant variety. A social act occurs in the presence of relevant stimuli and it has consequences that vary widely in predictability. A variety of terms that have come into usage—interest, purpose, value, choice, intention, attitude, and so forth—appear very different from a behavioral, or stimulus-response, description of the same behaviors. The principle difference between the two approaches, one cognitive and the other behavioral, lies in the extent to which the actual behavior is described and the extent to which it is referred to internal, mediating processes. We infer a person's interests and values on the basis of his activities; we retrospectively discern his purposes and intentions from his actual performances; we predict his choices from knowledge of how he has responded to similar alternatives in the past; we assign attitudes to him on the basis of his behavior with respect to certain classes of social stimuli. Behavioral descriptions have an advantage over mentalistic terms because they emphasize an objective analysis of specific performances and their outcomes.

Our purpose in this chapter is to present several examples of research in which the essential properties of social situations have been abstracted and where control has been exerted over the stimuli that both prompt and reinforce particular forms of social behavior. These experiments show how complex social processes can be studied in simpler versions, and how they may be rendered susceptible to a functional analysis through relatively precise manipulation and control of the relevant variables.

Basic Principles of Response Acquisition

The experiment reported by *Sidowski, Wyckoff, and Tabory* examines the proposition that social reinforcement can effectively modify the behavior of subjects without their understanding what is being done. Pairs of subjects, isolated from one another and unaware of each other's presence, pressed either one of two buttons in order to score points on an electrical counter. Actually, each subject delivered either a point or an electric shock to the other, depending on which of the two buttons he pressed. A strong and a weak shock were used to assess the effects of magnitude of punishment on behavior.

Under strong shock conditions the subjects quickly adjusted their choices so as to secure points rather than punishment nearly 65 per cent of the time. The authors analyze the findings in terms of the several possible combinations of responses that might be made by the two subjects. Of these several alternatives, the only one that is consistently reinforced for each subject is pressing the button that provides points rather than punishment to the other. The experimenters made no inferences concerning awareness or other mediating processes, since they had no information on which to base such inferences. The authors imply that social situations even more complex than this may also be interpretable in terms of reinforcement theory, without recourse to cognitive variables. As we shall see in subsequent articles, cognitive and mediating factors may refer to actual forms of conduct that occur in complex situations which can, in turn, be analyzed behaviorally.

5 *The Influence of Reinforcement and Punishment in a Minimal Social Situation*[1]

JOSEPH B. SIDOWSKI
L. BENJAMIN WYCKOFF
LEON TABORY

The study of conditioning in the laboratory, and the development of conditioning theory (Keller and Schoenfeld, 1950; Skinner, 1938, 1953), are justified in part by the hope that the principles derived will ultimately enhance our understanding of human behavior in complex situations, including social ones. The realization of such hopes is commonly relegated to some future time, and the path along which we expect to proceed is specified in the vaguest terms. In attempting to approach this problem, several questions may be raised: (*a*) Is it possible to handle social behavior within the framework of current conditioning theory, and if not, at what point along a scale of increasing complexity is it necessary to introduce additional concepts? (*b*) What new conceptual and analytical tools are necessary to handle the additional complexity encountered?

In the present study we attempt to re-evaluate the essential features of a social situation as viewed entirely within the framework of conditioning theory, and to investigate the simplest situation that could be considered truly social within this framework. In this way, we hope to lay the groundwork for a systematic investigation of social situations of increasing

From the *Journal of Abnormal and Social Psychology*, 1956, *52*, 115–119.

complexity, and to clarify methodological and theoretical problems. Analysis of social behavior in these terms implies that no assumption whatever is to be made regarding such concepts as attitude, understanding, awareness, etc. If such factors enter the picture at all, they are to be considered as manifestations of complex habits. Preferably, they will not be encountered at all in the minimal social situation, and in any event cannot be part of the definition of social behavior.

When restrictions such as these are accepted, we arrive at a conception of social behavior that will, no doubt, seem strange to most social psychologists. However, we gain the advantage of having a system that allows for a high level of objectivity in our definitions and principles, and one that is readily related to the mass of careful investigations of conditioning (Keller and Schoenfeld, 1950; McGeoch and Irion, 1952; Skinner, 1938, 1953). In this analysis we will assume that the main factors controlling social behavior are reinforcement (reward) and punishment. Within this framework, the essential features of a social situation may be expressed as follows: (*a*) Two or more Ss have at their disposal responses which result in reinforcing or punishing effects on other Ss. (*b*) The principal sources of reinforcement and punishment for any S depend on responses made by other Ss. (*c*) The responses controlling reinforcement and punishment are subject to learning through trial and error. We will assume that, whatever else may be involved, at least the above features are present in any social situation. At this point we may ask what learning would be predicted on the basis of these conditions alone, assuming only that the principles of conditioning theory are operating. In the present experiment an attempt was made to place Ss in a situation involving only these minimal features.

Two Ss isolated from each other were provided with push buttons by means of which each could give the other reinforcement or punishment (score or shock). The effects of previous social learning were minimized, since Ss were not told (nor did they guess) that they were in a social situation at all.

In this situation, if S makes a response, he does not "suffer the consequences" directly. An S can influence the reinforcing and punishing features of his environment only to the extent that his actions may change the behavior of the other S. Thus, if *A* makes a response which results in a reinforcement for *B*, we may expect *B* to continue with, or to repeat, his immediately preceding behavior. Similarly, if *A* makes a response which results in a punishment for *B*, we may expect *B* to tend to discontinue his immediately preceding activity. In addition, when *B* receives punishment, we will also expect an increase in his over-all activity level. These changes in *B*'s behavior have a direct effect on the reinforcement and punishment being received by *A*. Thus *A* does receive some consequences of his responses through an indirect but not entirely unlawful process.

It is not intended that this situation should be directly comparable to familiar everyday encounters. We generally enter social situations already equipped with a massive amount of prior learning relating to the effects of our behavior on others. For example, we have stylized ways of indicating approval or disapproval that are in effect methods of reinforcing or punishing others. On the other hand, in many situations, the responses we have learned are no longer appropriate. For example, an adult who has had little experience with children may find that his habitual ways of expressing approval and disapproval are completely ineffective when he first begins to interact with a child. As he gains experience he learns new responses. Other illustrations could be cited. One occasionally encounters adults who react negatively to conventional reinforcements or punishments. The process through which this learning and relearning takes place will be central to any extension of conditioning theory into the realm of social behavior. We may ask, is face-to-face contact and "understanding" of the relationship between Ss necessary for this learning or would such learning occur simply as a result of the operation of reinforcement and punishment? It is questions such as these which we hope to answer through the present research program. The first step in this program is an investigation of behavior in the minimal situation.

The Experiment. As indicated above, two Ss, isolated from each other, were given the opportunity to make responses which resulted in reinforcement or punishment (score or shock) for the other S. The general objective of the experiment was to discover what the course of learning would be under these conditions. It seemed likely that one of the most important parameters which would affect performance would be the magnitude of punishment used. Thus, two widely separated levels of shock were used for different groups of Ss.

Method

Subjects. The Ss were 40 members of elementary psychology courses at the University of Wisconsin who received class points for participating.

Apparatus. The two experimental rooms were each equipped with a control panel which provided two push buttons, an electrically operated counter, and a pair of electrodes. The right and left buttons in Room 1 controlled the counter and shock circuit in Room 2, and vice versa. Thus, pressing the right-hand button in Room 1 registered one point on the counter in Room 2, while pressing the left-hand button in Room 1 delivered an electric shock to the electrodes in Room 2. Similarly, the buttons in Room 2 controlled the counter and shock in Room 1, except that the right and left buttons had the opposite effect. A small red light also blinked each time the counter was activated, and a white light served as a signal that the experiment had begun. The white light remained on until the session ended. The *E*'s control board contained counters which indicated the number of times that each of the four buttons had been pressed.

An electronic circuit provided for regulation of the shock current and automatic compensation for changes in S's resistance. Separate controls were available for each of the two Ss.

Procedure. The 40 Ss, 20 pairs, were randomly assigned to two groups of 10 pairs each. The Strong-Shock group received shock current equal to 200 per cent of their absolute threshold, while the Weak-Shock group received 110 per cent of the threshold reading. Preliminary tests indicated that the absolute threshold was more reliable and more clearly defined than a "pain" threshold, so this measure was used as a basis for shock levels. The current used for the Strong-Shock group had a mean of .12 milliamp and a standard deviation of .05, while the current used for the Weak-Shock group had a mean of .12 milliamp and an *SD* of .07.

Although two Ss served during each experimental session, each S was led to believe that he was the only S serving in the experiment. At no time during or after the session were the Ss given any indication that another S had served in the experiment. Any questions concerning the current were ignored; however, each S was offered the opportunity to withdraw from the experiment before the session began. None of the Ss withdrew.

After the threshold readings were completed, S was taken to one of the two experimental rooms where he was seated before the S control board. Electrodes were attached to the first two fingers of his left hand. Instructions were then read to S, after which he was told to relax for a few minutes while the apparatus warmed up. During this time, *E* brought the second S before the *E* panel and went through the same procedure. The second S was taken to Room 2 and seated before the second control board. All Ss were given the following instructions:

"When the white light goes on, the experiment begins. The experiment is in progress as long as the white light stays on. You can press either of these buttons in any manner that you wish, and as frequently as you wish. Do not attempt to press both buttons at the same time and use only your right hand for pressing. You are to keep your left hand on the table. Do not hold a button down, but just press and release it. The object of the experiment is to make as many points as you can. Your point score will appear on this counter. The red light will blink and the counter will turn each time that you score a point. When the white light goes off, it is a signal that the experiment has ended. Remain seated until *E* comes into the room. Remember, you are to try to make as high score as you can in any manner that you can."

During the experiment, the four scores, a shock and a point score for each of the two Ss, were recorded by *E* every 30 seconds over a period of 25 continuous minutes. This gave a record of 50 scores for each button on the two S control boards.

At the conclusion of the experimental session, a series of questions was asked in order to determine whether or not any of the Ss were aware of the presence of another S in the experiment.

Results

In the initial analysis, scores over 5-minute intervals were tabulated for "score" and "shock" responses for each of the two groups. These data are presented graphically in Figure 1. An Alexander trend test (Alexander, 1946) was carried out on the data and the *F* was found to be significant beyond the .05 level of confidence. Duncan's test (Duncan, 1951) for differences between ranked treatments was carried out on the ranked means (presented in Table 1) of the four button responses. The differences between all ranked means were significant well beyond the .05 level of confidence (an exception was the nonsignificant difference between the Weak-Shock–Weak-Score means). In addition a ratio for each 5-minute interval was computed to give the proportion of the total responses which were "score" responses. These data are presented in Figure 2. An Alexander trend test showed an *F* significant beyond the .05 level of confidence.

These tests showed that the Strong-Shock group yielded significantly more "score" than "shock" responses, while no such difference for the Weak-Shock group was found. The tests did not indicate that the slope of the curves, which would have reflected gradual improvement, was significant. Inspection of the curves suggested that our failure to show significant slopes might have been due to the fact that much of the learning had occurred within the first

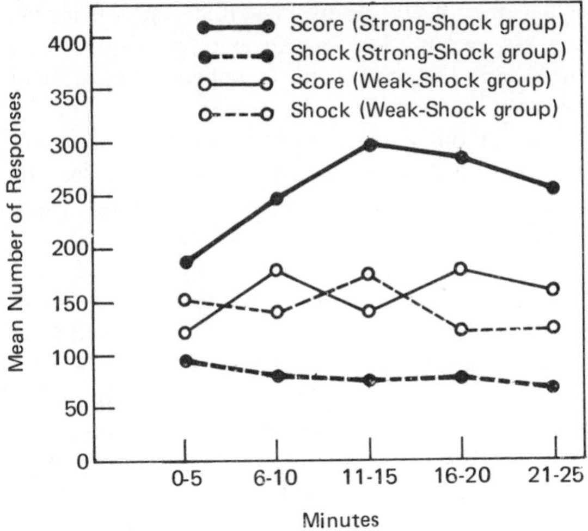

Figure 1 *Mean number of responses on the shock and score buttons by the Strong-Shock and Weak-Shock groups.*

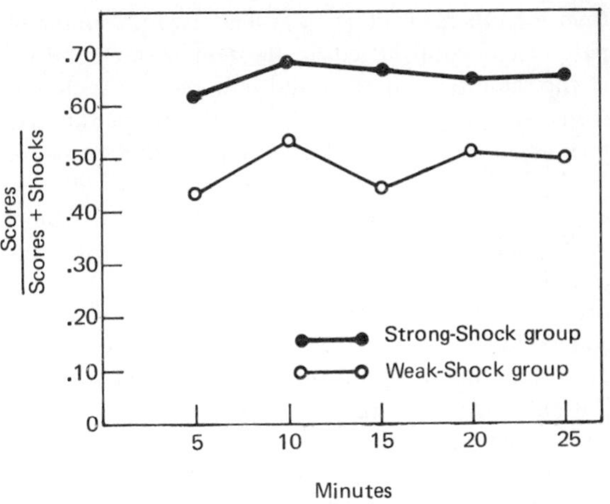

Figure 2 *Proportion of the total number of responses which were correct (score) responses during the 25-minute experimental session.*

Table 1 *Ranked Means for the Four-Button Responses*

Ranks	Means
Strong-Shock button	397.85
Weak-Shock button	719.95
Weak-Score button	786.75
Strong-Score button	1,288.65

five minutes. Therefore, the data for the first five minutes were divided into 1-minute intervals and analyzed. These data are presented in Figure 3. An Alexander trend analysis showed a significant difference between group slopes beyond the .05 level of confidence. This confirms our observation that learning took place within the first five minutes.

As a result of the preceding analyses, the major fact to be noted is that learning did occur in the Strong-Shock group, whereas no evidence of learning was obtained in the Weak-Shock group.

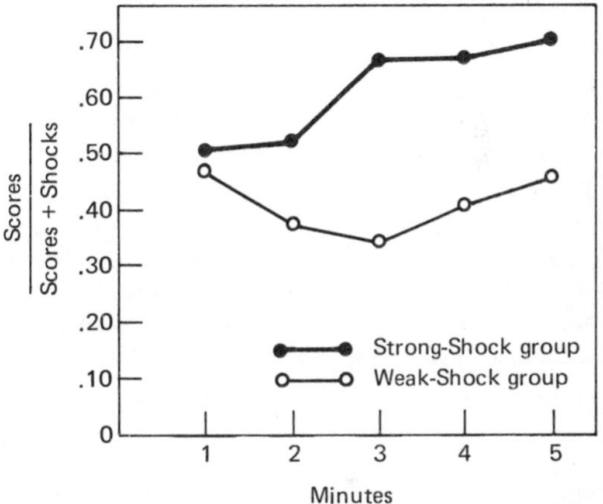

Figure 3 *Proportion of the total number of responses which were correct (score) responses during the first five minutes.*

Responses to the questions at the end of the experiment indicated that none of the Ss were aware that a second S was involved.

Discussion

Two major questions may be raised regarding the experimental findings: (*a*) Why did learning appear in the Strong-Shock group but not in the Weak-Shock group? (*b*) Why did learning occur at all under the conditions of this experiment?

In order to answer these two questions it is necessary to examine some of the sequences of responses which may have occurred during the course of the experiment. Examination of all possible sequences of events that might occur in the two groups becomes too cumbersome for our present purposes. However, it will be of interest to consider a few examples of possible beginning sequences and possible end states. Generally, we might assume random behavior by both Ss at the beginning of the experimental session. For example, let us suppose that each S made a response that shocked the other. It is not unlikely that this event might occur by accident early in the session. However, it is clear that some shift away from this behavior would soon appear, since neither S is receiving reinforcement and both are being punished. This shift would probably occur sooner under conditions of Strong Shock. The Ss might shift at the same time, or one might shift sooner than the other, resulting in at least two possible new patterns. If both shifted to the reinforcement button at the same time, both would now receive reinforcement, and we would expect a tendency for this pattern to continue. (In fact, the same prediction would be made if Ss commenced to reinforce each other at any time.) This pattern is perhaps the most obvious "self-sustaining" pattern which might emerge, and thus is one of the possible end states which might prevail. On the other hand, suppose that one S shifted to the reinforcement button before the other, or that, at any time, one S pressed the reinforcement button while the other pressed the shock button. The S who is pressing the reinforcement button should tend to shift to the shock button, with the result of reversion to the condition of both shocking each other. Since both of these patterns are "unstable," we might obtain a continual oscillation between the two states, with one S and then the other shifting temporarily to the reinforcement button. This oscillation itself would form a new pattern which could be stable under certain conditions, particularly if the magnitude of the shock were relatively small. If this magnitude were small enough, the intermittent reinforcement obtained by both Ss might sustain the over-all pattern. This oscillatory pattern thus represents another possible end state, one that would be most likely to occur under conditions of Weak Shock. Under conditions of Strong Shock, we might expect that the intermittent reinforcement obtained by both Ss would not sustain the over-all pattern of oscillation because of the punishing effects of the shock. Of course, many other sequences of responses could occur during the session, but it appears that most of these would be unstable.

Although the above considerations are not complete, they suggest a possible explanation for the occurrence of learning in the present experiment and the differential effect of the two levels of shock. It is suggested that under conditions of Strong Shock, the most probable stable pattern (end state) was that of both Ss reinforcing each other. Thus, Ss would tend to shift among patterns until they hit on this solution. (Some Ss could be expected to return to earlier responses, such as pressing the shock button from time to time due to the intermittent reinforcement which may have occurred early in the session following this type of response.) Under conditions of Weak Shock, the pattern of oscillation between the buttons was presumably the most probable stable state, since any of several initial sequences could lead into this pattern. It was not possible to analyze the sequential patterns in the present experiment, so further experimentation would be necessary to test these interpretations.

Within the framework of the present experiment, we can conclude that learning was demonstrated in a minimal social situation where: (*a*) the effects of previous social learning had been minimized, and (*b*) reinforcement and punishment were the only observable factors influencing the behavior of the Ss.

Summary

The present experiment investigates the influence of reinforcement and punishment in a minimal social situation. Two Ss, isolated from each other, were provided with two push buttons by means of which each could give the other a shock or score. The effects of previous social learning were minimized since Ss were unaware of the fact that they were in a social situation at all.

The Ss were divided into a Weak Shock and a Strong Shock group. All Ss were merely told that they could press the two buttons in any manner that they pleased (no information was given concerning the purpose of the buttons). Each S was also told that he was to make as many points as possible. His score was indicated on a counter which was mounted in front of S.

It was found that the proportion of the total number of responses (both score and shock) that were correct (score responses) was significantly higher for the Strong-Shock group. Learning occurred in the Strong-Shock group within the first 5 minutes of the 25-minute experimental session. Learning was not, however, evident in the Weak-Shock group.

Principles of reinforcement were used to interpret the results.

References

Alexander, H. W. A general test for trend. *Psychological Bulletin,* 1946, *43,* 533–557.

Duncan, D. B. A significant test for differences between ranked treatments in an analysis of variance. *Virginia Journal of Science,* 1951, *2,* 171–189.

Keller, F. S., and Schoenfeld, W. N. *Principles of psychology.* New York: Appleton-Century-Crofts, 1950.

McGeoch, J. A., and Irion, A. L. *The psychology of human learning.* New York: Longmans, Green, 1952.

Skinner, B. F. *The behavior of organisms.* New York: Appleton-Century, 1938.

Skinner, B. F. *Science and human behavior.* New York: Macmillan, 1953.

Another demonstration of social behaviors which occur because of specific reinforcement contingencies is provided in the article by *Azrin and Lindsley*. Pairs of children played a game that involved each child putting a stick into one of three holes in a tabletop. When the children inserted their sticks into opposite holes at the same moment, they were rewarded with a single jelly bean that dropped into a cup accessible to both. Without specific instructions, ten pairs of children learned to make cooperative responses within ten minutes.

The acquisition and extinction curves presented in this article show an orderly relationship between the cooperative behavior and the reinforcers it produced. When reinforcement no longer occurred, the frequency of cooperation declined. The results show that cooperative behavior need not be the result of either intention or instruction, but rather, can be shaped through the use of primary reinforcement.

6 | *The Reinforcement of Cooperation Between Children*[1]

NATHAN H. AZRIN
OGDEN R. LINDSLEY

Most methods for the development and experimental analysis of cooperation between humans require specific instructions concerning the cooperative relationship between the individual responses. Peters and Murphree (1954) have developed one of the most recent of these methods. Skinner has suggested (1953), and shown with lower organisms (1952), that cooperation between individuals can be developed, maintained, and eliminated solely by manipulating the contingency between reinforcing stimuli and the cooperative response.

The advantages of eliminating instructions concerning cooperation are that (*a*) the initial acquisition of cooperation can be studied, (*b*) subjects (Ss) that learn by demonstration and instruction with difficulty (i.e., infants, certain classes of psychotics, and lower organisms) can be studied, and (*c*) no problems involving the effects of instructions upon the behavior of the Ss are involved.

Some more general advantages of operant conditioning techniques are (*a*) a more continuous record of the cooperative process is obtained, (*b*) extraneous environmental variables are minimized, and (*c*) relatively long periods of experimental observation are possible.

Problem

Can cooperation between children be developed, maintained, and eliminated solely by the presentation or nonpresentation of a single reinforcing stimulus, available to each member of the cooperative team, following each cooperative response?

Cooperative Teams

Twenty children, seven to twelve years of age, were formed into ten cooperative teams of two children. The children in each team were matched as to age and sex. Seven teams were boys and three were girls.[2] Selection was made via the request, "Who wants to play a game?" The first two volunteers of the same age and sex were chosen for each team. The age given by the children was verified against available community center records. No information concerning the game was given during the selection. No teams were rejected.

Cooperative Response

Cooperation was assured by designing an apparatus that (*a*) could not be operated by one individual

[1] This paper was read at a meeting of the Eastern Psychological Association on April 10, 1954, New York City.

[2] We wish to thank the Harriet Tubman House and the South Bay Union of Boston, Mass., for providing the subjects and the use of their facilities.

alone (assuring group behavior), and (*b*) demanded that one individual respond to the behavior of the other individual in order to produce reinforcement (assuring cooperation).

Procedure

The two children of each cooperative team were placed at opposite sides of a table with three holes and a stylus in front of each child (see Figure 1). A wire screen down the center of the table prevented each child from manipulating the other child's stylus, which was on the other side of the table.

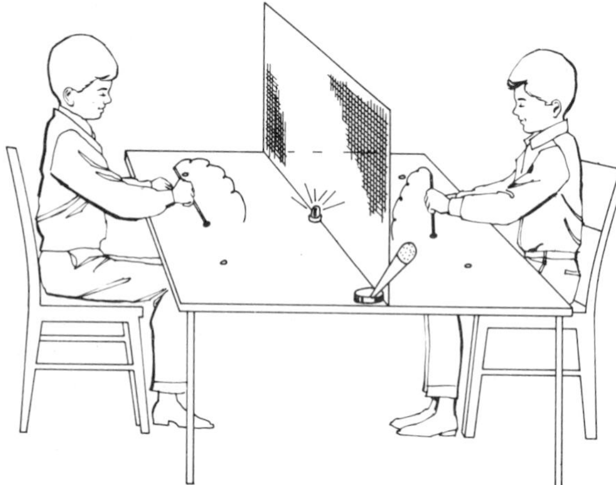

Figure 1 *Apparatus used for the reinforcement of cooperation between children.*

The following instructions were given: "This is a game. You can play the game any way you want to or do anything else that you want to do. This is how the game works: Put both sticks (styli) into all three of the holes." (This sentence was repeated until both styli had been placed in the three available holes.) "While you are in this room some of these [the experimenter (*E*) held out several jelly beans] will drop into this cup. You can eat them here if you want to or you can take them home with you." The instructions were then repeated without reply to any questions, after which *E* said: "I am leaving the room now; you can play any game that you want to while I am gone." Then *E* left the room until the end of the experimental session.

If the styli were placed in opposite holes within 0.04 seconds of each other (a cooperative response), a red light flashed on the table (conditioned reinforcing stimulus) and a single jelly bean (reinforcing stimulus) fell into the cup that was accessible to both children.[3] Cooperative responses were recorded on counters and a cumulative response recorder in an adjoining room.

Experimental Design

Each team was studied for one continuous experimental session divided into the following three consecutive periods without experimental interruption:

1. *First reinforcement period.* Every cooperative response was reinforced for over 15 minutes. If the rate of response was not steady at this time, the reinforcement was continued until five minutes passed with no noticeable change in the rate of cooperation.
2. *Extinction period.* The cooperative responses were not reinforced for a period of at least 15 minutes and until a steady rate of response for at least five minutes was observed.
3. *Second reinforcement period.* The cooperative responses were again reinforced until at least three minutes of a stable rate occurred. This was done to determine whether a reduction in rate during the extinction period was due to extinction, satiation, or fatigue.

Results

All teams learned to cooperate without specific instructions in the first 10 minutes of experimentation. Observation through a one-way vision screen disclosed that leader-follower relationships were developed and maintained in most cases. Almost immediately eight teams divided the candy in some manner. With two teams, one member at first took all the candy until the other member refused to cooperate. When verbal agreement was reached in these two teams, the members then cooperated and divided the candy. Most vocalization occurred during the initial acquisition period and throughout the extinction period. This vocalization was correlated with a higher variability in rate during these periods.

Figure 2 contains cumulative records of the cooperative responses of the three teams with the highest, the median, and the lowest number of cooperative responses for the experimental session. These curves show a large difference in the rate of acquisition of cooperation. One team took almost 10 minutes to acquire a high cooperative response rate. Stable rates of cooperation can be observed during the latter parts of the first reinforcement period. The gradual, rather than immediate, decline in cooperation during extinction suggests an orderly extinction of cooperative behavior, as is found with individual extinction curves. In all cases the variability of rate was greater during extinction than during reinforcement. Skinner has found this increased variability in rate during extinction with lower organisms and has described it as

[3] Skinner (1952) presented two reinforcing stimuli (one to each pigeon) following each cooperative response.

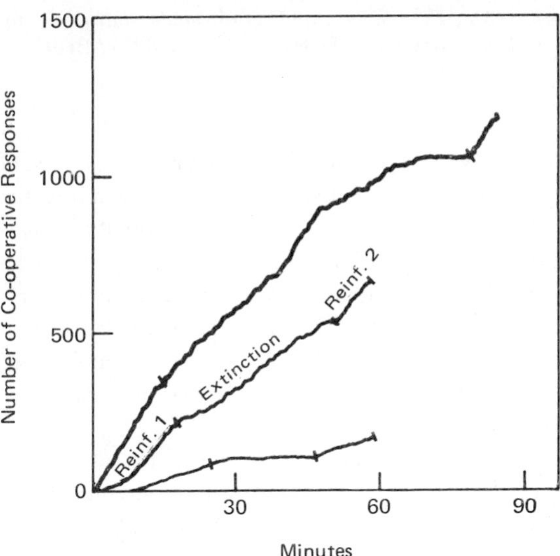

Figure 2 *Cumulative response records for the teams with the highest, median, and lowest rates of cooperation.*

Table 1 *Medians and Ranges of the Number of Cooperative Responses per Minute for the Critical Experimental Periods*

	Number of Cooperative Responses per Minute			
N 10	First Three Mins. of First Reinf. Period	Last Three Mins. of First Reinf. Period	Last Three Mins. of Extinction Period	Last Three Mins. of Second Reinf. Period
Median	5.5	17.5	1.5	17.5
Range	1–26	6–26	0–7	6–27

emotional behavior (1953, p. 69). The high rate of response following the first reinforcement of the second reinforcement period shows that reacquisition is almost immediate.

Table 1 contains a quantification of the records for statistical analysis. The median and range of the number of cooperative responses per minute for all 10 teams during the critical periods of the experiment are given. The number of cooperative responses per minute for the first three minutes of the first reinforcement period was significantly lower than the rate during the last three minutes of the first reinforcement period ($p < .02$).[4] This shows that the rate of cooperation was significantly lower during initial acquisition than during maintenance of cooperation. The number of cooperative responses per minute during the last three minutes of extinction was significantly lower than the rate during the last three minutes of the first reinforcement period ($p < .001$). This shows that the removal of reinforcement during extinction significantly lowered the rate of cooperation between these children.

The number of cooperative responses per minute during the last three minutes of the second reinforcement period was significantly above the rate during the last three minutes of the extinction period ($p < .001$). This shows that the rate of cooperation was significantly increased during the second reinforcement period and that the drop in rate during extinction was due to the absence of the reinforcing stimulus rather than satiation or fatigue. The rates of cooperation during the second reinforcement period and the last three minutes of the first reinforcement period were not significantly different and show that the rate was almost immediately restored to its pre-extinction value upon the presentation of reinforcement for the second time. The rate of cooperative responding during the first three minutes of the second reinforcement period was significantly higher than during the first three minutes of the first reinforcement period ($p < .02$). This again shows that the reacquisition of cooperation was not gradual, as was initial acquisition, but occurred almost immediately.

Conclusions

Operant conditioning techniques can be used to develop, maintain, and eliminate cooperation between children without the use of specific instructions concerning cooperation. The rate of a cooperative response changes in much the same way as a function of single reinforcements as does an individual response. In the reinforcement of cooperative responses, a reinforcing stimulus need not be delivered to each member of the cooperative team following each cooperative response. The presentation of a single reinforcing stimulus, available to each member of the cooperative team, is sufficient to increase the rate of cooperation. The cooperative response gradually increases in frequency when reinforced and gradually decreases in frequency when no longer reinforced (extinction). Cooperative responses are maintained at a stable rate during reinforcement but occur in sporadic bursts during extinction. Reinforcement following extinction results in an almost immediate restoration of the rate of cooperation to its pre-extinction value.

References

Peters, H. N., and Murphree, O. D. A cooperative multiple-choice apparatus. *Science*, 1954, *119*, 189–191.

Skinner, B. F. Classroom demonstration. Personal communication, 1952.

4 Wilcoxon's nonparametric *T* for paired associates was used in all statistical treatments (Wilcoxon, 1949).

SKINNER, B. F. *Science and human behavior.* New York: Macmillan, 1953.

WILCOXON, F. *Some rapid approximate statistical procedures.* New York: American Cyanamid Co., 1949.

In many textbooks of psychology, behavior is frequently "explained" in terms of drives, or motives. These terms refer to internal states that presumably impel the individual to engage in certain goal-related behaviors. Thus, an individual who eats voraciously is said to be exhibiting the effects of the hunger drive, and the person who seeks money, status, or power is said to be revealing achievement motivation. *Gewirtz and Baer* prefer to define a drive as ". . . the functional relation between deprivation (or satiation) for a reinforcer and responding for that reinforcer." This terminology emphasizes the antecedents and consequences of behavior rather than internal states that are not susceptible to direct observation or control.

In this experiment, children were either deprived, not deprived, or satiated on social approval before playing a game that involved dropping marbles into one of two holes. Following a four-minute period during which the experimenter observed the child's preference for one or the other hole, reinforcement in the form of "Good," "Mm-hmm," and "Fine" was given whenever the child dropped a marble into his least preferred hole. Social reinforcement was much more effective when the subjects had been deprived of social approval during a pre-experimental period of twenty minutes than under any of the other conditions. Thus, it appears that behavior reinforced socially is influenced by deprivation and satiation, just like behaviors reinforced by food.

7 Deprivation and Satiation of Social Reinforcers as Drive Conditions

JACOB L. GEWIRTZ[1]
DONALD M. BAER[2]

In an earlier study (Gewirtz and Baer, 1958) we received what appeared to be an affirmative answer to the question: Are there social drives that respond to reinforcer deprivation as do the primary appetitive drives? In this investigation we extend the question, asking in addition if the behaviors maintained by social reinforcers are responsive also to a condition of relative satiation for such reinforcers. Children are again employed as subjects (Ss).

In the earlier study it was found that when an adult made words and phrases like "Good!" and "Mm-hmm" contingent upon an arbitrarily chosen response in nursery school children, that response was reinforced (i.e., conditioned). This effect was similar to that found in several other studies using verbal stimuli appealing to the concept of *approval* as reinforcers (e.g., Chase, 1932; Greenspoon, 1955; Hurlock, 1924; Wolf, 1938). It was found, in addition, that this reinforcing effect of approval could be increased when the children experienced a preceding 20-minute period of social isolation, relative to its effectiveness for the same children when they had not been isolated. While this result held primarily for boys tested by a female (rather than male) experimenter, other aspects of the data clearly supported

[1] This study was carried out when the senior author was on the faculty of the University of Chicago, and was facilitated by a grant given to him by the Social Science Research Committee of that institution. The writers acknowledge with gratitude the discriminating assistance of Chaya H. Roth.

[2] At the time of this study, the junior author was a Public Health Service Predoctoral Research Fellow of the National Institute of Mental Health at the University of Chicago.

the equating of isolation to the deprivation of social reinforcers: *social isolation increased reliably the reinforcing power of adult approval for children as a positive function of the degree to which they typically sought such approval in other settings.* Approval was taken to be representative of the reinforcers which control the purely social initiations made by children to adults.

Deprivation implies a period of unavailability of a given reinforcer, which results in an increase in behaviors for it; *satiation* implies a period of availability of a reinforcer, sufficient to effect a decrease in behaviors for it. Thus, deprivation and satiation represent two statements of a single concept, a dimension characterized by the relative supply of a reinforcer in the recent history of an organism which determines the incidence of behaviors for that reinforcer. The concept of deprivation-satiation has considerable precedent as a drive operation in general behavior theory (e.g., Hull, 1952; Skinner, 1953), where it has been employed to order contemporary conditions which account for variance in reinforcer effectiveness. As such, drive is generally defined as the functional relation between deprivation (or satiation) for a reinforcer and responding for that reinforcer. Further, concepts like deprivation have been somewhat loosely applied in a number of speculative formulations of the antecedents of certain social behaviors (e.g., Bowlby, 1951; Goldfarb, 1945; Ribble, 1944; Spitz, 1945). Hence, laws relating social deprivation as an empirically defined dimension to certain basic characteristics of social behaviors would have considerable integrative value (Gewirtz, 1956). But first, the experimental operations of deprivation and its inverse, satiation, must be implemented effectively in social terms.

In the earlier study cited (Gewirtz and Baer, 1958), a beginning attempt was made to implement social deprivation: brief social isolation of a child was equated to a condition of deprivation of all social reinforcers (including approval), and the differential effects of that condition and of a comparison nonisolation (nondeprivation) condition were reflected in the reinforcing effectiveness of an adult's approval. The present study represents an attempt to simplify (and replicate) the social deprivation operation of the earlier study, as well as a beginning in the direction of establishing an operation of social satiation. Satiation will be equated to a condition in which an abundance of approval and social contact is supplied to a child by an adult. Experimental operations implementing the conditions of deprivation and of satiation for a class of social reinforcers are both reflected against an intermediate or nondeprivation (nonsatiated) condition. The hypothesis is that these conditions should enhance the effectiveness of the reinforcer in the order: Deprivation > Nondeprivation > Satiation.

Method

Sample

The Ss were 102 middle-class children selected from the classes of the first and second grades of a university laboratory school and randomly assigned to experimental conditions. Sixteen were Negro, the remainder white. Their mean age at the time of testing was seven years, six months, with a range from six and one-half to nine years. Their mean and median Stanford-Binet IQ score was 127 (the scores of only 3 Ss were below 100). One-half of the Ss under each condition were girls and one-half boys. The Ss were selected by their teachers according to the order in which their names appeared on alphabetical class lists. No S refused to participate.

Independent Variable

Deprivation. Seventeen boys and 17 girls were subjected to a condition of social isolation before playing the game. Each of these Ss was introduced to the experimenter (*E*) in the classroom by the teacher. The *E* was a young woman in her early twenties.[3] She walked with S a distance of several hundred feet through the school corridors to the experimental room. During this walk, *E* responded to S's questions and comments only when necessary, and maintained a somewhat distant but not unfriendly manner at all times. Upon reaching the experimental room, *E* showed S around the room, seated him and told him that someone else was using the game which he was to play and that she would have to fetch it but would be back in a little while. *E* then left the room and went (unobserved) to an adjacent observation booth from which S was observed during his isolation. She returned after 20 minutes with the toy. The game was then played in the usual fashion. The Ss, who occasionally accompanied adults in the school setting for tests, and who had experience in awaiting their turns, all accepted this condition without question.

Nondeprivation. Seventeen boys and 17 girls were subjected to a condition of nonisolation, i.e., they played the game immediately upon their arrival at the experimental room. (Since this condition represents both relative nondeprivation and relative non-

[3] This *E* served as one of the two *Es* in a companion study (Gewirtz and Baer, 1958).

satiation for approval, it served as an intermediate control condition for the other two conditions.) Until they entered the experimental room, Ss in this group were treated identically as were Ss in the Deprivation group.

Satiation. Seventeen boys and 17 girls were subjected to a condition of relative satiation for approval from the adult before playing the game. Again, each of these Ss was introduced to *E* in the classroom by the teacher, but during the walk to the experimental room, *E* maintained a very pleasant and interested attitude toward S, responding to all details of his comments and questions, asking questions to draw out more of S's conversation, and generally approving of anything about S which might reasonably be praised or admired. Upon reaching the experimental room, *E* showed S around the room, seated him, told him that the game was in use elsewhere and she would go fetch it in a little while when it would be free. She suggested that meanwhile S might like to draw pictures or cut out designs, and proffered the essential materials. Then, for 20 minutes S drew or cut out designs, while *E* maintained a stream of friendly conversation with him, inducing him to talk about himself if he did not do so naturally. The *E* alternated her praise and admiration of whatever S did with whatever he said about himself, all in an appropriate fashion, and attempted to dispense 30 such reinforcers during the 20-minute satiation period at an approximate rate of three every two minutes. In fact, *E* dispensed to the boys an average of 31.6 such reinforcers ($\sigma = 6.9$) and to the girls an average of 28.2 reinforcers ($\sigma = 8.1$).

The Game Setting

Following the experimental treatment, the central task for S (which was the same for all three groups) was to place marbles into either of the two holes of the toy (shown in Figure 1) while *E*, who sat beside him, looked on. (This procedure was identical to that employed in the earlier study [Gewirtz and Baer, 1958] and is only summarized here.) The *E* observed S's play for a "baseline" period of four minutes, during which *no* reinforcers were dispensed. Meanwhile, *E* responded to any of S's comments and questions in a friendly but brief manner. Without pause, the baseline period was followed by a 10-minute test of reinforcer effectiveness. That is, *E* proceeded at this point to dispense the reinforcer, consisting of words like "Good," "Mm-hmm," and "Fine," according to a schedule incorporating several, successively higher, fixed ratios, whenever S dropped marbles into the *correct* hole, defined as that preferred *least* during the last (fourth) minute of the baseline period.

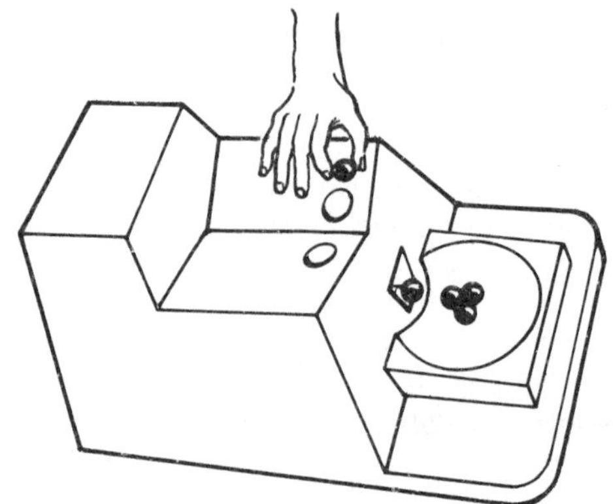

Figure 1 *A schematic diagram of the experimental apparatus (the "Game").*

Dependent Variables

Reinforcer Effectiveness Score. The determination of the effectiveness of approval as a reinforcer was made from the "game" which followed immediately the treatment condition (i.e., the 20 minutes of Deprivation or of Satiation, or in the Nondeprivation condition, the arrival at the experimental room). The basic data were the numbers of marbles dropped in the correct and incorrect holes during each minute of play. These generated four pairs of frequency scores for the baseline period, and 10 such pairs of scores for the reinforcer effectiveness test period. For each minute of play, the *relative frequency* of a correct response was the ratio of correct responses to total responses, i.e., number correct/(number correct + number incorrect). The score employed as dependent variable was taken as the difference, for each S, between the relative frequency of correct responses in the last (fourth) minute of the baseline period (when no reinforcers were dispensed) and the median relative frequency of correct responses of the 10 reinforcer test period minutes. This *reinforcer effectiveness score* represents the *gain* in relative frequency of the correct response attributable to the social reinforcer provided by the adult's approval.

Spontaneous Social Initiations. In addition, the verbal and purely social initiations of the child to the adult were tallied, but *only during the baseline period of the game,* before she began to dispense approval. The *E* treated the game as S's central task and, while permissive, generally discouraged lengthy initiations on the part of S, suggesting, when necessary, that they could converse at length after the game. Where a reply to an initiation of S was required, *E*'s response was always friendly, yet brief, leaving responsibility for continuing that interaction sequence in S's hands. All such responses by S were tallied by an observer in an observation booth. These responses took the form most frequently of Comments, less frequently of Questions, and least frequently of overt Attention-seeking.[4] They could be expected to represent behaviors by S for a variety of social reinforcers, in addition to approval. *Comments* were casual remarks which usually required no formal response from *E* (e.g., "We're going away for the holiday"). *Questions,* which were also casual, required only brief, token replies from *E* (e.g., "Do you think it will rain?"). When making a comment or asking a question, S typically continued responding in the game. *Attention-seeking* included responses characterized by urgency designed for active notice from *E*. Typically, S would pause to direct his complete attention to *E* while awaiting a response (e.g., "Watch me put the marble into this hole!"). Because of their generally infrequent occurrence in this study, these three behavior categories are scored in two different ways to produce two relatively independent response indices for the purpose of analysis:

a. The sum of the frequencies in the three social response categories, Comments, Questions, and Attention-seeking, which weights those categories in proportion to their frequency of occurrence (i.e., Comments contributes most and Attention-seeking least to that index).

b. The score of a *cumulative Guttman-like scale* (Guttman, 1950), indexing what appears to be the intensity of social contact, formed similarly as in the study by Gewirtz (1954), where the frequency scores for each verbal response category were dichotomized for each S into gross response alternatives, zero or nonzero frequency of occurrence.[5] A scale score of 3 indicated that an S had exhibited some of all three behaviors; a score of 2 indicated that some Comments and Questions were exhibited, but no Attention-seeking; a score of 1 indicated that only Comments were exhibited; and a score of zero indicated that no social response of any type was exhibited. Hence, the scale scores are weighted in favor of the less frequently occurring behavior categories, Questions and Attention-seeking.

Results

The hypothesis advanced is that the mean reinforcer effectiveness scores for the treatment groups would rank in the order Deprivation > Nondeprivation > Satiation. To test this, two relatively independent statistical procedures are followed: the first is sensitive to the rank-order of the treatment means but does not take account of the degree of overlap between the distributions upon which the means are based; and the second, which takes such information into account and allows parametric statements about the means, is somewhat less sensitive to the rank-order hypothesis.

Reinforcer Effectiveness Score

Rank-Order of the Means. In Table 1, it is seen that the rank-order predicted for the three means is found separately for Boys and for Girls. The sex variable may be taken as an independent replication of the experiment. The theoretical probability of obtaining a predicted rank-order of three independent means is $\frac{1}{6}$, and with one independent replication the probability of obtaining two such orders is $\frac{1}{6} \times \frac{1}{6}$ or $\frac{1}{36}$. On this basis, we can conclude that the null hypothesis, that all six rank-orders of the three means are equally likely, is rejected at $p < .03$. Hence, the alternative hypothesis, that the predicted rank-order of the three means prevails, is accepted.

Table 1 *Mean Reinforcer Effectiveness Scores*

Sex	Deprivation (D)	Satiation (S)	½ (D + S)	Non-deprivation
Boys	.36*	.18*	.27**	.21*
Girls	.33*	.07*	.20**	.23*
Combined	.34**	.13**	.23***	.22**

* 17 cases; S.E. of a mean difference is .068.
** 34 cases; S.E. of a mean difference is .048.
*** 68 cases.

Regression Analysis. For the purposes of the regression analysis (and for theoretical reasons as well), the three treatment conditions are considered

[4] These three observation categories are defined in detail by Gewirtz (1954). High agreement between observers was found there on these behavior categories, and they entered into similar patterns of relationship with the independent variables. Moreover, they were found by Gewirtz (1956) to have high loadings on a single factor and appeared to involve an active attempt to gain or to maintain the adult's attention, perhaps differing in the degree to which their initiations for attention were overt or direct.

[5] Of all 102 Ss in the four-minute baseline period, the proportion showing nonzero category frequencies was .71 for Comments, .53 for Questions, and .15 for Attention-seeking. When the response categories were arranged in the order of their decreasing popularities (the proportion of Ss exhibiting nonzero frequencies), it was concluded that, for present purposes, a satisfactory three-item Guttman-like scale was produced: only .03 of the 306 responses produced scale errors, the few scale errors found appeared random, and every observation category contained far less error than nonerror. Of the 68 Ss in the Deprivation and Nondeprivation groups, five each produced one scale error in his response pattern. Such response patterns were assigned scale scores corresponding to the higher pattern which would have been attained had there been no scale error.

as points along a single continuous dimension representing the degree of social deprivation. The analysis then proceeds from three working assumptions: (*a*) the units separating the treatments along this deprivation dimension are roughly equal in size, (*b*) their relationship to the reinforcer effectiveness means is linear, and (*c*) it is the *pattern* of the three means that is relevant to the rank-order hypothesis advanced, not the contrasts between mean pairs representing adjacent points on the postulated treatment dimension. On this basis, it appears most efficient to carry out the analysis of variance according to a regression model: in essence, to analyze the regression of the reinforcer effectiveness score means on the treatment dimension.

The reinforcer effectiveness scores of the Ss were classified in the six cells of a 3 × 2 factorial, there being three treatments and two sexes of Ss. After a Bartlett test indicated that the variances were homogeneous and an examination of the data suggested that the other assumptions underlying the analysis appeared to hold, the data were subjected to an analysis of variance. Table 2 indicates that there is no over-all sex difference, and that the treatment conditions do not affect the sex groups differentially. From Figure 2, it is seen that the group means corresponding to the three levels of the experimental variable rank-order according to the hypothesis. It is seen in Table 2 that the Deprivation vs. Satiation comparison is reliable and in the order predicted. In the case of three means, this comparison represents the regression of those means on the treatment dimension. A Nondeprivation vs. ½ (Deprivation + Satiation) comparison, which represents the deviation of the Nondeprivation mean from the regression line, indicates that that mean falls remarkably close to the regression line. Hence, the regression predicted was found. (This result provides presumptive evidence only for the effectiveness of either of the extreme treatments, Deprivation or Satiation, relative to the intermediate Nondeprivation treatment.)

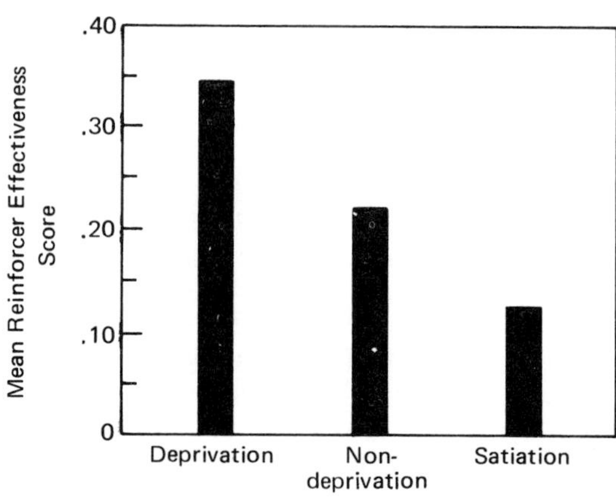

Figure 2 *Means for the three levels of the experimental variable (34 Ss per condition).*

Table 2 *Summary of Analysis of Variance of Reinforcer Effectiveness Scores*

Source of Variation	*df*	Mean Square	*F*
Boys vs. Girls (Sex)	1	.0412	.524
Treatments			
Total	(2)	(.4032)	(5.123)*
Deprivation (D) vs. Satiation (S)[a]	1	.8031	10.200**
Nondeprivation (N) vs. ½ (D + S)[b]	1	.0034	.043
Sex × Treatment			
Total	(2)	(.0356)	(.452)
Sex × D vs. S	1	.0268	.341
Sex × N vs. ½ (D + S)	1	.0444	.564
Error (within groups)	96	.0787	—

[a] Due to regression.
[b] Due to the deviation of the *N* mean from the regression line.
* $p < .01$.
** $p < .005$.

Approval as a Reinforcer. A question of interest is whether the reinforcer dispensed was effective as such under Nondeprivation, which would be comparable to the usual experimental case under which the effectiveness of the reinforcer would be examined, as well as following Satiation, when the reinforcer was relatively least effective in this experiment. The hypothesis is tested that the mean reinforcer effectiveness score under Nondeprivation is zero, employing an error term based only upon those 34 scores and a one-tail t test. That mean score (.22) is found to be reliably greater than zero at $p < .0005$. A similar test indicates that the Satiation condition of this study did not reduce the reinforcing effectiveness of approval to a zero level; the mean reinforcer effectiveness score following Satiation (.13) was reliably greater than zero at $p < .01$. Hence, it may be concluded that approval was effective as a reinforcer under all conditions, and that satiation was not complete but only relative.

Spontaneous Social Initiations

An examination of Ss' spontaneous verbal initiations to *E* during *only* the four-minute baseline period of the game can reinforce the conclusions drawn from the reinforcer effectiveness score (which reflects only the susceptibility of *Ss* to approval as a reinforcer). These initiations could be expected to represent behaviors by S for a variety of social reinforcers from *E* and, hence, might be sensitive as well to the treatments. It should be noted that *E* did not dispense approval during the baseline period, but merely looked on as S put marbles into the toy. (Because the Satiation treatment consisted of a period of intensive social contact between *E* and S, which could encourage S to continue to make social initiations during the game, only a comparison of the verbal social response scores between the Deprivation and Nondeprivation groups would be meaningful.)

The *total frequency of verbal initiation* scores was classified in a 2 × 2 factorial (Deprivation vs. Nondeprivation and Boys vs. Girls) and subjected to an analysis of variance. The mean number of verbal responses (Comments, Questions, and Attention-seeking) after Deprivation (4.4) was found to be reliably greater than that after Nondeprivation (2.3) at $p < .05$ ($F = 3.70$, 1 and 64 *df*, one-tail test). At the same time, the Treatment × Sex interaction effect was not reliable, indicating that the two treatments did not affect the sexes differentially.

The scale scores represent what appears to be the *intensity of social contact,* or the degree to which certain social reinforcers apart from approval (e.g., attention) are sought from the adult, and could take any one of the four values from zero to three. They were classified in a fourfold table, with *low* scores of zero and one taken to represent less intense social contact, and *high* scores of two and three taken to represent more intense social contact. It was found that 20 out of the 34 Ss exhibited high scale scores after Nondeprivation, indicating at $p < .05$ (chi square corrected for discontinuity = 2.89, 1 *df*, one-tail test) that a greater proportion of Ss exhibited more intense social contact scores after Deprivation than after Nondeprivation.

Hence, the two relatively independent indices derived from the three categories of spontaneous verbal initiations to *E both* reinforce the conclusions derived from the measure of the reinforcing effectiveness of *E*'s approval.

Discussion

In the earlier study cited (as in this study), the experimental operation of brief social isolation of the child was equated to a condition of deprivation[6] of all social reinforcers (including approval). Hence, it became important to demonstrate that this condition increases the incidence of behaviors for approval relative to an empirically defined level of satiation for that reinforcer. The results suggest that this has been accomplished. And since under the Nondeprivation condition Ss had just come from class, with no further experimental treatment, it seemed reasonable that it would represent some point intermediate between the other conditions. The rank-order of the mean reinforcer effectiveness scores for these three conditions followed this logic precisely and was uncomplicated by an interaction involving sex of Ss. Hence, the results replicate the finding of the earlier study concerning the greater effectiveness of approval after Deprivation, relative to Nondeprivation. While the mean difference between reinforcer effectiveness scores for Deprivation and Nondeprivation for the Ss in this study (ranging in age from 6-6 to 9-0) appears to be of the same order as that for the Ss in the earlier study (who ranged in age from 3-10 to 5-3), the absolute level of the means appears to be higher.

The two indices drawn from the three spontaneous verbal social initiation categories reinforced the conclusions based on the index of the reinforcing effectiveness of *E*'s approval for the Deprivation and Nondeprivation conditions (where a difference test was meaningful). It seems likely then, if the game-set were dispensed with and the natural or spontaneous social initiations to *E* were employed as the sole dependent variable, that similar conclusions would be drawn from the results. However, if the present establishing operation for satiation were to be employed in such a study, it would still be almost impossible to separate the social effects of satiation from the artifactual effects of Ss' greater familiarity with *E*.

The essence of the parallel between our use of the term drive for social reinforcers and the traditional use of the term for the deprivation of food and water reinforcers, as in hunger and thirst, lies in the definition of a drive as the functional relation between deprivation for a reinforcer and responding for that reinforcer. In that special sense, then, it would appear that there exist for children social drives that respond to social reinforcer deprivation as do many primary appetitive drives. Yet it should not be supposed that the results of this study validate decisively the conclusion that a social reinforcer follows a deprivation-satiation logic. The responsiveness of a reinforcer to relative values of both deprivation and satiation represents only one requirement under this logic. Social reinforcers may be supplied and deprived in a variety of ways, and it is important to discover their responsiveness to many of these ways. It would be especially important, for example, to implement the deprivation of a *single* social reinforcer, rather than of all social reinforcers. Further, it is essential to have some assurance that the social reinforcers are more or less homogeneous in this regard, for verbal approval may not be representative of the

[6] An analysis of some possible Deprivation condition artifacts is made in Gewirtz and Baer (1958).

reinforcers controlling the purely social initiations made by children to adults. Replications of these effects with other social reinforcers (e.g., attention) would strengthen the conclusions, as would parametric studies of the deprivation-satiation dimension. Another assumption is that approval had acquired reinforcing value for children through a history of conditioning. A stronger case would result if approval were demonstrated to be a more effective reinforcer than, say, a comparable nonsocial noise produced by a machine; or if that noise were shown to be less affected than approval by deprivation-satiation conditions like those employed here. Even so, the earlier finding (Gewirtz and Baer, 1958) that isolation enhanced the reinforcing power of adult approval for Ss as a positive function of the degree to which they sought adult approval in other settings would indicate against both these possibilities. And the difference in spontaneous social initiations following Deprivation and Nondeprivation supports the more general conclusions drawn here; those behaviors were very likely employed for social reinforcers other than approval.

While the results of this study can stand in their own right, several additional experimental conditions could help elucidate the processes at issue. Thus, it would be useful to separate the effects of some of the three components of the satiation condition employed, namely (*a*) *E*'s physical presence, (*b*) the social interaction between *E* and S, and (*c*) the approval reinforcers dispensed by *E* to S. To do this, it would be necessary to employ such conditions as, for example, one in which *E* sits with S for 20 minutes but says nothing, or one in which approval is dispensed without *E*, possibly out of "thin air." While some such conditions might be difficult to implement, the attempt to establish conditions like these would be worth while in the context of this experiment. Even so, the results of an experiment (Gewirtz, 1954) on related behavior (for attention) suggest that a condition in which *E* sits near S but interacts minimally with him (only upon request) functions more as a condition of social deprivation than as one of satiation (Gewirtz, Baer, and Roth, 1958).

Apart from these considerations, the standard primary-conditioned reinforcer issue in the study of animal drives cannot be involved as such in this case. We have assumed that some sort of conditioned reinforcer is at issue, but haven't separated out conclusively the effects of the several stimulus components of that conditioned reinforcer. At the very worst, then, it isn't clear that the social reinforcer dispensed is independent of *E*. We have already noted the possibility that noise, rather than social noise, might constitute the reinforcing stimulus. Apart from this, however, it does not seem significant to consider social reinforcers as separate from the person dispensing them: they are eminently social noises in our logic; and their social character refers not only to their presumed history but also to the method of their delivery.

Additional Considerations. In the earlier study, two *Es* were employed to dispense the social reinforcer, one male and one female. An interaction effect was found which indicated, among other things, that the increase in the effectiveness of approval as a reinforcer, brought on by Deprivation relative to Nondeprivation, was greatest for boys with the female *E*. This change was not reliable for the other three Sex of S × Sex of *E* groups. In this experiment, in which both boys and girls were tested by a female *E*, no Treatment × Sex interaction was found (although the Satiation mean of girls may not have differed from zero). Hence, to that extent, the previous results are not replicated, but the conclusions can be drawn more generally. (This finding could be referred to the postulate that Ss of this study are "latent" [in the Freudian sense], while those in the earlier study were "Oedipal." However, there exist other possibilities, including slight changes in method, to explain the discordant results of the two studies on this issue.)

Only one reinforcer-dispensing *E* was employed, and she was not unaware of the expected direction of the results. Her behavior was scored by objective and easily discriminated criteria and judged satisfactory. Still, there remains some reason for caution; for the findings of this experiment cannot be conclusive until they are widely replicated with similar and improved procedures. Nevertheless, the reliability of the results is supported by the difference between the Deprivation and Nondeprivation groups on the spontaneous social initiations made to *E* before she began to dispense the reinforcer: there, where it was even less likely that *E* could influence the outcome, the finding paralleled precisely that derived from the reinforcer effectiveness index.

Summary

On the assumption that approval is representative of the reinforcers controlling the purely social initiations of children to adults, the verbal approval of a female *E* was made contingent upon one response in a two-response game for 102 first- and second-grade children (Ss) of a university laboratory school. The change in relative response frequency from a baseline level following introduction of the reinforcer indicated the degree to which approval was reinforcing for an S.

Before playing the game, Ss were subjected to one of three experimental conditions: 34 *Ss* were subjected to a 20-minute period of isolation (conceived to be social *Deprivation*); 34 Ss played the game immediately upon coming from class (conceived to be an intermediate condition between deprivation and satiation, and called *Nondeprivation*); and 34 Ss devoted 20 minutes to drawing and cutting out designs, while *E* maintained a stream of friendly conversation with each of them and approved and admired their art efforts and statements in an appropriate fashion (conceived to be *Satiation* for approval and social contact). There were 17 boys and 17 girls in each experimental group.

Employing two independent tests (one on the order of the means, the other on the regression of the means on the treatment dimension), it was found that the rank-order hypothesis advanced was reliably supported (at $p < .03$ and $< .005$ respectively). The reinforcing effectiveness of approval was relatively greatest after Deprivation, intermediate after Nondeprivation, and least after Satiation. Approval functioned as a reinforcer after all conditions, even Satiation ($p < .01$). Boys and girls were affected similarly on this measure by the experimental conditions.

The spontaneous social initiations made by Ss to *E*, before she had begun to dispense approval in the game, supported the results based on the index of the effectiveness of approval as a reinforcer. Following the Deprivation condition, there resulted a greater mean frequency of social initiations ($p < .05$), and a larger proportion of Ss exhibiting apparently intense social interaction ($p < .05$), than following the Nondeprivation condition. (The nature of the establishing operation for the Satiation condition precluded a meaningful comparison of the other conditions with it on these social behaviors.)

Thus, a reinforcer appearing to be typical of those involved in children's social drives appears responsive to deprivation and satiation operations similar to those controlling the effectiveness of reinforcers of a number of the primary appetitive drives.

References

Bowlby, J. Maternal care and mental health. *Bulletin of the World Health Organization Monographs,* 1951, *3,* 355–533.

Chase, Lucille Motivation of young children: An experimental study of the influences of certain types of external incentives upon the performance of a task. *University of Iowa Studies in Child Welfare,* 1932, *5,* No. 3. P. 119.

Gewirtz, J. L. Three determinants of attention-seeking in young children. *Monographs of the Society for Research in Child Development,* 1954, *19,* No. 2 (Serial No. 59).

Gewirtz, J. L. A factor analysis of some attention-seeking behaviors of young children. *Child Development,* 1956, *27,* 17–36.

Gewirtz, J. L. A program of research on the dimensions and antecedents of emotional dependence. *Child Development,* 1956, *27,* 205–221.

Gewirtz, J. L., and Baer, D. M. The effect of brief social deprivation on behaviors for a social reinforcer. *Journal of Abnormal and Social Psychology,* 1958, *56,* 49–56.

Gewirtz, J. L., Baer, D. M., and Roth, Chaya H. A note on the similar effects of low social availability of an adult and brief social deprivation on young children's behavior. *Child Development,* 1958, *29,* 149–152.

Goldfarb, W. Psychological privation in infancy and subsequent adjustment. *American Journal of Orthopsychiatry,* 1945, *15,* 247–255.

Greenspoon, J. The reinforcing effects of two spoken words on the frequency of two responses. *American Journal of Psychology,* 1955, *68,* 409–416.

Guttman, L. The basis of scalogram analysis. In S. A. Stouffer et al., *Measurement and prediction.* Princeton, N.J.: Princeton University Press, 1950. Pp. 60–90.

Hull, C. L. *A behavior system.* New Haven: Yale University Press, 1952.

Hurlock, Elizabeth B. The value of praise and reproof as incentives for children. *Archives of Psychology, New York,* 1924, *11,* No. 71, 5–78.

Ribble, Margaret Infantile experience in relation to personality development. In J. McV. Hunt (Ed.), *Personality and the behavior disorders.* New York: Ronald Press, 1944. Pp. 621–651.

Skinner, B. F. *Science and human behavior.* New York: Macmillan, 1953.

Spitz, R. A. Hospitalism: An inquiry into the genesis of psychiatric conditions in early childhood. In Anna Freud et al. (Eds.), *The psychoanalytic study of the child.* Vol. 1. New York: International Universities Press, 1945. Pp. 53–74.

Wolf, Theta H. The effect of praise and competition on the persistent behavior of kindergarten children. *University of Minnesota Child Welfare Monograph Series,* 1938, No. 15. P. 138.

Dorwart, Ezerman, Lewis, and Rosenhan pick up the threads of the previous experiment by asking whether social or nonsocial reinforcers will more effectively maintain behavior following brief social deprivation. They cite research in which social reinforcement was found to be more effective than nonsocial reinforcement with younger boys. However, they point out that the experimenter's preliminary behavior in these studies could be described as relatively aloof, thereby providing a form of social deprivation similar to that induced in the experiment reported by Gewirtz and Baer. In their experiment, either social deprivation or social satiation was induced by having the experimenter behave in either aloof or friendly fashion as he was leading the child to the experimental room. In each instance, following this initial experience, the child was allowed to play a game, which consisted of pressing one of two toggle switches at the sound of a buzzer. Social reinforcement was provided for some of the children by the experimenter saying "Good" or "Fine" when the left-hand switch was pressed. Nonsocial reinforcement was provided for the remaining children in the form of a red light that went on after responses to the left switch.

The investigators report that the subjects who were socially deprived during the brief pre-experimental period performed more frequently when the reinforcement was social than when it was not. Deprivation or satiation did not produce any differential change in the subject's performance when a nonsocial reinforcer (light) followed the subject's behavior. Social reinforcement can, it would appear from these findings, be a powerful determinant of task behavior, especially when the setting operations of an experiment are such as to provide some measure of social deprivation.

8 The Effect of Brief Social Deprivation on Social and Nonsocial Reinforcement[1]

WILLIAM DORWART
ROBERT EZERMAN
MICHAEL LEWIS
DAVID ROSENHAN

It has been commonly observed that young children are more sensitive to direct social reinforcement—a smile or verbal encouragement—than they are to impersonal abstract reinforcers whose effects greatly depend upon self-mediating cognitive processes. Several theoretical treatments which have been concerned with the problem of internalized self-reinforcing patterns of behavior (Hill, 1960; Mowrer, 1960, Ch. 10; Sears, 1957) have incorporated this observation. These theories all point to the initial dependence of young children upon direct social reinforcement and, with increasing age, to their greater reliance on mediating cognitive processes.

Until recently, this progression from dependence upon external social reinforcers to self-reinforcement, which is more contingent upon own responses, lacked empirical test. Recently, however, Lewis, Wall, and Aronfreed (1963) demonstrated experimentally the relative effectiveness of these qualitatively different reinforcing events at different age levels. Specifically, the authors found that for 6-year-old boys, social reinforcement was more effective in probability learn-

[1] Data for these studies were collected by the first two authors, under the direction of the last two. The studies were partially supported by funds from the National Institute of Mental Health, United States Public Health Service, to Fels Research Institute (Grant M-1260) and to Rosenhan (Grant MH-07690–01).

The authors are indebted to the Lower Merion School District, and particularly to Elwood L. Prestwood, Assistant Superintendent, George L. Lutz, and Burns S. Best, Principals. The authors are also grateful to Molly Martin and Robert Fried who collected some of the pilot data referred to in this report. The manuscript benefited from suggestions by N. Kogan and L. J. Stricker.

From the *Journal of Personality and Social Psychology,* 1965, 2, 111–115.

ing than was nonsocial reinforcement, while among 11-year-olds, no difference obtained between the two reinforcement conditions.

The present study examines this process in greater detail. In the first place, pilot studies by the authors and their colleagues, which followed carefully the experimental protocols employed by Lewis et al. (1963), failed to replicate their findings on either female or male populations. This failure to confirm led to a careful inspection of the relationships established between the experimenter and the subject in the Lewis et al. study and in our experiments. Our attention was drawn to a difference in preexperimental conditions between these studies. Specifically, Lewis et al. established a taciturn preexperimental relationship with the subject; the experimenter was a stranger who, after a brief introduction to the class, led each subject to the experimental room. The experimenter did not attempt to establish a warm relationship with the subject on the way to the experimental room, but rather maintained a preexperimental environment best characterized as *aloof*. In our pilot studies quite the opposite environment existed. Prior to warmly introducing the experimenter to the class, the teacher informed the subjects reassuringly that they would be playing a game, that it would be fun, and that no one would do poorly or be marked according to his performance. The experimenter maintained the *reassuring* quality of the preexperimental environment by chatting with the subject on the way to the experimental room, addressing the subject by name, and inquiring into his interests.

These differences in preexperimental environment are strongly reminiscent of the studies by Gewirtz and Baer (1958a, 1958b) in which subjects who were relatively deprived of the presence of an adult were subsequently more responsive to reinforcers administered by that adult than were subjects who had been previously satiated with such reinforcers. True, the period of deprivation employed by Gewirtz and Baer was considerably longer (20 minutes) than it was in these studies, where approximately 2–3 minutes elapsed between the introduction of the subject to the experimenter and the time the actual experiment began. But the conditions were analogous enough to suggest that even brief interaction with a taciturn adult might have effects similar to the lengthier social deprivation. The analogy between social deprivation and social aloofness was buttressed by Gewirtz, Baer, and Roth (1958) who noted the similar effects of low social availability of an adult (defined as an adult present but paying no attention to the child's behavior) and the 20-minute social deprivation period.

In view of the above, the following hypothesis was suggested: the relative effectiveness of social over nonsocial reinforcement found by Lewis et al. (1963) is contingent upon the exposure of these children to a period of social deprivation, since social deprivation is antecedent to the need for social reinforcement. Under conditions of social satiation, however, no differences in the effectiveness of the reinforcer will be apparent. The hypothesis was tested with a male population in order to provide a replication of the Lewis et al. experiment.

In addition, the experiment served to answer the following question: Does a subject who has been socially deprived respond subsequently only to social reinforcers, or will a nonsocial reinforcer have the same effect?

Method

Subjects

Forty-nine boys from two middle-class elementary public schools participated in this experiment. Subjects from three first-grade classes in one school experienced a period of social satiation and were then rewarded either with social reinforcement (10 subjects) or nonsocial reinforcement (12 subjects). In the second school, subjects from four first-grade classes experienced a period of social deprivation and were subsequently rewarded with social reinforcement (17 subjects) or nonsocial reinforcement (10 subjects). Six subjects alternated responses for more than 75 trials. Their data were excluded because it had been previously determined that such alternation reflected subjects' failure to understand the experimental task. Data for an additional subject who failed to complete all of the training trials were also excluded.

Apparatus

The apparatus, identical to that used by Lewis et al. (1963), consisted of a mechanism with which each subject "played," and a monitoring device on which the experimenter could follow the course of the game. The mechanism was a black box (7 × 12 × 7 inches) with two toggle-type, automatic-return switches along the lower edge of the front panel. A large red light, which could be operated from the monitor, was centered on the front panel. The monitor also activated a signal buzzer inside the subject's machine.

Procedure

Social deprivation. Subjects were given no information about the experiment from their teacher. Rather, the teacher simply asked the subject to "go with this man" when the experimenter appeared in the classroom. During the walk to the experimental room, which took about 3 minutes, the experimenter engaged in minimal conversation with the subject.

Social Satiation. The teacher told the subjects that they would be playing a "fun" game in which no one could do poorly. She warmly introduced the experimenter to the class. On the way to the experimental room, the experimenter maintained this reassuring atmosphere by chatting with the subject in a quite friendly fashion, addressing the subject by name and inquiring into his interests.

Once in the experimental room, the procedure was identical to that employed in the Lewis et al. (1963) study. The subject was told that he would be playing a game in which he was to press one of the two levers each time the buzzer sounded. The instructions implied that the object of the game was to try to produce the reinforcing event, but not that there would always be a correct lever on every trial. Reinforcement, therefore, was contingent upon the subject's response.

Prior to the training trials, the subject was presented with four sample trials for which he was instructed to press the left lever for the first two trials and the right lever for the last two trials. Reinforcement was administered on the first and last trials. The subject then began the series of 150 training trials. Events were randomized within each block of 10 trials, with the probabilities of the left and right levers being correct in the ratio of 70:30, respectively. During the training period, a second experimenter, hidden entirely from the subject, monitored and recorded the subject's responses. Subjects were rewarded with one of the two reinforcers:

Social reinforcement—The experimenter, seated behind the subject during the entire series of trials, said either, "Good" or "Fine" whenever the subject's response was correct. The light was not used.

Nonsocial reinforcement—After the four sample trials, the experimenter told the subject that for the remainder of the game the subject was to respond when he heard the buzzer and the red light would indicate to the subject whether his response was correct. The experimenter then left the room, explaining that he had some other work to do and that he would return shortly.

Results

Figure 1 presents the mean proportion of responses to the more frequently reinforced side ($S_{.70}$) in blocks of twenty trials for all subjects. Inspection reveals a marked tendency by those subjects who experienced social deprivation to maximize the more frequently reinforced response. Among the remaining groups, no differential performance is evident. The Kruskal-Wallis test (Siegel, 1956), applied to the subjects' mean proportions of correct responses across all 150 trials, indicates that these four groups are not drawn from the same population ($p < .01$). The Mann-Whitney U test was applied (Siegel, 1956) to the asymptotic proportions of $S_{.70}$ responses over the last three blocks of 10 trials. These findings, presented in Table 1, confirm the need for social reinforcement on the part of those subjects who had been socially deprived prior to the learning task.

Table 1 *Comparisons of Experimental Conditions at Asymptotic Performance*

Trials	SD–SR	SD–NSR	SS–NSR
141–150			
SD-NSR	.01[a]		
SS-NSR	.001	*ns*	
SS-SR	.001	*ns*	*ns*
131–140			
SD-NSR	.01		
SS-NSR	.01	*ns*	
SS-SR	.01	.05	*ns*
121–130			
SD-NSR	.001		
SS-NSR	.01	*ns*	
SS-SR	.001	*ns*	*ns*

Note.—SR = socially reinforced, NSR = nonsocially reinforced, SD = socially deprived, SS = socially satiated.
[a] All p values are for one-tailed Mann-Whitney U tests.

Discussion

It is clear that the superior asymptotic performance found by Lewis et al. (1963) among young boys who had been socially reinforced was not due merely to the effectiveness of social reinforcement. Rather, it resulted from the combined effects of social deprivation followed by social reinforcement. And, while the data presented here do not permit extrapolation to older children, it would seem more reasonable to interpret their findings in terms of differential capacities to tolerate social deprivation among younger and older children, rather than in terms of the relative effectiveness of social and nonsocial reinforcement per se. Thus, it might be argued that for older children the need for social reinforcement is not so intense, perhaps because they have been satiated on that kind of reinforcement or because other reinforcements have become dominant in their reinforcement hierarchy. Older children would, then, be more able

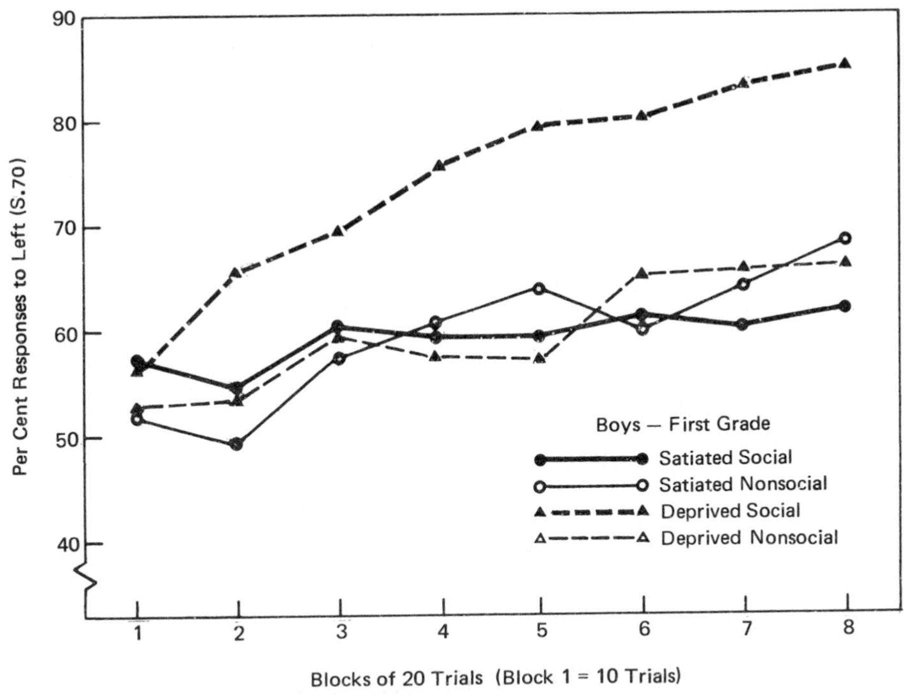

Figure 1 *Mean proportion of responses to the more frequently reinforced side.*

to tolerate social deprivation than younger children, for whom the need for, and consequently the potency of, social reinforcement is relatively greater.

These hypotheses are, of course, tentative formulations amenable to, and currently receiving, experimental verification. They are not, however, necessarily contradicted by the strong positive correlation found by Gewirtz and Baer (1958b) between deprivation and age, since in that study the authors used very young (nursery school) subjects. Conceivably, very young children show a marked responsiveness to social deprivation which tapers off and then actually decreases with increasing age.

Gewirtz and Baer (1958a), in discussing the implications of their study for a theory of social drives, suggest that the existence of such a theory would gain support if it could be shown that following social deprivation, subjects are more responsive to specifically social reinforcement than to other kinds of reinforcement. This experiment, along with Erickson's (1962), would appear to offer that support, in that a light, in this case, and marbles, in Erickson's —both nonsocial reinforcers—appear to have no differential effect following deprivation or satiation, while social reinforcements following deprivation do have their effects.

Indeed, these data and Erickson's (1962) invite some discussion regarding the controversy over whether the condition brought about by social deprivation is best seen as creating a social drive (Gewirtz and Baer, 1958a, 1958b) or anxiety. Walters and his co-workers (Walters and Karal, 1960; Walters and Quinn, 1960; Walters and Ray, 1960) have taken sharp issue with the concept of social *drive* (as opposed to the operationally defined social *deprivation*) on both theoretical and experimental grounds. As a matter of theoretical logic, they object to the evidential basis of any state whose existence is imputed solely from the behavior it is called upon to explain. Experimentally, they demonstrate that it may be to the anxiety component of social deprivation that the subsequent reinforcement is addressed, and they, therefore, prefer to interpret the findings in this area in terms of anxiety arousal and reduction.

The findings of this study and of Erickson's (1962) offer no support to the anxiety position, but implicitly support the interpretation of Gewirtz and Baer (1958a, 1958b). For if, indeed, it is anxiety that is at the root of the phenomenon elicited by social deprivation, then it must be an anxiety of a very special sort, one which is reduced not by all reinforcers but by a limited class of reinforcers of which, thus far, only the social reinforcer is known. And, while it may be argued that nonsocial reinforcement—lights or marbles—is not as powerful a reward as social reinforcement, it is certainly more powerful than no reward at all. The fact that these nonsocial reinforcements had no effect may indicate that the anxiety which arises from social deprivation requires a specific class (or kind) of reducer, to which nonsocial reinforcement does not belong, and to which, perhaps, only social reinforcers do belong. Further defining that class, that is, specifying which reinforcers affect social deprivation, is an interesting matter for future investigation.

The findings reported here are evidence for the operation of the social deprivation variable in a new experimental context—probability learning—and under conditions of considerably briefer deprivation than was previously employed. With regard to the latter, an issue of some methodological importance emerges, which is that apparently small and trivial differences in experimental procedure can yield large differences in experimental outcomes. The findings presented here, which indicate that preexperimental aloofness on the part of the experimenter produces effects similar to those of social deprivation, suggest that greater attention needs to be given to the preexperimental environment in which studies with human subjects take place. Certainly some comment regarding that environment might well be incorporated in the Method sections of research reports.

References

Erickson, Marilyn T. Effects of social deprivation and satiation on verbal conditioning in children. *Journal of Comparative and Physiological Psychology,* 1962, *55,* 953–957.

Gewirtz, J. L., and Baer, D. M. Deprivation and satiation of social reinforcers as drive conditions. *Journal of Abnormal and Social Psychology,* 1958, *57,* 165–172. (a)

Gewirtz, J. L., and Baer, D. M. The effect of brief social deprivation on behaviors for a social reinforcer. *Journal of Abnormal and Social Psychology,* 1958, *56,* 49–56. (b)

Gewirtz, J. L., Baer, D. M., and Roth, Chaya H. A note on the similar effects of low social availability of an adult and brief social deprivation on young children's behavior. *Child Development,* 1958, *29,* 149–152.

Hill, W. F. Learning theory and the acquisition of values. *Psychological Review,* 1960, *67,* 313–331.

Lewis, M., Wall, A. M., and Aronfreed, J. Developmental change in the relative values of social and nonsocial reinforcement. *Journal of Experimental Psychology,* 1963, *66,* 133–137.

Mowrer, O. H. *Learning theory and the symbolic processes.* New York: Wiley, 1960.

Sears, R. R. Identification as a form of behavioral development. In D. B. Harris (Ed.), *The concept of development.* Minneapolis: University of Minnesota Press, 1957. Pp. 149–161.

Siegel, S. *Nonparametric statistics for the behavioral sciences.* New York: McGraw-Hill, 1956.

Walters, R. H., and Karal, Pearl Social deprivation and verbal behavior. *Journal of Personality,* 1960, *28,* 89–107.

Walters, R. H., and Quinn, M. J. The effects of social and sensory deprivation on autokinetic judgments. *Journal of Personality,* 1960, *28,* 210–219.

Walters, R. H., and Ray, E. Anxiety, isolation and reinforcer effectiveness. *Journal of Personality,* 1960, *28,* 358–367.

Some Dimensions of Social Reinforcement

Although we are still far from understanding all of the reinforcement contingencies that shape and maintain social interaction, we can identify several of the more important variables. These include, of course, the several schedules of reinforcement that may apply in a given case, as well as a great many aspects of both the reinforcing agent and the person being reinforced. In the articles that follow, attention is given to several dimensions of the social reinforcement process. Specifically, these include immediate versus delayed reinforcement, characteristics of the reinforcing stimulus, and the age and family circumstances of the recipient of reinforcement. These experiments illustrate the manner in which these and other conditions of social reinforcement may be investigated.

The view that behavior is maintained by its immediate consequences seems to contradict the common observation that individuals make plans and forego immediate satisfactions for the sake of long-range goals and rewards. *Mischel* reports an interesting cross-cultural examination of this question. Studying two ethnic groups in Trinidad, he tested the hypothesis that preference for a small but immediate reward, as opposed to a large but delayed reward, is related to the presence or absence of a father in the home. Presumably, children living with their fathers would have been promised rewards which were delivered after varying periods of delay. Their reaction to a male experimenter, therefore, would more likely be to wait for a large reward than to settle immediately for a small one. On the other hand, children from fatherless homes would be less likely to have experienced the promise and delivery of delayed reinforcement, and they should be more inclined to accept a smaller, immediate reward. In general, Mischel's findings confirm these hypotheses. His results have implications for the role of personal history in the individual's reactions to various schedules of reinforcement.

9 *Preference for Delayed Reinforcement: An Experimental Study of a Cultural Observation*[1]

WALTER MISCHEL

This study is, in part, an attempt to validate, experimentally, an observation about cultural differences formulated during the course of a "culture and personality" field research in Trinidad, British West Indies. It may be of interest, therefore, not only for its specific findings but also as an example of experimentation in the cultural field.

On the basis of anthropological observation, a major personality difference between the Negro and East Indian ethnic groups of the island of Trinidad was suggested. This difference, as expressed by numerous informants, is that the Negroes are impulsive, indulge themselves, settle for next to nothing if they can get it right away, do not work or wait for bigger things in the future but, instead, prefer smaller gains immediately. In contrast to this, the Indian is said to deprive himself and to be willing and able to postpone immediate gain and pleasure for the sake of obtaining greater rewards and returns in the future. In effect, when given a choice, the Negro is said to be characterized by preference for relatively smaller, immediate reinforcements, whereas the Indian is said to prefer larger, delayed reinforcements.

Judgments centering about such a distinction of differential preference or tolerance for delayed reinforcement are, of course, also quite prevalent within our own culture. The widely observed preferences of children for immediate rewards has been commented on (Cole and Morgan, 1947; Faegre and Anderson, 1937; Harris, 1950) and is reflected in some theoretical formulations, e.g., the "pleasure principle" and the "reality principle" (Freud, 1922; Hendrick, 1948). In clinical applications, the inability to postpone immediate gratification for the sake of delayed rewards is often considered an important factor in immaturity, maladjustment, and "psychopathy." Mowrer and Ullman (1945), for example, consider the delay of reinforcements to be a critical factor in the development of neurotic and criminal behavior.

Although the research on delay of reinforcement in human conditioning has been vast (Wolfle's studies [1930, 1932] are representative), there has been comparatively little experimentation with human subjects on variables other than the effect of the time interval itself on learning rate or object preference (e.g., Brenner, 1934; Irwin, Armitt, and Simson, 1943; Irwin, Orchinik, and Weiss, 1946;

[1] This study was conducted while the author collaborated with Frances Mischel in an interdisciplinary project which was sponsored by the Wenner-Grenn Foundation for Anthropological Research. A report based on portions of this paper was read at the convention of the Rocky Mountain Psychological Association, April, 1957.

From the *Journal of Abnormal and Social Psychology,* 1958, *56,* 57–61.

Nagge, 1942; Saltzman, 1951) and outside the conditioning paradigm. A notable exception is Mahrer's (1956) attempt to apply Rotter's (1954) expectancy construct. Mahrer was able to make successful predictions about children's choices for immediate versus delayed reinforcements as a function of differential expectancies for obtaining positive reinforcement following delay. That is, the expectancy that reinforcement would follow from the social agent even after time delay was shown to be an important variable. In common sense terms, this kind of behavior may be thought of as "trust" or the belief that the agent promising delayed reinforcement will actually supply it. The emphasis in Mahrer's study, and in the present research, is on the expectancy for reinforcement to follow as a function of making a particular choice with a particular social agent in a given situation, rather than on the time interval itself.

One may assume that expectancies for reinforcement to follow from certain social agents, in spite of time delay, are learned in a manner fundamentally similar to the learning of any social behaviors, and are governed by similar principles of generalization. It seems probable, then, that a child's expectancies that delayed reinforcement will issue from new adult social agents are related to his past experiences in which promised reinforcement followed delay from such major adult sources of learning as the parental figures within the home. In a situation in which a child is confronted with a new male social agent, we would anticipate that his expectancies for promised reinforcement to follow from that social agent, in spite of time delay, are related to past experiences of this kind with the father or father figure in the home. Similarly, we would anticipate that the child's expectancies that promised reinforcement will follow, in spite of delay, from female social agents are related to past experiences of this kind with the mother or mother figure in the home. (Since in the present experiment the social agent (E) is male, our discussion and prediction center about expectancies for delayed reinforcement from male social agents.) We would further expect children who have had less of such experience with a male social agent in the home to show less "trust," or lower expectancy for reinforcement to follow in spite of time delay when promised by a new male social agent, than children who have had more of such experience. Presumably, a child whose father is absent in the home has had more limited experiences in which promised reinforcement follows in spite of time delay from a male social agent. We anticipate that such a child would have lower expectancy for delayed reinforcement from a male social agent than a child whose father is present within the home. Specifically, we would expect the "fatherless" child to show less preference for a larger but delayed reinforcement and more preference for a smaller but immediate reinforcement than the child whose father is present within the home.

The above prediction seemed, on the basis of tentative observation, to apply differentially to the two cultural groups we are considering; namely, examination of the family structures of the Negro and Indian groups within the particular culture and locale suggested that the Negro family seemed more frequently characterized by the absence of a temporally stable adult male figure in the home than was the Indian family. The presence or absence of a father within the family constellation was selected as a key variable influencing choice behavior with respect to delayed or immediate reinforcement and the aim of the experiment was: (*a*) to test the hypothesis of differential preference for larger, delayed as opposed to smaller, immediate reinforcement of the two ethnic groups, it being predicted that the Indian group would show greater preference for larger, delayed reinforcement than the Negro group; and (*b*) to test the hypothesis of differential preference for larger, delayed as opposed to smaller, immediate reinforcement, issuing from a male social agent, of children whose fathers are present or absent within the home, it being predicted that children having a father or father figure present within the home would prefer the larger, delayed reinforcement more than children lacking such a figure. Further, since age and socioeconomic level seemed potentially relevant variables for this kind of choice behavior, this information was included in the data collected, with the intent of relating it to the choice.

Method

Subjects. The subjects (Ss) included 53 male and female children between the ages of 7 and 9 in the elementary section of a rural Trinidad school. The school was located in the southern part of the island and seemed representative of rural schools within the colony. Thirty-five of the children were Negro and eighteen East Indian. The sex ratio was 29 males to 24 females. The children of the two ethnic groups attended the same large section or class and it was thus possible to administer the experimental test to the members of both ethnic groups at the same time.

The Reinforcements. Pre-experimental sessions were required to select two reinforcements of use for the experimental situation. Towards this end, 15 Negro and Indian boys and girls, representing the above ages, and selected from another rural Trinidad school, were seen in individual sessions and their preferences for various specific reinforcements were elicited. As a result, two reinforcements (both candy, but varying markedly in size, prize, and packaging, i.e., a one-cent and a ten-cent candy) were selected. These met the desired requirements inasmuch as the larger reinforcement was uniformly preferred in a straight choice situation ("which *one* of these two would you like to take"), but when the choice was "you can have this one (the smaller) today *or* this one (the larger) in one week" approximately 50 per cent of the group chose the former and approximately 50 per cent the latter.

Task and Measures. The Ss' task was to fill out a simple questionnaire. All the Ss were sufficiently literate for this. The questionnaire items of experimental interest were ethnic group, age, socioeconomic status, and presence or absence of the father within the household. Ethnic group was measured by S's checking either "Creole" or "Indian," and age by a "fill in" response. The measure of socioeconomic status was quite gross, and S merely checked "galvanized" (tin roof, comparatively expensive and generally a sign of relatively high socioeconomic status in the rural areas) or "carrat" (thatched leaf roof, inexpensive, and generally a sign of low socioeconomic status), in response to an item concerning the kind of house he lives in. This measure provided a crude dichotomization into relatively "high" and relatively "low" socioeconomic status. "Presence" or "absence" of the father in the home was measured by the response "yes" or "no" to the questions "does your father live at home with you," and "do your mother *and* father live at home with you." One S reported that father lived at home, mother lived at home, but that mother and father did not live at home and was eliminated from the analysis for this inconsistency. All but three Ss reported "yes" to the question "does your mother live at home with you." These three exceptions lived with their grandmothers and because of this deviation were omitted from the statistical analyses.

An informal check on the accuracy of the children's responses was attempted with the headmaster who was familiar with the home situations of most of the Ss. This check was undertaken on a sample of twenty of the protocols and indicated that, to the headmaster's best knowledge, the responses corresponded with his own information about the children.

Procedure. The experimenter (*E*) was introduced as an American interested in gathering information on children in the local schools of the island. To help with this the Ss were asked to fill out the questionnaire. When these were completed, *E* expressed his wish to thank the group for their cooperation. He displayed the two kinds of reinforcements and said: "I would like to give each of you a piece of candy but I don't have enough of these (indicating the larger, more preferred reinforcement) with me today. So you can either get this one (indicating the smaller, less preferred reinforcement) right now, today, or, if you want to, you can wait for this one (indicating) which I will bring back next Wednesday (one week delay interval)." To insure clarity, these instructions were repeated in rephrased form and both reinforcements were carefully displayed. The fact that getting the (smaller) candy today precluded getting the (larger) one next week, and vice versa, was stressed. Ss were asked to indicate their choice by writing "today" (T) or "next week" (W) on their questionnaires. The response made here was the measure of choice of a larger (or more preferred) delayed reinforcement or a smaller (less preferred) immediate reinforcement. Ss were seated sufficiently far apart from each other to insure reasonably that their choices were made independently in this group setting.

Results and Discussion

The data from the present experiment were analyzed in terms of differential preference for smaller, immediate reinforcement versus larger, delayed reinforcement in relationship to ethnic group, presence or absence of the father within the home, age, and socioeconomic status. All statistical analyses were made with the chi-square test. The data used for relating the experimental choice with ethnic group and presence or absence of the father within the home, are given in Table 1.

Comparison of the Negro and Indian groups on the experimental choice (Table 1) yielded a chi square of 4.17 (p between .05 and .02), a significantly larger proportion of the Negro Ss choosing immediate reinforcement. It should be noted, however, that if the Yates correction is applied (the expected frequencies within two of the cells are between eight and ten), the chi square is reduced to 3.06, having a p value of less than .10. Nevertheless, this difference between the ethnic groups on the experimental choice still seems sufficient to require caution in combining them on other analyses unless it can be shown that members of the two groups are in comparable proportions on the other relevant variables.

The comparison between ethnic groups with respect to presence or absence of the father does not indicate a difference at an acceptable probability level (chi square is 2.56 with $p < .20$ and $> .10$). Some ancillary evidence supporting the trend of differential fatherlessness within the two ethnic groups can be drawn from another source. Data, including the measure of presence or absence of the father within the home, were collected within the same school for older children, of both ethnic groups,

Table 1 *Relationships between Ethnic Group, Presence of the Father, and Experimental Choice*

Group	Number Choosing Immediate Reinforcement	Number Choosing Delayed Reinforcement	x^2	p
Negro	22 (18.49)[a]	13 (16.51)		
Indian	6 (9.51)	12 (8.49)	4.17 3.06[b]	< .05 < .10
Father present	17 (22.19)	25 (19.81)		
Father absent	11 (5.81)	0 (5.19)	10.13[b]	< .01
Negroes with father present	12 (15.71)	13 (9.29)		
Negroes with father absent	10 (6.29)	0 (3.71)	6.19[b]	< .02

[a] Figures in parentheses are expected frequencies.
[b] Chi square corrected with Yates correction, for continuity.

who were not included in the present study. If the data from these children ($N = 24$) on presence or absence of the father for the two ethnic groups are combined with data from the Ss of the present study, a chi square of 5.57 is obtained, which is significant beyond the .02 level, and in the direction expected from cultural observation.

In view of these findings, the relationship between presence or absence of the father and the experimental choice was tested for each of the ethnic groups separately as well as for the total combined sample. As there is only one "fatherless" S in the Indian group, such a test is not meaningful for that group. For the Negro group alone, and for the total sample, the comparison between presence or absence of the father and the experimental choice (Table 1) yielded chi squares of 10.13 and 6.19 respectively, which are significant beyond the .01 and .02 levels, and indicate, as predicted, a greater proportion of choices for immediate reinforcement on the part of "fatherless" Ss.

Before this relationship between presence of the father and preference for delayed, larger reinforcement can be generalized, it will of course be necessary to test other cultural groups in a similar experimental situation. The present research emphasized the relationship only between the "physical" presence of S's father in the home and preference for delayed reinforcement issuing from another male social agent. In view of the obtained significant finding, the relationship between the "psychological" presence of the father (e.g., degree of identification) and this kind of behavior merits further investigation. Such research would seem especially relevant for a further understanding of impulsive behavior and "psychopathy."

The presence or absence of the father may be significant not at, or just as, a causal factor in itself in relation to preference for delayed versus immediate reinforcement, but as an index of the extent to which the parents or the family participate in a delayed reward culture. That is, the presence of the father in the home (in contrast, for example, to a ready abandoning of the home) may, in turn, be related to the degree of family participation in a cultural pattern in which delayed, larger reinforcement is preferred or prized more than immediate, smaller reinforcement. Such participation may have many other impacts upon the child apart from, or in addition to, the paternal presence.

Neither the proportion of Negro and Indian Ss nor the proportion of Ss with father present and absent was significantly different for the three age groups or for their socioeconomic status groups (both p levels greater than .20). Therefore, tests of the relationship between age and the experimental choice, and between socioeconomic status and the experimental choice, can be made with all Ss combined. Table 2 shows the number of Ss in each age group choosing immediate versus delayed reinforcement. The chi-square test applied to this table yields a corrected chi-square value of 7.10 which is significant beyond the .05 level and indicates an increasing proportion of Ss choosing delayed reinforcement at the older age levels.

Table 2 *Relationship Between Age and Experimental Choice*

Experimental Choice	Age 7	Age 8	Age 9	x^2	p
Number choosing immediate reinforcement	13 (8.45)[a]	13 (14.27)	2 (5.28)		
Number choosing delayed reinforcement	3 (7.55)	14 (12.73)	8 (4.72)	7.10[b]	< .05

[a] Figures in parentheses are expected frequencies.
[b] Chi square corrected with Yates correction, for continuity.

This relationship between Ss' age and preference for delayed reinforcement is in accord with nonexperimental discussions of such a relationship to the effect that with increasing maturity comes the increasing ability to delay gratification. The finding is consistent with an interpretation of preference for delayed reinforcement as a learned behavior which is, in part, a function of the expectancy that the promised reinforcement will issue from the social agent in spite of time delay. With increasing age, the potentiality for developing a strong expectancy of this kind increase *if* the individual continues to gain reinforcing experiences within this area, thus building up the relevant expectancies, but not as a function of growing older or biological maturation per se.

Comparison of the "high" versus "low" socioeconomic groups on the experimental choice did not yield a significant difference (*p* value greater than .20). This lack of established relationship between socioeconomic level and the experimental choice cannot be considered definitive in view of the extreme crudeness of the measure of socioeconomic level employed.

Summary

This experiment tested an observation, made by anthropological field techniques, regarding personality differences between the East Indian and Negro populations of Trinidad, B.W.I. The primary results were significant differences between preference for immediate, smaller versus delayed, larger reinforcement and, first, the presence or absence of the father within the home, and second, age. The over-all findings appear to have implications not only for the two specific ethnic groups studied here but also for further research on relationships between personality variables of a less gross kind and this type of choice behavior within our own culture. If there are relationships between "maturity" or "adjustment" and tolerance, or preference, for larger, delayed as opposed to smaller, immediate reinforcement, then the isolation of major variables related to such preferences seems particularly important.

References

Brenner, B. Effect of immediate and delayed praise and blame upon learning and recall. *Teachers College Contributions in Education,* 1934, No. 620.

Cole, Luella, and Morgan, J. J. B. *Psychology of childhood and adolescence.* New York: Rinehart, 1947.

Faegre, Marion L., and Anderson, J. E. *Child care and training.* Minneapolis: University of Minnesota Press, 1937.

Freud, S. *Beyond the pleasure principle.* New York: Boni and Liveright, 1922.

Harris, D. B. How children learn interests, motives, and attitudes. In N. B. Henry (Ed.), *49th Yearbook, NSSE,* 1950, Part I, *Learning and instruction,* 129–155.

Hendrick, I. *Facts and theories of psychoanalysis.* New York: Alfred A. Knopf, 1948.

Irwin, F. W., Armitt, F. M., and Simson, C. Studies in object preferences: I. The effect of temporal proximity. *Journal of Experimental Psychology,* 1943, *33,* 64–72.

Irwin, F. W., Orchinik, C. W., and Weiss, Johanna Studies in object preferences: The effect of temporal proximity upon adults' preferences. *American Journal of Psychology,* 1946, *59,* 458–462.

Mahrer, A. R. The role of expectancy in delayed reinforcement. *Journal of Experimental Psychology,* 1956, *52,* 101–105.

Mowrer, O. H., and Ullman, A. D. Time as a determinant in integrative learning. *Psychological Review,* 1945, *52,* 61–90.

Nagge, J. W. *Psychology of the child.* New York: Ronald Press, 1942.

Rotter, J. B. *Social learning and clinical psychology.* New York: Prentice-Hall, 1954.

Saltzman, I. J. Delay of reward and human verbal learning. *Journal of Experimental Psychology,* 1951, *41,* 437–439.

Wolfle, H. M. Time factors in conditioning finger withdrawal. *Journal of Genetic Psychology,* 1930, *4,* 372–378.

Wolfle, H. M. Conditioning as a function of the interval between the conditioned and the original stimulus. *Journal of Genetic Psychology,* 1932, *7,* 80–103.

Zigler grapples with the question of what social reinforcement means to the child. He defines meaning in terms of the child's stage of development and his past experiences. But he takes issue with the view that reinforcers must be identified not independently but by their effect on some operant. This view implies, says Zigler, that each child will necessarily be influenced only by those particular events that have effectively become reinforcers for him. Zigler feels that the discovery and definition of a reinforcer in terms of the effects that a particular stimulus has upon the strength of a response is too mechanistic. This approach, he argues, forces us to catalogue the reinforcers that are effective for any given child and makes prediction of the behavior of children in general difficult if not impossible.

What Zigler suggests, in effect, is that we identify some class of behaviors and then determine what general consequences serve to increase the frequency of this behavior class. There is evidence, for example, that "praise" is an effective reinforcer for children of a certain age and socioeconomic standing, whereas being told that they are "correct" is more effective with other children. Presumably, these two contingencies have become differentially effective in maintaining behavior as a result of both the child's developmental level and his reinforcement history. Knowing something about each of these factors enables us to predict how a child with a particular background will react to the announcement that he is either "good" or "correct" for making a particular response. Zigler also questions whether deprivation operations, such as those described by Gewirtz and Baer, are not, in fact, mediated by other events in the child's life history. A child's behavior is seen by Zigler as determined not just by the immediate circumstances but rather by his total personality and life history.

10 *Social Reinforcement, Environmental Conditions and the Child*[1]

EDWARD ZIGLER

The view advanced herein is that social reinforcement, broadly defined, is a central construct in our understanding and prediction of the behavior of children. The full heuristic value of this concept will only be approached when certain present errors in our thinking concerning social reinforcement are corrected. Among these errors is the tendency to conceptualize social reinforcers as homogeneous entities acting upon the child in a mechanical manner.

Strong arguments can be mustered against such a view. The vast array of stimulus configurations that have been employed as social reinforcers, for example, human proximity, attention, nods, smiles, and verbal comments of various kinds, represent a much too heterogeneous collection of stimuli to be profitably conceptualized as equivalent referrents of some underlying conceptual entity. The practice of conceptualizing such stimuli as members of a common class rests upon the fact that such stimuli enter into a common general functional relationship with the responses of the child that precede the administration of such stimuli.

Stated in the simplest terms, what we have discovered is that, if a response of the child is followed by such stimuli, then the likelihood of occurrence of that response, its rate of emission, or its amplitude is increased. This simple functional relationship results in the construction of a two-category classificatory schema, the utilization of which allows us to label stimuli as either being or not being social reinforcers.

We will grant that such a twofold schema has an air of parsimony and if employed results in a modicum of predictability. It is this modicum of pre-

[1] The preparation of this paper was facilitated by National Institute of Mental Health Research Grant M-3945 (C1) United States Public Health Service.

dictability that has been capitalized on in those repeated studies employing social reinforcers that have done nothing more than demonstrate that the Law of Effect does indeed hold. Our faith in this simple view of social reinforcement has been replenished by such studies, and we have failed to move on to a more imaginative and refined classificatory schema that would allow for a more meaningful classification of social reinforcers.

I am suggesting here that we have been much too enthralled with the demonstration that a response of the child can enter into an easily plotted functional relationship with a social stimulus. But this concern with stimuli and responses, though scientifically respectable, appears to leave out the child as a functioning and adjusting organism and finally leads us into a maze from which it is impossible to escape. The demonstration that a social reinforcer strengthens a response sheds little light on the central issue of why this should be the case.

The answer to this theoretically more provocative question must inevitably involve an analysis of the social reinforcer from the viewpoint of the psychological structure of the child. The central question is what the social reinforcer means to the child, with such meaning ultimately being determined by the cognitive and motivational attributes of the child. There are those who would assert that this concern with internal structures and the meaning attributed to stimuli by the child must invariably involve us in a mentalistic or phenomenological morass. I do not believe this to be the case. How a child will experience any particular environmental configuration can in part be objectively assessed by gauging both the level of cognitive development and the gross experiential history of the child prior to his encounter with this particular configuration.

Furthermore, I would assert that it is the failure to concern ourselves with the internal processes and structures of the child that has eventuated in the sterile, two-category system mentioned earlier. This system, which is a natural outgrowth of the mechanistic approach to social reinforcement, does not actually possess the parsimony or predictive efficacy that has been attributed to it by its adherents. If we ask the simple question of how to classify social stimuli as being reinforcers or neutral in respect to reinforcement, we are told that we must in every instance observe some response, that is, an operant, and consistently present the social stimulus in question to the child as a consequence of his making that response. If the response increases in strength, we can then classify that stimulus as a social reinforcer on the basis of the functional relationship just outlined.

I fail to see the parsimony of such an approach, since such a cataloguing would involve an almost infinite number of stimuli and responses. The problem is made even more complex by the information that the degree of satiation or deprivation, which, when defined, is always in terms of variables external to the child, affects the functional relationship so that a social stimulus actually capable of affecting the child's behavior gives the appearance of being a neutral stimulus. We thus have social stimuli flitting from category to category in our twofold system, as a function of variables not involved in our basic definition of a social reinforcer.

Adding even further to our difficulty, the proponents of the mechanistic view (see Bijou and Baer, 1961) assert that differences in individual histories as well as differences in the current stimulus situation also determine what will be and what will not be a social reinforcer for any particular child. We thus see that our twofold category system must be constructed for each and every child with whom we intend to deal. Furthermore, employing this procedure, the most objectively negative social stimuli could be and in fact are defined as positive social reinforcers. Bijou and Baer tell us that such an approach will at last make the individual differences that we encounter in children understandable to us. It thus appears that the general principle of social reinforcement stemming from the mechanistic approach actually has little generality and in practice must be reduced to the individual case. Not even the strongest adherent of the idiographic position could support what essentially must become a nonpredictive psychology. This mechanistic view of social reinforcement instructs us that, if we are to understand and predict the behavior of the child, we must empirically catalogue the social reinforcers for that child, and we must repeat this process for every child that interests us. Such an impasse can only be avoided by introducing general principles of development and personality dynamics and thus attending to the central structures of the child, which are the actual mediating mechanisms between the stimuli and responses that have for so long enamored our mechanistic colleagues.

We agree that such structures and processes will have idiosyncratic components, but they will also be characterized by meaningful consistencies that would allow us a fuller and more meaningful understanding of the role of social reinforcers. When the wide range of social reinforcers is approached from such a child-centered viewpoint, we find that they often lend themselves to structural analyses.

One effort toward such an analysis is contained in a recent study conducted by Paul Kanzer and myself. We were struck by the tendency of many investigators to employ social reinforcers indiscriminately, their implicit assumption being that such reinforcers are homogeneous pellets being dispensed to equally hungry rats. We were interested in demonstrating that such an assumption is erroneous, even when applied to that narrower array of social stimuli represented by verbal reinforcers.

But how to proceed? Although one could randomly select some verbal reinforcers and empirically assess their relative efficacy, such a procedure would throw little light on why one such reinforcer was more effective than another. Furthermore, such a procedure would represent the gross empirical approach that I have been arguing against. Our own theoretical bias suggested that a more parsimonious approach would involve the designation of some classificatory principles whereby meaningful sub-classes of verbal reinforcers could be constructed. Optimally such a classificatory system would eventuate in specific predictions that reinforcers in one class would be more effective across all subjects than reinforcers in another class or that reinforcers in one class would be more effective with a particular type of subject than reinforcers in another class.

The investigations of child-rearing practices conducted by Davis (1944) and Erickson (1947) suggest that the degree to which a verbal reinforcer emphasizes correctness may constitute such a useful classificatory dimension. A number of investigators have suggested or reported that being correct is more reinforcing for middle- than for lower-class children. Obversely, in a study conducted by Zigler, Hodgden, and Stevenson, (1958), we found that, while verbal reinforcers having primarily a praise connotation lengthened the performance of retarded children drawn from the lower socio-economic class, they did not lengthen the performance of middle-class children.

Thus the prediction may be generated that reinforcers emphasizing praise will be more effective with lower-class children, while reinforcers emphasizing correctness will be more effective with middle-class children. The problem remains of how to classify verbal reinforcers on the praise-correct dimension. Although every verbal reinforcer conveys both an indication of praise and of correctness, it is possible on a priori grounds to designate certain verbal reinforcers as primarily in the praise category and others as primarily in the correctness category. In our study, the words "right" and "correct" were conceptualized as connoting correctness, while "good" and "fine" were conceptualized as connoting praise.

We employed groups of lower- and middle-class, seven-year-old children and utilized the Gewirtz-Baer procedure of reinforcing one of two holes into which the child could drop marbles, in order to assess the effectiveness of the reinforcers. As predicted, we found that praise reinforcers are more effective for lower- than for middle-class children, while correct reinforcers are more effective for middle- than for lower-class children.

Two views can explain this finding: The first is congruent with the mechanistic approach in which being praised and being correct would be conceptualized as tertiary reinforcers and the argument made that among middle-class seven-year-olds, being right has been more frequently associated with secondary and primary reinforcers, while, for lower-class seven-year-olds, being praised is more frequently associated with these reinforcers.

The second explanation would forego focusing on pairing frequency in favor of attending to the over-all cognitive development of the child. This approach would most centrally employ the concept of a developmentally changing reinforcer hierarchy. As has been suggested by Beller (1955), Gerwirtz (1954), and Heathers (1955) the effectiveness of attention and praise as reinforcers diminishes with maturity, being replaced by the reinforcement inherent in the information that one is correct. This latter type of reinforcer appears to serve primarily as a cue for the administration of self-reinforcement. Such a process would appear to be central in the child's progress from dependency to independence.

Of major importance here is not the particular social reinforcer that is paired with particular responses but rather the ability of the child to conceptualize a verbal stimulus as a cue for self-reinforcement and to be able to administer this type of reinforcement. Such a process involves a differentiated cognitive system in which the child has the ability to differentiate himself clearly from others and to comprehend clearly that his success is a direct outgrowth of his own efforts and the maturity involved in the rather complicated process of taking the self as an object that can be rewarded, with a resulting feeling of pride, or punished, with the resulting experience of shame or guilt.

Such a process is a far cry from that earlier period in life when the efficacy of a social reinforcer is probably dependent upon its close relationship to primary reinforcers and a period during which a wide array of social stimuli influences behavior in a relatively undifferentiated hedonistic way involving little or no central mediation. This would explain why a particular reinforcer is not equally effective for the infant, for the two-year-old and for the ten-year-old. We are again asserting that any real understanding of how social reinforcers affect the behavior of children can only come about through a careful analysis of the inherent characteristics of the particular social reinforcer in question and the full appreciation of the particular structure of the child to whom the reinforcer is being dispensed.

Employing such a view, such praise reinforcers as

"good" and "fine" would be conceptualized as conveying information to the child concerning the feelings of the social agent toward the responses that the child has made. It is these feelings that in the past have been associated with the availability of other reinforcers. For instance, when the parent feels that the child is good, other primary reinforcers may well be forthcoming. However, later in life the child becomes more liberated from the feelings of social agents, and the task of obtaining primary reinforcers becomes much less important. He becomes a more autonomous agent primarily interested in obtaining mastery over his world. The motive of effectiveness becomes central, and he becomes interested in the quality of his own performance. Here the concern is not limited to how social agents feel about him, but is extended to how he feels about himself. Furthermore, how he feels about himself is determined by the success he encounters in dealing with the continuous problems presented by the environment. What he is now interested in is whether he is doing things correctly, whether he is right. Thus, social agents and the social reinforcers they dispense take on new meaning.

At this stage it is the social reinforcer that signifies the successful coping of the child that is valued by him, and the feelings of the social agent as expressed in certain social reinforcers, though related, recede in importance. Approached in this way, certain central problems concerning social reinforcement emerge. For instance, we would be interested in discovering at what point in development the word "good" ceases to have inherent value and becomes instead a cue for self-reinforcement. That such a question has been glossed over can be demonstrated by referring to certain common practices in the general investigation of reinforcement effects. For instance, when we dispense the word "good" to children we refer to it as a social reinforcer. When we dispense the same word to adults we refer to it as a verbal reinforcer, emphasizing its cue properties and giving little or no attention to its social-reinforcement qualities.

But let us apply this thinking to the Zigler-Kanzer study that we have been discussing. It suggests that the lower-class seven-year-old child is developmentally lower than the seven-year-old middle-class child in that he has not made a transition in which reinforcers signifying "correct" replace praise reinforcers in the reinforcer hierarchy. Some support for this argument may be found in the recent work of Les Phillips and myself, which indicates that social class transcends economic and social considerations and reflects the global level of development attained.

Related to this argument is the suggestion of several investigators (Davis, 1941, 1943; Terrell, Durkin, and Wiesley, 1959) that the lower-class child is less influenced than the middle-class child by abstract, symbolic rewards. Such would be the case if the lower-class child were indeed developmentally lower than the middle-class child of the same CA. Thus, one would expect not only that correct reinforcers would be less effective than praise reinforcers for the lower-class child, but that all verbal reinforcers, due to their abstract quality, would be less reinforcing for lower- than middle-class children of the same CA. Some support for this, although not statistically significant, was found in the Zigler-Kanzer study. Studies by Terrell, Durkin, and Wiesley (1959) and by Zigler and deLabry (1962) have found statistically significant evidence that abstract reinforcers are less effective with lower- than with middle-class children.

This is not to say that the particular history of pairing of social reinforcers with responses does not influence the effectiveness of these social reinforcers, but rather to assert the view that other factors are involved as well. We are presently making longitudinal studies with groups of lower- and middle-class children, as well as studies in which we build in particular reinforcer histories and then test for the effectiveness of reinforcers. Hopefully, this body of work should cast further light on the issues we have been raising.

It thus appears that any real understanding of the social-reinforcement process demands an appreciation of the intricate relationship between the particular social reinforcer being dispensed and the developmental level of the child. However, it is abundantly clear that within any developmental level one finds marked differences in the effectiveness of various social reinforcers. Here we would agree with the general position of the mechanistic view that such differences reflect differences in the total social-reinforcement history of the child. Beyond a common recognition of this gross state of affairs, my views would have little similarity to those of my mechanistic colleagues.

To clarify this difference in viewpoint, consider an area of continuing concern, namely, the effect of social deprivation on the efficacy of social reinforcers. Let us first examine the mechanistic approach. Again the paradigm is a simple one. Once you know that a social reinforcer is effective, the theoretical assertion is made that satiating the child on that reinforcer results in the attenuation of its effectiveness, while depriving the child of that reinforcer results in increasing its effectiveness. Thus, social reinforcers are viewed as operating on the child in much the same way as such primary reinforcers as food and water.

In two of the most provocative studies of recent years, Gewirtz and Baer (1958a; 1958b) found that brief periods of social satiation or social deprivation did so effect the efficacy of social reinforcers as measured by performance on a simple two-hole learning task. Once one overcomes his uneasiness with the somewhat tautological definition in which deprivation means "the unavailability to the organism of a given reinforcer for a period sufficient to effect an increase in behaviors for it," he cannot help but admire the operational purity of the Gewirtz-Baer procedure. However, submerged beneath this purity there are views of the child and the effects of social deprivation that I cannot accept.

Implicitly, the child is seen as an automaton whose behaviors are almost unlimitedly shaped by his recent experiences. Is the child deprived of food? Give him a meal and the effects are gone. Is the child deprived of social reinforcement? Satiate him on social reinforcers until they are no longer effective in that situation, and the effects of social deprivation vanish. We are thus presented with a completely pliable organism whose behavior is continually a product of environmental factors external to him. While such a view may be appropriate for our understanding of Skinner's pigeons, it will hardly suffice for children.

The child must be viewed as an acting agent, a thinking, feeling, motivated organism who is not indiscriminately buffeted about by any wayward wind of experience. We are not dealing with an empty organism whom we may actually deprive or satiate through some simple experimental procedure. Rather, we are dealing with a programed organism who, although open to change, maintains an integrity or consistency in his interactions with his social world. Rather than viewing social deprivation as a phenomenon the effects of which are easily built into or out of the organism by external social agents, I have preferred to conceptualize it as a phenomenon that, once experienced, becomes built into the motivational structure of the child and there mediates the child's interaction with his environment. I certainly feel that, once the effects of social deprivation become a part of this mediational apparatus, it can be affected by subsequent environmental events, but the effect of such subsequent environmental events will not act upon the child in a mechanical manner. Rather, their effects will only be comprehensible if viewed from the mediational structure upon which such events are acting.

I, too, believe that social deprivation results in the enhanced effectiveness of social reinforcers, but as indicated above I feel not only that these effects are long-lasting, but that they color the subsequent social experiences of the child. Two related studies give evidence on this point. In the first study, done some years ago, I tested the hypothesis that the degree of preinstitutional social deprivation experienced by a group of institutionalized retardates would be positively related to the effectiveness of social reinforcers. The obvious problem here is that of defining such social deprivation. It is common knowledge that no concise, accepted definition of social deprivation is to be found.

At that time I concluded, with other investigators, that this concept has been loosely applied to certain events in early childhood, which, in turn, are characterized as antecedent to certain social behaviors. However, there has been little agreement on either the early events or the resultant behaviors. I could have designated such events arbitrarily, and then defined social deprivation in terms of their occurrence or nonoccurrence in the child's history. However, since that population of events which constitutes social deprivation has never been adequately delimited, such a procedure struck me as somewhat presumptuous. The procedure finally employed was that of asking judges to evaluate the entire preinstitutional social history of the child for social deprivation, while at the same time noting the specific factors in the history that determined their evaluation. The only instruction the raters were given was that social deprivation referred to the nature of the interactions that the child has had with the important adults in his life.

This procedure resulted not only in reliable ratings but also in the extraction of a universe of relatively objective factors, which now constitutes the major portion of a recently constructed social-deprivation scale. Included in this scale are such items as the economic circumstances of the home, the physical treatment accorded the child, the familial configuration, the adherence by the parents to social norms, the attitude of the parents toward the child and the general adjustment of the child.

On the basis of these ratings we divided our 60 subjects into two groups, "high" and "low" deprived. We employed a simple satiation game to assess the effectiveness of social reinforcers. The game was repetitive and monotonous, and was constructed to reduce relatively quickly the subject's desire merely to "play the game," thus allowing the assumed difference in motivation for interaction with the experimenter to become the dominant variable in determining performance. The game was extremely simple, and successful performance depended primarily upon compliance with the experimenter's instructions rather than upon learning. The rules of the game allowed the child to stop playing whenever he wished.

It should be emphasized that the two groups of children had been institutionalized for an average of two years and during this period had experienced identical environmental conditions. From the mechanistic viewpoint, such a two-year period of similar environmental conditions should result in the finding that social reinforcers are equally effective for both groups. However, the mediational viewpoint would suggest that the early social deprivation effects would continue to influence the child's performance even after two years of institutionalization. Such, indeed, proved to be the case. The high-deprived group manifested a more enhanced motivation for social reinforcers than did the low-deprived group, as measured by the time spent on the game.

Another interesting finding of this study was that in both groups the effectiveness of our primarily praise-connoting social reinforcers decreased as the mental age of the child increased. This is altogether in keeping with the view presented above. It indicates that, even in populations that have experienced rather severe degrees of social deprivation, there is no one-to-one relationship between the degree of social deprivation experienced and the effectiveness of particular social reinforcers. Even highly deprived children demonstrate an attenuation effect for social reinforcers of this type as they move on to higher developmental levels.

In a three-year follow-up study, Joanna Williams and I retested these same children on the same game. We were not surprised to find a general increase in the effectiveness of social reinforcers for all our subjects with this increased period of institutionalization. Furthermore, the simple relationship between amount of preinstitutional social deprivation and reinforcer effectiveness was not found after this average of five years of institutionalization. If we had terminated our analyses at this point we would have assumed that this common five-year period of institutionalization had homogenized our subjects and completely obliterated the effects of the differences in the degree of preinstitutional social deprivation experienced.

However, an analysis of the increase in the effectiveness of social reinforcers between the two testings revealed that the effects of the three added years of institutionalization were influenced by the degree of preinstitutional social deprivation experienced. We found that children with the better preinstitutional histories showed a significantly greater increase in motivation for social reinforcers between the two testings than did children with the poorer histories.

This finding points up the error of conceptualizing institutional living as if it affected all children in the same manner. It suggests that, for children who have suffered the greater amount of social deprivation prior to being institutionalized, institutional living adds relatively little to the already high motivation for social reinforcers. Indeed, in light of the extreme social deprivation experienced by many institutionalized children (Clarke and Clarke, 1954; Zigler, 1958, 1961), it would be surprising if institutional living were not less socially depriving for these subjects than their original homes, thus resulting in a lessened effectiveness of social reinforcers. Children who have had comparatively good homes, on the other hand, have less motivation for social reinforcers early in their institutionalization. However, the institution is a relatively depriving environment for these children, and, thus, longer institutionalization produces a greater increase in the effectiveness of social reinforcers.

I believe that, even as in the case of early social deprivation, an early history of satiation on social reinforcers has lasting effects. J. B. Gilmore and I became interested in the recent studies of Schachter (1959), who found that adult first-borns have a greater need for social contact and social reinforcers than do later-borns. In an effort to explain the enhanced effectiveness of social reinforcement for first-borns in the stress situations employed by Schachter, Gilmore and I hypothesized that first-borns were more likely than later-borns to have been continually satiated on social reinforcers early in their lives. We felt that the negative aspect of continually satiating a child's desire for contact and support was that it interfered with independence training. If the support, warmth and approval of social agents are continually available, there is little need for the child to develop mechanisms other than dependent ones in dealing with environmental stresses.

What is needed to support such an argument is a demonstration that first-borns are more satiated on social reinforcers during childhood than are later-borns. In an effort to provide such a demonstration, we employed groups of first-born and later-born children who played the simple satiation game referred to above. In this study we employed two reinforcement conditions. In one condition the child received a great deal of social reinforcement while playing the game. In the second condition the experimenter merely attended to the child's performance. Our view of first-borns' satiation led us to predict that when the game was played under a support condition, they would play our game for a shorter period of time than would later-borns. This prediction stems from the view that our first-borns were relatively sated on the social reinforcers that were being dispensed.

We also felt that the absence of social reinforcers would be more frustrating to children who are used to receiving them than to children who are not. We therefore predicted that in our nonsupport condition the first-borns would play the game longer than would first-borns who played in the support condition, in the hope that such play would eventually result in the usually administered social reinforcers. For the later-born children, nonsupport should not be a particularly frustrating condition, and they could be expected to view it as a relatively typical situation in which no social reinforcers were available. We therefore predicted that the later-borns would respond to the nonsupport condition by simply playing the game for a shorter period of time than did later-borns playing under a support condition. Our findings confirmed these predictions.

The intriguing problem remains as to the particular aspects in the caretaking of first-borns that produced these findings. The question whether the first-born child only received social satiation early in his childhood or was the recipient of social satiation as a preferred child throughout childhood is an open one. The fact that birth order effects are found in adults long after such subjects are being regularly satiated on early dependency needs suggests that the dynamics of birth order are established in a relatively early period of life. Such a view is not only in keeping with that advanced by several personality theorists, it is also consistent with the findings reported above, which indicated that both the effectiveness of social reinforcers later in life and differences in the enhanced effectiveness of social reinforcers with a constant length of institutionalization were related to the caretaking experienced during the first few years of life.

In conclusion, I hope that this brief review demonstrates that important questions are raised, and our knowledge concerning the social reinforcement process extended, when we turn our attention to the internal processes and structures of the child that mediate the observed relationship between the social reinforcer we dispense and the response we measure.

References

Beller, E. Dependency and independence in young children. *Journal of Genetic Psychology*, 1955, *87*, 25–35.

Bijou, S., and Baer, D. *Child development*. Vol. 1 *A systematic and empirical theory*. New York: Appleton-Century-Crofts, 1961.

Clarke, H., and Clarke, A. Cognitive changes in the feebleminded. *British Journal of Psychology*, 1954, *45*, 173–179.

Davis, A. American status systems and the socialization of the child. *American Sociological Review*, 1941, *6*, 234–254.

Davis, A. Child training and social class. In R. Barker, J. Kounin, and H. Wright (Eds.), *Child behavior and development*. New York: McGraw-Hill, 1943.

Davis, A. Socialization and adolescent personality. Adolescence, *43rd Yearbook, National Society for the Study of Education*, 1944, Part 1. Chicago, Illinois.

Erickson, M. Social status and child rearing practices. In T. Newcomb and E. Hartley (Eds.), *Readings in social psychology*. New York: Henry Holt, 1947.

Gewirtz, J. Three determinants of attention-seeking in young children. *Monographs of the Society for Research in Child Development*, 1954, *19* (2), Serial No. 59.

Gewirtz, J., and Baer, D. The effect of brief social deprivation on behaviors for a social reinforcer. *Journal of Abnormal and Social Psychology*, 1958, *56*, 49–56. (a)

Gewirtz, J., and Baer, D. Deprivation and satiation as drive conditions. *Journal of Abnormal and Social Psychology*, 1958, *57*, 165–172. (b)

Heathers, G. Emotional dependence and independence in nursery school play. *Journal of Genetic Psychology*, 1955, *87*, 37–57.

Schachter, S. *The psychology of affiliation*. Stanford, Calif.: Stanford University Press, 1959.

Terrell, G., Jr., Durkin, K., and Wiesley, M. Social class and the nature of the incentive in discrimination learning. *Journal of Abnormal and Social Psychology*, 1959, *59*, 270–272.

Zigler, E. The effect of preinstitutional social deprivation on the performance of feebleminded children. Unpublished Ph.D. dissertation, University of Texas, 1958.

Zigler, E. Social deprivation and rigidity in the performance of feebleminded children. *Journal of Abnormal and Social Psychology*, 1961, *62*, 413–421.

Zigler, E., and deLabry, J. Concept-switching in middle-class, lower-class, and retarded children. *Journal of Abnormal and Social Psychology*, 1962, *65*, 267–273.

Zigler, E., Hodgden, L., and Stevenson, H. The effect of support on the performance of normal and feebleminded children. *Journal of Personality*, 1958, *26*, 106–122.

The final paper in this section, by *Baer and Sherman,* deals with learning by imitation. Although we shall deal with this topic again in later sections, this article introduces us to an important aspect of social reinforcement, namely, the tendency of children to imitate certain behaviors of adults and other models. What this experiment demonstrates is that children can learn to imitate not just those performances for which they have been reinforced but, also, other nonreinforced performances displayed by the reinforcing agent. Baer and Sherman used a "talking" puppet as a model for preschool children. The puppet said "Good" or Fine" whenever the child imitated certain verbal responses. When the puppet pressed a bar, this response was also imitated by seven out of eleven subjects, even though no reinforcement was given. When the puppet ceased reinforcing the previously rewarded vocal behaviors, the children also showed a decreased frequency of imitative bar-pressing.

It is important to remember that in this experiment bar-pressing by the child was never reinforced directly. Nevertheless, the children mimicked this behavior as they did that for which they had received approval. Similarity of responding, rather than imitation of a particular performance, apparently is capable of being acquired as an indirect consequence of reinforcement for other behaviors. Whether similarity of responding must be discriminative for some reinforced behavior in order to be maintained is left as a matter for further research.

11 Reinforcement Control of Generalized Imitation in Young Children[1]

DONALD M. BAER
JAMES A. SHERMAN[2]

The term "imitation" has seen much use in the literature of child psychology. However, experimental work in this area has often failed to invoke its most powerful meaning. In experimental situations, behavior frequently has been called imitative because it resembled that of a model previously observed by the subject. But there rarely has been any guarantee that the *similarity* of the two behaviors was functional in producing the behavior in the observer. Instead, it has been common to require the observer to learn a reinforced response after having watched a model perform the same response and receive reinforcement for it. The observer often does profit from this observation of a correct performance. However, it is quite possible that he does so because certain stimuli of the situation have been paired with the sight of the reinforcement secured by the model. Since the sight of reinforcement should be a powerful secondary reinforcer, observational learning, not of a similar response, but of the cues which will facilitate that response may very well take place. When the observer is placed in the situation, his learning (of what typically is the only reinforced response in the situation) is speeded by his previously acquired sensitivity to the cues in the situation.

For example, a child may watch a model turn a crank on a green box and receive nothing, then turn a crank on a red box and receive reinforcement consistently and repeatedly. As a result of this observation, the observer subsequently may learn the same discrimination more quickly than a control subject. This may be due simply to the establishment of red as a discriminative cue for reinforcement. The observer is better reinforced for approaching red than

1 This research was supported in part by grant M-2208 from the National Institutes of Health, United States Public Health Service.

2 The authors are grateful to Miss Judith Higgins and Miss Sharon Feeney for their reliable and intelligent assistance as As. Appreciation is also due to Mrs. Mildred Reed, Director, and Mrs. Mildred Hall, Seattle Day Nursery Association, for their cooperation and assistance.

From the *Journal of Experimental Social Psychology,* 1964, *1,* 37–49. Reproduced by permission of Academic Press.

green as a consequence of his observation, and thereby is more likely to turn the crank on the red box and be reinforced for it. There is no need in this example to assume that the *similarity* of his crank-turning response and the model's is involved. The similarity may lie in the eye of the experimenter rather than in the eye of the observer, and, in this situation, only a similar response will be reinforced. Hence the similarity is both forced and (perhaps) irrelevant.

However, there can be a more powerful use of imitation in the experimental analysis of children's learning if it can be shown that similarity per se functions as an important stimulus dimension in the child's behavior. The purpose of the present study is to add another demonstration of this role of similarity to the small body of literature already produced (e.g., Bandura and Huston, 1961) and to show the function of certain social reinforcement operations in promoting responding along the dimension of similarity in behavior. Specifically, a response is considered which is imitative of a model but never directly reinforced. Instead, other responses, also imitative of a model, are controlled by reinforcement operations. The strength of the unreinforced imitative response is then observed as a function of these reinforcement operations. An animated talking puppet, used previously in studies of social interaction with children (Baer, 1962), serves both as a model to imitate and as a source of social reinforcement.

Method

Apparatus

The apparatus was an animated talking puppet dressed as a cowboy and seated in a chair inside a puppet stage. The puppet was capable of making four kinds of responses: (1) raising and lowering his head, or *nodding;* (2) opening and closing his mouth, or *mouthing;* (3) *bar-pressing* on a puppet-scaled bar-pressing apparatus located beside his chair, almost identical in appearance to a regular-sized bar-pressing apparatus located beside the child; and (4) *talking,* accomplished by playing *E*'s voice through a loudspeaker mounted behind the puppet's chair, while the puppet's jaw was worked in coordination with the words being spoken. (For a more complete description and a photograph, see Baer, 1962.)

First Sequence of Procedures

Introduction. The experiment was conducted in a two-room mobile trailer-laboratory (Bijou, 1958) parked in the lot of a day-care nursery. *E* observed the child and puppet through a one-way mirror from the other room. The child sat in a chair immediately in front of the puppet stage. An adult assistant, *A*, brought the child to the laboratory, introduced him to the puppet, seated him in his chair, and then sat in a screened corner of the room, out of the child's sight. The introduction for the first session was, "This is Jimmy the puppet. He wants to talk to you. And this (pointing) is your bar. See, it's just like Jimmy's bar, only bigger (pointing). Do you know how it works?" The usual answer was "No," in which case *A* demonstrated a bar-press, saying "Now you try it." (Some children pressed the bar without demonstration). *A* then said, "You can talk to Jimmy now." On all later sessions, *A* said simply, "Hello Jimmy, here's (child's name) to talk to you again," and, to the child, "Now you can talk to Jimmy again."

After *A*'s introduction, the puppet raised his head and began speaking to the child. He followed a fairly standard line of conversation, starting with greetings, and progressing through expressions of pleasure over the chance to talk with the child to alternating questions about what the child had been doing and colorful stories about what the puppet had been doing. This type of conversation was maintained throughout all the sessions; the social reinforcement procedures used as the independent variable in this study were interjected within the conversation according to the experimental design.

Operant Level. The first session was to acquaint child and puppet and to collect an operant level of the child's bar-pressing, imitative or otherwise. Shortly after the puppet began talking to the child, he began to press his bar, alternating between a slow rate of 1 response per 15 seconds and a fast rate of about 3 responses per second. The puppet's bar-pressing was recorded on a cumulative recorder.

The operant level period was interrupted after 5–10 minutes of the puppet's bar-pressing for a special procedure. The special procedure was designed to establish whether the child could generalize from the puppet's bar to his own. After the puppet had stopped bar-pressing, he would nod twice and say, "This is my head. Show me your head." Invariably, the child would move his head or point to it. The puppet then said, "Good," and began mouthing, saying, "This is my mouth. Show me your mouth." The child would move his mouth or point to it. Then the puppet said, "Good," and bar-pressing twice, said, "This is my bar. Show me your bar." Some children imitated the response; some pointed to their bar. A few did neither; of these, some appeared puzzled, and others tentatively reached for the puppet's bar. These were the children the procedure was designed to detect. In their cases, the puppet explained that they had a bar of their own and helped them find it, which usually sufficed to produce either a bar-press or a pointing toward the bar. The puppet gave no reinforcement for the bar-pressing response, and instead resumed the conversation about his adventures or the child's. With some subjects there then followed another 5–10 minutes of bar-pressing by the puppet to determine whether this procedure in itself had promoted imitative bar-pressing by the child. No imitative bar-pressing ever did develop as a result of this procedure alone in the children subjected to it. For the rest of the subjects, this extra portion of the operant level period was dropped.

Still another 5–10 minutes of bar-pressing by the puppet was sometimes displayed. On these occasions, the puppet took up a very approving line of conversation, dispensing a great deal of "Good," "Very good," and "You're really smart" to the child. This was to determine the effect of noncontingent social reinforcement on the child's imitative bar-pressing. However, no child subjected to this procedure ever developed imitative bar-pressing as a result. The other subjects had a similar kind of noncontingent approval incorporated into the earlier portions of their operant level periods.

The typical rate of imitative bar-pressing during operant level periods was zero. In fact, of 11 children seen in this study, only one showed a slight tendency to imitate the puppet's bar-pressing, but this disappeared early in her operant level period. Two others showed a non-imitative bar-pressing rate during the initial session.

Reinforcement of Some Imitative Responses. After collecting the child's operant level of bar-pressing, the puppet stopped bar-pressing and began to present a series of other responses, one after another at first, and then at scattered points in his conversation. Each time he would first ask the child, "Can you do this?" These responses consisted of nodding, mouthing, and a variety of nonsense statements (such as "Glub-flubbug," "One-two-three-four," or "Red robins run rapidly"). In each case, if the child imitated the responses, the puppet reinforced the child's response with approval, consisting mainly of the words "Good," "Very good," and "Fine." Almost without exception, the children did imitate virtually every response the puppet presented in this way, and after a few reinforcements, the puppet stopped asking "Can you do this?" in preface to the response.

After the child was consistently imitating each of these other responses without the prefatory "Can you do this?" the puppet resumed bar-pressing, alternating fast and slow rates. He continued to display nodding, mouthing, and verbal nonsense statements at scattered points in his conversation, and maintained a continuous schedule of reinforcement for every imitation of these by the child. The child's bar-pressing from this point on was the basic dependent variable of the study. An increase over operant level in this never-reinforced[3] bar-pressing by the child, especially insofar as it matched the puppet's bar-pressing, would be significant: It would be attributable to the direct reinforcement of the other responses (nodding, mouthing, and verbal). These responses have very slight topographical resemblance to bar-pressing; they are like it essentially in that they all are imitative of a model's behavior. Thus an increase in imitative bar-pressing by the child would indicate that similarity of responding per se was a functional dimension of the child's behavior, that is, similarity of responding could be strengthened as could responding itself.

This program of reinforcement for all imitative responding (other than bar-pressing) was usually begun during the first session. With some children, it was started early in their second session. Children were seen as many as 7 sessions in the course of the study. These sessions were separated by 3–7 days.

Results

In the design of this study, both individual and group performances are relevant to the central question. If any child showed a significant increase in imitative bar-pressing over his operant level, as a result of direct reinforcement of other imitative responses, this would demonstrate the functional role of similarity in behavior for that child. Hence each child represented an experiment in himself. As a group, the sample allows some estimation of the probability of the effect occurring in children from this population.

Of 11 children studied, 4 failed to show any development of an imitative bar-pressing response during the course of reinforcement of nodding, mouthing, and verbal imitations. Two of these were the only two children showing a high level of non-imitative bar-pressing during their operant level periods. The remaining 7 children showed varying degrees of increase in bar-pressing, as illustrated in Figure 1. This figure shows 4 records, selected to indicate the range of increase in bar-pressing obtained. A fact not always apparent in these records (necessarily compressed for publication) is that virtually every bar-pressing response by the child occurs closely following a response (or response burst) by the puppet, and hence is clearly imitative.

[3] On one occasion with one child, a bar-press was accidentally reinforced. This will be noted in the results.

Further Procedure and Results

The increased imitative bar-pressing by some of the children was brought about by reinforcement of other imitative responding by the child (nodding, mouthing, and verbal performances). Further procedures were developed to show the dependence of the generalized imitative bar-pressing on this reinforcement. These procedures were of two kinds: extinction of the other imitative responding, and time-out from the other imitative responding.

Extinction of Imitation. Extinction was instituted with two children, one of whom had developed a near-perfect rate of imitative bar-pressing, the other showing a low rate. After a stable rate of imitative bar-pressing had been established by each child, the puppet stopped giving any reinforcement for imitation of his nodding, mouthing, or verbal nonsense performances (imitation of which in the immediate past he had reinforced continuously). However, he continued performing these actions at the same rate. He also continued to reinforce the child at the same rate, but at appropriate points in the child's conversation rather than for imitation. This continued for several sessions, until the child had shown a stable or marked decrease in imitative bar-pressing. Then reinforcement was shifted back to imitations of nodding, mouthing, or verbal nonsense performances and maintained as before, until the child showed a stable or marked increase in imitative bar-pressing. As usual, bar-pressing was never reinforced.

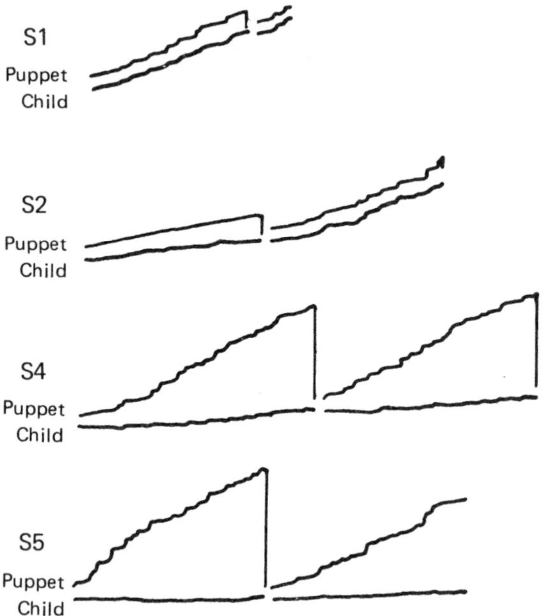

Figure 1 *The development of generalized imitative bar-pressing in four representative subjects.*

The subjects chosen for this procedure were S1 and S4 of Figure 1; both were girls. Their records (Figure 2) include the early sessions that show operant level and the development of generalized imitation, already seen in Figure 1, as a baseline against which the effect of extinction of other imitative responding is seen. (Sessions 4 and 5 are omitted from the record of S4 because they are virtually identical in procedure and performance to Session 3 and would needlessly enlarge Figure 2 if included.) It is clear that S1 was very responsive to the extinction and reinforcement operations: Her near-perfect rate of imitative bar-pressing weakened considerably after nearly one complete session of extinction for other imitative responding, but promptly recovered its near-perfect aspect when reinforcement was resumed.[4] The record of S4 shows the same pattern, but the differences are not so apparent. This may be due to the low rate of imitative bar-pressing induced in S4 under the previous reinforcement conditions. Sighting along the curve, however, will make clear the same pattern of rate changes apparent in the record of S1.

Time-out from Imitation. Time-out procedures were instituted with two other children, one of whom had a high rate of imitative bar-pressing, and the other only a modest rate. After a stable rate of imitative bar-pressing had been established by each child, the puppet ceased providing any nodding, mouthing, or verbal nonsense performances for the child to imitate, hence eliminating any reinforcement of imitation by eliminating the previously established cues for the occurrence of imitation. Social reinforcement was continued at the same rate, but was delivered for appropriate comments in the child's conversation rather than for imitation.

This time-out was continued until the child showed a stable or marked decrease in imitative bar-pressing. Then the puppet resumed performances of nodding, mouthing, and verbal nonsense statements, and shifted his reinforcement back to the child's imitations of these performances until the child showed a stable or marked increase in imitative bar-pressing. Then the whole cycle of time-out and reinforcement was repeated in exactly the same way. Bar-pressing, of course, was never reinforced.

The subjects chosen for this procedure were S2 of Figure 1 and S3, both girls. Their records are

[4] In the case of S1, it can be seen that the effects of extinction are markedly stronger with the beginning of session 4, and that the effects of resumed reinforcement, clear in the last half of Session 5, are even more pronounced with the beginning of Session 6. This interaction between session changes and experimental conditions remains an unexplained complication of the data; however, it need not greatly alter the conclusions drawn.

shown in Figure 3. (The early portion of the record of S2 has already been seen in Figure 1.) It is apparent that the time-out condition produced a quick and drastic weakening of imitative bar-pressing in these children, and that a resumption of reinforcement of other imitative responses, when these were again displayed by the puppet for the child to imitate, quickly generalized to the nonreinforced imitative bar-pressing. (By accident, S3 received one reinforcement for bar-pressing during Session 1. It is assumed that the effect of this single reinforcement was negligible.)

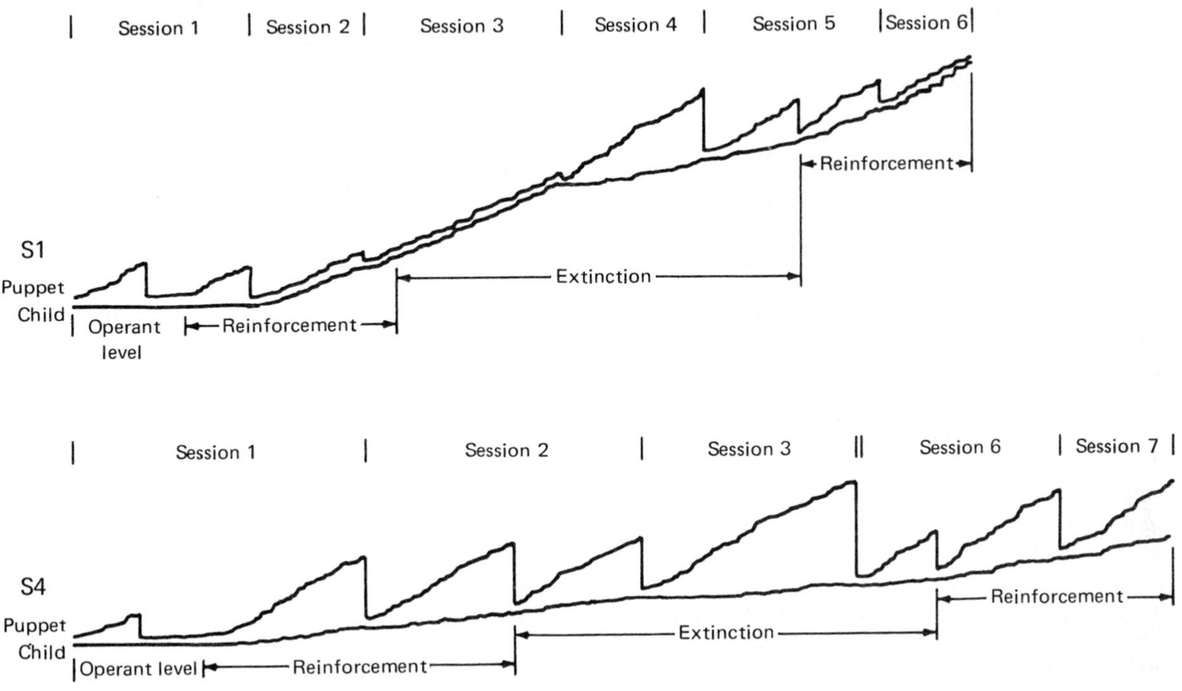

Figure 2 *The effects of extinction of previously reinforced imitation on generalized imitative bar-pressing in two subjects.*

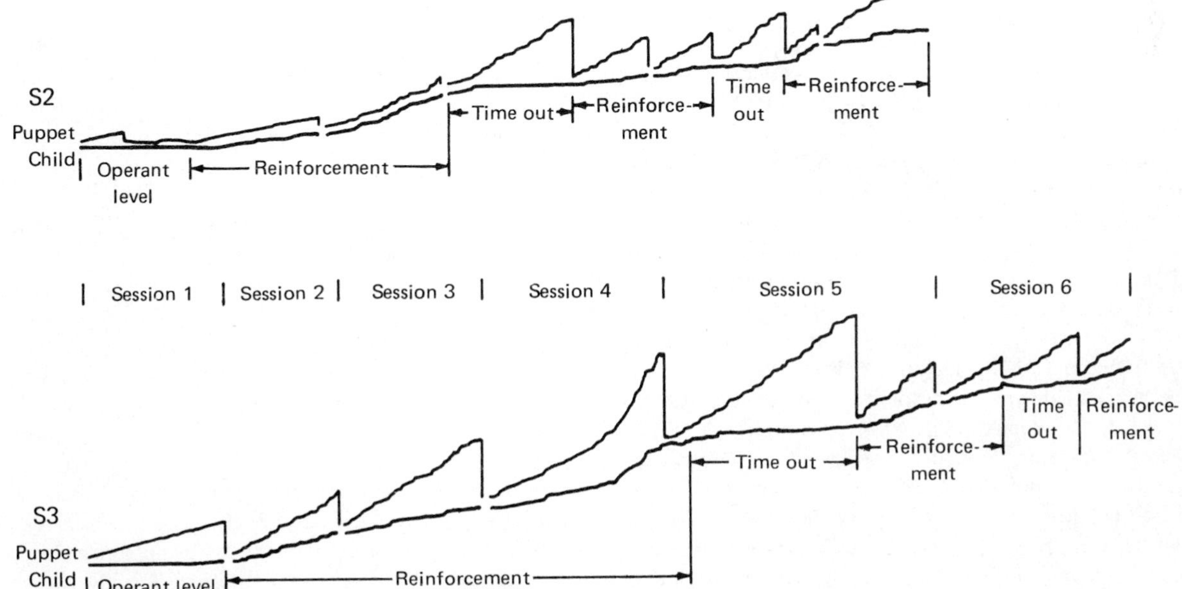

Figure 3 *The effects of time-out from reinforced imitation on generalized imitative bar-pressing in two subjects.*

Discussion

In this study, social reinforcement has been used to strengthen a set of behaviors directly. The responses of nodding, mouthing, and saying nonsense syllable chains have been established through instructions ("Can you do this?") and reinforcement, and maintained with reinforcement. These responses have in common the fact that they are all imitative of a model's behaviors and that the child does them only when the model does. It is in this context that the strengthening of imitative bar-pressing becomes significant. Bar-pressing was never reinforced directly; nor was the child ever instructed to bar-press imitatively. (The simple instructions dealing with the child's bar—"Show me your bar"—never promoted imitative bar-pressing in the children observed specifically for this possibility.) Bar-pressing has little physical or topographical resemblance to nodding, mouthing, and verbal nonsense chains. What it does have in common with these responses is the fact that it too is imitative of one of the model's performances. Hence its strengthening, following the direct strengthening of nodding, mouthing, and verbal responses, may be attributed to generalization along a dimension of similarity between the child's response and the model's response. In other words, the child is responsive to the stimulus of similarity between responses per se, apparently independently of the particular physical stimuli involved in specific responses.

It can be important to demonstrate that similarity between behaviors of model and child can be a functional stimulus dimension. Such a demonstration would be essential in at least some reinforcement analyses of imitation, especially in any analysis trying to show that imitation should be a strong response in a child, even when it does not produce extrinsic reinforcement. One such analysis might proceed as follows:

In the ordinary course of his early life, a child will form many hundreds of discriminations that involve the sight or sound of a model's behavior as a cue for a response by the child which achieves the same (or a similar) reinforcing outcome. In effect, in all such situations, the child is in a position to learn what response on his part reproduces the effect produced by the model's behavior. Many times, the world will be such that only a response similar in physical make-up or topography will reproduce the same effect. For example, many times a child will need to get through a latched door. He will often observe an older or more skillful model turn the knob and pass through. The child will eventually differentiate his own behavior to the point where it succeeds in opening the door. But doors are such that very few responses will succeed, and consequently the child's behavior will be very similar to the model's. In this situation, and in many others like it, the stimulus of similarity between the child's behavior and the model's is consistently programmed and sets the occasion for reinforcement of the child. Given enough of these situations, of adequate consistency and variety, the stimulus of similarity between behaviors in general may become discriminative for reinforcement. Since a stimulus which is discriminative for reinforcement becomes (secondarily) reinforcing in its own right, then responses which produce similarity between behaviors will thereby be strengthened. Responses of the child which "produce similarity" are those responses which have a topography that the child can compare to the topography of the model's responses, e.g., he can see both his response and the model's or can hear both. Hence the child will become generally "imitative," and, if similarity has great strength as a discriminative and therefore reinforcing stimulus, imitative behavior will be correspondingly more prevalent and apparently autonomous.

Certain details of procedure in this study may be worthy of note. One involves the fact that noncontingent social reinforcement given by the puppet to the child was not sufficient to induce imitation of the puppet. Furthermore, once a generalized imitation had been set up, noncontingent reinforcement was not sufficient to maintain it. Only when other imitative responses were being reinforced would imitative bar-pressing (never directly reinforced) remain at any strength. The puppet would, as the design required, shift his reinforcement from imitative responses to other appropriate moments in the interactions, but the general amount and spacing of this reinforcement remained the same. Hence the effects on imitative bar-pressing noted here cannot be attributed to the simple presence or absence of reinforcement, but rather are related to its contingent or noncontingent use. This is at some variance with the results of other studies (cf. Bandura and Huston, 1961), in which a prior condition of noncontingent social reinforcement from a model evoked more imitation of the model from the child than otherwise. This may be due to the particular response used in this study to observe generalized imitation, which was bar-pressing. Bar-pressing may be an unusual response for a young child and may have relatively little resemblance to the strong responses already in his repertoire. For this reason, it may be a relatively inefficient response with which to demonstrate a generalized imitation of the puppet. On the other hand, it may be that while similarity between behaviors is reinforcing for children, this reinforcing value is closely dependent on similarity remaining discriminative for at least some reinforcement in the situation. Possibly, when similarity clearly is no longer discriminative for reinforcement, it loses its own reinforcing function rather quickly. It will take an extensive program of research to provide useful data on this question, but the question may well be worth it, since such arguments about imitation can figure heavily in a conceptual account of socialization or "identification."

Another point, possibly important, is that all of the subjects showing imitation were girls. Since the group sampled was composed largely of girls, this may not be unusual. However, the puppet was clearly a male cowboy, and since cross-sex interactions are prevalent where social reinforcement is involved (especially with young children), it may be that later data will demonstrate that the sex of the subject and the model is an important variable. No conclusion is possible from the present data.

Finally, the increased imitative bar-pressing demonstrated here is not simply part of a generalized increase in activity; its clearly imitative nature denies that. Furthermore, it was apparent to the observers that there was no general increase of other observable activities as imitative bar-pressing developed in the child.

References

Baer, D. M. A technique of social reinforcement for the study of child behavior: Behavior avoiding reinforcement withdrawal. *Child Development,* 1962, *33,* 847–858.

Bandura, A., and Huston, Aletha C. Identification as a process of incidental learning. *Journal of Abnormal and Social Psychology,* 1961, *63,* 311–318.

Bijou, S. W. A child study laboratory on wheels. *Child Development* 1958, 29, 425–427.

Implicit and Vicarious Reinforcement

3

Most animal experiments deal with performances maintained by reinforcers which are explicit and definite consequences of the animal's behavior. Casual observation of much of human conduct, however, shows that many behaviors are influenced either indirectly or by consequences which occur much later. The fact that many human performances are not obviously reinforced by immediate and specific consequences, such as food, does not lessen the value of a functional analysis of these behaviors and their relationship to the environment. The papers in this section attempt to deal with some of these problems objectively. Implicit and vicarious reinforcement is intended to suggest that an individual's behavior may be influenced by related circumstances which are not an immediate product of his current conduct.

The point of an experimental analysis is to find out how a person may acquire a new or modified repertoire merely by observing another's behavior. This kind of transfer from a performer to an observer is called vicarious because, colloquially speaking, one person is benefiting indirectly from the experience of another. From a technical point of view, the problem is close to that posed by imitation. A child watching another child interact with a parent or teacher is influenced to the extent that behaviors in his repertoire can be either prompted or increased in frequency by the behavior he observes. This usually occurs, however, only if his existing repertoire shares common elements with that of the person he is observing. Thus, observing someone else's behavior is more likely to alter the frequencies of certain kinds of conduct or to recombine existing performances in the observer than to create new repertoires. Because so many of our child-rearing practices and even our legal customs are based on the assumption that a person is influenced when he observes someone else either enjoy or suffer certain consequences, the problem of vicarious and implicit reinforcement has importance for some of the broadest problems of human conduct. If a child sees someone injured by falling out of a tree, for example, will it influence his inclination to climb or his manner of climbing trees? At one time in England, petty criminals, such as pickpockets, were publicly hanged to deter others from such acts. We doubt today whether such displays serve the intended purpose. In fact, public hangings were said to be occasions for much pickpocketing and thievery. Many lawyers and judges maintain that the purpose of punishment in our legal system is to deter others from committing the same crimes. When we systematically observe the conditions under which implicit and vicarious reinforcement occurs, however, we see that learning in such situations is by no means automatic.

The experiments described in this section show beyond a doubt that an individual may be influenced by reinforcement contingencies that he observes influencing other people. These experiments also show that the details of this process are complex and that the special conditions under which modeling, imitation, or observational learning occur make a significant difference in how the observer is influenced by what he sees.

Learning by Observation

Bandura's article deals with one of the basic experimental paradigms for studying implicit and vicarious reinforcement in the laboratory. Both the methods section and the discussion of results illustrate the complexity of the problem and the range of circumstances that determine whether or not vicarious reinforcement and imitation will occur. Although Bandura describes some of the ways in which a child who observes the consequences of certain performances to other children will modify his own behavior accordingly, he acknowledges that "mere exposure to modeling stimuli does not provide the sufficient conditions for imitative or observational learning."

12 *Influence of Models' Reinforcement Contingencies on the Acquisition of Imitative Responses*[1]

ALBERT BANDURA[2]

It is widely assumed that the occurrence of imitative or observational learning is contingent on the administration of reinforcing stimuli either to the model or to the observer. According to the theory propounded by Miller and Dollard (1941), for example, the necessary conditions for learning through imitation include a motivated subject who is positively reinforced for matching the rewarded behavior of a model during a series of initially random, trial-and-error responses. Since this conceptualization of observational learning requires the subject to perform the imitative response before he can learn it, this theory evidently accounts more adequately for the emission of previously learned matching responses, than for their acquisition.

Mowrer's (1960) proprioceptive feedback theory similarly highlights the role of reinforcement but, unlike Miller and Dollard who reduce imitation to a special case of instrumental learning, Mowrer focuses on the classical conditioning of positive and negative emotions to matching response-correlated stimuli. Mowrer distinguishes two forms of imitative learning in terms of whether the observer is reinforced directly or vicariously. In the former case, the model performs a response and simultaneously rewards the observer. If the modeled responses are thus paired repeatedly with positive reinforcement they gradually acquire secondary reward value. The observer can then administer positively conditioned reinforcers to himself simply by reproducing as closely as possible the model's positively valenced behavior. In the second, or empathetic form of imitative learning, the model not only exhibits the responses but also experiences the reinforcing consequences. It is assumed that the observer, in turn, experiences empathetically both the response-correlated stimuli and the response consequences of the model's behavior. As a result of this higher-order vicarious conditioning, the observer will be inclined to reproduce the matching responses.

There is some recent evidence that imitative behavior can be enhanced by noncontingent social re-

[1] This investigation was supported by Research Grant M-5162 from the National Institutes of Health, United States Public Health Service.

[2] The author is indebted to Carole Revelle who assisted in collecting the data.

inforcement from a model (Bandura and Huston, 1961), by response-contingent reinforcers administered to the model (Bandura, Ross, and Ross, 1963b; Walters, Leat and Mezei, 1963), and by increasing the reinforcing value of matching responses per se through direct reinforcement of the participant observer (Baer and Sherman, 1964). Nevertheless, reinforcement theories of imitation fail to explain the learning of matching responses when the observer does not perform the model's responses during the process of acquisition, and for which reinforcers are not delivered either to the model or to the observers (Bandura, Ross, and Ross, 1961, 1963a).

The acquisition of imitative responses under the latter conditions appears to be accounted for more adequately by a contiguity theory of observational learning. According to the latter conceptualization (Bandura, 1965; Sheffield, 1961), when an observer witnesses a model exhibit a sequence of responses, the observer acquires, through contiguous association of sensory events, perceptual and symbolic responses possessing cue properties that are capable of eliciting, at some time after a demonstration, overt responses corresponding to those that had been modeled.

Some suggestive evidence that the *acquisition* of matching responses may take place through contiguity, whereas reinforcements administered to a model exert their major influence on the *performance* of imitatively learned responses, is provided in a study in which models were rewarded or punished for exhibiting aggressive behavior (Bandura, Ross, and Ross, 1963b). Although children who had observed aggressive responses rewarded subsequently reproduced the model's behavior while children in the model-punished condition failed to do so, a number of the subjects in the latter group described in postexperimental interviews the model's repertoire of aggressive responses with considerable accuracy. Evidently, they had learned the cognitive equivalents of the model's responses but they were not translated into their motoric forms. These findings highlighted both the importance of distinguishing between learning and performance and the need for a systematic study of whether reinforcement is primarily a learning-related or a performance-related variable.

In the present experiment children observed a film-mediated model who exhibited novel physical and verbal aggressive responses. In one treatment condition the model was severely punished; in a second, the model was generously rewarded; while the third condition presented no response consequences to the model. Following a postexposure test of imitative behavior, children in all three groups were offered attractive incentives contingent on their reproducing the models' responses so as to provide a more accurate index of learning. It was predicted that reinforcing consequences to the model would result in significant differences in the performance of imitative behavior with the model-rewarded group displaying the highest number of different classes of matching responses, followed by the no-consequences and the model-punished groups, respectively. In accordance with previous findings (Bandura, Ross, and Ross, 1961, 1963a) it was also expected that boys would perform significantly more imitative aggression than girls. It was predicted, however, that the introduction of positive incentives would wipe out both reinforcement-produced and sex-linked performance differences, revealing an equivalent amount of learning among children in the three treatment conditions.

Method

Subjects. The subjects were 33 boys and 33 girls enrolled in the Stanford University Nursery School. They ranged in age from 42 to 71 months, with a mean age of 51 months. The children were assigned randomly to one of three treatment conditions of 11 boys and 11 girls each.

Two adult males served in the role of models, and one female experimenter conducted the study for all 66 children.

Exposure Procedure. The children were brought individually to a semidarkened room. The experimenter informed the child that she had some business to attend to before they could proceed to the "surprise playroom," but that during the waiting period the child might watch a televised program. After the child was seated, the experimenter walked over to the television console, ostensibly tuned in a program and then departed. A film of approximately 5 minutes duration depicting the modeled responses was shown on a glass lenscreen in the television console by means of a rear projection arrangement, screened from the child's view by large panels. The televised form of presentation was utilized primarily because attending responses to televised stimuli are strongly conditioned in children and this procedure would therefore serve to enhance observation which is a necessary condition for the occurrence of imitative learning.

The film began with a scene in which the model walked up to an adult-size plastic Bobo doll and ordered him to clear the way. After glaring for a moment at the noncompliant antagonist the model exhibited four novel aggressive responses each accompanied by a distinctive verbalization.

First, the model laid the Bobo doll on its side, sat on it, and punched it in the nose while remarking, "Pow, right in the nose, boom, boom." The model then raised the doll and pommeled it on the head with a mallet. Each response was accompanied by the verbalization, "Sockeroo . . . stay down." Following the mallet aggression, the model kicked the doll about the room, and these responses were interspersed with the comment, "Fly away." Finally, the model threw rubber balls at the Bobo doll, each strike punctuated with "Bang." This sequence of physically and verbally aggressive behavior was repeated twice.

The component responses that enter into the development of more complex novel patterns of behavior are usually present in children's behavioral repertoires as products either of maturation or of prior social learning. Thus, while most of the elements in the modeled acts had undoubtedly been previously learned, the particular pattern of components in each response, and their evocation by specific stimulus objects, were relatively unique. For example, children can manipulate objects, sit on them, punch them, and they can make vocal responses, but the likelihood that a given child would spontaneously place a Bobo doll on its side, sit on it, punch it in the nose and remark, "Pow . . . boom, boom," is exceedingly remote. Indeed, a previous study utilizing the same stimulus objects has shown that the imitative responses selected for the present experiment have virtually a zero probability of occurring spontaneously among preschool children (Bandura, Ross, and Ross, 1961) and, therefore, meet the criterion of novel responses.

The rewarding and punishing contingencies associated with the model's aggressive responses were introduced in the closing scene of the film.

For children in the model-rewarded condition, a second adult appeared with an abundant supply of candies and soft drinks. He informed the model that he was a "strong champion" and that his superb aggressive performance clearly deserved a generous treat. He then poured him a large glass of 7-Up, and readily supplied additional energy-building nourishment including chocolate bars, Cracker Jack popcorn, and an assortment of candies. While the model was rapidly consuming the delectable treats, his admirer symbolically reinstated the modeled aggressive responses and engaged in considerable positive social reinforcement.

For children in the model-punished condition, the reinforcing agent appeared on the scene shaking his finger menacingly and commenting reprovingly, "Hey there, you big bully. You quit picking on that clown. I won't tolerate it." As the model drew back he tripped and fell, the other adult sat on the model and spanked him with a rolled-up magazine while reminding him of his aggressive behavior. As the model ran off cowering, the agent forewarned him, "If I catch you doing that again, you big bully, I'll give you a hard spanking. You quit acting that way."

Children in the no-consequences condition viewed the same film as shown to the other two groups except that no reinforcement ending was included.

Performance Measure. Immediately following the exposure session the children were escorted to an experimental room that contained a Bobo doll, three balls, a mallet and pegboard, dart guns, cars, plastic farm animals, and a doll house equipped with furniture and a doll family. By providing a variety of stimulus objects the children were at liberty to exhibit imitative responses or to engage in nonimitative forms of behavior.

After the experimenter instructed the child that he was free to play with the toys in the room, she excused herself supposedly to fetch additional play materials. Since many preschool children are reluctant to remain alone and tend to leave after a short period of time, the experimenter reentered the room midway through the session and reassured the child that she would return shortly with the goods.

Each child spent 10 minutes in the test room during which time his behavior was recorded every 5 seconds in terms of predetermined imitative response categories by judges who observed the session through a one-way mirror in an adjoining observation room.

Two observers shared the task of recording the occurrence of matching responses for all 66 children. Neither of the raters had knowledge of the treatment conditions to which the children were assigned. In order to provide an estimate of interscorer reliability, the responses of 10 children were scored independently by both observers. Since the imitative responses were highly distinctive and required no subjective interpretation, the raters were virtually in perfect agreement (99%) in scoring the matching responses.

The number of different physical and verbal imitative responses emitted spontaneously by the children constituted the performance measure.

Acquisition Index. At the end of the performance session the experimenter entered the room with an assortment of fruit juices in a colorful juice-dispensing fountain, and booklets of sticker-pictures that were employed as the positive incentives to activate into performance what the children had learned through observation.

After a brief juice treat the children were informed that for each physical or verbal imitative response that they reproduced, they would receive a pretty sticker-picture and additional juice treats. An achievement incentive was also introduced in order to produce further disinhibition and to increase the children's motivation to exhibit matching responses. The experimenter attached a pastoral scene to the wall and expressed an interest in seeing how many sticker-pictures the child would be able to obtain to adorn his picture.

The experimenter then asked the child, "Show me what Rocky did in the TV program," "Tell me what he said," and rewarded him immediately following each matching response. If a child simply described an imitative response he was asked to give a performance demonstration.

Although learning must be inferred from performance, it was assumed that the number of different physical and verbal imitative responses reproduced by the children under the positive-incentive conditions would serve as a relatively accurate index of learning.

Results

Figure 1 shows the mean number of different matching responses reproduced by children in each of the three treatment conditions during the no-incentive and the positive-incentive phases of the experiment. A square-root transformation $(y = \sqrt{f + \frac{1}{2}})$ was applied to these data to make them amenable to parametric statistical analyses.

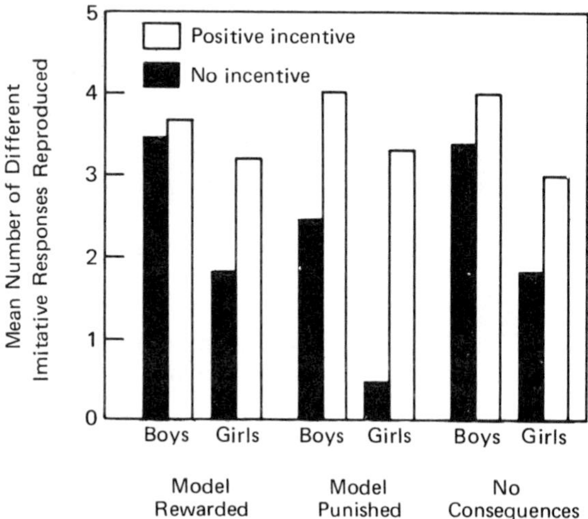

Figure 1 *Mean number of different matching responses reproduced by children as a function of positive incentives and the model's reinforcement contingencies.*

Performance Differences. A summary of the analysis of variance based on the performance scores is presented in Table 1. The findings reveal that reinforcing consequences to the model had a significant effect on the number of matching responses that the children spontaneously reproduced. The main effect of sex is also highly significant, confirming the prediction that boys would perform more imitative responses than girls.

Table 1 *Analysis of Variance of Imitative Performance Scores*

Source	*df*	MS	*F*
Treatments (T)	2	1.21	3.27*
Sex (S)	1	4.87	13.16**
T × S	1	.12	<1
Within groups	60	.37	

* $p < .05$.
** $p < .001$.

Further comparisons of pairs of means by t tests (Table 2) show that while the model-rewarded and the no-consequences groups did not differ from each other, subjects in both of these conditions performed significantly more matching responses than children who had observed the model experience punishing consequences following the display of aggression. It is evident, however, from the differences reported separately for boys and girls in Table 2, that the significant effect of the model's reinforcement contingencies is based predominantly on differences among the girls' subgroups.[3]

Table 2 *Comparison of Pairs of Means between Treatment Conditions*

Performance Measure	Treatment Conditions: Reward Versus Punishment *t*	Reward Versus No Consequences *t*	Punishment Versus No Consequences *t*
Total sample	2.20**	0.55	2.25**
Boys	1.05	0.19	1.24
Girls	2.13**	0.12	2.02*

* $p < .05$.
** $p < .025$.

[3] Because of the skewness of the distribution of scores for the subgroup of girls in the model-punished condition, differences involving this group were also evaluated by means of the Mann-Whitney U test. The nonparametric analyses yield probability values that are identical to those reported in Table 2.

Differences in Acquisition. An analysis of variance of the imitative learning scores is summarized in Table 3. The introduction of positive incentives completely wiped out the previously observed performance differences, revealing an equivalent amount of imitative learning among the children in the model-rewarded, model-punished, and the no-consequences treatment groups. Although the initially large sex difference was substantially reduced in the positive-incentive condition, the girls nevertheless still displayed fewer matching responses than the boys.

Table 3 *Analysis of Variance of Imitative Learning Scores*

Source	*df*	MS	*F*
Treatments (T)	2	0.02	<1
Sex (S)	1	0.56	6.22*
T × S	2	0.02	<1
Within groups	60	0.08	

* $p < .05$.

Acquisition-Performance Differences. In order to elucidate further the influence of direct and vicariously experienced reinforcement on imitation, the differences in matching responses displayed under nonreward and positive-incentive conditions for each of the three experimental treatments were evaluated by the *t*-test procedure for correlated means. Table 4 shows that boys who witnessed the model either rewarded or left without consequences performed all of the imitative responses that they had learned through observation and no new matching responses emerged when positive reinforcers were made available. On the other hand, boys who had observed the model punished and girls in all three treatment conditions showed significant increments in imitative behavior when response-contingent reinforcement was later introduced.

Table 4 *Significance of the Acquisition-Performance Differences in Imitative Responses*

Group	Treatment Conditions		
	Reward *t*	Punishment *t*	No Consequences *t*
Total sample	2.38*	5.00***	2.67**
Boys	0.74	2.26*	1.54
Girls	3.33**	5.65***	2.18*

* $p < .025$.
** $p < .01$.
*** $p < .001$.

Discussion

The results of the present experiment lend support to a contiguity theory of imitative learning; reinforcements administered to the model influenced the observers' performance but not the acquisition of matching responses.

It is evident from the findings, however, that mere exposure to modeling stimuli does not provide the sufficient conditions for imitative or observational learning. The fact that most of the children in the experiment failed to reproduce the entire repertoire of behavior exhibited by the model, even under positive-incentive conditions designed to disinhibit and to elicit matching responses, indicates that factors other than mere contiguity of sensory stimulation undoubtedly influence imitative response acquisition.

Exposing a person to a complex sequence of stimulation is no guarantee that he will attend to the entire range of cues, that he will necessarily select from a total stimulus complex only the most relevant stimuli, or that he will even perceive accurately the cues to which his attention is directed. Motivational variables, prior training in discriminative observation, and the anticipation of positive or negative reinforcements contingent on the emission of matching responses may be highly influential in channeling, augmenting, or reducing observing responses, which is a necessary precondition for imitative learning (Bandura, 1962; Bandura and Walters, 1963). Procedures that increase the distinctiveness of the relevant modeling stimuli also greatly facilitate observational learning (Sheffield and Maccoby, 1961).

In addition to attention-directing variables, the rate, amount, and complexity of stimuli presented to the observer may partly determine the degree of imitative learning. The acquisition of matching responses through observation of a lengthy uninterrupted sequence of behavior is also likely to be governed by principles of associate learning such as frequency and recency, serial order effects, and other multiple sources of associative interference (McGuire, 1961).

Social responses are generally composed of a large number of different behavioral units combined in a particular manner. Responses of higher-order complexity are produced by combinations of previously learned components which may, in themselves, represent relatively complicated behavioral patterns. Consequently, the rate of acquisition of intricate matching responses through observation will be largely determined by the extent to which the necessary components are contained in the observer's repertoire. A person who possesses a very narrow repertoire of behavior, for example, will, in all probability, display only fragmentary imitation of a model's behavior; on the other hand, a person who has acquired most of the relevant components is likely to perform precisely matching responses following several demonstrations. In the case of young preschool children their motor repertoires are more highly developed than their repertoires of verbal responses. It is, perhaps, for this reason that even in the positive-incentive condition, children reproduced a substantially higher percentage (67%) of imitative motor responses than matching verbalizations (20%). A similar pattern of differential imitation was obtained in a previous experiment (Bandura and Huston, 1961) in which preschool children served as subjects.

It is apparent from the foregoing discussion that considerably more research is needed in identifying variables that combine with contiguous stimulation in governing the process of imitative response acquisition.

It is possible, of course, to interpret the present acquisition data as reflecting the operation of generalization from a prior history of reinforcement of imitative behavior. Within any social group, models typically exhibit the accumulated cultural repertoires that have proved most successful for given stimulus situations; consequently, matching the behavior of other persons, particularly the superiors in an age-grade or prestige hierarchy, will maximize positive reinforcement and minimize the frequency of aversive response consequences. Since both the occurrence and the positive reinforcement of matching responses, whether by accident or by intent, are inevitable during the course of social development, no definitive resolution of the reinforcement issue is possible, except through an experiment utilizing organisms that have experienced complete social isolation from birth. It is evident, however, that contemporaneous reinforcements are unnecessary for the acquisition of new matching responses.

The finding that boys perform more imitative aggression than girls as a result of exposure to an aggressive male model, is in accord with results from related experiments (Bandura, Ross, and Ross, 1961, 1963a). The additional finding, however, that the introduction of positive incentives practically wiped out the prior performance disparity strongly suggests that the frequently observed sex differences in aggression (Goodenough, 1931; Johnson, 1951; Sears, 1951) may reflect primarily differences in willingness to exhibit aggressive responses, rather than deficits in learning or "masculine-role identification."

The subgroups of children who displayed significant increments in imitative behavior as a function of positive reinforcement were boys who had observed the aggressive model punished, and girls for whom physically aggressive behavior is typically labeled sex-inappropriate and nonrewarded or even negatively reinforced. The inhibitory effects of differing reinforcement histories for aggression were clearly reflected in the observation that boys were more easily disinhibited than girls in the reward phase of the experiment. This factor may account for the small sex difference that was obtained even in the positive-incentive condition.

The present study provides further evidence that response inhibition and response disinhibition can be vicariously transmitted through observation of reinforcing consequences to a model's behavior. It is interesting to note, however, that the performance by a model of socially disapproved or prohibited responses (for example, kicking, striking with objects) without the occurrence of any aversive consequences may produce disinhibitory effects analogous to a positive reinforcement operation. These findings are similar to results from studies of direct reinforcement (Crandall, Good, and Crandall, 1964) in which nonreward functioned as a positive reinforcer to increase the probability of the occurrence of formerly punished responses.

Punishment administered to the model apparently further reinforced the girls' existing inhibitions over aggression and produced remarkably little imitative behavior; the boys displayed a similar, though not significant, decrease in imitation. This difference may be partly a function of the relative dominance of aggressive responses in the repertoires of boys and girls. It is also possible that vicarious reinforcement for boys, deriving from the model's successful execution of aggressive behavior (that is, overpowering the noncompliant adversary), may have reduced the effects of externally administered terminal punishment. These factors, as well as the model's self-rewarding and self-punishing reactions followed the display of aggression, will be investigated in a subsequent experiment.

References

Baer, D. M., and Sherman, J. A. Reinforcement control of generalized imitation in young children. *Journal of Experimental Child Psychology,* 1964, *1,* 37–49.

Bandura, A. Social learning through imitation. In M. R. Jones (Ed.), *Nebraska symposium on motivation: 1962.* Lincoln: University of Nebraska Press, 1962. Pp. 211–269.

Bandura, A. Vicarious processes: A case of no-trial learning. In L. Berkowitz (Ed.), *Advances in experimental social psychology.* Vol. 2. New York: Academic Press, 1965. Pp. 1–55.

Bandura, A., and Huston, Aletha C. Identification as a process of incidental learning. *Journal of Abnormal and Social Psychology,* 1961, *63,* 311–318.

Bandura, A., Ross, Dorothea, and Ross, Sheila A. Transmission of aggression through imitation of aggressive models. *Journal of Abnormal and Social Psychology,* 1961, *63,* 575–582.

Bandura, A., Ross, Dorothea, and Ross, Sheila A.

Imitation of film-mediated aggressive models. *Journal of Abnormal and Social Psychology,* 1963, *66,* 3–11. (a)

BANDURA, A., ROSS, DOROTHEA, and ROSS, SHEILA A. Vicarious reinforcement and imitative learning. *Journal of Abnormal and Social Psychology,* 1963, *67,* 601–607. (b)

BANDURA, A., and WALTERS, R. H. *Social learning and personality development.* New York: Holt, Rinehart and Winston, 1963.

CRANDALL, VIRGINIA C., GOOD, SUZANNE, and CRANDALL, V. J. The reinforcement effects of adult reactions and non-reactions on children's achievement expectations: A replication study. *Child Development,* 1964, *35,* 385–397.

GOODENOUGH, FLORENCE L. *Anger in young children.* Minneapolis: University of Minnesota Press, 1931.

JOHNSON, ELIZABETH Z. Attitudes of children toward authority as projected in their doll play at two age levels. Unpublished doctoral dissertation, Harvard University, 1951.

MCGUIRE, W. J. Interpolated motivational statements within a programmed series of instructions as a distribution of practice factor. In A. A. Lumsdaine (Ed.), *Student response in programmed instruction: A symposium.* Washington, D.C.: National Academy of Sciences, National Research Council, 1961. Pp. 411–415.

MILLER, N. E., and DOLLARD, J. *Social learning and imitation.* New Haven: Yale University Press, 1941.

MOWRER, O. H. *Learning theory and the symbolic processes.* New York: Wiley, 1960.

SEARS, PAULINE S. Doll play aggression in normal young children: Influence of sex, age, sibling status, father's absence. *Psychological Monographs,* 1951, *65*(6, Whole No. 323).

SHEFFIELD, F. D. Theoretical considerations in the learning of complex sequential tasks from demonstration and practice. In A. A. Lumsdaine (Ed.), *Student response in programmed instruction: A symposium.* Washington, D.C.: National Academy of Sciences, National Research Council, 1961. Pp. 13–32.

SHEFFIELD, F. D., and MACCOBY, N. Summary and interpretation of research on organizational principles in constructing filmed demonstrations. In A. A. Lumsdaine (Ed.), *Student response in programmed instruction: A symposium.* Washington, D.C.: National Academy of Sciences, National Research Council, 1961. Pp. 117–131.

WALTERS, R. H., LEAT, MARION, and MEZEI, L. Inhibition and disinhibition of responses through empathetic learning. *Canadian Journal of Psychology,* 1963, *17,* 235–243.

Sechrest's experiment involved a situation in which a child working on a puzzle was influenced by observing how another child was either rewarded or punished for completing a similar puzzle. The significance of Sechrest's article will be more apparent to the reader after some comments on his terminology and on the behavior processes that he observed. Basically, the problem revolves around the use of the words punishment and negative reinforcement. Although some psychological writers have used the term negative reinforcement as a synonym for punishment, more recent usage defines punishment as the situation in which a performance is followed by an aversive stimulus. Negative reinforcement involves a performance which increases in frequency because it terminates or removes an aversive stimulus. The term "negative" has the implication of "removal of" a noxious stimulus rather than a decrease in the frequency of some behavior. Both definitions refer to the relation of a performance to the environment, but they do not specify the outcome of the procedure. Thus, punishment may or may not decrease the frequency of a performance, and in fact there are some circumstances in which a performance actually increases in frequency when it is punished. An attempt to increase some performance by terminating an aversive stimulus whenever the performance occurs (negative reinforcement) is not always successful. In short, negative reinforcement may or may not be effective, depending upon the circumstances. The reader therefore faces the difficult task of translating Sechrest's terms into those which specify the actual procedures. He must also distinguish between the procedure that was applied and the effect of the procedure on the child's performance.

For example, when the child completed a puzzle speedily as a result of seeing another child being punished, the result was labeled positive reinforcement because there was an increase in the frequency of the behavior. However, if we are to use a procedural terminology—distinguishing the procedure from its effect on the performance—this situation would properly be labeled "implicit negative reinforcement." We would hypothesize that the criticism of the other child's performance created a conditioned aversive stimulus which (by its removal) reinforced speedier completion of the puzzle (to avoid criticism). The terms positive and negative reinforcement refer to the procedures by which stimuli follow the performances. It is an independent issue as to whether the performances change in frequency as a result of positive reinforcements, negative reinforcements, or punishment. The child whose puzzle activity was criticized offers an example of punishment. In this experiment the punishment procedure did not alter the speed with which the child completed the puzzle. The observing child, however, revealed the effects of negative reinforcement in that he reacted to a conditioned aversive stimulus derived from this observation of the criticism of the other child. Sechrest speculates, in fact, that the reason the observer completed the puzzle rapidly was to avoid possible censure from the experimenter.

13 *Implicit Reinforcement of Responses*[1]

LEE SECHREST

There are many ways in which an organism, particularly a human, may gain information about the outcomes of responses which he makes or can make. The most obvious way is by making a response and then either enjoying or suffering its consequences. Such is what is meant by direct, explicit reinforcement. For the most part psychologists have devoted themselves to the study of the effect on an individual's behavioral dispositions of the reinforcements directly contingent upon his own responses. However, among the other ways in which response consequences may become evident is by the observation of the experiences of other persons (Campbell, 1961, 1963). Under some circumstances an individual may observe another person behaving, observe reinforcements being delivered to the other person in such a way that they seem contingent upon particular responses, and thereby have his own response tendencies altered in a congruent manner. Much of what has been called imitation or observational learning (Miller and Dollard, 1941; Rosenbaum, 1961) is of that general nature. Berger (1961), using the term "vicarious reinforcement" suggested by Lewis and Duncan (1958), has been able to demonstrate the learning of words and numbers on an incidental basis as a function of reinforcements delivered to a participant. More recently he has been able to demonstrate a conditioned GSR in subjects who were watching someone else receive what they thought was an electric shock (Berger, 1962).

On the other hand it is possible that under different circumstances an observer might watch the reinforcements being delivered to a model and have his own behavior tendencies altered in a direction opposite to the alterations produced for the model. Thus, for example, Briggs (1927, 1928) reported the retrospective accounts of early school experiences by high school and college students. He found that his respondents rather consistently reported having been adversely affected by sarcasm directed at them by a teacher. However, they also rather consistently reported that observing another pupil become the object of a teacher's sarcasm had a salutary effect on their own behavior. Thus the apparent effects produced for the observer and for the actual recipient of the reinforcement are opposites. If it is possible for an observer to make some inference about the adequacy of his own responses from the observations of reinforcements delivered to a model, then the observer may have his own response tendencies altered

[1] This investigation has been supported by Northwestern University's psychology-education project, sponsored by the Carnegie Corporation. The writer wishes to thank Nancy McKiernan for assistance in data collection and J. Wallace for a careful reading of the manuscript.

and we may say that he has been implicitly reinforced. For example, if a mother comes upon two of her children drawing a picture and says to one of them, "My that's a very nice picture you're drawing," and says nothing to the second child, it would not be surprising if the second child supposed that his own picture was by comparison inferior and if he then behaved as if he had been negatively rather than positively reinforced. In such a case we might say that the observing child was implicitly reinforced. It has been found that children are quite aware of verbal reinforcements administered to their classmates (Sechrest, 1962).

One type of situation in which implicit reinforcement of an observer is quite likely to occur, i.e., in which the effect produced on the observer is the opposite of that produced on the model, is one analogous to a zero-sum game, or in which the observer holds to a "depleted pool" hypothesis about available reinforcements. If a reinforcing agent has only so many reinforcements to dispense, then every reinforcement delivered to one person reduces the possibilities of reinforcement for every other person. For example, if a parent has only one piece of candy with which to reward two children, the dispensing of the candy to one child would not necessarily be expected to produce a congruent effect in an observing child.

In this paper an experiment is reported in which young school children were engaged in pairs in an experimental task during which the experimenter made a comment to one of the children which apparently made it possible for the other children to make some inference about the adequacy of his own performance and thus implicitly rather than explicitly be reinforced. For the sake of argument it is assumed that implicit positive reinforcement occurs in the pair in which explicit negative reinforcement is given. Similarly implicit negative reinforcement should occur when direct positive reinforcement is given.

Procedure

Preliminary work showed that it was possible to affect the speed with which children would work on a puzzle task by employing general verbal reinforcements. For this study the experimental task was the completion of a pair of wooden jigsaw puzzles of the type usually found in toy stores. The puzzles were of a moderate level of difficulty, having 18 and 21 pieces, respectively. The data for analysis were the difference scores between the log time scores (log transformation to correct for skewness) for the first and the second of the two puzzles.

In order for implicit reinforcement to occur the subjects must have the opportunity to make observing responses; therefore, children were run in pairs. Each child of a pair was given one of the two puzzles to work, and following completion by both children of their puzzles, each child was given the second one, i.e., they exchanged. Thus, all the subjects worked the same two puzzles, but in differing orders. The experimental manipulation occurred in the interval between the two puzzles. In the Explicit Reinforcement group one of the two children, randomly selected, was told,

> My, you did very well with your puzzle. That was good work. Now we are going to work another one.

In the Explicit Negative Reinforcement group one child of each pair, again randomly selected, was told,

> Well, that really wasn't so good. You seemed to have trouble with that one. Now we are going to work another one.

And finally in a control group the experimenter merely said,

> All right, now we are going to work another one.

Thus there were two experimental groups in which one of the children received either a positive or a negative verbal reinforcement and a control condition in which no evaluative comments were made. Time scores were recorded to the nearest 5 seconds, and surreptitiously, so that the children were not aware that speed was an issue.

Fifteen pairs of children were run in each experimental group, making 90 children in all. Children were selected in pairs by their teacher as being at about the same ability level, and all pairs were same-sex pairs. The children came from kindergarten, first, second, and third grade classrooms in the three schools in nearly equal proportions for the three reinforcement groups. Experimental procedures were conducted by a young female graduate student in education. The children were asked to go with the experimenter "to play some games." Every attempt was made to keep overt competition between the children at a minimum by using children at the same ability level, by having them work on different puzzles, by structuring the situation as a game session, etc. It will be noted that the verbal reinforcements used were quite general in nature and did not refer at all to time scores which were the measure of performance.

In the positive and negative reinforcement groups the children could be divided into those who had received explicit and those who had received implicit reinforcement. There were 15 of each. The 30 children in the control group were, of course, undifferentiated.

Results

The first analysis was a 2×2 analysis of variance for the two types (positive and negative) and the two conditions (explicit and implicit) of reinforcement, the data for which are given in Table 1. The results of the analysis are presented in Table 2. It can be seen that whether the reinforcement was explicit or implicit was of no consequence, but that positive and negative verbal reinforcements produced a significantly different effect, with positive reinforcement tending to have a facilitating effect on speed of performance on the second puzzle. There is no significant interaction between type and condition of reinforcement.

A comparison of the four experimental groups with the control group shows that only the implicit-positive group differs significantly from the controls ($t = 3.20$, $p < .01$). The explicit-positive and implicit-positive groups also differ from each other ($t = 2.05$, $p < .05$), although this finding is of questionable meaning in view of the lack of a significant main effect for condition of reinforcement.

Table 1 *Means and Standard Deviations of the Difference between Log Times of Two Puzzles for Four Experimental Groups and One Control Group*

Group	*N*	*M*	*SD*
Explicit positive	15	− .46	1.81
Implicit negative	15	.27	1.88
Explicit negative	15	.19	1.80
Implicit positive	15	−1.43	1.56
Control	30	− .12	2.11

Table 2 *Analysis of Variance of Log Time Scores for Four Experimental Groups and One Control Group*

Source	*df*	MS	*F*
Type of reinforcement (positive or negative)	1	21.14	6.32*
Condition of reinforcement (explicit or implicit)	1	2.90	< 1.00
Type × condition	1	4.07	1.22
Within groups	56	3.34	
Total	59		

* $p < .02$.

Discussion

We have seen that a negative reinforcement delivered to one child apparently operates as a positive reinforcement for another child who is participating in the same activity. Conversely, positive reinforcement intended explicitly for one child may have an implicitly negative effect on another. In fact in the experiment just described there was no overall difference attributable to the condition of administration of the reinforcement, i.e., whether it was explicit or implicit. The principal result in the experiment was the difference between positive and negative reinforcements in producing an improvement or a decrement in the speed of solution of the puzzles. However, the more detailed consideration of the results provided by *t* tests suggests that the implicit positive reinforcement was particularly likely to affect performance on the second puzzle. It will be remembered that none of the other three groups differed significantly from the control group, which showed a slight tendency toward improvement in time scores from Puzzle 1 to Puzzle 2. It is of interest to note that the results are somewhat reminiscent of the responses obtained by Briggs (1927, 1928), for his subjects reported being positively affected by negative verbal reinforcement administered to other persons. They also did not report being as susceptible to positive comments made to other persons, i.e., comments which in a competitive situation would be seen as implicitly negative. It should also be pointed out that Kounin and Gump (1958) and Gnagey (1960) have reported experimental findings suggesting the powerful effects on children of observing other children being subjected to a teacher's discipline.

We may ask what the conditions are under which subjects may act as if they had been vicariously reinforced, i.e., will act as if they themselves had received explicit reinforcement, and the conditions under which they will be expected to behave as if they had received an implicit, that is, an opposite, reinforcement. First of all it seems probable that subjects will behave as if they had received an implicit reinforcement when comparisons between performance are fairly evident. When the evaluative dimension of performance is not relevant, i.e., when there is no expectation on the part of the subject that his performance is to be evaluated, then there would seem to be no particular reason why he should respond to a positive reinforcement to a model as if he himself had received a negative reinforcement. It is to be noted in Berger's (1962) experiment as well as in some of the experiments of Rosenbaum (1961) and the experiment of Lewis and Duncan (1958) that the experimental procedures did not involve an evaluation of the responses of either the model or the observer. Hence, there was no reason for the subject to question the adequacy of his own performance.

Secondly, it would seem that implicit reinforcing effects would be more likely to be found in situations in which the observer and the model are engaged in some sort of competitive or quasi-competitive task. If the observer and the model are working on very different kinds of tasks, then an explicit reinforcement to the model would seem to have fewer implications for the adequacy of the performance of the observer. If one child is drawing a picture and the second child is jumping rope and an adult comes along and says, "My, that's very nice," to the child drawing a picture, the child jumping the rope might well not be affected in any way, at least in terms of his rope jumping. He might, however, decide that he would rather draw pictures than jump a rope. Third, implicit reinforcing effects would probably be minimized in groups of a large size. If in a classroom of 30 children a teacher tells one child that his paper is very good, the implicit invidious comparison of other children's papers is probably minimal.

References

BERGER, S. M. Incidental learning through vicarious reinforcement. *Psychological Reports,* 1961, *9,* 477–491.

BERGER, S. M. Conditioning through vicarious investigation. *Psychological Review,* 1962, *62,* 450–466.

BRIGGS, T. H. Praise and censure as incentives. *School and Society,* 1927, *26,* 596–598.

BRIGGS, T. H. Sarcasm. *School Review,* 1928, *36,* 685–695.

CAMPBELL, D. T. Conformity in psychology's theories of acquired behavioral dispositions. In I. A. Berg and B. M. Bass (Eds.), *Conformity and deviation.* New York: Harper, 1961.

CAMPBELL, D. T. Social attitudes and other acquired behavioral dispositions. In S. Koch (Ed.), *Psychology: A study of a science.* Vol. 6. *Investigations of man as socius: Their place in psychology and the social sciences.* New York: McGraw-Hill, 1963. Pp. 94–172.

GNAGEY, W. J. Effects on classmates of a deviant student's power and response to a teacher-exerted control technique. *Journal of Educational Psychology,* 1960, *51,* 1–8.

KOUNIN, J. S., and GUMP, P. V. The ripple effect in discipline. *Elementary School Journal,* 1958, *59,* 158–162.

LEWIS, D. J., and DUNCAN, C. P. Vicarious experience and partial reinforcement. *Journal of Abnormal and Social Psychology,* 1958, *57,* 321–326.

MILLER, N. E., and DOLLARD, J. *Social learning and imitation.* New Haven: Yale University Press, 1941.

ROSENBAUM, M. E. Imitation and observational learning. Colloquium given at Northwestern University, 1961.

SECHREST, L. The motivations of young children in school: Some interview data. *Journal of Experimental Education,* 1962, *30,* 327–335.

The experiment by *Bandura, Grusec, and Menlove* examines what happens when a child fearful of dogs observes other children playing with the dog positively and without aversive consequences. This experiment focuses on conditioned emotional reactions and avoidance behavior rather than on positively reinforced operant behavior as was done in the preceding two experiments. According to many theorists, lack of contact with the real situation is one of the reasons that feared and avoided objects continue to evoke conditioned reflexes and to maintain avoidance behavior, even though no aversive consequences are currently associated with them. If the child is not in frequent contact with the fear-provoking situation, the results of the previous reflex and avoidance conditioning cannot be reduced through extinction. Many experimenters have shown how direct exposure to previously aversive stimuli will eliminate their conditioned aversive effects, particularly if the subject is exposed to the stimuli in a gradual, progressive way. The desensitization procedure begins with stimuli slightly resembling the feared object and progresses to another only when the child no longer shows conditioned aversive effects.

These experimenters inquired whether extinction of the aversive properties of a previously conditioned stimulus situation could be carried out by allowing the child to observe another child who became less fearful each time there was a contact with the dog. Critical elements in the experiment were the use of positive and neutral contexts for the modeling performances and direct rather than vicarious exposure to the dog in a positive context. In the positive context—while a children's party was in progress—the model first saw the dog at a distance and then, in gradual steps, reached the point where he actually touched the dog. Another model performed the same approach sequences in neutral circumstances. In still another situation, the fearful children were exposed to the dog without first having observed a model. The experimenters found that observing a model interacting with the dog led to more extinction of fear than did direct, personal contact with the dog. They term this process vicarious extinction.

14 | Vicarious Extinction of Avoidance Behavior[1]

ALBERT BANDURA
JOAN E. GRUSEC
FRANCES L. MENLOVE

Recent investigations have shown that behavioral inhibitions (Bandura, 1965a; Bandura, Ross, and Ross, 1963; Walters and Parke, 1964) and conditioned emotional responses (Bandura and Rosenthal, 1966; Berger, 1962) can be acquired by observers as a function of witnessing aversive stimuli administered to performing subjects. The present experiment was primarily designed to determine whether preexisting avoidance behavior can similarly be extinguished on a vicarious basis. The latter phenomenon requires exposing observers to modeled stimulus events in which a performing subject repeatedly exhibits approach responses toward the feared object without incurring any aversive consequences.

Some suggestive evidence that avoidance responses can be extinguished vicariously is furnished by Masserman (1943) and Jones (1924) in exploratory studies of the relative efficacy of various psychotherapeutic procedures. Masserman produced strong feeding inhibitions in cats, following which the inhibited animals observed a cage mate, that had never been negatively conditioned, exhibit prompt approach and feeding responses. The observing subjects initially cowered at the presentation of the conditioned stimulus, but with continued exposure to their fearless companion they advanced, at first hesitantly and then more boldly, to the goal box and consumed the food. Some of the animals, however, showed little reduction in avoidance behavior despite prolonged food deprivation and numerous modeling trials. Moreover, avoidance responses reappeared in a few of the animals after the normal cat was removed, suggesting that in the latter cases the modeling stimuli served merely as temporary external inhibitors of avoidance responses. Jones (1924) similarly obtained variable results in extinguishing children's phobic responses by having them observe their peers behave in a nonanxious manner in the presence of the avoided objects.

If a person is to be influenced by modeling stimuli and the accompanying consequences, then the necessary observing responses must be elicited and maintained. In the foregoing case studies, the models responded to the most feared stimulus situation at the outset, a modeling procedure that is likely to generate high levels of emotional arousal in observers. Under these conditions any avoidance responses designed to reduce vicariously instigated aversive stimulation, such as subjects withdrawing or looking away, would impede vicarious extinction. Therefore, the manner in which modeling stimuli are presented may be an important determinant of the course of vicarious extinction.

Results from psychotherapeutic studies (Bandura[2]) and experiments with infrahuman subjects (Kimble and Kendall, 1953) reveal that avoidance responses can be rapidly extinguished if subjects are exposed to a graduated series of aversive stimuli that progressively approximate the original intensity of the conditioned fear stimulus. For the above reasons it would seem advisable to conduct vicarious extinction by exposing observers to a graduated sequence of modeling activities beginning with presentations that can be easily tolerated; as observers' emotional reactions to displays of attenuated approach responses are extinguished, the fear-provoking properties of the modeled displays might be gradually increased, concluding with interactions capable of arousing relatively strong emotional responses.

If emotion-eliciting stimuli occur in association with positively reinforcing events, the former cues are likely to lose their conditioned aversive properties more rapidly (Farber, 1948) than through mere repeated nonreinforced presentation. It might therefore be supposed that vicarious extinction would likewise be hastened and more adequately controlled by presenting the modeling stimuli within a favorable context designed to evoke simultaneously competing positive responses.

The principles dscussed above were applied in the present experiment, which explored the vicarious extinction of children's fearful and avoidant responses

[1] This research was supported by Public Health Research Grant M-5162 from the National Institute of Mental Health.
The authors are indebted to Janet Brewer, Edith Dowley, Doris Grant, and Mary Lewis for their generous assistance in various phases of this research.

[2] A. Bandura, "Principles of Behavioral Modification," unpublished manuscript, Stanford University, 1966.

toward dogs. One group of children participated in a series of modeling sessions in which they observed a fearless peer model exhibit progressively longer, closer, and more active interactions with a dog. For these subjects, the modeled approach behavior was presented within a highly positive context. A second group of children was presented the same modeling stimuli, but in a neutral context.

Exposure to the behavior of the model contains two important stimulus events, that is, the occurrence of approach responses without any adverse consequences to the performer, and repeated observation of the feared animal. Therefore, in order to control for the effects of exposure to the dog per se, children assigned to a third group observed the dog in the positive context but with the model absent. A fourth group of children participated in the positive activities, but they were never exposed to either the dog or the model.

In order to assess both the generality and the stability of vicarious extinction effects, the children were readministered tests for avoidance behavior toward different dogs following completion of the treatment series, and approximately one month later. It was predicted that children who had observed the peer model interact nonanxiously with the dog would display significantly less avoidance behavior than subjects who had no exposure to the modeling stimuli. The largest decrements were expected to occur among children in the modeling-positive context condition. It was also expected that repeated behavioral assessments and the general disinhibitory effects of participation in a series of highly positive activities might in themselves produce some decrease in avoidance behavior.

Method

Subjects. The subjects were 24 boys and 24 girls selected from three nursery schools. The children ranged in age from 3 to 5 years.

Pretreatment Assessment of Avoidance Behavior. As a preliminary step in the selection procedure, parents were asked to rate the magnitude of their children's fearful and avoidant behavior toward dogs. Children who received high fear ratings were administered a standardized performance test on the basis of which the final selection was made.

The strength of avoidance responses was measured by means of a graded sequence of 14 performance tasks in which the children were required to engage in increasingly intimate interactions with a dog. A female experimenter brought the children individually to the test room, which contained a brown cocker spaniel confined in a modified playpen. In the initial tasks the children were asked, in the following order, to walk up to the playpen and look down at the dog, to touch her fur, and to pet her. Following the assessment of avoidance responses to the dog in the protective enclosure, the children were instructed to open a hinged door on the side of the playpen, to walk the dog on a leash to a throw rug, to remove the leash, and to turn the dog over and scratch her stomach. Although a number of the subjects were unable to perform all of the latter tasks, they were nevertheless administered the remaining test items to avoid any assumption of a perfectly ordered scale for all cases. In subsequent items the children were asked to remain alone in the room with the animal and to feed her dog biscuits. The final and most difficult set of tasks required the children to climb into the playpen with the dog, to pet her, to scratch her stomach, and to remain alone in the room with the dog under the exceedingly confining and fear-provoking conditions.

The strength of the children's avoidant tendencies was reflected not only in the items completed, but also in the degree of vacillation, reluctance, and fearfulness that preceded and accompanied each approach response. Consequently, children were credited 2 points if they executed a given task either spontaneously or willingly, and 1 point when they carried out the task minimally after considerable hesitancy and reluctance. Thus, for example, children who promptly stroked the dog's fur repeatedly when requested to so received 2 points, whereas subjects who held back but then touched the dog's fur briefly obtained 1 point. In the item requiring the children to remain alone in the room with the dog, they received 2 points if they approached the animal and played with her, and 1 point if they were willing to remain in the room but avoided any contact with the dog. Similarly, in the feeding situation children were credited 2 points if they fed the dog by hand, but a single point if they tossed the biscuits on the floor and thereby avoided close contact with the animal. The maximum approach score that a subject could attain was 28 points.

On the basis of the pretreatment assessment, the children in each nursery school were grouped into three levels of avoidance behavior, with the corresponding scores ranging from 0 to 7, 8 to 17, and 18 to 28 points. There were approximately the same number of children, equally divided between boys and girls, at each of the three avoidance levels. The subjects from each of these groups were then assigned randomly to one of four conditions.

Treatment Conditions. Children who participated in the *modeling-positive context* condition observed a fearless peer model display approach responses toward a cocker spaniel within the context of a highly enjoyable party atmosphere.

There were eight 10-minute treatment sessions conducted on 4 consecutive days. Each session, which was attended by a group of four children, commenced with a jovial party. The children were furnished brightly colored hats, cookie treats, and given small prizes. In addition, the experimenter read stories, blew large plastic balloons for the children to play with, and engaged in other party activities designed to produce strong positive effective responses.

After the party was well under way, a second experimenter entered the room carrying the dog, followed by a 4-year-old male model who was unknown to most of the children. The dog was placed in a playpen located across the room from a large table at which the children were seated. The model, who had been chosen because of his complete lack of fear of dogs, then performed prearranged sequences of interactions with the dog for approximately 3 minutes during each session. One boy served as the model for children drawn from two of the nursery schools, and a second boy functioned in the same role at the third school.

The fear-provoking properties of the modeled displays were gradually increased from session to session by varying simultaneously the physical restraints on the dog, the directness and intimacy of the modeled approach responses, and the duration of interaction between the model and his canine companion. Initially, the experimenter carried the dog into the room and confined her to the playpen, and the model's behavior was limited to friendly verbal responses ("Hi, Chloe") and occasional petting. During the following three sessions the dog remained confined to the playpen, but the model exhibited progressively longer and more active interactions in the form of petting the dog with his hands and feet, and feeding her wieners and milk from a baby bottle. Beginning with the fifth session, the dog was walked into the room on a leash, and the modeled tasks were mainly performed outside the playpen. For example, in addition to repeating the feeding routines, the model walked the dog around the room, petted her, and scratched her stomach while the leash was removed. In the last two sessions the model climbed into the playpen with the dog where he petted her, hugged her, and fed her wieners and milk from the baby bottle.

It would have been of interest to compare the relative efficacy of the graduated modeling technique with bold displays of approach behavior from the outset. However, pretest findings showed that when modeled displays are too fear-provoking, children actively avoid looking at the performances and are reluctant to participate in subsequent sessions. The latter approach would therefore require additional procedures designed to maintain strong attending behavior to highly aversive modeling stimuli.

Children assigned to the *modeling-neutral context* condition observed the same sequence of approach responses performed by the same peer model except that the parties were omitted. In each of the eight sessions the subjects were merely seated at the table and observed the modeled performances.

In order to control for the influence of repeated exposure to the positive atmosphere and to the dog per se, children in the *exposure-positive context* group attended the series of parties in the presence of the dog with the model absent. As in the two modeling conditions, the dog was introduced into the room in the same manner for the identical length of time; similarly, the dog was confined in the playpen during the first four sessions and placed on a leash outside the enclosure in the remaining sessions.

Children in the *positive-context* group participated in the parties, but they were never exposed to either the dog or the model. The main purpose of this condition was to determine whether the mere presence of a dog had an adverse or a beneficial effect on the children. Like the third condition, it also provided a control for the possible therapeutic effects of positive experiences and increased familiarity with amiable experimenters, which may be particularly influential in reducing inhibitons in very young children. In addition, repeated behavioral assessments in which subjects perform a graded series of approach responses toward a feared object without any aversive consequences would be expected to produce some direct extinction of avoidance behavior. The inclusion of the latter two control groups thus makes it possible to evaluate the changes effected by exposure to modeling stimuli over and above those resulting from general disinhibition, direct extinction, and repeated observation of the feared object.

Posttreatment Assessment of Avoidance Behavior. On the day following completion of the treatment series, the children were readministered the performance test consisting of the graded sequence of interaction tasks with the dog. In order to determine the generality of vicarious extinction effects, half the children in each of the four groups were tested initially with the experimental animal and then with an unfamiliar dog; the remaining children were presented with the two dogs in the reverse order.[3] The testing sessions were separated by an interval of 1½ hours so as to minimize any transfer of emotional reactions generated by one animal to the other.

The unfamiliar animal was a white mongrel, predominantly terrior, and of approximately the same size and activity level as the cocker spaniel. Two groups of 15 children, drawn from the same nursery-school population, were tested with either the mon-

[3] The authors are especially indebted to Chloe and Jenny for their invaluable and steadfast assistance with a task that, at times, must have been most perplexing to them.

grel or the spaniel in order to determine the aversiveness of the two animals. The mean approach scores with the spaniel ($M = 16.47$) and the mongrel ($M = 15.80$) were virtually identical ($t = .21$).

Follow-up Assessment. A follow-up evaluation was conducted approximately one month after the posttreatment assessment in order to determine the stability of modeling-induced changes in approach behavior. The children's responses were tested with the same performance tasks toward both animals, presented in the identical order.

After the experiment was completed, the children were told that, while most dogs are friendly, before petting an unfamiliar dog they should ask the owner. This precautionary instruction was designed to reduce indiscriminate approach behavior by children who were in the modeling conditions toward strange dogs which they would undoubtedly encounter.

Measurement Procedure. The same female experimenter administered the pretreatment, posttreatment, and follow-up behavioral tests. To prevent any possible bias, the experimenter was given minimal information about the details of the study and had no knowledge of the conditions to which the children were assigned. The treatment and assessment procedures were further separated by the use of different rooms for each activity.

In order to provide an estimate of interscorer reliability, the performances of 25% of the children, randomly selected from pretreatment, posttreatment, and follow-up phases of the experiment, were scored simultaneously but independently by another rater who observed the test sessions through a one-way mirror from an adjoining observation room. The two raters were in perfect agreement on 97% of the specific approach responses that were scored.

A dog's actvity level may partly determine the degree of fear and avoidance exhibited by the children; conversely, timorous or unrestrained approach responses might differentially affect the animals' reactivity. Therefore, during the administration of each test item, the animals' behavior was rated as either passive, moderately active, or vigorous. The raters were in perfect agreement in categorizing the dogs' activity levels on 81% of the performance tests.

Changes in children's approach-response scores across the different phases of the experiment, and the number of subjects in each treatment condition who were able to carry out the terminal performance task served as the dependent measures.

Results

The percentages of test items in which the animals behaved in a passive, moderately active, or vigorous manner were 55, 43, and 2, respectively, for the model-positive context group; 53, 44, and 2 for children in the model-neutral context condition; 52, 45, and 3 for the exposure-positive context group; and 57, 41, and 2 for the positive-context subjects. Thus, the test animals did not differ in their behavior during the administration of performance tasks to children in the various treatment conditions.

Approach Responses. Table 1 presents the mean increases in approach behavior achieved by children in each of the treatment conditions in different phases of the experiment with each of the test animals.

The children's approach responses toward the two dogs did not differ either in the posttreatment assessment ($t = 1.35$) or in the follow-up phase ($t = .91$) of the study. Nor were there any significant effects ($t = 1.68$) due to the order in which the test animals were presented following completion of the treatment series. A t-test analysis also disclosed no significant change ($t = 1.50$) in mean approach scores between measurements conducted in the posttreatment and the follow-up phases of the experiment. Moreover, analysis of variance of the posttreatment scores revealed no significant Treatment × Dogs ($F = 2.15$) or Treatment × Order ($F = .30$) interaction effects. The data were therefore combined across phases and test animals in evaluating the major hypotheses.

Table 1 *Mean Increases in Approach Responses as a Function of Treatment Conditions, Assessment Phases, and Test Animals*

Phases	Treatment Conditions			
	Modeling–Positive Context	Modeling–Neutral Context	Exposure–Positive Context	Positive Context
Posttreatment				
Spaniel	10.83	9.83	2.67	6.08
Mongrel	5.83	10.25	3.17	4.17
Follow-up				
Spaniel	10.83	9.33	4.67	5.83
Mongrel	12.59	9.67	4.75	6.67
Combined data	10.02	9.77	3.81	5.69

An analysis of covariance, in which adjustments were made for differences in initial level of avoidance, was computed for mean approach responses performed by children in the various groups. The results reveal that the treatment conditions had a highly significant effect on the children's behavior ($F = 5.09$, $p < .01$). Tests of the differences between the various pairs of treatments indicate that subjects in the modeling-positive context condition displayed significantly more approach behavior than subjects in either the exposure ($F = 9.32$, $p < .01$) or the positive-context ($F = 8.96$, $p < .01$) groups. Similarly, children who had observed the model within the neutral setting exceeded both the exposure ($F = 6.57$, $p < .05$) and positive-context groups ($F = 4.91$, $p < .05$) in approach behavior. However, the data yielded no significant differences between either the two modeling conditions ($F = .04$) or the two control groups ($F = .76$).

Within-Group Analysis of Approach Responses. The approach scores obtained by the different groups of children in preexperimental and subsequent tests are summarized graphically in Figure 1. Within-group analyses of changes between initial performance and mean level of approach behavior following treatment disclose significant increases in approach behavior for children in the modeling-positive context group ($t = 7.71$, $p < .001$) and for those who observed the modeling performance within the neutral setting ($t = 5.80$, $p < .001$). Although the positive-context group showed an increment in approach behavior ($t = 5.78$, $p < .001$), children who were merely exposed to the dog in the positive context achieved a small, but nonsignificant ($t = 1.98$), reduction in avoidance responses.

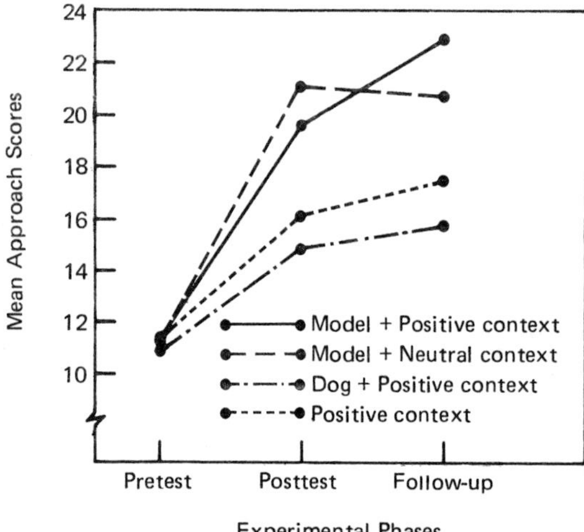

Figure 1 *Mean approach scores achieved by children in each of the treatment conditions in the three different periods of assessment.*

Terminal Performances. Another measure of the efficacy of modeling procedures is provided by comparisons of the number of children in each condition who performed the terminal approach behavior at least once during the posttreatment assessment. Since the frequencies within the two modeling conditions did not differ, and the two control groups were essentially the same, the data for each of the two sets of subgroups were combined. The findings show that 67% of the children in the modeling treatment were able to remain alone in the room confined with the dog in the playpen, whereas the corresponding figure for the control subjects is 33%. The χ^2 value for these data is 4.08, which is significant beyond the .025 level.

Within the control groups, the terminal performances were attained primarily by subjects who initially showed the weakest level of avoidance behavior. The differences between the two groups are, therefore, even more pronounced if the analysis is conducted on the subjects whose pretreatment performances reflected extreme or moderately high levels of avoidance behavior. Of the most avoidant subjects in each of the two pooled groups, 55% of the children in the modeling conditions were able to perform the terminal approach behavior following the experimental sessions, while only 13% of the control subjects successfully completed the final task. The one-tailed probability for the obtained $\chi^2 = 4.74$ is slightly below the .01 level of significance.

The relative superiority of the modeling groups is also evident in the follow-up phase of the experiment. Based on the stringent criterion in which the most fearful task is successfully performed with *both* animals, a significantly larger number of children in the modeling conditions (42%) than in the control groups (12%) exhibited generalized extinction ($\chi^2 = 4.22$, $p < .025$). Moreover, not a single control subject from the two highest levels of avoidance behavior was able to remain alone in the room confined in the playpen with each of the dogs, whereas 33% of the most avoidant children in the modeling conditions successfully passed both terminal approach tasks ($\chi^2 = 4.02$, $p < .025$).

Discussion

The findings of the present experiment provide considerable evidence that avoidance responses can be successfully extinguished on a vicarious basis. This is shown in the fact that children who experienced a gradual exposure to progressively more fearful modeled responses displayed extensive and stable reduction in avoidance behavior. Moreover, most of these subjects were able to engage in extremely intimate and potentially fearful interactions with test animals following the treatment series. The considerable degree of generalization of extinction effects obtained to the unfamiliar dog is most likely due to similar stimulus properties of the test animals. Under conditions where observers' avoidance responses are extinguished to a single animal, one would expect a progressive decrement in approach behavior toward animals of increasing size and fearfulness.

The prediction that vicarious extinction would be augmented by presenting the modeling stimuli within a highly positive context was not confirmed, although subjects in the latter condition differed more significantly from the controls than children who observed approach behavior under neutral conditions. It is entirely possible that a different temporal ordering of emotion-provoking modeling stimuli and events designed to induce anxiety-inhibiting responses would facilitate the vicarious extinction process. On the basis of evidence from conditioning studies (Melvin and Brown, 1964) the optimal treatment procedure might require repeated observational trials, in each of which aversive modeling stimuli are immediately followed by positively reinforcing experiences for the observers. These temporal prerequisites depend upon the abrupt presentation and termination of the two sets of stimulus events that cannot be readily achieved with live demonstrations. It would be possible, however, to study the effects of systematic variations in the temporal spacing of critical variables if modeling stimuli were presented pictorially. Apart from issues of economy and control, if pictorial stimulus material proved equally as efficacious as live modeling, then skillfully designed therapeutic films could be developed and employed in preventive programs for eliminating common fears and anxieties before they become well established and widely generalized.

Although children in both the exposure and the positive-context groups showed some increment in approach behavior, only the changes in the latter group were of statistically significant magnitude. Apparently the mere presence of a dog had some mild negative consequences that counteracted the facilitative effects resulting from highly rewarding interactions with amiable experimenters, increased familiarity with the person conducting the numerous tests of avoidance behavior, and any inevitable direct extinction produced by the repeated performance of some approach responses toward the test animals without any adverse consequences. As might be expected, the general disinhibitory effects arising from these multiple sources occurred only in the early phase of the experiment, and no significant increases in approach behavior appeared between the post-treatment and follow-up assessments.

The data obtained in this experiment demonstrate that the fearless behavior of a model can substantially reduce avoidance responses in observers, but the findings do not establish the nature of the mechanism by which vicarious extinction occurs. There are several possible explanations of vicariously produced effects (Bandura, 1965b; Kanfer, 1965). One interpretation is in terms of the informative value of modeling stimuli. That is, the repeated evocation of approach responses without any adverse consequences to another person undoubtedly conveys information to the observer about the probable outcomes of close interactions with dogs. In the present study, however, an attempt was made to minimize the contribution of purely cognitive factors by informing children in all groups beforehand that the test animals were harmless.

The nonoccurrence of anticipated aversive consequences to a model accompanied by positive affective reactions on his part can also extinguish in observers previously established emotional responses that are vicariously aroused by the modeled displays (Bandura and Rosenthal, 1966). It is therefore possible that reduction in avoidance behavior is partly mediated by the elimination of conditioned emotionality.

Further research is needed to separate the relative contributions of cognitive, emotional, and other factors governing vicarious processes. It would also be of interest to study the effects upon vicarious extinction exercised by such variables as number of modeling trials, distribution of extinction sessions, mode of model presentation, and variations in the characteristics of the models and the feared stimuli. For example, with extensive sampling in the modeled displays of both girls and boys exhibiting approach responses to dogs ranging from diminutive breeds to larger specimens, it may be possible to achieve widely generalized extinction effects. Once approach behaviors have been restored through modeling, their maintenance and further generalization can be effectively controlled by response-contingent reinforcement administered directly to the subject. The combined use of modeling and reinforcement procedures may thus serve as a highly efficacious mode of therapy for eliminating severe behavioral inhibitions.

References

Bandura, A. Influence of models' reinforcement contingencies on the acquisition of initative responses. *Journal of Personality and Social Psychology,* 1965, *1,* 589–595. (a)

Bandura, A. Vicarious processes: A case of no-trial learning. In L. Berkowitz (Ed.), *Advances in experimental social psychology.* Vol. 2. New York: Academic Press, 1965. Pp. 1–55. (b)

Bandura, A., and Rosenthal, T. L. Vicarious classical conditioning as a function of arousal level. *Journal of Personality and Social Psychology,* 1966, *3,* 54–62.

Bandura, A., Ross, D., and Ross, S. A. Vicarious reinforcement and imitative learning. *Journal of Abnormal and Social Psychology,* 1963, *67,* 601–607.

Berger, S. M. Conditioning through vicarious instigation. *Psychological Review,* 1962, *69,* 450–466.

Farber, I. E. Response fixation under anxiety and non-anxiety conditions. *Journal of Experimental Psychology,* 1948, *38,* 111–131.

Jones, M. C. The elimination of children's fears. *Journal of Experimental Psychology,* 1924, *7,* 383–390.

Kanfer, F. H. Vicarious human reinforcement: A glimpse into the black box. In L. Krasner and L. P. Ullmann (Eds.), *Research in behavior modification.* New York: Holt, Rinehart and Winston, 1965. Pp. 244–267.

Kimble, G. A., and Kendall, J. W., Jr. A comparison of two methods of producing experimental extinction. *Journal of Experimental Psychology,* 1953, *45,* 87–90.

Masserman, J. H. *Behavior and neurosis.* Chicago: University of Chicago Press, 1943.

Melvin, K. B., and Brown, J. S. Neutralization of an aversive light stimulus as a function of number of paired presentations with food. *Journal of Comparative and Physiological Psychology,* 1964, *58,* 350–353.

Walters, R. H., and Parke, R. D. Influence of response consequences to a social model on resistance to deviation. *Journal of Experimental Child Psychology,* 1964, *1,* 269–280.

Gewirtz and Stingle continue the discussion of implicit and vicarious reinforcement by bringing together many previous experiments and theoretical arguments to show that past reinforcement procedures are responsible for most imitation even though they are not obvious in the current situation. The authors argue that the observer has had many experiences in which imitative behaviors are reinforced and from which generalized imitaton emerges. The article is necessarily technical because the authors analyze the complex behavior processes from which generalized imitation develops. The basic process that Gewirtz and Stingle deal with is stimulus control. They return us to the proposition that the model can influence the observer through the behaviors that he prompts. Such a formulation naturally stresses the conditions under which the observer acquired the operant repertoire which now can be prompted.

Imitation and vicarious and implicit reinforcement naturally suggest the phenomenon of identification. The authors discuss identification from the point of view of several theories, particularly psychoanalysis, and then attempt to show how a functional analysis of the component behaviors in terms of the processes of reinforcement in stimulus control provides a simpler and more useful descriptive framework.

15 *Learning of Generalized Imitation as the Basis for Identification*[1]

JACOB L. GEWIRTZ
KAREN G. STINGLE[2]

After the response of another (a "model") has been witnessed, the observer will often exhibit a response resembling that of the model. This response class, termed *imitation,* does not consist of a specific set of responses classifiable by content or by similarity alone. Rather, a behavior is termed imitative if it is matched to the cues provided by the model's response and is similar to his behavior, but is not emitted because of common stimulus antecedents or environmental constraints. The term *generalized imitation* can be used when many different responses of a model are copied in diverse situations, often in the absence of extrinsic reinforcement. In contrast, the

[1] This paper is dedicated to the memory of Richard Haig Walters, who contributed so much to theory and research on social behavior and learning and whose recent passing cut short a most productive career.

[2] The authors wish to thank Donald M. Baer for his extensive comments on an early draft of this paper. Baer contributed to delineating our major theoretical difference with him and his associates and helped us to clarify our assumptions about responses that can comprise abstract values. Among others who have made thoughtful comments on this paper while it was in preparation, Roger Burton, Lawrence Kohlberg, and John Wright deserve special thanks.

term *identification* has usually referred to a person's taking on abstract psychological characteristics of a model like those termed motives, attitudes, values, roles, or affective states, rather than specific behavior patterns.

Our interest in generalized imitation stems from the awareness that much of the child's early learning is accomplished through that process. It has also evolved in reaction to the widely held view that this tendency to imitate as well as to identify is acquired *without* specific instrumental training (e.g., Aronfreed, 1967, 1969; Bandura, 1962, 1969; Sears, 1957). As an alternative to that position, we suggest that a simple instrumental learning model, with imitation representing one type of acquired stimulus control over responses, can encompass the complex behavior outcomes ordered under that concept and perhaps also many grouped under the heading of observational learning. A paradigm as elementary as the one presented here has not been fully developed as the basis for the acquisition and maintenance of either imitative behaviors or observational learning, much less as the basis for identification. This parsimonious paradigm, outlined in the first part of the paper, emphasizes intermittent extrinsic reinforcement of an instrumental response class containing a potentially unlimited number of responses, varied in content and matched to response-provided cues from many models (but which may be focused on one model), and often occurring in situations where the model is absent or where there is no extrinsic reinforcement for imitation. In the remaining portion of the paper, we consider the phenomena generally grouped under the rubric of identification and propose that they can be reduced to the simple conception of generalized imitation, and that this reduction can facilitate a research approach to identification.

There is a relatively large literature on imitation and identification, of which only selected references are listed here. Rather than attempt an extensive survey of this imitation and identification literature ourselves, we attend only to those conceptual themes in that literature that are basic to our case, which is to propose a parsimonious common learning basis for both imitation and identification phenomena.

Imitation

Miller and Dollard (1941) did much to bring imitation into a behavior-theory framework as "matched-dependent" behavior by suggesting that it is based on both the individual's capacity to learn to imitate and environmental conditions that have positively reinforced him for such learning. Copying, which by their definition involves the copier's knowing when his response is the same as the model's, is learned in a trial-and-error fashion when an external "critic" (reinforcing agent) rewards randomly occurring similarity and punishes dissimilarity, or when copying is followed by the same reinforcer that followed the model's response. Eventually, as the copier's discrimination improves, he emits anticipatory discrimination responses that produce anxiety if his copying response is different from the model's response or reduce anxiety if his copying response is the same. The copier in time becomes his own critic.

Also in a learning-theory framework, Mowrer (1950, 1960) advanced a theory of imitative learning in which he postulated that imitation (particularly of vocal behaviors) of a model occurs because cues from that model's behaviors have acquired reinforcing value through their pairing with primary reinforcers, and through generalization their imitation acquires secondary reinforcement value for the copier and is thereby maintained. Thus, imitation is learned through a process of self-contained instrumental learning, without direct (extrinsic) reinforcement for imitation. In a preliminary analysis, Skinner (1953) briefly sketched how the cues from models' responses can become discriminative for the extrinsic reinforcement of matching responses, but he did not develop the case for a functional matching-response class maintained by intermittent reinforcement.

The mechanism for the acquisition of imitative (-identificatory) behaviors stressed by Bandura (1962, 1965b, 1969) is that of *observational learning*, in which matching behaviors are acquired by an observer through simple exposure to a model's response, independent of the observer's overt response or of its reinforcement. Specifically, Bandura assumes that stimuli from the model's behavior elicit perceptual responses in the observer that become associated on the basis of the temporal contiguity of the stimuli provided by the environment (e.g., the model's behavior). After repeated contiguous stimulation, these perceptual responses come to form verbal or imaginal representations of the stimuli involved. These representational systems mediate response retrieval and reproduction, in that they provide cues which elicit or are discriminative for overt responses corresponding to those of the model. Thus, according to Bandura, it is primarily on the basis of stimulus contiguity and symbolic mediation that imitative behaviors are acquired.[3] The rate and

[3] Although there is a sense in which all organisms must somehow bridge the gap between relevant experience and later response outcomes, the means whereby this is accomplished is not obvious. Thus, theoretical approaches may differ not only on the means by which they explain this gap-bridging process (for instance, only with their theory or in addition

level of observational learning are conceived to be determined by a variety of what Bandura terms perceptual, motoric, cognitive, and incentive variables. Included under such categories are setting conditions (e.g., the saliency and complexity of modeling cues), the availability of necessary component responses in the observer's behavior repertoire, and overt and covert rehearsal of the matching response. However, Bandura assumes that performance of imitative responses, once they are learned, is primarily governed by extrinsic, self-administered, or vicariously experienced reinforcing events. Bandura's conceptualization of observational learning is considered further in a subsequent section.

Varying cognitive approaches to imitation (and identification) have also been put forth by Piaget (1951), and more recently in different ways by Kohlberg (1966) and Aronfreed (1967, 1969). Kohlberg rejects an S-R instrumental learning conception apparently on the basis of a narrow conception in which reinforcement is equated with organismic drive reduction. And although Aronfreed does not deny the role of instrumental learning for certain behaviors, he does qualify the learning mechanism with unindexed "representational" processes. Both theorists, however, minimize the importance of extrinsic reinforcement of the child subject's (S's) responses for imitative learning. Instead, they stress *observational learning* (as does Bandura) and *intrinsic reinforcement* of responses. Kohlberg assumes intrinsic reinforcement to result somehow from "motives" for "competence-mastery" and "interesting" consequences, while Aronfreed assumes that it derives from the child's observation of the model's behavior and the "affective" value that becomes attached (conditioned) to the model and his behavior as well as to the child's "cognitive representation" or "template" of the model's behavior.[4] This last-mentioned implicit response concept appears to be not dissimilar to the earlier-surveyed concepts of Bandura.

Explanations of imitative response acquisition in terms of observational learning or of S-R contiguity learning (Holt, 1931; Humphrey, 1921; Maccoby, 1959; Piaget, 1951) may have stemmed from the difficulty some have experienced in specifying some salient features of the imitative process, such as identifying a matching response class whose content changes from trial to trial or the reinforcing

---

with indexing operations), but also on the utility of even postulating such processes at all, particularly when operations are not employed to index successive aspects of a postulated process. For most heuristic purposes it has typically been assumed by conceptualizers of human and subhuman learning to be unnecessary to posit a special process over and above that implied in the functional relations of selected independent variables to overt response classes. For, unless an independent operation is specified and ultimately employed to index a postulated representational or cognitive process, the parsimony and utility of such an implicit process for bridging the time gap between experience and subsequent performance is questionable, both for infrahuman and human Ss.

Bandura has assumed that his implicit cue-producing response mediators can be independently manipulated, and that they are conditionable and extinguishable according to the same laws as those governing explicit forms of behavior. Thus, he has shown that various setting conditions, such as attentional highlighting or dimensional appreciation procedures, or even an observer's verbalizing or attempting to code visually the details of the behaviors of a model while he is viewing them, can be implemented during prior training (observation) to facilitate subsequent test performance (e.g., Bandura, Grusec, and Menlove, 1965, as cited in Bandura, 1965b). (Of course, the functional relations into which these setting operations enter with imitative behaviors constitute a contribution to the body of available data about the imitative process, and thus have a utility independent of Bandura's theory.) However, as the only indexes of implicit response processes are the very imitative-behavior outcomes those implicit responses are postulated to explain (or the differential operations that established them), it is difficult for us to see how the manipulation of such setting conditions (in what is termed an observational learning setting) can be conceived as the independent manipulation of implicit responses. Nor do such operations necessarily provide support for the notion that imaginal or representational processes mediate the recall of copying responses. Indeed, explaining the effects of such training conditions on behavior in terms of implicit representational or cognitive responses that remain unindexed, however intuitively plausible such processes might seem to the researcher operating within his prescientific context of discovery (e.g., as if he were S, human or not), is gratuitous and can often be detrimental to the search for the relevant functional relationships at issue. These comments apply as well to Aronfreed's (1967, 1969) assumptions about unindexed cognitive representations and affective mechanisms that are considered in the sections that follow, and several of the points raised in Footnote 4 apply also to Bandura's representational systems.

[4] Kohlberg (1966, p. 83) has termed this learning ". . . cognitive in the sense that it is selective and internally organized by relational schemata rather than directly reflecting associations of events in the outer world." Aronfreed (1967, 1969) has assumed that somehow children form a "cognitive template" of the model's behavior, which serves for storage and retrieval of performance and in accounting for how the child acquires a representation of the model's behavior. In cognitive-developmental approaches like these, intrapsychic cognitive-act euphemisms phrased in commonsense language are employed to characterize heuristically the bases for an S's behavior in a given context, and it is often difficult for the reader of such material to determine where the line is drawn to separate such heuristic variables from the required empirical variables, between observation and inference, or between interpretations and concepts. It is also difficult to determine whether the locus of those heuristic terms is meant to be the head of S or (the theory) of the scientist. In this process, the distinction between the statement of a problem and its explanation can be obscured, and empirical questions can lose their importance or appear to be solved simply by the application of cognitive labels to them. Our purpose here is to detail for the seemingly complex behavior systems of imitation and identification an instrumental learning model that is parsimonious, operational, and reasonably complete, and that readily lends itself to empirical test. Hence, it is appropriate for us to attend primarily to relevant learning approaches to this topic and to leave to a subsequent analysis the comparison of the simple conditioning theory presented here with particular cognitive theories. Such a confrontation would necessarily involve questions about the efficiency and parsimony of cognitive concepts relative to that of concepts like ours that are closely tied to stimuli, responses, and their sequential relationships. This issue has implications far beyond those of an analysis of imitation-identification.

stimuli for that response class when it has been specified. Possibly for these reasons also, covert rehearsal of the model's behavior has sometimes been suggested as essential in the learning of imitative behavior (Burton and Whiting, 1961; Maccoby, 1959; Sears, Maccoby, and Levin, 1957).

An experiment by Baer, Peterson, and Sherman (1965) provides a dramatic demonstration of imitation learning with implications for practical application, as well as a useful point of departure for the conceptualization of imitation which shall be proposed. By physically assisting the child to make the desired imitative responses initially and reinforcing each such response immediately, Baer et al. taught several imitative responses to retarded children whose behavior repertoires had been observed closely for a period and did not appear to include imitation. After training on a few such responses, each S could then imitate new modeled responses, and eventually response chains, without assistance. Further, the rate of a generalized imitative response that was never directly reinforced, but had been maintained when interspersed with reinforced imitative responses, declined when reinforcement was withdrawn from the imitative behaviors that were previously reinforced. Lovaas, Berberich, Perloff, and Schaeffer (1966) successfully used a similar paradigm for conditioning imitation of verbal responses in initially mute schizophrenic children.

Baer and his associates (Baer, Peterson, and Sherman, 1965; Baer and Sherman, 1964)[5] proposed that in their demonstrations the *similarity* between S's and the model's behaviors acquires stimulus value through the reinforcement of various directly imitative responses; and because the stimulus of similarity is programmed as discriminative for extrinsic reinforcement, it acquires (intrinsic) conditioned-reinforcement value. On this basis, further imitative responses that produce similarity (i.e., generalized imitative behaviors) will be strengthened and maintained in the *absence* of extrinsic reinforcement. This approach resembles those of Miller and Dollard and of Mowrer in its emphasis on the stimulus function acquired by the imitator's discrimination of similarity, and those of Aronfreed, Kohlberg, and Mowrer in its assumption of an intrinsic-reinforcement mechanism (for which no operational index is provided).

A Simple Mechanism for the Acquisition and Maintenance of Generalized Imitation

In this context, a simple mechanism for the acquisition and maintenance of generalized imitation will be detailed. The first imitative responses must occur by chance, through direct physical assistance, or through direct training (with shaping or fading procedures applied by a reinforcing agent to occurring responses). When such responses occur, they are strengthened and maintained by direct extrinsic reinforcement from environmental agents. After several imitative responses become established in this manner, a class of diverse but *functionally equivalent* behaviors is acquired and is maintained by extrinsic reinforcement on an intermittent schedule. Differences in response content of the imitative behaviors are thought to play a minimal role as long as the responses are members of the imitative response class as defined functionally *by reinforcing agents*. This process is thought to be the same as the way in which, for example, variations in the content of successively emitted plural nouns or first-person pronouns or even in the seemingly homogeneous free-operant bar-pressing output are irrelevant as long as most of the response variants are members of the response class reinforced.

Much past work on imitation (and even more on identification, as we shall see) has emphasized imitative responses as such, with only an implicit consideration of the relevant environmental stimuli that give that response class its functional meaning. The important difference between those approaches and the one presented here is that, in addition to an emphasis on the environmental stimuli (from the model's responses and discriminative settings) that cue the occurrence of imitative responses, we emphasize also those stimuli that maintain (reinforce) them as essential in the process. Thus, the term imitation implies for us just one type of stimulus control over responses. As with any functional response class under some kind of stimulus control, the response class has no special intrinsic value independent of the stimulus conditions controlling it. In a given context, an otherwise trivial response class like bar pressing can gain a functional status comparable to that of imitative responses in natural settings.

An even better analogy to the functional class of generalized imitation is provided by the matching-to-sample discrimination-learning paradigm, in which S is required on each trial to respond to the stimulus in an array of comparison stimuli that is the same as as (or similar to) a conditional standard stimulus. Through extrinsic reinforcement of the class of matching responses (i.e., those made to each matching comparison stimulus), S acquires the relevant matching-response class that then governs his responses to a wide range of stimuli differing in content. Some may term this a "concept" of identity or similarity, while, if a label must be used to provide historical context, we (with Cumming and Berryman, 1965) would favor Lashley's (1938) term "condi-

[5] In a paper which appeared after our analysis was submitted for publication, Baer, Peterson, and Sherman (1967) have modified their analysis at several points. Our concern in this analysis is therefore with the Baer and Sherman (1964) paper and the early Baer, Peterson, and Sherman (1965) paper.

tional discrimination."[6] On each trial, S's response to the comparison stimulus from the finite number in the array that matches the standard stimulus (the sample) is analogous to his selecting from a large set of alternatives (i.e., from his own repertoire) the response that matches the cues provided by the model's response, that is, the imitative response. As reinforced matching responses in the functional imitative class are diverse and under intermittent reinforcement, discrimination between matched behaviors that are reinforced and those that are not is unlikely to occur, and some copying responses that are never directly reinforced will therefore persist unless they are specifically punished or are incompatible with stronger responses in the child's repertoire. On this basis, new matching responses will continue to enter the functional imitation class in the child's repertoire.

This analysis updates an earlier analysis of generalized imitation (as the basis for identification) by Gewirtz (1961).

Some Issues Resolved by Our Generalized-Imitation Mechanism

Intrinsic versus Extrinsic Reinforcement. Our analysis with regard to the stimuli and responses in the imitative behavior chain was in part stimulated by earlier analyses by Baer and his associates (Baer, Peterson, and Sherman, 1965; Baer and Sherman, 1964). However, our analysis differs from theirs mainly in respect to which component details are emphasized, and in the fact that their heuristic account appears to emphasize an intrinsic-reinforcement mechanism and ours does not. In their analysis, conditioned-reinforcer value is assumed to become associated with the imitator's (unassessed) discrimination of similarity between his response and one previously emitted by the model, while the unit of our emphasis is the entire S-R chain, of which all elements are maintained by terminal extrinsic reinforcement.[7] (These elements could include the discrimination response and its assumed reinforcing value emphasized by Baer and his associates.) Our simpler assumption of a lack of discrimination between reinforced and nonreinforced members of the imitative response class serves the heuristic purpose equally well, is similar to the usual conceptual accounts of behavior, and does not necessitate the introduction of an additional construct. The functional value of each element in the imitative S-R chain is due entirely to its association with the terminal reinforcer. Thus, a key feature of our analysis is that the environmental agency (and not the imitator himself) determines the occasion for reinforcement.

In discussions in the literature of other functional classes, such as relatively simple bar pressing on an intermittent reinforcement schedule by nonverbal organisms, there is usually no special heuristic emphasis on S's discrimination that he has performed a response like those that have led to reinforcement in that setting in the past. Although such a discrimination may be involved, and its assumed conditioned-reinforcer value has occasionally been used to account for continued responding between reinforcements in intermittent schedules (e.g., Denny, 1946; Kimble, 1961), operations are rarely if ever introduced for its study. In the same vein, the singled-out unindexed conditioned reinforcer based on a judgment of similarity does not seem critical for Baer and his co-worker's analysis of what they consider to be a relatively complex case of imitative learning, and certainly not for an overall heuristic analysis. Indeed, as used by these authors, the intrinsic conditioned-reinforcer concept may carry surplus "cognitive" meaning. Even if the ultimate behavioral analysis of these implications proves more complex, for the moment at least Baer and his colleagues have made no case for treating the imitator's discriminative judgment any differently than analyses of the acquisition of other functional response classes would treat an organism's discrimination of the similarity between an emitted response and responses previously reinforced in that setting.[8]

[6] This is because unlike simple simultaneous or successive discrimination learning, in which the correct response is made on the basis of the presence or absence of a single discriminative stimulus that sets the occasion for the reinforcement of the response, in the (complex discriminated operant) matching-to-sample situation the correct response must be made in terms of the properties of two or more stimuli (the conditional or standard and the discriminative comparison stimuli). Thus, the significance of the discriminative stimulus varies with successive discrimination trials, changing relative to the conditional stimulus which preceded it, with the conditional stimulus coming to function more as a differential cue or selector of discriminations (or as a differential setting condition for them) than as a simple cue for individual responses.

[7] Reinforcing stimuli provided by the environment we have termed extrinsic. Even if the terminal stimulus has acquired its reinforcer value through conditioning, it differs from the conditioned-reinforcement value assumed to be associated with the stimulus of similarity in the Baer, Peterson, and Sherman (1965) analysis, in that it can be observed in the chain, measured along some dimension, and controlled by a reinforcing agent.

[8] Their stress on the conditioned reinforcer apparently had two purposes: to explain the emergence of new, topographically different imitative behaviors prior to any reinforcement of them; and to account for the continued strength of those behaviors thereafter despite consistent nonreinforcement of them. D. M. Baer (personal communication, February, 1967) has indicated that the emphasis on the role of the assumed conditioned reinforcer in the Baer, Peterson, and Sherman (1965) analysis represents a preliminary attempt to conceptualize the mode of acquisition of functional response classes, and is thus concerned with the general issue involving the formation of all such classes and not just with imitation. In this connection also, the argument that systematic improvement in the topography of an imitative response with extrinsic reinforcement operating (as reported, e.g., by Lovaas et al., 1966) requires a conditioned-reinforcer concept like that of Baer and his associates is not tenable, without ruling out many conditions confounded with practice that could be the basis for this improvement.

It is similarly difficult to see the value of some other intrinsic reinforcement concepts that have been postulated to account for imitation in the apparent absence of extrinsic reinforcement. Included among these concepts are Aronfreed's "affective value," Kohlberg's "motives" for "mastery" and "interesting" consequences, and the conditioned-reinforcement concept as used by Mowrer. As they have no independent operational status in the imitation context, these concepts as presently formulated can only be inferred from the very imitative behaviors they have been devised to explain. Therefore, in no way do such concepts advance the analyses or facilitate the research purposes of those theorists, for each of them still has the tactical problem of determining the environmental conditions that differentially affect acquisition and maintenance of the child's imitative responding.

In contrast, our functional analysis has assumed that many behaviors that appear to be acquired on the basis of observational learning in the presence of "intrinsic" reinforcement may in fact be functionally attributable to the operation of extrinsic reinforcers. It assumes also that mastery sequences and interesting consequences can (be isolated to) function as extrinsic reinforcers for child behavior. Hence, it represents one solution to the deficiencies noted in the above intrinsic reinforcement approaches. The simpler model proposed in this article appears to be the most parsimonious of the extant models to account for the original acquisition and the subsequent maintenance of the imitative response class. It is based on relatively few, well-defined concepts that are the same as those used in analyses of less complex animal behavior, and it does not single out for special emphasis concepts that in principle should be observable, without making independent provision in the experimental context to index such concepts operationally.

Observational Learning. Through the years, there has been considerable controversy among learning approaches, in the realms of both theory and research, as to whether or not (observational) learning can occur in the absence of appropriate responses by the viewing organism (and of reinforcement—Kimble, 1961). Comparative-psychological research with some subhuman species has also not been definitive on this issue. In this context Bandura (1962, 1965b, 1969) has catalogued evidence that children exhibit matching responses (even after delays) following observation of models' responses (whether reinforced or not), when there has been no apparent opportunity for the occurrence (practice) of the observing child's matching responses and therefore no extrinsic reinforcing stimuli provided contingent on those responses. On the basis of this evidence and the S-S learning assumptions he favors, Bandura has therefore opted to emphasize "no-trial" observational learning as the mechanism for the acquisition of imitative responses by children. In this context, he has faulted instrumental conditioning theories for requiring that matching responses be performed and reinforced before they can be acquired. It has been noted that Aronfreed (1967, 1969) and Kohlberg (1966) similarly emphasize, although perhaps on different grounds, observational learning as the basis for the acquisition of imitation.

Even so, Bandura (1965a) has noted that extrinsic reinforcement of matching responses is inevitable during human social development, where models typically exhibit responses from cultural repertoires proved effective in the stimulus settings. As he himself has observed, observational learning effects apparently demonstrated in experimental work with children may thus simply reflect prior instrumental learning, for which the requisite control conditions cannot be implemented practically. (In fact, Bandura believes that definitive tests of this theoretical issue may require the use of infrahuman Ss whose reinforcement histories can be readily controlled.)

Given the current theoretical indeterminacy of the issue of learning without response occurrence in instrumental life settings, and the fact that assumed observational learning effects that are clearly free of prior positive (or even negative) extrinsic reinforcement for responses matched to those of models are improbable in early-childhood contexts, we have chosen to emphasize how what Bandura and others have termed observational learning outcomes can be plausibly explained by the routine intermittent extrinsic reinforcement of overt matching responses that provides the basis for generalized imitation. Our heuristic concern is thus to illustrate, in a manner continuous with analyses in the literature of other functional response classes in simple organisms and settings, how basic instrumental conditioning procedures thought to be commonly involved in adult-child interaction can credibly account for the acquisition and maintenance of responses matched to (cues provided by) models' responses. That is, we attempt to show how one must *learn* to learn through exposure to models' responses.

It is our conception that intermittent extrinsic reinforcement for imitation of the varied responses of a range of models can account for the child's frequent (generalized) imitation of both the reinforced and nonreinforced responses of a model. The appearance that the child has not exhibited the response, and that he has not received extrinsic reinforcement when he did imitate, can be explained by the facts that: (*a*) There can be lengthy delays between the model's response and the child's imitation of it; (*b*) the functional, matching-response class will vary in content;

and (*c*) the reinforcement is intermittent. Both observational learning and our concept of generalized imitation involve S's matching his response to the response of a model in a given discriminative context and, in our view, therefore, may be functionally equivalent through the range of settings in which the two terms are used. As the generalized-imitation concept can account, in terms of a few key assumptions, for most or all of the phenomena grouped under the observational learning of young humans, and because extrinsically reinforced imitative performance is likely to characterize a child's experience in life settings prior to his exposure to a model in observational learning research designs where this factor has been typically uncontrolled, the generalized-imitation concept would seem to be a parsimonious one for approaching the general problem of explaining behavioral matching. This concept can provide a useful context for much of the research that remains to be done, and, at the very least, a context for the controls that remain to be implemented in research on the question of observational learning in young humans.

Vicarious reinforcement is a special case of observational learning, in which positive *reinforcement* administered *to a model* contingent upon a particular behavior is said to increase the likelihood that an observing child will copy that behavior (cf., e.g., Bandura, 1962; Bandura, Ross, and Ross, 1963; Hill, 1960). In our view a parsimonious (and plausible) explanation of this phenomenon is that the responses by the child that are similar to those for which a model is reinforced are likely frequently to be extrinsically reinforced in the same settings, whether emitted independently or matched to a model's responses; whereas the child's responses like those for which a model is not reinforced or for which he is punished are likely *not* to be reinforced. Often unknown to the viewer, therefore, the model's reinforced response is already in the child's repertoire due to its having been extrinsically reinforced earlier. This is possible particularly if the response is a likely one in the given context, and if extrinsic reinforcement is also likely there. Furthermore, after the child has been reinforced for imitation of several of a model's reinforced responses in a given context, reinforcement provided contingent upon a particular behavior of a model should come to function as a generalized cue for a high probability of extrinsic reinforcement to the child when he imitates that behavior. (Walters, Parke, and Cane, 1965, have similarly regarded reinforcement to the model in an experimental context as a cue indicating the "permissibility" of reproducing that behavior.) This conception would be one way to account for Bandura's (1965a) finding that, after observing a film in which various hostile-hurting behaviors of the model were reinforced, children emitted a greater variety of such imitative responses than did those children who saw the model's aggressive responses punished. Indeed, Bandura (1965b, 1969) and Aronfreed (1969) have noted this and several other ways in which reinforcing stimuli contingent upon the model's behavior could provide discriminative stimuli that facilitate or inhibit imitative behaviors, particularly in ambiguous settings.

From this analysis, it would be expected that if the child has not already learned this discrimination pattern, its acquisition depends only on the child's subsequent exposure to the proper discriminative occasions. Furthermore, if discriminative conditions were reversed, that is, if the observer were reinforced relatively less often for imitating behaviors for which the model is reinforced and more often for alternative behaviors, reinforcement to the model could come to serve as a discriminative stimulus for alternative behaviors, and vicarious reinforcement could thus be ineffective or its effects reversed in relation to the observer's behavior. Miller and Dollard (1941) demonstrated that children could learn nonimitation of a choice response for which a peer model was reinforced, and that this learning could generalize to other situations.

Life Conditions for Learning Generalized Imitation

Conditions in life settings make our analysis particularly appropriate in accounting for the rapid acquisition of topographically accurate imitative behavior sequences that typically occurs. Theorists like Mowrer (1960) and Bandura (1962) have argued that a trial-and-error process would be too slow to account for this rapid acquisition. However, that point does not seem cogent when one considers the abundance of extrinsic reinforcement occasions and efficient shaping processes during all stages of the child's development, particularly for response classes like imitation. Because these reinforcers come from a variety of sources, on an intermittent schedule overall, and for diverse imitative behaviors, generalized imitation will be acquired relatively early in the child's socialization, maintained at high strength, and relatively resistant to change. This is in keeping with the observation that gross imitative behaviors appear to occur early in life (Walters and Parke, 1965). Although, as a learned social behavior, imitation should be reversible, its extinction would rarely occur, since strict elimination of reinforcement for such pervasive response classes is unlikely to be implemented in complex life settings.

Parents often deliberately set out to teach the child to imitate, using direct tuition, shaping, and fading of the sort employed by Baer, Peterson, and Sherman (1965, 1967) or Lovaas et al. (1966). The child's imitation can be highly reinforcing *to* parents or models (when contingent on their behaviors). Sometimes a parent may himself imitate the child, either as a spontaneous response or as a step in the process of teaching him to imitate. Among other effects, this may facilitate the child's discrimination of the degree of similarity between his and the model's responses, and can constitute steps in a shaping procedure wherein the child's response is matched to the model's with increasing closeness through successive approximations. This procedure very likely plays an important role in the child's language learning.

Indeed, it is thought that generalized imitation constitutes a most important basis for the initial occurrence and acquisition of many language responses by the child, and for the subsequent expansion of his language repertoire, and may play an even more important role in this acquisition than does simple direct instrumental training without matching. Once such verbal responses are acquired, they will be maintained by responses made to them in conversational interchanges, according to the same principles that account for the maintenance of any other responses (Gewirtz, 1969).

Behaviors of the child that are in the direction of increasing competence and are thus reinforced by socializing agents are almost invariably behaviors the child has observed older models perform (e.g., walking, talking, writing), and his performance of those behaviors is frequently reinforced in the presence of models who are exhibiting them. In a sense, these behaviors are also imitative. Thus, reinforcement for progress toward increasing competence can at the same time be reinforcement for generalized imitation. As the child is subjected increasingly to the socialization process with age, the behaviors for which he is reinforced will change with his growing capacities. The agents reinforcing him will also vary and increase in number, each reinforcing on a different schedule and for different behaviors. In the face of this continual change, one thing remains constant for the child: The imitative response class continues to be reinforced at a high rate throughout his development.

Like other social behaviors, the appropriateness of imitative responses varies from one situation to another. Thus, the imitative behavioral unit usually includes a *discriminative occasion* indicating that an imitative response is likely to be reinforced. Reinforceable occasions may be preceded by an explicit verbal cue, like Baer, Peterson, and Sherman's "Susy, do this," or by a less explicit cue indicating that imitation is appropriate. The imitator learns to discriminate those cue stimuli from cues indicating that noncopying, complementary interactive responses—for instance, dependence—are appropriate. For example, based on differential reinforcement of the child's behaviors in the past, the model's *being oriented toward* the child (physically or otherwise), or his *not being occupied* in some ongoing activity, may acquire discriminative stimulus value for the child's emitting *complementary* interaction responses and for suppressing copying responses, which would be clearly inappropriate. Imitative behaviors are more likely to be reinforced when the model is busily engaged in a *solitary* activity and can more readily reinforce the child's parallel behaviors (like imitation) than his approach or interactive behaviors, as the model can then continue his activity without long interruption. If the child is frequently reinforced for making disruptive dependency initiations in this situation, he may not learn to discriminate that such behaviors are inappropriate and may interrupt the model at will, thus in extreme cases becoming what could be termed "spoiled." It is possible that such children do not learn to imitate to as great an extent as children whose models discourage interruptions of the model's task. It is also likely that at the same time they do not acquire autonomous task-oriented behavior patterns independent of frequent reinforcement from their socializing agents.

There remains a considerable need for a detailed analysis of the discriminative cues that indicate to the child, in specific and more general cases, when it is appropriate to imitate (i.e., when imitation is likely to be reinforced) and which model it is most appropriate to imitate when alternative models are available. An analysis from our intentionally simple approach would attend only in passing to developmental changes in imitative behaviors and learning that occur in typical life settings. Our conception of generalized-imitation learning in principle is not incompatible with cognitive-developmental analyses based on observation in life settings, like Piaget's (1951) conception of "stages" of imitation and other naturalistic approaches that stress change in the child's capacities during the early years as well as developmental differences in the organization of imitative behaviors. However, we assume that the basic mode of acquisition and maintenance of imitation is not altered by such developmental changes.

Focused Versus Nonfocused Generalized Imitation

The generalized-imitation paradigm as we have used it up to now has been relatively *non*focused with regard to the model imitated, summarizing imitation of diverse responses of *many* models. Yet an important case where such imitation appears to be *focused* more on one particular model than on others often occurs. This model is usually a parent, and the focused imitation involved is thought to provide an important basis for identification, as will be detailed later in this article. Such a selective imitation pattern can result from a combination of relatively frequent contact with one model and frequent reinforcement from the model and others when the child imitates a variety of the behaviors of that model. That model's behaviors will therefore acquire discriminative value for the child, indicating that his imitation of them has an even higher probability of being reinforced than does imitation in general.

Much of the child's early socialization takes place in the family setting, where he interacts with parents and siblings. Although a differential distribution of the child's interaction with the members of his family is bound to result, it should be less important for his generalized-imitation learning than should differential reinforcement for imitation of those members. Children of both sexes typically interact more with their mothers than with their fathers, but it is assumed the boy comes to imitate his father and the girl her mother because of differential reinforcement for copying each of them. As noted earlier, the child will be reinforced for imitating different models in diverse contexts. In the family setting, however, he will discriminate which single model it is usually most appropriate to imitate, on the basis of being differentially reinforced for such imitation; and because of frequent chances to observe that model, the child will imitate an extensive range of his behaviors. More will be said on this issue when we consider sex typing.

This distinction between focused and nonfocused generalized imitation is analogous to the one made by Gewirtz (1961) between focused attachment (to a particular object-person) and nonfocused social dependence (on a class of persons).

Generalized Imitation Extended

Thus far, we have shown that generalized-imitation learning based on extrinsic reinforcement can plausibly account for the acquisition and maintenance of imitative responses in the apparent absence of extrinsic reinforcement, can be facilitated by the heavy extrinsic reinforcement of developmental behavioral advances by the child in the presence of models performing those responses, can be focused on a single model under the proper circumstances, and can come under the discriminative control of gross behavioral settings in which the model is engaged. We will now see how the generalized-imitation concept can account for related behavioral phenomena that will be relevant to our analysis of identification. These include imitation of the model's behavior in his absence, imitation of a large portion of a model's behavior role in play settings, and wide-ranging similarities in abstract values or attitudes.

Imitation in the Model's Absence. Delayed imitation, including imitation of the model's behavior in his absence, can be regarded as a simple variant of the generalized-imitation paradigm. This point, which is also pertinent to observational learning, becomes clearer when one considers that all imitative behaviors occur *after* the model's performance that provides the relevant cue has terminated and often while the child is not even looking at the model, and in that sense they are always performed in the *absence* of the model. The delay between the model's performance and the imitative behavior may be further lengthened through shaping techniques, implemented either deliberately or in an unplanned way by reinforcing agents. Immediate direct reinforcement for delayed imitation in the model's absence may frequently be provided by agents other than the model, and sometimes in the form of statements like "you are acting just like your father" or "like a big boy." In addition, the agent may indicate explicitly that what is being reinforced is not only performance of the response, but its performance in the model's absence.

Imitation of the Model in Play. Imitation of large segments of a model's behavior role in play situations where the model is not present may also be facilitated by ecological factors. Props given to the child can be appropriate to the model's role, as in the case of toy kitchen utensils being made available to a young girl. Reinforcement can be provided through the reciprocal role play of other children, or through occasional direct reinforcement from the model or other adult witnesses. These toys may serve a dual purpose, in that they can also provide a sanctioned discriminable context for the child's imitation of a model's behaviors in his absence when these behaviors might be hazardous or inappropriate in their usual context.

Generalized Imitation of Values. The generalized-imitation concept can also be extended readily to account for wide-ranging similarities in abstract values (attitudes, life styles, or motives). For example, often a child will act as the model might in a situation even if he has not actually witnessed the model in that situation, or he will strive for the same goals as the model. (As we shall see in the next section, these behaviors are often termed identification.)

An example of a model's value is "tidy housekeeping." A mother's behavior may exemplify that value, and her daughter either may be extrinsically reinforced for nonimitative tidying responses or may exhibit these responses through simple generalized imitation (with or without extrinsic reinforcement), as we have been emphasizing. An important assumption for extending our analysis is that a daughter generally reinforced for acting like her mother may come to discriminate the common elements of responses exhibited by the model in a class of related stimulus contexts (such as housekeeping), which she might also inductively characterize with a statement like, "Mom keeps a tidy house." The child's value is based on her discrimination of such a functional class of the model's responses (some would term it a "concept"), which would then apply to situations in which the child, as generalized imitator, may not actually have seen the model perform. The daughter may also exhibit verbal responses that reflect the value, for instance, "It's good to keep the house tidy," which have been acquired together with tidy-housekeeping responses via generalized-imitation learning. Although some of the daughter's responses may be quite different in topography from those of her mother (because of changed climatic conditions, technological and socioeconomic levels, etc.), they will produce the same outcome: a tidy house. Once the value has been acquired in this manner, the mother is likely to reinforce the resulting responses, and the value will be maintained. As is true of all learned behaviors, however, the permanence of a value will depend on the continuation of the same reinforcement matrix for the class of responses implying that value, and thus it is potentially subject to change.

The analysis thus far has stressed primarily those situations in which cues from the model and extrinsic reinforcement to the child provide the context for the child's imitative behaviors. The above examples show the potential utility of the generalized-imitation paradigm in situations where some of the relevant discriminative and reinforcing stimuli for imitation are absent. In the next section we will argue that a substantial proportion of the phenomena grouped under the concept of identification may be ordered by the concept of generalized imitation and these extensions.

Identification

The child's acquisition of the motives, values, ideals, roles, and conscience of an important other person (the model), particularly of his parents and especially the same-sex parent, has been termed identification. The term has been used variously to refer to the process by which these characteristics are acquired, to the person's desire to possess the characteristics of the model and his belief that he does, and to the resulting similarity of behavior patterns of child and model. Several of these usages are often found in the same analysis. The identification term has also been used often as if it were a unitary concept that involves a single, incompletely specified complex paradigm with demographically defined independent variables (e.g., gender of S in an intact nuclear family) and no consensually valid dependent variable.

Psychoanalytic theory provided the earliest framework for the approach to the phenomena of identification, and much of identification theory still relies on those early attempts. While Freud dealt with identification in a scattered way through half a century of his writing, and there were apparent variations in his approach, he seems to have employed the term in at least two ways: as a *process* and as the behavior-similarity *outcome* of that process. Thus, Freud (1933, p. 90) regarded identification as the process by which "one ego becomes like another one, which results in the first ego behaving . . . in certain respects in the same way as the second; it imitates it, and as it were takes it into itself." And, in one of his writings, Freud's (1920) index of the outcome of identification was imitation of the model's behaviors. When assumed to result from complete instrumental dependence upon and an emotional tie to the model (typically the parent), identification has been termed "anaclitic" in Freud's approach and by Sears (1957; Sears, Rau, and Alpert, 1965) and "developmental" by Mowrer (1950); while "aggressive" or "defensive" identification (Freud, 1937; Mowrer, 1950) is assumed to result from fear of punishment from the model, with the child avoiding punishment by becoming like the model. The child's superego, the locus of self-observation, conscience, and ideals, has been assumed to be based largely on this latter type of identification and to be built upon the model of the parents' superego rather than on their actual behavior.

Although many would agree that the child can learn to imitate a range of behaviors on the basis of simple trial-and-error learning (as involved in generalized imitation), imitation has typically been treated in the literature as somehow distinct from identification. Thus, despite an early instance where Freud (1920) used imitation to index identification, the typical psychoanalytic view appears to be that the relatively precise matching to the model's overt behavior in imitation is a transient, surface, even symptomatic process, whereas the wider-ranging, less precise behavioral matching in identification results from a more fundamental or dynamic underlying process.

Kohlberg (1963) has proposed that identification

differs from imitation on three counts: (*a*) Identification is a "motivated disposition" because of the intrinsic reinforcing properties of perceived similarity to the model; (*b*) similarity between the behaviors of S and the model often occurs in the absence of the model; and (*c*) many aspects of the model's behavior are reproduced. These factors appear to have been the bases for many theorists' considering identification as a "higher-order" process than generalized imitation.

Within the learning-theory tradition, Miller and Dollard (1941) in a brief comment have suggested that imitation mechanisms are also involved in identification, while Seward (1954) has suggested that identification is a high-level abstraction from numerous imitative habits. Bandura (1962) and Bandura and Walters (1963) have noted that observational learning is often termed imitation in behavior-theory approaches to personality development and identification in more traditional personality theories, with no substantial differences between the two usages. In our similar view, often the only reason that generalized-imitation learning is assumed inadequate to account for identification phenomena is that factors like a "motivation" to be like, an "emotional attachment" to, or "envy" of the model that are assumed relevant for identification are just not considered at all relevant to generalized imitation, and, indeed, some even appear to think of them as outside the sphere of simple learning.

Generalized Imitation as the Basis for Identification

Such distinctions may have made the analysis of identification needlessly complex. They also point up the necessity for a more systematic approach to identification phenomena and their underlying mechanism(s). We have shown earlier that: (*a*) The seeming intrinsic reinforcing property of certain behavior classes, in particular imitation, depends entirely upon occasional extrinsic reinforcement of members of that class; and that (*b*) the performance of diverse imitative behaviors in the absence of the model is also accountable by straightforward application of the generalized-imitation paradigm, as is (*c*) the tendency to focus generalized imitation on one model and to imitate not only a range of his overt behaviors, but also behaviors implied in such general dispositions as are often termed motives, values, or attitudes. In this way, it has been automatically proposed under our functional approach that most if not all the phenomena usually grouped under identification may reasonably be assumed to be the direct consequences of generalized-imitation training, and thus can be reduced to that more parsimonious instrumental training conception.

It appears that another distinction implicit in most definitions of imitation and identification is that while both terms refer to behaviors matched to those of a model, the latter behaviors are maintained exclusively by social stimuli while the former may be maintained by both social and nonsocial ones. Thus, all identificatory acts may be imitative, but not all imitative acts may be identificatory. Because the specification of which stimulus contexts and reinforcers are social is often arbitrary, we contend that in a similar manner the distinction between identification and imitation is to a large degree an arbitrary semantic one, with no fundamental differences in the way in which they are learned. Under a learning analysis, the major reason we would prefer to use a single term like social imitation rather than both imitation and identification is that the use of both terms implies that such differences exist and are meaningful, an implication that can only cloud the issue. The use of more learning-oriented terms precludes such interpretations and facilitates the fitting of existing and future data on identification processes into a framework that allows us more easily to tie in other important aspects of the learning process.

Thus, it often appears that the only real distinction in use between identification and imitation may be that the identification process is typically defined in a less precise, more complex, and more inclusive way than is imitation. Further, a large number of loosely related and often overlapping terms at varying levels of conceptual analysis, like introjection, incorporation, internalization, modeling, role copying, and sex typing, all of which lead to similarities between the model's and the identifier's behavior patterns, are included under identification. This situation has further complicated the concept of identification and appears to have implied, as an artifact, a larger number of seemingly distinct processes than is warranted. The level from which such concepts typically are approached makes it difficult to make clear-cut differentiations between identification and overlapping concepts like introjection or sex typing. Reduction of these terms to the same level of analysis in basic paradigms open to a learning analysis is necessary and may show that apparent differences among them can be attributed to the methods of measurement, the segments of the stream of behavior emphasized, the particular stimuli evoking the responses, and the functional reinforcers available, factors that do not ordinarily justify separate paradigms. Such a reduction can be implemented by regarding identification concepts as based on the simpler generalized-imitation paradigm, with behavioral similarity as the outcome.

At this point in its evolution, the research area of identification can benefit from a deliberate approach, both theoretical and operational. In the context of a profusion of overlapping concepts and the need to reduce the frequently used demographic independent variables to component functional stimuli, the salient issues for our analysis must be operational, such as whether or not discriminative stimuli for imitation are present and whether or not functional extrinsic reinforcers follow imitative responses. In addition to reducing demographic variables to a more useful level of analysis, such factors can provide the basis for distinguishing among possibly diverse paradigms. By attending to the actual stimuli, responses, and the sequential details of their interaction, this level of analysis makes possible a flexible, individual-oriented approach to identification phenomena. Although in representative life settings some general outcomes do occur, for example, children typically do imitate behaviors appropriate to their sex category, this approach provides greater precision and flexibility in detailing the history of the individual child in question in terms of what similarity behaviors have been acquired and how they are evoked and maintained. But equally important, it can also highlight the conditions responsible for a failure to acquire particular identification behaviors and the conditions that may facilitate, extinguish, or otherwise modify such behaviors. Reversibility or change in identification-behavior patterns is almost never assumed or tested, yet is a perfectly reasonable corollary of the conception of learning, in representative life settings as in the laboratory. A functional analysis such as we propose would also make it possible to determine which antecedent process determines a particular behavior-similarity outcome and whether or not there are different combinations of antecedents that could lead to an identical outcome. The continuous-differentiation process involved would lead routinely to new concept groupings and labels, with previously unidentified but relevant phenomena brought under the identification concept and ordered by novel or derived paradigms.

Empirical research studies of identification, quite reasonably, have typically employed behavioral similarity between the child and his parents as a measure of identification (though often, when verbal reports have provided these indexes, the variables generated were at too removed a level to allow precise leverage on the process). At the level of analysis emphasized here, direct measures of similarity between the child's and the adult's responses (including those summarized as traits) in structured stimulus settings would be useful operational indexes of identification, with variations in discriminative and reinforcement parameters as independent variables. It will be necessary to show in such settings that the behaviors of the child that are termed identification are acquired under the control of the discriminative cues provided by the model's behaviors rather than being determined by environmental constraints or indepependent but parallel acquisition processes, and that they are, in the absence of the model, under the control of the same discriminative stimuli as were the model's behaviors.

The present approach, then, regards the development of identification behaviors as due to extrinsic reinforcement of the child's imitation of his parent's (or model's) behaviors. The degree to which a child is identified with a particular model is thus grossly determined by the value to the child of the reinforcers contingent upon his imitation of that person's behavior. His identification will also be a function of the amount of exposure to other potential models and reinforcement for imitating them, the frequency of reinforcement for original, nonimitative behaviors, and the value of the reinforcers provided for each of these behavior classes. Identification with the model at the level of abstract values may require finer discriminations by the child but, as we have already shown, should follow the same principles as simpler imitation.

The advantages of this functional approach are evident when one looks at such work as that by Lovaas (1967) with schizophrenic children. Besides teaching the children to imitate vocalizations and to converse, as was described earlier, Lovaas reinforced nonverbal imitation in order to teach behaviors in the areas of personal hygiene, games, drawing, and affectionate behavior, with the intention of eventually shifting the control of these behaviors (by fading procedures) away from the model to control by more appropriate or general stimuli. Noting that the behaviors learned by these children were neither as representative nor did they occur in as wide a range of settings as those covered by such terms as identification, Lovaas nevertheless implied that bringing about this more extensive imitation is not incompatible with the procedures he had been using and may primarily involve increasing the reinforcing value of stimuli from the model and others. Thus, besides permitting a more precise evaluation of the factors involved in the children's failure to identify, this approach suggests specific areas of attack to remedy the deficiencies.

Relationships of Other Identification Issues to the Learning Model

The Role of Motivation in Identification. Hindley (1957) has assumed that an acquired drive underlies imitation when, following acquisition based on extrinsic reinforcement, it continues to occur in the absence of extrinsic reinforcement. Bronfenbrenner (1960, p. 27) has argued that the identification concept cannot be reduced to a notion like "acquired similarity" because in the process one would risk losing sight of Freud's view of identification as what Bronfenbrenner terms a "sweeping and powerful phenomenon" involving the tendency of the child to take on a *total* pattern of the parental model's behavior with an emotional intensity that implies a powerful "motive in the child to become like the parent." Within a learning framework, Sears (1957) has written similarly of a motive to become like the model as the basis for the child's adopting total patterns of the parent-model's behavior without apparent specific training (although he later questioned the utility of the motive construct—Sears, Rau, and Alpert, 1965). As the mother's nurturant responses become secondary (conditioned) reinforcers for the child, he is conceived by Sears to acquire a secondary dependency drive and can partially gratify this drive by performing similar responses himself (an assumption not unlike Mowrer's, 1950).

Apart from these remarks, neither Bronfenbrenner nor Sears has detailed the implications of the use of a motivational concept for identification. They may intend it only to reflect the pervasiveness of imitative behaviors across many behavior contents and settings or, with Hindley (1957) and Kohlberg (1963), to reflect the apparent intrinsically reinforcing properties of such behaviors, or with Kohlberg to reflect its involving a particular model. However, the generalized-imitation response class discussed in this paper is also pervasive, can occur without apparent extrinsic reinforcement, and can be focused on one model. Because of their excess meaning, there is no advantage to introducing motivational terms in analyses such as these, when these terms can be replaced readily by concepts more coordinated to operations—like intermittently reinforced generalized imitation indexed by behavioral similarity.

The Role of Reinforcement in Identification. It has been seen that one issue on which our approach to identification differs from many others is the importance we assign to extrinsic reinforcement of imitative behaviors in the acquisition of identification. Our approach also differs from some others which implicitly or explicitly employ cognitive-flavored abstractions or intrapsychic euphemisms as mechanisms to account for identification phenomena, while we rely entirely on sets of responses maintained by extrinsic reinforcement. Thus, Kagan (1958) has assumed that the child identifies with an adult model whom he sees being rewarded because he *believes* that by possessing the model's characteristics and thus becoming similar to the model he too will command the attractive goal states that the model controls. In a similar vein, regarding the caretaker as the mediator of valued resources, Whiting (1960) and Burton and Whiting (1961) have assumed that the child's identification with the caretaker (as in learning his role) is motivated by *envy* of him because he can withhold the resources from the child or receive and consume them himself (implying control). In both analyses, extrinsic reinforcement of the child's imitative behaviors is only implied and is not considered essential for identification.

A basic assumption in our approach is that the child comes to copy diverse responses performed by his parent-models because he is consistently reinforced directly for that class of behaviors, perhaps even more consistently than for behaviors that he initiates on his own. The class of copying responses is highly likely to culminate in extrinsic reinforcers in a variety of settings and from many sources, both social and nonsocial. We assume that many imitative behaviors may occur without direct reinforcement, but only *after* the response class has initially been established in the child's behavioral repertoire by direct reinforcement and only if it is still being directly reinforced at least occasionally. Regardless of how often the model is rewarded in the presence of the child, we do not conceive of the child's imitating him (identifying) unless the child himself is at least occasionally rewarded for it. Likewise, the adult's withholding of reinforcement from the child can be effective only if in other situations or for other behaviors such reinforcement is not withheld. In the terms of our analysis, the model would make the withheld resources available to the child contingent upon various classes of behavior, one of which is likely to be imitation. What seems too little appreciated by many theorists is the ability of intermittent, even infrequent, extrinsic reinforcement to maintain an extensive class of behaviors, many of which are *never* reinforced, as has been well established by the research of Baer, Peterson, and Sherman, (1965, 1967) and Lovaas et al. (1966) and the context of behavioral technology from which these studies spring. At the same time, such research clearly demonstrates the necessity of at least occasional reinforcement in the acquisition and maintenance of a behavior.

The Role of Dependence-Attachment in Imitation Identification. In life settings, social dependence-attachment behaviors and imitative-identificatory behaviors may be acquired concurrently or sequentially from identical or similar stimulus conditions, as both behavior classes are emitted in the presence of many of the same discriminative stimuli and are maintained by many of the same reinforcers provided by the parents. Indeed, the latter behaviors may be considered a subset of the former, insofar as they are a means by which the child can obtain social stimuli from the parent (model). As changes in the social stimuli (and their efficacy) provided by the parents may be reflected in both imitative-identificatory and dependence-attachment behaviors, the acquisition of these two processes is not likely to be independent. Nevertheless, in our view, dependence-attachment is not necessary for the learning of generalized imitation; they are two separate response systems that can be represented by distinct paradigms, and are interdependent only in their use of some of the same stimulus elements for their acquisition and maintenance. Since a large number of imitative behaviors are maintained by social discriminative and reinforcing stimuli, the correlation between the strengths of imitative and attachment behaviors may be high, but this should not be taken to indicate that attachment is a precondition for generalized imitation, or vice versa. The search for such correlations, for example, by Sears, Maccoby, and Levin (1957), Payne and Mussen (1956), and others, may therefore provide information that is of limited theoretical consequence when both abstractions are reduced to their component functional relationships involving acquired stimulus control over responses.

Thus, from our approach the existence or strength of a dependence or attachment, the quality of a relationship, or the degree to which nurturance and affection were received earlier are gross abstractions, nurturance summarizing the social stimulus conditions provided to the child earlier, and dependence-attachment summarizing the efficacy for the child of social stimuli from a person or a class of persons. Such broad concepts will to some degree predict the effectiveness of social stimuli from the parent in functioning as discriminative stimuli and generalized reinforcers for the child's responses, including his imitative-identification ones, but will inevitably be nonspecific about the details of these contingencies. Further, there is no reason to expect that the person to whom the child is most strongly attached—that is, from whom discriminative and reinforcing stimuli (e.g., approval) should be most effective for his behaviors—will necessarily be the model for the child's behaviors. However, through differential reinforcement that person may determine who the model will be, as in the case of the mother who reinforces her young son for acting as his father does.

The Role of Fear in Identification. For heuristic simplicity, in this analysis we have avoided the use of concepts like "fear of rejection," "fear of punishment," or "anxiety" often used in identification theories, for example, as the assumed basis for defensive identification (Freud, 1937; Mowrer, 1950). We regard the paradigms for those concepts as compatible with ours for the acquisition and maintenance of generalized imitation, except that they may imply different classes of reinforcers, for example, removal or avoidance of a noxious stimulus. Self-critical responses and others labeled "guilt" or "resistance to temptation" reflecting "internalized controls" or "conscience" can undoubtedly be reinforced by such consequences, but they can also be acquired through the direct positive reinforcement processes we have emphasized.

Conclusions

In this paper, we have used only basic instrumental conditioning and S-R chaining concepts to order many of the assumed complexities of generalized imitation. We have proposed that the phenomena usually grouped under the rubric of identification can also be reduced, under a discriminated-operant learning model, to this more parsimonious conception of generalized imitation and its direct extensions. We have not advocated this approach for the sake of reduction per se, but rather to bring these phenomena to a level at which they will be dealt with more productively than they have been so far. Since identification phenomena involve systematic changes in behavior effected by recurring environmental conditions, a learning analysis is appropriate, and its use makes immediately available a wealth of knowledge about the functioning of stimuli and responses. Under a systematic learning approach to identification phenomena, the relevant behaviors are potentially subject to acquisition, discrimination, facilitation, extinction, and other modifications, according to well-established laws of behavior. The study of such modifications would be in contrast to the typical approach to identification, in which the effects are for the most part assumed to be long term, and reversibility or change in the process is never tested and almost never even assumed.

References

Aronfreed, J. Imitation and identification: An analysis of some affective and cognitive mechanisms. Paper presented at the biennial meeting of the Society for Research in Child Development, New York, March 1967.

Aronfreed, J. The concept of internalization. In D. A. Goslin (Ed.) *Handbook of socialization theory and research.* Chicago: Rand-McNally, 1969. Ch. 4. Pp. 263–323.

Baer, D. M., Peterson, R. F., and Sherman, J. A. Building an imitative repertoire by programming similarity between child and model as discriminative for reinforcement. Paper presented at the biennial meeting of the Society for Research in Child Development, Minneapolis, March 1965.

Baer, D. M., Peterson, R. F., and Sherman, J. A. The development of imitation by reinforcing behavioral similarity to a model. *Journal of the Experimental Analysis of Behavior,* 1967, *10,* 405–416.

Baer, D. M., and Sherman, J. A. Reinforcement control of generalized imitation in young children. *Journal of Experimental Child Psychology,* 1964, *1,* 37–49.

Bandura, A. Social learning through imitation. *Nebraska Symposium on Motivation,* 1962, *10,* 211–269.

Bandura, A. Influence of models' reinforcement contingencies on the acquisition of imitative responses. *Journal of Personality and Social Psychology,* 1965, *1,* 589–595. (a)

Bandura, A. Vicarious processes: A case of no-trial learning. In L. Berkowitz (Ed.), *Advances in experimental social psychology.* Vol. 2. New York: Academic Press, 1965. Pp. 1–55. (b)

Bandura, A. Social-learning theory of identificatory processes. In D. A. Goslin (Ed.), *Handbook of socialization theory and research.* Chicago: Rand-McNally, 1969. Ch. 3. Pp. 213–262.

Bandura, A., Ross, D., and Ross, S. A. Vicarious reinforcement and imitative learning. *Journal of Abnormal and Social Psychology,* 1963, *67,* 601–607.

Bandura, A., and Walters, R. H. *Social learning and personality development.* New York: Holt, Rinehart and Winston, 1963.

Bronfenbrenner, U. Freudian theories of identification and their derivatives. *Child Development,* 1960, *31,* 15–40.

Burton, R. V., and Whiting, J. W. M. The absent father and cross-sex identity. *Merrill-Palmer Quarterly,* 1961, 7, 85–95.

Cumming, W. W., and Berryman, R. The complex discriminated operant: Studies of matching-to-sample and related problems. In D. I. Mostofsky (Ed.), *Stimulus generalization.* Stanford: Stanford University Press, 1965. Pp. 284–330.

Denny, M. R. The role of secondary reinforcement in a partial reinforcement learning situation. *Journal of Experimental Psychology,* 1946, *36,* 373–389.

Freud, A. *The ego and the mechanisms of defense.* London: Hogarth, 1937.

Freud, S. *A general introduction to psychoanalysis.* Garden City, N.Y.: Garden City Publishing Co., 1920.

Freud, S. *New introductory lectures on psychoanalysis.* London: Hogarth, 1933.

Gewirtz, J. L. A learning analysis of the effects of normal stimulation, privation and deprivation on the acquisition of social motivation and attachment. In B. M. Foss (Ed.), *Determinants of infant behavior.* London: Methuen (New York: Wiley), 1961. Pp. 213–299.

Gewirtz, J. L. Mechanisms of social learning. In D. A. Goslin (Ed.), *Handbook of socialization theory and research.* Chicago: Rand-McNally, 1969. Pp. 57–212.

Hill, W. F. Learning theory and the acquisition of values. *Psychological Review,* 1960, *67,* 317–331.

Hindley, C. B. Contributions of associative learning theories to an understanding of child development. *British Journal of Medical Psychology,* 1957, *30,* 241–249.

Holt, E. B. *Animal drive and the learning process.* Vol. 1. Now York: Henry Holt, 1931.

Humphrey, G. Imitation and the conditioned reflex. *Pedagogical Seminary,* 1921, *28,* 1–21.

Kagan, J. The concept of identification. *Psychological Review,* 1958, *65,* 296–305.

Kimble, G. A. *Hilgard and Marquis' conditioning and learning.* New York: Appleton-Century-Crofts, 1961.

Kohlberg, L. Moral development and identification. In H. W. Stevenson (Ed.), *Child psychology: The sixty-second yearbook of the National Society for the Study of Education.* Chicago: University of Chicago Press, 1963. Pp. 277–322.

Kohlberg, L. A cognitive-developmental analysis of children's sex-role concepts and attitudes. In E. E. Maccoby (Ed.), *The development of sex differences.* Stanford: Stanford University Press, 1966. Pp. 82–173.

Lashley, K. S. Conditional reactions in the rat. *Journal of Psychology,* 1938, *6,* 311–324.

Lovaas, O. I. A behavior therapy approach to the treatment of childhood schizophrenia. In J. P. Hill (Ed.), *Minnesota symposia on child psychology.* Vol. 1. Minneapolis: University of Minnesota Press, 1967. Pp. 108–159.

Lovaas, O. I., Berberich, J. P., Perloff, B. F., and Schaeffer, B. Acquisition of imitative speech by schizophrenic children. *Science,* 1966, *151,* 705–707.

Maccoby, E. E. Role-taking in childhood and its consequences for social learning. *Child Development,* 1959, *30,* 239–252.

Miller, N. E., and Dollard, J. *Social learning and imitation.* New Haven: Yale University Press, 1941.

Mowrer, O. H. *Learning theory and personality dynamics.* New York: Ronald Press, 1950.

Mowrer, O. H. *Learning theory and the symbolic processes.* New York: Wiley, 1960.

Payne, D. E., and Mussen, P. H. Parent-child relations and father identification among adolescent boys. *Journal of Abnormal and Social Psychology,* 1956, *52,* 358–362.

Piaget, J. *Play, dreams and imitation in childhood.* New York: W. W. Norton, 1951.

Sears, R. R. Identification as a form of behavioral development. In D. B. Harris (Ed.), *The concept of development.* Minneapolis: University of Minnesota Press, 1957. Pp. 149–161.

Sears, R. R., Maccoby, E. E., and Levin, H. *Patterns of child rearing.* Evanston, Ill.: Row, Peterson, 1957.

Sears, R. R., Rau, L., and Alpert, R. *Identification and child rearing.* Stanford: Stanford University Press, 1965.

Seward, J. P. Learning theory and identification: II. Role of punishment. *Journal of Genetic Psychology,* 1954, 84, 201–210.

Skinner, B. F. *Science and human behavior.* New York: Macmillan, 1953.

Walters, R. H., and Parke, R. D. The role of the distance receptors in the development of social responsiveness. In L. P. Lipsitt and C. C. Spiker (Eds.), *Advances in child development and behavior*. Vol. 2. New York: Academic Press, 1965. Pp. 59–96.

Walters, R. H., Parke, R. D., and Cane, V. A. Timing of punishment and the observation of consequences to others as determinants of response inhibition. *Journal of Experimental Child Psychology*, 1965, 2, 10–30.

Whiting, J. W. M. Resource mediation and learning by identification. In I. Iscoe and H. W. Stevenson (Eds.), *Personality development in children*. Austin: University of Texas Press, 1960. Pp. 112–126.

B Internal and External Control

An important developmental process is internalization—a property of a repertoire which makes the individual less dependent upon a goad, a stimulus, or an impetus from the immediate external environment. Where behavioral processes are internalized, the behavior appears to be self-generated, in the sense that there is no immediate external antecedent. For example, the child, who picks up his toys to escape his parents' displeasure is emitting behavior that is reinforced by terminating an aversive stimulus. If the child picks up his toys even though the parent is not present, we say that his behavior is internally controlled. It is argued, theoretically, that the toys and the surrounding circumstances have acquired aversive properties because of the occasions when the child has been criticized for leaving them underfoot. Internalization resembles the Freudian concept of "superego," except that specific items of conduct and objective features of the environment are substituted for conscious and unconscious mental processes. The specific performances are those that are negatively reinforced by their instrumentality in avoiding or escaping from stimuli having conditioned aversive properties. Toys lying on the floor as provocation for the parent's wrath are examples of objects that may, under some circumstances, function as conditioned aversive stimuli.

Although internalization of control is most often discussed and studied in the context of punishment and avoidance, positively reinforced behaviors may also become internalized. We are more likely to refer to this process as self-control; internalization is involved, however, because there are no consequences in the immediate environment maintaining the behavior. An example of this is the child who works for money in the face of an opportunity to play because the long-term consequences of the earned money are prepotent over the immediate reinforcement of playing.

Rotter and Mulry tackle the problem of determining whether a performance is occurring because it has been reinforced in the past (internalized), or whether it occurs because of the demands of the immediate situation. In their experiment, subjects chose an angular shape that matched a standard one; but the differences were so small that the subject could not know whether his choices were correct. The experimenters determined whether the subjects were trying to match the sample or were simply conforming to the demands of the situation by recording how long it took them to make a decision (latency of the choice). In behavioral terms, a performance reinforced in the past by its differential consequences (whether the choice matched the sample) would take longer to occur than one reinforced because it complied with the request of the experimenter.

This article provides an example of the use of a functional analysis of two performances which appear topographically similar (same physical characteristics) but which are fundamentally different because they had been established by and are being maintained by different reinforcers. Physically, except for their latencies, the "internalized" and "externalized" performances appear identical. Functionally, however, one is a simple avoidance response, whereas the other comes from an internalized (generalized) reinforcer which is in the person's repertoire from a past history of reinforcement. To classify each subject before the experiment according to his "internal-external" characteristics, Rotter and Mulry measure how much of his past behavior has been reinforced by the consequences of "choosing." They call this an Internal-External Control Scale, because the person whose behavior is less frequently reinforced by its consequences (External) describes his achievements as due to luck (originating from the outside), while the person whose repertoire has many positively and differentially reinforced performances (Internal) sees his achievements (emitted behavior which influences the environment) as due to his own skill. This prior measurement of the subject's repertoire was then compared with his performance during the experiment, in which he had a chance to make a choice actively or passively.

16 *Internal Versus External Control of Reinforcement and Decision Time*[1]

JULIAN B. ROTTER
RAY C. MULRY

A series of previous investigations has demonstrated that the perception of a situation as controlled by chance, luck, fate, or powerful others will lead to predictable differences in behavior, in comparison to situations where a person feels that reinforcement is controlled by his own behavior (Holden and Rotter, 1962; James and Rotter, 1958; Phares, 1957, 1962; Rotter, Liverant, and Crowne, 1961). Other studies have indicated that individuals differ reliably in the degree to which they perceive reinforcement in a variety of ambiguous social situations to be controlled by their own characteristics and/or behavior versus by external forces. Such differences have been observed in children and adults and appear to be generalized over a wide variety of social situations.

Results of these investigations have shown that the individual who tends to perceive reinforcement as contingent upon his own behavior is more likely to take social action to better his life conditions (Gore and Rotter, 1963), is more likely to attend to, and to learn and remember information that will affect his future goals (Seeman, 1963; Seeman and Evans, 1962), and is generally more concerned with his ability, particularly his failures (Efram, 1964). The individual who seems to be more internal also appears to have a greater need for independence (Crowne and Liverant, 1963) and is resistive to subtle attempts at influence (Getter, 1963; Gore, 1963; Strickland, 1963). Ethnic, cultural, and social class differences among groups on this variable appear to be consistent with the above description (Battle and Rotter, 1963).

In social learning theory (Rotter, 1954), this characteristic is conceptualized as a generalized expectancy regarding the relationship between one's own behavior, efforts or characteristics and reinforcement. It is related to the sociological concept of alienation in the sense of "powerlessness" (Seeman, 1959).

Earlier studies of internal-external control as a personality variable have been concerned primarily with the generality of this characteristic and with construct validity. The present study is concerned with

[1] The data for this research were collected while both authors were at the Ohio State University. The investigation was supported in whole by the United States Air Force, under Contract No. AF49(638)–741 monitored by the Air Force Office of Scientific Research, Office of Aerospace Research.

a different aspect of this problem, namely, that of potential differences in the *value* or importance placed upon different kinds of reinforcements by individuals who can be characterized as more or less internal in their general attitudes.

Previous research by Barker (1946) and Lotsof (1956) has shown that if expectancy for receiving a reinforcement is held constant, then decision time for choosing one of a closely matched pair of possible reinforcements increases with the importance of the reinforcement. This research, along with commonsense considerations, suggests that individuals who place greater value on an outcome would take longer in making a difficult discrimination. Specifically, the study tests the hypothesis that internals will take longer to make a difficult discrimination in a task which they perceive to be skill determined and that, relative to others, externally oriented individuals will take longer to make a discrimination which they perceive to be determined by luck or chance. Essentially, it seems logical that an individual who felt that what happened to him depended on his own skills would place higher value on demonstration of skill (since it indicated a promise for future rewards) than would a person who felt that reinforcements were arbitrarily dispensed independently of his own actions. The latter individual might, on the other hand, regard "luck" as a personal although unstable attribute and would have greater concern with whether or not he was a lucky or unlucky person. Increased value in turn would lead to longer decision time in both cases. Since the discrimination was very difficult the person with more involvement in being correct would spend more time comparing the alternatives.

The measurement of individual differences has been accomplished primarily by a forced-choice questionnaire (the I-E Control Scale) which has evolved through a series of refinements to a 29-item test including 6 filler items.[2] The test has demonstrated adequate internal consistency and test-retest reliability.

The test primarily samples general attitudes. None of the items deal directly with the *values* placed upon skill reinforcements versus luck or chance reinforcements. A sample item follows:

a. In my case getting what I want has little or nothing to do with luck.
b. Many times we might just as well decide what to do by flipping a coin.

The score on this test is simply the number of "external" choices made by the subject. Typical college student means are approximately 8.5 and medians 8.0.

The present study was designed to provide subjects, dichotomized into internal and external control groups, with a difficult discrimination problem. Half the subjects were instructed that the discrimination was so difficult as to be a matter of luck. The other half were told that although the discrimination was difficult previous research had shown that some people are more skilled in making such discriminations.

To test the hypothesis it was necessary to control the frequency and order of reinforcement. Previous research by James (1957) has indicated that it was possible to control reinforcement and to have subjects accept the instructions of chance or skill control in an angle matching task. In this task there were actually no correct matches, but for every angle to be matched there were four equally close alternatives. After each trial the experimenter merely said right or wrong and subjects accepted the experimenter's statement without apparent questioning.

Method

Subjects. The subjects included 61 females and 59 males. The subjects were obtained from the elementary psychology course at the Ohio State University where all subjects were required to take part in some research but were able to choose, on the basis of minimal descriptions, the experiment they preferred.

Procedure. The subjects were tested by two experimenters.[3] The subjects were randomly assigned to either chance or skill groups. Half received the I-E Control Scale before the experiment, and the other half after the experiment. Without scoring the tests in the case of the former group the subjects were assigned on an alternating basis to either the chance or the skill group and given the angle matching tests. For the first eight trials, referred to as the training trials, all subjects received the same order of right and wrong reinforcements. They were told they were correct on 75% of the first eight trials. On the second and fourth trials they were told they were wrong. Following this sequence an extinction series was given on which they were told they were wrong on every trial. Fifty extinction trials were given and the experiment was terminated if the subjects did not extinguish before this point. Before each trial the subject was asked to state a probability from 0 to 10 as to whether or not he expected to be successful on the next trial. The points along this continuum were

[2] This scale was developed by S. Liverant, J. B. Rotter, M. Seeman, and D. Crowne. An article providing extensive data on the development, validity, and reliability of this test is now in preparation by J. B. Rotter.

[3] The subjects were tested by the junior author and by Mary Kay Moats. Grateful acknowledgment is made to Mary Kay Moats for her contribution to this study.

defined for the subject. During the extinction series if the subject stated an expectancy of 0 or 1 for two consecutive trials he was considered extinguished and the experiment terminated[4]

The task consisted of 28 standard cards mounted on a board. On each 6 × 6 inch card was an angle made by black tape. The standards were spaced at 5-degree intervals. The smallest angle was 40 degrees and the largest was 105 degrees. Two standards for each angle were made. The matching stimuli, referred to as samples, consisted of 13 angles mounted on 4 × 4 inch cards beginning with 42.5 degrees and spaced at 5-degree intervals so that the largest was 102.5 degrees. None of the samples matched any of the standards but for each sample there were four, nonadjacent equally close angles (2.5 degrees from the sample) with their apexes turned in different directions and the sides of unequal lengths. The task was so difficult, therefore, that the experimenter could say right or wrong on any trial and the subject did not apparently dispute his statement. Postexperimental interviews with pretest subjects indicated that subjects only rarely (1 or 2 of a group of approximately 20) questioned the accuracy of the experimenter's judgment during extinction only and none questioned whether or not a true match was possible.

Since there were only 13 sample angles and the experiment could continue for a maximum of 58 trials, standard samples were presented in order and after Trials 13, 26, 39, and 52 the standards were rotated 90 degrees and the same sequence repeated.

Decision time was measured on a running second hand, the experimenter standing slightly behind the subject so that the subject was not aware that he was being timed. Timing began when the subject was handed the sample card and ended as soon as he indicated which of the standards was the correct match.

Instructions. The verbatim instructions given to the subject are presented below:

> We are doing a series of experiments to test visual discrimination under conditions of perceptual confusion. In this experiment we are concerned with the judgments of degrees of angles when the differences between them are small and when there are a number of confusing elements present.
>
> [For skill groups only]: We have found that some people have a special skill at this and do consistently better than others.
>
> [For chance groups only]: We have found that under these conditions success is entirely a matter of chance. The way in which the test works is as follows:
>
> There are a number of angles on this board. They are of different degrees and are set in varying positions. As you can see, some of the angles on the board are very similar to each other.
>
> I also have here a series of cards such as this one [experimenter shows sample card] with various angles on them. The angles on these cards are of different degrees and are placed in varying positions on the cards.
>
> On each trial I will show you a card such as this. The idea is to look at the angle on the card and then to choose from the angles on this board, the angle which you think is the same degree as the one which I show you. Thus, if you think this angle [experimenter holds up sample card] is the same degree as this one on the board you would say [experimenter points to the M card] M. I have the set of answers here and I will let you know whether you are right or wrong. The idea is to concentrate only on the degree of the angle. All of the cards are of approximately equal difficulty.
>
> Do you have any questions so far? [If the subject asked a question, the relevant parts of the instructions were repeated to him.]
>
> The idea of the test, of course, is to get as high a score as you can. I will be keeping score and at the end of the experiment I will give you your total score and let you know how you did compared to other people.
>
> Now there is another factor which can affect your total score. Besides scoring the angles which you get right, I am also interested in how accurately you can predict how you will do on each trial. Before each trial I would like you to state what you feel the probability is of your being right on that trial. You can rate this on a scale going from 0 to 10. For example, if you feel sure that you will be right you would state a high number like 9 or 10. If you feel only moderately that you will be right, you would state a lower number like 5 or 6. If you feel that you won't be right, you would state the lowest numbers like 0 or 1. You might consider those numbers which you state as being estimates that you are making on the degree of confidence you have that you will be right. If you are right on the trial, the number you stated will be added to your total score; if you are wrong on the trial, the number you stated will be subtracted from your total score. From this you can see that it is very important that the estimates you make correspond closely with how you really feel you will do.
>
> Do you have any questions?
>
> [For skill groups only]: Although the discriminations required here are at a difficult level, we have found that some people are highly skilled at this and are able to get consistently high scores. The results depend entirely upon your ability. Do as well as you can and we will see if you have some skill at this.
>
> [For chance groups only]: Although the discriminations required here are at a level which makes it entirely a matter of chance, some people are lucky and get high scores. The results depend entirely upon guessing. Do as well as you can and we will see if you are lucky at this.

[4] Extinction is used throughout this article to refer to the reduction of a verbalized expectancy for success related to continuous failure trials. Holden and Rotter (1962) have previously shown that behavioral choice criteria (other than verbal) are affected in a similar fashion to verbalized expectancies with continuous failure experience.

Summary of Design. Four groups of subjects were compared on a series of dependent variables. To obtain these groups subjects were divided into "internals" and "externals" by splitting the groups at the median and then further subdividing on the basis of whether they were given chance or skill instructions. Since the determination of whether they were internals or externals was not made until after the experimental procedure was completed (thereby avoiding possible bias), the groups are slightly unequal. While the main comparison among groups was decision time, additional indices were computed to determine whether or not any other factors might be influencing decision time. These included the mean expectancy for the training trials and number of trials to extinction of the verbalized expectancy for success. In addition, the frequency of unusual shifts in expectancies was computed. The latter measure is simply a count of the number of times that a subject raises his expectancy after a failure or lowers it after a success. Previous studies have shown that externals tend to make more such unusual shifts than internals but findings have not always been consistent.

Results

The average I-E Control Scale score was 8.48 and the median was 8.0. Therefore, all subjects with scores of 9 or more were classed as externals and with 8 or less as internals. The four experimental groups, then, included 29 subjects classed as internals who were given chance instructions and 36 subjects classed as internals who were given skill instructions. There were 29 externals who had been given chance instructions and 26 externals who had been given skill instructions. The 59 males and 61 females were randomly distributed among the four groups.

Analysis of variance indicated that males and females did not differ significantly on any of the experimental measures and, consequently, sex did not appear to be a factor in accounting for any of the results. Analyses of variance were performed on all variables to determine whether data collected by the male experimenter differed in any way from data collected by the female experimenter. No significant differences were obtained. Similar analyses of variance were performed on the data obtained from the 60 subjects who took the test before in comparison with the 60 subjects who took the 1-E Scale after the experimental procedure. In this case a significant difference in decision time only was found. Subjects who took the test before the experimental procedure had significantly longer ($p < .01$) decision times on the first eight trials of the experimental procedure. Decision time for the extinction trials was also longer, but not significantly so, for those subjects who took the test before. There was no significant interaction in these effects with the chance and skill or internal-external control variables. That is, the effects were "across the board" and did not account for any of the differences between internals and externals or chance and skill groups. What these findings suggest is that by giving tests first the subjects became more involved in the experimental procedure than when the testing followed the angle matching task.

The major experimental results are given in Table 1. Decision time for the first eight trials and extinction trials are given in seconds and in logs. Conversion to logs of mean decision times was considered advisable to reduce the effect of a few extreme scores. While these subjects did not, on the whole, run counter to the rest of the group in the direction of their deviance, they tended to raise the variance for the group in which they appeared and therefore affected group differences to an unjustified degree. Analysis of the data was made using log conversions.

The main hypothesis of this study was that internals would place greater importance on whether or not they were correct in the skill instruction situation than in the chance instruction situation, and vice versa for externals. The most important test of the hypothesis was the decision time for the first eight trials in which all the subjects received the same order and number of positive reinforcements (75%). To be sure that differences in decision time were not dependent upon significant differences in mean expectancy for success, which could also influence decision time, a test was made of differences among the four groups on mean expectancies for success for the first eight trials. The means are presented in Table 1. Analysis of variance indicated no significant difference on any of the variables so that it may be concluded that differences in decision time among the four groups were not a function of differences of expectancy for success.

An analysis of variance for log decision times was computed. Neither internal versus external control nor chance versus skill alone was a significant variable on decision time, but the predicted interaction of these two was highly significant ($F = 6.6667$, $df = 1/116$, $p < .025$). The mean differences are shown in Table 1. Internals take much longer to decide on the correct match when they are instructed that the task is a matter of skill than when they are instructed that it is a matter of luck or chance. Externals, on the other hand, take longer to decide on the correct stimulus when they are told it is a matter of luck than when they are told it is a matter of skill but not significantly so. The Duncan range test for internals under chance versus skill is significant. The difference is not significant and is numerically smaller for externals under chance versus skill. It is clear that most of the variance is contributed by the internals who take much longer when they are told it is skill than do the other groups. Internals in the skill condi-

Table 1 *Means annd Standard Deviations of Major Dependent Variables for the Four Experimental Groups*

Decision Time	Internals		Externals	
	Chance ($N = 29$)	Skill ($N = 36$)	Chance ($N = 29$)	Skill ($N = 26$)
Training trials				
Seconds				
M	24.6500	37.7400	28.6800	26.2000
SD	16.4400	25.1100	17.0100	14.7300
Logs*				
M	1.2985_b	1.5090_a	1.3847_{ab}	1.3414_b
SD	.3020	.2440	.2500	.2504
Extinction trials				
Seconds				
M	29.2700	49.1000	35.4800	32.7900
SD	18.3600	30.5200	25.3200	18.4800
Logs*				
M	1.3850_b	1.5978_a	1.4591_{ab}	1.4379_b
SD	.2845	.3070	.3710	.2690
Mean expectancy, first 8 trials				
M	5.9400	6.1800	5.8700	5.7600
SD	1.5300	1.5200	1.6200	1.5400
Number of trials to extinction				
M	16.1700	18.3600	19.1000	16.7300
SD	14.2600	14.7400	14.7000	10.9800
Unusual shifts, first 10 trials				
M	.7590	.7770	1.2060	1.1920
SD	1.2700	1.4600	1.1630	1.8400

* Significant differences in means at the .05 level or better are indicated by letter subscripts, as determined by the Duncan range test. Means with the same subscript are not significantly different from each other.

tion are also significantly different from externals with skill instructions.

A further comparison on decision time could be made for the extinction trials if the number of such trials was not significantly different for the various groups. The mean trials to extinction are given in Table 1. Analyses of variance show that neither internal-external control, chance-skill, nor an interaction is significant. The number of trials to extinction was not significantly related to decision time ($r = -.16$).

Decision time for the extinction trials then could serve as a cross-validation of decision time for the training trials. An analysis of variance for log decision time was computed. The chance-skill variable approaches significance but only the interaction is clearly significant ($F = 6.850$, $df = 1/116$, $p < .025$). It can be seen from the means in Table 1 that the results were essentially the same as those for the eight training trials, but decision times in general were somewhat longer during extinction. The longer decision times in extinction could be expected, as Lotsof (1958) has shown that decision time increases with increased expectancy for failure. However, since the groups had approximately the same mean number of trials to extinction, one could assume that they had equivalent expectancies for failure. Again, according to the Duncan range test the internals took significantly longer to decide the correct match under skill instructions than under chance and significantly longer in the skill condition than externals in the skill condition.

Previous studies of internal-external control have shown that externals tend to make shifts in expectancy up after failure or down after success with greater frequency than do internals. The tendency is somewhat stronger with children (Battle and Rotter, 1963; Bialer, 1961) but has also been observed with adults (James, 1957; Phares, 1957). Mean tendencies in the present study are in the same direction. The mean unusual shifts for the four groups are shown in Table 1. Since all subjects had only the first 10 trials in common, unusual shifts for only the first 10 trials were calculated. The majority of subjects made no unusual shifts.

Analysis of variance of unusual shifts indicated no significant variable although internal versus external control was at the <.20 level. A chi-square analysis of those subjects who showed two or more unusual shifts versus one or none indicates a tendency for externals to more often have two or more unusual shifts ($p < .10$). The findings are consistent with previous research. Externals more often make unusual shifts in expectancy, presumably following the "gambler's fallacy" of raising the expectation after failure or dropping it after success. The trend is not strong, however, with college student subjects and only approaches significance.

Discussion

The findings of this study are relatively clear-cut. Individuals who can be characterized as internals from scores on the I-E Control Scale, take longer to decide in a matching task when the task is defined as skill controlled than when it is defined as chance controlled. The opposite tendency is found with subjects who are classed as externals. Externals tend to take longer to decide on the correct match when the task is defined as chance than when it is defined as skill controlled. The interaction is highly significant both for a predominantly positive reinforcement sequence of training trials and for a series of continuously negative extinction trials. Internals under skill conditions are significantly different from intervals under chance conditions, and internals under skill conditions are significantly different from externals under skill conditions. On the other hand, while externals differ under chance and skill conditions in the predicted direction, these groups are not significantly different. In other words, most of the difference is attributable to the longer time taken by internals under skill conditions. Perhaps this is not surprising since we are dealing with a select population which is probably more internal than the general population. The college students we are characterizing as externals, relative to the other subjects, are probably closer to the middle of a theoretical distribution. This study extends the construct validity of the internal-external control dimension and indicates that people distributed along this dimension not only differ predictably in expectancies regarding their own behavior-reinforcement contingencies but also in the degree to which they value chance determined and skill determined rewards.

These results have some interesting implications for the study of cultural differences. If it is true that groups who learn to expect chance or fate or powerful others to control the environment tend also to place value on reinforcements which they see as controlled by these outside influences than those which they perceive as a function of their own skill, it would imply that they would be less motivated towards an increase in skill or achievement. The findings also suggest support for Strodtbeck's (1958) hypothesis that differences in value placed upon achievement in Jewish and Italian subcultures relate to a generalized attitude concerning the individual's ability to control the environment which he felt differentiated these subcultures.

Internals may tend to select activities in which they can demonstrate skill, and externals activities in which they can demonstrate luck. This is a testable hypothesis. Studies of preference for games and different types of games and gambling activities could readily be accomplished. Similarly, the concern with superstitious signs of good and bad luck will be related, and we would expect to find that externals more frequently consult fortune-tellers, have their horoscopes read, etc.

This study also has implications for decision theory. Feather (1959) makes the assumption that reinforcement in a chance task is based on the value of the reinforcement alone but in skill tasks it is a combination of the value of the reinforcement and the value of success which he sees as based on achievement need. Presumably the ego involvement would always be higher in skill tasks when other factors are controlled. The finding that externally oriented individuals do not decrease decision time under chance instructions, but tend if anything in the opposite direction, suggests that Feather's results will obtain only in predominantly internally oriented samples.

References

Barker, R. An experimental study of relationship between certainty of choice and the relative valence of the alternative. *Journal of Personality*, 1946, *15*, 41–52.

Battle, Esther, and Rotter, J. B. Children's feelings of personal control as related to social class and ethnic group. *Journal of Personality*, 1963, *31*, 482–490.

Bialer, J. Conceptualization of success and failure in mentally retarded and normal children. *Journal of Personality*, 1961, *29*, 303–320.

Crowne, D. P., and Liverant, S. Conformity under varying conditions of personal commitment. *Journal of Abnormal and Social Psychology*, 1963, *61*, 547–555.

Efran, J. S. *Some personality determinants of memory for success and failure.* (Doctoral dissertation, Ohio State University) Ann Arbor, Mich.: University Microfilms, 1964, No. 64–4793–4794.

Feather, N. T. Subjective probability and decision under uncertainty. *Psychological Review*, 1959, *66*, 150–164.

Getter, H. *Variables affecting the reinforcement in verbal conditioning.* (Doctoral dissertation, Ohio State University) Ann Arbor, Mich.: University Microfilms, 1963, No. 63–3474.

Gore, Pearl M. *Individual differences in the prediction of subject compliance to experimenter bias.* (Doctoral dissertation, Ohio State University) Ann Arbor, Mich.: University Microfilms, 1963, No. 63–390–391.

Gore, Pearl M., and Rotter, J. B. A personality correlate of social action. *Journal of Personality,* 1963, *31,* 58–64.

HOLDEN, K. B., and ROTTER, J. B. A nonverbal measure of extinction in skill and chance situations. *Journal of Experimental Psychology,* 1962, *63,* 519–520.

JAMES, W. H. *Internal versus external control of reinforcement as a basic variable in learning theory.* (Doctoral dissertation, Ohio State University) Ann Arbor, Mich.: University Microfilms, 1957, No. 57–2314.

JAMES, W. H., and ROTTER, J. B. Partial and 100% reinforcement under chance and skill conditions. *Journal of Experimental Psychology,* 1958, *55,* 397–403.

LOTSOF, E. J. Reinforcement-value and decision-time. *Journal of Psychology,* 1956, *41,* 427–435.

LOTSOF, E. J. Expectancy for success and decision-time. *American Journal of Psychology,* 1958, *71,* 416–419.

PHARES, E. J. Expectancy changes in skill and chance situations. *Journal of Abnormal and Social Psychology,* 1957, *54,* 339–342.

PHARES, E. J. Perceptual threshold decrements as a function of skill and chance expectancies. *Journal of Psychology,* 1962, *53,* 399–407.

ROTTER, J. B. *Social learning and clinical psychology.* Englewood Cliffs, N.J.: Prentice-Hall, 1954.

ROTTER, J. B., LIVERANT, S., and CROWNE, D. P. The growth and extinction of expectancies in chance controlled and skilled tasks. *Journal of Psychology,* 1961, *52,* 161–177.

SEEMAN, M. On the meaning of alienation. *American Sociological Review,* 1959, *24,* 783–791.

SEEMAN, M. An experimental study of alienation and social learning. *American Journal of Sociology,* 1963, *49,* 270–284.

SEEMAN, M., and EVANS, J. W. Alienation and learning in a hospital setting. *American Sociological Review,* 1962, *27,* 772–782.

STRICKLAND, BONNIE R. *The relationship of awareness to verbal conditioning and extinction.* (Doctoral dissertation, Ohio State University) Ann Arbor, Mich.: University Microfilms, 1963, No. 63–2988.

STRODTBECK, F. L. Family interaction, values and achievement. In D. C. McClelland, A. L. Baldwin, U. Bronfenbrenner, and E. L. Strodtbeck (Eds.), *Talent and society.* New York: Van Nostrand, 1958. Pp. 138–195.

The paper by *Aronfreed and Reber* describes some of the specific conditions that bring about aversive control by the individual of his own repertoire (internalized control) rather than control by an external agent in the immediate environment. The experiment is based on the premise that punishing a child's performances makes the performance itself a conditioned aversive stimulus. This occurs because an aversive stimulus (shouting, criticism, or spanking) follows the emitted performance, thus meeting the requirements for reflex conditioning. The aversive stimulus that occurs in punishment is the unconditioned stimulus; and the punished behavior becomes a conditioned stimulus which elicits some of the same reactions elicited by actual punishment. No special difficulties are created by viewing the punished behavior as both a stimulus and a performance, because it is an observable change in the environment which can be observed as readily as any other kind of stimulus. Once the emitted, punished performance elicits conditioned responses (anxiety) because of pairing with the aversive stimulus, these conditioned stimuli will increase the frequency of any performances which terminate or avoid them. The process is called negative reinforcement. Because the avoidance performances are likely to be incompatible with the punished performances, the latter will tend to occur less frequently. Thus, the child who starts to giggle in class may learn to bite his lip, clap a hand over his face, or look away from the child who is inciting him. The giggling produces aversive stimuli because of past punishment by the teacher. Biting the lip, turning away, clapping a hand over the mouth, or other avoidance behaviors are reinforced because they are incompatible with laughing and hence prevent it.

The experimenters tested this formulation and measured some of the details of the behavior processes involved by determining how a delay between the emission of a performance and the occurrence of an aversive stimulus (punishment) influences the effectiveness of the punishment. If such a delay is a critical factor, then one can argue that the punished performance has, in fact, acquired the properties of a conditioned aversive stimulus. In one experimental group the punishment began as soon as the child emitted the performance, while in the other group the punishment was delayed until some time after the performance was concluded. Immediate punishment would be expected, on theoretical grounds, to impart conditioned aversive properties to the performance more readily than delayed punishment. Different groups of children were also given different amounts of punishment to determine whether more conditioned aversive effects would occur with higher frequencies of punishment. The greater magnitude of the conditioned aversive effects would then produce a higher frequency of performances incompatible with the punished behavior and, hence, would produce the greatest reduction in the frequency of such behavior.

17 *Internalized Behavioral Suppression and the Timing of Social Punishment*[1]

JUSTIN ARONFREED
ARTHUR REBER

Many forms of conduct tend to become internalized as they are acquired in the course of social learning. They can then be elicited, and maintained to some extent, in the absence of surveillance or reinforcement. Developmental conceptions of conscience (Bronfenbrenner, 1960; Miller and Swanson, 1960, Ch. 5; Sears, Maccoby, and Levin, 1957, Ch. 10) and theoretical approaches to the social psychology of conformity (Kelman, 1958; Thibaut and Kelley, 1959, Ch. 13) commonly appear to assume that this kind of intrinsic control over behavior requires the individual's adoption of the values or standards of others. It seems very doubtful, however, that either moral or other kinds of evaluative processes are indispensable to the stability of conduct in the absence of external monitors. Preverbal children and even animals are capable of suppressing previously punished behavior, for example, over significant periods of time during which punishment contingencies are no longer present. Recent studies of older children (Aronfreed, 1961, 1964) indicate that their internalized reactions to already committed transgressions also can be established and maintained with little evidence that they are applying evaluative standards to their own behavior. And common observation suggests that adults likewise have many durable patterns of social behavior which are remarkably independent of external outcomes and yet do not call upon their evaluative resources.

Much of the intrinsic control of behavior which human beings show is, of course, mediated by evaluative cognition. But the experimental socialization paradigms which will be described in this paper are designed to provide a relatively simple context for examining the motivational and reinforcement mechanisms through which internalized behavioral suppression is established. These mechanisms are presumed to be fundamentally constant, regardless of the complexity of the cognitive structures which may intervene between a stimulus situation and the individual's ultimate behavior. Accordingly, the paradigms minimize the place of cognitive structure in the internalization process and emphasize the role of intrinsic cues which are closely tied to behavior itself. Even under these conditions, there is a problem in specifying the operational criteria for internalization. The degree to which conduct is internalized may be indeterminate even though it is maintained without direct social observation. For example, its maintenance may be controlled by the individual's expectations of rewards or punishments which will be eventually contingent on his alternative actions. Whiting's (1959) cross-cultural observations illustrate that control over behavior in the absence of socializing agents remains dependent, in many societies, on perceived external surveillance and sanctions. The rationales which children of different ages offer as justification for specific acts of conduct (Kohlberg, 1963; Piaget, 1948) also reveal how the evaluative processes which support internalization may vary in the extent of their reference to external outcomes.

[1] This investigation was supported in part by Research Grant MH-06671 to the senior author from the National Institute of Mental Health, United States Public Health Service.

From the *Journal of Personality and Social Psychology,* 1965, *1,* 3–16. Copyright 1965 by the American Psychological Association, and reproduced by permission.

A proper criterion of internalization might specify that an act is internalized to the extent that it can be maintained in the absence of external outcomes which have directly reinforcing consequences for the actor (and, one might wish to add, in the absence of the actor's anticipation of such outcomes). A more pragmatic extension of this criterion, to be used in the present study, is that conduct be considered internalized if it can be reliably elicited in the absence of socializing agents, after having been acquired under the control of either direct response outcomes which were mediated by the agents or the display of similar conduct by the agents. Whatever the precise meaning to be assigned to internalization, its demonstration clearly requires evidence that the maintenance of conduct has shown some movement from external to intrinsic control. We may conceive of the intrinsic control as being mediated by changes of affective state which have become partially contingent on the stimulus properties of behavior itself (response-produced cues) or on the cognitive representations of the behavior. In the case of internalized suppression, the relevant affective changes are the induction and attenuation of anxiety, which were originally controlled by the aversive social outcomes of particular forms of behavior. These aversive outcomes can be roughly assumed under the heading of social punishment, since they usually occur in a context where they are perceived as being transmitted by an agent who specifically intends to introduce them in response to one's actions. It is unlikely that any substantial repertoire of behavior becomes independent of external outcomes, in the course of naturalistic socialization, through interaction that is exclusively punitive. But the distinct contribution that response-contingent punishment makes to internalization can be examined in experimental situations where the effects of positive reinforcement have been reduced to a minimum.

The experiment to be reported here attempts to test a conception of internalized behavioral suppression that specifies a two-step acquisition process. It can be most conveniently illustrated in terms of the socialization of the child. The first acquisition mechanism is the attachment of anxiety to stimuli which are intrinsically produced. The most general common effect of all types of socially mediated punishment is their induction of an aversive affective state in the child. This state may have a number of qualitative variations (such as fear, guilt, or shame) which are dependent on the cognitive setting in which it is embedded. But its invariant motivational properties may be broadly designated as anxiety. Once the child has had some experience with a punished act, the role of punishment in eliciting anxiety can be easily displaced to social cues which have acquired secondary aversive value through their previous association with punishment. The incipient and even ongoing actions of children are frequently brought under the control of warning signals which are provided by their socializing agents.

Although the aversive social consequences of a child's behavior do not always reflect the violation of recognized norms of conduct, they do always imply some form of behavioral constraint between the child and the agent of punishment. It is therefore convenient to refer to any act as a transgression, when it is followed by social punishment of sufficient consistency and intensity to produce suppression of the act. If the punishment does have some minimally consistent relationship to the child's act, then a component of anxiety will necessarily become attached to the intrinsic stimulus correlates of the act. These intrinsic stimuli may be cues directly produced by the performance of the act itself. They also may be the cue properties of cognitive or verbal representations of the act—in the form, for example, of intentions or evaluative processes. Thus, certain kinds of actions, and their intrinsic representations, become capable of eliciting anxiety both during their performance and before they are even carried out, without the benefit of any external surveillance or objective threat of punishment.

The second mechanism in the internalization of behavioral suppression follows from the motivating properties of anxiety. Children quickly discover that they can avoid or attenuate social punishment and aversive warning stimuli by terminating an ongoing transgression or by arresting a transgression while it is still in an incipient stage. A variety of alternative nonpunished behaviors, including simple suppression of the transgression, consequently acquire instrumental value for them in reducing the anxiety elicited by aversive external events. At the same time, these suppressive behavioral modifications (and their representative cognitive processes) eliminate the intrinsic stimulus correlates of transgression and attenuate whatever anxiety may have been already independently attached to such correlates. Anxiety reduction will then gradually become attached directly to the intrinsic response-produced and cognitive correlates of suppression. And it will serve to reinforce the suppression, regardless of whether or not there are external consequences of the kind associated with surveillance and punishment. This entire two-step formulation is consistent with phenomena which are readily observable in naturalistic socialization, and also with the findings of extensive experimentation on the effects of punishment learning in animals (Estes, 1944; Mowrer, 1960a, Ch. 2; Solomon and Brush, 1956). It can also be extended to the learning of internalized reactions to transgressions which have already been committed (Aronfreed, 1963, 1964; Hill, 1960).[2]

Temporal Locus of Internalized Anxiety

Most of the acts which are defined by social punishment as transgressions are not punished indiscriminately without reference to the conditions of their occurrence. Ordinarily, an act has been punished in some situations, but not in others. The suppression of a transgression therefore cannot be viewed as being entirely mediated by intrinsic cues merely because it occurs in the absence of surveillance. The changes of affective state which motivate and reinforce suppression must rather be dependent on stimulus complexes which consist of both intrinsic and external cues, even though the external cues may not include the presence of a socializing agent. In order to examine the function of intrinsic cues in the mediation of suppression, it is necessary to have an experimental method in which these cues are given a variable relationship to the course of anxiety, while the role of external situational cues remains constant. One such method is to observe the effects of variation in the timing of punishment with respect to the initiation and completion of a punished act. The rationale for this procedure is implicit in the common finding that punishment is less effective in suppressing the behavior of animals when it follows an act only after a relatively long temporal interval (Bixenstine, 1956; Kamin, 1959; Mowrer, 1960a, Ch. 2). The particular variant of the procedure used here was suggested by an informal report on work in progress with dogs by R. L. Solomon (see Mowrer, 1960b, pp. 399–404). Solomon's observations of 6-month-old puppies tentatively indicated that punishment upon approach to a forbidden food resulted in more prolonged suppression, during a test in which the experimenter was absent, than did punishment after a considerable portion of the food had been eaten. There was also some indication that puppies who did trangress during the test were more likely to show reactive signs of distress if they had been punished originally after having eaten part of the food.

Any act may be regarded as having a number of distinguishable components. In addition to intentions or other implicit precursors of the act, there are intrinsic cues which occur as the act is initiated. When the act is fully committed, there will be other intrinsic stimulus correlates which have some duration in time, and they may actually extend beyond the point of its completion. If we assume that internalized suppression requires some mediation of anxiety by the sequence of intrinsic cues associated with a punished act, then we would expect the temporal locus of the original social punishment to have a significant impact on the effective motivation for subsequent suppression when the child is no longer under surveillance. Punishment used at initiation of a transgression would attach maximal anxiety to the intrinsic cues which occur at that point. In contrast, punishment administered only when a transgression has been already committed would tend to produce greater intensity of internalized anxiety at the point where subsequent transgressions have also been completed.

The difference in the effects of these two temporal loci of punishment would be limited by generalization or spread of anxiety to elements of the act other than those immediately present at the point of punishment. But to the extent that responses alternative to transgression (including its suppression) are motivated by anxiety and reinforced by anxiety reduction, they should have a greater probability of being elicited by the incipient cues of transgression—before the transgression is actually carried out—if punishment originally occurred at its initiation. If punishment occurred only after the commission of a transgression, the anxiety generalized to the point of onset might not be intense enough to motivate subsequent suppression when the child has been removed from the external presence of the punitive agent. Moreover, if punishment were to occur consistently after a transgression was socially perceived as having been already committed, suppression would not acquire much anxiety-reducing value at the point where maximal internalized anxiety would eventually be concentrated. When a child has completed a transgression, suppression is ordinarily no longer instrumental to the avoidance or attenuation of punishment.

Method

Two experimental socialization paradigms were constructed to require children to choose, on each of nine training trials, between a punished class of responses and a nonpunished class of active alternative responses (rather than between punished responses and passive suppression). This technique insured that there would be some opportunity for punishment training among all of the children, since they could not reduce their anxiety about the entire situation by resorting to a generalized suppression of all active responses. Consequently, the suppression

[2] The anxiety induced by punishment may disrupt punished responses not only because it motivates alternative responses but also because it serves in itself as a competing response.

to become evident during training appeared not simply as absence of the punished response, but rather as the positive choice of a nonpunished alternative. The children were confronted with a relatively simple discrimination. They were asked to choose between two small toy replicas of real objects commonly found in their social environment, to pick up the chosen toy, and to describe its function if they were asked to do so. The pair of toys varied from trial to trial, but one was always quite attractive, while the other was relatively unattractive. Punishment was consistently administered for choice of the attractive toy, and the child was not permitted to describe its function. Choice of the unattractive toy was not punished, but was also not rewarded, except for the minimal social reinforcement inherent in being permitted to describe its function and in the experimenter's noncommittal recognition of the child's verbal statement (in the form of a casual "uh-huh").

The experimenter's role as a socializing agent was predominantly punitive and provided in itself no model for the behavioral changes which the child was to acquire. A very limited cognitive context for punishment was provided by telling the children that certain of the toys were supposed to be chosen only by older children. This restriction was imparted during instructions and was repeated each time that the child was punished. In one training condition, punishment was administered as soon as the child's hand approached the attractive toy, and before the child picked it up. In the other training condition, the child was permitted to pick up the attractive toy and hold it for a few seconds (but not to handle it), and then punishment was given and the toy was removed from the child's hand. A control condition without explicit punishment was also devised, primarily to control for any possible effects of the difference between the two punishment conditions in habituation to picking up the toys during punished choices.

Following the nine trials used under each of these conditions, the children were tested for internalized suppression of the punished behavior. The experimenter set out a tenth pair of toys, one of which was highly attractive, and then left the room on a pretext. When he returned, he was able to discern whether the attractive toy had been picked up or even moved. The experiment was not designed to assess the effects of timing of punishment upon internalized reactions to completed transgressions, because of the difficulty of eliciting overt evidence of such reactions without disclosing the hidden monitoring of the children's behavior during the test for internalization. However, an attempt was made to get a tentative index of responses which the children might have used to reduce their anxiety following transgressions in the test situation.

Subjects

The subjects used in the experiment were 88 boys from the fourth and fifth grades of two public schools in a large urban school system.[3] The subjects were divided as follows among the three conditions: Punishment at Initiation, 34; Punishment at Completion, 34; Control, 20.

Procedure

Each child was taken individually from his classroom to the experimental room by the experimenter, who was a male. The child was asked to sit at a small table, and the experimenter seated himself across from the child. A rectangular wooden presentation board, roughly 12 × 18 inches in size, lay centered on the table. At the experimenter's right was a second table, upon which lay a black compartmentalized box and the experimenter's recording materials. The box had 24 compartments, each of which held a pair of toy replicas. Only the first 10 pairs were actually used for the nine training trials and the test trial. The toys were all quite small, and varied in their outer dimensions from roughly .5 inch to 2.5 inches. The attractive member of each pair was always somewhat larger, had more detailed fidelity to its realistic prototype, and had a higher relevance to masculine interests (for example, a tiny electric motor, a camera with moving parts, etc.). The unattractive items were, in contrast, smaller, shabbily designed, and more generally associated with feminine interests (for example, a barrette, a thimble, etc.). The pairs of items were used in a fixed order under all conditions.

Punishment at Initiation. The experimenter's instructions were given as follows:

> I'm going to put some toys down here on this board. Each time I'll put down two toys. Here's what you do —pick up the one you want to tell about, hold it over the board [the experimenter indicated appropriate action with his hand, using his fingers to show that the item was to be easily visible when held], look at it for a while, and just think about what you're going to say. Then, if I ask you, tell me what it's for or what you do with it. Do you understand?

Following the child's indication of understanding, the experimenter continued:

> Now some of the toys here are only supposed to be for older boys, so you're not supposed to pick them. When you pick something that's only for older boys, I'll tell you.

[3] The experiment was made possible through the cooperation of a number of administrators and teachers in the Philadelphia public school system.

The experimenter then began the first trial by placing the initial pair of toys on the board and saying: "All right, now pick up the one you want to tell about, look at it for a while, and just think about what you're going to say." To indicate subsequent trials, the experimenter said: "All right, pick up the one you want to tell about," or simply "All right." The position of the attractive toy was consistently alternated over the nine training trials, so that it appeared at the child's left on odd-numbered trials and at his right on even-numbered trials (thus providing another cue, in addition to attractiveness, to simplify the discrimination).

After the experimenter initiated each trial by placing a pair of toys, he dropped his hands lightly to an apparently casual resting position just behind the toys. When the child reached for the unattractive toy, he was permitted to pick it up and hold it over the board, in accordance with the instructions. After 2 or 3 seconds, the experimenter said: "All right, tell me about it." Following the subject's description of the toy's function (usually rather brief), the experimenter simply said "uh-huh" (quite flatly) and removed both toys from the board after the child had put down the toy he had chosen. When the child reached for the attractive toy, the experimenter said: "No—that's for the older boys" (firmly, though not very sharply), and raised the fingers of his hand behind the toy as though to slightly cover it. The experimenter's verbal disapproval was always given before the child actually touched the toy, but when the child's hand was rather close to it. The disapproval was almost always immediately effective in causing the child to withdraw his hand without even touching the toy. The experimenter then first removed the attractive toy, leaving the unattractive one for a few seconds, in the event that the child would want to pick it up and thus correct its original transgression. But very few children ever used the opportunity to pick up an unattractive toy, once they had already been punished for their choice of the attractive one.

Punishment at Completion. The instructions and general procedure for the training condition, and the experimenter's behavior when the child chose an unattractive toy, were identical to those described above for the Punishment at Initiation condition. The only difference was in the timing of punishment when the child chose an attractive toy. Here, the child was permitted to pick up the attractive toy and hold it over the board, just as in the case of an unattractive toy. Then, after 2 or 3 seconds, the experimenter said: "No—that's for the older boys," and gently but firmly removed the toy from the child's hand (the position in which the children had been instructed to hold the toys was such that the toy was never actually handled and was readily removable). As in the first condition, the unattractive toy was removed from the board a few seconds later, so as to give the child an opportunity to correct himself.

Control. The Control condition was constructed to observe the effects of lack of opportunity to pick up the attractive toys, during training in which there was no response-contingent punishment. Instructions and procedure were similar to those used for the punishment conditions, but had to be slightly modified to define a situation in which the child would never actually pick up the toys, without the necessity of using explicit punishment. A statement was also added to specifically indicate which of the toys were intended only for older boys, since the general prohibition on choosing such toys, imparted in the instructions, was concretized in the other training conditions by the information conveyed on punishment trials.

The experimenter's modified instructions were as follows:

> I'm going to put some toys down here on this board. Each time I'll put down two toys. Here's what you do —you just point to the one you want to tell about [the experimenter demonstrated with his hand], look at it for a while, and just think about what you're going to say. Then, If I ask you, tell me what it's for or what you do with it. Do you understand?

Following the child's indication of understanding, the experimenter continued:

> Now some of the toys here are only supposed to be for older boys, so you're not supposed to pick them up. The nicer-looking, more interesting toys are for the older boys.

The experimenter then initiated the training trials. On each trial, the child was asked to indicate his choice by pointing. When the child pointed to an unattractive toy, the experimenter said: "All right, tell me about it." After the child had finished describing the toy's function, the experimenter said "uh-huh" and removed both toys. When the child pointed to the attractive toy, the experimenter simply removed both toys without saying anything (a procedure which, while it was not explicitly punitive, may well have been frustrating or otherwise aversive to the child).

Test situation. The two objects used on the tenth (test) trial were related to one another in the same way as were the members of previous pairs used during training. But they were somewhat less toy-like. There was visible action within the attractive object, whereas the other object was not only unattractive but also relatively difficult to identify. Consequently, some generalization had to be exercised by the child in carrying his response tendencies to the test situation. The attractive object was a two-chambered glass timer in which an enclosed quantity of salt ran down from the upper to the lower chamber in a period of 1 minute (previous pilot work had suggested that the tendency to turn the timer, or at least to handle it, was difficult to resist). The unattractive object was a dingy, yellow, 2-inch square of terry cloth, folded into an approximation of a piece of toweling. As the tenth trial began, the experimenter was about to place these objects, but then turned hesitatingly to his folder of papers, in which he had been recording the child's choices, and said (in a halting and distracted fashion, while looking into the folder):

> It looks like I forgot some of the papers I need . . . I must have left them in my car . . . I'll have to go outside on the street and get them.

The experimenter then placed the pair of toys. The presentation board was unfinished and had on its surface a number of scratches. One of these was actually a faint marker inserted for the test situation, a straight line about .5 inch in length. A barely visible scratch line had also been made on each of the timer's two hexagonal rubber bases, running from their edges along their upper surfaces. The experimenter placed the timer so that the scratch line on one of its bases was exactly orthogonal to the faint line on the board. As the experimenter placed the item, he also rose and said:

> I'll be gone for about 5 or 10 minutes . . . while I'm gone, you can be deciding which one of these toys you want to tell about.

The experimenter then took his folder and left the room, closing the door firmly behind him. The experimenter remained out of the room for 5 minutes, and then reentered, first rattling the doorknob, so as to give the child time to replace either of the toys which he might have picked up. While the experimenter was walking over to the table where the child was sitting, he asked: "While I was gone, were you thinking about the toys?" Then the experimenter continued, after sitting down and opening his folder to his recording sheet: "Well, I don't want you to choose yet, but tell me what you were thinking while I was gone." Following the child's response to this inquiry, the experimenter asked: "While I was gone, did you decide on which one you want to tell about?" The child's responses to each of these questions were recorded verbatim. The experimenter also noted whether the timer had been moved during his absence.

After the inquiry described above was completed, the experimenter closed the procedure on the pretext that the remaining toys in the box could not be used because he could not find his misplaced papers. A further statement was added to put the child at ease about his performance and to invoke his cooperation in not discussing his experience with other children.

Results

The primary observations were of whether or not the children picked up or handled the attractive minute-glass in the experimenter's absence, an index of the internalized effectiveness of the suppression acquired during training. Table 1 shows, for each of the training conditions, the numbers of children who did and did not transgress. Chi-square values for the 2×2 contingency tables which compare each two of the three training conditions, with respect to frequencies of transgression and nontransgression during the test, are as follows: Punishment at Initiation versus Punishment at Completion: $\chi^2 = 11.54$, $p < .001$; Punishment at Initiation versus Control: $\chi^2 = 12.44$, $p < .001$; Punishment at Completion versus Control: $\chi^2 = .19$, *ns*.[4]

These differences in the effectiveness of internalized suppression, during the test situation, were complemented by the behavior of the children during training. Despite the mild prohibition conveyed in the instructions, the children in the Control condition persistently pointed to the attractive toys, even though this behavior resulted in no opportunity to describe the function of the toys. The great majority of these children chose the attractive toy on six to eight of the nine trials. More than a few chose it on all nine trials. The discriminability of the toys within

Table 1 *Frequency of Test Transgression and Nontransgression following Each of Three Training Paradigms*

Behavior During Test Situation	Training Paradigms		
	Punishment at Initiation ($N = 34$)	Punishment at Completion ($N = 34$)	Control ($N = 20$)
Transgression	9	24	16
Nontransgression	25	10	4

[4] All values shown here are for one-tailed tests and incorporate a correction for continuity.

Table 2 *Frequency of Transgression and Punishment during Training among Test Transgressors and Nontransgressors Trained under Each of Two Variations in Timing of Punishment*

Experimental Group	Frequency of Punishment During Training							
	0	1	2	3	4	5	6	7
Punishment at Initiation								
Transgressors	1	3	2	2		1		
Nontransgressors	1	11	7	5		1		
Both test groups	2	14	9	7		2		
Punishment at Completion								
Transgressors	1	5	10	4	1	2		1
Nontransgressors		2	3	3		1	1	
Both test groups	1	7	13	7	1	3	1	1

each pair, and the consistent difference in their attractiveness, was also apparent in the responses of children in the punishment training conditions, but in a very different way that clearly showed the effects of the punishment. Under punishment training, the typical sequence of behavior was to choose the attractive toy on the first one, two, or three trials, and then to fairly consistently choose the unattractive toy thereafter. A single punishment was sufficient, for 21 of the children, to inhibit further choices of the attractive toys. Occasionally, a child would revert once, near the middle of the series of trials, to choosing an attractive toy, but would then return immediately to choosing the unattractive ones.

It is particularly interesting to note that children punished at initiation of transgression exposed themselves to punishment *less* frequently than did those punished at completion. Table 2 shows the distribution of frequencies of punishment in the two punishment training paradigms, separately for those children who transgressed and those who did not transgress in the test situation. The two total training groups are significantly different from one another ($\chi^2 = 3.16$, $p < .05$), if we compare the number of children who received less than two punishments with those who received two or more punishments.[5] Clearly, it is not the number of punishments during training that makes punishment at initiation more effective as a paradigm for inducing internalized suppression. A comparison of all transgressors with all nontransgressors also indicates that behavior in the test situation is not attributable to frequency of punishment during training.

For reasons already set forth, it might be expected that children trained under punishment at completion would experience more anxiety *following* a transgression in the test situation than would children trained under punishment at initiation. Since the anxiety was not likely to be so intense as to overflow into an overt display of affect, the only evidence of its presence would be in certain responses which might be instrumental to its reduction. In the present experiment, it was important that the experimenter's knowledge of the child's transgression not be revealed, and consequently it was not possible to employ techniques which would directly elicit observable responses such as confession and reparation. It appeared, however, that some of the children might be using a quasi-confessional response, predispositionally available from past experience, to reduce their anxiety following a transgression in the experimenter's absence. When the experimenter returned to the room, there were virtually no spontaneous responses from the children which could be easily classified as internalized reactions to transgression. But there were some interesting variations of response to the inquiry about their thoughts during the test situation. Children who had been in the Control condition almost invariably indicated that they had been "thinking" about the attractive test object, a verbal response that agreed with their behavior during the test. In contrast, a substantial majority of the children exposed to the two punishment conditions reported that they had thought about the unattractive object (a few indicated that they had not thought about either one). However, roughly one third of the punished children did admit thinking about the attractive object. Closer inspection of the data, shown in Table 3, revealed that these latter children were predomi-

[5] The value shown is for a one-tailed test and incorporates a correction for continuity. The comparison given results in the least disproportionate division possible along the frequency scale. Separate analogous comparisons of the two punishment conditions, within the transgressor and nontransgressor groups, would not be meaningful because of the extremely small samples which would appear in some cells of the relevant frequency tables.

The effects of differential timing of punishment are also visible in the occurrence of reversals. Seventeen of the children punished at completion reverted momentarily to choosing an attractive toy afer suppression had begun to be established during training, but this behavior was shown by only nine of the children punished at initiation.

Table 3 *Frequency of Admission and Nonadmission Reactions following Test Situation among Transgressors and Nontransgressors Trained under Each of Two Variations in Timing of Punishment*

Experimental Group	Reaction following Test Situation	
	Admission	Nonadmission
Punishment at Initiation		
Transgressors	4	5
Nontransgressors	1	24
Both test groups	5	29
Punishment at Completion		
Transgressors	16	8
Nontransgressors	2	8
Both test groups	18	16

nantly those trained under punishment at completion, and that they were almost entirely transgressors. In view of the overall contrast between the Control and punishment groups, it seemed that their response to the inquiry might be regarded as a reaction of "admission."[6]

Comparison of the total numbers of transgressors and nontransgressors who showed admission and nonadmission reactions shows a highly significant difference ($\chi^2 = 18.29$, $p < .001$). The same difference appears when the comparison is made only among children trained under punishment at completion ($\chi^2 = 4.44$, $p. < .05$; $p < .02$ for the Fisher exact test). And a similar tendency is apparent among children punished at initiation (though it does not attain statistical significance in the latter case). If the admission of having thought about the attractive test object did serve to reduce the anxiety that followed transgression, then we would expect to find it more commonly among transgressors trained under punishment at completion than among transgressors trained under punishment at initiation. Inspection of Table 3 does reveal a tendency in this direction, but it does not attain statistical significance, in part because of the restricted number of children who transgress following punishment at initiation.[7]

Discussion

The difference between the effects of the Punishment at Initiation and the Punishment at Completion paradigms indicates that timing of punishment is a very significant determinant of internalized behavioral suppression, at least when the punishment is accompanied by only minimal cognitive structure. This finding strongly supports the view that the suppression is some positive function of the intensity of the anxiety which is mobilized at the onset of a transgression, and that the anxiety is in turn a function of the original temporal relationship between this locus and the occurrence of punishment. It also supports the broader conception of the internalization of social control through punishment as resting first on the attachment of anxiety to intrinsic cues associated with transgression, and secondly on the attachment of anxiety reduction to intrinsic cues associated with alternative nonpunished behavior.

The great majority of the children who were exposed to the Control paradigm picked up the attractive toy during the test, even though they were never permitted to pick up any toys during training. This last observation clearly indicates that transgressions had to be specifically punished in order to induce internalized suppression, and that the differential effects of the two punishment paradigms cannot be attributed to lack of opportunity to pick up attractive toys during training with punishment at initiation. Effects which are similar to those of the Control paradigm are commonly observed in naturalistic socialization. In the absence of external surveillance, previous mild injunctions and prophylactic restrictions of opportunity to transgress are often insufficient, without the addition of punishment, to suppress behavior which may have other highly reinforcing consequences for the child.

It will be observed that the experimentally induced suppression, during the test for internalization, cannot be attributed simply to "generalized" anxiety that might have become attached to the external cues which remain when the socializing agent has left the situation. Nor is it reasonable to suppose that the suppression is mediated by variable expectations about the risk of punishment. The difference in the effects of the two variations in the timing of punishment was apparent not only during the test, but also while the socializing agent was still present during training. And during both training and test, external cues and conditions of risk were identical for children who were exposed to either of the two punishment paradigms. It is likewise implausible to attribute the experimental findings to differences between the two paradigms in whatever positive reinforcement may have been as-

[6] The term guilt is unwarranted in reference to the effects of this kind of experimental situation, if one regards guilt as a phenomenon of rather specific cognitive properties interwoven with an affective base of anxiety (Aronfreed, 1964). The situation does not provide the kind of evaluative processes through which the perception of transgression can properly be said to arouse a moral affect (for example, cognitive focus on intentions or on the consequences of action for others).

[7] The values shown are for one-tailed tests and incorporate a correction for continuity.

sociated with the act of choosing (but never being able to tell about) an attractive toy. The children who were trained under punishment at completion were permitted to pick up attractive toys, but they were required to do so in such a way that they could not handle them. They were also subjected to an additional period of uncertainty while they awaited the experimenter's punitive response (particularly during the early training trials), and to the possibly enhanced frustration entailed in having the toys removed from their hands. Moreover, it should be noted that children trained under the Control paradigm transgressed even more freely during the test than did children trained under punishment at completion, even though they were prevented from picking up any toys during training.

There may well have been some cognitive mediation of the experimental effects, despite the attempt to minimize cognitive structure. If the two variations in timing of punishment induced different temporal patterns of arousal and reduction of anxiety, these patterns might have become intrinsically mediated by intentions or other cognitive representations of the sequential elements in the acts of choice. Such cognitive interventions would tend to restrict the mediational role of cues which were directly produced by the punished and nonpunished acts. But they would not require any change in the more general view that behavioral suppression becomes internalized when the course of anxiety begins to be monitored by intrinsic stimuli. If one were to assume that the primary difference between the two experimental groups, at the point of decision between transgression and nontransgression, was cognitive rather than motivational —for example, that the perceived determinant of punishment was reaching for the attractive toy in one group, but was picking it up in the other group—it would be difficult to account for the observed effects. Such an assumption would make no reference to the variable intensity of anxiety, which might precede or accompany a punished act. It would lead us to expect that children in the Punishment at Completion group would be more likely than those in the Punishment at Initiation group to *reach for* the attractive test toy. It would also lead, however, to the prediction that the Punishment at Completion group would not go so far as to *pick up* the attractive toy. But the observations during both training and the test for internalization indicate that children in this group do pick up the attractive test toys more frequently than do children trained under punishment at initiation.[8]

[8] The assumption that the experimental groups differ in their cognition of the determinants of punishment is perhaps not very credible in any case. The common general instructions to the children clearly convey the idea that "picking" a toy (i.e., the act of choice) is the relevant determinant.

The acquisition and maintenance of internalized suppression are not determined only by the intensity of the anxiety that becomes attached to the intrinsic cues associated with an incipient transgression. They are also affected by the reinforcement of behavioral alternatives to the punished act (including suppression). When the timing of social punishment is predictable to a child, as it is in the experimental paradigms, it may result in a delay-of-reinforcement effect upon suppression. The direction of this reinforcement effect would be parallel to the direction of the motivational effect that timing of punishment exercises upon suppression through its impact on the intrinsic temporal locus of anxiety. When children are confronted with choices between punished and nonpunished acts, they will experience some anxiety in connection with any choice, particularly early in the learning process before discriminant cues are firmly established. And the temporal relationship between nonpunished behavior and the reinforcement inherent in anxiety reduction will tend to be a direct function of the timing with which punishment predictably occurs for transgressions. In the Punishment at Initiation paradigm, for example, the external cues which signal that the child will not be punished begin to become apparent to him as soon as his hand reaches an unattractive toy without a punitive interruption. The anxiety reduction that reinforces the suppression of attractive choices thus soon becomes virtually immediate. In the Punishment at Completion condition, however, the anxiety reduction that follows nonpunished behavior is considerably more delayed, since the external safety signals do not occur until the child has been asked to tell about the toy. A possible implication of this analysis for naturalistic socialization is that children who are closely supervised by their parents may tend to experience more immediate reinforcement for their suppression of transgressions. It is also interesting to note that children may be forced to rely too heavily on the external outcomes of their behavior, if anxiety reduction cannot easily become discriminately attached to the intrinsic correlates of nonpunished behavior. This difficulty might arise if they were faced with complex discriminations in which they could not distinguish between punished and nonpunished responses, or if the anxiety induced by punishment were so intense as to disrupt the discrimination of relevant cues.

Some Further Theoretical Implications

The Punishment at Completion paradigm seems to be hardly more effective than the Control paradigm in producing internalized suppression. This finding suggests that the anxiety mobilized by an incipient transgression during the test situation was not sufficient to motivate suppression, when its intensity was attenuated across a gradient of generalization from the total complex of cues which were originally present at punishment of a completed transgression during training. The relative lack of effectiveness of the Punishment at Completion paradigm presents an instructive contrast to the observations made in a similar experiment conducted by Walters and Demkow (1963). These investigators used reaching for attractive toys versus touching the toys as their two temporal positions of punishment, and found that these training conditions produced only a tenuous difference in the subsequent effectiveness of the child's behavioral suppression in the experimenter's absence. The limitation on the effect which they observed was very probably due to the fact that their variation in timing cut a rather fine difference into the topography of the punished act and into the generalization gradients of the anxiety induced at the two points of punishment. A comparison of their findings with the findings of the present study indicates that the anxiety induced by the social punishment of an act does generalize from the intrinsic stimuli which are immediately present at the point of punishment to closely surrounding stimulus components of the punished act.

It may appear to be somewhat surprising that so many transgressions occur in the test situation following the Punishment at Completion paradigm, since naturalistic socialization commonly produces effective internalized suppression, even though it is very dependent on the punishment of already committed transgressions. Although the punishment of parents and socializing agents may be extremely variable in its timing, the ecology of socialization does not present too many opportunities to introduce punishment when a child is only on the threshold of transgressions. Part of this apparent discrepancy between naturalistic and experimental socialization may be an artifact of the use of a gross index of suppression in the test situation—the occurrence or nonoccurrence of transgression in a limited time period. A more sensitive index, such as elapsed time before the occurrence of transgression, might have revealed differences in the strength of the internalized suppression induced by the two punishment training conditions, without implying that the small variation in timing was so powerful as to determine whether a transgression could be elicited at all. The use of an elapsed time measure might have disclosed, for example, that transgressions following the Punishment at Completion paradigm occurred later in the test period than transgressions following the Control paradigm. Conversely, a longer test period might have raised the attractiveness of the forbidden toy, or might have resulted in extinction of some of the anxiety attached to intrinsic cues of incipient transgression, so that transgression would have been more common following training under punishment at initiation.

Variation of the precise timing of punishment, within the microstructure of a punished act, may be a convenient method for teasing out the specific mechanisms through which behavioral suppression becomes acquired and internalized. But naturalistic socialization has a number of other features which would tend to dilute the significance of timing, and to facilitate internalization even when punishments typically follow transgressions at temporal intervals well beyond these used in the experimental paradigms. The anxiety aroused by the punishment of agents to whom the child has strong positive attachments (particularly the parents) may be substantially greater than the anxiety aroused by an experimenter's verbal disapproval. And even if punishment follows a committed transgression, a greater intensity of anxiety at its point of application will be more likely to insure enough generalization to motivate suppression at the point of subsequent incipient transgressions. The punishment and warning signals emitted by parents are also often patterned in accordance with the continuous or intermittent character of many of a child's transgressions. Parents sometimes punish in the midst of a committed but sustained transgression, or after a discrete repeatable act that the child has completed but is about to initiate again. Under these conditions, substantial anxiety can become directly attached to the intrinsic cues associated with an incipient transgression, even though punishment is originally contingent on visible commission of the transgression. Moreover, the child may be given the opportunity to avoid or escape punishment by introducing its own behavioral control in the course of an ongoing transgression—a corrective option that is not available in the experimental paradigms—with the result that suppression may acquire instrumental, anxiety-reducing value even when it does not initially prevent the occurrence of transgression.

In the social interaction between parents and children, the reinforcement of behavioral suppression is not entirely defined, of course, by the presence or absence of aversive outcomes. Parents often react with affection, praise, or other forms of positive reinforcement, when they are aware of evidence of suppression in their children's behavior. A significant component of the intrinsic reinforcement that supports internalized suppression may consequently be derived from positive affect which was originally induced by social rewards, rather than from the reduction of the anxiety which is elicited by incipient transgression. It is for this reason that situational assessments of children's already acquired dispositions to suppress socially prohibited behavior are ambiguous with respect to the motivational antecedents and reinforcing consequences of the suppression. Such dispositions will be the resultants of a complex history of interaction of the effects of direct punishments and rewards (and also, perhaps, of the effects of modeling). Two well-designed surveys (Burton, Maccoby, and Allinsmith, 1961; Grinder, 1962) have, in fact, uncovered only tenuous and inconsistent relationships between children's internalized suppression of social transgressions and the discrete practices of punishment or reward which are used by their parents.

Probably the feature of naturalistic socialization that most effectively insures internalized suppression, regardless of the temporal locus of punishment, is the extensive verbal mediation used by parents. A verbal medium of punishment makes it possible for the child's anxiety to become monitored by intentions, conceptual labels, and other cognitive processes. Such cognitive processes may act as common mediators of anxiety. They can become attached to any of the concrete patterns of proprioceptive and external cues which emerge sequentially in the performance and after-effects of a transgression. And they can consequently bridge the microstructure and temporal separation of these concrete cues, so that the cues retain only a negligible function in governing the course of anxiety. The intensity of the anxiety that is elicited at the point of an incipient transgression would thus become independent of the original temporal relationship between the cues which are immediately present at that point and the occurrence of punishment. When a child is enabled to represent its intentions to itself, for example, in close conjunction with punishment that occurs long after a transgression has taken place, then its intentions may elicit sufficient anxiety to motivate suppression when they subsequently intercede before a transgression is carried out.

A number of surveys (Bandura and Walters, 1959; Maccoby, 1961; Sears, 1961; Sears, and Maccoby, and Levin, 1957, Ch. 7) have reported some evidence that children's internalized control over socially prohibited actions is positively associated with the closeness of supervision exercised by their parents. As was pointed out earlier, it is unlikely that close supervision affects suppression merely through the opportunity that it affords to punish the child's incipient transgressions. The association is more probably generated by the tendency of parents who closely control their children's behavior to also use verbal mediation and to be more attentive to the intrinsic cognitive and motivational precursors of transgression. Support for this observation can be found in the correlates of the different disciplinary methods to which parents in our society are disposed (Aronfreed, 1961; Bronfenbrenner, 1958; Davis and Havighurst, 1946; Kohn, 1959; Maccoby and Gibbs, 1954). Middle-class parents tend to be more oriented toward their children's intentions. They are likely to use reasoning and explanation to induce an internal governor in their children, and not merely to sensitize them to the punitive external consequences of transgression. They also often actively induce their children to initiate their own self-corrective processes. Working-class parents are more prone to react to the concretely visible consequences of their children's transgressions, and to sensitize their children to the threat of punishment. Their methods of punishment are more direct and occur in a less verbal medium. And they are less oriented toward reinforcing signs of internally mediated control in their children. Middle-class children do show more of a corresponding orientation toward internal monitors in the control of behavior, while working-class children show more of an external orientation (Aronfreed, 1961; Boehm, 1962; Kohlberg, 1963). Some surveys (Allinsmith, 1960; Bandura and Walters, 1959; MacKinnon, 1938; Sears, Maccoby, and Levin, 1957, Ch. 7) have found direct relationships between the internal versus external orientation of parental discipline and parallel differences of orientation in children's suppression of socially prohibited behavior.

Children do acquire highly general and integrative evaluative systems for some areas of social behavior. Such value systems may affect internalized control over behavior in ways which are not apparent from the effects of direct response outcomes in a simple discrimination situation. It is possible, for example, that more massive and cognitive forms of internalization can occur through acquisition processes of the kind implied in theories of identification. Certainly, stable behavioral changes can be induced in children through their tendency to reproduce the behavior of models (Bandura and Walters, 1963) without the initial support of direct external reinforcement. But the experimental findings reported in this paper show that internalized suppression can be acquired through a form of aversive learning that is highly sensitive to the timing of punishment, a parameter of social learning that is not readily translatable into the child's disposition to adopt the role of a model. A general conception of mechanisms of internalization must take into account, then, that some forms of internalized control over behavior can be established through the direct reinforcement and punishment of the child's overtly emitted responses.

References

Allinsmith, W. The learning of moral standards. In D. R. Miller and G. E. Swanson (Eds.), *Inner conflict and defense.* New York: Holt, 1960. Pp. 141–176.

ARONFREED, J. The nature, variety, and social patterning of moral responses to transgression. *Journal of Abnormal and Social Psychology,* 1961, *63,* 223–240.

ARONFREED, J. The effects of experimental socialization paradigms upon two moral responses to transgression. *Journal of Abnormal and Social Psychology,* 1963, *66,* 437–448.

ARONFREED, J. The origin of self-criticism. *Psychological Review,* 1964, *71,* 193–218.

BANDURA, A., and WALTERS, R. H. *Adolescent aggression.* New York: Ronald Press, 1959.

BANDURA, A., and WALTERS, R. H. *Social learning and personality development.* New York: Holt, Rinehart, and Winston, 1963.

BIXENSTINE, V. E. Secondary drive as a neutralizer of time in integrative problem-solving. *Journal of Comparative and Physiological Psychology,* 1956, *49,* 161–166.

BOEHM, LEONORE The development of conscience: A comparison of American children of different mental and socioeconomic levels. *Child Development,* 1962, *33,* 575–590.

BRONFENBRENNER, U. Socialization and social class through time and space. In Eleanor E. Maccoby, T. M. Newcomb, and E. L. Hartley (Eds.), *Readings in social psychology* (3rd ed.). New York: Holt, 1958. Pp. 400–425.

BRONFENBRENNER, U. Freudian theories of identification and their derivatives. *Child Development,* 1960, *31,* 15–40.

BURTON, R. V., MACCOBY, ELEANOR E., and ALLINSMITH, W. Antecedents of resistance to temptation in four-year-old children. *Child Development,* 1961, *32,* 689–710.

DAVIS, A., and HAVIGHURST, R. J. Social class and color differences in child-rearing. *American Sociological Review,* 1946, *11,* 698–710.

ESTES, W. K. An experimental study of punishment. *Psychological Monographs,* 1944, *57*(3, Whole No. 263).

GRINDER, R. E. Parental childrearing practices, conscience, and resistance to temptation of sixth-grade children. *Child Development,* 1962, *33,* 803–820.

HILL, W. F. Learning theory and the acquisition of values. *Psychological Review,* 1960, *67,* 317–331.

KAMIN, L. J. The delay-of-punishment gradient. *Journal of Comparative and Physiological Psychology,* 1959, *52,* 434–437.

KELMAN, H. C. Compliance, identification, and internalization: Three processes of attitude change. *Journal of Conflict Resolution,* 1958, 2, 51–60.

KOHLBERG, L. Moral development and identification. In H. W. Stevenson (Ed.), *Yearbook of the National Society for the Study of Education.* Part I. *Child psychology.* Chicago: University of Chicago Press, 1963. Pp. 277–332.

KOHN, M. L. Social class and the exercise of parental authority. *American Sociological Review,* 1959, *24,* 352–366.

MACCOBY, ELEANOR E. The taking of adult roles in middle childhood. *Journal of Abnormal and Social Psychology,* 1961, *63,* 493–503.

MACCOBY, ELEANOR E., and GIBBS, PATRICIA K. Methods of child-rearing in two social classes. In W. E. Martin and Celia B. Stendler (Eds.), *Readings in child development.* New York: Harcourt, Brace, 1954. Pp. 380–396.

MACKINNON, D. W. Violation of prohibitions. In H. A. Murray (Eds.), *Explorations in personality: A clinical and experimental study of fifty men of college age.* New York: Oxford University Press, 1938. Pp. 491–501.

MILLER, D. R., and SWANSON, G. E. (Eds.) *Inner conflict and defense.* New York: Holt, 1960.

MOWRER, O. H. *Learning theory and behavior.* New York: Wiley, 1960. (a)

MOWRER, O. H. *Learning theory and the symbolic processes.* New York: Wiley, 1960. (b)

PIAGET, J. *The moral judgment of the child.* Glencoe, Ill.: Free Press, 1948.

SEARS, R. R. Relation of early socialization experiences to aggression in middle childhood. *Journal of Abnormal and Social Psychology,* 1961, *63,* 466–492.

SEARS, R. R., MACCOBY, ELEANOR E., and LEVIN, H. *Patterns of child rearing.* Evanston, Ill.: Row, Peterson, 1957.

SOLOMON, R. L., and BRUSH, ELINOR S. Experimentally derived conceptions of anxiety and aversion. In M. R. Jones (Ed.), *Nebraska symposium on motivation: 1956.* Lincoln: University of Nebraska Press, 1956. Pp. 212–305.

THIBAUT, J. W., and KELLEY, H. H. *The social psychology of groups.* New York: Wiley, 1959.

WALTERS, R. H., and DEMKOW, LILLIAN. Timing of punishment as a determinant of response inhibition. *Child Development,* 1963, *34,* 207–214.

WHITING, J. W. M. Sorcery, sin, and the superego: Some cross-cultural mechanisms of social control. In M. R. Jones (Ed.), *Nebraska symposium on motivation: 1959.* Lincoln: University of Nebraska Press, 1959. Pp. 174–195.

The experiment by *Mischel and Grusec* investigates some of the ways in which the prior relationship of a model to a child influences the child in later interaction with the model. The experiment concerns internalization because the model's influence on the child comes from the history of their interaction as well as from some consequence provided by the model in the child's current environment. Behaviorally, we are concerned with the properties of the parent or model as a generalized reinforcer. The experiment attempts to establish in the laboratory some of the conditions that are responsible for generalized conditioned reinforcement by a model or parent. The parent becomes a generalized reinforcer in the natural environment, because so many important consequences in the child's life are provided by the parent. The parent also provides differential occasions for the reinforcement of much of the child's conduct. In short, the parent not only reinforces requests for food, attention, play, or privilege, he also establishes the conditions under which these reinforcers can occur. The child's ability to influence his social and physical environment by observing the way the parent acts is another large factor contributing to the generalized reinforcing properties of the parent. Hence, it is hypothesized that any behaviors the child carries out which resemble those of the parent or model will increase in frequency because they produce consequences that act as a generalized reinforcer.

This experiment also tests the hypothesis that all of the models' activities, including those performances that punish the subject or withdraw positive reinforcers from him, will be copied. A critical property of the parent as a generalized reinforcer is that he is a link in the chain between the child's behavior and the consequences in the social and physical environment that maintain it. The process is enhanced and heightened because so much of the reinforcement of the child's behavior is not only mediated by the parent but often is impossible without him.

18 *Determinants of the Rehearsal and Transmission of Neutral and Aversive Behaviors*[1]

WALTER MISCHEL
JOAN GRUSEC

Recent investigations have demonstrated that children and adults who observe a model's behavior may reproduce that behavior even when they are not directly reinforced for it by social agents (Bandura and Walters, 1963). In these studies models exhibited a variety of behaviors which had no direct consequences for the subject. For example, children observed an adult aggress against a doll but they themselves were not the objects of aggression. However, in many life situations the behaviors exhibited by social models do have direct positive or negative consequences for the observer of the behaviors because he is also their recipient. Thus, during much of his socialization the child is the object, as well as the witness, of the behavior of parental and other models and receives direct consequences from the behaviors they display. The child who is spanked observes the parental disciplinary style but also experiences it.

It has been commonly noted, anecdotally and in clinical observation, that individuals rehearse and transmit to others behaviors which had aversive consequences for them. For example, parents often claim they unwillingly behave towards their children in

[1] This study was supported by Research Grant M-6830 from the National Institutes of Health, United States Public Health Service. Acknowledgment is also made to the Stanford University Nursery School.

ways similar to those that produced pain for them when performed by their own parents. At present the factors governing the reproduction of a model's novel behaviors which were aversive to the individual in his interactions with that model remain ambiguous. Several theories (e.g., Maccoby, 1959; Sears, 1957; Whiting and Child, 1953), including the well-known theory of "identification with the aggressor" (Bettelheim, 1943; Freud, 1946) have been invoked to account for this reproduction and transmission of social punishments, and the difficulties of a secondary positive reinforcement interpretation have been noted (e.g., Aronfreed, 1964). Relevant data, however, have been primarily clinical and informal, and the very occurrence of the phenomenon itself has been rarely demonstrated in laboratory research.

Notable exceptions are Aronfreed's (1964) recent investigations into the origins of self-criticism which illustrate that the timing of punishment is an important determinant of the acquisition of self-critical labels. These studies led Aronfreed to conclude that

> The reproduction of social punishment appears to be acquired only when the relevant components of punishment have a circumscribed temporal relationship to an anticipatory aversive state [and that] the reproduction of social punishment cannot be subsumed under the consequences of a model's rewarding characteristics (pp. 212–213).

However, this cannot be accepted as a firm conclusion because in Aronfreed's study on the effect of the model's social characteristics the manipulations of the model's rewarding characteristics were confined to expressions of verbal and physical approval (e.g., patting the child on the head) during the experimental procedure. It should also be noted that these studies did not involve the transmission of aversive behaviors by the subject to another person but only their reproduction in the experimenter's presence, usually in response to the experimenter's direct probes.

There is considerable evidence that the characteristics of the model, such as his rewardingness and power or control over resources, affect the extent to which some of his displayed behaviors are imitated by an observer (e.g., Bandura and Huston, 1961; Mussen and Distler, 1959). The unresolved question is whether the characteristics of the model can affect the reproduction of social punishments which the individual not only observed but also directly received from the model. The two characteristics of the model which were manipulated in the present study are considered major determinants of imitation in several prominent theories of identification. The conceptualizations of Sears (1957), Mowrer (1950), and Whiting and Child (1953) all give the rewarding characteristics of the model a central role for the development of identification. For example, in Mowrer's formulations, if the model's behavioral attributes are paired with positive reinforcements they acquire secondary reinforcing properties on the basis of classical conditioning and, through stimulus generalization also become rewarding when performed by the child. After the model's behaviors have been paired with positive reinforcement the child can self-administer secondary reinforcers by reproducing components of the behavior. In addition, Maccoby (1959) and Mussen and Distler focus on the model's control of resources as well as his rewardingness, stressing the model's social power as the characteristic which enhances identification. Maccoby, for example, suggests that the control exercised by a model over resources important for the needs of the child will determine the amount of role practice in which the child engages. He will rehearse both the rewarding *and* the punishing characteristics of the model since both are relevant to him in guiding his plans about future actions. Because these behaviors have been well rehearsed they are more likely to be performed when relevant eliciting stimuli evoke them by contiguity.

In the present study rewardingness was manipulated by varying the degree to which the model provided the child with both material and social noncontingent reward. Power or control over both positive and negative outcomes was manipulated cognitively by varying the model's role. For half the children the model was introduced as a visiting teacher who would never reappear while for the other half she was introduced as the child's new teacher.

Thus, the present study investigated the effects of the model's rewardingness or use of noncontingent reinforcement, and his control over the subject's future resources, on the degree to which behaviors displayed by the model without direct consequences for the subject ("neutral" behaviors) and those directed at the subject with negative consequences for him ("aversive" behaviors) are rehearsed and transmitted. The main purposes of this study were to: demonstrate the occurrence of both rehearsal and transmission of aversive behavior; investigate the relative effectiveness of noncontingent reinforcement by the model and his control over future resources in producing this rehearsal and transmission; and compare the determinants of the rehearsal and transmission of such initially aversive behaviors with those of neutral behaviors displayed by the model.

Preschool children were exposed to an adult female model whose noncontingent rewardingness and future control over the child were varied. Thereafter, the children participated with the model in a "special game" which involved playing with a cash register, making change with play coins and bills, etc. The model included the following behaviors during this interaction: she was aversive to the child in novel ways (aversive behavior) and she exhibited novel behaviors with no direct reinforcement consequences for the child (neutral behavior). More specifically, the aversive acts consisted of imposing delay of reward, removal of reward, and criticism. The modeling of neutral behaviors consisted of emitting distinctive verbal and motor behaviors (e.g., marching around the room while saying "March! March! March!"). The aversive behaviors were designed to have direct negative consequences for the subject whereas the neutral behaviors were merely modeled without direct reinforcement consequences for him. In the former instances the child was the object of the behavior whereas in the latter he was only the observer of the displayed behaviors. Following these treatments, the subject's task was to show another person who was dressed as a clown how to play the cash register game in the model's absence. Measures were taken of the rehearsal and reproduction of novel behaviors in the model's presence, and of the transmission of neutral and aversive behaviors to the "clown" in her absence.

In accord with the above-mentioned theories of identification which stress both the model's rewardingness and power, it was anticipated that the reproduction of both neutral and aversive behaviors would be more frequent when the model's noncontingent reinforcement was high than when it was low. The combination of noncontingent reinforcement and future control over resources was expected to result in the most frequent reproduction of the model's behaviors. Conversely, it was expected that reproduction would be least frequent when the combination of non contingent reinforcement and future control is lowest. The other combinations of rewardingness and control were expected to fall between these extremes, with no prediction made concerning their relative strengths.

Method

Subjects

The subjects were 56 Stanford nursery school children ranging in age from 37 months to 64 months with a mean age of 52 months. There were 31 boys and 25 girls, and the same adult female experimenter was used with all children. The children were assigned randomly to each treatment, with separate assignments for each sex to assure that similar proportions of boys and girls were included in each condition.

The Model's Rewardingness and Control

Four manipulations were used to vary the model's rewardingness and control:

High noncontingent reward (high reward). Attractive toys were available (e.g., a bowling set, battery-operated cars and planes, musical tops, hand puppets) and the model and subject played together with them, the model showing interest, affection, and warmth, and frequently praising the child. In addition, she dispensed attractive stickers and cookies to the child. The intent was to establish the model as noncontingently rewarding, with highly attractive resources at her disposal. These operations were similar to those usually labeled "nurturance" (e.g., Bandura and Huston, 1961).

Low noncontingent reward (low reward). There were less attractive toys available (e.g., coloring book, used crayons, broken toys) and the model informed the child that she had some work to complete saying, "I don't have too many toys here, but you can play with them for awhile. I'll be right over here working [pointing to corner of room]." The model responded minimally but pleasantly to attention bids, indicating that she had to finish her work.

High future control (high control). The model structured her role as that of the child's new nursery school teacher, and she commented that they would therefore be seeing a lot of each other.

Low future control (low control). The model structured her role as that of a visiting teacher who was leaving the nursery school in an hour to take the bus back home to Milwaukee. She commented that they would therefore not be seeing each other again.

Experimental Groups

Each of the four experimental treatment groups contained 14 children and consisted of these combinations of the above-described operations: high reward-high control, high reward-low control, low reward-high control, low reward-low control. Each involved a 20-minute interaction between the adult and child. There were 6 girls and 8 boys in each group except the low reward-high future control condition in which there were 7 boys and 7 girls.

Procedure

The experimenter introduced herself to the child, identifying herself either as his new nursery school teacher or as a visiting teacher who was leaving that same day (high or low control). The 20-minute play session followed in which she displayed either high-or low-reward behavior. The experimenter again reminded the subject of her future role, and then took him to another experimental room to "play a special game with a toy cash register." On entering the room the subject was shown a large container of toys and was allowed to select the one he wanted most. This toy was placed in a bag and given to the child and he was told that he could take it home.

Presentation of Neutral and Aversive Behavior

The experimenter and child seated themselves in front of the toy cash register. The game involved playing store with a cash register, making change, opening and closing the register drawer, hitting the register keys, etc. During the game, all subjects were exposed to the following two kinds of behaviors:

1. Neutral behaviors. The model hit a key on the cash register and said "Bop," marched around the table saying "March, march, march, march, march," and repeated this sequence two more times.

2. Aversive behaviors. (*a*) Imposed delay—When the child touched the cash register for the first time, the model said that if one wants to play with anything badly enough one ought to be able to wait for it, and instructed the subject to sit still with his hands in his lap until she finished counting. She then very slowly and methodically repeated the numbers "1, 2, 3" 15 times. (*b*) Criticism and removal of reward—The cash register was constructed so that, unknown to the subject, the model could make the drawer come all the way out when it was opened, giving the appearance that it was broken. When this happened, as the child "broke" the drawer the experimenter exclaimed sharply, "Oh my! Do you know what this makes you? It makes you a storewrecker, and when you're a storewrecker, you lose your toy." She then removed the toy the child had received previously, saying sternly "You try not to be a storewrecker again."

The model performed the neutral behaviors and the counting at two different times in the course of playing cash register with the child whereas the drawer was broken once. The children's reactions to the aversive behaviors varied from tears to silent but obvious tension and indicated that the behaviors had painful consequences for them. This was further substantiated by the fact that seven subjects (not included in the total *N*) had to be eliminated because they cried and became too upset to continue participating. This occurred with similar frequency across treatment conditions. At the conclusion of the learning session the child was left alone to play with the cash register in the experimental room for 3 minutes during which he was observed through a one-way mirror by the experimenter and her confederate. The purpose of this interval was to reduce any immediate emotional arousal stemming from the interaction and to observe any additional practice of the model's behaviors during her absence.

Transmission

The experimenter returned to the experimental room and led the child back to the room in which the play session had taken place. She informed him that, as a special treat, he was going to be allowed to show someone else how to play the cash register game. All the events that had occurred during the game, including the neutral and negative behaviors, were reviewed verbally by the experimenter who also reminded the child again of her future role (high or low control). The subject was told that the person he was going to teach was a girl dressed up as a clown. The adult and child then returned to the experimental room where an adult female experimental confederate was seated in front of the cash register. The confederate was dressed as a clown to disinhibit children who might be reluctant to relate with a strange adult in novel and aversive ways. As the subject and the model came into the room the clown began to play with the cash register. The model playfully tapped the clown's hand and told her not to play until she was told what to do by the subject. The model then left the subject and clown together, and observed them through a one-way mirror in an adjoining room.

The clown behaved in a pleasant way to the subject, nodding and bowing occasionally. When asked any questions about her background she answered minimally, for example, she was just pretending to be a clown, she lived down the road, she did not have any age when she was a clown. If the subject did not immediately show the clown how to play, the clown attempted twice to elicit this behavior by saying, "Can you show me what to do" and "I really want to learn how to play." If the subject still made no response the clown began to play with the cash register and money by herself. Always, in the course of the transmission session, the clown broke the drawer and exclaimed, "Oh look what happened!" When the subject stopped demonstrating the clown said, after 10 seconds had elapsed, "It there anything else? Can you show me what else to do?"

Measures of Rehearsal and Transmission

"Behavior rehearsal" refers to reproduction of any aspects of the model's distinctive neutral or aversive behaviors either in her presence while she participated with the children in the cash register game or during the interval in which the child was alone before his interaction with the clown. "Behavior transmission" was scored when the child enacted any aspects of the model's neutral or aversive behaviors directly towards the clown while showing her the game. Because the referents for behavior rehearsal and transmission involved the presence or absence of clear overt behaviors (e.g., marching, counting) scoring was unambiguous. Independent scoring was done by the experimenter and the confederate who served as clown and yielded perfect agreement with only one exception. In the transmission phase the confederate recorded her independent scoring of the child's behavior at the end of her interaction with him. After the experimental procedure was completed each child obtained toys and warm approval for his performance in a brief play session.

Results

Twenty-six children, or almost 50% of the total, did not rehearse or transmit either neutral or aversive behaviors. The percentage of children in each treatment condition who reproduced none of the model's behaviors was 21 in the high reward-high control group, 50 in the high reward-low control group, 64 in the low reward-high control group, and 50 in the low reward-low control group. Because of this highly skewed distribution the data were analyzed with chi-square tests.[2] Inspection of the data for sex differences indicated no trends, and scores for males and females were therefore combined. Chi-square comparisons between treatment conditions were computed separately for neutral and aversive behaviors and for behavior rehearsal and behavior transmission. In view of the lack of appropriate eliciting stimuli during the rehearsal phase it was not expected that "storewrecker" would be repeated, and indeed only one child did so, all other rehearsals of aversive behaviors consisting of slowly counting "1, 2, 3," aloud in the manner modeled by the experimenter during the imposed delay periods. In contrast, during the transmission phase, children called the clown a storewrecker and imposed delay periods on him by counting repetitiously with approximately equal frequency.[3] With the exception of the virtual absence of "storewrecker" responses during rehearsal, inspection of the data for reproduction of each separate aspect of the model's neutral behaviors on the one hand, and her aversive behaviors on the other, revealed no systematic pattern differences within these two classes of behavior. Therefore these separate aspects were combined, and the four final scores assigned to each child indicated the presence or absence of imitative neutral behavior, and imitative aversive behaviors, respectively, computed for the rehearsal phase and the transmission phase separately.[4]

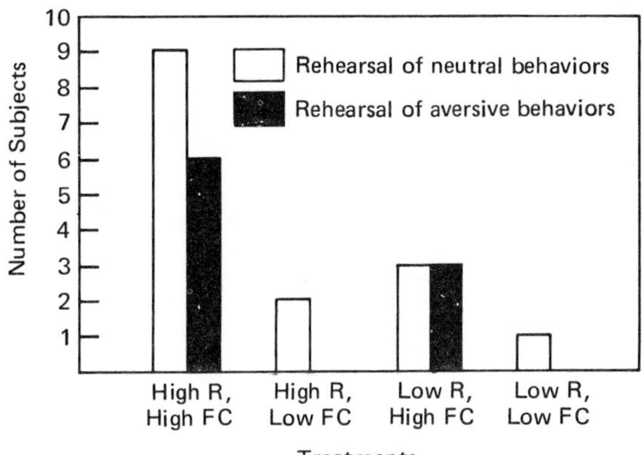

Figure 1 *Number of subjects rehearsing neutral and aversive behaviors as a function of the model's rewardingness (R) and future control (FC).*

Behavior Rehearsal

Figure 1 shows the number of subjects in each treatment condition who rehearsed neutral and aversive behaviors. Chi-square tests comparing the relevant treatment groups and treatment combinations on rehearsal of each class of behavior are included in Table 1. As predicted, significantly more children rehearsed both aversive ($p < .025$) and neutral ($p < .005$) behaviors when the model was both highly rewarding and had future control than when her rewardingness and control were low.

Comparisons of the two high-control groups showed that rewardingness significantly affected the rehearsal of neutral ($\chi^2 = 3.65$, $p < .05$) but not aversive behavior ($\chi^2 = .65$), although the trend was in the same direction for aversive behavior. That is, with high control, high as opposed to low rewardingness produced greater rehearsal of neutral behavior but the effect was not significant for aversive behavior. Likewise, significantly more subjects in the two high-reward groups combined rehearsed neutral ($p < .05$) but not aversive ($\chi^2 = .53$) behaviors than in the two low-reward conditions combined.

In the high reward-high control group, more subjects rehearsed both aversive ($\chi^2 = 5.30$, $p < .025$)

[2] Chi squares were corrected for continuity whenever *df* was 1 and the expected frequency in any cell was less than 10. All *p* values are based on one-tailed tests.

[3] During the transmission phase the clown was not given a toy and therefore subjects did not have an opportunity to remove it in the manner used by the model towards the child during the initial interaction. The clown's script was designed only to elicit imitation of the model's aversive verbal behaviors, namely, the use of the label "storewrecker" and repetitious counting in the style employed by the model when she imposed delay periods on the child.

[4] The data on behavior rehearsal are based primarily on rehearsal in the model's presence. During the rehearsal phase, only four children imitated the model's behavior while alone. Of these, three rehearsed both neutral and aversive behavior whereas one rehearsed only aversive behavior. None of these four children rehearsed the model's behaviors in her presence.

Table 1 *Between-Treatment Chi-Square Comparisons of Subjects Reproducing Aversive and Neutral Behavior in Each Phase*

Treatment Comparisons	Rehearsal		Transmission	
	Aversive	Neutral	Aversive	Neutral
High reward-high control *versus* low reward-low control	5.30**	7.62****	.16	.21
High *versus* low reward	.53	3.28*	2.87*	.11
High *versus* low control	8.47****	5.83***	.32	.11

Note.—$df = 1$, p one-tailed.
* $p < .05$
** $p < .025$.
*** $p < .01$.
**** $p < .005$.

and neutral ($\chi^2 = 5.39$, $p < .025$) behaviors than in the high reward-low control group. That is, with equally high rewardingness, high as opposed to low control produced greater rehearsal of both aversive and neutral behavior. The potency of future control, with reward constant, is further demonstrated by the fact that, as predicted, significantly more children in the two high-control groups combined rehearsed both aversive ($p < .005$) and neutral ($p < .01$) behaviors than in the two low-control conditions combined. Thus, rewardingness significantly increased the rehearsal of neutral but not aversive behaviors whereas control affected the rehearsal of both aversive and neutral behaviors. It is striking that in the two low-control treatments not a single subject rehearsed aversive behavior (Figure 1).

It should also be noted that when either reward or control were low the other variable did not produce significant differences in the rehearsal of either aversive or neutral behaviors. That is, when the model's rewardingness was low, differences in her control did not affect behavior rehearsal and, conversely, when her control of the child's future was low, variations in her rewardingness did not result in significant differences in behavior rehearsal. Likewise, there were no significant differences in behavior rehearsal between treatments in which either reward or control was high when the other variable was low and the condition in which both reward and control were low. If it were possible to measure an interaction effect in these data, it would probably be sizable.

Behavior Transmission

The number of subjects in each group who transmitted neutral and aversive behaviors to the clown is shown in Figure 2. Comparison of the combined high-reward conditions with the combined low-reward groups, presented in Table 1, shows that the model's rewardingness led to greater transmission of aversive behaviors ($p < .05$) but did not affect the transmission of neutral behaviors.[5] Table 1 also shows that the model's future control did not affect the extent to which the children transmitted any of her behaviors. Likewise, the condition in which the model was both rewarding and had high control did not produce more behavior transmission than the treatment in which the model's rewardingness and control were both low.

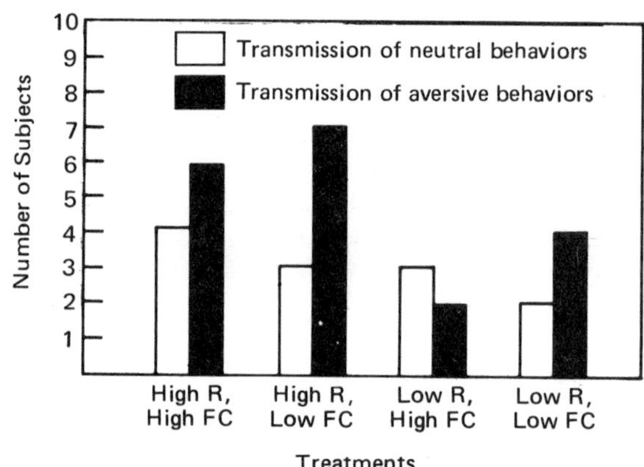

Figure 2 *Number of subjects transmitting neutral and aversive behaviors as a function of the model's rewardingness (R) and future control (FC).*

Discussion

The results demonstrate that observed behaviors may be reproduced and transmitted to others without external reinforcement for their performance, even when the observer was the object of the modeled behaviors and received aversive consequences from them. Moreover, the extent to which the model's behaviors were reproduced was affected by her rewardingness or use of noncontingent reinforcement and her future control over the subject.

The present data suggest that the degree to which subjects reproduce components of the aversive, as well as the neutral, behavior which they observed and

[5] It is possible that a fatigue factor was operative because children rarely reproduced the model's behaviors in more than one phase. Only 22% of the children who rehearsed the model's aversive behaviors and 33% who rehearsed her aversive behaviors subsequently transmitted these behaviors. Such a fatigue factor may account for the lack of differences between treatments in the transmission of neutral behaviors.

whose outcomes they directly experienced, is determined, in part, by the characteristics of the social agent who initially performed the behaviors. It is noteworthy that the percentage (34) of transmitted aversive behavior exceeded the percentage (21) of transmitted neutral behavior.

The obtained results support theoretical formulations stressing the rewardingness of the model and his power as determinants of the degree to which his behavior is adopted and indicate that both variables are useful for an adequate theory of imitation. The findings indicate, however, that these two variables have somewhat different effects as a function of the type of behavior displayed by the model and the stimulus situation in which the subject reproduces it. Both reward and control significantly affected the rehearsal of neutral behavior. Aversive behaviors were rehearsed only when the model had high control, and even with a highly rewarding model not a single child rehearsed them if the model's control was low. Both neutral and aversive behavior rehearsal were rare in all conditions in which either reward or control was low (see Figure 1). Indeed, when reward was low, variations in control did not significantly affect behavior rehearsal; conversely, when control was low, variations in reward did not produce differences in rehearsal. The fact that the differences produced in behavior rehearsal by one variable were enhanced by the presence of the other suggests that reward from the model may be a necessary condition for the effectiveness of his control and likewise that a rewarding model who has little control over the subject's future resources is no more effective than one who is not rewarding and does not have control.

In contrast, the transmission of the model's behavior by the child to another person was affected only by the model's rewardingness and not by his future control. Children who had been exposed to a noncontingently rewarding model transmitted components of her aversive behavior to another person more frequently than those who had received little noncontingent reinforcement. Although not impressively strong, this result was significant, whereas there was no indication that the model's future control over the child affected the extent to which he transmitted the model's behavior. Indeed, rewardingness and future control may have opposite effects on the transmission of aversive behavior, and these antagonistic effects may have tended to cancel each other. Exposure to a noncontingently rewarding model may have disinhibited the children about transmitting aversive behaviors to another person, whereas exposure to a model who had great control over the child's future may have served to inhibit the transmission of such aggressive behavior, even in the physical absence of the model. Calling an adult, albeit one dressed as a clown, a "storewrecker" and making him wait while the child repetitiously counts "1, 2, 3" is unlikely to incur the pleasure of a "new nursery school teacher" even if the same behavior was originally displayed by her. To be sure, the model was absent in this phase of the study but it is not unlikely that the child's behavior was influenced by expectations concerning what would please her. Subjects may also have feared that the clown would report their behavior to the teacher. Fear of negative consequences from the model for aggression to the other adult would inhibit children who believed the model was their new teacher more than those who believed she was about to leave their school forever. Although the differences were not significant, children transmitted aversive behaviors must frequently when the model had been rewarding and had low control and least frequently when she was not rewarding but had high control (see Figure 2). These trends support the interpretation that rewardingness disinhibited the children, thus enhancing transmission of aversive behaviors, whereas control over the children's future inhibited the transmission of aversive behaviors because of the greater likelihood of delayed negative consequences from the powerful model.

The results on transmission of aversive behaviors are in direct opposition to those anticipated by theories of defensive identification with the aggressor. Such formulations predict that the punitive behaviors displayed by a highly powerful, and thus potentially threatening, model would be transmitted most frequently. Instead, the data indicate that such transmission was facilitated by the model's rewardingness, irrespective of her control over the subject. The effects of high control when the model himself strongly encourages and disinhibits the subjects about transmitting punitive behaviors remain unknown and merit investigation.

An attempt was made in the present study to determine whether the two variables of rewardingness and control affect only the child's performance of a model's behavior or whether they affect the acquisition or learning of those behaviors. If the obtained treatment effects were due to differences in learning, these were probably mediated by differences in the amount of attention given the model as a function of her manipulated social characteristics. It is plausible that a new teacher or rewarding adult was more closely observed than a stranger or nonrewarding adult. Immediately after the transmission phase the child was asked by both the model and the clown to recall what had happened when the model had first showed him how to play store. For each item of the model's behavior which the child correctly recalled he was given an attractive sticker and warmly praised. There were no differences between the groups in the number of children recalling either aversive or neutral behaviors, although there was a slight, but not significant, trend for more children in the low reward-high control group to recall neutral behavior. These data were considered unsatisfactory, however, since many of the children who reproduced behavior did not recall it. This was true of 40% of the children with respect to aversive behavior and 50% of the children with respect to neutral behavior. In spite of their obvious inadequacy as a measure of total learning, it is clear from these data that the behaviors which the children learned considerably exceeded those which they performed. Thus 21% of the subjects recalled aspects of the model's aversive behavior that they did not perform while 25% recalled aspects of the model's neutral behavior that they did not perform. In addition, of the 26 subjects who performed none of the model's behaviors, only 11 were unable to recall any of her behaviors. The discrepancy between performed and acquired behaviors was most striking in the low reward-high control group. Whereas only 5 subjects performed aspects of the model's behavior, 6 who did not perform it recalled it. The deficiencies of the measure prevent firm conclusions, but these data are suggestive that the obtained differences between the experimental groups reflect differences in performance and not in acquisition.

References

ARONFREED, J. The origin of self-criticism. *Psychological Review*, 1964, *71*, 193–218.

BANDURA, A., and HUSTON, ALETHA C. Identification as a process of incidental learning. *Journal of Abnormal and Social Psychology*, 1961, *63*, 311–318.

BANDURA, A., and WALTERS, R. H. *Social learning and personality development.* New York: Holt, Rinehart and Winston, 1963.

BETTELHEIM, B. Individual and mass behavior in extreme situations. *Journal of Abnormal and Social Psychology*, 1943, *38*, 417–452.

FREUD, ANNA *The ego and the mechanisms of defense.* (Originally published in 1936) New York: International Universities Press, 1946.

MACCOBY, ELEANOR E. Role-taking in childhood and its consequences for social learning. *Child Development*, 1959, *30*, 239–252.

MOWRER, O. H. *Learning theory and personality dynamics.* New York: Ronald Press, 1950.

MUSSEN, P. H., and DISTLER, L. Masculinity, identification, and father-son relationships. *Journal of Abnormal and Social Psychology*, 1959, *59*, 350–356.

SEARS, R. R. Identification as a form of behavioral development. In D. B. Harris (Ed.), *The concept of development.* Minneapolis: University of Minnesota Press, 1957. Pp. 149–161.

WHITING, J. W. M., and CHILD, I. L. *Child training and personality.* New Haven: Yale University Press, 1953.

Bandura and Perloff compare reinforcement delivered by the experimenter's decision with reinforcement whose conditions are set by the subject himself. As in the previous paper, the experimental conditions focused on the subject's social history as the variable responsible for the efficacy of the reinforcing system. The experimenters discovered that each subject came to the experiment with an existing disposition to do certain amounts of work for a given amount of reinforcement. Those that set their own standards sustained their effort at the same level as those whose standards were set for them by the experimenters.

The experiment makes use of an experimental technique called "yoked control," frequently used in animal experiments to separate the effects of the contingency of reinforcement from its frequency. The use of this technique in semi-naturalistic experiments with children illustrates one of the ways in which animal laboratory experiments have contributed to the study of human behavior.

19 Relative Efficacy of Self-Monitored and Externally Imposed Reinforcement Systems[1]

ALBERT BANDURA
BERNARD PERLOFF

It has been abundantly documented by research that behavior is governed to some extent by its consequences. However, investigations of reinforcement processes have involved limited forms of reinforcing feedback, characteristically produced by externally controlled operations in which an experimenter imposes a particular contingency upon an organism and delivers reinforcing stimuli whenever the appropriate responses are displayed. While this system of behavioral control may be adequate in accounting for responsivity in infrahuman organisms, it is considerably less efficacious when applied to human functioning which is self-regulated to a greater degree. Unlike rats or chimpanzees, persons typically set themselves certain standards of behavior, and generate self-rewarding or self-punishing consequences depending upon how their behavior compares to their self-prescribed demands.

In recent years there have been numerous investigations of the conditions governing the acquisition of behavioral standards and self-reinforcing responses (Bandura, Grusec, and Menlove, 1967; Bandura and Kupers, 1964; Bandura and Whalen, 1966; Marston, 1965; Mischel and Liebert, 1966). Although these studies have shown that after persons adopt a self-monitoring system their performances arouse positive and negative self-evaluative reactions, there has been no adequate demonstration that self-administered consequences do, in fact, possess reinforcing capabilities. The major purpose of the present study was therefore to test the efficacy of self-monitored reinforcement, and to compare it to that of an externally imposed system of reinforcement.

A self-reinforcing event includes several subsidiary processes, some of which have been extensively investigated in their own right. First, it involves a *self-prescribed standard of behavior* which serves as the criterion for evaluating the adequacy of one's performances. The standard-setting component has received considerable attention in studies of aspiration level.

[1] This research was supported by Public Health Research Grant M-5162 and by Predoctoral Fellowship FI-MH-34,248 from the National Institute of Mental Health.

In the case of most performances, objective criteria of adequacy are lacking and hence, the attainments of other persons must be utilized as the norm against which meaningful self-evaluations can be made. Thus, for example, a student who achieves a score of 120 points on an examination, and whose aspirations are to exceed modal levels, would have no basis for either positive or negative self-reactions without knowing the accomplishments of others. A self-reinforcing event, therefore, often involves a *social comparison process.*

Third, the *reinforcers are under the person's own control;* and fourth, *he serves as his own reinforcing agent.* These various defining characteristics guided both the form of the self-monitored reinforcement system and the types of controls that were instituted.

The capacity to maintain effortful behavior over time is perhaps the most important attribute of a reinforcement operation, and consequently it was this property that was tested in the present investigation. Children performed a task in which they could achieve progressively higher scores by turning a wheel on a mechanical device. Subjects in the self-monitored reinforcement condition selected their own performance standard and rewarded themselves whenever they attained their self-prescribed criterion. Children assigned to an externally imposed reinforcement condition were yoked to the self-reward group so that the same performance standard was set for them and the reinforcers were automatically delivered whenever they reached the predetermined level.

In order to ascertain whether subjects' behavioral productivity was due to the operation of contingent self-reinforcement or to gratitude for the rewards that were made available, children in an incentive-control group performed the task after they had received the supply of rewards on a noncontingent basis. A fourth group worked without any incentives to estimate the response maintenance value of the task itself.

It was predicted that both self-monitored and externally imposed reinforcement systems would sustain substantially more behavior than conditions in which rewards were bestowed noncontingently or were ab-

From the *Journal of Personality and Social Psychology,* 1967, *7,* 111–116.

sent altogether. No hypothesis was put forward concerning the relative efficacy of the two systems of reinforcement, since there exists no adequate theoretical basis for a differential prediction.

Method

Subjects. The subjects were 40 boys and 40 girls drawn from two elementary schools in a lower middle-class area. The children's ages ranged from 7 to 10 years.

Apparatus. The apparatus consisted of a rectangular box, the front face of which contained a vertical plastic-covered aperture ½ inch wide by 16 inches high divided into four equal sections. Contained within this upright column were four score-indicator lamps, each one capable of illuminating one and only one of the translucent sections. Directly adjacent to the sections were mounted, in ascending order, the corresponding numbers 5, 10, 15, and 20, signifying four performance levels.

The score indicator lamps were activated in an ascending order by turning a wheel located at the bottom of the apparatus. It required eight complete rotations of the wheel to advance 5 points, so that a total of 32 cranking responses was necessary to attain a 20-point score.

A criterion-selector switch, which could be turned to any one of four positions corresponding to the scores next to the lights, was mounted on the front panel of the apparatus. The electrical circuit was so designed that whenever the selected performance standard was attained a chime sounded and the lights were automatically extinguished, signifying the completion of the trial. For example, in the case where a 20-point standard was chosen, the lamps adjacent to the numbers 5, 10, 15, and 20 would be illuminated after 8, 16, 24, and 32 rotations of the wheel, respectively, and then all of them would simultaneously extinguish.

Contained within the upright section was an automatic chip dispenser which delivered plastic tokens into a bowl mounted in front of the apparatus. The bountiful supply of tokens was hidden from view since their public display would not only provide children with a basis for comparing their earned rewards with the maximum possible, but it might also produce erroneous hypotheses about normative performance on this task. These factors, if uncontrolled, could have served as extraneous determinants of responsivity in the contingent-reinforcement conditions.

Located above the chip receptacle was a button which, when pressed, released a token into the bowl. A remote control device was constructed that was capable of performing the same operations as the selector switch and the token delivery button, and when necessary, rendering them inoperative.

Procedure. The introductory phase of the experiment was the same for all subjects. The children were brought individually to a mobile laboratory, ostensibly to test some game equipment. After the experimenter explained and demonstrated the operation of the apparatus, the children were given a practice trial to familiarize themselves with the task.

Small plastic tokens served as the reinforcers or incentives in those treatment conditions that required them. Children who received contingent reinforcement—either self-administered or externally applied—were informed that the tokens would later be exchanged for prizes, and the more tokens they obtained the more valuable the redeemable prizes. The incentive control subjects, who were given tokens on a noncontingent basis, were also informed that the chips they possessed would be traded later for prizes.

Several procedures were instituted in order to remove any extraneous social influences on subjects' responsivity. It was explained to children in all groups that they would perform the task alone in the room because the experimenter had some other work to do, and they might work at it as long as they wished. They were asked to notify the experimenter, who was in another room of the mobile laboratory, after they no longer wished to continue the activity. Moreover, children in the self-reinforcement condition selected their performance standard after the experimenter had departed to remove any concern that the experimenter might evaluate their behavioral productivity from the number of tokens accumulated, the children were instructed to place the banks in which they deposited their tokens in a sealed paper bag; a second experimenter would collect the banks later that day and return with the prizes in a few weeks. Finally, to control for the possibility that children's response output might be partly determined by the classroom activities they were missing, subjects in all four conditions were tested during the same instructional periods.

Children in the *self-monitored reinforcement* condition were informed that they would have to decide which performance standard they wished to set for themselves, and then to turn the selector switch to that level. In addition, they were instructed to treat themselves to tokens whenever they attained their self-imposed standard. Since these subjects had full control over the token rewards, they were free to choose their own magnitude of self-compensation on any given trial.

The children were further told that after they had selected the performance level they desired to attain, they could, if they wished, change it once, but only once, during the remainder of the session. This procedure was employed for two reasons: first, observation of self-reinforcing behavior occurring under naturalistic conditions reveals that individuals rarely shift their behavioral standards capriciously. Rather, persons usually adhere to their adopted standards and change them only as a result of cumulative feedback experiences. Therefore, an effort was made to elicit from children criterion-selection behavior which could be somewhat analogous to that occurring in everyday life.

The second reason for allowing the self-reinforcement group only one modification in their standards was related to the yoking requirement of the experiment. In order to control for the influence of behavioral standards upon responsivity across the four treatments, the performance requirements adopted by a child in the self-reward group were applied to the subject paired with him in each of the remaining conditions. Thus, for example, if a particular child in the self-monitoring group initially selected a criterion of 15 and after 20 trials lowered it to 10, this same pattern of standards was set for his yoked counterpart in each of the three comparison groups.

It is possible that any one of the children in the other conditions might persist longer than the self-reward subject to whom he was matched. If the standard selection had been highly changeable, there would be no basis for deciding that criterion to impose upon him for the remainder of the session. The limitation that standards be modified only once created a situation in which most self-reward children effected their allotted change before terminating the session, thus establishing the final performance requirement. In fact, 16 of 20 subjects had made the change before discontinuing the task. Therefore, it was meaningful to apply the standard last employed by the self-reward subject to children in the other conditions who might display more endurance than their matched partner.

After the instructions were completed, the children were handed a token bank, and left alone to perform the task as long as they wished.

Children in the *externally imposed reinforcement* system were yoked according to the procedure described above, so that the performance standard was fixed for them and the tokens were automatically delivered by the machine whenever they reached the prescribed performance level. They also received the same magnitude of reward as children in the self-reinforcement condition, that is, if a subject in the self-reward group treated himself to two tokens on a given trial, the machine would dispense two chips on the same trial to the paired counterpart in the external-reinforcement condition.

Subjects in this group were told that the machine determined the performance standard, and upon reaching it the tokens were automatically delivered. The token dispenser and the standard setting were, in fact, controlled by the experimenter from a remote console in an adjoining observation room.

Children in the "inheritance" or *incentive-control* condition were given at the beginning of the session the entire amount of tokens accumulated by their partner in the self-reward group. As in the previous treatment, the children were told that the machine regulated the performance standards operative at any given time. Another *control group* of subjects performed the task without receiving any tokens whatsoever to evaluate the response maintenance capacity of the game itself.

There are two important elements within a self-reinforcing event whose independent effects must be assessed before persistence of self-reinforced behavior can be meaningfully interpreted. These are (*a*) the self-imposition of an achievement standard, and (*b*) the self-administration of rewards. In order to examine the performance increments, if any, due to imposing a standard alone, a second study was conducted. The behavioral output of 10 children allowed to select the performance standard for which they endeavored was compared to that of 10 yoked subjects for whom the same standard was externally imposed; neither group, however, received any token rewards.

Dependent Measures. The number of cranking responses performed by the children, which constitutes the major dependent variable, was mechanically recorded. In addition, the experimenter recorded the performance standards selected by the self-reward children, and the number of reinforcers that they administered to themselves on each trial. A second observer, who scored independently the latter responses of 15 subjects, was in perfect agreement with the experimenter.

Results

Behavioral Productivity. Figure 1 presents the mean number of effortful cranking responses performed by boys and girls in each of the four conditions of the main experiment. Analysis of variance of these data disclosed a highly significant main effect due to reinforcement conditions ($F = 15.56$; $p < .001$).

In order to determine the specific differences contributing to the overall treatment effect, separate t tests were computed for pairs of conditions. These analyses revealed that self-monitored and externally imposed reinforcement were equally efficacious ($t = 1.62$), but both reinforcement systems sustained substantially more behavior than either noncontin-

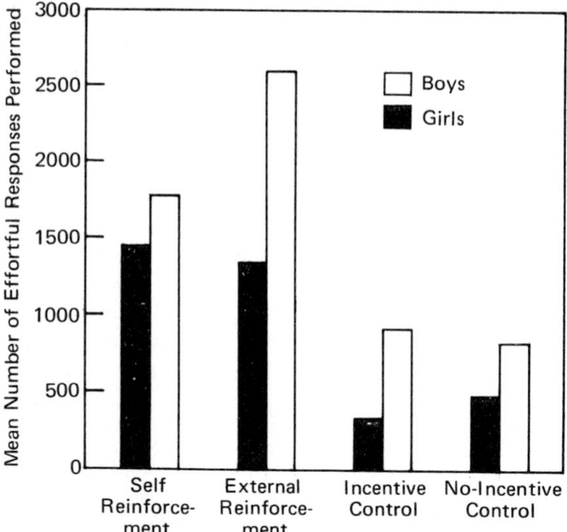

Figure 1 *Mean number of responses performed as a function of sex and type of reinforcement system.*

gent rewards or a nonreward condition. Children who reinforced their own behavior generated significantly more responses than children in the incentive-control group ($t = 3.91$; $p < .001$), or the no-incentive condition ($t = 3.87$; $p < .001$). The corresponding t values for comparisons between external reinforcement and the incentive-control and no-incentive-control groups were $t = 5.53$ ($p < .001$) and $t = 5.49$ ($p < .001$), respectively. It is also interesting to note that rewarding subjects noncontingently did not produce a significant increment in performance as revealed by comparison with the behavior of children who performed the task without any external incentives ($t = 0.04$).

The analysis also revealed that boys generated more responses than girls ($F = 13.09$; $p < .001$). Although no significant interaction effect was obtained between sex and treatment conditions, external reinforcement produced more behavior in boys ($t = 2.45$; $p < .05$) than the self-monitored system.

Children who set their own performance standards without engaging in self-reinforcement produced a mean number of 369 cranking responses, whereas the corresponding mean for the yoked controls was 586. Statistical analysis of these scores yielded no significant difference ($F = 1.56$) between the groups, thus indicating that self-imposition of a standard alone has response maintenance value.

Self-Imposition of Performance Demands. The four performance standards employed in the present experiment essentially correspond to advancing fixed-ratio schedules of 8, 16, 24, and 32 responses for each self-reinforcement. Table 1 presents the standards initially adopted by children in the self-monitoring condition, the performance demands that

Table 1 *Self-Imposed Standards and Associated Magnitude of Self-Reward*

Ss	First Standard	Mean Number of Rewards	Second Standard	Mean Number of Rewards
Boys				
1	10	1.00	No change	
2	10	1.00	5	1.09
3	15	1.00	20	1.18
4	15	1.00	20	1.00
5	15	0.98	No change	
6	20	1.11	5	1.02
7	20	1.00	10	1.06
8	20	1.00	10	0.90
9	20	1.00	15	1.00
10	20	1.00	No change	
Girls				
1	10	1.00	15	1.00
2	10	1.11	20	1.14
3	15	1.00	5	1.04
4	15	1.00	20	1.00
5	15	1.04	20	1.12
6	15	1.00	No change	
7	20	1.00	5	1.05
8	20	1.00	5	0.93
9	20	1.21	5	1.02
10	20	1.00	10	1.00

they imposed upon themselves in later phases of the experiment, and the average magnitude of self-reward associated with the achievement of each standard.

It is apparent from these data that the children did not behave in ways that would maximize rewards. Not a single child chose the lowest ratio schedule, and approximately half the children self-prescribed the most austere schedule of self-reinforcement (i.e., 32 responses for each self-reward). Moreover, a third of the children subsequently altered their initial standard to a higher level, without a significant commensurate increase in amount of self-reward, thereby imposing upon themselves a more unfavorable work-to-reinforcement ratio.

It is also interesting to note that three children occasionally did not reward themselves after attaining their chosen criterion. In two of the three cases this occurred after they had reduced their performance standard drastically. At times these children apparently did not regard their low performances as sufficiently meritorious to warrant self-reward.

Discussion

Results of this study disclose that self-monitored reinforcement possesses considerable behavior maintenance value. Moreover, the high response productivity engendered by this system was not due to merely the self-imposition of a performance standard, or availability of positive incentives.

Although self-regulated and externally imposed reinforcement did not differ in their capacity to sustain behavior, there was some suggestive evidence that, within the age range studied, boys might be more responsive under conditions of externally determined than of self-governed reinforcement, while for girls both systems are equally efficacious. These findings are consistent with those of developmental studies (Sears, Rau, and Alpert, 1965), showing that sex differences in adult-role-behavior and various indexes of self-control generally favor the girls. The obtained sex difference in response productivity under all treatment conditions is most likely due to the fact that the task required some physical effort, and consequently the boys' higher output simply reflects their greater strength.

A supplementary finding of considerable interest is the prevalence with which children imposed upon themselves highly unfavorable schedules of reinforcement. This behavior is all the more striking considering that the self-imposition of high performance demands occurred in the absence of any social surveillance and under high permissiveness for selfreward. Evidence obtained from experiments investigating the acquisition of self-reinforcing behavior (Bandura and Kupers, 1964; Bandura and Whalen, 1966; Bandura, and Grusec, and Menlove, 1967) throws some light on the probable mechanism governing this apparently irrational behavior.

The above studies demonstrate that after a person has adopted a standard of what constitutes a worthy performance, attainments that fall short of self-prescribed norms generate negative self-evaluative reactions, whereas those that match or exceed the guiding standard give rise to positive self-evaluations. Hence, under conditions where persons are provided with ample opportunities to optimize their material outcomes by engaging in behavior which has low self-regard value, strong conflicting tendencies are likely to be aroused. On the one hand, individuals are tempted to maximize rewards at minimum effort costs to themselves, but on the other hand, low quality performances produce negative self-evaluative consequences which, if sufficiently strong, may inhibit generous self-compensation. Indeed, many of the children in the experiment set themselves performance requirements that incurred high effort costs at minimum material recompense. These findings are at variance with predictions from reward-cost theories unless these formulations are extended to include the self-esteem costs of rewarding devalued behavior.

The foregoing discussion has been primarily concerned with conflicts that might arise between two forms of self-reinforcing tendencies and how their resolution results in selective self-reinforcement under the discriminative control of performance standards. Of equal importance is the recurring phenomenon in which self-generated consequences conflict with externally occurring outcomes, as when certain behaviors are reinforced by particular social agents, but if carried out would give rise to self-critical reactions. Conversely, response patterns may be effectively maintained by self-reinforcement operations under conditions of minimal external support. It is perhaps due to the stabilizing effects of self-reinforcement that persons do not ordinarily behave like weathervanes in the face of conflicting patterns of external contingencies which they repeatedly encounter in their social environment.

In view of the demonstrated efficacy of self-monitored systems, it would be of interest to explore further the extent to which self-reinforcement may substitute for, supplement, or override the effects of externally occurring outcomes. It would likewise be of considerable import to determine the degree to which overt behavior can be regulated by convert self-reinforcing operations which rely upon self-generated symbolic consequences in the form of self-satisfaction, esteem-enhancing reactions, or self-deprecation.

Although many children selected unusually high performance standards for themselves and did not lower them to enhance their fortunes, other children self-imposed equally lofty standards of achievement but later settled for a relatively mediocre level of productivity. Further research is needed to establish the conditions determining both the initial imposition of behavioral requirements for self-reward and the direction in which self-reinforcement contingencies might subsequently be altered.

References

BANDURA, A., GRUSEC, J. E., and MENLOVE, F. L. Some social determinants of self-monitoring reinforcement systems. *Journal of Personality and Social Psychology,* 1967, *5,* 449–455.

BANDURA, A., and KUPERS, C. J. The transmission of patterns of self-reinforcement through modeling. *Journal of Abnormal and Social Psychology,* 1964, *69,* 1–9.

BANDURA, A., and WHALEN, C. K. The influence of antecedent reinforcement and divergent modeling cues on patterns of self-reward. *Journal of Personality and Social Psychology,* 1966, *3,* 373–382.

MARSTON, A. R. Imitation, self-reinforcement, and reinforcement of another person. *Journal of Personality and Social Psychology,* 1965, *2,* 225–261.

MISCHEL, W., and LIEBERT, R. M. Effects of discrepancies between observed and imposed reward criteria on their acquisition and transmission. *Journal of Personality and Social Psychology,* 1966, *3,* 45–53.

SEARS, R. R., RAU, L., and ALPERT, R. *Identification and child rearing.* Stanford: Stanford University Press, 1965.

Early Socialization

4

In recent years, a great deal of research with children has involved not just observations but actual experimental control of the child's behavior. This chapter samples some of those studies which emphasize the conditions that prompt and maintain social behaviors in children.

Sigmund Freud was one of the first to draw attention to the profound impact that early life experiences have upon later personality development. The pattern of social influences that shapes the child's behavior may be called the early socialization process. We are in agreement with Freud that early socialization represents a period during which the more enduring aspects of the individual's behavioral repertoire are developed. Whether one can account verbally (consciously) for these early experiences at a later time is the issue to which psychoanalysis is addressed. Regardless of the conceptual terms we use to describe the development of the child, however, almost all psychologists believe that what a person learns in adulthood consists mainly of an overlay upon the behaviors that he has acquired through the early influence of parents, friends, and teachers. For this reason alone, it is important to understand the early social interactions that shape the individual's behavior.

The explanation of a child's early behavior in reinforcement terms is not as simple as it may at first appear. Not only may reinforcers be delivered on simple as well as compound schedules, but characteristics of both the agent and the recipient, such as age, sex, and socioeconomic status, interact to determine the effectiveness of the reinforcing process. The papers in this section deal with several such variables as they relate to social reinforcement with children.

Characteristics of the Social Agent and Recipient

Stevenson draws an interesting parallel between some principles of Freudian psychology and the influence of age and sex on social behavior and its reinforcement. As children progress through the several stages of what Freud called "psychosexual development," they react differently to their mothers and their fathers. The Oedipal period, in particular, is one in which the child becomes strongly attracted to the parent of the opposite sex. Reinforcers provided by the father during these years should more effectively influence certain behaviors of girls in the family, whereas those provided by the mother should be more effective with boys.

In Stevenson's experiment, children between the ages of three and ten played a game of dropping colored marbles through holes in a flat surface. Following a period in which the experimenters observed each child's base rate without attempting to influence it, male and female experimenters reinforced the child's performance verbally. The frequency of dropping marbles into the holes was the dependent variable of the experiment. As predicted, reinforcement by females enhanced the performances of both three- and four-year-old boys and girls. At six and seven years, however, the experimenters were most effective when they were reinforcing a child of the opposite sex. Although the results elaborate Freud's theory, the author chooses to explain them in terms of social learning.

20 *Social Reinforcement with Children as a Function of CA, Sex of E, and Sex of S*[1]

HAROLD W. STEVENSON[2]

The purpose of this study is to investigate the effectiveness of social reinforcement in modifying children's performance in a simple game. The variables of primary concern are the sex of the adult providing the social reinforcement, and the sex and age of the child being studied.

In two recent studies with preschool children (Gewirtz, 1954; Gewirtz and Baer, 1958), women were found to have a significantly greater effect on the performance of boys than of girls, and men were found to have a greater effect on the performance of girls than of boys. Two types of tasks were used: easel painting in the presence of a permissive adult and a simple game in which one of two alternative responses was socially reinforced by the adult. A significant interaction between sex of adult and sex of child was found for amount of attention seeking while painting and for the frequency with which the socially reinforced response was made. Although, as the authors indicate, other interpretations may account for the results, the Oedipal theory of Freud

[1] This study was supported by Grant M-3519 from the National Institute of Mental Health.

[2] The assistance of Richard Strate in the conduct of this study, and of Raymond Collier in the analysis of the data, is gratefully acknowledged.

From the *Journal of Abnormal and Social Psychology*, 1961, *63*, 147–154.

provides perhaps the most meaningful focus about which to view the data.

The results of these two studies lead one to speculate further about the possible effects of social reinforcement by adults on the performance of children of different ages. Again, even though other views may lead to similar predictions, Freudian theory provides the most integrated series of hypotheses for making such predictions.

During the early years of childhood the principal caretaker of both boys and girls is usually the mother. Through her role in satisfying the child's basic needs, the mother becomes the primary love-object of the young child, and her presence and comments acquire the capacity for reinforcing behaviors not associated with primary drives. Assuming the relationship with the mother generalizes to other women, social reinforcement provided by women should be more effective in modifying the performance of both young boys and girls (2–4 years) than social reinforcement provided by men. As the girl grows older and enters the Oedipal period a shift in object-choice from the mother to the father begins to occur. During this period the boy not only fails to change his love-object from the mother to the father, but comes to view the father negatively. Results such as those found in the Gewirtz studies are predicted for this stage (4–7 years); that is, women are predicted to have a significantly greater effect on the performance of boys than of girls, and men are predicted to have a significantly greater effect on the performance of girls than of boys. Later, the Oedipal relationships decrease in strength and the pattern of object-choice changes. The girl re-establishes a close affective relationship with the mother, and the boy shifts his object-choice from the mother to the father. During late childhood (7–11 years), women should be more effective reinforcing agents for girls' behavior than for boys', and men should now be more effective reinforcing agents for boys' behavior than for girls'.

The present study attempts to investigate the validity of such predictions by testing children at three age levels (3–4 years, 6–7 years, and 9–10 years) in a simple game in which either a male or female experimenter (*E*) makes supportive comments during the subject's (S's) performance. In order to reduce the problems resulting from having only one male and one female *E*, six *Es* of each sex were employed. The use of more than one *E* also makes it possible to determine whether there are significantly different effects associated with different *Es*.

Method

Subjects. The *Ss* were 252 boys and 252 girls selected on the basis of CA. One-third of the *Ss* of each sex were within the CA range from 3–0 to 5–0 years, one-third from 6–0 to 8–0 years, and one-third from 9–0 to 11–0 years. The children were attending preschools or elementary schools in Minneapolis and St. Paul, and all of the children of the appropriate CAs in each group or class visited were used as Ss.[3] The schools in general enrolled children of average socioeconomic and intellectual level and were selected on the basis of availability rather than any other criteria.

Experimenters. The *Es* were 12 persons who were willing to perform as *Es* and who were involved in some phase of the Institute of Child Development program. The female *Es* included two graduate students in psychology, three graduate students in child development, and a secretary. The male *Es* included a graduate student in psychology, a graduate student in child development, a postdoctoral research associate in child development, and undergraduate students in psychology, sociology, and industrial education. The age range for the *Es* was 19–25 years, with a mean CA of 22.8 years.

Apparatus. The apparatus has been described in detail elsewhere (Stevenson and Fahel, 1961). It consisted essentially of a table of adjustable height with two bins, 8 × 10 inches, and a short transverse upright panel to shield *E*'s recording from S. The left bin contained approximately 1,600 orange, blue, and green marbles. The right bin was covered by a plate with six ⅝-inch holes placed randomly about the surface. Below the right bin was a mechanism whereby each marble was counted as it fell to the bottom of the bin.

Procedure. The Ss were tested individually. Each S was obtained from the classroom by *E* and taken to the experimental room, which in practically all of the schools visited was a quiet, isolated room. The *E* engaged S in friendly conversation and seated S at the table. The *E* affirmed S's age and name, and said:

> We're going to play a game. Let me tell you about it. This is called the Marble Game. See the marbles? We have blue ones and orange ones and this color green ones and this color green ones. Let me show you how to play it. The marbles go in these holes. [*E* indicated the marbles in the left bin and the holes of the plate covering the right bin.] You can put any

[3] The writer wishes to thank Judith Rosen, Barbara Knight, Kristin Arnold, Stephanie Grossman, Evelyn Stern, Norma McCoy, Richard Strate, Norman Kass, Gerald Peterson, Peder Johnson, Mervyn Bergman, and Edward Dowd who served as *Es*, and the principals and teachers of the nursery schools and elementary schools visited for their cooperation in providing children for the study.

> color marble in any hole. These are the marbles and these are the holes. Pick the marbles up one at a time and put them in the holes. Let me show you how to do it. [*E* demonstrated how the marbles could be dropped in each hole.] O.K.? I'll tell you when to stop. Now you can play the game.

The first minute of the game was used to establish a baseline rate of response for each S. During this minute *E* played the role of an attentive but nonreinforcing observer of S's performance. Care was taken not to smile or to nod approval of S's behavior during this period. After the first minute *E* continued to be attentive to S's performance and did not avoid smiling and nodding when delivering one of the statements of verbal support. Twice a minute for the next 5 minutes *E* made a supportive statement about S's performance. The statements were made after approximately 15 seconds and 45 seconds within each minute, and immediately following one of S's responses. Five statements were used: "You're doing very well," "That's very good," "You know how to play this game very well," "That's fine," "You're really good at this game." These statements were made in a predetermined random order established separately for each S. Any attempts by S to engage *E* in conversation were not responded to by *E*.

Three departures from this procedure were allowed. First, if S stopped responding for 30 seconds during the course of the game, *E* said, "I'll tell you when to stop." If S failed to resume response or if S later stopped again for 30 seconds, the game was terminated. Second, if S picked up a handful of marbles, *E* said, "Put them in one at a time." If S did not heed this instruction, S was dropped from the experiment. Third, if S stopped responding during the first minute before a supportive comment was made, S was discarded. In addition to the last two criteria, *Ss* were also discarded if there were mechanical difficulties in the apparatus, or if any difficulties arose in the experimental procedure, such as someone's interrupting the game. A total of 35 Ss were eliminated from the experiment and replaced by other Ss on these bases.

Each *E* tested seven boys and seven girls at each of the three age levels. Most of the *Es* tested children from several schools within an age level. This was desirable from the standpoint of increasing the randomness of the sample of children tested by each *E* and was necessary because of the small number of children in some of the classes or groups visited. The children were obtained either alphabetically, according to seat order, or according to which children happened to be unoccupied or not engaged in group activities at the time *E* visited the class. There was no tendency for the first *E* visiting a group to obtain a different set of children from *Es* visiting the group later. When large groups were visited, several *Es* were available so that all children in a group were tested in a fairly uninterrupted sequence.

Before beginning to test children, each *E* practiced the procedure several times with an experienced *E* as the S.

Response Measures. The number of marbles inserted during each minute of the game was recorded by *E*. The number inserted during the first minute when *E* made no supportive comments was used as an index of S's base rate of response. The base rate was subtracted from the number of marbles inserted during each subsequent minute for each S and the mean of these difference scores was used as an index of the effectiveness of the social reinforcement in modifying S's rate of response. The two measures used in the major analyses of the results were, therefore, the base rate and the mean difference score.

Results

The first prediction was that women would have a significantly greater effect than men on the performance of both boys and girls at the 3–4 year level. The mean difference score for boys and girls tested by men was −.04, and for boys and girls tested by women it was 1.38 (see Figure 1). This difference is significant at the .005 level ($t = 2.97$, $df = 166$).

In order to determine whether this difference might also be characteristic of the performance of *Ss* at the other age levels, the same comparison was made for the other ages. The mean difference score for *Ss* tested by women at the 6–7 year level was 1.29 and for Ss tested by men, .90. The difference is not significant ($t = 1.08$). The mean difference score for Ss tested by women at the 9–10 year level was .80, and for Ss tested by men, 1.55. The difference is in the opposite direction from that found for younger Ss, but is not significant ($t = 1.68$, $df = 166$, $p > .10$).

The first prediction is therefore confirmed. Social reinforcement in the present setting is more effective in modifying the rate of response of boys and girls at the 3–4 year level when it is provided by women than when it is provided by men. The difference is significant at the 3–4 year level and at none of the other CA levels.

The second prediction was that for children of 6–7 years women would have a greater effect on the performance of boys than of girls, and men would have a greater effect on the performance of girls than of boys. The mean difference score for boys tested by women was 2.18, and for girls tested by women, .40. The difference is significant at less than the .025 level ($t = 2.37$, $df = 82$). The mean difference score for girls tested by men was 1.15, and for boys tested

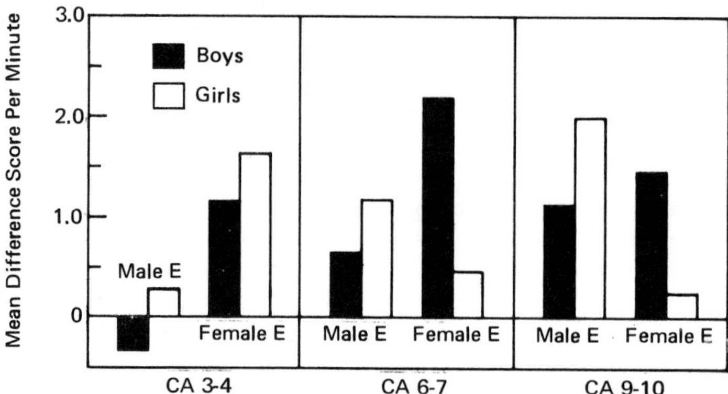

Figure 1 *The average difference score obtained for each minute of the game for each CA and for each subject sex and each experimenter (E) sex.*

by men, .64. The difference is in the predicted direction, but is not statistically significant ($t = .66$).

Again, to determine whether this effect occurs only at the 6–7 year level, the same comparisons were made at the other age levels. The difference between the mean difference scores at the 3–4 year level for boys and girls tested by women was not significant ($t = .50$). The difference between the mean difference scores for boys and girls tested by men was also not significant ($t = .54$). At the 9–10 year level, the different between the mean difference scores for boys and girls tested by women was not significant ($t = 1.27$), nor was the difference between the mean difference scores for boys and girls tested by men ($t = 1.13$).

The second prediction was thus only partly confirmed. At the 6–7 year level, and only at this CA level, women were more effective in modifying the behavior of boys than of girls. Social reinforcement provided by men did not have a significantly greater effect in modifying the behavior of girls than of boys at any of the CA levels.

The third prediction was that at the 9–10 year level boys tested by men would show a greater increment in response than would girls tested by men, and conversely, girls tested by women would show a greater increment in response than would boys tested by women. This prediction was not supported. The tendency was for the cross-sex effect suggested by the results at the 6–7 year level to be maintained at the 9–10 year level, but by the 9–10 year level the variability among Ss was so great that the differences were not statistically significant.

The average difference scores obtained for all Ss tested by men showed a consistent increase across the three age levels from −.04 to .90 to 1.55, while the average difference scores obtained for Ss tested by women showed a decrease across the three age levels from 1.38 to 1.29 to .80. The increase for the men from the 3–4 to the 9–10 year levels is highly significant ($t = 4.17$, $df = 166$, $p < .001$), but the corresponding decrease for the women is not significant ($t = 1.23$). Social reinforcement delivered by men therefore became increasingly effective as the Ss' CA increased, but no significant changes in the general effectiveness of social reinforcement delivered by women as a function of Ss' CA was found.

Base Rate. The question may be raised whether differences in performance among the various subgroups may not also have been manifest during the base rate period. The *E*s may have induced different levels of motivation during the initial stages of the task which would be reflected in different base rates of response. The data in Table 1, which presents the average base rate for each of the subgroups, indicate that this was not the case. Although, as might be expected, the rate of response increased with increasing CA, the values for the subgroups within an age range are remarkably similar. None of the tendencies found in the analysis of the difference scores is seen.

An analysis of variance of the base rates was performed to determine whether the apparent similarities in performance were indeed nonsignificant, as well as to determine whether the mean rates of response of Ss tested by different *E*s differed signifi-

Table 1 *Mean Base Rate for Each Subgroup*

Sex of *E* and *S*	3–4 yrs.	6–7 yrs.	9–10 yrs.
Male *E*			
Boys	12.4	26.0	36.0
Girls	14.4	27.1	34.0
Female *E*			
Boys	11.6	24.3	34.3
Girls	12.3	26.1	35.7

Table 2 *Analysis of Variance of Base Rate Scores*

Source	*df*	MS	Error	*F*
Sex *E* (A)	1	110.50	D	.64
Sex S (B)	1	97.78	B×D	2.01
Age S (C)	2	21137.50	C×D	1265.72**
Individual *E* (D)	10	173.66		5.25**
D_M	5	235.05		7.11**
D_F	5	112.27		3.40*
A×B	1	24.90	B×D	.51
A×C	2	34.68	C×D	2.08
B×C	2	42.03	B×C×D	.50
B×D	10	48.69		1.47
C×D	20	16.70		.50
A×B×C	2	51.10	B×C×D	.61
B×C×D	20	83.20		2.52**
B×C×D_M	10	41.63		1.26
B×C×D_F	10	124.78		3.78**
Within	432	33.05		

* $p < .01$.
** $p < .001$.

cantly. This analysis is summarized in Table 2. There was no significant difference between the base rates of boys and girls, nor between the base rates of Ss tested by men and women. The difference associated with CA is highly significant, with each age level showing an increase in rate of response.

There is a highly significant difference in the average base rates of Ss tested by different *Es*. Significant differences occur among the base rates of Ss tested both by men and by women. Since the Ss tested by each *E* were determined at random, these differences in base rates cannot be attributed to characteristics of Ss. It must be concluded that the *Es* differed in ways which had significant effects on the rate with which Ss responded.

Finally, there is a highly significant interaction between Sex of S, Age of S, and Individual *E*. It is evident in the breakdown of this interaction according to sex of *E* that the major contribution to this interaction is derived from the women *Es*. The average base rates of Ss tested by men were rather evenly distributed within each age and sex grouping. For Ss tested by women, however, the dispersion of average base rates was similar for boys and girls at the 3–4 year level, but increased more for girls than for boys at the 6–7 and 9–10 year levels.

Difference Scores. An analysis of the changes in difference scores through the period in which social reinforcement of Ss' responses occurred indicates an increase in the average difference score from .35 for the second minute to 1.30 for the sixth minute. This increase is highly significant ($t = 4.62$, $df = 503$, $p < .001$). The difference scores increased from the second through the sixth minute in 11 of the 12 subgroups. The only group in which a decrease through this period occurred was for girls at the 9–10 year level tested by women. Here the change was minimal; the average difference score for the second minute was .14, and for the sixth minute, .01.

Since the effect of social reinforcement was greatest during the sixth minute of the game, an analysis of variance was performed on the difference scores obtained for this period. Because of the lack of homogeneity of variance, a logarithmic transformation of the data was performed. The analysis is summarized in Table 3.

There was no significant difference in the sixth-minute difference scores for boys and girls or for Ss tested by men and women. There was a significant difference in the difference scores of Ss tested by individual *Es*, a significant double interaction between Individual *E* and Age of S, and a significant triple interaction between Individual *E*, Age of S, and Sex of S.

The tendency was for the dispersion of the average difference scores to increase with increasing CA. The range tended to be more restricted, however, for boys than for girls at the youngest age level and the increase in range from one age level to the other tended to be greater for boys than for girls. In general, the findings are similar to those, obtained in the analysis of the base rates in that the dispersion of average difference scores obtained for Ss tested by women tended to be greater than that obtained for Ss tested

Table 3 *Analysis of Variance of Difference Scores for Sixth Minute*

Source	*df*	MS	Error	*F*
Sex *E* (A)	1	.002	D	.15
Sex S (B)	1	.006	B×D	2.14
Age S (C)	2	.014	C×D	.14
Individual *E* (D)	10	.013		6.84***
D_M	5	.010		5.26***
D_F	5	.015		7.89***
A×B	1	.012	B×D	4.28
A×C	2	.031	C×D	.31
B×C	2	.015	B×C×D	1.78
B×D	10	.003		1.47
C×D	20	.099		52.10***
C×D_M	10	.005		2.63**
C×D_F	10	.015		7.89***
A×B×C	2	.010	B×C×D	1.19
B×C×D	20	.008		4.42***
B×C×D_M	10	.004		2.10*
B×C×D_F	10	.013		6.84***
Within	432	.002		

* $p < .05$.
** $p < .01$.
*** $p < .001$.

by men and in that the dispersion tended to be greater for girls than for boys at all ages.

An inspection of the sixth-minute difference scores indicates that there was some consistency in the ordering of the average difference scores of Ss tested by individual *Es* at the 3–4 and 9–10 year levels. Although the number of *Es* is small, rank order correlations were computed to give an indication of the degree of consistency found. The correlation for boys at the 3–4 and 9–10 year levels tested by men was .81 ($p < .05$), and for boys tested by women, .60. The correlation for girls tested by men was −.71, and for girls tested by women, −.76. In other words, the ordering of *Es* tended to be similar at the early and late ages for boys, while the ordering for girls indicated that women who produced high difference scores at the younger age levels tended to produce low difference scores at the highest age levels and vice versa.

The correlation between the number of marbles inserted during the first minute of the game and the difference score for the sixth minute was −.40. This r is highly significant ($p < .001$) and indicates a tendency for Ss with low base rates to have high increments in response and for Ss with high base rates to have lower increments in response.

Discussion

The results at the 6–7 year level are similar to those reported by Gewirtz, Baer, and Roth (1958) for 4- to 6-year-old children tested following a 20-minute period of social isolation. Since the index of the effectiveness of social reinforcement differs in the two studies, it is possible to compare the results only in terms of direction and not in terms of the absolute changes in behavior. In both studies social reinforcement provided by women had a significantly greater effect on the behavior of boys than of girls, and there is a tendency, not significant in either study, for social reinforcement provided by men to have a greater effect on the behavior of girls than of boys. The major discrepancy between the results from the two experiments is that the cross-sex effect was reliable in the Gewirtz, Baer, and Roth study only following social isolation and was not reliable when Ss were tested without such isolation. The basis of this difference is not clear, and the present data indicate that deprivation immediately prior to testing is not a necessary condition for the effect to emerge.

The results provide some support for the predictions derived from psychoanalytic theory. There is clear support of the prediction that women are more effective than men in modifying the performance of boys and girls at the 3–4 year level in this type of task. As discussed above, the results are also in line with the prediction that adults should have a greater effect on children of the opposite sex at the 6–7 year level. The results for Ss tested by men are in the appropriate direction, but are not reliable. The strong effect of women on boys' performance at this age level, as contrasted with the more moderate effect of men on girls' performance, has some basis in the Freudian assumption that the Oedipal relationship is more intense with boys than with girls. The results do not support the prediction that the behavior of children at the 9–10 year level would be modified to a greater degree by social reinforcement provided by adults of the same sex as S compared to adults of the opposite sex. The view that the 9- to 10-year-old children's close affective relationship with the like-sex parent results in adults of this sex having a greater effect on the performance of the child is not supported.

The question arises as to whether other positions than the Freudian one may not provide a more satisfactory account for the results. Gewirtz and Baer (1958) have hypothesized that the effectiveness of social reinforcement is increased by social deprivation. A simple extension of this hypothesis may account for the cross-sex effect discussed above. It may be hypothesized that the effectiveness of social reinforcement provided by an adult in modifying children's performance is a function of the degree of social deprivation children have for contacts with members of the adult's sex.

It must be assumed that during the early years of the child's life the parent functions more frequently as a caretaker than as a source of social satisfaction for the child. As discussed earlier, the effectiveness of the mother as a reinforcing agent during the early years of the child's life may be posited as being a result of her gaining in secondary reinforcing value because of her presence in the satisfaction of the child's basic needs. The father has a relatively less important role at this time and only later does he begin to play a significant part in the child's daily activities. The increased effectiveness of the male *Es* with increasing CA of the child was found in this study. As the child grows older and becomes capable of satisfying his own basic needs or of delaying gratification of his needs, the importance of both parents as social agents increases.

Social forces begin to operate after the first years to direct boys' activities towards those of other boys and men and to direct girls' activities towards those of other girls and women. Masculine contacts and behavior are reinforced for boys and not for girls, and feminine contacts and behavior are reinforced for girls and not for boys. The boy is relatively more deprived of contact with females than with males and the girl is relatively more deprived of contact with males. This is assumed to be maximal during the early school years, for it is perhaps at this time that there is the greatest emphasis placed upon the child's adopting an appropriate sex role. Because of this deprivation, the effectiveness of women as reinforcing agents for boys and of men as reinforcing agents for girls is assumed to increase. The strength of the cross-sex deprivation is assumed to be greater for boys than for girls. Feminine activies and contacts are more likely to be discouraged for boys than masculine activities and contacts are for girls. Further, the boy has had a closer relationship and more frequent contact with the mother during the first years of life than the girl has had with the father, thus being forced to decrease or relinquish such relationships and contacts should have a greater effect on boys than on girls.

This general argument leads to an odd paradox, for it would be predicted that during these years the more effective reinforcement of masculine behavior for boys would be derived from the mother and the more effective reinforcement of feminine behavior for girls would be derived from the father. It may be important, therefore, to distinguish between the model for identification and the source of reinforcement for adopting behavior congruent with this model. Although the father may provide the model for masculine behavior for the young boy, the degree to which the boy identifies with this model may be a function of the degree to which the mother reinforces masculine behavior.

The results give several indications that there are differences between boys and girls in the degree to which the characteristics of individual adults influence their performance. The adults who were effective with younger girls tended to be less effective with older girls, while the adults who were effective with younger boys tended to remain effective with older boys. In view of the fact that the performance of 3- to 4-year-old boys tested by different *Es* did not differ to so great a degree as did the performance of the young girls, it may be hypothesized that boys and girls differentiated the characteristics of the particular *Es* equally well, but that the performance of the young girls was influenced to a greater degree by the characteristics of particular *Es* than was the performance of young boys. The fact that the average difference scores obtained by the various groups of girls tended to differ to a greater degree at all age levels than did those obtained by the groups of boys indicates that the performance of girls in general was affected to a greater degree by particular characteristics of the individual *Es* than was the performance of boys. An examination of such factors as *E*'s age, appearance, experience with children, scholastic status, or scores on the MMPI gave no indication of what characteristics of the *Es* produced these differences in base rates and difference scores. Further, there are no data which clarify why men in general tended to produce more homogeneous grouping of performance in children than did women.

Summary

Six male and six female *Es* tested seven boys and seven girls at each of three age levels (3–4, 6–7, and 9–10 years) in a simple game. Following an initial minute during which a baseline for performance was established, *E* made two of five standard supportive comments about *S*'s performance each minute for the next 5 minutes. The increment in response occurring after the first minute of the game was used in the analysis of the results. The average difference score was greater for Ss tested by women than by men at the 3–4 year level, and was significantly greater for boys than for girls tested by women at the 6–7 year level. The increment was greater at the 6–7 year level for girls than for boys tested by men, but the difference was not significant. At the 9–10 year level the differences in performance associated with sex of *E* and sex of *S* were not statistically significant. An analysis of the increment of response during the sixth minute of the game indicated significant differences in the scores obtained by Ss tested by different *Es*, and significant interactions between individual *Es* and *S*'s CA, and between individual *Es*, *S*'s CA, and *S*'s sex. The results were interpreted in terms of the hypothesis that the effectiveness of social reinforcement provided by an adult is a function of the degree to which children are deprived of contact with members of the adult's sex.

References

Gewirtz, J. L. Three determinants of attention-seeking in young children. *Monographs of the Society for Research in Child Development*, 1954, *19* (2), No. 59.

Gewirtz, J. L., and Baer, D. M. The effect of brief social deprivation on behaviors for a social reinforcer. *Journal of Abnormal and Social Psychology*, 1958, *56*, 49–56.

Gewirtz, J. L., Baer, D. M., and Roth, C. H. A note on the similar effects of low social availability of an adult and brief social deprivation on young children's behavior. *Child Development*, 1958, *29*, 149–152.

Stevenson, H. W., and Fahel, Leila S. The effect of social reinforcement on the performance of institutionalized and noninstitutionalized normal and feebleminded children. *Journal of Personality*, 1961, *29*, 136–147.

Social reinforcement is a two-way street; each party to an interaction is both prompted and reinforced by the actions of the other. In most experiments, attention is focused on the behavior of the subject. The effects that the subject's performance has on the experimenter's behavior are seldom noted. The experimenter generally schedules contingencies, whereas the subject reacts to the contingencies in ways that depend upon his own characteristics. Socioeconomic status is one variable that *Sgan* hypothesizes will influence social reinforcement.

Sgan used a game situation in which the children indicated their preferences for one of two pictures and the experimenter provided either (a) continuous positive reinforcement of the child's choice, (b) a period of positive reinforcement followed by a period of disagreement with the child's choice, or (c) neutral reactions to choices made by the child. Following one of these three kinds of interactions, the children played another game in which the experimenter first indicated her own preferences among the original pictures before asking the child for his choice. The child's susceptibility to the adult's influence was measured by the number of times the child changed his previous choice to one that accorded with the choice made by the adult.

Sgan reports that both socioeconomic status and sex of subject were significant variables. The boys from working-class homes were less affected by the experimenter's preferences than either boys or girls from middle-class homes. Among the children as a group, a previously rewarding experience with the adult experimenter tended to increase the frequency with which they made later choices that corresponded to those of the adult. This tendency was less when the previous experience had included withdrawal of the adult's supportive behavior.

21 *Social Reinforcement, Socioeconomic Status, and Susceptibility to Experimenter Influence*[1]

MABEL L. SGAN

The effects of adult nurturance and its subsequent withdrawal on children's behavior has long been a topic of interest in theoretical accounts of the socialization process and retrospective studies of parent-child relationships (e.g., Bronfenbrenner, 1960, 1961; Dollard and Miller, 1950; Mussen and Distler, 1959; Payne and Mussen, 1956; Sears, Maccoby, and Levin, 1957; Whiting and Child, 1953). Results from recent experimental investigations of this issue parallel in a provocative manner some of the findings and theoretical analyses reported earlier. Thus, a number of researchers have demonstrated that the experimental introduction of nurturance enhances both imitative and simple motor learning (Bandura and Huston, 1961; Bandura, Ross, and Ross, 1961; Rosenblith, 1961; Stevenson, 1965). While nurturance has been found to be a salient factor in the modification of children's behavior, observed relationships are typically qualified by sex of the subject as well as sex of the experimenter.

Less certain is the case for the withdrawal of nurturance or social isolation. Gewirtz (1954) observed that children displayed more attention-seeking behavior in the presence of a nonresponsive adult than in the presence of an adult who devoted his complete attention to the child. In addition, the experimenters were found to be more effective with chil-

[1] This article is based on a dissertation submitted to the Graduate School of Cornell University in partial fulfillment of the requirements for the PhD degree. The author wishes to express her appreciation to the members of her dissertation committee for their generous counsel and encouragement: Urie Bronfenbrenner, chairman, Robert B. MacLeod, and Henry N. Ricciuti. The valuable assistance of Carol A. Millsom in the execution of the experiment is also gratefully acknowledged.

dren of the opposite sex than with children of the same sex as themselves. Using female experimenters, Hartup (1958) found that among nursery school children, nurturance withdrawal stimulated faster learning than consistent nurturance for girls. Results for boys were not significant, although there were indications that highly dependent boys responded to the withdrawal of nurturance in the same fashion as did the girls. The findings supplied by Rosenblith (1959, 1961) on imitative learning in kindergarten children support partially Hartup's results, but are again complicated by sex differences between subject and experimenter. For boys only, withdrawal of attention by a male model was found to produce more imitation than consistent attention. Girls, on the other hand, displayed more imitation when they were exposed to consistent attention, regardless of sex of the model. An interesting study by Stein and Wright (1964) attests to the complexity of the effects of nurturance manipulations. Increases in imitation were observed when the child reacted to nurturance withdrawal with increased dependency or when he responded to continuous nurturance with decreased dependency. Although the findings on the effects of nurturance withdrawal thus far are ambiguous, the trends reported by these investigators are intriguing and invite further research on the issue.

The experiment reported here was aimed primarily at extending social reinforcement research to children's behavior in a contrived influence situation. With the notable exception of the work of Janis and his colleagues (Janis and Hovland, 1959), comparatively few studies have examined the developmental aspects of conformity and persuasibility in young children despite the vast amount of research conducted on adults. The lag is surprising, since the latter studies indicate that exploration of this fundamental social process among young children may prove to be a fruitful source of hypotheses concerning the important features of socialization, as well as of the phenomenon in question. Specifically, the present investigation sought to determine the relative effectiveness of three different kinds of social reinforcement in inducing shifts in children's preferences toward agreement with an adult: consistent nurturance, withdrawal of nurturance, and unresponsive attention. In line with the previous research cited, it was expected that, in general, children who had previously experienced consistent nurturance from a female adult on a simple preference task would subsequently be more susceptible to that adult's influence on a similar task than children who had experienced merely unresponsive attention. Further, it was predicted that withdrawal of nurturance would be more effective than either consistent nurturance or unresponsive attention in inducing susceptibility to experimenter influence. These expectations take as their point of departure the social learning formulations developed by the Yale group (e.g., Dollard and Miller, 1950; Mowrer, 1950; Sears, 1957). The view begins with the familiar argument that the nurturant responses of parents and other adults acquire generalized secondary reinforcing properties for the child through association with primary reinforcers (Dollard and Miller, 1950; Sears, 1957). Such affectional rewards are presumed to predispose the child to imitate the behavior of the adult model for the satisfaction these cues provide (Mowrer, 1950). Once the parental characteristics have acquired positive reinforcing properties, the threat or the actual withdrawal of approval and support by an otherwise nurturant adult is believed to further stimulate the child to perform imitative responses. Thus, the child reinforces himself by continued support and a reduction in anxiety over the loss of nurturance. The child will respond with behavior that will, in his judgment, secure for him the desired warmth, approval, and support. He will tend to alter his behavior in an attempt to assure himself continued nurturance (Sears, 1957; Whiting and Child, 1953). Some empirical support for this prediction is available in the reported relationship between the use of discipline techniques involving the parent's withdrawal of love after the child's transgression and "high conscience" (Sears, Maccoby, and Levin, 1957). In summary, the present study predicted that the relative effectiveness of the three treatments in inducing susceptibility to experimenter influence would be as follows; nurturance withdrawal > nurturance > neutral.

Another variable which may contribute to differential behavior in the experimental situation is the socioeconomic background of the subject. Few studies have made explicit attempts to determine possible differences in the effect of social reinforcers as a function of social class membership. What little data exist on the issue are equivocal. Zigler and deLabry (Zigler, 1962) have observed that lower-class children were generally less responsive to verbal reinforcement in a marble-sorting task than were middle-class children. In a further analysis of two classes of verbal reinforcers, Zigler and Kanzer (1962) have reported that praise was less effective with middle-class children than were statements implying correctness of response, while the reverse relationship appeared with lower-class children. A replication of this study by Rosenhan and Greenwald (1965) failed to substantiate the major finding, although a significant interaction was found between sex of subject and socioeconomic status. Specifically, middle-class girls and lower-class boys were found to be more responsive to both kinds of reinforcers from a male experimenter than were middle-class boys and lower-class girls.

One explanation for the discrepant findings may lie in the different sampling procedures employed by the two sets of investigators. The Rosenhan-Greenwald results may possibly reflect interactions between the race and sex of examiners and subjects, inasmuch as Negro subjects were used for the lower-class group. In any event, the general social susceptibility of children of the two social classes remains an open issue. Surveys of child-rearing practices (Bronfenbrenner, 1958; Sears, Maccoby, and Levin, 1957) lead one to expect, however, that lower-class children would be less susceptible to influence attempts than their middle-class counterparts and, by inference, less responsive to nurturance and its withdrawal.

Method

Subjects. The subjects were 36 boys and 36 girls drawn from the entire first-grade population of two public schools in Ithaca, New York. Two major subgroups were counterbalanced with respect to sex of subject and socioeconomic status (SES) as determined by a modification of Warner's scale of occupational status (Warner, Meeker, and Eells, 1949). The middle-class group was composed primarily of professional, business, and managerial occupations, together with other white-collar occupations such as salesmen and clerical workers. The working-class group included blue-collar workers, ranging from carpenters and plumbers to unskilled laborers; the largest number were semiskilled workers who were not self-employed. Children who were repeating the first grade were excluded from the sample. All subjects came from intact homes of white, native-born parents. Assignment to the three treatment conditions was random.

Experimenters. Each of two female graduate students majoring in child development served with one random half of the sex-SES subgroups under each of the experimental conditions. Although they were of similar age, one of the experimenters was Caucasian, the other was Oriental. Neither of the women had had previous contact with any of the subjects.

Measure of Susceptibility to Experimenter influence. The susceptibility series was designed specifically to measure the dependent variable in this experiment. Drawn from a pool of approximately 100 pictures taken from current issues of American magazines, the 18 pairs of objects constituting the series were selected so as to be similar enough to preclude strong preference for one member of the pair over the other, but not so similar as to destroy the reliability of preferences under noninfluence situations.

The items in the susceptibility series and the 14 pairs of a supplementary reinforcement series were selected from among the items which survived an item analysis of 56 pairs of pictures administered in several pretests. Subjects of the preliminary studies were the entire first-grade population of the public school systems of three towns in upstate New York. Items which showed significant sex differences were eliminated, as were those which were too similar to be discriminated reliably, as indicated by the children's verbalizations. All but three pictures each in the susceptibility and reinforcement series were in color.

Procedure. Employing a before-after design, the experiment consisted of three phases conducted in the following sequence: Phase I was administered in a morning session, Phases II and III in an afternoon session. The mean time interval between the two sessions was 3½ hours. Each subject was tested individually and participated once under only one of the experimental conditions. In each of the two schools from which the samples were drawn, the experimental room was a quiet, isolated office, customarily used by visiting specialists, including school psychologists, remedial reading instructors, and nurses.

Phase I consisted of a neutral administration of the susceptibility series. In an informal session aimed at providing a gamelike atmosphere, the subject was introduced to the experimental task with the following instructions:

> I would like to play a game with you. We call the game: which do you like best? I will show you two pictures and you will tell me which you like the best. Then I will show you two other pictures, and you will tell me which you like the best. We will do this until the game is over. All right? Let's begin. Here are the first two pictures: which do you like the best?

During this session the experimenter played the role of an attentive but nonreinforcing observer. She displayed an interested but undemonstrative manner and recorded each of the child's preferences without comment. However, in order to set the subjects at ease in this situation, each child was told that he was "playing the game very nicely" after he had expressed his preference on the second item of the series. Except for this standard remark, no additional verbal support was given, and the experimenter took care to avoid nodding or saying "um-hmmm." At the completion of the preference task, the subject was thanked for playing the game and sent back to his classroom. Subjects were asked to promise not to tell any other child about the game they played.

Phase II, administered after an interval of approximately 3½ hours, consisted of the experimental manipulation of reinforcement conditions immediately preceding attempts at influence. Subjects were first introduced to the reinforcement series as follows:

> Do you remember the game we played this morn-

ing? I have another game just like it. I will show you some pictures and you will tell me which you like the best and why you like it best. Okay? Let's begin. Here are the first two pictures: which do you like the best? Why do you like it best?

Then one of the three treatments was administered in the following manner:

1. Under the nurturance condition, the experimenter was rewarding, supportive, and encouraging throughout the treatment. She agreed with each of the child's preferences with verbal reinforcement and paraphrased in a supportive manner the reasons the child gave for his choices. In addition, she leaned toward the subject, looked directly at him, smiled, nodded, and made other approving comments at appropriate intervals. In each of the treatment conditions, attempts by the subject to engage the experimenter in conversation were pleasantly but quickly terminated.

2. Under the nurturance-withdrawal condition, the experimenter's behavior was similar to that displayed in the nurturance condition, but was limited to the first half of the treatment only; that is, during the administration of the first seven items of the reinforcement series. On the remaining items, the experimenter displayed nonsupportive behavior: she disagreed with each of the child's preferences and withheld all supportive paraphrases of the reasons offered by the child. In contrast to the nurturance condition, she leaned away from the subject, refrained from smiling and nodding, and avoided eye contact with the child.

3. Under the neutral condition, the experimenter's behavior was identical with that shown during the administration of the susceptibility series in Phase I. She provided no form of social reinforcement other than her attentiveness to the subject's preferences. She made no comments and avoided nodding or murmuring "um-hmm."

Although an attempt was made to keep constant the amount of time spent with each subject, the nature of the social interaction prescribed for each of the experimental conditions precluded complete achievement of this aim. In anticipation, therefore, of a possible significant regression of the dependent variable upon treatment time, a record was kept of the total length of time spent by each subject in Phase II.

Phase III, the critical influence situation, began immediately after the completion of the experimental manipulation of social reinforcement. The susceptibility series was readministered to all subjects and introduced with the following transitional remarks:

Now, this time, I will go first, I will tell you which picture I like best and then you tell me which one you like best. Okay?

The experimenter then presented each pair of pictures, saying, "I like this one [pointing to one member of each pair], which one do you like?" The experimenter's stated preferences actually consisted of contradictions of 15 of the child's 18 preferences expressed in Phase I. In order to allay suspicion, the experimenter agreed with the subject's initial preferences on three dummy items. Throughout the session, the experimenter carefully avoided reinforcing the child's agreement or disagreement with the experimenter's preferences by withholding all forms of verbal and nonverbal reinforcement.

A procedural postscript. While it was the consensus of the experimenters that the nurturance-withdrawal condition did not evoke stressful reactions in the children, indirect cues provided by changes in voice quality, gross bodily movements, and hesitation before expressing preferences and verbalizing reasons suggested that the treatment probably did arouse a mild degree of anxiety or discomfort in some of the children. A repair measure was thus instituted at the end of the experiment in order to alleviate any residual anxiety in the subject which may have resulted from the previous experimental treatment. Accordingly, all subjects who had received withdrawal of nurturance were renurtured by the experimenter through a final administration of five pairs of items similar to those in the susceptibility and reinforcement series. The child was again instructed to indicate his preferences and to verbalize the bases of his choices; in each instance, the experimenter expressed agreement, made supportive comments, and interacted with the subject in a warm and friendly manner.

Results

Examination of the overall means and standard deviations for the separate sexes and for the combined sexes in the two schools revealed no differences approaching statistical significance. Consequently, the data from the two schools were combined for all subsequent analyses.

As another preliminary step, the relationship between the dependent variable and time spent in treatment (Phase II) was ascertained. Clearly, if time were correlated significantly with susceptibility scores, differences found for this variable could be spuriously determined by differences in the length of time spent in the experimental condition. Inspection of the relevant data indicated that although boys and girls did not spend significantly different amounts of time under each condition, there was, nevertheless, a tendency for time to increase from the neutral through the nurturance withdrawal to the nurturance conditions for both sexes. Product- moment correlations between susceptibility scores and treatment time for boys, however, did not differ significantly from chance

($r = .05$, $p > .05$); on the other hand, the obtained correlation for girls barely attained significance ($r = .32$, $p = .05$) thereby suggesting a tendency for those subjects who had spent more time in the treatment phase of the experiment to shift their preferences toward agreement with the experimenter more frequently than those who had spent less time.

Further analyses of the experimental data for girls by means of the covariance adjustment technique demonstrated that the differences in susceptibility scores for girls were significant beyond the .01 level even when scores were adjusted for differences in treatment time. The findings therefore permit one to conclude that any variations which may emerge between the experimental groups on the dependent variable cannot be attributed to differences between the subjects in the length of time spent in the reinforcement condition.

The difference in the ethnic backgrounds of the two experimenters prompted the decision to include the experimenter as an additional dimension in the analysis of data, although it was not initially offered as one of the major experimental variables. Since it was conceivable that the differences in ethnicity could have operated to produce differential effects quite apart from the experimental manipulation of social reinforcement and social influence, and in the light of the literature on experimenter effects (e.g., Rosenthal, 1963, 1964; Stevenson, 1961), the separate data for the experimenters were evaluated independently by means of the analysis of variance.

Table 1 presents a summary of the analysis of the effects of experimenter, experimental condition, sex of subject, and SES level on susceptibility scores. The results indicated that the main effect of experimental condition was a highly significant source of variation. The F value of 8.01 ($df = 2$, $p < .01$) provides support for the inference that susceptibility to experimenter influence was affected by the preliminary social interaction. Table 2 shows that mean susceptibility scores tend to decrease from the nurturance to the neutral conditions. The more specific differences contributing to the significant F for the experimental condition were investigated by one-tailed t tests, whose error variances were based on the error term ($df = 48$) of the analysis of variance. The results summarized in Table 2 indicate that the mean of the neutral condition differs significantly from the means of both nurturance ($p < .0005$) and nurturance withdrawal ($p < .025$). The difference between the means for the latter conditions is significant at the .05 level, but contrary to prediction, nurturance was associated with higher susceptibility scores than nurturance withdrawal. Thus, while the data support the hypothesis of the greater effectiveness of consistent nurturance from the experimenter as compared with unresponsive attention, they are less obliging with respect to the predicted superiority of withdrawal of nurturance in inducing subsequent susceptibility in these subjects. However, it is of interest to note the differential responses of the middle-class girls. For the neutral treatment, the mean susceptibility score was 2.33 ($SD = 1.49$); for nurturance and nurturance withdrawal, the means were virtually identical ($M = 6.00$, $SD = 2.58$; $M = 6.33$, $SD = 2.50$, respectively). This pattern of responses did not appear in any of the remaining sex-SES groups and suggests that the intent of the nurturance withdrawal treatment came closest to being realized among the middle-class girls.

The main effects for the experimenter and SES and the simple interaction between these two were of borderline significance ($p < .10$), reflecting a tendency for the overall susceptibility scores obtained by the Oriental experimenter (E_1) to be higher than

Table 1 *Analysis of Variance of Susceptibility Scores according to Experimenter, Experimental Condition, Sex and Socioeconomic Status*

Source	*df*	MS	*F*
Experimenter (*E*)	1	26.88	2.98
Experimental condition (EC)	2	72.35	8.01**
Sex of subject (S)	1	9.39	1.04
Socioeconomic status (SES)	1	29.38	3.25
E×EC	2	12.35	1.37
E×S	1	6.73	1.00
E×SES	1	29.40	3.26
EC×S	2	10.59	1.17
EC×SES	2	2.26	<1
S×SES	1	56.89	6.30*
E×EC×S	2	15.99	1.77
E×EC×SES	2	17.12	1.90
E×S×SES	1	.21	<1
EC×S×SES	2	27.21	3.01
E×EC×S×SES	2	13.24	1.47
Error (within)	48	9.03	
Total	71		

* $p < .05$.
** $p < .01$.

Table 2 *Comparison of Mean Susceptibility Scores for Experimental Conditions*

Experimental Condition	*M*	*SD*	*t*
Nurturance (N)	6.42	4.35	N vs. NW: 1.68*
Nurturance withdrawal (NW)	4.95	2.77	N vs. 0: 3.99***
Neutral (O)	2.96	2.51	NW vs. 0: 2.31**

Note.—Bartlett test of homogeneity of variance yielded a nonsignificant chi square of 2.58, $p > .20$.
* $p = .05$, 1-tailed.
** $p < .025$, 1-tailed.
*** $p < .0005$, 1-tailed.

those of the Caucasian experimenter (E_2). There was, moreover, a tendency for middle-class children to have somewhat higher scores than working-class children and, in addition, to be slightly more susceptible to E_1 than to E_2.

Table 1 also shows a significant first-order interaction effect between sex and SES ($p < .05$). The finding is clarified by an inspection of the means shown in Table 3 and by the results of *t* tests which reveal that working-class boys have a significantly lower mean susceptibility score than working-class girls ($p < .05$), middle-class boys ($p < .02$), and middle-class girls ($p < .05$), irrespective of experimental condition; the means of the latter three groups do not differ significantly from one another. Inspection of the primary data indicated that the means for the three experimental conditions for working-class boys showed little variation ($M = 2.67$, $SD = 2.13$ for nurturance; $M = 3.50$, $SD = 2.81$ for nurturance withdrawal; $M = 2.50$, $SD = 2.63$ for neutral). Furthermore, there was no significant difference between the two experimenters in their effectiveness with working-class boys (for E_1, $M = 3.11$, $SD = 3.00$; for E_2, $M = 2.67$, $SD = 2.05$). This finding eliminates the possibility that working-class boys were reacting differentially to the Oriental experimenter because of greater prejudice.

Table 3 *Mean Susceptibility Scores according to Sex and Socioeconomic Status*

SES Level	Boys	Girls	Combined Sexes
Middle class	5.94_a	4.89_a	5.41
Working class	2.89_b	3.39_a	4.14
Combined SES	4.41	5.14	

Note.—Cells containing the same subscript are not significantly different at the .05 level by 2-tailed test.

Reliability of the Susceptibility Series. Evidence for the reliability of the susceptibility series was obtained by correlating each subject's susceptibility score on the odd items with his score on the even items. The corrected odd-even reliability coefficients for the nurturance, nurturance withdrawal, and neutral conditions were .78, .68, and .83, respectively; for the combined groups the overall reliability coefficient was .72. All of the reliability coefficients were significant at the .01 level. It is interesting to note that the reliability coefficient was lowest for the nurturance withdrawal condition. This finding may reflect the slightly unsettling effect of the previous social interaction resulting in mild discomfort and instability of choice behavior during the influence attempts.

Discussion

That susceptibility to adult influence is enhanced by previous social reinforcement is clearly supported by these findings: children who had been exposed to consistent nurturance and rewarding interaction with the experimenter shifted their initial preferences to agree with that experimenter to a significantly greater degree than children who had been exposed to unresponsive attention. This finding is in accord with previous experimental demonstrations of the effectiveness of nurturance in the modification of children's behavior. It should be emphasized that the manipulation of this investigation (Phase II) did not involve reinforcement of imitative responses; what was reinforced was the state of agreement and supportiveness between the adult and the child. The intent of the nurturance treatment was to achieve a certain degree of positive reinforcement for the adult-child interaction.

In demonstrating the effect of nurturance on susceptibility to experimenter influence, the present study also reveals the operation of the tendency for interpersonal behavior to be reciprocated. Thus, the degree of generosity evoked in subjects by another person's behavior is a function of the subject's perception of that person's own benevolent or malevolent intentions (Lambert, 1959). Dominative behavior on the part of one child induces domination in his partner; integrative behavior in one child elicits integrative behavior in his companion (Anderson, 1939). And in the present instance, agreement on the part of the adult induces agreement in the child.

It should be noted that while the explicit influence attempts of the experimenter in Phase III involved neither coercion nor reinforcement for agreement rewards were not entirely absent from the influence situation. The experimenter with whom the child could agree or disagree was not only prestigeful by virtue of age and size, but also her identification with teachers and other school authorities was emphasized by the fact that the experiment was being conducted within the school setting, where compliance to adult figures typically receives positive reinforcement. Yet the significantly lower degree of susceptible behavior displayed by the children in the neutral condition suggests that the influence of these additional reinforcers was minimal and points instead to the differential social reinforcement manipulated by the experimenter as the critical variable.

The failure of the experimental results to support the predicted relation between consistent nurturance and the withdrawal of nurturance requires further comment, in view of the positive results reported by previous investigators. Underlying the prediction was the assumption that an implied threat to the relationship between the child and the experimenter following a period of nurturance would arouse a certain amount of anxiety in the child which, in turn, would motivate shifting to agree with the experimenter. The finding that nurturance and nurturance withdrawal were equally effective with middle-class girls is suggestive in light of previous studies which show that it is these girls, rather than working-class children or middle-class boys, who are most likely to be exposed to "love-withdrawal" discipline techniques (Bronfenbrenner, 1961; Sears, Maccoby, and Levin, 1957).

One explanation for the failure of the nurturance-withdrawal hypothesis to find confirmation may lie in the form of threat employed. It is quite possible that disagreement with 7 out of 14 choices and the withholding of supportive paraphrases, comments, and smiles by the experimenter had only mildly threatening implications for these children. Moreover, the fact that the experimenter remained in close view may have mitigated the treatment and may even have constituted a condition of mild support. The subtle nature of the technique used to imply withdrawal of nurturance in this experiment becomes apparent when it is examined against the methods employed in previous investigations of social deprivation and inconsistent nurturance on children's behavior. The latter techniques are characterized by a sharp termination of social reinforcement, including physical absence of the reinforcing figure for a specified period of time. Thus, the relatively mild and superficial nature of the treatment may have vitiated the experimental manipulation of nurturance withdrawal.

On the other hand, the work of Crandall and her associates (Crandall, 1963; Crandall, Good, and Crandall, 1964) on the sequence effects of social reinforcement raises the possibility that the treatment was not necessarily as mild or as superficial as has been suggested. Crandall found that the experimenter's silence following positive reinforcement had the effect of lowering the expectancy of success in an ambiguous situation, whereas negative reactions followed by silence led to the raising of expectancy. She posits a contrasting process whereby the child interprets an adult's silence as containing information opposite to that of the preceding reaction.

More plausible explanations for the discrepant results obtained in this study may be found in other dissimilarities in methodology. The difference in the chronological age of the subjects—preschoolers (Hartup, 1958; Stein and Wright, 1964) and kindergarteners (Rosenblith, 1961) as opposed to first graders in this study—may be relevant, if one considers the possibility that the withdrawal of motherly nurturance has less threatening implications for 6- to 7-year-old children than for 3- to 4-year-old subjects. Finally, there was a significant difference in the criterion task used in this experiment. Stein and Wright (1964) and Rosenblith (1961) used simple imitation, whereas in this study, an imitative response demanded that the child change his original preference. In addition, the criterion tasks of previous research were designed to elicit adult approval; in this experiment, social reinforcement was explicitly withheld from the criterion task.

The predicted difference between the two social classes was confirmed by the behavior of the working-class boys only. As indicated earlier, these subjects showed little variation in their responses to the three experimental conditions. This fact, coupled with their significantly lower mean susceptibility score in comparison with the other three sex-SES sub-groups, suggests the hypothesis that the working-class boys may have been actively resisting the experimental manipulation of both social reinforcement and social influence. The present study would have been strengthened methodologically by the inclusion of a control group in which children were administered the susceptibility series twice without any intervening reinforcement condition or influence manipulation. Such a control would not only have provided data on the test-retest reliability of the series, but would also have furnished a base level against which the experimental effects could be assessed more systematically. Had such a group been included, it would be expected that the change score of the working-class boys would be significantly less than that of the unrun control group, if they were, indeed, consciously resisting experimenter influence.

This experiment was not originally designed to assess the relative adequacy of the social drive (Berkowitz, 1964; Erickson, 1962; Gewirtz and Baer, 1958a, 1958b) as opposed to the valence position (Berkowitz, Butterfield, and Zigler, 1965; Berkowitz and Zigler, 1965; McCoy and Zigler, 1965; Shallenberger and Zigler, 1961) in accounting for the differential effectiveness of social reinforcers following different types of social interaction. Nevertheless, the present findings do appear to lend some post hoc support to the valence position. Within the social drive framework, interaction with a highly nurturant adult is viewed as satiating social drive and leading to a decrease in the child's responsiveness to the social reinforcers which the adult dispenses, whereas deprivation of social reinforcers is seen as increasing social drive and enhancing the adult's effectiveness as a reinforcing agent. According to the valence interpretation, the child's responsiveness to the social reinforcers which the experimenter dispenses is a direct function of the valence which the experimenter has for the child. This valence, or the child's attitude toward the experimenter, is, in turn, determined by the nature of the social contact. A positive interaction is thus viewed as increasing the experimenter's effectiveness and a negative interaction as reducing it. In line with the valence position, the present study suggests that it was the magnitude of the dose of nurturance the child received rather than the sequence of nurturance followed by its withdrawal which enhanced the experimenter's effectiveness as an influencing agent.

References

ANDERSON, H. H. Domination and social integration in the behavior of kindergarten children and teachers. *Genetic Psychological Monographs,* 1939, *21,* 287–385.

BANDURA, A., and HUSTON, A. C. Identification as a process of incidental learning. *Journal of Abnormal and Social Psychology,* 1961, *63,* 311–318.

BANDURA, A., ROSS, D., and ROSS, S. A. Transmission of aggression through imitation of aggressive models. *Journal of Abnormal and Social Psychology,* 1961, *63,* 575–582.

BERKOWITZ, H. Effects of prior experimenter-subject relationships on reinforced reaction time of schizophrenics and normals. *Journal of Abnormal and Social Psychology,* 1964, *69,* 522–530.

BERKOWITZ, H., BUTTERFIELD, E. C., and ZIGLER, E. The effectiveness of social reinforcers on persistence and learning tasks following positive and negative interactions. *Journal of Personality and Social Psychology,* 1965, *2,* 706–714.

BERKOWITZ, H., and ZIGLER, E. Effects of preliminary positive and negative interactions and delay conditions on children's responsiveness to social reinforcement. *Journal of Personality and Social Psychology,* 1965, *2,* 500–505.

BRONFENBRENNER, U. Socialization and social class through time and space. In E. E. Maccoby, T. M. Newcomb, and E. L. Hartley (Eds.), *Readings in social psychology* (3rd ed.). New York: Holt, Rinehart and Winston, 1958. Pp. 400–425.

BRONFENBRENNER, U. Freudian theories of identification and their derivatives. *Child Development,* 1960, *31,* 15–40.

BRONFENBRENNER, U. Some familial antecedents of responsibility and leadership in adolescents. In L. Petrullo and B. M. Bass (Eds.), *Leadership and interpersonal behavior.* New York: Holt, Rinehart and Winston, 1961. Pp. 239–272.

CRANDALL, V. C. Reinforcement effects of adult reactions and nonreactions on children's achievement expectations. *Child Development,* 1963, *34,* 335–354.

CRANDALL, V. C., GOOD, S., and CRANDALL, V. J. Reinforcement effects of adult reactions and nonreactions on children's achievement expectations: A replication study. *Child Development,* 1964, *35,* 485–497.

DOLLARD, J., and MILLER, N. E. *Personality and psychotherapy.* New York: McGraw-Hill, 1950.

ERICKSON, M. T. Effects of social deprivation and satiation on verbal conditioning in children. *Journal of Comparative and Physiological Psychology,* 1962, *55,* 953–957.

GEWIRTZ, J. L. Three determinants of attention-seeking in young children. *Monographs of the Society for Research in Child Development,* 1954, *19*(2, Whole No. 59).

GEWIRTZ, J. L., and BAER, D. M. Deprivation and satiation of social reinforcers as drive-conditions. *Journal of Abnormal and Social Psychology,* 1958, *57,* 165–172. (a)

GEWIRTZ, J. L., and BAER, D. M. The effect of brief social deprivation on behavior for a social reinforcer. *Journal of Abnormal and Social Psychology,* 1958, *56,* 49–56. (b)

HARTUP, W. W. Nurturance and nurturance-withdrawal in relation to the dependency behavior of preschool children. *Child Development,* 1958, *29,* 191–201.

JANIS, I. L., and HOVLAND, C. I. (Eds.) *Personality and persuasibility.* New Haven: Yale University Press, 1959.

LAMBERT, N. W. An experimental study of benevolence and malevolence. Unpublished doctoral dissertation, Cornell University, 1959.

MCCOY, N., and ZIGLER, E. Social reinforcer effectiveness as a function of the relationship between child and adult. *Journal of Personality and Social Psychology,* 1965, *1,* 604–612.

MOWRER, O. H. Identification: A link between learning theory and psychotherapy. In *Learning theory and personality dynamics.* New York: Ronald Press, 1950. Pp. 573–616.

MUSSEN, P., and DISTLER, L. Masculinity, identification, and father-son relationships. *Journal of Abnormal and Social Psychology,* 1959, *59,* 350–356.

PAYNE, D., and MUSSEN, P. Parent-child relations and father identification. *Journal of Abnormal and Social Psychology,* 1956, *52,* 358–367.

ROSENBLITH, J. F. Learning by imitation in kindergarten children. *Child Development,* 1959, *30,* 69–80.

ROSENBLITH, J. F. Imitative color choices in kindergarten children. *Child Development,* 1961, *32,* 211–223.

ROSENHAN, D., and GREENWALD, J. A. The effects of age, sex, and socioeconomic class on responsiveness of two classes of verbal reinforcement. *Journal of Personality,* 1965, *33,* 108–121.

ROSENTHAL, R. Experimenter attributes as determinants of subjects' responses. *Journal of Projective Techniques and Personality Assessment,* 1963, *27,* 324–331.

ROSENTHAL, R. The effect of the experimenter on the results of psychological research. In B. A. Maher (Ed.), *Progress in experimental personality research.* New York: Academic Press, 1964. Pp. 79–114.

SEARS, R. R. Identification as a form of behavioral development. In D. B. Harris (Ed.), *The concept of development.* Minneapolis: University of Minnesota Press, 1957. Pp. 149–161.

SEARS, R. R., MACCOBY, E. E., and LEVIN, H. *Patterns of child rearing.* Evanston, Ill.: Row, Peterson, 1957.

SHALLENBERGER, P., and ZIGLER, E. Rigidity, negative response tendencies, and cosatiation in normal and feebleminded children. *Journal of Abnormal and Social Psychology,* 1961, *63,* 20–26.

STEIN, A. H., and WRIGHT, J. C. Imitative learning under conditions of nurturance and nurturance withdrawal. *Child Development,* 1964, *35,* 927–938.

STEVENSON, H. W. Social reinforcement with children

as a function of CA, sex of *E*, and sex of S. *Journal of Abnormal and Social Psychology*, 1961, *63*, 147–154.

STEVENSON, H. W. Social reinforcement of children's behavior. In L. P. Lipsitt and C. C. Spiker (Eds.), *Advances in child development and behavior*. Vol. 2. New York: Academic Press, 1965. Pp. 97–126.

WARNER, W. L., MEEKER, M., and EELLS, K. *Social class in America*. Chicago: Science Research Associates, 1949.

WHITING, J. W. M., and CHILD, I. L. *Child training and personality: A cross-cultural study*. New Haven: Yale University Press, 1953.

ZIGLER, E. Rigidity in the feebleminded. In E. P. Trapp and R. Himelstein (Eds.), *Research readings on the exceptional child*. New York: Appleton-Century-Crofts, 1962.

ZIGLER, E., and KANZER, P. The effectiveness of two classes of verbal reinforcers on the performance of middle- and lower-class children. *Journal of Personality*, 1962, *30*, 157–163.

McGrade's brief report also examines social class as a determinant of the subject's reactions to different kinds of reinforcers. Her subjects were children from working-class and upper-middle-class homes in England. Two types of reinforcers were used in this experiment, verbal and nonverbal. For all of the children the light and candy used as reinforcers were clearly superior to the experimenter's saying either right-correct or good-fine. There was some indication that the middle-class children learned more quickly under all conditions. This article also gives us some insight into the way hypotheses concerning the relative effectiveness of different types of reinforcers are tested.

22 *Social Class and Reinforcer Effects in Discrimination Learning*[1]

BETTY JO McGRADE

Terrell, Durkin, and Wiesley (1959) have reported that reinforcer effectiveness is a function of Ss' social class background. Using a signal light in one condition and light plus candy in another, they found middle-class children more responsive to light alone while lower-class Ss learned more quickly with candy. In a later study using two types of verbal reinforcers, Zigler and Kanzer (1962) also found an interaction with social class. Lower-class Ss were more influenced by "good" and "fine" while middle-class Ss were more responsive to "right" and "correct." Zigler and Kanzer suggested that their "right-correct" condition was analogous to a signal light furnishing knowledge of results, while "good-fine" conveyed approval, a direct reinforcer similar to candy. The present study used these four reinforcer conditions to investigate the similarity suggested.

Two recent studies have failed to replicate the interaction reported by Zigler and Kanzer (Rosenhan and Greenwald, 1965; McGrade, 1966), and with a broad range of incentives, Witryol, Tyrrell, and Lowden (1965) have found few social class effects. Since no replication of Terrell et al. has been reported, the

1 The author is indebted to the late Michael Blake, of the Medical Research Council, applied Psychology Research Unit, Cambridge, for his assistance during this study, and to Ruth Blake, who served as experimenter. The kind cooperation of the headmasters, teachers and students of St. Luke's School and Newnham Croft School is gratefully acknowledged.

From *Psychonomic Science*, 1968, *12*, 140. Reproduced by permission.

present study follows their general procedure. One change was the present study's use of a naive *E*, who had been thoroughly trained in the experimental procedure but did not know the hypotheses under study.

Method

The Ss were 80 boys, seven and eight years old, attending state supported schools in Cambridge, England. Half were supplied by a school in a heavily working-class neighborhood. The remainder came from an upper-middle-class area.

The "game" consisted of a wooden box, 18 × 12 × 5 inches, and a stand 10 inches tall on which was mounted a red light bulb. When light was to be the reinforcer, this stand was placed immediately behind the box and wired to two pairs of permanently mounted push buttons: one pair on the top surface of the box accessible to Ss and a second pair on the back visible only to *E*. The stimuli were three-dimensional shapes, triangular prisms and rectangular prisms, each in two sizes, with sides 1-¼ × ⅝ or 2-½ × 1-¼ inches.

One woman *E* was used. After bringing the child to the experimental room she said: "I'm going to put two blocks up on this box. You pick one and push the button in front of the block you've chosen." In the light condition only, she continued, "If you pick the correct one, this light will go on." After the first trial, *E* said: "Now I'll put up two more and you choose again."

On each trial a small and a large block of the same shape were presented. Alternate Ss were reinforced for choosing the large block or the small. The order of presentation randomized the occurrence of triangles and rectangles over trials and the position of large and small blocks on the left or right. Every correct response was reinforced to a criterion of 9 out of 10 correct, or until the S had made 60 responses. In verbal conditions, the two words were used alternately. For candy reinforcement, *E* placed a single M&M on the table near S with no verbal comment. In the light condition, the bulb went on automatically when S pushed a button corresponding to one *E* depressed behind the box.

Results and Discussion

The dependent variable was trials to criterion, and mean scores for the groups on this measure are shown in Table 1. An analysis of variance was performed on these scores, two social classes by four reinforcement conditions. Only the *F* for reinforcement conditions approached significance ($F = 2.20$, $df = 3/72$, $p < .10$). Comparisons among the reinforcement conditions showed a significant dichotomy between the two verbal reinforcers on one hand and light and candy on the other ($F = 5.99$, $df = 1/72$, $p < .025$). The suggested dichotomy, light and right-correct vs. good-fine and candy, was insignificant ($F < 1$). The residual from these two orthogonal comparisons was also insignificant ($F < 1$).

Table 1 *Mean Trials to Criterion for Social Class Groups* (N = 10 Per Cell)

Social Class	Reinforcement Conditions			
	Light	Right–Correct	Good–Fine	Candy
Middle class	17.1	32.5	33.5	21.2
Lower class	22.5	36.9	35.8	29.4

Scores for the four reinforcement conditions fail to support Zigler and Kanzer's suggestion that "right-correct" functions like a signal light, "good-fine" like candy. The present results can be handled more easily by a distinction between verbal and nonverbal reinforcers, and agree with a previous report that the nonverbal are more effective at this age level (Witryol et al. 1965).

These data show no indication of the social class by reinforcer interaction reported by Terrell et al. The major difference in procedure between studies is the use, by Terrell et al. of a signal light with its accompanying instructions in all conditions, while the present study separated light and candy. It is, however, difficult to see why reducing the overlap between conditions should eliminate this interaction. Possibly English boys are different from their American counterparts in some way which accounts for the negative finding, or the use of a naive *E* may be crucial, but at least the present results suggest limitations on the generality of previously reported social class by reinforcer interactions.

References

McGrade, B. J. Effectiveness of verbal reinforcers in relation to age and social class. *Journal of Personality and Social Psychology,* 1966, *4,* 555–560.

Rosenhan, D., and Greenwald, J. A. The effects of age, sex and socioeconomic class on responsiveness to two classes of verbal reinforcement. *Journal of Personality,* 1965, *33,* 108–121.

Terrell, G., Durkin, K., and Wiesley, M. Social class and the nature of the incentive in discrimination learning. *Journal of Abnormal and Social Psychology,* 1959, *59,* 270–272.

Witryol, S. L., Tyrrell, D. and Lowden, L. Development of incentive values in childhood. *Genetic Psychology Monographs,* 1965, *72,* 201–246.

Zigler, E., and Kanzer, P. The effectiveness of verbal reinforcers on the performance of middle- and lower-class children. *Journal of Personality,* 1962, *30,* 157–163.

Perhaps one of the most potent variables influencing a person's reaction to social influence is his history of reinforcement in similar circumstances. Specifically, it has been suggested that adults who have had punitive, rejecting, or restrictive parents show a tendency to identify with (imitate) threatening individuals. Those who have had loving, accepting, and permissive parents, on the other hand, tend to identify with supportive individuals. These relationships are examined experimentally in the article by *Baxter, Lerner, and Miller.* Using a questionnaire, they obtained information from college subjects about the attitudes of their parents toward conformity and discipline in the home. The subjects were then told that they were taking part in a language learning task in which they would either be (a) punished by an instructor for mistakes, (b) rewarded by an instructor for rapid learning, or (c) simply told how well they were doing. The procedures were intended to establish the language instructor as either a threatening figure, a rewarding figure, or a relatively neutral figure.

All that the subjects were required to do, however, was to rate both themselves and the "instructor" on a series of adjectives, descriptive of personality. Similarities in the two sets of ratings provided a measure of the degree to which they identified with the instructor. In general, it was found that those subjects who had described their parents as restrictive and authoritarian tended to rate the threatening instructor as more similar to themselves. However, those subjects who reported a permissive, democratic home environment tended to rate themselves and the rewarding instructor as more similar. The terms *defensive* and *anaclitic* identification are used to describe the differences among the subjects. Behaviorally, this means that the words one uses to describe oneself are often similar to those one uses to describe his parents. Individuals whose performances resemble those of one's parents may be described in like fashion; their functional similarity to the parents causes them to prompt reactions similar to those prompted by the parents. Thus, identification may generalize from an original reinforcing agent to agents encountered at a later time who exhibit equivalent behaviors.

23 *Identification as a Function of the Reinforcing Quality of the Model and the Socialization Background of the Subject*[1]

JAMES C. BAXTER
MELVIN J. LERNER
JEROME S. MILLER

Since the time of Freud's (1938) initial writing on the topic of identification, the concept has been regarded as a central variable in personality development (Bandura and Walters, 1963; Bronfenbrenner, 1960; Kagan, 1958). Two major processes of identification have been described: anaclitic identification, or the imitation of a highly valued and positively regarded model; and identification with the aggressor, or the defensive imitation of a threatening model. These two processes have been

[1] This study was supported in part by a small grant from the University of Kentucky Research Fund. The authors would like to express their appreciation to the University of Kentucky Computing Center for assisting with the data analysis. The views expressed are those of the authors and do not necessarily reflect an official position of the United States Public Health Service.

From the *Journal of Personality and Social Psychology,* 1965, 2, 692–697. Copyright 1965 by the American Psychological Association, and reproduced by permission.

related to qualitative differences in the relationship between subject and model by a number of authors in subsequent writings (e.g., Bronfenbrenner, 1960; Carlson, 1963; Freud, 1960; Mowrer, 1950; Sanford, 1955; Sarnoff, 1962; and others). A considerable amount of research has been reported to corroborate the anaclitic process (e.g., Bandura and Huston, 1961; Helper, 1955; Mussen and Distler, 1959, 1960; Payne and Mussen, 1956; Sears, 1953; Sears, Maccoby, and Levin, 1957). The process of identification with the aggressor, on the other hand, has stimulated less research. Anecdotal accounts of the imitation of threatening models have been described (Balint, 1945; Freud, 1954), and an extensive naturalistic report of threat-based behavior in a German concentration camp has appeared (Bettelheim, 1943). Two studies have also been reported which describe stable individual differences in patterns of identification in response to threat (Carlson, 1963; Sarnoff, 1951). However, no experimental studies of the process have been reported.

Sarnoff (1951) has argued that three basic conditions are necessary for the occurrence of identification with the aggressor: an aggressor who is determined to impose his hostility upon another individual; a victim who is socially dependent upon the aggressor and who thus makes a convenient target for the aggressor's hostility; and a system of social constraints such that the victim cannot completely escape the influence of the aggressor. Anaclitic identification, on the other hand, is based on the rewarding qualities of the model, and thus would be expected to occur in a situation in which the individual is socially dependent upon a model who is supportive and nonthreatening toward him, and who makes these behaviors conditional upon the individual's behavior (Bandura and Huston, 1961).

It has been proposed that individual differences in childhood experiences affect the process of identification and influence the type of imitation shown by a person. In particular, Balint (1945) has suggested that children reared in homes in which the parents take a punitive and restrictive attitude toward pleasure-seeking activities show a decreased tolerance for frustration and anxiety. As a consequence, the children show an increased tendency to identify with available models, especially those posing a threat to their self-esteem.

Sarnoff (1951) has provided data which tend to support one aspect of Balint's position by showing that people who identify with an aggressor more strongly (e.g., anti-Semitic attitudes in Jews), do in fact ascribe more rejecting, frustrating, and hostile attitudes to their parents than do people who resist such identification. The latter report more accepting and love-oriented parental attitudes.

The present study was aimed at investigating identification in an experimental setting designed to encourage either an anaclitic (support-based) or defensive (threatbased) relationship between young adults and a model. In addition to the experimental manipulation, subjects were also differentiated for their reports of the parents' child-rearing attitudes: rejecting and hostile versus accepting and supportive. Under these conditions both anaclitic and defensive identification were expected to occur. Individual differences in degrees of identification as well as type of identification were also predicted.

Method

Subjects. Subjects were drawn from male introductory psychology students at the University of Kentucky. All subjects were unpaid volunteers and received course credit for their participation. Only those subjects, who reported having been reared in an intact parental home were eligible. Also, since other studies involving similar experimental procedures were being conducted during the same semester, only subjects who had not participated in similar studies were used. A total of 69 subjects participated, although 15 were later excluded from the sample due to failure to cooperate with the experimental instructions or failure to accept the experimental ruse (described below).[2] The remaining 54 subjects represent the final sample.

Apparatus. The room in which the experiment was conducted contained two chairs and a table, on which a microphone and one set of earphones were placed in full view. Wires from the communication equipment led to a terminal box in the wall. The earphones were connected to a tape recorder in the adjoining room. Depending on the experimental condition to which the subject had been assigned, there was also present in the room additional experimental apparatus. For one arrangement of the room, an imposing looking "shock" apparatus was placed next to the subject's chair, on an electrical apparatus rack, standing about 3 feet high. The apparatus contained a large stimulator unit with the words "shock stimulator" painted on it, a row of six patch panels above the stimulator to which a network of variously colored wires were attached, and a small unit of dials below the stimulator. Colored lights located on the stimulator and the dial unit were turned on at all times. Electrodes leading from the apparatus were resting on the table in front of the subject. Wires leading from a different outlet on the apparatus went to the adjoining room under a connecting door. A

[2] The identification scores (described below) of all 15 subjects omitted from the sample were compared with the scores of those included in the study. In 11 out of 15 cases the scores fell within 1 standard deviation of their corresponding cell means, and in all 15 cases the scores were within 1.31 standard score units of their corresponding cell means.

second arrangement of the room involved the chairs, table, and communication equipment, but without the shock apparatus. In this condition three rolls of quarters wrapped in standard orange-colored bank rolls with $10 and the word Quarters printed on the side in large characters were displayed on the table. One roll was "broken open," with 10 quarters piled next to the filled rolls. A pad of receipts with the words University of Kentucky printed at the top was placed next to the quarters. The third arrangement of the room included only the chairs, table, and communication equipment.

Procedure. Subjects were contacted during the laboratory period of their class and asked to volunteer for an experiment in learning. When they appeared at their appointed time, they were accompanied to the experimental room by a male undergraduate experimenter. All subjects were run individually by the same experimenter, who was carefully supervised in the conduct of the study, but who was naive with respect to experimental hypotheses.

Upon entering the room, the experimenter seated the subject and told him that before beginning the main experiment he would be asked to fill out a brief questionnaire for another purpose and at the request of another experimenter. He was told that since it would take only a short time, it could be "gotten out of the way" before the main experiment. The experimenter read the instructions with the subject, answered any questions raised, and then permitted him to complete the ratings on the form while the experimenter busied himself with other papers. The questionnaire items were actually an abbreviation of the Traditional Family Ideology (TFI) Scale (Levinson and Huffman, 1955), which was obtained for the purpose of later differentiating subjects into levels of parental authoritarianism and restrictiveness toward child socialization. Fifteen items were chosen from the full scale which represented parental attitudes of authoritarian submission, conventionalism, exaggerated reliance on masculinity and femininity, moralistic rejection of impulse life, and extreme emphasis on discipline. Items were selected (or in several cases rephrased) to apply to both parents and to balance the direction of responding. A 6-point scale, ranging from very strong agreement to very strong disagreement, was provided for each item. Subjects were instructed to recall the period when they were growing up and answer the items the way they thought their parents would have responded to them.

Following completion of the TFI, the questionnaire was put aside and the subject was told that the main experiment was beginning. The experimenter read to the subject the instructions to the experiment in a standard and conversational manner. The experiment was presented as an investigation of the effectiveness of a particular method of learning an artificial language, Esperanto. He was told that he would receive a number of basic principles about the language through the earphones, and then, after he had become familiar with the principles, he would be given a list of 35 words in Esperanto one at a time and at a constant rate, to which he was to respond with the English translation.

Subjects were assigned on a random basis to one of three experimental treatments. A punishment group (run in the presence of the shock apparatus) was told that the method of learning being studied was the use of punishment as a learning technique. The subject was told that the electrodes would be attached to his left hand just before starting, and that each time he made an error in translation or failed to report the correct translation within 5 seconds, the instructor in the other room would push a button and he would receive a shock through the electrodes. He was told that the shock would be quite strong, and would probably hurt a little. He was also told that most people tend to get 15–20 shocks under these conditions, and that some get more or less, depending on how quickly they learn. Finally, he was told that he would be able to ask any questions he had later, but that there was another part to the study that he was to be told about first.

The reward group (run in the presence of the quarters and receipt pad) was given comparable instructions which stressed the expectation that the instructor in the other room would press a button after each correct translation within the time period, and the subject would be given a quarter. The experimenter demonstrated how quarters would be moved to the subject's reward pile on his side of the table, and the experimenter said that the quarters would be his winnings, and would be his to keep. The subject was also told that a receipt for his winnings would be requested, and he was led to believe that most people tend to get 15–20 quarters under these conditions, with some getting more or less, depending on how quickly they learn. The control group (run in the absence of supporting equipment) was given comparable instructions which stressed the expectation that the instructor in the other room would say "right" after each correct translation within the time period, and would say "wrong" if the translation were incorrect or too slow. Subjects were also told that most people tend to get about 15–20 correct translations under these conditions and about the same number incorrect.

The experimental treatments, then, were designed to place the subject in a dependent relationship with the instructor in the adjoining room, who was characterized as specially trained in the material to be learned, and who was to be either punishing, rewarding, or informative while teaching the subject the language.

To measure the degree of identification present, an additional manipulation was introduced. Following the instructions concerning the task and the nature of the relationship between the subject and the instructor, the experimenter indicated that another aspect of learning was also being studied. This aspect was "what the student knows about his instructor." The subject was informed that experts think that knowing one's instructor is an important factor in learning. He was told that this was also being investigated, and that he was to overhear an interview in the adjoining room between the professor conducting the study and the subject's instructor. He was told that both the professor and the instructor knew he would be listening. He was also told that he should try to form as clear a picture of his instructor as possible while listening.

The interview was actually a 4-minute tape recording which the experimenter started in the next room by leaving the experimental room briefly, ostensibly to inform the professor and instructor that the subject was ready to begin. The content of the interview was quite general and dealt with impressions the instructor, who was identified as a graduate student, had gained of the University, Lexington, and the surrounding horse farms.

After the subject had heard the interview, he was asked to make a series of ratings about his instructor from impressions he had gained. When the ratings of the instructor were completed, the sheet was withdrawn and he was asked to rate himself on another sheet containing the same items. Finally, the self-ratings were withdrawn, and he was asked to rate the average male student at the University of Kentucky, using the same items. The ratings were made on 22 bipolar adjectival dimensions, each of which was judged on a 7-point equal-appearing interval scale. The dimensions used were obtained from Cattell's (1950) rating scale items.

Following completion of the three sets of ratings, the subject was given a booklet containing four questions about the experiment which were rated on either 31- or 36-point scales. The specific items referred to: how pleased he felt about participating in the experiment; how much he would like to be an instructor for this kind of task in a future experiment; how many correct (incorrect) responses he thought he would get in translating the words; and how valuable he felt research of this kind is. Results of the ratings on the four items proved to be unreliable, and thus were not considered further.

After the subject had completed all the ratings, he was informed that the experiment was over and he was interrogated briefly concerning his acceptance of the experimental use. Only those 54 subjects accepting the ruse were included in the sample. Finally, subjects were asked to avoid discussing the experiment with other students and were dismissed.

Results and Discussion

Subjects were classified into six experimental groups by dividing each of the three treatment groups at the median TFI score. Six groups of nine subjects each were obtained. Comparison of TFI scores across experimental conditions was done in order to evaluate the comparability of the experimental groups with respect to the degree of authoritarianism ascribed to their parents. The three experimental groups were found to be quite comparable in levels of TFI ($Fs < 1.00$).

Product-moment correlations between the ratings of the instructor, the self, and the average male student were computed for each subject. Partial correlations between self and instructor were then obtained, with the average male student ratings controlled. In this way, characteristics attributable to male college students in general were partialed out, and a more direct measure of perceived similarity between the subject and the particular instructor was obtained. This measure was adopted as an index of identification. Transformation of these correlations to z scores was done in order to allow parametric analyses. An analysis of the variance of the transformed identification scores was then done. Table 1 summarizes these results.

Table 1 *Analysis of Variance of Transformed Identification Scores*

Source	*df*	MS	*F*
Between cells	5		
Conditions (C)	2	.264	1.28
Socialization (S)	1	.123	<1.00
C×S	2	1.042	5.08*
Error	48	.205	
Total	53		

* $p = .01$.

It can be seen that both the experimental conditions and the individual differences in severity of childhood socialization considered separately show no reliable relation to identification scores. The interaction of the experimental conditions and levels of severity of socialization did reach significance at the .01 level, however. Mean transformed identification scores for the six groups are reported in Table 2. It can be seen from these scores that more identification occurred in high TFI subjects under the punishment condition, while the low TFI subjects tended to show more identification under both the reward and control (information) conditions. This difference

Table 2 *Mean Transformed Identification Scores (TFI)*

Severity of Socialization	Condition		
	Punishment	Reward	Control
High TFI	.89	.27	.26
Low TFI	.24	.48	.42

in patterns of identification between TFI groups is significant at the .01 level by two-tailed t test ($t = 2.75$, $df = 48$). Individual comparisons indicate that the differences are primarily attributable to the unusually high degree of identification shown by the high TFI subjects in the punishment condition. The high TFI punishment group differed from the other high TFI groups and from the low TFI punishment group at the .01 level, and tended to differ from the remaining low TFI groups (p's $< .10$). Considered alone, the three low TFI groups did not differ reliably between experimental conditions.

The overall pattern of results indicates rather persuasively that differences in the type of identification obtained in the present situation depend on individual differences in perceived childhood socialization experiences. Subjects who report being reared in restrictive, authoritarian homes show significantly more identification with the aggressor while subjects who report being reared in permissive, democratic homes tend to show more anaclitic identification. These results are consistent with previous data reported by Sarnoff (1951) and tend to confirm Balint's (1945) hypothesis that more severely socialized children develop tendencies to identify defensively. The absence of an overall difference in identification as a function of differences in severity of socialization alone is at variance with the second aspect of her hypothesis, however. If such differences in adjustment can be said to exist after the subjects have reached maturity, they appear to be secondary to predispositions to respond selectively to the affective quality of the situation encountered.

On the basis of the present findings a more tenable hypothesis appears to be that individuals reared in an authoritarian atmosphere, which required the development of tendencies toward defensive identification in childhood, will be more likely to identify with an aggressor as an adult. On the other hand, individuals whose patterns of identification developed in relation to supportive democratically oriented parents will be more responsive to situations which engender anaclitic identification. Such an interpretation appears to be related to differences in conformity and submission training in childhood socialization which have been emphasized in the authoritarian ideology research (Adorno, Frenkel-Brunswik, Levinson, and Sanford, 1950). On the basis of their interview data, these authors have concluded that "much of the submission to parental authority in the [extremely high scoring] prejudiced subject seems to be induced by impatience on the part of the parents and by the child's fear of displeasing them" (p. 385).

This threat-based training, often accomplished at the hands of extremely harsh and arbitrary parents, appears to be coextensive with the present concept of identification with the aggressor. Accordingly, the results of the high TFI groups in the present experiment are congruent with earlier clinical finding vis-à-vis the authoritarian personality.

The problem of why the conditions favoring identification were not different from the control condition in the present experiment raises an unanswered question. This result is somewhat surprising, since at least the anaclitic process of identification has been demonstrated previously by several investigators under different conditions (e.g., Bandura and Huston, 1961; Mussen and Distler, 1959, 1960). One possible explanation for the present, somewhat anomalous result appears to be that the control (information) condition was not actually as neutral as it was intended to be. That is, it may have been that the provision of information by the instructor established the anticipation of a supportive relationship. There is some evidence to support this possibility. As can be seen in Table 2, the subjects in the control condition responded quite similarly to the subjects in the reward condition. In any event, alternative control procedures appear warranted for further research using this situation.

References

Adorno, T. W., Frenkel-Brunswik, Else, Levinson, D. J., and Sanford, R. N. *The authoritarian personality.* New York: Harper, 1950.

Balint, Alice. Identification. In S. Lorand (Ed.), *The yearbook of psychoanalysis.* Vol. 1. New York: International Universities Press, 1945. Pp. 317–338.

Bandura, A., and Huston, Aletha C. Identification as a process of incidental learning. *Journal of Abnormal and Social Psychology,* 1961, *63,* 311–318.

Bandura, A., and Walters, R. H. *Social learning and personality development.* New York: Henry Holt, 1963.

Bettelheim, B. Individual and mass behavior in extreme situations. *Journal of Abnormal and Social Psychology,* 1943, *38,* 417–452.

Bronfenbrenner, U. Freudian theories of identification and their derivatives. *Child Development,* 1960, *31,* 15–40.

Carlson, R. Identification and personality structure in preadolescents. *Journal of Abnormal and Social Psychology,* 1963, *67,* 566–573.

Cattell, R. B. *Personality: A systematic, theoretical, and factual study.* New York: McGraw-Hill, 1950.

Freud, Anna. *The ego and the mechanisms of defense.* (Originally published in 1936) London: Hogarth Press, 1954.

Freud, S. Three contributions to the theory of sex.

In A. A. Brill (Ed.), *The basic writings of Sigmund Freud.* (Originally published in 1905) New York: Modern Library, 1938. Pp. 553–632.

FREUD, S. *Group psychology and the analysis of the ego.* (Originally published in 1921) New York: Bantam Books, 1960.

HELPER, M. M. Learning theory and the self concept. *Journal of Abnormal and Social Psychology,* 1955, *51,* 184–194.

KAGAN, J. The concept of identification. *Psychological Review,* 1958, *65,* 296–305.

LEVINSON, D. J., and HUFFMAN, PHYLLIS E. Traditional family ideology and its relation to personality. *Journal of Personality,* 1955, *23,* 251–273.

MOWRER, O. H. Identification: A link between learning theory and psychotherapy. In *Learning theory and personality dynamics.* New York: Ronald Press, 1950. Pp. 573–616.

MUSSEN, P., and DISTLER, L. Masculinity, identification, and father-son relationships. *Journal of Abnormal and Social Psychology,* 1959, *59,* 350–356.

MUSSEN, P., and DISTLER, L. M. Child-rearing antecedents of masculine identification in kindergarten boys. *Child Development,* 1960, *31,* 89–100.

PAYNE, D. E., and MUSSEN, P. Parent-child relationships and father identification among adolescent boys. *Journal of Abnormal and Social Psychology,* 1956, *52,* 358–362.

SANFORD, R. N. The dynamics of identification. *Psychological Review,* 1955, *62,* 106–118.

SARNOFF, I. Identification with the aggressor: Some personality correlates of anti-Semitism among Jews. *Journal of Personality,* 1951, *20,* 199–218.

SARNOFF, I. *Personality dynamics and development.* New York: Wiley, 1962.

SEARS, PAULINE S. Child-rearing factors related to playing of sex-typed roles. *American Psychologist,* 1953, *8,* 431. (Abstract)

SEARS, R. R., MACCOBY, ELEANOR E., and LEVIN, H. *Patterns of child rearing.* Evanston, Ill.: Row, Peterson, 1957.

Parents and Caretakers as Reinforcers

In the previous group of papers we dealt with the concept of identification. The first article in this section, by *Mussen and Parker,* treats identification behaviors as cases of incidental learning. Children often tend to identify with their parents; that is, they describe themselves as like their parents and they imitate much of what their parents do. Imitation of the parent need not be directly reinforced to be learned; just observing the parent often enables the child to imitate his conduct. Whether or not the child then incorporates any of these behaviors into his own repertoire depends upon such factors as the extent to which the adult has been a source of either punishments or rewards. As we saw in the article by Baxter, Lerner, and Miller, a child from a punitive family may learn to identify with threatening rather than rewarding adults.

Nevertheless, it appears that children are more likely to imitate parents who use positive reinforcement than those who are punitive and threatening. In short, the child who is socialized by positive reinforcement will probably identify positively with his parents. This means that he will come to exhibit more of their behaviors, regardless of whether such imitative performances have ever been reinforced. This hypothesis was tested in the experiment by Mussen and Parker, who used five-year-old girls as subjects and their mothers as models. The children learned how to solve a maze problem by watching their mothers. They could also see and hear other activities of the mother which were to be the test of the child's imitation. Some of the mothers had been identified, on the basis of prior interviews, as being relatively more nurturant (warm, supportive) than others.

The results showed that the nurturant mothers engendered the most imitation. The daughters of the less-nurturant mothers were less inclined to imitate, although they did as well in solving the problem. Identification is thus revealed in part as a process by which an agent of positive reinforcement prompts more generalized imitative behavior than an agent that has less often provided positive control.

24 Mother Nurturance and Girls' Incidental Imitative Learning[1]

PAUL H. MUSSEN
ANN L. PARKER

It has been demonstrated experimentally that the child's incidental imitative learning of a model's behavior increases immediately after nurturant interaction between the model and the child. There is also considerable evidence from correlational studies that a high degree of nurturance toward the child by the same-sex parent is conducive to the child's acquisition of appropriately sex-typed interests and attitudes (Mussen and Distler, 1959; Mussen and Rutherford, 1963). In these studies, it is assumed that the appropriate sex typing is a consequence of identification with the parent of the same sex, or in behavioral terms, the result of incidental imitative learning of that parent's behavior. If this assumption is correct, it follows that parents who are generally warm and nurturant will have a facilitating effect on their children's imitation of parental behavior, even in the absence of specific instruction or of reward for such imitation.

The research reported in this paper was designed to test this hypothesis directly. Mothers served as the experimenter-models, paired with their own daughters, the subjects, in a problem-solving situation involving imitation.

Method

Subjects. The subjects were 30 girls between 5 and 6 years of age enrolled in two kindergarten classes of a predominantly middle-class school. Their mothers had volunteered their daughters' and their own participation in the study. Each mother was interviewed and each child was seen for two sessions, one with one of the investigators (A.L.P.) and, for the second session, with this investigator and the mother.

During the first session, the procedure was essentially like Rosenblith's (1959, 1961). After being seated in the room with the investigator, the child was told that she would play a paper and crayon game, and she could choose any crayon she wanted to draw with from the four (red, orange, green, and blue) in front of her. The Porteus Maze Test (Porteus, 1950) was then administered, slightly modified in instructions and procedure to render them more suitable to the age of the children. The test consists of a series of mazes, one maze for each year from ages 3 to 12, two trials being allowed for each maze. Testing is discontinued when the subject fails two consecutive age levels.

Between 3 and 4 weeks after the first session, the child was again called from her classroom by the investigator, who explained that they would "have a second turn at the game." Before entering the room where the testing was conducted, the child was told, "Today we have someone else here to play our games with us." Upon entering the room, the child met her mother and was asked to sit next to her at the table. The mother and child each had her own set of crayons, arranged in identical order on the table, and they were given identical sets of mazes.

Before she met with the subject in the experimental room, the mother had been given explicit instructions about the procedure to be followed. She had been carefully coached to draw slowly and to hesitate at the choice points, to make certain comments before each trial ("hm, hm, let's see now," and upon starting the maze, "here we go") and to make some irrelevant marks while tracing the maze (a loop at any point in her tracing and, a definite final mark such as ⊗).

After instructions were given to the pair, the mother began by "casually" picking up a crayon of the color least frequently selected by the child in the first session, using this crayon to trace the first maze correctly at a deliberately slow pace. The child watched and then was given her own turn on her copy of the same maze. The same procedure was followed for each of the 10 mazes, two trials being allowed for each maze.

Any improvement in maze-test performance between the first and second sessions presumably resulted from direct imitation of the mother's responses, and thus could be used as a measure of the child's tendency to imitate the mother's task-relevant performance. The major hypothesis of the study involved another type of imitation, however—incidental imitation learning, that is, duplication of the model's

[1] This study was supported by the National Institute of Mental Health, United States Public Health Service, under Research Grant M-3217, and the University of California Institute of Social Science.

responses that were not relevant to solving the problem. This type of imitation was scored in terms of the number of times the child picked up a crayon of the same color as the one her mother picked, repeated the mother's irrelevant utterances, and made loops or final marks like the mother's in tracing the maze.

Interviews. Testing the hypothesis required some basic data on child-rearing practices, and more specifically, on the degree of the mother's nurturance of the child. It was also essential to determine the extent of maternal fostering of dependent behavior in the child, for, according to some theories of identification, dependency itself facilitates imitative learning (Sears, Maccoby, and Levin, 1957). These data were obtained from maternal interviews conducted at the mothers' homes between the children's first and second sessions. The interviews consisted of 15 open-ended questions taken from the Sears et al. interview schedule. The questions were related to maternal warmth and hostility, fostering of dependency, restrictions and demands on the child, permissiveness, democracy in the home, and child-centeredness of the home. The interviews were tape recorded. Overall ratings of both nurturance and dependence were made on the basis of the analysis of these interview protocols. These ratings were made by the junior author after she had been trained in rating comparable interviews and had achieved 85% agreement with an experienced rater.

The distribution of the rating on nurturance was dichotomized as nearly as possible to the median, and the mothers above the median were considered nurturant ($N = 17$), while those below were considered nonnurturant ($N = 13$).

It should be noted that the ratings of the mother's interaction with the child were made before there was any knowledge of whether, or how much, the child would imitate the mother in the second session. Thus, there was no contamination of maternal rating and the child's tendency to imitate.

Teacher Ratings. Further assessment of the children's dependency came from teacher ratings of the children on four scales: frequency of attention-getting behavior, tendency to cling to the teacher, need for praise and approval, seeking help with tasks child is capable of doing. A rating of 1 on each scale represented the lowest degree of dependency, and a rating of 4, the highest. The child's dependency score was the sum of his ratings on all four scales.

It will be recalled that the subjects were in two kindergarten classes and had different teachers. Each teacher rated only her own pupils, of course, and, since the teachers probably had different standards of evaluating the children, their ratings had to be handled separately. One teacher rated 20 girls (10 in each group), while the other rated 10 girls (7 daughters of nurturant mothers and 3 others).

Results and Discussion

The major hypothesis was tested by comparing the imitation scores of two groups of girls, those with nurturant and those with nonnurturant mothers. The groups did not differ from each other in average age, ordinal position, number of siblings, or socioeconomic status. Since they did not differ significantly in their first session maze-test performance, it may be inferred that there were no significant intellectual differences between the two groups.

Since maternal nurturance may foster dependency in the child, and this in turn may promote imitative behavior, it was important to establish that maternal nurturance and child dependency were not closely correlated variables in this population. Analysis of the interview data revealed that the highly nurturant mothers in this study did *not* encourage dependency in their daughters. On the contrary, interview ratings of nurturance and encouragement of dependency, were slightly, though significantly, negatively correlated ($r = -.33$, $p = .05$). Apparently in this group, maternal nurturance was accompanied by some encouragement of independence in the child.

There is also some evidence that this encouragement of independence was, in fact, associated with a relatively low level of overt expression of dependency. According to teachers' ratings, the daughters of nurturant mothers were significantly less dependent than the other girls. The average dependency score, based on the teacher's ratings, of the 10 subjects with nurturant mothers was 8.2, the average for the other 10 was 10.1 ($t = 2.2$, $p < .05$). In the other class, the 7 subjects with nurturant mothers had an average dependency score of 10.5; the other 3 averaged 12.0 ($t = 1.6$, $p = .10–.15$).

Table 1 shows that the mean scores of the two

Table 1 *Mean Imitation Scores of Girls with Highly Nurturant and Nonnurturant Mothers*

Variable	Highly Nurturant Group ($N = 17$)	Non-Nurturant Group ($N = 13$)	U
Imitation of goal-related responses (improvement in maze test performance)	5.2	6.4	54.5[a]
Incidental imitation	17.8	12.9	65*

[a] In calculating U for this variable, we eliminated the scores of six girls who scored 16 or more (highest possible score = 20) in the first testing.

* $p < .05$.

groups on two types of imitation—imitation of goal-related responses and incidental imitation learning. Since the number of subjects in each group was small, and distributions of the scores were nonnormal, *U* tests were used to compare rank transformation scores on all these measures of subjects in the two groups. The results of these tests and their significance are summarized in Table 1.

The table shows that the two groups did not differ significantly in imitation of behavior directly related to achievement of the goal in the maze test. The finding is analogous to the findings of Bandura and Huston (1961) that the experimenter-model's nurturance did not significantly affect the children's tendency to imitate his choice (the correct and rewarded box) in a discrimination learning task. Children imitate the model's operant responses that lead to the solution of problems, regardless of the degree of the model's nurturance. Perhaps this is attributable to the power of the direct rewards involved, extrinsic (e.g., a prize for learning a discrimination task), intrinsic (such as the feeling of satisfaction derived from successful maze tracing), or both.

As Table 1 shows, the major hypothesis was confirmed. Maternal nurturance was found to be related to the child's incidental imitation learning, that is, to her tendency to match or imitate the mother's behavior that was incidental or irrelevant to solving the problem or achieving the goal. These results are clearly consistent with the conclusions of Bandura and Huston (1961) that "children display a good deal of social learning of an incidental imitative sort, and that nurturance is one condition facilitating such imitative learning" (p. 316). Either an immediately preceding nurturant interaction between the model and the child or a long-standing nurturant relationship between the two may have this facilitating effect. Thus, if the parent is generally nurturant toward the child, there is an increased tendency for the child to imitate aspects of that parent's behavior spontaneously, that is, in the absence of an immediately preceding experience of nurturance or of direct tuition or specific rewards for this imitation.

It may be inferred that the child's assumption of certain aspects of his parent's behavior may be explained in terms of the principles underlying imitation of a model's incidental behavior, the model's (or parent's) secondary reward value, and the self-rewards that consequently arise from this imitation. The child's acquisition of appropriate sex-typed behavior, which is related to nurturance by the same-sex parent (Mussen and Distler, 1959; Mussen and Rutherford, 1963) may be considered a result of this kind of imitation that occurs without teaching or direct, immediate rewards. In short, it may be concluded that the data support the notion that "the process subsumed under the term 'identification' may be accounted for in terms of incidental learning, that is, learning that apparently takes place in the absence of an induced set or intent to learn the specific behaviors or activities in question . . ." (Bandura and Huston, 1961, p. 311).

References

Bandura, A., and Huston, Aletha C. Identification as a process of incidental learning. *Journal of Abnormal and Social Psychology,* 1961, *63,* 311–318.

Kagan, J., and Mussen, P. H. Dependency theme on the TAT and group conformity. *Journal of Consulting Psychology,* 1956, *20,* 29–32.

Miller, N. E., and Dollard, J. *Social learning and imitation.* New Haven: Yale University Press, 1941.

Mowrer, O. H. *Learning theory and personality dynamics.* New York: Ronald Press, 1950.

Mussen, P. H., and Distler, L. Masculinity identification and father-son relationships. *Journal of Abnormal and Social Psychology,* 1959, *59,* 350–356.

Mussen, P. H., and Rutherford, E. Parent-child relations and parental personality in relation to young children's sex-role preferences. *Child Development,* 1963, *34,* 589–607.

Porteus, S. D. *The Porteus Maze Test and intelligence.* Palo Alto, Calif.: Pacific Books, 1950.

Rosenblith, Judy F. Learning by imitation in kindergarten children. *Child Development,* 1959, *30,* 69–80.

Rosenblith, Judy F. Imitative color choices in kindergarten children. *Child Development,* 1961, *32,* 211–223.

Sears, R. R., Maccoby, Eleanor E., and Levin, H. *Patterns of child rearing.* Evanston, Ill.: Row, Peterson, 1957.

How does the socialization process develop when the parent provides mostly aversive stimuli to the child? In these cases the child's behavior is shaped more through negative than through positive reinforcement; that is, the parents have tended to punish undesirable behavior rather than to reward desirable behavior. Negative reinforcement is involved because the aversive stimulus used in punishment will increase the frequency of any performance that removes it. Children who are punished frequently and strongly may simply become intransigent or rebellious. On the other hand, given a sufficient degree of identification with the parent, the child may actually become more responsive to the type of treatment to which he has become accustomed. The article by *Patterson* deals with the behaviors prompted in boys and girls by parents who provided disapproval for a performance.

The experimental situation is similar to that described earlier by Gewirtz and Baer (see Article 7). The boys and girls who served as subjects played a game in which they dropped marbles through one of two holes in a box. On signal from the experimenter, the child's parent made comments indicating disapproval of the child's choice of hole. Continuous recording of the child's responses later revealed how often the child changed his preference for one hole or the other as a function of the parent's reactions. Interviews with both the parents and children gave the experimenters information with which to rate the degree of restrictiveness and punitiveness imposed on the child at home.

Results of the study revealed that boys from punitive-restrictive homes were more influenced by disapproving reactions from their parents than were boys from supportive-permissive homes. No such conclusion could be reached in the case of girls, although the girls who were most responsive to disapproval by their fathers were described by their teachers as being poorly adjusted in school. The boys who were most influenced by disapproval were also described as exhibiting inefficient classroom behavior. Although they are not definitive in every respect, the data from this study suggest that some children react more effectively to approval in a learning situation, whereas others are more responsive to disapproval. The basis for this difference appears to lie in their relationships with their parents.

25 | *Parents as Dispensers of Aversive Stimuli*[1]

G. R. PATTERSON

There is extensive experimental literature which shows that aversive social stimuli are more effective than positive social reinforcers in controlling the behavior of both adults (Ferguson and Buss, 1959) and children (Brackbill and O'Hara, 1958; Meyer and Seidman, 1961; Starr and Patterson[2]). These findings taken in conjunction with the fact that aversive stimuli are rather frequent occurrences in the life of the child (Fawl, 1963; Simmons and Schoggin, 1963) would imply that the child's responsiveness to aversive stimuli is a variable which is crucial to the socialization process.

It is assumed here that the child who has been repeatedly exposed to aversive stimuli will be more responsive to social disapproval than will the child who has been exposed to a lesser degree. More specifically, children from punitive-restrictive homes will be more responsive to social disapproval than will children from nonpunitive homes. This hypothesis

[1] This study was supported by Grant M-5429 from the United States Public Health Service. The writer gratefully acknowledges the assistance of D. Anderson and H. Hawkins in collecting the data, and to Beverly Fagot for her assistance in the data analysis.

[2] "Use of Criticism and Praise in Operant Conditioning of a Simple Motor Response," undergraduate National Science Foundation paper, 1961.

From the *Journal of Personality and Social Psychology,* 1965, *2,* 844–851.

will be tested by relating current parental practices in the home to a laboratory task assessing the responsiveness of the child to social disapproval dispensed by the parent.

A pilot study by Williams[3] showed that (neutral) adults with high anxiety scores on the MMPI tended to be more effective with children in dispensing both positive and aversive social stimuli. This leads to the second hypothesis that parents describing themselves as anxious on the MMPI would be more effective than nonanxious parents in dispensing aversive stimuli.

The research by Kagan (1956) and Emmerich (1961) would suggest that the father is seen by the child as being more punitive and fear arousing than is the mother. These findings lead to the third hypothesis that fathers will be more effective in dispensing social disapproval than will mothers.

The review by Church (1963) of the effect of punishment upon animal behavior strongly suggests a dichotomy of effects. The research literature shows that in addition to the general effect of punishment in suppressing responding, there may also be an emotional consequence attached to the use of punishment. These findings lead to the very tentative hypothesis that the same parental punitiveness which results in a child's being overly responsive to disapproval will also be related to the child being described as "overly emotional." More specifically, it was predicted that the child found to be most responsive to parental disapproval in the laboratory would also be described by the teachers as being poorly adjusted in the classroom.

The apparatus used in this study was an adaptation of the operant conditioning device described by Gewirtz and Baer (1958). Parental disapproval is made contingent upon one of the responses available in a simple two-choice game played by the child. The magnitude of the child's change in preference for these two choices constitutes a measure of his responsiveness to parental disapproval. Following the conditioning trial, the mother was interviewed to assess current child-rearing practices. The teachers were also asked to provide ratings of the child's current classroom adjustment behaviors.

Procedure

Sample. Sixty families volunteered to participate in the study; each family contributed one parent and one child for a conditioning trial. The 30 boys and 30 girls were taken in approximately equal numbers from the second, third, and fourth grades of the local public schools.

Data obtained from the interview with the mother showed that the sample was drawn largely from the middle class. Only those families were used in the study in which both the mother and father could be present for the conditioning trial. A table of random numbers was used to determine which of the parents would serve as social agent in the conditioning trial.

Apparatus. To facilitate the cooperation of the families, the equipment was mounted in a 15-foot house trailer which was taken to the home. A soundproof partition separated the electronic equipment and the experimenters from the subjects. To reduce distracting sounds, the recording equipment was mounted in insulated cabinets.

The apparatus was an adaptation of the marble box described by Gewirtz and Baer (1958). The box was approximately 8 inches high and 18 × 10 inches wide. The two holes at the top were .75 inch in diameter and placed 1 inch apart. In a tray at the base of the box were 250 blue glass marbles. The box was located on a level platform adjusted so that the base was approximately at waist level for the subject. The subject faced the reinforcing agent who sat on a bench 3 feet to the front and right of the subject. The apparatus was automated to the extent that frequency of response to either hole was recorded along a time line on a multiple channel event recorder. A programmer was used to signal the reinforcing agent through an earphone. Upon receiving a signal, the reinforcing agent read a statement from a list given to him by the experimenter. The statements were: not too good, huh-uh (with head movement), not yet, no that's not right, nope, guess not, huh-uh, wrong.

Procedure. Parents who consented to participate in the study were contacted about a week in advance and arrangements were made for the laboratory to be brought to their home. The majority of the appointments were on Saturday mornings and afternoons, the remainder being scheduled between 7:00 and 8:30 weekday evenings. At the appointed time, the trailer was brought to the home and approximately 10 minutes were taken to introduce the research team (at least two experimenters) and to set up the apparatus. Invariably, the staff were well received by the family.

One of the parents (randomly assigned) was taken into the trailer first and given the following instructions:

> Your child will be playing a simple game of dropping marbles into this box. We would like you to be in this room with him [or her] part of the time, and listen for signals that we will send you over this earphone. [The experimenter demonstrates how earphone is worn, then sends a few signals to test apparatus

[3] Unpublished manuscript entitled "Personality Characteristics of the Adult in Operant Conditioning of Children," 1962.

and make sure parent can hear the signal clearly.] Whenever you hear a signal, we would like you to make one of the following remarks from this sheet. [Hands parent sheet.] Use only these words, and do not say them when you do not hear a signal over the earphone. OK, if we could practice that now a couple of times.

The experimenter then dropped some marbles and checked to make sure that the parent's discrimination of signals and his behavior were in accord with the instructions. The parent was then cautioned not to give his child any other information during the experimental session other than to speak the appropriate comments. The parent was ushered out and the child was brought into the laboratory and given the following instructions:

Would you stand here behind this blue box. OK, now here you see a whole bunch of marbles and up here are two holes. What I want you to do is to pick up the marbles, one at a time, and drop them into the holes. You can drop as many as you like, in any order, into either hole [experimenter demonstrates]. Just use one hand at a time, and remember not to pick up more than one at a time. Would you like to try a few? OK. Now you can wait until I give you the signal to start by tapping on this window from outside. Then just keep on dropping them one at a time until I tell you to stop.

The first 100 responses constituted the base operant level. The frequency of responses was tabulated on both an event recorded and cumulatively on two electric counters. The latter could quickly be scanned by the experimenter. When the counters showed a total of 100 responses, the experimenter identified the hole which was most preferred; he then activated the programmer so that each time a response to that hole occurred the parent would receive a click in his earphone. A 1 : 1 schedule of aversive stimuli was maintained for 10 responses to the preferred hole. Following this, the child received 20 aversive stimuli on a 4 : 11 variable ratio schedule.

At the end of the trial, the parent was given a note instructing him to dispense a positive reinforcer each time he heard a click in the earphone. Although the data from this phase of the trial were not used in the analysis, the procedure was introduced to counteract the effect of a long period of disapproval by the parent.

Dependent Variables. The data were tabulated for the frequency of occurrence of responses A and B for each 15-second interval through the experiment. The measure of preference change was obtained by computing $X/A + B$ for each 15-second interval where X was the frequency of the least preferred response. The median of this relative frequency score was calculated for both the base operant phase and the conditioning phase of the experiment. The difference between these two medians provided a measure of the magnitude of shift in preference. From previous studies, the test-retest reliability of this score was .75 (Patterson and Hinsey, 1964).

Previous studies have also shown that the magnitude of the difference score is significantly determined by the magnitude of the position preference shown during the base operant period (Patterson and Hinsey, 1964). In the present study the correlation between position preference during the base operant period and the magnitude of preference change was .50 ($p < .001$). This would indicate that it is necessary to partial out the effect of base operant position preference before subjecting the data to intensive analysis. To meet this problem, data have been analyzed for several hundred children who have participated in conditioning trials with a variety of social agents using both positive and aversive social stimuli. Frequency distributions of preference change scores were calculated for three base operant levels of position preferences. Deviation scores were computed for each of these distributions; the deviation scores were then converted to T scores by using McCall's T score transformation. The correlation between base operant position preference and the T scores for preference change was not significant (−.17).

Interview with Mother. Tape recordings were made of a 30-minute structured interview with the mother. The mimeographed form used by the interviewer contained both the questions and the rating scales; the latter were filled out by the interviewer as soon as he felt he had obtained enough information to make a judgment. The tape recordings of one half the families were listened to by a second experimenter, who made independent judgments on each of the 33 scales. The reliabilities for the individual items will be presented in a later section. The data specific to each item ranged from .18 to .91 with a median correlation of .74.

The questions and ratings scales were based partially upon a procedure developed by Patterson, Littman, and Hinsey (1964). Many of the original questions and scales were based upon material published by Bandura and Huston[4]; Becker (1960), Roff (1949), Sears, Maccoby, and Levin (1957). Although these latter studies do not show factor identity, they all identify the following two bipolar factors: warm versus hostile and permissiveness versus restrictiveness. Approximately one half of the items used in the present interview were taken from these studies.

4 "Identification as a Process of Incidental Learning," progress report to the National Institute of Mental Health, United States Public Health Service, 1961.

Each parent who served as the social agent in the conditioning trial filled out the items of the *L* and *K* scales of the MMPI in addition to the items forming the Taylor Manifest Anxiety (*MA*) scale.

Interview with the Child. Following the conditioning trial, the child was interviewed to determine his awareness of the various contingencies. The interview first identified whether the child was attending to the behavior of the parent, or to changes in his own behavior. Finally, he was told that dropping a marble into one of the holes elicited the comments from the parent; the child was asked to guess which hole it was. The interview and rating scale for awareness were described in detail elsewhere and will not be reproduced here (Patterson et al., 1964).

In previous studies with the present operant procedure and its very complex ratio schedules, there have been no significant correlations between ratings of awareness and changes in preferences. In the present study the correlations for the subsamples ranged from .03 to .40, none of which were significant.

Each child was also interviewed with a series of questions designed by Kagan (1956) to determine the child's perception of parental roles in the family. These questions were: If you were in an argument at home with your mother and father, who would be on your side, your mother or your father? Let's make believe you were bad and your mother and father were both home. Who would punish you, your mother or your father? Who is the boss in your house, your mother or your father? Who are you scared of more, your mother or your father? For the correlation analysis reported in a later section of the paper, the answer to any given question was scored as 1 if the child replied "father" and scored 2 if the child replied "mother."

Teachers' Ratings. After an interval of from 3 weeks to 4 months following the conditioning trial, each child was rated by his classroom teacher. The 47 bipolar items used in the rating schedule were taken from a schedule developed by Becker (1960). Becker's pool of items were intended to sample the factor domain outlined by Cattell. The items were designed to be appropriate to the behavior of nursery school children. Becker derived six factors by a centroid factor analysis of a large sample of teachers' ratings using this scale. The items in the present study sample the variables with the highest loadings on each of these six factors.

Results

Parents dispensing disapproval were highly effective in changing the child's choice behavior. The total number of responses occurring in a 15-second interval ranged from 4 to 8. The mean increase in the least preferred response was 15.5% of the response occurring in a 15-second interval. The *t* test of these difference scores was significant, $p < .001$. Although the studies are not directly comparable, it is of interest to note in passing that the parents dispensing disapproval were more effective in changing preference behavior than were parents dispensing social reinforcers ($M = .070$) or peers dispensing social reinforcers ($M = .098$) (Patterson and Anderson, 1964; Patterson et al., 1964).

Preference Change, Controlling for Sex and Age of Child and Sex of Parent. The mean *T* score for preference change and the sample size of the various subgroups are presented in Table 1.

The analysis of variance followed a 2 × 2 × 3 design controlling for sex of the child, sex of the parent, and age of the child. The analysis of variance and correlation for unequal cell frequencies was based upon the procedures outlined by Winer (1962). Neither the analysis of main effects nor interactions were significant. Although, for most of the subgroups, fathers tended to be more effective than mothers, the effects are not significant. The lack of significance for main effects for sex of child and sex of parent were also found in the study by Patterson et al. (1964). In this latter study, parents dispensed positive social reinforcers.

Parental Practices Correlated with Responsiveness. Earlier in the discussion, it was hypothesized that

Table 1 *Mean T Scores and Sample Sizes*

Subjects	Age of Child: 7		8		9		Overall
	M	*N*	*M*	*N*	*M*	*N*	*M*
Boys reinforced by fathers	55.1	4	58.0	5	49.8	7	53.6
Boys reinforced by mothers	48.7	4	46.5	4	47.5	6	47.6
Girls reinforced by fathers	63.2	4	44.8	4	51.1	4	53.0
Girls reinforced by mothers	51.7	5	56.2	7	51.0	6	53.2
Overall *M*	54.5		52.4		49.7		
Total *N*		17		20		23	

Table 2 *Parental Practices Correlated with Preference* T *Scores*

Reliability	Interview Variable	Boys		Girls	
		Fathers	Mothers	Fathers	Mothers
	Parental practices				
.80	Frequency mother explodes	.64**	.16	−.46	−.43
.74	Use deprivation of privileges	−.60**	−.34	−.18	.01
.38	Restrictions outside of the home	.09	.52**	.36	.07
.91	Frequency parent spanks, slaps	.13	.58**	−.40	.41
.63	Use of reasoning	.57**	.18	.38	−.12
.90	Frequency scolding, nagging	.03	.39	−.49*	−.05
.44	Mother tends to give socially desirable responses in interview	−.61**	.04	−.37	.23
	In argument, mother is on child's side[a]	−.52*	−.41	.75**	−.01
	Child behaviors				
.88	Attention seeking	.59**	.26	−.10	−.20
.81	Seeks tangible rewards	.35	.12	−.58**	.36
.85	Seeks affection	.44	−.36	−.08	.51**
	Parents' self-description				
	MMPI, *K* scale	−.36	.18	−.57**	.02
	MMPI, Manifest Anxiety Scale	.49*	−.02	.67**	.20

[a] These data from (Kagan, 1956) interview with the child.
* $p < .10$.
** $p < .05$.

the responsiveness of the child to social disapproval would be correlated with use of punitive-restrictive parental practices in the home. To test this assumption, the 33 rating scales from the interview were correlated with the preference *T* scores. To minimize confounding effects, the data are presented separately for boys-fathers, boys-mothers, girls-fathers, and girls-mothers. Only variables with a Pearson product-moment correlation significant at $< .10$ are presented in Table 2. The reliability correlations represent the agreement between judges in filling out the rating scales.

The data for boys supported the hypothesis that responsiveness to parental disapproval will be associated with homes described as restrictive and punitive.

Boys were most responsive to fathers who described themselves as being rather tense individuals. These fathers tended to support the boy during periods of family discord. In these homes, although deprivation of privileges was not used with any great frequency, the mother tended to explode frequently as a technique for controlling the child and both parents made intensive use of reasoning. The boys themselves were described as seeking attention and rewards and affection; the correlations for these last two variables were not significant, however.

The significant correlations relating to boys' responsiveness to their mothers are so limited in number that this number of correlations could have occurred by chance. In general, the more frequent the punishments and restrictions, the more responsive the boys were to maternal disapproval.

The significant correlations relating childrearing practices to girls' responsiveness to fathers' and mothers' disapproval were too limited in number to permit interpretation. It seems quite probable that the variables relating to the child's responsiveness to maternal disapproval were not being sampled in the present procedure. The fathers of girls most responsive to paternal disapproval described themselves as being rather tense, retiring, inhibited individuals.

Adjustment Behaviors Associated with Responsiveness to Disapproval. It was hypothesized that the child's responsiveness to parental disapproval would be related to poor adjustment behaviors in the child. The relevant data for boys are presented in Table 3. The correlations are Pearson product-moment correlations between the preference *T* scores and both the teachers' and the parents' ratings of personality trait behaviors. Because the ratings from the parents were collected only during the last half of the experiment, the resulting sample size was too small to permit analyzing the data separately for mothers and fathers as social agents. Combining the data from the two parents will introduce some confounding and lower the correlations. Only those items significant at $p < .10$ are presented here. The significant variables are grouped according to the factor dimensions derived by Becker (1960).

The number of significant correlations with the

Table 3 *Boys: Personality Ratings Correlated with Preference* T *Scores*

Personality Trait Behaviors	Correlations with Teachers' Ratings: Mother as Punishing Agent ($N = 14$)	Correlations with Teachers' Ratings: Father as Punishing Agent ($N = 12$)	Correlations with Parents' Ratings ($N = 15$)
Schoolroom intelligence			
Dull minded-intelligent	−.32	−.10	−.43*
Poor memory-good memory	−.40	−.48*	−.14
Ineffective-effective	−.23	.01	−.67***
Meaningless-meaningful	−.24	.29	−.52**
Hostile-withdrawn			
Interesting-boring	.30	−.24	.45*
Relaxed disposition			
Fluctuating-stable	−.24	−.61**	−.15
Lack of aggression			
Impatient-patient	−.32	−.19	−.45*
Submission			
Strong willed-weak willed	.20	.41	.48*
Dominant-not dominant	−.02	.64**	
Conduct problems			
Obedient-disobedient	.52**	−.05	−.04
Responsible-irresponsible	.46*	.42	.45*
Cooperative-obstructive	.52**	.21	.07
Easily disciplined-difficult to discipline	.64**	.11	−.03
Adult like-infantile	.42	−.30	.50**

* $p < .10$.
** $p < .05$.

teachers' ratings did not exceed chance expectations. However, there are a significant number of high correlations with the parents' ratings of personality trait behaviors. In addition, there is some general agreement between teachers' and parents' ratings in terms of the factors within which the significant correlations are found and the signs of the correlations. The boys most responsive to parental disapproval were described by parents and by teachers as manifesting behaviors which would be inefficient in the classroom setting, for example, dull-minded, ineffective, and meaningless. The responsive boy was also described by his parents and teachers as being irresponsible and infantile. The correlations from both the parents' and the teachers' ratings would suggest that the most appropriate label for the boy responsive to parental disapproval would be "immature." The data offer rather weak support for the hypothesis that boys most responsible to parental disapproval would be characterized as poorly adjusted.

The corresponding data for girls are presented in Table 4.

Only the data for teachers' ratings correlated with girls' responsiveness to fathers produced more significant relations than would be expected by chance.

In general, these data support the hypothesized relation between responsiveness to disapproval and poor adjustment. As in the case of boys, both teachers and parents seemed to agree in describing girls responsive to parental disapproval as showing inefficient classroom behaviors, for example, dull-minded and subject to distraction. The girls most responsive to disapproval by the father are particularly described by the teachers as being poorly adjusted. These girls are described as being tense, anxious, fearful, demanding, and jealous.

Discussion

The data for boys support the hypothesis that the punitive-restrictive home is most likely to be associated with the child who is most responsive to parental disapproval. Previous research by Patterson et al. (1964) shows that this type of home is also associated with boys who are most responsive to social reinforcers dispensed by the mother. This would suggest that parental practices which are punitive and restrictive may be related to rather high potential for the control of the boy. Taken together the two studies would suggest that in such a home the boy would be highly responsive to disapproval dispensed by either parent and also highly responsive to social approval dispensed by the mother. If this is true, it would suggest some significant implications for the socialization in the child. At the present time a study is being initiated in which the boy is reinforced by the mother and punished in a second task by the

Table 4 *Girls: Personality Ratings Correlated with Preference* T *Scores*

Personality Trait Behaviors	Correlations with Teachers' Ratings: Mother as Punishing Agent ($N = 14$)	Correlations with Teachers' Ratings: Father as Punishing Agent ($N = 12$)	Correlations with Parents' Ratings ($N = 15$)
School intelligence			
Dull minded-intelligent	−.34	−.39	−.49*
Subject to distraction-able to concentrate	−.29	−.74***	.12
Slow-quick	.02	.21	−.68***
Bored-interested	−.24	.48*	−.28
Hostile-withdrawn			
Responsive-aloof	−.43*	.09	.20
Extraverted-introverted	−.51**	.25	.04
Trusting-distrusting	−.17	.52*	−.16
Relaxed disposition			
Tense-relaxed	−.04	−.48*	.11
Anxious-nonchalant	−.32	−.57**	00
Fearful-not fearful	−.02	−.65**	00
Lack of aggression			
Demanding-not demanding	−.10	−.58**	−.29
Jealous-not jealous	.35	−.48*	−.40
Submissive			
Noisy-quiet	−.56**	.08	.16

* $p < .10$.
** $p < .05$.
*** $p < .01$.

father. This study will provide a necessary check upon the assumption that the restrictive-punitive home has implications for the boys' responsiveness to both social approval and disapproval.

The data for girls do not provide support for the hypothesis that parental practices relate to responsiveness to disapproval. The correlations between responsiveness to either of the parents and parental practices are too limited in number to permit any interpretation. This would suggest that, in the case of girls, the hypothesis should be changed.

Bronfenbrenner (1960) and Hoffman (1960) suggest an alternate hypothesis which might relate to responsiveness to disapproval by girls. These writers indicate that some combination of parental affection *and* parental authority would lead to be the best prediction about the child's responsiveness to social cues. In the present case, the sample is too small to permit such an analysis. Data from a study now underway will, however, provide a test of this hypothesis, the prediction being that parental restrictiveness will again relate to responsiveness in boys but that a combination of affection and restrictiveness will be required to account for responsiveness in girls.

The second hypothesis predicted that the parent describing himself as anxious and tense (*MA* scale) would be associated with the child most responsive to parental disapproval. Although the hypothesis was in part based upon earlier data by Williams,[5] it also seemed reasonable to suppose that the anxious parent would tend to be rather unpredictable in his punitive reactions to the child. This should lead in turn to his being seen as a more threatening figure. The data show that the hypothesis is supported only for fathers. The more anxious the father described himself to be, the more responsive are both the boys and the girls to paternal disapproval. These data suggest that it is not the general role played by the parent, for example, mother or father, which determines the responsiveness of the child to disapproval but rather *specific* characteristics of the parent. In the present study, anxiety proved to be a significant variable. This would suggest that further studies of this type include a broader coverage of personality characteristics in patients.

The preliminary impression from the present data is that girls most responsive to paternal disapproval tend to be seen as emotionally disturbed and inefficient in the classroom setting. Boys who are responsive to parental disapproval are described by the parents as immature. If these findings are replicated, they could be of major significance in explicating the nature of some cases referred to child guidance outpatient settings. For example, research (Levine and

[5] See Footnote 3.

Simmons, 1962; Patterson et al., 1964) showed that nonresponsiveness to social approval was associated with maladjusted behaviors in children. The present data suggest that many of these children, while relatively nonresponsive to social approval, might be more responsive to social disapproval than would normal children.

References

BECKER, W. C. The relationship of factors in parental ratings of self and each other to the behavior of kindergarten children as rated by mothers, fathers, and teachers. *Journal of Consulting Psychology,* 1960, *24,* 507–527.

BRACKBILL, YVONNE, and O'HARA, J. The relative effectiveness of reward and punishment for discrimination learning in children. *Journal of Comparative and Physiological Psychology,* 1958, *51,* 747–751.

BRONFENBRENNER, U. Toward a theoretical model for the analysis of parent-child relationships in a social context. In *Parental attitudes and child behavior.* Springfield, Ill.: Charles C. Thomas, 1960. Pp. 90–109.

CHURCH, R. M. The varied effects of punishment on behavior. *Psychological Review,* 1963, *70,* 369–402.

EMMERICH, W. Family role concepts of children ages 6 through 10 years. *Child Development,* 1961, *32,* 609–624.

FAWL, C. L. Disturbances experienced by children in their natural habitats. In R. G. Barker (Ed.), *The stream of behavior.* New York: Appleton-Century-Crofts, 1963. Pp. 99–126.

FERGUSON, ELSIE, and BUSS, A. Supplementary report: Acquisition, extinction, and counterconditioning with different verbal reinforcement combinations. *Journal of Experimental Psychology,* 1959, *58,* 94–95.

GEWIRTZ, J. L., and BAER, D. M. The effect of brief social deprivation on behaviors for a social reinforcer. *Journal of Abnormal and Social Psychology,* 1958, *56,* 49–56.

HOFFMAN, M. L. Power assertion by the parent and its impact on the child. *Child Development,* 1960, *31,* 129–143.

KAGAN, J. The child's perception of the parent. *Journal of Abnormal and Social Psychology,* 1956, *53,* 257–258.

LEVINE, G. R., and SIMMONS, J. T. Response to praise by emotionally disturbed boys. *Psychological Reports,* 1962, *11,* 10.

MEYER, W. J., and SEIDMAN, S. B. Relative effectiveness of different reinforcement combinations on concept learning of children at two developmental levels. *Child Development,* 1961, *32,* 117–127.

PATTERSON, G. R., and ANDERSON, D. Peers as reinforcers. *Child Development,* 1964, *35,* 951–960.

PATTERSON, G. R., and HINSEY, C. Investigations of some assumptions and characteristics of a procedure for instrumental conditioning in children. *Journal of Experimental Child Psychology,* 1964, *1,* 111–123.

PATTERSON, G. R., LITTMAN, R., and HINSEY, C. Parents as reinforcers. *Journal of Personality,* 1964, *32,* 182–199.

ROFF, M. A factorial study of the Fels parent behavior scales. *Child Development,* 1949, *20,* 29–45.

SEARS, R. R., MACCOBY, ELEANOR E., and LEVIN, H. *Patterns of child rearing.* Evanston, Ill.: Row, Peterson, 1957.

SIMMONS, H., and SCHOGGIN, P. Mothers and fathers as sources of environmental pressure on children. In R. G. Barker (Ed.), *The stream of behavior.* New York: Appleton-Century-Crofts, 1963. Pp. 70–77.

WINER, B. J. *Statistical principles in experimental design.* New York: McGraw-Hill, 1962.

The reader should not let himself be put off by the rather formidable title of the article by *Etzel and Gewirtz.* This is actually a straightforward and readable account of the procedures that were effective in reducing the amount of operant crying of two infants, one six weeks old and the other twenty weeks old. The authors point out how adults often unwittingly reinforce in young children the very behaviors that they would like to terminate. Crying, in particular, may easily become an operant performance that is maintained by the attention it prompts from parents or other caretakers. Modification of this particular behavior, when it becomes sufficiently aversive to others, is accomplished by subjecting it to extinction procedures and, at the same time, reinforcing some behavior that is incompatible with crying.

Etzel and Gewirtz describe how an adult reinforced smiles by smiling and talking. Crying, frowning, and fussing by the child prompted only an expressionless gaze. The younger child was not influenced by the same method of reinforcement, and so they supplied additional stimuli, such as bells, hand puppets, and whistles, when the child smiled. Reinforcement for smiling was discontinued, as the final experimental procedure, thus demonstrating that smiling indeed occurred because of the reinforcement. In general, this experiment illustrates the careful use of both descriptive and manipulative procedures in arranging the environment of an infant so that certain specified behaviors may be brought under experimental control.

26

Experimental Modification of Caretaker-Maintained High-Rate Operant Crying in a 6- and a 20-Week-Old Infant (Infans tyrannotearus): *Extinction of Crying with Reinforcement of Eye Contact and Smiling*[1]

BARBARA C. ETZEL[2]
JACOB L. GEWIRTZ

Infant crying behaviors can be evoked by a large variety of stimuli but occasionally occur in the absence of an identifiable stimulus. Thus, pinpricks, head bumps, and gas pain can evoke crying, and, in principle, various social stimuli which precede or follow crying can acquire discriminative or reinforcing control of that response, regardless of the basis for its initial occurrence. At least two classes of crying behavior in children have been identified, respondent and operant (Hart, Allen, Buel, Harris, and Wolf, 1964). These classifications depend on the stimulus variables which precede or follow crying. We shall emphasize operant crying in our experimental analysis.

In life settings operant crying usually comes under the close control of social stimuli provided by the environment, possibly because of its strong noxious quality for caretakers and the fact that the maintaining contingencies are often not obvious ones. Operant crying may begin to acquire strength when an infant's crying results in his being picked up, talked to, or given a bottle. When such crying occurs in connection with some event like the passage of time or the appearance of a passing caretaker, cues provided by that event can become discriminative for the infant and he may begin to cry. Such contingent events, when repeated, can maintain the response. Operant crying often terminates when the caretaker approaches the crib, and may resume more loudly than before when the caretaker departs. Tears may more commonly accompany crying brought on by a noxious stimulus, but wails may be indiscriminable between the two classes of crying.

Hart et al. (1964) demonstrated successful modification of operant crying in two 4-year-old preschool children. Two systematic procedures were used to study operant crying in a nursery school: extinction of crying by removal of contingent "attention," and social reinforcement of consensually valued behaviors that are incompatible with crying. Wolf, Risley, and Mees (1964) applied similar procedures to the behavior of a 3½-year-old autistic child and successfully reduced his rate of temper tantrums (which included crying). The youngest operant crier "treated" to date was a 21-month-old S whose temper tantrums were reduced by the use of an extinction procedure alone (Williams, 1959). It is thought that operant crying may be demonstrated early in infant life, perhaps even within the first few weeks. The reinforcing stimuli provided by the environment at this early age may not be conditioned or even social.

This paper reports the experimental extinction of operant crying in two young infants. The procedures differ slightly from similar studies. An experimental room was used to modify the crying behavior, since control of the caretaking staff in the nursery was not possible in this study. It was determined before and during the course of the study that crying was being regularly reinforced in the nursery. Therefore the smile, a response incompatible with crying, was reinforced for both infants at the same time that crying was being extinguished. For one S, both eye contact and smiling were reinforced. Extinction of crying and reinforcement of an incompatible response were employed jointly to facilitate establishing a discrimination between nursery and experimental settings.

Method

Subjects. William and Anthony were Negro infants in the nursery of the well-baby boarders unit of a children's hospital. Infants remain there in the charge of Negro and white caretakers until institutional or family placement is arranged for them. The woman

1 We express our thanks to Dr. Allen E. Marans and Dr. Reginald Lourie of the Division of Psychiatry, and to the staff of the Boarders Unit, Children's Hospital, Washington, D.C., for their cooperation during the course of the study. The writers appreciate the help of Mrs. Rita Verkouteren, who served as the second observer, and of Mrs. Deborah G. Singer and Mr. E. J. Haupt, who made helpful editorial suggestions in the preparation of this report.

2 This study was carried out when the first author, on leave of absence from the Department of Human Development, University of Kansas, held a special NICHD Fellowship to work with the second author in the Section on Early Learning and Development, Laboratory of Psychology, National Institute of Mental Health.

who served as *E* with both Ss had helped in the nursery for several weeks prior to this study.

William was 20 weeks 3 days old at the beginning of the study and had been in the nursery for 7 weeks 2 days. His medical chart indicated that he was in good health. William had been selected for inclusion in another of our studies, but his crying behavior did not abate after several days of adaptation procedures in the experimental room, during which he was presented with *E*'s unresponding and unchanging Caucasian face. He would typically smile to the face within the first five seconds, then begin to frown, fuss, and finally cry. Crying would continue until *E*'s face was removed. When the face was again presented, the same sequence of behaviors ensued. During the adaptation period of the other study, William's rate of eye contact with *E* (as opposed to looking away) was recorded. These data allow an examination of the direction of William's visual response at the time he started to cry. William started to cry when he was in eye contact with *E* 91% of the time during three daily 12-minute sessions of observation. This can be further compared with his spending about half (55%) of each session in eye contact with *E*. Thus, it appeared that William's crying behavior came under the close control of the appearance of *E*'s face. Following the three days of observation, William was transferred to this study.

In the nursery, William generally exhibited a high rate of crying. His crying was louder than that of other infants and attracted the attention of aides and volunteers. Someone often sat and held or rocked William, apparently in response to his crying. When he was held, William often smiled at adults near him, and they would stop to respond to him. In spite of his appealing qualities when held, aides described him as being "normally fussy" when *E* asked regularly about his health during the previous 24 hours. Often when he was taken for his daily experimental session, caretakers indicated that they were glad to get him out of the nursery for a while. Although the aides said that William cried to "get attention," there were no examples noted of a caretaker attempting to remove the attention contingencies that appeared to maintain his crying.

Anthony was 6 weeks of age when the study began. He had been in the nursery for 4 weeks 2 days. His medical chart noted some rapid breathing earlier in life, but otherwise he was considered healthy. During the period Anthony was being studied, three to four crying "checks" (randomly timed) were made each morning in the nursery to obtain systematic observations of nursery behavior. The crying behavior of three other infants of approximately the same age and in the same section of the nursery was also observed. The total number of crying episodes recorded for Anthony was approximately equal to the combined total for the three comparison infants. The total number of times he was held in an aide's or volunteer's arms because of crying was twice that of the total for the three comparison infants. The experimenter did not mention to the staff her interest in crying behavior, since the tactic was to attempt extinction of crying in the experimental setting rather than in the maintaining environment. Extinction should have been easier to effect in the nursery than in the separate room we used, for a simpler discrimination would have been involved.

Apparatus and Responses. When an S was to be taken to the experimental room, he was lifted from his crib and placed in a seated position in a plastic baby seat which was put into a baby carriage. The subject was wheeled through the corridors, and taken via elevator to the experimental room on the floor below the nursery. The subject was not handled further until he was returned to the nursery at the completion of the session, some 15 minutes later.

In the well-lit experimental room, the carriage was placed in the "center" of a U-shaped (three-panel) screen. The subject faced a rectangular opening in the screen's center panel. The experimenter sat on a chair on the opposite side of the panel from S behind the opening. Her face and shoulders were presented when a window shade, covering the opening, was raised. A white cloth hanging behind *E* masked other stimuli from being seen through the opening. The daily 15-minute sessions were divided into six 2-minute stimulus presentation intervals with a 30-second rest interval between the 2-minute presentations. During the 30-second interval the shade was down. Timer lights observable only to *E* signaled the start and end of the intervals. Responses were recorded by *E*'s depressing keys mounted on a box on her lap. Slight pressure on the keys activated event pens on an Esterline Angus recorder. Response duration and frequency were simultaneously but independently recorded.

With William, the four responses observed were *cry, fuss, frown,* and *smile*. The definitions are similar to those of Gewirtz (1963).[3] The three responses

[3] This 1963 Social Test Manual constitutes a refined and slightly modified version of the 1961 definitions published in Gewirtz (1965). An abbreviated version of the definitions used are: *cry*—*S* emits loud rhythmic wails accompanied by tears and redness of face: *full*—*S* emits a loud rhythmic wail, whimper, whine or screech which is not accompanied by tears but does include a "frown-like" facial expression; *frown*—eyebrows lower, folds appear above nose, vertical lines appear on forehead, eyes narrow, mouth elongates downward (frown is scored only when there is no vocalization that would usually accompany a cry or fuss); *smile*—an elongation of the mouth outward and upward, a deepening of the naso-labial folds (lines) from the corners of the mouth to the wings of the nose, mouth may be open, wrinkles may form at the outer corners of the eyes as the eyes narrow, and the cheeks may bulge under the eyes.

recorded for Anthony were *cry, smile,* and *eye contact* when not crying. The latter response was defined as S's eyes (or one eye when S had temporarily covered the other eye) in apparent direct eye-to-eye (pupil) contact with *E*, or S's eyes scanning *E*'s face. Crying and eye contact were scored for *duration* of response; frown, fuss and smile were *frequency* scores. Reliability of the five responses to standard presentations of *E*'s face was determined by aligning *E*'s record with the simultaneous record of another observer (*O*).[4] The observer was seated adjacent to *E* and slightly behind her. The white masking cloth behind *E* hung in front of *O*. Two small holes in the cloth allowed *O* to see S's face.

General Procedure. The general procedure for both Ss included baseline (operant level), conditioning and extinction periods respectively. Cries, fusses, and frowns were *always* under base line (i.e., extinction) conditions regardless of the experimental procedure being applied to S at the moment. The responses reinforced for both Ss during the second (Reinforcement) phase were smiles, and for Anthony also eye contact. Because the definitions of these responses are incompatible with crying (and fussing), changes in smile rate should tend to vary inversely with the incidence of crying and fussing. Even though crying, fussing, and frowning are never reinforced, when smiling and eye contact decrease in rate as extinction progresses, the former responses might rise again to baseline. This expectation was based on the maintenance through regular reinforcement of crying in the nursery environment for both Ss.

Procedure for William. Three days of baseline data on cries, fusses, frowns, and smiles were collected for William. Each experimental day's session was divided into six 2-minute presentations of *E*'s sober and unresponsive face. A 30-second rest interval with the blind pulled down separated each 2-minute period.

During the Reinforcement phase of the experiment (Days 4, 5, and 6) *E* reinforced smiles, while cries, frowns, and fusses were continued on extinction. When reinforcing smiles, E would immediately say (after S smiled) "Good boy, William," and nod her head up and down twice during this verbalization. This was followed by a 2-second full smile by *E*. Compared with several studies that have used reinforcement procedures with such young infants, the reinforcer of this study was more similar to that of Rheingold, Gewirtz, and Ross (1959) and Weisberg (1963) than to the one used by Brackbill (1958). The main exception to all of these studies is that the reinforcer we employed did not contain a physical contact component. The experimenter did not respond to fusses, frowns, and cries, and continually presented an expressionless face during all other behaviors except when S's smiles were being reinforced.

On Day 7, the Extinction phase began and reinforcement for smiling was discontinued. The procedure returned to baseline conditions. The original plan was for the Extinction phase to continue for several sessions, after which smiling would be reconditioned. Unknown to the caretaking personnel, arrangements for the outside placement of William were completed, and he was removed from the boarders unit several hours after the session on Day 7. William's experimental days were successive, except for one free day between sessions 4 and 5.

Procedure for Anthony. The baseline phase (Days 1 through 6) for Anthony was the same as with William. Smiles, cries, and eye contact while not crying were recorded each day for six 2-minute periods while Anthony was presented with a neutral face.

During the Reinforcement phase (Days 7 through 15) the two responses of smiling and eye contact when not crying were first shaped through the reinforcement of successive approximations to the defined response, and were then reinforced regularly. The neutral face was presented whenever Anthony cried. Eye contact while not crying was shaped by withholding reinforcement until the amplitude of S's crying began to decrease and he was looking at *E*. On subsequent occasions *E* did not provide the reinforcer until she judged that the amplitude of crying dropped from that of the preceding trial. The final stage of shaping involved S's not crying but maintaining eye contact. This procedure was necessary in Anthony's case, because once he started to cry, his crying would increase and decrease in volume but never totally stop to qualify for the receipt of reinforcement. Thus, eye contact in the absence of crying was defined as the necessary response so that S would be "attending" to E. In this context S's smiles could be evoked more easily.

Anthony's smiling was very infrequent during the Baseline phase. As Gewirtz's (1965) age norms for smiling to an unresponsive adult face indicate, this low rate may be associated with Anthony's relatively

[4] The formula used for calculating percentage observer agreement for each behavior category was: [No. agreements/(No. agreements + No. disagreements)] × 100. An agreement was defined as the simultaneous recording of a response by both *E* and *O*. A disagreement was scored when *E* recorded either frequency or duration of a response and *O* did not, or vice versa. An agreement about the nonoccurrence of a response by both *E* and *O* was not counted as an agreement. Such instances tend to raise markedly percentage agreement figures. The agreement percentage and total number of instances on which each figure was based for crying, fussing, frowning, smiling, and eye contact when not crying were 80% (42), 80% (5), 76% (17), 87% (53), and 88% (235), respectively. Reliability figures were derived from 132 minutes of *E*'s and *O*'s simultaneous observations.

young age. The smile Anthony exhibited would fit Gewirtz's (1963, 1965) definition of a "partial" smile. Even this partial smile was not exhibited often by S during the first day of reinforcement. Therefore, several stimuli were used on the first Reinforcement day to evoke the smile. Some expressions of the human face other than a neutral expression (whether or not mixed with motion and sound) could be most effective in evoking smiles. However, because it would be difficult to implement these conditions without variation, the tactic of employing an object to evoke smiles (so they could be reinforced) was used. On the second Reinforcement day a shiny gold-colored child's tea saucer which reflected the overhead lights was found to be effective in evoking smiles. The experimenter slowly moved the saucer both up and down and sideways so that it would reflect the light. Anthony's smiles to the saucer were reinforced. The saucer was presented only when S was in eye contact with *E* and not crying. Fuller smiles were then required on successive occasions to attain reinforcement. The metal saucer was discontinued once a broad full smile was established during the second 3-day block of smile reinforcement. After this point only smiling to *E*'s neutral face was reinforced.

The attempt was made to provide the same social reinforcer complex to Anthony as was used with William. This reinforcer used on the first Reinforcement day did not increase the rate of the few partial smiles or eye contacts emitted by Anthony that were to be conditioned. On the second Reinforcement day a set of complex reinforcing stimuli (both auditory and visual) were used. Bells of varying tones, hand puppets, toy crickets and whistles were presented singly in random order but always paired with *E*'s face, voice and smile. Whenever Anthony looked away or cried, the stimulus was withdrawn immediately and *E*'s face became expressionless. At first a continuous schedule of reinforcers was given for S's coming into eye contact with *E*. Toward the end of the conditioning period eye contact was reinforced more on a "quasi" variable ratio schedule. However, the smile response was reinforced each time it occurred.

The Extinction phase (Days 16 through 31) was the same as the Baseline phase. The experimenter presented a neutral face to all responses so that smiling and eye contact were no longer reinforced. Meanwhile, crying continued on extinction. An increase in crying might be expected if this response were maintained in the nursery and if the rates of the incompatible responses of smiling and eye contact were decreasing due to nonreinforcement. The Extinction phase was divided into two segments. From Days 16 through 24 the nursery environment was still reinforcing Anthony's crying. However, from Days 25 through 31 extinction of crying occurred both in the experimental setting and nursery. This procedural tactic had not been planned, but on Day 25 the head nurse announced that a new plan for Anthony was in effect, and requested that no one pick him up if he cried. She informed *E* that this plan was devised because Anthony had become "spoiled."

After Day 31 the nursery was quarantined due to a case of chickenpox and the study was terminated. The 31 experimental days were spread over 48 calendar days. Only once was there an interval of more than one nonexperimental day between experimental sessions.

Results

William. Figure 1 shows the percentage of total time spent by William in crying during each 4-minute period. Smiles, fusses, and frowns are shown in frequency of occurrence per 4-minute period. The seven days of the study along the abscissa are divided into Baseline (Days 1, 2, and 3), Reinforcement of smiling (Days 4, 5, and 6), and Extinction of smiling (Day 7). Each day's scores are plotted as three 4-minute blocks.

During the three Baseline days, William cried during every 4-minute period. When all Baseline days are considered together, he cried about 75% of his total time in the experimental sessions. By Day 3 he cried during most of the experimental session (11 minutes 21 seconds out of a possible 12 minutes). The frequency of smiles, frowns, and fusses declined across the three Baseline days. During the last eight minutes of Day 3, it is seen that only crying was emitted.

It had been decided that shaping procedures for smiling might be needed on the first Reinforcement day (Day 4), since it was suspected that William's smile response may have been nearly extinguished in the experimental setting. When William did not emit any full smiles in the beginning of the first 2-minute period of Day 4, *E* first reinforced a slight broadening of the lips. Reinforcement was then withheld until after a more complete partial smile was emitted and ultimately until after a full smile was emitted. This shaping procedure required only three steps between a broadening of the lips and a full smile. The three shaped responses are included in the data for Day 4. Smiling increased under Reinforcement until the frequency of smiles on Day 6 was more than four times the Baseline rate. As smiles increased, crying decreased. During the first Reinforcement of smiling day (Day 4), crying occurred only during the last 4 minutes, a period when there were no smiles. There was no crying at all on Days 5 and 6, the last two smile Reinforcement days. Also, as crying decreased, there was a short-lived increase in fussing. Finally, decreases in fussing appear to

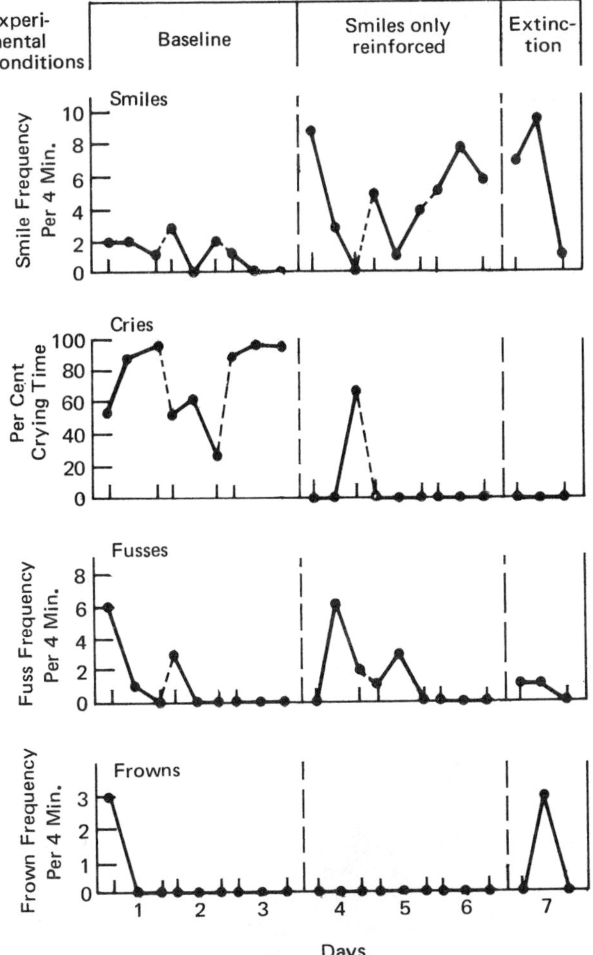

Figure 1 *Four concurrent response curves under three experimental phases for William, age 20 weeks, whose crying was being reinforced in the nursery environment. Baseline measurements were made on Days 1–3. On Days 4–6, smiles were reinforced while crying, fussing, and frowning were extinguished. On Day 7 all four responses were extinguished.*

parallel increases in smiling. By Day 6 William was a very "smiley" infant with no cries, fusses, or frowns during the entire 12 minutes of that session.[5]

Figure 1 shows that on Day 7 (Extinction of smiles) smile rate increased during the first 8 minutes and then decreased precipitously during the last 4 minutes of that session. This pattern of increase followed by decrease is typical of response patterns in the early phases of extinction when the response has been on a continuous schedule of reinforcement. Although William did not cry during that first day of Extinction of the smile response, he did exhibit frowns and fusses again. It is thought that, had the study been continued, William would have exhibited crying again in the experimental setting, since the nursery environment was regularly reinforcing his crying.

Anthony. In Figure 2, the ordinate for smiles is plotted in *average frequency per day,* while cries and eye contact are presented in *average minutes per day.* The 31 days of the study are divided into 3-day blocks under the successive conditions of Baseline, Reinforcement of smiling, Extinction with nursery reinforcement of crying, and Extinction with nursery extinction of crying. Absolute scores rather than averages for Anthony's three responses are presented for Day 31.

During Baseline (Days 1 through 6), Anthony maintained a fairly steady and moderate rate of crying, while his smiling rate was very low or absent. He engaged in eye contact with *E* for less than half (39%) of the total time of the 12-minute experimental sessions.

During the 9 days of Reinforcement of smiles and eye contact (Days 7 through 15), crying duration decreased rapidly. Crying was totally absent on the last 3 days (Days 13 through 15). Smile rate increased to an average of 14 smiles per session on the last 3 days of Reinforcement and paralleled the decrease in crying. By then only full smiles were reinforced and the metal plate stimulus was no longer used. Eye-contact duration increased to more than 10½ minutes per 12-minute session for the last 3 days of Reinforcement. By the end of the Reinforcement phase, Anthony was an "accomplished smiler" who spent most of the experimental periods looking at *E*.

The Extinction of smiling and eye contact (which started on Day 16) resulted in crying and eye contact approaching their Baseline rates within the first 3 days (Days 16 through 18). That is, crying duration increased while eye contact duration decreased. Smiles continued to increase in frequency during the first 3 days of their extinction, after which they showed a steady drop during the six remaining Extinction days. However, by Day 24 the smiling rate was still far from the baseline, and extinction was planned for several more days. Although extinction was continued in the experimental setting, the change in the caretaking tactic in the nursery in connection with S's crying resulted in changes in his crying in

[5] The effects of the Reinforcement and Extinction procedures are not as apparent in the 4-minute-score curve for William's data as they are in the 3-day-mean-score curves for Anthony's data. Therefore, two simple nonparametric tests of differences in the proportion of scores above the pooled-score medians to compare the first two experimental conditions were performed, using Fisher's exact test for fourfold tables. Nine baseline and nine smile-reinforcement scores for crying and smiling were involved, as is seen in Figure 1. Compared with the magnitude of baseline scores, more crying scores were found lower during Extinction when smiles were reinforced ($p < .005$, one tail), while more smile scores were found higher during this period of smile reinforcement ($p < .01$, one tail).

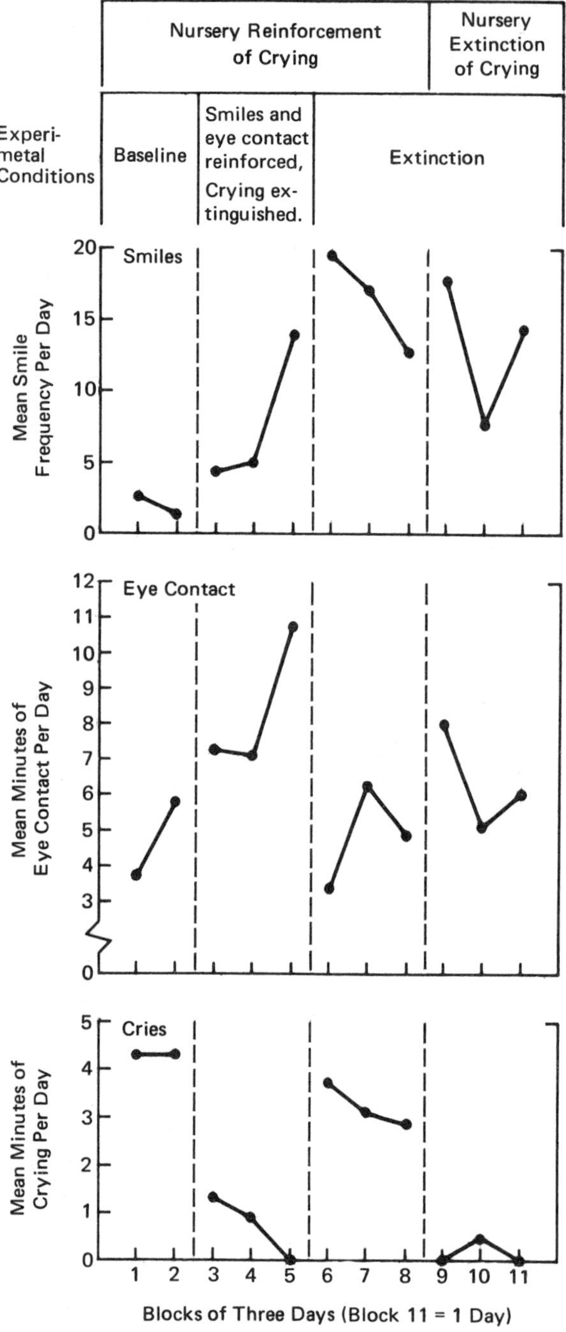

Figure 2 *Three concurrent response curves under three experimental phases for Anthony, age 6 weeks, whose crying was being reinforced in the nursery environment until the last portion of the experimental Extinction phase. Baseline measurements were made on Days 1–6. On Days 7–15, smiling and eye contact were reinforced while crying was extinguished. Experimental extinction of the three responses occurred on Days 16–31.*

the experimental setting. This practice of not picking up or attending to Anthony in other ways when he was crying in the nursery correlated with a sharp decrease in his crying in the experimental sessions. In 7 more days of experimental Extinction and nursery Extinction of crying (Days 25 through 31), Anthony exhibited only one short crying episode. Nursery Extinction of Anthony's crying also resulted in a temporary increase in his smiling and eye contact during the first 3 days of nursery Extinction. Although eye contact again approached the baseline level, smiling never decreased to baseline, since the study was ended by the quarantine.

Discussion

The procedures chosen to modify William's and Anthony's crying, involving both extinction of crying and reinforcement of incompatible responses, appear to have been successful. Our experience in this study indicates that successful modification would have been unlikely if only extinction procedures were employed, as was done, e.g., by Williams (1959). This is because the extinction was effected by us in an environment separate from the maintaining nursery environment, whereas Williams worked in the home setting and could effect complete extinction. The tactics of the study took account of the continued reinforcement of crying behavior in the nursery, a fact which accounted for the return of crying when the responses incompatible with it were extinguished. The results indicate also that infants can make a discrimination like that between a maintaining and an experimental setting where different contingencies are in effect, and that this is rapidly established for operant behavior. The results support a conclusion of operant crying in infants as young as six weeks. A descriptive observation of Anthony's behavior at the beginning of extinction of both smiling and eye contact can add a bit of flavor to this interpretation. Anthony would look at *E*, smile, receive no reinforcement, wrinkle up his face as if to cry but without vocalizing, look at *E* again and smile, and so on. This shift from one behavior to another happened too rapidly to be readily explained by the conventional emotion constructs like those of "sheer happiness" or "utter misery." Yet, this rapid change is explicable in terms of the dynamics of instrumental conditioning and extinction. This then would illustrate the limited utility of conventional "state" concepts in explaining such everyday behavior conditions as those dealt with in this paper.

Although both infants exhibited similar crying behavior patterns, they presented quite different experimental problems. William was an accomplished smiler before the study began, and the utility of social reinforcement with him could be taken for granted from observations in the nursery. On the other hand, Anthony who was younger than William was far from a "social smiler." His case illustrates that the technique of *evoking* behavior so that it can be shaped and reinforced, which has been successful in other studies, can be a useful method when the behavior to be reinforced (because of its incompatibility with the prepotent behavior) occurs infrequently and with low amplitude.

Although the study with Anthony was unavoidably terminated by the quarantine before his smiling could be returned to baseline level, a question is in order as to why his smile response was more resistant than eye contact to extinction. Aside from Anthony's being older at the study's end and smiling rate is known to increase during this age period, a plausible reason (even if not the only one) may be that by the time extinction procedures were used with Anthony, his smile may have come under the control of social stimuli in his environment. This appeared not to be the case at the beginning of the study. One caretaking aide remarked near the study's end, "Anthony now has many mothers." They spent much of their time with him responding to his smiles. Just as the nursery was maintaining Anthony's crying until Day 25, so, too, was it now reinforcing his smiling. It would very likely have taken a bit longer for his final discrimination between nursery (reinforcement for smiling) and experimental (extinction of smiling) settings to have occurred, since this shift in reinforcing contingency constituted a reversal in both settings.

The study also illustrates that there may be individual differences in the potency of reinforcing stimuli, even for such young infants. Hence, the selection of reinforcers for infant's behavior must be made on the basis of what stimuli do in fact function as reinforcers for *each* individual infant (Gewirtz, 1961; Bijou and Baer, 1965).

Despite our finding that crying was modified for both infants, there remain several questions still to be answered. The precise identities of the discriminative and reinforcing stimuli that operated in the nursery where crying started and was maintained can only be guessed at. In the experimental setting, the sober, unresponsive human face appeared to provide the discriminative stimulus for William's crying. It is unclear which stimulus(i) functioned in a comparable role for Anthony. Different complexes of stimuli were found to operate as reinforcers for the smiling and visual contact behaviors for both infants in the experimental setting. However, which elements of these stimulus complexes actually functioned as reinforcers for smiling remains to be determined.

Even though our method was adapted to the individual infant, these generalizations seem warranted from our results: (1) a social response (smiling and eye contact) can be conditioned in a life setting according to the operant paradigm in the first months of life, thus replicating Brackbill's (1958) work with $3\frac{1}{2}$- to $4\frac{1}{2}$-month-old Ss, the work of Rheingold, Gewirtz, and Ross (1959), and that of Weisberg (1963) with 3-month-old Ss; (2) the smile response appears conditionable at 16 weeks, which replicates Brackbill's result with Ss of comparable age; and (3) the smile response appears to be conditionable on an instrumental basis with the procedures used as early as the eighth week of life.

One conceptual issue involved in analyses such as ours is that the operant and Pavlovian paradigms overlap at critical points and can converge for the purposes of a particular analysis. There is also the basic issue of whether narrowly defined crying is evoked repeatedly by discretely presented, narrowly defined stimuli, as are those unconditioned reflexes (e.g., pupillary, knee jerk, eyelid) typically unquestioned as bases for acquisition under the classical conditioning paradigm. (These responses are usually thought to involve the autonomic nervous system.) Gewirtz (1965) raised these issues while surveying the difficulties of placing the smile under the conception of an unconditioned elicited reaction, and on this basis questioned the utility of conceptualizing smiling under the classical conditioning paradigm. These questions also apply to crying, for as with the smile, a wide range of stimuli (or no identifiable stimulus) also appear to evoke that response, and specific reflexes like the pupillary do not provide a ready model for its being conditioned on a Pavlovian basis. Thus, there is at present some question about the utility of the Pavlovian paradigm in ordering the acquisition by environmental stimuli of control over crying and smiling. While the operations controlling conditions usually ordered under the classical conditioning paradigm are not precluded for infant crying and smiling, the assumptions underlying operant learning appear easier to fit with those behavior classes. This is one basis for our emphasis on instrumental concepts in the heuristic analysis we have presented.

The results of this study have implications for infant-care practices, both in home and institution environments. A number of these implications are considered in detail elsewhere (Gewirtz and Etzel[6];

[6] Gewirtz, J. L., and Etzel, Barbara C. Contingent caretaking as a solution for some child-rearing paradoxes. In preparation.

Gewirtz, 1968). The results also can have implications for the infancy researcher. Perhaps more than any other response (except sleeping), crying seems to constitute a frequent reason for tardily beginning or prematurely terminating experimental sessions or for discarding a subject. Many infancy researchers would say they exercise more effective control over sleep behavior than over crying. When infants are routinely screened for physical problems, it might be useful also to collect crying data systematically. Thus, when "rehabilitation" is too expensive and an infant can be excluded from a study because his crying behavior is maintained by his environment, that fact would make the reason for his exclusion from a study more reasonable, and could save the investigator much time.

Identification of a high-rate *operant crier* appears simple when baseline data are collected. As indicated, the crying rates of neighboring infants of comparable age were also observed when data were being collected on Anthony. Although one such infant did not yet respond at a rate which was highly annoying to the caretaking staff, he did show a fairly high rate of fusses and cries. This infant generally received attention when he began to cry, particularly from volunteer aides. (The duties of these aides were not as exacting as for regular staff members, for they came with charitable intentions to help infants; hence, they could respond readily to infants who began to cry.) It was thought that in the proper circumstances that infant could become an operant crier. About one month later the "critical" occasion arose when he was innoculated. As a result, during that day he had a fever and showed most noticeable crying and fussing, which led to his being held and comforted by the sympathetic staff. Although his physical reaction to the innoculation subsided within a day, his crying continued and appeared increased in rate, as did the correlated incidence of reinforcement of his crying provided by the caretakers. The experimenter might have witnessed the first stages in the shaping by the environment of a tyrannical infant crier (*Infans tyrannotearus*).

References

Bijou, S. W., and Baer, D. M. *Child development.* Vol. 2: *Universal stage of infancy.* New York: Appleton-Century-Crofts, 1965. Pp. 122–141.

Brackbill, Yvonne. Extinction of the smiling response in infants as a function of reinforcement schedule. *Child Development,* 1958, *29,* 115–124.

Gewirtz, J. L. A learning analysis of the effects of normal stimulation, privation and deprivation on the acquisition of social motivation and attachment. In B. M. Foss (Ed.), *Determinants of infant behavior.* London: Methuen (New York: Wiley), 1961. Pp. 213–299.

Gewirtz, J. L. *Social test observation manual.* Section on Early Learning and Development, National Institute of Mental Health, Bethesda, Maryland, 1963. Mimeographed.

Gewirtz, J. L. The course of infant smiling in four child-rearing environments in Israel. In B. M. Foss (Ed.), *Determinants of infant behavior III.* London: Methuen (New York: Wiley), 1965. Pp. 205–260.

Gewirtz, J. L. On designing the functional environment of the child to facilitate behavioral development. *In* Laura L. Dittmann (Ed.), *New perspectives in early child care.* New York: Atherton, 1968. Chapter 8.

Hart, Betty M., Allen, K. Eileen, Buel, Joan S., Harris, Florence R., and Wolf, M. M. Effects of social reinforcement on operant crying. *Journal of Experimental Child Psychology,* 1964, 1, 145–153.

Rheingold, Harriet L., Gewirtz, J. L., and Ross, Helen W. Social conditioning of vocalizations in the infant. *Journal of Comparative and Physiological Psychology,* 1959, *52,* 68–73.

Weisberg, P. Social and non-social conditioning of infant vocalizations. *Child Development,* 1963, *34,* 377–388.

Williams, C. D. The elimination of tantrum behavior by extinction procedures. *Journal of Abnormal and Social Psychology,* 1959, *59,* 269.

Wolf, M. M., Risley, T. R., and Mees, H. I. Application of operant conditioning procedures to the behavior problems of an autistic child. *Behaviour Research and Therapy,* 1964, *1,* 305–312.

A great deal of interest has been aroused among social scientists by the apparent success of the *kibbutz* in Israel, not only as a model for group living under exceptional circumstances but as a novel setting for the rearing of children. Unlike the average American home, where parents are in virtually constant contact with their children, the kibbutz provides for the professional care of infants and children in a communal setting where the parents play a supporting but subsidiary role. The following report by *Gewirtz and Gewirtz* is interesting to us mainly because it details a method of accounting accurately and systematically for the various activities and events that constitute the child's day in a kibbutz. Under these circumstances the parents are not the sole, nor even the most important agents of reinforcement for the child.

The method of observation provides for the simultaneous recording of both behavioral and situational variables. Data derived from these detailed records give a more precise picture of the proportions of time consumed by various activities than could be obtained from casual or unsystematic observation. Some interesting differences emerged with respect to the differential amount of caretaking devoted to boys and to girls. Although the writers offer no interpretation of these differences other than to suggest that they might be either the causes or the effects of other behavioral differences between the two sexes, the method illustrates the first steps that must be taken in trying to understand the impact of the early social environment on behavior. It is possible, as this article shows, to obtain a reasonably complete and objective description of behavior in a circumscribed environment. Such an ecological description is a necessary precursor to a functional analysis of selected behaviors. This procedure could undoubtedly be used with appropriate modification in a variety of settings—with adults as well as children.

27 *Visiting and Caretaking Patterns for Kibbutz Infants: Age and Sex Trends*[1]

HAVA B. GEWIRTZ
JACOB L. GEWIRTZ

This report is based on a segment of a large-scale study of infant behavior and caretaking environment in which full-day observations were conducted on 2- to 8-month-old Israeli infants in diverse child-rearing environments. The environments included the residential institution, the middle-class town family, and the collective settlement (kibbutz) (Gewirtz, 1965; Rabin, 1965; Spiro, 1958). The observations were focused on catching the sequential flow of behavioral interchange between the infant and his caretakers within the contexts of caretaking routines and patterns of social contact available to the infants.

Observation was usually conducted in two sessions, morning and afternoon, on successive days. A trained woman observer sat at a reasonable distance from the infant throughout the observation period, and followed him to other locations when necessary. She recorded ongoing events and discrete behaviors in coded form, using predetermined observation categories. A timer (heard only by the observer) signaled the marking off of the continuous observation record into half-minute units. Thus it became possible to describe the observed events in terms of their duration, the sequence of their appearance in time, and

1 This research was supported in part by U.S. Public Health Service Grant MH-06779 to the first author. Both authors wish to thank Deborah Singer and Leslie Zebrowitz for editorial assistance and for help in the data analysis.

even the actual hours of the day at which they occurred.

Our theoretical approach, the complete method of observation, and the definition of the observation categories have been outlined in detail elsewhere. Two aspects, however, are unique to this segment of the study: (1) the inclusion of female infants in the sample selected for analyses, and (2) the use of the structural aspects of the environment as dependent variables.

Sample

The sample consists of 24 kibbutz infants in four age-by-sex groups: four 4-month-old girls, four 8-month-old girls, eight 4-month-old boys, and eight 8-month-old boys.[2] Our original decision was to use only male infants as subjects for the full study because we wished to control for possible effect of the sex variable without having to complicate the analyses by dealing with it directly. However, a number of kibbutz females were observed in the early phases of data collection, so rather than discard these observation records, a small but proportionate subsample of eight kibbutz girls was established to serve as an occasion for comparing the caretaking features of the environments of male and female infants.

Such comparisons, we thought, might be of particular interest in the kibbutz where child-rearing is guided by an explicit ideology of sex equality, and where we would therefore expect the treatment of boys and girls to be relatively homogeneous, particularly during infancy. Boys and girls at the same age level share their living quarters and their *metapelet* (caretaker). The principles which guide caretaking routines for both sex groups are also identical. As compared to town-family infants, kibbutz infants are less dependent on their parents as exclusive agents of socialization, and therefore might reflect less their parents' differential treatment according to sex, should it exist. If no such treatment differences were found, we could justify the pooling of the female Ss with the male kibbutz Ss for some purposes of our larger study. However, if the sex-group comparisons were to show that boys and girls in the kibbutz receive differential treatment in some life sectors, we might expect even more sex differentiation in those child-rearing environments that have neither an explicit ideology of equality of the sexes nor standardized caretaking practices. Under such circumstances, we might reserve the sex-group comparisons for separate analyses, instead of including the female Ss in the analyses of the full study. The current report represents such a preliminary examination of sex differences in connection with selected features of a caretaking environment.

The Dependent Variables

While the ultimate focus of our study is on the interchange of behaviors between the infant and his environment, we believe it is important to define and outline the context within which behaviors occur, prior to the analysis of the behaviors themselves. For example, the interpretation of an infant's fussing would depend upon knowledge of his recent feeding schedule, the presence of caretakers in his vicinity, etc. This thematic context might also be termed the ecology or structural frame of an environment. Specifically, it refers to the pattern of caretaking routines and social contacts available to the infant.

The day of the infant is bounded by a cycle of sleep, eating, and elimination activities. This cycle is correlated with caretaking events such as feeding, diaper-changing, and the like. These caretaking routines, in turn, define the minimal limit of social contact to which the infant is exposed, although the availability of such contacts can extend far beyond mere caretaking, both in terms of the variety of persons entering the infant's vicinity and the pattern of each person's visits. Moreover, the infant's physical environment can be expanded by exposure to different locations. We have classified and defined these ecological themes in terms of setting events (mostly caretaking) and background events (social presence).

In this report, such ecological trends are outlined as they relate to the four age-by-sex groups (cells). Caretaking routines and social contacts serve to generate dependent variables, without further-reduction to the behavioral elements with which they are correlated. It is in this respect that the data summarized in this report constitute only a segment of our larger study. While complete in itself, this segment represents but an intermediate stage of analysis under our theoretical approach. (Subsequently, it is our intention to employ the ecological contexts as independent variables in terms of which the behavioral interchanges will be assessed.) Thus, our primary concern at this point is not to prepare an ethnography of child-rearing in the kibbutz, nor is it to compare sex groups. Rather, we have chosen to study this subsample because, as a compact unit, it allows us to explore some methods of data organization and data analysis, and to test the utility of

[2] These infants were observed in 1961 in eleven kibbutzim, representing the three main kibbutz federations. During the intervening years, both practice and theory of kibbutz child-rearing have undergone some changes, on top of the variations which have existed all along within and between kibbutzim of the three federations. These modifications appear primarily to affect children older than one year of age. Hence, they would qualify minimally the data being presented here.

our observational methodology, prior to the analysis of the data of the larger study. Our dependent variables are described in the sections that follow.

Settings

Setting events reflect onsets and durations of general states or caretaking themes. They do *not* represent discrete behaviors of either S or his attendants (which are recorded in a separate section and are not presented in this report). Definitions of the settings considered in this report follow:

Sleep was used in two ways to provide: (1) (by subtraction) the duration of S's Time Awake during the observation day, and (2) the sleep patterns in the infant's day. Very brief sleep episodes (of one- to two-minute duration) were excluded from the calculations of sleep periods.

Feeding referred to S's meal periods, but did not include short pauses in the actual feeding process, as when a mother left the room to warm a bottle of milk or when diaper-changing took place during a meal. Likewise, occasional drinking of water between meals was not scored as a Feeding event. However, when an adult "burped" S as part of the feeding procedure, it was considered part of the Feeding setting, even when it was prolonged and no additional food was offered S.

Eating referred to S's feeding himself, as when he held and chewed a piece of bread or fruit. Unlike Feeding, once Eating was initiated by a caretaker, it did not require her continuous presence. Even so, Eating has been included in our observation categories, because of its relationship to Feeding as a source of supplemental food.

Diaper-changing referred only to the actual process of changing diapers. Any changes of clothing which did not clearly follow elimination were recorded as Dressing.

Dressing referred to changes of clothes (other than diaper-changing), as before S was taken outdoors and preceding and/or following a bath or sunbath. The cosmetic routines which typically follow the bath (e.g., oiling, nose-cleaning, combing) were scored as part of the Dressing setting.

Bathing covered the period when S was at least partially immersed in the bath water. "Bathing" the infant by wiping him with a washcloth on the dressing table was considered part of Dressing, not Bathing.

Medicating referred to diverse caretaking events relating to health and illness, such as handling by a physician, giving vitamins or medicines, applying medications, thermometer insertion, etc. Such activities all require the continuous presence of a caretaker.

Other noncaretaking settings which were recorded during the observation period (e.g., sunbathing, play situations, being in locations other than the infants' crib room) are not dealt with in this report.

Background Events

Background events refer to the presence or visits of different persons in S's vicinity during the observation day. A visit is defined in terms of the duration of a particular person's presence in S's room from the time of his entry to the time of his departure. Durations of visits may range from less than a minute to several hours, and their frequency of occurrence for each person can vary considerably.[3]

Kibbutz infants are regularly in the company of several other infants with whom they share their room in the infants' house. Because this is a constant condition for all kibbutz Ss, the other "peer" infants were not routinely recorded as persons in background. In this report, we attend primarily to the visits of three persons: the infant's mother, father, and main caretaker. A brief description of their weekday roles as they apply to infants of the ages we observed follows.

Mother. Kibbutz parents reside in quarters separate from their children. During the first six to eight weeks of the infant's life, his mother is on full maternity leave from her regular work assignment. After this period, she resumes her work routines gradually. Even so, the mother plays the major caretaking role for her infant. During the early months, when nursing is the common mode of feeding, the mother's contact with her infant is typically determined by his feeding schedule. In the intervals between these nursing visits, she leaves the infants' house to return either to her own room or to her kibbutz work duties. However, all kibbutz locations are within short walking distance of each other, and a mother may look in at the infants' house several times during the day.

Father. The kibbutz father does not usually see his children until late in the afternoon after he has completed his work day. Typically, the weekday afternoon visiting period is spent in the parents' quarters (or outdoors with them), when their children come to visit for the customary period of one to two hours before returning to the children's houses at bedtime. The father rather than the mother will often be the one to call for his child from the infants' house for the afternoon visit with the family.

Main Caretaker. The main caretaker is a trained

[3] Specific background activities performed by the visitors are not summarized in this report. Background events consisting of nonsocial stimuli, such as noises, are also excluded.

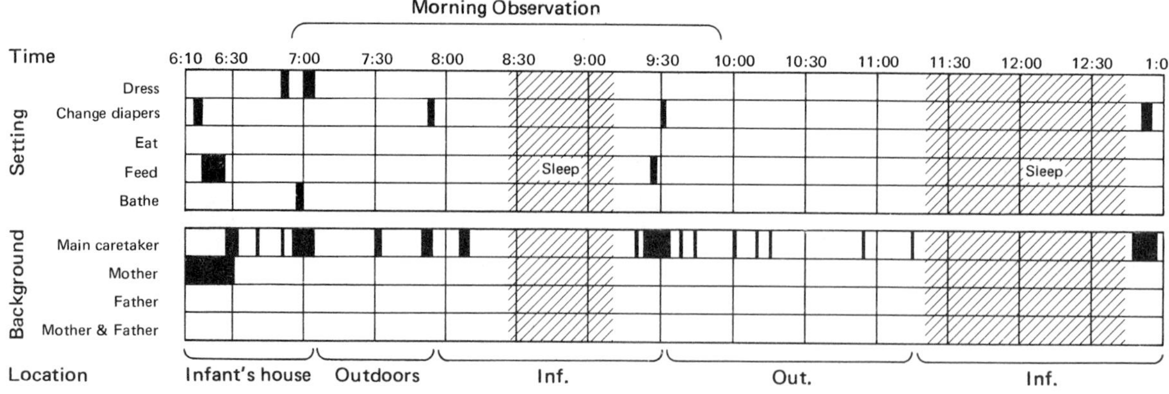

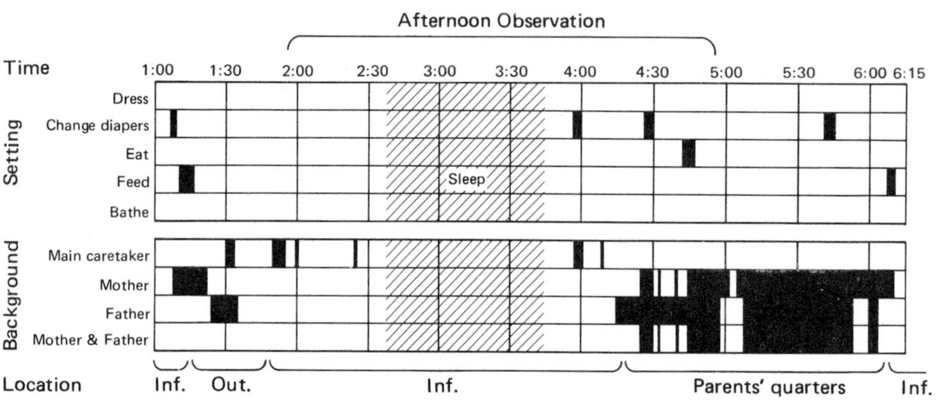

Figure 1 *Chronological log for one 8-month-old kibbutz boy's day.*

kibbutz member who is in charge of the infants' house or peer group. Her duties range from helping and instructing the mothers in the handling of their infants to keeping the rooms in the infants' house clean. She shares with the mother such caretaking activities as diaper-changing, bathing, and some supplementary feeding. The main caretaker is typically assisted by another caretaker assigned to replace her for a few hours during the day. However, the main caretaker is generally more highly trained or experienced than her assistant and has more direct and continuous contact with the infant and his parents.

Data Analysis

Individual Chronological Logs. Our observation method made it possible to catch the onset and termination of each event at the actual time of its occurrence, providing a score for its duration.[4] Thus, at the simplest descriptive level we have generated chronological logs of setting and background events for each S, showing their distribution in time during the observation day. For some settings these seem to comprise regular cycles. The individual logs are useful for demonstrating graphically the interplay between caretaking activities and presence of various persons which characterizes the infant's day.

Figure 1 illustrates such a log for an 8-month-old S. Selected setting and background events are plotted independently along the scale of the actual hours of this S's observation day. Inspection along the horizontal dimension allows assessment of the pattern of occurrences for each event separately (e.g., feeding schedule, father's visits, periods of S being "alone"). At the same time, the vertical dimension shows the interrelationship between setting and background events (e.g., which person is typically present at feeding time). Figure 1 shows that for this S the morning and afternoon observation periods (conducted on separate days) ended and began, respectively, at 1 P.M. However, a time gap or an overlap between the two observation sessions did occur for many of our Ss, for there was no attempt made to observe all Ss for precisely the same durations nor to start and end all observations at identical

[4] Formal computations of reliability level were not made for setting and background event categories, as the pilot observations indicated that observers could easily reach complete agreement on the recording of these events.

hours. Such a requirement for identical hours of observation was disregarded not only because it was difficult to carry out but also because "psychological time" appeared to be a more relevant determinant of observation periods than absolute time. Thus, for the purpose of catching a "typical day" routine, it appeared more meaningful to start a morning observation using a criterion such as S's "awakening," or to end it "after his noon meal," than to adhere to standard absolute time criteria for the observation sessions with every S.

Results and Discussion

We shall precede the presentation of age- and sex-group differences in caretaking and background-visit themes with a brief outline of the infants' daily schedule as it applies to all kibbutz Ss in our sample. Some of the trends described would be unique to the kibbutz while others could be equally applicable to infants of similar ages in other child-rearing environments. However, no between-environment comparisons are attempted at this point. Rather, the purpose of this outline is, first, to examine whether a meaningful ecological picture of kibbutz child rearing could be derived entirely from summaries of the observational data, and, second, to use this picture to highlight the subsequent presentation of group differences within the kibbutz sample.

Overall Ecological Trends. Each infant was observed for about 12 hours, typically from around 6 A.M. to around 6 P.M. About one-third of that time was spent in sleep, with the remaining eight hours of wakefulness divided between Time Alone, Caretaking Time, and Pure Social Time. This division of the waking day is shown graphically in Figure 2, where mean-percentage data are presented separately for each of the four age-by-sex cells.

The daily cycles of events (Figure 1), show a pattern of caretaking routines which is fairly homogeneous for the kibbutz infants: Ss are given meals regularly, at around 6 A.M., 10 A.M., 2 P.M., and 6 P.M. Feeding is the predominant caretaking setting. Eating was never observed fully to replace Feeding, but sometimes occurred between meals during the day. Diaper-changing occurred at irregular intervals during the observation day, and seemed to be geared more to each S's state than to some external schedule. Dressing was restricted routinely to the periods immediately preceding and following bath time, or prior to the daily outing to the parents' rooms. Bathing was even more uniform, in that it lasted between two and three minutes, and of the 22 Ss bathed, all but two had their daily bath between 7 and 9 in the morning. In contrast, Medicating occurred for only six Ss and for variable durations.

With the exception of two Ss who remained in the infants' house during the entire observation day, the visit to the parents' quarters typically lasted between one and two hours. Although the periods of stay in the parents' room showed a considerable range (from 20 minutes to over three hours), the duration of the P.M. visit with the parents was actually quite uniform when account is taken of locations other than the parents' room, for Ss, in the company of a parent, often visited the garden and farm areas of the kibbutz and the quarters of grandparents or other kibbutz members.

Our data for the entire observation day suggest that during the first eight months of his life the infant in the kibbutz sees his mother for at least twice as much time as he sees his father or the main caretaker. But, if the mother's time or role is divided into a "caretaking" (A.M.) period and a "social" (P.M.) period, her predominance in any *one* period diminishes: in the A.M. period her presence overlaps with that of the main caretaker; in the P.M. period her presence overlaps the father's. However, there is minimal overlap between the main caretaker and the father who, as it were, each "specialize" in a separate period of the day. Only the mother's presence occurs throughout the day.

Age-Group Trends. No differences are found between the two age groups in Total Duration of Sleep. Thus, we have some assurance that the distribution of events within the waking time was not contaminated by an artifact of differential durations of sleep among these groups. Within these homogeneous periods awake, however, total caretaking activities for the younger Ss take up between two and three times as much as they do for the older Ss. While the finding that older infants require less caretaking was not unexpected, we did not quite expect this difference to result in the older Ss spending almost twice as much Time Alone as the younger Ss, and in the younger Ss having a proportionately greater amount of Social Time (with someone in their vicinity).

Two aspects of kibbutz practices may clarify the meaning of Time Alone for kibbutz infants. The first is that by the time infants are eight months old, their mothers have usually returned to full-day work assignments, and although their work schedule is flexible, it is geared to their child's caretaking needs rather than to leisurely interaction with him.

The second practice concerns the infants' living arrangements. In the town-family apartment, the infant is typically kept within visible distance of his mother. He may watch her from his playpen even when she attends to her housework, or, if able to crawl, he may follow her from room to room. But in

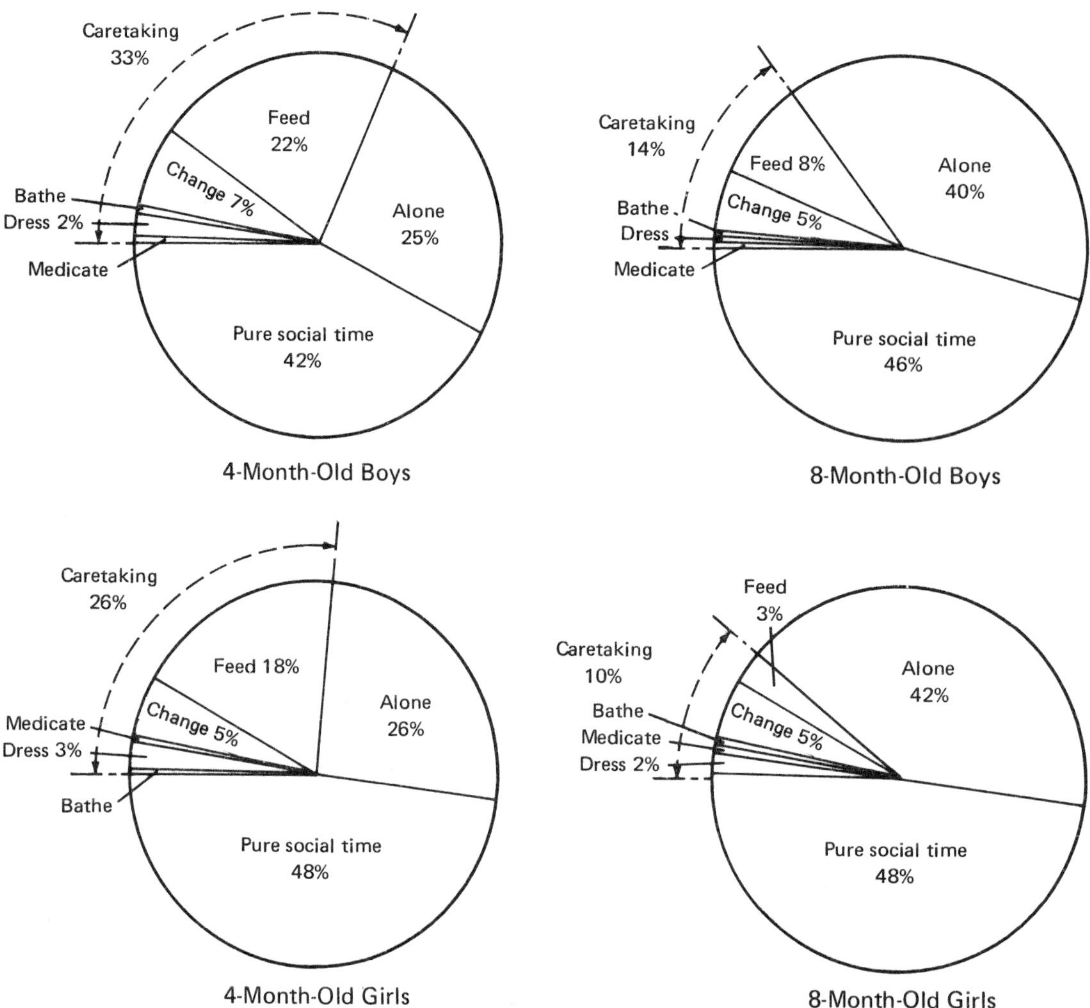

Figure 2 *Mean distribution of setting duration for age-by-sex cells of kibbutz infants as a proportion of observed time awake.*

the kibbutz, locations have more differentiated functions: infants are either put down to rest in their sleeping rooms (which contain little else but cribs) or placed outdoors in large playpens, while caretakers attend to tasks indoors. In terms of our observation categories, therefore, the kibbutz infant is more likely to be found "alone" in a specified location during the periods not designated for either caretaking or socializing.[5]

While the duration of Social Time declines between four and eight months, the proportion within it of Pure Social Time increases. Thus, the reduction of caretaking time between the ages of four and eight months affects two aspects of the infant's day: he spends more of his time without adults around him; and when there are visitors in his vicinity, their presence is more social than instrumental in character, being less associated with caretaking.

With respect to particular caretaking settings, the most noteworthy difference between the two age groups is in the pattern of Feeding. The percentage of time spent in Feeding is more than three times as long for the younger as it is for the older Ss, although the reliable difference in frequency of Feeding involves only one more meal for the younger Ss. Our inspection of Feeding durations within each of the sex groups shows similar dramatic decreases

[5] Kubbutz infants spend a great deal of time outdoors during the warm months, perhaps as much as 40% of the day. While they are outdoors, tractors, cows, pets, and people may pass near them, providing continuous visual and auditory stimulation as well as some interaction with those passing by. Moreover, there are always other infants in the vicinity. Therefore, being "alone" outdoors is quite different from being alone in a bedroom.

from four to eight months of age. For instance, boys' mean duration scores decline from 28 to 9.2 minutes, while girls' decline from 16 to 4.6 minutes. Median duration, total duration, and other Feeding indices follow a similar trend. It is thought reasonable that feeding takes less time for older than for younger infants. For example, the feeding procedure can be simplified with the older infant by permitting him to handle some food by himself. Such a trend is suggested by the Eating data which clearly differentiate between the proportion of infants who fed themselves at each age level. In addition, the marked discrepancy between the Feeding durations of the two age groups can be accounted for by two practices characteristic of kibbutz child rearing, namely the mothers' schedule and the mode of feeding: first, mothers of younger infants are enabled and even explicitly encouraged by kibbutz child-rearing ideology to spend long and relaxed periods feeding their infants, whereas the mothers of older infants return to their work duties following caretaking; and second, the longer feeding periods could be partly explained by the predominance of breast feeding for the younger infants (for breast feeding appears to be a slower process than are other feeding modes): 10 of the 12 younger Ss were breast-fed, compared to only two of the 12 older Ss ($p < .005$). Moreover, the greater attention given to the proper "burping" of younger infants (especially following bottle and breast feeding) might also contribute to the difference in duration scores between the two age groups.

Dressing appeared to be slightly more frequent and to last longer for the younger Ss. It is possible that the routines which follow the daily bath, such as body-oiling, ear- and nose-cleaning, etc., are carried out more carefully with younger than with older infants, and are consequently more time-consuming.

No age differences were found in any of the duration indices for the Sleep setting, but the younger infants showed more frequent sleep periods ($p < .05$) than did the older ones. Inspection of individual sleep patterns (as illustrated for one S in Figure 1) suggests that the older Ss seem to have developed a rather stable cycle of two or three uninterrupted sleep periods at regular hours during the day, compared to the irregular pattern which characterizes the younger Ss' sleep.

As the pattern of total caretaking activities differentiated between the two age groups, it is not surprising that visits by the adults who are involved in caretaking showed corresponding differences. For example, during the A.M. period, mothers of younger Ss were with their infants almost three times as long as were mothers of older Ss, while caretakers spent equivalent amounts of total time with both age groups. In addition to these indices, we also compared directly the visit durations of every pair of adults (in terms of difference scores). Such a comparison between mothers' and caretakers' A.M. visits can illustrate the age effect even more sharply than does the preceding analysis: mothers spent more time (76 minutes or 23% of the child's A.M. time awake) than did the main caretaker with their 4-month-old infants, but the main caretaker spent more time (29 minutes or 7%) than did mothers with their 8-month-old infants ($p < .005$). Background (and setting) trends which involve age-by-sex interactions are considered in the next section on sex-group differences.

Sex-Group Trends. The expectation of finding differences between younger and older infants in caretaking and background events appeared to be a reasonable one. In contrast, there were no strong a priori reasons for expecting the sexes to differ in these experiences, especially within the egalitarian environment of the kibbutz. In keeping with these expectations, our analyses resulted in but few reliable sex differences, most of which were further qualified by interactions with age. Nevertheless, because of the exploratory nature of this report, the sex differences that were detected are considered in some detail.

The one outstanding difference between the sex groups is in Total Caretaking duration. In absolute time and as a percentage of time awake, cumulative caretaking activities were found to be of longer duration for boys than for girls. This tendency was present at both age levels (Figure 2), despite the marked reduction in caretaking time between four and eight months.

The difference in cumulative caretaking time itself was due mainly to differences in the Feeding pattern. Boys had reliably higher scores than girls for Feeding duration as a percentage of Time Awake and for other Feeding indices (e.g., median duration). However, in still other Feeding indices a reliable sex-by-age interaction qualified the sex-group differences: while the mean Feeding periods was longer for boys within each age group, the greatest discrepancy between the sex groups was found at the younger level, where the mean Feeding duration for the boys was 28 minutes as compared to 16 minutes for the girls.

The Feeding picture would be incomplete without an examination of the Eating index pattern. Although the discrepancy between the sex groups is reduced when the Eating and Feeding duration indices are added together, it appears that within the

8-month-old Ss the proportion of that combined index that is made up of Eating duration is twice as large for girls as it is for boys (52% compared to 24%). (It is to be recalled that among the 4-month-olds, the Eating durations are negligible for both sexes.) This result and its relation-ship to age corresponds to those showing that less time is spent on the caretaking of girls (and older infants) than on the caretaking of boys (and younger infants).

Intervals between Diaper Changing occasions were reliably shorter for boys than the girls. This result may reflect nothing more than anatomical differences between boy and girl infants in a society where the use of protective rubber pants is not the rule. Nevertheless, these scores (together with other isolated scores not reported here in detail, e.g., Medicating) contribute to the cumulative duration of caretaking activities which differentiates between the sexes (Figure 2).

None of the background indices showed a clear-cut difference between caretakers' or parents' visits to boys and to girls. Mothers of boys and of girls spent approximately equal total durations with their infants during the entire observation day and during its two parts. The main caretaker's visiting pattern was similarly identical for boys as for girls.

In contrast, fathers' visits to boys are generally longer than their visits to girls, due mostly to their longest visits being with the older boys. This is reflected in near-reliable sex-by-age interactions for several P.M. visit indices, in all of which fathers' highest visit scores are to 8-month-old-boys. These indices are: total duration of fathers' visits (92 minutes or 75% of Ss' Time Awake); and mother-minus-father score, which reflected the smallest difference (7.6 minutes) between the two parents' visits. The group receiving lowest visit scores from fathers are either 4-month-old boys or girls, depending on the index.

No differences in the duration of mothers' visits to boys and girls was detected. Even so, considering the entire day or the A.M. period alone, there is a tendency for mothers to visit their older boys and younger girls most often, and their older girls least often.

Our investigation has pointed up several trends which suggest a different pattern of caretaking for boys than for girl infants. But this pattern is not a simple one. It emerges mostly in the form of sex-by-age interactions, where relative to girls' scores, those of boys are characteristically in the same direction as those of younger Ss. More caretaking activities (Feeding, Diapering) are directed to the boys and particularly to the younger boys. Similarly, mothers attend more frequently to the boys, and especially to the younger ones. Fathers are not as involved in caretaking. While mothers busy themselves more with their younger infants, fathers spend more time with their older infants, and predominantly with their older boys. Moreover, while the discrepancy between the boys' and girls' scores is greater at the younger age level, it diminishes as the infants grow older. It is typically the boys' curve that shows the steeper drop between the 4-month and 8-month points, suggesting that boys who may start off discrepant from the girls tend to "catch up" with them eventually.

One way of looking at these patterns is to think of infant boys as initially less "mature" developmentally than infant girls. Boys' states may be more variable or more dependent on immediate gratifications than those of girl infants. Such constitutional "immaturity" could result in more caretaking (e.g., more feeding), reflecting directly actual needs or indirectly a heightened activity level or restlessness (e.g., fussing) which may be manifestations of such unrequited states. On the other hand, if boys are in fact more restless, that could be looked upon as an outcome of the greater amount of caretaking attention showered on them, rather than as its cause. Infant boys may have learned to be more vocal or generally active, because such responses may be more likely to be followed by adult attention than the placid behaviors of the content baby.

The research literature is replete with biological and environmental hypotheses about the bases of differences in caretaking patterns of boy and girl infants. There is no need to refer to these studies or to offer alternative explanations to those we have mentioned. Any interpretations we might venture at this point would have to be highly speculative. Some clarification might be obtained subsequently from comparisons with similar data we have collected on infants in other age groups and in other child-rearing environments. Even more critical leverage on this issue will come from our analyses of the actual behaviors of the infants, parents and caretakers, and of the interaction sequences constituted by the interchange between the behaviors of the infant Ss and those of the persons visiting them.

Conclusion

In closing, let us recall that the purpose of this report was to make use of a small kibbutz sample, in which Ss of both sexes are represented, to explore some methods of data organization and analysis. Because sex category is not an independent variable in our larger investigation (where only boys are studied), data derived from this sample has made possible a partly independent test of the utility of our ecological descriptions of caretaking patterns, based on direct observation of infants in their natural environment, prior to our dealing with the extensive body of observation data of our larger study. Probability levels derived from inferential statistical methods have been used only to help us to identify, in a preliminary way, some contextual dimensions of the environment that could provide independent variables for subsequent analyses. We preferred not to rely on casual data comparisons for that end. For this reason, also, we have refrained from bringing into the analysis assumptions from our theoretical approach. Apart from the required methodological assumptions, made explicitly or implied, our analysis in the main has remained close to the level of the data.

Insofar as the simple setting and back-ground categories we have used are meaningful for the reader, therefore, this report can at the very least provide potentially useful ethnographic data about some conditions of child care in the kibbutz environment for the first year of life. For our longer-term research aims, the first-level summaries presented can pave the way for data analyses which will be used specifically to test directional hypotheses. Hence, this report represents the beginning stages of the required functional analysis of child-rearing environments, which will deal with the systematic impact of conditions of stimulation (provided for the most part through caretaker behaviors) on actual child-behavior patterns.

References

GEWIRTZ, HAVA, and GEWIRTZ, J. Caretaking settings, background events, and behavior differences in four Israeli child-rearing environments: Some preliminary trends. In B. M. Foss (Ed.), *Determinants of infant behavior IV*. London: Methuen, in press.

GEWIRTZ, J. The course of infant smiling in four child-rearing environments in Israel. In B. M. Foss (Ed.), *Determinants of infant behavior III*. London: Methuen (New York: Wiley), 1965. Pp. 205–260.

RABIN, A. *Growing up in the kibbutz.* New York: Springer, 1965.

SPIRO, M. *Children of the kibbutz*. Cambridge, Mass.: Harvard University Press, 1958.

Conformity and Deviance

5

Reinforcement analysis proceeds on the basic assumption that the individual is shaped by the consequences of his behavior in the environment. Some of these consequences are effective because of the changes they produce in the physical environment, and some are effective by virtue of their influence on other individuals. A new phenomenon appears to emerge, however, when more than one person reacts in concert to an individual's behavior. This section deals with experiments in which the conduct of individual subjects is influenced, determined, or changed by contingencies of reinforcement applied by a group.

The topics of social conformity and deviance are very similar to those in which judgment and perception are influenced by social pressure, as in the type of experiments carried by Solomon Asch and Muzafer Sherif. Asch had subjects judge the lengths of lines with a group of people who distorted their reports in accordance with instructions from the experimenter. In the study of conformity and deviance, however, our concern is not so much the change in a single performance, such as the perception of the length of a line or the magnitude of the autokinetic effect, but whether the subject is inclined to adjust his conduct in a wide variety of ways to conform to that of some group. We are also interested in knowing whether any deviation from the patterns of conduct of the group decrease in frequency because they are punished, fail to be rewarded, or are incompatible with other kinds of conduct required by the group. Thus, while the general paradigm of the experiments involves a group that differentially reinforces a subject—depending upon whether the subject's performance is the same as the group's—the test of conformity is whether the individual subsequently conforms without explicit consequences from the group. Thus, in each of the experiments reported in this section, there are two phases: (a) the development of conformity in an individual as a result of a group's reaction to his performance, and (b) determination of the subject's general inclination to conform during a subsequent period of nonreinforcement.

The uniquely social quality of these phenomena is indicated by an almost exclusive use of the verbal behavior of confederates to differentially reinforce the behavior of the subjects. The conformity involved in wearing a tie, for example, can come about by a person's having been excluded from a restaurant, but it may be restricted to this particular situation and performance. Situations involving verbal interaction extend the basic phenomenon to a large variety of situations in the natural environment where social interchange is verbal rather than physical or gestural. Conformity in the verbal sense appears as an increase in the frequency of certain broad classes of language behavior. General tendencies to conform or to deviate in situations involving nonverbal interactions may also occur, of course.

The conformity of a subject to a group practice implies many contingencies of reinforcement which are implicit but frequently unstated. As Skinner has suggested, there are two classes of behavior to be accounted for: (a) the behavior of the group members that is reinforced by the conformity or deviance of the individual they are attempting to influence, and (b) the behavior of the individual who conforms to or deviates from the group. Many experiments have dealt only with the behavior of the individual who conforms or deviates. The group activities which provide the reinforcers for the individual are simulated by using confederates of the experimenter. In the natural environment for which these experiments are a paradigm, however, the situation is much more complex, because we have to account for the behavior of the group as well as the behavior of the conforming or deviating member.

In general the group can provide three kinds of consequences to an individual member: (a) *Punishment and other kinds of aversive control.* The aversive stimulus usually consists of the withdrawal of important reinforcers. For example, acceptable speech forms are reinforced by the group's attention and reaction. Unacceptable speech forms tend not to be answered and, in extreme cases, lead to various degrees of ostracism. This type of punishment or extinction of vocal interaction is "natural" in the sense that the reinforcers involved are the same ones that normally maintain the performances. Aversive stimuli frequently have no relation to the behavior that the group is trying to reduce. For example, the stones that a crowd throws at a radical speaker are related only indirectly to the reinforcers which maintain the speaker's conduct. (b) *Positive reinforcement.* A group may use positive reinforcement to shape conformity behavior or to maintain its frequency. (c) *Differential reinforcement.* In the kind of verbal shaping that occurs in natural interactions between an individual and a group, the reinforcement processes are intrinsic to the actual verbal performances. Conformity arises as a result of the fine-grain, detailed, interaction between the speaker and the listener. Since the essence of verbal reinforcement lies in the behaviors prompted in the listener by the speaker, any mismatch in the verbal repertoires between the listener and the speaker will result in nonreinforcement of the speaker's performance. Thus, a speaker with a repertoire very different from that of his listener cannot prompt behaviors relevant to the variables that caused him to speak. In more general terms, the speaker doesn't get any place whenever his behavior fails to prompt the required forms or frequencies of verbal performances in the listener. Because every speaker is also his own listener, verbal interactions can occur within the individual's own repertoire. Such interactions within a single individual's verbal repertoire have been described as "cognitive dissonance" by Leon Festinger and others. The effectiveness of attempts to reinforce behavior, as in persuasion and other forms of social influence, is limited by the compatibility of the new performances with related verbal behavior already in the subject's repertoire.

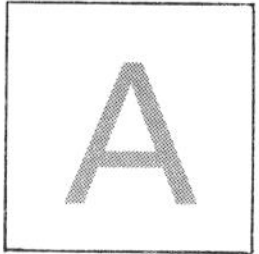

Some Experimental Paradigms

Endler's procedure, a prototype in this area, influenced a subject by having him answer questions after he had already heard the responses of three other subjects who were confederates of the experimenter. The questions were presented to the subjects on projected slides, which asked questions of fact, required a decision about the difference between two stimuli, or prompted a statement of attitude. Two conditions operated on the subjects' answers to the questions: one, the social pressure by the other "subjects" who had answered first, and the other, the experimenter's approval or disapproval of the subject's answer. In one group, the experimenter approved (reinforced) the subject whenever his answer conformed to that of the other three subjects. In another group the experimenter approved of the subject's answer to a question only when it deviated from the replies of the other three "subjects." Thus, under one condition the experimenter joined the other three "subjects" and in the other condition he opposed them.

The results of the experiment showed that approval or disapproval by the experimenter was the critical factor—increasing the number of times the subject conformed to the confederates when conformity was reinforced and decreasing the number of times the subjects conformed when deviance was reinforced. Endler also discovered that the experimenter's reinforcement influenced the subject differently depending upon the kind of problem posed by the slides. Simple facts and perceptual items were most resistant to the experimenter's influence, whereas statements of attitude were more easily influenced. This result suggests that attitudes involve performances which have a more variable reinforcement history than statement of facts or judgments of stimuli. The main experimental result was further buttressed by the finding that the amount of conformity increased in proportion to the number of times that the experimenter agreed or disagreed with the subject.

28 *The Effects of Verbal Reinforcement on Conformity and Deviant Behavior*[1]

NORMAN S. ENDLER

Introduction

There are a number of factors that influence conforming behavior. These include (*a*) the stimulus variables used to elicit the conforming behavior; (*b*) group properties: i.e., group structure and function; and (*c*) individual differences or personality factors. A fourth phenomenon related to both (*a*) and (*b*), yet operating as a factor in its own right, is (*d*) the situational factor or the conditions under which conforming behavior occurs.

Conformity is not a general factor that occurs indiscriminately, but is partially determined by the situational context in which it occurs. If, in a group situation, the individual is reinforced for conform-

[1] The author wishes to express his thanks to Herbert Kee, Clayton Ruby, and Douglas Rutherford who served as confederates and to Larry Snyder and Helen Penner who assisted in the analysis of the data.

ing, his conforming behavior will increase. If he is reinforced for being deviant, his conforming behavior will decrease. As Oliver and Alexander state, ". . . conforming responses are seen as voluntary behavior whose occurrence is under the control of reinforcing stimuli that follow them, and discriminative stimuli or cues that precede them" (1963, p. 3). They go on to say that "In social interaction, the behaviors of individuals or groups may serve as reinforcing stimuli, or they may serve as discriminative stimuli" (1963, p. 3).

Conforming behavior can be manipulated like any other class of behavior. (Walker and Heyns, 1962). It is an instrumental act that leads to need satisfaction and goal attainment, with reinforcement playing a crucial role in the need → instrumental act → goal, behavioral sequence (Walker and Henys, 1962). If conforming behavior is followed by positive reinforcement, the probability of its reoccurrence is increased; if deviation from a group norm is followed by positive reinforcements, the probability of nonconformity is increased. Reinforcement is an important force in shaping (i.e., in forming and altering) social behavior, including conformity.

In a conformity situation there are a number of sources of social reinforcement, including the individuals comprising the group and the experimenter (*E*). Crutchfield (1956), for example, had *E* inform the Ss of the correct answers (i.e., the false group consensus) to various items immediately after the responses to each slide. The reinforcement by *E* (an authority figure) in conjunction with the group consensus increased the degree of conformity. Schein (1954) found that reward facilitated learned imitation, but that this did not generalize to all types of problems. Jones, Wells, and Torrey (1958) found that feedback by *E* in terms of group consensus had little or no effect on conformity, but that feedback in terms of objective reality reduced conforming behavior. However, when *E* stressed the importance of group accuracy and social conformity, feedback by *E* in terms of group consensus increased conforming behavior; and reinforcement by *E* of independence still reduced conformity but to a lesser extent.

The present study was designed to study the effects on conforming behavior of feedback by *E*. The proposition tested was that verbal reinforcement for agreeing with a contrived group consensus increases conformity, while reinforcement for disagreeing increases deviant behavior (i.e., decreases conformity).

Furthermore, because a number of investigators (Applezweig and Moeller, 1958; Asch, 1956; Beloff, 1958; Crutchfield, 1956; Tuddenham, 1958) have found that females conform more frequently than males, sex differences in conforming behavior were also examined. Bass (1961) attempts to explain these differences in terms of motivational orientation, stating that men are more task-oriented while women are more social-interaction oriented. Because women are more concerned than men with receiving social approval from other individuals, women tend to conform more.

As a side issue, the present study also investigated the effects of the type of stimulus on conforming behavior. There are at least two dimensions to the stimulus factor: (*a*) ambiguity and (*b*) personal commitment. Luchins (1944), Asch (1951), Blake, Helson, and Mouton (1956), and Endler (1960) have shown that the more ambiguous the stimulus the greater proportion of Ss conforming to the objectively incorrect judgment of the confederates. Crutchfield (1956) found that conformity is least common for items involving personal commitment, such as personal preferences and attitudes.

In the present study, three types of stimulus items were used: verbal (obscure facts), perceptual (geometrical forms), and attitudes. Because the obscure facts (verbal items) would be most ambiguous for S, and because the attitude items involve personal or emotional commitment, we would expect most conformity to the verbal items, least conformity to the attitude items, and an intermediate degree of conformity to the perceptual items.

This study deals primarily with the effects of the situational factor on conformity (reinforcement) and secondarily with the effects of individual differences (sex) and stimulus factors.

Method

Subjects. Forty male and 35 female college freshmen were randomly assigned to one of three experimental conditions: conformity reinforcement (CR), 14 males and 12 females; neutral (N), 12 males and 10 females; and deviancy reinforcement (DR), 14 males and 13 females. There were three approximately equal groups of males; and three, of females.

Three male college sophomores served as confederates, and *E* (Ss' psychology instructor) served as the source of verbal reinforcement. The three confederates had prestige value in that one was the president of the students' council and was majoring in psychology, a second was editor of the student periodical, and the third was majoring in psychology.

Procedure. Each S was tested separately by *E*, but in the presence of the three male confederates. A series of 36 slides, consisting of 20 critical (conformity) items and 16 buffer items was used to measure conforming behavior. The 20 critical items, which were of the multiple-choice type, included eight information (verbal), nine perceptual, and three attitude items. The series of slides was programmed so that after the first three buffer items there were never more than two consecutive buffer items or two consecutive critical items. Slide Numbers 4, 5, 7, 8, 10, 12, 13, 15, 17, 18, 20, 22, 23, 25, 27, 28, 30, 32, 33, and 35 served as the critical items. Base rates in responding to these items were determined by administering them to a control group.

The 36 two-inch by two-inch slides were projected (one at a time) on a screen six feet in front of the respondents. The confederates and S were seated behind tables, and each individual had a pencil and a data recording sheet on which to record his answers. *E* projected the slide onto the screen and then told each individual when to respond. Each individual was required to announce his response. For the buffer or neutral items, *E* randomized the order in which the individuals responded. For each critical item, S was required to respond after hearing the responses of the three confederates. Previously, the confederates had been instructed how to respond to the critical items. The conformity score for each S was the number of times he agreed with the contrived consensus of the confederates on the critical items.

Ss were randomly assigned to one of three experimental conditions: conformity reinforcement (CR), neutral (N), and deviancy reinforcement (DR). Ss in the CR group were verbally reinforced by *E* saying, "*Good*, that is right," every time they *agreed* with the contrived consensus of the confederates on the critical items. Ss in the DR group were similarly reinforced by *E* every time they *disagreed* with the confederates on the critical items. Ss in the N group were not explicitly reinforced by *E*. Nothing was said after the buffer items, nor did the confederates at any time comment on an S's responses. The independent variable was the experimental treatment; the dependent variable was the S's conformity score.

Results

To test the hypotheses of differences in conforming behavior due to experimental conditions and sex, the data were analyzed by means of a two-way (conditions-by-sex) analysis of variance with unequal *N*s (Johnson and Jackson, 1959, pp. 234–245). Table 1 shows that the observed differences among the several subclasses are significant ($p < .01$), indicating that at least one of the components (experimental conditions, sex, or interaction) is significant. Therefore, specific tests of the hypotheses concerning conditions, sex, and interaction were made, and the analysis of variance for this also appears in Table 1. The only significant factor is that among conditions CR, N, and DR ($F = 15.56$, $p < .01$). There are no significant sex or interaction differences. Since there were no significant sex differences, the male and female samples were combined, and Tukey's (1949)

Table 1 *Two-way (Experimental Conditions-by-Sex) Analysis of Variance of Conformity Scores (for Unequal Ns)*

Source	Sum of Squares	*df*	Mean Square	*F*	*p*
Experimental conditions*	375.69	2	187.85	15.56	<.01
Sex	14.88	1	14.88	1.23	
Interaction	16.53	2	8.26	.68	
Among subclasses	407.10	5	81.42	6.75	<.01
Within subclasses	833.03	69	12.07		
Total	1240.13	74			

* The experimental conditions are conformity reinforcement (CR), neutral (N), and deviancy reinforcement (DR).

Table 2 *Means and Standard Deviations of Conformity Scores for Male, Female, and Combined Samples under Three Experimental Conditions*

Sample	Conformity Reinforcement			Neutral			Deviancy Reinforcement		
	N	*M*	*SD*	*N*	*M*	*SD*	*N*	*M*	*SD*
Male	14	10.43	3.79	12	6.17	3.08	14	4.14	1.96
Female	12	8.25	3.27	10	6.20	4.85	13	3.62	2.17
Combined	26	9.42	3.72	22	6.18	3.99	27	3.89	2.08

gap tests for comparing means in the analysis of variance reveal that Ss in the CR group conformed significantly more ($p < .01$) than those in the N group, who conformed significantly more ($p < .01$) than those in the DR group. Table 2 contains the means and standard deviations for the various subgroups.

To test the hypothesis that the verbal items elicit the greatest degree of conformity, that attitude items elicit the least degree of conformity, and that the perceptual (geometrical) items elicit an intermediate degree of conformity, the Jonckheere (1954) distribution-free k-sample test against ordered alternatives—was performed for the CR, N, and DR conditions separately, yielding Z values of 3.64, 6.94, and 12.08, respectively ($p < .01$).

Discussion

The results indicate that verbal reinforcement for *agreeing* with a contrived group consensus increases the degree of conforming behavior. Similarly, reinforcement for *disagreeing* with a contrived group consensus decreases the degree of conformity (i.e., increases deviant behavior).

Verbal reinforcement is a potent force in shaping social behavior, often more potent than the objective state of affairs. From an early age, when a child is undergoing the socialization process, he is rewarded for imitating others and is often punished for attempting to be different: e.g., for not listening to his parents. Much of the individual's behavior (as he goes through grade school, high school, and college) is similarly shaped by reward and punishment. Likewise, the individual's behavior outside of classes is shaped by reward and punishment. Campbell (1961) has pointed out that the more an individual is rewarded for nonconformity, the less often he will conform; and the more he is punished for nonconformity, the more he will conform.

In the experimental conformity situation the individual is faced with a discrepancy between the confederates' responses and what he knows or believes to be true. This discrepancy induces a conflict or a state of cognitive dissonance for S (Festinger, 1957). (Another potential source of dissonance is between what a person privately believes to be true and what he publicly expresses.) The individual can reduce his dissonance via rationalizing: i.e., by redefining the situation and conforming.

In the neutral (N) situation, there are only two sets of opposing forces: the responses required by the stimulus materials and the responses required by the group pressure. For the Conformity-reinforcement (CR) and Deviancy-reinforcement (DR) groups, a third force is present: the reinforcing responses of the experimenter.

In the CR Group, the group pressures summate or interact with the pressures created by *E*'s verbal reinforcement for conforming; and this tends to maximize conformity pressure and produce the greatest amount of conforming behavior. In the DR Group, the group conformity pressures oppose those created by *E*'s verbal reinforcement for disagreeing with the group. Furthermore, in this case, *E*'s reinforcements are congruent with what S believes to be the objective state of affairs. This tends to minimize conformity pressure and produce the least amount of conforming behavior. In the N Group, there is no reinforcement from *E*. The only pressures to conform come from the confederates, and the only pressures to deviate come from S himself. There is still conforming behavior because S, in his previous life history, has been reinforced for conforming and punished for nonconformity. However, the conforming behavior is less than that for the CR Group, but greater than that for the DR Group.

Sex differences in conforming behavior did not occur. Most other investigators (Asch, 1956; Crutchfield, 1956) have found that females conform more than males do. However, in most of these cases the sex of the S has been the same as that of the confederates. In this present study, all the confederates were males while there were both male and female Ss. It is possible that females conform less to male confederates than they do to female confederates. This may be because they identify more with other females and are more concerned with receiving social approval from females as a group than from males as a group. The presence of male confederates, therefore, may have reduced the conforming behavior of the females to the conformity level of the males.

In terms of the amount of conforming behavior, the type of stimulus material was also a factor. For all three experimental groups (CR, N, and DR), there was the greatest amount of conformity to the verbal items; the least amount to the attitude items; and an intermediate amount to the perceptual (geometrical) items. The verbal items were composed primarily of obscure facts, and S was not expected to know or be able immediately to verify the correct answers. Therefore S, presumably, would be willing to conform to the answers of the confederates who had both prestige value and more educational experience than Ss. Since individuals have a strong emotional or personal commitment to their attitudes, these would be most resistant to change and, for these items, pressure would produce the least amount of conforming behavior. Since Ss, presumably, could verify the perceptual items via visual inspection these items would also be resistant to change. However, S would have no strong personal or emotional commitment to these items and, therefore, would be more likely to conform to these than to the attitude items. The results of the relative effects of the different kinds of stimuli on conforming behavior can be considered only as exploratory, since there were only eight verbal, nine perceptual, and three attitude items.

In general, conformity is found to be greatest when Ss are verbally reinforced (by *E*) for agreeing with a contrived group consensus and is least when Ss are reinforced for disagreeing with the group. It is intermediate when Ss are not reinforced by *E*. There were no sex differences in conformity, but the type of stimulus material affects the amount of conforming behavior.

References

APPLEZWEIG, M. H., and MOELLER, G. Conforming behavior and personality variables. Technical Report No. 8, Contract No. NR 996 (02), Connecticut College, New London, Conn., 1958.

ASCH, S. E. Effects of group pressure upon the modification and distortion of judgments. In H. Guetzkow (Ed.), *Groups, leadership and men.* Pittsburgh: Carnegie Press, 1951.

ASCH, S. E. Studies of independence and conformity: I. A minority of one against a unanimous majority. *Psychological Monographs,* 1956, *70,* Whole No. 416.

BASS, B. M. Conformity, deviation and a general theory of interpersonal behavior. In I. A. Berg and B. M. Bass (Eds.), *Conformity and deviation.* New York: Harper, 1961. Pp. 38–100.

BELOFF, H. Two forms of social conformity: Acquiescence and conventionality. *Journal of Abnormal and Social Psychology,* 1958, *56,* 99–104.

BLAKE, R. R., HELSON, H., and MOUTON, J. The generality of conformity behavior as a function of factual anchorage, difficulty of task and amount of social pressure. In R. R. Blake and H. Helson (Eds.), *Adaptability screening of flying personnel: Situational and personal factors in conforming behavior.* Randolph Field, San Antonio, Texas: School of Aviation Medicine, USAF, 1956. Pp. 27–34.

CAMPBELL, D. T. Conformity in psychology's theories of acquired behavioral dispositions. In I. A. Berg and B. M. Bass (Eds.), *Conformity and deviation.* New York: Harper, 1961. Pp. 101–142.

Crutchfield, R. S. Conformity and character. *American Psychologist,* 1956, *10,* 191–198.

ENDLER, N. S. Social conformity in perception of the autokinetic effect. *Journal of Abnormal and Social Psychology,* 1960, *60,* 489–490.

FESTINGER, L. *A theory of cognitive dissonance.* Stanford, Calif.: Stanford University Press, 1957.

JOHNSON, P. O., and JACKSON, R. W. B. *Modern statistical methods: Descriptive and inductive.* Chicago: Rand-McNally, 1959.

Jonckheere, A. R. A distribution-free k-sample test against ordered alternatives. *Biometrika,* 1954, *41,* 133–145.

JONES, E. E., WELLS, H. H., and TORREY, R. Some effects of feedback from the experimenter on conformity behavior. *Journal of Abnormal and Social Psychology,* 1958, *57,* 207–213.

LUCHINS, A. S. On agreement with another's judgment. *Journal of Abnormal and Social Psychology,* 1944, *39,* 97–111.

OLIVER, B., and ALEXANDER, S. Reinforcing effects of congruent group judgments on conforming behavior. Paper read at the annual meeting of the Midwestern Psychological Association, Chicago, May 4, 1963.

SCHEIN, E. H. The effect of reward on adult imitative behavior. *Journal of Abnormal and Social Psychology,* 1954, *49,* 389–395.

TUDDENHAM, R. D. Some correlates of yielding to a distorted group norm. Technical Report No. 8, Contract NR 170–159, University of California, Berkeley, Calif., 1958.

TUKEY, J. W. Comparing individual means in the analysis of variance. *Biometrics,* 1949, *5,* 99–114.

WALKER, E. L., and HEYNS, R. W. *An anatomy for conformity.* Englewood Cliffs, N.J.: Prentice-Hall, 1962.

Successful replication of Endler's findings has increased their generality by showing that his procedures will produce conformity or deviance regardless of variations in some of the details. The experiment by *Tolman and Barnsley* replicated the procedures of Endler's experiments almost exactly, except that the interaction between the subjects was simulated rather than actual. The fact that identical results were obtained despite the variations in details of procedure strengthen Endler's main finding.

29 Effects of Verbal Reinforcement on Conformity and Deviant Behavior: Replication Report[1]

C. W. TOLMAN
R. H. BARNSLEY

Endler (1965) recently demonstrated that in a typical Asch-type group-pressure situation conformity or deviance of S's responses from the contrived group consensus can be manipulated by *E* with verbal reinforcement. The present experiment was very similar to Endler's, variations being minor.

As Endler found no difference between males and females, only 35 female Ss from an introductory psychology class were shown materials identical to those used by Endler except for some minor changes in geographic names made necessary by regional differences. There were 36 multiple-choice items of which 20 were critical items and 16 were buffer items.

The procedure was identical to Endler's except that the group was simulated rather than face-to-face. A script[2] for *E* and three group members, leaving blank spaces for S's responses, was taped (see Blake and Brehm, 1954). *S* interacted with this group via intercom. *S* could be observed by *E* through a one-way window. *E* controlled the progress of the tape and, when appropriate, could insert verbal reinforcements such as "very good" and "that's right." All Ss were interviewed following the experiment to determine their awareness of the real nature of the experiment. Only two gave evidence of suspicion that the situation was somehow rigged. These Ss were discarded and replaced. The conditions ($ns = 9$) were reinforcement for conformity, no reinforcement, and reinforcement for deviancy. There was also a baseline condition which involved only *E* and Ss without reinforcement.

Mean per cent of critical items on which conformity occurred are as follows: for the group reinforced for conformity, 44.96 ± 12.5; for no reinforcement, 23.89 ± 6.97; for reinforcement for deviancy, 15.40 ± 8.89; and for the baseline Ss, 10.56 ± 5.49. [For the reinforcement groups this percentage is based on the responses after and including the first reinforced response.] An analysis of variance of these data yielded an F of 24.95 ($df = 3/33$, $p < .01$). This result confirms that of Endler and supports his conclusion that verbal reinforcement can be a potent force in shaping social behavior.

1 The data reported here were collected by P. G. Arnold, G. Booth, D. Louie, and Marlene Farmer under the supervision of the authors.

2 A copy of the script can be obtained by writing to the American Documentation Institute, Auxiliary Publications, Project, Photoduplication Service, Library of Congress, Washington, D.C. 20540. Remit $1.25 for Document No. 9082 (photocopies or 35-mm. microfilm).

References

BLAKE, R. R., and BREHM, J. W. The use of tape recording to simulate a group atmosphere. *Journal of Abnormal and Social Psychology,* 1954, *49,* 311–313.

ENDLER, N. S. The effects of verbal reinforcement on conformity and deviant behavior. *Journal of Social Psychology,* 1965, *66,* 147–154.

From *Psychological Reports,* 1966, *19,* 910. Reprinted by permission.

Endler and Hoy report an experiment in which they attempted to measure separately the factors underlying conformity and deviance. They set out to discover how much the experimenter's reinforcement influenced the subject apart from the social pressure by the confederates. The original experiment by Endler had confounded these two factors, because the experimenter's agreement or disagreement always occurred in the context of the social pressure from the confederate's replies. Endler and Hoy therefore used procedures by which they could evaluate the effect on the subject of social pressure alone.

Although the experimenter's approval or disapproval seems to be defined as reinforcement and the contingencies provided by the confederates as social pressure, these definitions appear too restrictive. Behaviorally, both situations may be viewed as ones in which the subject's behavior is modified by the differential social consequences it produces in other persons. The reinforcement of the subject's behavior by the prior report of the confederates is not so obvious as that provided by approval or disapproval from the experimenter. This is probably because many of the relevant contingencies of reinforcement have occurred in the past. Thus, if the three confederates said that New York City was the capital of the state of New York, the subject's inclination to say Albany would be weakened because behavior about New York City acquired in the past would be prepotent.

The conformity of the subjects' statements to those of the group is a reinforcer, because under most circumstances statements of fact by a group have been correct. Most individuals have a history of experiences in which statements at variance with those of the group have tended to be incorrect. For example, an individual adding a column of numbers is more likely to report an incorrect sum than a group of people who can check their answers with each other. Herein, perhaps, lies the basis for the reinforcing power of group consensus.

30 | *Conformity as Related to Reinforcement and Social Pressure*[1]

NORMAN S. ENDLER

ELIZABETH HOY

The socially learned response of conforming behavior (agreement with a contrived group consensus) can be modified via reinforcement. In general, reinforcement for agreeing increases conforming behavior, and reinforcement for disagreeing (Endler, 1965; Tolman and Barnsley, 1966) decreases it. Furthermore, the extent of the conforming behavior is a function of the amount of reinforcement (Endler, 1966a).

Most of the reinforcement studies in this area have focused on the acquisition of conforming responses under various experimental conditions and have ignored their resistance to extinction (durability). Endler (1966a) found that both the acquisition and extinction of conforming behavior were a function of different reinforcement schedules during the acquisition trials. Reinforcement for agreement elicited more conformity than reinforcement for disagreeing, with the extent of the effect being a function of the amount of reinforcement. Conformity was significantly higher in the reinforcement social pressure (experimental) session than during the nonreinforcement nonpressure posttest. The procedure differed in the two sessions in that both the social pressure and reinforcement present during the experimental session were removed during the posttest. Therefore

[1] This study was supported in part by Grant APA 109 from the National Research Council of Canada, in part by Grant MH-08987 from the United States Public Health Service, and in part by a grant from York University. The authors wish to thank Ken Koffer and Corinne Wilks for their assistance in the collection of data.

From the *Journal of Personality and Social Psychology,* 1967, 7, 197–202.

differences in conforming between these two sessions may be due to either or both of these sources of pressure.

The present study was designed to investigate the effects of removing only one of the sources (reinforcement, but not social pressure) during the posttest. It was hypothesized that there would be significantly less conformity in the posttest (extinction trials) than in the experimental session (acquisition trials) and that conforming behavior during both sessions would be a function of the reinforcement schedules of the experimental session; that is, conformity differences between sessions are primarily due to the removal of reinforcement (but not social pressure) during extinction trials.

A further purpose of this study was to separate the effects of social pressure and reinforcement. Endler (1966a) partially confounded the effects of social pressure and reinforcement by including the control group in his analysis. (All other groups received social pressure, but differed from one another in terms of reinforcement schedules. The control group received neither social pressure nor reinforcement.) Therefore, to rule out this possible contamination the control group was excluded from the analysis in this study, thereby permitting a direct test of the effects of reinforcement. To determine the efficacy of social pressure per se, the control group was compared to a social pressure-no reinforcement group. This study also provides some basis for the generality of Endler's findings by replicating the social pressure-reinforcement session. The procedures for the two studies differ only in the posttest.

Endler (1966a) found that females conformed more than males, but found no differences due to type of stimulus material (verbal or perceptual). The present study also examined these two factors.

Method

Apparatus

A conformity apparatus (see Endler, 1966a) consisting of a master control panel and five subject booths all containing appropriate toggle switches and lights was used to simulate social pressure. This electronic signaling device enabled the experimenter to communicate contrived responses (to multiple-choice items) and reinforcements (true or false) to the subject, and the subject to transmit his responses to the experimenter, by depressing one of five toggle switches which lit up the appropriate light in the experimenter's master control panel. The subjects were led to believe that they could communicate with one another, but in fact all communications were controlled by the experimenter. For a more detailed description of the apparatus, see Endler (1966a).

Subjects and Procedure

One hundred and twenty college subjects randomly assigned to six different experimental conditions were tested in groups of five in the conformity apparatus. There were 10 males and 10 females for each experimental condition, and the sexes were tested separately. The six conditions (explained in detail below) were called: true-agree 100% (1), true-agree 50% (2), neutral (3), true-disagree 50% (4), true-disagree 100% (5), control (6).

Groups 1–5 were subjected to social pressure via the conformity apparatus and responded to 36 slides (five alternative multiple-choice items) projected on a screen in front of them. Of the 16 critical items used, 8 were verbal (obscure facts) in which subjects were asked such questions as, "The most popular beverage in Laos is"; and 8 were perceptual (geometrical forms) in which they were asked to tell, for example, which of five figures (circles, triangles, squares, etc.) had the largest area, or which of five lines was the longest.

Subjects were tested in two sessions: a *reinforcement* session and a posttest *nonreinforcement* session 2 weeks later. They were subjected to social pressure in both sessions.

Session 1 (reinforcement). All groups except control (6) and neutral (3) were subjected to the following true-false reinforcement schedules administered by the experimenter via the apparatus—if the experimenter pressed the true switch on the master panel, the blue (true) light lit up on the subject's panel; for the false switch, the red (false) light lit up: Group 1, true-agree 100%, was positively (true) reinforced for agreeing and negatively (false) reinforced for disagreeing with the contrived group consensus (simulated by the experimenter) on all 16 critical items. Group 2, true-agree 50%, was reinforced as above on 8 critical items. Group 4, true-disagree 50%, and Group 5, true-disagree 100% were analogous to Groups 2 and 1, respectively, except that subjects were *positively* reinforced for *disagreeing* and *negatively* reinforced for *agreeing*.

Group 3, the neutral group, was subjected to social pressure, but not to reinforcement (i.e., did not receive experimenter feedback). Group 6, the control group, responded to the stimulus items in the absence of both social pressure and reinforcement. The subject's conformity score was the number of times he agreed with contrived consensus on the critical items.

Session 2 (nonreinforcement). Two weeks later

all subjects were tested again in the conformity apparatus. All groups except the control group were subjected to social pressure but not to reinforcement. The control group received the same treatment they did in Session 1.

The procedure for Session 1 is identical to that used by Endler (1966a) in Session 1. The procedure for Session 2 differs from Endler's (1966a) in that in the present study all subjects (except the control group) were subjected to social pressure, but not to reinforcement, whereas in Endler's (1966a) study subjects were neither subjected to social pressure nor to reinforcement.

Conformity responses of neutral and control-group subjects were compared for both sessions. Separate two-way analyses of variance (Reinforcement Conditions × Sex) were conducted for each session (with the control-group subjects excluded), and in addition an overall four-way classification analysis of variance was computed on all the data, excluding the control-group subjects (Reinforcement × Sex × Stimulus Item × Session).

Results

To determine whether social pressure per se had any effect, the mean conformity responses for the neutral and control groups were compared for Sessions 1 and 2, yielding t values of 5.63 ($p < .01$) and 3.68 ($p < .01$), respectively.

Table 1 presents two-way classification analyses of variance (Reinforcement Conditions × Sex) of subjects' conformity scores (excluding the control group) for both the experimental reinforcement session (1) and the posttest nonreinforcement session (2). The main effect of reinforcement was significant at the .01 level for both sessions. The main effect of sex and the interaction were not significant for either session.[2]

Table 1 *Two-Way Classification (Reinforcement Conditions × Sex) Analyses of Variance (Fixed-Effects Model) of Conformity Scores for Reinforcement and Posttest Nonreinforcement Sessions*

Source	*df*	Experimental Reinforcement		Posttest Nonreinforcement	
		MS	*F*	MS	*F*
Reinforcement condition (A)	4	245.80	25.47*	181.79	12.78*
Sex (B)	1	2.89	.30	7.84	.55
A × B	4	2.54	.26	10.17	.72
Within	90	9.65		14.22	
Total	99				

* $p < .01$.

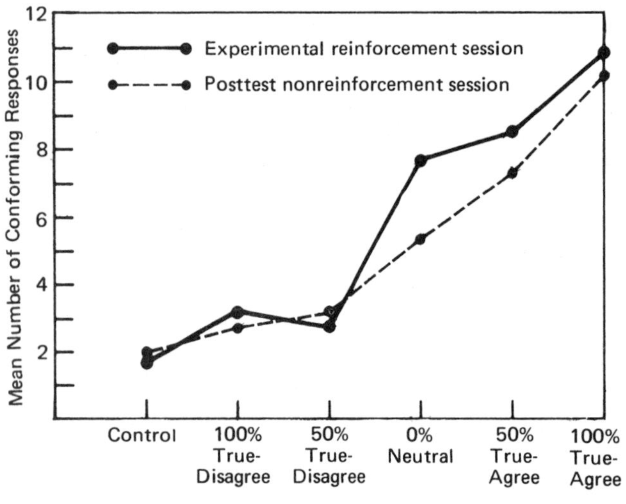

Figure 1 *The effects of different reinforcement conditions on conforming responses for reinforcement and posttest nonreinforcement sessions.*

Table 2 presents the means and standard deviations of the conformity scores (for male, female, and combined samples) in both sessions for the various treatment conditions (including the control group).

Note that in Session 1, the rank order of the mean conformity scores for females (from highest to lowest) was as follows: true-agree 100%, true-agree 50%, neutral, true-disagree 50%, true-disagree 100%, and control. For males in Session 1 the order was the same except for the fact that conformity scores for the true-disagree 100% group were higher (though not significantly) than those for the true-disagree 50% group. For the posttest (Session 2), the magnitude of the conformity scores for the various groups was in the order predicted for both sexes.

Figure 1 is a graph comparing the mean conformity scores (for males and females combined) of the different reinforcement conditions for Sessions 1 and 2 (see Table 2). Note that for all of the *experimental conditions* (excluding the control group), except the true-disagree 50% the conformity scores were higher for Session 1 than for Session 2. These differences, however, are only significant for the true-agree 50% and neutral groups.

Some subjects conformed more to perceptual items

2 There were no essential differences in the results of the present study, when the control group was *included* in the analyses; that is, whether or not the control group is included in the analyses of variance does not basically affect the results nor the resulting conclusions.

Table 2 *Means and Standard Deviations of Sessions 1 and 2 Conformity Scores for Male, Female, and Combined Samples under Different Reinforcement Conditions*

Reinforcement Conditions	Experimental Reinforcement Session (1)			Posttest Nonreinforcement Session (2)		
	Male ($N = 10$)	Female ($N = 10$)	Combined ($N = 20$)	Male ($N = 10$)	Female ($N = 10$)	Combined ($N = 20$)
True-agree 100%						
M	11.0	10.9	10.95	11.4	8.7	10.05
SD	1.95	2.77	2.40	4.52	4.65	4.86
True-agree 50%						
M	8.8	8.4	8.60	7.0	7.6	7.30
SD	4.51	3.29	3.90	4.71	4.54	4.62
Neutral						
M	7.0	8.2	7.60	6.0	4.7	5.35
SD	4.52	3.87	4.25	3.87	3.26	3.64
True-disagree 50%						
M	2.4	3.4	2.90	3.0	3.6	3.30
SD	0.80	2.01	1.61	1.67	2.94	2.41
True-disagree 100%						
M	3.2	3.2	3.20	2.7	2.7	2.70
SD	1.83	0.90	1.44	1.49	1.95	1.73
Control						
M	1.4	2.2	1.80	2.0	2.0	2.00
SD	1.02	1.66	1.44	1.34	1.79	1.58

than to verbal items. These differences were significant for the true-agree 100% group in Session 1 and for the true-disagree 50% and true-disagree 100% groups in Session 2. Trend analyses of conformity to individual items, for Session 1, for both males and females were performed. Both male and female true-disagree 100% groups and the male true-disagree 50% group indicated a significant downward trend; that is, for the true-disagree groups there was significantly less conformity at the end of the series than at the beginning. The trends for the true-agree groups were not significant.

Table 3 presents a four-way fixed-effects analysis of variance (multifactor repeated-measurements design) of the conformity data, excluding the control group[3] (see Winer, 1962). The four factors are reinforcement conditions, sessions (experimental reinforcement versus posttest nonreinforcement), sex, and type of stimulus item (verbal versus perceptual).

The effects due to reinforcement conditions, type of stimulus item, and sessions were significant ($p <$ .01). The effect due to sex was not significant. There were no significant interactions.

The variance components derived from the mean squares of the analysis of variance (see Endler, 1966b) in Table 3 (after pooling the nonsignificant sources), indicated that reinforcement conditions accounted for 14.63% of the variance; type of item, .41%; session, .59%. The pooled residual of subjects within groups (Sex plus Sex × Reinforcement plus subjects within groups) accounted for 52.55% of the variance.

Table 3 *Analysis of Variance of Conformity Scores for Reinforcement Conditions, Males and Females, and Verbal and Perceptual Stimulus Items*

Source	*df*	MS	*F*
Between Ss			
Sex (A)	1	.31	.03
Reinforcement condition (B)	4	209.00	22.38*
A × B	4	3.19	.34
Ss within groups (C)	90	9.34	
Within Ss			
Type of stimulus item (D)	1	14.83	8.62*
A × D	1	1.55	.90
B × D	4	.64	.37
A × B × D	4	.06	.03
D × C	90	1.72	
Session (E)	1	21.21	10.82*
A × E	1	4.55	2.32
B × E	4	4.67	2.30
A × B × E	4	3.29	1.68
E × C	90	1.96	
D × E	1	1.89	1.09
A × D × E	1	.64	.37
B × D × E	4	.55	.32
A × B × D × E	4	1.64	.94
D × E × C	90	1.74	
Total	399		

* $p < .01$.

[3] See Footnote 2.

Discussion

Since subjects in the neutral group conformed more than those in the control group for both Sessions 1 and 2, the results clearly indicate that social pressure per se is effective in producing conforming behavior. Reinforcement, however, has additional effects on conformity. The greater the degree of reinforcement (100% versus 50% versus 0%) for agreeing with others, the more frequent the conforming behavior, and, with one exception, the greater the degree of reinforcement for disagreeing, the less frequent the conforming behavior. This one exception occurred during Session 1 where male subjects in the true-disagree 100% group conformed more (not significantly) than those in the true-disagree 50% group. Otherwise the relative magnitude or rank order (from high to low) of conforming responses for both Sessions 1 and 2 was as follows: true-agree 100%, true-agree 50%, neutral, true-disagree 50%, and true-disagree 100%. These results replicate and confirm those found by Endler (1966a). For both the reinforcement and posttest sessions the true-agree 100% (males and females combined) conformed significantly more and the true-disagree 100% group significantly less than the neutral group, as determined by Dunnett's (1955) test for multiple comparisons. Furthermore, for the reinforcement session the true-disagree 50% group conformed significantly less than the neutral group.

Table 3 indicates that in this study conformity was a function of reinforcement conditions, session (greater in reinforcement than in posttest session), and type of stimulus item (greater for perceptual than for verbal items), but was not related to sex. Sessional and item differences were localized only in certain groups. Trend analyses of conformity to individual items during Session 1 indicated significantly less conformity at the end of the series than at the beginning for the true- disagree 100% group (both sexes) and the true-disagree 50% group (males only). There were no other significant trends. Endler (1966a) found both (significant) downward and upward trends for the true-disagree and true-agree groups, respectively.

Endler (1965, 1966a) has suggested that conforming behavior can be explained in terms of social reinforcement learning theory and cognitive dissonance (see Festinger, 1957). The discrepancy between the social pressure (contrived consensus) and the subject's perceptions or beliefs creates cognitive dissonance which may be reduced via conformity. During Session 1, the reinforcements (experimenter feedback) for the true-agree groups are congruent with the social pressure, thereby increasing conformity; for the true-disagree groups the reinforcements are opposite from the social pressure, thereby reducing conformity.

Social learning occurs during the reinforcement session (acquisition trials), and this carries over to the posttest nonreinforcement session (extinction trials). During the postsession the reinforcement is absent (removed), but the social pressure is still present. Although there is a significant drop in the level of conformity during Session 2 (extinction), there are significant differences in conformity among the various groups as a function of the treatment they received during Session I (acquisition). This indicates that the effects of reinforcement are relatively stable. Earlier reinforcement experiences influence subsequent conforming behavior. If this were not the case, there would be no differences among the various groups (all of whom were subjected to social pressure but not reinforcement) during Session 2. However, the fact that conformity is significantly lower in Session 2 than Session 1 (see Table 3) indicates that in the absence of reinforcement some extinction occurs. The rate of extinction is a function of prior reinforcement experiences. These findings are analogous to those found by Hollander, Julian, and Haaland (1965, p. 587) that "prior conditions of group support do yield differential consequences for subsequent conforming behavior."

The present study found no sex differences with respect to conforming behavior, but Endler (1966a) found that females conformed more than males.[4] However in the present study females served as the experimenter more frequently than in the previous one. It may be that females conform less for a female experimenter than for a male experimenter, or possibly the sex difference in conformity is not stable.

Another difference between the present study and the Endler (1966a) study is that in the latter conformity was not a function of the type of stimulus item, while in the present study subjects in some groups (true-agree 100% in Session 1 and true-agree 50% and true-disagree 100% in Session 2) conformed more to perceptual (geometrical forms) items than to verbal items (obscure facts). However, Endler (1965) found that subjects conformed more to verbal items than to perceptual items. Possibly differences in conformity as a function of type of stimulus represent an unstable phenomenon.

[4] The analyses of variance for Sessions 1 and 2 and the overall analyses in the Endler (1966a) study indicated that females conformed significantly more than males. However, in attempting to localize the differences between the sexes for the various experimental groups, it was found that the only significant difference between the sexes occurred between the true-agree 100% groups in Session 1. Therefore the sex differences found by Endler (1966a) with respect to conforming behavior may have been an unstable or chance finding.

The major and most stable finding of this study was that the situational factor of reinforcement is an important determinant of conforming behavior, affecting both its acquisition and extinction. In Session 1 it accounted for 56.04% of the variance; in Session 2, for 37.48%; and in the overall analysis, 14.63%. These results confirm Endler's (1966a) findings. Furthermore, they clearly indicate that reinforcement influences conforming behavior over and above the effects of social pressure per se. The individual differences (sex) factor was insignificant.[5] Our interpretation of conformity would be congruent with that of Appley and Moeller (1963) and Moeller and Applezweig (1957), who suggest that conformity is situationally bound and is a means to an end rather than a personality variable. Work now in progress is aimed at determining the relative influence of situational (reinforcement) and personality factors on conformity. The present results suggest that conforming behavior is a form of social learning, modifiable via reinforcement.

[5] Since the sex and Sex × Reinforcement sources were insignificant (see Table 3), they were pooled with the subject's within-groups source to form a pooled residual which was used in estimating variance components. Therefore it was not possible to determine the variance due to the sex factor per se, since the pooled residual contains variance due to Sex, Sex × Reinforcement, and within-group or error variance.

References

Appley, M. H., and Moeller, G. Conforming behavior and personality variables in college women. *Journal of Abnormal and Social Psychology,* 1963, *66,* 284–290.

Dunnett, C. W. A multiple comparison procedure for comparing several treatments with a control. *Journal of the American Statistical Association,* 1955, *50,* 1096–1121.

Endler, N. S. The effects of verbal reinforcement on conformity and deviant behavior. *Journal of Social Psychology,* 1965, *66,* 147–154.

Endler, N. S. Conformity as a function of different reinforcement schedules. *Journal of Personality and Social Psychology,* 1966, *4,* 175–180. (a)

Endler, N. S. Estimating variance components from mean squares for random and mixed effects analysis of variance models. *Perceptual and Motor Skills,* 1966, *22,* 559–570. (b)

Festinger, L. A. *A theory of cognitive dissonance.* Stanford: Stanford University Press, 1957.

Hollander, E. P., Julian, J. W., and Haaland, G. A. Conformity process and prior group support. *Journal of Personality and Social Psychology,* 1965, *2,* 852–858.

Moeller, G., and Applezweig, M. H. A motivational factor in conformity. *Journal of Abnormal and Social Psychology,* 1957, *55,* 114–120.

Tolman, C. W., and Barnsley, R. H. Effects of verbal reinforcement on conformity and deviant behavior: Replication report. *Psychological Reports,* 1966, *19,* 910.

Winer, B. J. *Statistical principles in experimental design.* New York: McGraw-Hill, 1962.

The experiment by *Hollander, Julian, and Haaland* has the same direction as the preceding ones except for a different experimental paradigm to measure conformity. The subject's task was to report which of three lights came on first. A major independent variable concerned the influence of three confederates of the experimenter. During the first part of the experiment, the subject made his choice *before* observing those made by the confederates. By manipulating the number of times the confederates agreed or disagreed, the experimenter caused the subject to sometimes be at variance with the majority. During the second part of the experiment, the subject registered his choice only *after* he had observed the choices by the other subjects. During the final 20 trials of the experiment, when the confederates consistently disagreed with the subject's judgments, the subjects persisted in making independent judgments only if they had the previous experience of making choices which conflicted with those of the group.

Hollander, Julian, and Haaland's use of the concept of expectancy provides an opportunity for us to comment on this term which is used so widely in psychological theory. Expectancy is generally taken to mean the probability that someone will do one thing rather than another as a result of his past experience. Thus, these authors say, "We look on group support as a reinforcer of the implicit expectancy that one's judgment of an ambiguous stimulus is shared by others." In this case, "the subject's expectancy" is inferred from the frequency with which he chooses one light or the other. In behavioral and reinforcement language, we predict the frequency of a performance as a result of its past history of reinforcement. Thus, when a performance has been reinforced, there is a high probability that it will occur frequently, even during extinction. In the present experiment the performance that the authors are dealing with is the choice of the light reported by the rest of the group as likely to go on first. The presumption here is that "consistency with the rest of the group" is the reinforcer that maintains the subjects' behavior. The results indicate that the frequency of conformity is highest when it has been reinforced consistently and lower when it has been reinforced intermittently. The advantage of describing behavior by its frequency of occurrence rather than by what a subject expects is that frequency is easily and objectively observed, while expectancy leads us to unobservable characteristics of behavior. In almost every case, very little is lost by substituting frequency or probability of occurrence for expectancy.

31 | *Conformity Process and Prior Group Support*[1]

E. P. HOLLANDER
JAMES W. JULIAN
GORDON A. HAALAND

The study of conforming behavior involves the identification of behavior change where more than a single response alternative exists. Typically, a "conforming response" matches the relevant normative information provided by the group while, in the absence of this norm, the choice of other alternatives would be expected.

There have been at least three noteworthy historical developments in experimentation on this phenomenon. Variations on these constitute a good share of the work done in this area today. Sherif (1935) demonstrated normative effects on behavior in an ambiguous stimulus situation. Asch (1951) initiated the use of the unambiguous stimulus with social influence pressures produced by a contrived group norm at variance with subjects' perceptions. Crutchfield (1955) modified and mechanized aspects of both approaches with the introduction of simultaneously controlled feedback to all subjects by means of signal lights; he also sought personality correlates of yielding under a variety of stimulus conditions.

Though these three methods differ in stimulus type and the extent of the effect produced, they all have in common the consideration of the group as an influence source which prescribes norms on which persons might or might not depend. They also share the failing, however, of not accounting for sources of dependence which grow out of processes of interaction, including the significance of prior conditions of exposure to the group. A more process-oriented approach to conformity emphasizes neither structural properties of the situation nor personality dispositions of the participants (cf. Hollander, 1958, 1960). Rather, it studies conformity as an ongoing commerce between parties which these factors can only partially determine. This is in line with a number of contemporary movements, including conceptions of social exchange (Homans, 1958, 1961; Thibaut and Kelley, 1959) and of reciprocity (Gouldner, 1960).

Clearly, a central feature of conformity resides in the significance persons come to attach to others as a relevant group on which to depend in solving problems. In terms of process, therefore, dependence can be related to factors in interaction producing influence effects on behavior (see Hollander and Willis, 1964; Willis, 1963, 1964; Willis and Hollander, 1964a, 1964b). What is learned in a given influence situation is a weighting of feedback from others

[1] Presented to the 1965 Eastern Psychological Association Convention at Alantic City, New Jersey. This study is part of a program of research supported under ONR Contract 4679 from the Group Psychology Branch, Office of Naval Research.

such as to produce a greater or lesser dependence upon their judgments as against one's own impressions.

Such a process approach is illustrated in the experiment of Pepinsky, Hemphill, and Shevitz (1958), in which they studied social behavior as a function of prior conditions prevailing between the individual and the group. Where an individual was low in the initiation of activity within the group they found that such responses could be encouraged by the group's positive support of suggestions offered by that individual; alternatively, those who had been high in initiating activity were found to give a far lower level of such response by a pattern of discouragements from the others. In a related way, Bachrach, Candland, and Gibson (1916) have similarly demonstrated the effects of "support" by a group on the verbal conditioning of individuals. The significance of work of this kind lies in the linkage it affords between social behavior and the prior reinforcement experience provided by the group.

A different approach, exemplified in the research of Kelman (1950), Mausner (1954), and Luchins and Luchins (1961), provides feedback to subjects by having the experimenter report their accuracy or correctness in advance of being confronted with a conflicting position from one or more other subjects. Generally, it is found that conformity to the alternative position is reduced by such prior reinforcement or support by authority. While this research appears to have a similarity to the work just noted, it has quite the opposite cast in that it makes for greater *independence* vis-à-vis others in the group and hence less conformity.

It seems to us that one meaningful approach which builds upon this earlier work is to study the dependence on the group arising from immediately preceding encounters. In particular, our focus is upon prior group support as a source of "reinforcement of expectancy" leading to later elicitations of conformity behavior in that group. Consequently, in the present study we employ the standard Crutchfield apparatus with the essential difference that subjects initially respond in the *first* of the five positions where, to varying degrees, they appear to receive uniform support or agreement from the others. Only after this initial background experience of receiving some level of group agreement are the subjects then shifted to the usual last position. There other members of the group appear to disagree with the accurate response to the unambiguous stimulus event. Conformity is inferred from those instances where the erroneous group report is given by a subject as his own response. A separate measure of perceived dependence is obtained from the postinteraction questionnaire.

Problem

Within a learning framework, conforming responses can be considered to reflect a dependence upon the group, varying as a function of the previous levels of support the group provides. We therefore hypothesize that conforming behavior after a shift to the last response position will be significantly related to the prior agreement or support from the group. We look upon group support as a reinforcer of the implicit expectancy that one's judgment of an unambiguous stimulus is shared by others. We use the term "expectancy" in the sense conveyed by Rotter (1954) in his model of social learning.

Four patterns of group support were chosen for the present study. An initial condition of 100% support or agreement was predicted to have the most pronounced effect in producing dependence upon the group, and that therefore it would yield the highest initial conformity response; furthermore, learning theory would lead us to predict the greatest dropoff over trials in the absence of any continuing confirmation of a high expectancy. Two variable levels of group support (a 70% and a 50% condition) should produce the effects associated with intermittent reinforcement under conditions of "extinction," that is, nonconfirmation of a lower expectancy. Such effects include less dependence on the group and lower initial conformity, yet a greater persistence of the conformity response. Finally, the control condition, which provides no feedback of the group's response in the first trials, should produce little or no dependence and therefore less conformity in the last set of trials.

Method

Equipment. The equipment consisted of the five panels of signaling lights and switches. Each panel presented 15 lights, arrayed in three columns of five lights each. In addition, a mercury switch was mounted beneath each column of signaling lights. These switches corresponded with one of three stimulus lights mounted on the wall. These stimulus lights were controlled by two Hunter timers; one light went off first and the other two simultaneously .05 second later. The sequence of extinguishing was randomly determined. Three blue candelabra screw-mount lights were used. Previous pilot work indicated this to be an unambiguous stimulus insofar as the correct order of extinguishing was identifiable 95% of the time.

Subjects and Procedure. The subjects were 76 females and 36 males drawn from lower level psychology courses at the State University of New York at Buffalo. Many weeks prior to the experiment itself, these students had been administered the social desirability scale, as modified by Ford (1964). With no reference to that administration, subjects were later recruited from courses for the experiment. They reported to the laboratory in groups of four or five, and each was escorted to one of the signaling panels which were arranged in cubicles to shield the subjects from one another's view. There they found instructions before them, which were also read aloud, as follows:

> This is an experiment on perceptual ability. The task is relatively simple, requiring only that you judge which of the three blue stimulus lights on the wall goes *off first*. This experiment is supported in part by a Navy grant and is thus interested in the ability to coordinate various colors of lights with relatively complex readings of panel lights. This is the reason for the extensive equipment.
>
> In front of you there is a panel of red lights. These show which blue stimulus light people judge to go off first. This permits you to see how your judgment matches the judgment made by others, as the experiment proceeds.

Each subject was told that the bottom row of lights would show his response and the other four rows would show the responses of the other subjects. The instructions also went on to indicate that they were to close the mercury switch which corresponded to their judgment of the first light to go off. For the initial 20 trials, all subjects responded in what they believed to be the first position after which they all shifted positions and this time each believed that he or she was responding in the fifth position, that is, last. They were also instructed to maintain the proper sequence of responding, that is, first position answers first, second next, and so forth.

Design. During the first 20 trials the independent variable took the form of the number of times the subject was led to believe the group uniformly agreed with his own response. There were four conditions: 100% support (all 20 trials), 70% support (14 randomized trials), 50% support (10 randomized trials), and a control condition involving no feedback of the group's responses. Nine males and 19 females were run for each condition, always in same-sex groups. For all of the last 20 trials, when they were in the last position, subjects received information appearing to indicate a uniform group response *opposite* to the accurate perception of the stimulus. A willingness to accept this manifestly incorrect group response as one's own was taken as the behavioral measure of conformity on each trial. A postexperimental questionnaire was employed to supplement this measure of conformity for the last 20 trials. Responses to this questionnaire were checked for any indications of suspiciousness by the subjects regarding the true intent of the experiment; no evidence of awareness in this regard was found. This was corroborated by interviews.

Table 1 *Responses to the Question "In Which Position Was It Easier for You to Make Your Judgments?" for Prior Support Conditions*

Prior Support Condition	Position		No Response
	First	Second	
100%	23	2	3
70%	22	5	1
50%	16	5	7
0 control	10	9	9
Total	71	21	20

Results

Induction of Effects. As expected, the postinteraction questionnaire reflected important differences in the effects of the prior support conditions. Revealing this, Table 1 demonstrates that the treatments produced varying responses regarding the position in which subjects reported they found it easier to make their judgments. A chi square comparing the first two columns in this table yields a value of 10.42 ($p < .01$). Clearly, the subjects evidenced a marked tendency to report the first position as the easier of the two for the three experimental conditions of support; for the control condition, however, a roughly equal split is found between the positions. This pattern was unaltered when the sexes were compared. Looking at the total frequencies with which the positions were chosen as easier, the distribution of choices for the 100% and for the 70% support conditions was significantly different ($p < .02$) from the control condition.

In general, the magnitude of the conformity response was in keeping with past research utilizing subjects in anonymous circumstances (cf. Deutsch and Gerard, 1955) and supported the inference that little suspicion had been aroused. Sex differences in the amount of total conformity also were found when a median test was applied to the total conformity scores for the two sexes. The chi-square value of 6.81 was significant ($p < .01$) for $df = 1$. Accordingly, analyses of variance of the conformity response measure were performed separately for the two sexes. Because of the nonnormal nature of its distribution, the cell means were used as synthetic cases in these analyses. Such a procedure, though drastically reducing the degree of freedom, permitted application of a parametric model to the conformity data.[2]

[2] This trend analysis (see Winer, 1962, pp. 353–369) entailed the necessary assumption that the cubic component of the residual sum of squares was zero. Although such an assumpion could be unfounded in the analysis of the data for females, if it were to be so the residual component would act to provide an even more conservative test of the null hypothesis.

Table 2 *Analysis of Variance of Mean Conformity for Females*

Source	*df*	SS	MS	*F*
Support conditions (A)	3	1.251	.417	18.13*
Trial blocks (B)	3	.365	.122	
Linear component	1	.262	.262	11.39*
Quadratic component	1	.050	.050	2.17
Residual	1	.053	.053	
A × B	9	.167	.018	
Linear component	3	.071	.024	1.04
Quadratic component	3	.027	.009	.39
Residual (error)	3	.070	.023	

* $p < .05$.

Table 3 *Analysis of Variance of Mean Conformity for Males*

Source	*df*	SS	MS	*F*
Support conditions (A)	3	.6722	.2240	149.33**
Trial blocks (B)	3	.7361	.2454	
Linear component	1	.4320	.4320	288.00**
Quadratic component	1	.2782	.2782	185.47**
Residual	1	.0257	.0257	
A × B	9	.2786	.0310	
Linear component	3	.2170	.0723	48.20**
Quadratic component	3	.0570	.0190	12.66*
Residual (error)	3	.0045	.0015	

* $p < .05$.
** $p < .01$.

Tables 2 and 3 present the summaries of these analyses for females and males, respectively. As predicted, the prior support conditions did yield significant differences in the total number of conforming responses elicited. This was true for both sexes.

Sequential Conformity. Of central interest is the sequence of conformity responses following the conditions of prior support or "reinforcement." In Figures 1 and 2 these differences by conditions are shown for female and male subjects, respectively. In keeping with our prediction, the 100% support condition yielded the highest initial level of conforming behavior for both sexes. Intermittent group support produced more complex effects but these were generally in harmony with the anticipated persistence of conforming behavior revealed in the inclination found in both the 50% and 70% conditions for each sex. The trend analyses, indicated in Tables 2 and 3, showed the statistical significance of some of these features. For each of the sexes there was a clear negative linear trend across blocks of conformity trials. In addition, the significant interaction component for males indicated that the simple trends across

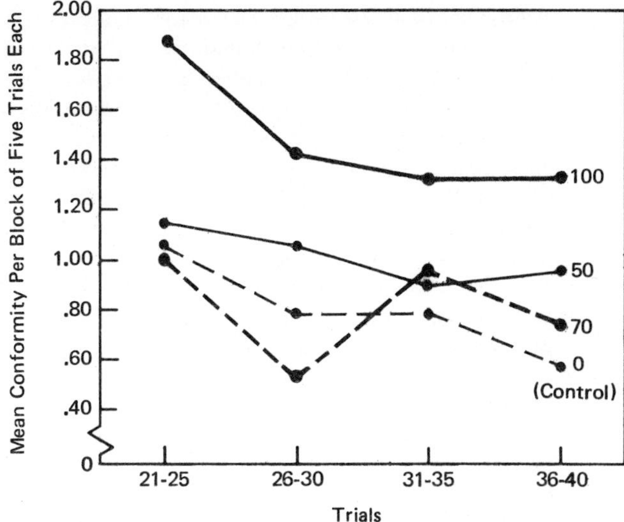

Figure 1 *Sequential conformity of female subjects as a function of prior support conditions (N = 19 in each group).*

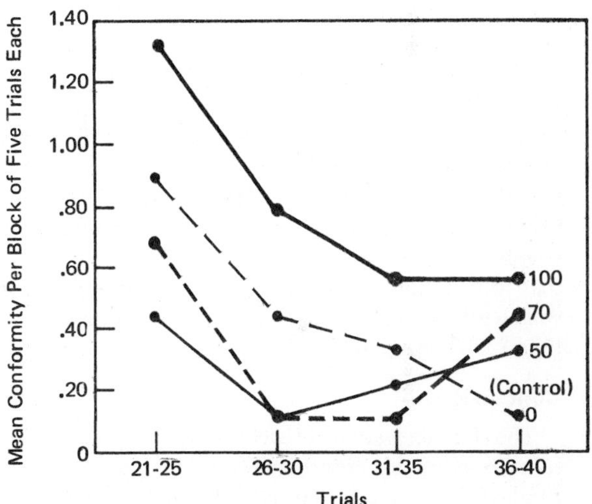

Figure 2 *Sequential conformity of male subjects as a function of prior support conditions (N = 9 in each group).*

trials differed for the different conditions of group support. The pattern of trends for females, however, can apparently be well described by the overall linear component. Thus, for the men and women, analyzed separately, a clear shift is evident in conforming from the first to the second trial blocks. Similarly, the "extinction" process is evident for each of the sexes in the linear decline in response for the 100% support condition.

Relation between Conformity Response and Perceived Dependence. A measure of dependence was developed from two questions on the postinteraction questionnaire. These called for answers indicating to what degree the subjects found the judgments of other members useful or hindering in making their own responses. Summing these led to a simple index of the degree of perceived dependence-independence from the group. A tetrachoric correlation analysis, based on roughly equalizing splits for this measure and for the total number of conformity responses in the last 20 trials, yielded a value of .46 ($p < .01$) each for females and males, independently calculated. Leaving out the control condition, on the expectation that it should not yield dependence in association with conformity, the recalculated values were raised to .53 for females and .67 for males. Thus, the omission of the control condition has the effect of raising the correlations for the experimental treatments where support is provided. In every instance, these correlations reveal a significant relationship between conformity behavior and the postinteraction measure of dependence.

Conformity Response and Social Desirability. Previous work has shown that conformity in an Asch situation is significantly correlated with scores on social desirability, measured by the Marlowe-Crowne Social Desirability scale (Crowne and Liverant, 1963). In our study, however, we do not find this strong relationship holding with a similar social desirability measure (Ford, 1964). The correlation between total conformity and social desirability for women was .17 and for men, .15. It appears then that the conditions of prior group support were sufficiently salient to override any substantial effects from social desirability.

Conclusions

The findings are consistent with the theoretical framework of this experiment and indicate that prior conditions of group support do yield differential consequences for subsequent conforming behavior.

The curves presented in Figures 1 and 2 reveal sequential patterns of conformity which are in line with expectation. There are, of course, sex differences in level of conformity which require further study. Crutchfield (1955) has long since noted the tendency for women to be more accepting of the group's normative response than are a comparable group of men. We also have the suggestion of variable effects of intermittent support or "partial reinforcement" upon responses of men and women under the same conditions. Additional research is needed to amplify and test for this differential effect.

It may be noted, further, that for both sexes, considered separately, the control condition appears to yield a pattern which is quite parallel in the main to that produced by 100% reinforcement. Bearing in mind that the control condition is closest in character to that found in research following the usual Asch-Crutchfield procedure, this finding can be interpreted to indicate the possibility of an implicit expectancy that others in the group should see an unambiguous stimulus as the subject does, even in the absence of confirmation.

The question inevitably to be considered is whether prior support gives persons a greater credence in the group judgment, or a sense that they themselves are better judges for having had group support. On analysis of our postinteraction measures, both of these processes appear to be at work. Indeed, in either instance they resolve down to an implicit dependence relationship. In one case the group's view is adopted as a standard of judgment regarding the stimulus task, and in the other the group's view is adopted as a standard for assessing one's own judgment. The fact that in the present data, and for each sex, such a high relationship obtains between dependence and frequency of conforming gives evidence of both these processes.

In sum, it seems plain that the concept of dependence growing out of interaction leads to another fruitful line of study regarding conformity process. In this respect, one evident outcome of the present study is to demonstrate the different *sequential* effects produced by varying levels of prior support, apart from establishing the broader linkage between prior experience and subsequent levels of conformity. Viewing conformity, then, as a process involving learning experiences in groups lends greater richness to the study of this phenomenon.

References

Asch, S. E. Effects of group pressure upon the modification and distortion of judgments. In H. Guetzkow (Ed.), *Groups, leadership, and men.* Pittsburgh: Carnegie Press, 1951. Pp. 177–190.

Bachrach, A. J., Candland, D. K., and Gibson, Janice T. Group reinforcement of individual response experiments in verbal behavior. In I. A. Berg and B. M. Bass (Eds.), *Conformity and deviation.* New York: Harper, 1961. Pp. 258–285.

Crowne, D. P., and Liverant, S. Conformity under varying conditions of personal commitment. *Journal of Abnormal and Social Psychology,* 1963. *66,* 547–555.

Crutchfield, R. S. Conformity and character. *American Psychologist,* 1955, *10,* 191–198.

Deutsch, M., and Gerard, H. B. A study of normative and informational social influence upon individual judgment. *Journal of Abnormal and Social Psychology,* 1955, *51,* 629–636.

Ford, L. H., Jr. A forced-choice, acquiescence-free social desirability (defensiveness) scale. *Journal of Consulting Psychology,* 1964, *38,* 475.

Gouldner, A. W. The norm of reciprocity: A preliminary statement. *American Sociological Review,* 1960, *25,* 161–179.

HOLLANDER, E. P. Conformity, status, and idiosyncrasy credit. *Psychological Review,* 1958, *65,* 117–127. (Reprinted: E. P. Hollander, *Leaders, groups, and influence.* New York: Oxford University Press, 1964, Pp. 161–178.)

HOLLANDER, E. P. Reconsidering the issue of conformity in personality. In H. P. David and J. C. Brengelmann (Eds.), *Perspectives in personality research.* New York: Springer, 1960. Pp. 210–225. (Reprinted: E. P. Hollander, *Leaders, groups, and influence.* New York: Oxford University Press, 1964. Pp. 179–193.)

HOLLANDER, E. P., and WILLIS, R. H. Conformity, independence, and anticonformity as determiners of perceived influence and attraction. In E. P. Hollander, *Leaders, groups, and influence.* New York: Oxford University Press, 1964. Pp. 213–224.

HOMANS, G. C. Social behavior as exchange. *American Journal of Sociology,* 1958, *63,* 597–606.

HOMANS, G. C. *Social behavior: Its elementary forms.* New York: Harcourt, Brace, 1961.

KELMAN, H. C. Effects of success and failure on "suggestibility" in the autokinetic phenomenon. *Journal of Abnormal and Social Psychology,* 1950, *45,* 267–285.

LUCHINS, A. S., and LUCHINS, EDITH H. On conformity with judgments of a majority or an authority. *Journal of Social Psychology,* 1961, *53,* 303–316.

MAUSNER, B. The effect of prior reinforcement on the interaction of observer pairs. *Journal of Abnormal and Social Psychology,* 1954, *49,* 65–68.

PEPINSKY, PAULINE, HEMPHILL, J. K., and SHEVITZ, R. N. Attempts to lead, group productivity, and morale under conditions of acceptance and rejection. *Journal of Abnormal and Social Psychology,* 1958, *57,* 47–54.

ROTTER, J. B. *Social learning and clinical psychology.* New York: Prentice-Hall, 1954.

SHERIF, M. A study of some social factors in perception. *Archives of Psychology,* 1935, *27,* No. 187.

THIBAUT, J. W., and KELLEY, H.H. *The social psychology of groups.* New York: Wiley, 1959.

WILLIS, R. H. Two dimensions of conformity-nonconformity. *Sociometry,* 1963, *26,* 499–513.

WILLIS, R. H. Conformity, independence, and anticonformity. *Human Relations,* 1965, *18,* 373–388.

WILLIS, R. H., and HOLLANDER, E. P. An experimental study of three response modes in social influence situations. *Journal of Abnormal and Social Psychology,* 1964, *69,* 150–156. (a)

WILLIS, R. H., and HOLLANDER, E. P. Supplementary note: Modes of responding in social influence situations. *Journal of Abnormal and Social Psychology,* 1964, *69,* 157. (b)

WINER, B. J. *Statistical principles in experimental design.* New York: McGraw-Hill, 1962.

B Two Theoretical Analyses

The following excerpt by *Skinner,* from *Science and Human Behavior,* discusses the mechanism by which a group of people exert special control over an individual through the contingencies of reinforcement provided by the members of the group. Skinner discusses the ways in which the group reinforces the individual's behavior, the reinforcers that maintain the behavior of people who do the reinforcing, and the balance that results between the motives of the group and the needs of the individual.

32 | Group Control

B. F. SKINNER

The individual is subjected to a more powerful control when two or more persons manipulate variables having a common effect upon his behavior. This will happen if two or more persons are moved to control him in the same way. The condition is usually fulfilled when the members of a group compete for limited resources. A social system is then established in which one man's positive reinforcement is another man's negative. In the expression, "the spoils of war," the reinforcement of the conqueror is named for its aversive effect upon the conquered. The child who takes a toy from another is thereby reinforced, but the loss of the toy is aversive to the other child. The successful suitor inevitably creates an aversive condition for other suitors.

Since an individual may affect all other members of a group in this way, their countercontrol may be undertaken in concert. All the other members become what we may designate as the controlling group. The group acts as a unit insofar as its members are affected by the individual in the same way. It need not be highly organized, but some sort of organization usually develops. Controlling practices acquire a certain uniformity from the cohesive forces which lead individuals to take part in group action and from their mode of transmission from one generation to another.

The principal technique employed in the control of the individual by any group of people who have lived together for a sufficient length of time is as follows. The behavior of the individual is classified as either "good" or "bad" or, to the same effect, "right" or "wrong" and is reinforced or punished accordingly. We need not seek far for a definition of these controversial terms. The behavior of an individual is usually called good or right insofar as it reinforces other members of the group and bad or wrong insofar as it is aversive. The actual practices of the group may not be completely consistent with these definitions. The initial classification may have been accidental: a conspicuous bit of behavior which was only adventitiously correlated with reinforcing or aversive events came to be classed as good or bad accordingly. Our definition applies literally to the origin of such a superstitious practice but does not fit any current effect. A classification of behavior may also continue in force long after it is out of date: behavior often continues to be branded good or bad although, through some change in conditions, it is no longer reinforcing or aversive.

The classification may also be defective because of the faulty structure of the group. All members may not participate to the same extent. Since an act may have different effects upon different members, some of whom may, therefore, classify it as good and others as bad, subdivisions of the group may conflict with each other in the direction of their control. For example, the use of physical force is generally aversive to others and hence called bad, but it may be classified as good by those who exhibit similar behavior in controlling a third party, either within or outside the group. Behavior which is immediately reinforcing may have a long-term aversive effect. The behavior of seduction or of exerting "undue influence" is often effective through positive reinforcement, but the ultimate consequences may lead the victim, as well as others, to classify it as bad.

The group as a whole seldom draws up a formal classification of behavior as good or bad. We infer the classification from our observations of controlling practices. A sort of informal codification takes place, however, when the terms themselves come to be used in reinforcement. Perhaps the commonest generalized reinforcers are the verbal stimuli "Good," "Right," "Bad," and "Wrong." These are used, together with unconditioned and other conditioned reinforcers such as praise, thanks, caresses, gratuities, favors, blows, blame, censure, and criticism, to shape the behavior of the individual.

The actual controlling practices are usually obvious. Good behavior is reinforced, and bad behavior punished. The conditioned aversive stimulation generated by bad behavior as the result of punishment is associated with an emotional pattern commonly called "shame." The individual responds to this when he "feels ashamed of himself." Part of what he feels are the responses of glands and smooth muscles recorded by the so-called lie detector. The relevance of this instrument to lie detection is based upon the fact that lying is frequently punished. Another part of the reaction of shame is a conspicuous change in normal dispositions—the social offender acts in a shamefaced manner. Any or all of these emotional conditions may be directly or indirectly aversive, in which case they combine with other conditioned aversive stimulation in providing for the reinforcement of behavior which displaces or otherwise reduces the probability of the punished response. The best example of such behavior is self-control. The group also directly reinforces practices of self-control.

Why the Group Exerts Control

In explaining any given instance of group control we have to show how the behavior of the controller is interlocked with that of the controllee in a social system. We must also show that both are adequately accounted for by the specified variables. In a given instance, good behavior on the part of *A* may be positively reinforced by *B* because it generates an emotional disposition on the part of *B* to "do good" to *A*. This explanation is not very satisfactory because it simply appeals to a standing tendency to do good. But it seems clear, simply as a matter of observation, that the behavior of favoring another is modified by appropriate emotional circumstances and that good behavior on the part of another is a case in point. The mother reinforces her child in a burst of affection when the child's behavior is especially good or right.

Another possibility is that the group appropriately reinforces good behavior just because the probability of similar behavior in the future is thus increased. The gratuity may be given to guarantee similar service in the future; it then has nothing to do with gratitude as an emotional disposition to favor others. The community also teaches each member to thank or praise the individual who has behaved well and to do so even when the member himself is not directly affected. An act of heroism is acclaimed by many people who have not, in this instance, been positively reinforced. The educational practice generates good behavior in the individual by assuring the proper reinforcing behavior on the part of the group.

The emotional dispositions which lead the members of a group to punish bad behavior are, unfortunately, more obvious. Anyone who injures others, deprives them of property, or interfers with their behavior generates a heightened inclination toward counterattack. This statement is again merely an appeal to an observed increase in the tendency of individuals to act aggressively under certain circumstances, but there are variables outside the field of emotion which work in the same direction. If *A*'s aggression is momentarily reduced through *B*'s counter-aggression (we have seen, of course, that the long-term effect is different), *B* will be reinforced. *B*'s behavior in punishing *A* may thus be due simply to operant reinforcement. It is sometimes argued that an emotional disposition to counterattack is the basic variable—that we always "strike a child in anger," and that any interpretation of the behavior as "intellectual" is a mere rationalization. But the practice could arise in the absence of an emotional variable; one could punish objectionable behavior simply to reduce the probability that it will recur. Educational agencies also encourage the use of punishment to control bad behavior, and they generate a tendency to exert the control even though the individual himself is not at the moment involved. The agency may work through emotional variables—for example, by generating resentment or indignation with respect to dishonesty, theft, or murder—or through operant reinforcement by appeal to the consequences.

The Effect of Group Control

The control exercised by the group works to at least the temporary disadvantage of the individual. The man who has been positively reinforced for giving his possessions and services to others may find himself thoroughly despoiled. The group has generated behavior which, although it achieves the positive reinforcement accorded good behavior, also creates strongly aversive conditions for the individual. Among the forms of good behavior strengthened by the community are practices of self-control in which behavior which might result in extensive reinforcement is weakened. That the individual suffers when bad behavior is punished is more obvious. Punishment itself is aversive, and behavior which works to the advantage of the individual at the expense of others is, temporarily at least, suppressed. Punishment is also the principal variable responsible for the behavior of self-control, which, as we have just seen, also reduces primary reinforcement.

In short, the effect of group control is in conflict with the strong primarily reinforced behavior of the individual. Selfish behavior is restrained, and altruism encouraged. But the individual gains from these practices because he is part of the controlling group with respect to every other individual. He may be subject to control, but he engages in similar practices in controlling the behavior of others. Such a system may reach a "steady state" in which the individual's advantages and disadvantages strike some sort of balance. In such a state a reasonable control over the selfish behavior of the individual is matched by the advantages which he gains as a member of a group which controls the same selfish behavior in others.

The power of the group is, of course, great. Even the political tyrant, the despotic father, the bully in the street gang, or any other exceptionally strong individual usually yields eventually to the group as a whole. The less talented may be wholly submerged by it. Fortunately, the group seldom acts efficiently enough to press its advantage to the limit, and its full power is probably never felt. Classifications of behavior as "good," "bad," "right," or "wrong" are seldom clear-cut. And they are not consistently supported by all members of a group. Certain organized subdivisions of the group, however, may make better use of their power.

Justification of Group Control

Certain familiar questions in the field of ethics may have occurred to the reader. What do we mean by the Good? How may we encourage people to practice the Good Life? And so on. Our account does not answer questions of this sort in the spirit in which they are usually asked. Within the framework of a natural science certain kinds of behavior are observed when people live together in groups—kinds of behavior which are directed toward the control of the individual and which operate for the advantage of other members of the group. We define "good" and "bad," or "right" and "wrong," with respect to a particular set of practices. We account for the practices by noting the effects which they have upon the individual and in turn upon the members of the group, according to the basic processes of behavior.

Ethics is usually concerned with *justifying* controlling practices rather than with merely describing them. Why is a particular bit of behavior classed as good or bad? The question is sometimes answered by asserting that "good" and "bad" have been defined by supernatural authorities. Although a science of behavior might help in designing educational practices which would encourage people to be good and dissuade them from being bad according to a given authority, it can scarcely pass upon the validity of such a definition. When it can be shown that a classification leads to results which are positively reinforcing to the individual who reveals the word of authority, another sort of explanation is available. Such an explanation need not question the ultimate, possibly beneficial, effect of a classification.

Attempts have been made to avoid an appeal to authority by finding other bases for a definition. It has been argued that a particular form of individual behavior, or the controlling practice which produces it, is to be recommended if it can be shown to work for the "greatest good of the greatest number," to increase the "sum total of human happiness," to maintain the "equilibrium" of a group, and so on. The original problem remains, however, because we still have to justify the criteria. Why do we choose the greatest good or the sum total of human happiness or equilibrium as a basis for a definition? A science of behavior might be able to specify behavior which would or would not make for happiness, but the question remains whether it can decide that happiness is "best" in the ethical sense. Here again we may be able to show that practices which are justified in terms of happiness have consequences which are reinforcing to the proponents of such a justification. It is *their* happiness which is primarily affected. But this is also irrelevant to the ultimate effect of the classification.

Such a criterion as the "greatest good of the greatest number" represents a type of explanation, based upon the principle of maxima and minima, which has often proved useful in the physical sciences. In the field of behavior, however, the definition of what is being maximized or minimized is unsatisfactory—as we might suspect from the enormous amount of discussion which terms like "the greatest good" have provoked. Even if these terms could be defined, the practice of characterizing a controlling practice as maximizing or minimizing some such entity is very different from an analysis in terms of relevant variables. It is not impossible that the two could be shown to be compatible if physical dimensions could be assigned to the thing maximized, but this has not been done in the traditional study of ethics. The program of a functional analysis offers a course of action in which the problem of the definition of such entities may be avoided.

The final article in this chapter, by *Weiss*, is an example, in a theoretical framework somewhat different from Skinner's, of how reinforcement concepts may be extended to complex social phenomena. Weiss discusses the conditions under which an individual defects from one organization and joins another. The social phenomena that he describes, however, are used only to illustrate the usefulness of reinforcement concepts in understanding social behavior.

The theoretical positions of Hull and Skinner, although very different in many important ways, have broad common features. Both analyze the behavior of an organism in terms of performances and their consequences in the environment, and both stress the consequences of a performance as the variable responsible for its reoccurrence. Probably the biggest difference between the conceptual approaches of Skinner and Hull is the extent to which inferred, conceptual explanatory devices (Skinner would say "explanatory fictions") are used. Skinner, on the one hand, limits his descriptions to the behavior of the organism, the frequency of the various items of conduct, the occasions in the environment which prompt them, and the changes they produce in the environment. Hull, on the other hand, deals with terms like inhibition, strength of response, and motivation—intervening variables which are inferred from observations of behavior.

33 *Defection from Social Movements and Subsequent Recruitment to New Movements*[1]

ROBERT FRANK WEISS

Social movements recruit members and lose some of them. Adherents defect in small numbers or *en masse,* in organized groups or without organization. It can scarcely be doubted that when alternative movements are already available, or can be newly formed, some defectors will tend to join them (e.g., Neal, 1956; Heberle, 1945). The dependent variables with which this paper is concerned are the strength of the tendency to join a new movement, following defection, and the choice of a particular social movement. The determinants of such new recruitment, considered here, are the social variables which produced the original defection together with certain social characteristics of the alternative movements. This paper will not concern itself with individual personality traits which may conceivably predispose some individuals to the indiscriminate joining of social movements. The present analysis may thus be characterized as stimulus-response (S-R), in that it seeks to relate the behavior (R) of the defector to certain aspects of his social environment (S). Such an approach shares some of the assumptions of social institutional and historical materialist approaches, and may be contrasted with the response-response approach found in *The True Believer* (Hoffer, 1958) or *The Authoritarian Personality,* (Adorno, Frenkel-Brunswik, Levinson, and Sanford, 1950), in which joining social movements (R) is regarded as largely dependent upon individual personality traits (R).

The S-R analysis conducted here is based on extrapolation from simple learning laws and Hullian learning theory. (See, for example, Hull, 1952; Miller and Dollard, 1941; Spence, 1956). This theory has been developed primarily to predict the actions of individual subjects in highly controlled experimental situations. The theory has, nevertheless, been extended, with a considerable measure of success, into more complex areas (e.g., Dollard and Miller, 1950; Miller and Dollard, 1941). The explanatory power of learning theory stems, in part, from two sources. First, Hullian theory includes a number of principles which may be combined in a determinate manner. Principles which may seem relatively trivial when taken singly become powerful explanatory tools when the manner of their interaction can be specified. Secondly, Hullian theory is quantitative, with the usual advantages that attend scientific quantification.

Four processes underlying defection and new recruitment may be enumerated at this point and discussed later. They are (*a*) *simple stimulus generalization,* related to the similarity and availability of social movements; (*b*) *extinction,* related to the concept of non-reward; (*c*) *displacement* (owing to inhibition by approach-avoidance conflict), a more complex form of stimulus generalization related to the concepts of similarity and punitive social sanctions, and (*d*) *counterconditioning,* related to multiple participation and reward. A discussion of these four processes in defection and recruitment forms the next section of the paper. These four processes do not necessarily represent any kind of an exhaustive classification. The purpose of the theory is to explain and predict defection and re-recruitment, and only such distinctions as appear useful in this theoretical context have been made. It is clear that such terms as "similarity of social movements" and "non-reward" will require further elucidation. The next section will also clarify the meaning of these terms at a verbal level, while the final section will briefly discuss the problems (and possible solutions) involved in their measurement.

[1] This investigation was supported, in part, by grant M-4523 from the National Institute of Mental Health, U.S. Public Health Service.

From *Sociometry,* 1963, *26,* 1–20. Reprinted by permission.

Theory of Defection and Re-Recruitment

Some Major Boundary Conditions

Before passing on to these topics it seems necessary to briefly note some of the phenomena specifically excluded from a detailed consideration. The theory is primarily concerned with people who join a movement and make a commitment to it. One group of people thus excluded from detailed analysis are those complying under duress. Such people may generally be expected to defect when the threat is mitigated, and revert to their former institutional allegiances. Thus, Baron Rosenberg reluctantly allied himself with the Hussite revolutionaries, when he felt himself menaced by the revolutionary armies of Prague and Tabor, reasserting his loyalty to the Emperor Sigismund and the Church at the first safe opportunity. Similarly excluded from detailed consideration is the purely opportunistic association with social movements. The opportunist remains with the successful social movement—the "November revolutionaries" remained in the Stalin apparatus long after Old Bolsheviks had quit in disgust or been purged. When the movement founders, the opportunists leap to the nearest or most profitable refuge—thus the opportunist Kuomintang leader Wang Ching-wei concluded his career as a Japanese puppet (see, for example, Isaacs, 1951). The theory developed here is also best suited to those circumstances in which defection does not take place in organized factions. To the extent that defection is organized, additional analysis would probably be necessary to do any justice to the data. Actually, relatively unorganized defection is considerably more common than might be expected. Anabaptists defected *en masse* (but without organization) when John of Leyden's regime collapsed, and a steady stream of worker-Bolsheviks tore up their party cards during the NEP (Cohn, 1957; Deutscher, 1959). When defection does take place in organized groups or factions the principles elucidated here probably would provide a *partial* explanation.

Simple Stimulus Generalization

The effects of learning in one situation transfer to other situations; the less similar the situation the less transfer occurs. Thus, in a simple learning situation, a response may be conditioned to a particular stimulus (e.g., a 1000-cycle tone), and the strength of the tendency to make the conditioned response may then be assessed when the stimulus is the original tone, a somewhat dissimiliar tone (say, 900 cycles), a more dissimilar tone, etc. Figure 1 shows the results which have been obtained in numerous learning studies: in the absence of the original stimulus, the individual will tend to respond (with lesser strength) to similar stimuli.

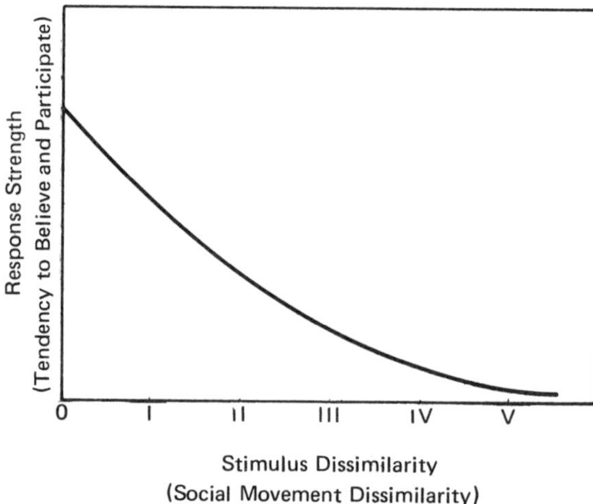

Figure 1 *Simple stimulus generalization. Point O represents the stimulus (social movement) to which the response (tendency to believe and participate) was originally conditioned. Points I–V represent stimuli (social movements) which are progressively more dissimilar to the original stimulus (social movement).*

Now let us consider the situation in which a social movement becomes unavailable to some or all of its members. One way in which this has happened is through emigration of members. Under such circumstances the stimulus complex to which the person's loyalties are attached is no longer available. Extended to this situation, the principle of stimulus generalization implies that such people would tend to transfer their loyalties to the available movement most nearly similar to the one they formerly belonged to. A re-examination of Figure 1, using "social movement dissimilarity" as the independent variable and "tendency to believe and participate" as the dependent variable shows this process more clearly. If several movements are available, the strongest tendency will be to believe and participate in the most immediately similar movement. The tendency to believe and participate in alternative movements decreases as similarity to the old movement decreases. Thus when several alternative movements are available, the movements which are most similar to the old movement will be joined in the greatest numbers, and the others in decreasing numbers. When there is only one alternative movement to be joined, the strength of the tendency to join at all will depend on the similarity to the old movement. An illustration of this kind of situation is afforded by the immigration to the United States, during the early part of this century, of members of European Social Democratic movements. When they joined any movement at all, they tended distinctly to join the foreign language federations of the Socialist

Party. Thus, a member of the Social Democracy of the Kingdom of Poland and Lithuania (SDKPL) would join a Polish or Lithuanian language local of the Socialist Party of the U.S.A. (Draper, 1957).[2]

A second way in which the movement may become unavailable to the individual is the collapse or destruction of the movement. Not infrequently, the forces which bring about the destruction or collapse of a social movement do *not* operate directly on the majority of its members.[3] Colonial administrators in Melanesia have typically reacted to cargo cult movements among the natives by jailing or exiling the leaders of the movement. The remaining members have sometimes been unable to replace these leaders (often limited to a prophet and a single organizer) and the movement has collapsed (Worsley, 1957). The apparent continuity of membership in successive cargo movements in some areas of Melanesia is probably due, in part, to generalization of habits of belief and participation from a given movement to its successor.

Analysis of the role of stimulus generalization in re-recruitment can be deepened by consideration of the interaction of stimulus similarity with other variables. A generalized habit remains no more than a *predisposition* to act unless motivation is present.[4] Thus the tendency of the cargo cult members to join a new movement, when one becomes available, was due not only to stimulus generalization, but also to the fact that the social deprivations and stresses, which motivated the original belief and participation, were not ameliorated by the colonial administrators. Moreover, an increase in motivation raises the entire gradient of generalization (Brown, 1942, 1948). An examination of Figure 2 indicates that "raising the gradient" would encompass the following: (*a*) the tendency to join alternative movements similar to the old one is increased; (*b*) the more similar the alternative movement is to the old one, the greater the increase; (*c*) movements which had no chance of being joined because they were too dissimilar to the old movement now have some (relatively small) tendency to be joined. This last point may acquire particular significance when there are no "highly similar" alternatives available: an increase in motivation might then, for the first time, induce some ex-members to join a new movement.

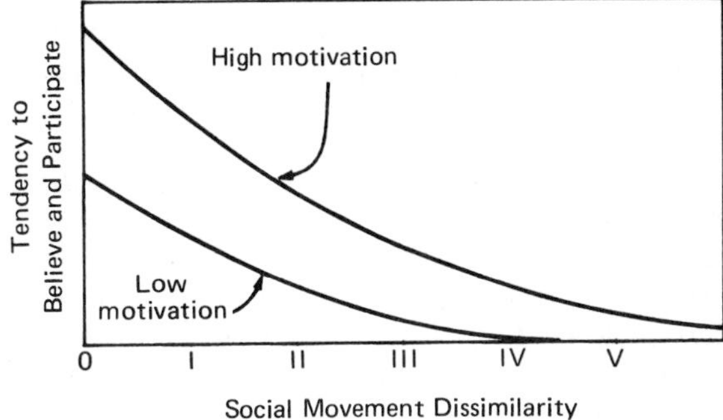

Figure 2 *Raising the level of motivation raises the entire gradient of generalization. (Point O represents the movement to which the person originally belonged; Points I–V represent increasingly dissimilar movements.)*

Extinction

Reward is essential to the maintenance of learned behavior. When a learned response is repeated without reward, the strength of the tendency to perform that response undergoes a progressive decrease. This process is called extinction, and a response which has been decreased to "negligible" strength by nonreward is said to be extinguished. There is also a tendency (spontaneous recovery) for an extinguished habit to reappear (in a substantially weakened form) after an interval of time during which no non-rewarded trials occur. After each extinction, there will be less spontaneous recovery. These laws of learning, first discovered by Pavlov, are very well established.

In order to apply this to defection and subsequent behavior, it is necessary to specify which responses (or classes of responses) are undergoing extinction. It seems useful to distinguish between non-reinforcement for *participation* and non-reinforcement for *belief* (opinions, convictions). ("Belief" is used here to refer to the member's own convictions regarding the aims, etc., of his movement, which are not necessarily identical with the officially promulgated ideology). This distinction is crude, but appears helpful, and also corresponds roughly with the common and convenient distinction between overt and covert-verbal behavior.

[2] The defection of foreign language locals from the Russian Empire areas (e.g., Russian, Finnish, Lettish, Ukranian) to the new Communist parties, following the October revolution, appears to represent a striking example of mediated generalization.

[3] New affiliations following defections induced by punitive social sanctions or termination of reward will be discussed later.

[4] Learning theory makes a distinction between learning (habit) and performance. Performance depends on the interaction of habit with motivation (also called drive) and the effects of magnitude and delay of reward (incentive). Habit depends on the number of times an action has been performed (and then rewarded), and also upon stimulus similarity. Motivation depends on such factors as deprivation, pain, and fear. Motivation (drive) and incentive combine additively to determine response strength. Habit combines multiplicatively with both motivation and incentive to determine response strength. This multiplicative relation between habit and motivation is the basis of point *b* in the discussion of Figure 2 which follows.

Extinction of Both Belief and Participation. When people are continuously nonrewarded for both belief and participation, we would expect them to lose both their opinions and their tendency to participate, and consequently to defect. There would be no greater susceptibility to alternative social movements than other people have. Indeed, since the effects of extinction generalize to similar stimuli, there would actually be somewhat greater resistance to recruitment to similar movements than would be found in people who had not been movement members. If a new recruitment did take place, it would most likely be to the old movement (spontaneous recovery).

Differential Extinction of Belief or Participation. When reward for participation is terminated, but the members continue to be rewarded for belief, they will lose the habit of participation but retain their beliefs. It seems likely that such people would be extremely difficult to recruit for a new movement. In addition to the generalization of the extinction of participation to similar movements, the defector retains the ideology of his old movement—and this ideology may conflict in some regards with that of a new movement. An increase in motivation can increase the strength of the participation response so that the defector may once again be willing to participate. In such an instance, the defector would be most likely to rejoin his old movement (since he retains its beliefs, and participation is still most strongly conditioned to the old movement).

When reward for belief is terminated, but the members continue to be rewarded for participation, defection is not likely, since loss of belief does not necessarily imply the acquisition of new convictions incompatible with continued participation. What is to be expected, rather, is degeneration (if these conditions affect many members) into social clubism or opportunist manipulation, depending on the member's position in the movement. Those highly placed in the movement will become opportunist manipulators, while rank-and-file members will find themselves members of a club, rather than a movement. Repeated examples may be drawn from the history of reformist political parties.

Displacement (Due to Inhibition by Conflict)

In simple stimulus generalization the person is prevented from responding to the original stimulus because it is absent. In displacement, as discussed here, the person is prevented from responding to the original stimulus because there is a conflicting response of avoidance, based on punishment and sustained (for a time) by fear. An experimental method of producing such a conflict might involve training a rat to run down an alley for food, and then, on one trial, giving him an electric shock instead of food. The result of such a procedure is usually referred to as approach-avoidance conflict. As Figure 3 indicates, the stimulus generalization gradient of avoidance drops off more *steeply* than the stimulus generalization gradient of the original response. (The steepness of the gradient can be regulated by special conditions of learning, but the above

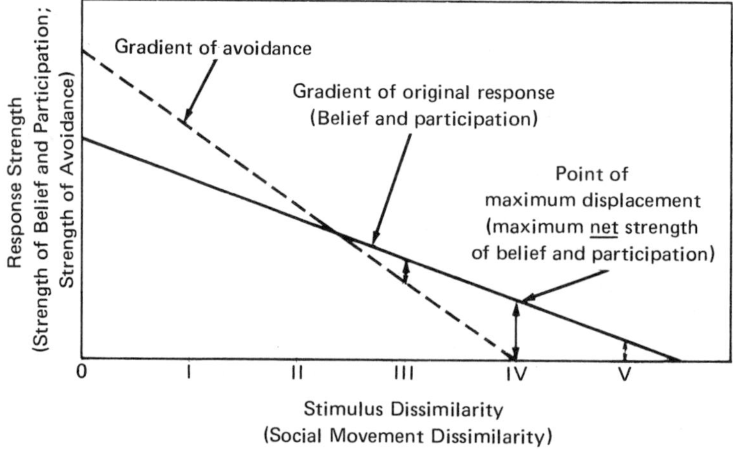

Figure 3 *Displacement due to inhibition by approach-avoidance conflict. As in previous graphs, Point O represents the stimulus (social movement) to which the response (belief and participation) was originally conditioned. Points I–V represent increasingly dissimilar movements. The gradients of generalization of avoidance and of belief and participation are actually curved, as in Figures 1 and 2, but straight lines have been used here for clarity in exposition.*

difference in steepness can usually be expected to hold even when the exact conditions of learning are not known to the investigator.) If it is assumed that the *net* strength of a response will be its strength minus the strength of a simultaneously elicited directly conflicting response, then the following are among the implications of Figure 3. Where the conflicting (avoidance) response is stronger (higher) than the original response, as at points I & II, the original response will not occur. Where the original response is stronger than the conflicting response (Points III, IV, & V), the original response will occur, and the point where the net strength of the original response (original R minus conflicting R) is greatest, is the point where the response is most likely to occur (point of strongest displacement, Point IV). As can be seen, this means that inhibition by conflict results not in the person responding to the stimulus to which he was originally conditioned (O) and not to the most similar stimulus (I), nor, of course, to a radically dissimilar stimulus, but to a stimulus of intermediate similarity.[5]

As in the previous discussion, it seems advisable to distinguish between punishment for participation and punishment for belief. Punitive sanctions for both participation and belief will be discussed in some detail, following which punishment for belief alone and for participation alone will be briefly considered.

Punishment for Both Participation and Belief. (a) Where punishment is not sufficient to raise the avoidance gradient above the gradient of participation and belief at any point, then both participation and belief continue. Thus, small difficulties do not lead to displacement when belief and participation are relatively strong.

(b) When punitive sanctions are so severe that the gradient of avoidance is always higher than the gradient of participation and belief, then there will be no displacement. Members will defect and will be distinctly unrecruitable for the old movement or similar movements. The Canton Commune incident in the Chinese Revolution of 1925–27 represents an example of this process (Isaacs, 1951). In the course of this revolution, the General Labor Union had seized power in Canton. The Chinese Communist Party, following a Stalin-dictated policy of close alliance with the Kuomintang, induced the workers to welcome Chiang Kai-shek's forces, and even to lay down their arms. A general massacre of the workers, accompanied by tortures, followed. Some time later the Communists, following a new turn in their opportunist line, attempted to stir the Cantonese to a second rising. There was no response. The Cantonese workers looked on in indifference while a handful of predominantly non-Cantonese Communists were easily defeated by the Kuomintang forces. It would be absurd to suggest that the principle described above represents a full explanation of the failure of the abortive Communist rising known as the Canton Commune. Many leaders and militants had been killed, and were hence not available for the second rising. More importantly, the workers' organizations had been destroyed or transformed into instruments of Kuomintang control. But in order to do justice to the remarkable *indifference* of the workers at the time of the Canton Commune (as contrasted with the first rising) a principle such as that introduced here seems essential.

(c) When punishment produces crossing gradients, as in Figure 3, the *strongest* displaced response will occur to movements which have an intermediate degree of similarity to the original one. Defection to more or less dissimilar movements is still possible, but the tendency is to choose the movement located at the point of strongest displacement.

(d) The tendency to join a new movement is weaker for defectors whose participation and belief in the original movement is blocked by approach-avoidance conflict than it is for people whose participation has been prevented by the unavailability of the original movement. That is to say, simple stimulus generalization leads to a greater tendency to join than displacement does, all other things (including the range of new movements available) equal. As shown in Figure 3, the movements of intermediate similarity (chosen in displacement) do not arouse as much generalized tendency to believe and participate as does the movement of greatest similarity (chosen by those who are prevented from participation by the absence of the original movement).

(e) The greater the punishment which led to defection, the less similar to the original movement is the new movement most likely to be chosen. As shown in Figure 4, as the gradient of avoidance is raised, the point of strongest displacement shifts in the direction of movements which are less similar to the movement from which the defection occurred. This point should help to make comprehensible the fact that defectors from the Communist Party of the U.S.A. have joined a variety of movements and ideologically oriented institutions ranging from the Trotskyites and Lovestoneites to the Quakers and the Catholic Church. Rather than indicating a complete and irrational interchangeability of social movements, such choices may reflect the interaction of differing degrees of initial belief and participation, punish-

[5] For further elucidation of the general principles, their experimental basis and application to psychopathology and psychotherapy, see especially Dollard and Miller (1950; Miller, 1948; Miller and Kraeling, 1952; Miller and Murray, 1952; Murray and Berkun, 1955; Murray and Miller, 1952).

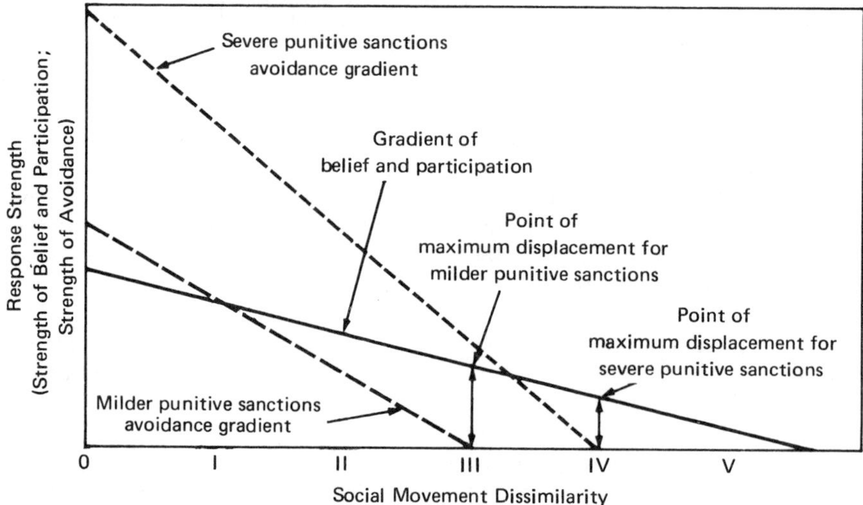

Figure 4 *Increasing the severity of punitive sanctions against belief and participation shifts the point of strongest displacement toward movements which are less similar to the original movement. When punitive sanctions have been severe, Movement IV is the movement most likely to be joined, but when punitive sanctions have been milder, Movement III is most likely to be joined.*

ment and similarity. It should be further noted that the tendency to join is weaker the further the point of strongest displacement is from the original movement. Thus, the more punished, the less likely to join *anything,* the limiting case of this being the Canton Commune type of situation discussed in *b,* above.

(f) If the motivation underlying commitment to the original movement increases the height of the entire gradient of belief and participation increases more than the avoidance gradient, and the strength of the tendency to join a new movement is increased (Figure 5). A continued worsening of the social conditions which motivated the commitment to the original movement could lead to such an increase in motivation, as could deprivation of the satisfactions (e.g., unemployment benefits) provided by adherence to the original movement.

(g) If the motivation underlying belief and participation increases, it will be possible for increasingly dissimilar movements to attract some of the defectors (Figure 5). This effect is of particular interest when movements of an intermediate degree of similarity to the original movement are not available to the defector. An increase in motivation might then, for the first time, induce some defectors to join a new movement.

(h) If the motivation underlying belief and participation increases, the more similar to the original movement is the new movement most likely to be chosen. (In Figures 3, 4, and 5 the gradients have been depicted as linear since this improves clarity of presentation. The shape of the gradients actually specified by learning theory is an exponential function, such as is shown in Figures 1 and 2. This last deduction—Point *h* above—can only be made if the more exact quantitative specification of the gradient shape is employed.)

Punishment for Participation Only. A fairly extensive discussion of the effects of punishment of both belief and participation has been given above. Since most aspects of differential punishment of belief and participation can be easily inferred from the above, discussion of this problem will be limited to a few points of particular interest.

(a) When punishment for participation (but not for belief) has been so severe that the gradient of avoidance is always higher than the gradient of participation, there will be a tendency to withdraw from participation in the movement, while maintaining belief. This kind of social phenomenon is characteristic of certain traditionalist dictatorships (e.g. the Horthy and Salazar regimes) which suppress organized opposition but are relatively unconcerned with private expression of belief.

(b) When punitive sanctions for participation produce crossing gradients (in the manner of Figure 3), there will be a displacement of participation (membership) and maintainance of belief. One clear example is afforded by the loss of the Menshevik mass support to the Bolsheviks, between February and October, 1917. The continuation of the war (supported by the Menshevik leaders), the increasing incidence of industrial lockouts (which the Menshevik

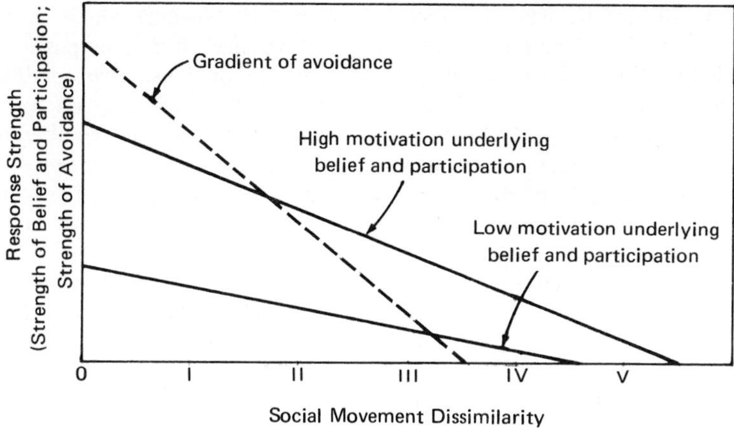

Figure 5 *An increase in the motivation underlying belief and participation makes it possible for more dissimilar new movements to recruit the defector. Movement V would have no chance of being joined when motivation is low.*

leaders did not prevent), etc., represented severe punishments to the Menshevik workers, and the smaller number of Menshevik soldiers and sailors. The actions of the Menshevik leadership did not correspond to the beliefs of their mass membership. The Menshevik mass membership displaced their allegiance to the Bolsheviks, retaining their beliefs (which were in accord with Bolshevik ideas) (Trotsky, 1957).

(c) If the motivation underlying belief and participation increases, it will be possible for increasingly dissimilar movements to attract some of the defectors (in the manner of Figure 5), while, at the same time, there is an intensification of the original belief. This appears to be a characteristic schismatic phenomenon —the pure doctrine, held with greater fervor, in a new sect or splinter party. This kind of phenomenon acquires a particular significance when movements of an intermediate degree of similarity to the original movement are not available to the defector.

Punishment for Belief Alone. Suppression of social movements by agencies of the established order involves, primarily, an effort to weaken or eliminate participation in the movement. A more totalitarian and demanding state or church may also seek to suppress deviant beliefs through punishment, while a less scrupulous authority may not trouble itself to differentiate between belief and participation, even where this is possible. Where punishment is resorted to on behalf of the established order, participation is the first target and belief is the second. It would not ordinarily be expected, therefore, to find the authorities neglecting punishment of participation while practicing punishment of belief. However, social movements have their own internal social control systems, which, in hierarchically structured movements, may be employed by the leaders in order to change the beliefs of the members, without, if possible, impairing participation. Punishment for belief, but not for participation, was therefore employed in the Anabaptist movement when John of Leyden promoted himself from prophet to messiah (Cohn, 1957). More familiar examples may be drawn from successive shifts in party line in various Communist Parties.

(a) When punitive sanctions directed against belief (but not against participation) have been so severe that the gradient of avoidance is always higher than the gradient of belief, there will be a tendency to lose belief while maintaining participation. While new beliefs may be learned through internal propaganda, or the old beliefs may recover in time (as fear is gradually extinguished), permanent loss of belief together with retention or organizational loyalty does not appear to be an uncommon phenomenon.

(b) When punishment for belief produces crossing gradients of belief and avoidance (in the manner of Figure 3), there will be a displacement of belief and a maintenance of participation. This could conceivably lead directly to a relatively uniform change of belief among members. However, in the more likely case that punishment is unequally applied or initial strength of belief differs among members, a more likely possibility is the formation of factions within the movement. The Yugoslav Communist Party was instructed by the Comintern in 1935 to switch from its current beliefs (e.g., no cooperation with the Social Democrats, self-determination for the non-Serbian minorities) to Popular Front beliefs (e.g., cooperation with all anti-fascists, a strong united Yugoslav state). Yugoslav Communists were assailed and reprimanded for their beliefs. The short-term consequence of this was dissension in the Yugoslav central committee (Comintern quip: "Two Yugoslavs—three factions") and, it appears, consequent dissension in the rest of the Party. Until the repression was intensified, some members retained their old beliefs, while others displaced their beliefs in the direction of those advocated by the Comintern (e.g., Maclean, 1957).

Counterconditioning

In the preceding analyses, participation or belief in the original movement ceases because (*a*) the movement becomes unavailable to the member (generalization); (*b*) the strength of belief or participation is decreased by non-reward (extinction); (*c*) the net strength of belief or participation is decreased by punishment-induced avoidance (displacement). A fourth possible cause of defection from the original movement is an *increase* in the strength of participation in an alternative movement (and/or adherence to its beliefs). The circumstances in which this fourth process, counterconditioning, can occur are probably less common than the circumstances underlying each of the other three processes, and the conditions required for making it predictable are also more stringent. Counter-conditioning occurs, when, in addition to his rewarded participation (and belief) in the original movement, the member also participates in an alternative movement and is rewarded for the participation (and/or when the member adhers to the beliefs of the alternative movement and is rewarded for that adherence). This multiple participation need not culminate in defection from the original movement unless participation and belief in the one are highly incompatible with participation and belief in the other, *and* the member is confronted with the necessity for a final choice. If the member is never faced with the necessity for a *final* choice, the probability of his participation in one movement or the other when faced with various less drastic choices remains a topic of considerable interest. While the analysis presented here has focused on social movements, a particularly apt example of this general kind of phenomenon may be found in the case of two ideologically-oriented organizations which are, perhaps, too bureaucratic and routinized to be called social movements: the participation and belief of many southern Italians in both the Catholic Church and the Communist Party.

The conditions required for making counterconditioning predictable in the laboratory are so stringent as to make it very doubtful whether the analysis can be properly carried beyond the description given above. If, however, three conditions are reasonably well satisfied, it may be possible to hazard some tentative predictions. Two conditions refer to the prediction of a particular choice: (1) the member is confronted with the two alternatives simultaneously; (2) the member may make the decision on an ideological basis or on any basis other than a conscious calculation of the rewards he has derived from belief or participation. The third condition refers to the background of decisions leading up to the particular choice to be predicted: once having chosen a course of action (such as between attending a Church or Party function held at the same time on a particular day) circumstances have compelled the member to adhere to that choice until the course of action is completed.

If these conditions are satisfied, a number of interesting relations may be tentatively expected. Any useful discussion of the principles of learning theory which permits the derivation of these relations would require considerably more space than would be appropriate for this paper. Since an exposition of learning theory can be found elsewhere (Spence, 1956, especially pp. 199–220, 237–244) (though in terms appropriate for controlled experiments with non-articulate organisms, rather than the present social phenomena), only the specific predictions will be given here. The first two of these are fairly obvious from common sense, the others much less so.

(a) The greater the magnitude of the rewards typically derived from belief and participation in one movement, the greater will be the tendency to choose that movement.

(b) The greater the number of occasions on which the member has been rewarded for belief and participation in one movement the greater will be the tendency to choose that movement.

(c) The effects of motivation and magnitude of reward are independent, except when the strength of belief and participation in both movements is weak. If the strength of belief and participation in both movements is not weak, and motivation increases, there will be no effect on the tendency to choose the movement from which the member derived the greater magnitude of reward. If the strength of belief and participation in both movements is weak, and motivation *increases,* there will be a *decreased* tendency to choose the movement from which the member derived the greater magnitude of reward.

(d) If motivation increases, and the number of occasions on which the member has been rewarded for belief and participation is the same for both movements, the increase in motivation will have no effect on choice (all other things equal).

(f) Information which supports a belief tends to have the same effects as a reward for espousing that belief. (Weiss, Rawson, Pasamanick, 1963; Weiss, 1962).

Counterconditioning is sometimes so effective that belief and participation in the original movement are completely replaced by belief and participation in the new movement. The original habits of belief and participation are not lost, but are merely overridden by the greater strength of the new beliefs and actions. If reward for the new beliefs and participation is terminated, extinction may weaken the tendency to believe and participate in the new movement to the point where the tendency to believe and participate in the original movement is able to compete successfully with allegiance to the new movement. Such a sequence of complete counterconditioning followed by extinction of the new response is probably involved in the return to childhood religion shown by some defectors.

Measurement Problems

Similarity of Social Movements

In simple learning situations, similarity of stimuli is generally varied along a physical continuum (brightness, loudness, pitch, etc.). Physical similarity is of lesser importance in the case of similarity of social movements. Here similarity is verbally mediated. Labeling physically similar stimuli with different words can lead to acquired distinctiveness, and labeling physically different stimuli with the same word can lead to acquired similarity e.g., (Miller and Dollard, 1941). This kind of mediated generalization has also been studied under laboratory conditions, but accurate prediction depends on knowledge of the verbal responses involved in the particular situation. Moreover, generalization in the defection situation may very well take place along more than one continuum of similarity. Such diverse continua as, say, radicalism-conservatism, and friendliness-impersonality might be involved. A rather good solution to the problem may be found in the statistical technique known as multi-dimensional scaling. In this method, subjects are asked to judge pairs of stimuli (e.g., names of social movements) with regard to their similarity. The subjects are asked only "how similar are these two," the criteria of similarity *not* being specified in advance. The multi-dimensional scaling extracts from these judgments the dimensions along which the subjects do their judging, though the subjects may be unable to verbalize these underlying dimensions themselves. The movements are thus arrayed along a dimension and the distances between them are known. (It remains for the researcher to give the dimensions a name, but the name is irrelevant to prediction in this case, the distances between movements being adequate for this.) If there is only one underlying dimension, prediction is obvious. If there is more than one underlying dimension, it is possible to estimate the generalization along each dimension separately. If the estimates of generalization along several dimensions do not agree in predicting the movement most likely to be chosen, it is possible to estimate the prominence of each dimension (amount of variance explained) and to arrive thereby at the probability of the subject's responding in terms of any given dimension alone. If any one dimension is distinctly more prominent than the remaining dimensions combined (a not unlikely outcome), it would again be possible to treat the results as if there were only a single dimension along which generalization took place.

While an adequate technique for the measurement of social movement similarly exists, the problem of when to apply the technique remains. It is possible that the events leading to defection, as well as experiences following recruitment to a new movement, could lead to changes in the defector's evaluation of the similarity of different movements. Ultimately, this remains a question to be answered by research, though the dimensional structure of perception is likely to be quite resistant to change.

Reward and Punishment

It is difficult to determine adequately the manner in which rewards or punishments have impinged on members of social movements from historical records or from contemporary studies of social movement structure. Estimates of the numbers and magnitude of rewards or punishments may be obtained by several conventional methods. Among these would be questionnaires administered to the defectors as well as to members and ex-members of the movement who might be informed on the experiences of the defector. It would be possible to identify different dimensions of reward through factor analysis or multi-dimensional scaling. Probably such an elaborate form of analysis would be unnecessary. The major reason for identifying dimensions of reward would be to relate them to differences in the motivations of the defectors. However, laboratory studies of simple learning phenomena indicate that a given reward has the same effect when motivation is high as it does when motivation is low (Weiss, 1960;

Reynolds and Pavlik, 1960). As previously indicated, information which supports a belief tends to have the same functional properties as a reward for holding that belief. The results in this situation agree with the results from simple learning experiments in indicating that the effects of belief-supporting information ("reward") on the strength of a belief are independent of level of motivation (Weiss, Rawson, and Pasamanick, 1963).

Summary

A theoretical analysis of recruitment to social movements, following defection from a movement, was developed. The theory was concerned both with the strength of the tendency to join a new movement and choice of a particular social movement. The determinants of re-recruitment considered by the theory were limited to the social variables which produced the original defection and certain characteristics of the social environment at the time of re-recruitment. A social-institutional and learning-theory approach was utilized, and the effect of individual personality traits was therefore excluded from consideration.

Four social causes of defection affecting subsequent recruitment were identified: (a) the movement becomes unavailable to the member, (b) the strength of belief or participation is decreased by non-reward, (c) the net strength of belief or participation is decreased by punitive social sanctions, and (d) the strength of belief and participation in an alternative movement is increased until defection from the original movement takes place. Four psychological processes were systematically related to each of these four social causes of defection: (a) simple stimulus generalization, (b) extinction, (c) displacement owing to approach-avoidance conflict, and (d) counterconditioning (corresponding to social causes a, b, c, and d, respectively). Prediction (actually, postdiction, since historical illustrations were used) depends on which process is involved, whether both belief and participation are equally affected, and the social conditions at the time of re-recruitment (especially the characteristics of the new movement). For example, when the movement becomes unavailable to the member (e.g., through emigration) simple stimulus generalization leads to recruitment into the available movement most nearly similar to the original movement. However, when punishment for belief and participation in a social movement causes defection, displacement through approach-avoidance conflict leads to recruitment into a social movement of moderate similarity to the original movement, *not* to the most nearly similar movement available. Moreover, displacement yields a weaker tendency to join a new movement than does stimulus generalization.

In the course of the analysis of re-recruitment, certain aspects of such phenomena as faction-formation and defection were also discussed. For example, when social movement members continue to be rewarded for participation, but reward for belief is terminated, the consequent extinction of belief leads not to defection but to degeneration into social clubism or opportunist manipulation, depending on the members' position in the movement. Those highly placed in the movement become opportunist manipulators, while rank-and-file members find themselves to be members of a social club rather than a movement.

A brief discussion of measurement problems involved in such concepts as "similarity of social movements" was included in the paper. Illustrations of the processes involved were drawn from a variety of movements and incidents including the Canton Commune, Melanesian cargo cult movements, Bolshevik re-recruitment of Menshevik defectors, and forced recruitment in the Hussite revolution.

References

Adorno, T., Frenkel-Brunswik, Else, Levinson, D. J., and Sanford, R. N. *The authoritarian personality.* New York: Harper, 1950.

Brown, J. S. The generalization of approach responses as a function of stimulus intensity and strength of motivation. *Journal of Comparative Psychology,* 1942, 33, 209–226.

Brown, J. S. Gradients of approach-avoidance responses and their relation to level of motivation. *Journal of Comparative and Physiological Psychology,* 1948, *41,* 450–465.

Cohn, N. *The pursuit of the milennium.* Fairlawn, N.J.: Essential Books, 1957.

Deutscher, I. *The prophet unarmed.* New York: Oxford University Press, 1959.

Dollard, J., and Miller, N. E. *Personality and psychotherapy.* New York: McGraw-Hill, 1950.

Draper, T. *The roots of American Communism.* New York: Viking, 1957.

Heberle, R. *From democracy to Nazism.* Baton Rouge, La.: Louisiana State University Press, 1945.

Heymann, F. G. *John Zizka and the Hussite revolution.* Princeton: Princeton University Press, 1955.

Hoffer, E. *The true believer.* New York: Mentor Books, 1958.

Hull, C. L. *A behavior system.* New Haven: Yale University Press, 1952.

ISAACS, H. R. *The tragedy of the Chinese revolution.* Stanford, Calif.: Stanford University Press, 1951.

MACLEAN, F. *Disputed barricade.* London: Jonathan Cape, 1957.

MILLER, N. E. Theory and experiment relating psychoanalytic displacement to stimulus-response generalization. *Journal of Abnormal and Social Psychology,* 1948, *43,* 155–178.

MILLER, N. E., and DOLLARD, J. *Social learning and imitation.* New Haven: Yale University Press, 1941.

MILLER, N. E., and KRAELING, DORIS. Displacement: Greater generalization of approach than avoidance in generalized approach-avoidance conflict. *Journal of Experimental Psychology,* 1952, *43,* 212–217.

MILLER, N. E., and MURRAY, E. J. Displacement and conflict: Learnable drive as a basis for the steeper gradient of avoidance than of approach. *Journal of Experimental Psychology,* 1952, *43,* 227–231.

MURRAY, E. J., and BERKUN, M. M. Displacement as a function of conflict. *Journal of Abnormal and Social Psychology,* 1955, *51,* 47–56.

MURRAY, E. J., and MILLER, N. E. Displacement: Steeper gradient of generalization of avoidance than of approach with age of habit controlled. *Journal of Experimental Psychology,* 1952, *43,* 222–226.

NEAL, A. G. The interchangeability of social movements. Unpublished Master's Thesis, Ohio State University, 1956.

REYNOLDS, W. F., and PAVLIK, W. B. Running speed as a function of deprivation period and reward magnitude. *Journal of Comparative and Physiological Psychology,* 1960, *53,* 615–618.

SPENCE, K. W. *Behavior theory and conditioning.* New Haven: Yale University Press, 1956.

TROTSKY, L. The history of the Russian revolution. Ann Arbor, Mich.: University of Michigan Press, 1957.

WEISS, R. F. Deprivation and reward magnitude effects on speed throughout the goal gradient. *Journal of Experimental Psychology,* 1960, *60,* 384–390.

WEISS, R. F. Persuasion and the acquisition of attitudes: Models from conditioning and selective learning. *Psychological Reports,* 1962, *11,* 710–732.

WEISS, R. F., RAWSON, H. E., and PASAMANICK, B. Argument strength, delay of argument and anxiety in the "conditioning" and "selective learning" of attitudes. *Journal of Abnormal and Social Psychology,* 1963, *67,* 157–165.

WORSLEY, P. *The trumpet shall sound.* London: MacGibbon and Kee, 1957.

Perceptual and Judgmental Processes

6

It is sometimes asserted that behaviorism does not effectively come to grips with the phenomena of perception and judgment, because they are, by their very definition, implicit and private. Perception and judgment are made explicit and public only through some overt motor, verbal, or glandular reaction which can be directly observed or recorded on sensitive measuring devices, such as blood pressure, pupillary dilation, or the galvanic skin response. The subtlety of the indicators that we select is determined by the degree of sophistication of our behavioral analysis measuring instruments and observational techniques. Thus, even thought processes are potentially susceptible to direct scrutiny through the use of electronic probes such as the electroencephalogram.

For practical purposes, however, it is probably true, as Skinner has suggested, that "Our 'perception' of the world—our 'knowledge' of it—is our *behavior* with respect to the world."* We interpret the term "behavior" to include motor performances as well as those physiological reactions that can be detected and recorded. It is possible to talk meaningfully about perceptions, thoughts, and judgments with the understanding that our actual data are the behavior of the organism.

A perceptual experience is not, it may be argued, identical with the verbal response that it prompts. This is conceded; but we are nevertheless left with the verbal behavior as the only public event capable of scientific treatment. To the extent that we care to make inferences about the implicit processes that have preceded certain verbal operants, we must be careful to distinguish between what we observe and what we explain. This is not to argue that such inferences are impossible to make, nor that they are not useful in understanding certain complex behaviors, but rather that we should not confuse implicit processes with their explicit *indicators*.

The articles in this chapter report several experiments in which reinforcement variables have been manipulated within the context of situations requiring perceptual discriminations on the part of observers. The first four reports deal with the perception of lengths of lines and autokinetic movement and with the selective perception of words. The last two articles are concerned with the perceptions of persons, a relatively new area of research. In each of these experiments we attempt to identify the controlling stimuli for the observers' performances as well as the consequences that have served to increase the frequency of certain responses over others. Although inferences are made about perceptual events, each experimenter makes it clear that his primary data consist of verbal reports. One of the problems to which these studies are addressed is that of making appropriate inferences about perceptual responses from the several indicators that are used.

* B. F. Skinner, *Science and Human Behavior.* New York: Macmillan, 1953, p. 140.

Group Consensus Effects

A number of experimental findings have shown that subjects who are asked to make judgments about stimuli in one another's presence tend to converge toward a common norm; that is, they tend to report similar experiences. The fact that such a concordance of verbal reports is not perfect, however, suggests that some individuals are less influenced in a group situation than others. If some persons conform less to a group standard than others, then one is inclined to look for differences in their histories of reinforcement in similar situations.

Mausner attempted to manipulate the consequences to subjects of rendering judgments about the lengths of lines. Some were told they were "right" 82 per cent of the time, whereas others were told they were "Wrong" on the same proportion of trials. Pairs of observers, formed so as to include either similar or dissimilar prior reinforcement experiences, then judged the same lines together. The results demonstrate rather convincingly that the prior social reinforcement of each individual was an important factor determining how much he could be influenced by the other person. Whether the subjects really believed what they were saying about the lines is a question that cannot be answered from the data.

34 *The Effect of Prior Reinforcement on the Interaction of Observer Pairs*[1]

BERNARD MAUSNER

The study of the manner in which groups of observers arrive at perceptual norms has been a central problem in experimental social psychology since Sherif's work (1935). In his experiment, subjects (*Ss*) whose previous judgments of the extent of autokinetic movement had differed tended to approach a norm when they worked in groups. Subsequent investigations using a similar design have disclosed that this phenomenon of convergence toward group norms is not restricted to judgments of autokinetic effect (Luchins, 1945; Mausner, 1950; Schonbar, 1945), and that its occurrence will be affected by a number of factors. Among these are: (*a*) the nature of the stimulus field (Luchins, 1945),

[1] Number two in a series entitled Studies in Social Interaction. The present report is based on a dissertation (Mausner, 1950) submitted to the Faculty of Pure Science, Columbia University, in partial fulfillment of the requirements for the Ph.D. The writer is indebted to Professors Otto Klineberg and W. N. Schoenfeld for guidance in the design and conduct of this investigation. Apparatus and facilities for the experiment were made available by the Department of Psychology, Washington Square College, New York University, of which the writer was formerly a member.

(*b*) the past history of contact among members of the group (Bovard, 1951), (*c*) attitudes towards group membership of partners (Berenda, 1950; Bray, 1950), and (*d*) the personalities of the Ss (Kelman, 1950).

It is probable that in the group situation each S has some conflict between opposing response tendencies. The S may have a tendency to continue to make the responses he has previously made toward the stimuli being presented; he may also have a tendency to be influenced by his partner or partners. The S's personality, his impression of the partner, and any past experiences they may have had in common may affect the strength of this latter tendency. If a population of Ss is so chosen that the tendency to agree can be assumed to be randomly distributed, it may be possible to affect the extent of convergence by varying the opposing tendency, i.e., the tendency to continue in the former judgment range. Random distribution of the tendency to agree may be assumed (*a*) if the population Ss is relatively homogeneous, and (*b*) if, in addition, coacting Ss have not been previously acquainted.

Laboratory studies of learning suggest that one possible determinant of the strength of the tendency to maintain the former range of judgments may be the degree to which previously made judgments have been reinforced. In the present experiment the following specific hypothesis was tested: for any given type of judgment, if the responses of S have a history of past positive reinforcement, they will show less tendency to converge than if they have a history of nonreinforcement or of negative reinforcement.

This hypothesis has been tested independently by Kelman (1950). Although his work is not directly comparable to the present study, since he used a different procedure and treatment of data, Kelman's results do furnish support of the above hypothesis.

Method

The task in this experiment was judgment of lengths of lines. The apparatus has been described elsewhere (Mausner, 1950). The Ss were 38 members of undergraduate psychology classes. All Ss were naive regarding the purpose of the present experiment and previous work in the field.

In an alone session 200 judgments were made: 20 lines varying in length from 8 inches to 18.5 inches in steps of .5 inch were each presented 10 times. The judgments were made in inches or fractions of an inch. The S was told that he would be informed whether he was right or wrong after each judgment. The supposed criterion of "right" was accuracy within one inch. Each series of 20 trials contained the entire group of stimuli in a different order so that no one line followed any other more than once in the total sequence. The same order of stimuli was followed for all Ss. Half the Ss were told they were right on 82 per cent of the trials (group R); half were told they were wrong on 82 per cent (group NR). Alternate Ss were assigned to groups R and NR at the first sessions.

The position of the "wrongs" for group R and "rights" for group NR was the same in the entire series of trials. Lines from 8 inches to 9.5 inches, and from 17 inches to 18.5 inches were consistently "right" for group R and "wrong" for group NR. This was done to avoid a tendency which appeared in a pilot study for group NR to continue to make "right" judgments of the easily identified longest and shortest lines.

For the second session Ss made their judgments in pairs. The Ss in each pair, previously unacquainted with each other, were so chosen as to minimize overlap between frequency distributions of judged lengths of any single line in the first session. Pairs were of three kinds: seven consisted of two Ss from group R (R-R), six of one S from each group (R-NR), six of two Ss from group NR (NR-NR). The Ss were told that two Ss would work concurrently in order to complete the experiment within the scheduled time. Each S judged every stimulus. The members of the pair alternated as first to judge. The order of presentation of stimuli was the same as in the first session, but now S was not told whether he was right or wrong.

Treatment of Data

The following procedure was used to measure change in judgment: the frequency with which each "number" response (e.g., "10 inches") was made by S was obtained separately for alone (A) and together (T) situations. For each of the number-response categories the difference in frequency of occurrence between alone and together situations was calculated ("T – A" score). All number-response categories which occurred in either of the two situations were then arranged in order of "magnitude." The midpoint of the series of "magnitudes" was found. Algebraic sums of the T – A scores were obtained separately for the group of response categories above and below the midpoint of the series of categories. The two sums of T – A scores were then added without respect to sign to give a score which represents the amount of shift in response frequency from alone to together situations. This henceforth will be referred to as the D score.

The direction of shift was measured as follows: the number of plus and minus signs of the T – A scores was taken separately for response categories above and below the midpoint. Where no systematic shift occurred, the number of plus and minus T – A

Table 1 *Calculation of D and C Scores from 200 Judgments of Lengths of Lines (Hypothetical Data for One Subject)*

Judgment Category (Inches)	Frequency Alone (A)	Frequency Together (T)	T − A	Subtotal T − A
3	2	0	−2	
4	18	0	−18	
5	24	0	−24	−106
6	43	0	−43	+7
7	43	24	−19	——
8	38	45	+7	−99
		Midpoint		
9	22	38	+16	
10	8	33	+25	
11	2	26	+24	
12	0	14	+14	−0
13	0	12	+12	+99
14	0	8	+8	——
	200	200		99

Calculation of D score		Calculation of C score	
Σ(T−A) above midpoint	99	No. + T−A below midpoint	+1
Σ(T−A) below midpoint	99	No. − T−A below midpoint	−5
D score	198	Reverse sign, subtotal	+4
		No. + T−A above midpoint	+6
		No. − T−A above midpoint	−0
		Retain sign, subtotal	+6
		C score	+10

scores should be equal in each half of the judgment category series. Where shift occurred, two possibilities are present: if shift was "up," there were more high-number responses in the together series; there was, therefore, a preponderance of negative T − A scores below the midpoint and of positive T − A scores above it. If shift was "down," the reverse obtained. All signs in the lower half of the response category series were reversed, and the total algebraic sum of positive and negative T − A signs then taken. This total will be referred to as the C score. A positive C score indicates movement "up" in the number category series; a negative C score shows movement "down." In summary, the D score gives a measure of degree of shift in judgment, the C score of direction. For examples of calculation of D and C scores see Table 1.

Results and Discussion

Table 2 gives C and D scores for all Ss, and mean and σ of the distribution of D scores for each group. Only one S in group NR, and three in group R, had D scores more than 1.5 σ from the means of their respective groups. Comparison of mean D scores for the two groups shows that group NR has a D score significantly higher than group R ($t = 4.15$, $df = 33$, $p < .01$). Thus, the nonreinforced Ss showed a significantly greater tendency than the reinforced Ss to shift judgments from the alone to the together situation, substantiating the hypothesis presented above.

Of the three Ss in group R with D scores more than 1.5 σ from the means of their group, the preponderance of judgments of two moved away from those of the partner, as demonstrated by C scores opposite in sign from those of their partners (TYL and BRU, see Table 2). The results for the third S (HOG) are not in accord with the experimental hypothesis, since this S, although his judgments were previously reinforced, had a high D score, and converged toward his partner. The S in group NR with a D score more than 1.5 σ lower than the group mean was a member of an NR-NR pair which did arrive at a group norm.

Examination of the C scores to indicate direction of shift shows that what shift did occur among the 12 Ss in R-R pairs was more often away from the partner than toward him: seven Ss showed this tendency, one had a zero C score, and four shifted towards the partner. All of the NR Ss in R-NR pairs converged toward the partner, high Ss giving negative C scores and low Ss positive C scores. The R Ss in these pairs had two zero C scores, two C scores showing tendency to shift toward the partner, and two away from him. Nine of the 12 Ss in NR-NR pairs showed a tendency to converge toward the partner. Here, however, in all cases a group norm was reached, as can be demonstrated by graphs showing median judgments for each 20 trials in the course of the experiment.

These plots of median responses through the course of the experimental sessions permit comparison of the results of this study with Sherif's (1935). The predictions advanced in this experiment were that the convergence by both Ss, as found in Sherif's work, would occur only in the NR-NR pairs; that in an R-NR pair only the NR member would converge; and that neither member of an R-R pair would converge. Partial confirmation of these predictions was found in the characteristics of the C scores discussed above. In Figure 1, the median graphs for the R-R group show that in all but one case neither S converged toward his partner. The plots of R-NR pairs

Table 2 *D* and C Scores for Subjects of Each Pair. (Reinforced Ss indicated by (R), nonreinforced Ss by (NR), high S (H), low S (L); negative C shows movement "up," positive C "down.")*

Subject	D	C	Subject	D	C	Subject	D	C
MEY (R, H)	39	+1	MAR (R, H)	31	−8	ABR (NR, L)	91	−11
GRE (R, L)	72	+12	FEI (NR, L)†	—	—	ROD (NR, H)	201	−17
KRA (R, L)	18	0	FRA (R, H)	13	−4	SLA (NR, L)	212	+13
BAT (R, H)	25	+3	MAK (NR, L)	199	+21	ROS (NR, H)	78	−12
LEV (R, H)	5	+2	NAD (R, H)	31	0	KLE (NR, L)	204	+10
ERU (R, L)	104	−2	BER (NR, L)	95	+8	MCC (NR, H)	159	−16
WEI (R, L)	7	−1	RUO (R, L)	26	−2	COF (NR, H)	103	−19
HOG (R, H)	107	−14	LEW (NR, H)	87	−17	AMS (NR, L)	30	−8
TYL (R, H)	104	+16	COH (R, L)	14	−2	FER (NR, H)	97	−22
LUR (R, L)	38	−9	MOL (NR, H)	260	−25	FLE (NR, L)	117	+11
MEE (R, L)	7	+6	UNG (R, H)	2	0	TEP (NR, H)	229	−26
FEL (R, H)	17	−4	STE (NR, L)	84	+9	PLI (NR, L)	81	−10

* Mean D score, group R, 37, $\sigma = 34$; group NR, 142, $\sigma = 100$.
† D and C scores for three Ss, FEI, RAN, and VAL, were not computed because of incomplete data. Graphic treatment shows all three responded according to the experimental hypothesis (Mausner, 1960).

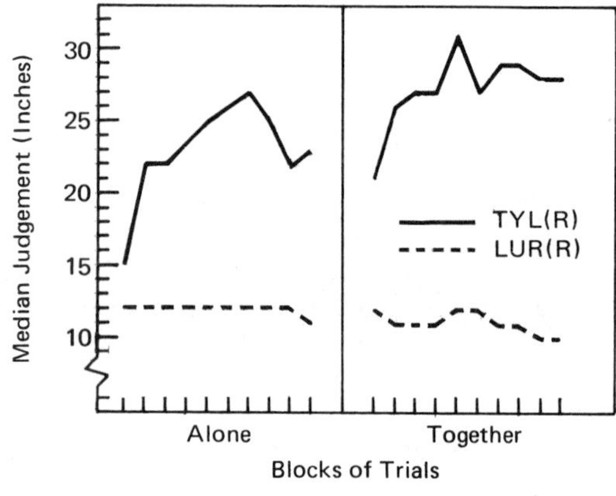

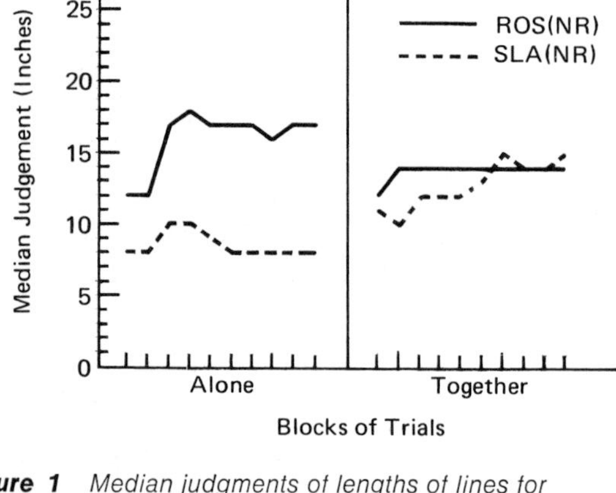

Figure 1 *Median judgments of lengths of lines for groups of 20 trials. Subjects TYL, LUR, and COH were positively reinforced (R). Subjects MOL, ROS, and SLA were negatively reinforced (NR).*

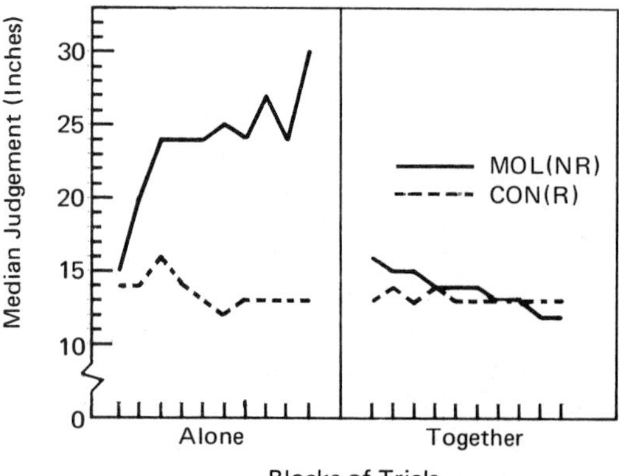

confirm the previously noted trend for the NR member to converge toward the judgments of the reinforced partner, and for the latter to maintain his judgment range. The characteristic funnel-shaped curves which denote convergence by both partners can be found only for subject pairs in which both members came from the NR group.[2]

[2] The data of the subjects in Figure 1 are representative of their respective groups. Complete graphs for all Ss are available in microfilm form (Mausner, 1950).

Summary and Conclusions

The hypothesis that the interaction of observer pairs is a function of the degree of prior reinforcement of the judgment responses was tested on 38 Ss who first made judgments of lengths of lines when alone, and then in pairs. The pairs were so chosen that the alone judgments of the two Ss overlapped minimally. In the alone situation half of the Ss were told they were right on 82 per cent of the trials (group R); half were told they were wrong on 82 per cent of the trials (group NR).

Mean D score (a measure of shift in judgment) was significantly higher at the .01 level for group NR than for group R. This indicates a greater tendency for NR Ss to be influenced by their partner's judgments in the group situation.

Graphic and quantitative measures of direction of shift show that Ss in group NR tended to converge toward their partners; Ss in group R maintained their former judgment ranges or shifted away from those of their partners.

On the basis of these findings it is concluded that Ss with a past history of positive reinforcement in a given type of judgment are less influenced by their partners in a group judgment situation than Ss with a history of negative reinforcement.

References

Berenda, Ruth W. *The influence of the group on the judgments of children.* New York: Kings Crown Press, 1950.

Bovard, E. W., Jr. Group structure and perception. *Journal of Abnormal and Social Psychology,* 1951, *46,* 398–405.

Bray, D. W. The prediction of behavior from two attitude scales. *Journal of Abnormal and Social Psychology,* 1950, *45,* 64–84.

Kelman, H. Effects of success and failure on "suggestibility" in the autokinetic situation. *Journal of Abnormal and Social Psychology,* 1950, *45,* 267–285.

Luchins, A. S. Social influences on perception of complex drawings. *Journal of Social Psychology,* 1945, *21,* 257–273.

Mausner, B. The effect of prior reinforcement on the interaction of observer pairs. Ann Arbor, Mich.: University Microfilms publication No. 2118, 1950.

Schonbar, R. A. The interaction of observer pairs in judging visual extent and movement: The formation of social norms in a structured situation. *Archives of Psychology,* 1945, No. 299.

Sherif, M. A study of some social factors in perception. *Archives of Psychology,* 1935, No. 187.

Autokinetic movement is the apparent movement of a point source of light against an otherwise dark background. It has been shown in several experiments that the amount of movement reported by persons in a group tends to converge toward a common norm. When these persons later view the effect alone, their judgments of movement are more like those they made in the group than those made when judging originally by themselves.

Stone's experiment demonstrates that autokinetic movement can be influenced by social reinforcement much as it can by a group. Stone's subjects were first divided into three groups. They reported on the autokinetic effect either alone, with one other person, or with three other persons present. On the next day, all the subjects were treated alike: At first, they were reinforced verbally for reporting extreme movement, and later the experimenter made no comment following their reports of movement (extinction). The results showed that the members of four-person groups were less susceptible to the apparent movement effect than subjects in groups of two or alone. All the subjects, however, were influenced by the conditioning procedure; that is, their estimates increased in size. The autokinetic effect persisted longest with the subjects who were first alone and then conditioned. Thus, it appeared that social reinforcement from the experimenter had as profound an effect on the behavior of the subjects as that produced by judging with others.

The results of this study do not necessarily tell us whether perceptual or reporting behavior is being influenced. They do suggest, however, that a group provides social reinforcement of the autokinetic effect in a manner analogous to an experimenter's reinforcement procedures.

35 Autokinetic Norms: An Experimental Analysis[1]

WILLIAM F. STONE

Although there has been controversy (Gibson, 1953) concerning the generality of his results, Sherif's (1935) study of norm formation in the autokinetic situation has been a continuing stimulus to research in social cognition. A peculiar advantage is that the judgment of autokinetic movement is a task new to most subjects. Thus, it is possible to observe the formation of novel opinions in the laboratory. Elaborations on the use of the autokinetic situation in the study of social judgment have been made by Sherif and Hovland (1961), Jacobs and Campbell (1961), and others.

There is evidence that social ("group") reinforcement is operative in the autokinetic situation. Sherif (1935), for instance, demonstrated that perceptual norms are more stable when formed with another person or persons. Subsequent investigators have found that autokinetic judgments are more likely to remain centered on the same value if the subject is told that his judgments are accurate (Harvey and Rutherford, 1958; Kelman, 1950; Mausner, 1954). These findings accord well with the assertion that reward serves to fix perceptual responses (Solley and Murphy, 1960). Although Solley and Murphy also suggest that perceptual responses are self-reinforcing, there seems to be little evidence concerning the effects of practice (i.e., the number of self-reinforcements) in setting perceptual norms.

The present study examined the effects of practice and group size on perceptual norm formation. It was hypothesized that:

1. When autokinetic norms are learned in the absence of external reward, there is an increment of habit strength associated with each response, because "the achievement of percepts is reinforcing to a perceptual act" (Solley and Murphy, 1960, p. 82).
2. With the addition of other observers habit increments will be larger, owing to "group reinforcement." That is, hearing other persons make responses similar to his own will be reinforcing and hence will increase the strength of the subject's response. As the habit strength of the responses near the norm increases, it is expected that the norm will become stronger. The strength of norms formed under the various conditions was expected to be reflected in the subject's behavior in an operant conditioning situation (Kanfer, 1954; Spivak and Papajohn, 1957) imposed on the day following the formation of his norm.

Method

Subjects

The subjects were 150 male undergraduates enrolled in psychology classes at the University of Miami. They received course credit for participation.

Apparatus

The autokinetic light was mounted at the rear of a light-tight plywood box, 4 feet high × 5½ feet wide. Four cloth-hooded viewing ports were provided on the four panels (which were set at angles of 135 degrees to each other) which comprised the front of the box. The spot of light was produced by means of a ⅛-inch diameter lucite rod, which protruded ⅛ inch upward from a small metal box. A ¼-watt neon bulb in the metal box was operated at 132 volts to illuminate the rod, which presented a ⅛-inch square target 2½ feet from each subject. Timing relays provided 7-second exposures alternating with 13-second dark periods.[2]

The experimental room was dimly illuminated by two red 25-watt bulbs, and an air-conditioner to the rear of the apparatus ran constantly.

Design of the Experiment

The experiment was conducted in two periods, on

[1] Based upon a dissertation submitted to the graduate school, University of Florida. Partial support was afforded by a Veterans Administration Traineeship held by the author, and by a grant from the Research Committee, Veterans Administration Hospital, Coral Gables, Florida. Marvin E. Shaw, who directed the dissertation, also read a draft of this article and made many helpful suggestions. Appreciation is expressed to J. McDavid and other faculty at the University of Miami for subjects and use of facilities. W. B. Webb, H. D. Kimmel, and J. Sandler gave valuable assistance in the design and execution of the study. This article was prepared while the author was at Lafayette College.

[2] A sketch and more detailed instructions for construction of the apparatus may be obtained from the author.

From the *Journal of Personality and Social Psychology*, 1967, *5*, 76–81. Copyright 1967 by the American Psychological Association, and reproduced by permission.

successive days. On the first day, the subjects formed norms under the various experimental conditions (the norm session). On the second day, subjects were run individually in the conditioning and extinction sessions.

The main experiment consisted of nine conditions, representing all possible combinations of three group sizes (one, two, and four) and three numbers of practice trials during norm formation (20, 40, and 80). That is, during the norm session on Day 1, subjects made judgments of autokinetic movement either alone, with another person, or with three other persons, and made either 20, 40, or 80 judgments. On Day 2, all subjects were treated alike. They were given up to 40 conditioning trials during which 10 reinforcements for high responses were given, followed by 40 extinction trials.

In addition to the experimental groups, two control groups were run. Control groups made 40 judgments alone in the norm session. Control Group A also formed norms alone, but received random reinforcements from the experimenter, who said "right" following 50% of the judgments. This group was treated the same as the experimental groups during the conditioning and extinction sessions. Control Group B received no reinforcements during the norm session. During the conditioning session, subjects in this group received 10 noncontingent reinforcements, determined by yoking each subject with a subject in the comparable experimental condition, 40–1 (group size, 1; 40 judgments). Extinction was the same as in other groups.

Procedure

The subjects were recruited for the "night vision experiment." It was announced, in the call for volunteers, that the experiment involved "making judgments of the movement of a small light in a dark field."

Day 1 (*norm session*). The subjects entered the laboratory, chose seats at one of the portholes, and during the 5-minute dark-adaptation period were told:

> This is an experiment in visual discrimination. After I tell you what to do, and you take your places at the apparatus, I will turn on a small light inside. After a short while, the light will start to move. Then it will go off. After the light is off I want you to tell me the distance the light has moved. Make your estimates in full inches or half inches. For example, say "5½ inches," or "7½ inches," or "10 inches," and so on. (Give your estimates one at a time, beginning with the person at the left.) The light will move no less than 1 inch and no more than 24 inches. Report only the distance that the light moves. Do not report the direction of movement (adapted from Kanfer, 1954).

After a practice trial the stimulus was presented periodically, and the subjects reported their estimates in turn during the 13-second intertrial interval. A 1-minute rest period followed every twentieth exposure. Upon completion of the trials, individual appointments were made for the following day.

Based upon the distribution of his last 20 estimates, the high response class for each subject was defined as any response above his median class.

Day 2 (*conditioning and extinction sessions*). The subject entered the laboratory alone, dark adapted for 5 minutes, and was told: "I want you to make estimates as you did yesterday. At the start, I'll say 'right' when you guess within ½ inch of the correct distance. Otherwise, I'll say nothing. . . ."

The first 10 high responses emitted by the subject were reinforced, on a continuous schedule. The session was terminated after the tenth reinforcement, or the fortieth trial, whichever came first. Subjects who did not make 10 high responses within 40 stimulus presentations were discarded. After a 2-minute rest period the extinction session began. No additional comments, instructions, or verbal reinforcements were given. Forty extinction trials were run (2 blocks of 20 estimates each, separated by a 1-minute rest period). Following the fortieth trial, a brief interview was held with the subject, and two paper-and-pencil questionnaires were administered.

The conditioning and extinction procedure for Control Group A was the same as for the experimental groups. Group B was also treated the same, except that the reinforcements for Group B subjects were not contingent on their responses. Each subject in Group B was "yoked" with one subject in Group 40–1, in that the B subject was given reinforcements on the same trials as had his yokemate.

Results

A total of 138 subjects returned for the second day's sessions out of 150 who participated in the norm-formation procedure. Of these, 9 failed to meet the conditioning criterion (4 from Group 40–1, 1 each from 5 other groups). Seven additional subjects were over the preset age limit of 30 years and were dropped, and data from 12 subjects were randomly discarded to maintain equal cell frequencies in each of the 11 groups.

The session-by-session estimates for the 10 subjects in each of the experimental groups are shown in Figure 1. Norm-session (N) scores are means of the subject's last 20 estimates, C scores are means of all of his estimates in the conditioning session,

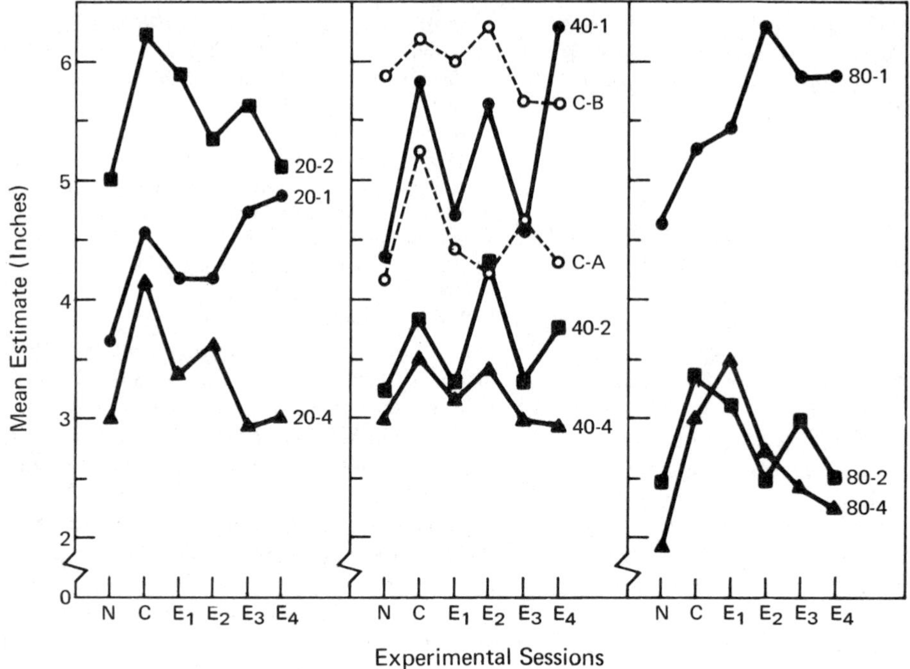

Figure 1 *Conditioning and extinction of autokinetic judgments as functions of the learning conditions. (See text for explanation of symbols.)*

and E scores are means of successive 10-trial blocks of estimates in the extinction session.

Norms. Although the norms for individual subjects are the basis for subsequent analyses, it should be noted that those who formed norms together did form *group* norms, as expected. For example, the mean difference between N scores of members of the two-man groups was .77 inch, as compared with 3.50 inches for random pairs formed from subjects who judged alone.

It is apparent (Figure 1) that there were large differences among the various groups in mean N scores, and that these between-group differences in norms were perpetuated throughout the experimental sequence. Means and *SD*s of N scores for the experimental groups are shown in Table 1. Initial differences in norms were tested by the between-subject terms of a mixed analysis of variance of the N and C data. A significant group-size *F* ratio ($F_{2,\ 81} = 5.81$, $p < .01$) demonstrated that mean estimates (norms) of individual subjects are inversely related to size of group in which they formed their norms. Changes over sessions were not, however, correlated with N scores. Therefore the absolute differences between groups were ignored in subsequent analyses, and attention was focused on within-subject changes over sessions.

The *SD*s of the experimental group means which are reported in Table 1 also reflect between-group differences in variability. This heterogeneity tended to be perpetuated through all experimental periods, and to allow for it, apparent significance levels were doubled in making interpretations (Lindquist, 1953, p. 83). *F* ratios having a probability of .025 or less were considered statistically significant.

Conditioning. The within-subject analyses of the N-C data showed quite conclusively that: (*a*) The conditioning procedure was effective in changing the subjects' mean estimates (trend $F_{1,\ 81} = 57.76$, $p <$

Table 1 *Mean Estimates (in Inches) for Norm Session (Based on Means of Subjects' Last 20 Judgments)*

Practice Trials	Group Size		
	1	2	4
20			
M	3.65	5.02	2.99
SD	2.95	1.72	1.30
40			
M	4.37	3.25	2.97
SD	1.60	1.26	0.69
80			
M	4.65	2.43	1.95
SD	2.73	1.18	0.72

Note.—$N = 10$ subjects per group.

.001); and (*b*) there were no differential changes among groups from N to C (no trend interactions). Thus there was no evidence of between-group differences in conditionability. (This finding is not affected by the initial differences in norms, since the correlations between individual norms and changes from N to C do not differ from zero.)

Extinction. The differential changes in slope of the extinction curves of the experimental groups were reflected in the trend interactions of the analysis of variance presented in Table 2. In general, subjects who form norms alone show greater resistance to extinction than do those who form norms in groups of two or four, as shown by the significant Group Size × Trend interaction. In fact, analysis of trend effects for the three group sizes taken separately shows that subjects who form their norms alone show an increasing trend in their estimates over the extinction session ($F_{3,\ 243} = 4.37$, $p < .01$). Subjects

Table 2 *Summary of Analysis of Variance of Extinction Data (Four 10-Trial Blocks)*

Source	*df*	MS	*F*
Between Ss	89		
Practice (P)	2	12.12	0.71
Group size (G)	2	141.37	8.36***
P × G	4	46.52	2.75
Error (b)	81	16.91	
Within Ss	270		
Trend (T)	3	1.44	1.35
P × T	6	2.86	2.67*
G × T	6	3.35	3.13**
P × G × T	12	0.44	0.41
Error (w)	243	1.07	
Total	359		

* $p < .025$.
** $p < .01$.
*** $p < .001$.

from the two-man groups show a downward, though not significant, trend ($F_{3,\ 243} = .47$). Those who form norms in the four-man groups show near significant decreases ($F_{3,\ 243} = 2.78$, $p < .05$), a tendency to return to their norms.

The Trend × Practice interaction shown in Table 2 seems to be accounted for entirely by the periodic vacillation in estimates of subjects in the 40-trial groups, as shown by the extinction trend for the combined 40-trial groups, tested against error (w) ($F_{3,\ 243} = 5.46$, $p < .005$). Neither the 20-trial nor the 80-trial groups showed significant trends over the extinction session.

Control groups. Means for the two control groups, A and B, are plotted in the center panel of Figure 1. Comparison of these groups with 40–1 was made by an analysis over all six blocks. This analysis shows that: (*a*) the absolute differences between groups were not significant ($F < 1$); and (*b*) the trend for all three groups combined approached significance ($F_{5,\ 135} = 2.25$, $p < .10$). When the trend for each group was tested against error (w), neither Group A nor Group B showed *F* ratios greater than 1. The trend for 40–1 was significant ($F_{5,\ 135} = 3.81$, $p < .005$). Neither Group A, in which the subjects' norm-session estimates were randomly reinforced by the experimenter, nor Group B (noncontingent reinforcement in the conditioning session) showed changes from their own norms. These analyses, plus the striking resemblance of the control-group curves to those for 40–2 and 40–4, suggest that: (*a*) Reinforcement by the experimenter during norm formation produces resistance to change similar to that produced by judging with others; and (*b*) changes in estimates which occur during conditioning are produced by the contingency of the reinforcements on high responses, and do not result from "encouragement" or the like from the experimenter's vocalizations.

Discussion

Norm formation. Subjects in the group norm-formation conditions (in addition to the oft-noted convergence of estimates) showed a decided tendency to report less movement than do subjects judging alone. This phenomenon is of interest, since it suggests a tendency for the observers to be influenced in the direction of "reality" (the light actually does not move). Subjects who experience relatively less movement seem to have more influence in determining the group norm. A somewhat similar finding was reported by Jacobs and Campbell (1961), who found that an arbitrary norm of 15 inches gradually decayed to about 3 inches as naive subjects replaced those who had been indoctrinated by confederates. These authors postulate the existence of a natural norm for autokinetic movement, averaging about 3 inches in their experimental setting (8-foot viewing distance, 5-second exposure).

The shift toward zero in groups judging autokinetic movement, together with the findings concerning shifts of member opinion toward riskier positions (Wallach, Kogan, and Bem, 1962), brings into question certain assumptions about opinion convergence in groups. French (1956), for example, suggests that the most probable value for the "final common opinion" reached in a group will be the arithmetic mean of the initially divergent opinions. It seems more probable that in a given situation opinions at certain positions on the continuum carry more weight than others. In general, when initial opinions are well distributed, there will be convergence, but with some polarization toward one or the other extreme (in the autokinetic situation, toward zero).

Practice and reinforcement. The present study confirms previous findings (Harvey and Rutherford, 1958; Kelman, 1950) concerning the strength of autokinetic norms as a function of prior reinforcement. Subjects who form norms in groups retain them longer than do those who judge alone initially. Maximum strength appears to be attained in the four-man groups, whose members' norms are somewhat stronger than those of subjects in the two-man groups. The major behavioral differences in extinction, however, are in the contrast between subjects who form norms alone and those who had at least one other person judging with them.

Surprisingly, amount of practice has no demonstrable relationship to norm strength. This finding if of interest since two considerations lead us to predict increased strength of autokinetic norms with practice. First, the hypothesized "self-reinforcement" of perceptual responses is expected to contribute to habit strength in proportion to the number of responses. Second, within-subject variability of autokinetic estimates decreases over trials, and subjects who gave more variable estimates (i.e., who had fewer learning trials) should be more influenceable (Bovard, 1948).

Group reinforcement. The present study has demonstrated that norm responses made in the presence of others are strengthened over those made alone. Further, it was shown that the "judging-with-others" effect can be duplicated by delivery of verbal reinforcements to solitary respondents. These findings appear to confirm the notion that autokinetic norms are formed through the reinforcement of "reporting responses" (Schoenfeld and Cumming, 1963). However, the manner in which the subjects reinforce one another's responses is not altogether clear, since the order of response and reinforcement is not always that specified by the instrumental learning model. While the existence of an empirically defined group reinforcement has been demonstrated, its mediating mechanism remains to be explicated.

References

Bovard, E. W., Jr. Social norms and the individual. *Journal of Abnormal and Social Psychology,* 1948, *43,* 62–69.

French, J. R. P., Jr. A formal theory of social power. *Psychological Review,* 1956, *63,* 181–194.

Gibson, J. J. Social perception and the psychology of perceptual learning. In M. Sherif & M. O. Wilson (Eds.), *Group relations at the crossroads.* New York: Harper, 1953. Pp. 120–138.

Harvey, O. J., and Rutherford, J. Gradual and absolute approaches to attitude change. *Sociometry,* 1958, *21,* 61–68.

Jacobs, R. D., and Campbell, D. T. The perpetuation of an arbitrary tradition through several generations of a laboratory microculture. *Journal of Abnormal and Social Psychology,* 1961, *62,* 649–658.

Kanfer, F. H. The effect of partial reinforcement on acquisition and extinction of a class of verbal responses. *Journal of Experimental Psychology,* 1954, *48,* 424–432.

Kelman, H. C. Effects of success and failure on "suggestibility" in the autokinetic situation. *Journal of Abnormal and Social Psychology,* 1950, *45,* 267–285.

Lindquist, E. F. *Design and analysis of experiments in psychology and education.* Boston: Houghton-Mifflin, 1953.

Mausner, B. The effect of prior reinforcement on the interaction of observer pairs. *Journal of Abnormal and Social Psychology,* 1954, *49,* 65–68.

Schoenfeld, W. N., and Cumming, W. W. Behavior and perception. In S. Koch (Ed.), *Psychology: A study of a science.* Vol. 5. New York: McGraw-Hill, 1963. Pp. 213–252.

Sherif, M. A study of some social factors in perception. *Archives of Psychology,* 1935, No. 187.

Sherif, M., and Hovland, C. I. *Social judgment.* New Haven: Yale University Press, 1961.

Solley, C. M., and Murphy, G. *Development of the perceptual world.* New York: Basic Books, 1960.

Spivak, M., and Papajohn, J. The effect of schedule of reinforcement on operant conditioning of a verbal response in the autokinetic situation. *Journal of Abnormal and Social Psychology,* 1957, *54,* 213–217.

Wallach, M. A., Kogan, N., and Bem, D. J. Group influence on individual risk taking. *Journal of Abnormal and Social Psychology,* 1962, *65,* 75–86.

B Perceptual Selection vs. Selective Report

A dramatic turn was given to research on social factors in perception by a series of experiments in which subjects were required to report words exposed for very short durations of time. Attempts were made in these studies to select stimulus words that bore some meaningful relationship to certain values and attitudes of the subjects. Personal values, for example, can be measured by means of a standardized questionnaire. An individual's score on an inventory of values can then be used to predict the exposure durations at which he will be able to perceive words relating to these values. An alternative experimental situation is one in which stimulus words are selected so as to represent certain cultural taboos (sex, aggression, excretion). These words are then mixed randomly with neutral words, and the minimum exposure time required for an unselected group of subjects to recognize the words is determined. A more precise way of getting at what has been called "perceptual defense" under such circumstances is to determine for each subject, by means of interview or questionnaire procedures, his areas of personal conflict or emotional arousal. Words symbolic of these areas can then be presented to him, along with neutral or control words, to determine which ones he perceives with greater alacrity.

A major problem in all such experiments is whether the verbal report of the subject is an accurate indicator of his perceptual response. Or, stated otherwise, there is a serious question as to whether the subject's explicit verbal response occurs contiguously with his implicit verbal response. Does he report what he *sees,* or does he report what he thinks will be more acceptable to the experimenter, or what he thinks will reflect more favorably upon himself? Still another problem concerns whether the perceptual threshold is determined by the meaning of the stimulus word, or whether the threshold reflects the operation of more mundane factors, such as the frequency with which a particular word appears in print. If the natural frequency of the words were the important factor, subjects would have an expectancy, or be "set," to perceive certain classes of words rather than others.

The two articles that follow illustrate some of the problems and methods of attack in this interesting and controversial area. They ask why recognition thresholds (perceptual defense) increase for certain classes of visual stimuli.

The experiment by *McGinnies and Sherman* is an outgrowth of an earlier study in which subjects revealed higher thresholds of recognition for taboo words than for neutral words of the same length. Other investigators later pointed out that the subjects may have encountered the taboo words less frequently and therefore were not likely to guess in that direction. In view of this criticism, and because of the possibility that the subjects in the earlier experiment may have been reluctant to report the taboo words as they gradually became recognizable under increasing exposure durations, McGinnies and Sherman designed an experiment in which the subjects would be required to report neutral words all having the same frequency of occurrence. Some of the neutral words to be recognized by the subjects, however, were preceded on each exposure by a taboo word that could be clearly recognized.

The remaining neutral task words were regularly preceded by exposure of other neutral words. Assuming that the aversive properties of the taboo words would elicit conditioned emotional reactions from the subject, it was predicted that recognition thresholds for the neutral words following taboo words would be delayed through generalization, or spread, of this inhibitory process.

The results of the experiment are interpreted not in terms of any special cognitive mechanisms but in the language of reinforcement theory. When the taboo words were shown clearly and ambiguously, the resulting emotional response, it is assumed, delayed recognition of subsequently presented stimuli that were not themselves aversive. Here we speak not of reinforcement but simply response interference.

36 | *Generalization of Perceptual Defense*

ELLIOTT MCGINNIES
HOWARD SHERMAN

The importance of the meaning, or connotation, of stimuli used in perceptual research has been amply demonstrated in recent years. Words, for example, which contain the same number of letters, which differ only randomly in structure, and which are shown to observers under identical conditions of distance and illumination require, for recognition, exposure durations which vary systematically as a function of their motivational significance. In general, recent findings indicate that words representing areas of little interest (Postman, Bruner, and McGinnies, 1948) as well as words having "taboo" associations (McGinnies, 1949) require longer exposures for recognition by most observers than do words representing areas of high interest value or having nonemotional connotations.

One interceptation of these findings has been that the delay in correct verbal report of visually-presented words of a "taboo" or "contra-valuant" nature represents a genuine interference, or repression, at the perceptual level of response rather than a voluntary refusal by the observer to communicate verbally his perceptual experience. This inferred interference process has been termed *perceptual defense* and is operationally defined by the report thresholds of the observer.

As in all perceptual research, we are confronted with a situation in which we presume to have information about an aspect of behavior which, by definition, occurs at the level of implicit, or private, response. It must be admitted that a degree of uncertainty in our description of perceptual behavior does exist to the extent that we fail to differentiate convincingly between perceptual response and verbal response. Perceptual defense, as suggested by Howes and Solomon (1950), may simply be a case of suppressed verbal report. The present writers, however, are inclined to the opinion that a process of emotional selectivity does operate in perception and that the term "perceptual defense" may be useful as a description of the events underlying delayed report of certain socially relevant stimuli. What is obviously needed in the field of empirical reporting before an adequate theory of perceptual defense can be formulated is an experimental demonstration of behavior that is clearly a reflection of differential perceptual organization rather than of selective verbal report. The experiment presently to be reported was designed to demonstrate the generalization of perceptual defense, or interference, to words which observers would have no reluctance to verbalize.

The Experiment

In a previous study (McGinnies, 1949), the senior author has shown that the recognition thresholds of observers are significantly elevated for taboo words as compared with their thresholds for neutral words. The interpretation of these findings in terms of "perceptual defense," or conditioned avoidance operating below the threshold of conscious awareness, is defended in a later paper (McGinnies, 1950). Assuming that such a mechanism actually does operate to delay the recognition of "taboo" words, we might expect that the response processes mediating this effect will persist long enough to declay recognition

From the *Journal of Abnormal and Social Psychology*, 1952, *47*, 81–85.

of neutral stimuli immediately following exposure to an anxiety-arousing word. Such an effect would be closely allied with the well-known phenomenon of associative inhibition.

Our experiment tested the prediction that the duration thresholds of affectively-neutral words would be raised when these words followed immediately upon the perception of others having socially-taboo connotations.

Experimental Procedure. We were particularly concerned with using task words that would arouse no reluctance to verbalization on the part of the observers. Eighteen five-letter words with no apparent emotional significance were selected on the basis of their having approximately the same frequency listings in the Thorndike-Lorge (1944) semantic frequency lists (1944). In addition to these, four of the socially-taboo words employed in a previous experiment by McGinnies (1949) were selected as being adequately representative of the type of verbal stimulus that will arouse autonomic reactivity and perceptual defense on the part of most individuals. All words used in the experiment are presented alphabetically in Table 1.

The experimental material, then, consisted of 22 words. All were typed singly, in capital letters, on sheets of white paper spaced so that the word would appear in the center of the visual field. The apparatus employed for presentation of the words was a Gerbrands Mirror Tachistoscope which permits variation in the exposure duration of stimulus objects by the activation of fluorescent tubes for intervals of .01 second and upward. By means of a one-way screen, it is possible in this apparatus to present the observer with two different stimuli in rapid succession. A toggle switch connected in series with the pre-exposure source of illumination enabled us to control the exposure duration of the initial stimulus word as well as the interval separating it from the timer-controlled exposure of the second, or task, word.

Eight pairs of words were presented to each observer. In four of these pairs, the first, or *pre-task* word, was one of the four taboo words previously noted. The second, or *task* word, in each of these four pairs was one of the eighteen neutral words selected from the Thorndike-Lorge tables. In the remaining four pairs, both words were affectively neutral in connotation.

When seated at the viewing window of the tachistoscope, the observer fixated the center of a dark 8- by 10-inch field at a distance of 22 inches from his eyes. He was instructed that following a "ready" signal from the experimenter, a word would appear at this central position at a duration sufficient for full recognition. This word would then disappear and be replaced immediately by another word of a much shorter duration. The observer was to attempt identification of the *second* word. Illumination of the fields surrounding both the pre-task and task words was equated for brightness, the value of each being approximately 0.40 foot-candle as measured by a Weston Master II exposure meter.

Table 1 *Words Used in the Experiment**

bitch	*penis*
brand	phone
cable	quest
flush	ranch
frock	*raped*
glide	rider
grind	scent
hound	spray
legal	towel
lucky	weave
outer	*whore*

* All have approximately the same frequency listings in the Thorndike-Lorge tables. Critical, or taboo, words are in italics.

By manual operation of a toggle switch, the pre-task word (either neutral or critical) was first shown the observer for approximately two seconds. (A check on the duration actually achieved by manual operation of the switch showed the error to be insignificant.) The neutral task word was then exposed for .01 second. If the observer did not recognize it, the pre-task word was again illuminated for two seconds followed this time by exposure of the task word for .02 second. Repeated exposure of the task word, preceded each time by a two-second presentation of the pre-task word, was continued until it was reported correctly. Duration of exposure of the task word was controlled by an electric timer which permitted an increase in exposure time of .01 second on successive trials. Hypotheses, or guesses, made by the observers were recorded together with their duration thresholds for the eight neutral task words. Before commencing the experiment proper, the experimenter followed the above procedure with three pairs of neutral words in order to accustom the observer to the apparatus and to allow a leveling-off of practice effect.

Pairing of the words was done randomly, a different randomization being used with each observer. Order of presentation of the word-pairs was also determined randomly. A different order obtained for each observer. Subjects in the experiment were twenty male undergraduates all of whom were naive as to the problem under investigation.

Results and Discussion

Threshold Data. Assuming that some centrally-

Table 2 *Total Number of Exposures Required for Each Observer to Report Correctly Task Words in the Critical Pairs and in the Control Pairs*

Observer	Critical	Control	Difference
1	10	12	−2
2	49	28	21
3	9	9	0
4	10	7	3
5	21	9	12
6	8	8	0
7	25	12	13
8	56	18	38
9	6	9	−3
10	5	5	0
11	8	13	−5
12	8	7	1
13	14	6	8
14	21	13	8
15	31	32	−1
16	17	13	4
17	14	12	2
18	75	65	10
19	46	6	40
20	68	20	48
Mean difference = 9.85		$t = 2.87$	$p < .01$

mediated interference effect would be generated by the taboo words, and that this effect would persist long enough to influence recognition time for the neutral words, we predicted that the duration thresholds of the task words following *critical* pre-task words would be higher than the thresholds of those following *neutral* pre-task words. To test this prediction, we first computed the total number of exposures required for each observer to correctly report the four task words in the *critical-neutral* pairs and in the *neutral-neutral* pairs.[1] A difference score between these two values was determined for each observer. These results are presented in Table 2. As may be noted in the table, the group trend was in the predicted direction. An obtained t of 2.87 computed from the data is significant at the .01 confidence level and justifies rejection of the null hypothesis of no difference between recognition thresholds for task words in the two groups. The findings may be interpreted as supporting beyond reasonable doubt the hypothesis that perceptual interference, or defense, may generalize to neutral stimulus words when these are temporally contiguous with affectively-toned words.

Although the observers demonstrated higher thresholds for the task words in the "critical" pairs than they did for those in the "control" pairs, they volunteered approximately the same proportion of hypotheses in both cases. The number of hypotheses, or perceptual "guesses," that an observer made to each stimulus word was divided by the total number of exposures required for recognition of that word. A distribution of differences between per cent hypotheses per exposure was thus obtained for the task words in both the "critical" and "control" pairs. The mean per cent difference did not deviate significantly from zero.

[1] This procedure is equivalent to computing the mean threshold of recognition of each observer for the two sets of task words and eliminates decimals from the data.

Table 3 *Contingency Table Showing Tabulation of Hypotheses According to their Structural Resemblance to the Pretask or Task Words**

	Neutral Pretask	Critical Pretask	
Resembled Pretask	11(5.41)	4(9.59)	15
Resembled Task	108(111.37)	201(197.63)	309
Combination	5(3.96)	6(7.04)	11
Neither	18(21.26)	41(37.73)	59
Total	142	252	394
Chi square = 10.40	$p < .02$		

* The columns in the table represent the number of hypotheses made when the pretask words were neutral or critical (taboo). The rows represent the coding categories. Theoretical frequencies are in parentheses.

Nature of Hypothesis Formation. An attempt was made to break down the perceptual hypotheses of the observers into meaningful categories. It seemed apparent that most of the "guesses" made by the subjects during the prerecognition period could be coded according to whether they exhibited structural similarities to: (a) the *pre-task* word, (b) the *task* word, (c) a *combination* of the two, or (d) *neither* the pre-task nor the task word. The resulting breakdown of hypotheses for the group of observers is shown in Table 3. When the task word followed presentation of a neutral pre-task word, there was a slightly greater tendency on the part of the observers to make hypotheses resembling the pre-task word than the task word followed a taboo word. Conversely, there was a somewhat greater tendency for hypotheses based on task words following critical words to resemble the task word itself than when the task word followed a neutral word. Proportionately more *combination* hypotheses were made to task words following neutral pre-task words, and relatively more hypotheses bearing a structural resemblance to *neither* the pre-task nor the task words occurred when the former were emotionally toned.

Although chi square computed from Table 3 is large enough to reach statistical significance, it must be regarded as highly suspect inasmuch as the observed trends were caused by the prerecognition behavior of only six of the observers. The same tendencies with respect to hypothesis formation just reported, however, were noted in a similar experiment in our laboratories by Talantis (1948). Other investigations have also shown that the nature of prerecognition hypotheses relates meaningfully to the stimulus word (McGinnies, 1949; Postman, Bruner, and McGinnies, 1948). The present findings, therefore, are included as suggestive of the manner in which the cues for making perceptual hypotheses to an as-yet-unrecognized neutral word are more frequently based upon the structure of that word when it is preceded by a taboo word than when it is preceded by another neutral word. In the latter case, structural elements of the pre-task word are more likely to influence hypothesis formation.

Theoretical Implications. By indirection, our results support the assumption that the threshold of perceptual recognition, not merely the threshold of veridical report, is subject to elevation by stimuli which customarily elicit reactions of embarrassment or anxiety. There is little reason to suspect that deliberate delay in reporting a neutral stimulus word should result from prior viewing by the observer of an emotionally-toned word. We shall assume, therefore, that the elevated thresholds of report of the observers for the task words following taboo words reflect a genuine elevation in their recognition thresholds to these words. Why should this "defensive" reaction generalize from taboo words to subsequent stimuli which are not of a threatening character?

To answer this question, we must first interpret the concept of perceptual defense in more precise terms. In a previous paper, McGinnies and Bowles (1949) have expressed a preference for reenforcement theory as a framework within which the data from perceptual experiments might be discussed. Other investigators have shown a similar leaning (Lambert, Solomon, and Watson, 1949; Proshansky and Murphy, 1942; Schafer and Murphy, 1943). It may be useful, then, to state the adaptive significance of perceptual defense in reenforcement terms. Such an interpretation is not difficult. Without diverging at this point into a discussion of the acquisition of language habits, we may make the limited assumption that verbal responses involving taboo symbols have, for most individuals, been punished by parents and parent-surrogates. The taboo words thus become *secondary negative reenforcing agents.* When operating as stimuli, they signal a state of approaching punishment and consequently become cues for eliciting the anxiety associated with actual punishment. That the threshold for anxiety may be lower than the threshold of recognition of the taboo word has been demonstrated by the elevated magnitude of galvanic skin responses prior to correct perception of taboo symbols (McGinnies, 1949). Certain autonomic cues apparently are adequate to initiate perceptual avoidance of the stimulus. The avoidance is accomplished by distortion of the stimulus(as evidence by hypothesis formation) or by an elevation of the recognition threshold—or by both.[2]

The paradox involved in explaining avoidance behavior by means of reenforcement principles has been examined by Mowrer and Lamoreaux (1942). They resolve the problem by assuming that the avoidance response, by preventing occurrence of the punishing stimulus, reduces anxiety and is thereby reenforced. This explanation finds ready application to the phenomenon of perceptual defense, or perceptual avoidance as it might have been termed. A perceptual response involving either distortion of a noxious stimulus or vague awareness of that stimulus serves to delay recognition and thus reduce the anxiety aroused by a potentially threatening situation.

When, as in the present experiment, the observer is confronted suddenly with a taboo word at a duration sufficient for accurate recognition, he is unable to avoid perceiving it correctly. The defensive mechanisms, which ordinarily would operate below the report threshold, are overridden. Consequently, the observer reacts with a complex cognitive and autonomic pattern that, for economy of description, may be termed "anxiety" or embarrassment." The emotional reactions thus aroused serve as additional sources of stimulation to the observer at the succeeding moment when he is confronted with a neutral word exposed at a duration below his threshold of accurate perception. So the observer is responding not only to the neutral task word, but also to a pattern of stimulation aroused by the taboo word that signifies a "state-of-affairs-to-be-avoided." The autonomic and associative responses initiated by the emotionally-toned word trip off a pattern of perceptual avoidance ordinarily accompanying such reactions. This "set" for avoidance then persists long enough to interfere with recognition of the immediately following neutral word which, by itself, has no characteristics that would initiate defensive behavior.[3]

Those who would search the present discussion for implications in the field of social behavior may

[2] Of course, the prevalence of socially taboo expressions in the verbal behavior of many conversing adult males raises the possibility that avoidance behavior with respect to such responses operates only under conditions of social restraint. Given an appropriate stimulus context, that of isolation, or of an all-male "bull session," such responses are readily evoked. Obviously, the situational context must be considered in designating the probability of evoking taboo verbal response patterns.

[3] The authors are indebted to Dr. Paul Siegel for critical reading of this discussion and for many suggestions that have influenced its final form.

well discover analogies to our experimental situation in the argumentative and persuasive endeavors of individuals. An emotionally aroused person may be literally unable to perceive meanings in situations that under less stressful circumstances would be well above his threshold of awareness. An *ad hominum* argument, for example, may induce in a listener emotional reactions the effects of which carry over to influence adversely his perception of otherwise neutral aspects of an issue. Similarly, an individual attempting to learn under stress may suffer from an elevated threshold of recognition for aspects of a problem that have no intrinsic capacity for arousing avoidance or resistance. Description of such commonplace events as these should be possible in less discursive fashion than is frequently resorted to by social theorists. A reduction of complex behavioral adjustments to concepts capable of operational definition should do much to reduce the multiplicity of theoretical constructs currently employed to explain such behavior. The present discussion has attempted to indicate how such a reduction might be attempted by applying reenforcement principles to a laboratory perceptual situation that finds counterparts in everyday experience.

Summary

The recognition thresholds of twenty male undergraduates were determined for eight five-letter words, approximately equal in frequency of occurrence and of apparently neutral connotation. Four of these task words were always presented to the observer following full exposure of a "taboo" word. The remaining four were always preceded by exposure of a neutral word. Duration thresholds of the observers for the task words following critical, or taboo, words were significantly higher than their thresholds for task words following neutral words. An attempt has been made to interpret these findings in terms of reenforcement of an avoidance reaction that has generalized from the taboo to the neutral stimuli.

References

Howes, D. H., and Solomon, R. L. A note on McGinnies' "Emotionality and perceptual defense." *Psychological Review*, 1950, *57*, 229–234.

Lambert, W. W., Solomon, R. L., and Watson, P. D. Reenforcement and extinction as factors in size estimation. *Journal of Experimental Psychology*, 1949, *39*, 637–641.

McGinnies, E. Emotionality and perceptual defense. *Psychological Review*, 1949, *56*, 244–251.

McGinnies, E. Discussion of Howes and Solomon's "A note on McGinnies' 'Emotionality and perceptual defense.'" *Psychological Review*, 1950, *57*, 235–240.

McGinnies, E., and Bowles, W. Personal values as determinants of perceptual fixation. *Journal of Personality*, 1949, *18*, 224–235.

Mowrer, O. H., and Lamoreaux, R. R. Avoidance conditioning and signal duration: A study of secondary motivation and reward. *Psychological Monographs*, 1942, *54*, Whole No. 247.

Postman, L., Bruner, J. S., and McGinnies, E. Personal values as selective factors in perception. *Journal of Abnormal and Social Psychology*, 1948, *43*, 142–154.

Proshansky, H., and Murphy, G. The effects of reward and punishment on perception. *Journal of Psychology*, 1942, *13*, 295–305.

Schafer, R., and Murphy, G. The role of autism in a visual figure-ground relationship. *Journal of Experimental Psychology*, 1943, *32*, 335–342.

Talantis, Billie S. Perceptual interference induced through spatial and temporal association of verbal stimuli. Unpublished Master's thesis, University of Alabama, 1948.

Thorndike, E. L., and Lorge, I. *The teacher's word book of 30,000 words*. New York: Teachers College, Columbia, University, 1944.

The second experiment in this section, conducted fifteen years after McGinnies and Sherman's experiment, replicated and extended that study. Three British investigators, *Forrest, Gordon, and Taylor,* found, as McGinnies and Sherman had, that prior exposure of a taboo word will, indeed, delay recognition of a neutral word presented immediately afterward. These researchers, however, questioned whether the result should be interpreted in terms of a generalization of perceptual defense. Although they agree that the elevated recognition thresholds could not be explained by response probability or response suppression, they suggested still another interpretation. They hypothesized that presenting the taboo words just before the task (neutral) words leads to an interruption of "set," which interferes with recognition of the second, or task word.

Forrest, Gordon, and Taylor were able to show that not only taboo words but also nonsense words interfered with the report of neutral words that followed. They also were able to eliminate the inhibitory effect of taboo words by advising the subjects what kinds of words they were about to see. This result was not compatible with the "generalization of avoidance behavior" hypothesis, because the nonsense words were as effective as taboo words and because practicing the taboo words eliminated the inhibitory effect. These investigators do not disallow the possibility that a spread of avoidance may operate in perceptual situations where the subjects have not been given practice in seeing taboo words, and that such an effect may occur over and above the interference generated by a change in set. However, they believe that an interpretation in terms of set is more parsimonious.

37 *Generalization of Perceptual Defense: An Interpretation in Terms of Set*[1]

DEREK FORREST
NICOLA GORDON
ANN TAYLOR

McGinnies and Sherman (1952) performed an experiment which appeared to demonstrate the generalization of the perceptual defense effect. Their experiment entailed the initial presentation of taboo and neutral words for periods of 2 seconds. Each of these "pretask" words was followed by the rapid exposure of a "task" word, always of neutral connotation, which the subject attempted to recognize. They found that the subjects took longer to recognize those neutral words that followed taboo words than those that followed neutral words. Thus, perceptual defense was said to have "generalized," that is, the avoidance reaction triggered off by a taboo word persisted long enough to interfere with the recognition of the neutral word which immediately followed.

Although criticism of this explanation appeared soon after (Postman, Bronson, and Gropper, 1953) on the grounds that it was premature to hypothesize the generalization of an effect before that effect had been definitely demonstrated, no alternative explanation was offered, and further research appeared to lend support to McGinnies and Sherman's position. Walters, Banks, and Ryder (1959) obtained similar results when the pretask words were presented three times in succession and subliminally. Although they request replication of their experiment in view of an uncertainty in their timing procedure, this deficiency does not seem likely to be a potent source of error, and their results can be taken to support the findings of McGinnies and Sherman.

In recent years the whole concept of perceptual defense has been seriously challenged by those investigators who claim that differential threshold effects should be attributed not to a directly perceptual process but to the response bias of the observer (e.g., Ericksen and Browne, 1956; Goldiamond, 1958). In experiments on the generalization of perceptual defense the familiarity and emotional tone of the task words are rigidly controlled, only the pretask words being varied. Thus, the data cannot be reinterpreted in terms of response suppression or response probability, and it would seem that the original conception of perceptual defense as an avoidance response, autonomic in nature and capable of persistence over time, must be retained.

It was the purpose of the present series of experiments to test a third possible explanation: namely, that the appearance of taboo words in a series of neutral words led to an interruption of "set" and that this interruption in turn was responsible for the difficulty experienced in recognizing the subsequent task words. We considered the interruption of set brought about by the introduction of dissimilar material to be crucial to the effect, rather than the emotional nature of that material. Thus, we supposed that the same effect would be produced by the introduction of dissimilar material which was not taboo in nature.

First, an attempt was made to replicate McGinnies and Sherman's results in another laboratory.

From the *Journal of Personality and Social Psychology,* 1965, 2, 137–141.

Experiment I

Method

Subjects. Twenty undergraduate women volunteered for Experiment I. Although some were first-year students of psychology, none was aware of the purpose of the experiment.

Apparatus. The words used by McGinnies and Sherman served as material. Twenty-two words in all were used, 18 neutral and 4 taboo words: neutral —BRAND, CABLE, FLUSH, FROCK, GLIDE, GRIND, HOUND, LEGAL, LUCKY, OUTER, PHONE, QUEST, RANCH, RIDER, SCENT, SPRAY, TOWEL, WEAVE; taboo—BITCH, PENIS, RAPED, WHORE.

The neutral words had been equated by McGinnies and Sherman for frequency of usage on the Thorndike-Lorge (1944) word count (between 18 and 28 per million).

The words were printed singly on slides and projected onto a screen, where they appeared in block capitals 2 inches high. The subject sat at a distance of 5 feet from the screen which was illuminated at all times at an intensity of 1 footcandle when the projectors were off and 3 footcandles when a pretask word was being shown.

Two Liesegang projectors were used, each fitted with a timing device which enabled the experimenter to present the pretask word via one projector for a period of 2 seconds; immediately this shutter closed, a shutter on the other projector was simultaneously opened to expose the task word for .75 second. The brightness of the latter projector could be altered by means of a Variac.

Procedure. Three pairs of words were chosen at random for each subject from the neutral series and used to determine the subject's approximate recognition threshold. The shutter speed was held constant at .75 second and the brightness adjusted to a point at which the subject was just able to identify the words.

Four of the remaining 12 neutral words were chosen at random for each subject and with the 4 taboo words made up the pretask series. The remaining 8 neutral words served as task words and were paired with the pretask words at random. The order of presentation of the 8 pairs was again determined randomly for each subject.

For the experiment proper the task words were initially presented at a Variac setting 8 volts lower than the threshold value, an increase of 2 volts occurring on each trial until the words were correctly recognized.

Certain differences between our procedure and that of McGinnies and Sherman should be noted. During a series of pilot trials in which the apparatus was tested, it became apparent that an after-image of the pretask word frequently interfered with the attempt to recognize the task word. In order to overcome this the task word was projected 2 inches above the position where the pretask word had occurred. A fixation point was provided here.

Second, thresholds were estimated by alterations in voltage, and therefore indeterminately in brightness, and not in exposure time. Both these changes from McGinnies and Sherman's procedure were necessitated by the unavailability of a mirror tachistoscope.

A third change was introduced after observations of the pilot subjects had convinced us that they were not bothering to read the pretask words at all but were concentrating solely on the task words. These subjects were frequently unable to report the pretask word at the end of a trial. We attempted to overcome this difficulty by first presenting the pretask word alone and asking the subject to read it silently to herself. It was then presented again 2 seconds later while the subject watched the fixation point where the task word would appear. This double presentation of the pretask word occurred on each trial of the experiment.

Instructions to the subject were as follows:

> When I say "Ready" a word will appear in the center of the screen here for a long enough period for you to recognize it easily. I want you to read it silently to yourself; there is no need to read it aloud. It will then disappear and soon afterwards reappear again on the signal "Ready." This time, as soon as it disappears, another word will flash on here (indicating the fixation point) and remain only for a very brief second. I want you to try and identify this second word and tell me what you see. Is that clear? Have you any questions? We will begin with one or two practice trials to show you what happens.

Table 1 *Exposures Required to Recognize Task Words in the Three Experiments*

	Following Neutral Pretask Word M	Following Taboo (or Nonsense) Pretask Word M	$SE_{diff.}$	t
Experiment I	19.55	23.55	1.34	2.99**
Experiment II	18.83	21.39	0.95	2.68*
Experiment III	19.4	19.3	0.78	0.19

* $p < .05$.
** $p < .01$.

Results

Table 1 gives the mean number of exposures required to report correctly the task words. It can be seen that more trials were required to report words that followed taboo pretask words. A t test of the difference gives a t value of 2.99, $p < .01$. This statistical procedure is similar to that employed by McGinnies and Sherman, who also used 20 subjects, and in spite of the differences between our procedure and theirs the main finding is the same. Thus, the effect appears to be a robust one, not unduly dependent on procedural niceties.

Having demonstrated the phenomenon with our technique, we proceeded in a second experiment to explore the effects produced by the use of nonsense instead of taboo pretask material.

Experiment II

Method

Subjects. Eighteen women drawn from the same population served as subjects.

Apparatus. The material used was similar to that of Experiment I except that the four taboo words were replaced by four 5-letter nonsense words. These were obtained by choosing at random eight nonsense syllables with an associative value of less than 15% from the Trapp and Kausler (1959) lists. The nonsense syllables were then combined in pairs by dropping the first letter of one syllable and adding the remainder as a suffix to another. By this procedure the following four words were obtained: BIWUJ, MEFIV, WOJUB, ZAHIV.

Procedure. Approximate thresholds were determined in a manner exactly similar to that of Experiment I. In the presentation proper the pretask items consisted of four neutral words and four nonsense words, the task words all being neutral. The pairing was done at random as before. Instructions were identical.

Results and Discussion

Table 1 shows the mean number of trials required to identify the task words in Experiment II. More trials were needed to recognize words that followed nonsense words than words following neutral words. A t test of the difference gives a t value of 2.68 and a $p < .05$.

The results of this experiment are very similar to those of the previous experiment in which taboo material was used. Yet in the present case the difficulty in recognition was consequent on the pretrial exposure of a nonsense word. It does not seem feasible to ascribe this raised threshold to the generalization of an avoidance response. On the other hand, it is not all clear that it can be ascribed to an interruption of the observer's set as intimated earlier. If a set to see neutral words was disrupted by the occurrence of a nonneutral word, whether of the taboo or nonsense variety, it might be expected that the first example of the contraset material would have a greater disrupting effect than later occurrences (Bitterman and Kniffin, 1953; Postman and Leytham, 1951). Accordingly we examined the number of exposures required to recognize each of the critical words (i.e., those following a nonsense pretask word) in their order of presentation, but found no significant differences and no evidence of a trend. It might be argued that as only 4 of the 22 words were contraset the subject had not time to become accustomed to them, but it cannot be confidently maintained that an explanation in such terms is entirely satisfactory. A more direct attack on the set hypothesis was provided by the third experiment in which the subjects were warned beforehand and given practice with the contraset material.

Experiment III

Method

Subjects. Twenty subjects were employed; they were undergraduate women taken from the same population.

Apparatus. The same material used in Experiment I was utilized. Six additional words were used in the practice trials when the subject's approximate threshold was determined. Three of these words were neutral—BASIN, DWARF, LEMON; three were taboo—BELLY, PUBIC, SEMEN. The neutral words all occur in the Thorndike-Lorge word count between 25 and 27 per million, while of the taboo words belly only is included, at 10 per million.

Procedure. In two respects the procedure differed from that of the earlier experiments. The practice trials now consisted of six pairs of words. Three of the pretask words in these trials were neutral and three taboo, while in all cases the task words were neutral. Each subject thus had experience of taboo words as pretask material.

Second, additional instructions were given to the

subject after the practice trials. She was told to expect during the remainder of the experiment words of the same kind as those she had just seen.

Results

From Table 1 it can be seen that words following taboo pretask words were not appreciably more difficult to recognize than those following neutral pretask words; a *t* test of the difference gives an insignificant value of .19. Repetition of Experiment I with the addition of three taboo words in the practice trials and with additional instructions has produced no evidence for the generalization of defense.

It can also be seen from Table 1 that the thresholds following the exposure of neutral pretask words are very similar in the three experiments. This finding indicates that the samples of subjects did not differ in their perceptual ability and that our assumption of their comparability is justified.

Discussion

There appear to be two possible explanations of the generalization effect reported by McGinnies and Sherman and confirmed here in Experiment I: either it was due to the persistence (generalization in time) of an autonomic avoidance reaction to threatening stimuli, or it represented the disruption of a set to perceive neutral rather than taboo material. In Experiment II we demonstrated that the phenomenon still occurs, and with equal magnitude, in a situation where the explanation in terms of an avoidance reaction is inappropriate and the alternative explanation applies. Finally, Experiment III showed that under conditions to which the former explanation would be appropriate and an explanation in terms of set inappropriate, the phenomenon does not occur. Thus, our data indicate that an adequate explanation of the generalization effect can be made in terms of set. The findings of Walters et al. (1959) present no additional difficulties for this explanation since there is no reason to suppose, and indeed good reason to deny, that a set must be consciously established in order to be effective (Luchins, 1942).

The exact nature of the set which is disrupted remains unclear. It may be, as Freeman (1954) and others have claimed, that in the experimental situation naive subjects are generally set to perceive neutral rather than taboo words. However, the sets commonly demonstrated in the laboratory are highly specific and there are difficulties in assuming that a class of stimuli as broad as that comprising neutral words could be thus benefited. Alternatively it might be argued that subjects in this situation are set to perceive a task word which is similar in kind to the pretask word: thus, if the pretask word is neutral, or meaningful, subjects expect a neutral, or meaningful, task word. Such an effect would perhaps be analogous to the finding of Cofer and Shepp (1957) that visual recognition of a stimulus word is facilitated by prior, suprathreshold presentation of a synonymous word. A set of this type may be either a relatively stable characteristic of the subject's expectation in an appropriate situation, or, more simply, it may have been induced by the uniform pairing of the practice words. The results of Experiment III do not invalidate either of these possibilities since the practice trials included taboo pretask words paired with neutral task words. Thus, the set to perceive a task word similar in nature to its pretask companion would not arise, or if such a set were held to be already present it would immediately be invalidated. Any decisive statement of the nature of the set involved must therefore await further evidence.

It is possible that the effect observed in Experiment II, although identical with that observed in Experiment I, has a different cause: the occurrence of raised thresholds following nonsense words might represent the disruption of set, while the raised thresholds following taboo words might represent the operation of perceptual defense. Such a viewpoint is tenable but lacks the advantage of parsimony. It can also be argued that perceptual defense cannot be expected to occur in Experiment III, as when taboo words are made socially acceptable through their presentation in practice trials with encouragement to report them they become no longer taboo and a defensive reaction becomes no longer necessary.

Thus, we do not claim from the present series of experiments to have demonstrated beyond controversy that the apparent generalization of perceptual defense is a phenomenon of set. But it is now apparent that the evidence supplied by McGinnies and Sherman is capable of explanation in other terms and therefore does not, through lack of alternatives, enforce acceptance of the hypothesis of a conditioned avoidance response which through its persistence in time renders more difficult the subsequent recognition of neutral material.

References

Bitterman, M. E., and Kniffin, C. W. Manifest anxiety and "perceptual defense." *Journal of Abnormal and Social Psychology*, 1953, *48*, 248–252.

Cofer, C. N., and Shepp, B. E. Verbal context and perceptual recognition time. *Perceptual and Motor Skill*, 1957, *7*, 215–218.

ERIKSEN, C. W., and BROWNE, C. T. An experimental and theoretical analysis of perceptual defense. *Journal of Abnormal and Social Psychology,* 1956, *52,* 224–230.

FREEMAN, J. T. Set or perceptual defense? *Journal of Experimental Psychology,* 1954, *48,* 283–288.

GOLDIAMOND, I. Indicators of perception: I. Subliminal perception, subception, unconscious perception: An analysis in terms of psychophysical indicator methodology. *Psychological Bulletin,* 1958, *55,* 373–411.

LUCHINS, A. S. Mechanization in problem solving: The effect of *Einstellung. Psychological Monographs,* 1942, *54* (6, Whole No. 248).

MCGINNIES, E., and SHERMAN, H. Generalization of perceptual defense. *Journal of Abnormal and Social Psychology,* 1952, *47,* 81–85.

POSTMAN, L., BRONSON, W. C., and GROPPER, G. L. Is there a mechanism of perceptual defense? *Journal of Abnormal and Social Psychology,* 1953, *48,* 215–224.

POSTMAN, L., and LEYTHAM, G. Perceptual selectivity and ambivalence of stimuli. *Journal of Personality,* 1951, *19,* 390–405.

THORNDIKE, E. L., and LORGE, I. *The teacher's word book of 30,000 words.* New York: Teachers College, Columbia University, Bureau of Publications, 1944.

TRAPP, E. P., and KAUSLER, D. H. A revision of Hull's table of associative values for 320 selected nonsense-syllables. *American Journal of Psychology,* 1959, *72,* 423–428.

WALTERS, R. H., BANKS, R. K., and RYDER, R. R. A test of the perceptual defense hypothesis. *Journal of Personality,* 1959, *27,* 47–55.

C Interpersonal Judgment

The final problem to which we turn in this chapter is that of judgments made by individuals about each other. This area of research, sometimes referred to as person perception, has generated relatively little in the way of a comprehensive theory. But a number of empirical generalizations have found support, among them the fact that persons tend to use the same terms to describe persons whom they like as they use to describe themselves. This may, of course, simply reflect the fact that individuals associate with those whom they perceive as similar to themselves. Although a host of other variables operate to determine the nature of interpersonal judgments, the critical underlying factor is probably the individual's history of reinforcement in situations where other persons have either prompted or reinforced his behaviors. The two articles in this section describe techniques for setting up models of these reinforcement histories in the laboratory.

James and Lott devised a play situation in which children were given nickels as reinforcers for playing a game. Through the use of sociometric questionnaires, they determined whether interpersonal preferences within three-member groups were related to the amount of money (reinforcement) the children had received in their particular groups. The results indicated that sociometric choice, or liking, for other children was a function of the amount of reward that the recipient had experienced in their presence. Generalization from these results to other situations would suggest that how much one likes a person depends upon how much that person has been associated with positive reinforcers.

38 Reward Frequency and the Formation of Positive Attitudes Toward Group Members[1]

GALE JAMES
ALBERT J. LOTT

Problem

In the second edition of *Group Dynamics* (1960), Cartwright and Zander have again pointed out, as they did in 1953, that there is "very little systematic knowledge about the conditions which heighten cohesiveness" (p. 79). The present experiment focuses directly on this problem. It was designed to replicate, and extend, an investigation by Lott and Lott (1960) in which it was found that members of three-person groups who were rewarded in the presence of other group members tended to develop positive attitudes toward these members more than did those who were not rewarded. This finding is fundamental to a formulation of group cohesiveness in which the concept is defined as that *group property which is inferred from the number and strength of mutual positive attitudes among group members,* and in which the development and consequences of such attitudes are predicted on the basis of learning-theory principles (Lott, 1961). The hypothesis that positive attitudes toward group members will result from being rewarded in their presence is based on the principle of secondary reinforcement as well as on assumptions outlined in the earlier papers mentioned above.

While, in the first experiment, only reward and nonreward were manipulated, the present study investigates the effect of varying reward frequency. Specifically, it is predicted that, in a small group situation, individuals whose performance on a task is rewarded each time they perform it in the presence of other group members will be more likely to develop positive attitudes toward them than will persons who are rewarded a fewer number of times, and that these latter individuals will be more likely to develop positive attitudes toward the other members than will those who receive no rewards at all.

As in the previous investigation, positive attitudes were inferred from choices made on a sociometric test outside of, and subsequent to, the experimental situation. In addition, the present study required a subject to choose between one person whom he had chosen on an earlier sociometric test and another who had been a member of his experimental group.

Method

Sixty children from Linlee Elementary School in Lexington, Kentucky, served as subjects (*Ss*): 18 from Grade 3; 24 from Grade 4; and 18 from Grade 5.

The *Ss* were divided into 20 three-member groups, following the administration of two sociometric tests which were given by the regular classroom teacher, on two consecutive days, several days before the actual experimental situation. Each test required S to choose four classmates with whom he would like to participate in a hypothetical space venture, and to name two whom he would prefer not to take part. On the basis of the children's responses, the groups were formed so that each was made up of children who had *not chosen each other* and had *not rejected each other* on either of the tests: that is, children who had relatively "neutral" feelings toward one another. Some of the groups were same-sex and some were mixed-sex, but all were composed of members of the same class.

To produce a situation in which frequency of reward could be manipulated, every group played a board game called "Rocket Ship," which was designed for, and utilized in, the previous study. The object of the game is to land cardboard rocket ships on planetary objectives, each of which is reached by separate paths containing "danger zones" at which a choice must be made between a "safe" and a "dangerous" subpath. A group tried for three objectives in the morning and three more in the afternoon. In the present investigation a child received one nickel for every planet he reached. Twenty Ss received six nickels, 20 received three, and 20 received zero. The determination of reward condition for each S was predetermined on a random basis.

Groups differed in the pattern of reward administered to their members. There were 10 such patterns, one of which was randomly assigned before the experiment to two groups. The patterns were as fol-

[1] This paper is based upon the first author's thesis for the Master of Arts degree at the University of Kentucky. The authors are grateful to Miss Susan Gabby, Principal of Linlee School in Lexington, Kentucky, for providing subjects and facilities for the investigation.

lows: 6–6–6 (that is, each of the group members received six nickels); 3–3–3; 0–0–0; 6–6–3; 3–3–6; 6–6–0; 3–3–0; 0–0–6; 0–0–3; 6–3–0.

Shortly before the close of the school day, approximately one hour after the last group played the game, the classroom teacher administered Sociometric Test III, which asked Ss to list four children they would invite for a trip to a nearby star, and two children they would rather not have go.

Following collection of the responses, the teacher administered a Ranks Test. She handed each child a slip of paper containing the name of a child with whom he had played the game (chosen randomly from the two group members other than himself), and also the name of the child he had chosen as number 1 on Sociometric Test I. The children were then told:

> Pretend that you may go on a private vacation to a star with only one person. You may choose just one of these children to go and no one else. Which one would you choose first? Put number 1 beside his (her) name and number 2 beside your second choice.

Results and Discussion

The hypothesis was tested by comparing the number of subjects in the three different reward categories who chose one or more play group members on Sociometric Test III with the number who chose only other classmates: i.e., who chose no one from his play group. These results are presented in Table 1.

A chi-square analysis revealed a significant difference among the basic reward treatments at the .02 level of confidence ($\chi^2 = 9.04$). Additional chi squares (using Yates' correction) indicated that there were significant differences between Ss receiving six nickels and those receiving either three or so nickels. The chi-square values were 5.38 and 3.84, respectively, and were significant at the .025 and .05 levels. No reliable difference was found between the choices made by Ss receiving three nickels and those receiving none.

There were only two instances of a play group member being rejected on Sociometric III; in both cases the rejection was made by zero reward Ss.

Table 1 *Choices Made by Subjects on Sociometric Test III*

Subjects	Number Choosing at Least One Play-Group Member	Number Choosing No Play-Group Member	*N*
6 rewards	11	9	20
3 rewards	3	17	20
0 rewards	4	16	20
Total	18	42	60

Table 2 *First Choices Made by Subjects on the Ranks Test*

Subjects	Play-Group Member Ranked First	"Friend" Ranked First	*N*
6 rewards	8	12	20
3 rewards	1	19	20
0 rewards	2	18	20
Total	11	49	60

The data yielded by the Ranks Test permitted another comparison among the three reward conditions. In Table 2 is shown the number of Ss in each condition who ranked play-group members first, over a nonmember "friend" (first sociometric choice on Test I), after the game had been played. A chi-square analysis revealed a significant overall relationship between S's reward condition and his choice of play-group members ($\chi^2 = 9.51$, $p = .01$). The choices of Ss rewarded with six nickels differed reliably from those of Ss rewarded with three nickels ($\chi^2 = 5.16$, $p = .025$), but again no difference was found between Ss who were rewarded three times and those who were not rewarded at all. The difference in choices between Ss rewarded six times and those not rewarded at all was in the predicted direction, but just short of the acceptable significance level ($\chi^2 = 3.33$; $p = .10$).

That three- and zero-reward conditions did not produce reliably different consequences indicates that three rewards were insufficient to strengthen a new response (positive attitudes toward other group members) to the degree required by our technique for measuring it. This suggests that a more fruitful test of the predicted positive relationship between frequency of reward experienced in the presence of group members and the probability of developing positive attitudes toward these members must provide individuals with the opportunity for receiving different, but sizable, numbers of rewards, as we assume is the case within naturally existing groups with a duration history of weeks, months, or years, instead of minutes.

The lack of difference in effect between the three- and zero-reward conditions may, possibly, be explained in still another way. The three-reward condition may be interpreted as a partial reinforcement situation (and the six-reward condition as 100 per cent reinforcement), and it is known (Jenkins and Stanley, 1950; Lewis, 1960) that under conditions of partial reinforcement the acquisition of a response is particularly slow during the early trials in a series.

This study extends the scope of the original findings of Lott and Lott (1960) since similar results have been obtained under different conditions: a choice had to be made here between a play-group member and an out-group friend; money rewards instead of small toys were used; and children with negative feelings toward one another (i.e., those listed on the preexperimental sociometric test as "unwanted") were eliminated from the play groups.

Summary

Three-member groups of children played a game in which some members were rewarded with six nickels, others with three nickels, and others with zero nickels. On a sociometric test and a ranking test, outside of the game situation, significantly more Ss in the six-reward condition chose their fellow group members than did those receiving either three or zero rewards. There were no differences in the preferences of the three-reward condition and the zero-reward condition. This latter finding was discussed in terms of partial reinforcement.

The results offer additional support for an S-R approach to group cohesiveness, from which predictions were derived.

References

CARTWRIGHT, D., and ZANDER, A. *Group dynamics* (2nd ed.). Evanston, Ill.: Row, Peterson, 1960.

JENKINS, W., and STANLEY, J. Partial reinforcement: A review and critique. *Psychological Bulletin,* 1950, *47,* 193–234.

LEWIS, D. Partial reinforcement: A selective review of the literature since 1950. *Psychological Bulletin,* 1960, *57,* 1–28.

LOTT, B. E. Group cohesiveness: A learning phenomenon. *Journal of Social Psychology,* 1961, *55,* 275–286.

LOTT, B. E., and LOTT, A. The formation of positive attitudes toward group members. *Journal of Abnormal and Social Psychology,* 1960, *61,* 297–300.

We suggested earlier that persons holding similar or compatible attitudes tend to be attracted to each other. This hypothesis has been put to experimental test by *Byrne and Nelson,* who define positive reinforcement in this instance as similarity of attitude. They manipulated this type of reinforcement by giving their subjects the answers to an attitude questionnaire purportedly filled out by an anonymous stranger. The subject's task was to evaluate the stranger with respect to several personality variables and to indicate how strongly he felt attracted to him.

They manipulated the scores on the attitude scale to vary both the number and the proportion of attitudes presumably held in common by the subject and the stranger. For example, they might have agreed on 8 items and disagreed on 16, an agreement proportion of .33. The experimenters wanted to know whether the subjects' attraction to the stranger depended upon the absolute number of agreements or upon the proportion. That is, 16 agreements out of 32 is more than 8 out of 16, but the proportion of agreement is the same. Their results indicated that attraction was a linear function of the proportion rather than the number of positively reinforcing attitudes attributed to a stranger.

The reader might wish to glance ahead to the study by Golightly and Byrne, in Chapter 10, where evidence is presented to show that attitude statements can function as reinforcers in a visual discrimination task. It is not surprising to find that they can also act as reinforcers in a situation requiring judgments about another person.

39

Attraction as a Linear Function of Proportion of Positive Reinforcements[1]

DONN BYRNE
DON NELSON

It is a well-established finding that the attraction of a subject toward a stranger is a function of the similarity or dissimilarity of the latter's attitudes and values to those of the subject. When similarity is manipulated experimentally, attraction is found to increase as the similarity of the stranger increases (Byrne, 1961a; Jones and Daugherty, 1959; Schachter, 1951; Smith, 1957). In order to proceed beyond these empirical findings to build a genuine theory of attraction, it would be helpful to obtain a clearer identification of the stimulus which evokes differential attraction responses and a more precise specification of the relationship between this stimulus and attraction.

In a series of papers, Newcomb (1953, 1956, 1959, 1961) has dealt with the antecedents of interpersonal relationships. Along with other principles he has proposed that attraction between individuals is a function of the extent to which reciprocal rewards are present in their interaction. As an extension of this conceptualization, it was further suggested (Byrne, 1961a, 1962) that attraction toward a person is determined by the number of rewards relative to the number of punishments received from him. Various types of reward and punishment have been utilized experimentally, but the major portion of attraction research has utilized similarity and dissimilarity of attitudes, opinions, beliefs, and values as the stimulus. The rationale is that the learned drive to be logical and to interpret incoming information correctly is reinforced by consensual validation and frustrated by consensual invalidation (Dollard and Miller, 1950; Festinger, 1950, 1954; Newcomb, 1953, 1956, 1959, 1961).

Investigations of the effects of varying proportions of similar and dissimilar attitudes have, unfortunately, involved a confounding of the number of positive reinforcements with the proportion of positive reinforcements. For example, Byrne (1962) varied seven items of similarity-dissimilarity in the eight possible combinations ranging from 7–0 to 0–7. The highly significant effects on attraction toward the stranger to whom the attitudes were attributed could have been a function of either the proportion or the number of similar attitudes. The present investigation is designed to test the proposition that attraction toward a stranger is a positive function of the proportion of positive reinforcements received from that stranger.

Procedure

Utilizing attitude similarity-dissimilarity, the design permits the comparison of the effects of number of positive reinforcements (16, 8, and 4) with the effects of proportion of positive reinforcements (1.00, .67, .50, and .33) on attraction in a 4 × 3 factorial design as shown in Table 1. Each cell contained 14 subjects, divided approximately evenly with respect to sex. Subjects were asked to read an attitude scale supposedly filled out by another student of their same sex and then make several judgments about him or her including the ratings that constitute the measure of attraction.

The subjects consisted of 168 students enrolled in the introductory psychology course at the University of Texas. In their classrooms, each student responded to one of several forms of an attitude scale (ranging in length from 4 to 48 items) in which they indicated their opinions about each topic on a 6-point scale.

Table 1 *Number of Items on Which the Stranger Held Similar/Dissimilar Attitudes*

Proportion of Similar Attitudes	Number of Similar Attitudes		
	4	8	16
1.00	4/0	8/0	16/0
.67	4/2	8/4	16/8
.50	4/4	8/8	16/16
.33	4/8	8/16	16/32

[1] This research was supported in part by the United States Air Force under Grant AF-AFOSR 261–63 from the Air Force Office of Scientific Research of the Air Research and Development Command.

The authors wish to thank June Goldberg, Rex Golightly, Nancy Johnson, Patricia Yale, and Betsy Young for their assistance on this project.

Table 2 *Means and Standard Deviations of Attraction Scores toward Strangers with Varying Numbers and Varying Proportions of Similar Attitudes*

Proportion of Similar Attitudes	Number of Similar Attitudes							
	4		8		16		Total	
	M	*SD*	*M*	*SD*	*M*	*SD*	*M*	*SD*
1.00	11.14	1.68	12.79	1.01	10.93	2.28	11.62	1.93
.67	10.79	2.46	9.36	2.64	9.50	2.47	9.88	2.60
.50	9.36	2.52	9.57	2.53	7.93	3.20	8.95	2.86
.33	8.14	3.02	6.64	1.99	6.57	2.02	7.12	2.50
Total	9.86	2.74	9.59	3.05	8.73	3.01		

On the basis of a pilot study with another group of 138 subjects, each scale was balanced with respect to the importance of the topics; in addition, items which yielded extremely uniform responses in the population were omitted in favor of items yielding as close as possible to 50–50 splits. The latter control was an attempt to avoid the possible confounding of dissimilarity of attitudes with deviancy of attitudes on the part of the stranger. The attitude items covered a variety of topics including fraternities and sororities, integration, science fiction, welfare legislation, tipping, discipline for children, community bomb shelters, and gardening.

In the experiment itself, subjects were brought into a special room in small groups. As has been described previously (Byrne, 1962) they were told that the experiment concerned the accuracy of interpersonal judgments based on limited information. They were to receive an attitude scale filled out by an anonymous stranger, read the responses carefully, and then make several judgments about him or her. Each subject received a spurious scale containing responses which constituted the appropriate number of similar and dissimilar attitudes depending on the cell to which he was assigned.

The stranger was rated on 7-point scales (Byrne and Wong, 1962) with respect to intelligence, knowledge of current events, morality, adjustment, and then on the two attraction scales (probable liking for the stranger and probable enjoyment of working with him). In previous investigations, responses to the latter two scales have been analyzed separately as alternate measures of the dependent variable. It seems advantageous, however, to combine the ratings on the two scales into a single attraction index with a possible range of 2–14. With the two scales conceptualized as forming a two-item measuring device, data from 10 different samples totaling 1,010 subjects yield an average corrected split-half reliability of .85 for the attraction measure.

Results

The means and standard deviations of the attraction scores are shown in Table 2. Before computing the analysis of variance, Hartley's maximum *F* ratio test for heterogeneity of variance (Walker and Lev, 1953) was employed. The F_{max} of 10.04 indicated a significant departure from homogeneity. Even though it has been found (Young and Veldman, 1963) that heterogeneity of variance has a negligible effect on both the alpha level and the power of the *F* test, the data were transformed into the square of each number in order to obtain acceptable homogeneity. There was no difference in significance levels between the analysis based on the raw data and that based on the transformed data; the summary shown in Table 3 is based on the raw data. Since the only significant *F* is that for the proportion of similar attitudes, the hypothesis is confirmed.

Table 3 *Analysis of Variance of Attraction Scores toward Strangers with Varying Numbers and Varying Proportions of Similar Attitudes*

Source	*df*	MS	*F*
Proportion (A)	3	158.71	23.34*
Number (B)	2	11.11	1.63
A × B	6	8.49	1.25
Within	156	6.80	

* $p < .001$.

Discussion

The positive relationship between proportion of similar attitudes held by a stranger and attraction toward him appears to be a firmly established one. The nature of that relationship can be described somewhat more precisely at this point. Data were available to the author from five published studies (Byrne, 1961a, 1961b, 1962; Byrne and McGraw, 1964; Byrne and Wong, 1962),[2] the present investigation, and two unpublished studies; in each instance attraction was the dependent variable and various proportions of similar attitudes the independent vari-

[2] In two of the studies some of the strangers were identified as Negroes, but for the purpose of the present paper only the data involving white strangers have been utilized.

able. The subjects totaled 790, and 11 different values of the proportion of similar attitudes held by the stranger were represented. A plot of the mean attraction scores for these 11 points suggested linearity, and a straight-line function was fitted to the data by the least-squares method. The solution yielded the formula $Y = 5.44X + 6.62$, and the plot is shown in Figure 1.

While the linear relationship between proportion of similar attitudes and attraction appears to be a lawful phenomenon, more evidence is needed to support the more general proposition that attraction is a linear function of the proportion of positive reinforcements. Attraction has been found to be influenced by various types of reward and punishment, including high and low ratings of creative productions (McDonald, 1962), facilitation of success at an experimental task (Kleiner, 1960), and insulting and frustrating behavior (Worchel, 1958). Only in McDonald's experiment, however, was proportion of positive reinforcements represented by a series of values. His subjects were asked to create seven stories in response to a set of stimulus cards; a confederate posing as another subject rated each story on a 10-point scale with respect to creativity. Each of the 192 subjects was assigned to one of eight possible conditions (seven high ratings, six high and one low, etc.). Attraction toward the peer who made the ratings was found to increase as a function of the proportion of high ratings. McDonald made his data available to the author, and they were plotted as shown in Figure 2. Again, a linear function was found to fit the data: $Y = 2.98X + 8.47$. Thus, linearity of the relationship is evident across two different experimental conditions but the values of the constants differ. Presumably, the similarity across stimulus conditions is attributable to the common element of positive and negative reinforcements involved. A tentative law of

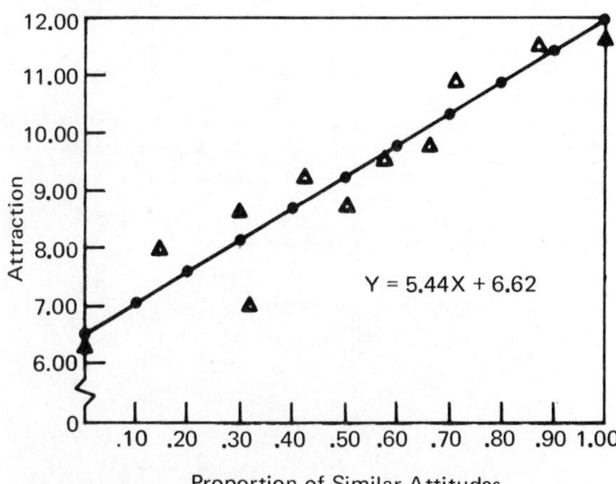

Figure 1 *Attraction toward strangers as a linear function of proportion of similar attitudes.*

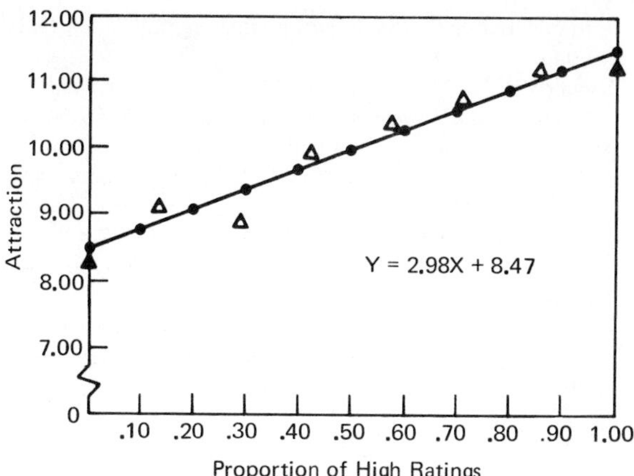

Figure 2 *Attraction toward strangers as a linear function of proportion of high creativity ratings.*

attraction is proposed as $A_x = mPR_x + k$ or attraction toward X is a positive linear function of the proportion of positive reinforcements received from X. The explanation for the differences between the two situations in terms of the slope of the line and the Y intercept must be sought in subsequent research.

References

Byrne, D. Interpersonal attraction and attitude similarity. *Journal of Abnormal and Social Psychology,* 1961, *62,* 713–715. (a)

Byrne, D. Interpersonal attraction as a function of affiliation need and attitude similarity. *Human Relations,* 1961, 3, 283–289. (b)

Byrne, D. Response to attitude similarity-dissimilarity as a function of affiliation need. *Journal of Personality,* 1962, *30,* 164–177.

Byrne, D., and McGraw, C. Interpersonal attraction toward Negroes. *Human Relations,* 1964, *17,* 201–213.

Byrne, D., and Wong, T. J. Racial prejudice, interpersonal attraction, and assumed dissimilarity of attitudes. *Journal of Abnormal and Social Psychology,* 1962, *65,* 246–253.

Dollard, J., and Miller, N. E. *Personality and psychotherapy.* New York: McGraw-Hill, 1950.

Festinger, L. Informal social communication. *Psychological Review,* 1950, *57,* 271–282.

Festinger, L. A theory of social comparison processes. *Human Relations,* 1954, *7,* 117–140.

Jones, E. E., and Daugherty, B. N. Political orientation and perceptual effects of an anticipated interaction. *Journal of Abnormal and Social Psychology,* 1959, *59,* 340–349.

Kleiner, R. J. The effects of threat reduction upon interpersonal attractiveness. *Journal of Personality,* 1960, *28,* 145–155.

McDonald, R. D. The effect of reward-punishment and affiliation need on interpersonal attraction. Unpublished doctoral dissertation, University of Texas, 1962.

Newcomb, T. M. An approach to the study of communicative acts. *Psychological Review,* 1953, *60,* 393–404.

NEWCOMB, T. M. The prediction of interpersonal attraction. *American Psychologist,* 1956, *11,* 575–586.

NEWCOMB, T. M. Individual systems of orientation. In S. Koch (Ed.), *Psychology: A study of a science.* Vol. 3. *Formulations of the person and the social context.* New York: McGraw-Hill, 1959. Pp. 384–422.

NEWCOMB, T. M. *The acquaintance process.* New York: Holt, Rinehart, and Winston, 1961.

SCHACHTER, S. Deviation, rejection, and communication. *Journal of Abnormal and Social Psychology,* 1951, *46,* 190–207.

SMITH, A. J. Similarity of values and its relation to acceptance and the projection of similarity. *Journal of Psychology,* 1957, *43,* 251–260.

WALKER, HELEN M., and LEV, J. *Statistical inference.* New York: Holt, 1953.

WORCHEL, P. Personality factors in the readiness to express aggression. *Journal of Clinical Psychology,* 1958, *4,* 355–359.

YOUNG, R. K., and VELDMAN, D. J. Heterogeneity and skewness in analysis of variance. *Perceptual and Motor Skills,* 1963, *16,* 588.

Leadership

7

The three experiments on leadership included here bear some resemblance to those on language and communication. In each instance, the experimenter arranges an environment which reinforces the speech of one participant in a group while punishing the others. This has the effect of giving a selected individual the dominant role in carrying out some group task. The proposition that emerges is that leadership is a consequence of social reinforcement.

Most of the experiments in which specific reinforcement procedures are used do not deal with the kinds of activities that allow one member of a group actually to lead the others. As suggested by the literature on group dynamics, the topography of the component behaviors in a leader-follower relationship is very complex. Under some circumstances—as in group therapy or nondirective discussion—the leader of the group may not even be the one who behaves the most frequently. But in order to maintain his status in the group, the leader needs to provide effective reinforcers for the conduct of the other group members, no matter how little or how much he acts. Thus, in a functional analysis of the behavior of a group, the leader is the one whose reaction is the reinforcer that maintains the conduct of the group members.

We now have ample evidence that principles of reinforcement are relevant to the processes by which the members of a group go about a task, and that an outside authority (the reinforcement conditions set by the experimenter) can determine which members will be dominant and which will be submissive. Dominance and submission, in many social experiments, refer to how frequently the members act. As we have noted, however, the sheer frequency of behavior is not the only criterion of leadership. Perhaps a more meaningful index is the number of times the group members refer to one person. Nominations, or peer ratings, in fact, have proven to be among the more valid and reliable measures of leadership status. This method of sociometric choice, therefore, is sometimes used to determine the effectiveness of selective reinforcement in establishing or modifying leadership patterns in a group.

An Analysis of Authority

Adams and Romney analyze some simple verbal interactions in which one person makes a request or a demand of another. These interactions are put in the domain of authority because the reply to the demand or request is instrumental in avoiding or terminating a threat. The authors analyze a variety of simple interactions stressing the observability and manipulability of all the component performances. They stress that the relationship is a reciprocal one. Not only does the person in authority prompt compliance with the request or demand, but the compliance also reinforces the behavior of the "authority." When we say that Person A controls Person B, we must distinguish two aspects of their interaction. The first is the functional relation between their performances in the sense that the behavior of one depends upon (is controlled by) the behavior of the other. The second involves A's ability to coerce B's reply by using aversive stimulation or by creating a state of deprivation. To the extent that he is able to do this, A can be said to have more reinforcers at his disposal than B and, hence, to possess greater authority. The significance of a command lies more in its functional relation to the listener's behavior than in a formal description of what the speaker does. The critical dimension of a command, whatever form it takes, is the negative reinforcement of the listener's compliance.

40 | *A Functional Analysis of Authority*[1]

J. STACY ADAMS
A. KIMBALL ROMNEY

An important segment of social interaction that requires systematic analysis is the behavioral control of one person over another: in other words, authority. The purpose of this paper is to analyze this type of interaction for the dyad, showing of what variables it is a function.

Authority, as defined below, is seen as a special case of verbal behavior as analyzed by Skinner (1957), and is consonant with his definition of the "mand." Thus, the analysis of authority will make fundamental use of the concept of the reciprocal reinforcement of behavior. The general aim is to carry through an analysis of the dyadic situation, and simple extensions of it, that specifies the conditions that are relevant to the occurrence of "authority behavior" and the variables of which such behavior is it is a function.

We begin with a definition of authority. A basic paradigm of an authority sequence will then be given and the variables of which such an authority sequence is a function will be discussed in detail. Finally, functional relationships between authority sequences will be analyzed.

[1] This paper was written at the Interdisciplinary Program in the Behavioral Sciences at the University of New Mexico, Summer, 1958, sponsored by the Behavioral Sciences Division, Air Force Office of Scientific Research, under Contract AF 49 (638)–33. We gratefully acknowledge their support.

Definition of Authority

We define authority as follows: Person A has authority over Person B, in a given situation, when a response of A, under the control of deprivation or aversive stimulation and specifying its own reinforcement, is reinforced by B.

This definition implies that authority is a social relation under the dual or reciprocal control of both A and B. It is social in the sense that it requires behavior on the part of both A and B and that the behavior of A constitutes a stimulus for B and vice versa. For the relation to be maintained, B's behavior must be reinforcing for A and A's behavior must be reinforcing for B. As will be discussed later, the controlling relation of A over B may be enduring or temporary, and it may extend over a large or small range of B's responses.

The relation of authority is asymmetrical in that A's initial response (such as a command, request, suggestion, etc.) specifies its own reinforcement, whereas B's does not. The reinforcement is provided by B's response, if the response reduces the state of deprivation or withdraws aversive stimuli for A. For the maintenance of the relationship B's response must be likewise reinforced by A, but the reinforcement is not specified as in the case of A.

The phrase, "in a given situation," indicates that the authority relation is not assumed to be a general one between individuals regardless of time and place. Authority is learned in specific situations, although it may later be transferred to other situations by such processes as stimulus induction. The phrase also implies the reversibility of the relation from one situation to another. This reversibility may violate the usual definition of and feeling for "authority." For example, one readily accepts the notion of a father's authority over his son, while one would balk at a statement of a child's "authority" over his father. Yet, precisely the same functional relationships may hold in both cases, as we shall demonstrate. It is, therefore, both rigorous and useful to speak of a person's having "authority" over another whenever the same relationships are found, even though this practice might do violence to everyday usage.

The clause, "under the control of deprivation or aversive stimulation," indicates that it is not sufficient to know only the topography of the response of A, but that it is also necessary to specify the controlling variables of the response of A. For example, if A says, "Water, please," in the presence of B, we must know whether the controlling variable of that response is water deprivation or some other deprivation, or whether it is aversive stimulation.

When it is said that the response of A specifies its own reinforcement, we assume that there is "communication" between A and B. Not only does the presence of B, in part, set the occasion for the response of A, but the reinforcement of A's response is contingent upon a response by B. Thus authority behavior is necessarily verbal behavior as defined by Skinner (1957), i.e., behavior the reinforcement of which is contingent upon stimulation of and response by another individual. The definitions of all other terms used in the analysis closely follow the behavioral, empirical definitions given by Verplanck (1957).

Basic Paradigm of an Authority Sequence

The central idea in authority relations is that of the reciprocal control and reinforcement of behavior of two persons. Basically, the paradigm is that a response of one person, A, is reinforced by another person, B, and that, in turn, the reinforcing response of B is, itself, reinforced by A. Such an interaction will be called an *authority sequence*. An example is the situation in which Person A asks B for water and B complies by giving A water. Figure 1 gives an illustration of the process. The figure is divided into two parts, the top half representing stimuli and responses directly related to Person A, while the lower half pertains to Person B. The interaction between A and B begins at the far left of the figure with A in a state of deprivation and in the presence of a discriminative stimulus, S_d and $S_B{}^D$. These stimuli set the occasion for the response R_{A1}, "Give me water." S_d is the stimulus, presumably physiological in the example, that results from water deprivation. $S_B{}^D$ is the discriminative stimulus resulting from B's presence in A's environment. $S_B{}^D$ is a discriminative stimulus with respect to R_{A1} in this illustration by virtue of previous conditioning. The response, "Give me water," would not occur unless A were thirsty; nor would it occur unless someone were present to give A water. In some sense, R_{A1} is "appropriate" only in the presence of S_d and $S_B{}^D$, and these stimuli may therefore be viewed as "setting the occasion for" and as having control over R_{A1}. As will be seen, this control is not exclusive, however, for it is the reinforcement of R_{A1} in the presence of the two stimuli that is crucial for the demonstration of authority.

Once the verbal command, "Give me water," has been emitted, it is a stimulus to B. Specifically, it is a discriminative stimulus, $S_{A1}{}^D$, in that it sets the occasion for a response by B that is later reinforced.

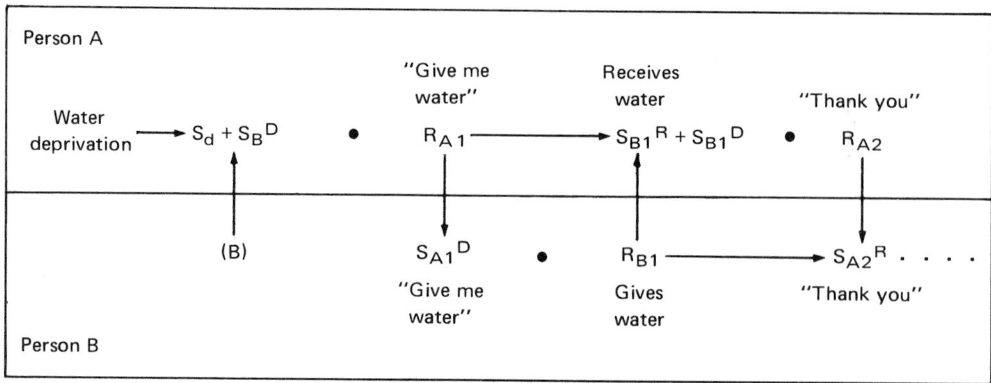

Figure 1 *Authority sequence with initial response under control of deprivation.*

The major characteristic of R_{A1} is that it specifies how B can reinforce it. B is in fact "told" that the response, "Give me water," will be reinforced by giving water to A. When B gives water to A, his response, R_{B1}, constitutes the reinforcement, $S_{B1}{}^R$ of response R_{A1}. In addition, R_{B1} is also a discriminative stimulus, $S_{B1}{}^D$, that sets the occasion for a further response by A. The response in this example is, "Thank you," R_{A2}. In turn, R_{A2}, a generalized reinforcer, constitutes a reinforcement of R_{B1}. Although the reciprocal reinforcement of responses on that part of A and B is terminated arbitrarily in the present example, R_{A2} itself would need to be reinforced by a further response of B, perhaps the verbal response, "You're welcome," or a nod or smile. As the dots to the far right of Fig. 1 suggest, the sequence is theoretically infinite, though in practice it is finite.

The use of only one discriminative stimulus ($S_B{}^D$) is greatly simplifying a situation encountered in "real life." The essence of the model is in no way affected by this simplification, however. Quite complex stimuli could be made discriminative—i.e., given "sign" status—in an experimental situation, and an authority sequence from "real life" could be replicated.

In the illustrative sequence of behavior presented, it is important to note that if the sequence is interrupted at any point, predictable consequences follow. Assume, for example, that B does not give water to A, after A has said, "Give me water." This might be because R_{A1} did not result in a discriminative stimulus for B, i.e., it had no "meaning" for B because of lack of previous learning. Or it may be that R_{A1} resulted in a discriminative stimulus that set the occasion for a response other than giving water, perhaps telling A to get his own water. Whatever the reason for not giving water to A, the consequence would be for R_{A1} to undergo some extinction. Similarly, if the sequence were interrupted by A's not emitting R_{A2}, B's response, R_{B1}, giving water, would undergo some extinction, with the result that the probability of R_{A1}'s being reinforced would be decreased. As before, the probability of A's emiting R_{A1} would then be smaller. In both instances where the sequence is interrupted, it is evident that A's authority over B is decreased, at least in this particular situation. It is interesting to note that in the first instance the decrease in A's authority is primarily "because" of a failure attributable to B. In the second instance, however, A's authority is affected "because" of his failure to reinforce B's response, R_{B1}. The use of "because" here is very loose, of course; no attribution of causality to A and B as persons is intended. Their responses are completely determined, except on their very first occurrence, by their previous reinforcement history and by antecedent stimulus conditions.

In Figure 1, A's initial response was partly under the control of deprivation. Instead it could have been under the partial control of aversive stimulation. For example, B might have been making some disturbing noise and this aversive stimulus might have set the occasion for the response, "Keep quiet!" It is also true that B's response, R_{B1}, need not necessarily be reinforced by the presentation of a positive reinforcing stimulus. It could have been reinforced by the withdrawal of an aversive stimulus or conditioned aversive stimulus. Figure 2 shows how aversive stimuli might exercise control in an authority interaction.

An aversive noise stimulus, $S_n{}^{av}$, and a discriminative stimulus, $S_B{}^D$, set the occasion for the responses R_{A1} and $R_{A1}{}^{av}$, constituted by the verbal response, "Keep quiet!" and an implied threat carried by the accentuation and intonation of the verbal response. Thus B is presented with a discriminative verbal stimulus, $S_{A1}{}^D$, and a conditioned aversive stimulus, $S_{A1}{}^{av}$. These stimuli set the occasion for stopping the noise, indicated in the figure as R_{B1}. This response consists of the withdrawal of the aversive noise stimulus, $S_n{}^{av}$, and constitutes a negative rein-

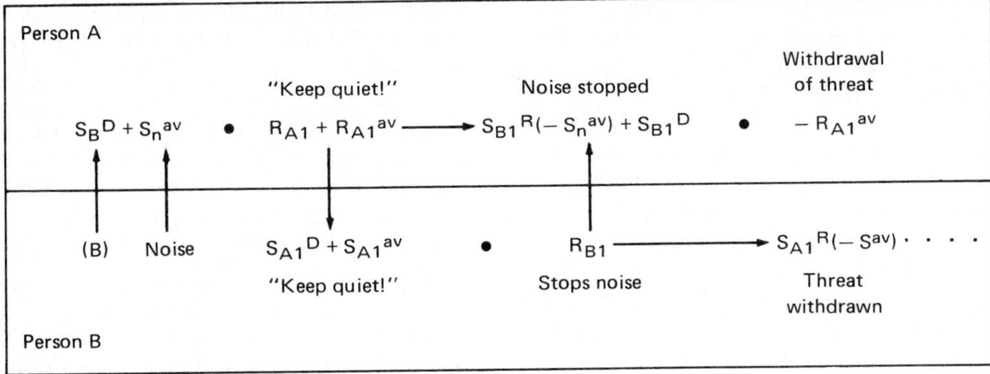

Figure 2 *Authority sequence with initial response under control of aversive stimulation.*

forcing stimulus for A, as well as a discriminative stimulus, $S_{B1}{}^D$, setting the occasion for a further response. The response, in this example, is the withdrawal of implicit threat and is labeled,—$R_{A1}{}^{av}$. This, in turn, is an appropriate negative reinforcing stimulus for B's response, R_{B1}. As in the previous example, the sequence of behavior is stopped at this point. Thus, we have here an interesting case of escape conditioning, with an implied threat as a conditioned aversive stimulus, as well as one of avoidance conditioning with respect to the negative reinforcing stimulus inferred from the threat.

In a manner analogous to that presented earlier, interruption of the behavioral sequence has implications for the authority A has over B. If B, for example, does not stop making noise (perhaps because of the inadequate control of $S_{A1}{}^D$ and $S_{A1}{}^{av}$), A's response, "Keep quiet!" will undergo some extinction and A's authority over B will be weakened under the particular circumstances described. However, B's lack of compliance may of itself constitute additional aversive stimulation for A and thus set the occasion for a new response, perhaps, "If you don't stop that noise, you'll suffer the consequences," which may generate enough additional aversive stimulation for B to make him stop the noise. If this occurred, A would maintain his authority over B, though at some additional expense. A could, of course, alternatively "leave the field," in which case there would be no question of authority over B.

The sequence in Figure 2 would also be interrupted if A did not withdraw aversive stimulation after B had complied with his command. The consequence would be that R_{B1} would have less likelihood of occurring in the future, a fact which would tend to reduce the probability of occurrence of R_{A1} and $R_{A1}{}^{av}$ and, therefore, would tend to reduce A's authority over B in this illustrative situation. As was pointed out before, the resulting loss of control of A over B might set the occasion for new responses by A.

In both the illustrations given thus far, certain assumptions have been made which need to be made explicit before the implications of the paradigm are further explored. Some of the assumptions concern the discriminative status of stimuli. For example, it is assumed in Figure 1 that B is a discriminative stimulus ($S_B{}^D$) setting the occasion for the response, "Give me water." But by definition a discriminative stimulus is one in the presence of which a response is reinforced and in the absence of which it is unreinforced. Since A's response, R_{A1}, is not reinforced until some time later, B cannot initially be a discriminative stimulus in the sense of setting the occasion for R_{A1}. What is assumed, then, is some previous learning, i.e., some previous temporal contiguity of response (R_{A1}) and reinforcing stimulus ($S_{B1}{}^R$) in the presence of B. The assumption is, however, only one of convenience, and what has been said applies to the free operant situation as well. If A had merely emitted spontaneously the response, "Give me water," in the presence of B (and in the context of deprivation), and if B had responded appropriately to reinforce A's response, the behavioral consequences would have been the same as previously discussed. The only difference is that B would have been a mere stimulus without discriminative properties. However, on *subsequent* occasions B would have discriminative characteristics, assuming further that A's responses had been unreinforced on some occasion when B was absent. The same line of reasoning applies to other stimuli which appear as discriminative stimuli in the figures.

Another assumption is that the reciprocal reinforcement of behavior is a finite sequence. It was stated earlier that the reciprocal reinforcement sequence in the authority relation may be theoretically infinite but that we assumed it was finite in practice. The assumption is difficult to substantiate even though everyday observation suggests that persons in an authority relation do not reinforce each other's responses ad infinitum. There are, of course, cases where reinforcement continues for considerable lengths of time, for example the endless exchange of bows that occurs when a Westerner visits a Japanese home. Nevertheless, the fact is that in our culture the interaction usually stops at approximately the point indicated n Figures 1 and 2, and that extinction is not a consequence. The reason for this may be that terminating an interaction sequence at a certain point is of itself reinforcing in that it avoids aversive consequences which would be forthcoming were the sequence not terminated. Thus, for example, in our own culture there are conventions about the termination of an interaction sequence beyond which further responding is punished by the use of conditioned aversive stimuli. As an illustration, it is commonly observed that after compliance with a request, anything beyond a "Thank you" and "You're welcome" results in raised eyebrows, a sardonic smile, or a look of impatience, which may be discriminative stimuli for stopping the interaction. When the stimuli for stopping are not known to one of the parties in the interaction (i.e., are not discriminative), responding may continue for some time, as in the bowing example above. In some situations responding beyond a given point may have the aspect of impertinence and have appropriate aversive results. Alternatively, responding beyond a certain point is unreinforced by society, and an agreed-upon sequence of reciprocal reinforcement becomes a discriminative stimulus for stopping further responding.

Controlling Variables

Thus far it has been shown how an authority relation between two persons can evolve and either be maintained or be destroyed. The external events (independent variables) of which responses (dependent variables) in an authority interaction are a function will now be discussed. This will be done by grouping variables into general classes and discussing instances under class headings. The basic A-B interaction paradigm will be used throughout.

Reinforcing Stimulus Variables

Stimulus events that have the property of increasing the probability of recurrence of a preceding response are fundamental controlling variables. B's giving water to A and A's saying "Thank you" in Figure 1 are such events in that they increase the probability of A's again asking B for water when he is later water-deprived, and of B's giving A water, respectively, other variables remaining constant. In other words, certain responses such as "Give me water" have consequences which empirically increase their probability of recurrence and thus in part determine the authority A has over B.

The importance of reinforcing stimuli is more pervasive than has been suggested above, however. The discriminative character of other stimuli is dependent upon their being paired with reinforcement. Thus, for example, in Figure 1, B's presence would not constitute a discriminative stimulus for A's demanding water, unless it had been temporally contiguous with the reinforcement of A's response. Nor, in Figure 2, would A's verbal command "Keep quiet!" be a discriminative stimulus for B's stopping noisiness, unless stopping noise-making had been reinforced following the occurrence of the stimulus resulting from A's response. It can therefore be seen that a reinforcing contingency is *necessary* before a stimulus can acquire discriminative properties. This is, of course, not a *sufficient* characteristic: It is also required that the absence of a stimulus be associated with nonreinforcement before it can be a discriminative stimulus. For example, with respect to Figure 1, it would be necessary that A's response, "Give me water," be unreinforced in the absence of B.

The withholding of reinforcing stimuli following a response is the operation resulting in experimental extinction and, as an observable consequence, produces a decreased probability of response. Illustrations of this have been given previously.

The general properties and the importance of reinforcing stimuli having been pointed out, A and B as the agents or mediators of reinforcement must now be considered.

A as a reinforcer. A can act as a direct mediator of reinforcement or as a conditioned reinforcer. As a direct mediator he can both present positive reinforcers (or conditioned reinforcers) and withdraw negative reinforcers (or conditioned negative reinforcers). A father can reinforce his child for obeying a command by givng it candy. The business executive can reinforce his secretary's compliance with an order by withdrawing an implied threat, much as in the example of Figure 2. In a similar fashion the traffic policeman reinforces stopping at his gestured command by lowering his arm and, hence, removing conditioned negative reinforcers.

It is evident that, as a direct mediator of reinforcement. A can exercise considerable control over B's behavior. But it is also true that, indirectly, he exercises control over his *own* responses, for the probability of recurrence of his own responses is in part a function of the extent to which he is successful in reinforcing B's responses. Other things being equal, then, A is in some sense the master of his own authority over B. This notion is not a new one, but in the present case it has the advantage of being systematically derivable from the basic model.

A further derivation is that A's probability of successfully developing or maintaining an authority relation over B will in part be a function of the amount and variety or range of reinforcers he has available. The person who can mediate reinforcements appropriate to several states of deprivation can exercise more authority than one who can, say, provide only food (e.g., a parent versus a neighbor). The person who has access to a large range of aversive stimuli can have more authority than one who has not (e.g., a company commander versus a corporal). From a similar consideration it also follows that the greater the amount and range of reinforcers available to A, the greater the range of B's responses he can control, other variables remaining constant. Thus a parent can have wider authority than an older sister who can mete out limited punishment only and who has no money for material rewards.

As a conditioned reinforcer, either positive or negative, A may also exercise control over B's behavior, as well as indirectly over his own. Before he can act as a conditioned reinforcer, however, it is necessary that he have acted on previous occasions as a direct mediator of reinforcement, or, at least, that he be similar to someone who acted as a reinforcer. The important thing to consider is that the mere presence of A can reinforce some of B's responses, no direct reinforcement being given. For example, using the illustration of Figure 1, it is possible for A to omit saying, "Thank you," and for B's response to remain at considerable strength, provided stimulus attributes of A have become conditioned or generalized reinforcers by virtue of A's having previously, and frequently, reinforced B's responses. However, in order for the attributes of A to remain effective conditioned reinforcers (and discriminative stimuli as well), it is necessary that on occasion A mediate direct reinforcement; otherwise B's operant will undergo extinction. The same applies to A qua A as a negative conditioned reinforcer.

B as a reinforcer. The distinguishing characteristic of B as a reinforcer is that his reinforcing response has no, or only a few, degrees of freedom, as contrasted with A as a reinforcer. His reinforcing response is specified by A, by definition. To be sure, the discrete topography of his response may vary, but its net effect on A is specified. Thus, for example, B may get and bring water to A in a variety of ways, but the giving of water is the essential property of the response that will reinforce A's request and, therefore, establish or maintain the authority relation.

In a manner similar to A, B may also act as a conditioned reinforcer or negative conditioned reinforcer, in that the authority relation between the two will be maintained or strengthened. This presumes, of course, that B, or someone similar to B, will have appropriately reinforced A's behavior in the past under similar circumstances.

Generalization of A and B as conditioned reinforcers. It has been pointed out that A and B may exercise control over each other's behavior, and thus maintain or strengthen an authority relation, in their capacities as conditioned reinforcers. It is also true that conditioned reinforcement may be effected by individuals other than A and B who have physical properties similar to A and B. Thus, an officer never before encountered may act as a conditioned reinforcer of an enlisted man's compliance with an order, by virtue of the fact that he has properties similar to those of other officers who have reinforced the same response. The dimensions of similarity in this example might be the uniform and emblems of office; or the relevant dimension might be physical characteristics of verbal operants, e.g., "'ten shun!" Similarly, the authority of policemen is partially maintained, even though never before seen personally, through stimulus induction. How often has one slowed down at the sight of an unknown policeman whose back was turned?

Deprivation and Aversive Stimulus Variables Affecting A

As stated in the definition of authority, A's initial response (order, command, request, demand, etc.) is partially under the control of deprivation or aversive stimulation, other control being exercised by discriminative stimuli (e.g., the presence of a B). This results from the fact that certain responses of the human organism are typically followed by specific consequences under certain conditions agreed upon by the social community, and that when this occurs the probability of occurrence of these responses will be a function of the deprivation or aversive stimulation paired with the reinforcing consequences. Thus the response, "Give me water," has a greater probability of occurrence under water deprivation than under satiation because other organisms are more likely to have provided water when A emitted this response and was thirsty. It should be noted that deprivation and aversive stimulation do not *necessarily* exercise control over the response. The control results from the fact that other organisms are predisposed by "societal consensus," so to speak, to respond in certain characteristic ways. This predisposition of other organisms is analogous to certain automatic consequences of the nonanimal environment. For example, picking and eating an apple is automatically reinforcing when the organism is food-deprived, though not if he is satiated. Thus, food deprivation would come to control picking and eating an apple. A similar line of reasoning applies to aversive stimulation, though in this case reinforcement consists in the withdrawal of an aversive stimulus.

The relations holding between deprivation (or aversive stimulation), response topography of A, and reinforcing response by B are stated in idealized terms. This is especially true with regard to A's response topography "specifying" its reinforcement. It is conceivable, for example, that the response, "Give me water," specified not a state of water deprivation which could be reinforced by water but rather a demand for submissiveness on the part of B, the state of deprivation being for something other than water. In such a case the content of A's response does not clearly specify the appropriate reinforcing stimulus—at least the words used do not clearly convey the state of A's deprivation. However, other aspects of the verbal response than the words may serve as appropriate discriminative stimuli for submissiveness (i.e., sheer compliance). The imperative mood of the response, for example, may serve this function. Whether it does this effectively on a particular occasion is, of course, a function of appropriate previous differential reinforcement. To put it somewhat loosely, it is a function of whether B has learned that use of the imperative mood is a "sign" for compliance regardless of the specific content of A's response.

Discriminative Stimulus Variables

In the discussion of Figures 1 and 2 the role of discriminative stimuli was made explicit. We wish to expand the discussion at this point and focus specifically on the discriminative stimuli that control A's initial response. The discriminative stimulus characteristics of responses by A and B will be omitted, as they are evident.

Two general groups of discriminative stimulus variables controlling A's initial response may be considered, stimulus characteristics of B and situational stimuli, excluding B. A general characteristic of B that may serve as a discriminative stimulus is his being an organism with the potentiality of responding. Without another person's being present, a response by A cannot be reinforced, and A cannot exercise any authority. There are, however, other relevant aspects of B. One is B as a particular individual, i.e., the stimulus characteristics of a B who has previously reinforced A's response, as opposed to a B who has not. A second is B as the incumbent in a particular role, as an office boy or corporal, for example. In this instance characteristics of B serve as discriminative stimuli for a comparatively narrow range of responses by A. In other instances characteristics of B may set the occasion for one class of responses only; for example, the elevator boy is a discriminative stimulus for the response, "Take me to the sixth," only. Thus we may think of B as having discriminative stimulus characteristics that exercise control over A's responses with different degrees of specificity. The specificity of control exercised is a function of the extent of differential reinforcement carried out in the presence of particular characteristics.

The second group of discriminative stimulus variables are situational variables. They include virtually all relevant stimuli not directly pertaining to B. Some situational variables are part of the purely physical environment. Thus, the request, "Take me to the sixth," has a low probability of being reinforced in the absence of an elevator. Similarly, "Give me water," will usually have a low probability of occurring without a source of water in the immediate environment. However, in an instance of this sort, deprivation may become so severe that it exercises almost exclusive control. The "Water, water!" of the wounded soldier on the deserted battlefield is an example. Other situational variables are of a more "social" character in that the presence of other persons, or of persons having particular types of interaction, has a controlling discriminative stimulus function. Certain kinds of commands or requests are not issued to one's wife at home in the context of a cocktail party (and would go unreinforced, if issued), though they are issued and reinforced when just family members are present. Orders may be successfully given to an employee at the office, though not at the country club.

Whether discriminative stimulus control is exercised by B proper or by situational variables, it will be achieved only after differential reinforcement. The controlling stimulus variables may, of course, be of great complexity and require considerable training. For example, an authority response, R_{A1}, will be reinforced only if Stimuli I, J, . . . , *or* N are present, *and* if Stimuli B and C are present, *and* if Stimulus R is absent. The situation is analogous to those encountered in concept formation studies (e.g., Bruner, Goodnow, and Austin, 1956). In the present instance a response is reinforced only in the presence of particular stimuli, whereas in concept formation studies a response is said to be "correct" in the presence of some stimulus combinations and "incorrect" in the presence of other combinations.

Since complex stimulus control of this type requires considerable training with differential reinforcement, it follows that in early stages of training control will be imperfect. Some variables, in the absence of others which are necessary for reinforcement, will exercise some control over a response, even though it will not be reinforced. It is also possible that during the course of differential training "irrelevant" variables would exercise some control over an authority response. This inappropriate control of stimuli results when a response is reinforced in the presence of both appropriate discriminative stimuli and irrelevant other stimuli. These stimuli then acquire some discriminative stimulus capacity. Their control is eventually weakened and abolished during further differential training.

The Functional Interrelation of Authority Sequences

The classes of variables of which authority is a function have been specified for a two-person situation. In large groups new problems arise with respect to the arrangement of authority sequences within the group. The problems associated with relating authority sequences arise from the basic characteristics of authority and the presence of more than two persons in the total situation. This section is addressed to these problems and consists of an analysis of the ways in which authority sequences are patterned within the limitations imposed by the assumptions of authority as outlined in the preceding section.

In order for two authority sequences to be functionally related, one of the following conditions must be met: (*a*) authority sequence, K, or some part of it, controls authority sequence, L, or some part of it; (*b*) all or some part of authority sequences, K and L, are under the control of a common (or similar) variable (variables); and (*c*) two simultaneous initial responses are made that specify incompatible reinforcement responses by B.

For purposes of exposition, these will be regarded as distinct cases of authority sequence interrelationships and will be discussed separately.

Case I: One Sequence Exercises Functional Control over Another

There are a number of ways in which an authority sequence exercises control over a succeeding sequence, but it is important to note that an all-or-none relationship of control is not implied. The whole or any part of an authority sequence may control a succeeding sequence. This control may be either partial or complete and affect all or part of the succeeding sequence. Discussion will be limited to two basic ways in which two sequences may be functionally related.

Situation where a response in Sequence K controls a response in Sequence L. Authority sequence are frequently related by virtue of the fact that a response in the first sequence controls a response in the second. Generally speaking, with exceptions to be noted, the response by B in the first sequence is the initial response in the second sequence. For example, when a father orders his daughter to tell baby to be quiet, the response of daughter saying "quiet" to baby is B's response in the sequence father-daughter, and also the initial response in the sequence involving daughter-baby. Figure 3 gives an illustration of how the process might operate.

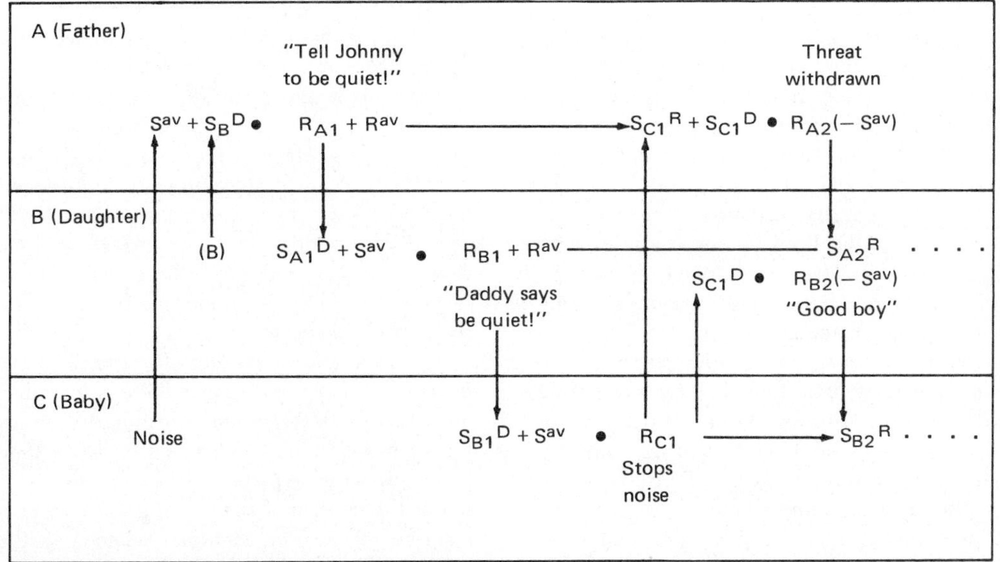

Figure 3 *Response-related authority sequences.*

A's response, "Tell Johnny to be quiet," is under the control of aversive stimuli from noise being made by the baby and of B as a discriminative stimulus. B's response of going and telling baby, "Daddy says, 'be quiet,'" is under the control of the stimuli of A's initial response, i.e., of a discriminative stimulus ($S_{A1}{}^{D}$) and of a conditioned aversive stimulus (S^{av}) consisting of an implied threat of punishment for noncompliance. B's response, R_{B1}, unlike responses in the dyadic situation, does not directly reinforce A's initial response, R_{A1}. Rather, it constitutes stimuli for C to stop making noise, R_{C1}. It is C's response, R_{C1}, that reinforces the original response of A, i.e., R_{A1}. This in turn sets the occasion for A to make a response that reinforces B's response; i.e., $R_{A2}(-S^{av})$ constitutes reinforcement for R_{B1}. The form of this response might be the removal of the implied threat. In order for the behavior to be maintained, C's response, R_{C1}, must also be reinforced. In the figure this response is a discriminative stimulus for B, who makes a response something like "Good boy," R_{B2}, which reinforces the response of stopping noise, R_{C1}, by removing an aversive stimulus.

Functionally related series of this general sort take many different forms. For example, in Figure 3, it would be possible for the second response of the father, $R_{A2}(-S^{av})$, to take the form "Thank you, children" and constitute reinforcement for not only the response of the daughter, R_{B1}, but also for the response of the baby, R_{C1}. In such an event it would be unnecessary for the daughter to reinforce the baby. Another very common situation in command chains arises when, for example, the president of a company asks the vice-president for a report, and the vice-president asks a department, head for the report. In this case the department head gives the report to the vice-president, who in turn gives it to the president. Here the action of the department head, C, does not directly reinforce any response by the president, but rather of the vice-president.

An inherent characteristic of situations involving a chain of command is that there is some delay in the reinforcement of A's initial response. This delay in reinforcement has implications for the readiness with which such responses are conditioned. Generally, conditioning of the response is a decreasing function of the delay between response and reinforcement. In practical situations there are techniques available to "help A across" such a time lag by presenting conditioned reinforcers during the delay period. For example, B can supply comments such as, "The report will be ready at three," "Yes, sir," "Right away, sir," "I'll attend to it immediately," and so on. Periodic "progress reports," frequent personal communications, and verbal reassurances are probably manifestations of the utility of supplying some supplementary conditioned reinforcement to A where the situation involves a long delay in reinforcement. This is in accord with the findings of Perin (1943a, 1943b) and Grice (1948) on the effects of removing conditioned reinforcers upon the delay of reinforcement gradient.

Situation where a response in Sequence K is under control of Sequence L. In this situation the whole of one sequence constitutes part of the situation for a second sequence. When the second sequence can be shown to be, at least in part, under the control of the first sequence, then the two sequences are functionally related. Consideration is limited here to the situation in which no individuals who are in the first sequence are also in the second.

An authority sequence frequently controls a response in another sequence either through "imitative" mechanisms—that is to say, by serving as a discriminative stimulus—or by increasing deprivation or aversive stimulation. Consider, for example, a group of mothers and children, where the children are playing in the mud. The first mother tells her child to stop playing in the mud. The child complies and is rewarded. This authority sequence may constitute a conditioned aversive stimulus for the second mother. The aversive stimulus may be social disapproval of not following the first mother's "example." The first sequence may also be a discriminative stimulus setting the occasion for the second mother's telling her child to stop playing in the mud. If the child complies, the aversive disapproval (perhaps only implied) of the first mother is withdrawn, and the second mother's behavior is reinforced.

Case II: A Common Variable Exercises Functional Control over Two or More Sequences

Probably the simplest manner in which authority sequences are functionally related is by sharing a common controlling variable. Sequences interrelated in this way are found most commonly in large groupings of face-to-face interactions where more complex ways of arranging authority sequences becomes unwieldy. Two types may be considered: (*a*) where an initial response by A specifies the behavior of several people, and (*b*) where two or more initial responses specify a single reinforcing response on the part of one person.

Situation where an initial response specifies behavior of several individuals. The situation in which one individual, A, directs a response to a large number of individuals, B, C, . . . , N, is a common one. The authority sequences in such an event are all under the control of the variables affecting the initial response of A. For example, when a drill sergeant calls a company of soldiers to attention we have a situation where the response, "Attention!" specifies

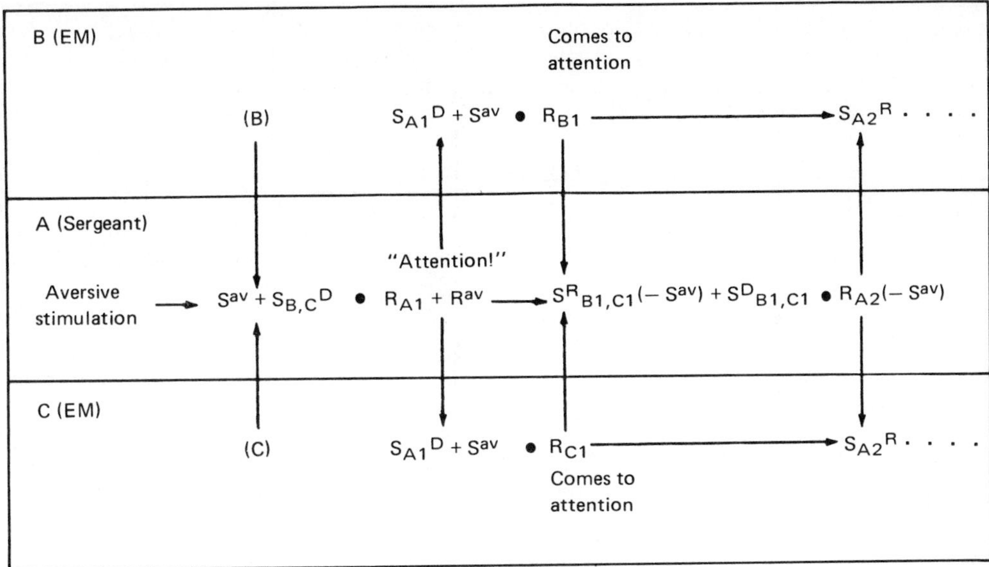

Figure 4 *One-to-many authority sequences.*

as its reinforcement the behavior of several individuals. Each pair formed by the sergeant and an individual soldier may be thought of as an authority sequence, assuming, of course, that they all come to attention and are reinforced by some behavior of the sergeant. These authority sequences are functionally related by the fact that they are all under the control of whatever variables determine the response of the sergeant, namely, calling the company to attention. The situation is illustrated in abbreviated form in Figure 4. An interesting implication of this type of authority situation is that the authority response of A is likely to remain in considerable strength and to be very resistant to extinction by virtue of the fact that the more other persons his response is addressed to, the more likelihood there is for some compliance and, hence, the more likely he is to get some reinforcement. In some limiting cases, of course, it is possible that the compliance of *all* Bs is the sole effective reinforcement for A. In such cases, the Bs can be treated as a single entity. It could be predicted, then, that certain military men, certain types of supervisors and foremen, teachers, housewives with large families, etc., would on the average have greater strength of authority responses in these situations than others, because there is a greater probability of their being reinforced. These are in fact persons who are often labeled "bossy."

Situations where two or more initial responses specify a single reinforcing response. Under certain circumstances to be specified below, two or more individuals may simultaneously initiate an authority sequence (give a command, request, suggest, etc.) with a third party, in which both of their responses specify the same behavior on the part of the third party as reinforcement. The example of a father and mother both saying, "Keep quiet" to their noisy child at the same time is diagramed in Figure 5.

The sequences are here functionally related by the fact that R_{C1} is part of both sequences. Since every response in a sequence exercises some control over the sequence, these sequences are under the control of the common variables related to the common response. The sequences are also related by the fact that the aversive stimulation in partial control of R_{A1} and R_{B1} is from the same source.

This type of relation between authority sequences is subject to more restrictions than any of those previously discussed. The most important restriction is that the two initial responses by A and B must specify a response on the part of C that will reinforce both initial responses. A and B, of course, need not specify an identical response, though in practice this may often be the case. It is only necessary that the responses specified be equivalent in their effects. Figure 5 illustrates a common way in which this arises, namely, A and B are under the control of a common aversive stimulus, the noise of a child. Under other circumstances A and B could be under the control of a common deprivation. Other more complex and subtle relations are not uncommon. For example, an audience in the presence of a good performer may be under the control of common stimuli so that they all applaud and shout "Bis!" and the performer complies with an encore. Here the exact specification of the controlling variables for the

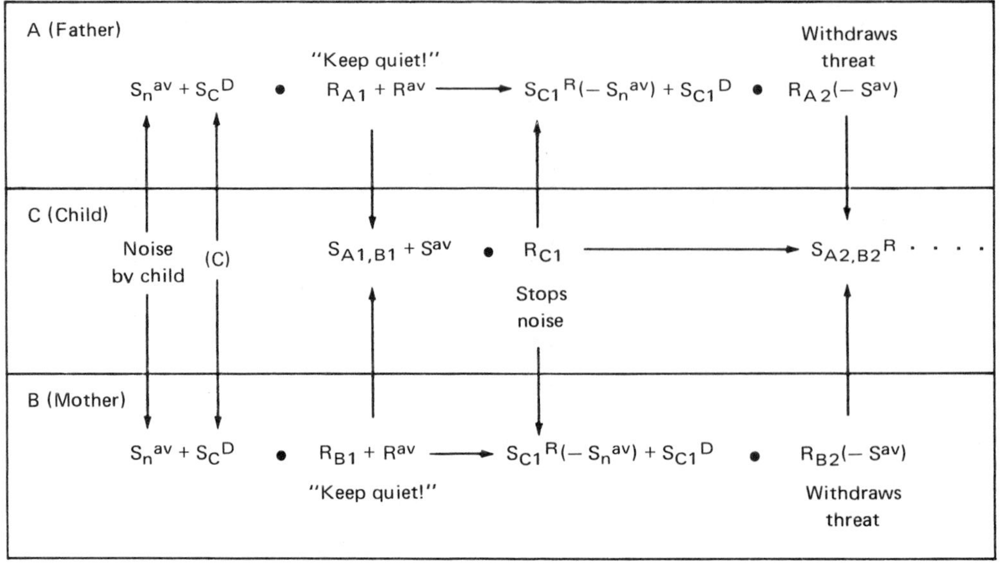

Figure 5 *Many-to-one authority sequences.*

audience is somewhat difficult, and there may be a variety of variables operating on different members of the audience.

Other things being equal, C is under more aversive stimulation than in the simple authority sequence by virtue of the fact that he is under multiple aversive stimulation, as shown in Figure 5 by the two implied threats symbolized by $S_{A1}{}^{av}$ and $S_{B1}{}^{av}$. Making the assumption that degree of control and amount of aversive stimulation (or of deprivation), up to a limit, are positively correlated, it follows that compliance will be an increasing function of aversive stimulation (or of deprivation).

Another feature to note in these types of relationships between sequences is that A and B may be viewed as a "coalition" under the control of common deprivation or aversive stimulation. When they do not act as a coalition, i.e., when they are not under common deprivation or aversive stimulation so that the initial responses specify incompatible responses on the part of C, the total relation becomes impossible to complete. That is to say, contradictory behavior may be required of C such that it is impossible for him to reinforce the responses of A and B simultaneously. We call such a situation one of *authority conflict*.

Case III: Authority Conflict

Two or more authority sequences may be functionally related in that one sequence is associated with the interruption of another or that the sequences mutually preclude the completion of each other. Specifically, sequences interfere with terminal reinforcements. In such cases there exists *authority conflict*.

Figure 6 provides an illustration. The situation is that of two bosses descending simultaneously upon their joint secretary late in the day with rush jobs. The typing jobs are of such a nature that only one can be completed. The two bosses, A and C, issue requests, R_{A1} and R_{C1}, with implied threats for noncompliance. These, let us assume, constitute discriminative stimuli plus aversive stimulation for the secretary, B. (The consequences to be discussed do not require this assumption, but it is made for the sake of reality.) Since B can comply with only one of the requests, there exist for her two incompatible (conflicting) response tendencies. These response possibilities exist for her: (*a*) she can comply with A's request and thus reinforce his response; (*b*) she can comply with C's request and thus reinforce his response; or (*c*) she can comply with neither request and therefore reinforce neither A's nor C's response. The consequences of the first two possibilities are analogous, while those of the third are different.

If B complies with A's request and therefore reinforces his initial response, A's response will have an increased probability of recurrence in the future under similar circumstances and C's response will tend to undergo extinction. If we now assume further that when C alone—that is, in the absence of A—makes a request of B, she complies and his behavior is reinforced, it follows that A will become a negative discriminative stimulus for C. In sum, if B reinforces

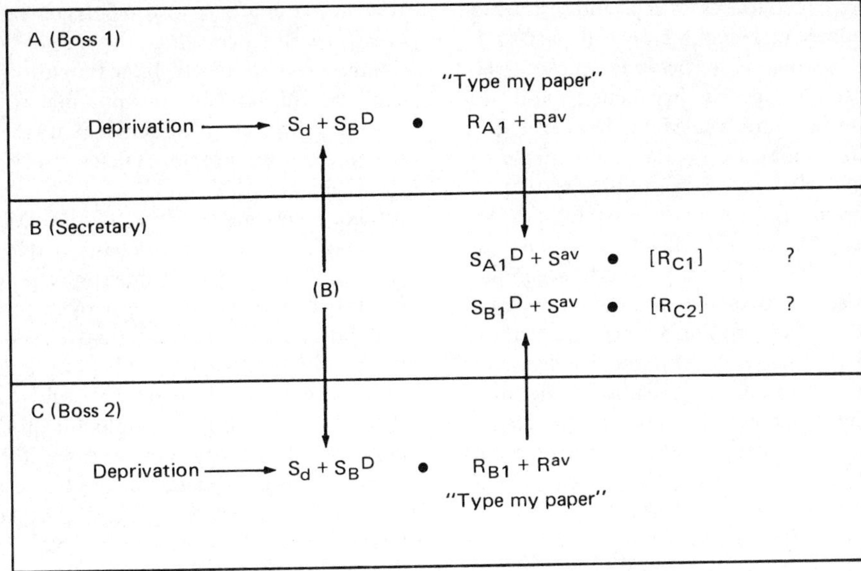

Figure 6 *Authority conflict situation.*

C in the absence of A and does not reinforce him in the presence of A, C will "learn" to make his requests in the absence of A. In practice, this may lead to a scheduling of authority responses, as when Boss 1 directs the secretary mornings and Boss 2 directs her afternoons.

The factors which result in B's reinforcing A's behavior in preference to C's are of interest. One factor is that A may have reinforced B more frequently than had C in the past for the same or similar responses, with the result that A's response exercised greater control over B. Another possibility is that A, perhaps because of powers associated with his rank or position, could give B greater reinforcement than could C, frequency of reinforcement by A and C being equal. It might also be that, even though having reinforcing powers equal to those of C, A made greater (and "better") use of generalized reinforcers. His expression of thanks, for example, might generally be more reinforcing (it might be less perfunctory). Another factor may be that A, as opposed to C, has acquired conditioned reinforcing properties under circumstances quite different from the boss-secretary relation. Finally, if we assume a completely free operant situation and no previous learning histories, it could be that B's response to A merely has a higher operant level than the conflicting response to C.

The second case to consider is when B complies with and reinforces neither A's nor C's request. In such an instance it is clear that both A's and C's initial authority responses will undergo extinction. However, it is clearly possible for the secretary's inactivity to set the occasion for new responses on the part of A or C or both which will be reinforced. Thus, A and C might say, "Type A's paper now and C's tomorrow." Furthermore, it is possible that, if A and C, when interacting alone with B, are reinforced in their requests, they will come to make their requests only in the absence of the other. This follows from the operation of differential reinforcement and of the resultant control exercised by a negative discriminative stimulus.

What the antecedents are for nonresponse on the part of B are many and need not be enumerated. Generally, however, the situation is that both A's and C's responses and situational stimuli exercise the same degree of control over B's responses. To use a vector analogy, the vectors representing B's two response tendencies are of equal length and at 180 degrees to each other.

In the discussion of authority conflict, attention has thus far been limited to the consequences of B's responses upon the behavior of A and C. It is evident, however, that the types of conflict envisaged will have effects upon the behavior of B. One effect is that, when B reinforcers the behavior of A in preference to C's and is in turn reinforced by A, her response to A will have an increased probability of recurrence, whereas any response tendency toward compliance with C's request will be weakened under similar circumstances. When B responds neither to A nor C, whatever response tendencies existed at the time will undergo extinction since they will not be reinforced. In both of these cases it is interesting to note that the conflict of responses on the part of B is self-reducing, in one case because one of the two response tendencies is weakened and in the other because both are weakened. However, the existence of conflict may have other side-effects.

If it is assumed that being in conflict results in aversive stimulation, certain consequences can be predicted. Under this assumption the secretary in the illustration will be subjected to aversive simulation. Furthermore, this aversive stimulation will be contingent upon her responding or tending to respond to A and C. That is to say, the conflict and consequent aversive stimulation exist solely *because* of her competing responses (of course, phenomenally, B may perceive A and C as being instrumental in her conflict). It follows, then, that A and C, as well as other aspects of the total situation, will become conditioned negative reinforcers and that B will tend to *avoid* them. Making the further assumption that degree of conflict and resulting aversive stimulation are positively correlated, it also follows that the strength of B's avoidance response will increase with increasing degree of conflict. Since degree of conflict will be a function of the strength similarity of B's two incompatible response tendencies, it may be concluded that the more nearly equal the response tendencies, the greater will be the avoidance of A and C.

The preceding analysis of authority conflict has dealt exclusively with the case in which only one of two (or more) incompatible responses can be emitted by B. It can, however, also happen that one response will be emitted first and that a second will subsequently be emitted upon the completion of the first. Thus, the fictional secretary could have typed A's letter first and, upon completion of that job, could have typed C's. In such a case both A's and C's authority responses will be reinforced. However, it is evident that some delay is entailed in the reinforcement of C's responses. The consequence of this will be to weaken the effect of the reinforcement, the magnitude of the net effect being inversely proportional to the amount of delay.

Summary

We have suggested the following definition of authority: A person A has authority over B, in a given situation, when a response of A, under the control of deprivation or aversive stimulation and specifying its own reinforcement, is reinforced by B. Authority, so defined, has been analyzed as a function of the following variables:

1. Reinforcing stimulus variables
   (*a*) A as a reinforcer
   (*b*) B as a reinforcer
   (*c*) Generalization of A and B as conditioned reinforcers
2. Deprivation and aversive stimulus variables affecting A
3. Discriminative stimulus variables.

A paradigm of an authority sequence was analyzed in terms of these variables. Series of functionally related sequences were defined as sequences under the control of one another or of common variables. Three classes of functionally related sequences were analyzed:

1. Where one sequence exercises functional control over another
2. Where a common variable exercises functional control over two or more sequences
3. Authority conflict.

The functional analysis of authority that has been presented places primary emphasis upon the reciprocal nature of authority interactions and, by so doing, suggests how authority evolves, is maintained, and may be weakened.

As the analysis suggests, it is actually improper to speak of the locus of authority, except perhaps for "shorthand" purposes. Authority is behavior and is a function of certain operationally defined variables. By adopting this functional approach, it should be possible not only to account for observations that have been made about authority, but to deduce systematically the consequences of manipulating variables in specified ways.

References

Bruner, J. S., Goodnow, J. J., and Austin, G. A. *A study of thinking.* New York: Wiley, 1956.

Grice, G. R. The relation of secondary reinforcement to delayed reward in visual discrimination learning. *Journal of Experimental Psychology,* 1948, *38,* 1–16.

Perin, C. T. A quantitative investigation of the delay-of-reinforcement gradient. *Journal of Experimental Psychology,* 1943, *32,* 37–51. (a)

Perin, C. T. The effect of delay of reinforcement upon the differentiation of bar responses in white rats. *Journal of Experimental Psychology,* 1943, *32,* 95–109. (b)

Skinner, B. F. *Verbal behavior.* New York: Appleton-Century-Crofts, 1957.

Verplanck, W. S. A glossary of some terms used in the objective science of behavior. *Psychological Review,* 1957, *64* (6), Part 2.

B Modification of Leadership Behavior

Blum and Kennedy were able to influence dominance in pairs of children who were given two tasks—choosing pictures and matching lights. First, they observed the children in order to determine which child normally took the dominant role. Then they reinforced the performances of the child who had shown less dominance during the preliminary tests in order to increase the frequency of his leadership behavior. A second task provided an opportunity to determine whether the reinforced child would continue to be dominant in a new situation. Although the overall design of the experiment is relatively simple, it provides an example of the kind of complex statistical analyses sometimes used by psychologists to analyze experimental results.

41 *Modification of Dominant Behavior in School Children*

ELLIOT R. BLUM
WALLACE A. KENNEDY

Psychologists generally have embraced learning-theory viewpoints to account for the development, maintenance, and modification of individual human behavior. Indeed, hundreds of studies have supported the contention that reinforcement principles govern and regulate the responses of subjects in all highly structured situations. Recently attention has been directed toward extending these findings to more complex interpersonal social behavior.

Initially most of these studies examined the effects of reward and punishment on specific social responses. For example, studies on aggressive behavior have demonstrated the effectiveness of reinforcement (Bandura and Walters, 1963; Walters and Brown, 1963).

Other social behaviors have also been shown to be affected by various reinforcement conditions: dependency (Heathers, 1953), cooperative responses (Azrin and Lindsley, 1956), infant vocalizations (Rheingold, 1956), smiling response (Brackbill, 1958), positive attitudes toward group members (Lott and Lott, 1960), sharing behavior (Fisher, 1962), group decision making (Wolfgang, Banta, and Pishkin, 1964), and two-person conversational patterns (Levin and Shapiro, 1962).

In contrast, the effects of reinforcement on the development and modification of interpersonal dominant behavior have rarely been studied in controlled laboratory situations. Indeed, the overwhelming majority of the studies of dominant behavior have been correlational, emphasizing factors such as leadership (Krech and Crutchfield, 1948), vocational choice (Beaver, 1954), emotional responsivity (Cervin, 1957), age (Scott and Ball, 1957), delinquent adolescents (Fitzhugh, 1958), interpersonal choice (Altrocchi, 1959), extroversion and neuroticism (Bronzaft, Hayes, Welch, and Kottuv, 1960), and schizophrenic offspring (Farina, 1960).

The few which have been concerned with actually modifying dominant behavior through experimental operations have not been conclusive (Anderson, 1937; Chittenden, 1942; Gellert, 1962; Jack, 1934; Mummery, 1947; Page, 1936). The vehicles by which modification had been achieved were not clearly specified, nor were important variables delineated, for example, training "to build up con-

From the *Journal of Personality and Social Psychology*, 1967, 7, 275–281.

fidence." The gross behavioral units of analysis were highly susceptible to observer bias and lack of objectivity.

Reinforcement could be assumed to be a critical component of dominant behavior, in light of the vital role it plays in other social behavior. Yet those studies on dominance which have included some reward-type training have done so quite unsystematically. None has been concerned with punishment or has investigated clearly generalization or transfer effects.

Problem

The present study was concerned with the modification and generalization of dominance behavior in school children as a function of different combinations of reward and punishment. Three questions of primary concern were: (*a*) Could initial dominant behavior exhibited in a two-person game situation be modified by the dispensing and/or withdrawal of rewards contingent upon a specific dominant or nondominant response? (*b*) If so, would this change generalize to another, similar dyadic situation? (*c*) Which reinforcement combinations would be most effective?

For this study, dominance was defined in terms of the contributions made by the individual members of a dyad toward a joint decision. That is, on any given trial, the subject whose individual preference prevailed in the final collective answer was considered to have made a dominant response on that trial. Mann (1959), in a recent review article, reported that the number of task contributions by a member of a group correlated highly with other measures of dominance for that member.

Method

The subjects, from three elementary schools in Tallahassee, Florida, were 128 third- and fourth-grade children between 8 and 10 years of age. The children in each class were randomly assigned into same-sex pairs, the 64 dyads then randomly assigned to four experimental treatment groups: reward-nonreward (R-N), reward-punishment (R-P), nonreward-punishment (N-P), and control (C-C). There were thus 16 dyads in each treatment group.

Each dyad remained together during an entire experimental session lasting approximately 40 minutes and including four phases presented in the following sequence: pregeneralization (PG), preconditioning (PC), conditioning (C), and postgeneralization (G) phases. A teacher-selection task was utilized in the PG and G phases; a light-matching task in the PC and C phases.

The teacher-selection task consisted of 20 × 8-inch white index cards upon which were mounted seven photographs of women's faces clipped from a collegiate yearbook. Individual pictures had been preselected so as to reduce the marked preference that some children had initially displayed for particular faces.

In the PG phase each dyad member was instructed to select from each of the 20 seven-picture cards the one "teacher's" face he liked best. After both subjects had made separate individual choices, they were given 10 of the 20 cards from which together they were to decide which "teacher's" face they liked best. On each of these 10 joint decisions a dominant response was recorded for the team member whose independent choice was the team's decision. Whenever both subjects contributed equally, that is, their individual choices were the same or the team's decision reflected neither of their individual selections, a half-dominant response was credited to each team member. The total number of dominant responses made by a subject to these 10 cards constituted the pregeneralization measure, which was later compared to the postgeneralization measure, the number of dominant responses made to the remaining 10 cards at the end of the testing period.

The light-matching apparatus, designed expressly for this study, consisted of an aluminum panel board (13 × 5 × 3 inches) fitted on an aluminum chassis (17 × 3 × 7 inches). Two horizontal rows of seven neon lights, alternately encased in red, green, and amber plastic shells, faced the children. The top row was controlled in the rear by the examiner; the bottom row was activated by the subjects with switches below each bottom-row light.

Both conditioning phases involved the light apparatus and utilized both the individual and joint responses of the dyad. The PC phase was introduced to the subjects as a guessing game. The top row of seven lights flashed intermittently for several seconds, culminating with one light remaining on. The subjects, first individually by writing the number of the light they expected to remain on, and then jointly by agreeing on which button to press, guessed which light would remain on, following which the examiner activated the apparatus. The impression conveyed to the subjects was that the pattern of flashing lights, including the one light remaining on, was determined by a set number sequence from a table of random numbers clearly visible to the subjects and which the examiner readily consulted while depressing the push-button switches concealed in the rear of the apparatus. Actually which light remained on depended upon the subjects' responses and experimental treatment group.

During the 10 trials of the PC phase no reinforcement was given. That is, the dyads were not permitted to make a correct light-matching choice.

The dominant response was scored in the same manner as in the PG phase.

At the end of the 10 PC trials, the team member adjudged nondominant, the one with fewer dominant responses, was the one whose subsequent behavior controlled the experimental treatment. In the few cases where both team members were equally dominant, randomly one member was considered nondominant for the subsequent treatment during the C phase, which consisted of 20 trials identical to the PC phase with the addition of the various reinforcement conditions.

During the 20 conditioning trials, the R-N group was rewarded with two pieces of candy and correct light matching when the nondominant member made the dominant response. When the dominant member made the dominant response, the light matching was incorrect and the team received no candy.

The dyads in the R-P group were given six candies at the beginning of the C phase. Thereafter, every time the nondominant partner made the dominant choice the team received two pieces of candy and correct light matching. When the dominant partner made the dominant response, the team not only received an incorrect light matching and no candy, but had one piece of candy taken away from them.

The N-P group received 20 candies at the beginning of the C phase. Thereafter, when the nondominant partner made the dominant response, the team received correct light matching but no candy. When the dominant member of the team made the dominant response, the team gave up one piece of candy and received an incorrect light matching.

The control group never received correct light matching or any candy.[1]

At the end of the 20 conditioning trials, the subjects were administered the 10 last seven-picture cards in the postgeneralization phase. Dominant responses were recorded in the same manner as in the pregeneralization phase.

Results

The dependent measure of this study was the number of dominant responses made by the nondominant member of each dyad. Several analyses of the results were permitted by the experimental design. The major focus was on the conditioning phase of the experiment and the between-group differences across blocks of trials within this phase. To this end, an analysis of variance with repeated measures was performed on the data after Hartley's F_{max} test demonstrated that the variance between the four treatment groups was homogeneous (Winer, 1962, pp. 92–96).

In order to determine that the four groups were initially similar during the PC phase, a simple analysis of variance was performed on the number of dominant responses made by the nondominant dyad members. A second analysis of variance was performed on the preconditioning data means. Neither of these analyses demonstrated significant differences between the treatment groups. Table 1 presents the means and standard deviations of the 10 PC trials.

Table 1 *Means and Standard Deviations of Dominant Responses by Nondominant Dyad Members during 10 Preconditioning Trials*

Group	*M*	*SD*
R-N	4.34	.59
R-P	4.22	.79
N-P	3.78	1.22
C-C	4.16	.72

Table 2 *Analysis of Variance of Dominant Responses Made by Nondominant Dyad Members during 20 Conditioning Trials*

Source	*df*	SS	MS	F
Incentive groups (A)	3	32.97	10.99	6.54*
Blocks of trials (B)	3	7.33	2.44	4.28*
A × B	9	7.94	.88	1.54
Ss within groups (C)	60	100.99	1.68	
B × C	180	103.48	.57	
Between Ss	63	133.96		
Within Ss	192	118.75		

* $p < .01$.

Table 2 presents the analysis of variance of the dominant responses made by the nondominant dyad members during the 20 conditioning trials. These trials are divided into four blocks of five trials and both incentive group and blocks of trials were significant at the .01 level. The groups by blocks were not significant, indicating that the curves for each group could be considered parallel.

Table 3 indicates the mean number of dominant

[1] It could be argued here that this procedure might be conceived as a condition of punishment for both members. The authors contend that it did not make a difference to the basic study, in that a pure baseline was not essential in evaluating the effectiveness of the various reinforcement combinations. The C-C group was established in an attempt to demonstrate the stability of the dominant-nondominant response pattern of a dyad in the absence of any differential reinforcement. Of course, one could conjecture as to possible differential effects on nondominant and dominant members. However, taking the group as a whole, if we assume a normal distribution of dominant and nondominant behavior, we would expect no group bias.

Table 3 *Mean Numbers of Dominant Responses Made by Nondominant Dyad Members during 20 Conditioning Trials*

Trials	R–N		R–P		N–P		C–C	
	M	*SD*	*M*	*SD*	*M*	*SD*	*M*	*SD*
Block 1	2.50		2.41		2.75		1.78	
Block 2	2.53		3.03		2.81		2.16	
1st half	5.03	1.21	5.44	1.73	5.56	1.38	3.94	1.29
Block 3	2.35		2.94		2.91		2.31	
Block 4	2.56		3.59		3.09		2.09	
2nd half	4.91	1.40	6.53	1.99	6.00	1.39	4.40	1.46
Total	9.94	2.30	11.97	2.67	11.56	2.93	8.34	2.47

responses made by nondominant dyad members during the 20 conditioning trials, divided into blocks of five and giving the mean and standard deviation for the first half, second half, and total conditioning phase.

The two punishment groups contained the highest mean responses from the nondominant team members. The control group contained the lowest. During the conditioning trials variability tended to be greatest for the R-P group. This trend is partially consistent with previous findings that punishment increases variability. However, the N-P group did not show this variability increase.

Across groups the mean number of dominant responses by the nondominant team member increased over the four successive blocks of trials, except for blocks 2 and 3, which were equal. However, Scheffe's test (Winer, 1962, pp. 85ff) for multiple comparisons between blocks showed only the difference between Blocks 1 and 4 to be statistically significant ($p < .01$).

The Scheffe test was also employed in comparing the group differences on each block of trials. On Block 1 the difference between the N-P and C-C groups was significant ($p < .05$). On Blocks 2 and 3 none of the groups significantly differed from each other. On Block 4, the final five conditioning trials, the P-P group made significantly more dominant responses than the R-N group ($p < .05$) and the C-C group ($p < .01$), while the N-P group performance was significantly greater than that of C-C ($p < .05$).

The *t*-test results on these group differences for the mean number of dominant responses made by nondominant dyad members during conditioning appear in Table 4. All three of the treatment groups responded significantly differently from the control group. The punishment groups responded significantly differently from the R-N group, but not from each other.

The *t*-test results of the assessment of the learning or modification effects as a function of the group reinforcement combinations are presented in Table 5. Comparison was made between the 10 preconditioning trials and the last 10 conditioning trials. Significant differences were found for the two punishment groups.

Table 4 *t-test Comparisons of the Differences between Experimental Treatment Groups on the Mean Number of Dominant Responses Made by Nondominant Dyad Members during 20 Conditioning Trials*

Group Comparisons	Mean Difference	t^a
R-N vs. C-C	+1.60	3.49*
R-P vs. C-C	+3.63	7.93*
N-P vs. C-C	+3.22	7.03*
R-N vs. R-P	−2.03	4.43*
R-N vs. N-P	−1.62	3.54*
R-P vs. N-P	+ .41	.89

[a] Two-tailed test; $df = 59$.
* $p < .01$.

Table 5 *t-test Comparisons of the Differences within Experimental Treatment Groups on the Mean Number of Dominant Responses Made by Nondominant Dyad Members during 10 Preconditioning Trials and Last 10 Conditioning Trials*

Group	Preconditioning	Conditioning	Mean Difference	t^a
R-N	4.34	4.91	+ .57	1.50
R-P	4.22	6.53	+2.31	5.23*
N-P	3.78	6.00	+2.22	4.58*
C-C	4.16	4.41	+ .25	.67

[a] Two-tailed test; $df = 15$.
* $p < .01$.

The further comparison of the relative effectiveness of the various treatments is illustrated in Table 6, which shows the *t*-test results comparing the differences between the groups on the preconditioning trials and the last 10 conditioning trials. The two punishment groups showed significantly greater mean changes from preconditioning to the last 10 conditioning trials than did the control group or the reward-nonreward group, but were not significantly different from each other.

Turning to the secondary focus of this study, the generalization or transfer effects, the analysis of variance performed on the differences between the mean number of dominant responses made by the dyad members during the pre- and postgeneralization phases in each of the experimental treatment groups was nonsignificant. However, since *t* tests could not

Table 6 *t-test Comparisons of the Differences between Experimental Treatment Groups on the Responses Made by Nondominant Dyad Members during 10 Preconditioning Trials and Last 10 Conditioning Trials*

Group Comparison	Difference Between Mean Differences	t^a
R-N vs. C-C	+ .32	.60
R-P vs. C-C	+2.06	3.56**
N-P vs. C-C	+1.97	3.22**
R-N vs. R-P	−1.74	2.98**
R-N vs. N-P	−1.65	2.68*
R-P vs. N-P	+ .09	.14

a Two-tailed test; $df = 30$.
* $p < .05$.
** $p < .01$.

be applied appropriately to the generalization data in the absence of significant main effects, a sign test, used to determine if a significant number of subjects who were initially adjudged nondominant on the basis of the preconditioning performance also were nondominant on the pregeneralization measure, was significant at the .01 level. This finding seems to show that the generalization and conditioning tasks were similar to the extent that each reflected the stability of the initial disposition of the subjects to be dominant or nondominant.

Discussion

This study was an empirical attempt to demonstrate, rather than merely to assume, that reinforcement principles apply within interpersonal situations and govern social behavior of humans in a way similar to that which regulates the responses of human and infrahuman subjects under highly structured, nonsocial laboratory conditions.

The numerous studies which have investigated the effects of different reward and punishment combinations in individual learning tasks have generally shown that reward for correct responses with punishment for incorrect responses and punishment alone for incorrect responses are more effective than reward alone (Brackbill and O'Hare, 1958; Buss, Braden, Orgel, and Buss, 1956; Buss and Buss, 1956; Penny and Lupton, 1961; Warden and Aylesworth, 1927). Furthermore, the Brackbill and O'Hare study, as well as others (e.g., Baer, 1960, 1961), has demonstrated that the withdrawal of positive reinforcement serves as a punishing technique with children. In this regard, Bandura and Walters (1963, p. 14) noted, ". . . from a child's point of view, active confiscation is usually seen as punishment, simple nonreward as mere disinterest."

The authors attempted to make the reinforcement operations in this present study comparable to those utilized in experiments with single individuals, that is, a subject's "correct" responses are either rewarded or nonrewarded and his incorrect responses punished or nonrewarded. Accordingly, "candy given" was defined as reward, "candy withdrawn" defined as punishment, and "candy not withdrawn" defined as nonreward, or neutral. These incentive combinations were investigated to determine their relative effectiveness in modifying interpersonal dominant behavior.

However, since these conditions were superimposed upon incorrect and correct light matching, which conceivably had reinforcing properties, the absolute effects of the reinforcement combinations in this study were obscured; only the relative effects could be examined.

The results of the present study not only indicated that interpersonal dominant-nondominant behavior could be significantly modified through the withdrawal or dispensing or reward when made contingent upon the desired response, but they also appear to have corroborated the findings, from nonsocial learning experiments, concerning the effectiveness of certain reinforcement combinations, in which punishment alone and punishment in conjunction with reward are the most effective in producing change.

The oft-repeated question, which punishment combination, R-P or N-P, is the more effective one, has not been resolved by this study. To ultimately make a proper determination of this, operations are needed which are first independently established as having neutral effects.

In this study nondominant dyad members in each of the three experimental treatment groups made more dominant responses in the 20 conditioning trials than did their control counterparts. Both of the punishment groups were more effective than the R-N group, although neither was more efficient than the other.

The nondominant members in the R-P and N-P groups, who hitherto gave 50% or less dominant responses in the preconditioning phase, averaged significantly more than 50% during the subsequent conditioning phase. The nondominant members of both the R-N and C-C groups continued to give less than 50% during the conditioning trials, although the two groups differed significantly from each other.

That significant differences were not found between treatment groups except on the final block of trials suggests that perhaps more trials would be needed before the complete effects of specific group reinforcement combinations could be adequately evaluated. Certainly other studies which have examined reinforcement effects in individual learning, such as discrimination, have utilized many more trials. Before one can conclude that specified reinforcement combinations are equally effective across social and nonsocial learning situations, more studies are needed which focus on interpersonal learning over longer time periods. Perhaps uniquely characteristic changes and patterns of reinforcement effects might be revealed.

The limited number of conditioning trials probably contributed to the failure in obtaining significant generalization effects. In this study, that data showed that even though a nondominant dyad member will make more dominant responses under certain conditions, he retains his nondominant position in a subsequent task. That the conditioning and generalization tasks were at least partly functionally related seems supported by the sign-test results.

Few studies have focused on the important issue of generalization of social behaviors learned under various conditions. The extent to which reinforcement and other variables control the amount and degree of generalization needs to be thoroughly investigated.

The authors contend that correlational approaches to the study of social behaviors, while often yielding information suggestive of pertinent functional relationships, have not measurably increased our understanding of the variables involved in its development, maintenance, modification, or generalization. Social responses, such as dominance, must be made amenable to more useful experimental analyses by limiting study to small aspects of the desired behavior and directly searching for and manipulating the relevant variables involved.

This study not only shows that dominant behavior, like other social responses, can be controlled and modified in an interpersonal setting by arranging specifiable reinforcing consequences, but also that, at least under the conditions of this study, behavior in a dyadic group situation seems subject to the same laws of conditioning that have been found to hold for single individuals. Continued efforts need to be made to discover and clarify the role that reinforcement plays in complex social situations. One approach could be directed toward investigating the parameters governing those studies under which the effects of reinforcement on group and individual behaviors are similar.

References

ALTROCCHI, J. Dominance as a factor in interpersonal choice and perception. *Journal of Abnormal and Social Psychology,* 1959, *59,* 303–308.

ANDERSON, H. H. Domination and integration in the social behavior of young children in an experimental play situation. *Genetic Psychology Monographs,* 1937, *19,* 341–408.

AZRIN, N. H., and LINDSLEY, O. R. The reinforcement of cooperation between children. *Journal of Abnormal and Social Psychology,* 1956, *52,* 100–102.

BAER, D. M. Escape and avoidance response of preschool children to two schedules of reinforcement withdrawal. *Journal of Experimental Analysis of Behavior,* 1960, *3,* 155–159.

BAER, D. M. Effect of withdrawal of positive reinforcement on an extinguishing response in young children. *Child Development,* 1961, *32,* 67–74.

BANDURA, A., and WALTERS, R. H. *Social learning and personality development.* New York: Holt, Rinehart and Winston, 1963.

BEAVER, A. P. Dominance in the personality of student nurses as measured by the A-S reaction study. *Journal of Psychology,* 1954, *38,* 73–78.

BRACKBILL, Y. Extinction of the smiling response in infants as a function of reinforcement schedules. *Child Development,* 1958, *29,* 115–124.

BRACKBILL, Y., and O'HARE, J. The relative effectiveness of reward and punishment for discrimination learning in children. *Journal of Comparative and Physiological Psychology,* 1958, *51,* 747–751.

BRONZAFT, A., HAYES, R., WELCH, L., and KOTTUV, M. Relationships between extraversion, neuroticism, and ascendance. *Journal of Psychology,* 1960, *50,* 279–285.

BUSS, A. H., BRADEN, W., ORGEL, A., and BUSS, E. H. Acquisition and extinction with different verbal reinforcement combinations. *Journal of Experimental Psychology,* 1956, *52,* 288–295.

BUSS, A. H., and BUSS, E. H. The effect of verbal reinforcement combinations on conceptual learning. *Journal of Experimental Psychology,* 1956, *52,* 283–287.

CERVIN, V. B. Relationship of ascendant-submission behavior in dyadic groups of human subjects to their emotional responsibility. *Journal of Abnormal and Social Psychology,* 1957, *54,* 241–249.

CHITTENDEN, G.E. An experimental study in measuring and modifying assertive behavior in young children. *Monographs of the Society for Research in Child Development,* 1942, *7,* 1 (Serial No. 31).

FARINA, A. Patterns of role dominance and conflict in parents of schizophrenic patients. *Journal of Abnormal and Social Psychology,* 1960, *61,* 31–38.

FISHER, W. F. Sharing in preschool children as a function of amount and type of reinforcement. *Dissertation Abstracts,* 1962, *22,* 2871–2872.

FITZHUGH, K. B. Yielding behavior of delinquent and non-delinquent adolescents. *Dissertation Abstracts,* 1958, *19,* 1108.

GELLERT, E. The effect of changes in group composition on the behavior of young children. *British Journal of Social and Clinical Psychology,* 1962, *1,* 168–181.

HEATHERS, G. Emotional dependence and independence in a physical threat situation. *Child Development,* 1953, *24,* 169–179.

JACK, L. M. An experimental study of ascendant behavior in preschool children. *University of Iowa Studies in Child Welfare,* 1934, *9,* 3–65.

KRECH, D., and CRUTCHFIELD, R. S. *Theory and problems of social psychology.* New York: McGraw-Hill, 1948.

LEVIN, G., and SHAPIRO, D. The operant conditioning of conversation. *Journal of Experimental Analysis of Behavior,* 1962, *5,* 309–316.

LOTT, B. E., and LOTT, A. J. The formation of positive attitudes toward group members. *Journal of Abnormal and Social Psychology,* 1960, *61,* 297–300.

MANN, R. D. A review of the relationships between personality and performance in small groups. *Psychological Bulletin,* 1959, *56,* 241–270.

MUMMERY, D. V. An analytical study of ascendant behavior of preschool children. *Child Development,* 1947, *18,* 40–81.

PAGE, M. L. The modification of ascendant behavior in preschool children. *University of Iowa Studies in Child Welfare,* 1936, *9,* 3–65.

PENNEY, R. K., and LUPTON, A. A. Children's discrimination learning as a function of rewards and punishment. *Journal of Comparative and Physiological Psychology,* 1961, *54,* 449–451.

RHEINGOLD, H. L. The modification of social responsiveness in institutional babies. *Monographs of the Society for Research in Child Development,* 1956, *21,* 2 (Serial No. 63).

STOTT, L. H., and BALL, R. S. Consistency and change in ascendance-submission in the social interaction with children. *Child Development,* 1957, *28,* 259–272.

WALTERS, R. H., and BROWN, M. Studies of reinforcement of aggression. III. Transfer of responses to an interpersonal situation. *Child Development,* 1963, *34,* 563–572.

WARDEN, D. J., and AYLESWORTH, M. The relative value of reward and punishment in the formation of a visual discrimination in the white rat. *Journal of Comparative Psychology,* 1927, *7,* 117–127.

WINER, B. J. *Statistical principles in experimental design.* New York: McGraw-Hill, 1962.

WOLFGANG, A., BANTA, T. J., and PISHKIN, V. Conditioning of group decisions as a function of need for social approval. *Journal of Clinical Psychology,* 1964, *20,* 68–73.

In a further demonstration of behavior modification in a group situation, *Hastorf* analyzes the "why" and "how" of the reinforcement procedures that influenced the relative participation of each member. The experimenters, who turned on the lights signifying either reinforcement or punishment, attempted to increase the verbal leadership of one person in the group. Their success provides confirmation of many other experiments on verbal reinforcement, in which similar procedures of differential control have been shown to be effective.

The procedure of reinforcing "leadership" without defining it explicitly is an example of differential reinforcement where the natural reactivity of the experimenter defines the reinforced and nonreinforced classes of behavior. The generic nature of leadership behavior was defined by the selectivity of the experimenters, who decided when someone was leading the discussion and when he was not. One control experiment was conducted to find out whether the "natural reactivity" of the experimenters was the critical factor in the experiment rather than the occurrence of reinforcing events. Such an artifact was not found. Another control experiment demonstrated that the lights themselves had no effect when they were not specifically contingent on a verbal performance. The results also showed that the group members' evaluations of one another conformed to the behavioral changes produced by the reinforcement procedures. That is, those persons whose verbal outputs increased during the discussion were also accorded higher rankings in terms of overall leadership demonstrated.

42 The "Reinforcement" of Individual Actions in a Group Situation

ALBERT H. HASTORF

The experiments described in this report are characterized by two major conditions: a group of four men discuss, in one sitting, three problem cases; and during the discussion of the second case, each group member receives, privately, evaluations of his behavior from "experts" who are watching and listening in an adjoining observation room.

The four men sit around a table which is unobstructed except for a microphone and four small boxes all grouped at the center of the table. The boxes are radially oriented, each one pointing at one of the participants. Each box houses two small lights, which are the means by which the experts' evaluations are made known. The boxes are so built that only the person at whom they point can see the lights, and they are visible to him without peering into the box.

The central question in each of the experiments is whether the evaluations received during the discussion of the second case will affect the behavior and the perceptions of the participants. Will they talk more or less? Will their views of their own and the others' behavior change? Will their estimates of their own and the others' effectiveness of participation change? And if changes occur during the discussion of the second case, will they persist into the discussion of the third case?

The primary data, therefore, are measures of verbal activity, rankings of effectiveness of participation which each group member makes of himself and of the others, and the answers to a number of questionnaire items concerning the over-all process.

Experimental Procedure

The typical experimental procedure went as follows. Four subjects arrived to participate in a study of group problem solving. The subjects were seated around a circular table and were instructed that they would work as a group on the solution of some human relations problems. They were allowed 10 minutes for the discussion and solution of the first case. No intrusions were made during their discussion, but they were observed from behind one-way mirrors and records were kept of the total number of times each individual talked and the total length of time that he talked. This provided us with a measure of the number of outputs per subject, and the total amount of time consumed by each subject. At the end of this discussion a brief sociometry questionnaire was distributed and each subject was asked to rank-order the group, including himself, on four questions: (a) Who would you say talked the most? (b) Who would you say had the best ideas? (c) Who would you say did the most to guide the discussion? (d) Who would you say was the group's leader? It was not especially surprising to us that these four sociometric questions were highly correlated; after all, it had only been a 10-minute discussion. We therefore combined them into a general measure of the perceived status hierarchy in the group. We also had available to us the previously mentioned measures of behavioral output. In general the behavioral output data correlated quite highly with the sociometric data. This enabled us to obtain a general status ranking in the group.

While this ranking was going on, group members were reading the next case. Our procedure was to select the individual who ranked third in the hierarchy, that is, next to the bottom. He was selected as the *target person*. His selection was quite naturally not announced to the group. The group members were then instructed as follows: "You've now discussed one case. This research is concerned with the influence of feedback on group discussion." There then followed a statement concerning the fact that in many group discussions the chairman does not really give the members any feedback on how they are doing; all he does is direct the discussion, call on people, and maintain proper order. They were told that they were to be a feedback group and that they were going to be given evidence as to how they were doing. Each subject, as they sat in a circle, had a little box in front of him with a green light and a red light. The subjects were told that they were going to be given feedback concerning their performance in the group and that there were "human relations experts" in another room, who were very skilled in the general phenomena of group discussion.

Abridged and condensed from "The 'Reinforcement' of Individual Actions in a Group Situation" by Albert H. Hastorf, from *Research in Behavior Modification* edited by Leonard Krasner and Leonard P. Ullmann.

The experts were going to give the subject feedback of the following sort. "Whenever you make a contribution to the discussion which is helpful or functional in facilitating the group process your green light will go on. Whenever you behave in a way which will eventually hamper or hinder the group process your red light will go on." The contingency was vague since it was clearly possible that one could say something that would receive a red or a green light, but that might be because the expert deemed that it would help or hinder later activity. But the subject's directions clearly implied some contingency between what they did in the group and the presence of either red or green lights. There seemed to be no doubt that the subjects believed the instructions.

Subjects were further instructed that they should not mention the fact that they had received either a red or green light. It should be kept in mind that they were unable to see the other people's lights, because the lights were placed in boxes which shielded any one subject's lights from the view of the other participants. We therefore have a situation where the subjects are prepared to engage in a 20-minute case discussion, where they expect to receive reasonable and frequent feedback on their participation.

What is special about the whole situation is that the experts back of the one-way mirrors are actually the experimenters, and they were going to follow somewhat different rules than the subjects had been told. An experimenter controlled the distribution of red and green lights given to the subject who ranked third in the status hierarchy (the target subject). The experimenters also tried to influence the behavior of the other participants. The experimenter who was going to try to control the behavior of the target person had the task of trying to make him the leader of the group. The experimenters also had the task of trying to make the other three subjects followers. Only the most informal rules were agreed to by the experimenters. We did not attempt to formally define leadership. We did not attempt to prescribe just what behaviors should be reinforced or punished on the part of the target person or on the part of the followers.

During the first trials of this procedure the experimenter who was hooked up with the target person usually said things like, "My fellow was awfully quiet during the first discussion; I've clearly got to get him talking." By the same token, the experimenter who was hooked up to the Number 1 man in the status hierarchy usually said something like, "I'm going to have to try and shut this fellow up." During the first trial there was a general feeling on the part of the experimenters that the natural tendency on the part of some people to talk and engage in leadership acts, and on the part of others to be quiet and submissive, was very great. In fact, they were very doubtful that they could alter behavior in a mere 20-minute acquisition period. We shall soon see that they were surprisingly successful.

There was one bit of informal evidence that it might be possible to bring about change of this kind. Researchers had explored the technique of inviting one member of a group to "try and act important" in a group discussion. The evidence was that although subjects were very hesitant about trying this, sociometric evidence indicated considerable success.[1] Beyond this, there is an investigation by Oakes, Droge, and August (1960) that reports changes in the verbal output in four-person groups as a function of two subjects receiving positive reinforcement and two subjects receiving punishment. In that situation, however, the subjects were unable to see each other and their concern was primarily with change in verbal output.

Our acquisition session lasted for 20 minutes. We again made records of total number of outputs and talking time consumed by each subject; and at the conclusion of this session, the same sociometry questionnaire was distributed. Subjects were asked to rank the group on the same four questions. We were interested in not only the question as to whether we could change behavior, but also the question as to whether this behavior change was reflected in the perceptions of group members.

Reference to Table 1 under Condition B, which is the condition we have been describing, indicates the rather dramatic change in both the number of outputs and the amount of time consumed on the part of the target person or "leader." We will return to this table in more detail later, but the rather dramatic improvement that occurred in the sociometric status of the target person should be noted. In fact, a colleague, upon learning of our first results, described our procedure as "the mouse that roared."

There then followed a third session that lasted for ten minutes. At the start of the session the subjects were told that there would be no feedback lights. We again took measures of actual performance and obtained sociometric rankings. Following this, the subjects were given a brief questionnaire regarding their total experience, and the entire procedure was explained to them.

Before going to some general questions that might be asked, it might be helpful to make a few informal observations. First of all, the experimenter hooked up with the target person found that he had to use red lights early in the acquisition session; in essence, he had to punish silence on the part of the target person. He found a rather quick response to this.

[1] Richard E. Farson, a personal communication, 1963.

The target person said something which he immediately reinforced with a green light. As time went along the target person increased output and this output could be maintained with an occasional green light. Experimenters attempting to control the behavior of the first and second persons in the status hierarchy found that they had to punish talking early in the acquisition session, but that in time they could give some green lights to reinforce agreement with the target person. We even noticed postural changes on the part of our subject. The target person appeared to be slouched down in his chair at the beginning of the acquisition session; halfway through the session he was actually quite upright and looking rather attentive and eager.

Objectives of Studies

Let us now turn to some general questions that might be asked, the answers to some of which have already been implied. One might first question whether the lights really would make a difference, and could we really change the verbal output of our subjects? Secondly, one might ask just what the import is of the rather vague instructions given to the experimenters. The experimenters were all social psychologists, and we might assume that they could apply their sophistication concerning group behavior and be especially adept at selecting out the behavior that is to be reinforced or punished. In other words, is it really important that qualified experimenters select the behavior that is reinforced? Perhaps a machine that gives reinforcements where the only contingency was on verbal output would do just as well. One can push this a little further and raise the question as to whether the reinforcements need be contingent on verbal output. Perhaps one can preset a certain number of reinforcements and punishments for each subject and have them contingent on nothing but time.

Note that we have been operating on all four members of the group. Perhaps one can get the same effect by only reinforcing and punishing the target person and doing nothing to the other three members; or we may be able to raise the status of the target person by doing nothing to him but encouraging the other three members to be followers, so that the target person is almost forced to act like a leader because everyone else is acting like a follower. These are questions that we shall return to shortly with some data that bear on their answers.

Another question that we might ask relates to the perservance and generalization of this effect. If we do get some behavior change, does it carry over to the nonfeedback session? Reference to Table 1 indicates that there is some carry-over in the third session. Beyond this, one might ask if it would carry over to another group? Can we employ this therapeutic technique on a quiet person and have it carry over to other social situations? This and the above questions all relate to the technology of behavior change.

Another set of questions are concerned with the ways people perceive this behavior change. What is the target person's perception of the situation? Does he notice a change in his own behavior? Does this change go above or below his own adaptation level? Does he say, "I talked more"? Does he like talking more? There are psychologists who believe that people have their own adaptation level toward participation in group discussion and if forced above or below their adaptation level they become unhappy. In general, the evidence is that target persons whose behavioral output was stepped up seemed to be pretty pleased with talking more. A second and possibly more interesting question concerns the reaction of the other subjects to the target person. If behavior change occurs, do the others notice it? If they do notice it, what do they make of it?

Behavior change would appear to be a rather significant stimulus for our perception and evaluation of others. Heider (1958) has stressed the fact that in order to make an evaluation of another person's behavior we must make certain inferences as to the causality of the behavior. His primary distinction has been between internal and external causality. For example, if one perceives another's behavior as having been internally caused and it happens to have been "good" behavior, we will evaluate that individual as being a "good" person; whereas, if we perceive another person as behaving in the way he did for external reasons, that is, because some external force made him behave that way, then we are not in a position to necessarily infer that he is a "good" person; we cannot be sure.

It would appear that this issue applies rather directly to inferring the quality of "leadership." More specifically, if our group members notice an increase in the verbal output of the target person and also raise that person's status on such dimensions as best ideas and leadership, one would have to guess that they experience him as talking more because he wanted to. Compare this with the perception that another person is talking more only because some external force is making him do it. It should be noted at this point that the group members under condition B raised the status of the target person on all the sociometric dimensions. They appeared to be willing to make certain attributions concerning his behavior change. We shall return to this issue after a discussion of the experimental conditions that have been run and the data that have been obtained.

Table 1 *Output and Sociometric Status of the Target Person (TP)*

Condition	Number of Groups	Average Sociometric Rankings (1 to 4) Received by TP from Other Group Members			Total time talked by TP expressed as percentage of length of session			Total utterances by TP expressed as percentage of total group utterances		
		OPER 1	ACQ	OPER 2	OPER 1	ACQ	OPER 2	OPER 1	ACQ	OPER 2
C	9	3.05	2.81	2.80	15.3	18.2	18.1	19.5	22.5	22.9
		p. 01	p. 06		p. 01	p. 01		p. 02	p. 01	
B	9	3.23	1.70	2.30	13.4	35.5	24.6	17.2	31.2	25.4
			p. 01			p. 01			p. 01	
		p. 02			p. 10					
D	7	3.18	2.13	2.36	15.4	26.9	28.6	22.6	30.9	29.4
			p. 02			p. 02				
E	7	3.12	2.80	2.75	17.5	18.7	18.8	22.0	21.6	20.5
V	7	3.08	2.66	2.82	16.4	21.4	20.6	20.4	26.0	27.2
W	7	3.24	2.95	3.11	18.6	20.5	17.0	20.7	22.6	24.3

Only *p* values of .10 or less are indicated. All tests are two-tailed.

OPER 1–ACQ differences for all experimental conditions are compared with OPER 1–ACQ differences for control (C) groups by the Mann-Whitney test.

Significance levels for ACQ–OPER 2 and OPER 1–OPER 2 differences were computed by the Wilcoxon matched-pairs, signed-ranks test.

Results

Table 1 presents our results. Note that six conditions have been run, and that for each condition data are presented for both sociometric rankings and for length and frequency of talking. All values refer to the behavior of the target person and to the sociometric rankings given him by the other three group members. The target person's own sociometric ratings are excluded. The three case discussions are referred to as: operant 1 (10 minutes), acquisition (20 minutes), and operant 2 (10 minutes).

Condition C refers to the control condition in which four subjects discussed cases 1, 2, and 3 under instructions that they were a nonfeedback group. In other words, the lights were not operated at all. There were no significant changes in either output or sociometric status in this situation. It should be noted that there is a small increase in the target person's output and sociometric status at the end of the acquisition period. These changes do not approach statistical significance. This may well be some sort of a regression effect. The changes in all other conditions were compared with the control condition.

Condition B is the experimental condition that was described earlier in the report. Group members participated in a 10-minute case discussion followed by a 20-minute acquisition period in which they were given red and green lights. The meaning of these lights, from the standpoint of the participants, was that they were evaluative of their contributions to the group; however, the experimenters operating the lights were attempting to raise the level of participation of the target person and to lower the level of participation and encourage follower-type behavior on the part of the other three group members.

The operant 2 session immediately followed in which no lights were given and no lights were expected. Reference to Table 1 indicates that the acquisition period led to a significant increase in both the output and the sociometric status of the target person. In the operant 2 session, there was a significant drop in both the output and the sociometric status of the target person. However, it should be noted that the target person's output and status do not fall to their original position, but remain significantly above the original position.

The effects of the acquisition experience appear to carry over to an immediately following discussion.

Two things should be stressed in regard to this finding. First of all, we have not only succeeded in bringing about behavioral change, but we have found that group members are aware of the change. Secondly, an experimentally increased incidence of talking is correlated with an increase in sociometric status on the leadership dimension. Previous research has usually demonstrated a high correlation between talking and leadership, but one could never be quite sure how this came to be. Was it that people who were perceived as having "leadership qualities" were encouraged or permitted to talk a lot, or did the sheer amount of talking create an impression of leadership? These findings appear to indicate that if one can increase the incidence of any person's talking, it will increase the likelihood that that person will be seen as a leader.

One comment should be noted in regard to these data. It is conceivable that the increase in the target person's status could be the result of the other three group members reducing their self-ranking because they had received red lights. However, if we eliminate their self-ranking, they still increase the status of the target person.

Condition D was run in order to explore the importance of selecting specific behaviors to be reinforced or punished. The directions to the subjects were exactly the same as under condition B; however, a preprogramed machine was responsible for giving red and green lights to the participants. The experimenters' job was to let the machine know that a participant had talked. The machine was programed so that the target person would get quite a few green lights and very few red lights; the other three participants would get a greater incidence of red lights for talking and a small number of green lights. The program was set so that if all subjects talked about the same amount as they had under condition B, each of the participants would get about the same number of lights as he had under condition B.

The program was set so that the target person received three green lights for each five outputs and a red light at the end of a 45-second period of continuous silence. The other participants received seven red lights and two green lights for each 25 outputs. Note that under this condition the experimenter was allowed to make no selection of the verbal behavior that would be rewarded or punished. Surprisingly enough, the results of condition D are remarkably similar to those of condition B. This is especially remarkable in that the increase of talking on the part of the target person was not quite as great as it was in condition B. This of course reduced his chances of getting green lights and, as it turned out, more green lights were given to the target person under condition B. Even with this reduction in the incidence of controlling stimuli, sociometric status follows the same general pattern as in condition B. Interestingly enough, in condition D the target person appears to maintain his gains of the acquisition period during the operant 2 session.

It appears that the primary difference between the two conditions was in the first 2 minutes. It is at this time that the experimenters under condition B worked most heavily on the target person in order to "get him started." With a preprogrammed machine, this was not possible under condition D.

Condition E was run in order to determine whether the effect could be obtained when the lights were not contingent on verbal output. Again, the subjects were instructed in the same manner as before; however, this time in the acquisition period the lights were preprogramed on the basis of time. In other words, the target person was going to receive about the same number of green lights that he had received under condition B, but they were to be given at certain times and contingent on nothing but time.

Reference to Table 1 indicates that there were no significant changes in either the output or the sociometric status of the target person. Quite obviously the phenomenon of increase in output and increase in status is not a function of merely the number of reinforcements given. Quite clearly there must be some contingency between the lights and talking in order to get the effect.

Conditions V and W are similar enough so that they will be discussed at the same time. They represent our preliminary explorations into reinforcing only certain members of the group. Condition V entailed an exploration of the effect on the target person of the attempt to create a leadership vacuum in the group. The target person was instructed by private written directions that he was in a nonfeedback group and that there would be no lights during the acquisition period. The other three group members were instructed by private written directions that they would receive lights. The experimenters attempted to suppress the verbal output of the other three group members to see if the target person would increase his behavior in order to fill the vacuum we had created. Reference to Table 1 indicates that this was not successful. There was a slight tendency for the target person to talk somewhat more, and there was a slight increase in his sociometric status; these changes did not approach significance.

Interestingly enough, there was a slight increase in the amount of "dead air" during the acquisition period. By this we mean there was an increase in the amount of time when no one in the group was talking. This seems to imply that we had made the other group members somewhat more hesitant about talking, but apparently the target person did not leap in to fill the gap.

Condition W is essentially the mirror image of condition V. One might describe it as a wedge. In this condition the target person received written instructions indicating that he would receive lights during the acquisition period and he was given a regular "leadership" schedule of lights, just as in the B condition, whereas the other group members were given private instructions that they would not receive lights. We were curious to see if we could create the effect by merely operating on the target person. Reference to Table 1 indicates that we were not successful. It is worth noting that if you conceive of adding together condition V and W, you get condition B. However, if you add together the behavioral effects of conditions V and W you do not approach the size of effect that you get in condition B. It would appear that one must have the operations combined at the same time.

Summary

Let us summarize what we now know. The procedure that has been described permits us to bring about rather dramatic behavior changes when we use lights as both rewards and punishments. We also know that these lights must in some way be contingent on talking, although it does not seem to be necessary for the experimenters to make decisions as to what classes of talking should be reinforced. We also know that it appears to be necessary to influence all group members to get the effect. Beyond this, it is apparent that the group members notice the behavior change on the part of the target person, and that they appear to be willing to alter their perception of this status. It is also clear that if the lights are removed, the output and the sociometric status of the target person tends to fall, but they do not fall to their original position. The target person maintains some of his gain.

This all seems to imply that in a very short period of time we can take a person of fairly low status and make him a leader, at least in the eyes of the members of his group.

It would seem important to explore the evaluations people make of behavior change in a situation such as this when they are in the role of observers, having been told just what the participants have been told, and not being aware of the experimenters' rules. They ought to perceive the situation essentially as the participants themselves do. What if observers are informed about the experimenters' rules? Would they have a tendency to perceive the behavior change as externally caused (the lights made him talk), and thus not positively evaluate his ideas? What if the observers actually operate the lights? An important facet of this situation may be the active conscious attempt to influence another person's verbal output. It is possible that this situation could lead to an even less positive evaluation of an individual's ideas and leadership activity. Exploration of these situations are of considerable theoretical importance to social psychology. They also strike us as being of overwhelming concern to the clinical psychologist. The clinical psychologist is in the business of behavior change, and it would seem crucial to understand how he perceives and evaluates the changes that he brings about.

Verbal Behavior

8

Verbal behavior is usually defined as a performance whose reinforcement is mediated by the action of another person. Thus, most verbal behavior has little effect on the environment other than to vibrate some air or make marks on paper. The significance of verbal activity lies in the way it influences another person who, in turn, acts on the environment in a way important for the speaker or the writer. The mediation of the second person (listener or reader) is what makes language and verbal behavior such a critically important element in the social process.

The reactivity of the listener to the verbal stimulus from the speaker is the major reinforcer we are dealing with, and this is obviously very complex. After all, speech in its simple form is an auditory stimulus which operates on the listener's eardrum. Its effectiveness lies not so much in the complexity of the speaker's repertoire as in the potential behaviors which can be prompted in the listener. Thus, the listener is best conceived of as a potentially large repertoire of performances. The auditory stimuli produced by the speaker's behavior will be effective if they prompt forms of conduct already existing in the listener's repertoire. Despite our ordinary concepts of persuasion and education, it is the listener who shapes the speaker rather than the reverse. From the speaker's point of view, his verbal utterance will be effective if it prompts actions in the listener that are relevant to the reasons for his utterance in the first place.

To deal with verbal conduct behaviorally it is necessary to separate the behavior of the listener from that of the speaker. The behavior of the listener is already in his repertoire, and it increases in frequency when it is prompted by the speaker. In analyzing the significance of a "word," therefore, it is critical for us to know whether we are dealing with the speaker or the listener. Our common language usage about communication is misleading when we say that "someone has an idea, the idea is clothed into words, the words are coded into air vibrations which impinge upon the sense organ of the listener who then retranslates them back into the original idea." Behaviorally, nothing could be further from the truth. The major reasons that the behavior of the speaker has anything at all to do with the behavior of the listener is that the speaker's performance is reinforced by the way it changes the listener's conduct. Therefore, he tends to emit those behaviors that produce stimuli capable of increasing or decreasing the frequency of the behaviors in the listener which are of interest to him as a speaker. This functional significance of an auditory stimulus may be completely different for the speaker who produces it than for a listener whose current repertoire it prompts.

Verbal Conditioning

The first two articles in this section describe how the basic phenomena have been approached in experimental studies and compare two conflicting theoretical approaches. The article by *Kanfer* compares operant conditioning experiments on verbal behavior with operant laboratory experiments with animals. Many of the research workers who have done verbal conditioning experiments were strongly influenced by their experience with animal operant laboratory studies or their knowledge of the literature. The relevance of animal research to problems of human conduct is most easily seen in experiments which deal with one abstract property of behavior, such as frequency. The study of intermittent reinforcement, for example, can be carried out with a simple arbitrary performance such as a pigeon pecking a key. Analysis of this relatively simple situation helps us to understand more complex behaviors, such as one person persuading another or a student studying. These behaviors are also intermittently reinforced, and their frequency is changed as a result of the schedule of reinforcement. In moving from animal experiments to human situations we can deal with the frequency of the more complex behavior without having to analyze its content. The problem is much more difficult in verbal behavior, of course, because the very content and complexity of the behavior lies at the heart of our inquiry.

In this article, Kanfer comments on some of the ways that research on verbal behavior has carried over from the procedures and concepts of the animal laboratory. He also points out several ways in which verbal research with humans differs from animal studies. Probably one of the biggest differences lies in the nature of the reinforcer. As Kanfer points out, many of the verbal conditioning experiments are literal analogs of animal paradigms which attempt to increase the frequency of some verbal performance by reinforcing it. The basic procedure resembles that in which food pellets are used to increase the frequency with which a rat presses a bar. The relationship between the rat and the experimenter has at least some of the characteristics of a verbal interchange, in that the bar-press produces a signal for the experimenter to effect the rat's reinforcement by dropping a pellet into the tray. In effect, the two have communicated with one another.

Psychologists who carry out experiments on verbal behavior have engaged in a lively argument about the relative usefulness of a behavioral approach or a cognitive approach. Kanfer concludes his article with a comparison of these competing theoretical positions. Although Kanfer prefers the behavioral approach, he concludes that theoretical arguments are less important than the discovery and description of facts from behavioral experiments.

43 | Verbal Conditioning: A Review of Its Current Status[1]

FREDERICK H. KANFER

Stages in Verbal Conditioning Research

It is possible to categorize verbal conditioning studies with regard to four major purposes. Although there is continuing overlap between studies, the bulk of experiments show a trend of increasing shifts toward the latter categories. It seems that research on verbal conditioning has undergone the following four stages:

(1) a *Demonstration* stage;
(2) a *Re-evaluation* stage;
(3) an *Application* stage; and
(4) an *Expansion* stage.

(1) *Demonstration stage.* Studies of the early 1950's mainly purported to demonstrate that various modifications of the basic operant conditioning paradigm can be fruitfully applied to human behavior and that response classes of varying complexity are sensitive to reinforcing operations. These studies attempted to show that at least some of the variables found to be effective in modifying animal behavior might be applied to human verbal responses. The repeated demonstrations of the modifiability of verbal behavior by systematic application of stimuli known to have reinforcing properties can leave no doubt that such a demonstration has been successful. While it is always possible to use an endless variety of verbal response classes, with innumerable variations in the setting and in the reinforcing operations, the continued demonstration of the effectiveness of conditioning techniques with different verbal behaviors is no longer of great significance.

(2) *Re-evaluation stage.* Verbal conditioning paradigms originally had been hailed for their apparent simplicity in an approach to understanding human verbal behavior. The accumulating evidence made it clear that the typical verbal conditioning experiment, despite its minimal requirements of materials, equipment or experimenter skill, is highly sensitive to the influence of a wide variety of variables.

(3) *Application stage.* With little direct interest in the theoretical problems created by the re-evaluation of the original verbal conditioning paradigm, investigators have gone on to use the procedures for the evaluation of hypotheses about social behavior, personality, or other topics of their interest. In these studies, the verbal conditioning procedure has simply been used as a tool, as might be other learning procedures, to establish differences between values of independent variables. The potential for tests of specific and limited hypotheses about the effects of many independent variables is enhanced by the fact that the very ambiguity of the paradigms and the sensitivity of response measures to clinically relevant factors parallels many clinical interactions. In this sense, verbal conditioning methods represent excellent laboratory analogues to the clinical interview and to other psychotherapeutic procedures.

(4) *Expansion stage.* The researcher who has become interested in verbal conditioning because of its promise to approach verbal behavior within a simple S-R framework has discovered that the procedure also lends itself to investigation of theoretical issues related to the capability of human Ss for self-regulation. This human characteristic tends to attenuate predictability of behavior from simple knowledge of input-output relationships. Therefore, some researchers have used the verbal conditioning procedure as a starting point for the study of complex verbal processes. Others have seen the richness of problems encountered in verbal conditioning not as a challenge to their solution but as an opportunity to attack once again the feasibility of an S-R approach to complex behavior. Still others have made the point that the discovery of effective variables, not currently under *E*'s control in the verbal conditioning paradigm, is sufficient ground for rejecting all the empirical relationships which had been demonstrated in the verbal conditioning literature, on the basis of the fact that the paradigm did not turn out to be a simple, "automatic" procedure for behavior modification.

[1] This paper was written in conjunction with research supported in part by Research Grants MH 06921–04 and MH 06922–04 from the National Institute of Mental Health, United States Public Health Service.

From: Frederick H. Kanfer, "Verbal Conditioning: A Review of Its Current Status," in Theodore R. Dixon and David L. Horton, Eds., *Verbal Behavior and General Behavior Theory,* © 1968. Reprinted by permission of Prentice-Hall, Inc., Englewood Cliffs, N.J. [Portions of this selection—concerning theoretical issues and clinical implications of verbal conditioning research—have been omitted from the original, with the permission of the author and the publisher.]

In this stage, experimenters have increasingly modified the original paradigms to study such processes as vicarious learning, the role of awareness in learning, variables affecting self-reinforcing and self-control, the associative relationship of words, and many others. Eventually, this phase should lead to efforts toward integration of the verbal conditioning literature with other verbal learning paradigms.

Verbal and Animal Conditioning Compared

When a laboratory phenomenon is the basis of an analogue for further research exploration in a different species, it is essential to recognize that inherent species differences may necessitate methodological and conceptual adjustments. Before the general principles of the underlying theoretical framework can be extended, it must be first ascertained whether or not the necessary changes or transformations can be accommodated. This adjustment may create new problems for the more limited theoretical framework, but the expansion can hold the promise for increased coverage and for more stringent tests of the framework.

In verbal conditioning research the parallel to animal work rested mainly on the following elements of operant conditioning:

1. Operant conditioning is characterized by an initial lack of congruence of the response with a particular eliciting stimulus. Therefore, any response class can be chosen if it has a moderate rate of occurrence in an environment, even when the eliciting stimulus is unknown.
2. Response classes of varying sizes can be chosen with reference to their functional similarity, as long as it is known that they have the potential for increase.
3. Response frequencies can be changed by administration of any stimulus known to have reinforcing properties, closely following emission of the critical response.
4. Empirical relationships can be described in terms of the systematic application of reinforcing stimuli and response rate, generally with the assumption that no other systematic organismic changes occur in S during acquisition.

In applying this paradigm to verbal behavior, additional considerations are required because of the species differences between rats, pigeons, and men, and because human experimentation requires certain methodological changes due to the characteristics of Ss. It is obvious that the greater the number of modifications made in the human study, the more variables need to be accounted for, and the more distant becomes the comparison with the animal analogue. A point may be reached where sufficient differentiation between the two experimental methods may tax the underlying theory to the degree that drastic changes become necessary. In fact, as has been the case in the area under discussion, entirely new research areas may develop out of the problems posed by the expansion of the analogy. A review of verbal conditioning studies suggests the following among the main differentiating features of the verbal procedure.

Habituation

In animal work Ss are usually exposed to the experimental apparatus for several sessions before the actual experimental design is introduced. During this habituation period animals manifest individual differences in their preferences for various motor responses, for various locations of a cage, or for activities involving different parts of their bodies. Upon their first experience in a Skinner box, many animal Ss also show a somewhat higher rate of "emotional" responses, including rapid movement, bar-biting, defecation, and urination. While we do not know to what specific stimuli these animals are responding, nor what their behavioral intentions may be, the habituation period serves to reduce individual differences and behavior fluctuations in order to permit observation of a stable base rate prior to introduction of independent variables. If animals seem to be oriented away from the manipulandum, some shaping often is carried out to speed up the response to the manipulandum and the food trough. If any consistent response-reinforcement contingencies are set up at all during this pretraining phase, they are not identical to training conditions. With simultaneous extinction of many initial exploratory or emotional responses, the animal is better prepared and more easily controlled by the subsequent experimental manipulations.

In the human experiment, the habituation procedure is usually absent or of brief duration. Considerable variability in verbal behavior has often been noted during the initial few minutes of the experiment. However, only a few studies parallel the essential preparation of an animal for an acquisition experiment by use of repeated sessions with human Ss over an extended period of time. To preserve a closer analogy to animal conditioning, it would be more appropriate to conduct verbal conditioning procedures only after variability has been reduced and S has shown relatively stable behaviors, in an environment which he has had time to evaluate, scrutinize, and test out. As it stands, although animal studies involve organisms with a much more limited response repertoire, a relatively simple history, and less potential for interaction with the environment, animal Ss are carefully handled in soundproofed, air-conditioned, humidity-controlled, and light-controlled boxes to avoid adventitious learning. In contrast, human Ss with their rich verbal and motor repertoire and great sensitivity to environmental stimuli are seen in offices, laboratories, home environments, or called over the telephone, and observation of operant rate is often begun at once and followed immediately by an acquisition procedure.

When care is taken to pretrain human Ss, much of the variability and the problems of self-instructions, hypothesis testing, or other "game playing" disappear and S's behavior comes under increased control of *E*'s experimental manipulation. In verbal conditioning, cumulative records of S's working under different reinforcement schedules after six hourly sessions on consecutive days show highly regular response curves and greatly reduced inter-individual differences (Kanfer and Marston, 1962). In fact, S's attitudes toward *E*, his awareness of the response-reinforcement contingency and many other interesting but tangential variables seem to lose their impact. It is only under such conditions of sustained performance that verbal response measures may approximate the regular patterns obtained with nonverbal operant responses reported by Lindsley (1960) with psychotics, by Long, Hammack, May, and Campbell (1958) with children, and by many other investigators.

Available Reinforcers

In tests of particular hypotheses in animal operant conditioning, stimuli are used which have such well-established reinforcing properties as food or shock, in conjunction with operations insuring their effectiveness, e.g., food deprivation. If a study tests the effectiveness of differing stimuli as reinforcers, care is taken to select response classes and experimental parameters which have been well explored in other studies to provide easy comparability of findings and to avoid ambiguity of conclusions due to interactions among other variables. Frequently, a new reinforcing stimulus is first tested for its effectiveness in a close replication of a widely accepted basic experiment. With human Ss this rigorous procedure has usually not been followed. On the basis of Skinner's theoretical analysis (1953) and the early findings of the effectiveness of minimal verbal cues in group data, many researchers have continued to presuppose that simple verbal responses by *E* can equally serve as reinforcers for all Ss.

Mandler and Kaplan (1956) were among the first to point out that human Ss differ greatly in their responsiveness to the reinforcing properties of verbal stimuli. It is of interest to note that these studies have not led to efforts toward *independent* verification of S's responsivity to the experimental reinforcing stimulus. While assessment of reinforcing properties of a stimulus *post hoc* may be better than total disregard of this variable, this practice raises serious methodological problems. The conduct of a preference test for different food substances as a basis for splitting experimental groups with animals who have just completed experimental runs in which food reward was offered would parallel the postexperimental inquiry. This difference of *prior* testing of the reinforcing stimulus versus *post* testing is one notable factor encountered in comparing the animal and human research paradigms.

Task Requirements

In an effort to provide comparability with animal research, verbal conditioning studies usually have given Ss limited or misleading instructions about the task. In a sense, both animal and human Ss are informed of the task by *E*'s manipulation of their environment. It is pretty clear, however, that the analogue breaks down rapidly when one considers the propensity of human Ss for defining their job not only on the basis of environmental cues, but also on the basis of their diverse past experiences. In contrast to animal work, the human S appears to be faced with the problem of discovering what *E* wishes him to do, with the task of following instructions, and with other self-imposed tasks which affect the result, often in unknown ways. The complexity of variables controlling the behavior of human Ss in a one-hour experiment, with a strange *E*, in a novel experimental setting, and with an ambiguous task further attenuates direct and simple comparison with animal research.

Verbal Response Classes

In animal work the critical response is usually defined with sufficient clarity so that its occurrence can trigger off a mechanical reinforcing mechanism. The selection of verbal behavior for modification immediately carries with it the problem of analysis of such a behavior along some dimensions. Difficulties of defining a verbal response class have been extensively discussed by Salzinger (1965) and others. The choice of the verbal response mode is further complicated by the fact that verbal conditioners seek to isolate *functional* response units. In distinction to other areas of verbal learning, this choice limits use of structural (grammatic or semantic) word categories. The richness of the verbal repertoire may also affect the rate of learning and the case of forming conditionable response classes. Salzinger, Feldman, and Portnoy (1964) found that verbal members conditioned as a single response class and at a faster rate than nonverbal members, which tended to be conditioned separately. The importance of the characteristics of other items in which the class is embedded on presentation has been demonstrated by Kanfer and McBrearty (1961), and Marston, Kanfer, and McBrearty (1962), and McBrearty, Kanfer, Marston, and Evander (1963).

Some Comments on the Cognitive Position

The main contributions of the cognitive view have been to stress the central role of awareness in verbal conditioning, to propose the use of verbal reports as the measuring instruments of awareness, and to offer theoretical models aimed at remedying the insufficiencies of S-R approaches with respect to mediational constructs. This section attempts to show that some of the problems remain unsolved because of the questionable status of verbal reports and the complexity of cognitive constructional frameworks.

The Verbal Report

When S's verbal or written reports are treated as indices or correlates of hypothesized internal processes, the full range of problems associated with introspectionism again beclouds the issue. There is much merit in gaining information from Ss about their attitudes and descriptions of the experimental procedures. This information can provide a rich field for hypotheses to be tested in subsequent studies and yields many insights useful for the design of fresh experiments. The major difficulty lies in the temptation to handle these verbal reports as substitutes for the events which they describe. It is for these reasons that most researchers in other areas of verbal learning have avoided their use.

In a thoughtful and detailed analysis of this problem, Spielberger and DeNike (1966) summarize the main criticism by noncognitive researchers of the use of verbal reports under four headings:

1. the procedure suggests awareness;
2. awareness follows learning;
3. awareness facilitates later learning during acquisition; and
4. awareness may be a behavior concurrently strengthened during acquisition.

Partial remedies are proposed by the authors and have been utilized in studies coming from their laboratories. The first criticism can be attenuated by careful phrasing of questions or use of written questionnaire responses, although Spielberger and DeNike note that a standardized written procedure may not be sufficiently complete or clear to elicit full reports. We would be inclined to question whether or not a change in the written mode of response eliminates the influence of the experimental setting on the content of these replies, even though the personal interaction with *E* is reduced.

The criticism of the use of the verbal report should not be construed to deny that relationships can be established between specific experimental operations (such as giving information about the task or about the response-reinforcement contingency in instructions) and performance. There is good evidence that such information does, in fact, facilitate learning. The crux of the behavioristic criticism of the cognitive position, however, lies in the fact that such information cannot be inferred to mediate learning when it is obtained in postlearning reports.

Another problem encountered in the use of verbal reports lies in the fact that it demands a special verbal repertoire. Accurate discriminations of complex problems often occur in the absence of S's ability to verbalize the characteristics of the two discriminated classes. On the response side, differences in S's histories, training in stimulus predifferentiation, and other variables affect the emission of the verbal report. In verbal conditioning, the particular stimulus dimensions selected for discrimination may affect not only S's performance, but also his verbalizations (Martin and Dean, 1965).

The problem of acceptance of verbal reports as awareness indices is illustrated in Dulany's categorization of verbal reports for measuring behavioral intentions (BI). One response category (Dulany, 1962, p. 114) classifies an S who reports intentions to produce some response class that is negatively correlated with the correct response class. If one performs experimental manipulations producing such a report, e.g., by asking S not to cooperate with *E*, or by a hostile set, it would logically follow that such an S might respond with falsehoods to the questionnaire. If he does so, such a stated intention should also affect his response to the questionnaire (e.g., by denying knowledge of the response-reinforcement contingency or misrepresenting his attitudes), as well as his performance on the conditioning task.

The case of the "lying subject" raises the problem of categorizing the verbal report by its content when suppressive factors may be operating. One could argue that other conditions not as extreme as lying, such as the induction of a hostile set or personality variables associated with hostility, would influence the report in a predetermined nonveridical or *E*-antagonistic direction. It is interesting to note that Krasner, Weiss, and Ullmann (1961) found that college Ss who had undergone hostility induction by a pre-experimental negative interaction with the examiner reported fewer awareness responses than those Ss who had not been made hostile. Further, Ss who did not report awareness were significantly more hostile on two different test measures of hostility than Ss who did report awareness.

The criticisms concerning the status of verbal reports should not be interpreted to suggest that they have no heuristic value in generating new research hypotheses. However, when a theoretical position is strongly anchored in these reports and their use becomes a base for rejecting other research strategies, it is most critical to avoid building a theoretical formulation mainly on response dimensions which have equivocal status.

Some Comments on the Non-cognitive Position

Much of the controversy in the verbal conditioning literature has resulted from the limitations of the operant conditioning paradigm to account for variability among Ss due to factors not under *E*'s control. While such issues as the role in learning of S's covert verbalizations can be temporarily postponed, the problems cannot be resolved by ignoring them. At this time the behavioristic approach cannot offer adequate experimental support for a description of human self-regulatory processes, their development, or their relationship to thinking and problem-solving. The statement that response learning and learning of rules or other verbal behaviors occur concurrently and may be parallel or interdependent is a tentative formulation until the conditions are worked out which describe these relationships and provide a basis for higher-order generalization.

The early experiments in verbal conditioning had hoped to avoid the very problem of inference from verbal reports by introduction of the operant conditioning paradigm. And the approach has been, and can continue to be, of value in examining empirical relationships without attempting to resolve the process issue. This approach has faith in the feasibility of eventually attacking these "processes" directly as behavioral events which can be observed, at least under special laboratory conditions, and related to other variables. Progress in this direction has been made in several research areas, growing out of the Skinnerian system. For instance, the relationship of verbal and nonverbal behavior has been studied by Lovaas (1961; 1964), who found evidence for increase in aggressive nonverbal behavior following reinforcement of aggressive verbal behavior. Lovaas also demonstrated a change in food selection as a result of conditioning of food-denoting verbal responses. Verbal control over a motor response (squeezing a dynamometer) has also been reported by Krasner, Knowles, and Ullmann (1965) by means of conditioning attitudes toward medical research. This inductive route may be more tedious because of the requirement for accumulation of a large body of data before generalizations can be formed. Preference for this strategy is based on the conviction that premature theorizing may be more hazardous than acceptance of several temporary and limited descriptive hypotheses.

The operant-conditioning model has fallen short of expectations because too much has been expected too soon. In addition to the puzzling problem of handling covert links in a complex chain of verbal responses, the introduction of hypotheses from the clinical and social areas has yielded a mixture of findings with pragmatic clinical value in which the substantive contributions to a Skinnerian framework tend to be overlooked. For example, such variables as reinforcement schedules (Simkins, 1962; McNair, 1957; Webb, Bernard, and Nesmith, 1963; Kanfer, 1954, 1958), or delay of reinforcement (Lublin, 1965; Hare, 1965), and others of traditional interest in learning have not been separated from studies in which personality or interactional variables are examined.

In attacking the behavioristic approach to verbal conditioning, Spielberger (1965) quotes Chomsky's review to bolster the argument that "lack of interest in internal processes is strikingly evident in the proportion of verbal conditioning experiments in which the awareness issue is simply ignored, and in the operations by which awareness is evaluated in most of the remaining studies." The arguments by Spielberger and his colleagues are based heavily on the assumption that verbal conditioning in the hands of Skinnerians presumes an "empty box" organism. This oversimplification can easily be remedied by reference to Skinner's own view that the individual does take an active role with regard to the variables affecting him. Specifically referring to such behaviors which have often been called "self-determination" Skinner writes,

> any comprehensive account of human behavior must, of course, embrace the facts referred to in statements of this sort. But we can achieve this without abandoning our program. When a man controls himself, chooses a course of action, thinks out the solution to a problem, or strives toward an increase of self-knowledge, he is behaving. He controls himself precisely as he would control the behavior of anyone else—through the manipulation of variables of which behavior is a function. His behavior in so doing is a proper object of analysis and eventually it must be accounted for with variables lying outside the individual himself (1953, pp. 228–229).

Skinner devotes an entire section of *Science and*

Human Behavior to an analysis of the manner in which "the individual acts to alter the variables of which other parts of his behavior are functions."

Skinner's solution has its difficulties. The philosophical weaknesses of behaviorism *and* phenomenology are well illustrated in a recent Rice University Symposium (Wann, 1964). The crux of the problem is presented perhaps most clearly by Malcolm who notes that

> the notion of verification does not apply to a wide range of first person psychological reports and utterances. Another way to put the point is to say that those reports and utterances are *not based on observations*. The error of introspectioninsm is to suppose that they are based on observations of the inner, mental events. The error of behaviorism is to suppose that they are based on observations of outward events or physical events inside the speaker's skin. These two philosophies of psychology share a false asumption, namely, that a first person psychological statement is a report of something the speaker has, or thinks he has, observed (p. 151).

It seems proper to criticize both the behavioristic and phenomenological positions for their failure to have resolved the puzzle on how to deal with "subjective" verbal content. However, it is not proper to contrast behavioristic and cognitive approaches to verbal conditioning on the basis that the former denies that complex processes may intervene between stimulus input and response, while the latter offers an adequate account of these processes.

The area of verbal conditioning has introduced Skinner's functional analysis to verbal learning, but it has not contributed significantly to the construction of a good model for analysis of verbal content, verbal associations, and the semantic aspects of language. The Skinnerian schema (1957) for classifying verbal operants into tacts and mands and his analysis of the autoclitic and of the variables of self-control in verbal behavior has remained a guiding framework, but it has not stimulated the massive research efforts which would demonstrate its contribution to the traditional areas of verbal learning. While the interest of the Skinnerian approach is avowedly in "natural" verbal interactions and not in understanding either the serial or paired-associates learning to nonsense syllables or specific language units, it would be very comforting to see both the traditional associationistic and the Skinnerian view attacking similar problems in human learning.

Staats (1961) has made an interesting attempt to integrate operant conditioning into a Hullian model for the development of meaning and intraverbal associations. Staats appears to accept operant conditioning as a method by which response emission can be modified, but classical conditioning is involved in the learning of (implicit) meaning responses, and reinforcement of a given response affects both the meaning response (rm) as well as the verbal response itself. It is the strengthening of the common anticipatory meaning response in the habit-family that mediates strengthening of the responses in the class defined by *E*. This view suggests that effectiveness of verbal conditioning procedures is related to S's particular verbal habit-families and to variables associated with meaning components of a given word class. Lack of congruence between *E*'s and S's response classes could occur when reinforcement of a subset in a class strengthens all the meaning components so that only the subset responses are given.

This view of "what is reinforced" in verbal conditioning differs from Salzinger's (1959) suggestion that verbal response classes can be defined on a functional basis, i.e., by the variables controlling the class members, and that generalization accounts for strengthening of other response class members which share some property with the reinforced response. Among some of the dimensions for categorizing verbal responses are the communalities of effects on the environment, controlling stimuli, response topographies, etc.

Concluding Remarks

Our review of verbal conditioning is an attempt to show the development of a research area which had as its intent the demonstration of the utility of a functional-behavioral analysis for verbal interactions. The implications of the effectiveness of social reinforcement in modifying verbal responses were quickly grasped by the clinical researcher. Not inconsistent with the spirit of other work growing out of Skinner's system, the verbal conditioning paradigm was extensively used in the area of engineering verbal behavior, especially for attack on clinical problems. This significant contribution can be measured only by its heuristic value.

For purposes of theorizing, even at the level of limited inductive generalizations, the research findings have been difficult to evaluate. Even though only two basic procedures have been used, studies are not often comparable because of the differences in several variables, in addition to the specific treatment variable under experimental investigation. Among these are:

1. population differences: inclusion of psychiatric patients, college students, children or "normal" volunteer Ss;
2. the stimulus and response content, method of

presentation, timing, and other parameters of the task;
3. the financial or other type of compensation for Ss and the method of recruitment and selection;
4. the instructions;
5. the criteria for learning;
6. the degree of control over the reinforcing stimulus; and
7. the presence, manner and use of postperformance inquiries.

Contrasting findings such as the ones cited here appear to be sufficient reason to view the current research in verbal conditioning as pretheoretical. The data do warrant the conclusion that the paradigm covers a complex human activity, related to the areas traditionally subsumed under problem-solving rather than conditioning. However, it is also clear that a "conditioning" or S-R approach, wiser and older by a half a century than Watson's view (with which it is often compared) may now be able to attack these complex behaviors more effectively. Serving as a point of departure, the introduction of a functional Skinnerian approach has already had its impact not only in clinical research but also in the study of self-regulatory behavior, which is undoubtedly involved in verbal conditioning.

The problem of dealing with personal, covert, or self-observed experiences has slipped into the area by way of the "awareness issue." That this issue has not yielded to solution by decrees of exclusion, or dualism, or operational definitions is a well-known and often deplored fact. However, it would be burdening the limited verbal conditioning procedure too much to make it the arena for testing these philosophical issues. The same issues are encountered in much of human psychology. As Feigl (1959) has suggested, the very definition of psychology's subject matter is painfully uncertain until there is some resolution of the "nothing but" vs. the "something more" view of behavior. The choice of research strategy is partly determined by the investigator's interest and his estimate of the ultimate utility of his approach. In verbal conditioning the wider contributions so far seem to have come from the behavioristic camp, if the disclosure of new research areas is taken as a criterion.

Neither the cognitive nor the S-R views have answered the question of "what is learned" or "how is it learned," but these questions also underlie a large proportion of the research in contemporary American psychology. What contribution has been made by verbal conditioning studies comes from isolation of some relevant variables, not from any new theoretical formulations. It is probable that verbal conditioning will gradually be absorbed into the psychology of verbal behavior as a useful laboratory procedure. Greater interest in nonclinical variables might also lead to several modifications in procedure which would reduce S's variability, the importance of prior experiences, and the problem-solving behavior of Ss. These changes could make the paradigm more manageable for research on basic verbal learning principles. The contributions to the structure of interverbal associations has been limited, as has been the use for the study of language acquisition. Perhaps some progress toward a comprehensive behavior theory has been made, after all, when we note that the simple conditioning paradigm (derived from the animal laboratory, at that) has been of service in testing the wide range of hypotheses and empirical relationships represented by the literature in this area.

References

Dulany, D. E., Jr. The place of hypotheses and intentions: An analysis of verbal control in verbal conditioning. In C. W. Eriksen, (Ed.), *Behavior and awareness*. Durham, N.C.: Duke University Press, 1962.

Feigl, H. Philosophical embarrassments of psychology, *American Psychologist,* 1959, *14,* 115–128.

Hare, R. D. Suppression of Verbal Behavior as a Function of Delay and Schedule of Severe Punishment, *Journal of Verbal Learning and Verbal Behavior,* 1965, *4,* 216–221.

Kanfer, F. H. The effect of partial reinforcement on acquisition and extinction of a class of verbal response, *Journal of Experimental Psychology,* 1954, *48,* 424–432.

Kanfer, F. H. Verbal conditioning: Reinforcement schedules and experimenter influence, *Psychological Reports,* 1958, *4,* 443–452.

Kanfer, F. H., and Marston, A. R. Control of verbal behavior by multiple schedules, *Psychological Reports,* 1962, *10,* 703–710.

Kanfer, F. H., and McBrearty, J. F. Verbal conditioning: Discrimination and awareness, *Journal of Psychology,* 1961, *52,* 115–124.

Krasner, L., Knowles, J. B., and Ullman, L. P. Effect of verbal conditioning of attitudes on subsequent motor performance, *Journal of Personal and Social Psychology,* 1965, *1,* 407–412.

Krasner, L., Weiss, R. L., and Ullman, L. P. Responsivity to verbal conditioning as a function of "awareness," *Psychological Reports,* 1961, *8,* 523–538.

Lindsley, O. R. Reduction in rate of vocal psychotic symptoms by differential positive reinforcement, *Journal of Experimental Analysis of Behavior,* 1960, *2,* 269.

Long, E. R., Hammack, J. T., May, F., and Campbell, B. J. Intermittent reinforcement of operant behavior in children, *Journal of Experimental Analysis of Behavior,* 1958, *1,* 314–339.

Lovaas, O. I. Interaction between verbal and nonverbal behavior, *Child Development,* 1961, *32,* 329–336.

LOVAAS, O. I. Control of food intake in children by reinforcement of relevant verbal behavior, *Journal of Abnormal and Social Psychology,* 1964, *68,* 672–678.

LUBLIN, I. Sources of differences in effectiveness among controllers of verbal reinforcement. Paper presented at APA, Chicago, 1965.

MANDLER, G., and KAPLAN, W. K. Subjective evaluation and reinforcing effect of a verbal stimulus, *Science,* 1956, *124,* 582–583.

MARSTON, A. R., KANFER, F. H., and MCBREARTY, F. J. Stimulus discriminability in verbal conditioning, *Journal of Psychology,* 1962, 53, 143–153.

MARTIN, R. B., and DEAN, S. J. Word familiarity and avoidance conditioning of verbal behavior, *Journal of Personality and Social Psychology,* 1965, *1,* 496–499.

MCBREARTY, J. F., KANFER, F. H., MARSTON, A. R., and EVANDER, DEANNE. Focal and contextual stimulus variables in verbal conditioning, *Psychological Reports,* 1963, *13,* 115–124.

MCNAIR, D. M. Reinforcement of verbal behavior, *Journal of Experimental Psychology,* 1957, 53, 40–46.

SALZINGER, K. Experimental manipulation of verbal behavior: A review, *Journal of General Psychology,* 1959, *61,* 65–94.

SALZINGER, K. The problem of response class in verbal behavior. Paper presented at the Verbal Behavior Conference, New York City, September, 1965.

SALZINGER, K., FELDMAN, R. S., and PORTNOY, STEPHANIE. The effects of reinforcement on verbal and nonverbal Responses, *Journal of General Psychology,* 1964, *70,* 225–234.

SIMKINS, L. Scheduling effects of punishment and nonreinforcement on verbal conditioning and extinction, *Journal of Verbal Learning and Verbal Behavior,* 1962, *1,* 208–213.

SKINNER, B. F. *Science and human behavior.* New York: Macmillan, 1953.

SKINNER, B. F. *Verbal behavior.* New York: Appleton-Century-Crofts, 1957.

SPIELBERGER, C. D. Theoretical and epistemological issues in verbal conditioning. In S. Rosenberg (Ed.) *Directions in psycholinguistics.* New York: Macmillan, 1965.

SPIELBERGER, C. D., and DENIKE, L. D. Descriptive behaviorism versus cognitive theory in verbal operant conditioning, *Psychological Review,* 1966, *73,* 306–326.

STAATS, A. W. Verbal habit-families, concepts, and the operant conditioning of word classes, *Psychological Review,* 1961, *68,* 190–204.

WANN, T. W. (Ed.) *Behaviorism and phenomenology.* Chicago: University of Chicago Press, 1964.

WEBB, R. A., BERNARD, J. L., and NESMITH, C. C. Reinforcement ratio, spontaneous recovery and suggestibility as a control in verbal conditioning, *Psychological Reports,* 1963, *12,* 479–482.

Because there has been so much argument in the psychological literature about the relative usefulness of behavioral and cognitive explanations of verbal behavior, the article by *Spielberger and DeNike* examines this problem further. These writers, however, emphasize cognition as a critical variable. The cognitive approach to verbal conditioning emphasizes that the subject's awareness (the behaviorists would say the subject's description of his own behavior) has a critical influence on the effect of verbal reinforcement contingencies. The differences between the cognitive and behavioral approaches to verbal behavior are not insurmountable, however, if one makes a behavioral analysis of "awareness." Psychologists who utilize the concepts of consonance and dissonance to explain verbal interaction use an approach similar to that of the cognitive psychologists. The cognitive theorists criticize verbal reinforcement experiments which purport to produce conditioning without awareness. They argue for the importance of mediating events which occur when a subject becomes aware of the contingencies of reinforcement. It seems established beyond doubt, however, that an effective reinforcer can influence the frequency of verbal behavior under almost any conditions, as, for example, in a group discussion. Yet it also seems clear that many important examples of verbal reinforcement are those in which the subject interacts with his own repertoire. In these cases he is both speaker and listener within the same skin, and this interaction appears to be what the cognitive psychologists and others who postulate mediating mental events are dealing with.

44 Descriptive Behaviorism Versus Cognitive Theory in Verbal Operant Conditioning[1]

CHARLES D. SPIELBERGER
L. DOUGLAS DeNIKE

Operant behavior generally refers to responses which an organism in a given environment displays spontaneously without special training. Operant conditioning usually implies a variety of experimental techniques wherein a subject is rewarded after engaging in operant behavior of a selected kind. The successful conditioning of an operant response is inferred from an increase in its rate of occurrence as a function of reward (reinforcement) administered by the experimenter. Through the efforts of those who have used operant conditioning procedures, significant advances in our knowledge of animal learning have been made possible, and widespread interest has been generated in the use of such procedures for investigating human learning. The purpose of the present paper is to examine theoretical and methodological issues which have arisen in recent applications of operant conditioning techniques to verbal learning.

In verbal operant conditioning, hereafter termed verbal conditioning, the subject is typically instructed to speak in accordance with a particular task. He is not told that this task involves reinforcement or learning. The experimenter attempts to change the rate of emission of certain responses by the systematic application of a reinforcing stimulus, usually some form of social reward, such as the experimenter saying "Mmm-hmm" or "Good." Studies of verbal conditioning originated in close connection with the concepts and procedures developed by Skinner (1938) with infrahuman species. Greenspoon, a pioneer in verbal conditioning research, maintains that

> . . . it should be possible to work with verbal behavior in much the same way that experimenters have worked with the behavior of rats, pigeons, etc. It should also be possible to investigate the same kinds of variables that have been investigated with the non-verbal behavior of humans and infrahumans (1962, p. 511).

Thus, the Skinnerian (1957, 1963a, 1963b) approach has been clearly apparent both in the methods employed and the variables investigated in most verbal conditioning experiments.

In keeping with Skinner's emphasis on the "experimental analysis of behavior," many verbal conditioners have largely ignored the possibility that subjects' awareness of response-reinforcement contingencies might influence their conditioning performance. Investigators who have examined subjects' verbal reports in relation to their conditioning performance have discovered considerable evidence suggesting that cognitive processes mediate performance gains in verbal conditioning. But descriptive behaviorists have been quick to rejoin that the relationships between awareness and performance observed by cognitively oriented researchers have arisen from artifacts associated with the verbal report procedures from which awareness was inferred. Thus, in verbal conditioning, broadly opposed theoretical systems lock horns: Descriptive behaviorists argue for learning without awareness, those of cognitive persuasion argue against it, and proponents of each point of view generate methodological criticisms of the experimental work carried on in the opposing camp.[2]

It would appear that radically different epistemologies underlie the theoretical differences between

[1] Work on this paper was supported in part by grants to the first author from the National Institutes of Mental Health (MH 7446) and Child Health and Human Development (HD 947), United States Public Health Service. We are indebted to Norman Cliff, Jum C. Nunnally, Henry Slucki, and Donald L. Thistlethwaite for their critical comments on the manuscript.

[2] It should be noted that S–R behavior theorists in the Hull-Spence tradition are not a party to this controversy. The model developed by these theorists was designed to account for the behavior phenomena exhibited by nonarticulate organisms or by humans in simple learning situations in which the operation of higher mental processes was minimal, for example, in eyelid conditioning and rote learning. A major difference between the views of descriptive behaviorists and those of Hull and Spence is that the latter never claimed that their theoretical concepts would hold for complex verbal processes. In his discussion of the postulates and methods of behaviorism nearly two decades ago, Spence (1948, p. 76) noted that:

> . . . in dealing with the more complex types of animal and human behavior, implicit emotional responses, covert verbal responses and not easily observable receptor-exposure and postural adjustments will have to be postulated . . .

and that:

> It is in this realm of theorizing that the verbal reports of human subjects are likely to be of most use to the behavior theorist, for presumably these reports can be made the basis on which to postulate the occurrence of these inferred activities.

Skinnerian and cognitive researchers. The epistemological issues, which revolve around the admissibility of conscious awareness as a desideratum for psychological science, have been discussed in detail elsewhere (Spielberger, 1965). Therefore, rather than restating these issues here, a simple analogy may better serve to illustrate how varying pretheoretical assumptions about the general nature and scope of science can lead to highly disparate approaches to a concrete scientific problem.

It seems reasonable to conjecture that biologists of an earlier generation who did not believe in protozoa probably contended at times that objects too small to be observed by the naked eye were *irrelevant to scientific analysis* (of disease, for instance). Attempts to explore the domain of the microscopic world might have been disdained by such observers as revealing only illusory effects traceable to light diffusion in the microscope, and so on. Similarly, we might expect that present-day psychologists who consider thoughts and hypotheses to be beyond the limits of "scientific" inquiry would not vigorously search for them in experimental subjects. Furthermore, we should not be surprised to find that such psychologists were uninterested and unskilled in evaluating cognitive phenomena which for them do not exist. On the other hand, early biologists who believed in protozoa might occasionally have "seen" them when they were not there. Similarly, we might expect, as has been suggested by Farber (1963), that cognitively oriented verbal conditioning researchers, in their eagerness to attribute behavior to mediating conscious processes, would sometimes inadvertently suggest (or erroneously infer) awareness in questioning subjects who show performance gains.

One obvious implication of the above analogy is that competing scientific theories lead to different experimental procedures and often to observational errors which support the theoretical predilections of the investigator (Rosenthal, 1963). In most cases, however, such methodological differences and observational errors are eventually resolved since competing theories generally lead to more sensitive experiments. Furthermore, good experiments contribute to the accumulation of a composite set of facts which facilitate the convergence of theoretical schools and the establishment of an organized body of scientific knowledge (Campbell, 1963). But, if the epistemological assumptions which underlie competing scientific theories differ, the methodological consequences of such differences may lead to the collection of noncomparable data about which pointless theoretical controversy is generated. Unfortunately, this seems to be the case in verbal conditioning.

In this paper, we propose to examine the relative merits of cognitive and Skinnerian interpretations of verbal conditioning annd the methodological assumptions on which these interpretations are based. The organization of the paper is as follows: In Section I the use of verbal report measures as indexes of awareness (mediating cognitive processes) will be discussed, and the various objections which investigators of a Skinnerian bent have raised concerning these measures will be enumerated and analyzed. In Section II methodological problems associated with the assessment of awareness from postconditioning interviews will be considered, and procedures for assessing awareness during conditioning will be described along with the results of two experiments in which such procedures were utilized. A theoretical analysis of verbal conditioning in terms of cognitive concepts will be presented in Section III. In Section IV the significance of the verbal conditioning paradigm for the more general question of learning without awareness will be taken up.

I. Can Verbal Reports Be Interpreted as Indexes of Mediating Cognitive Processes?

Methodological criticism has been associated with attempts to condition verbal behavior since Thorndike's early experiments in this area. In these Thorndike was interested in determining whether the law of effect operated when the subject was unaware of the contingency of reinforcement. Utilizing a word-association task, Thorndike and Rock (1934) reinforced sequential as opposed to denotative associations (OVER-the hill, as opposed to OVER-above). They reasoned that if subjects gained sudden insight (awareness) into the response-reinforcement contingency, the number of sequential responses which they gave would rise sharply. Hence, they regarded the gradual increase in sequential responses, which they in fact obtained, as providing evidence for learning without awareness. This interpretation, however, was immediately challenged by the demonstration that similar gradual performance gains ensued even when subjects were informed of the basis of reinforcement (Irwin, Kauffman, Prior, and Weaver, 1934). It is perhaps an unfortunate commentary on the narrow, behavioristic zeitgeist then prevailing that the simple procedure of questioning subjects was not utilized in either of these studies. Irwin et al. (1934), while they did not fill the need for measures of insight or awareness that are operationally independent of performance, helped at least to make the need evident. More recently, the quest for such measures has generally led to the use of systematically obtained verbal reports.

Now Skinnerian verbal conditioners do not hold that subjects should never be asked questions, nor do they assert that reliable relationships between verbal reports and performance measures cannot be found. They do argue that such relationships when found do not constitute adequate evidence that awareness plays a *causal* intervening role. However, descriptive behaviorists have not attempted to investigate the adequacy of verbal report procedures. Thus, their criticisms of them appear to stem chiefly from the implicit assumption that consciousness is in principle unknowable and/or that it is unnecessary to consider it. These epistemological bases are not often made explicit, but under their influence criticisms of cognitive interpretations of verbal conditioning phenomena are made on methodological and theoretical grounds. It is to such criticisms[3] that we now turn.

1. The first group of objections advanced by descriptive behaviorists to the interpretation of verbal reports in cognitive terms is concerned with the possibility that awareness is *suggested* by the procedures which are employed to assess it. Questioning techniques used to evaluate awareness may, it is argued, differentially suggest the contingency of reinforcement to subjects who condition as compared to those who do not. When both the conditioning task and the awareness interview are conducted by the same experimenter, it is certainly plausible that the experimenter might inadvertently ask questions and/or record answers in such a way as to suggest and/or impute awareness to those subjects who showed performance gains. A related way in which the interviewer might artifactually bring about a relationship between performance and awareness is through cues provided by the wording of interview questions. Questioning subjects about their experiences and possibly also to develop hypotheses about the response-reinforcement contingency.

2. A second general class of criticism contends that subjects condition without awareness, notice their increasing outputs of the critical response class, and then *label* the response-reinforcement contingency. In other words, it is argued that the subjects' knowledge of the contingency emerges as a result of an automatic conditioning process, and those subjects who indicate in a postconditioning interview that their performance was mediated by their hypotheses are merely rationalizing their performance gains. This line of criticism calls into question correspondences between performance and awareness based on measures taken after performance gains have ensued and points up the theoretical significance of the temporal sequence of events in verbal conditioning, that is, whether in fact performance gains precede awareness or occur subsequent to the subjects' development of awareness.

3. A more complicated variant of the point of view indicated in 2 above has been suggested by Postman and Sassenrath (1961)[4] who state that "awareness as reflected in verbalization may represent an advanced stage in the development of a habit under conditions of reinforcement" (p. 124). They go on to suggest that the verbalization of a response-reinforcement contingency *"may be considered at the same time a result of past improvement and a condition for further improvement"* (p. 124). The tenability of this formulation, which ascribes a secondary mediational role to awareness, rests upon the demonstration of significant amounts of learning prior to the subjects' verbalization of a correct or partially correct contingency.

4. Another line of criticism contends that awareness is merely a covert response which is conditioned over trials, in an automatic fashion, at the same time as the reinforced response class is strengthened. Postman and Sassenrath (1961), in discussing symbolic mediators, have posited this sort of mechanism to explain the acquisition of hypotheses in instrument learning. They state: "The differential reinforcements administered for the overt instrumental responses will at the same time selectively strengthen the correct mediating responses" (p. 132). In this view, awareness is assigned the properties of an operant response, and it is hypothesized that covert verbalizations of the reinforcement principle (awareness) are directly and automatically strengthened by the same reinforcement process through which other instrumental responses are conditioned.[5]

The formulations described above are presented as schematic diagrams in Figure 1. These diagrams are not intended to represent particular viewpoints

[3] These criticisms have not been listed and treated in detail in any single article. What follows is an attempted coverage of relevant objections to interpretations of verbal reports in verbal conditioning in terms of mediating states. These have been adapted from friendly and unfriendly sources, including Dulany (1961, 1962), Eriksen (1958, 1960, 1962), Greenspoon (1962, 1963), Kanfer and his colleagues (Kanfer and Marston, 1961, 1962; Kanfer and McBrearty, 1961), Krasner (1962), Krasner and Ullmann (1963), Postman and Sassenrath (1961), Salzinger (1959), Spielberger (1962, 1965), and especially Dulany (1963).

[4] It should be noted that although Postman and Sassenrath cite findings of verbal conditioning investigations as relevant to this interpretation, their conclusions are based primarily upon Thorndikian experiments in which gradual increments in performance typically precede the point of verbalization.

[5] A similar interpretation is suggested by Kanfer and McBrearty (1961) who contend that:

> . . . verbalization of the response-reinforcement contingency may be independently affected by *different* antecedent conditions than the acquisition rate of the (reinforced verbal) response class, even though experimental conditions may sometimes facilitate an interaction between these two events (p. 116).

1. **Suggestion**

$R --- S_R \rightarrow R\uparrow$ $\langle S_I, S_Q \rangle \rightarrow$ Awareness

2. **Labeling**

$R --- S_R \rightarrow R\uparrow \rightarrow S_{R\uparrow} \rightarrow$ Awareness

3. **Secondary mediation**

$R --- S_R \rightarrow R\uparrow \rightarrow S_{R\uparrow} \rightarrow$ Awareness $\rightarrow R\uparrow$

4. **Joint conditioning effects**

Figure 1 *Schematic diagrams depicting noncognitive interpretations of verbal reports of awareness in verbal conditioning.*

in detail, but are offered only tentatively as an aid in expressing interpretations of verbal conditioning which consider verbal reports primarily as responses rather than as indexes of mediating states. In each schematic, the temporal sequence of events is from left to right. Events which are merely temporally contiguous are indicated by dotted lines; presumed causal relationships between events are represented by solid arrows.

Schematic 1 illustrates the two possibilities whereby awareness might be suggested by questioning procedures to subjects who showed performance gains. The symbol R stands for the subject's verbalization of responses belonging to the reinforced response class. S_R refers to the reinforcing stimulus administered by the experimenter for each R. $R\uparrow$ indicates performance gains. S_I represents biasing stimuli that might be transmitted unwittingly to the subject by an interviewer who had knowledge of the subject's conditioning performance. S_Q stands for possible cues conveyed by the wording of questions which might lead subjects who showed performance gains to construct correct hypotheses after the fact by reflecting on their performance.

Schematic 2 diagrams the hypothetical automatic strengthening-labeling sequence in which subjects are said to condition without awareness and then to become aware of the response-reinforcement contingency after noticing their increasing output of reinforced responses, $S_R\uparrow$.

Schematic 3 depicts the hypothetical operation of mediating processes subsequent to automatic conditioning. As described in Schematic 2, the subject becomes aware as a result of increments in performance brought about by the automatic effects of reinforcement and utilizes this awareness further to enhance performance gains. In this diagram, $R\uparrow$ symbolizes augmented performance consequent upon the subject becoming aware of the correct contingency.

Schematic 4 illustrates the view that reinforcement acts simultaneously to condition both the reinforced response class and verbalization of the reinforcement principle. Presumably, reinforcement would operate in this paradigm to strengthen covert verbalizations of the correct response-reinforcement contingency, R_A.

Underlying all of the above formulations is the epistemological viewpoint mentioned earlier. It would appear that what descriptive behaviorists object to basically is the use of verbal reports as a Trojan horse for the reintroduction of private experiences into psychology. Since private experience does not meet positivistic canons of interobserver reliability, they argue largely on epistemological grounds that interest in it remains but a vestige of discredited introspectionism. However, the heuristic value of operationally defined awareness variables in verbal conditioning has been demonstrated empirically, and the numerous instances in which such measures have been found to relate consistently and meaningfully to other variables provides strong justification for their use, irrespective of how they are interpreted. Over and above this pragmatic value, the utilization of awareness as a systematic concept has led to experimental findings which the Skinnerian approach would not have predicted and can explain only with piecemeal augmenting assumptions (Dulany, 1962; Spielberger, 1962).

In this paper we will contend that the descriptive behaviorists' rejection, on epistemological grounds, of verbal reports as indexes of mediating states has retarded the convergence of empirical findings and the development of adequate theory in verbal conditioning. We will argue moreover that this general approach has contributed little to the understanding of verbal behavior because, as Guttman (1963, p. 119) has recently suggested with respect to perception:

> . . . the effort to speak the language of behavior *only* is just inefficient, and to do so leads to bad experiments . . . , to a truncated set of laws of behavior, and to wide misinterpretation as to what our current knowledge of behavioral laws portends, theoretically and practically.

Having stated these goals and claims, we may now proceed to a discussion of procedures used for assessing awareness in verbal conditioning.

II. The Use of Verbal Reports in Verbal Conditioning

The questioning techniques employed to assess awareness in verbal conditioning studies have included both oral interviews and written-response questionnaires. These have been utilized both during and after conditioning trials. In this section, we will first consider methodological factors associated with the assessment of awareness from postconditioning interviews. We will then describe procedures developed for assessing awareness during conditioning and the findings of two experiments in which such procedures were employed. Finally, the noncognitive formulations developed in Section I will be reviewed in the light of these studies.

The Assessment of Awareness after Conditioning

The assessment of awareness from postconditioning interviews is influenced by the style of questioning, the wording of questions and the number of questions asked, the interpolation of extinction trials, and the experimenter's concern with correlated hypotheses. Each of these factors will be discussed below in terms of its potential effect on reports of awareness obtained in post-conditioning interviews.

Oral Interview Versus Written Questionnaire Procedures. Both oral interviews and written-response questionnaires have been utilized for assessing awareness after the completion of conditioning trials. Either style of questioning would appear to have certain characteristic advantages and disadvantages. Written-response questionnaires eliminate the potential biasing influence of the experimenter who conducts an oral interview. However, the responses elicited by this procedure may not be as complete as those obtained from questions asked and answered orally, and clarification of unclear replies through additional inquiry is not generally feasible. Furthermore, some subjects may be inclined to avoid being incorrect by not responding when they are unsure of their hypotheses.

Number and Wording of Questions. In early verbal conditioning studies, awareness interviews were very brief, and the questions were vaguely worded. For example, in one study (Sidowski, 1954) the postconditioning interview consisted of only two questions: (*a*) "Were you aware of the purpose of the experiment?" and (*b*) "Were you aware of the purpose of the light?" (the contingent reinforcing stimulus). In response to these questions, a subject who might have been perfectly aware of the response-reinforcement contingency might not have had any idea of the "scientific purpose" of the experiment nor of the reinforcing stimulus. Furthermore, questions asked in this form make it easier to say "No" than "Yes" since the latter response will obviously require elaboration. A series of questions in which subjects were asked to state their thoughts about when and why the light was blinking would have been more satisfactory.

Given minimal questioning, subjects tend to respond according to their own preconceptions about what is important and refer to the reinforcing stimulus only when asked about it. For example, after the conclusion oof a pseudo-ESP verbal conditioning experiment, Krieckhaus and Eriksen (1960) held informal conversations with subjects who showed performance gains, but failed to verbalize a correct response-reinforcement contingency in a structured interview. They reported:

> Two (subjects) verbalized very clearly their awareness of the effects of reinforcement upon their behavior. When asked why they had not stated this in response to the post-conditioning interview questions, both of them commented that they hadn't understood that this was what *E* was asking. They both stated that they thought *E* was concerned with whether or not they were getting ESP messages, rather than trying to find out whether the reinforcement of "good" had affected their choice of responses (p. 515).

Thus, the requirement of asking for information with clear and adequately worded questions is coordinate with the necessity of asking a sufficient number of questions.

Although more detailed questioning might be thought to increase the likelihood of suggesting awareness indiscriminately (Farber, 1963), a series of questions of gradually increasing specificity enables the interviewer to assess awareness and motivation while providing minimal *surplus* information. Furthermore, in studies in which such interviews were employed (see Spielberger, 1962), it has been demonstrated that: (*a*) Substantial numbers of subjects were identified as aware of correct response-reinforcement contingencies who were not so classified on the basis of brief interviews; and (*b*) performance gains were limited essentially to aware subjects and specific to those responses for which the individual subject was aware of a correct contingency.

Extinction Trials. In verbal conditioning, the practice of interpolating extinction trials (e.g., Cohen, Kalish, Thurston, and Cohen, 1954; Greenspoon, 1955) or other tasks (Gergen, 1965; Sassenrath, 1959) between acquisition trials and the interview in which awareness is assessed probably reduces the likelihood that awareness will be detected. Subjects who are aware of a correct contingency during conditioning may either forget their hypotheses, interpret the withdrawal of the reinforcing stimulus during extinction as a sign that they were wrong, or both. We have observed that, even during acquisition trials, instances of *accidental* nonreinforcement due to experimenter error sometimes suffice to disconfirm subjects' hypotheses (Spielberger and DeNike, 1963).

Correlated Hypotheses. The problem of assessing correlated hypotheses in learning experiments was first raised by Postman and Jarrett (1952). In verbal conditioning, a subject is considered to have a correlated hypothesis if he verbalizes a contingency which is different from, but correlated with, the reinforcement principle employed by the experimenter (Dulany, 1961). Thus, a subject need not be aware of the *experimenter's* definition of the contingency in order to show performance gains through conscious pursuit of his *own* hypotheses. For example, suppose one spring a whimsical millionaire were to emplace a few gold nuggets on some fertile ground on his estate and announce magnanimously to the townsfolk that all were welcome to come there and shovel around on the surface. Anyone inquiring among these townsfolk as they labored would find them highly aware that they were "digging for gold" and highly unaware that they were "spading a garden."

In the traditional verbal conditioning task in which plural nouns are reinforced (Greenspoon, 1955), a subject would receive 100% reinforcement if he said serially, "apples, oranges, peaches," etc. When interviewed, he might report as his hypothesis that reinforcement is contingent upon his naming "fruits." While the response class "fruits" is formally different from "plural nouns," the subject who named fruits would be reinforced for acting on this hypothesis and would be likely to develop the conviction that he was being encouraged to say words of similar meaning, as Dulany (1961) has convincingly shown. That subjects sometimes develop and pursue correlated ideas in response to less than 100% reinforcement points up the importance of *random* reinforcement rather than *no* reinforcement for control groups in verbal conditioning experiments (DeNike and Spielberger, 1963; Spielberger, DeNike, and Stein, 1965). And as Adams (1957) has pointed out, correlated hypotheses are typically *not* evaluated in investigations which have reported evidence for learning without awareness.

Thus far, we have discussed methodological factors which influence reports of awareness obtained from interviews or questionnaires conducted after the completion of the conditioning task. As previously noted, in recent verbal conditioning experiments in which such factors were taken into account, performance gains were limited essentially to subjects who verbalized a correct or correlated contingency. However, in these experiments, awareness was inferred from responses to interview questions asked *after* performance measures had been taken. Therefore, it could be argued that the performance gains of aware subjects were automatically produced by reinforcement and the awareness-performance relationship could be accounted for by any of the noncognitive explanations described in Section I. The assessment of awareness during conditioning would provide a firmer basis for evaluating the temporal relationship between performance and awareness in verbal conditioning. Such procedures will now be considered.

The Assessment of Awareness during Conditioning

Most noncognitive explanations of verbal conditioning implicitly assume that increments in performance initially result from the direct and automatic effects of reinforcement and that performance gains occur prior to the time that the subject becomes aware of a correct response-reinforcement contingency. On the other hand, it is argued in cognitive explanations of verbal conditioning that awareness precedes performance increments. Thus, reinforcement theory and cognitive theory lead to differential predictions with regard to the temporal relationship between the development of awareness and the inception of performance gains. But in order to evaluate temporal factors in verbal conditioning, a procedure is required which will permit determination of whether or not subjects become aware of a correct contingency *during conditioning,* and if so, when. The results of two studies in which awareness was assessed during conditioning are discussed below.

Experiment I. DeNike (1964) reinforced female college students for giving *human-noun* responses in a word-naming task (Matarazzo, Saslow, and Pareis, 1960). His subjects were required to write down their "thoughts about the experiment" after each block of 25 response words. As a signal for the subject to record her thoughts, a light was turned on which remained lit until the subject indicated she was ready to resume saying words. No reinforcement was given during the first two word blocks, which provided a measure of operant rate. Beginning with the third word block, subjects in the Experimental Group were reinforced with "Mmm-hmm" for each human-noun response; those in the Control Group were reinforced with "Mmm-hmm" for 10% of their response words, according to a predetermined random schedule.

Awareness of the contingency between human-noun responses and the experimenter's "Mmm-hmm" was inferred from the thoughts (notes) which each subject recorded during conditioning. On the basis of these notes, subjects were independently rated by four judges as either *aware* or *unaware* of a correct contingency. Agreement between pairs of judges ranged from 90 to 95%, and there was unanimity or a 3–1 consensus among the judges with respect to the classification of 59 of the 61 subjects in the Experimental Group. For each aware subject the judges also indicated the word block on which a correct contingency was first recorded.

If performance gains in verbal conditioning are automatically produced by reinforcement, it would be expected that gradual increments in performance would occur for all subjects, and that performance gains for aware subjects would occur prior to the word block on which they recorded a correct contingency in their notes. However, if acquisition of the reinforced response class in verbal conditioning is mediated by awareness, performance gains would be expected only for aware subjects, and these should occur on or subsequent to the word block on which such subjects recorded a correct contingency. The performance curves of DeNike's Aware, Unaware, and Control Groups are presented in Figure 2A. It may be noted that the output of human nouns for the Aware Group increased markedly over the reinforced word blocks and that the Unaware and Control Groups failed to show any performance gains. However, although only subjects who recorded correct contingencies in their notes gave more human nouns, it cannot be determined from the data as arrayed in Figure 2A whether or not aware subjects showed increments in performance prior to the word block on which they recorded a correct contingency.

In order to evaluate the temporal relationship between performance gains and awareness, the conditioning data for the aware subjects were examined as a function of the word block on which each first recorded a correct contingency in her notes. This word block was designated the "0" block. Word blocks prior to and subsequent to Block 0 were designated the preverbalization and postverbalization blocks and were labeled respectively with negative and positive integers, after the practice of Philbrick and Postman (1955). The 0 blocks of the aware subjects were then aligned, and the data for the preverbalization and postverbalization blocks were separately Vincentized (Munn, 1950). The Vincentized conditioning curve for the Aware Group is given in Figure 2B in which it may be noted that performance on the conditioning task: (*a*) remained at essentially

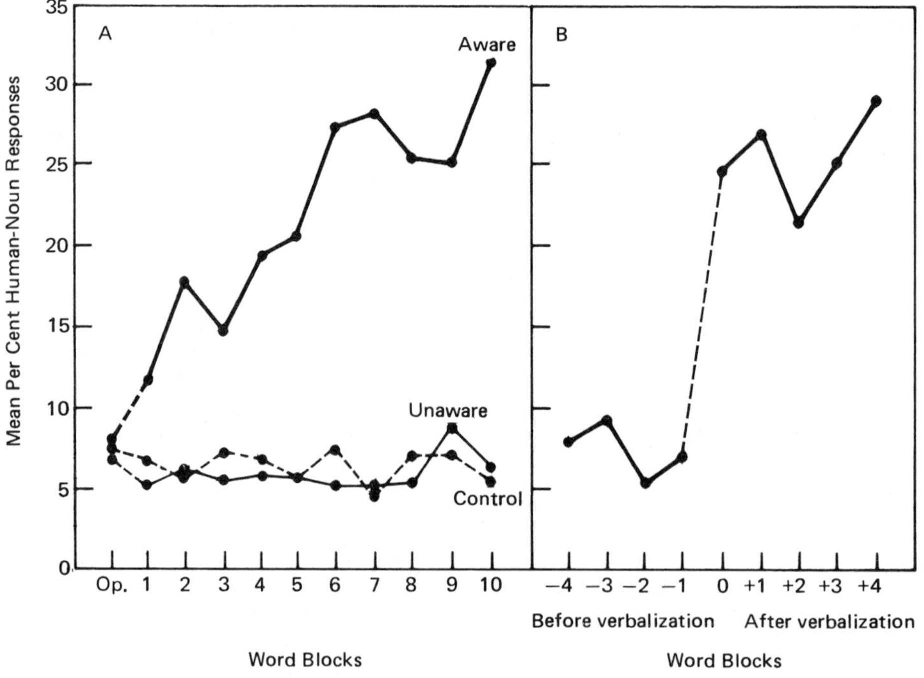

Figure 2 *Conditioning curves. A: Mean percentage of human-noun responses given by the Aware, Unaware, and Control Groups on the conditioning task. B: Conditioning curve for the Aware Group in which the data for preverbalization and postverbalization word blocks have been separately Vincentized. (Adapted from DeNike, 1964.)*

the same level in the preverbalization blocks as in the operant blocks, (*b*) increased markedly on the 0 block, and (*c*) was maintained at a relatively high level during the postverbalization blocks. The finding that the performance increments of aware subjects first occurred during the word block in which they first recorded a correct contingency in their notes would appear to indicate that their increased output of human-noun responses was cognitively mediated. The absence of preverbalization performance gains would appear particularly difficult to explain by the use of learning theories which ascribe automatic trans-situational reinforcing effects to verbal stimuli.

Although it was possible, according to a cognitive theoretical interpretation of verbal conditioning, for aware subjects in DeNike's study to give essentially 100% human-noun responses on each postawareness word block, it may be noted in Figure 2 that the mean number of such responses given by these subjects never exceeded 35%. Interview data obtained by DeNike after the conclusion of the conditioning task revealed some aware subjects for whom the reinforcing stimulus had no incentive value, and these subjects failed to show performance gains (DeNike, 1965). In contrast, aware subjects who reported that they wanted to receive reinforcement showed a marked increase in their output of human nouns on postawareness word blocks. In the next study to be reported, a uniformly high level of motivation to receive reinforcement was induced during conditioning in all subjects.

Experiment II. Using similar conditioning procedures to those described for Experiment I, female college students were reinforced with "Mmm-hmm" for giving human-noun responses (Spielberger, Bernstein, and Ratliff, 1966). Also, as in Experiment I, awareness of a correct response-reinforcement contingency was evaluated from the thoughts about the experiment (notes) which subjects recorded after each word block. However, the procedures differed from those of the previous experiment in that, between the seventh and eighth reinforced word blocks of the conditioning task, each subject was told: "As you may have noted, there is a rule under which I say 'Mmm-hmm.' Try to act on that rule so as to make me say 'Mmm-hmm' as often as you can." The purpose of this instruction was to increase the incentive value of the reinforcing stimulus. Immediately after conditioning a different experimenter conducted an interview which checked on the incentive manipulation and provided additional data on subjects' awareness.

The notes which subjects recorded during conditioning were rated by two judges who had neither contact with the subjects nor knowledge of their performance on the conditioning task. The judges agreed perfectly in classifying each subject as either aware or unaware of a correct contingency. For the subjects rated aware, the judges also indicated the work block in which a correct contingency was first reported. Those subjects who recorded a correct contingency prior to the incentive-inducing instruction were designated the Aware-Pre Group; those who did so subsequent to this instruction were designated the Aware-Post Group; subjects who failed to record a correct contingency during conditioning were called the Unaware Group. The mean percentage of human-noun responses given by the three groups in the operant blocks and the reinforced blocks prior to the incentive-inducing instruction are given in Figure 3A, in which the Aware-Pre Group's conditioning data have been Vincentized. Statistical analyses of these data indicated that :(a) The three groups did not differ during the operant blocks; (*b*) the per-

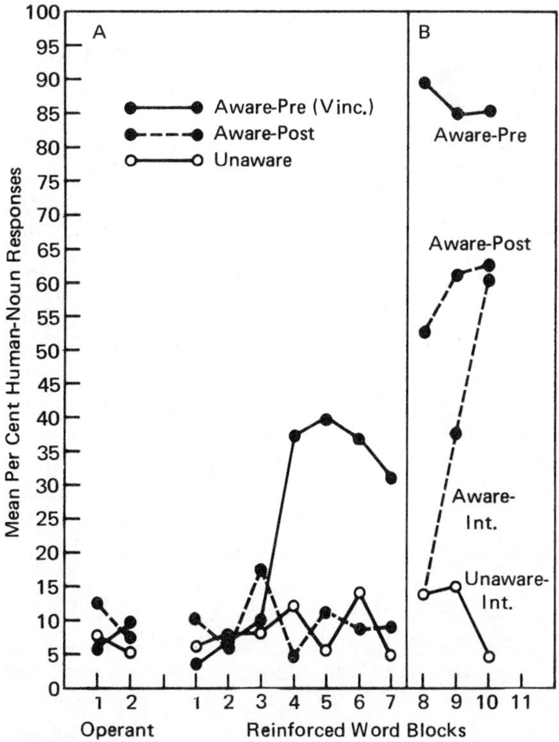

Figure 3 *Conditioning curves. A: Mean percentage of human-noun responses given by the Aware-Pre, Aware-Post, and Unaware Groups on the operant word blocks prior to the incentive-inducing instruction. B: Mean percentage of human-noun responses given by the Aware-Pre, Aware-Post, Aware-Interview, and Unaware-Interview Groups on the word blocks subsequent to the incentive-inducing instruction. The latter two groups were rated unaware on the basis of their notes. (Adapted from Spielberger et al., 1966.)*

formance gains of the Aware-Pre Group first occurred on the word block on which these subjects first recorded a correct contingency; and (*c*) the Aware-Post and Unaware Groups failed to show performance gains. Thus, prior to the incentive-inducing instruction, aware and unaware subjects performed much as did their counterparts in DeNike's study (see Figure 2).

Data obtained in the post conditioning interview indicated that the instruction to try to make the experimenter say "Mmm-hmm" had the desired effect on the subjects' motivation to receive reinforcement. Almost all the subjects indicated that, as a consequence of the instruction, they wanted more for the experimenter to say "Mmm-hmm," and they tried harder to make him say it. The performances of the Aware-Pre, the Aware-Post, and Unaware Groups in the word blocks subsequent to the instruction are indicated in Figure 3B. The immediate marked increase in the number of human nouns given by the Aware-Pre Group on Block 8 suggested that the incentive manipulation increased the motivation of these subjects to receive reinforcement and that their prior awareness of a correct contingency permitted them at once to give more human-noun responses. The somewhat less marked increase in human nouns for the Aware-Post Group subsequent to the instruction may be interpreted as indicating that these subjects, most of whom recorded a correct contingency in their notes on Block 8, had to become aware before heightened motivation induced by the instruction could influence their performance. Consistent with this interpretation, examination of the conditioning data for individual subjects in the Aware-Post Group revealed that initial performance increments tended to occur on the word block on which a correct contingency was first recorded.

The mean percentage of human-noun responses given by the Unaware Group increased gradually in the postinstruction word blocks, from 15% on Block 8 to 30% on Block 10 (not shown in Figure 3B), suggesting that these subjects conditioned without awareness. In order to evaluate this possibility further, the postconditioning interview protocols of all subjects who failed to record a correct contingency in their notes were examined by two judges who had neither contact with the subjects nor knowledge of their performance on the conditioning task. The judges agreed perfectly in rating approximately half of these subjects as aware of a correct contingency solely on the basis of their verbal reports in the interview.

The performance of subjects rated aware on the basis of their interview responses, but unaware on the basis of their notes (Aware-Int. Group), is compared, in Figure 3B, with the performance of subjects rated unaware on the basis of *both* their interview responses and their notes (Unaware-Int. Group). For the latter group, the output of human-noun responses subsequent to the instruction did not increase. Indeed, by the final word block, the number of human nouns given by the Unaware-Int. Group was below what it had been prior to the instruction. In contrast, the conditioning curve for the Aware-Int. Group showed a significant rise subsequent to the instruction, and performance increments for individual subjects tended to correspond with the word block on which they claimed they became aware. Furthermore, several of these subjects spontaneously reported that they had not recorded a correct response-reinforcement contingency in their notes because they did not become aware of it until the final word block and did not have sufficient confidence in their hypothesis to report it.

In sum, the findings in Experiments I and II are consistent with the hypothesis that "what is learned" in verbal conditioning is awareness of a correct response-reinforcement contingency. These findings would also appear to indicate that the reinforcing stimulus in verbal conditioning has both information and incentive value (Dulany, 1962), and that the latter influences the degree to which subjects who are aware of a correct contingency act on their awareness. The adequacy with which noncognitive explanations of verbal conditioning can account for the results in these experiments is considered below.

Noncognitive Interpretations of the Findings in Experiments I and II

The findings in Experiments I and II would appear difficult to account for in terms of a theory which does not include a concept of awareness as a mediating cognitive state or process. In these investigations, only subjects who were judged to be aware of a correct response-reinforcement contingency showed performance gains, and these tended to correspond with the word block on which each aware subject first recorded a correct contingency. However, the question remains whether the obtained relationships between performance gains and operational indexes of awareness can be explained without recourse to cognitive variables. The possibility that these relationships arose artifactually will now be examined in terms of each of the noncognitive formulations described in Section I (see Figure 1).

Suggestion. The possibility that awareness might have been suggested to subjects who showed conditioning through cues provided by a biased experimenter was practically eliminated in Experiments I and II. In these studies, awareness was inferred primarily from notes recorded during conditioning, and these notes were *not* written in response to potentially biasing questions. The signal for the subject to record her thoughts, a light presented at uniform intervals, was a completely impersonal nonverbal stimulus which was in no way contingent upon the subject's conditioning performance. For those subjects in Experiment II whose awareness was inferred from their responses to the postconditioning interview, the experimenter who conducted this interview had neither prior contact with the subjects nor knowledge of their performance on the conditioning task.

Labeling. The findings in Experiments I and II do not support the interpretation that reinforcement automatically produced increments in performance and that the subjects' knowledge of a correct response-reinforcement contingency subsequently resulted from their noticing and labeling the relationship between the critical response class and the reinforcing stimulus. As may be noted in Figure 2B and 3A the performance gains of aware subjects first occurred on the word block on which these subjects recorded a correct contingency in their notes. Thus, the reinforcing stimulus had no apparent influence on performance prior to the subjects becoming aware of a correct contingency. And while it still might be argued that automatic reinforcement effects produced performance gains during the 0 word block, the absence of performance gains on the preceding word blocks would remain unaccounted for. Only the performance of the small group of subjects ($N = 4$) in the Aware-Int. Group of Experiment II might be interpreted as consistent with the labeling hypothesis. But even these subjects, who failed to record a correct contingency in their notes but reported it in the postconditioning interview, tended spontaneously to explain this discrepancy in terms of insufficient opportunity to test their hypotheses.

Secondary Mediation. The secondary-mediation hypothesis assumes that automatic performance increments precede the development of awareness of a correct contingency, and that awareness then facilitates further performance gains. This view is contradicted by the same findings in Experiments I and II which led us to challenge the labeling interpretation. The demonstration of automatic reinforcement effects prior to the verbalization of awareness would appear crucial in order to support the hypothesis of secondary mediation. No such evidence was found, except possibly for the subjects in the Aware-Int. Group in Experiment II. Thus, at the very least, the secondary-mediation hypothesis would require extensive modification if it is to account for *all* of the findings in Experiments I and II.

Joint Conditioning Effects. According to the joint conditioning hypothesis, gradual gains in performance on the conditioning task would be expected along with the simultaneous strengthening of the covert "awareness response." The absence of performance increments in Experiments I and II prior to the word block on which aware subjects recorded a correct contingency, and the striking temporal correspondence of the inception of performance gains with the verbalization of awareness would seem to dictate the additional assumption of a "threshold" concept in order to support the view that the reinforced response class and a covert awareness response were simultaneously and automatically strengthened. Moreover, it would also appear necessary to assume that the threshold at which awareness was verbalized corresponds to the threshold at which the cumulative effects of reinforcement influence performance on the conditioning task, and that performance and covert awareness responses were practically identically susceptible to influence by reinforcement in *each individual subject*. While such assumptions might provide tenuous post-hoc explanations for the findings obtained in Experiments I and II, the conclusion appears inescapable that a theory of automatic strengthening of verbal response by reinforcement requires extensive modification and radical augmentation before it can account for such findings. In the next section, a theoretical analysis of verbal conditioning in terms of the concepts of cognitive learning theory will be proposed.

III. An Analysis of Verbal Conditioning in Terms of Cognitive Concepts

The schematic diagram presented in Figure 4 reflects a general formulation of the sequence of hypothetical events which we believe mediate performance gains in verbal conditioning for subjects who show "conditioning" effects. The diagram is not intended to represent any particular cognitive theory in detail. Rather, it is offered to account for the findings of recent investigations of verbal conditioning, such as those described in Section II, at the same level of specificity as the noncognitive formulations presented in Figure 1. A similar more detailed and sophisticated theoretical analysis of verbal conditioning has been recently advanced by Dulany (1962).

The temporal sequence of events in Figure 4 is from left to right. Those events which are merely temporally contiguous are indicated by dotted lines;

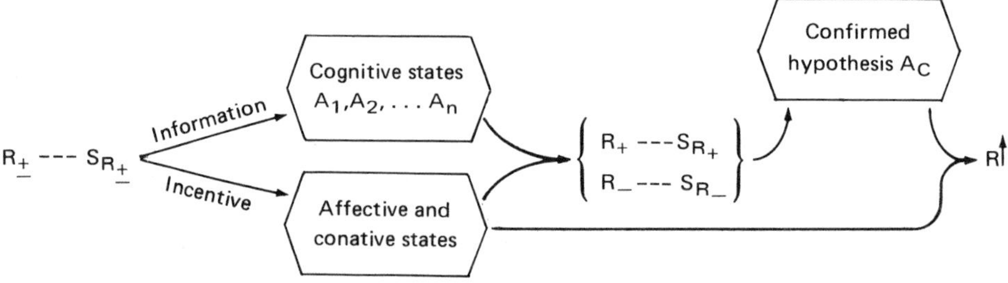

Figure 4 *Schematic diagram indicating the hypothetical processes which are assumed to mediate performance gains in verbal conditioning for subjects who show "conditioning" effects.*

presumed causal relationships between events are represented by solid arrows. The symbol $R_{\pm}$ indicates that in verbal conditioning the subject initially emits a variety of responses, some of which belong to the reinforced class, R_{+}, and some of which do not, R_{-}. These are followed respectively by reinforcement, S_{R+}, and nonreinforcement, S_{R-}, which convey differential information and provide differential incentive to the subject.

The information provided by the reinforcing stimulus gives rise to one or more cognitive states, represented as A_1, A_2, . . . A_N. For example, the sequence of cognitive states developed by a subject in a word-naming verbal conditioning task might be: "The experimenter sometimes says 'good' after some of my words" (A_1); "Perhaps his saying 'good' depends on what words I say" (A_2); "Perhaps he wants me to figure out what words he is saying 'good' to, and give more of those" (A^3), etc. Depending upon the pattern and amount of reinforcement which they receive and recall, some subjects may be able to skip some of these early logical steps and go directly to a tentative formulation of the correct hypothesis, A_N: "Perhaps he is saying 'good' when I say words denoting people." We have observed that subjects who verbalize a correct hypothesis approach the experiment essentially as a problem-solving task. Furthermore, in verbal conditioning experiments in which subjects are given explicitly a problem-solving set, they proceed more directly to test out their hypotheses, and a larger proportion verbalize a correct contingency (DeNike and Spielberger, 1963; Spielberger and Levin, 1962).

Concurrent with the concept-formation activity involved in arriving at a correct hypothesis, subjects also develop affective and conative states based on the *incentive* provided by the reinforcing stimulus. For example, if the reinforcing stimulus has positive incentive value for a particular subject, he will *want* to receive reinforcement, and generally will *try* to elicit it from the experimenter. On the other hand, if the reinforcing stimulus has neutral or negative incentive value for the subject, he may be indifferent to it or attempt to avoid it (Mandler and Kaplan, 1956). Thus, the subject's affective and conative states in conjunction with his cognitive states (hypotheses) lead him to give responses, R_{+}, which he believes are in the reinforced response class, intermixed with a few responses, R_{-}, which are not expected to elicit reinforcement. Following these responses, the selective administration of the reinforcing stimulus, S_{R+}, or the absence of the reinforcing stimulus, S_{R-}, either confirms the subject's hypothesis, A_C, or leads him to modify it. The confirmed hypothesis, if accompanied by appropriate affective and conative states, results in increased output of the reinforced response class, $R\uparrow$.

It should be noted that the schematic diagram in Figure 4 massively oversimplifies our view of verbal conditioning. In it, we have treated affective and conative states as essentially constant and independent of cognitive states; there is much reason to suspect that these fluctuate and interact with the subjects' hypotheses. We have diagramed the process for the successful subject and ignored the numerous blind alleys explored by both successful and unsuccessful subjects; such processes should receive consideration in any theory which claims completeness. The nature of the conditioning task, the status of the experimenter, the instructions given to the subject, the characteristics of the subject population—all of these have demonstrable influence on mediating states and performance in verbal conditioning. In the final section of this paper, the significance of the verbal conditioning paradigm for the more general question of human learning without awareness will be considered.

IV. Verbal Conditioning and the Question of Learning Without Awareness

Few persons doubt that behavior occurs without awareness, as in, for example, shifting gears, finger-nail biting, facial tics, etc. (Eriksen, 1960). Of theoretical interest, however, is the extent to which such behaviors are initially *learned* without the mediation of cognitive processes. Kimble (1962) has suggested that the question of whether learning without awareness is possible may not have the same answer for all forms of learning. In classical eyelid conditioning, according to Kimble, it would appear that the subject need only be aware of the unconditioned stimulus for learning to take place.

In verbal conditioning, the evidence for learning without awareness reported in early experiments (e.g., Cohen et al., 1954; Greenspoon, 1955; Taffel, 1955) now appears suspect because of shortcomings in the evaluation of awareness in these studies. In recent experiments in which awareness was more carefully and thoroughly assessed (e.g., DeNike, 1964; Dulany, 1961, 1962; Spielberger, 1962), the absence of learning-without-awareness effects all but compels the conclusion that performance gains in verbal conditioning are consciously mediated.[6] However, for the reasons indicated below, the verbal conditioning paradigm may not provide an appropriate framework for clarifying the more general question of whether human operant learning can occur without awareness.

Subject Vigilance

Most subjects in psychological experiments, as Orne (1962) has pointed out, tend to be alert to manipulations that the experimenter may impose upon them and vigilant vis-a-vis their own behavior. In almost all verbal conditioning research, the subject is aware that he is participating in a psychological experiment. Thus, subjects in verbal conditioning experiments ordinarily notice the reinforcing stimulus and attempt to ascribe some meaning to it, making learning without awareness unlikely.

Response Monitoring

Despite reinforcement and no admonition to the contrary, reinforced words are rarely repeated in word naming verbal conditioning tasks. This almost universal tendency not to repeat words would be difficult to explain by automatic reinforcement theories. When asked why they did not repeat reinforced words, subjects usually indicate that they believed they were supposed to give a variety of words. It would appear that the subject keeps both his past responses and their consequences in mind and monitors new responses according to his hypotheses about the experiment. Thus, on the assumption that selective responding is guided by response monitoring in accordance with the subjects' hypotheses, the tendency not to repeat reinforced words in verbal conditioning becomes understandable, and learning without awareness seems improbable.

Response Sets

Some subjects approach verbal conditioning with a problem-solving set, while others interpret the conditioning task as either a personality test or an attempt to make them "conform." When a problem-solving set is combined with response monitoring in a vigilant subject, the subject notices the reinforcing stimulus, proceeds to test out successive hypotheses about the experiment, and is likely to become aware of a correct or correlated response-reinforcement contingency. In contrast, subjects with a personality-test set may get so involved in their free associations (on a word-naming verbal conditioning task) that they are oblivious to the reinforcing stimulus or tend to regard it as annoying and disruptive. Other subjects with personality-test sets devote considerable effort to the selection of "innocuous" or "unrevealing" words or otherwise defensively edit their responses so that they will not reveal personal secrets or shortcomings. Subjects who believe the experimenter is attempting to manipulate their behavior often report that they deliberately ignored the reinforcing stimulus or tried to avoid it. Thus, while a "conformity" or "personality" interpretation of the verbal conditioning task tends to prevent learning without awareness by causing subjects to ignore or avoid the reinforcing stimulus and/or to perceive it as unpleasant, a problem-solving approach tends to preclude learning without awareness by making it easier for the subjects to become aware.

The foregoing analysis of the "demand characteristics" (Orne, 1962) of verbal operant conditioning suggests that it is unlikely that learning without awareness will be found in laboratory experiments which employ the methods traditionally associated with the verbal conditioning paradigm. Under such conditions, it might be expected on a priori grounds that subjects will be particularly vigilant about their own verbal responses which are likely to be more carefully monitored than most other behavior. Or, in Eriksen's (1960) words, ". . . any situation where the cues and the reinforcements are salient enough to produce learning, will not escape detection by awareness" (p. 298).

It would appear more plausible to seek evidence of learning without awareness in situations where subjects are not aware that they are participating in a psychological experiment and on tasks which do

[6] It should be noted, however, that some subjects who are unaware of a correct contingency may nevertheless show slight gains in performance in verbal conditioning if they develop what may be termed a *correlated set.* For example, subjects (patients) who regard the Taffel (1955) sentence-construction task as a personality test sometimes assume they are supposed to make up sentences about themselves and their families. In response to either *random or systematic* reinforcement, subjects with such response dispositions may interpret the reinforcing stimulus as a sign of the experimenter's approval or encouragement and therefore give increasingly more sentences beginning with "I" or "We" (Spielberger, DeNike, and Stein, 1965).

not induce intensive response monitoring or defensive response sets. A likely place to look for such evidence might be in settings where subjects are motivated not to be aware, as, for example, in experimental situations involving processes such as repression, dissonance reduction, conformity, and ingratiation. At present, only scattered attempts have been made to investigate human operant learning with research designs representative of some of the forenamed conditions (e.g., Centers, 1963; Gergen, 1965; Goldiamond, 1965; Hefferline, Keenan, and Harford, 1959; Kimmel and Baxter, 1964; Verplanck, 1956; Vogel-Sprott, 1964). In such studies, however, the role of awareness has ordinarily not been the focus of investigation, and, consequently, the methods employed to assess awareness are subject to the criticisms discussed earlier. Therefore, where learning-without-awareness effects have been found, little confidence may be placed in such results. This in no way implies that human operant learning cannot take place without awareness, but merely affirms Adams' (1957) observation that such learning has not been demonstrated convincingly in the laboratory.

Some Final Considerations

We have endeavored in this paper to compare the relative adequacy with which descriptive behaviorism and cognitive learning theory can account for the findings of verbal operant conditioning experiments. We have argued that the descriptive behaviorists' implicit rejection of awareness as a concept has had serious methodological consequences which have retarded the convergence of empirical findings and the development of adequate theory. We have also contended that the utilization of awareness as a systematic concept has led to experimental findings which the Skinnerian approach would not have predicted. Finally, we have presented evidence to support the view that the reinforcing stimulus in verbal conditioning has both information and incentive value and that "what is learned" in verbal conditioning is awareness of a correct (or correlated) response-reinforced contingency.

With respect to whether human operant learning can occur without awareness, it should be noted that although this question would appear to have an empirical answer, in verbal conditioning the answer turns out to be inextricably tied to an investigator's theoretical orientation and, more fundamentally, to his epistemological assumptions concerning awareness as a concept (Spielberger, 1962, 1965). The issue is further complicated by the fact that different learning theories imply different operational definitions of the learned response (Campbell, 1954), leading in verbal conditioning to the collection of noncomparable data and to fruitless theoretical controversy. This controversy, which revolves about the role of awareness in verbal conditioning, is reminiscent of earlier disagreements among S-R and cognitive theorists concerning the role of reinforcement in learning. It has since been recognized that much of the controversy and confusion with respect to reinforcement stemmed from the failure of learning theorists to differentiate conceptually between the law of effect as an empirical statement and as a general theory of reinforcement (Spence, 1951).

On an empirical level, most would agree with the observation that performance in a variety of tasks is facilitated by reinforcement, but S-R and cognitive learning theories are still sharply divided on the question of whether reinforcement is required for learning to take place. Similarly, it is generally accepted that performance will be facilitated by the presence of appropriate cognitive states; that is, an "empirical law of cognition" is as supportable as the empirical law of effect,[7] but whether cognitive processes mediate any and all forms of learning is as dubious as a general theory of reinforcement. Thus, while a "theoretical law of cognition" might well serve to explain the findings in verbal conditioning experiments with human adults, it is quite another matter to demonstrate the role of cognitive processes in the learning of animals and preverbal children.

Nevertheless, the careful investigation of subjects' awareness in relation to other behavior is, we believe, requisite to the development of an adequate theory of human learning. Progress in this direction will depend upon the general acceptance of experimental procedures which permit sensitive evaluation of cognitive processes. These procedures must surely include subjects' verbal reports and must provide necessary safeguards against biasing or distorting such reports. Furthermore, it must be clearly recognized that the validity of verbal reports in any experimental context rests upon the willingness and linguistic competence of subjects to describe their mediating states when properly questioned (Dulany, 1961), and that verbal reports are but imperfectly related to the subjects' internal states (Eriksen, 1960). Paradoxically, perhaps the most significant contribution of verbal conditioning research has been the stimulation of interest in verbal report procedures and in concepts such as awareness among psychologists who are inclined to insist that thoughts and ideas are beyond the limits of scientific inquiry.

[7] We are grateful to Donald L. Thistlethwaite for suggesting the analogy between an empirical law of cognition in verbal conditioning and the empirical law of effect in traditional discussions of learning theory.

References

ADAMS, J. K. Laboratory studies of behavior without awareness. *Psychological Bulletin,* 1957, *54,* 383–405.

CAMPBELL, D. T. Operational delineation of "what is learned" via the transposition experiment. *Psychological Review,* 1954, *61,* 167–174.

CAMPBELL, D. T. Social attitudes and other acquired behavioral dispositions. In S. Koch (Ed.), *Psychology: A study of a science.* Vol. 6. New York: McGraw-Hill, 1963. Pp. 94–172.

CENTERS, R. A. Laboratory adaptation of the conversational procedure for the conditioning of verbal operants. *Journal of Abnormal and Social Psychology,* 1963, *67,* 334–339.

COHEN, B. D., KALISH, H. J., THURSTON, J. R., and COHEN, E. Experimental manipulation of verbal behavior. *Journal of Experimental Psychology,* 1954, *47,* 106–110.

DENIKE, L. D. The temporal relationship between awareness and performance in verbal conditioning. *Journal of Experimental Psychology,* 1964, *68,* 521–529.

DENIKE, L. D. Recall of reinforcement and conative activity in verbal conditioning. *Psychological Reports,* 1965, *16,* 345–346.

DENIKE, L. D., and SPIELBERGER, C. D. Induced mediating states in verbal conditioning. *Journal of Verbal Learning and Verbal Behavior,* 1963, *1,* 339–345.

DULANY, D. E. Hypotheses and habits in verbal "operant conditioning." *Journal of Abnormal and Social Psychology,* 1961, *63,* 251–263.

DULANY, D. E. The place of hypotheses and intentions: An analysis of verbal control in verbal conditioning. In C. W. Eriksen (Ed.), *Behavior and awareness.* Durham: Duke University Press, 1962. Pp. 102–129.

DULANY, D. E. How can we speak of awareness and volition as instrumental? In H. D. Kimmel (Chm.), Awareness as a factor in verbal operant conditioning. Symposium presented at Southeastern Psychological Association, Miami Beach, April 1963.

ERIKSEN, C. W. Unconscious processes. In M. R. Jones (Ed.), *Nebraska symposium on motivation: 1958.* Lincoln: University of Nebraska Press, 1958. Pp. 169–228.

ERIKSEN, C. W. Discrimination and learning without awareness: A methodological survey and evaluation. *Psychological Review,* 1960, *67,* 279–300.

ERIKSEN, C. W. Figments, fantasies, and follies: A search for the subconscious mind. In C. W. Eriksen (Ed.), *Behavior and awareness.* Durham: Duke University Press, 1962. Pp. 3–26.

FARBER, I. E. The things people say to themselves. *American Psychologist,* 1963, *18,* 185–197.

GERGEN, K. J. The effects of interaction goals and personalistic feedback on the presentation of self. *Journal of Personality and Social Psychology,* 1965, *1,* 413–424.

GOLDIAMOND, I. Stuttering and fluency as manipulable operant response classes. In L. Krasner and L. P. Ullmann (Eds.), *Research in behavior modification: New developments and their clinical implications.* New York: Holt, Rinehart and Winston, 1965. Pp. 106–156.

GREENSPOON, J. The reinforcing effect of two spoken sounds on the frequency of two responses. *American Journal of Psychology,* 1955, *68,* 409–416.

GREENSPOON, J. Verbal conditioning and clinical psychology. In A. J. Bachrach (Ed.), *Experimental foundations of clinical psychology.* New York: Basic Books, 1962. Pp. 510–553.

GREENSPOON, J. Reply to Spielberger and DeNike: "Operant conditioning of plural nouns: A failure to replicate the Greenspoon effect." *Psychological Reports,* 1963, *12,* 29–30.

GUTTMAN, N. Laws of behavior and facts of perception. In S. Koch (Ed.), *Psychology: A study of a science.* Vol. 5. New York: McGraw-Hill, 1963. Pp. 114–178.

HEFFERLINE, R. F., KEENAN, B., and HARFORD, R. A. Escape and avoidance conditioning in human subjects without their observation of the response. *Science,* 1959, *130,* 1338–1339.

IRWIN, F. W., KAUFFMAN, K., PRIOR, G., and WEAVER, H. B. On "learning without awareness of what is being learned." *Journal of Experimental Psychology,* 1934, *17,* 823–827.

KANFER, F. H., and MARSTON, A. R. Verbal conditioning, ambiguity and psychotherapy. *Psychological Reports,* 1961, *9,* 461–475.

KANFER, F. H., and MARSTON, A. R. The effect of task-relevant information on verbal conditioning. *Journal of Psychology,* 1962, *53,* 29–36.

KANFER, F. H., and MCBREARTY, J. F. Verbal conditioning: Discrimination and awareness. *Journal of Psychology,* 1961, *52,* 115–124.

KIMBLE, G. A. Classical conditioning and the problem of awareness. In C. W. Eriksen (Ed.), *Behavior and awareness.* Durham: Duke University Press, 1962. Pp. 27–45.

KIMMEL, H. D., and BAXTER, R. Avoidance conditioning of the GSR. *Journal of Experimental Psychology,* 1964, *68,* 482–485.

KRASNER, L. The therapist as a social reinforcement machine. In H. Strupp and L. Luborsky (Eds.), *Research in psychotherapy.* Vol. 2. Washington, D.C.: American Psychological Association, 1962. Pp. 61–94.

KRASNER, L., and ULLMAN, L. P. Variables affecting report of awareness in verbal conditioning. *Journal of Psychology,* 1963, *56,* 193–202.

KRIECKHAUS, E. E., and ERIKSEN, C. W. A study of awareness and its effect on learning and generalization. *Journal of Personality,* 1960, *28,* 503–517.

MANDLER, G., and KAPLAN, W. K. Subjective evaluation and reinforcing effect of a verbal stimulus. *Science,* 1956, *124,* 582–583.

MATARAZZO, J. D., SASLOW, G., and PAREIS, E. N. Verbal conditioning of two response classes: Some methodological considerations. *Journal of Abnormal and Social Psychology,* 1960, *61,* 190–206.

MUNN, N. L. *Handbook of psychological research on the rat: An introduction to animal psychology.* Boston: Houghton Mifflin, 1950.

ORNE, M. T. On the social psychology of the psychological experiment: With particular reference to demand characteristics and their implications. *American Psychologist,* 1962, *17,* 776–783.

PHILBRICK, E. B., and POSTMAN, L. A further analysis of "learning without awareness." *American Journal of Psychology,* 1955, *68,* 417–424.

POSTMAN, L., and JARRETT, R. F. An experimental analysis of "learning without awareness." *American Journal of Psychology,* 1952, *65,* 244–255.

POSTMAN, L., and SASSENRATH, J. M. The automatic action of verbal rewards and punishments. *Journal of General Psychology,* 1961, *65,* 109–136.

ROSENTHAL, R. On the social psychology of the psychological experiment: The experimenter's hypothesis as unintended determinant of experimental results. *American Scientist,* 1963, *51,* 268–283.

SALZINGER, K. Experimental manipulation of verbal behavior: A review. *Journal of General Psychology,* 1959, *61,* 65–94.

SASSENRATH, J. M. Learning without awareness and transfer of learning sets. *Journal of Educational Psychology,* 1959, *50,* 205–212.

SIDOWSKI, J. B. Influence of awareness of reinforcement on verbal conditioning. *Journal of Experimental Psychology,* 1954, *48,* 355–360.

SKINNER, B. F. *The behavior of organisms: An experimental analysis.* New York: Appleton-Century-Crofts, 1938.

SKINNER, B. F. *Verbal behavior.* New York: Appleton-Century-Crofts, 1957.

SKINNER, B. F. Behaviorism at fifty. *Science,* 1963, *140,* 951–958. (a)

SKINNER, B. F. Operant behavior. *American Psychologist,* 1963, *18,* 503–515. (b)

SPENCE, K. W. The postulates and methods of "behaviorism." *Psychological Review,* 1948, *55,* 67–78.

SPENCE, K. W. Theoretical interpretations of learning. In S. S. Stevens (Ed.), *Handbook of experimental psychology.* New York: Wiley, 1951. Pp. 690–729.

SPIELBERGER, C. D. The role of awareness in verbal conditioning. In C. W. Eriksen (Ed.), *Behaviorism and awareness.* Durham: Duke University Press, 1962. Pp. 73–101.

SPIELBERGER, C. D. Theoretical and epistemological issues in verbal conditioning. In S. Rosenberg (Ed.), *Directions in psycholinguistics.* New York: Macmillan, 1965. Pp. 149–200.

SPIELBERGER, C. D., BERNSTEIN, I. H., and RATCLIFF, R. G. Information and incentive value of the reinforcing stimulus in verbal conditioning. *Journal of Experimental Psychology,* 1966, *71,* 26–31.

SPIELBERGER, C. D., and DENIKE, L. D. Implicit epistemological bias and the problem of awareness in verbal conditioning: A reply to Greenspoon. *Psychological Reports,* 1963, *12,* 103–106.

SPIELBERGER, C. D., DENIKE, L. D., and STEIN, L. S. Anxiety and verbal conditioning. *Journal of Personality and Social Psychology,* 1965, *1,* 229–239.

SPIELBERGER, C. D., and LEVIN, S. M. What is learned in verbal conditioning? *Journal of Verbal Learning and Verbal Behavior,* 1962, *1,* 125–132.

TAFFEL, C. Anxiety and the conditioning of verbal behavior. *Journal of Abnormal and Social Psychology,* 1955, *51,* 496–501.

THORNDIKE, E. L., and ROCK, R. T. Learning without awareness of what is being learned or intent to learn it. *Journal of Experimental Psychology,* 1934, *17,* 1–19.

VERPLANCK, W. S. The operant conditioning of human motor behavior. *Psychological Bulletin,* 1956, *53,* 70–83.

VOGEL-SPROTT, M. E. Response generalization under verbal conditioning in alcoholics, delinquents, and students. *Behaviour Research and Therapy,* 1964, *2,* 135–141.

Differential Reinforcement

This section contains four experiments which evaluate, under controlled conditions, the effectiveness of reinforcers that change the form and frequency of a subject's speech. The general procedure in these experiments is to observe a baseline frequency under the experimental conditions but without reinforcement; then, some class of verbal utterances is reinforced according to the experimental design, and the increase in frequency that results is compared with both the baseline and a subsequent period in which reinforcement is discontinued.

The experiment by *Adams and Hoffman* demonstrates the effectiveness of attention as a reinforcer. The experimenter, in a face-to-face interview with each subject, literally ignored him while he was talking, except when a statement of self-reference was made—then he looked up and listened attentively. Even though the listener's reaction was contrived, such a reinforcer is very similar to those that normally maintain speech in the natural environment. Although we speak of the experimenter (listener) as having manipulated the behavior of the speaker in this experiment, the comparable interaction in the natural environment is best described as one in which a speaker, by his utterances, prompts the reactions of a listener. The attention of the listener depends upon the speaker uttering statements which can increase the frequency of verbal behaviors in which the listener is interested (behaviors having a high frequency in the listener's repertoire). Thus, differential reinforcement comes about because some utterances of the speaker prompt existing repertoires, whereas others do not. The reactivity of the listener's potential repertoire to prompts by the speaker is the differential reinforcement which shapes the speaker's behavior into a form that makes it effective for the listener. This inter-reactivity between the speaker and the listener defines verbal reinforcement in its full complexity.

Attention by a listener also illustrates the dual function of a conditioned reinforcer. That is, attention, besides increasing the frequency of the statement which it follows, also functions as a discriminative stimulus. It is an occasion when further reinforcement of the speaker's utterances is highly probable. In contrast, the speaker is not likely to influence the listener when the latter is not paying attention. It is difficult in the present experiment to disentangle the increase in frequency of the subject's utterances that comes from the "audience effect" of the speaker's attention from that of the reinforcing effect. The "audience effect" occurs because the listener's attention is an occasion when he is likely to reply. When the listener is not attentive, requests for something or attempts to prompt reaction will be ineffective. It is for this reason that our verbal repertoires contain so many items reinforced by producing the listener's attention—such as saying the person's name with a rising intonation. The attention of the listener reinforces the performance requesting it. The patois that adults develop with infants is a simple example of this kind of shaping. On the other hand, the situation is complicated because the listener's reaction can also reinforce the speaker's current behavior.

It is instructive to compare the reinforcer in this experiment with the procedure in the classical verbal reinforcement experiment, where the experimenter says "Mm-hmm" following each utterance whose frequency he wishes to increase. The reply "Mm-hmm" has some of the dimensions of attention, because the listener who replies is also likely to be paying attention. The two functions do not go together completely, however.

45 | *The Frequency of Self-Reference Statements as a Function of Generalized Reinforcement*[1]

J. STACY ADAMS
BROWNING HOFFMAN

Recent experiments have demonstrated applications of operant conditioning in the realm of verbal behavior (e.g., Hildum and Brown, 1956; Verplanck, 1955; see Krasner, 1958, for review). Stimuli demonstrated to be reinforcing have been verbalizations of assent, agreement and approval, nods, smiles, paraphrases and impersonal events such as buzzer and

[1] The assistance of Beverly A. Brown, George E. Dunn, Ben V. Hole, Frank B. Krause, Lillian Lauer, Jack Lyle, and Aline Spivock is gratefully acknowledged.

From the *Journal of Abnormal and Social Psychology,* 1960, *60,* 384–389.

bell tones and colored lights. Attention, although hypothesized by Skinner to be a generalized reinforcer (Skinner, 1953, 1957) has not been specifically investigated.

The purposes of this study were (*a*) to determine whether a combination of attention and assent constituted a reinforcing event, (*b*) to explore the effects of prolonged extinction on the occurrence of self-reference statements and other behavior such as emotional reactions and escape behavior, and (*c*) to determine what are the implications of the use of common events (attention-assent) in free, unstructured interview situations. In most previous studies extinction has not been carried out at length. In Verplanck's investigation, for example, extinction was carried out for only 10 minutes, a period too brief to uncover any effects other than those upon the class of operants considered (Verplanck, 1957).

Method

General Experimental Plan. The experiment was conducted under the guise of being a survey of student opinion with two groups of 31 Ss, one experimental group and one control group. The survey interview was divided into four consecutive periods, the first three each lasting 10 min., while the last varied in length up to a maximum of 20 min. Each period was further subdivided into 2-minute intervals during each of which S's self-reference statements and other statements were counted. After the introduction of the "survey" and after S understood what was wanted of him, the first 10 minute period began and the operant level of statements containing self-references was determined, no reinforcement being given in either group.

During the second 10 minute period *E* reinforced all statements containing self-references made by experimental Ss by following their occurrence by a combination of attention and assent. A precise description of reinforcing events is given below. Control Ss received no reinforcement in Period II, nor in any other period.

Extinction was conducted during the third 10-minute period and during the subsequent 20-minute period. As will be seen, some Ss stopped responding entirely during the course of extinction. Extinction consisted of withholding from experimental Ss the reinforcement previously given in Period II.

If at any time during the course of the experiment S's over-all rate of responding fell to zero, nondirective probes such as "What else can you think of?", "Can you think of anything else?", or "Do you have any other ideas?" were used. These were infrequently necessary except during extinction and then they were often unsuccessful in maintaining continued responding.

Subjects. The experimental Ss were 31 male and female, graduate and undergraduate students at Stanford University, who were "interviewed" in the spring of 1958. Control Ss were drawn from the same population but were "interviewed" in the spring of 1959. It was ascertained at the conclusion of the experiment, when the real purpose of the "interview" was explained, that all Ss were naive to the extent that they had no training in conditioning and had never before participated in an experiment on operant conditioning.

Experimenters. The *Es* were advanced undergraduate and graduate students in two of the senior author's courses on language and verbal behavior. Seven of these collected the experimental group data; two collected the control group data. One *E* collected data from both groups. In addition to having some theoretical sophistication in verbal operant conditioning, each *E* had a minimum of four complete practice sessions followed by a detailed critique period. The *E* who collected data from both groups had, in addition, one year's intensive practice in verbal conditioning in connection with a number of other studies. He acquired considerable sensitivity in identifying statements and self-reference statements and imparted this skill to the other *E* who collected control data and for whose training he was responsible. As a consequence, to which reference will be made below, rates of response show an elevation in the control group data as compared to the experimental group data.

In view of the fact that there is a difference in the sensitivity of the experimental and control group *Es*, it would have been desirable to obtain interexperimenter reliability data. Unfortunately, any useful reliability data would have had to be based on the reinterview of the same Ss by different *Es* and this, of course, would have had an effect on the observed responses. Our feeling is that *Es* of equivalent training would have yielded acceptably high reliabilities. Since the seven *Es* who collected the experimental group data had comparable training and the two who collected control group data had equivalent training, the inter-*E* reliabilities within the two groups are probably acceptable. And this is really the important point, for we are especially concerned with change or lack of change *within* each group.

Procedure. The experiment was conducted at the convenience of Ss in their living quarters or other quiet place at a time when only *E* and S were present and when S had one full hour available. When the experiment proper began, *E* was seated in front of S and recorded the frequency of self-reference statements and all statements at the end of each 2-minute period.

In his introduction to S, *E* told him that he was doing a "survey" for the psychology department, that the purpose was to find out students' "frank and honest personal opinions and ideas about conformity and education in America," and that S could talk for about an hour or more on the subject. S was further told that *E* would not enter into the interview except to take notes. S was then reminded that the interview would be most fruitful if a complete, detailed and exhaustive expression of his ideas and opinions were obtained.

The topic "conformity and education in America" was selected for several reasons. First, it was a topic students frequently discussed and about which they held quite definite opinions. Thus, it was felt that there would be some motivation to express views on it. Secondly, the subject was broad enough to permit sustained talking. Thirdly, it was a topic which neither imposed an upper nor a lower limit on the use of statements of self-reference.

Except during the 10-minute reinforcement period for the experimental Ss, *E* kept his entire attention on his notebook and was silent. He did not lift his head, shift his line of regard to S, or make any verbal responses, unless S stopped talking. When the latter occurred *E* used a general, nondirective probe in order to try to maintain S's output.

Reinforcing Stimulus Events. A single class of stimulus events was hypothesized to have reinforcing properties. The event consisted of *E*'s (*a*) lifting his head, (*b*) shifting his line of regard from his notebook to S, and (*c*) murmuring "mm-hmm" simultaneously. After a reinforcement (which took about 1 second) *E* returned to his original position and composure until S emitted another statement containing a self-reference. As previously indicated, it is only among experimental Ss in Period II that reinforcement of self-references was used. Among control Ss, *E* was silent throughout the experiment and kept his attention on his notebook.

The Class of Operant Responses Conditioned. The verbal operants selected for conditioning were all statements containing one or more references to S personally. Thus, statements having "I," "me," "my," "mine," "myself" and like words were considered self-reference statements, except in those instances when the pronoun had someone else than S as a referent (e.g., "my roommate thinks . . ."). Statements containing the first person plural pronoun, "we," were also counted as self-reference statements if they pertained to an activity in which S himself had participated, or a belief he shared.

Statements were defined as units of "thought," containing a complete idea. Statements, therefore, were complete sentences as defined in standard dictionaries, although in speech they might not be clearly punctuated as a written sentence. Such a definition is not entirely satisfactory, for the sufficient and necessary criteria are not enumerated, and there is, therefore, room for subjective variability on the part of *Es*. *Es*, however, become more proficient with experience and there is a tendency for them to identify more self-reference statements as their proficiency increases.

Results

Effects of Reinforcement. The basic index of responding used in the analysis is the ratio of self-reference statements to total statements made (called SR ratio hereafter). The mean SR ratios for each period and the mean SR ratio over all periods are plotted in Figure 1 for the experimental and control Ss.

The first point to be noted is that the mean over-all SR ratio in the experimental group is .305, whereas it is .408 in the control group. The difference is significant beyond the .001 level and represents increased proficiency by one *E* in identifying statements and self-references as he gained experience, during a period of approximately one year, as previously related.

As Figure 1 shows, the size of the SR ratio increases during reinforcement and drops during extinction in the experimental group, as predicted under the hypothesis that attention-assent constitutes a reinforcing state of affairs. To determine the significance of the observed change in SR ratios two analyses were performed. First, Cochran's *Q* test (Siegel, 1956) was applied to determine whether the values of SR deviated significantly from the mean over-all SR value of .305. This required a determination of whether each individual ratio deviated above or below that value. The *Q* value obtained was 9.38, which is significant beyond the .05 level.

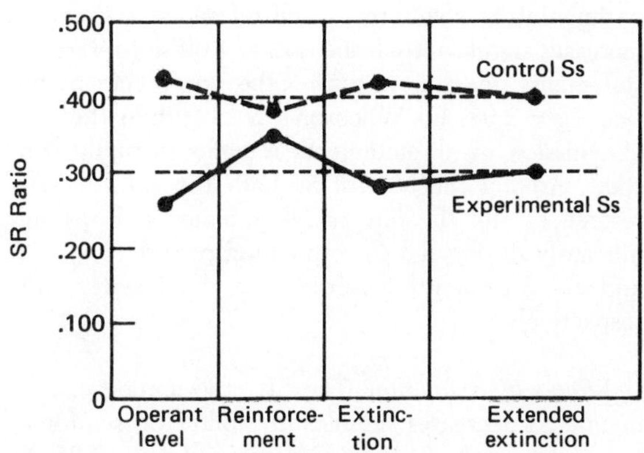

Figure 1 *SR (self-reference) ratios by periods for experimental and control subjects.*

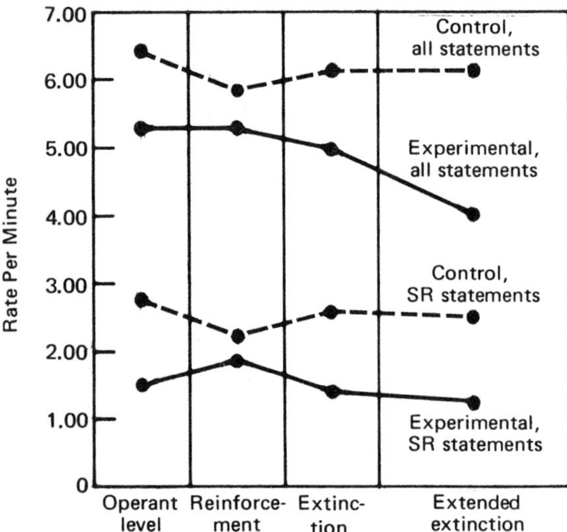

Figure 2 *Rates of emitting self-reference and all statements for experimental and control subjects.*

Among the controls the SR values during each period did not differ significantly from the over-all mean SR value of .408 ($Q = 2.68$).

The second analysis, Friedman's nonparametric analysis of variance (Siegel, 1956), reveals that the treatments contributed significantly to the variance among experimental Ss ($\chi_r^2 = 16.7$) but not among control Ss ($\chi_r^2 = 5.15$). Further analysis of the data for the experimentals revealed that the reinforcement treatment is the major contributor. Wilcoxon's signed-ranks analysis for matched pairs (Siegel, 1956) indicated that the SR ratio during reinforcement among experimental Ss was significantly greater (*a*) than the SR ratio during the operant level period ($z = 2.5$), (*b*) than the SR ratio during the first extinction period ($z = 2.9$), and (*c*) than the SR ratio during the second extinction period ($z = 3.1$).

The rate of emitting self-reference statements and all statements is shown in Figure 2. Among the experimental Ss the rate of self-reference statements increases significantly from 1.42 to 1.90 self-reference statements per minute during the reinforcement period ($z = 2.98$, by Wilcoxon's test), while the rate of emission of all statements remains virtually constant. Among the control Ss both the rate of self-references and the rate of all statements drops significantly during the corresponding period ($z = 3.20$ and $z = 3.13$, for self-reference and all statements, respectively).

Effects of Extinction. The SR ratio among experimental Ss decreases significantly following reinforcement, during the first extinction period ($z = 2.9$). In the second extinction period, lasting up to 20 minutes, there is no further decrease in the SR ratio Figure 1). However, the rate of self-reference statements decreases continuously during extinction, as may be seen in Figure 2. By Wilcoxon's test, the rate of self-reference statements during the first extinction period is significantly smaller than during reinforcement ($z = 3.4$) and is significantly smaller during the second extinction period than during the first ($z = 3.08$). The rate of making all statements is not significantly smaller during the first extinction period than during the reinforcement period ($z = 1.27$). However, the rate is significantly smaller during the second extinction period than during the reinforcement period, ($z = 4.3$). Furthermore, the rate during the second extinction period is smaller than during the first extinction period ($z = 3.96$). Therefore, although the SR ratio during the second extinction period is not smaller than during the first extinction, the rate of emitting self-references and total statements decreases during successive extinction periods.

The rates of self-reference and all statements for control Ss do not vary significantly after the first 10-minute period of the "interview." The extinction effects noted among experimental Ss are in no way evident among the controls. Hence, the observed experimental extinction effects are attributable to withdrawal of generalized reinforcement.

Many experimental Ss displayed general disturbance, emotionality, and, in some instances, downright anger and hostility toward *E* during extinction. This was especially noticeable in the late stages of extinction. In her report on her "interviews," one of the experimenters wrote: ". . . many Ss found the interview to be a stress situation (during extinction)." This finding is in accord with reports by Verplanck (1955). There was further evidence that some Ss "left the field"—i.e., refused to continue speaking, despite prompts—because the discontinuance of reinforcement was aversive to them. It is as though nonreinforcement constituted *punishment* for them. However, it is not possible to say that all Ss whose verbal behavior stopped before the end of the second extinction period did so because of aversion. In only one S was there evidence of emotionality among the controls, though a number of them stopped responding before the end of the 50-minute experimental session, despite the use of probes, apparently having run out of comments on the subject of conformity.

In Figure 3 the number of Ss who continued to respond during each 2-minute interval of the extinction period is plotted. At the beginning of the extinction period all experimental Ss were responding; during the corresponding period twenty-eight of the thirty-one controls were responding. The difference is not significant by Fisher's exact test

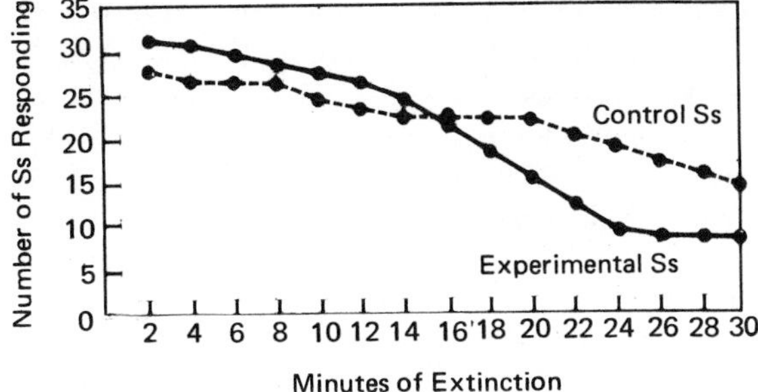

Figure 3 *Number of experimental and control subjects continuing to respond at two-minute intervals during extinction.*

($P = .12$, one-tailed). At the end of the extinction period, however, nine experimental Ss and sixteen control Ss were responding. The difference is significant beyond the .05 level ($\chi^2 = 3.28$, one-tailed).

Evidence of Awareness. Upon questioning at the end of the experiment not one experimental or control S reported that the "interview" situation was other than was related to him. Some experimental Ss reported "awareness" of change in *E*'s behavior during the reinforcement and extinction periods, this change being one of "interest" and "attention." None, however, were able to report on what these changes were contingent—i.e., emitting self-reference statements. We may conclude, therefore, that the observed experimental effects were not a function of knowledge or awareness of the experimental manipulations.

Discussion

The evidence is unequivocal that the frequency of emitting self-references can be controlled by making attention-assent contingent upon their occurrence. When attention and assent follow, self-references increase (relative to total output); when attention and assent are withdrawn, the relative frequency of self-references decreases. The same is true for the rate of emitting self-reference statements. These effects are not observable among the controls, whose self-reference statements were not reinforced at any time. Further evidence of the effects of the experimental manipulations comes from the fact that *all* verbal behavior is extinguished in significantly more experimental than control Ss.

Four explanations of the latter over-all extinction phenomenon suggest themselves. First, it is plausible that Ss stop responding because they have exhausted all that they can say on the subject of conformity and education in America. Though this is undoubtedly true in the case of some Ss, since a number of control Ss stopped responding, such an explanation does not account for the fact that the experimental Ss are more likely than the control Ss to stop responding before the termination of the experiment. Nor does it account for the experimental Ss' greater emotionally during extinction. Second, it is possible that statements without self-references were extinguished along with those containing self-references because of generalization. Both types of statements are quite similar in that both are verbal responses and it is therefore possible that extinction of self-reference statements generalizes to other statements. However, in the present instance the explanation appears improbable because, if there were stimulus generalization, it should have been evident during reinforcement. But there was no evidence for stimulus generalization during reinforcement, for only the frequency of self-reference statements and rate of emitting them increased, while total output and rate of total output remained constant.

A third possibility is that a minimum number of self-reference statements is necessary if talking on the selected topic is to be possible. There is no direct evidence in support of this explanation. However, the data in Figure 1 indirectly suggest that it may have validity. After prolonged extinction the SR ratio among experimental Ss drops only to the operant level in those Ss who continue talking. Thus, approximately .270–.300 may be the *minimum* possible ratio if talking is to continue. If the proportion of self-references drops below this level (because of extinction), talking may become impossible or at least very difficult. Further support for this hypothesis comes from the fact that while the SR ratio remains constant during extinction, the *rate* of self-references and total output steadily decreases. Among the controls, on the other hand, both the SR ratio and the rate of self-reference statements and of total output remain constant during the corresponding periods.

A fourth possible explanation of the extinction of all verbal behavior is that withdrawal of reinforcement constitutes punishment and that this punishment has the effect of arresting all verbal behavior (and perhaps other behavior) in the presence of *E*. If punishment is defined as "an operation in which an aversive or conditioned aversive stimulus is made contingent upon a response" (Ferster and Skinner, 1957, p. 731), the explanation seems reasonable, for silence is probably used by the verbal community as a conditioned aversive stimulus. As Skinner points out, remaining silent when the occasion usually gives rise to speech constitutes punishment (Skinner, 1957). Thus, in the present experiment the *E*'s withholding of attention and assent, following reinforcement, may have had an effect very similar to the silence following the commission of a verbal *faux pas* in a social group. That some experimental Ss who stopped responding may have perceived the situation in precisely this way is evidenced by their reporting that they felt the *E* had become uninterested in or even annoyed at what they were saying and by the fact that they frequently became visibly tense, angry, and hostile.

Of the four possible explanations suggested, the data rule out that relating to the generalization of extinction. Running out of comments to make may partially account for the Ss stopping to respond altogether, for some Ss in the control group, as well as in the experimental group, stopped before 50 minutes elapsed. However, it could not account for the significantly greater proportions of experimental Ss who stopped. This disparity may be accounted for by either the third and fourth explanations offered, or, perhaps, by both. The data do not permit a choice between the two, however.

With respect to interviewing of the free, unstructured type, the findings of this study have clear implications. Attention and assent—both common interviewer responses—can produce significant changes in the content of a respondent's verbalizations. In this study, the effect was to increase the frequency of self-reference statements. When one member of a dyad differentially reinforces specific verbal response classes of the other participant, he gains some control over the conversation. Such control has obvious advantages. Psychotherapists may use verbal reinforcement techniques to guide their patients toward significant insights; these procedures may be of considerable importance, for instance, when applied to self-reference, affect, or other statements where therapeutic circumstances preclude direct requests for such information from the patient. Similarly, survey interviewers can control the content of a respondent's verbalizations in a direction consonant with the purpose of an interview by use of differential reinforcement. Or, a physician might find it useful to reinforce differentially in his patients' verbal descriptions of symptoms, as opposed to diagnostic inferences.

Perhaps more importantly, interviewers should be aware of the possible undesirable influence which verbal reinforcement may have upon the responses of interviewees. Inappropriate use of such techniques may easily lead to selective biases in the data or clinical evaluations based upon reflected idiosyncrasies of the interviewer which have been reinforced in a respondent or patient. Furthermore, the withdrawal of reinforcement, as in the present study, may result in emotionality that might have undesirable consequences, particularly in psychotherapeutic situations.

Summary

An experiment was conducted to determine whether the use of a combination of attention and assent by an "interviewer" constituted a reinforcing event and to find out the effects of prolonged extinction. Following a 10-minute period during which the operant level of self-reference statements was measured, all self-reference statements by experimental Ss were reinforced by *E*'s showing attention-assent for a period of 10 minutes. The Ss' responses were then extinguished for a period of as long as 30 minutes. The same procedure was followed with control Ss with the exception that they received no reinforcement.

It was found that attention-assent constituted a reinforcing state of affairs since the relative frequency and rate of self-reference statements significantly increased during conditioning among the experimental Ss, while control Ss showed no change. Extinction of self-reference statements produced a significant decrease in their relative frequency and rate of occurrence among experimental Ss, but not among control Ss.

During extinction most experimental Ss showed emotional disturbance; in some cases anger and hostility. The verbal behavior of significantly more experimental than control Ss was totally extinguished before the end of the 30-minute extinction period. In some instances it was evident that Ss were leaving an aversive field. Possible explanations of the observed extinction phenomena were offered.

There was no evidence that any *S* was aware or had knowledge of the experimental manipulations.

References

Ferster, C. B., and Skinner, B. F. *Schedules of reinforcement.* New York: Appleton-Century-Crofts, 1957.

Hildum, D. C., and Brown, R. W. Verbal reinforcement and interviewer bias. *Journal of Abnormal and Social Psychology,* 1956, *53,* 108–111.

Krasner, L. Studies of the conditioning of verbal behavior. *Psychological Bulletin,* 1958, *55,* 148–170.

Siegel, S. *Nonparametric statistics.* New York: McGraw-Hill, 1956.

Skinner, B. F. *Science and human behavior.* New York: Macmillan, 1953.

Skinner, B. F. *Verbal behavior.* New York: Appleton-Century-Crofts, 1957.

Verplanck, W. S. The control of the content of conversation: Reinforcement of statements of opinion. *Journal of Abnormal and Social Psychology,* 1955, *51,* 668–676.

The study by *Reynolds and Risley* provides an example of a verbal situation in which the reinforcer bears a very different relationship to the behavior of the speaker from that of simple attention. The experimenters used material reinforcers, such as the blocks, stencils, paper, paste, and paints needed for ordinary nursery school activities. Only if the child asked for the materials were they given. Such a relationship between a verbal request and the material object it produces is called a "mand," because the speaker specifies the reinforcer that relates to his current state of deprivation. This form of verbal behavior contrasts with the verbal performances reinforced in the previous experiment by Adams and Hoffman, where the reinforcement was generalized rather than a particular thing the speaker was currently requesting.

Reynolds and Risley carried out several control procedures to determine which part of the teacher's reaction to a child was critical for an increase in the frequency of the child's behavior. The actual contingency between the child's request and the reply it produced could have been the critical element in the procedure; or just the occurrence of the teacher's remarks, unconnected with the child's requests, could have stimulated the child's increased verbal activity. The DRO (Differential Reinforcement of Other Behavior) provided a very useful technique to prove that the contingency of reinforcement between the teacher's reaction and the subject's behavior, rather than just the occurrence of the teacher's remarks, was responsible for the change in performance. In DRO, the reinforcing stimulus occurs with the same frequency as it would have normally, but its delivery is delayed so that it always follows some other behavior than the one which had previously been reinforced. This control procedure showed, very clearly, that the contingency between the reinforcer and the performance was the critical element.

Control experiments also proved that the actual reinforcers maintaining the child's behavior were the teacher's replies to the child's requests (asking for more information) rather than the praise or attention also given to the child for asking for the materials. Thus, the experimenters effectively separated two components of the teacher's reply—praise and the verbal interactions leading to receipt of the materials. The experimental findings again suggest two functions of the verbal reinforcer: (1) the reinforcing function, which produces an increase in the frequency of requests for material, and (2) the subsequent behavior that becomes possible when the teacher supplies materials and replies verbally to clarify the use of the materials.

This experimental paradigm is an alternative to the statistical designs used in many of the other experiments we have reported. Statistical analysis is absent in this experiment because of the careful control of conditions with a single subject, the use of a baseline, and repeated manipulation of the same verbal behaviors.

46 The Role of Social and Material Reinforcers in Increasing Talking of a Disadvantaged Preschool Child[1]

NANCY J. REYNOLDS
TODD R. RISLEY

Children in an economically deprived area lack many skills which would enable them to function effectively in the public schools or in the middle-class society, of which public schools are an integral part. The most damaging deficiency appears to be a lack of verbal and language skills (Bereiter and Engelmann, 1966), whereby the child learns what the school has to teach and communicates what he has, or has not, learned. Consequently, most people interested in remedying the effects of cultural deprivation are concerned with increasing the language skills of these children. In view of this concern with the value of verbal skills for economically deprived children, it was felt that an especially low frequency of verbal behavior by one such preschool child should be altered. Previous studies utilizing operant conditioning procedures have demonstrated how a manipulation of this nature could be undertaken. The pioneering studies from the University of Washington Preschool have investigated the applicability of operant principles to changing the problem behavior of normal children in naturally occurring situations (summarized in Harris, Wolf, and Baer, 1964). These studies, which investigated the relationship between the behaviors of teachers and the behaviors of preschool children, have indicated that the "attention" of the teacher can function as a strong reinforcer to establish, modify, and maintain the behavior of preschool children.

This development has provided information about principles of behavior and how these principles affect human behavior. It has also provided a technology for therapeutic intervention in human problems and for increasingly more sophisticated analyses of human behavior. The present study was undertaken to increase the frequency of verbalization of a child in a preschool setting and subsequently to analyze the controlling components of the teacher-child interaction in producing the behavior increase, as well as to assess some of the changes in the content of verbalizations in relation to changes in the frequency of verbalizations.

Method

Subject and Setting

The study was conducted at the Turner House preschool of the Juniper Gardens Children's Project in Kansas City, Kansas. The subject was a 4-year-old girl who exhibited a low frequency of verbal behavior well after the period considered normal for adaptation to the preschool routine and setting. She was one of 15 children, all Negroes from a lower-class community, selected from large families with extremely low incomes. The subject's Peabody Picture Vocabulary Test I.Q. was 59, slightly below the average (79) of the group, but she did not appear retarded. She gave appropriate answers in structured teaching situations if the teachers could get her to speak loud enough to be heard. She was particularly skilled in motor activities, and despite her non-verbal method of obtaining play materials from other children ("grabbing"), appeared well-liked by the other children.

The preschool ran from 8:30 to 11:30 A.M. five days a week. During the first 45 minutes of the morning, special training programs and individual tasks for the children were combined with breakfast. The remainder of the morning consisted of an approximately 45-minute period of free play inside, a 30-minute snack and instruction time, a 45-minute period of free play outside, and a story time inside just before going home.

1 This study is based upon a thesis submitted by the senior author to the Department of Human Development in partial fulfillment of the requirements for the Master of Arts degree. The authors express appreciation to Dianetta Coates, Maxine Preuitt, and, especially, Betty Hart for their able assistance in all aspects of the study. This research was supported by Grants (HD 03144) from the National Institute of Child Health and Human Development and (CG-8474) from the office of Economic Opportunity, Headstart Research and Demonstration to the Bureau of Child Research, and the Department of Human Development at the University of Kansas.

During free-play periods, the children could move from one to another of the unstructured activities usually found in preschool programs such as a block area, a doll area, a painting area, or a sand box. Some materials such as blocks were available to the children, and others such as paint were dispensed by the teachers. During the free-play periods, the three teachers always attended to, talked to, and interacted with the children and occasionally provided snacks (fruit, cookies, crackers, etc.) contingent upon generally appropriate play behavior.

Procedures and Results

Recording

Three observers recorded data during the morning free-play periods, and although present in the preschool room and yard with the children, did not interact with or respond to them. Observations of the subject were made at sample intervals only during free-play periods. During these periods the child's speech was sampled using two different recording procedures, one recording how often she spoke and one recording what she said.

Frequency of Verbalization. Verbal frequency data were collected simultaneously by all three observers. They carried data sheets similar to those described by Allen, Hart, Buell, Harris, and Wolf (1964) and Hall, Lund, and Jackson (1968). Each row of the data sheet contained 30 squares representing a 10-second interval per square, or 5 minutes per row. Two adjacent rows were used for each 5-minute observation. The top row was used to record talking or verbalization by the child. Whenever the child verbalized during a 10-second interval a (T) was written in the square corresponding to that interval. Only one (T) was marked in any interval during which the child verbalized irrespective of the amount of talking that occurred in that 10-second period. If the child's verbalization began in one 10-second interval and extended into the next, a (T) was noted in both intervals. Frequency of verbalization was therefore recorded as the per cent of 10-second intervals of the sample during which verbalization occurred. The bottom row was used to record teacher attention by placing the initial of the attending teacher in the square corresponding to the 10-second interval in which teacher attention occurred. Teacher attention was counted in the same way as verbalizations by the child.

Starting at the same time, using stopwatches, the three observers simultaneously but independently recorded the frequency of the child's verbalizations for 5-minute periods. Usually, three such 5-minute samples were taken each day during the two free-play periods: two during the first free-play period and one during the second, although occasionally only one or two 5-minute samples were taken during a day.

Verbalizations were defined as any speech from the child heard by the observers, except random noises such as shrieking, humming, or laughing. During rate samples, speech which was too low for the observers to understand fully was counted, though this was not true of the content samples. Teacher attention was counted as any time a teacher spoke to, gave equipment to, or touched the child.

The correspondence between the three observers' data on frequency of verbalization is shown in Figure 1, where the top line represents the highest rate and the bottom line the lowest rate obtained by an observer on a given sample. The product-moment correlation coefficients between the frequency data of the three observers on all observations throughout the year were:

0.97 for observers A and B (64 samples)
0.96 for observers A and C (59 samples)
0.99 for observers B and C (59 samples).

The product-moment correlation coefficients between the teacher attention data over the same samples were:

0.85 for observers A and B (64 samples)
0.90 for observers A and C (59 samples)
0.97 for observers B and C (59 samples).

Content of Verbalization. The content of verbalization samples were collected over the same portions of the year as the frequency of verbalization samples, but not necessarily on the same days. The verbal content samples were recorded during free play by one of three observers, who wrote down in longhand "everything" that the child said while following her from one activity to another during a 15-minute period. Twenty-nine such samples were taken on different days during the baseline condition (Days 1 to 29), 7 by observer A, 13 by observer B, and 9 by observer C. During the experimental conditions (Days 130 to 164) observer A recorded all 30 verbal content samples, with observer B simultaneously recording on two occasions (Days 157 and 162). These verbalization records were then transcribed, and content was categorized and counted from the transcribed phrases by one teacher. As observers recorded the data, they also put a check in one column if the verbalization was directed toward a child, and

Table 1 *Comparison Between the Three Observers' Records of the Content of the Child's Speech during Baseline (Average Frequency Per Sample)*

		Observer	
	A	B	C
Nouns and Verbs			
Total	10.0	8.6	12.3
Different	4.6	5.5	6.9
Verbalizations			
To teacher	3.8	2.8	5.3
To child	4.8	11.0	5.8
Verbalizations			
Mands	6.6	3.6	5.4
Non-mands	0.02	3.4	1.0

a check in a second column if it was directed toward a teacher (immediately following a recorded verbalization). General grammatical rules were used to categorize roughly the content of the verbalizations. As the nouns and verbs were counted, the first appearance of a noun or a verb was added to the count of *different* nouns and verbs. Each subsequent time the child said that noun or verb in the same content sample, it was counted as a repetition. The phrases were also defined as sentences if they included a subject (or implied subject) and a verb. These sentences were then categorized as *mand,* generally a request, demand, or question which specified the reinforcer (Skinner, 1957), or *non-mand* sentences. Sixteen of these verbalization records (randomly selected but including at least two from each condition) were independently categorized and counted by the second teacher.

The averages of the content measures from each observer's records during the baseline period are compared in Table 1. The correspondence between the measures taken from the three observer's records indicates the reliability of the low frequencies of the content measures between different observers on different days. On the two occasions of simultaneous recording, observer A recorded 12 different nouns and verbs with 37 repetitions and observer B recorded 11 different and 22 repetitions on Day 157; observer A recorded 16 different and 58 repetitions and observer B recorded 14 different and 43 repetitions on Day 162. On the 16 samples categorized by the second teacher, the product-moment correlation coefficients between the scores of the two raters were 0.99 for nouns and verbs, and *mand* sentences and 0.95 for *non-mand* sentences.

Experimental Conditions

The following contingencies and experimental manipulations were in effect throughout the entire free-play periods, which usually totaled close to 1.5 hours each day:

A. Baseline.	(Days 1 to 129)
B. Teacher attention contingent on verbalization.	(Days 130 to 142)
C. Teacher attention contingent on non-verbalization; differential reinforcement of other behavior (DRO).	(Days 143 to 148)
B. Teacher attention contingent on verbalization.	(Days 149 to 154)
D. Modified teacher attention contingent on verbalization.	(Days 155 to 161)
B. Teacher attention contingent on verbalization.	(Days 162 to 163)

A. *Baseline.* During the first 129 days that the child was in school, verbalizations occurred during an average of 11% of the 10-second intervals of each sample, ranging between 1% and 32% on individual samples. Teacher attention during that time ranged between 0% and 36% with an average of 11%. Data between Days 31 to 45, 65 to 78, and 119 to 129 are shown in Condition A of Figure 1.

B. *Teacher Attention Contingent upon Verbalization.* From Day 130 through 142, the teachers' at tention to the child was contingent upon her verbalizations and was maintained while she was talking. Teacher attention consisted of a variety of stimuli which included one or more of the following: praising the child, asking her questions, giving her equipment, assisting her, attending to, talking to, and providing a requested object or material. The form of the teacher attention varied according to the context of the child's verbalizations and the nature of the situation. However, whenever the child's verbalization was in the form of a request for materials, the teacher would ask questions about the materials or the child's projected use of the materials. The material itself would only be given contingent upon the child's responding to one or more such questions. For example, if the child said that she wanted to paint, the teacher would praise her for saying what she wanted, and then ask her what she was going to paint or what other things she needed in order to paint, e.g., brush, paper. Again they praised her for any verbal responses she made and perhaps asked her another question. This was continued as long as the teacher could ask reasonable or logical questions concerning the situation; it usually ranged between one and three questions per request for materials, though occasionally no questions were asked. Thus, while teacher attention in the form of social interaction was given contingent upon each instance of verbalization, whenever the verbalization was a re-

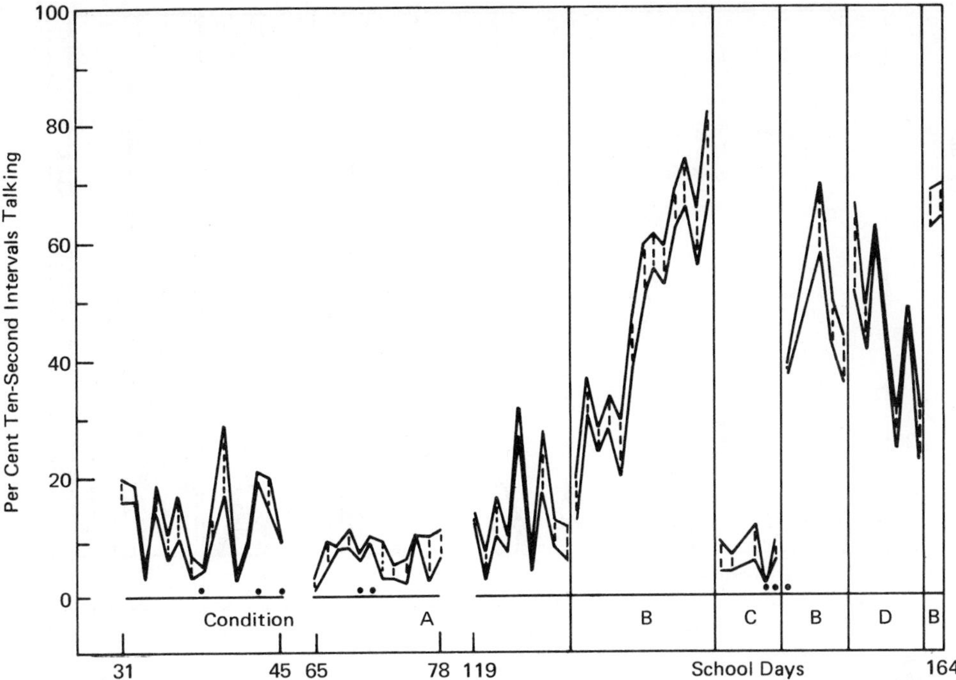

Figure 1 *The per cent of 10-second intervals during which talking occurred. The experimental conditions were: A, Baseline. B, Teacher attention contingent upon any verbalization. (Social interaction immediately contingent upon all verbalizations; access to materials contingent upon responding to variable number of questions whenever verbalizations were requests for materials.) C, Teacher attention contingent upon silence (DRO). D, Teacher attention contingent upon any verbalization. (Social interaction immediately contingent upon all verbalizations; materials immediately contingent upon requests.) The two curves represent the highest and lowest scores of the three observers. The dots along the abscissa mark those days when observations were made by only two observers.*

quest for materials, teachers' interactions were in the form of asking questions about the materials and the materials were dispensed on a small variable ratio for answering questions. When possible, teachers required the child to ask for materials by preventing her free access to them.

During the 13 days of these conditions, the frequency of the child's verbalization increased from 11% to 75% of the 10-second intervals (Condition B, Figure 1). The number of nouns and verbs used increased from an average of 15 (range 3 to 25) to an average of 46 (range 14 to 73) per 15-minute content sample. The number of different nouns and verbs used per sample increased from an average of seven to an average of 16 while the frequency of repetitions increased nearly twice as much from an average of seven to an average of 30 (Condition B, Figure 2).

The number of verbalizations directed to a child remained approximately constant (changing from an average of 7.6 to 7.9) while the number of verbalizations directed to a teacher increased from an average of 4.2 to 26.8 during this period (Condition B, Figure 3). The number of *non-mand* sentences remained approximately constant (changing from an average of 2.3 to 2.6) while the number of *mand* sentences increased from an average of 4.2 to 19.5 during this period (Condition B, Figure 4).

In summary, the marked increases in frequency of verbalizations were almost entirely a function of an increase in the frequency of requests (*mands*) to the teacher (usually for materials). These increased requests involved the use of a slightly greater vocabulary than before but a proportionately greater increase in repetitions of the same words.

C. Teacher Attention Contingent on Non-verbalization (DRO). Since the frequency of teacher attention was now higher, it became necessary to investigate whether the increased instance of teacher attention, *per se*, or the contingency of presenting teacher attention immediately after the child verbalized was maintaining the verbal rate. It might be said that the child verbalized at a higher frequency simply because the

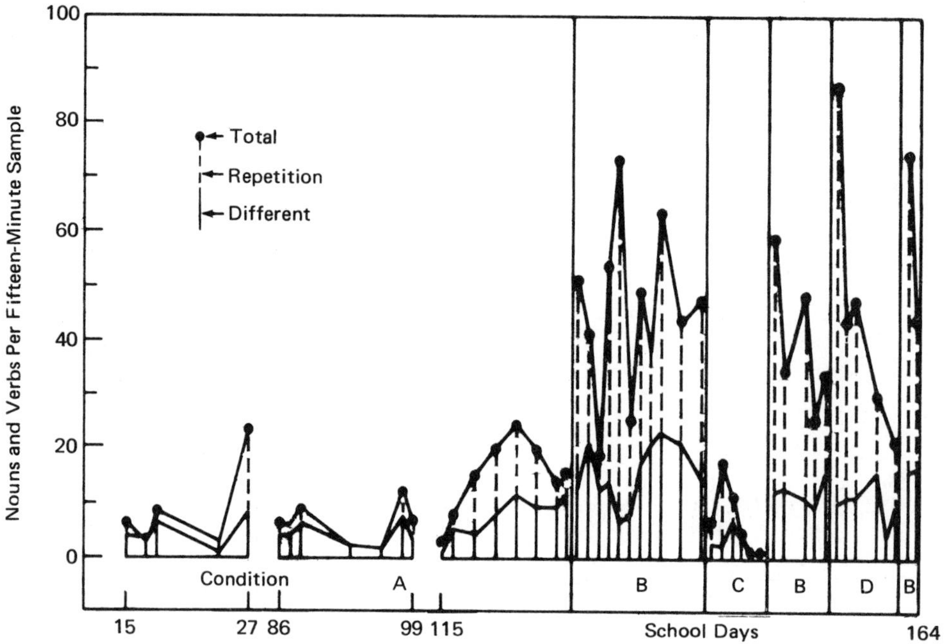

Figure 2 *Frequency of nouns and verbs during periodic recording of the child's speech. The conditions correspond to the conditions described in Figure 1.*

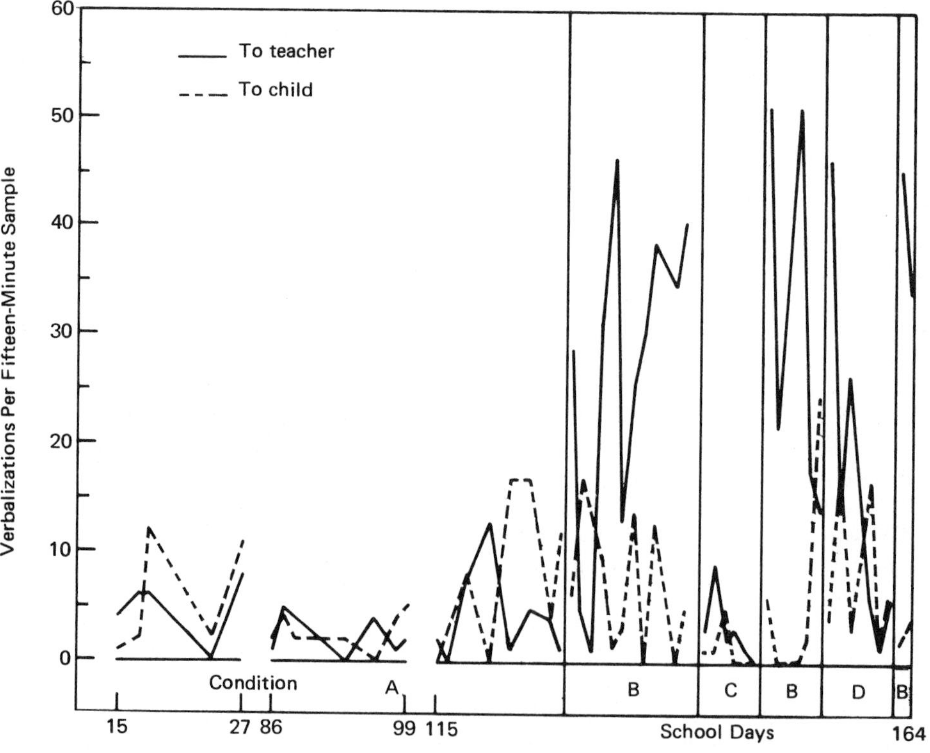

Figure 3 *Frequency of statements to teachers and to other children during recording of the child's speech. The conditions correspond to the conditions described in Figure 1.*

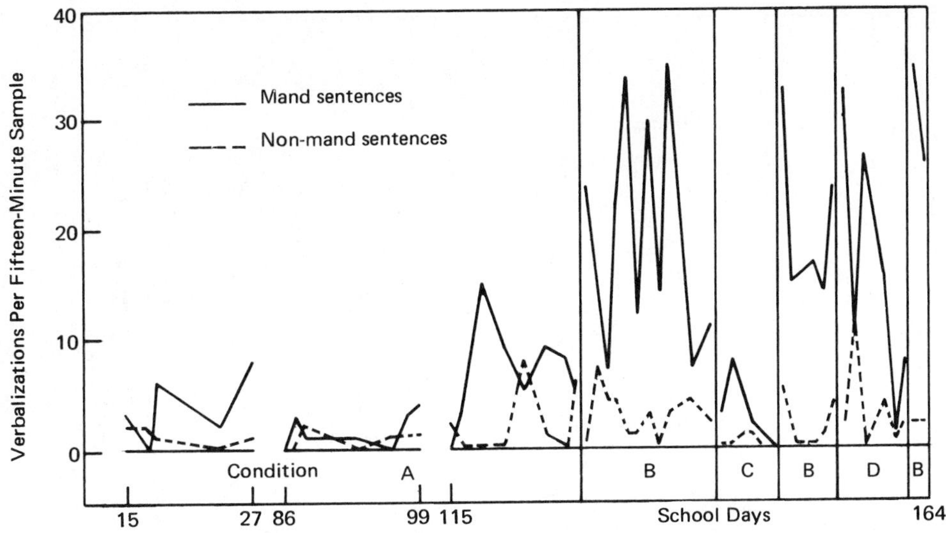

Figure 4 *Frequency of* mand *and* non-mand *sentences during periodic recordings of the child's speech. The conditions correspond to the conditions described in Figure 1.*

teachers were attending and talking to her more, indicating that the higher incidence of teacher attention rather than its contingency of following the child's verbalizations was maintaining this frequency. Therefore, the teacher attention was maintained at as high a rate but was now made contingent upon nonverbalization by the child. Typically the teachers would attend to the child, praising her and providing her with materials while she was silently engaged in activities. For example, if the children near the child were asking for water and she picked up a cup, the teacher would reinforce the child's behavior of not asking by pouring water into her cup and keeping it filled as long as she was silent, and praising her for pouring from her cup, working hard, and keeping busy. The teachers removed their attention and the supplying source of materials for 15 to 30 seconds immediately following a verbalization by the child. (This procedure is often described as differential reinforcement of other behaviors) [DRO], since teacher attention is presented contingent upon any behavior except the behavior being measured, in this case talking.)

During six days of DRO, the rate of verbalization dropped from an average of 46% to 6% while the rate of teacher attention was maintained at an average of 67% (Condition C, Figures 1 and 5). At this point, teacher attention was again given contingent upon verbalization by the child. Her frequency of verbalization immediately increased to an average of 51% during the four days of this condition, while the rate of teacher attention averaged 47% (Condition D, Figures 1 and 5).

During DRO, several aspects of the child's verbal content dropped well below the baseline level. The number of total nouns and verbs used dropped to an average of four per day. The amount of talking decreased to the point that little verbalization was made to either teachers or children, though the amount of talking to teachers was higher at an average of three per day, but only one per day to children.

D. Modified Teacher Attention Contingent on Verbalizations. The DRO condition demonstrated the function of the gross category of teacher attention in maintaining the child's increased rate of verbalization. However, the analysis of the content of the verbalizations, which revealed that the increase was primarily in repeated requests to the teachers for materials, indicated that the praise and social interaction components of the teachers' attention might not be functional. Therefore, a further manipulation was made to analyze experimentally the functions of the two components of teacher attention: the teachers' praise and social interaction, and the teachers' questioning the child and requiring additional verbalizations before providing a requested material.

After recovery from DRO, for six days social interaction with the teacher remained exclusively contingent upon verbalization, but questioning the child and requiring further verbalization before providing any requested material to the child was discontinued. Now she could immediately acquire materials by asking for them, rather than being required to respond verbally to questions in order to get them. Under these conditions, the child's frequency of verbalization gradually declined from 61% to 28% of the 10-second intervals (Condition D, Figure 1).

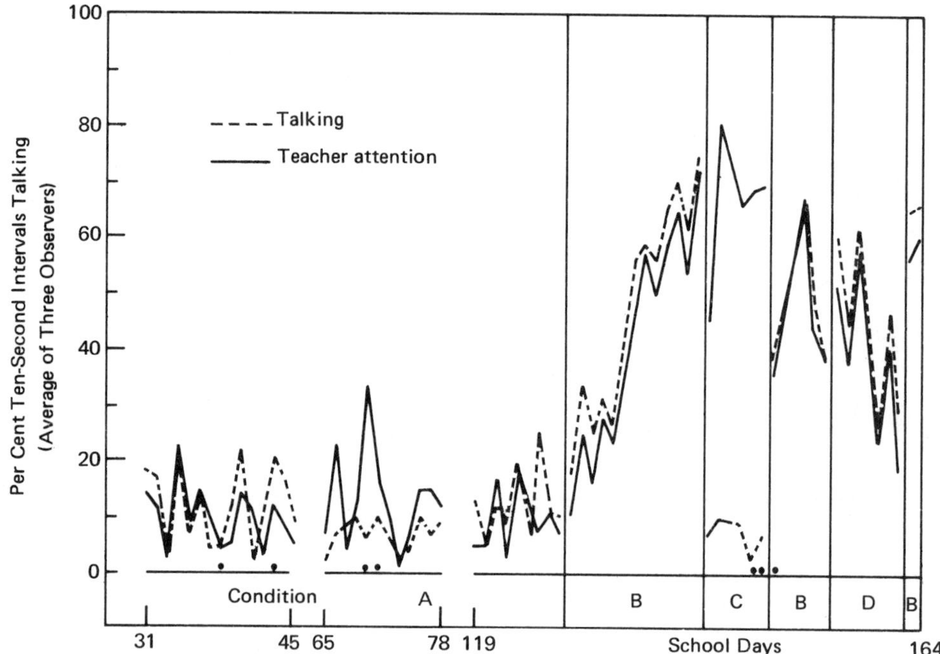

Figure 5 *The relationship between teacher attention and talking by the child. The conditions correspond to the conditions described in Figure 1.*

Since teacher attention was given only after verbalization by the child, it too dropped along with the frequency of verbalization (Condition D, Figure 5). *Non-mand* sentences, different nouns and verbs used, and verbalizations to children remained relatively stable, while *mand* sentences, repetitions of nouns and verbs, and verbalizations to teachers decreased systematically (Condition D. Figures 2, 3, and 4).

When the teachers again asked questions and required several responses from the child before providing her with requested materials during the following two days (the final two days of school), the rate of verbalization immediately increased from 29% on the last day of Condition D to an average of 67% (Figures 1 and 5). The number of repetitions of nouns and verbs, verbalizations to teachers, and *mands* all increased to a level comparable to the previous periods in which these conditions were present (Figures 2, 3, and 4).

Discussion

In the present study, a child's low frequency of verbal behavior was increased, utilizing the techniques of consequent teacher attention. This increase was reversed and recovered by altering the contingent relationship between teacher attention and verbalization. Thus, this study consisted in part of a replication of prior preschool studies showing that contingent teacher attention can effectively alter yet another behavior of the preschool child.

Teacher attention includes a variety of behaviors such as looking at, smiling at, talking to, touching, providing materials for, and assisting the children, only some of which may be functional in altering or maintaining the behavior of a child. In studies utilizing teacher attention as a consequence for children's behavior, the form of the teacher attention varies from instance to instance according to the activity in which the child is engaged and the content of the child's verbalizations. Therefore, to a large extent, the child's behavior determines the form of the teacher's attention. In the present study, the criterion behavior, verbalization, appeared primarily in the form of a request for materials. The teacher's attention, therefore, almost always included providing the child with materials.

Both the DRO procedures and the fact that the majority of the child's verbalizations were directed toward teachers indicated that the teachers were in fact controlling the relevant reinforcers. However, the fact that the majority of the child's verbalizations were *mands* (primarily, requests for materials) indicated that the strictly social interaction components of teacher attention were perhaps not the functional components. The DRO contingency provided no information on this question since social interactions, questions, and access to materials were simultaneously altered. The subsequent manipulation, in which access to materials no longer entailed answering a series of the teacher's questions, resulted in a steady decline in the child's frequency of verbalization. This decline occurred in spite of the fact that social interaction was still contingent upon each instance of the child's verbalization and materials were immediately contingent upon those verbalizations which were requests for materials. This demonstrated that the social interaction per se was not the reinforcing component of teacher attention that maintained the high rate of verbalization. The important component of teacher attention was questioning the child and requiring several verbal responses before allowing access to materials. Time did not permit a further experimental analysis to separate the two obvious aspects of this functional component of teacher attention: the questioning per se and the ratio scheduling of access to materials. However, the facts that the questioning occurred only when the child requested materials and the child usually responded to the questions by simply repeating her original request rather than "answering" the question, and that most of her increased verbalizations were *mands* indicate that the ratio scheduling of access to materials through the teacher was critical to establishing and maintaining a higher rate of verbal behavior. This child could get few materials or equipment without first obtaining the teachers' attention. Only when the teacher's attention "mediated" access to materials did it function as a reinforcer for this child's verbalization. A similar procedure (of allowing access to materials contingent upon certain forms of speech) but without the prompts or questions proved to be functional in altering the speech of the other children in the preschool (Hart and Risley, 1968).

In work with culturally deprived preschool children, the teachers have informally observed that these children's verbalizations contain relatively few descriptive or informative statements, but a large proportion of commands and requests. Bereiter and Engelmann (1966) have reported similar observations. The high frequency of requests may indicate that material reinforcers are disproportionately strong, or that social interaction with adults is a disproportionately weak reinforcer, and that adults may be important primarily as dispensers of material reinforcers. Such appeared to be the case for this child. However, since the previous studies utilizing adult attention as a reinforcer (summarized in Harris, Johnston, Kelley, and Wolf, 1964) did not analyze the components of attention which were functional in producing changes in the behavior of middle-class preschool children, material reinforcers may have, in fact, been the functional aspect of the teacher attention for those children as well.

In an analysis of the effect of a behavioral manipulation, usually the rate of only one aspect of the behavior is considered. A concurrent analysis of other aspects of the studied behavior allows a more detailed specification of the effect of the functional variables. In this study, as the frequency of the child's talking increased, the data on the content of verbalization revealed that the increase involved primarily an increase in verbalizations to teachers in the form of repetitions of the same nouns and verbs in *mand* sentences.

With additional time, access to materials might have been applied to alter the content of this child's speech. However, before considering differential reinforcement of the content of verbalization, it seems essential to obtain a high stable frequency of verbalization. The data indicated that the teachers could control the rate of verbal behavior. Once this high frequency was obtained, it would have been possible to provide access to materials differentially contingent upon *non-mands*, child directed speech, or variety of nouns and verbs. The nature of such differential reinforcement procedures, their success, or even their necessity, are questions for further investigation.

References

ALLEN, K. EILEEN; HART, BETTY M., BUELL, JOAN S., HARRIS, FLORENCE R., and WOLF, M. M. Effects of social reinforcement on isolate behavior of a nursery school child. *Child Development,* 1964, *35,* 511–518.

BEREITER, C. and ENGELMANN, S. *Teaching disadvantaged children in the preschool.* Englewood Cliffs: Prentice-Hall, 1966.

HALL, R. V., LUND, DIANE, and JACKSON, DELORES. Effects of teacher attention on study behavior. *Journal of Applied Behavior Analysis,* 1968, *1,* 1–12.

HARRIS, FLORENCE R., JOHNSTON, MARGARET K., KELLEY, C. SUSAN, and WOLF, M. M. Effects of positive social reinforcement on regressed crawling of a nursery school child. *Journal of Educational Psychology,* 1964, *55,* 35–41.

HARRIS, FLORENCE R., WOLF, M. M., and BAER, D. M. Effects of adult social reinforcement on child behavior. *Young Children,* 1964, *20,* 8–17.

HART, BETTY M., ALLEN, K. EILEEN; BUELL, JOAN S., HARRIS, FLORENCE R., and WOLF, M. M. Effects of social reinforcement on operant crying. *Journal of Experimental Child Psychology,* 1964, *1,* 145–153.

HART, BETTY M. and RISLEY, T. R. Establishing use of descriptive adjectives in the spontaneous speech of disadvantaged preschool children. *Journal of Applied Behavior Analysis,* 1968, *1,* 154–165.

JOHNSTON, MARGARET K., KELLEY, C. SUSAN; HARRIS, FLORENCE R., and WOLF, M. M. An application of reinforcement principles to development of motor skills of a young child. *Child Development,* 1966, *37,* 379–387.

SKINNER, B. F. *Verbal behavior.* New York: Appleton-Century-Crofts, 1957.

In *Kanfer's* experiment we see a shift away from the individual toward a social group whose interaction is influenced by the intervention of a third party, whereas in the preceding experiments the speech of only a single speaker was modified. The experimental procedure involved two subjects operating as a team to describe pictures from the Thematic Apperception Test. These are ambiguous scenes which can prompt a wide range of discussion and description. Although the money that was given to the subjects as a result of their talking about the cards accrued to them as a team, the actual delivery of money followed the behavior of either one or the other. The results showed that the reaction of the listener influenced the pattern of speech within the dyad more than the amount of money the team earned.

Furthermore, despite the money which was used to increase the frequency of the subject's speech, the effective reinforcers were actually the social and other implicit effects of the experimenter's reactions. The difference between the reinforcers in this experiment and the preceeding one lies in the arbitrary relationship between money and the subject's speech, in Kanfer's experiment, and the natural relationship observed by Reynolds and Risley between the child's request for play materials and its consequences—the materials received.

47 | *Control of Communication in Dyads by Reinforcement*[1]

FREDERICK H. KANFER

Traditional psychotherapy is a dyadic interaction which has a long-range purpose and special rules for its participants. Studies of therapeutic interviews have mainly confined themselves to naturalistic observations, or to partial standardization by control of either a temporal or content dimension in the therapist's speech. Notable among the former are studies by Lennard and Bernstein (1960) who reported that patient-therapist communications tend to become more similar over interviews in content and duration of utterances; and Goldman-Eisler (1952) who found that the average speech duration among psychiatrists tended to vary inversely with the talkativeness of their patients. Matarazzo, Weitman, Saslow, and Wiens (1963) found evidence that length of interviewer utterances affects the duration of those by the interviewee in a systematic and predictable way when duration of the interviewer's comments is controlled. Content of the interviewer's comments was shown to influence the temporal pattern of interviewee behavior (Kanfer, Phillips, Matarazzo, and Saslow, 1960).

In interviews, communication between the partners can occur by verbal and non-verbal means. Since it has been repeatedly demonstrated that minimal cues emitted by an audience may affect the speaker's behavior (Kanfer and McBrearty, 1962; Salzinger and Pisoni, 1960), *E*'s emphasis on *verbal* communication does not prevent mutual influences by non-verbal cues. The degree of correlation between verbal and non-verbal cues could influence the results of a study even though *E* focuses solely on speech behavior. The second problem encountered in this research area lies in the fact that each participant has innumerable subtle ways of changing his role from speaker to listener, by content, intonation or accompanying gestures of his comments. For example, the speaker may invite a response from his partner by making some outrageously inaccurate statement, by pausing tentatively, or by relaxing his posture. In the face-to-face interview situation it is difficult to be sure that the interviewer responds only to cessation of talk and that a brief pause signifies that the speaker has relinquished his role to his partner.

In several studies (Kanfer, Bass and Guyett, 1963; Elwood, 1963) we have attempted to explore dyadic interactions in a paradigm which partially overcomes these difficulties. Kinesic and other non-verbal cues were eliminated by separating the two partners into adjacent booths. Further, by using a one-way inter-

[1] This study was supported in part by Research Grant MH 06922–02 from the National Institute of Mental Health, United States Public Health Service.

From *Psychological Reports*, 1964, *15*, 131–138. Reprinted by permission.

com one member could be given full control over the communication system. This paradigm permits the study of S's distribution of available time to his role as a listener or a speaker, and the frequency with which he shifts such roles as a function of various conditions.

The particular variables which affect the distribution of time S spends in the speaker or listener role may have their locus in extra-dyadic factors (e.g., the purpose of the interaction), in the behavior of one of the dyadic members, or in the relationship between the two participants. Kanfer, Bass, and Guyett (1963) found that agreement or disagreement by a partner who was *E*'s confederate did not affect distribution of talking time between the two members, while S's personality did. It was pointed out that the effects of reinforcement on a speaker by his dyadic team member may be difficult to evaluate because it allows two contradictory predictions. It is possible that agreement by a partner can be considered as reinforcement, enhancing the probability of continued *talking* by the speaker. On the other hand, such agreement might reinforce the speaker's tendency to *listen*. Any reinforcement for S's performance delivered by some agent other than the group partner is likely to have more uniform effects on S. But even under these conditions the partner's success may further modify S's behavior. In a dyad in which the team is rewarded as a unit it would be expected that S attempt to maximize the probability of pay-off, participating more when his actions are reinforced and participating less when his partner's behavior is instrumental in procuring reinforcement.

The purpose of this experiment was to examine the effects of varying the ratio of reinforcements for speaking, in dyadic members, on S's tendency to act as a speaker or listener. In the present study S was reinforced by *E* either for speaking or for listening. Ss should increase their participation when their rate of reinforcement exceeds that of their partners, and decrease their talk (or increase their listening) when their partners are reinforced for talking at a higher rate than they.

Method

Subjects. Ss were 56 female student nurses who were paid volunteers. Eight Ss were discarded, 5 because they failed to participate minimally as speakers during the pre-acquisition blocks, and 3 Ss because of equipment malfunction.

Apparatus. Each S was seated at a table. Before her was a signal board, a Masco intercom unit, a three-way control switch for the intercom, and a tray containing a series of TAT cards arranged face down in predetermined order. On the signal board were three lights mounted at S's eye level. A white light was labeled "Point," a red light was labeled "Listen," and a green light was labeled "Talk." S's control switch was wired to the intercom unit. In the resting position the intercom was non-operational. S could depress the switch to the side marked "Talk" which opened the intercom so that she could communicate with her partner. When the switch was pressed to the side marked "Listen," the intercom was open so that the partner could talk. This switching arrangement permitted one-way communication only when S depressed the switch in either direction. The intercom and control switch were wired to the signal board so that activation of the key lit up either the talk or listen light in front of S. A similar unit was located in the adjacent room which housed *E* and S's partner, who was *E*'s confederate (*C*). The light marked "Point" was controlled by *E* for administration of the reinforcing stimulus.

In the control room the same equipment was duplicated for *C* except that *C* had no control over the intercom system and could speak only when S placed the control switch in a "Listen" position. The intercom system was also wired to a Gerbrand recorder. Two channels recorded the time during which S had the control switch in the talk or listen positions. An additional channel recorded the administration of a point to the speaker. Reinforcements were delivered by hand by *E*. From S's viewpoint a reinforcement was given to her when she was speaking. When the point light flashed during *C*'s talk, this indicated a reinforcement administered to *C*. The beginning and end of a trial was indicated by a buzzer which was controlled by chronoscopes.

The stimulus material consisted of 15 TAT cards. The cards were divided into five blocks of three cards each. One block was designated as the operant period, three blocks made up the acquisition period, and one block made up the extinction period. The card order was fixed within blocks but the order of presentation of blocks of cards was rotated and balanced for the experimental groups. After running several pilot Ss, the TAT cards were so arranged in each block that the first and last card containing two human figures and the middle card contained the picture of one person.

Procedure. Appointments were individually arranged by telephone for each S. When S arrived she was given the impression that another girl who was to be her partner had already been seated in an adjacent room. S could not see *C*, nor the equipment in the control room. S was told that the purpose of the study was to find out how well two people, working together as a team, can describe the actions and motives of others from the information they get from a picture. E continued: "You are going to be the leader of this team. Your partner is already seated on the other side of the partition. She is a student from ________ College, interested in nursing as a career. You and your partner will be conversing through the intercom in front of you. As a team leader you will be able to regulate the discussion by operating this switch. Your partner has a speaker and a light panel like yours but she does not have a control switch. She can talk and listen over the intercom only as you direct her." E demonstrated the equipment and continued: "You can interrupt your partner at any time during the discussion by simply flipping the switch back to *talk*. Why don't you try it now? Ask your partner if she can hear you through her speaker." E then allowed S and C to interact briefly. E instructed both partners to turn over the first TAT card which was a demonstration card. E then pointed to a white card on the signal panel which listed the following points: (1) What is going on in the picture, (2) What might have led up to it, (3) What the people in the picture are thinking and feeling, and (4) How the story might end. E told S: "Do not feel restricted by the order of suggestions, the card is there only to make it easier for you to talk. Basically, your task is to exchange ideas about the people you see depicted so that *as a team* you come up with the best description of the actions and motives of the people you see on each card." E indicated that S would be able to earn points for the team for insightful statements and that S would be paid according to the *team's score*. S was reminded: "(1) You must talk *only* about the pictures, (2) you must not ask each other questions while you are exchanging ideas, and (3) you must not talk to each other between discussion periods." S was told that the trials would be marked by a buzzer signal. Each TAT card was presented for 3 minutes, constituting a trial.

To be sure that S understood the instructions a brief practice trial was given. S was then told "Now remember you are in charge. During the discussion one of your two lights must be on at all times except for the brief second it takes for you to switch." After presentation of three cards which constituted the operant block, S was told "from now on the white light will flash whenever you make a statement which corresponds to those judged by psychologists to be insightful and revealing of your understanding of people's actions and motives. Every time your white light flashes it means your team has earned a point. Remember that these points are earned *as a team*. Individual scores do *not* count. Each of you will receive a nickel for every three points earned by your team. There is no limit to the number of points you can earn. I will keep score on a counter. You will each be paid at least one dollar no matter what your team score is, but above that there is no limit to how much money your team can make." After presentation of nine cards an extinction period followed. S was told "your team is doing very well. Continue the same way. From now on the white light will no longer flash when your team earns a point for an insightful statement. However, I will continue to keep score and you will continue to be paid at the same rate as before." After three extinction cards the experiment was terminated and S was asked to fill out a post-experimental questionnaire. This questionnaire contained 6 multiple-choice questions, designed to elicit attitudes toward her partner and toward S's participation in the group.

Two female *E*s were used as confederates.[2] They had previous experience with this task with a number of pilot Ss. They were instructed to talk only about the pictures, to follow the main theme that S had decided to talk about, to maintain "the same level of emotionality for all Ss and for all stories," and to continue talking all the time that S's listen light was on.

Experimental Design. Ss were randomly assigned to three groups with 16 Ss in each. The groups differed only in the rate at which the two members were reinforced. In Group SH (Subject-high), S was reinforced at an average rate of 1 point for each 15 seconds of talking. *C*s were reinforced for talking at the rate of 1 point for 45 seconds. In Group CH (Confederate-high) Ss were reinforced at an average rate of 1 point for 45 seconds of talking while *C*s were reinforced at the rate of 1 point for 15 seconds of talking. In Group HH (high-high) both *Ss* and *C*s were reinforced at an average rate of 1 point per 15 seconds for their respective talking. To avoid temporal conditioning both high and low reinforcement rates were varied about the values indicated.

The treatment groups were split, and half of each group was run by each of the two confederate *C*s. In addition, in each treatment group five card orders of TAT card presentations were used.

The event recorder yielded the following measurements: (1) frequency and duration of S's depression of her *talk* switch, (2) frequency and duration of S's depression of her *listen* switch, and (3) number of reinforcements administered to S and *C*, respectively. Durations were measured by two *E*s who were consistent and reliable within 1 mm. of tape measurement.

Results

The difference in the delivery rate of reinforcement represented the main independent variable in this study. Since administration of reinforcements

[2] The author wishes to acknowledge the assistance of M. Cosgrove and D. Moore who served as confederates in this study, and B. M. Wolland who served as *E*.

was contingent upon S's maintenance of a sufficiently long utterance to permit reinforcement, *E* could not control the exact number of reinforcements delivered to S and *C*. Therefore an analysis of the actual number of reinforcements delivered to S and *C* was computed for Ss over the three acquisition blocks. In Group SH the mean number of delivered reinforcements was 57.6 for S and 20.3 for *C*. In Group HH it was 53.4 for S and 73.7 for *C*, and in Group *CH* it was 15.6 for S and 71.3 for *C*. In congruence with the prescribed schedule Ss received significantly more reinforcements in SH than CH ($t = 14.0$), and significantly fewer reinforcements in CH than in HH ($t = 11.1$). In SH and HH ($t = 0.93$), the number of reinforcements was not significantly different. Comparisons of reinforcements for *Cs* showed similar results with HH > SH ($t = 2.82$), CH > SH ($t = 2.64$), and HH not significantly different from CH ($t < 1.0$). The respective ratios of S/*C* reinforcements were: 2.90 in S, 0.71 in HH, and 0.22 in CH. These results indicate that the actual number of reinforcements delivered followed the predetermined treatment plan for the groups.

To determine whether Ss initially behaved similarly in all groups and with the two *E*s, an analysis of variance was run on the amount of time spent talking by Ss on the initial three TAT cards in the operant phase. The analysis indicated that neither groups, nor *E*s, nor card order, nor their respective interactions differed significantly. On the basis of this finding, card order and *E*s were pooled for all subsequent analyses. During the operant phase, Ss spent approximately 61% of their allotted time listening to *C*. Of the available time, 37.8% was spent in talking. The amount of silence, i.e., the time during which S activated neither her talk nor her listen switch was negligible.

The mean frequency of requests for *C* comments showed little variation over blocks and groups. The number of mean requests per block ranged from 7.4 to 8.6. Thus, Ss invited their partners to talk during the 3 minutes for each card between 2.4 and 2.9 times on the average. Neither reinforcement schedules nor trials influenced this interactional pattern.

The change in the amount of time spent by S as a speaker is presented in Figure 1 as a function of the different reinforcement rates in the three groups. The curves indicate that Ss in all groups tended to increase their contributions as speakers as acquisition progressed. The groups started at different levels during the operant phase and the amount of change in talking-time may be correlated with the initial amount of time which S spent speaking. Therefore an analysis of variance was carried out on the difference between S's score on a trial block and her score on the preceding block for all acquisition blocks, e.g., the first score consisted of S's score on the first acquisition block minus her score on the preceding (operant) block, etc. This repeated measures analysis yielded an *F* of 4.48 (2 and 45 *df*) for groups ($p < .05$). This finding indicates that the change in duration of S's talking time was significantly affected by reinforcement. Ss in Group SH increased most and Ss in Group CH showed the least increase. Blocks effect was also significant ($F = 3.11$, $df = 2/90$, $p < .05$). This significant blocks effect suggests that increments differed over the acquisition blocks. As can be seen from Figure 1, the greatest increment was shown on the first acquisition block. An *F* of 1.91 for the Groups × Blocks interaction indicates no significant change in different scores over blocks as a function of group treatments. As shown in Figure 1, all groups increased during the first acquisition block and continued to increase on subsequent blocks except for Group HH in the second acquisition block.

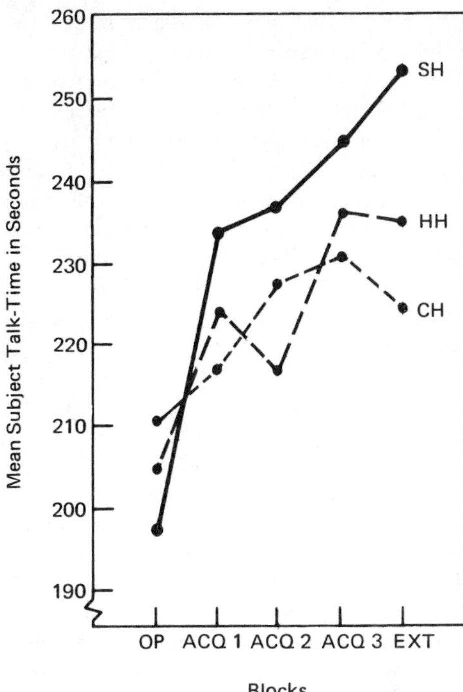

Figure 1 *Comparison of mean time spent talking by the subject, for all groups, in operant, acquisition, and extinction blocks.*

In order to assess the over-all effectiveness of the acquisition procedure, an analysis of variance was also carried out on the difference between the last (third) acquisition block and the operant block for each S. This analysis on difference scores yielded a significant *F* (3.45, $df = 2/45$, $p < .05$), indicating that the groups differed significantly in the over-all change from the operant block to the end of acquisition. Group SH showed the greatest change, HH was second, and Group CH showed the least change.

It is noteworthy that the difference scores in all groups showed an increase, suggesting that reinforcement of the partner in Group CH did not result in the expected decrease of time spent by S as a speaker.

An analysis of covariance on extinction, covarying for the last acquisition block, yielded no significant differences between the groups. Further, difference *ts* between the last acquisition block and extinction were not significant. Therefore, any differences in extinction as seen in Figure 1, can be attributed primarily to the group differences on the final acquisition block.

On the post-experimental questionnaire, the responses to the six questions were combined into three groups of two questions each. On the first and second question, each S's score was summed. A Mann-Whitney *U* test was then carried out on the data for the three groups. The first two questions inquiring about S's satisfaction with the team revealed no significant difference among the three groups. The third and fourth question inquired about S's perception of his relative contribution to the team. A significant Mann-Whitney *U* test suggests that Ss in Group SH felt that they had contributed most and showed most psychological insight, while Ss in Group CH felt that they had made a lesser contribution. Finally, the groups did not differ with regard to their answers to the question "To what extent did you feel that you changed in insight as you had more practice on the pictures?" and the related question, "Did you feel that you gained in psychological insight through this experiment?"

Discussion

The results support the hypothesis that reinforcements delivered by an extra-dyadic source can affect the amount of talk by one member in a dyad. The data show some effects of reinforcement even though Ss tended to increase their participation in all groups. Compared to an earlier study, differential reward by *E* had a greater effect than agreement or disagreement by a partner in a similar task (Kanfer, Bass, and Guyett, 1963). The present effect still falls short of the results one might have expected if other variables had not also exerted strong effects on S's behavior. Ss in Group CH obviously did not follow a strategy for maximizing their rewards. Minimal talking by S could have increased considerably the monetary pay-off for Ss in CH. In answers to post-experimental questions many Ss said they thought that they had "caught on" by listening to their partner. Therefore, they believed, they talked about the pictures themselves rather than allot time to *C*. Since the difference between groups can be seen to lie in the increase of S's talking in Group SH as compared with the other two groups (Figure 1), it is possible that the results are mainly due to *C*'s lower reinforcement rate rather than S's higher rate in Group SH. Thus, if Ss were competitive despite their instructions and pay-off contingencies, reinforcement to the *partner* may have had a direct effect on their own behavior.

Competitive attitude apparently persisted despite our efforts to reduce them by asking Ss to work as a team and by emphasizing the shared pay-off. Azrin and Lindsley (1956) conditioned and extinguished cooperative responses in children. Ss were given one piece of candy for a joint cooperative response, and "almost immediately eight teams (out of ten) divided the candy in some manner" (Azrin and Lindsley, 1956, p. 101). The adults in our study were less effective in achieving maximum cooperation, even though *both* were rewarded. Possibly, the reward was less immediate and the competitive set was stronger in the present study. The challenge to S to test her psychological insight may have been sufficient to conflict with the incentive value of the money reward. Further, it is likely that Ss saw themselves as participants in a test situation in which communication was ultimately directed toward a prestigeful *E*. In Group SH, there is another interesting deviation from the maximum pay-off strategy. Ss failed to speak for most of the time, as they should if monetary reinforcement were the main determinant of their participation. Histories of social reinforcement for politeness in sharing conversation with a partner and S's personal involvement may be parameters which limited the effectiveness of the reinforcing operations during this laboratory study.

The relative invariance of S's invitation for *C* to talk is rather surprising. These stable values in all groups and over trial blocks suggest that the changes which took place consisted primarily of lengthening or shortening the average duration of S's own utterances and that of *C*'s, and not in a variation of the frequency of utterances with a fixed pattern of duration. The data suggest that the reinforcing stimuli primarily the *duration* of S's output rather than the tempo of his social interactional pattern. Since S's roles as speaker and listener are mutually exclusive, we cannot differentiate between these two explanations.

On the post-experimental question none of the Ss indicated awareness of the precise response-reinforcement contingency. They accepted the correlated hypothesis as stated in the instructions, and reported trying to "express insight" to gain points. Instructions giving the actual purpose of the experiment might enhance the effects of reinforcement, although it would be interesting to see whether S would deviate totally from the expected social interaction pattern, even under these conditions.

While these findings shed no immediate light on

psychotherapeutic processes, the study suggests the problems encountered in efforts to modify behavior in any adult dyad. The monetary loss to a patient and failure to resolve his problem may be no greater incentive for changing his habitual social pattern at the beginning of psychotherapy than was the monetary loss for our Ss. The study also suggests that the effects of widely used reinforcers on adult behavior may be greatly modified once they are introduced into a social group in which many other incentives are also operative.

References

AZRIN, N. H., and LINDSLEY, O. R. The reinforcement of cooperation between children. *Journal of Abnormal and Social Psychology.* 1956, *52,* 100–102.

ELWOOD, D. L. Modification of talking in dyadic interactions. Unpublished doctoral dissertation, Purdue University, 1963.

GOLDMAN-EISLER, F. Individual differences between interviewers and their effect on interviewees' conversational behavior. *Journal of Mental Science,* 1952, *98,* 660–671.

KANFER, F. H., BASS, B. M., and GUYETT, I. Dyadic speech patterns, orientation, and social reinforcement. *Journal of Consulting Psychology,* 1963, *27,* 199–205.

KANFER, F. H., and MCBREARTY, J. F. Minimal social reinforcement and interview content. *Journal of Clinical Psychology,* 1962, *18,* 210–215.

KANFER, F. H., PHILLIPS, J. S., MATARAZZO, J. D., and SASLOW, G. Experimental modification of interviewer content in standardized interviews. *Journal of Consulting Psychology,* 1950, *24,* 528–536.

LENNARD, H. L., and BERNSTEIN, A. *The anatomy of psychotherapy: Systems of communication and expectation.* New York: Columbia University Press, 1960.

MATARAZZO, J. D., WEITMAN, M., SASLOW, G., and WEINS, A. N. Interviewer influence on durations of interviewee speech. *Journal of Verbal Learning and Verbal Behavior,* 1963, *1,* 451–458.

SALZINGER, K., and PISONI, S. Reinforcement of verbal affect responses of normal subjects during the interview. *Journal of Abnormal and Social Psychology,* 1960, *60,* 127–130.

Aiken's experiment extends the laboratory reinforcement of verbal behavior to a group situation. In this study, the experimenter signaled approval or disapproval to each member of four-person discussion group teams. This was done by using a light for each subject so that they could be signaled independently. A forty-minute baseline discussion showed that some of the subjects spoke much less than the others. A blue light was then used as a reinforcer to increase the verbal frequency of the subject who had spoken the least. For the remaining members of the group the light was designated as punishment. The result was a large increase in the speech of the subject who had spoken least during the baseline condition. Punishment of the others had the effect of reducing their speech, a result consistent with our knowledge of the effects of aversive control.

48 Changes in Interpersonal Descriptions Accompanying the Operant Conditioning of Verbal Frequency in Groups[1]

EDWIN G. AIKEN

The extensive literature on operant verbal conditioning is currently being expanded by the application of these procedures to group situations (Bachrach, Candland, and Gibson, 1961: Cieutat, 1959, 1962,

[1] This investigation was supported, in part, by research grand RD 892 p from the Vocational Rehabilitation Administration, Department of Health, Education, and Welfare to the Western Behavioral Sciences Institute, La Jolla, California.

From the *Journal of Verbal Learning and Verbal Behavior,* 1965, *4,* 243–247. Reprinted by permission of Academic Press.

1964; Hastorf, 1967; Liederman and Shapiro, 1963; Levin and Shapiro, 1962; Oakes, 1962a, 1962b; Oakes, Droge, and August, 1960, 1961). Data indicate that response classes generated during group interaction can be readily brought under stimulus control. Whether the response changes brought about are apparent to the group participants, and if so whether these changes exert control over the perceptions of the group members has received little attention. It is possible that when changes in verbal behavior are largely under the control of an external *E* they appear quite different from similar changes emerging from the reinforcement contingencies within the group itself; particularly if the controlled S would ordinarily have been the least verbal participant. Hastorf (1967) has reported some studies on this question. However, pilot studies prior to the present research indicated that the duration of time Hastorf used for establishing operant talk levels for the group members was too short for reliable prediction of their subsequent verbal output. In addition, the length of the conditioning session was doubled over that used by Hastorf to establish a more reliable behavior sample from which the participants made their interpersonal judgments. Conditioning procedures used were an adaptation of those reported by Oakes et al. (1960). A balanced number of male and female groups was employed, as this factor has been reported to influence the outcome in somewhat similar settings (Cieutat, 1962, 1964). Specifically, the research here reported had the goal of manipulating verbal frequency in small groups through *E*-controlled reinforcement and punishment contingencies, and assessing modifications in intra- and interpersonal descriptions of the group members on dimensions of behavior expected to correlate with the verbal frequency changes.

Method

Subjects. The Ss were 64 San Diego State College undergraduates. They were assigned to four-person groups on the basis of available time. Members of any group were of the same sex and there were an equal number of male and female groups in the experimental and control conditions.

Procedure. The Ss were seated alphabetically at the corners of a knee-high table approximately 36 inches square. On the table in front of each S was a megaphone-shaped box with the flaring-end directed at him, and with a 7½-watt blue light at the narrow end.

The procedure for the experimental Ss was as follows: Instructions for the first discussion, together with two of four discussion topics were distributed. The instructions indicated that techniques in group problem solving were being studied, and that each S would have a trained observer assigned to watch and listen to him from the other side of a one-way vision window. It was indicated that they would have 40 minutes for the discussion and would be allowed to distribute their time over the two topics as they chose. They were told to disregard the light boxes during the first discussion. The topics for discussion concerned: (a) the use of grading in higher education, (b) college student sexual conduct, (c) restrictions on teenagers, and (d) political extremists as faculty members. Topics (a) and (b) were always paired as were (c) and (d), and the frequency of occurrence of the two pairs was counterbalanced between the first and second discussions. After the reading of the instructions, if Ss had no questions, Calrad CC-1 contact microphones were strapped around their throats and *E* left the room. The signal to begin the discussion was a tap on the one-way mirror.

Four *Es* observed the groups and monitored their discussions through an intercom. The throat microphones led to a four-channel voice-keyed relay which actuated four Hunter Model 120, Series D Klockounters, producing continuous records of the time talked by each S. The Klockounters were photographed at 10-minute intervals during the discussion. The total time talked in the first discussion by each S provided the measure of free operant verbal output.

At the end of 40 minutes, the discussion was stopped and a discussion questionnaire distributed. It required the Ss to rank one another, including themselves, on: (a) leadership, (b) quality of ideas, (c) participation, and (d) self-confidence. New discussion topics were distributed together with the instructions for the second discusion. The instructions indicated that the purpose of the second discussion was to evaluate the relative benefits of reward and punishment on the learning of group problem-solving skills. Each S was told that when the light in the box in front of him began flashing, it would either signal approval or disapproval of his behavior by the observers. The S who had registered the lowest verbal output in the first discussion was instructed to attach approval significance to his light, while the other three Ss were instructed to attach disapproval significance to theirs, and all were instructed to avoid indicating to the other group members when their light was flashing or its significance. After answering any questions, *E* left the room and signaled for the discussion to begin. Each *E* was assigned to observe one S. At each *E* position was a switch which when closed completed a circuit through a timer to his S's light, which then flashed on for 1 second and off for 1 second until the switch was turned off.

A series of pilot investigations was required to

establish the precise rules for the utilization of the reward and punishment lights. The principal problem involved just how much freely emitted speech to allow before either rewarding or punishing it. It became clear that different rules would have to govern the two contingencies. The very low verbal rate of the Ss with approval instructions made it necessary to intervene with rewards quite early in their speech emissions. On the other hand, too early a use of punishment with the more verbal Ss tended to elicit disbelief on their part that the light stimuli were in any way relevant to what they were saying. The rules finally settled on were as follows: The *E* assigned to the S who had received approval instructions (henceforth called the rewarded S) actuated his switch if 5 seconds of speech was emitted with no more than a 3-second break. The *E*s assigned to Ss who had received disapproval instructions (henceforth called punished Ss) turned their switches on if 20 seconds of speech was emitted by their S with no more than a 3-second break.

The discussion was stopped after 40 minutes, and the discussion questionnaire was administered again.

The groups of control Ss were treated in the same way, except that reinforcing stimuli were not employed in either session. Their instructions for both sessions were essentially the same as those for the experimental Ss' first discussion.

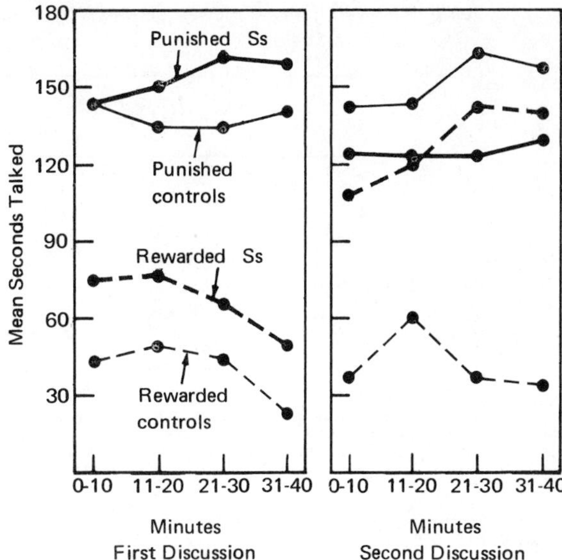

Figure 1 *Time spent talking during the two discussion periods.*

Results

For purposes of comparing verbal output, the data from the three punished Ss in each experimental group were combined, and similarly those from the rewarded Ss. Data from the Ss acting as controls for the punished Ss (henceforth called the non-punished Ss) and those from the Ss acting as controls for the rewarded Ss (henceforth called the non-rewarded Ss) were similarly combined. Figure 1 presents the mean number of seconds talked in 10-minute intervals for the two discussion periods. Little change between sessions is seen in the control Ss data, while a clear rise is shown in the output of the rewarded Ss and a slight decline in that of the punished S*s*.

Summed over the 40-minute periods, the mean differences in time talked for the second discussion minus the first discussion were: punished Ss, −120.21 seconds; non-punished Ss, 46.63 seconds; rewarded Ss, 243.38 seconds; non-rewarded Ss, 7.75 seconds. An analysis of variance was run on this measure, extracting variance attributable to the four treatments and the sex of the groups. Because of heterogeneous variance, the analysis was performed on a $X^{\frac{1}{2}} + (X + 1)^{\frac{1}{2}}$ transformation of the data. The transformation succeeded in stabilizing the variances. The F (3, 56) for treatments was 9.14, $P < .001$. Neither Sex nor the Sex x Treatment interaction was significant, though the latter F reached a level of significance between the .05 and .10 levels. Examination of the means involved in this near-significant interaction indicates it is attributable to the greater responsiveness to both punishment and reward contingencies of the female groups. A closer examination of the significant main effects for treatments was made by means of the Newman-Keuls test for ordered mean comparisons described in Winer (1962, pp. 238–239). The test indicated that the rewarded Ss differed at better than the .05 level from the other three conditions, but that no reliable mean differences existed among the latter.

Kolmogorov-Smirnov two-sample tests were run between the rewarded and non-rewarded Ss for the two discussions, based both on the summed ranks assigned them by the other members of their group (henceforth called O judgments) and their self-rankings(henceforth called S judgments). Table 1 summarizes the results of these tests. All significant differences are one-tailed probabilities in the direction of superior rankings for the rewarded Ss. The expected mean rank is 2.5 for all scales. The smaller the rank value obtained, the greater the amount of the behavior judged as present. Following the first discussion, rewarded Ss and their controls obtained mean ranks on O and S judgments greater than the expected values on all scales, and did not differ reliably from one another. After the second discussion, control Ss continued to obtain mean O and S judgment mean ranks above expectation on all scales, while the rewarded Ss obtained mean ranks below expectation on all scales. With the exception of S

Table 1 *Mean Ranks of Rewarded and Non-rewarded Subjects on the Post-discussion Questionnaire Scales*

Scale	Rank Source	First Discussion		Second Discussion	
		Non-rewarded	Rewarded	Non-rewarded	Rewarded
Leadership	Self	3.38	3.13	3.38	2.13*[a]
	Others	3.58	3.58	3.63	2.42*
Quality of ideas	Self	2.63	3.50	2.63	2.13
	Others	3.50	3.29	3.42	2.08**
Participation	Self	3.78	3.25	3.50	2.25**
	Others	3.63	3.71	3.75	2.33*
Self-confidence	Self	3.38	2.88	3.13	2.20*
	Others	3.33	3.13	3.46	2.21**

a Kolmogorov-Smirnov tests between rewarded and non-rewarded mean ranks.
* $p < .05$.
** $p < .01$.

judgments on quality of ideas, the differences between rewarded and non-rewarded Ss were all significant.

A similar analysis of punished Ss versus non-punished Ss indicated that they differed only on S judgment of leadership after the second discussion, where the punished Ss were higher in mean rank.

Discussion

It is clear that the operations employed served to bring one aspect of the verbal behavior of these four-person groups under stimulus control; i.e., Ss with the lowest operant output in the first discussion were significantly above their non-rewarded controls following the second discussion. This behavior change was apparently noted by the group members, since significant differences were obtained on seven out of eight behavioral dimensions judged, both in terms of rankings assigned by the other group members and the rewarded Ss' self-rankings. The fact that only one out of eight of these differences was significant for the punished versus non-punished Ss is consistent with the absence of a significant difference in talk-score change. This failure of punishment significantly to depress talk time is in accord with the highly variable response often observed with this sort of contingency. Some investigators have even reported increases in the response class punished (Church, 1963). Something of this sort was observed in several of the groups, when some Ss receiving punishment stimuli emitted more verbal behavior in an apparent attempt to find a response class which did not produce the punishing stimuli. In addition, some punished Ss were observed limiting the length of their statements, thereby avoiding punishment while at the same time maintaining a relatively high total verbal output. However, the nearly significant sex-by-treatment interaction indicates that had only female groups been employed a significant verbal suppression from punishment might well have been obtained.

Because the conditioning procedures involved both punishment and reward stimuli, it is unclear how much of the resulting changes can be attributed to reward-induced increases and how much to punishment-induced decreases. The non-significant difference in talk-time change between punished and non-punished Ss implies that the reward stimuli principally accounted for the significant difference between rewarded and non-rewarded Ss, but is not conclusive. Hastorf (1967) presents some evidence that reward alone is inadequate. It is safer at this point simply to indicate that the experimental operations resulted in a significant modification in the pattern of verbal output in the groups, and that this change was accompanied by significant changes in interpersonal descriptions.

References

Bachrach, A. J., Candland, D. K., and Gibson, J. T. Group reinforcement of individual response: Experiments in verbal behavior. In I. A. Berg and B. M. Bass (Eds.), *Conformity and deviation.* New York: Harper, 1961, pp. 258–285.

Church, R. M. The varied effects of punishment on behavior. *Psychological Review,* 1963, *70,* 369–402.

Cieutat, V. J. Surreptitious modification of verbal behavior. *Psychological Reports,* 1959, *5,* 648.

Cieutat, V. J. Sex differences and reinforcement in the conditioning and extinction of conversational behavior. *Psychological Reports,* 1962, *10,* 467–474.

Cieutat, V. J. Sex differences in verbal operant conditioning, *Psychological Reports,* 1964, *15,* 259–275.

Hastorf, A. H. The reinforcement of individual actions in a group situation. In L. Krasner and L. P. Ullman (Eds.), *Research in behavior modification.* New York: Holt, Rinehart and Winston, 1967.

LEIDERMAN, P. H., and SHAPIRO, D. A physiological and behavioral approach to the study of group interaction. *Psychosomatic Medicine*, 1963, *25*, 146–157.

LEVIN, G., and SHAPIRO, D. The operant conditioning of conversation. *Journal of Experimental Analysis of Behavior*, 1962, *5*, 309–316.

OAKES, W. F. Reinforcement of Bales' categories in group discussion. *Psychological Reports*, 1962, *11*, 427–435. *a*

OAKES, W. F. Effectiveness of signal light reinforcers given various meanings on participation in group discussion. *Psychological Reports*, 1962, *11*, 469–479. *b*

OAKES, W. F., DROGE, A. E., and AUGUST, B. Reinforcement effects on participation in group discussion. *Psychological Reports*, 1960, *7*, 503–514.

OAKES, W. F., DROGE, A. E., and AUGUST, B. Reinforcement effects on conclusions reached in group discussion. *Psychological Reports*, 1961, *9*, 27–34.

WINER, B. J. *Statistical principles in experimental design*. New York: McGraw-Hill, 1962.

C The Effectiveness of Verbal Reinforcement

The papers in this section show how verbal reinforcers are different for children of different sex and social class. The experiments answer questions about how the child's total repertoire, cultural and familial, determine what kinds of changes in the social environment are effective reinforcers.

Zigler and Kanzer test the hypothesis that praise is a more effective reinforcer with lower-class children than knowledge of the correctness of their answer. They hypothesize that "correctness" rather than praise would be an effective reinforcer for upper-class children. The results confirm the hypothesis and suggest that lower-class children have had fewer experiences in which intellectual accomplishment has been a link in a chain (and hence a conditioned reinforcer) which allowed the child to do other things that were, in turn, reinforcing. Praise, on the other hand is an effective reinforcer with simpler repertoires—those that occur first developmentally. Parental approval and praise are conditions under which many simple performances are reinforced at almost any developmental stage of the child's life. Even if a child had never had a sequence of successful experiences in arithmetic from addition to multiplication and finally to division, he is likely to have been in many situations where adult approval followed many elements in his current repertoire.

49 The Effectiveness of Two Classes of Verbal Reinforcers on the Performance of Middle- and Lower-Class Children[1]

EDWARD ZIGLER
PAUL KANZER

Considerable evidence has been presented to indicate that verbal reinforcers affect performance. Since such reinforcers are usually dispensed by another person, they are included within the rubric of social reinforcement. Although energy continues to be expended in demonstrating that positive social reinforcers heighten or improve performance while negative social reinforcers attenuate performance, little in the way of a careful analysis of the effectiveness of particular reinforcers within these broad reinforcement categories has been carried out. Armed with the knowledge that social reinforcement affects performance, most investigators have been content to conceptualize any particular positive social reinforcer as the functional equivalent of any other positive social reinforcer. This practice of treating social reinforcers as if they were homogeneous pellets dispensed to equally hungry rats was recently called into question by Zigler.[2]

An expanding body of literature has now shown that the effectiveness of a social reinforcer is related to: the type of social reinforcement previously received (Shallenberger and Zigler, 1961; Stevenson and Snyder, 1960); a previously experienced condition of social isolation or social satiation (Gewirtz and Baer, 1958a, 1958b); long-term social deprivation experienced (Stevenson and Fahel, 1961; Zigler, 1961; Zigler, Hodgden, and Stevenson, 1958); anxiety level of the subject (Walter and Ray, 1960); the particular sex of the *E* in relation to the sex of the S (Gewirtz and Baer, 1958a; Stevenson, 1961); and the CA or MA of the S (Gewirtz and Baer, 1958a; Stevenson, 1961; Zigler; 1958). Of special interest is the finding that verbal reinforcement is more effective in shaping the performance of middle-class than lower-class children (Douvan, 1956; Zigler, 1962).

All of these studies either have evaluated the effectiveness of a particular social reinforcer in Ss differing in short- or long-term experiences or have evaluated the effectiveness of a particular verbal reinforcer as compared to some tangible reinforcer, e.g., toys, money. While some headway has been made in scaling the reinforcement value of various tangible reinforcers (Clifford, 1959; Witryol and Fischer, 1960), as noted above little effort has been made to evaluate the effectiveness of various verbal reinforcers. Although one could randomly select some verbal reinforcers and empirically assess their relative efficacy, such a procedure would throw little light on why one such reinforcer was more effective than another. A more parsimonious approach would appear to involve the designation of some classificatory principle whereby meaningful subclasses of verbal reinforcers could be constructed.

Optimally, such a classificatory system should eventuate in specific predictions that reinforcers in one class would be more effective across all Ss than reinforcers in another class or that reinforcers in one class would be more effective with a particular type of S than reinforcers in another class. Several of the studies noted above as well as some work done on child-rearing practices (Davis, 1944; Ericson, 1947) suggest that the degree to which a verbal reinforcer emphasizes correctness may constitute such a useful classificatory dimension. A number of investigators have suggested or reported that "being correct" is more reinforcing for middle- than for lower-class children. This has been attributed to the middle-class emphasis on being right for right's sake alone. Obversely, it has been shown (Zigler et al., 1958) that while verbal reinforcers having primarily a praise connotation lengthened the performance of retarded children generally drawn from the lower socio-economic class, they did not lengthen the performance of middle-class children.

Thus the prediction may be generated that reinforcers emphasizing praise will be more effective with lower-class children, while reinforcers emphasizing correctness will be more effective with middle-class children. The problem remains of how to classify verbal reinforcers on the praise-correct di-

[1] This research was supported by Research Grant M-3945 from the National Institute of Mental Health, United States Public Health Service.

[2] In a paper presented at SRCD symposium, March, 1961. ("The effect of social reinforcement on normal and socially deprived children.")

From the *Journal of Personality*, 1962, *30*, 157–163. Reprinted by permission of Duke University Press.

mension. While every verbal reinforcer conveys both an indication of praise and of correctness, it is possible on a priori grounds to designate certain verbal reinforcers as primarily having a praise connotation with others having primarily a correctness connotation. In the present study "right" and "correct" were conceptualized as connoting correctness, while "good" and "fine" were conceptualized as connoting praise.

Method

Subjects. The Ss consisted of a group of 20 middle-class and a group of 20 lower-class children matched on the basis of CA. All the Ss were obtained from second grade classes of public schools in New Haven, Connecticut, and Harrison, New York. Warner's Index of Social Characteristics (Warner, Meeker, and Eells, 1949) was used to define socio-economic class membership.

Procedure. The experimental game used was quite similar to the one employed by Gewirtz and Baer (1958a). It was a large wooden box having two holes in the side facing the player into which a marble could be dropped and an opening in the bottom through which the marble returned.

The male *E* brought each *S* into a vacant classroom containing two chairs and a table holding the game. The *S* was informed that he was going to play a fun game called Marble-in-the-Hole. He was told that the game was played by picking the marble out of the chute and putting it into either hole. Each S played the game for 10 minutes. The first three minutes was a baseline period during which the verbal reinforcers were not dispensed. Following this period in which the preferred hole was noted, the *E* immediately began reinforcing responses made to the hole preferred least during the last minute of the baseline period. The reinforcement schedule employed and its qualifications were identical to those employed by Gewirtz and Baer (1958a). Generally, after the onset of reinforced play every correct response was reinforced until 10 consecutive correct responses had been made. During the next 10 correct responses a reinforcer was delivered after every second correct response. During the next 15 correct responses a reinforcer was delivered after every third correct response. Finally, a reinforcer was given for every fifth correct response until the game ended.

For half of the Ss in each group the reinforcers dispensed were "good" and "fine." The remaining Ss were reinforced with "correct" and "right." Each word was used an equal number of times in each reinforcement condition. Care was taken to dispense each of the reinforcers with an equal amount of enthusiasm. Employing these two conditions of reinforcement four groups were formed: middle-class, praise; middle-class, correct; lower-class, praise; lower-class, correct.

The major dependent variable was the reinforcer effectiveness score devised by Gewirtz and Baer (1958a). For each of the 10 minutes of play the percentage of responses to the hole reinforced following the baseline period was computed. The reinforcer effectiveness score employed was the median percentage during the reinforced period minus the percentage during the third minute of the baseline period.

Results and Discussion

The mean social-effectiveness score and a description of each group are presented in Table 1. A preliminary analysis revealed that the mean reinforcer effectiveness scores under the combined conditions were reliably greater than zero ($t = 4.79$; $p < .001$). As can be seen in Table 1, the onset of verbal reinforcement resulted in all groups increasing the percentage of responses to the reinforced hole. In order to investigate whether the reinforcer effectiveness score was related to the type of S or to the particular class of social reinforcers dispensed, a 2 × 2 analysis of variance was run. Neither the F associated with type of subject ($F = 2.40$; $p < .20$) nor with reinforcement condition ($F < 1$) reached the .05 level of significance. However, the interaction effect was significant ($F = 6.21$; $p < .02$). As can be seen in Table 1, this interaction effect reflects the finding that praise reinforcers are more effective for lower- than for middle-class children, while correct reinforcers

Table 1 *Composition of the Groups by Sex, Mean Chronological Age (CA), and Social Effectiveness Scores*

Groups ($N = 10$)	Sex		CA (in years)		Social Effectiveness Scores	
	Boys	Girls	Mean	Range	Mean	Range
Middle-class, praise	5	5	7.9	7.4–8.6	35.0	13–60
Middle-class, correct	5	5	7.8	7.3–8.3	54.6	4–93
Lower-class, praise	4	6	7.7	7.3–8.7	42.6	− 1–69
Lower-class, correct	4	6	7.5	7.2–8.3	22.0	− 1–75

are more effective for middle- than for lower-class children.

This finding would appear to have both practical and theoretical import. It suggests that in experimental work with children care must be taken to employ verbal reinforcers that are optimal for the particular type of child being investigated. As was found with tangible reinforcers (Brackbill and Jack, 1958), such a procedure should decrease the variance in children's performance beneath that found when some particular verbal reinforcer is arbitrarily employed for all children. The findings of this study also suggest that studies which purport to demonstrate cognitive differences between various types of children (e.g., Kounin, 1941) may actually be demonstrating the differential effectiveness of the reinforcer employed. The present findings also appear to be immediately applicable to the everyday problem of motivating middle- and lower-class children and offer support for the view that being right is more rewarding for the middle- than for the lower-class child.

Why being right is more reinforcing than being praised for middle-class seven-year-olds while the reverse is true for lower-class seven-year-olds is not immediately clear. If being praised and being correct are conceptualized as tertiary reinforcers, the possibility presents itself that among middle-class seven-year-olds being right has been more frequently associated with secondary and primary reinforcers, while in lower-class seven-year-olds being praised is more frequently associated with these reinforcers.

The concept of a developmentally changing reinforcer hierarchy may also be applied to the findings of this study. As has been suggested (Beller, 1955; Gewirtz, 1954; Heathers, 1955) the effectiveness of attention and praise as reinforcers diminishes with maturity, being replaced by the reinforcement inherent in the information that one is correct. This latter type of reinforcer appears to serve primarily as a cue for the administration of self-reinforcement. This process is central in the child's progress from dependency to independence.

This thinking applied to the present study suggests that the lower-class seven-year-old child is developmentally lower than the seven-year-old middle-class child in that he has not made a transition in which reinforcers signifying correct replace praise reinforcers in the reinforcer hierarchy. Some support for this argument may be found in recent work[3] which indicates that social class transcends economic and social considerations and reflects the global level of development attained. Related to this argument is the suggestion (Davis, 1941; 1943; Terrell, Durkin, and Wiesley, 1959) that the lower-class child is less influenced than the middle-class child by abstract, symbolic rewards. Such would be the case if the lower-class child were indeed developmentally lower than the middle-class child of the same CA. Thus, one would expect not only that correct reinforcers would be less effective than praise reinforcers for the lower-class child, but that all verbal reinforcers, due to their abstract quality, would be less reinforcing for lower- than middle-class children of the same CA. Some support for this, albeit not statistically significant, was found in the tendency ($p < .20$) in the present study for all verbal reinforcers to be more effective for middle- than for lower-class children. Other studies (Terrell et al., 1959; Zigler, 1962) have provided statistically significant evidence that abstract reinforcers are less effective with lower- than with middle-class children. The experimental investigation of these ideas would appear to be a fertile area for further research.

[3] Phillips, L. "Studies in social competence." Paper read at Eastern Psychological Association, New York, April, 1960.

Summary

Two types of verbal reinforcers, those emphasizing praise and those emphasizing correctness, were dispensed to groups of middle-and-lower-class children equated on CA. A significant interaction was found between the type of reinforcer used and the social class of the S. The praise reinforcers were more reinforcing than the correct reinforcers with lower-class children, while the correct reinforcers were more effective than the praise reinforcers with middle-class children. The practical and theoretical import of this finding was discussed.

References

Beller, E. Dependency and independence in young children. *Journal of Genetic Psychology,* 1955, *87,* 25–35.

Brackbill, Y., and Jack, D. Discrimination learning in children as a function of reinforcement value. *Child Development,* 1958, *29,* 185–190.

Clifford, E. Ordering of phenomena in a paired comparisons procedure. *Child Development,* 1959, *30,* 381–388.

Davis, A. American status systems and the socialization of the child. *American Sociological Review,* 1941, *6,* 345–354.

Davis, A. Child training and social class. In R. G. Barker, J. S. Kounin, and J. F. Wright (Eds.), *Child behavior and development.* New York: McGraw-Hill, 1943.

Davis, A. Socialization and adolescent personality. *Adolescence, Forty-third Yearbook,* Part 1. Chicago: National Society for the Study of Education, 1944.

Douvan, E. Social status and success striving. *Journal of Abnormal and Social Psychology,* 1956, *52,* 219–223.

ERICSON, M. Social status and child rearing practices. In T. M. Newcomb and E. L. Hartley (Eds.), *Readings in social psychology.* New York: Holt, 1947.

GEWIRTZ, J. Three determinants of attention seeking in young children. *Monographs of the Society for Research in Child Development,* 1954, *19,* No. 2 (Serial No. 59).

GEWIRTZ, J., and BAER, D. The effect of brief social deprivation on behaviors for a social reinforcer. *Journal of Abnormal and Social Psychology,* 1958, *56,* 49–56. (a)

GEWIRTZ, J., and BAER, D. Deprivation and satiation of social reinforcers as drive states. *Journal of Abnormal and Social Psychology,* 1958, *57,* 165–172. (b)

HEATHERS, G. Emotional dependence and independence in nursery school play. *Journal of Genetic Psychology,* 1955, *87,* 37–57.

KOUNIN, J. Experimental studies of rigidity. I. The measurement of rigidity in normal and feebleminded persons. *Character and Personality,* 1941, *9,* 251–273.

SHALLENBERGER, P., and ZIGLER, E. Rigidity, negative reaction tendencies, and cosatiation effects in normal and feebleminded children. *Journal of Abnormal and Social Psychology,* 1961, *63,* 20–26.

STEVENSON, H. Social reinforcement with children as a function of CA, sex of *E,* and sex of S. *Journal of Abnormal and Social Psychology,* 1961, *63,* 147–154.

STEVENSON, H., and FAHEL, L. The effect of social reinforcement on the performance of institutionalized and noninstitutionalized normal and feebleminded children. *Journal of Personality,* 1961, *29,* 136–147.

STEVENSON, H., and SNYDER, L. Performance as a function of the interaction of incentive conditions. *Journal of Personality,* 1960, *28,* 1–11.

TERRELL, G., JR., DURKIN, K., and WIESLEY, M. Social class and the nature of the incentive in discrimination learning. *Journal of Abnormal and Social Psychology,* 1959, *59,* 270–272.

WALTERS, R., and RAY, E. Anxiety, isolation, and reinforcer effectiveness. *Journal of Personality,* 1960, *28,* 358–367.

WARNER, W., MEEKER, M., and EELLS, K. *Social class in America.* Chicago: Science Research Associates, 1949.

WITRYOL, S., and FISCHER, W. Scaling children's incentives by the method of paired comparisons. *Psychological Reports,* 1960, *7,* 471–474.

ZIGLER, E. The effect of pre-institutional social deprivation on the performance of feebleminded children. Unpublished doctoral dissertation, University of Texas, 1958.

ZIGLER, E. Social deprivation and rigidity in the performance of feebleminded children. *Journal of Abnormal and Social Psychology,* 1961, *62,* 413–421.

ZIGLER, E. Rigidity in the feebleminded. In E. P. Trapp and P. Himelstein (Eds.), *Research readings on the exceptional child.* New York: Appleton-Century-Crofts, 1962.

ZIGLER, E. HODGDEN, L., and STEVENSON, H. The effect of support on the performance of normal and feebleminded children. *Journal of Personality,* 1958, *26,* 106–122.

The previous experiment was replicated and extended by *Rosenhan and Greenwald.* Their achievement of the same results in replication strengthens our confidence in Zigler and Kanfer's basic findings and enlarges their generality by providing variation in certain of the background conditions such as race of subjects, place, and procedure. This experiment also clears up some ambiguity in the original experiment that came from the confounding of race and economic class. The lower-class children in the Zigler and Kanzer study were also Negro, so that it was impossible to know whether the reinforcing property of praise was due to the cultural differences accruing from their race or from their economic class. Still another experiment did confirm the basic finding that older children were more influenced than younger children by "correctness" as a reinforcer. According to the developmental hypothesis, older children would have acquired more behavioral components from which "correctness" could become a reinforcer than would be the case with young children.

50 The Effects of Age, Sex, and Socioeconomic Class on Responsiveness to Two Classes of Verbal Reinforcement[1]

DAVID ROSENHAN
JEAN A. GREENWALD

In a recent paper, Zigler and Kanzer (1962) have shown that children from two different socioeconomic strata respond differentially to the two classes of verbal reinforcers. Specifically, they demonstrated that lower-class children are more responsive to reinforcers connoting praise, such as "good" and "fine" (called here person reinforcers), while middle-class children respond more to reinforcers implying accuracy, such as "right" and "correct" (performance reinforcers).

The Zigler and Kanzer findings have stimulated interest for at least two reasons. In the first place, it is somewhat surprising that children actually differentiate between person and performance reinforcers. Parents quite commonly use these reinforcers interchangeably: they themselves do not appear to distinguish between these classes of reinforcers, and it is thus difficult to imagine that children would. Even if parents did make the distinction, the subtle differences involved in the words "right" (performance) and "good" (person) might reasonably be expected to elude young children. The fact that they too can sense such differences implies a semantic sensitivity not commonly ascribed to seven-year-olds.

Secondly, the very fact that there were social class differences is of interest since remarkably little experimental work has been done in this area. Douvan (1956) found that in a situation where reward was merely the personal satisfaction derived from good performance (as opposed to concrete, material rewards) lower-class children produced less achievement imagery after a failure experience than did children from the middle class. Zigler (1962) reported that lower-class children are in general less responsive to verbal reinforcement than are middle-class children. However, that socioeconomic class should be related to responsiveness to particular classes of verbal reinforcement constitutes an interesting elaboration of this finding.

[1] This study was supported by Research Grant No. MH 07690–01 from the National Institute of Mental Health. The authors are grateful to Robert Fried who collected the data for Experiment I, to Henrietta Gallagher who analyzed the data from both experiments, and to Rodney Skager and Anthony Greenwald for critical comments.

It should be noted that it was not entirely clear from the Zigler and Kanzer study whether socioeconomic class alone accounted for the obtained differences or whether the different racial compositions of the samples were responsible for the results. Since Negro children tend more often to be found in the lower classes and white children in the upper classes, the Zigler and Kanzer findings might have resulted from either racial or socioeconomic class differences.

One interpretation that Zigler and Kanzer (1962) offer for their data is that lower-class children are developmentally retarded relative to middle-class children. The interpretation derives from conceptualizations of internalized self-reinforcing behavior which hold that the young child is initially dependent upon externally administered reinforcements and with increasing age comes to rely more heavily on reinforcers intrinsically related to his own responses (Beller, 1955; Gewirtz, 1954; Heathers, 1955; Mowrer, 1960, Chap. 10). Since the latter reinforcers are more abstract, more directed to the performance than to the performer, responsiveness to them is viewed as relatively more mature.

Attempts to verify the maturity hypothesis experimentally have produced ambiguous results. Lewis, Wall, and Aronfreed (1963) administered social (verbal) and signal reinforcers to younger and older children in a binary choice game. Younger children were more responsive to social reinforcers than were older children. However, Dorwart, Ezerman, Lewis, and Rosenhan (1965) failed to replicate these findings, except when the children were briefly socially deprived prior to the experiment. Thus, they argued that the greater responsiveness of younger children to social reinforcement was a function of an experimentally induced drive for sociality rather than the relative attractiveness of the two classes of reinforcement per se. The distinction between person and performance reinforcers as relatively more concrete or abstract permits a re-examination of the maturation hypothesis.

The present report describes two experiments that were performed concurrently and that were de-

From the *Journal of Personality*, 1965, *33*, 108–121. Reprinted by permission of Duke University Press.

Table 1 *Composition of the Sample by Age, Sex, Socioeconomic Class and Performance Scores*

Subject Group ($N = 5$)	CA (yrs:mos)		Socioeconomic Class		Reinforcer Effectiveness Score (per cent)	
	Mean	Range	Mean	Range	$\bar{X}$	Range
Middle-class white						
Boys-Person	7:5	7:2 -7:10	1.4	1–2	10.2	– 3–23
Boys-Performance	7:6	7:0 -8:2	1.4	1–2	4.0	–23–46
Girls-Person	7:3	6:11–7:7	1.4	1–2	33.7	0–100
Girls-Performance	7:2	6:10–7:6	1.4	1–3	7.2	–21–21
Lower-class white						
Boys-Person	8:0	7:5 -9:0	6.4	6–7	21.6	9–37
Boys-Performance	7:10	7:6 -8:1	5.8	5–7	31.6	0–100
Girls-Person	7:4	6:6 -7:9	6.4	6–7	– 5.8	–35–5
Girls-Performance	7:11	7:7 -8:6	6.0	5–7	3.6	0–16
Lower-class Negro						
Boys-Person	7:6	7:2 -8:3	6.2	5–7	– 8.0	–13–46
Boys-Performance	7:1	6:1 -7:11	7.0	7	44.9	8–55
Girls-Person	7:5	6:11–8:1	6.0	5–7	30.0	– 9–65
Girls-Performance	7:7	7:0 -7:10	6.4	5–7	17.4	0–52

signed to answer three questions: (*a*) Are children from lower and middle socioeconomic classes differentially influenced by person and performance reinforcers?—a replication of the Zigler and Kanzer experiment. If so (*b*) are the differences genuinely attributable to socioeconomic class, or are the racial differences between the Ss the more likely source of the performance differences? (*c*) Finally, are there age differences in responsiveness to person and performance reinforcers such that one might argue that a greater responsiveness to performance reinforcers, being more abstract, reflects a higher level of developmental maturation. In addition to examining these issues, both studies investigated the potentially differential effects of verbal reinforcers according to the sex of the S.

Experiment I

The first experiment was a replication of the Zigler-Kanzer (1962) study. In order to distinguish the effects of socioeconomic class from those of race, the present study employed two lower-class samples, one white and the other Negro. Only a middle-class white sample was available.

Method

Subjects. A total of 20 middle-class and 40 lower-class children were drawn from four public schools.[2] Half of the lower-class children were Negro, while the other half were white. Within each class and racial group, half of the Ss were boys and half were girls. All Ss were drawn from the second grade.

While the socioeconomic class of each S was determined after he was examined, on the basis of his parent's occupation (Warner, Meeker, and Eells, 1949, p. 140), in only two of the four schools were the two socioeconomic classes present in large proportions. Of the other two schools, one was predominantly lower class while the other was almost entirely populated by middle-class children. There was no overlap in socioeconomic class between the two samples.

Data from an additional six Ss whose parent's occupation could not be determined with certainty were excluded from the analysis. So too were the data from the last three middle-class children examined, in order to obtain comparison groups of equal size. A summary of the composition of the sample is shown in Table 1. A male *E* conducted the experiment with all Ss.

Apparatus. The experimental apparatus (Marble-in-the-Hole) was similar to that used by Gewirtz and Baer (1958) and Zigler and Kanzer (1962). It consisted of a large wooden box with two holes in the top into which S could drop marbles. The marbles were returned to an open container situated at the front of the apparatus. The chutes through which the marbles traveled were lined with foam rubber in order to reduce auditory feedback. Six marbles were available to S in the container. When S dropped a marble into one of the holes a microswitch was activated which, in turn, pulsed an event recorder located in another room. *E* was provided with a

2 We are grateful to the following individuals and school systems for their co-operation in the research: in the Lawrence Township School System, Mr. Robert Schremser, Assistant Superintendent, Mrs. Esther Updike and Mr. Lawrence Ksanznak, Principals, Mr. Irwin Hyman, School Psychologist; in the Trenton School System, Miss Olive Brown, Director of Instruction, Mr. Lester Blinn and Miss Merle Lloyd, Principals.

hand switch which he depressed each time he administered a reinforcement; this also pulsed the event recorder. Thus, a continuous record of S's responses and *E*'s reinforcements was obtained.

Procedure

Each S was accompanied from his classroom by *E* who introduced himself and explained that S was going to play a game called Marble-in-the-Hole. S was told that he could pick up only one marble at a time and drop it into either hole. Each S played the game for 10 minutes. The first three minutes constituted the baseline period during which *E* noted S's preferred hole but did not dispense any reinforcement. Following this baseline period, *E* reinforced the responses which S made to the hole he had *least* preferred during the last minute of the baseline period. The reinforcement schedule and its qualifications were identical to that employed by Zigler and Kanzer (1962) and Gewirtz and Baer (1958). Every correct response was reinforced until S emitted 10 consecutive correct responses. After this, a reinforcement was delivered for every other correct response until five reinforcements were administered. Then, a reinforcement was delivered for every third correct response until 15 reinforcements had been delivered. Following this a reinforcement was delivered for every fifth correct response until the seven-minute conditioning period was over.

Half of the Ss in each group received performance reinforcers ("right" and "correct") and half received person reinforcers ("good" and "fine"). Each reinforcer in a particular class was used an equal number of times during each reinforcement condition. An attempt was made to deliver each reinforcement with equal emphasis and enthusiasm.

Results

The major dependent variable was the *reinforcer effectiveness score* devised by Gewirtz and Baer (1958) and employed in the Zigler and Kanzer (1962) study. The percentage of S's responses to the reinforced hole was computed for each minute of the conditioning period. The median percentage of each S's responses for this seven-minute period minus the percentage of his response to that hole during the third minute of the baseline period constituted the reinforcer effectiveness score.

The usefulness of the reinforcer effectiveness score is predicated on the assumption that there is no correlation between performance during the base rate and conditioning periods. Patterson (1963) has questioned this assumption and has shown that children who demonstrate little preference for one hole over the other during the base rate period (such as response alternators) may be relatively unresponsive to reinforcements administered during the conditioning period relative to children who evidence marked preferences during the base rate period.

We examined the relationship between baseline and conditioned performance in our experiments. We anticipate ourselves somewhat and present the data from Experiments I and II in Table 2. Because the *N*s in each experimental subgroup were small, the

Table 2 *Correlations between Performance during the Third Minute of Base Rate and Median Performance during the Conditioning Period*

Subject Classification	*N*	*r*
All Ss	100	.02
Performance reinforcement	50	.09
Person reinforcement	50	−.06
All males	50	−.05
All females	50	.04
All second-grade Ss	80	.04
Middle-class second-grade Ss	40	−.02
Lower-class second-grade Ss	40	.10

Table 3 *Analysis of Variance for White Middle- and Lower-Class Children*

Source		*df*	MS	*F*
Person vs. performance	(A)	1	.0112	<1.00
Sex	(B)	1	.0517	<1.00
Lower vs. middle class	(C)	1	.0011	<1.00
A×B		1	.0272	<1.00
A×C		1	.1700	2.56
B×C		1	.4199	6.32*
A×B×C		1	.0246	<1.00
Within cells		32	.0664	
T		39		

* $p < .02$.

Table 4 *Analysis of Variance for Lower-Class White and Negro Children*

Source		*df*	MS	*F*
Person vs. performance	(A)	1	.1188	2.20
Sex	(B)	1	.2320	4.30*
Negro vs. white	(C)	1	.1525	2.83
A×B		1	.1567	2.91
A×C		1	.0015	<1.00
B×C		1	.1550	2.88
A×B×C		1	.1503	2.79
Within cells		32	.0539	
T		39		

* $p < .05$.

subgroups were combined in various ways: according to Ss' sex, age, socioeconomic class, and the type of reinforcement administered. It will be seen that for these samples, no substantial correlation existed between base rate and conditioned performance.

We turn now to the further analysis of the data from Experiment I. Because a middle-class Negro sample was unobtainable, and in order to distinguish the effect of S's race from his socioeconomic status, two analyses of variance were performed. The first (Table 3) compared the performance of white boys and girls from the lower and middle classes with regard to their responsiveness to the two classes of verbal reinforcers. No main effects were obtained with either the variables of sex, socioeconomic class, or type of reinforcement, nor was there a significant interaction between type of reinforcement and socioeconomic class. Thus, the Zigler-Kanzer study, which reported socioeconomic interactions with responsiveness to the two classes of reinforcers, was not replicated. However, an interaction between sex of S and socioeconomic class was obtained, such that middle-class girls and lower-class boys were more responsive to both kinds of verbal reinforcers than were middle-class boys and lower-class girls (Table 1).

The second analysis of variance compared the performance of white and Negro lower-class children (Table 4). Here, only the main effects of sex attained statistical significance, with boys more responsive than girls to both classes of reinforcement. Differential performance according to class of verbal reinforcement or according to color of Ss was not clearly evident in these data. An interpretation of the findings from both analyses of variance follows Experiment II.

Table 5 *Composition of Sample by Age, Sex, and Reinforcer Effectiveness Score*

Subject Group	CA (yrs:mos)		Reinforcer Effectiveness Score	
	Mean	Range	Mean	Range
Sixth grade				
Boys-Person	11:4	10:11–11:10	35.3	0–91
Boys-Performance	11:3	10:10–11:7	19.6	− 6–72
Girls-Person	11:2	10:11–11:8	13.1	−30–50
Girls-Performance	11:0	10:9 –11:4	39.9	13–55
Second grade				
Boys-Person	6:11	6:1 – 7:7	23.6	−13–57
Boys-Performance	7:4	7:1 – 7:8	−12.0	−54– 5
Girls-Person	7:2	6:11– 7:8	24.9	2–55
Girls-Performance	7:0	6:8 – 7:4	16.7	0–42

Table 6 *Analysis of Variance for Age, Sex, and Class of Reinforcer*

Source	*df*	MS	*F*
Second vs. sixth grade (A)	1	.1613	2.09
Sex (B)	1	.0637	<1.00
Person vs. performance (C)	1	.0841	1.09
A×B	1	.0489	<1.00
A×C	1	.1623	3.10
B×C	1	.3423	4.43*
A×B×C	1	.0227	<1.00
Within cells	32	.0773	
T	39		

* $p < .05$.

Experiment II

The second experiment examined the hypothesis that older children are more influenced by abstract reinforcers than are younger children.

Method

Subjects, Apparatus, and Procedure. Twenty second-grade and 20 sixth-grade middle-class children, drawn from one predominantly middle-class school and equally divided among boys and girls within each grade, served as Ss in this experiment. The composition and performance of these samples is shown in Table 5. A female *E* tested all Ss. The apparatus and procedures were identical to those used in Experiment I.

Results

Once again, the dependent variable was the reinforcer effectiveness described above. A 2 × 2 × 2 factorial analysis of variance was applied to the data with two levels of sex, age, and class of reinforcer constituting the factors (Table 6). There were no significant main effects for any of the variables. However, a significant interaction obtained between sex of S and class of reinforcer, reflecting the fact that boys were more responsive to person reinforcers, while girls responded more to performance reinforcers (Table 5).

A marginally significant interaction was found between the age of the children and their responsiveness to the two classes of reinforcement ($F = 3.10$; $.05 > p < .10$). Comparison of the means obtained by younger and older children for the two classes of reinforcers, is shown in Table 5. No differences in responsiveness to person reinforcers were found between second- and sixth-grade children. However, the older children were more responsive than the

Table 7 *Analysis of Variance for Sex of E, Sex of S, and Class of Reinforcer*

Source	*df*	MS	*F*
Sex of *E*	1	.0003	<1.00
Person vs. performance	1	.3665	5.11*
Sex of S	1	.1998	2.79
A×B	1	.0076	<1.00
A×C	1	.0007	<1.00
B×C	1	.0032	<1.00
A×B×C	1	.1429	1.99
Within cells	32	2.2954	
T	39		

* $p < .05$.

younger ones to performance reinforcers ($t = 2.36$; $p < .05$; two-tail).

In order to compare the responsiveness of middle-class Ss to the male and female *Es*, the middle-class second-grade data from Experiments I and II were combined. A further 2 × 2 × 2 analysis of variance was then performed (Table 7) with sex of *E*, sex of S, and class of reinforcer constituting the factors. Only the main effects of class of reinforcer were significant; Ss were more responsive to person reinforcers than to performance reinforcers. Neither the sex of S nor the sex of *E* significantly affected responsiveness to reinforcement. Neither first- nor second-order interactions were evident in the data.

Discussion

In some respects the findings of these experiments differ substantially from those presented by Zigler and Kanzer (1962). In others, the data support their notions. In Experiment I, no differences were found between middle- and lower-class children in their responsiveness to the two classes of verbal reinforcement. Thus, no further basis could be found for the argument that, relative to middle-class children, lower-class children may be developmentally retarded in their responsiveness to abstract reinforcers.

On the other hand, the experiments described here offer tentative evidence that children do differentiate between person and performance reinforcers. In Experiment II, older children appeared to be more responsive than younger children to performance reinforcers, while boys in general appeared more sensitive to person, and girls to performance reinforcers. Moreover, the combined analysis of the data obtained in Experiments I and II from middle-class second-grade children indicated that these children are more influenced by person than performance reinforcers.

Let us consider some of the differences between the Zigler and Kanzer data and those presented here, with an eye to the methodological and theoretical issues that both studies raise. In the first place, there is evidence that our *Es* were, in general, less effective as reinforcing agents than the *E* in the Zigler and Kanzer study. In both studies there were individuals who failed to "learn" the task, but in our experiments there were three entire subgroups that obtained negative scores, and three others where learning was, at best, marginal. These findings indicate that there may have been considerable variability in the effectiveness of the respective *Es* and that reinforcer effectiveness is as yet an elusive variable. The data are consistent with Stevenson's finding (1961) that different *Es* using identical reinforcement procedures, have differential impacts upon children. In this same vein, our previous work (Dorwart et al., 1965) has shown that seemingly trivial encounters between *E* and S, such as the amount and quality of pre-experimental contact between them, can massively influence *E*'s subsequent effectiveness as a reinforcing agent. It is conceivable that such apparently trivial (and, as yet, unspecifiable) experimental differences contributed to the varying findings.

It is also possible, of course, that the varying results obtained by Zigler and Kanzer and by us derived from the differing hypotheses we held regarding the performance of lower- and middle-class children (cf. Rosenthal, 1963). Zigler and Kanzer appear to have been convinced by previous studies (cf. Douvan, 1956; Terrell, Durkin, and Wiesley, 1959; Zigler, 1962) that such socio-economic class differences exist and might be demonstrable in differential responsiveness to classes of verbal reinforcers.

We were, and continue to be, rather skeptical of the findings. The basis of our skepticism is twofold. In the first place, we were doubtful that such differences, if they existed, would manifest themselves within the narrow meaning bands that person and performance reinforcers connote. Secondly, such differences as have been reported between the performance of lower- and middle-class children have been obtained by middle-class *Es* in middle-class environments. Although the differences are always interpreted to reflect deficiences, as it were, in lower-class children, in fact the differences were obtained by an *E*, and in a context with which lower-class children were less familiar and hence less comfortable than were middle-class children.

Consider the Zigler-Kanzer experiment as a case in point. Quite apart from being less abstract than performance reinforcers, person reinforcers are probably also more anxiety reducing because they are personally reassuring. Lower-class children, feeling more anxious than their middle-class counterparts with a middle-class *E*, might be more responsive to person reinforcers because they reduce anxiety. By the same token, had the *E* been distinctly lower-class, it is conceivable that middle-class Ss, finding themselves with a person whose characteristics were relatively unfamiliar, might be more responsive to person rather than to performance reinforcers.

This point has been made at some length in order to suggest a different theoretical view of experimentally obtained social class differences and to illustrate a methodological error in our experiment and previously reported ones. It is not to argue that there are no differences between children of various social strata. Rather, the interpretation of the experiments themselves is in question, for it is hard to know whether the obtained findings are directly a function of subject characteristics or the interaction between subject characteristics and special circumstances. Situational conditions (cf. Abelson, 1962) make a crucial theoretical and methodological difference for the interpretation of social-class data. At the very least, the issues require the use of both lower-and middle-class *Es* with lower- and middle-class Ss, in order to establish whether the findings are social-class-specific or are the result of social-class interactions. Attempts to implement such experiments are currently being explored. With these problems firmly in mind, let us examine further the findings of these experiments.

Effects of Sex and Socioeconomic Status. Previous studies in the area of social reinforcement have reported that women have significantly greater effects on the performance of boys than of girls, while men have greater effects on the performance of girls than of boys (Gewirtz, 1954; Gewirtz and Baer, 1958; Stevenson, 1961). The findings presented here are at variance with those reports. Such sex effects as are found are limited to either lower-class children or to interactions with variables other than sex of *E*. Thus, in Experiment I, middle-class girls and lower-class boys were more responsive to verbal reinforcement than either middle-class boys or lower-class girls, while within the lower class, boys were more responsive than girls to verbal reinforcement. In Experiment II, middle-class boys were more responsive than girls to person reinforcers, while girls were more influenced by performance reinforcers. However, the combined analysis of date obtained in Experiments I and II among middle-class second-grade children failed to reveal interactions with either sex of *E* or sex of S. We have no ready explanation for the fact that the sex of S interactions "washed out" in the combined analysis. Perhaps a broader spectrum of age needs to be present in an experiment before the sex of S interactions appear consistently.

Implications for a Developmental Hierarchy of Reinforcers. The evidence from both experiments would suggest that children are indeed sensitive and responsive to the semantic nuances connoted by person and performance reinforcers. It is possible that parents, as primary reinforcing agents, employ these reinforcers differentially, particularly according to the age and sex of the child.

We noted earlier that theories of self-reinforcement have held that the process of development is marked by the gradual decrement in responsiveness to more primitive kinds of reinforcement (i.e., concrete, personal) and a corresponding increment in responsiveness to more mature (abstract, impersonal, performance) kinds of reinforcement. The data from Experiment II do not entirely support this formulation but rather suggest that in growing older, children do indeed become more responsive to performance reinforcers, but not at the expense of person reinforcers. A somewhat different view of maturation is offered in this regard: that maturation involves increasing sensitivity to a broader class of reinforcers, perhaps more specifically to abstract reinforcers. But no decrement in responsiveness to person or concrete reinforcers is implied in maturation. Further evidence for this hypothesis will have to be obtained across a wide variety of experimental tasks and populations.

Summary

The effects of two classes of verbal reinforcers, one more abstract (performance reinforcers) and the other less abstract (person), were examined among lower- and middle-class children. Previous work that had shown lower-class children to be relatively unresponsive to abstract reinforcers was not substantiated. The experiment suggested serious deficiences in the experimental methodology (and hence in conceptualization) for examining the psychological properties of lower-class children.

A second experiment examined the developmental implications of responsiveness to person and performance reinforcers. The results suggested that, in growing older, children become more sensitive to a broader band of reinforcers, and particularly to abstract reinforcers, without declining in their responsiveness to concrete ones.

References

Abelson, R. P. Situational variables in personality research. In S. Messick and J. Ross (Eds.), *Measurement in personality and cognition.* New York: Wiley, 1962.

Beller, E. K. Dependency and independence in young children. *Journal of Genetic Psychology,* 1955, *87,* 25–34.

Dorwart, W., Ezerman, R., Lewis, M., and Rosenhan, D. The effect of brief social deprivation on social and nonsocial reinforcement. *Journal of Personality and Social Psychology,* 1956, 2, 111–115.

DOUVAN, ELIZABETH. Social status and success striving. *Journal of Abnormal and Social Psychology,* 1956, *52,* 219–223.

GEWIRTZ, J. L. Three determinants of attention seeking in young children. *Monographs of the Society for Research in Child Development,* 1954, *19,* No. 2 (Serial No. 59).

GEWIRTZ, J. L., and BAER, D. M. The effect of brief social deprivation on behaviors for a social reinforcer. *Journal of Abnormal and Social Psychology,* 1958, *56,* 49–56.

HEATHERS, G. Emotional dependence and independence in nursery school play. *Journal of Genetic Psychology,* 1955, *87,* 37–57.

LEWIS, M., WALL, A. M., and ARONFREED, J. Developmental change in the relative values of social and nonsocial reinforcement. *Journal of Experimental Psychology,* 1963, *66,* 133–137.

MOWRER, O. H. *Learning theory and the symbolic processes.* New York: Wiley, 1960.

PATTERSON, G. R. Responsiveness to social stimuli. Paper presented at a symposium entitled "Current research in behavior modification," Palo Alto, Calif., 1963.

ROSENTHAL, R. On the social psychology of the psychological experiment: The experimenter's hypothesis as an unintended determinant of experimental results. *American Scientist,* 1963, *51,* 268–283.

STEVENSON, H. W. Social reinforcement with children as a function of CA, sex of *E,* and sex of S. *Journal of Abnormal and Social Psychology,* 1961, *63,* 147–154.

TERRELL, G., JR., DURKIN, K., and WIESLEY, M. Social class and the nature of the incentive in discrimination learning. *Journal of Abnormal and Social Psychology,* 1959, *59,* 270–272.

WARNER, W. L., MEEKER, MARCIA, and EELLS, K. *Social class in America.* Chicago: Science Research Associates, 1949.

ZIGLER, E. Rigidity in the feebleminded. In E. P. Trapp and P. Himelstein (Eds.), *Research readings on the exceptional child.* New York: Appleton-Century-Crofts, 1962.

ZIGLER, E., and KANZER, P. The effectiveness of two classes of verbal reinforcers on the performance of middle- and lower-class children. *Journal of Personality,* 1962, *30,* 157–163.

9

Communication in the Group

Some of the more important instances of social communication occur in groups, where plans are discussed and decisions are reached. Communication in a group differs from ordinary conversation in several important respects. First, and most obviously, the number of different patterns of interaction increases sharply as new members are added to the group. Many of the events that transpire in a group discussion are similar to those that occur in a conversation between two individuals. However, certain products of the group setting, such as the development of a consensus or the increased persuasion directed toward a deviate, could not occur in a simple dyad relationship. To this extent, groups have "emergent" properties that require special techniques of investigation.

A basic problem confronting researchers studying small groups is that of developing appropriate and reliable methods for recording and evaluating communication among the members. Procedures have been devised for handling the content of discussion in a group, the volume and direction of communication, and the nonverbal concomitants of group discussion. The use of one-way observation screens, movie cameras, and tape recorders makes it possible to obtain observations that are relatively uncontaminated by the presence of an observer. Computer technology offers a means of handling large masses of data and complex statistical analyses that would otherwise be tedious and difficult, if not unmanageable.

But procedural niceties and analytical elegance alone do not reveal the most significant dimensions of group interaction. If we assume that the individual participants prompt and maintain each other's behaviors in ways that are susceptible to both manipulation and functional analysis, examination of these functional relationships requires skillful manipulation of the consequences of interaction. Techniques developed within the past twenty years, for example, have enabled social psychologists to control both the channels and the content of communication in groups of various sizes. Manipulation of communication among the members of a group has now become feasible, so techniques of observation no longer hold center stage. Although the nature of the social reinforcers that operate under such circumstances has only recently been a subject of inquiry, a number of experimenters are attempting to deal directly with reinforcement variables. In this chapter, we consider several studies in which reinforcement effects in group communication have been examined.

Controlled Networks

Although seemingly complex, the experiment reported by *Butler and Miller* is actually rather simple in execution. Five individuals, separated by partitions, pass slips of paper to one another through slots. Each has a number of *A* messages, which are valuable, and *B* messages, which are worthless. The proportion of *A* to *B* messages in a total of 100 varies from subject to subject, and the power structure of the several groups is also varied. Thus, one group might contain four persons with 90 *A* messages and one person with only 50 *A* messages. Another group would have four persons possessing 10 *A* messages each and one person possessing 50 *A* messages. It was predicted that those subjects having a greater power to reinforce others, by virtue of having more *A* messages at their disposal, would also be the recipients of more messages from the other group members. The assumption is that an individual will be more inclined to communicate with someone who reinforces him. The results bear out this general notion, with the number of messages received by the various individuals being a monotonic increasing function of their power to reinforce others. Any social situation in which leaders, who are in a position to dispense reinforcements to others, are also the targets of more communications may be understood in these terms. Social reinforcement, apparently, can both prompt and maintain communication in a group.

51 "Power to Reinforce" as a Determinant of Communication[1]

DONALD C. BUTLER
NORMAN MILLER

In line with a current movement toward simplified and controlled experiments on social interaction (Church, 1961; Kelley, Thibaut, Radloff, and Mundy, 1962; Rosenberg, 1960; Sidowski, 1957; Suppes and Atkinson, 1960) a simplification of the well known Bavelas (1951) procedure has been developed. In the typical Bavelas experiment 5 *Ss* pass each other written messages while *E* varies the number of channels through which messages can be passed. *S*'s major concern is efficient solution of a problem confronting the group, a reinforcing event over which *E* has little control. Usually there are no rules curtailing the content of messages, the rate of sending, or the frequency of sending. Thus, both behavior and its consequences are dishearteningly heterogeneous.

The present simplified method increases *E*'s control and correspondingly reduces *Ss*' freedom in the following manner: (a) there is no "group problem," only an "individual problem"; (b) messages have one of two contents, *A* or *B;* (c) each *S* sends one message per trial; (d) there is a fixed number of trials for all Ss; (e) Ss neither know nor control the content of the message they send on any trial. *S* is free only to choose *to whom* he communicates on each trial throughout the experiment. The major dependent variable is the number of messages received by each S from all other Ss.

Although much of the realism of verbal interaction vanishes under this procedure, it enables *E* to control message content and the effects of a unit message

[1] Supported in part by grants to Yale University from the National Institute of Mental Health (Grant M-4840) and the National Science Foundation (Grant GS-428). We thank Hiroshi Ono for aid in conducting the experiment.

From *Psychological Reports*, 1965, *16*, 705–709. Reprinted by permission.

on the receiver. For example, if all Ss are instructed to try to receive as many *A* messages as possible and that *B* messages are worthless, it seems reasonable to assume that the receipt of an *A* message will act as a reinforcer. Thus, by pre-determining the ratio of *A* to *B* content of a given S's supply of messages, *E* can manipulate his *power to reinforce* other Ss. The pattern or frequency of communication to a given S can be examined as a function of that S's *power to reinforce*. By providing each group member with a fixed proportion of *A* and *B* messages, one can examine the extent to which the frequency of response to a given power position varies when that position is embedded in different power structures.

In the social situation, the term *power* has been used to describe a person's ability to control the behavior of others, and through that, his own outcomes (Thibaut and Kelley, 1959, pp. 101–102). *Power to reinforce* fits well as a sub-class of power in this sense, since reinforcement is one of the major techniques of social control (Skinner, 1953, pp. 298–312). Stogdill finds it "reasonable to conclude that power resides in the hands of those group members who are able to control reinforcement" (1959, p. 138). Of course, other kinds of power have been defined corresponding to the employment of other control techniques, such as aversive stimulation, deprivation, and physical restraint (Thibaut and Kelley, 1959, pp. 100–110), or corresponding to the *perception* that another person has the ability or knowledge necessary for such control (Thibaut and Kelley, 1959, pp. 122–127; French and Raven, 1959, pp. 155–156). In addition, *influence* has been defined in terms of power. French and Raven (1959, pp. 152–153) speak of the influence of one person upon another as "actualized power," that is, the product of the sending S's power and his probability of sending to the receiver.

If the receipt of an *A* message does result in an increased tendency to communicate with the sender, then those who send more *A* messages should end up receiving more messages. Since this factor works for all persons at once, a person's relative advantage should depend on the power of the others in the group who are competing with him for messages. In the absence of a more specific quantitative theory to predict the differentiation in frequency of communication to different members of a group, the simplest assumption is that a person's rate of communication to a target person is a monotonically increasing function of the target person's power to reinforce. To explore this relation, five different group power structures were investigated.

Method

Two groups of 5 male undergraduates were assigned to each of 5 conditions. The 5 conditions were different group power structures, each specified by listing the 5 members' proportions of messages with content *A*. The conditions were .5.9.9.9.9, .1.1.1.1.5, .1.3.5.7.9, and .1.1.5.9.9. These structures were selected as simple representations of several different dimensions along which power structures in the natural social environment might actually vary: a single low-power member (.5.9.9.9.9), a single high-power member (.1.1.1.1.5), low total group power (.1.1.1.1.5), moderate total group power (.1.5.5.5.9, .1.3.5.7.9, .1.1.5.9.9), high total group power (.5.9.9.9.9), low power variance (.1.5.5.5.9), moderate power variance (.1.3.5.7.9), high power variance (.1.1.5.9.9). Obviously, among the power structures employed, these dimensions are not orthogonal to one another. Nevertheless, they permit some suggestive comparisons.

A standard Bavelas apparatus was used, with all channels open. Each S was provided with 100 strips of cardboard of the same color as his portion of the apparatus (red, yellow, white, blue, or brown). A 1-inch fold at the end of each strip concealed the symbol *A* or *B* from the sender, but the receiver was permitted to look under the fold and determine the message content. Ss were instructed to acquire as many *A* messages as possible, but they neither knew nor controlled the content of their own messages.

All groups received 100 trials with an intertrial interval of about 5 seconds. On every trial each S simultaneously sent a single message to the person of his choice. The order of *A* and *B* messages in each S's output was predetermined by sampling without replacement from a 100-element supply with a fixed proportion of *A* messages. The messages were numbered from 1 to 100, corresponding to the trial on which they were to be sent. The receivers collected messages in two piles, one for those of type *A* and one for type *B*. At the end of the experiment the color and trial number of messages received were recorded according to their frequency and source for blocks of 10 trials.

Results

Figure 1 shows the effect of power on message sending in each of the 5 power structures. Pooling the two groups run under each structure, the figure presents the mean number of messages received on the last 10 trials by Ss at each power level. Inspection of the figure shows monotonic increases in frequency to a target-subject as a function of the target-subject's power. The same invariant relation between power of a target-subject and number of messages received by that S also holds for means based on the last 30 trials. This suggests that there is some stability in the differentiation of responding, even after as few as 70 trials.

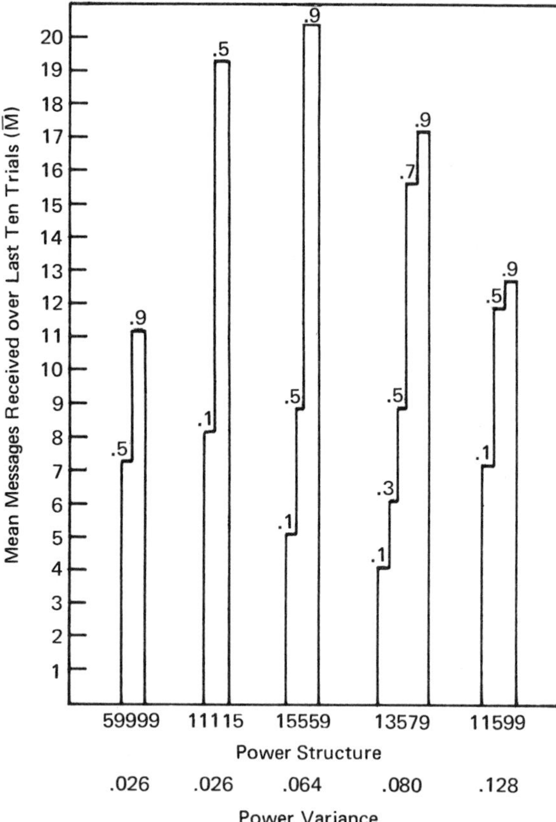

Figure 1 *The number of messages received over the last 10 trials by subjects in different power positions in each group. (See text for explanation of power structure and power variance.)*

Differences in number of messages received by the power positions within each structure were tested by 5 analyses of variance, each based on two replications (see Table 1). In each analysis, the number of subgroups and their sizes depended on the number of different power levels within that structure. Thus, for the analysis of the .1.5.5.5.9 structure there were 3 subgroups having 2, 6, and 2 Ss, respectively, whereas for the .1.3.5.7.9 structure there were 5 subgroups with 2 Ss in each. For all 5 analyses, a pooled within-structure error term was used based on the data from all 5 structures. Use of this pooled within-structure error term was supported by Bartlett's test comparing the 5 separate within-structure variances ($\chi^2 < .50$). Significant power effects were found for four of the structures. The one insignificant structure (.5.9.9.9.9) possessed a high average power (.82) which may have hindered differentiation.

Inspection of Figure 1 shows that going from groups .1.5.5.5.9 to .1.3.5.7.9 to .1.1.5.9.9, which all had the same total power within the group (2.5), there is a decreasing differentiation between the top and bottom power levels in each structure. The difference among these 3 power structures appears to be inversely related to the degree of variation of power within them. The variance of power in each structure is presented in Figure 1 below the power structures.

This suggests that, given a fixed total power, the difference in frequency of response to fixed high- and low-power individuals increases as the over-all variation of power in the group decreases. This generalization can be extended to the .1.1.1.1.5 group. There, the difference between the extremes of power was less than that in the .1.5.5.5.9, .1.3.5.7.9, and .1.1.5.9.9 groups (.1 and .5 as opposed to .1 and .9) and the power variance was even smaller. In spite of the smaller difference between the extremes of power, there was substantial differentiation between frequency of response to high- and low-power positions. However, with the .5.5.5.5.9 group in which power variance was equally small, the generalization clearly breaks down. A plausible interpretation of this exception is that with power variance constant, high total power (.5.9.9.9.9) retards differentiation while low total power (.1.1.1.1.5) enhances it. However, this interpretation ignores the direction of the nonhomogeneous group member's deviation in power. Since direction of deviation is confounded with total group power in these two groups, the effect of total group power must remain a conjecture pending further research.

Table 1 *Analyses of Variance of Number of Messages Received by Power Positions Within Each Structure*

Power Structure	Variance Between	Variance Within*	*df*	*F*	*p*
.5.9.9.9.9	22.50	7.94	1	2.64	$.25 > p > .10$
.1.1.1.1.5	180.62	14.30	1	21.20	.01
.1.5.5.5.9	122.00	4.29	2	14.32	.01
.1.3.5.7.9	60.75	3.40	4	7.13	.01
.1.1.5.9.9	30.38	10.46	2	3.57	$.05 > p > .01$

* In computing the F ratios, the pooled within-structure variance of 8.52, with 35 *df*, was used as the best estimate of error.

References

Bavelas, A. Communication patterns in task-oriented groups. In D. Lerner and H. D. Lasswell (Eds.), *The policy sciences*. Stanford, Calif.: Stanford University Press, 1951. Pp. 193–202.

Church, R. M. The effects of competition on speed of response. *Journal of Comparative and Physiological Psychology*, 1961, *54*, 162–167.

French, J. R. P., and Raven, B. The bases of social power. In D. Cartwright (Ed.), *Studies in social power*. Ann Arbor, Mich.: Institute for Social Research, 1959. Pp. 150–167.

Kelley, H. H., Thibaut, J. W., Radloff, R., and Mundy, D. The Development of cooperation in the "minimal social situation." *Psychological Monographs*, 1962, *76*, No. 19 (Whole No. 538).

Rosenberg, S. Cooperative behavior in dyads as a function of reinforcement parameters. *Journal of Abnormal and Social Psychology*, 1960, *60*, 318–333.

Sidowski, J. B. Reward and punishment in a minimal social situation. *Journal of Experimental Psychology*, 1957, *54*, 318–326.

Skinner, B. F. Science and human behavior. New York: Macmillan, 1953.

Stogdill, R. M. *Individual behavior and group achievement*. New York: Oxford University Press, 1959.

Suppes, P., and Atkinson, R. C. *Markov learning models for multiperson interactions*. Stanford: Stanford University Press, 1960.

Thibaut, J. W., and Kelley, H. H. *The social psychology of groups*. New York: Wiley, 1959.

Various patterns of communication that might exist among the members of a group have been studied in some detail. In the wheel network, for example, all messages must be transmitted through one individual who is centrally located. In the circle, each person may communicate only with the two individuals on either side of him. Although the wheel type of communication net has been found to yield the fastest solution to a problem, group members seem to obtain greater satisfaction from the circle. Generally, no specific reinforcers have been made contingent upon performances in any of the communication patterns that have been used. Moreover, the results from different experiments are not always consistent. *Burgess* argues that the absence of any significant consequences to the subjects for their performance in these experiments constitutes neglect of one of the most basic properties of social life.

The experiments reported by Burgess made use of both the wheel and the circle communication networks. Rather than simply have his groups solve a few problems, however, Burgess kept them working until their performances had reached a steady state. This enabled him to make more accurate comparisons of problem-solving behavior in the two different networks, as well as to determine the effect of introducing both positive and aversive consequences for efficient performance. He discovered that introducing contingencies of reinforcement eliminated differences between the two networks that could otherwise be observed. Without reinforcement, the wheel yielded faster rates of solution; but this advantage was reduced as soon as the subjects were able to obtain some benefit from more efficient performance. Differences between the two networks disappeared entirely during steady-state periods when reinforcement was contingent upon a rapid rate of solution.

52 | Communication Networks: An Experimental Reevaluation

ROBERT L. BURGESS

Social psychology is often defined as the study of social interaction (Swanson, 1965). In view of this fact, it is not surprising that many social psychologists have been concerned with exploring the effects of different patterns or forms of interaction upon other features of group processes such as member satisfaction or group productivity. These patterns of interaction are usually termed *networks* or *structures*. Alex Bavelas and his associates contributed probably the most elegant operationalization of interaction networks or structures yet available (Bavelas, 1950). In his design, each individual in a group is given certain information. The group is given the task of assembling this information, using it to make a decision, and then issuing orders based on this decision. The critical feature of the design is that the group members are separated from one another and can communicate only through channels which may be opened or closed by the experimenter.

Research employing this design has been in progress for the past 18 years. Unfortunately, the research has not produced consistent and cumulative results. Indeed, the results are contradictory as well as inconclusive. Table 1 summarizes some major experiments conducted to date with regard to the dependent variable, productivity or solution rate. One independent variable which many experimenters have considered to be important is problem-complexity. Hence, the results are presented for both "simple" and "complex" problems.[1] Looking first at those studies that employed the "simple" task, we see that seven out of thirteen reported that the Wheel network produced the highest solution rate. The *Wheel* is a net in which organizational problems are kept to a minimum. All information is directed toward the individual occupying the central position. Typically, this individual, upon receiving the information provided by the other group members, solves the problems and sends out directives to the other group members. However, the All-channel network was found to produce the highest rate in three cases. The All-channel is a net which permits direct communication between all members. In three instances there were found to be no significant differences between the networks. With those studies that used the "complex" task we see that one of ten reported the Wheel to be the most proficient, six the All-channel, and three found no significant differences between the networks. The most obvious conclusion is that the variables underlying the relative effectiveness of different communication networks have not been isolated as yet. While this conclusion is difficult to avoid, it is quite simple to articulate; the more difficult task, yet the one which must be accomplished if we are to further our knowledge of social structure, is to specify and improve upon the deficiencies of previous studies. We shall take up this issue in the next section.

Experiment I

Method. The present investigation was designed in the anticipation that these inconsistent and contradictory findings could be resolved. In this experiment, the four members composing a group were separated from one another by partitions. They could communicate with one another by means of interconnected slots in the partitions through which written messages could be passed. These slots could be closed at any time by the experimenter in order to create any desired communication structure. As with earlier studies, the practice here was to permit free and continuous communication within the limits imposed by the various networks under investigation. Two networks were investigated. One network, the *Wheel*, has been described above. The other net, the *Circle*, makes imperative some sort of relay system within the group; no member has channels open to all other members. This is a net which permits the emergence of one or several forms of patterned communication. Yet, unlike the All-channel net, it is not possible for the members in the Circle to simulate completely the pattern found in the Wheel. The comparison of these two rather extreme networks should provide us with a crucial test of the effects of different communication networks.

Several criticisms may be leveled against com-

[1] The "simple" problem, sometimes called the Leavitt-type problem, is utilized in this study and described below. The "complex" problem refers to a variety of arithmetic problems such as the following:

A small company is moving from one office building to another. It must move: (a) chairs, (b) desks, and (c) typewriters. How many trucks are needed to make the move in one trip? For a three-member group, six items of information would be needed to solve the problem and these would usually be equally divided over the group members. For example, the company owns 12 desks, 48 chairs, and 12 typewriters, and one truckload can take 12 typewriters, or 3 desks, or 25 chairs.

From the *Journal of Experimental Social Psychology*, 1968, *4*, 324–337.
Reprinted by permission of Academic Press.

Table 1 *Synopsis of Communication-Network Findings*

Author	Date	Group Size	Network Solution Rate (in Descending Order)	Task
Leavitt	1951	5	Wheel (fastest trial)	Simple
Heise and Miller	1951	3	All-channel: Wheel	Simple
			Wheel: All-channel	Complex
Hirota	1953	5	No significant difference	Simple
Shaw	1954a	4	No significant difference	Complex
Shaw	1954b	3	No significant difference	Complex
			No significant difference	Simple
Guetzkow and Simon	1955	5	Wheel: All-channel: Circle	Simple
			(stable nets—no significant difference)	
Shaw	1956	4	All-channel: Wheel	Complex
Shaw and Rothschild	1956	4	All-channel: Wheel	Complex
Guetzkow and Dill	1957	5	All-channel: Circle	Simple
Shaw, Rothschild, and Strickland	1957	4	All-channel: Wheel	Complex
Shaw	1958	4	All-channel: Wheel	Complex
Mulder	1959	4	Wheel	Simple
Mulder	1960	4	No significant difference	Simple
			No significant difference	Complex
Mohanna and Argyle	1960	5	Wheel	Simple
Cohen, Bennis, and Wolkon	1961	5	Wheel	Simple
Cohen, Bennis, and Wolkon	1962	5	Wheel	Simple
Lawson	1964a	4	(NR)[a] All-channel, Wheel:Circle	Simple
			(R) Wheel, All-channel: Circle	
Lawson	1964b	4	(NR) All-channel, Circle: Wheel	Complex
			(R) All-channel, Circle: Wheel	

[a] NR = nonreinforced; R = reinforced.

munication-network experiments. For example, data from psychology have indicated that during individual learning there is an initial transition or acquisition period, a period marked by an acceleration in the response rate, leading to a "steady state." Once the steady state is reached, the behavior typically remains stable for long periods of time. None of the previous communication-network experiments was designed in such a way that we could observe steady-state periods. This state of affairs is, unfortunately, typical of most social-psychological investigations. By being overly concerned with tests of significance, we incorporate large samples with short periods of observation. The reverse strategy is called for if, as the data of individual psychology suggest, such transitional states are the rule rather than the exception. In the present investigation, a small number of groups (15) was investigated for a relatively extended duration of time. In previous experiments, groups were required to solve only from 25 to 60 problems. As a consequence, the groups were still learning to organize and solve the tasks presented *when the experiments were terminated.* In the present investigation, the groups were required to solve from 900 to 1100 problems.

Another defect in previous studies is that, with one or two exceptions, they relied entirely upon control by randomization. It may be argued that this method increases rather than decreases random error variance (Sidman, 1960). Here, control by constancy was employed wherever possible; all groups were run under both experimental conditions. Each group was "its own control." One half of the groups began under the Circle net, and were subsequently changed to a Wheel net and back again in an A-B-A design. For the other half of the groups the pattern was Wheel-Circle-Wheel.

Another major criticism of previous studies is that they failed to include one basic property of social life; namely, behavioral consequences, either positive or negative. This is particularly critical since recent research seems to indicate that most social behavior exists precisely because of its environmental, especially social, consequences (Staats and Staats, 1964). Hence, in this experiment "reinforcement" was provided contingent upon correct problem solving, and "punishment" was provided contingent upon errors.

Apparatus. In front of each member was a panel on which five letters of the alphabet were placed vertically with a light and a banana-jack next to each letter. For each problem a different light was illuminated on each member's panel. The task was to determine, through written communication, which light was not illuminated on any subject's panel. Once the group had determined the answer, all members inserted their plugs into the selected answer jacks. If the answer was correct an amber light on the panel was illuminated. The subjects then took their plugs out of the answer jacks and inserted them into a neutral jack below the amber light. With this accomplished, electro-mechanical relays automatically set up the next problem and the process began all over again.

Procedures. For Experiment I, 20 subjects volunteered from the experimenter's Introductory Sociology class for 10 hours of experimental work in lieu of an assigned term paper. The groups were randomly assigned to either the Circle or the Wheel network.

Each experimental session began with the subjects' being ushered into the experimental room and seated around a table. It will be recalled that they were separated from one another by four vertical partitions. Their communications were restricted to written messages which they could pass through slots in the partitions. During the operating trials, they interchanged messages on precoded cards. Blank cards were provided also, for organizational purposes or for any other reason the subjects might have. The first session for each group was preceded by a training period, during which they worked through two problems to make sure the basic mechanics were understood.

Results[2]

During the first sessions especially, but also during succeeding sessions, there was a gradual, yet steady, acceleration in solution rates. Eventually, all groups reached a steady state. An example can be seen in Figures 1 and 2. By hour 6 this group had reached a steady state. It took the five groups in this experiment, on the average, some 500 problems to reach a steady state. Consequently, one must question the generalizability of the findings from previous investigations, particularly since the maximum number of required solutions before this was 60. If it took this long to reach a steady state with the "simple" problems, the findings from studies incorporating "complex" problems should be especially questionable. One would expect the attainment of a steady state in those circumstances to be attenuated drastically. These results strongly suggest that in order to compare properly the effects of communication structures, a group should have enough experience as an operating group to reach a steady state.

Observation of the five groups in this experiment

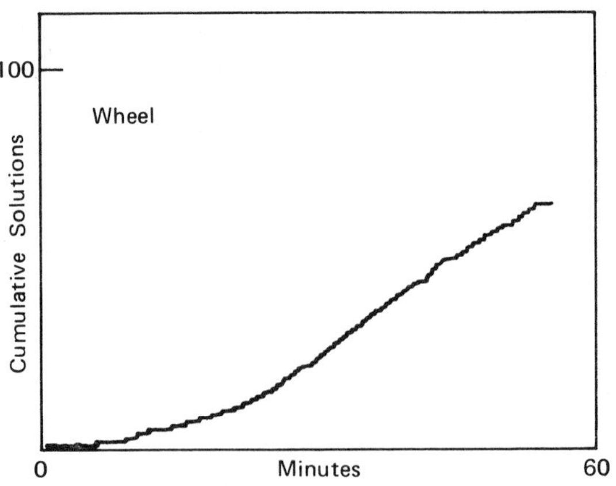

Figure 1 *Cumulative record of Hour 1 for a group under the Wheel network. Note the positively accelerating slope.*

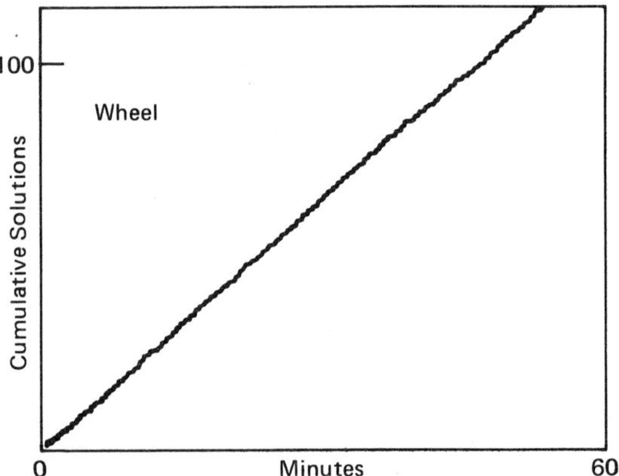

Figure 2 *Cumulative record of Hour 6 for the group seen in Figure 1. It can easily be seen that the group no longer is exhibiting the erratic, relatively slow, and accelerating solution rate. The group has reached a "steady state."*

revealed wide differences in motivation. One group, for example, was very concerned with working as quickly as possible, even though the experimenter's instructions were only to "work at your own speed." But by being so concerned with speed, this group was making a remarkable number of errors. In contrast to this group, another was concerned not with speed but with minimizing errors. As a consequence this group worked at a steady but slow rate. Still another group was concerned with maximizing speed as well as minimizing errors. It became quite apparent that, despite random assignment, this motivational factor would confound the evaluation of the effects of the communication-network variable.

In an attempt to reduce this variability, control by constancy was employed. The error-rate dimension was tackled first. Now whenever an error occurred,

[2] For a more detailed presentation of the data from this study see Burgess (1968).

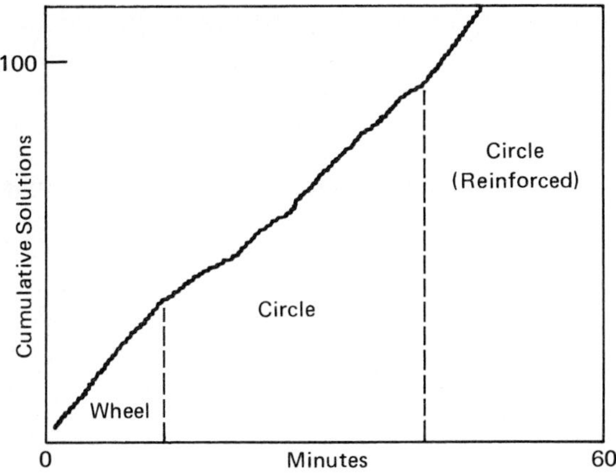

Figure 3 *The behavior of a group under three experimental conditions: the Wheel net, the Circle net, and the Circle net with reinforcement. The pattern is typical. Upon having the network changed to a Circle pattern, there is a noticeable deterioration in the group's performance. After reinforcement is introduced, the behavior becomes much less erratic and the solution rate increases, even surpassing the rate under the Wheel network.*

a raucous buzzer would sound for 15 seconds and the subjects' panels would be shut off for the same period of time. Upon the onset of the buzzer and the "time-out" period, there was an immediate decline in the solution rate as well as in the error rate. But, whereas the error rate remained at a low level, the solution rate recovered. The other major effect of this manipulation was that the error rates declined to a level which mitigated against their previous contaminating effects. The error rates for the five groups also became much more comparable. For Groups 1 through 5 the number of errors per hundred problems was, before the manipulation, 24, 40, 11, 15, and 30, respectively. After the change the rates were 2.2, 4.3, 2.3, 3.0, and 3.2 errors per hundred problems.

The other aspect of behavioral consequences involves positive reinforcement or incentives, contingent upon solution performance. In this case, the experimental situation was altered so that the groups could reduce their time in the experiment by working quickly. This turned out to be a substantial incentive, as can be seen in Figure 3. Looking at this figure we see a very typical pattern. At the beginning of this session the group was operating under the Wheel network. During this period they were working at a relatively high and steady rate, 2.7 solutions per minute. But, upon having the net changed to the Circle, there was an immediate deterioration in performance, both in terms of solution rate, now 1.9 per minute, as well as in overall consistency in performance. But note the effects of the onset of the reinforcement contingency: there was an immediate increase in the solution rate to 3.1 per minute, and an elimination of the variability in the group's behavior. This pattern was observed in each of the five groups; only before the introduction of the reinforcement variable was the solution rate lower and more erratic under the Circle net.

Two major findings have emerged so far from Experiment I. First, as with individual learning, groups exhibit an initial transition period during which their response rates steadily increase until a steady state is reached. Second, the introduction of reinforcement and punishment consequences, contingent upon group behavior, alters the behavior in the predicted directions.

But what are the effects of the two networks upon a group's solution rate? Here we find that without reinforcement in effect, the Wheel is significantly faster than the Circle initially. But, once a steady state has been reached *and* contingencies of reinforcement are in operation, there are no significant differences between the two networks with regard to the variable, solution rate. Indeed, under these conditions the solution rates are, for most purposes, identical. An example can be seen in Figure 4.

This experiment, however, leaves certain issues unresolved. For while there may be no *ultimate* differences in solution rates for the two networks, there do appear to be some *initial* differences between the networks. The communication structure may affect the behavior of groups indirectly, by either handicapping or facilitating the group members in their attempts to organize themselves for efficient task per-

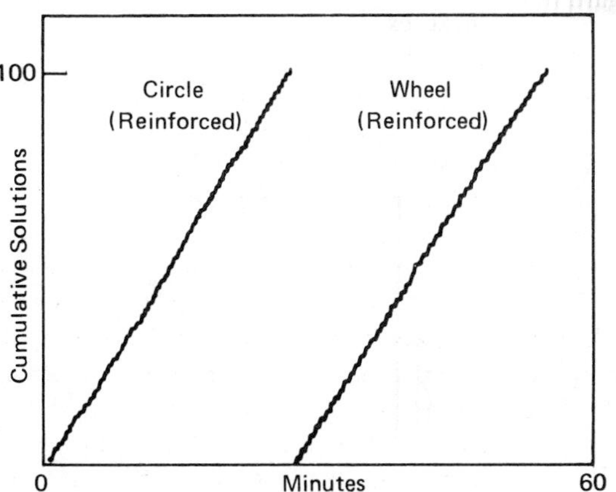

Figure 4 *The last two sessions of a group. These cumulative records highlight one important finding in this study; that is, once groups have reached a steady state, and there are events contingent upon their behavior, there are no differences in solution rates for the two networks under investigation.*

formance. There may be, for example, a difference in the networks with regard to the time it takes to reach a steady state.

In this connection, certain structural characteristics stand out. For instance, the Wheel net is structured in such a way that all "unnecessary" channels are blocked. The very structure itself largely determines who the group leader will be. Furthermore, the other members of the group cannot communicate directly with anyone but the person in the centralized position. Thus, it is not surprising that the behavior of the group members operating under such a structure is devoted entirely to the problem-solving task. That the solution rate under the Wheel net is relatively stable was seen in both Figures 2 and 3. The Circle net, at least before contingent reinforcement is introduced, produces a very different pattern, as also was seen in Figure 3. This particular communication structure, besides requiring a relay system of some sort, is of such a nature that it permits the group members to communicate directly and at will with their respective "neighbors." Such a structure increases the possibility of nontask-related behavior. And in the absence of behavioral consequences, this is precisely what happens.

The major problem yet to be answered is whether there are differences between the two networks in the transitional stages leading to the steady states. To answer this question would require one to look in detail at the developmental behavior of such task groups. The next experiment was designed in an attempt to answer this question, as well as to provide a replication of the results of the first experiment with regard to the failure to find any difference in the solution rates during the steady-state periods for the two networks.

Experiment II

Method. For this experiment 40 additional subjects were recruited and divided into ten groups. After random assignment, half of the groups began under the Circle net and were kept there until they reached a steady state. Once they had attained a steady state, the network was changed to a Wheel. And after they had solved at least 100 problems at a steady rate, the network was changed back to a Circle. For the other five groups this procedure was reversed to a Wheel-Circle-Wheel pattern. From the very beginning, contingencies were in operation in this experiment. Though the subjects volunteered for ten 1-hour sessions, they were instructed at the beginning of the experiment that they could reduce this time by working quickly. A session would be terminated upon the completion of 100 problems. In actuality, it took a few of the groups slightly longer than 1 hour to complete 100 problems at first; but with practice they were able to solve the required number of problems in less than half an hour. They were, in effect, getting back almost 5 of the 10 hours for which they had volunteered.

Results

The entire experimental history of a group under these conditions can be seen in Figure 5. Here we see under the Circle net a transitional stage of almost 500 problems leading to a steady-state period. Then, upon having the network changed to a Wheel, there is a decrease in the solution rate. But after this tran-

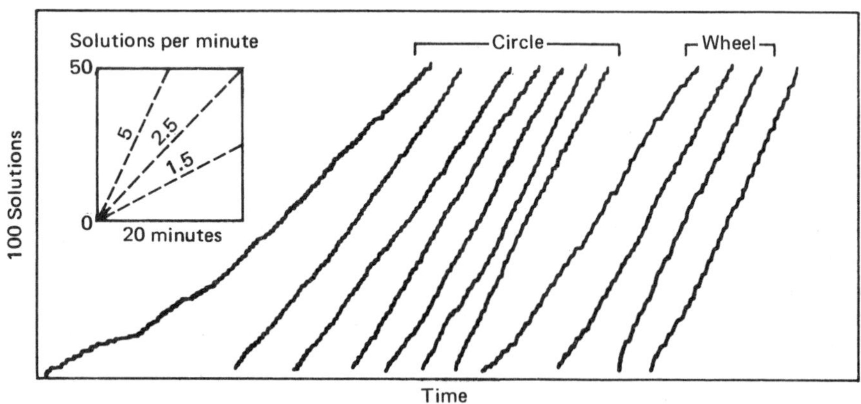

Figure 5 *The entire experimental history of a group under both networks. They reached a steady state under the Circle network during the sixth and seventh sessions. At that point, the network was changed to a Wheel. Note the decline in their solution rates and their subsequent recovery during the next two sessions. The rates under the two networks during the steady-state periods were essentially identical.*

sition period a steady state again is reached. The network was then changed back to the Circle. As in the previous experiment, the rates for the two nets during the steady-state periods are for all purposes identical. This was true for each of the ten groups investigated.

Theoretically, Wheel and Circle groups can be equally efficient. That is, there are no *physical* limitations favoring one net over another. If there were, any observed *behavioral* differences would result from this experimental artifact and, hence, would be social-psychologically uninteresting. As it stands, if the groups were to perform optimally, they could solve problems using a minimum of only six message units under both networks. One way to compare the networks is, then, to measure how long it takes the groups to reach an optimally efficient organization. And here we find that all of the groups that began under the Wheel net immediately used only the minimum number of message units. In contrast, none of the Circle groups developed such an organization at the very beginning. Indeed, one group never did reach this level of efficiency. Four of the five groups that began operation under the Circle net required, on the average, 40 problems to reach an optimum message-unit system. Consequently, one possibly important and significant difference between the networks during the transitional period is the amount of experience it takes to attain an optimally efficient organization. It should be remembered, however, that each of these four groups eventually attained an optimum organization.

The fifth group is an interesting case in itself. Throughout the entire experiment, it employed an each-to-each communication pattern while operating under the Circle net. What evolved within this group is essentially a three-step flow of information *for each member*. In other words, the members of this group developed a very complex relay system. This group took much longer to reach a steady state than any other group. But once the group did reach a steady state it performed as well as it did under the Wheel net. If this experiment had not been designed to allow groups to reach steady states, we never would have been able to determine that this particular difference between the networks is only temporary in nature.

Though the groups that began under the Wheel network were from the very beginning using only the minimum number of message units, it still took them on the average over 200 problems to reach a steady state. In contrast, it took groups under the Circle net a little over 300 problems to reach a steady state. Something more than simply minimizing redundant messages is involved here. In actuality, the solution of this group tasks involves a wide range of component behaviors. The group members, for example, must *learn* how to manipulate the experimental apparatus properly and efficiently; how to organize and collate the incoming information; and how to transfer messages efficiently to the position or positions with whom they are linked. In short, there is not just one behavior here. Rather, there are a number of relatively complex interconnected behaviors; and these behaviors must be learned. This is one reason why the contingent-reinforcement variable is so important. These behaviors, in other words, are subject to the principles of learning, and the experimenter can ignore such principles only at the expense of inconclusive, artificial, and inaccurate results.

One final point should be made: Steady states and optimum organizations may vary independently of one another. For example, a group may reach a steady state that fails to employ an optimum organization, as we found to be the case with one group. Likewise, a group can attain an optimum organization before reaching a steady state, as was the case for a time with nine groups.

Conclusion

Four-member groups under two rather extreme networks were studied. One network, the Wheel, is a net in which the communication restrictions reduce the difficulty of organizational problems to a minimum. The other net, the Circle, makes imperative some sort of relay system within the group.

In Experiment I, it was determined that group problem-solving behavior within such communication networks exhibits a substantial transition period evidenced by an acceleration in the solution rate leading to a steady state. It also was determined that contingencies of reinforcement substantially increase the solution rate for such groups. The reinforcement variable was introduced by altering the experimental situation so that groups could reduce their time in the experiment by working quickly. It was also found that punishment for errors effectively reduced the error rate and eliminated a large portion of the intergroup variability along this dimension. Finally, it was discovered that only without contingencies of reinforcement in effect does the Wheel network produce a significantly higher solution rate than the Circle. But, groups in natural settings invariably will have some form of reinforcement system in operation. Any experiment not incorporating this variable would be needlessly artificial.

Experiment II was designed to explore systematically the transition periods leading to the steady states. The two networks were found to differ during these transition periods. For example, the Wheel initially performed at a slightly higher rate than the

Circle net; the Circle net generally required more problems to reach a steady state than the Wheel; and it took the Circle longer than the Wheel to reach an optimum organization.

Looking at the entire experimental history of these task-groups, there was an orderly progression toward smaller differences between the networks. The differences between the nets are greatest during the acquisition period without reinforcement in effect; less with reinforcement in effect; still less during the nonreinforced steady-state period; and, finally, during the steady-state periods, with reinforcement in effect, there are no differences between the networks.

On the methodological side, these findings argue for the design of social-psychological experiments to permit the observation and analysis of the entire developmental histories of groups from their transition periods to their steady-state periods. The findings also suggest that one important variable which must be included in order to explore properly the effects of various communication networks, and possibly social structures in general, is motivation. This can be appreciated especially in light of the fact that the introduction of reinforcement eliminated previous differences in solution rates between the networks.

One conclusion which is suggested by these data is that previously asserted "differences" in solution rates between communication structures, in which there were no physical limitations favoring one network over the other, were a function of experimental artifacts. Had previous experimenters included reinforcement contingent upon performance, and had they observed their experimental groups over sufficient time periods, the collection of a vast array of contradictory findings could have been avoided. It remains to be seen whether presumed differences in member satisfaction under such networks also are temporary phenomena.

References

BAVELAS, A. Communication patterns in task-oriented groups. *Journal of the Acoustical Society of America*, 1950, *22*, 725–730. Reprinted in D. Cartwright and A. F. Zander (Eds.), *Group dynamics: Research and theory* (2nd ed.). New York: Row, Peterson, 1960. Pp. 660–683.

BURGESS, R. L. Communication networks and behavioral consequences. *Human Relations* (1968) in press.

COHEN, A. M., BENNIS, W. G., and WOLKON, G. H. The effects of continued practice on the behaviors of problem-solving groups. *Sociometry*, 1961, *24*, 416–432.

COHEN, A. M., BENNIS, W. G., and WOLKON, G. H. Changing small-group communication networks. *Administrative Science Quarterly*, 1962, *6*, 443–462.

GUETZKOW, H., and DILL, W. R. Factors in the organizational development of task-oriented groups. *Sociometry*, 1957, *20*, 175–204.

GUETZKOW, H., and SIMON, H. A. The impact of certain communication nets upon organization and performance in task-oriented groups. *Management Science*, 1955, *1*, 233–250. Reprinted in A. H. Rubenstein and C. J. Haberstroh, *Some theories of organization*. Homewood, Ill.: Richard D. Irwin, and The Dorsey Press, 1960. Pp. 259–277.

HEISE, G., and MILLER, G. Problem solving by small groups using various communication nets. In A. P. Hare, E. F. Borgatta, and R. F. Bales (Eds.), *Small groups: Studies in social interaction*. New York: Alfred A. Knopf, 1955. Pp. 353–367.

HIROTA, K. *Japan Journal of Psychology*, 1953, *24*, 105–113.

LAWSON, E. D. Reinforced and non-reinforced four-man communication nets. *Psychological Reports*, 1964, *14*, 287–296. (a)

LAWSON, E. D. Reinforcement in group problem-solving with arithmetic problems. *Psychological Reports*, 1964, *14*, 703–710. (b)

LEAVITT, H. Some effects of certain communication patterns in group performance. In E. E. Maccoby, T. M. Newcomb, and E. L. Hartley (Eds.), *Readings in social psychology* (3rd ed.). New York: Holt, 1958. Pp. 546–564.

MOHANNA, A. I., and ARGYLE, M. A cross-cultural study of structured groups with unpopular central members. *Journal of Abnormal and Social Psychology*, 1960, *60*, 139–140.

MULDER, M. Group-structure and performance. *Acta Psychologica*, 1959, *16*, 356–402.

MULDER, M. Communication structure, decision structure and group performance. *Sociometry*, 1960, *23*, 1–14.

SHAW, M. E. Group structure and the behavior of individuals in small groups. *Journal of Psychology*, 1954, *38*, 139–149. (a)

SHAW, M. E. Some effects of problem complexity upon problem solution efficiency in different communication nets. *Journal of Experimental Psychology*, 1954, *48*, 211–217. (b)

SHAW, M. E. Random versus systematic distribution of information in communication nets. *Journal of Personality*, 1956, *25*, 56–69.

SHAW, M. E. Some effects of irrelevant information upon problem-solving by small groups. *Journal of Social Psychology*, 1958, *47*, 33–37.

SHAW, M. E., and ROTHSCHILD, G. H. Some effects of prolonged experience in communication nets. *Journal of Applied Psychology*, 1956, *40*, 281–286.

SHAW, M. E., ROTHSCHILD, G. H., and STRICKLAND, J. F. Decision processes in communication nets. *Journal of Abnormal and Social Psychology*, 1957, *54*, 323–330.

SIDMAN, M. *Tactics of scientific research: Evaluating experimental data in psychology*. New York: Basic Books, 1960.

STAATS, A. W., and STAATS, C. K. *Complex human behavior: A systematic extension of learning principles*. New York: Holt, 1964.

SWANSON, G. E. On explanations of social interaction. *Sociometry*, 1965, 28, 101–123.

B

Verbal and Nonverbal Reinforcement

Oakes reports a series of experiments which come even closer to "real life" situations than those just considered. Subjects engaging in free discussion were either reinforced or punished for emitting certain classes of verbal responses. In one situation, for example, some subjects were told that a signal light would flash each time they made a remark that demonstrated "psychological insight." Others were advised that a light would flash whenever they said something that showed "lack of psychological insight. Actually, the lights were flashed for the two groups of subjects whenever they offered an opinion, regardless of whether it revealed insight. As predicted, the response rate of the rewarded subjects increased, whereas that of the punished subjects declined.

Using this general technique, Oakes has also managed to shape the discussion behavior of experimental subjects so that they will emit certain kinds of statements with greater than chance expectancy. And by attributing the reinforcing signal to various reference groups (i.e., experts versus novices), he has been able to vary its effectiveness. This clearly written article describes how the content of an individual's contribution to a group discussion may be manipulated by making specific stimulus events contingent upon his utterances.

53 | *Reinforcement Effects in Group Discussion*

WILLIAM F. OAKES

The research to be discussed in this paper concerns the effect of reinforcers on the behavior of participants in group discussion. The term *reinforcer* as used here refers to stimuli that increase the probability that one of a particular class of responses will be made by a subject. Stimuli which increase this probability when they are *presented* closely following the occurrence of a member of the response class are called *positive reinforcers,* and stimuli which increase this probability when they are *removed* or terminated closely following the occurrence of a member of the response class are called *negative reinforcers.* This increase in response probability as a function of the presentation of positive reinforcers or the removal of negative reinforcers is what is referred to as *operant conditioning.* Thus the present research involves the operant conditioning of verbal and other behavior in a group discussion situation.

There have been a great many studies of verbal operant conditioning since Greenspoon's (1955) original one in 1950, but most of those studies have involved at most the interaction of a single subject with an experimenter, and have usually been conducted under highly artificial conditions. In the Greenspoon technique, for example, the subject is brought into a room and told to "say words," with the experimenter murmuring "mm-hmm" unobtrusively when the subject emits a member of the response class preselected for reinforcement, e.g., "animal" words, or adverbs. The reinforcement effect is then an increase in the frequency with which the subject emits "animal" words, or adverbs.

The verbal operant conditioning procedure of Taffel (1955) has most frequently been used. The subject is brought into a room, presented with a series of cards on which he finds four or six pronouns

From *Readings in General Psychology,* edited by W. Edgar Vinacke. Copyright © 1968 by Litton Educational Publishing, Inc., reprinted by permission of Van Nostrand Reinhold Company. Figures 1 and 2 used by permission of *Psychological Reports.* [Portions of this selection have been omitted or changed slightly from the original, with the permission of the author and the publisher.]

and a verb, and is instructed to construct a sentence upon presentation of each card, beginning with one of the pronouns and using the verb. The experimenter again murmurs "good" when the subject uses the preselected pronoun, and the reinforcement effect is seen in the subject's increased usage of the pronoun or pronouns reinforced.

As indicated above, these situations are highly artificial and quite unlike situations that the subject is likely to encounter in the course of his everyday activities. This, of course, does not make them any less valuable as objects of scientific inquiry, but it does limit the direct generalizability of the results to everyday situations. As far as the conditioning paradigm is concerned, the Taffel procedure, and most verbal operant conditioning studies, have employed what is called the "instrumental conditioning paradigm," i.e., involving discrete trials. Relatively few studies have utilized what is called the free operant conditioning paradigm (or, sometimes, the operant conditioning paradigm), in which the subject responds freely, "at will" as it were, and the experimenter chooses a class of responses from this ongoing stream of behavior for reinforcement. This latter procedure, in which the subject verbalizes freely, with the experimenter reinforcing members of preselected response classes, is adopted in the present research. Thus in these studies the subjects meet in groups and engage in group discussion, and the experimenter selectively reinforces certain responses during the discussion, in order to observe the effect of the reinforcement on the verbal and other behavior of the subjects.

Various reinforcers have been used in verbal operant conditioning studies. Greenspoon and Taffel chose as a reinforcer verbalization by the experimenter, such as murmuring "mm-hmm" or "good." This kind of stimulus qualifies as a *generalized reinforcer*, i.e., one which in the past history of the subject has accompanied a great many different primary reinforcers under a wide variety of conditions, and thus has become relatively independent of the present state of deprivation or satiation of the organism, or of any special environmental conditions. Verbal operant conditioning studies have almost exclusively employed such generalized social reinforcers—typically various sorts of indications of approval. Relatively little has been done with negative reinforcers, i.e., stimuli whose removal strengthens the response that precedes their removal. The presentation of such a negative reinforcer is called *punishment*. The present series of studies investigates the effect of the presentation of both positive and negative reinforcers —that is, rewards and punishments.

Effects on Participation

The first study in the series (Oakes, Droge, and August, 1960) dealt with the effect of reinforcement on the amount of participation by individuals in group discussion. More specifically, the investigators determined the effect of the presentation of presumed positive and negative reinforcers on rate of verbalization in a situation of the free operant type.

Four-person groups were established, with the subjects seated around a table in a small semi-soundproof room, in which was located only a table, four chairs, and the equipment used in the experiment. There was a one-way vision window between the subjects' room and the experimenters' room next door. The experimenters could see the subjects, but they could not see the experimenters. Cardboard screens 24 inches high were set up on the table, so that the subjects could not see each other during the experiment. These screens were not used in some of the later experiments, but they were introduced in the early studies to eliminate the interfering reinforcing effects on the speaker of inadvertent and unwitting head nodding, eyebrow lifting, smiling, etc., by other group members. Thus in this first study the subjects sat around the same table and talked, but they could not see each other.

On the table before each subject, and hidden by the screens from each of the other subjects, was a hooded panel containing a signal light, which could only be seen by the individual subject. Each of the four hooded panels was painted a different color. The signal lights were all controlled from the experimenters' room. There was a microphone in a connection box in the center of the subjects' table, and the experimenters could monitor the discussion as it was being recorded on tape. The tape also contained a record of each time the experimenter flashed the signal light for one of the subjects.

When a group of subjects arrived, they were met in a waiting room by the experimenter and escorted to the subjects' room. There they were seated around the table and given some instructions to read. Actually, the subjects had to *read* the instructions because different instructions were given to the subjects within the same group. The instructions stated that the group was participating in a study to assess the degree of "psychological insight" of psychology students.

In each group two subjects were rewarded and two were punished by means of the signal lights. Those who were to be positively reinforced were told that they were going to discuss a case history taken from the files of a team of professional psychologists and psychiatrists. They were to discuss the causes of the patient's problem, the development of the problem, and suggestions as to what might be done with the patient. They were told that the experimenter was a professional psychologist who would monitor the discussion from another room, and that he would flash a subject's signal light each time he made a statement that showed "psychological insight" into the patient's problem. It was explained that the statements would be judged on the basis of "the insights into the case discovered by the professional team that originally worked with the patient." The subjects were volunteers from psychology classes.

The punished subjects were told essentially the same thing, except that the experimenter would flash a subject's signal light whenever he made a statement that showed a "lack of psychological insight" into the patient's problem.

After reading the instructions, the subjects read the case history, which was a rather ambiguously described case about a girl with an Oedipus problem. They then began their discussion, which lasted thirty minutes. Every time any one of them stated an opinion about any aspect of the case his light was flashed, regardless of whether or not he made an insightful statement. For two of the subjects in each group the light flash indicated that the statements they had just made indicated insight. For the other two subjects in each group the light indicated that their statements lacked insight.

In this experiment we have a group discussion situation in which subjects verbalize freely. Since they are students in psychology classes we would expect them to be motivated to demonstrate their understanding of the dynamics of behavior, as discussed in their psychology classes. The experimenter then proceeds to present signals whose meaning has been established through instructions as relevant to the motivation of the subjects. It would be expected that such signals would function as reinforcers, appropriate for influencing the verbal output of the subjects.

As a measure of verbal output, the experimenters counted the number of words spoken by each subject in each successive ten-minute period of the discussion. They then compared this measure for the subjects receiving positive light flashes and those receiving the negative ones. Figure 1 presents this comparison.

It can be seen that there was a strong differential effect of the direction of reinforcement during the first ten-minute period, and that the effect increased throughout the thirty-minute discussion.

The reversal of the operant conditioning process is called extinction, a return of the preconditioning level resulting from the nonreinforced occurrence of the response. In the present experiment, then, a reversal of the reinforcement effect would be expected, if the situation for the subjects whose verbalization had been influenced by the signal lights remained the same but the experimenter did not flash the lights.

In order to investigate this extinction effect, the same groups of subjects were brought back and run

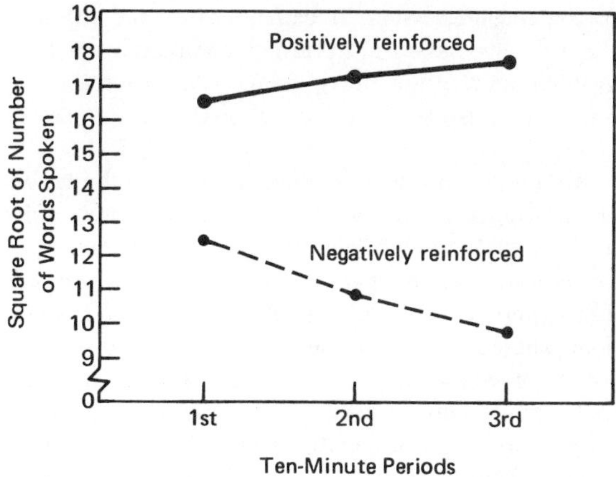

Figure 1 *Effects of positive and negative reinforcement on number of words spoken in group discussion. (Adapted from Oakes, Droge, and August, 1960.)*

through the procedure a week later. This time they were seated in the same positions as before, given the same instructions they had received before, but were presented with a different case history. The procedure was exactly the same as in the first session, except that the light was never flashed for any subject. Here the positive subjects are told that their lights will flash when they show insight, but the lights never flash. The negative subjects are told that their lights will flash when they exhibit a lack of insight, but their lights never flash. The absence of the light flash should result in a reversal, with the subjects originally reinforced positively talking less and less, and those who originally received the negative lights talking more and more.

Figure 2 shows the amount of verbalization of the positive and negative subjects in the last ten minutes of the first session and the last ten minutes

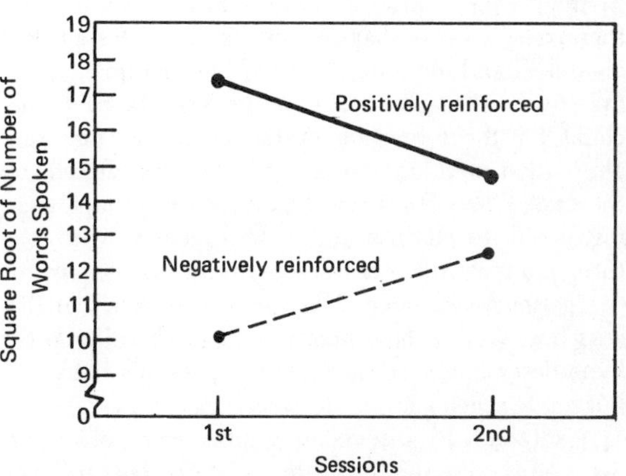

Figure 2 *Extinction of verbal output during group discussion in a session one week after the reinforcement session. (Adapted from Oakes, Droge, and August, 1960.)*

of the second session. It can be seen that although the subjects have not returned completely to their original level after thirty minutes of nonreinforcement, there is clearly a reversal of the reinforcement effect.

Although considerable intersubject variability occurred, nevertheless in this first study it was quite obvious that the light signifying insight or lack of it had a powerful effect on the subjects' verbalizations. The experimenters could see it during the discussion. Some subjects who were positively reinforced reached the point where they seemed to be saying anything that came to mind just to keep talking, while most subjects getting the negative lights exhibited a great deal of hesitancy in their speech and were quite bothered by the light. One person, for example, received a negative light flash, stopped in the middle of a sentence, and remained silent for the next twenty minutes while his face turned red and he fidgeted. These were psychology students who were strongly motivated to show "psychological insight," and the signal indicating insight or lack of it had a very potent influence on their behavior.

Effects on Conclusions Reached

The above study demonstrated the effect of the reinforcers on amount of participation of subjects in group discussion. The response class reinforced included all case-relevant verbalizations by the subjects. In the next experiment (Oakes, Droge, and August, 1961) a more limited class of verbal responses was selected for reinforcement, to see if the conclusions reached in group discussion could be influenced and controlled through the presentation of reinforcers.

The subjects in the discussion groups in this study were given a problem situation, presented in a case history. The case involved a female client who came to the therapist after having been to several other therapists with unhappy results. She forgot her cigarettes and requested them of the therapist on her first two visits. Three alternative hypotheses to account for the forgetting of the cigarettes provided alternative solutions to the problem presented by the case. The subjects in the discussion groups were instructed to discuss the case together with the three alternative hypotheses advanced to account for the patient's behavior. They were instructed to discuss how well or how poorly each of the alternative hypotheses might account for the patient's behavior, but not to reach a group decision.

A total of 18 discussion groups were observed. Six groups were reinforced for all statements in favor of each of the three hypotheses. Thus, in each group the subjects were reinforced, with a light flash indi-

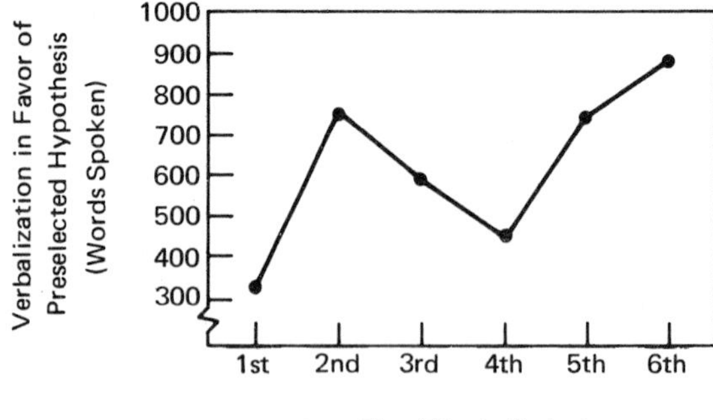

Figure 3 *Effect of reinforcement for statements pertinent to preselected hypotheses.*

cating "psychological insight," for all favorable comments about one of the three hypotheses —that is, all suggestions as to why that particular hypothesis might account for the patient's behavior or why they might not be as good as the other hypothesis. In other words, for each group the experiments had predetermined the hypothesis that was to be favored by the group. Then they set about reinforcing every statement that they thought would bring the subjects to decide that it was the best hypothesis, to see if the light flash reinforcer would be effective in that way.

At the close of the thirty-minute discussion each subject individually was asked to make a check mark on his instruction sheet beside the hypothesis he thought best accounted for the patient's behavior. This choice was thus made individually and privately, not as a group. The subjects' choices significantly departed from chance ($p < .001$) in the reinforced direction. The influence of the reinforcement during the discussions was shown by taking the statements during the discussion in favor of the preselected hypothesis as a proportion of all statements made. This measure showed a significant increase, then decrease, then increase during the thirty-minute session over all groups. It is presented in Figure 3.

The experimenters could see these changes occurring as the groups were run. The subjects seemed to begin by exploring all three hypotheses and then would shortly begin to favor the reinforced hypothesis. Then they would remember that they were to discuss all three. And then after the nonreinforced alternatives had been well explored they would come to dwell more and more on the preselected one.

The results of this study thus indicated that the subjects tended to make more statements in favor of the hypothesis that had been preselected for reinforcement, and they also significantly tended to choose that one as the best alternative. In short, the experimenters were able to influence the subjects' choice by the reinforcement technique.

Effects of Different Meanings of the Light

In the next study (Oakes, 1962b) the effectiveness of signal lights with various meanings was investigated. In this experiment some subjects were told that their lights would flash when their statements indicated "insight" or "lack of insight" based on the analysis of the case by some reference group. Other subjects were told that their lights would flash for statements that "agreed" or "disagreed" with statements about the case made by the reference group. The experiment also compared three presumed "sources" of the reinforcement—that is, presumed reference groups. For some subjects the "agreement" or "disagreement" or "insight" or "lack of insight" was based on the analysis of the case made by "the original panel of experts that handled the case." For others the insight (or agreement) or lack of it was based on "statements by a group of students like yourselves" who had discussed the case, and for other subjects it was based on "statements made by a group of laymen with no psychological training" who had discussed the case. Apart from the comparison of the various meanings of the light flash, the procedure for the present study was the same as for the first study of reinforcement effects on individual participation.

The results indicated the greatest reinforcement effect for insight or lack of it where the source was a team of experts. In general, "insight" reinforced better than "agreement," and the greater the prestige of the presumed source the greater the reinforcing effect. The group of laymen had the least influence for these psychology students.

Effects on Different Response Classes

The fourth study in the series (Oakes, 1962a) was an attempt to compare the conditionability of a variety of classes of responses in group discussion. Bales (1950) has developed a system of categories into which the responses occurring in group interaction or discussion may be sorted. The Bales system consists of twelve categories of response, including responses that show solidarity, show tension release, agree, give suggestions, give opinions, give orientation, ask for orientation, ask for opinions, ask for suggestions, disagree, show tension, and show antagonism.

For each of the twenty-four discussion groups in the study the experimenters reinforced, with a light flash for the speaker indicating "insight," each instance of a response falling into the category preselected for that group. There were thus two groups reinforced for each of the twelve categories of response. The experimenter's task was to listen to the discussion and detect each instance of the occurrence of a response falling into the particular category that had been assigned to that group for reinforcement. Accordingly, he flashed the lights for that speaker.

Working from the tape recordings of the discussion, the experimenters then classified each statement into one of the twelve Bales categories or a thirteenth category, unclassifiable. To control for possible unwitting experimenter bias, the experimenter classifying the statements did not know which category had been reinforced for any particular group.

Analysis of the results indicated that only one category, *gives opinion,* exhibited an effect of the reinforcement. Of course it is not possible to conclude on the basis of this evidence that the other categories are not conditionable. Theoretically, it should be possible to condition any class of response, the members of which have some behavioral disposition in common. But the results of this study do suggest that with groups engaged in this kind of discussion, with an "insight" reinforcer, the *gives opinion* category is the easiest of the Bales categories to condition.

References

Bales, R. F. *Interaction process analysis: A method for the study of small groups.* Reading, Mass.: Addison-Wesley, 1950.

Greenspoon, J. The reinforcing effect of two spoken sounds on the frequency of two responses. *American Journal of Psychology,* 1955, *68,* 409–410.

Oakes, W. F. Effectiveness of signal light reinforcers given various meanings on participation in group discussion. *Psychological Reports,* 1962, *11,* 469–470. (a)

Oakes, W. F. Reinforcement of Bales' categories in group discussion. *Psychological Reports,* 1962, *11,* 427–435. (b)

Oakes, W. F., Droge, A. E., and August, B. Reinforcement effects on participation in group discussion. *Psychological Reports,* 1960, *7,* 503–514.

Oakes, W. F., Droge, A. E., and August, B. Reinforcement effects on conclusions reached in group discussion. *Psychological Reports,* 1961, *9,* 27–34.

Taffel, C. Anxiety and the conditioning of verbal behavior. *Journal of Abnormal and Social Psychology,* 1955, *51,* 496–501.

The final article in this chapter, that by *Rosenfeld,* deals with an aspect of social reinforcement that has been largely neglected until recently, namely, nonverbal behavior. Perhaps because they are difficult to measure and to quantify, gestures and other expressive movements are often ignored in research on verbal conditioning. Some nonverbal reactions, however, are relatively easy to observe and to record. These include smiles, head nodding, and broad hand movements. Two adults interviewed junior high school students on matters of general interest and, while doing so, employed four classes of nonverbal reactions: approving, disapproving, mixed, and noncommittal.

Rosenfeld reports that the student interviewees smiled and nodded much more frequently when the interviewer emitted these behaviors than when he was nonresponsive, disapproving, or mixed in his reactions. In fact, negative gestures from the interviewers depressed the frequency of smiling and nodding by the students and at the same time increased the frequency of such indicators of anxiety as nervous self manipulation, i.e., scratching, tugging the ear, and so forth. When the content of a verbal interaction provides insufficient cues for either party to determine the other's approval or disapproval, nonverbal performances apparently may supply discriminative stimuli for reactions in kind. That is, individuals normally engage in a process of reciprocal nonverbal reinforcement; when one smiles, the other smiles, when one nods, the other tends to nod also. Initiation of these gestures by one participant may not be reciprocated, however, in which case, as this experiment shows, they undergo extinction. They may even be replaced by gestures indicative of anxiety.

Perhaps the greatest significance of nonverbal cues in communication is that they may prompt changes in the participants' verbal repertoires. Approving gestures by a listener probably increase the frequency of those classes of verbal operants that have prompted them. Disapproving gestures, on the other hand, may prompt the speaker to modify either the manner or the content of his remarks. If he is uncertain about whether to proceed verbally in a particular fashion, he may use nonverbal probes to determine the reactions of the listener. Verbal and nonverbal performances in a discussion are thus interrelated in a complex but meaningful fashion.

54 *Nonverbal Reciprocation of Approval: An Experimental Analysis*[1]

HOWARD M. ROSENFELD

Several classes of verbal and nonverbal response have been employed effectively as social reinforcers in experiments on verbal conditioning (Krasner, 1958). Recent research on three such categories—smiles, positive head nods, and brief verbal recognitions such as "mm-hmm"—has indicated that they play similar roles in free social interaction (Rosenfeld, 1966; in press). These responses were more often emitted by subjects motivated to seek approval from peers than by control groups; and the responses tended to bring about approving reactions from the peers to whom they were directed. A less expected finding was that when pairs of unacquainted peers

[1] The research reported herein was supported by Public Health Service Program Grant HD 00870, and conducted through facilities of the Bureau of Child Research. The author wishes to acknowledge the assistance of Pam Gunnell, Duane Smith, Richard Vogle, Edith Anderson, and Colleen Burch. Part of the study was reported at the 1966 annual convention of the Midwestern Psychological Association, Chicago, Illinois, May, 1966.

From the *Journal of Experimental Social Psychology,* 1967, *3,* 102–111.
Reprinted by permission of Academic Press.

were observed in free interaction, the rates of performance of the nonverbal approval-related responses by the two members of dyads were significantly intercorrelated. Smiles occurred at highly similar levels within the dyad during initial acquaintance periods and maintained this high similarity over repeated encounters. Positive head nods gradually increased in their intra-dyadic similarity with repeated encounters. Gesticulations of the hand, interpreted as an indicator of intensity of motivation, also showed evidence of intra-pair similarity.

Given such findings, it is tempting to speculate that approving responses are normatively reciprocated in our society, and that this process provides interpersonal feedback which may play a significant role in the maintenance of free interaction. However, several alternative explanations of the evidence obtained so far are plausible. For example, rather than directly reciprocating smiles or nods, two persons may express them simultaneously in response to the content of a verbal statement. Or similarity between persons on a given response dimension could be confounded with similarity in total output of responses. Thus, the current study was designed to rule out these alternatives and to determine if reciprocation of the approval-related responses could be demonstrated.[2]

To vary rates of presentation of the approval-related responses by a stimulus person, while controlling the rate and content of his other responses, an interview procedure was constructed. For efficiency, the three approval-related responses and gesticulations were varied simultaneously. It was predicted that these responses would be expressed more often by subjects whose interviewers regularly emitted such responses than by subjects whose interviewers either withheld such responses or who displayed disapproving responses instead.

Two other classes of behavior of the subjects were of particular interest in the present study—self-manipulatory responses and verbal disfluencies. These two response classes, which have been interpreted as indicators of anxiety (Boomer and Goodrich, 1963; Kasl and Mahl, 1965), were expected to be less common in subjects interviewed by an approving interviewer than in any other condition.

Method

Subjects. Subjects were 48 students, ranging in age from 14 to 16 years, selected to fall within one standard deviation of the mean I.Q. score of their ninth-grade class. The sample consisted of an equal number of males and females.

Experimental Procedures. The interviewer presented questions from a standard list to the subject over a 5-minute period. The interview consisted in brief inquiries, and follow-up probes, into events relevant to the daily lives of the subjects. The standard items included requests for descriptions and evaluations of classes the subjects were taking in school and their after-school activities, and opinions about teaching practices, discipline problems, and institutions in the community. An interviewer of each sex was randomly assigned half of the subjects of each sex. Two interviewers were employed primarily to reduce the potential effect of idiosyncratic personal characteristics.[3]

Four different modes of interviewer response to the answers of the subject comprised the experimental treatments of the study. In the *approving condition* the interviewer immediately followed each utterance[4] of the subject with as many of the following four responses as he (or she) could perform in a natural fashion: smile, positive head nod, gesticulation, and brief verbal indication of attention. In the *disapproving condition,* the interviewer followed each utterance of the subject with as many of the following responses as he could appropriately perform: frown, negative head nod, and short disparaging comment. In the *mixed condition* the interviewer used the approving responses in the first half of the interview, and switched to the disapproving responses in the second half. In the *nonresponsive condition* the interviewer failed to respond to the subject's answers in either the approving or disapproving modes, remaining as nonresponsive as possible both verbally and gesturally. In each condition, a new question or probe was introduced by the interviewer at the end of a brief but noticeable silence on the part of the subject. During a short training period, the various approving and disapproving response classes were described to the interviewers in common-sense terms. The interviewers were permitted to perform the responses in the manner that was most natural to them. They were not informed of the hypotheses.

[2] The term "reciprocation" is used here merely to label the temporal causal contingency between members of a dyad in the performance of a given response class. No further explanatory mechanisms are implied at this time.

[3] The design also provided an opportunity for "cross-sex" effects to appear (cf. Stevenson, 1965). However, an adequate test of consequences of the interaction of sex of subject and sex of interviewer would require a sample of experimenters of each sex.

[4] In our formal analyses of data, "utterance" was defined linguistically in terms of pause, change in inflection, and grammatical completion (Davis, 1937, p. 44). However, the interviewers, who were not trained in linguistic analysis, were asked only to attend immediately to each completed response of the subject.

Subjects were transported in small groups from their school to a laboratory conveniently located in a research department of a local institution for retarded children. While a given subject was in the interview room, the remaining subjects waited in a separate room. Sessions were run in 1 day to prevent information about the task from reaching untested subjects. Questions about the institution were included in the interview schedule to make the subjects' presence there appear plausible to them. Subjects were randomly assigned to conditions, which were run repeatedly in the sequence described above.

Recording of Responses. Smiles, positive head nods, and gesticulations emitted by subjects were recorded by an observer who had established high reliability in marking their occurrence in the earlier studies. He also marked two additional responses for which he was trained—negative head nods and self-manipulations, the latter referring to any motion of the hands or fingers in contact with the body. Working definitions of the nonverbal responses and the simple observational procedures for recording them are presented elsewhere (Rosenfeld, 1966). The observer also operated a tape recorder from which transcriptions could be made of verbal responses in the interviews. To reduce bias in observation, the observer was assigned the ostensible task of gathering normative data on the frequency of occurrence of the nonverbal responses (which he previously had observed only among college students) in the younger population sampled in the current study.

The tape-recorded verbal responses were transcribed by a typist who was asked to note every verbalization of interviewer and subject, including mispronunciations and lengthy pauses. The transcriptions were then compared with the tapes, corrected, and content-analyzed by an assistant who was previously trained in the reliable scoring of speech disturbances (Kasl and Mahl, 1965) and various grammatical and lexical categories (Rosenfeld, in press). The verbal response of subjects of greatest interest was "recognition," which may be summarized here as a broad class of usually brief responses to an utterance which indicate attentiveness to the other person, but apparently add no other information to the conversation. Recognitions include commonly-used "verbal reinforcers" such as "mm-hmm," and less commonly researched attentional responses such as "I see," "no kidding?" and "really?" when no other communicative functions are apparent.

Results

All of the verbal and nonverbal response categories of interviewers and subjects that provided adequate frequency distributions were submitted to a $4 \times 2 \times 2 \times 2$ analysis of variance—treatments, by sex of subject, by sex of interviewer, by time period.[5] More specific analyses were made by applying Duncan's multiple comparison test (Edwards, 1960) to differences between cell means. While there were occasional effects of sex of subject and sex of interviewer on particular responses, these sex variables seldom interacted with each other or with the experimental treatments. Also, the design did not permit unconfounded interpretations of causal direction of sex effects, since both interviewers and subjects could vary in their responses to each other. For the sake of clarity, the presentation of results will be limited to the effects of treatments and time periods within treatments. Time periods are included primarily because each half of the mixed condition comprised a different treatment.

Responses of Interviewers. Except for withholding responses to subject utterances in the nonresponsive condition, the interviewers were expected to keep their amount of verbal participation relatively constant across treatments. Analyses of variance of frequencies of interviewer utterances and words indicated no significant effect of treatments on either measure of verbal output. A comparison of treatment means, however, did show one significant difference: in the nonresponsive condition the interviewers made fewer utterances than in any of the other three conditions. When interviewer utterances were subclassified into questions, recognitions, and a residual category, the only significant finding by analysis of variance was that recognitions were affected by treatments and by the interaction of treatments and time periods. Multiple comparison tests revealed that interviewer recognitions were significantly higher in the two time periods of the approving condition and in the approving half of the mixed condition than in any of the other treatment periods.

Responses of Subjects. Subjects were expected to smile, nod positively, gesticulate, and verbally "recognize" the interviewer more in both halves of the approving condition and the approving half of the mixed condition than in any other treatment period. Recognitions by subjects occurred too infrequently to permit analysis. Gesticulations were relatively uncommon, although they were significantly more frequent in the approving and in the mixed conditions than in either the disapproving or the nonresponsive

[5] Non parametric statistics were also used to analyze treatment effects on positive head nods and gesticulations because of their infrequent occurrence in some conditions. The results were identical in p-levels to those obtained by analysis of variance. A "significant" statistical finding in this report refers to the .05 or less probability level, two tails, unless otherwise qualified.

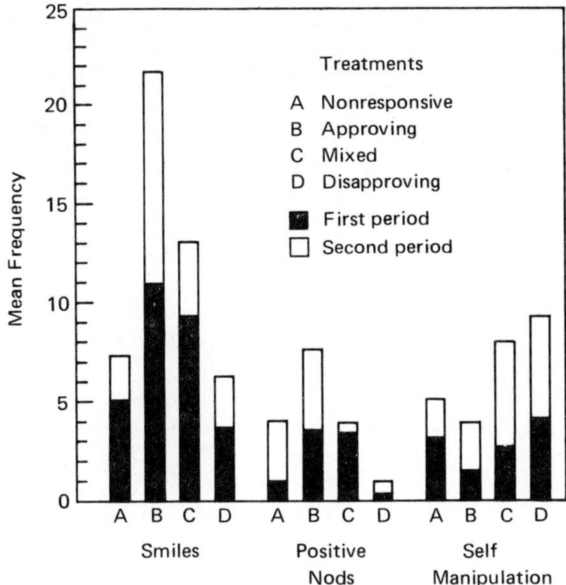

Figure 1 *Effects of experimental treatments on frequencies of nonverbal responses.*

conditions. Smiles and positive head nods both showed significant treatment effects and significant interactions of treatments and time periods. Multiple comparison tests revealed that each of these two responses operated as predicted. As Figure 1 indicates, they were significantly more frequent in the three approving periods than in any other period.

Significant effects of treatments were also found on *total* nonverbal responses, which was significantly correlated with the specific category frequencies. To eliminate this possible confounding, the nonverbal response categories were also analyzed as percentages of total nonverbal responses of the subject. Table 1 shows that the treatment effect, and the treatment-by-time interactions, remained significant for percentage of smiles and, to a weaker degree, for percentage of positive head nods. Again, these two responses were distributed precisely as predicted—significantly higher in each of the three approving periods than in any other period. The percentage of gesticulations was significantly higher in the approving condition than in the nonresponsive condition.

The treatments did not have significant effects on the raw frequencies of self manipulation ($p < .20$), although Figure 1 shows that the predicted order of treatment effects occurred. Analysis of variance of percentages of self manipulations (Table 1) showed a significant main effect of treatments. Comparisons of the four treatment means revealed that subjects in the approving condition engaged in a significantly lower percentage of self manipulations than did subjects in any other condition.

A more extensive analysis of verbal responses of subjects showed no significant effect of treatments on total utterances or words, although subjects tended to talk most in the approving periods. Of particular interest was the effect of treatments on aspects of speech disturbance (Kasl and Mahl, 1965). Analyses of variance showed no significant effect of treatments on the total ratio of speech disturbances to words spoken. However, when the speech disturbance ratio was divided into "ah" and "non-ah" subcategories the latter was found to be affected by treatments at the .10 level of confidence. The non-ah ratio was significantly higher in the disapproving condition than in any other condition.

Discussion

Although the nonverbal responses of the interviewers were not observed formally during the experimental sessions, some indirect objective evidence of the validity of the roles played by the interviewers was available from transcriptions of the tape recordings. Recognitions—conceived as a broad class of

Table 1 *Analyses of Variance of Interviewee Nonverbal Responses as a Function of Interviewer Treatment and Time Period*

Source[b]	*df*	*F* Scores for Nonverbal Responses[a]			
		All Nonverbal Responses	% Smiles	% Positive Head Nods	% Self Manipulations
Treatment	3	4.58***	6.49***	5.79***	3.98**
Time period	1	0.56	18.65***	3.66	2.04
Treatment × period	3	2.72*	3.98**	2.57*	2.59*

[a] Percentages of negative head nods and gesticulations are not shown because of their low frequency distributions.
[b] Sex of interviewer, sex of subject, and their interactions are omitted here (see text).
* $p < .10$.
** $p < .05$.
*** $p < .01$.

social reinforcers expressed in conversation—should have been emitted more often by interviewers when they were attempting to express approval than at any other time. This proved to be the case. No other subcategory of interviewer utterance significantly differentiated the four roles of the interviewers. Total interviewer utterances were comparable across treatments except, as expected, for their somewhat reduced level in the nonresponsive condition. Thus, the attempt to prevent the amount and content of interviewer responses from confounding their various treatment-roles appears to have been successful.

Several response classes of subjects occurred too infrequently to permit meaningful statistical analysis. One of these—negative head nods—also had occurred at a similarly low level in previous observations of college student dyads in free interaction (Rosenfeld, 1966). Gesticulations and recognitions were less frequent in the current study than in the earlier studies. The rare occurrence of recognitions by subjects may have been due to the structure of the interviews, a large portion of which consisted in asking the subject questions calling for particular informational content in response. The gesticulation rate, which tends to indicate general motivational level (Ekman, 1965; Rosenfeld, 1966; Rosenfeld, in press), may have been unexpectedly low because of the relative passivity of the role of interviewee. However, the distribution of gesticulations across treatments was consistent with the reciprocation hypothesis.

The two approval-related responses of subjects that did occur regularly—smiles and positive head nods—were emitted precisely as predicted. They were significantly more common in the approving periods of the interviews than in the disapproving or nonresponsive periods; and this effect was upheld both between and within subject groups. Given that smiles and positive head nods were relatively uncommon among subjects in the disapproving condition, in which the interviewer was gesturally active, it is unlikely that the subject's rate of smiling or nodding can be attributed to the sheer nonverbal activity of his interviewer. Also, there were no differences in frequencies of utterances between the approving and disapproving periods. Thus, assuming that the interviewers smiled and nodded primarily in the approving periods, and that the amount and content of conversation was approximately equivalent across conditions, it is concluded that the subjects were indeed reciprocating forms of approval expressed by the interviewers. The fact that smiles apparently were more highly reciprocated than were positive head nods coincides with the finding of an earlier study that in free interaction smiles were more similar in frequency of occurrence between members of dyads than were nods, especially during early acquaintance (Rosenfeld, 1966).

Previous research also indicated that a subject's self manipulations were disapproved of by the person with whom he was conversing (Rosenfeld, in press). In the present study self manipulations were most common among subjects in the disapproving periods and least common in the approving periods. Thus it would appear that not only do self manipulations by a subject lead to disapproval from others, but also that disapproval from others leads to self manipulations by the subject.

Another potential indicator of anxiety was available at the spoken level—the non-ah speech disturbance ratio (Kasl and Mahl, 1965). The non-ah ratio was significantly higher in the disapproving condition than in any other condition. Thus disapproving responses by the interviewer produced an increase in anxiety-related responses at both the vocal and gestural levels.

Thus, a person motivated to gain or maintain another individual's approval can receive immediate feedback about his effectiveness in several ways. If the person's responses are followed by a high or increasing level of smiling, nodding, and perhaps gesticulating by the other, then the person's response style should be reinforced. If the other withholds such feedback after having provided it earlier, the person's response style should be extinguished. If the other fails to provide smiles and positive head nods throughout the interaction, the person may not know whether the other disapproves of his behavior or whether he just is habitually nonreinforcing. Thus, the person may emit smiles and nods to determine if reciprocation will occur. If it does, the person may continue his style of interaction, assuming covert approval from the other.[6] If not reciprocated, the person may change his tactics to determine if a new approach will increase approving gestures by the other, or increase the likelihood of reciprocation of approving responses. Besides the failure to obtain reciprocation of normatively reciprocated responses, the person may interpret changes in other classes of response by the other individual as negative feedback. One of these is self manipulation; another is the non-ah speech disturbance ratio.

Many questions about the responses that were reciprocated in this study remain to be answered. What topological and contextual constraints are necessary for smiles and positive head nods to be perceived as approving? How common is the use

[6] It is recognized that certain forms of smiles and positive head nods, and their expression in certain contexts, may function as aversive stimuli.

of such responses across social groups, and how consistent are their approval-related functions? How is the reciprocation process related to different mechanisms of behavioral contagion (cf. Wheeler, 1966)? The role of awareness, which has been raised in the area of verbal conditioning in particular (Spielberger and DeNike, 1966), also may be raised with regard to nonverbal reciprocation processes. From their rate of occurrence and their positive evaluation in American advertising, one would surmise that we are very conscious and concerned about the expression of smiles. On the other hand, previous research and informal observations by the author have quite consistently indicated that persons other than professional operant conditioners are seldom aware of either their own rates of positive head nodding or those of the persons they converse with. Most of these problems can be approached by objective behavioral procedures. The direct study of the approval-seeking process in free social interaction has some obvious advantages over research that is focused primarily on personality assessment in situations removed from social interaction, or experimental studies that limit response possibilities to the degree that they bear little resemblance to common varieties of human social behavior.

References

BOOMER, D. S., and GOODRICH, D. W. Speech disturbance and body movement in interviews. *Journal of Nervous and Mental Diseases,* 1963, *136,* 263–266.

DAVIS, EDITH A. *The development of linguistic skill in twins, singletons with siblings, and only children from age five to ten years.* Minneapolis: University of Minnesota Press, 1937.

EDWARDS, A. *Experimental design in psychological research.* New York: Holt, 1960.

EKMAN, P. Differential communication of affect by head and body cues. *Journal of Personality and Social Psychology,* 1965, *2,* 726–735.

KASL, S. V., and MAHL, G. F. The relationship of disturbances and hesitations in spontaneous speech to anxiety. *Journal of Personality and Social Psychology,* 1965, *1,* 425–433.

KRASNER, L. Studies of the conditioning of verbal behavior. *Psychological Bulletin,* 1958, *55,* 148–170.

ROSENFELD, H. M. Instrumental affiliative functions of facial and gestural expressions. *Journal of Personality and Social Psychology,* 1966, *4,* 65–72.

ROSENFELD, H. M. Approval-seeking and approval-inducing functions of verbal and nonverbal responses in the dyad. *Journal of Personality and Social Psychology,* in press.

SPIELBERGER, C. D., and DENIKE, L. D. Descriptive behaviorism versus cognitive theory in verbal operant conditioning. *Psychological Review,* 1966, *73,* 306–326.

STEVENSON, H. W. Social reinforcement of children's behavior. In L. P. Lipsitt and C. C. Spiker (Eds.), *Advances in child development and behavior,* Vol. 2. New York: Academic Press, 1965. Pp. 97–126.

WHEELER, L. Toward a theory of behavioral contagion. *Psychological Review,* 1966, *73,* 179–192.

Attitude Formation

10

Attitudes have been variously conceived as implicit responses, overt responses, or merely dispositions to respond. Those who attribute some latent or covert reality to attitudes generally also acknowledge that this reality is not susceptible to direct observation or to direct measurement. What is both observable and measurable is some performance, that is, a behavioral event that is public rather than private and, hence, potentially manipulable. When we talk about someone's attitude toward democracy or government, what we actually observe is the range of comments and reactions he makes to political figures and political issues, the frequency with which he reads about political matters, his inclination to vote or to support a candidate, the occasions on which he either prevents someone else from expressing unpopular opinions or complains about the free expression of opinion, and so forth. Because these performances have a common theme, tend to vary together, and are predictable one from the other, we speak of them as an attitude.

This rigorously behavioral approach to attitude formation and change may seem unacceptably parochial to those who would prefer to stress the cognitive, or mental, aspects of an attitude. In reply to this charge we would simply reiterate the obvious fact that cognitive events are accessible only through introspection and are measurable only through their behavioral manifestations. A statement of the functional relationship between the antecedents and the consequences of a performance enables us to predict the behavior with greater certainty than does endless speculation about cognitive mediators. Doubtless individuals do have private experiences that defy veridical report; and doubtless they engage in implicit verbalizations that may act as the controlling stimuli for overt behavior. Because of the extensive and complex repertoire that each person brings with him to an experimental setting, we can probably never achieve more than a modicum of experimental control over such covert processes. But this does not mean that our ability to predict a behavioral outcome is equally indeterminate. On the contrary, it matters little what private events transpire in the interim between stimulus and response so long as a reasonably consistent relationship can be established between two. We are left ultimately with a stimulus-response contingency as the basis for our theories and our predictions about attitudinal behavior. Often it would be nice to know what a person has "said to himself" before he responds overtly, and frequently it would be very useful to know whether what he says publicly is correlated in any systematic fashion with what he does in nonverbal situations. We shall probably never learn with confidence much about the correspondence between private and public speech, but we can determine the extent to which a verbal performance is related to other behavior.

Some psychologists, such as Staats,* have viewed an attitude essentially as a conditioned emotional response. We prefer, however, to define an attitude as a class of behaviors under the control of some social referent, such as a group, a religion, or a political party. Staats has suggested that the measure of the strength of an attitude is the physiological, "emotional" response that the subject makes. Actually, if we take a behavioral approach toward attitudes, recognizing them as comprising an operant repertoire, then the physiological signs to which Staats points are concomitants or symptoms rather than the attitude itself. Thus, the strength of an attitude is reflected in the frequency of the component performances. It only incidentally happens to be true that high frequency behaviors that are either positively or negatively reinforced also tend to be accompanied by physiological changes. Attitudinal behavior has an emotional component that is probably conditioned in the manner described by Staats; but the attitude as commonly measured consists of a performance, or group of related performances. These performances are usually under rather narrow stimulus control, such as that represented by an attitude scale or a face-to-face encounter with a member of a minority ethnic group. Behavior under two such different conditions may or may not be highly correlated.

Staats has argued that the emotional reactions triggered by attitudinal stimuli may act to reinforce other instrumental behaviors. Thus, the word *dangerous* may acquire the capacity to arouse an emotional response, and it can also serve as a discriminative stimulus controlling a number of performances, such as keeping away from deep water while swimming. The behaviors prompted by the word *dangerous* are negatively reinforced through their instrumentality in avoiding aversive consequences. Attitudes are an important part of our social behavior repertoires, and their acquisition can be understood in much the same terms that we use to understand the learning of many other complex performances. A distinguishing feature of attitudes, however, is the affect, or emotion, that ordinarily accompanies them. The procedures used in respondent conditioning provide us with a framework for understanding the manner in which the emotional component of an attitude comes to be elicited.

* A. W. Staats, An outline of an integrated learning theory of attitude formation and function. In M. Fishbein (Ed.), *Readings in Attitude Theory and Measurement.* New York: Wiley, 1967.

Respondent Conditioning Procedures

This section introduces us to the analysis of attitude formation in terms of the principles of classical, or respondent, conditioning. Staats' analysis makes the assumption that attitudinal behavior, such as rating the pleasantness or unpleasantness of a nationality label or designation, is mediated in part by the evaluative meaning that this social referent has acquired. Evaluative meaning, as defined by such negative words as "bitter, ugly, failure" or such positive words as "gift, sacred, happy" can, he argues, be conditioned to other, more neutral words. In his experiment, it is demonstrated that the evaluative ratings assigned by subjects to nationality designations, such as Dutch and Swedish, varied as a function of the positive or negative appellations with which these nationalities had previously been paired in a learning situation. Although he does not claim that behavior toward the designated nationalities had been altered by this conditioning procedure, Staats does assert that the subjects had acquired an "implicit attitudinal response" which mediated their behavior in scoring the rating scales.

The attitudinal repertoire in this experiment consists of all the performances (connotations) controlled by a verbal stimulus such as "Dutch" or "Swedish." Thus, when prompted by the stimulus "Dutch," a person can make a large number of relevant statements. What *Staats and Staats* really showed is that when the word "Dutch" is paired with unpleasant words (aversive stimuli), it becomes a conditioned aversive stimulus which reinforces verbal performances of the sort that terminate, avoid, or assault the stimulus. The entire process falls in the area of the compatibility of behaviors. If the word "Dutch" evokes the conditioned reactions "ugly," "bad," and "failure"—and also prompts the corresponding operant behaviors —then the performances which may subsequently be emitted in the presence of "Dutch" will tend to be incompatible with those kinds of performances which we call favorable. The difficulty in evaluating and describing this experiment behaviorally is that the actual behaviors with which Staats and Staats dealt are not described in sufficient detail in his account of the experiment.

55 | *Attitudes Established by Classical Conditioning*[1]

ARTHUR W. STAATS
CAROLYN K. STAATS

Osgood and Tannenbaum have stated, ". . . The *meaning* of a concept is its location in a space defined by some number of factors or dimensions, and *attitude* toward a concept is its projection onto one of these dimensions defined as 'evaluative'" (1955,

[1] This article was written and the theoretical-experimental method developed by the first author as the principal investigator of a research project supported by the Office of Naval Research under Contract NONR-2305(00). The second author assisted in the conduct of the study and was responsible for the method of statistical analysis of the data.

p. 42). Thus, attitudes evoked by concepts are considered part of the total meaning of the concepts.

A number of psychologists, such as Cofer and Foley (1942), Mowrer (1954), and Osgood (1952, 1953), to mention a few, view meaning as a response —an implicit response with cue functions which may mediate other responses. A very similar analysis has been made of the concept of attitudes by Doob, who states, "*An attitude is an implicit response . . . which is considered socially significant in the individual's society*" (1947, p. 144). Doob further emphasizes the learned character of attitudes and states, "The learning process, therefore, is crucial to an understanding of the behavior of attitudes" (p. 138). If attitudes are to be considered responses, then the learning process should be the same as for other responses. As an example, the principles of classical conditioning should apply to attitudes.

The present authors (1957), in three experiments, recently conditioned the evaluative, potency, and activity components of word meaning found by Osgood and Suci (1955) to contiguously presented nonsense syllables. The results supported the conception that meaning is a response and, further, indicated that word meaning is composed of components which can be separately conditioned.

The present study extends the original experiments by studying the formation of attitudes (evaluative meaning) to socially significant verbal stimuli through classical conditioning. The socially significant verbal stimuli were national names and familiar masculine names. Both of these types of stimuli, unlike nonsense syllables, would be expected to evoke attitudinal responses on the basis of the pre-experimental experience of the Ss. Thus, the purpose of the present study is to test the hypothesis that attitudes already elicited by socially significant verbal stimuli can be changed through classical conditioning, using other words as unconditioned stimuli.

Method

Subjects. Ninety-three students in elementary psychology participated in the experiments as Ss to fulfill a course requirement.

Procedure. The general procedure employed was the same as in the previous study of the authors (1957).

Experiment I. The procedures were administered to the Ss in groups. There were two groups with one half of the Ss in each group. Two types of stimuli were used: national names which were presented by slide projection on a screen (*CS* words) and words which were presented orally by the *E* (*US* words), with Ss required to repeat the word aloud immediately after *E* had pronounced it. Ostensibly, Ss' task was to separately learn the verbal stimuli simultaneously presented in the two different ways.

Two tasks were first presented to train the Ss in the procedure and to orient them properly for the phase of the experiment where the hypotheses were tested. The first task was to learn five visually presented national names, each shown four times, in random order. Ss' learning was tested by recall. The second task was to learn 33 auditorily presented words. Ss repeated each word aloud after *E*. Ss were tested by presenting 12 pairs of words. One of each pair was a word that had just been presented, and Ss were to recognize which one.

The Ss were then told that the primary purpose of the experiment was to study "how both of these types of learning take place together—the effect that one has upon the other, and so on." Six new national names were used for visual presentation: *German, Swedish, Italian, French, Dutch,* and *Greek* served as the *CS*s.

These names were presented in random order, with exposures of 5 seconds. Approximately one second after the *CS* name appeared on the screen, *E* pronounced the *US* word with which it was paired. The intervals between exposures were less than one second. Ss were told they could learn the visually presented names by just looking at them but that they should simultaneously concentrate on pronouncing the auditorily presented words aloud and to themselves, since there would be many of these words, each presented only once.

The names were each visually presented 18 times in random order, though never more than twice in succession, so that no systematic associations were formed between them. On each presentation, the *CS* name was paired with a different auditorily presented word, i.e., there were 18 conditioning trials. *CS* names were never paired with *US* words more than once so that stable associations were not formed between them. Thus, 108 different *US* words were used. The *CS* names, *Swedish* and *Dutch,* were always paired with *US* words with evaluative meaning. The other four *CS* names were paired with words which had no systematic meaning, e.g., chair, with, twelve. For Group 1, *Dutch* was paired with different words which had positive evaluative meaning, e.g., gift, sacred, happy; and *Swedish* was paired with words which had negative evaluative meaning, e.g., bitter, ugly, failure.[2] For Group 2, the order of *Dutch*

[2] The complete list of *CS-US* word pairs is not presented here, but it has been deposited with the American Documentation Institute. Order Document No. 5463 from ADI Auxiliary Publications Project, Photoduplication Service, Library of Congress, Washington 25, D.C., remitting in advance $1.25 for microfilm or $1.25 for photocopies. Make checks payable to Chief, Photoduplication Service, Library of Congress.

and *Swedish* was reversed so that *Dutch* was paired with words with negative evaluative meaning and *Swedish* with positive meaning words.

When the conditioning phase was completed, Ss were told that *E* first wished to find out how many of the visually presented words they remembered. At the same time, they were told, it would be necessary to find out how they *felt* about the words since that might have affected how the words were learned. Each *S* was given a small booklet in which there were six pages. On each page was printed one of the six names and a semantic differential scale. The scale was the seven-point scale of Osgood and Suci (1955), with the continuum from pleasant to unpleasant. An example is as follows:

German

pleasant:—:—:—:—:—:—:—:unpleasant

The Ss were told how to mark the scale and to indicate at the bottom of the page whether or not the word was one that had been presented.

The Ss were then tested on the auditorily presented words. Finally, they were asked to write down anything they had thought about the experiment, especially the purpose of it, and so on, or anything they had thought of during the experiment. It was explained that this might have affected the way they had learned.

Experiment II. The procedure was exactly repeated with another group of Ss except for the *CS* names. The names used were *Harry, Tom, Jim, Ralph, Bill,* and *Bob.* Again, half of the Ss were in Group 1 and half in Group 2. For Group 1, *Tom* was paired with positive evaluative words and *Bill* with negative words. For Group 2 this was reversed. The semantic differential booklet was also the same except for the *CS* names.

Design. The data for the two experiments were treated in the same manner. Three variables were involved in the design: conditioned meaning (pleasant and unpleasant); *CS* names (*Dutch* and *Swedish,* or *Tom* and *Bill*); and groups (1 and 2). The scores on the semantic differential given to each of the two *CS* words were analyzed in a 2 × 2 latin square as described by Lindquist (1953, p. 278) for his Type II design.

Results

The 17 Ss who indicated they were aware of either of the systematic name-word relationships were excluded from the analysis. This was done to prevent the interpretation that the conditioning of attitudes depended upon awareness. In order to maintain a counter-balanced design when these Ss were excluded, four Ss were randomly eliminated from the analysis. The resulting *N*s were as follows: 24 in Experiment I and 48 in Experiment II.

Table 1 presents the means and standard deviations of the meaning scores for Experiments I and II. The table itself is a representation of the 2 × 2 design for each experiment. The pleasant extreme of the evaluative scale was scored 1, the unpleasant 7.

The analysis of the data for both experiments is presented in Table 2. The results of the analysis indicate that the conditioning occurred in both cases. In Experiment I, the *F* for the conditioned attitudes was significant at better than the .05 level. In Experiment II, the *F* for the conditioned attitudes was significant at better than the .01 level. In both experiments the *F* for the groups variable was significant at the .05 level.

Table 1 *Means and Standard Deviations of Conditioned Attitude Scores*

Experiment I	*Dutch*		*Swedish*	
	Mean	*SD*	Mean	*SD*
Group 1	2.67	.94	3.42	1.50
Group 2	2.67	1.31	1.83	.90
Experiment II	*Tom*		*Bill*	
	Mean	*SD*	Mean	*SD*
Group 1	2.71	2.01	4.12	2.04
Group 2	3.42	2.55	1.79	1.07

Note.—On the scales, pleasant is 1, unpleasant 7.

Table 2 *Summary of Analysis of Variance for Each Experiment*

Source	Experiment I			Experiment II		
	df	MS	*F*	*df*	MS	*F*
Between Ss						
Groups	1	7.52	4.36*	1	15.84	5.00*
Error	22	1.73		46	3.17	
Within						
Conditioned attitude	1	7.52	5.52*	1	55.51	10.47**
Names	1	.02	.01	1	.26	.05
Residual	22	1.36		46	5.30	
Total	47			95		

* $p < .05$.
** $p < .01$.

Discussion

It was possible to condition the attitude component of the total meaning responses of *US* words to socially significant verbal stimuli, without Ss' awareness. This conception is schematized in Figure

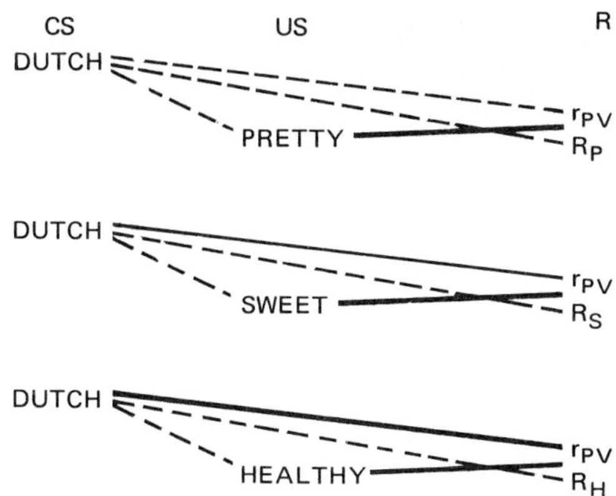

Figure 1 *The conditioning of a positive attitude. (Line weight represents strength of association.)*

1, and in so doing, the way the conditioning in this study was thought to have taken place is shown more specifically. The national name *Dutch,* in this example, is presented prior to the word *pretty. Pretty* elicits a meaning response. This is schematized in the figure as two component responses; an evaluative response r_{PV} (in this example, the words have a positive value), and the other distinctive responses that characterize the meaning of the word, R_P. The pairing of *Dutch* and *pretty* results in associations between *Dutch* and r_{PV}, and *Dutch* and R_P. In the following presentations of *Dutch* and the words *sweet* and *healthy,* the association between *Dutch* and r_{PV} is further strengthened. This is not the case with associations R_P, R_S, and R_H, since they occur only once and are followed by other associations which are inhibitory. The direct associations indicated in the figure between the name and the individual words would also in this way be inhibited.

It was not thought that a rating response was conditioned in this procedure but rather an implicit attitudinal response which mediated the behavior of scoring the semantic differential scale. It is possible, with this conception, to interpret two studies by Razran (1938, 1940) which concern the conditioning of ratings. Razran found that ratings of ethnically labeled pictures of girls and sociopolitical slogans could be changed by showing these stimuli while Ss were consuming a free lunch and, in the case of the slogans, while the Ss were presented with unpleasant olfactory stimulation. The change in ratings could be thought to be due to the conditioning of an implicit evaluative response, an attitude, to the CSs by means of the lunch or the unpleasant odors. That is, part of the total response elicited by the food, for example, was conditioned to the pictures or slogans and became the mediation process which in turn elicited the positive rating.

It should be stated that the results of the present study do not show directly that Ss' behavior to the object (e.g., a person of Dutch nationality) has been changed. The results pertain to the Ss' attitudinal response to the signs, the national names themselves. However, Kapustnik (1934) has demonstrated that a response generalized to an object when the response had previously been conditioned to the verbal sign of the object. Osgood states,

> The aggressive reactions associated with *Nazi* and *Jap* on a verbal level certainly transferred to the social objects represented under appropriate conditions. Similarly, prejudicial behaviors established while reading about a member of a social class can transfer to the class as a whole . . . (1953, p. 704).

The results of this study have special relevance for an understanding of attitude formation and change by means of verbal communication. Using a conception of meaning as a mediating response, Mowrer (1954) has suggested that a sentence is a conditioning device and that communication takes place when the meaning response which has been elicited by the predicate is conditioned to the subject of the sentence. The results of the present study and the previous one of the present authors (1957) substantiate Mowrer's approach by substantiating the basic theory that word meaning will indeed condition to contiguously presented verbal stimuli. In the present study, the meaning component was evaluative, or attitudinal, and the CSs were socially significant verbal stimuli. The results suggest, therefore, that attitude formation or change through communication takes place according to these principles of conditioning. As an example, the sentence, "Dutch people are honest," would condition the positive attitude elicited by "honest" to "Dutch"—and presumably to any person called "Dutch." If, in an individual's history, many words eliciting a positive attitude were paired with "Dutch," then a very positive attitude toward this nationality would arise.

The reason for the group differences in each of the experiments is not clear. These differences could have arisen because there were actual differences in the Ss composing each group, or in some condition of the procedure occurring to one of the groups. Nothing the authors were aware of seem to indicate this as the explanation, and in the previous experiments of the authors (1957) there were no group differences. Since in a 2×2 latin square the interactions are entirely confounded with the main effects, the group differences could also have arisen as a result of the interaction of the other two main effects (i.e., direction of conditioning and names).

Summary

Two experiments were conducted to test the hypothesis that attitude responses elicited by a word can be conditioned to a contiguously presented socially significant verbal stimulus. A name (e.g., *Dutch*) was presented 18 times, each time paired with the auditory presentation of a different word. While these words were different, they all had an identical evaluative meaning component. In Experiment I, one national name was paired with positive evaluative meaning and another was paired with negative evaluative meaning. In Experiment II, familiar masculine names were used. In each experiment there was significant evidence that meaning responses had been conditioned to the names without Ss' awareness.

References

Cofer, C. N., and Foley, J. P. Mediated generalization and the interpretation of verbal behavior: I. Prolegomena. *Psychological Review,* 1942, *49,* 513–540.

Doob, L. W. The behavior of attitudes. *Psychological Review,* 1947, *54,* 135–156.

Kapustnik, O. P. The interrelation between direct conditioned stimuli and their verbal symbols. (Translated from Russian title) *Psychological Abstracts,* 1934, *8,* No. 153.

Lindquist, E. F. *Design and analysis of experiments in psychology and education.* Boston: Houghton Mifflin, 1953.

Mowrer, O. H. The psychologist looks at language. *American Psychologist,* 1954, *9,* 660–694.

Osgood, C. E. The nature and measurement of meaning. *Psychological Bulletin,* 1952, *49,* 197–237.

Osgood, C. E. *Method and theory in experimental psychology.* New York: Oxford University Press, 1953.

Osgood, C. E., and Suci, G. J. Factor analysis of meaning. *Journal of Experimental Psychology,* 1955, *50,* 325–338.

Osgood, C. E., and Tannenbaum, P. H. The principle of congruity in the prediction of attitude change. *Psychological Review,* 1955, *62,* 42–55.

Razran, G. H. S. Conditioning away social bias by the luncheon technique. *Psychological Bulletin,* 1938, *35,* 693.

Razran, G. H. S. Conditioned response changes in rating and appraising sociopolitical slogans. *Psychological Bulletin,* 1940, *37,* 481.

Staats, C. K., and Staats, A. W. Meaning established by classical conditioning. *Journal of Experimental Psychology,* 1957, *54,* 74–80.

Another situation in which a contingency was arranged between the responses of subjects to social objects and verbal reinforcers is reported by *Singer.* Briefly, he asked subjects who had been selected three months previously on the basis of their moderately prodemocratic responses on the California F (authoritarian) and E (ethnocentrism) Scales to agree or disagree vocally to the F Scale items when these were read aloud to them. For some of the subjects, the experimenter said "Good" or "Right" following all prodemocratic responses, while for others he simply recorded the answers without comment. It should be noted that Singer's selection of subjects who were already moderately prodemocratic assured him that the operant level of their replies to the F Scale items would be sufficiently high to make differential reinforcement possible. At the same time, they were not so prodemocratic that they could not move even further in this direction. Following this conditioning procedure, the experimenter read items from the E Scale aloud to all of the subjects and recorded their agreement or disagreement without comment. It was found that those subjects who had been positively reinforced for prodemocratic responses to the F Scale gave significantly more prodemocratic responses to items from the E Scale than the control subjects who had not been differentially reinforced. This effect, however, was observed only if the experimenter remained in the room. The results suggest that the modification of the subject's performance was so narrowly under the control of the experimenter's presence that it did not constitute what we conventionally call a change in attitude. That is, the subject's inclination to emit prodemocratic statements occurred in a special situation rather than on those more general occasions where it would be appropriate to talk about ethnocentrism and authoritarianism.

In short, the conditioning effect was observed when the testing situation resembled the learning situation. Thus, it appears that the change in the subject's performance by the reinforcement procedure was under the control of the experimenter, who was conspicuously present when the differential reinforcement took place. One might guess that the efficacy of a specific reinforcement procedure in changing a person's attitude would be in proportion to the number of situations in which the new attitudinal performance can be similarly reinforced.

56 *Verbal Conditioning and Generalization of Prodemocratic Responses*[1]

ROBERT D. SINGER[2]

Skinner (1953) has suggested that verbal behavior may be conditioned by arranging a contingency between a verbal response, which is a unit of verbal behavior, and a "generalized conditioned reinforcer." The verbal responses most frequently conditioned have been uttered specific words, numbers, or categories of these such as plural nouns (Greenspoon, 1955), and three-digit numbers or verbs (Sarason, 1957). In a few studies, the verbalizations to be reinforced have been "statements describing or evaluating the state of the patient by himself," or statements of opinion used as a measure of a particular, relatively simple, attitude (Ekman, 1958).

This study concerns itself with the question of whether the responses of subjects to a complex, multifactorial attitude scale (the F Scale) can be altered by means of verbal reinforcement and whether such change, if obtained, generalizes to a related attitude scale (the E Scale). A further point of interest is whether generalization takes place if the source of original reinforcement is no longer present. Since the prestige of the experimenter is an important variable in the effectiveness of conditioning (Verplanck, 1955), one may speculate that his presence or absence should be important in obtaining or failing to obtain generalization.

The study has practical relevance to the general area of behavior change. Psychotherapists may transmit their own values, beliefs, and theoretical orientations to the patient by means of verbal and gestural conditioning. For both theoretical and practical reasons, it therefore seems important to know the practicability of verbally conditioning complex attitudes, the nature and extent of the generalization of such conditioning, and whether these phenomena represent the effects of simple automatic reinforcement or whether they are more complex examples of social influence processes.

Method

Materials. The California F Scale was chosen as a complex, multifactorial attitude scale individual items of which bear only an indirect relationship to each other. The 30-item California scale was combined with the 30-item reversed Christie scale (1958) to exclude the influence of acquiescence set. Combining these two sources, a 60-item scale was constructed with items arranged in random order. The California E Scale of 30 items, which according to Adorno, Frenkel-Brunswik, Levinson, and Sanford (1950) is ideologically and historically related to the F Scale, was chosen as the measure of generalization.

Subjects. Twenty-four pairs of female subjects (48 subjects in all) were chosen from a sample of 250 subjects who completed the combined F Scale and the E Scale, and who were taking the introductory psychology course at the University of Pennsylvania. To be chosen a subject had to have at least 30, but no more than 45 F Scale items answered in the prodemocratic direction, and between 12 and 24 in the prodemocratic direction on the E Scale. This insured that all subjects were already relatively prodemocratic. Subjects were matched on the basis of their scores on both scales to form the 24 pairs.

Experimenter. The experimenter was a 28-year-old male who was presented to the subjects as an experimental psychologist from a research institute con-

1 This paper is based on a dissertation submitted to the Graduate School of the University of Pennsylvania in partial fulfillment of the requirement for the degree of Doctor of Philosophy.

2 The writer is deeply indebted to Seymour Feshbach under whose supervision the study was conducted and to Francis W. Irwin whose suggestions and criticisms proved to be an invaluable aid. Special thanks go to Harold A. Rashkis of Eastern Pennsylvania Psychiatric Institute who made the time available to do this study while the author was in his employ.

ducting some studies at the university (which was in fact true).

Procedure. The experiment was conducted three months after the initial F and E Scales were filled out. Half of the subjects (one from each of the 24 pairs) were randomly assigned to the experimental procedure and the other half (their matched pairs) to the control procedure. After the learning session, one-half of the 24 pairs responded to the E Scale (generalization procedure) with the experimenter in the room and one-half with him absent.

In the experimental group the experimenter read all 60 items of the combined F Scale aloud and asked the subjects to state whether she "agreed" or "disagreed" with each item. Every time the subjects gave an answer in the prodemocratic direction the experimenter said either "good" or "right" ("good" and "right" were alternated in an irregular order but with about equal frequency). For each control subject, the experimenter merely read the items aloud and recorded the subject's answers without comment.

For one-half of the pairs, after completing the F Scale procedure, the experimenter went on to read aloud all 30 items of the E Scale and recorded the subject's "agree" or "disagree" answers without comment (*experimenter present generalization condition*). For the other half of the subjects, the experimenter excused himself from the room after the conditioning period and had the subjects fill out the E Scale by themselves (*experimenter absent generalization condition*). This procedure was identical for the control group.

The experimental paradigm may be characterized thus:

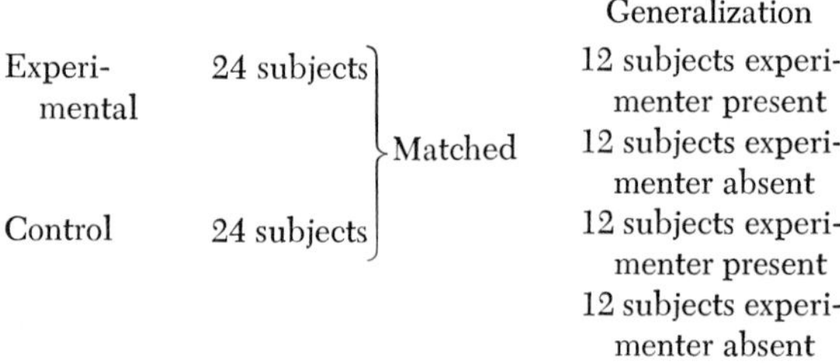

Finally, all experimental subjects were questioned by the experimenter (experimenter absent subjects were spoken to in the hall after leaving) as to their degree of awareness of the experimental contingency between prodemocratic responses and "good" and "right."

Results

The results of the 60-trial conditioning period were divided for purposes of analysis into three blocks of 20 trials for both the experimental and control subjects. The data may be treated by t tests. Although the data lend themselves to a trend analysis based on analysis of variance, such a procedure does not take into consideration the matching of subjects (but in this case it yields results identical to those found by t tests).

Table 1 shows the total and mean number of prodemocratic responses for the experimental and control groups.

Table 2 deals with the question of the significance of the obtained differences between the experimental and control groups. It shows that learning, that is, a shift in a more democratic direction, took place in the experimental group.

Table 1 *Total and Mean Number of Prodemocratic Responses for Each Set of Twenty Learning Trials*

	1st 20 Trials		2nd 20 Trials		3rd 20 Trials		All 60 Trials
	Total	*M*	Total	*M*	Total	*M*	Total
Experimental ($N = 24$)	306	12.75	318	13.25	379	15.79	1003
Control ($N = 24$)	304	12.66	299	12.45	293	12.20	8.96

Table 2 *t Tests for Matched Pairs for Experimental versus Control Group Overall and for Each of Three Pairs of Twenty Trials*

	Mean Difference	Variance	t	p
Overall (60 trials)	1.49	.53	2.81	<.01
1st 20 trials	.08	.5	.016	>.05
2nd 20 trials	.79	.51	1.54	>.05
3rd 20 trials	3.6	.6	6.00	<.01

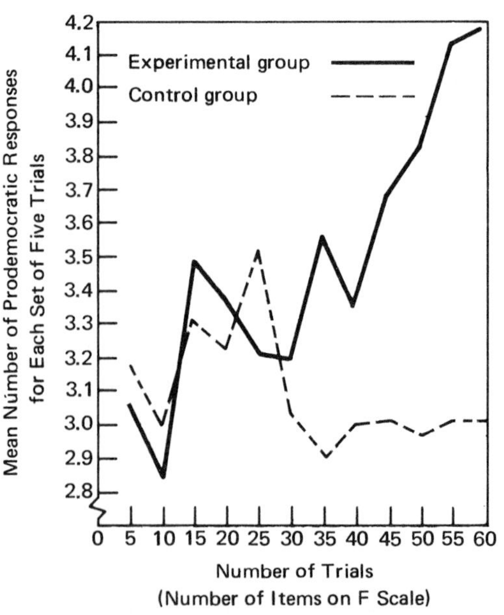

Figure 1 *Learning curves by groupings of 5 trials.*

Table 3 *Mean E Scale Scores (Mean Number of Anti-Ethnocentric Responses)*

	Experimenter Present	Experimenter Absent
1st 10 trials	7.9	7.1
2nd 10 trials	7.0	6.1
3rd 10 trials	6.8	6.1
Overall Means	7.2	6.4
	Control Present	Control Absent
1st 10 trials	5.5	6.1
2nd 10 trials	6.1	6.1
3rd 10 trials	6.1	6.4
Overall Means	5.7	6.2

Table 4 *t Tests for Generalization Comparisons*

	Mean Difference	Variance	t	p
Experimenter present vs. Control present: Overall	4.6	1.23	3.73	<.01
Experimenter absent vs. Control absent: Overall	.66	1	.66	>.05
Experimenter absent vs. Control absent: 1st 10 trials	1 $M_1 - M_2$[a]	.41	2.43	<.05
Experimenter present vs. Experimenter absent: 1st 10 trials	.8 $M_1 - M_2$[a]	.201	3.92	<.01

[a] Based on nonmatched subjects.

The t tests clearly indicate that there is an overall learning effect, although the difference is statistically significant only for the last block of 20 trials. Figure 1 illustrates the course of learning as shown by blocks of 5 trials (learning appears to occur rapidly somewhere after the 30th trial).

In regard to generalization, Table 3 presents the data for the generalization conditions, showing both the total means and means obtained by dividing the 30 trials of the E Scale into three blocks of 10 trials. Table 4 represents the statistical analysis of these data.

The first t test indicates that the subjects do show an overall generalization effect in terms of more prodemocratic responses when the experimenter remains in the room. The second t test demonstrates that if the experimenter leaves the room it is *not* possible to show significant overall generalization. The third t test suggests that even though no *overall* generalization effect can be shown when the experimenter leaves the room, there is some generalization over the first of 10 trials even under this condition. Such

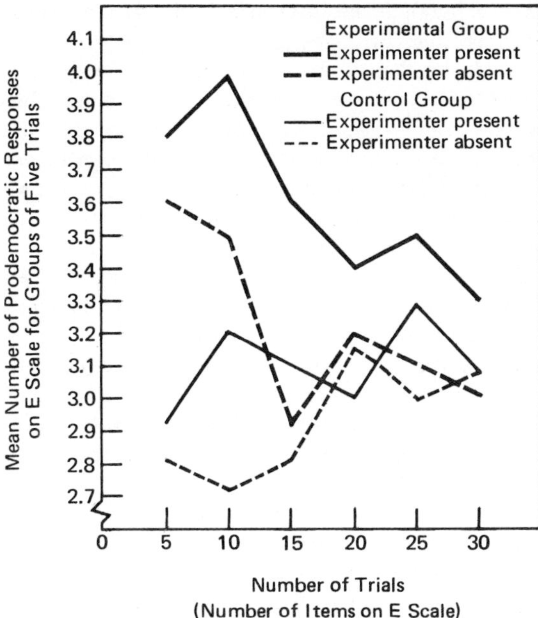

Figure 2 *Generalization data by groupings of 5 trials.*

generalization is greater when the experimenter is in the room than when he is absent. Figure 2 shows the course of the generalization by groups of 5 trials.

Certain other data warrant brief mention. The initial correlation before conditioning between the combined F Scale and the E Scale for the 48 subjects was quite low ($r = + .23$, not significant). It is noteworthy that generalization from the F to the E Scale did take place in spite of the low common variance between the two scales. However, r between the F Scale and the E Scale for the 12 subjects of the experimenter present condition, after conditioning, increased to + .60 ($p < .05$). Despite the originally low pre-experimental correlation (+ .22 for these 12 subjects) these subjects not only gave more democratic responses on the E scale, after repeated reinforcement on the F Scale for prodemocratic responses, but the shared variance of the two scales markedly increased. A conceptual change may have taken place in which the subjects learned the hypothesis of Adorno et al. (1950) that these two scales ought to be related!

There was a tendency short of significance for the more aware subjects to show a greater change in the prodemocratic direction. Generally, however, the subjects had a low level of awareness and the differences were small.

Discussion

This study demonstrates that at least one complex attitude scale is amenable to influence by means of verbal reinforcement. Since the responses studied involve stated opinion rather than action, it is problemactic whether such changes would affect the subjects' overt behavior. It was also shown that change on one attitude scale can produce change on another attitude scale. Indeed the results suggest that the verbal reinforcement procedure may be capable of bringing about conceptual changes that alter preexisting relationships between components of the subject's cognitive structure.

There is an indication that changes brought about by verbal reinforcement depend on the experimenter's physical presence. At least in the initial phases of generalization, the subjects' altered verbal behavior is dependent on the presence of the experimenter. As in Rogers' (1960) study, there is the implication that changes may be specific to the interpersonal situation in which they take place.

A strictly Skinnerian (1953) explanation of the findings seems to run into difficulty in accounting for discrimination of the similarity between scale items when they bear such little physical resemblance to each other. Osgood's (1957) theory, in terms of "mediated generalization," seems to be more powerful in explaining the basis for the subject's discriminations, but the explanation rests on speculation about past experiences which are far from easy to demonstrate. At present it seems simpler and safe, particularly in light of the findings about the experimenter absent condition, to view the results as reflecting the dependence of learning (whatever the nature of the learning mechanism) on social influence phenomena.

Summary

This investigation found that verbal reinforcement was effective in shifting subjects to a more democratic position on a combination of the California and Christie F Scales. Further, the change generalized to the E Scale under conditions in which the experimenter was present, even though he was no longer reinforcing the subject. The experimenter evidently has social influence value.

References

Adorno, T. W., Frenkel-Brunswik, Else, Levinson, D. J., and Sanford, R. N. *The authoritarian personality.* New York: Harper, 1950.

Christie, R., Havel, J., and Seidenberg, B. Is the F Scale irreversible? *Journal of Abnormal and Social Psychology,* 1958, *56,* 143–159.

Ekman, P. A comparison of verbal and nonverbal behavior as reinforcing stimuli of opinion responses. Unpublished doctoral dissertation, Adelphi College, 1958.

Greenspoon, J. The reinforcing effects of two spoken sounds on the frequency of two responses. *American Journal of Psychology,* 1955, *68,* 409–416.

Osgood, C. E. A behavioristic analysis of perception and language as cognitive phenomena. In *Contemporary approaches to cognition.* Cambridge: Harvard University Press, 1957.

Rogers, J. M. Operant conditioning in a quasi-therapy setting. *Journal of Abnormal and Social Psychology,* 1960, *60,* 247–252.

Sarason, Barbara R. The effects of verbally conditioned response classes on post-conditioned tasks. *Dissertation Abstracts,* 1957, *12,* 679.

Skinner, B. F. *Science and human behavior.* New York: Macmillan, 1953.

Verplanck, W. S. The operant, from rat to man: An introduction to some recent experiments on human behavior. *Transactions of the New York Academy of Science,* 1955, *17,* 594–601.

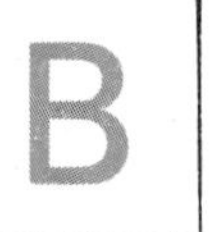

B Operant Conditioning Procedures

A somewhat different approach to the role of attitudes in behavior is described by *Golightly and Byrne,* who used statements of attitudes as reinforcers for the "correct" response in a visual discrimination task. Whenever a subject named the larger (or, for half the subjects, the smaller) of two geometric figures, he was presented with a card on which was printed a statement. Depending upon the correctness of his response, this statement either confirmed or disconfirmed the subject's previously determined attitudes on such topics as birth control or belief in God. Other subjects were simply told, in the more usual fashion, that their responses were "Right" or "Wrong." A group of control subjects were shown cards bearing neutral statements following each trial. The subjects for whom appropriate attitude statements were made contingent upon a correct or incorrect discrimination did not learn as rapidly as those who were told "Right" or "Wrong," but they did much better than the control subjects.

In a sense, the Golightly and Byrne experiment is the reverse of the others so far reported, because the properties of an attitude are used to define a reinforcer. Thus, when we say that a subject's attitudes were determined in advance, we know what inclination he has to perform in particular ways or, in this case, to make certain kinds of statements and to discuss certain themes. The reason that a statement of attitude confirmation is a reinforcer is that it provides stimuli which prompt further behavior of the same kind. Thus, the attitude reinforcer might be thought of as a conditioned reinforcer, or as part of a chain, in that it prompts more behavior appropriate to that already in the subject's repertoire. It has the element of a chain in that it provides a condition under which there can be further emission of reinforced behavior. An analogous link in a chain of performances is that of a rat going to the right fork in a maze, this being the only condition in which the subject can emit the next performance, which leads to the food.

The results of the experiment demonstrate that simply reading an attitude-related statement with which one agrees can effectively reinforce a related performance. The high degree of redundancy that occurs in the conversations of persons who agree with one another thus becomes understandable in simple reinforcement terms.

57 | *Attitude Statements as Positive and Negative Reinforcements*[1]

CAROLE GOLIGHTLY
DONN BYRNE

Attitude is a construct which refers to an enduring, learned readiness to behave in a consistent way along an affective dimension toward a given object or class of objects. On the basis of a variety of antecedent experiences, each individual holds a large number of beliefs, opinions, values, and judgments which involve attitudinal components. The relative similarity or dissimilarity of the attitudes of any two individuals has been found to exert a significant effect on their mutual attraction.

In the typical experimental study of attitude-similarity and attraction, the investigator obtains a sample of the attitudes of a group of subjects, later presents the subjects with the real or purported attitudes of a stranger, and measures the subject's attraction toward this stranger. It is a consistent finding that attraction toward the stranger is a positive linear function of the proportion of that stranger's attitudes similar to those of the subject (Byrne and Nelson, 1965).

[1] This research was supported in part by the U.S. Air Force Office of the Air Research and Development Command grant AF-AFOSR 261–64.

In accounting for this relationship, one approach has been to interpret the effects of attitude similarity-dissimilarity as a special case of the effect of positive and negative reinforcements on attraction (Byrne, 1962; Newcomb, 1956; McDonald, 1962). Briefly, the rationale is that there is a learned drive to be logical and to interpret the environment correctly. With respect to the physical world, objective criteria are available to denote correct and incorrect behavior. Positive and negative reinforcements are usually provided immediately in terms of direct perceptual feedback (for example, fire is hot, stones are hard). There also exists, however, a complex social environment in which there are equal demands to be logical and correct but for which the only criterion is that of consensual validation. Thus, agreement by others concerning political affiliations or religious practices or morality acts as a reward in that it provides evidence that one is functioning in a logical and correct manner. Consensual invalidation and hence punishment occurs when there is disagreement by others. To date, there has been no direct test of the proposition that similar and dissimilar attitude statements act as reinforcing stimuli.

In the investigation described here, a simple discrimination learning task was employed in which the traditional reinforcements were replaced by statements of attitudes. If the reinforcement interpretation of attitude similarity-dissimilarity is correct, such statements should act to change behavior. Specifically, it was hypothesized that the probability of the occurrence of a response increases if that response is followed by the presentation of a statement consonant with an attitude held by the responder and decreases if that response is followed by the presentation of a statement dissonant with an attitude held by the responder.

A 45-item attitude scale was administered to over 100 students enrolled in introductory psychology at the University of Texas. The items concerned such topics as birth control, political parties, and belief in God. Subjects responded to each item on a six-point scale. For the experiment itself, 60 subjects who had relatively extreme views (1, 2, 5, or 6 on the scale) on at least 20 topics were selected.

The learning task consisted of a simple discrimination problem. The subjects sat in front of a large wooden apparatus which contained a window for the presentation of the stimulus cards. A total of 96 cards was used, one for each trial, each containing a circle and a square of which one was black and one white, one large and one small. Each of the eight possible combinations of shape, size, color, and position appeared in random order in each block of eight trials. All subjects, run individually, were told that the experiment dealt with learning. When a stimulus card appeared in the window, the subject chose one of the two figures and said it aloud. Immediately afterward, a card was presented through a slit. The subject read the information printed on the card and then disposed of it in a discard box.

The 60 subjects were randomly assigned to one of three experimental conditions. The discrimination to be learned was small-large. In each group, small was correct and large incorrect for half of the subjects with the reverse for the other half. In the traditional reward-punishment group, the choice of the correct stimulus was followed by a card saying "RIGHT"; choice of the incorrect stimulus was followed by "WRONG." The attitude similarity-dissimilarity group received cards containing statements agreeing or disagreeing with their own position on one of the 20 topics about which they had strong views, depending on whether they gave correct or incorrect responses. Examples are: "There is definitely a God," or "There is no God"; "The Democratic Party is best," or "The Republican Party is best." Regardless of the correctness of each response, the control group received cards containing neutral statements relevant to one of the 20 topics about which they held extreme attitudes. Examples are: "Most modern religions are monotheistic"; "Political conventions are held in large cities." Trials were continued until the subject reached a criterion of eight consecutive correct responses or until 96 trials were completed. Responses were scored according to the number of correct responses per block of eight trials.

The results are depicted in Figure 1. Analysis of variance yielded a number of significant F ratios. Two findings were critical in confirming the hypothesis. Both in terms of overall performance scores [$F = 14.35$, degrees of freedom $(df) = 1/54$, $p < .001$] and in terms of the linear trend ($F = 16.38$, $df = 1/54$, $p < .001$), the attitude similarity-dissimilarity group was superior to the control group. The presentation of statements with attitudes similar and dissimilar to those of the subject acted to change response probability; hence, the reinforcement interpretation of similar and dissimilar attitudes is on considerably firmer theoretical ground. The particular research design employed in this investigation makes it impossible to determine if similar and dissimilar attitudes are both necessary to bring about learning or if just one of these conditions would be sufficient.

None of the other significant findings is directly relevant to the hypothesis under investigation. The traditional reinforcement group performed better than the other two groups ($F = 26.78$, $df = 1/54$, $p < .001$), but this is hardly surprising. In addition, there was a small but significant difference ($F = 5.04$, $df = 1/54$, $p < .05$) between the small and

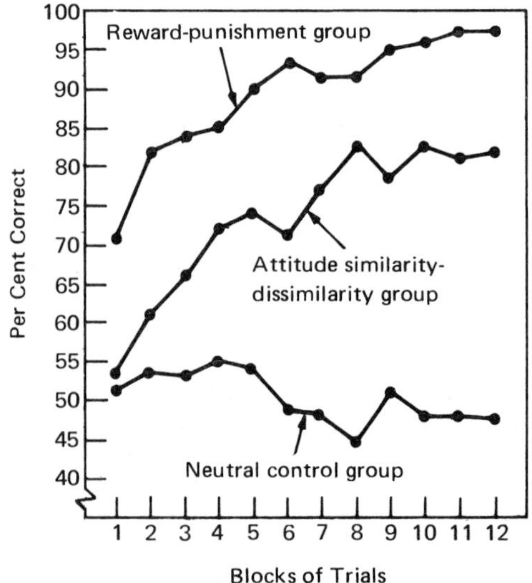

Figure 1 *Learning curves for the three groups of subjects showing percentage of correct responses over blocks of 8 trials as a function of experimental conditions.*

large condition; large was easier to learn as the correct response than small. Since this variable was controlled across groups, it could have no effect on the major findings.

References

BYRNE, D. Response to attitude similarity-dissimilarity as a function of affiliation need. *Journal of Personality,* 1962, *30,* 164–177.

BYRNE, D., and NELSON, D. Attraction as a linear function of proportion of positive reinforcements. *Journal of Personality and Social Psychology,* 1965, *1,* 659–663.

McDONALD, R. D. The effect of reward-punishment and affiliation need on interpersonal attraction. Unpublished doctoral dissertation, University of Texas, 1962.

NEWCOMB, T. M. The prediction of interpersonal attraction. *American Psychologist,* 1956, *11,* 575–586.

Insko's paper deals with the selective reinforcement of students' attitudes toward a neutral issue. The experimenters contacted students by telephone, read them statements concerning the creation of a Springtime Aloha Week in Honolulu, and said "Good" whenever the respondents agreed (or, in half the cases, disagreed) with those statements that favored such an event. One week later, the same students responded to an opinion questionnaire that contained an item dealing with this issue. Not only did the subjects tend to give more reinforced responses in the telephone interview, they also showed the effects of this treatment in their answers to the critical item on the opinion schedule. We may conclude that making agreement by a listener contingent upon a particular attitudinal response class increases the frequency with which members of that response class will be emitted. It is likely, however, that such an effect would be generated only where new or relatively unimportant attitudes are involved. We should not expect attitudes on more significant issues to be so readily manipulated.

58 | Verbal Reinforcement of Attitude

CHESTER A. INSKO

Numerous studies of the effect of reinforcement upon attitudes have been reported (Das and Nanda, 1963; Ekman, 1958; Hildum and Brown, 1956; Maccoby, Maccoby, Romney, and Adams, 1961; McGuire, 1957; Scott, 1957, 1959a, 1959b; Staats and Staats, 1958; Staats, Staats, and Heard, 1960; Weiss, Rawson, and Pasamanick, 1963). Of these studies two, Ekman, and Hildum and Brown, were concerned with the effect of verbal reinforcement. Ekman found that "good" was an effective reinforcer for modifying agree-disagree responses to a series of opinion and attitude statements regarding capital punishment. The reinforcements were delivered during a structured interview situation. Hildum and Brown reported that "Good" but not "Mm-hmm" was an effective reinforcer for modifying agree-disagree responses to a series of opinion statements regarding the Harvard philosophy of general education. The reinforcements were delivered via a telephone interview. For both of these studies there is a question as to whether verbal reinforcement actually produced attitude change or simply modified the immediate responses in the interview situation. The present study was undertaken in an attempt to gain some information on this question.

Method

Six male graduate assistants[1] each contacted by telephone 12 randomly assigned students (6 male and 6 female) from the experimenter's course in introductory psychology at the University of Hawaii

[1] The author is indebted to Richard A. Haag, John W. James, Creighton U. Mattoon, Paul O. McGaffey, Clarence M. Souza, and Frances C. Wong for their assistance in collecting the data.

From the *Journal of Personality and Social Psychology,* 1965, *2,* 621–623.

($N = 72$). The subjects were asked to either strongly agree, agree, disagree, or strongly disagree with a series of 14 statements regarding the creation of a Springtime Aloha Week.[2] The statements, which were so phrased that agreement with one half and disagreement with the other half indicated a positive attitude, were assertions of opinion and not attitude. The statements did not say that the creation of a Springtime Aloha Week was good or bad, but simply that it would lead to certain ends such as more tourists dollars or growing traffic congestion. Each graduate assistant reinforced responses indicating positive attitudes for 6 subjects (3 males and 3 females) and responses indicating negative attitudes for 6 subjects (3 males and 3 females). Reinforcement was given by saying "good" after the appropriate agree or disagree response.

Approximately one week after the telephone interviews were completed the experimenter passed out a "Local Issues Questionnaire" in his introductory class, and requested that the 225 students in the class cooperate in giving him some information on student attitudes toward various local issues. The questionnaire contained a series of 15-point attitude scales dealing with such issues as the creation of a state subsidized interisland ferry, and higher salaries for public school teachers. The attitude scales ranged from "definitely in favor of" to "definitely opposed to." The key item concerned with the creation of a Springtime Aloha Week occurred two-thirds of the way through the questionnaire.

Results

Each response to each statement in the telephone interview was given a score between 0 and 3, with high scores indicating a favorable attitude. An analysis of variance of the three independent variables, type of reinforcement, sex, and assistants, is presented in Table 1.

As predicted the total between-groups F and reinforcement F are significant. The mean positive reinforcement score is 28.22 and the mean negative reinforcement score is 20.69. The only other significant F is the interaction between assistants and sex. This interaction indicates that regardless of the type of reinforcement some assistants obtained more positive opinion responses from males and some more positive opinion responses from females.

Twelve of the 72 subjects contacted by telephone were not present in class when the attitude questionnaire was passed out the first time. The experimenter attempted to get these 12 subjects to fill out the questionnaire by requesting during the next class period that anyone who had not previously filled out the questionnaire do so after class. It was truthfully explained that this was necessary in order to have a non-biased sample. By this method completed questionnaires from 10 more subjects were obtained giving a total N of 70. One of the missing subjects was a male, reinforced for positive attitude, and the other a female, reinforced for negative attitude. Due to the existence of unequal Ns in the 24 cells and the nonsignificance of the reinforcement interactions in the previous analysis, the data were simply analyzed with a t test. A comparison of the mean positive reinforcement score of 10.40 with the mean negative reinforcement score of 8.20 resulted in a significant t of 2.03 ($p < .05$). The mean positive reinforcement score is in the area of the scale labeled "somewhat in favor of," and the mean negative reinforcement score is in the area labeled "uncertain."

[2] Aloha Week is a festival in Hawaii occurring annually every fall.

Table 1 *Analysis of Variance of the Telephone Interview Data*

Source	*df*	MS	*F*
Reinforcement (R)	1	1020.01	15.31**
Sex (S)	1	110.01	1.65
Assistants (A)	5	51.69	0.78
R × S	1	11.69	0.18
R × A	5	45.78	0.69
S × A	5	207.58	3.12*
R × S × A	5	60.98	0.92
Total between	23	129.21	1.94*
Within	48	66.63	
Total	71		

* $p < .05$.
** $p < .01$.

Discussion

The finding of an effect for reinforcement in the interview situation is consistent with the results of Hildum and Brown (1956) and of Ekman (1958). The additional finding of an effect for reinforcement on the attitude questionnaire gives support to the assertion that verbal reinforcement results in attitude change and not just in a temporary modification of responses in the interview. From a strictly operational point of view what has been demonstrated is response generality. The experiment demonstrates generality across time, experimenters (the experimenter or graduate assistant), situational context (home or classroom), media of stimulation (oral or written), media of response (oral or written), and type of response (agreement-disagreement with opinion statements or favorability-unfavorability to an attitude object).

References

Das, J. P., and Nanda, P. C. Mediated transfer of attitudes. *Journal of Abnormal and Social Psychology*, 1963, *66*, 12–16.

EKMAN, P. A comparison of verbal and nonverbal behavior as reinforcing stimuli of opinion responses. Unpublished doctoral dissertation, Adelphi College, 1958.

HILDUM, D. C. and BROWN, R. W. Verbal reinforcement and interviewer bias. *Journal of Abnormal and Social Psychology,* 1956, *53,* 108–111.

MACCOBY, ELEANOR E., MACCOBY, N., ROMNEY, A. K., and ADAMS, J. S. Social reinforcement in attitude change. *Journal of Abnormal and Social Psychology,* 1961, *63,* 109–115.

MCGUIRE, W. J. Order of presentation as a factor in "conditioning" persuasiveness. In C. I. Hovland et al., *The order of presentation in persuasion.* New Haven: Yale University Press, 1957. Pp. 98–114.

SCOTT, W. A. Attitude change through reward of verbal behavior. *Journal of Abnormal and Social Psychology,* 1957, *55,* 72–75.

SCOTT, W. A. Attitude change by response reinforcement: Replication and extension. *Sociometry,* 1959, *22,* 328–335. (a)

SCOTT, W. A. Cognitive consistency, response reinforcement and attitude change. *Sociometry,* 1959, *22,* 219–229. (b)

STAATS, A. W., and STAATS, CAROLYN K. Attitudes established by classical conditioning. *Journal of Abnormal and Social Psychology,* 1958, *57,* 37–40.

STAATS, A. W., STAATS, CAROLYN K., and HEARD, W. Attitude development and ratio of reinforcement. *Sociometry,* 1960, *23,* 338–350.

WEISS, R. F., RAWSON, H. E., and PASAMANICK, B. Argument strength, delay of argument, and anxiety in the "conditioning" and "selective learning" of attitudes. *Journal of Abnormal and Social Psychology,* 1963, *67,* 157–165.

One of the more firmly established generalizations from the experimental literature on instrumental conditioning is that response frequency declines as the interval between performance and reinforcement increases. *Weiss* devised a instrument to record the speed with which a subject responds to statements of opinion. The subject's opinion was reinforced by the reply of the experimenter, who argued persuasively with him. However, the reply did not occur immediately after the subject expressed the opinion. Delay was achieved by interposing neutral material not relevant to the subject's opinion just before the persuasive argument. When an opinion was supported promptly, it was expressed more frequently and sooner than when support was delayed. Thus, a prediction based on Hull-Spence learning theory appears relevant to the instrumental conditioning of attitudes.

59 *A Delay of Argument Gradient in the Instrumental Conditioning of Attitudes*[1]

ROBERT FRANK WEISS

In terms of the empirical law of effect, an event which follows a response and increases the strength of that response on the next trial is called a reinforcer. In this experiment Ss read aloud persuasive communications designed so that S says the opinion to be learned, followed by an opinion-supporting argument. (The argument consists of information supporting the opinion, and specifically excludes repetitions of the opinion.) It seems reasonable to expect that an opinion which is followed by a convincing argument will be strengthened more than an unsupported opinion. Such an argument would then function as a reinforcer of the opinion response and might perhaps exhibit other functional properties of reinforcers. One such property is the inverse relationship between delay of reinforcement and response strength, and a logical development of the paradigm outlined above indicates that the delay of argument (time interval between the opinion response and the reinforcing argument) may be regarded as analogous to delay of reinforcement. Research in instrumental conditioning (e.g., Perin, 1943; Logan, 1960) indicates that conditioned response strength (as measured by response speed) is a negatively accelerated decreasing function of delay of reinforcement. Theoretically, then, attitude strength (as measured by response speed)

[1] Research supported by grant MH-12402, National Institute of Mental Health.

From *Psychonomic Science,* 1967, *8,* 457–458. Reprinted by permission.

should be a negatively accelerated decreasing function of delay of argument (Weiss, 1962).

Method and Procedure

The "instrumental conditioning" procedure of Weiss et al. (1963) was employed. In order to study attitude "conditioning" rather than "habit reversal" all Ss selected had no initial opinion, as measured by a questionnaire 2–8 weeks before the experiment.

Under the impression that he was participating in a study of "speech patterns and decision making," each S twice read the communication (and three other passages) into a tape recorder. The persuasive communication consisted of two passages; the first passage ended with the opinion to be learned, and the second passage was the opinion-supporting argument. Delay of argument was varied by inserting neutral reading material between the opinion and argument passages of the persuasive communication. The mean time to read the delay material is given below (reading times were normally distributed). There were five levels of delay: 0, 3.5, 8.5, 23.0, and 55.5 seconds, with 22 Ss in each delay condition ($N = 110$).

The attitude measuring apparatus assessed each S's speed of agreement with the opinion after S had been exposed to the persuasive communication. A statement of the opinion (preceded by 14 buffers) was projected on a screen and S signified his agreement (if he agreed) by moving a lever toward the statement. When an opinion was projected on the screen, an electric timer automatically began to measure latency of agreement (to .01 second). When the lever was moved ¼ inch, a photobeam silently stopped the timer (speed = 1/latency). The timing equipment was not visible to the Ss, who did not know they were being timed. If an S did not respond within 45 seconds, his speed of agreement was considered to be zero. Ss who did not agree did not move the lever.[2]

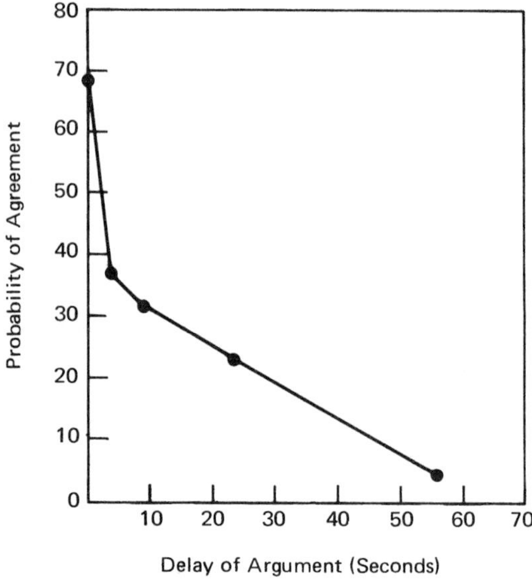

Figure 1 *Probability of agreement as a function of delay of argument.*

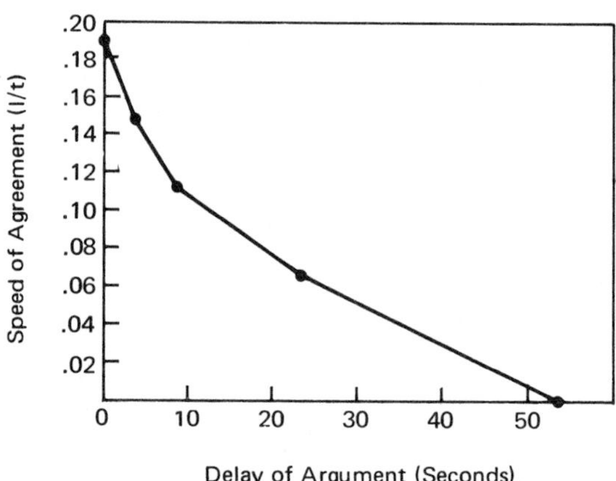

Figure 2 *Speed (1/latency) of agreement as a function of delay of argument.*

Results

Probability of agreement was a negatively accelerated decreasing function of delay of argument (Figure 1) (Chi square = 14.56, $df = 4$, $p < .01$). The powerful effect of delay on probability of agreement makes it difficult to find an adequate representation of speed data for the entire sample. Since Ss who do not agree have a speed of zero, and probability of agreement exceeds 50% only in the shortest delay condition, the median is very insensitive, while the mean is little more than a weighted probability score. In order to obtain a measure of delay effects on speed which would minimize these difficulties, the upper (fastest) quartile of each of the five groups ($N = 30$) was examined. Median speed of agreement was a negatively accelerated decreasing function of delay of argument (Figure 2). A Kruskal-Wallis test indicates that this effect was highly significant, even with the reduced sample size ($H = 15.82$, $p < .005$).

Figure 3 shows the interaction between delay (zero vs. 2.8 seconds) and number of persuasion trials (one vs. two readings of the communication). The diverging curves suggest a multiplicative relationship be-

[2] Following the typical animal conditioning procedure meant that the time from the end of the *response* (rather than the *reinforcement*) to the response-measurement was 55 sec. longer for the 55-sec. delay group than for the 0-delay group. Since 15 min. elapsed between the second reading of the opinion response and testing on the 15th slide, it was not expected that the 55-sec. difference would result in differential forgetting of the opinion, and a control experiment confirmed this.

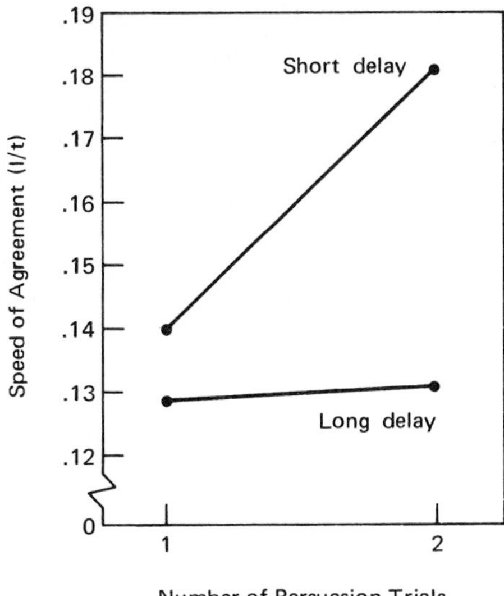

Figure 3 *Speed (1/latency) of agreement as a function of number of persuasion trials at two levels of delay of argument.*

tween delay and trials. The data are assembled from the upper quartiles ($N = 40$) of two exploratory experiments, run at different times, and therefore not susceptible to combined statistical treatment. Even though the long delay groups show little improvement from one to two trials, the one-trial long-delay group was significantly superior to a comparable no-persuasion control.

Discussion

The research reported here derives from a theory of attitude learning (Weiss, 1962) which is based on systematic analogies with learning research and Hull-Miller-Spence learning theory. The analogy between delay of argument and delay of reinforcement appears to hold in some detail. (a) In the present study of attitude "conditioning" a delay of argument gradient of the same shape as a delay of reinforcement gradient was discovered (speed measure). (b) The probability gradient also agrees with theory, although it does not afford a test over the full range of probability values; if the curve began with 100% agreement at zero delay (instead of 68%) then the curve would be expected to exhibit a brief positive acceleration, since probability is related to excitatory potential ($\dot{\bar{E}}$) by a normal integral function (e.g., Spence, 1956). (c) Again, as in conditioning, delay appears to combine multiplicatively with the number of persuasion trials to determine speed. (d) In a previous study (Weiss et al., 1963) of the "selective learning" of attitudes, the Ss learned to choose the opinion response which had been reinforced with the shorter delay, and (e) the interaction of drive with delay was similar to these effects in selective learning.

References

Logan, F. A. *Incentive.* New Haven: Yale University Press, 1960.

Perin, C. T. A quantitative investigation of the delay of reinforcement gradient. *Journal of Experimental Psychology,* 1943, *32,* 37–51.

Spence, K. W. *Behavior theory and conditioning.* New Haven: Yale University Press, 1956.

Weiss, R. F. Persuasion and the acquisition of attitudes: Models from conditioning and selective learning. *Psychological Reports,* 1962, *11,* 709–732.

Weiss, R. F., Rawson, H. E., and Pasamanick, B. Argument strength, delay of argument, and anxiety in the "conditioning" and "selective learning" of attitudes. *Journal of Abnormal and Social Psychology,* 1963, *67,* 157–165.

Attitude Modification

11

In their recent critical review of theories and research in attitude change, Kiesler, Collins, and Miller* voice several of the misgivings that some psychologists have had about the usefulness of reinforcement (S-R) theory for understanding how attitudes are formed and modified. They discuss the hypothetical case where expression of a favorable opinion, say toward capital punishment, is reinforced by a smile from the listener. What, they ask, do we conclude if we discover that the smiling does not increase the frequency of favorable opinions about capital punishment? There seem to be two possible explanations. One is that a smile is not a reinforcer in this situation. The other is that reinforcing events do not necessarily change attitudes. According to these writers, "There are considerable data that suggest, in fact, that the delivery of verbal or monetary incentives for the overtstatement of an attitude does not necessarily produce any consequent attitude change."

Reinforcement theory, to be sure, postulates that the frequency of a performance is functionally related to its consequences. It does not follow from this assumption, however, that a reinforcer can be specified without qualifying some of the circumstances. For example, candy is normally an effective reinforcer for a six-year-old boy, but not just after he has eaten five chocolate bars. Nor is candy a reinforcer to a boy who doesn't eat candy. If I react each time someone speaks, and his frequency of speaking increases as a result, then my reply is a reinforcer. On the other hand, if his frequency of speaking does not increase, it does not necessarily follow that my reply could not be an effective reinforcer on some other occasion. The same would be true if money were to be used either as a reinforcer or as an incentive. There are several reasons for this. First, money is a reinforcer only if it controls the behavior of the person whose performance it follows. For example, if a waiter is working for incentives other than the money he earns, then it will be impossible to influence his performance with tips. Second, there are often performances which are prepotent over or perhaps incompatible with the behavior that we are attempting to reinforce. If the waiter is not giving us adequate service, then he must be doing something else. Whatever these activities may be, they are, we assume, being more effectively reinforced than his table service. In short, we must look elsewhere than to the incentive of a tip for the con-

* C. A. Kiesler, B. E. Collins, and N. Miller, *Attitude Change*. New York: Wiley, 1969. Quotation from p. 91.

tingencies that are effectively determining the waiter's behavior. Theoretically, the problem may be stated as the difference between reinforcement as a *procedure* and as a *process*. As a procedure, reinforcement designates a stimulus that follows a performance. If such an operation does not effectively increase the frequency of the performance, however, then it has failed as a process.

This analogy can help us to understand what is happening in instances of attitude modification. If a subject fails to make a response that we would consider indicative of attitude change, even when we are providing what we assume to be either an incentive or a reinforcer for such change, we need not conclude that reinforcement is irrelevant in this situation. Quite the contrary, we should try to identify the alternative behaviors that *are* being strengthened and which are interfering with the changes that we are attempting to induce. Having accomplished this, we may then be able to discover what the effective reinforcers are for the subject's behavior. The fault with many experiments in persuasion and attitude change is that the investigators have been more concerned with what the subject is *not* doing than with what he *is* doing. For example, it is frequently reported that subjects have not changed certain attitudes, opinions, or judgments as a result of the experimenter's manipulation of incentives. In such instances, our attention should perhaps be directed to the persistence of other attitudes or opinions that are of long standing and that are prepotent over any that we may be attempting to instill in the subject as a result of some brief and perhaps superficial experimental manipulation. As we have noted, it has often been assumed that money and agreement are intrinsically reinforcing when presented following some attitudinal performance. This violates one of the cardinal postulates of reinforcement theory, namely, that a reinforcer is identified by its functional relationship to some performance. True, the theory assumes that *some* stimulus event is supporting any given behavior; and this assumption may be open to challenge. But any theory, as Hull* has pointed out, is built upon certain antecedent statements. Only the empirical outcomes of deductions from these statements can validate or invalidate the theory. A theory is not weakened when its postulates are either misstated or misused.

* C. L. Hull, *Principles of Behavior.* New York: Appleton-Century-Crofts, 1943.

The Use of Reinforcement

The first series of articles in this chapter deals with attitude modification as a function of various reinforcement contingencies. *Scott* regards attitudes as implicit anticipatory responses that mediate overt behavior. He invokes an inner condition to account for the increased frequency of the specific class of operant performances that defines the attitude. In his experiment, students in several large psychology classes wrote out their opinions on several issues of interest to them. Their statements were scored by the experimenter on seven-point scales with alternatives ranging from very favorable to very unfavorable on each issue. Several weeks later, arrangements were made for the students to debate these issues in pairs. In some cases, a subject was assigned a position with which he initially disagreed, in others he defended a position with which he agreed, while in others subjects who were initially neutral on an issue were given an extreme position to argue. Three professors and a graduate student acted as judges of the debates, and they arbitrarily accorded victories to one or the other of the two contestants according to a prearranged schedule. When assessing attitudes again after this experience, Scott found, as he had in an earlier study, that students who were designated as "winners" in the debates changed their attitudes more in the direction of the position they had defended than did the "losers." This occurred regardless of whether they had initially indicated agreement, disagreement, or neutrality on the question. The results suggest that selective social reinforcement can effectively modify an individual's attitudes on social issues. Behaviorally, what can be observed in this experiment is that certain frequencies of verbal performances on attitude scales tend to accompany related kinds of overt behaviors. The selective reinforcement of speaking during a debate altered the frequency of related verbal behavior prompted by the experimenter's attitude scale.

60 *Attitude Change by Response Reinforcement: Replication and Extension*[1]

WILLIAM A. SCOTT

Within the framework of *S-R* learning theory an attitude may be regarded, like a habit, as an implicit anticipatory response which mediates overt behaviors, and arises out of them through response reinforcement (Doob, 1947). Such a conception provided the basis for an earlier study (Scott, 1957) of the effect on attitudes of rewarding relevant verbal behaviors. The purposes of the present experiment were to substantiate the earlier results with different operations, to investigate the effects of response reinforcement on subjects with neutral as well as extreme attitudes, and to determine whether or not the induced attitude changes were "permanent."

Briefly, the design of the earlier study (Scott, 1957) was as follows: Pairs of students were selected from a number of general psychology classes and asked to debate any of three different issues on which they had previously expressed their opinions. However, both members were required to defend sides of the issue opposite to those which they actually held. The excellence of their presentations was to be judged

[1] The research reported in this article was supported by a grant from the Foundation for Research on Human Behavior, Ann Arbor, Michigan.

From *Sociometry*, 1959, *22*, 328–335. Reprinted by permission.

by class vote, but this vote was falsified so that a predetermined member of each pair won. Posttests of subjects' attitudes showed that the "winners" had changed in the direction of debate significantly more than the "losers" and more than a group of control Ss, while the "losers" did not change significantly more than the controls.

This study had used only Ss with initially extreme attitudes, and no provision had been made for a second posttest to determine the extent to which the attitude changes persisted. Therefore, a new experiment was designed to fill these gaps. Although the design was conceptually similar to the previous one, the actual operations differed in several respects: different issues were presented. Ss debated under different conditions, and the nature of the reinforcing stimuli was different. Given these innovations in operations (not in conceptualization), it was felt that corroborative results would better serve to substantiate the theory on which the experiments were based than would replication by identical operations.

Method

Attitudes of students toward three different controversial issues were assessed in several General Psychology classes, by the following open questions:

1. *Curriculum.* If you had the job of laying out a curriculum of required courses for all undergraduates at CU, what kinds of courses would you lay most emphasis on—those related to the study of scientific facts and research methods, or courses dealing with social problems and courses which help the student learn more about people?

2. *Fraternities and sororities.* Some people feel that fraternity and sorority life contributes a great deal to the development of the student during his college career. Others feel that fraternities and sororities work to the detriment of students by taking their attention away from more important academic matters. What do you think about this?

3. *Ideal husband or wife.* If you were thinking of getting married, which kind of a husband or wife would you rather have: One who is mainly interested in people and enjoys being with people, or one who has a wide variety of interests and creative talent in some area?

Immediately after this pretest, a general invitation was addressed to the classes to participate in an elimination debate contest, the winners of which would share a $100 cash prize. The investigator's interest was reported to be "to find out what kinds of people hold what kinds of attitudes." A couple of weeks later volunteers were contacted by phone and asked to take a particular side of one of the three issues for debate. The sides were assigned irrespective of Ss' initial positions, so that some debaters defended their own opinions, some the opposite opinions, and some debated "off-neutral" (they expressed no clear opinion on the pretest, but were assigned a definite position in the debate). The only restrictions were to keep these three groups (same, opposite, and off-neutral) approximately equal and to give equal representation to each of the three issues. Ss were told that debate positions were being assigned irrespective of actual attitudes, because "the purpose of the study is to see how well people can present opinions they don't actually hold, and how well their opponents can judge their own true attitudes."

The debates took place in a small research room, with the two Ss seated at one end of a long table, and three judges at the opposite end. For every debate, two of the judges were professors of psychology, and the third was a mature graduate student; *E* was one of the judges at every debate, but the other judging professor and the graduate student were changed several times throughout the experiment. Introductions were formal, as was the decorum of the entire procedure. None of the Ss had known his opponent prior to that time. It was explained that the winner of this first debate would be contacted for a second debate, and if he won that, as well as a third debate, he would receive a $20 prize. Ss presented their initial arguments for five minutes each, followed by two-minute rebuttals in reverse order.

Each judge, in turn, rendered his decision on the relative merits of the two performances. The reasons he offered for his decision were confined to the manner of presentation (style, clarity, convincingness, etc.), rather than to the content of the talk, in order to minimize the possible influences of prestige suggestion which might be entailed if the judgment referred to the substance of the argument (e.g., "That was a good point"). The winner in each case had been predetermined in systematic fashion, so that all the judges had to do during the debate was to jot down plausible reasons for their decisions.

Following the judgment, Ss were led to small individual rooms near the debate room, where they filled out questionnaires on the three issues, identical with those from the pretest. *E* indicated that "we are interested in seeing how you feel about these matters at this time," without explicitly indicating that opinions were expected either to change or to remain constant. In addition there was the question, "How do you think your opponent *really* feels about this issue?" included simply to maintain the pretext previously offered for the study.

Winning Ss were called back about ten days later to debate a different issue. Their positions were again

Table 1 *Mean Attitude Changes of Winners, Losers, and Controls*

Group of Subjects	*N*	Mean Change*	*SD* of Change	Difference in Mean Changes
First debate				
(A) Winners	20	+1.67	1.55	A vs. B: $t = 2.76$; $p < .01$
(B) Losers	20	+0.15	1.83	A vs. C: $t = 3.80$; $p < .001$
(C) Controls	15	+0.24	0.47	B vs. C: $t = -0.20$; *ns*
(D) Winners ten days later	20	+1.20	1.66	D vs. C: $t = 2.40$; $p < .05$
Second debate				
(A) Winners	10	+1.40	1.80	A vs. B: $t = 1.29$; *ns*
(B) Losers	10	+0.36	1.62	
Third debate				
(A) Winners	5	+2.80	1.72	A vs. B: $t = 2.88$; $p < .05$
(B) Losers	5	−0.20	1.17	

* A positive sign indicates a mean change in the direction of debate, or, for control *Ss*, a mean change opposite to their original position. For control *Ss* with initially neutral attitudes, alternate positive and negative directions of changes were assigned. One-tailed tests of significance were used throughout.

assigned irrespective of their true attitudes, and the debating situation was as before, except that judgments of win or lose were based on merit (as the judges saw it).[2] There were no predetermined winners or losers, so occasionally there was a split vote among the three judges; but *E* always voted last, in order to make the decision as clear and definite as possible. A second posttest of attitudes toward the three issues was obtained. (*S*s wrote in separate rooms.)

Winners of the second debate were recalled for a third time, to debate the remaining issue of the three. The consequences of this contest were made clear, and *S*s were given the choice of "winner take all" ($20) or "split the prize" ($15 and $5). Three pairs chose the former division; two, the latter. Again the voting of judges was genuine; a third posttest of attitudes toward all three issues was obtained.

Attitudes expressed in the pretest and on the three posttests were typed on 3″ x 5″ cards, numbered in such a way as to disguise their sources (see Scott, 1957). These were then coded by *E* on a seven-point attitude scale, representing a neutral position and three degrees of intensity toward each extreme of the issue—e.g.:

1. Greek organizations are very definitely a help.
2. Greek organizations are a help.
3. Greek organizations are mainly a help, but also some hindrance.
4. Don't know; not ascertained; equally a help and a hindrance; depends on the individual.
5. Greek organizations are mainly a hindrance, but also some help.
6. Greek organizations are a hindrance.
7. Greek organizations are very definitely a hindrance.

Check-coding, by an independent judge of a sample of these attitudes showed their coding reliability to be .87.

Results

Of principal interest is the comparison of winners and losers on the first round of debates, for in that series they were randomly determined. The results are presented in the top part of Table 1, which shows that winners tended to change toward the side debated more than did losers or controls. (The control group was composed of those volunteers who could not be scheduled during the first debate series. Their posttest attitudes were assessed just after the third debate series, approximately one month after the pretest.)

Attitude changes following the second and third debates were comparable to those in the first debate (see bottom of Table 1). It will be recalled that, here, the decisions were not predetermined, but depended on performance as estimated by the judges.

Also of interest are the findings concerning "permanence" of the effects of reinforcement. As previously noted, all 20 *S*s who participated in the second debate were tested concerning their attitudes toward the issue of the first debate. From their responses it is possible to estimate the degree of "sav-

[2] This shift in the basis for determining winners was largely for ethical reasons. Though a random choice of winners was necessary for purposes of experimental control, once this had been achieved on the first round of debates, there appeared to be no reason why virtue should not be rewarded.

ings" from the first posttest to the second posttest —approximately ten days later. It is clear from the data in Table 1 ("First debate: Winners ten days later") that attitudes expressed on the second posttest are different, both from the pretest attitudes, and from the first posttest attitudes. Thus, there is a significant degree of savings from the first reward experience, even though the reinforcement is not explicitly repeated; but the amount of savings is less than the amount of initial change.

Since Ss were assigned debate positions regardless of their own true attitudes, it is possible to see whether or not the response reinforcement was effective when it operated in the same direction as Ss initial attitude, or when it aimed at moving him from a neutral position. Table 2 shows the results of the debates, grouped according to the relationship between Ss initial attitude and his debate position. When Ss debated "opposite sides," the absolute change of winners was largest (2.77 on a seven-point scale). When debating "off-neutral," the mean change was 1.47, and the mean change of winners debating their "own sides" was 0.63 toward a more extreme position in the same direction. A comparison of absolute changes in position is deceptive, however, since Ss debating "opposite sides" had the greatest room for movement, and those debating "own sides" had the least. Relative to the amount of movement (in the direction of reinforcement) possible, the three groups showed changes of 55 per cent, 49 per cent, and 63 per cent, respectively. But since there is no way of comparing scale intervals at various points on the dimension, it would be mere sham to conclude anything about the relative effects of response reinforcement under the three circumstances.

Table 2 *Mean Attitude Change as a Function of the Relationship between S's Pretest Attitude and Debate Position*

Group of Subjects	*N*	Mean Change*	*SD* of Change	Difference in Mean Changes
Debating opposite side				
(A) Winners	10	+2.77	1.97	A vs. B:
(B) Losers	10	+0.90	1.05	$t = 2.53; p < .05$
Debating off-neutral				
(A) Winners	11	+1.47	1.25	A vs. B:
(B) Losers	13	+0.54	1.44	$t = 1.62; p < .10$
Debating own side				
(A) Winners	7	+0.63	0.86	A vs. B:
(B) Losers	13	−0.77	1.89	$t = 2.15; p < .05$

* A plus sign indicates a mean change in the direction of debate. One-tailed tests of significance are reported.

All one can say is that winners tended to change in the direction of debate more than losers did, regardless of whether they debated their own positions, opposite positions, or off-neutral.

Discussion

The results of this study suggest, first of all, that the effects of response reinforcement on attitude change are not necessarily transitory but may be preserved up to periods of at least ten days. On the one hand, this may seem surprising, since, during the interval between tests, Ss were presumably living within the same social contexts that had supported their initial attitudes. Thus one might expect them to revert to their old positions as soon as they were removed from the reinforcing situation. On the other hand, the occasion for the second posttest was so nearly identical with that for the first posttest that the cues present could well have served to reintegrate the former response, even though it did not conform to S's true attitude at that time. In a more imaginative study, one might attempt a follow-up assessment of S's attitudes in a completely different context, with someone other than *E* eliciting the relevant response.

A second result suggests that response reinforcement can be effective either in strengthening previously held attitudes, in changing them, or in creating new ones (if those Ss who debated "off-neutral" can be said to have developed "new" attitudes). There was no evidence to indicate that Ss with neutral attitudes were more amenable to change than those with more extreme views. Such an outcome might have been expected in the light of the frequently reported finding that people who hold intense attitudes, oor who are quite certain of their opinions, are relatively resistant to pressures to change (Birch, 1945; Burdick, 1956; Carlson, 1956; Hochbaum, 1954; Osgood and Tannenbaum, 1955). However, with less than interval-scale measures, it is difficult to compare relative movements at different positions on the attitude scale. Moreover, the status of the initially "neutral" attitudes is by no means clear, since that category included Ss who expressed balanced opinions on both sides of the issue as well as those who replied "no opinion." It seems to this writer that neutrality of an attitude as such is probably not the critical feature for predicting susceptibility to change, but rather it is the degree to which the attitude, of whatever direction or strength, is embedded in a cognitive structure of other supporting attitudes and cognitive elements. (This quality of "embeddedness" has been referred to elsewhere as *cognitive consistency* [Scott, 1958, 1959]).

The major significance of the study, however, would seem to lie in its confirmation of previously obtained results (Scott, 1957) not by exact replication, but by "methodological triangulation" (Campbell, 1953). Whereas the earlier experiment required Ss to debate in front of their fellow classmates and "rewarded" them by class vote, the present procedure involved debates in a private setting with reinforcement by judges' decisions and monetary reward. Moreover, the judges debated were different from those previously used. Thus one can safely maintain that the hypothesized relationship is not exclusively dependent on the particular methods chosen to assess it. When a number of different sets of empirical operations yield comparable results, it is reasonable to presume that they reflect a valid relationship (i.e., one that is independent of the measuring procedures) rather than just a reliable relationship (one that depends on a particular instrument or experimental design) (cf., Campbell and Fiske, 1959).

Summary

Ss were invited to participate in a series of debates, in which they defended positions on three different issues irrespective of their own opinions. Comparison of their pretest attitudes with those expressed immediately following the debates indicated that Ss who "won" (by judges' decision) tended to change their attitudes in the direction of the positions presented. This result confirmed that of a previous experiment in which Ss debated under different conditions and were reinforced by vote of their classmates. The effect on "winners" in this study occurred regardless of whether they debated their own side of the argument, the opposite side, or from an initially neutral position. Some permanence of the change was evidenced on a second posttest about ten days after the initial winning. "Losers" in the debate did not change their attitudes significantly more than a control group of nondebaters.

References

Birch, H. G. The effect of socially disapproved labelling upon well-structured attitudes. *Journal of Abnormal and Social Psychology,* 1945, *40,* 301–310.

Burdick, H. A. The Relationship of attraction, need achievement, and certainty to conformity under conditions of a simulated group atmosphere. *Dissertation Abstracts,* 1956, *16,* 1518–1519.

Campbell, D. T. *A study of leadership among submarine officers.* Columbus: Ohio State University, Personnel Research Board, 1953.

Campbell, D. T., and Fiske, D. W. Convergent and discriminant validation by the multitrait-multimethod matrix. *Psychological Bulletin,* 1959, *56,* 81–105.

Carlson, E. R. Attitude change through modification of attitude structure. *Journal of Abnormal and Social Psychology,* 1956, *52,* 256–261.

Doob, L. W. The behavior of attitudes. *Psychological Review,* 1947, *54,* 135–156.

Hochbaum, G. M. The relation between group members' self-confidence and their reactions to group pressures to uniformity. *American Sociological Review,* 1954, *19,* 678–687.

Osgood, C., and Tannenbaum, P. H. The principle of congruity in the prediction of attitude change. *Psychological Review,* 1955, *62,* 42–55.

Scott, W. A. Attitude change through reward of verbal behavior. *Journal of Abnormal and Social Psychology,* 1957, *55,* 72–75.

Scott, W. A. Rationality and non-rationality of international attitudes. *Conflict Resolution,* 1958, *2,* 8–16.

Scott, W. A. Cognitive consistency, response reinforcement, and attitude change. *Sociometry,* 1959, *22,* 219–229.

Goldstein and McGinnies report an experiment in which subjects were selected on the basis of their scores on a Likert-type scale measuring attitudes toward the church. Some time later, twelve subjects who had demonstrated very pro-church attitudes were asked to read an essay highly critical of the church to three-person audiences. Unknown to any of the speakers, some of the audiences were composed of subjects whose attitudes were very favorable toward the church, others contained subjects who were neutral toward the church, while still others consisted of subjects holding negative attitudes toward the church. There were four speakers and four audiences in each of these conditions. Following each speaker's presentation of the anti-church document, the groups engaged in short discussions of the points raised. Following this experience, all of the subjects responded again to the attitude scale. Those speakers who had confronted either neutral or anti-church audiences moved significantly toward the anti-church end of the scale, whereas those who had engaged in discussion with pro-church audiences were virtually unmoved form their initial positions. The results suggest strongly that the audience members whose attitudes were congruent with those of the speaker behaved in such a manner as to reinforce the speaker's original viewpoint toward the church, thereby negating any persuasive effect that the anti-church essay may have had. Such reinforcement was not provided by either the neutral or the anti-church audiences, so that the speakers were swayed by the anti-church arguments that they had presented, as well as by assent given to these arguments by the audience members, especially in the anti-church groups.

61 Compliance and Attitude Change under Conditions of Differential Social Reinforcement[1]

IRWIN GOLDSTEIN
ELLIOTT McGINNIES

It seems clear that social attitudes are formed in deference to the same learning principles that govern the acquisition of other verbal and motor responses. In general, it can be assumed that individuals acquire those attitudes that are positively reinforced by the contingent behavior of other persons. By the same reasoning, it may be postulated that attitude change occurs when different reinforcement contingencies come to operate upon the individual. A learning-theory interpretation of persuasion and attitude change has, of course, been introduced by Hovland, Janis, and Kelley (1953) and has been elaborated in subsequent studies emanating from the Yale group. Festinger (1957) and his co-experimenters, on the other hand, have argued for a theory of attitude change based upon assumptions of incompatible cognitions and resulting pressures toward consistency or congruence among these cognitions. This approach stresses the role of inner tensions in achieving consonance between conflicting attitudes rather than the operation of external reinforcers which might increase the probability of one attitudinal response over another. In the present experiment, we have borrowed Festinger's basic procedure of "forced compliance" as a vehicle to induce attitude change but have relied upon differential social reinforcement as the major variable controlling the direction of such change.

That individuals are influenced by exposure to a persuasive communication and, even more, by active rehearsal of an argument, is well established. King and Janis (1956) found that subjects who improvised a speech were more inclined to change their own opinions to agree with it than subjects who read it aloud, who, in turn, changed more than those who read it silently. What is not clear at present is the extent to which such persuasive influences might be rendered more or less effective when accompanied by appropriate reinforcing behavior from other persons. Several tangential approaches to this problem have been made. Brodbeck (1956) had groups listen to a taped speech presenting a viewpoint toward wire tapping with which most members of the groups disagreed. She reports that when later permitted to discuss the communication, the group members tended to listen preferentially to persons who agreed with them and to find confirmation of their original views through such discussion. Steiner (1962) reaches exactly the opposite conclusion from Brodbeck's data and suggests that much additional research is needed on this point.

Maccoby, Maccoby, Romney, and Adams (1961) have further reported that following exposure to a persuasive communication, people do indeed tend to discuss it more frequently with persons who agree with their own initial attitudes. A failure of majority pressure in discussion to influence the attitudes of individual members on the issue of nationalism versus internationalism, however, was reported by Lawson and Stagner (1957).

Mitnick and McGinnies (1958) formed groups of high school students having similar scores on the California E Scale, ranging in different groups from high to low, and showed them a mental health film designed to reduce ethnocentrism. They found that highly ethnocentric students who were allowed to discuss the film showed less reduction in E Scale scores than did ethnocentric students who viewed

[1] This paper is based upon a master's dissertation submitted by the first author to the University of Maryland. The second author directed the research and prepared the present report. Nancy Anderson provided helpful advice at all stages of the experiment.

From the *Journal of Abnormal and Social Psychology*, 1964, *68*, 567–570.

the film without discussion. Analysis of the discussions revealed that the subjects had used this opportunity to reiterate and, hence, to reinforce their original convictions. This study supports the contention that social reinforcement is a critical variable determining attitude change, or lack of change.

If kind and amount of social reinforcement are conceived as the principal variables governing attitude change, it should be possible to control the extent of such change by manipulating these reinforcement contingencies. In the present experiment, contrived audiences with predetermined attitudes toward the church were used to provide either positive, neutral, or negative social reinforcement (both verbal and nonverbal) for prochurch individuals who delivered an anti-church argument. In line with reinforcement principles, it was hypothesized that speakers whose own attitudes were supported by a group discussion would be less influenced by the communication than where group members agreed with the position taken by the communication in opposition to the speaker's viewpoint. Stated somewhat differently, the experiment tested the prediction that induced compliance of the type described would sway the subject in the direction of the communication more when followed by positive reinforcement in discussion than when followed by neutral or negative social reinforcement.

Method

Subjects. A 23-item Likert-type scale measuring attitudes toward the church and based on Thurstone and Chave's (1929) statements, was administered to approximately 600 students in the introductory psychology course at the University of Maryland. Each statement provided five scale positions for indicating extent of agreement or disagreement with statements relating to the church, so that scores could range from 23 (extremely prochurch) to 115 (extremely antichurch). Twelve subjects were selected from each of three segments of the total distribution so as to represent prochurch ($M = 35.0$), neutral ($M = 67.4$), and antichurch ($M = 94.1$) viewpoints. The 12 individuals representing each of these attitudes toward the church were then formed into groups of three, designated as the "audiences." Twelve such audience groups provided positive, neutral, or negative reinforcement for the speakers, four groups being assigned to each reinforcement category.

An additional 12 subjects were chosen at random from the prochurch end of the distribution to serve as speakers and as objects of the differential social reinforcement effects that were anticipated from the contrived audiences. These 12 individuals had a mean score on the attitude scale of 36.1, nearly the same as that of the 12 prochurch audience members. Since the total distribution was badly skewed toward the higher scores, it was not possible to select additional speakers with negative attitudes toward the church. We worked, therefore, with individuals who were exposed to three different types of social reinforcement for compliance in reiterating an antichurch communication.

Communication. The vehicle used both to influence the speaker's attitudes and to serve as a basis for group discussion was a 300-word essay strongly critical of the church. The communication incorporated some of the antichurch items in the scale as well as additional antichurch material calculated to have logical as well as emotional appeal.

Procedure. Each of the 12 prochurch "speakers" was induced to read the antichurch essay to a group of three listeners under the pretext of engaging in an experimental study of the group-discussion process. To further enhance the plausibility of this explanation of the task, a preliminary discussion was actually held on such topics as college regulations, student problems, the college curriculum, and fraternity life.

The speakers, although known to the experimenters as positively oriented toward the church, were ostensibly selected at random. Neither the speakers nor the audience members knew in advance what each other's proclivities were toward the church, although all had interacted sufficiently during the "warm-up" period to facilitate discussion of the antichurch communication. Each speaker was allowed to study the communication briefly before reading it aloud, and each audience member was asked to make at least one comment about the speech as a prelude to general discussion of it. Following the discussions, each of which lasted 12 minutes, all of the subjects were asked to fill out the attitude scale as well as two short questionnaires designed to elicit their reactions to the communication and to the discussion.

In summary, 12 prochurch subjects complied in reading to three-person audiences an antichurch communication. Four of the speakers faced audiences with prochurch views, four had neutral audiences, and four were confronted with audiences having antichurch attitudes. Short discussions following the communication permitted these various viewpoints to be expressed, thus providing the speakers with positive, neutral, or negative reinforcement of their compliant behavior.

Results

Attitude Change as a Function of Compliance. The experimental conditions were such that both the speakers and the audiences were exposed to the persuasive communication, the speakers actively and the listeners passively. Both, therefore, might have been expected to show attitude change as a result of their common experience. The discussions were expected to determine the direction and amount of such change by providing differential reinforcement for subjects in the different groups.

Since pre- and postexperimental scores on the attitude scale were available for all subjects, *t* tests for difference scores obtained from these correlated measures were performed to test the null hypothesis that the mean change for the 12 speakers and the three groups of individuals who comprised the pro, neutral, and antichurch audiences would not differ significantly from zero. The speakers, as a group, showed a mean change of 6.83 scale points toward the antichurch end of the attitude continuum. With a standard deviation of 8.29, this change yielded a *t* of 2.86, significant beyond the .01 level (one-tailed test). None of the mean changes for the listeners, grouped according to initial attitude toward the church, reached significance at the .05 level. It is apparent that only the speakers' attitudes were influenced significantly by the experimental procedure.

Differential Reinforcement Effects. Did change in attitude toward the church among the speakers occur differentially according to the type of discussion in which they participated? It had been hypothesized that attitude change consistent with the compliance experience would be greater when the other discussants supported the communication and would be less following a discussion with individuals who supported the church and disagreed with the communication.

The four speakers in the prochurch groups changed an average of 1.75 scale points, the four speakers in the neutral groups showed a mean change of 9.25 scale points, and the speakers in the antichurch groups moved an average of 9.50 scale positions in an antichurch direction. Since the speakers who interacted with neutral and antichurch discussants showed approximately the same amount of attitude change, their scores were combined and compared with the mean change of speakers with prochurch discussants. A Mann-Whitney *U* test showed the difference to be significant at the .05 level. The compliance experience apparently was more strongly reinforced for those speakers who were exposed to neutral and antichurch audiences than for the speakers exposed to prochurch audiences.

As a check upon the validity of the attitude scale, every subject was asked to indicate how often he attended church, using five categories ranging from "very frequently" to "almost never." The average attendance indicated by the prochurch subjects was 4.67 (very frequently), for the neutral subjects 2.67 (every now and then), and for the antichurch subjects 1.33 (almost never).

Discussion

Some light was thrown on the operation of the social reinforcement process by examination of replies to the postexperimental questionnaires. Although the small *N*s would have made statistical treatment meaningless, it was found that the speakers in the prochurch, neutral, and antichurch groups were progressively less certain that the discussion had provided them with an opportunity to express their initial opinions about the church.

The fact that the speakers "disagreed" with the communication following discussions in the antichurch groups contrasts with their reactions of "strongly disagree" after discussions with other prochurch individuals. This is consistent with their behavior on the postexperimental administration of the attitude scale. A similar consistency is found in the fact that the speakers judged the members of the prochurch groups as having "disagreed" with the communication and as having failed to defend it in discussion. They were "undecided" about both of these questions in the neutral and antichurch discussion groups. The listeners also responded to interrogation in a manner consistent with their own attitudes and the experimental situations to which they had been exposed. All "agreed" that the speakers had not adequately defended the position taken by the communication, and all recognized that the speaker was not actually in agreement with the argument that he had presented. Perhaps this is why the listeners were relatively uninfluenced by the communication. Members of the prochurch discussion groups also perceived that the other group members shared their views, whereas the neutral and antichurch discussants were undecided about this. This may reflect a degree of awkwardness created in these two types of groups by their perception that the speakers neither agreed with what they had said nor had defended it adequately.

Finally, it may be pointed out that the results could have been predicted from cognitive dissonance theory as well as from reinforcement theory. Dissonance probably was greatest for those speakers participating in discussion with individuals whose attitudes toward the church were antagonistic to their own. Pressures to achieve greater consonance between their privately held convictions and their public reading of the antichurch communication, which had received additional support during discussion, would have resulted in their observed shifts in attitude. This interpretation, however, seems to involve additional assumptions about cognitive processes that are circumvented by a reinforcement-theory approach.

References

BRODBECK, MAY. The role of small groups in mediating the effects of propaganda. *Journal of Abnormal and Social Psychology,* 1956, *52,* 166–170.

FESTINGER, L. *A theory of cognitive dissonance.* Evanston, Ill.: Row, Peterson, 1957.

HOVLAND, C. I., JANIS, I. L., and KELLEY, H. H. *Communication and persuasion.* New Haven: Yale University Press, 1953.

KING, B. T., and JANIS, I. L. Comparison of the effectiveness of improvised versus nonimprovised role-playing in producing opinion change. *Human Relations* 1956, *9,* 177–186.

LAWSON, E. D., and STAGNER, R. Group pressure, attitude change, and autonomic involvement. *Journal of Social Psychology,* 1957, *45,* 299–312.

MACCOBY, ELEANOR E., MACCOBY, N., ROMNEY, A. K., and ADAMS, J. S. Social reinforcement in attitude change. *Journal of Abnormal and Social Psychology,* 1961, *63,* 109–115.

MITNICK, L. L., and MCGINNIES, E. Influencing ethnocentrism in small discussion groups through a film communication. *Journal of Abnormal and Social Psychology,* 1958, *56,* 82–90.

STEINER, I. D. Receptivity to supportive versus nonsupportive communications. *Journal of Abnormal and Social Psychology,* 1962, *65,* 266–267.

THURSTONE, L. L., and CHAVE, E. J. *The measurement of attitude.* Chicago: University of Chicago Press, 1929.

In their reading of an essay critical of the church, the speakers observed by Goldstein and McGinnies could be said to have played "roles." Additional evidence for the reinforcing effects of audience feedback upon a person enacting a role that is not characteristic of him is presented in the study by *Sarbin and Allen.* They examined an additional variable, namely, the person's "need" for reinforcement as inferred from his answers to a questionnaire dealing with the value that he places upon close and affectionate relations with others. On the pretext that they were being observed for debating ability, subjects who had been classified as either high or low in need for social reinforcement were asked to argue a position which they actually opposed. Ten-person audiences, acting on instructions from the experimenter, provided either positive or negative feedback to the speakers during their presentations. Unexpectedly, those subjects who were subjected to negative audience reactions changed more in the direction of the position they were presenting than did the subjects who were positively reinforced for their speaking efforts. The authors suggest that these subjects may have engaged in more improvisation and thereby played their roles more effectively than the subjects who received positive audience feedback. Whether they evoked reactions of approval or disapproval from their audiences, the reinforced subjects showed greater attitude change in the direction of the positions they had advocated than did control subjects. Although not statistically significant, there was a tendency for the subjects high in need for social reinforcement to be more influenced by audience reactions than those low on this measure. This experiment emphasizes the necessity of determining empirically the consequences of a performance that increases its frequency before attempting to specify what stimuli will act as effective reinforcers. What we take to be negative consequences may, in fact, prompt more behaviors of a particular class than consequences that ostensibly are more positive.

62 | Role Enactment, Audience Feedback, and Attitude Change

THEODORE R. SARBIN
VERNON L. ALLEN

Frequent observations from "real life" attest to the influence of role enactment on other aspects of behavior. Anecdotes abound of the person whose attitudes, values, and perceptions tend to shift toward greater congruence with the norms of his role. These observations support the general proposition advanced by role theory that prolonged occupancy of any position in the social structure affects the individual's total cognitive structure, including the self (Sarbin, 1954).

Among the data offered to support this proposition are the early studies of Merton (1940) on bureaucrats, and Waller (1932) on teachers. These data are, however, subject to alternative explanations. Occupancy of a position may cause the change in attitude, or a selective factor may operate so that persons having attitudes congruent with a role are more often chosen to enact that role. Several recent experimental studies have attempted to clarify the relation between role enactment and attitudes by manipulation of the relevant variables. The studies of Culbertson (1957), King and Janis (1956), Janis and King (1954), and Lieberman (1956) lend convincing experimental support to the hypothesis that role enactment is conducive to a change in attitude and opinion. Various explanations have been offered to account for the phenomenon: cognitive dissonance (Festinger, 1957), reinforcement (Scott, 1957), and improvisation and involvement (King and Janis, 1956). These theoretical statements have all been shown to have some utility in accounting for attitude change produced by role enactment.

Implicit in the concept of role and role enactment is the assumption of reciprocal role-others or, in other words, an audience for the actor. Hence, during role enactment there is usually available feedback in the form of social reinforcement from other persons. It is to this component of the process of attitude change—audience effects—that we address ourselves. We asked the question: what effects follow from role enactment before audiences that provide positive social reinforcement, compared with those that provide negative social reinforcement? We recognize the fact of individual differences in responsiveness to social reinforcement (Krasner, 1958), and for this reason included in the design a face-valid measure of "need for social reinforcement."

Our first general hypothesis is that the enactment of a role which supports an attitude contrary to one's private belief will lead to change in that belief. We further predict as a second hypothesis that when positive social reinforcement is given, the direction of attitude change will be toward the position expressed publicly during role enactment; this change will be greater when positive social reinforcement is given than when negative social reinforcement is given. Our third general hypothesis is that persons who are characterized as high on the variable "need for social reinforcement" will change their private attitudes in the direction of role enactment to a greater extent than persons who are low on this variable. The present study constitutes an attempt to test these hypotheses experimentally by using a realistic role enactment situation in which the social reinforcement received by the subject is under experimental control.

Method

Subjects. Subjects for the experiment were 64 students from an undergraduate course in abnormal psychology. Participation as experimental subjects fulfilled part of the requirements of the course.

Design. Two experimental samples ($N = 23$ and $N = 16$) and two control samples ($N = 12$ and $N = 13$) were used. The audience provided positive social reinforcement to one experimental sample and negative social reinforcement to the other. Each experimental sample contained an approximately equal number of subjects who scored high and low on a scale measuring "need for social reinforcement." About half the subjects were male and half were female.

Materials. Two weeks before the study began, two questionnaires were administered to students in the undergraduate course taught by the senior author. Attitude scales consisting of six items, stated alternatively positively and negatively, were constructed for each of five attitude domains. Responses were scored on a six-point scale, ranging from "strongly agree" to "strongly disagree." The subjects also rated

From *Sociometry*, 1964, *27*, 183–193. Reprinted by permission.

the importance of each item by using a six-point scale.

From inspection of the frequency distributions of responses to the five attitude areas, two were chosen for use in the experiment: allowing controversial persons to speak on campus, and giving federal aid to parochial schools. Most subjects held strongly the opinion that controversial persons should be permitted to speak on campus, and strongly opposed federal aid to parochial schools.

The class was also administered a face-valid questionnaire measuring "need for social reinforcement." Two scales were selected from Schutz's (1958) FIRO-B (Fundamental Interpersonal Relations Orientation—Behavior) instrument, "Wanted Inclusion," and "Wanted Affection." The scales measure how much one wants other people to include him, and to be close and personal with him, respectively.

Procedure

Experimental Sample. The following instructions were read to the experimental subjects:

> This experiment is part of a research project designed to study the psychological factors involved in debating ability. I would like each of you to give an informal five-minute talk to an audience of 10 other students. You will take a definite position on a contemporary issue. From several available topics you may choose one at random by taking one of the sheets in this large manila envelope. The sheet will state a topic and your position on the topic, along with some suggestions that you might use as an outline for your talk. You may use the outline as a basis for your talk, but you do not have to restrict your talk to these points. You may elaborate, improvise, or bring in facts and examples of your own. Try to present any kind of arguments, illustrations, and types of appeals that you think will be most convincing. You are to support the position suggested on your paper. Make as strong an argument as possible, and make your talk as convincing as possible. Your object is to do your utmost to convince the audience of your viewpoint. We will determine from the audience how much you have influenced their opinions. The audience will rate your performance in terms of overall effectiveness, and on several specific points such as sincerity, convincingness, poise, logic, and so on.

The experimental subjects were selected prior to the experiment on the basis of having either a high or a low score on the two FIRO-B scales. The subject "randomly" chose a topic from a large envelope; in the envelope were preparatory arguments for an extreme position on only one attitude—a position strongly opposed personally by the subject receiving it. In each experimental sample the two topics were assigned alternately to the subjects. After the five-minute preparation, the subject went into an adjoining room. The experimental subjects stood behind a rostrum and spoke to the audience for five minutes. When the subject returned to a waiting room, the teaching assistant for the course gave him a questionnaire concerning evaluation of and reaction to his speech. The assistant then pretended to search through his records, explaining that some questionnaires filled out earlier in class had been lost. A fictitious check appeared to disclose that one of the subject's questionnaires was missing, and he was asked to take it again. In this manner, a second administration of the attitude questionnaire was obtained.

Control Samples. Two control samples were used. Control sample "A" received the same instructions as the experimental samples. At the end of the five-minute preparation the experimenter told the subjects in this group that there would be a slight delay because the experiment was not ready to begin. On the pretext that several earlier questionnaires had been lost, all subjects were asked to fill out the attitude questionnaire again while waiting.

Control sample "B" did not prepare arguments. They were told that several questionnaires had been lost, and were requested to take them again while waiting for the experiment to begin. This group was, therefore, a before-after control sample.

Audience. The 10 subjects composing the audience were seated in a natural manner among the first five rows of seats in a large lecture room. A different audience was used at each two-hour experimental session. Members of the audience were given two instruction sheets, one for positive responses and one for negative responses, explaining how to react during the speech. Each member of the audience received an instruction sheet describing several specific responses to give to the speaker. Most members of the audience were told to give different responses. A signal from the experimenter—presence or absence of a large card on the blackboard—informed the audience whether to respond to the speaker with positive or negative social reinforcement.

The audience was given general instructions to act naturally, not to overdramatize, and to space their reactions at reasonable intervals. With the experimenter as speaker, the audience always practiced reacting with positive and negative social reinforcement until he was satisfied with their performance.

The positive reinforcement condition included such responses from the audience as: alertness and undivided attention, nodding head in agreement and writing a note, nodding head in agreement when points are made, looking directly at the speaker, smiling, looking pleasant and pleased. The negative reinforcement condition included such responses as: averting eyes from speaker, looking down at desk instead of speaker, shaking head slowly in disagreement, shuffling feet and fidgeting, looking out window during speech, yawning, looking around room, frowning.

Results

Effectiveness of Manipulation. Effectiveness of the manipulation of feedback from the audience was ascertained from a questionnaire dealing with the subjects' perception of the audiences' reactions to their speech. Data for the positive and negative reinforcement groups, as shown in Table 1, provide evidence that the audience's reactions were detected by the subjects and were perceived as intended. Experimental subjects in the negative reinforcement condition perceived various negative responses from the audience significantly more often than the subjects in the positive condition. Similarly, the subjects in the positive reinforcement condition perceived positive responses from the audience significantly more often than the subjects in the negative condition.

To determine whether the subjects were aware that reactions of the audience were planned, responses to several open-ended questions were analyzed. Nine subjects seemed to suspect that the audience's reactions were partially contrived. Since these subjects were evenly distributed in the two conditions (four in the positive and five in the negative), it was considered advisable to retain their data.

Table 1 *Subjects' Perception of Audience's Reaction to Their Arguments*

Item[a]	Reinforcement	
	Positive[b] (per cent)	Negative[c] (per cent)
1. Was convinced of my arguments.	30	06*
2. Seemed bored.	17	69**
3. Was attentive.	87	25**
4. Thought I did well.	31	27
5. Seemed restless.	04	50**
6. Was sympathetic and considerate.	87	19**
7. Remembered my main points.	22	38
8. Affected my presentation.	56	44
9. Was ignored by me.	22	06
10. Agreed with me.	36	06**
11. Seemed sleepy sometimes.	04	50**

[a] Each per cent was obtained by combining the two most extreme points ("All the time" and "Most of the time") from the six-point rating scale.
[b] N equals 23. [c] N equals 16.
* $p < .05$. ** $p < .01$.

Reinforcement Conditions. Possible scores on each attitude area ranged from 6 to 36. Data consisted of net change in attitude as measured by difference between the pre-experimental and post-experimental questionnaires. Change was scored positive when in the direction advocated by the role enactment.

Mean change in attitude for experimental conditions, combining both attitude areas, is shown in Table 2. It can be seen that change scores for the experimental conditions are toward the position advocated by subjects during the role enactment. It was found that negative reinforcement caused greater mean change than positive reinforcement (3.13 to 2.78). Combining the reinforcement conditions, results showed that subjects high on need for social reinforcement changed more than subjects who were low (3.59 to 2.41). Statistical evaluation of the difference between means in the experimental conditions was conducted by the t test; differences did not approach accepted levels of statistical significance.

A small difference was found between the two attitudes employed: a slightly greater change occurred on the free speech topic than on the federal aid to parochial schools topic (3.00 to 2.86). Examination of the experimental conditions for differences according to sex of the subjects disclosed that males changed more as a result of role enactment than did females (3.33 to 2.27). Analysis by sex and type of reinforcement showed that males changed more under negative reinforcement, while females changed more under positive reinforcement. None of these differences met our minimal criteria of statistical significance.

An interesting regularity can be seen in the data in Table 2. The largest change occurred for subjects high on need for social reinforcement who were in the negative reinforcement group, and next highest for subjects who were high in need for social reinforcement and in the positive reinforcement sample. Smallest change occurred for subjects low on need for social reinforcement and in the sample receiving positive reinforcement; the next to lowest change occurred with subjects low on need for social reinforcement and in the negative reinforcement sample.

Subsequent to the role enactment, the experimental subjects were administered a questionnaire dealing with evaluation of their performance. Inspection of responses revealed that subjects in the negative reinforcement sample, as compared with the positive reinforcement sample, thought their arguments helped the speech (50% to 22%), and that their arguments were reasonable (62% to 48%); nevertheless, more subjects in the negative reinforcement sample thought they would have done better taking the opposite position (69% to 44%). Moreover, the subjects in the negative reinforcement sample, when

Table 2 *Mean Attitude Change for Experimental and Control Groups*

Type of Group	Net Attitude Change
Experimental groups	
High FIRO-B, Negative reinforcement ($N = 7$)	3.71
High FIRO-B, Positive reinforcement ($N = 10$)	3.50
Low FIRO-B, Negative reinforcement ($N = 9$)	2.67
Low FIRO-B, Positive reinforcement ($N = 13$)	2.23
Control groups	
Argument prepared ($N = 12$)	1.96
Before—after ($N = 13$)	0.50

compared with the positive group, perceived themselves as being more sincere (50% to 39%), as feeling more secure and at ease (37% to 26%), and as doing better in their overall performance (50% to 26%).

Effect of Role Enactment. To determine the effect of audience reactions as distinguished from the effect of speech preparation, two control samples were used. It can be seen in Table 2 that, combining both attitude areas, the prepared control sample showed greater mean change than the before-after sample. Yet the amount of change found in the experimental sample was higher in all conditions than change in the prepared control sample. Since the experimental samples that received positive and negative reinforcement did not differ significantly, they were combined for the statistical tests.

Difference between the before-after control subjects and the total mean for the experimental subjects was significant at less than the .02 level of confidence by a one-tail t test. Because the prepared control sample did not differ significantly from the before-after control sample, they were combined to provide a larger control sample. Use of such a sample provides a more rigorous test of the effect of role enactment, since the prepared control subjects showed greater attitude change than the before-after control subjects. Difference between the combined experimental subjects and the combined control subjects was less than the .05 level by a one-tail t test.

Discussion

One aspect of this study that should be considered in evaluating the results is that the attitudes used for the role enactment were important and particularly salient to the subjects. Almost all rated the two attitude areas as extremely important to them, and the topics were objects of controversy on campus during the time the study was conducted. It is to be expected that such topics will be relatively resistant to change.

The finding that role enactment is effective in changing attitudes agrees with results of previous studies (Culbertson, 1957; Janis and King, 1954; Lieberman, 1956). Earlier studies did not, however, control for the variable of audience reinforcement. It is not known to what extent attitude change in other studies might be due to role enactment, and to what extent to reinforcement from an audience. In the present study, the primary interest was in the relative effect of positive and negative reinforcement during role enactment, and control subjects that enacted the role without an audience were not included. It should be remembered, however, that subjects were told that their task was to convince the audience of their views, and that the audience would later rate them. It may be assumed, then, that the subjects tried to impress the audience and were sensitive to any responses forthcoming from the audience. The subjects' perceptions of the audience do indicate that the differential reinforcement was noticed. At any rate, it seems reasonable that one of the important variables operating was reinforcement from the audience.

The difference found between the positive and the negative reinforcement samples suggests that social reinforcement probably operates in producing some of the attitude change associated with role enactment. Though not statistically significant, the difference is worth discussing briefly. Straightforward application of reinforcement theory would lead one to predict greater change in attitude for the positive reinforcement condition than for the negative condition. If reinforcement operates simply by strengthening the verbal behavior emitted by the subject, then receiving positive reinforcement during role enactment should cause a change in attitude toward the position receiving reinforcement. Similarly, negative reinforcement by the audience should cause the subject's attitude to move away from the position taken during role enactment. This prediction was not confirmed by the present results: more change occurred in the negative reinforcement group.

At least two explanations can be advanced for this

finding. An explanation according to cognitive dissonance theory (Festinger, 1957) might be that the negative reinforcement produces greater dissonance than positive reinforcement, because receiving such unpleasant reactions from others is dissonant with the subject's enacting the role. Reduction of the dissonance could be accomplished by the subject's changing his attitude toward greater agreement with the role.

Pursuing the implications of supplementary data obtained from the post-experimental questionnaires leads to another explanation. It was clear from the questionnaire data that the behavior of the negative reinforcement subjects differed from that of the positive reinforcement subjects. The negative reinforcement subjects seemed to be *more involved* and to engage in more improvisation. These two factors probably contributed to the greater attitude change for the negative reinforcement group. This interpretation agrees with Janis and King's (1954) finding concerning the effect of improvisation on attitude change. The variable, role-involvement (Sarbin, 1954), seems to be central in this interpretation.

Greater role-involvement for the negative reinforcement group seems plausible. Given the task of convincing an audience on an issue, the subject was confronted by unmistakable signs of disapproval and boredom. Such an unexpected reaction could cause such responses as doubt and hostility, which might lead the subject to exert more effort to convince his audience. Some techniques that the subject could try might include using his own arguments and examples, delivering the speech in his own style, and being more "dramatic." Improvisation could thus be a result of the subject's increased role-involvement.

It should be pointed out, while discussing the difference between the experimental groups, that a greater number of different kinds of responses were used for negative reinforcement than for positive reinforcement. The effect on the subjects' attitude change, if any, of this difference between the groups cannot be determined.

In connection with differences between the experimental and the control groups, it is possible that the greater attitude change in the experimental groups may be only indirectly due to social reinforcement. Social reinforcement, whether positive or negative, may create greater emotional involvement. Thus, social reinforcement might contribute to attitude change in the experimental samples in one or both of the following ways: directly, by strengthening the attitude that was publicly verbalized; and, indirectly, by causing involvement and improvisation, which in turn is associated with attitude change.

Results of the present study showed that the control subjects who practiced arguments but did not enact the role exhibited slightly greater attitude change than the before-after control subjects. Commitment to defend a position may be one of the critical variables in the sequence of behaviors comprising role enactment. Evidence from this study is only suggestive, but it is very likely that review of contemplated arguments and preparation of the speech could cause some attitude change in the direction of the anticipated speech. Data have been reported by Brehm (1960) indicating that commitment to a position is sufficient under certain conditions for attitude change.

Some evidence is available from the present study to indicate that subjects who are discriminated on the basis of their need for social reinforcement respond differently to social reinforcement, in terms of resultant attitude change. The questionnaire assessing need for social reinforcement was selected for apparent relevance to the concept "need for social reinforcement." This area of individual differences is an important one, and experiments using an instrument constructed specifically to measure need for social reinforcement should be especially fruitful.

In conclusion, results of the present study again demonstrate that role enactment creates a corresponding change in attitude, and further suggest that social reinforcement may be one of the means by which the change occurs. Many additional factors are present in any complex social situation, and further research is needed to elucidate fully the mechanisms by which role enactment affects attitude change.

Summary

The present experiment investigated one of the factors hypothesized to contribute to the attitude change that has often been observed to accompany enactment of a social role. Specifically, the effect on attitude change of positive and negative social reinforcement of role enactment was examined.

Subjects spoke for five minutes to a small audience of their peers and advocated a position on an attitude opposite to their privately expressed opinion. In each condition subjects were selected to have either high or low need for social reinforcement. While S spoke, the audience responded in various contrived ways: the audience had been previously instructed by the experimenter to respond to the speaker with either positive or negative reinforcement. Positive reinforcement included various responses indicating attention and social approval (e.g., nodding of head); negative reinforcement included various responses indicating boredom and disapproval (e.g., looking out of window). One control sample received the same instructions as the experimental subjects but did not speak; a second control sample merely filled out the attitude scales twice.

Results disclosed that the experimental samples showed more attitude change toward the position advocated by the role enactment than did the control samples. The experimental condition of negative reinforcement resulted in slightly greater attitude change than did positive reinforcement, and high need for social reinforcement was associated with slightly greater attitude change than low need for social reinforcement. One explanation for the somewhat greater attitude change for the negative reinforcement condition was based on findings which suggested that negatively reinforced subjects were more involved and used more improvisation than the positively reinforced subjects.

References

BREHM, J. W. A dissonance analysis of attitude-discrepant behavior. In M. J. Rosenberg, C. I. Hovland, W. J. McGuire, R. P. Abelson, and J. W. Brehm, *Attitude organization and change.* New Haven: Yale University Press, 1960.

CULBERTSON, F. M. Modification of an emotionally held attitude through role playing. *Journal of Abnormal and Social Psychology,* 1957, *54,* 230–233.

FESTINGER, L. A theory of cognitive dissonance. Evanston, Ill.: Row, Peterson, 1957.

JANIS, I. L., and KING, B. T. The influence of role playing on opinion change. *Journal of Abnormal and Social Psychology,* 1954, *49,* 211–218.

KING, B. T., and JANIS, I. L. Comparison of the effectiveness of improvised versus non-improvised role-playing in producing opinion change. *Human Relations,* 1956, *9,* 177–186.

KRASNER, L. Studies of the conditioning of verbal behavior. *Psychological Bulletin,* 1958, *55,* 148–170.

LIEBERMAN, S. The effects of changes in roles on the attitudes of role occupants. *Human Relations,* 1956, *9,* 385–402.

MERTON, R. K. Bureaucratic structure and personality. *Social Forces,* 1940, *18,* 560–568.

SARBIN, T. R. Role theory. In G. Lindzey (Ed.), *Handbook of social psychology.* Vol. I. Reading, Mass.: Addison-Wesley, 1954. Pp. 223–258.

SCHUTZ, W. C. FIRO: *A three-dimensional theory of interpersonal behavior.* New York: Rinehart, 1958.

SCOTT, W. A. Attitude change through reward of verbal behavior. *Journal of Abnormal and Social Psychology,* 1957, *55,* 72–75.

WALLER, W. W. *The sociology of teaching.* New York: Wiley, 1932.

The final article in this section, by *Janis, Kaye, and Kirschner,* examines the proposition that a primary reinforcer, such as food, may enhance the effectiveness of a persuasive communication, even when the donor of the food is explicitly absolved from sponsorship of the communication. Subjects were asked to read articles containing viewpoints with which they were known (on the basis of previous interrogation) to disagree. Some of the subjects were offered peanuts and PepsiCola while engaged in this task, others were offered nothing, and still others were subjected to an unpleasant odor from a hidden bottle of butyric acid. In general, those subjects who ate and drank while reading changed their opinions more in the direction advocated by the printed material than did subjects to whom no snack was offered. The unpleasant odor produced no significant change in the responsiveness of the subjects in this condition as compared with subjects in the no-food condition. The reasons for the facilitating effects of eating upon receptiveness to persuasion are undoubtedly complex. However, the basis for the observed result is probably not classical conditioning, even though the communication could be viewed as a conditioned stimulus and the food as an unconditioned stimulus. It is possible that the presentation of food sets the occasion for those kinds of agreeable or acquiescent behaviors that have come, through past experience, to be associated with eating. If so, then we would expect a similar effect to be found wherever persuasion is attempted under circumstances that permit the emitting of positively reinforcing behaviors, such as eating and drinking.

63 Facilitating Effects of "Eating-While-Reading" on Responsiveness to Persuasive Communications[1]

IRVING L. JANIS
DONALD KAYE
PAUL KIRSCHNER

It is commonly assumed that people are more likely to yield to persuasion at a time when they are eating or drinking than at a time when they are not engaged in any such gratifying activity. Salesmen, business promoters, and lobbyists often try to "soften up" their clients by inviting them to talk things over at a restaurant or cafe. Representatives of opposing economic or political groups, when unable to settle their disputes while seated formally around a conference table, may find themselves much more amenable to mutual influence, and hence more conciliatory, while seated comfortably around a dinner table.

Little systematic research has been done, as yet, to determine the conditions under which pleasant stimulation will augment the acceptance of persuasive communications. One might expect that when the communicator is the perceived source of the gratifying stimulation, a more favorable attitude toward him will ensue, which would tend to lower the recipient's resistance to his persuasive efforts (see Hovland, Janis, and Kelley, 1953, pp. 19–55). But a more complicated situation often arises at educational symposia, political conventions, cocktail parties, and informal dinners where: (*a*) the donor (that is, the person who is perceived as being responsible for the gratification) is *not* the communicator and (*b*) the donor does *not* endorse the persuasive communications that happen to be presented at the particular time when the recipients are being indulged. If a positive gain in effectiveness is found to occur under these conditions, where the gratifying activity is entirely extraneous to the content, source, or endorsement of the communications, a number of important theoretical questions will arise—questions concerning some of the basic processes of attitude change which will require systematic experimental analysis. For example, when eating has a facilitating effect on acceptance of persuasive messages, does it always depend entirely upon the heightened motivation of the recipients to conform with the donor's wishes? If so, a positive outcome under nonendorsement conditions will be paradoxical unless it turns out that there is a general tendency for people to assume, consciously or unconsciously, that the donor would like them to be influenced by whatever communications are presented (even though he explicitly says that he does not endorse the point of view being expressed). Or does the extraneous gratification operate as a source of reinforcement independently of the recipient's attitude toward the donor? If this is the case, we might be led to assume that the food corresponds to an "unconditioned stimulus," and its facilitating effects might be accounted for in terms of the laws of conditioning.

The latter theoretical possibility is suggested by Razran's (1940) brief research note, published 25 years ago, in which he gave a summary statement of the following two experimental observations: (*a*) an increase in ratings of "personal approval" occurred when a series of sociopolitical slogans were presented to experimental subjects while they were enjoying a free lunch and (*b*) a decrease in such ratings occurred when the slogans were presented while the subjects were being required to inhale a number of unpleasant, putrid odors. In his report, however, Razran does not mention certain important details, such as whether the experimenter was the donor of the free lunch and whether he said anything to the subjects about his personal attitude toward the slogans.

So far as the authors have been able to ascertain, no subsequent experiments have been published pertinent to checking Razran's observations. Nor has any published research been found bearing on the related questions of whether or not (and under what limiting conditions) extraneous pleasant or unpleasant stimulation can affect the degree to which a recipient will accept a series of persuasive arguments that attempt to induce him to change a personal belief or preference.

As a preliminary step toward reopening experimental research on the above-mentioned set of

[1] This experimental investigation was conducted under the auspices of the Yale Studies in Attitude and Communication, which is supported by a grant from the Rockefeller Foundation.

theoretical problems, the present study was designed to investigate the alleged phenomenon of enhanced communication effectiveness arising from "eating-while-reading." The research was designed primarily to answer the following question: If an experimenter gives the subjects desirable food and drink but states explicitly that the persuasive messages to be presented are ones with which he does not necessarily agree, will there be a significant increase in acceptance from the gratifying activity of eating that accompanies exposure to the communications?

Method and Procedure

Experimental Design. The basic design involved randomly assigning the subjects to two different experimental conditions. One was a condition in which a substantial quantity of food was offered to the subjects during the time they were engaged in reading a series of four persuasive communications. Upon entering the experimental room, the subjects found the experimenter imbibing some refreshments (peanuts and PepsiCola) and they were offered the same refreshments with the simple explanation that there was plenty on hand because "I brought some along for you too." The contrasting "no-food" condition was identical in every respect except that no refreshments were in the room at any time during the session.

The same measures of opinion change were used in the two experimental groups and also in a third group of *unexposed controls,* who were included in the study in order to obtain a baseline for ascertaining the effectiveness of each communication per se. The subjects randomly assigned to the control condition were given the same pre- and postcommunication questionnaires, separated by the same time interval as in the other two experimental conditions, but without being exposed to any relevant communications.

The Communications and the Opinion Measures. On the basis of extensive pretesting, we prepared four communications, each of which advocated an unpopular point of view and had been found to be capable of inducing a significant degree of opinion change. These communications were attributed to fictitious authors who were described as journalists or news commentators. The main conclusions, all of which involved quantitative predictions or preferences about future events, were as follows:

1. It will be more than 25 years before satisfactory progress can be expected in the search for a cure for cancer.
2. The United States Armed Forces do not need additional men and can be reduced to less than 85% of their present strength.
3. A round-trip expedition to the moon will be achieved within the next decade.[2]
4. Within the next 3 years, three-dimensional films will replace two-dimensional films in practically all movie theaters.

In order to assess opinion changes, four key questions were included in both the pre- and the postcommunication questionnaires, each of which asked the subject to express his opinion in the form of a quantitative estimate (for example, "How many years do you think it will be before an extremely effective cure is found for cancer so that cancer will no longer be a major cause of death? About —— years.")

Experiments I and II: Similarities and Differences. The same experimental design, described above, was used in two separate experiments, during successive semesters at the same college. In all essential features the first (Experiment I) was identical with the second (Experiment II) in that exactly the same experimental variations were used along with the same instructions, the same communications, and the same pre- and postcommunication questionnaires. But the two experiments differed in several minor ways. The main difference was that in Experiment I the time interval between the precommunication questionnaire and exposure to the communications was about 2 months; whereas in Experiment II the precommunication questionnaire was given at the beginning of the experimental session, immediately preceding the communications.

In Experiment I, the initial questionnaire was administered in regular undergraduate class sessions. It was introduced as a "survey of student opinions" and the key questions were embedded among numerous filler questions on a variety of other controversial issues. After a period of 2 months, the subjects were contacted by telephone and asked to be unpaid volunteers for a study on reading preferences. The vast majority volunteered and each subject was seen in a private interview session, at the beginning of which he was randomly assigned to the "food with communication" condition or the "no food with communication" condition or the unexposed control condition. After answering the final set of postcommunication questions, each subject was briefly interviewed concerning his reactions to the experimental situation.

In Experiment II, the same essential procedures

[2] This study was carried out before the major developments in space flights had occurred, at a time when few people were optimistic about the rate of technical progress in this field. In response to the moon-flight question on the initial questionnaire, almost all the students gave estimates of 10 years or more before a successful round-trip flight could be expected.

were used except for the fact that the precommunication questionnaire was given at the beginning of the experimental session. Another minor difference was that the unexposed controls were given some extracts from a popular magazine on irrelevant topics, which took approximately the same reading time as the four persuasive communications. Moreover, unlike the unexposed controls in Experiment I, those in Experiment II were given the same food in the same way as in the main experimental condition, so that they too were eating while reading the (irrelevant) articles.

In addition to the three conditions that were set up to replicate the essential features of Experiment I, a fourth experimental condition was introduced in Experiment II in order to investigate a subsidiary problem, namely, the effects of extraneous *unpleasant* stimuli. The fourth experimental group, while reading the four persuasive communications, was exposed to an unpleasant odor (produced by a hidden bottle of butyric acid), for which the experimenter disclaimed any responsibility.

In both experiments, the experimenter explained that the purpose was to assess the students' reading preferences. He asserted that he did *not* endorse the communications and casually mentioned that he happened to agree with certain of the ideas expressed and not with others (without specifying which). He asked the subjects to read the articles as though they were at home reading a popular magazine. In line with the alleged purpose, the postcommunication questionnaire in both Experiments I and II included 20 filler questions asking for interest ratings of the articles (for example, ratings of how much interest they would expect the average college student to have in each topic).

Subjects. A total of 216 Yale undergraduate students were used in the two experiments. In Experiment I, 35 men were in the unexposed control group, 32 in the "no food with communication" condition, and 33 in the "food with communication" condition. In Experiment II, the corresponding numbers were 23, 31, and 31, respectively. There were also 31 subjects in the fourth experimental group exposed to the "unpleasant" condition.

Results

In both experiments, observations of the subjects' eating behavior in the "food" condition showed that every one of them ate at least one handful of peanuts and drank at least one-half glass of the soft drink. The main findings concerning the effects of eating desirable food on the acceptance of the four persuasive communications are shown in Table 1.

In general, the results indicate that "eating-while-reading" has a facilitating effect on the amount of opinion change. In Experiment I, the differences between the food and no-food conditions are consistently in the predicted direction for all four communications, two of which are significant at the .05 level. (All p values are one-tailed and were obtained on the basis of the formula for assessing the difference between two net percentage changes, given by Hovland, Lumsdaine, and Sheffield, 1949.) The results for Experiment II show differences in the same direction for three of the four communications, two of which are significant at the .10 level. There is a very small, nonsignificant difference in the reverse direction on the fourth communication.

The p values based on the combined data from both experiments, shown in the last column of Table 1, can be regarded as a satisfactory summary of the overall outcome inasmuch as: (*a*) the numbers of cases in each experiment are almost equal; and (*b*) the two experiments differed only in minor features that are irrelevant to the main comparison under investigation. The combined data show that all four communications produced differences in the predicted direction and for three of them the differences are large enough to be statistically significant. Thus, the results support the conclusion that, in general, the extraneous gratification of eating while reading a series of persuasive communications tends to increase their effectiveness.

That each communication was effective in inducing a significant degree of opinion change, whether presented under food or no-food conditions, is indicated by the comparative data from the unexposed controls. In both experiments, the control group showed very slight positive changes, if any, on each of the four key questions and the amount of change was always significantly less than the corresponding net change shown by the food and no-food experimental groups.[3] There were no consistent differences

[3] In all but one instance, the net change shown by the unexposed controls was not significantly different from zero. The one exception occurred in the control group in Experiment I with respect to the first issue (cancer cure), on which a significant net change of −34% was found. This change, however, was in the reverse direction from that advocated by the communication (probably as a consequence of optimistic publicity concerning new advances in cancer research that appeared in the newspapers during the months between the before and after questionnaires). Thus, on this item, as well as on the other three, the control group showed significantly less change in the expected direction than the two experimental groups.

An analysis of responses to the precommunication questionnaire from both experiments showed that initially, on each of the four key opinion questions, there were only very slight, nonsignificant differences among the experimental and control groups. None of the results in Table 1 and none of the other observed differences in amount of opinion change are attributable to initial differences.

Table 1 *Per Cent Opinion Changes Induced by Exposure to Four Persuasive Communications under Two Different Conditions: "Food" versus "No Food" Given by the Experimenters*

Communication Topic	Experiment I		Experiment II		Combined Data from Experiments I and II	
	No food ($N = 32$)	Food ($N = 33$)	No food ($N = 31$)	Food ($N = 31$)	No food ($N = 63$)	Food ($N = 64$)
1. Cure for cancer						
Positive change	68.7	81.8	80.7	93.5	74.6	87.4
Negative change	21.8	12.1	3.2	0.0	12.7	6.3
No change	9.5	6.1	16.1	6.5	12.7	6.3
Total	100.0	100.0	100.0	100.0	100.0	100.0
Net change	46.9	69.7	77.5	93.5	61.9	81.1
	$p = .11$		$p < .10$		$p < .05$	
2. Preferred size of United States armed forces						
Positive change	65.6	81.8	29.0	51.6	47.6	67.2
Negative change	9.4	0.0	0.0	0.0	4.8	0.0
No change	25.0	18.2	71.0	48.4	47.6	32.8
Total	100.0	100.0	100.0	100.0	100.0	100.0
Net change	56.2	81.8	29.0	51.6	42.8	67.2
	$p < .05$		$p < .05$		$p < .01$	
3. Round-trip to moon						
Positive change	53.2	75.9	48.4	58.0	50.8	67.2
Negative change	21.9	12.1	19.4	12.9	20.6	12.5
No change	24.9	12.0	32.2	29.1	28.6	20.3
Total	100.0	100.0	100.0	100.0	100.0	100.0
Net change	31.3	63.8	29.0	45.1	30.2	54.7
	$p = .05$		$p = .20$		$p < .05$	
4. Three-dimensional movies						
Positive change	68.7	75.9	74.2	77.4	71.5	76.6
Negative change	21.8	12.1	0.0	6.5	11.1	9.4
No change	9.5	12.0	25.8	16.1	17.4	14.0
Total	100.0	100.0	100.0	100.0	100.0	100.0
Net change	46.9	63.8	74.2	70.9	60.4	67.2
	$p = .20$		$p = .40$		$p < .20$	

between the control group in Experiment I and the one in Experiment II, which indicates that the different time intervals between the before and after measures and the other minor procedural differences between the two experiments had no direct effect on the opinion measures.

The condition of unpleasant stimulation introduced into Experiment II had no observable effect on the amount of opinion change. The net changes obtained from the group exposed to the foul odor ($N = 31$) were as follows: cancer cure, 67.7%; size of armed forces, 25.8%; round trip to moon, 38.7%; three-dimensional movies, 64.5%. These values differ only very slightly from those obtained from the group exposed to the no-food condition in Experiment II (see Table 1); none of the differences are large enough to approach statistical significance. As expected, however, all the net changes for the unpleasant odor condition are smaller than those for the food condition and in two of the four instances the differences are statistically significant at beyond the .05 level.

Discussion

Our finding that the extraneous gratifying activity of eating tended to increase the degree to which the accompanying persuasive messages were accepted may prove to have important implications for the psychology of attitude change, especially if subsequent research shows that the gains tend to be persistent, giving rise to sustained modifications of personal beliefs or preferences. Since the control group in Experiment II (which received food along with irrelevant communications) showed net opinion changes that were practically zero and were significantly less than those shown by the main experimental group, the food alone appears to have had no direct effect on any of the opinion measures. Hence the observed outcome seems to implicate psychological processes involved in the *acceptance* of persuasive influences.

Our results on the positive effects of food are similar to Razran's (1940) findings on the increase in favorable ratings of sociopolitical slogans induced by a free lunch. Razran has indicated that he regards his observations as evidence of Pavlovian conditioning, resulting from the contiguity of the conditioned stimuli (the slogans) and the unconditioned pleasant stimuli (food). Before accepting any such interpretation, however, further investigations are needed to check systematically on the possibility that the change in acceptability is brought about by creating a more favorable attitude toward the donor. We attempted to minimize this possibility in both Experiments I and II by having the experimenter give the subjects an introductory explanation in which he clearly stated that he was not sponsoring the persuasive communications. Despite this attempt, however, the subjects may have ignored or forgotten his remarks and assumed that he was sponsoring them. We have no evidence bearing directly on this matter, but we did note that in the informal interviews conducted at the end of each experimental session, many more favorable comments about the experimenter were made by the subjects who had been in the food condition than by those who had been in the no-food condition.

Our failure to confirm Razran's findings on the negative effects of *unpleasant* stimulation might be accounted for in terms of attitude toward the experimenter. In Razran's experiment, the experimenter "required" the subjects to sniff the putrid odors, and hence he might have been directly blamed for the unpleasant stimulation; whereas in our Experiment II, the unpleasant odor was presented as an accidental occurrence for which the experimenter was not responsible. Further experimental analysis is obviously needed to determine if the effects of pleasant and unpleasant stimulation observed in our experiment are dependent upon whether or not the experimenter is perceived as the causal agent.

The fact that the experimenter himself participated in eating the food might have influenced the subjects' perceptions of the general atmosphere of the reading session and hence needs to be investigated as a possible variable, independent of the subjects' food consumption. The limiting conditions for positive effects from "eating-while-reading" also require systematic investigation, particularly in relation to unpleasant interpersonal stimuli, such as those provoking embarrassment, outbreaks of hostility, or other forms of emotional tension that could counteract the positive atmosphere created by the availability of desirable food.

It is also important to find out whether variations in the experimenter's endorsement of the communications play a crucial role in determining the facilitating effects of the proferred food. For example, if subsequent research shows that the experimenter's positive versus negative endorsements make a difference, then an explanation in terms of increased motivation to please the donor will be favored, rather than a simple conditioning mechanism, and a more complicated explanation will be required to account for the positive effects obtained under conditions where the experimenter explicitly detaches himself from sponsorship of the communications.[4] These implications are mentioned to illustrate the new lines of research suggested by comparing the results from the present experiment with those from Razran's earlier study.

References

Hovland, C. I., Janis, I. L., and Kelley, H. H. *Communication and persuasion.* New Haven: Yale University Press, 1953.

Hovland, C. I., Lumsdaine, A. A., and Sheffield, F. D. *Experiments on mass communication.* Princeton: Princeton University Press, 1949.

Razran, G. H. S. Conditioned response changes in rating and appraising sociopolitical slogans. *Psychological Bulletin,* 1940, *37,* 481.

[4] The potential importance of positive versus negative endorsement by the experimenter as an interacting variable was suggested by some unexpected results obtained in a pilot study by Dabbs and Janis, which was carried out as a preliminary step toward replicating the present experiment under conditions where the experimenter indicates that he personally *disagrees* with the persuasive communications. The pilot study results led us to carry out a new experiment in which we compared the effects of eating-while-reading under two different endorsement conditions (the experimenter agreeing or disagreeing with the communications). A report on the effects of the interacting variables, as revealed by the data from the Dabbs and Janis experiment, is currently being prepared for publication.

B

The Use of Incentives

A great deal of research in persuasion has been stimulated by the notion that a person experiences "cognitive dissonance" when he is induced to behave publicly in a manner inconsistent with his privately held beliefs or attitudes. Attitude change is thus seen as a device for reducing dissonance, which by definition is an aversive stimulus. Three conditions seem to be essential in an experimental test of dissonance predictions. First, the subject must be induced to take a position that is *discrepant* from his private convictions. Second, he must perceive any incentive offered him for compliance as clearly *insufficient*. Third, he must make his *decision* to comply only after having considered the magnitude of the incentive. These three elements—insufficient incentive, choice, and counterattitudinal behavior—are the hallmarks of a situation involving cognitive dissonance. Where one or more of these conditions is not fulfilled, dissonance theory provides no clear-cut basis for predicting different outcomes.

The article by *Linder, Cooper, and Jones* summarizes some of the more provocative research that has been reported by dissonance theorists and, in addition, presents the results of an experiment in which the incentives for attitude change were manipulated in a setting where the subjects could choose to participate or not. A critical element in cognitive dissonance theory is the decision or choice made by the subject to comply by expressing an opinion with which he actually disagrees. Seldom acknowledged in such experiments, however, is the fact that choosing to comply is a performance that is also under stimulus control. The same operations that make the subject "choose" to comply, therefore, may determine the impact of the persuasive manipulation as well. Thus, an individual who agrees to voice a dissonance-arousing viewpoint may already have been persuaded to adopt portions of that viewpoint as his own. Why differing incentives should influence the extent to which he is persuaded, however, is a matter still under investigation.

Linder, Cooper, and Jones actually paid their subjects—either $.50 or $2.50—in advance of a counterattitudinal task but after the subjects had committed themselves to engage in it. So the subjects were offered an incentive before agreeing to write the essay and then were reinforced for their decision to comply. The longer time taken by the low-incentive subjects to decide whether to write the essay or not is cited as evidence for the greater dissonance under which they labored. The subjects who were given no opportunity to refuse the task, of course, experienced no such conflict and, presumably, experienced less dissonance as well. Interestingly, the experimenters do not report that any of the subjects in the choice condition elected not to participate. We must conclude that the incentives of receiving experimental credit and cooperating with the experimenter were sufficient to induce their compliance. The subjects who were given no choice showed more attitude change when paid $2.50 than when paid $.50. The subjects who were offered an opportunity to refuse, however, changed more when they were paid $.50 than when paid $2.50. The authors interpret these findings as supportive of predictions from reinforcement theory in the case of the subjects given no choice, and of predictions from dissonance theory in the case of the subjects given a choice. However, note that the subjects in the low-incentive, free-choice condition took significantly longer to make their decision to write the essay than the high-incentive, free-choice subjects. This suggests that since they had already been informed of the nature of the required essay, any modification of their attitudes on the issue may have occurred even *before* they began to write. The subjects who were offered more money to comply, on the other hand, took less time to decide and, consequently, may well have engaged in less preliminary self-admonishment about the merits of the position they would have to defend. Such an interpretation, to be sure, involves speculation about implicit processes that are not subject to direct observation. But it also emphasizes the verbal behavior in which subjects are apt to engage as a result of direct manipulation rather than states-of-feeling that are adjusted through some subsequent performance.

64 Decision Freedom as a Determinant of the Role of Incentive Magnitude in Attitude Change[1]

DARWYN E. LINDER
JOEL COOPER
EDWARD E. JONES

If a person can be induced to behave publicly in a manner that does not follow from his private attitudes, he will experience cognitive dissonance. The magnitude of dissonance will be greater when there are few reasons for complying than when there are many reasons (Festinger, 1957). This dissonance may be reduced by an accommodating change in private attitude if other ways of reducing dissonance are not available. Thus a person who has been induced to behave in a counterattitudinal fashion will change his private attitude more the less he has been rewarded for complying. Festinger and Carlsmith (1959) found support for this proposition in a study in which subjects were persuaded (for $1 or $20) to extol the attractiveness of a dull and tedious task for the benefit of the next subject. Also, Cohen (1962) found that Yale students who were induced to write essays in favor of the New Haven police later showed more positive attitudes the smaller the incentive they had been offered to write the essay.

Rosenberg (1965) has recently questioned the generality of this proposed relationship and has suggested that subjects in the Festinger and Carlsmith (1959) and the Cohen (1962) experiments must have considered the incentive excessive and, because of the "evaluation apprehension" that subjects in psychology experiments commonly feel, those in the high-incentive conditions may have interpreted the experiment as one testing their honesty and autonomy. To resist influence in the face of a substantial bribe, therefore, would cause the experimenter to evaluate them favorably. Alternatively, Rosenberg suggests that the subjects may have suspected deception in the high-incentive condition and angrily resisted confirming the perceived hypothesis. Either reaction might conceivably account for the obtained inverse relationship between incentive amount and degree of ultimate congruence between attitude and behavior.

Rosenberg proceeded to conduct an experiment loosely replicating Cohen's (1962), the major difference being that one experimenter provided the incentive for essay writing and another measured the subsequent attitude. The two tasks were presented to the subjects as unrelated, and thus there was presumably no chance for evaluation apprehension to affect the results. Rosenberg found that attitude and behavior were most congruent when subjects were offered $5 for writing essays and least in line when they were offered $.50. Rosenberg's results are clearly at variance with the apparent dissonance prediction and with the findings obtained by Cohen and by Festinger and Carlsmith. Instead,

[1] This experiment was facilitated by National Science Foundation Grant 8857. We are indebted to H. B. Gerard for his valuable suggestions.

From the *Journal of Personality and Social Psychology,* 1967, *6,* 245–254.

the results seem to favor a reinforcement position or, as Rosenberg would prefer, a theoretical position that considers the effects of reinforcement in the context of an affect-cognition consistency model. In Rosenberg's view, either the expectation or the receipt of reward strengthens and stabilizes the cognitions associated with the counterattitudinal statement—the greater the reward, the greater the stabilizing effect. There is then a change in attitudinal affect in the interests of cognitive-affective consistency.

Nuttin (1964) carefully replicated Rosenberg's experiment and found that—even with evaluation apprehension removed in the same manner—inferred attitude change varied inversely with the amount of incentive offered. While Nuttin's results were of only borderline significance, they clearly offered more support for the dissonance proposition than for the counterproposition reflecting reinforcement theory. Aronson (1966) has criticized Rosenberg's reasoning and his conclusions on many different grounds. Perhaps his most telling criticism was that Rosenberg should have tried to reproduce the inverse incentive effects previously attributed to dissonance theory by adding conditions to his design in which the same experimenter called for the essay and measured the subsequent attitude. Aronson argued that there were many differences between the Cohen experiment and the Rosenberg replication, and to assume that his results reversed the dissonance proposition solely because evaluation apprehension was removed is unwarranted.

The fact remains that Rosenberg (1965) was able to obtain a positive relationship between amount of incentive and inferred attitude change, and the intriguing empirical and theoretical problem is how to account for the fact that both dissonance and reinforcement effects have been found within the forced-compliance paradigm. Carlsmith, Collins, and Helmreich (1966) have predicted and successfully produced these opposing effects in a context approximating the original Festinger and Carlsmith (1959) study. When the subject was induced to describe the task as attractive to the next "unsuspecting subject," the former's subsequent task-attractiveness ratings were more positive in low- than in high-incentive conditions. When the subject was instead asked to write an essay praising the task, portions of which might later be used by the experimenter, rated attractiveness varied directly with the amount of incentive offered. Carlsmith et al. argued that amount of incentive will relate directly to attitude change (a reinforcement effect) whenever the dissonance involved in a counterattitudinal act is minimal. The subject who complied in the essay-writing conditions of their experiment had a number of legitimate reasons for doing so, and the experimenter, the only person to read the essay, knew full well that the essay did not express the subject's private opinion. Dissonance should be much greater in the conditions requiring the subject to dupe another person like himself.

The Carlsmith et al. (1966) experiment is especially important because of the care with which it was conducted, the clear replication of the Festinger and Carlsmith (1959) results it provides, and the separate elicitation of both dissonance and reinforcement effects within the same general design. But while they may account for the Rosenberg reinforcement effect, Carlsmith et al. are left without any clear explanation for Cohen's (1962) results. After all, he required an essay rather than a deceitful confrontation with another subject and obtained dissonance rather than reinforcement effects. One could argue that attitudes toward the New Haven police are likely to be more central and important than attitudes toward a boring task, and thus a counterattitudinal essay is more inherently dissonant in the former case. Or, one could argue that the subjects in Cohen's experiment were not really assured anonymity (as in Carlsmith et al.'s). Nevertheless, the empirical discrepancies existing in the forced-compliance literature are not entirely reconciled by the Carlsmith et al. study.

The major focus of these studies has been the relationship between the amount of incentive offered and subsequent attitude change, but a clear prediction from dissonance theory cannot be made unless the subject makes his decision to comply *after* considering the incentive magnitude. The incentive must be one of the conditions potentially affecting the decision to comply rather than a reward for having already so decided.

Both Cohen (1962) and Rosenberg (1965) reported that they took care to assure subjects that the decision to write the essay was entirely their own. It may be argued, however, that Rosenberg's major alteration of Cohen's procedure, the separation of the compliant-behavior setting from the attitude-measurement setting to eliminate evaluation apprehension, reduced his subjects' freedom not to comply. When Rosenberg's subjects arrived for the experiment, they found him busily engaged and were given the option of waiting for "15 or 20 minutes" or, as an afterthought, participating in "another little experiment some graduate student in education is doing." Professing to know little about this other experiment except that it "has to do with attitudes" and "I gather they have some research funds." Rosenberg did not pressure the subject into a decision, but let him decide for himself whether he wanted to participate or wait. Having made the decision to participate, each subject further strengthened his commitment by walking to the location of the second experiment. The choice then offered by the second experimenter was considerably less than a free one. Being already effectively committed, the subject would be more likely to treat the subsequent monetary offering as a bonus for prior compliance than as one of the conditions to be considered in making a free choice.

If the preceding argument is correct, Rosenberg's findings cannot be compared with Cohen's because different conditions prevailed in the two experiments when the counterattitudinal essays were written. Rosenberg inadvertently made it difficult for subjects not to comply and found that degree of attitude change was positively related to incentive magnitude, in support of a reinforcement position or an affective-cognitive consistency model (Rosenberg, 1960). In contrast to this, Cohen's procedure presented the choice not to comply as a more viable alternative and found that attitude change was inversely related to incentive magnitude, in support of a derivation from dissonance theory. A meaningful resolution of these discrepant findings would be to show that the effects of incentive magnitude on attitude change are either direct or inverse, depending on the presence or absence of freedom not to comply. The first experiment to follow was conducted as a direct test of the role of such freedom to choose not to engage in counterattitudinal behavior.

Experiment I

Method

Attitude Issue and Subjects. At the time of the first experiment a rather heated controversy was raging in the state of North Carolina concerning the wisdom of a law that forbade Communists and Fifth Amendment pleaders from speaking at state-supported institutions. On the basis of informal opinion sampling, fortified by the plausible expectation that students deplore implied restrictions on their own freedom to listen, we assumed that college-student subjects would be strongly opposed to speaker-ban legislation. The issue thus seemed comparable to "the actions of the New Haven police" (Cohen, 1962) and to a ban on Ohio State's participation in the Rose Bowl (Rosenberg, 1965).

Fifty-five introductory psychology students at Duke University served as subjects in the experiment. Forty subjects (15 males and 25 females) were randomly assigned to four experimental conditions[2]; 13 were subsequently assigned to a control condition. All experimental subjects were asked to write a "forceful and convincing essay" in favor of the speaker-ban law. After writing the essay each subject was asked to indicate his opinion about the speaker-ban law by checking a point on a 31-point scale comparable to Cohen's (1962) and Rosenberg's (1965) measure. The scale read, "In my opinion the Speaker Ban Law of North Carolina is . . . ," followed by 31 horizontal dots with seven labels ranging from "not justified at all" to "completely justified." Subjects in the control condition merely filled out the scale without having previously written a pro-speaker-ban essay.

[2] Two more experimental subjects were actually run whose data were not analyzed. One of these was obviously in favor of the speaker-ban law at the outset, and the other was the victim of experimenter error in presenting instructions.

Procedure and Design

The basic procedure was closely modeled after that of Cohen (1962) except that the subjects were recruited from the introductory psychology course and came individually to the laboratory, rather than being approached in their dormitory rooms. The experimenter introduced himself as a graduate student in psychology. In the *free-decision condition* he immediately said, "I want to explain to you what this task is all about. I want to make it clear, though, that the decision to perform the task will be entirely your own." In the *no-choice condition* he merely said, "I want to explain to you what this task that you have volunteered for is all about." He then proceeded in both conditions to provide the following rationale for the essay-writing task:

> The Association of Private Colleges of the Southeast, of which Duke is a member, is considering the adoption of a uniform speaker policy that would be binding on its member schools. Before they can decide what kind of policy to adopt, if indeed they decide to adopt one, they have undertaken a large-scale research program in order to help them understand what the issues really are. This study is part of that program. The APCSE is working through the Department of Psychology here at Duke and through the departments of psychology at other private schools in the area because of the access which the department has to a wide cross-section of students such as yourself who must participate in psychological experiments and because of the number of graduate students that are available to conduct research. We have found, from past experience, that one of the best ways to get relevant arguments on both sides of the issue is to ask people to write essays favoring only one side. We think we know pretty much how you feel about the student's rights in this matter. [Here the experimenter paused and waited for a comment that would confirm the subject's initial opinion opposing the speaker-ban law. Only one subject expressed a favor-

ing opinion at this point; see Footnote 2.] Nonetheless, what we need now are essays favoring the speaker ban.

At this point, the free-decision and no-choice conditions again diverged. In the free-decision condition the subjects were told that the APCSE was paying $.50 (low incentive) or $2.50 (high incentive) in addition to the standard experimental credit given to all subjects. The experimenter again stressed that the decision to write the essay was entirely up to the subject and that he would receive experimental credit in any case. In the no-choice condition the experimenter acted as if, naturally, the subject in volunteering for the experiment had committed himself to its requirements. He simply pointed out that the experiment involved writing a strong and forceful essay favoring the speaker-ban law. After the subject was handed a pencil and some paper, but before he began to write, the experimenter broke in: "Oh yes, I almost forgot to tell you. . . . The APCSE is paying all participants $.50 [or $2.50] for their time."

In all conditions subjects were paid, *before* they wrote the essay, the amount of money promised them. The experimenter then left the room and allowed the subject 20 minutes to complete his essay. When he returned, the experimenter collected the essay, administered the brief attitude scale, and interviewed the subject concerning his perceptions of the experiment. No subject indicated any suspicion regarding the true purpose of the experiment. The purpose was then explained to each in detail, and all deceptions were revealed. None of the subjects recalled having any doubts about the existence of the fictitious APCSE. Each subject was ultimately allowed to keep $1.50. Because they were made to realize that they were assigned by chance to the high-inducement condition, those who had initially received $2.50 were quite agreeable when asked to return $1 of their money. Subjects in the low-inducement condition were delighted to learn of their good fortune—that they would receive $1 more than they had bargained for.

Results

Before the results bearing on the central hypothesis are presented, it is of interest to note the difference in decision time in the two free-decision conditions. After the experimenter began to notice that *free-decision* subjects in the low-incentive condition took much longer to make up their minds about writing the essay than *free-decision* subjects in the high-incentive condition, he started to record decision times with a hidden stopwatch. The last seven subjects in the low-incentive condition took an average of 25.29 seconds to reach a decision; the comparable mean for the last seven subjects in the high-incentive condition was 11.00 seconds. In spite of the reduced n, this difference is significant ($p < .025$, U test). This evidence strongly suggests that there was greater predecisional conflict in the low-incentive condition, and thus the conditions are appropriate for testing the dissonance hypothesis: since predecisional conflict leads to postdecisional dissonance (Festinger, 1964), more dissonance and hence more attitude change should occur in the free-decision–low-incentive condition.

After establishing that the means for female and male subjects were nearly identical ($t = .18$), the posttreatment attitude scores were placed in a simple 2 (for Degree of Decision Freedom) ×2 (for Level of Incentive) factorial design. The means for each condition are presented in Table 1. Scale values could range from 1.0 (anti-speaker ban) to 7.0 (pro-speaker ban). Table 2 summarizes the analysis of variance and appropriate orthogonal comparisons. The prediction that the amount of inferred attitude change would relate positively to inducement level in the no-choice conditions and negatively in the free-decision conditions is clearly confirmed ($F_{1, 36} = 8.70$; $p < .01$). The dissonance effect in the free-decision condition was itself significant; the reinforcement effect in the prior-commitment condition was not. The control subjects, who checked the scale without writing an essay, were about as much against the speaker ban as subjects in the conditions where little or no change was predicted.

In an effort to shed light on possible mechanisms underlying these findings, the essays themselves were examined. The average number of words per essay was 192.3, and there were no significant differences among the four conditions in essay length. The essays were evaluated in a manner similar to that described by Rosenberg (1965). Two independent

Table 1 *Attitude-Scale Means Obtained in the Five Conditions: Experiment I*

	Incentive		
	$.50		$2.50
No choice	1.66[a]		2.34
Free decision	2.96		1.64
Control[b]		1.71	

Note.—$N = 10$ under both incentives for free-choice and free-decision conditions. For the control condition, $N = 13$.

[a] The higher the number, the more the speaker-ban law was considered to be justified.

[b] Since subjects in the control condition were all run after the main experiment was completed, the mean for this condition is presented only as an estimate of student opinion toward the issue in the absence of dissonance or incentive effects. The data from the control condition were not included in the statistical analysis.

Table 2 *Summary of Analysis of Variance: Experiment I*

Source of Variation	MS	F
Choice (A)	0.90	<1
Incentive (B)	1.02	<1
A × B	10.00	8.70**
Error	1.15	
Low incentive vs. high incentive within free-decision conditions	8.71	7.57**
Low incentive vs. high incentive within no-choice conditions	2.31	2.01*

Note.—Two-way analysis of experimental conditions
* $p < .20$, $df = 1/36$.
** $p < .01$, $df = 1/36$.

raters, blind as to the subject's condition, rated the essays in terms of the degree of organization manifested and the degree of "intent to persuade." Each of these ratings was made in terms of a 5-point scale. The judges agreed or were 1 point discrepant in 72% of the organization ratings and 85% of the persuasiveness ratings. These percentages of agreement were comparable to those obtained by Rosenberg (1965), but two independent judges using 5-point rating scales should, by chance, be no more than 1 point discrepant on more than 50% of their ratings. When a more traditional estimate of the reliability of the ratings was calculated (Winer, 1962, pp. 124 ff.), it was found that the reliability coefficient for the ratings of degree of organization was .54, and the coefficient for the ratings of persuasiveness was .55 These coefficients estimate the reliability of the ratings that result from averaging over the two judges. When these ratings were submitted to an analysis of variance, there were no differences among conditions in either organization or persuasiveness.

Since the reliability of the ratings discussed above was quite low, an attempt was made to obtain ratings of acceptably high reliability. Two varsity debate partners agreed to rate the essays. General criteria to be used in determining the ratings were discussed, but the ratings were made independently. Each essay was rated for the persuasiveness of the presentation on a 7-point scale. Sixty per cent of these ratings were no more than 1 point discrepant; the reliability coefficient was .48. (The chance percentage for agreements or 1-point discrepancies is 39% when a 7-point scale is used by two independent judges.) There were again no differences among the conditions in the rating received. Also, no between-condition differences appeared on the ratings made by any individual judge.

Discussion

The major purpose of the present experiment was achieved: to show that dissonance and reinforcement effects can be obtained within the same forced-compliance paradigm by varying the degree to which the subject is committed to comply before learning about the monetary incentive. Subjects who commit themselves after weighing the unpleasantness of the essay-writing task against the amount of incentive offered show the effects predicted by dissonance theory. The decision-time data strongly suggest that the subjects do in fact consider the essay-writing task unpleasant. Subjects who are not free to decide against compliance and then learn about a financial "bonus" produce results in line with reinforcement theory (that which is associated with something of value itself takes on value) or in line with the more complex affective-cognitive consistency model espoused by Rosenberg.

The present study was stimulated by Rosenberg's (1965) experiment, but the relevance of the results to a critique of Rosenberg's conclusions rests on the claim that his way of removing evaluation apprehension precommitted the subject to an unpleasant task before he had a chance to weigh the incentive for compliance. If this criticism is valid, then it should be possible to reproduce Rosenberg's results by closely replicating his procedures, and to obtain the converse of these results (confirming the dissonance prediction) by insuring that the subject does not commit himself before being confronted with the incentive for compliance. A second experiment was planned in an attempt to do precisely this.

Experiment II

Method

Attitude Issue. As we prepared to run the second experiment, certain paternalistic policies of the Duke University administration were being challenged by the undergraduates, and there was a movement toward liberalization of *in loco parentis* social regulations. It was assumed, therefore, that undergraduates who were induced to write forceful and convincing essays in support of strict enforcement of *in loco parentis* policies would be performing a counter-attitudinal task.

Subjects. Fifty-nine male introductory psychology students volunteered to participate for experimental credit in a study described as an "Attitude Survey." The data of 50 of these students, who were randomly assigned to the four experimental conditions and the control condition, were used in the reported analysis. Six subjects were eliminated because they did not complete the experimental procedure. Usually, they chose to read or study while waiting for the first experimenter rather than go to the second experimenter. Another subject was eliminated because he was initially in favor of strict *in loco parentis* policies, and writing the essay would not have been counterattitudinal for him.

Only two subjects who had completed the procedure were eliminated from the analysis. The first of these was excluded when it was discovered during the final interview that he had misinterpreted the attitude questionnaire. The second was eliminated because he accurately perceived the true purpose of the experiment. Both subjects had been assigned to the *free-decision–high-incentive condition.* The results of the study are not changed if these two subjects are included in the analysis.

Procedure and design. The procedure was a close approximation to that used by Rosenberg (1965). All subjects reported to the office of the first experimenter (E_1) where they found E_1 engaged in conversation with another student and were told, "I'm sorry, but I'm running late on my schedule today, and I'll have to keep you waiting for about 15 or 20 minutes. Is that all right?" All subjects agreed to wait.

Each experimental subject was then told:

> Oh, I've just thought of something; while you're waiting you could participate in another little experiment that some graduate student in education is doing. This fellow called me the other day and said he needed volunteers in a hurry for some sort of study he's doing—I don't know what it's about exactly except that it has to do with attitudes and that's why he called me, because my research is in a similar area as you'll see later. Of course, he can't give you any credit but I gather they have some research funds and they are paying people instead. So, if you care to do that, you can.

At this point, one-half of the experimental subjects (*prior-commitment condition*) were allowed to leave for the second experiment without further comment by E_1. Since it was believed that Rosenberg's procedure restricted subjects' freedom not to comply with the task of the "little experiment," it was decided to manipulate degree of choice by removing this restriction. Thus, for subjects in the *free-decision* condition, after the subject had agreed to participate in the second experiment, E_1 added:

> All I told this fellow was that I would send him some subjects if it was convenient but that I couldn't obligate my subjects in any way. So, when you get up there, listen to what he has to say and feel free to decide from there.

All experimental subjects then reported to the second experimenter (E_2). To control for the effects of experimenter bias, E_2 was not informed whether the subject was in the prior-commitment condition or the free-decision condition. E_2 presented himself as a graduate student in the Department of Education and introduced the essay-writing task using a procedure that, as in Experiment I, very closely approximated Cohen's (1962).

Rather than the free-decision versus no-choice manipulation of Experiment I, E_2 began by saying to all subjects, "At the present time, Duke University is beginning to question the wisdom of assuming the role of 'substitute parent' to its students." From that point, the instructions paralleled those of Experiment I with the substitution of *in loco parentis* regulations for the speaker-ban law. After confirming that the subject held an opinion opposed to rigid *in loco parentis* regulations, E_2 concluded:

> What we need now are essays favoring a strict enforcement of *in loco parentis.* So, what we would like you to do—if you are willing[3]—is to write the strongest, most forceful and most convincing essay that you can in favor of a strict enforcement of the substitute parent concept here at Duke.

It was then explained that the sponsoring agency was offering either \$.50 (*low-incentive* conditions) or \$2.50 (*high-incentive* conditions) for participation in the study. When the subject agreed to write the essay, he was paid the money promised to him and then began the task.

After completing the essay and being thanked and dismissed by E_2, all experimental subjects returned to E_1's office. To introduce the dependent measure, E_1 explained:

> What I had wanted you to do was participate in a continuing study I carry on every semester as a sort of Gallup poll to keep a check on opinion patterns on different University issues. I'd like you to fill out this questionnaire as an objective indication of your opinions and when you've finished I'd like to chat for a while about various issues on campus. OK?

E_1 was not informed of the amount of money the subject had received, and in no case did he find out until after the subject had completed the dependent measure.

The dependent measure consisted of an eight-item questionnaire dealing with various university issues.

[3] This vague statement of choice was given to all subjects in order to keep the instructions constant across experimental groups and to enable E_2 to remain "blind" as to the condition of each subject. It was assumed that the crucial manipulation of free decision versus prior commitment had already been accomplished by E_1.

The critical item read, "How justified is the University's policy of assuming parental responsibilities for its students?" and was accompanied by the familiar 31-point scale. When the subject had completed the questionnaire, E_1 put it aside (without looking at the responses) and began a structured interview that included probes for suspicion and checks on perceptions of the manipulations. When E_1 was satisfied that the subject had not perceived the true purpose of the experiment, he revealed the deceptions and explained the necessity for them. As in Experiment I, all experimental subjects agreed to accept $1.50 for their time.

Subjects assigned to the control condition also found E_1 engaged in conversation and were asked if they could return in 15 or 20 minutes. Upon their return they were treated exactly as experimental subjects.

These procedures resulted in five conditions: two levels of incentive magnitude under a condition of free decision, the same two levels under a condition of prior commitment, and the control condition.

Results

The mean attitude-scale scores on the critical item for each of the five conditions are presented in Table 3. It can be seen that the results are very similar to those of Experiment I. The data were submitted to a one-way analysis of variance, summarized in Table 4. The overall treatment effect was significant ($F_{4,\ 45} = 4.02$; $p < .01$). The two comparisons reflecting the hypotheses of this study were also significant: Within the free-decision conditions a low incentive produced more inferred attitude change than a high incentive ($F_{1,\ 45} = 6.82$; $p < .025$). Within the prior-commitment conditions this effect was reversed and a high incentive produced more inferred attitude change than a low incentive ($F_{1,\ 45} = 4.90$; $p < .05$). The position of the control group indicates that differences between the experimental conditions resulted from positive attitude change rather than a combination of positive and negative changes.

Once again we attempted to investigate the possibility that these effects were mediated by some aspect of the counterattitudinal performance. Two raters, working independently and without knowledge of the experimental conditions, rated each essay on 7-point scales for the extremity of attitudinal position advocated, the persuasiveness of the essay, and its degree of organization. The two raters agreed or were within 1 point of each other for 65% of the essays when estimating the attitudinal position, 60% when rating them for persuasiveness, and 52.5% when rating them for organization. The reliability coefficient for the estimated attitudinal position (Winer, 1962, pp. 124 ff.) was .67, the coefficient for the persuasiveness ratings was .51, and the coefficient for the organization ratings was .38. There were no differences among conditions on any of these ratings. The essays were then rated for the persuasiveness of the presentation on a 7-point scale by the same varsity debaters as had rated the essays from Experiment I. The debaters agreed or were within 1 point of each other for 65% of the essays, and the reliability coefficient was a somewhat more acceptable .71. Again, however, there were no differences among conditions on these ratings, whether the judges' ratings were averaged or each judge's ratings were examined separately. In a final attempt to find a performance difference among the conditions the number of words in each essay was counted; the conditions were compared on this measure of performance and were found not to differ from one another.

Table 3 *Attitude-Scale Means Obtained in the Five Conditions: Experiment II*

	Incentive		
	$.50		$2.50
Prior commitment	2.68[a]		3.46
Free decision	3.64		2.72
Control		2.56	

Note.—$N = 10$ in all conditions.
[a] The higher the number, the more strict application of *in loco parentis* regulations was considered justified.

Table 4 *Summary of Analysis of Variance: Experiment II*

Source of Variation[a]	MS	F
Treatment	2.49	4.02***
Error	.62	
Low incentive vs. high incentive free-decision conditions	4.23	6.82**
Low incentive vs. high incentive prior-commitment conditions	3.04	4.90*

Note.—One-way analysis of five conditions.
[a] The control condition differs significantly from both the prior-commitment–high-incentive and the free-decision–low-incentive conditions.
* $p < .05$, $df = 1/45$.
** $p < .025$, $df = 1/45$.
*** $p < .01$, $df = 4/45$.

Discussion

The results of Experiment II support the argument that Rosenberg's (1965) procedure for the elimination of evaluation apprehension committed his subjects to perform the essay-writing task before they learned of the nature of the task and the amount of reward offered. The positive relationship between incentive magnitude and attitude change in the prior-commitment conditions of the present experiment replicates the no-choice results of Experiment I and the relationship found by Rosenberg (1965). It could be argued on this basis alone that such procedures as Rosenberg's have the same effect as allowing the subject no choice concerning performance of the counterattitudinal act. The argument becomes much more convincing, however, if it can be shown that appropriate alteration of Rosenberg's procedure, reducing the prior commitment of the subject, leads to an *inverse* relationship between incentive magnitude and attitude change. The free-decision conditions of Experiment II demonstrate precisely this point: when the subject does not feel that he has previously committed himself to performance of the counterattitudinal action requested by E_2, attitude change is an inverse function of incentive magnitude.

It should be noted here that a "balanced replication" (Aronson, 1966) of Rosenberg's (1965) study was required. Had Experiment II included only the free-decision conditions it would be possible to argue that our procedure was not successful in eliminating evaluation apprehension and that the results reflected once again the effect of this contaminant in research on forced compliance. The results of the prior-commitment conditions of Experiment II, however, counter this criticism. A persistent critic might still argue that the free-decision manipulation reintroduced evaluation apprehension. Perhaps the comment added to create the free-decision condition in some way increased the chances that subjects would see the experiments as related. However, the structured interview conducted by E_1 revealed no differential level of suspicion between the prior-commitment and free-decision conditions. In the absence of a reliable and valid measure of evaluation apprehension, we can do no more than contend that our interview was sensitive enough to detect suspicion and that we found no indication of differential suspicion among the conditions.

The results of the two studies reported above imply that the discrepancy between Cohen's (1962) findings and the results of Rosenberg's (1965) experiment may indeed be resolved in the manner indicated earlier in this paper. For Cohen's subjects the decision not to comply was a viable alternative at the time they were confronted with the essay-writing task and offered an incentive of certain value. Under such conditions dissonance will be induced whenever the incentive is not large enough to justify performance of the task, and incentive magnitude will be inversely related to subsequent attitude change. However, if a subject's freedom not to comply has been restricted before he is confronted with the task and with a clear description of the incentive, dissonance cannot be induced by an incentive of insufficient magnitude. Under these conditions, the reinforcing properties of the incentives will lead to a positive relationship between incentive magnitude and attitude change. Although Rosenberg (1965) demonstrated such a relationship, his assertion that it may be obscured by failure to remove evaluation apprehension seems no longer tenable. No attempt was made in the procedure of Experiment I to remove evaluation apprehension, and yet the results are very similar to the results of Experiment II.

Rosenberg (1966) has more recently advanced two additional hypotheses intended to resolve discrepancies in the forced-compliance literature. The first of these is that we must distinguish counterattitudinal actions that are simple and overt from those featuring the elaboration of a set of arguments. Supposedly a performance of the former kind (e.g., eating a disliked food) will lead to the inverse relationship between attitude change and incentive magnitude, while an act of the latter kind (e.g., writing a counterattitudinal essay) will result in a positive relationship. The second hypothesis is that we must distinguish between two kinds of counterattitudinal performances: (*a*) those carried out under instructions that lead the subject to believe his performance will be used to deceive others, and (*b*) those following from instructions to elaborate, for some reasonable and legitimate purpose, a set of arguments opposite to his private opinion. It it hypothesized that even if the actual task is the same, say essay writing, the first type of instruction will lead to an inverse relationship between incentive magnitude and attitude change, and the second type of instruction will lead to a positive relationship.

In the studies reported above the subject's task was presented with no hint that his performance would be used to deceive anyone, and the task in all cases was to elaborate a set of arguments opposite to his own opinion. It follows from the two hypotheses suggested by Rosenberg (1966) and presented above that we should not have been able to obtain the inverse relationship between incentive magnitude and attitude change using our procedures. However, in both experiments, we obtained the positive *and* the inverse relationship. We are forced to conclude that neither the "simple versus complex" hypothesis nor the "duplicity versus legitimate" hypothesis can account for the present results.

In place of these hypotheses we conclude that at least some of the discrepancies in the forced-compliance literature may be resolved by close attention to the role of decision freedom at the time the incentive is offered. A barely sufficient incentive for making counterattitudinal statements *does* result in dissonance and subsequent attitude change if the subject feels he is quite free not to comply. When the freedom not to comply is removed or markedly decreased, on the other hand, attitude change is greater the greater the incentive for compliance.

References

ARONSON, E. The psychology of insufficient justification. In S. Feldman (Ed.), *Cognitive consistency: Motivational antecedents and behavioral consequents.* New York: Academic Press, 1966. Pp. 115–133.

CARLSMITH, J. M., COLLINS, B. E., and HELMREICH, R. L. Studies in forced compliance: I. The effect of pressure for compliance on attitude change produced by face-to-face role playing and anonymous essay writing. *Journal of Personality and Social Psychology,* 1966, *4,* 1–13.

COHEN, A. R. An experiment on small rewards for discrepant compliance and attitude change. In J. W. Brehm and A. R. Cohen, *Explorations in cognitive dissonance.* New York: Wiley, 1962. Pp. 73–78.

FESTINGER, L. *A theory of cognitive dissonance.* Evanston, Ill.: Row, Peterson, 1957.

FESTINGER, L. *Conflict, decision, and dissonance.* Stanford: Stanford University Press, 1964.

FESTINGER, L., and CARLSMITH, J. M. Cognitive consequences of forced compliance. *Journal of Abnormal and Social Psychology,* 1959, *58,* 203–210.

NUTTIN, J. M., JR. Dissonant evidence about dissonance theory. Paper read at second Conference of Experimental Social Psychologists in Europe, Frascati, Italy, 1964. (Mimeographed)

ROSENBERG, M. J. An analysis of affective cognitive consistency. In C. I. Hovland and M. J. Rosenberg (Eds.), *Attitude organization and change.* New Haven: Yale University Press, 1960. Pp. 15–64.

ROSENBERG, M. J. When dissonance fails: On eliminating evaluation apprehension from attitude measurement. *Journal of Personality and Social Psychology,* 1965, *1,* 28–42.

ROSENBERG, M. J. Some limits of dissonance: Toward a differentiated view of counter-attitudinal performance. In S. Feldman (Ed.), *Cognitive consistency: Motivational antecedents and behavioral consequents.* New York: Academic Press, 1966. Pp. 135–170.

WINER, B. J. *Statistical principles in experimental design.* New York: McGraw-Hill, 1962.

In *Gerard's* experiment, it is pointed out that the *decision* to comply for an insufficient reward is critical to the production of dissonance. But Gerard himself acknowledges the difficulty of manipulating an individual's decision. Logically, we might add, there is no reason why someone should engage in either an effortful or a distasteful task without sufficient incentive. The very fact that he does engage in the task implies either that the task was intrinsically interesting, thus providing its own incentive, or that some extrinsic reinforcement was provided. In short, the conditions required to test dissonance theory, namely insufficient justification for compliance, may be not only artificial but self-contradictory. Gerard handled this dilemma by offering his subjects a sum of money that was sufficient to induce their compliance in a counterattitudinal task, and then giving some of them less than they had been promised. The reinforcement was thus insufficient only in terms of the subjects' expectations. As controls, some of the subjects were given no prior expectations of amount of money to be paid them for complying.

Unfortunately for the resolution of the dissonance-reinforcement controversy, Gerard's findings do not unequivocally support either viewpoint. Whether or not they had been led to expect a particular sum for writing an essay supporting a position with which they did not agree, the subjects changed more in the advocated direction for payments of $2.00 and $5.00 than they did for $.50. This would seem to confirm predictions from incentive, or reinforcement, theory. However, the subjects who had been led to expect $2.00, but received only $.50, changed their opinions significantly more than those who had been promised $2.00 and received $2.00. This finding could be interpreted as supporting a dissonance prediction, since $.50 would have been perceived as insufficient justification to those subjects who were initially offered a larger sum. Although Gerard suggests a way to control this variable more carefully, the fact remains that cognitive dissonance, whatever it may be, is a fragile commodity that waxes and wanes with slight variations in the experimenter's instructions.

We are inclined to suggest that any experiment in which subjects are given the choice of whether to engage in or not engage in some counterattitudinal performance usually provides varying degrees of incentive for compliance. Rather than look to the effects of choice on dissonance, we suggest that more attention be paid to the setting operations that may have led to a particular result. These, in nearly all reported instances, consist of instructions from the experimenter, and slight differences in these instructions may prompt the kinds of performances that are judged as reflecting dissonance reduction.

65 | *Compliance, Expectation of Reward, and Opinion Change*[1]

HAROLD B. GERARD

An issue about which there is currently a good deal of controversy concerns the relationship between the amount of reward offered a person for advocating an opinion that is discrepant from his private opinion and the amount of his subsequent opinion change in the direction of the opinion he advocated. In the experiment described here the role of expectation of reward as it affects opinion change under these conditions will be examined. The person's expectation is a feature of the situation that is acknowledged as being important but one that has as yet not been examined systematically.

The experiment by Festinger and Carlsmith (1959) which started the controversy was based upon a derivation from dissonance theory that predicts an inverse relationship between the amount of reward offered to a person for publicly advocating an opinion that is discrepant from his actual opinion and the subsequent change in his actual opinion in the direction of the opinion he advocated. This relationship appears, at first glance, to be paradoxical; the less justification the person has for advocating the discrepant opinion, the greater will be the amount he changes his opinion toward the stand advocated and hence away from his own private conviction. There is no paradox, however, when we consider that opinion change is itself an after-the-fact way of justifying having taken the discrepant stand in the first place. After deciding to advocate an opinion he initially does not agree with, the person comes to find this opinion more acceptable and thus provides justification for his decision. The theory entertains a variety of ways in which the person may reduce dissonance in this type of situation other than opinion change, but we shall not consider these other avenues here. Festinger and Carlsmith confirmed the prediction within a context where a subject, after participating in a very boring task, was paid either $1 or $20 to lie to another subject by telling him that the task was interesting. A postmeasure of the subject's attitude toward the boring task indicated that he found it less boring in the $1 than in the $20 condition. This was offered as evidence for the theory. In the $1 condition the subject had less justification for lying than he did in the $20 condition and hence experienced greater dissonance which he subsequently reduced by justifying his lie; he came to believe that the task was indeed not as boring as he originally thought it was.

A number of criticisms were raised regarding this interpretation of the results, one of these being that the effect was not due to the need for justification in the $1 treatment but to possible suspicion aroused in the $20 treatment. The payment, that is, was far beyond the subject's *expectation.* The argument is that a subject would be suspicious about being offered $20 to tell such a harmless lie and would therefore be negatively disposed toward the experiment in general, resulting in less of a tendency for him to change in the direction of the opinion he was asked to advocate.

In a subsequent experiment Cohen (reported in

[1] This study was conducted with support from Grant MH 118170 from the National Institute of Mental Health and Grant GS 392 from the National Science Foundation. I would like to thank Edward F. O'Connor, Jr. for serving as the experimenter and helping with the data analysis.

From the *Journal of Personality and Social Psychology,* 1967, *6,* 360–364.

Brehm and Cohen, 1962) attempted to answer this criticism by introducing four levels of reward: $.50, $1, $5, and $10. His subjects were college students, and the issue they chose was a very salient "town" versus "gown" dispute, concerning which the students were unanimously (or nearly so) on the gown side. Each subject was asked to write an essay favoring the town position on the issue. A measure of the subjects' subsequent attitudes toward the issue showed an inverse relationship between amount of payment and favorableness toward the town side of the argument, thus adding strong confirmation to the findings in the Festinger and Carlsmith experiment and effectively putting to rest the "suspicion" interpretation of the original results.

Two recent experiments, one modeled after the Festinger and Carlsmith procedure and the other after the one by Cohen, have reopened the issue as to whether a dissonance interpretation of the earlier experiments is appropriate. Janis and Gilmore (1965) resurrected the "suspicion" interpretation of the Festinger and Carlsmith results. The subject in their experiment was asked to write an essay in favor of the proposition that a year of physics and a year of mathematics should be required of all college students. As in the Festinger and Carlsmith experiment, the subject was offered either $1 or $20 if he agreed to write the essay. In the Festinger and Carlsmith experiment the subject agreed not only to lie to the next subject but also to be on call to lie to other subjects in the future. A $20 payment for all these tasks would not tend to arouse as much suspicion as the procedure used by Janis and Gilmore of merely writing an essay. Subjects were indeed found to be more suspicious in their $20 treatment than in the one used by Festinger and Carlsmith. They might have contrasted a condition in which $20 was *clearly* a justified reward with the procedure used by Festinger and Carlsmith, where there is certainly some doubt about how justified that large a reward might have seemed to the subject. They found a statistically insignificant trend in the opposite direction; that is, there was a slightly greater tendency for the subject in the $20 treatment to end up more favorably disposed toward adding science and math to the curriculum than in the $1 treatment. This is certainly not evidence for the suspicion hypothesis which Janis and Gilmore presumably started out to test. It is also probably true that their manipulation did not provide an adequate test of the hypothesis.

Nowhere in their report do Janis and Gilmore mention what their subjects' private convictions were initially. The inverse relationship between attitude change and reward predicted by dissonance theory requires that the subject take a *discrepant* stand. If he writes an essay that agrees with his conviction, we would, on the basis of an incentive effect, expect a positive relationship between attitude change and reward. There is no way of knowing, at least from the report of the procedure given by Janis and Gilmore, how many subjects were pro science and math and how many were anti to start with. Their procedure assumes that all subjects were initially anti science and math. From the standpoint both of a failure to test the suspicion hypothesis and the possibility that a number of subjects were not advocating a discrepant stand, the Janis and Gilmore results must be considered inconclusive.

Rosenberg (1965) has offered another interpretation of the inverse relationship between amount of reward and counterattitudinal opinion change. He argues that since the typical subject is probably concerned with the experimenter's evaluation of him he would not like to be judged as immature, maladjusted, or dishonest. In an experimental treatment where the subject is offered a large reward for engaging in certain behavior, ". . . he may be led to hypothesize that the experimental situation is one in which his autonomy, his honesty, his resoluteness in resisting a special kind of bribe, are being tested" (p. 29). To the extent that he entertains this hypothesis, the subject will be likely to show stalwart resistance to exhibiting the behavior he perceives the bribe was intended to elicit. In the case of forced-compliance studies he may perceive that in addition to advocating the discrepant stand for the reward offered, the experimenter is bribing him to change his attitude. It follows from this argument that the larger the reward, the more resistant the subject will be to indicating that he had changed his attitude.

In testing this hypothesis, Rosenberg repeated the Cohen experiment using a different issue but one on which student opinion was polarized. A significant difference between the two procedures was that in the Cohen study the request to write the essay was made by the same experimenter who took the final attitude measurement, whereas in the Rosenberg experiment the request was made by one experimenter and the measure taken by another. This should make no difference as far as the dissonance-theory prediction is concerned, but should make a difference as far as "evaluation apprehension" is concered. Rosenberg found, using rewards of $.50, $1, and $5, a *positive* relationship between attitude change and the size of reward, which supports his interpretation.

Rosenberg did not run a set of conditions paralleling his own which exactly replicated Cohen's procedure. Since he did use a different subject population, these conditions would have provided an important control. Also, his notion about evaluation apprehension does not explain the Festinger and Carlsmith results, since in that experiment the post-measure of opinion *was* taken by someone other than the experimenter who offered the reward.

One must also raise questions about specific aspects of Rosenberg's procedure that differed from the procedure used by Cohen, and that might therefore account for the results which were opposite to those of Cohen. One such difference between the Cohen and Rosenberg experiments, which may be a key to the discrepancy in results, is the difference in degree of affluence of the two subject populations used. Cohen's experiment was conducted with Ivy League students, where as Rosenberg used students at a state university. Perhaps for a state university student $.50 would seem a perfectly adequate payment for writing a brief essay, $1 would seem generous, and $5 more than generous. A typical Ivy League student, on the other hand, might consider anything less than $10 an insufficient reward for the effort required of him. If there were such a difference in the perceived value of money, it would account for the difference in results. Dissonance is aroused only when the reward for compliance is perceived as *insufficient*, a condition which may not have been satisfied in the Rosenberg experiment where the results might have been due to an incentive effect, since a reward greater than $.50 may have provided further inducement. When replicating an experiment, the important thing is not necessarily to repeat the experiment in exact detail, but to create the conditions required to test the hypothesis even if it may mean altering certain aspects of the procedure in order to do so. In the case of this series of experiments, a proper test of dissonance theory ultimately hinges on whether or not sufficient and insufficient reward conditions are being contrasted. With a change in subject population, rewards may have to be altered or certain other techniques employed in order to produce the psychological states required to test the hypothesis. Cohen may have made a felicitous choice of reward levels and Rosenberg may not have. Lacking further information as to the perceived sufficiency or insufficiency of the rewards in both experiments, this interpretation of the difference in results can only be a tentative guess.

Since the perception of insufficiency of reward is crucial, the subject's expectation as to what is a sufficient reward must somehow be violated. Offering him a smaller reward than he expected would produce dissonance and a subsequent tendency to reduce this dissonance by attempting to justify having engaged in the discrepant behavior. On the other hand, offering him a more than sufficient reward would tend to produce an incentive effect.

Method

An Overview of the Design. Two experimental treatments were compared, one in which the subject was led to expect a $2 honorarium for participating in a "survey of student opinion" on a current campus issue, and one in which no expectation of a sufficient reward was induced. Within each of these treatments, the subject was given either $.50, $2, or $5 to write an essay advocating the side of the issue he disagreed with. The subject's subsequent opinion on the issue was measured to determine the amount of his opinion change away from his original stand on the issue.

Procedure. The subjects were 48 male undergraduates at the University of California, Riverside, who were approached individually in their dormitory rooms and assigned randomly to the experimental conditions. The experimenter introduced himself as a fellow student who was working for the Survey Research Institute of Los Angeles, a (fictitious) research organization which was doing a study of various aspects of the free speech movement which had been active at the University during the school year. If the subject agreed to let the experimenter into his room, he was handed a sheet of paper briefly describing the purpose of the survey and indicating that the topic of particular interest at the moment was the controversial issue of whether or not the student government should be able to act or take positions on non-University-related issues. The regulations that were in force prohibited such action. The Survey Research Institute, he was told, was involved in finding out the pros and cons on the issue.

In the expectation treatment there was an additional paragraph to the effect that each student participating in the survey would receive a $2 honorarium. This paragraph was omitted in the no-expectation treatment.

In the expectation treatment, the subject in the $.50 condition was handed $.50 and was told, "unfortunately, we have had some unanticipated expenses and we can only afford to pay $.50 instead of the $2 that we had planned to give each student." In the $2 treatment the experimenter handed the subject $2. In the $5 condition he was handed $5 and was told, "fortunately we have had fewer expenses than we had anticipated and we can afford to pay $5 rather than $2 to all the students who help us in this survey. Since we would have had money left over, we thought this was an equitable way of distributing that money." In the no-expectation treatment the subject was given either $.50, $2, or $5 and was told that he was being given the money in return for his help with the survey.

At this point the subject was handed a sheet of paper on which to indicate whether or not he was in favor of the present regulation that forbids the student government to take a position on off-campus issues. After having done this, he was asked to write an essay supporting the side of the issue he opposed. The excuse given for asking him to do this was that the Institute had a sufficiently large number of essays that favored the position he believed in, and arguments were needed on the other side. These essays were to be seen by the staff of the Institute. Only one subject refused to comply with this request. He was replaced in the design. After the subject completed his essay, he stated his present opinion on the issue by checking a point on a scale 15 centimeters long. The true purpose of the experiment was then revealed, and the subject was asked to keep this information in strictest confidence. Very little difficulty was experienced in asking subjects in the $5 treatment to return the money. Each subject was given $2 for participating in the experiment.

Summary of the Design. The experiment used a 2 × 3 factorial design; three levels of monetary reward were run under a treatment where a prior expectation was induced or under a treatment where there was no prior expectation. In the expectation condition the reward was less than, equal to, or more than the subject expected to receive. This was done in an attempt to induce psychological states of insufficient, sufficient, or oversufficient reward. Eight subjects were assigned to each treatment.

Results

The data from the experiment consisted of the subject's attitude position on the issue as measured by a postexperimental questionnaire. He checked a point on the 15-centimeter bipolar scale indicating the extent of his agreement or disagreement with the present campus regulation. One end of the scale was labeled "the regulation is completely justified," and the other end was labeled "the regulation is completely unjustified." It was assumed that the subject's initial position on the issue was at either one of the two extremes, depending upon how he responded to the premeasure. The distance from this extreme to the point he checked on the scale was taken as the change measure; the larger this distance, the greater the assumed change. For the purposes of measurement the scale was divided into 24 equal units.

The data, which are presented in Table 1, show a curvilinear relationship between attitude change and reward under both expectation and no expectation. The difference between expectation and no expectation is not significant. There is, however, an overall effect of reward level ($p < .05$, F test). Further analysis indicates a significant difference between the $2 and $.50 treatments ($p = .01$, t test). The difference between the $2 and $5 treatments is not statistically significant.

Table 1 *Effect of Expectation and Reward on Opinion Change*[a]

Reward Level	Expectation	No Expectation
$ .50	4.56	1.62
$2.00	7.25	6.81
$5.00	5.19	5.12

[a] The larger the number, the greater the change away from the subject's original opinion.

Discussion

If we assume that there is no reliable difference between the $2 and $5 treatments, and this is probably a safe assumption to make since the edge that appears to favor the $2 treatment is due primarily to one large score under each of the two expectation conditions, the data neither confirm dissonance theory nor do they show a clear effect of incentive. For dissonance theory to have been confirmed there should have been an inverse relationship between opinion change and reward under the expectation treatment. Assuming that our subjects and those of Rosenberg enjoy the same degree of affluence, we would have expected results similar to Rosenberg's under the no-expectation treatment, although we had no clear prediction of the direction of the relationship. If the direction of the relationship between opinion change and reward had been positive under no expectation and negative under expectation, our intuition as to the discrepancy between the Cohen and Rosenberg experiments would have been confirmed, namely, that the difference was due to a difference in affluence of the two subject populations.

The results do suggest the operation of incentive if the $.50 and $2 treatments are compared. For an incentive theory to have been unequivocally supported, however, the $5 treatment should have produced more opinion change than the $2 treatment. There was nothing like a "ceiling effect" since the subjects in the $5 treatment could have changed considerably more than they did.

When the two $.50 conditions are compared, there is a suggestion that dissonance was operating since the change in the expectation condition was greater than in the no-expectation condition ($p = .05$, t test). There is amazingly little overlap (only 4 cases out of 16) between the two $.50 conditions ($p < .05$, chi-square test). This interpretation assumes that a feeling of insufficient justification was induced in the $.50-expectation condition.

Thus, we find partial evidence for the operation of both dissonance and incentive. Part of the problem may be due to the unexpected importance of one aspect of the procedure. You will recall that when the subject was approached in his dormitory room the experimenter entered the room, introduced himself, and stated his purpose. Once the subject had invited the experimenter into his room this was tantamount to complying with nearly any reasonable request the experimenter might make that pertained to the opinion survey. The subject at that time did not expect to receive any monetary reward. When the reward was offered it may have served as an additional incentive. This is likely to have happened in the no-expectation treatment and possibly in the expectation treatment as well. Thus, we may not have produced the basic conditions necessary for testing a dissonance versus incentive interpretation of the earlier experiments since it may be necessary to get the subject to commit himself for what he believes to be an insufficient reward *before* he permits the experimenter to enter his room. It is the *decision* to comply for an insufficient reward that presumably produces the dissonance.

Upon examining the Cohen and Rosenberg procedures we find that they did differ in this respect. Cohen used the monetary reward in order to get the subject to commit himself to writing the essay, whereas Rosenberg followed the procedure used in the present experiment by having the subject essentially commit himself to cooperating with the experimenter and then offering him the monetary reward. The fact that our results do tend to resemble Rosenberg's rather than Cohen's suggests that this may be a crucial aspect of the procedure and one that should be given special attention in future research in this area. The difference we found between the two \$.50 conditions suggests that in spite of the possible flaw in our procedure we did induce a psychological state of insufficient reward under the expectation treatment.

A procedure that might be used to realize a more exacting test of the two interpretations would be to somehow create an expectation of a specific monetary reward in one treatment and not in the other. Then, with only one foot barely in the door of the subject's dormitory room, offer him one of three reward levels for writing a discrepant essay—one less than, one equal to, and one greater than the reward promised in the expectation treatment.

References

BREHM, J. W., and COHEN, A. R. *Explorations in cognitive dissonance.* New York: Wiley, 1962.

FESTINGER, L., and CARLSMITH, J. M. Cognitive consequences of forced compliance. *Journal of Abnormal and Social Psychology,* 1959, *58,* 203–210.

JANIS, I. L., and GILMORE, J. B. The influence of incentive conditions on the success of role playing in modifying attitudes. *Journal of Personality and Social Psychology,* 1965, *1,* 17–27.

ROSENBERG, M. J. When dissonance fails: On eliminating evaluation apprehension from attitude measurement. *Journal of Personality and Social Psychology,* 1965, *1,* 28–42.

C Consonance and Dissonance

The two articles in this section pursue further the theoretical predictions about persuasibility that have been derived from cognitive dissonance theory. Although the authors of these articles prefer to interpret their findings in reinforcement terms, they place a great deal of stress on the subject's interpretation of the experimental conditions. If he is suspicious or anxious about the behaviors required of him, then any inducements offered him by the experimenter may take on a different tone than if he were more positively disposed toward the procedures. Again, this amounts to saying that the particular setting operations employed by the experimenter alter in significant ways the stimulus complex to which the subject is responding. A positive incentive such as money may, thus, become a negative incentive if it is introduced in such a way as to generate suspiciousness or hostility on the part of the subject. Absolute size of an incentive may be less critical than the conditions under which it is proffered.

Consonance may be construed as referring either to stimuli or to performances that are consistent with the subject's existing repertoire. A consonant argument, used as a stimulus, is one that the subject might readily voice himself. A consonant performance by the subject is one that is predictable from his previously observed behaviors. Dissonant arguments, on the other hand, are those that the subject would emit spontaneously either rarely or never. A dissonant performance is one that would be predicted *not* to occur on the basis of previously observed behaviors. Whether or not we can speak meaningfully of states of conscious experience that reflect consonance and dissonance among stimuli and performances is a moot question. The experiments described here may help clarify this problem.

Elms and Janis take the position that attitude change is a process involving conflict between positive and negative incentives. They see the expression of a counterattitudinal viewpoint as involving self-persuasion occurring when the subject verbalizes incentives that follow from acceptance of a position heretofore rejected by him. In short, the individual who "role-plays" a position with which he is not in agreement is said to be engaging in dissonant behavior. He may, however, modify his position as a result. Does he do so because of certain favorable consequences of adopting the new position, or is his change of attitude simply a means of reducing the dissonance between his past and his current attitudinal behaviors? Dissonance theory, as we have seen, predicts greater attitude change with decreased inducement for such change. Presumably, this is because the amount of dissonance to be reduced through attitude change is an inverse function of what the subject perceives as justification for engaging in counterattitudinal behavior; the less the justification, the greater the dissonance, and the greater the attitude change. This assumes, of course, that alternative modes of dissonance resolution, such as rejecting the argument or its source, are not used.

In the experiment by Elms and Janis, subjects were required to write essays favoring a position with which they disagreed, namely, sending American students to study for four years in the Soviet Union. Sponsorship of this task was attributed either to the U.S. State Department (favorable source) or to the Soviet Embassy (unfavorable source). Under each sponsorship condition, the subjects were paid either $.50 or $10.00 for writing the essay. A group of control subjects filled out the post-experimental attitude questionnaire immediately following this phase of the procedure, without actually writing the essays. The results were as predicted, namely, greater attitude change among those subjects who actually wrote the essays, and did so under favorable sponsorship, and who received the larger sum of money. Dissonance theory would predict greater change under unfavorable sponsorship and with a small reward, since the pressures to achieve consonance through attitude modification would be greater.

66 | Counter-Norm Attitudes Induced by Consonant Versus Dissonant Conditions of Role-Playing[1]

ALAN C. ELMS
IRVING L. JANIS

"Dissonance" Theory Versus "Incentive" Theory Predictions

Social scientists have long taken account of the strong social pressures that are exerted on men and women to live up to the demands of prescribed norms whenever they enter a new occupational role, advance to a more responsible position in an organizational hierarchy, or acquire a new social status in the community. It has been observed that many people, when complying to role demands, express the prescribed attitudes and values even though they do not privately accept them. Less frequently observed has been the transformation from outer to inner compliance that seems to be a central feature of role adaptation—a gradual change whereby the person comes to accept privately the beliefs and value judgments that he has expressed publicly while playing the expected social role. During the past decade, a number of experimental studies have begun to present systematic evidence concerning the effects of role-playing on attitude change. Janis and King (1954; King and Janis, 1956) found that when college students were induced to improvise a talk, in order to fulfill the demands of a public-speaking task which required them to express opinions that differed from their private beliefs, they showed more opinion change than an equivalent control group exposed to the same informational content. Kelman (1953) found a similar increase in opinion change when school children were given a mild incentive to write essays in support of an arbitrarily assigned position; but he observed no such gain in an equivalent group of children put under strong pressure to conform with the role-playing task, many of whom showed signs of constriction, resentment, and negativism.

The present study was not designed merely to see if the role-playing phenomenon could be replicated with a counter-norm attitude. Our main purpose was to test opposing predictions from two theories of attitude change, both of which have testable consequences concerning the ways in which justifications and rewards for the role-playing performance will influence the amount of attitude change. One of the rival theories in question, known as "dissonance" theory, predicts that when very weak incentives are used to induce someone to play the role of an advocate of an unaccepted position (e.g., unfavorable sponsorship and low financial reward), the amount of dissonance will be greater than if strong incentives are used, and hence the person will show more attitude change (Brehm and Cohen, 1962; Festinger, 1957). As will be seen shortly, exactly the opposite prediction follows from an "incentive' 'theory of attitude change.

Festinger (1957, p. 112) gives the following explanation of the role-playing effects observed in the Janis and King experiments:

> These studies lend support to the idea that attitude or opinion change is facilitated if a person finds himself in a situation where, by showing compliant behavior, he is engaged in actions which are dissonant with his private opinions. The changes in private opinion which ensue are the end result of a process of attempting to reduce or eliminate this dissonance.

"Dissonance" theory postulates that the amount of attitude change is proportional to the total magnitude of dissonance, which, in turn, is an inverse function of the number and importance of the pressures, rewards, and justifications used to induce the person to present arguments in favor of attitudes and beliefs that differ from his own.

A carefully executed experiment by Festinger and Carlsmith (1959) appears to give clear-cut support to the dissonance theory prediction that a small monetary reward ($1) for role-playing will elicit more opinion change than a large monetary reward ($20), but there are ambiguities in this study which make it plausible to consider alternative interpretations of the findings. For example, *E* told Ss that he, as a re-

[1] This experiment was conducted under the auspices of the Yale Studies in Attitude and Communication, which is directed by I. L. Janis and supported by a grant from the Rockefeller Foundation. A. C. Elms is now at Southern Methodist University in Dallas, Texas. The authors wish to express their thanks to Dean Robert Evans of Quinnipiac College for his helpful cooperation, which enabled us to conduct the experiment with students at that college.

From the *Journal of Experimental Research in Personality*, 1965, *1*, 50–60. Reprinted by permission of Academic Press. [Portions of the original have been omitted, with the permission of the authors and the publisher.]

search investigator affiliated with the University's Psychology Department, was interested in obtaining knowledge about human behavior; he then gave each S an hour-long series of monotonous tasks designed to induce negative attitudes about the experiment, explaining immediately afterward that he had a hidden purpose which involved a deliberate deception. Then, with "some confusion and uncertainty . . . [and] with a degree of embarrassment," *E* asked each of the male Ss (who had up to that point had been required to serve in this experiment as part of his course work) to take on the job of a laboratory assistant, which involved playing the role of a "stooge" to help carry out the deception with a young woman who was alleged to be the next S. Under these somewhat ambiguous and even negative circumstances, the extraordinarily large reward of twenty dollars might have functioned as a *negative* incentive and reduced the amount of attitude change by unintentionally generating some degree of suspicion (about being exploited by *E*) or some degree of guilt (about being paid handsomely to lie to a fellow student).

Unfortunately, the *E*s have provided no information as to how the Ss perceived the large versus small reward, and consequently there is no way of knowing whether E's explanation operated primarily as a positive or negative incentive. If the latter type of incentive were to predominate, an alternative interpretation of the Festinger and Carlsmith findings could be constructed on the basis of "incentive" theory. This theory postulates that attitude change is a process involving conflict between positive and negative incentives (Janis, 1959) and explains role-playing effects in terms of "self-persuasion" from focusing predominantly on the positive incentives supporting the hitherto rejected position (see Hovland, Janis, and Kelley, 1953, pp. 223–237).

Janis and Gilmore (1965) point out that this alternative theoretical approach specifies several conditions for inducing maximal attitude change via role playing that are quite different from those specified by dissonance theory:

> According to this "incentive" theory, when a person accepts the task of improvising arguments in favor of a point of view at variance with his own personal convictions, he becomes temporarily motivated to think up all the good positive arguments he can, and at the same time, suppresses thoughts about the negative arguments which are supposedly irrelevant to the assigned task. This "biased scanning" increases the salience of the positive arguments and therefore increases the chances of acceptance of the new attitude position. A gain in attitude change would not be expected, however, if resentment or other interfering affective reactions were aroused by *negative* incentives in the role playing situation. Among the obvious instances of negative incentives would be information that lowers the prestige of the sponsor or that leads to his being perceived as a manipulative person who is trying to influence people for his own personal aggrandizement or for other alien purposes. Any signs of exploitative intentions in the behavior of the sponsor would also be expected to operate as negative incentives, evoking responses that conflict with the positive incentive value of improvising arguments in support of the conclusion assigned by the sponsor.

One of the predictions from this theory, tested by Janis and Gilmore, is that role-playing will give rise to more attitude change under favorable rather than unfavorable sponsorship conditions, i.e., when the sponsor who induces S to engage in the role-playing task is perceived as being affiliated with an organization or cause that promotes public welfare rather than one that has commercial, exploitative, or other objectionable purposes. Confirmatory results were obtained when they compared two groups of role-players who wrote essays in favor of an unpopular educational policy (that of requiring all undergraduates in the United States to have additional courses in mathematics and science). Less personal approval of the role-played position was found under unfavorable sponsorship conditions (*E* presenting himself as a representative of a commercial company that was hiring Ss to help prepare advertising copy to promote the sale of science textbooks) than under favorable sponsorship conditions (*E* presenting himself as a representative of a public welfare organization that was hiring Ss to help prepare for a nationwide educational survey). These findings tend to support incentive theory and contradict dissonance theory since they show that overt role-playing was more effective when the sponsors' affiliations and goals were regarded by Ss as consonant with their own values than when they were regarded as being relatively dissonant. Additional findings from the same experiment showed that (a) under favorable sponsorship conditions, *overt* role-playing (actually writing an essay in which S improvises arguments in favor of an opposed point of view) was more effective in inducing attitude change than *nonovert* role-playing (merely agreeing to write such an essay without actually having the opportunity to do so); and (b) there were no significant differences between role-players who were paid \$20 in advance and those paid \$1 in advance for writing the essays (although the largest amount of attitude change occurred in the subgroup given the large amount of money under favorable sponsorship conditions). The latter finding fails to confirm the outcome of the Festinger and Carlsmith (1959) experiment in which exactly the same amounts of money were compared.

Janis and Gilmore report observations indicating that the large financial reward of $20 elicited mixed feelings in the Ss and all of them expressed a great deal of puzzlement about the inordinately large sum they were being paid for their services.

Incentive theory predicts that the amount of attitude change induced by role-playing will *increase* if a large monetary reward generates positive feelings of satisfaction, but will *decrease* if the same large reward generates negative affects, which tend to interfere with the type of open-minded set needed to be influenced by one's own improvised arguments as they are being scanned during the role-playing performance. Janis and Gilmore point out that an interaction effect might therefore be expected on the basis of incentive theory: *With positive sponsorship, a large monetary reward will have a predominantly positive incentive effect and thus make for an increase in the amount of attitude change; whereas with negative sponsorship, a large reward will tend to induce guilt, suspicion, or other negative affects that would give rise to interfering responses during the role-playing performance and therefore lead to less attitude change.* They point out that their finding that the $1 versus $20 payment had no effect does not necessarily tend to disconfirm this hypothesis because the ambivalent reactions evoked by the over-payment in the high-reward condition could obscure any such interaction effect. Moreover, in the unfavorable condition used in their experiment, the purpose of the role-playing task, despite the commercial motives of the sponsors, might have been regarded as socially accepted, since it involved helping to develop a legitimate advertising campaign. On the basis of these considerations, Janis and Gilmore point out that, in order to test the interaction hypothesis, the effects of a small reward should be compared with the effects of a more *plausible* large reward, and, in addition, a favorable sponsorship condition for the role-playing task should be compared with a more objectionable condition in which a distrusted sponsor asks Ss to violate important social norms by deceiving their peers (as in the Festinger and Carlsmith experiment) or by helping a despised out-group to spread its propaganda.

With these considerations in mind, we designed the present experiment in a way that would enable us to investigate the same variables as in the Janis and Gilmore experiment, but with a role-playing task that requires Ss to advocate a counter-norm attitude under conditions that are appropriate for testing the above-stated interaction hypothesis derived from incentive theory. Accordingly, we selected as the unfavorable (high-dissonant) condition, a role-playing situation that was defined as *helping the Soviet Union to prepare for a propaganda campaign to be directed to American students,* in contrast to the more favorable (low-dissonant) condition of *helping the United States government to prepare for a survey in order to take account of current attitudes among American students.* In both favorable and unfavorable sponsorship conditions, we used a plausible large monetary reward in contrast to a small one and, as in the Janis and Gilmore experiment, we also compared the effects of overt role-playing with a control condition in which the same information was given. In the latter condition, Ss agreed to perform the role-playing task and were paid for it, but the attitude effects were assessed before any overt role-playing took place. Thus, the present experiment involved a three-dimensional factorial design to investigate the amount of attitude change as a function of (1) overt vs. non-overt role-playing; (2) favorable vs. unfavorable sponsorship of the role-playing task; and (3) large vs. small monetary reward for the role-playing performance.

Method

The experiment was conducted in a New England teacher's college with both male and female undergraduates, all of whom volunteered for the experiment following class announcements which promised payment to students who volunteered to participate in a new research project requiring less than 1 hour of time. The Ss were assigned, according to chance, to one of the eight experimental conditions within

Table 1 *Mean Net Attitude-Change Scores*[a]

Sponsorship of Role-playing Task		Control Groups: No Overt Role-Playing			Experimental Groups: Overt Role-Playing		
		Small payment, \$0.50	Large payment, \$10.00	Total	Small payment, \$0.50	Large payment, \$10.00	Total
Favorable: U.S. Government	*N*	5	5	10	18	16	34
	M	+0.2	+0.8	+0.5	+0.9	+2.4	+1.7
Unfavorable: Soviet Union	*N*	5	5	10	17	19	36
	M	−2.0	+1.6	−0.2	+0.6	−0.1	+0.3

[a] Positive scores indicate change in counter-norm direction.

the three-dimensional factorial design. (The number of cases in each subgroup is shown in Table 1.)

All Ss were given an initial pretreatment questionnaire of ten items which asked them to express their personal attitude toward a new proposal that would involve sending American students to the Soviet Union to take their entire four years of college education in a Soviet university. They were assured that their answers would be kept anonymous.

After the initial questionnaire, all Ss were given the same instructions concerning the role-playing task, which was introduced in all conditions by the following standard background information:

> Negotiations have been under way for some time between the Soviet Union and our Government, involving a joint program to send qualified U.S. students to study in the Soviet Union for 4 years. These American students would go through a complete 4-year course in a Russian university, where they would study the Soviet system of government and the history of Communism. Our Government is somewhat skeptical about the value of this training and will not agree to the program unless it can be shown that a significant number of eligible U.S. students favor the plan. The Soviet Government wishes to go ahead with the plan for obvious reasons. Although our State Department believes the program might have some serious disadvantages, in addition to any advantages, it is withholding final judgment until an accurate evaluation of student sentiment can be made.

In the *unfavorable sponsorship* condition, Ss were informed by the interviewer (*E*) that he was a representative of a private attitude-research firm which had contracted to carry out this study for the Soviet Embassy (after the firm had checked with the U.S. State Department and obtained permission to do so). The *E* asserted that the Soviet government had hired his firm to collect the materials needed to produce a pamphlet which representatives of the Soviet Union would distribute to all U.S. college campuses, presenting arguments in favor of the proposed program that would be appealing and convincing to American students. The Ss were then instructed to outline the most convincing arguments they could think of to use in the Soviet propaganda pamphlet aimed at students like themselves.

The Ss in the *favorable-sponsorship* condition, after being given exactly the same background information (quoted above), were told that the interviewer's firm had a contract with the U.S. State Department to help find out the attitudes of American students toward the program. The *E* said that his firm was getting ready to conduct a large-scale survey of U.S. students, whose opinions would be assessed after asking them to examine a pamphlet containing arguments on *both sides* of the question, which would make them fully aware of the issues involved. The Ss were then told that *E* had already gathered sufficient arguments *against* the program, and therefore he was now asking a few students to outline some arguments in *favor* of the program, to be inserted in the pamphlet.

Thus, the information presented in the unfavorable and favorable sponsorship conditions was identical, except for assertions about (a) the employer's being the Soviet Union vs. the U.S. State Department, and (b) the purpose of S's role-playing performances being to help the Soviet Union conduct a propaganda campaign vs. helping the U.S. State Department obtain information about the attitudes of American students.

Anonymity was again assured for both conditions, and, in order to make the financial reward plausible, all Ss were told: "Please consider the arguments carefully and express them as clearly as possible, since our survey groups are small and the arguments you write down will almost certainly be included in the pamphlet." Within both sponsorship conditions, half the Ss were told that every participant would be paid a large amount of money ($10.00), which our pretesting results indicated would be regarded as a plausible large reward. The other half were offered a small reward ($0.50).

Before beginning the task, all Ss were paid the large or small reward in cash, *in advance,* and signed a receipt at *E*'s request, after which they were assigned on a stratified random basis to the overt role-playing condition or the control condition. Those in the former condition were asked to write down their arguments and, after 2 minutes, *E* mentioned four general questions to consider, in order to stimulate their thinking about cogent arguments (e.g., "How would this program affect relations between the U.S. and the U.S.S.R., particularly with regard to world peace?"). After Ss had written for 5 minutes more, their outlines were collected and they were given the final (post-treatment) questionnaire. In the control (nonovert role-playing) condition, the same four "stimulating questions" were asked immediately after S agreed to perform the role-playing task. Then, instead of allowing the control S to write down his arguments, he was told that before beginning to think of arguments, there was one other thing to be done —to fill out another brief questionnaire.

The Ss in both the overt and nonovert role-playing conditions were given exactly the same rationale for the post-treatment questionnaire: Whereas the previous questionnaire had dealt with student opinion about study in Russia in general, the second questionnaire was to be used as part of an initial survey of student opinion concerning the specific "students-to-Russia" program, about which they had just been informed. The final questionnaire contained the same questions as the first one, except that the opening item made it clear that the students were to evaluate the new Soviet-sponsored proposal.[2] The other nine questions, which were worded in exactly the same way on both questionnaires, asked each S to indicate his personal desire to participate in the program, his expectations concerning its potentially favorable or unfavorable consequences, his judgments of its importance, and his anticipations of how it would be regarded by most other American students and by his parents.

After completing the final questionnaire, each of the overt role-players was asked to rate the quality of the arguments he had written in his essay. Then, after all the data were collected from each S, *E* carefully went through a dehoaxing procedure, correcting the misinformation given earlier and explaining that the procedure was part of a psychological study completely unconnected with the Soviet Embassy or the State Department. The Ss who had been given $10.00 returned the money and were paid the same standard amount as the controls ($1.50) for their participation.

Just before being dehoaxed, every S was asked several open-ended questions to find out whether he had accepted the various explanations *E* had given concerning the experimental procedures. The Ss' answers (as well as their spontaneous comments following the "dehoaxing" information, at the very end of the session) indicated that the information *E* had presented was generally regarded as genuine and valid. The comments by Ss in the favorable sponsorship condition indicated that they fully accepted *E*'s statement that the study was being done as part of an educational survey for the U.S. State Department. Similarly, none of the Ss given the information about the unfavorable sponsorship expressed any disbelief about the alleged fact that the job was being done for the Soviet Union. Some of their answers in fact, indicated that they perceived the purpose as being even more malignant than *E* had asserted. One S, for example, said he believed the real purpose was to try to pick up new recruits for the Communist Party and to help the Soviet Union in ways that would be just within the law.

[2] On the pretreatment questionnaire, the opening item was worded as follows: "Certain educators have proposed a program to send qualified American students to study in Russian Universities for a period of 4 years, beginning as freshmen and continuing through their complete undergraduate training there. If this program were permitted by the U.S. Government, would you favor or oppose the proposal?" On the final questionnaire, the opening item was modified in the following way, so as to provide the appropriate context for the post-treatment questions: "United States and Soviet governmental authorities are negotiating on a program to send qualified American students to Russian universities to study the Soviet system of government and the history of Communism for a period of 4 years. Would you favor or oppose this program?"

The Ss in the unfavorable sponsorship condition, all of whom eventually complied, showed considerable hesitation, tension, and other manifestations of dissonance or conflict about writing an essay to help the Soviet Embassy conduct a propaganda campaign. Signs of disturbance were noted in their overt behavior at the time the purpose of the study was being described as well as in their written answers to the open-ended questions asked at the end of the session. For example, when we made completely blind ratings of the attitudes expressed in their responses to questions about how they thought their essays would be used, we found that none of the 36 Ss in the unfavorable sponsorship condition expressed any personal approval whatsoever; seven of them took pains to make it clear that they felt strong opposition or resentment, as compared with only one S in the favorable sponsorship condition. Moreover, at the beginning of the session, a number of additional Ss in the unfavorable sponsorship–low payment group showed open reluctance to participate in the study. Several asked if they should take part even if they did not approve of the program or raised other questions that delayed their decision about whether or not to accept the job.

At the end of the session, when *E* told the truth about the purpose of the study, three Ss in the unfavorable sponsorship condition who had been paid $10.00 were disinclined to return any of the money, arguing that they had agreed to do the job because of the high pay. No such difficulties were encountered among the Ss who had been given the large payment in the favorable sponsorship condition. Another distinctive reaction, which was observed in most Ss in the unfavorable sponsorship condition, was the marked relief displayed when they were given the dehoaxing information.

Although the behavioral signs and the written answers to the post-treatment questions indicate that the high-dissonance condition succeeded in generating a relatively high degree of disturbance and conflict about engaging in the role-playing task, the amount of dissonance was nevertheless not so great as to interfere with the research by leading to a high incidence of outright refusals to participate in the study. Only one man (in the unfavorable sponsorship–low payment condition) refused to write the essay, and hence the differential loss of Ss was negligible among the various treatments to be considered.[3]

[3] Two other Ss who wrote the essay were eliminated from the tabulations of the results because they expressed some vague suspicions that the large ($10.00) payment might entail something more than *E* had asserted. One of the Ss was in the favorable sponsorship condition and the other in the unfavorable sponsorship condition of the overt role-playing treatment.

Results and Discussion

The appropriateness of regarding the role-played position as a counter-norm attitude is indicated by results from the pretreatment questionnaire, which revealed that the Ss generally shared the widespread negative attitude of U.S. citizens toward Soviet institutions. The majority of students expressed strong opposition to the proposed educational policy of having American students receive their entire college education in the Soviet Union and asserted that their peers and their parents would also be opposed. There were no significant differences among any of the subgroups on the pretreatment attitude measures ($p >$ .20, two-tailed, for every pair of means).

The attitude changes induced by the various conditions of role-playing were assessed by scoring the changes on each of the ten items in the attitude scale in terms of 0, +1 or −1, depending on whether the responses remained unchanged or shifted in the direction of favoring or opposing the Soviet-sponsored proposal. A net attitude-change score was computed for each S, and represented the total number of questions on which he changed positively from the "before" to the "after" questionnaire minus the total number of those on which he changed negatively. (This measure was selected in advance because in our prior research on attitude change we have noted that a total score based on the presence or absence of change on each item generally entails less error variance than a score that summates the *amount* of change shown on every item.) The *mean* net attitude-change score for each condition is shown in Table 1.

It will be noted that the largest amount of attitude change occurred in the *overt* role-playing group that was exposed to the *least* dissonant condition, i.e., favorable sponsorship with large monetary reward. The mean net change of +2.4 shown by this group was found to differ significantly at beyond the 5% confidence level from each of the other groups of overt role-players (when t tests were computed in two different ways, one basing the standard error of the mean differences solely on the two distributions being compared and the other using an overall error estimate obtained from an overall $2 \times 2 \times 2$ analysis of variance). These findings indicate that overt role-playing is most effective when the inducements for performing the task are consonant with the Ss' personal values. The outcome clearly contradicts the dissonance-theory prediction and supports the incentive-theory prediction.

The large mean attitude-change score noted in the group of overt role-players given the favorable sponsorship information and the large monetary reward indicates that attitude change can be induced by role-playing even for a counter-norm type of attitude. Quite aside from the implications this finding has for opposing theories of attitude change, it helps to substantiate an empirical generalization inferred from prior role-playing experiments dealing with more innocuous types of opinion changes. The generalization in question is that the technique of improvised role-playing can exert a powerful influence to modify existing attitudes, including those anchored in social norms, which ordinarily are highly resistant to the usual forms of persuasive pressures.

According to "incentive theory," the attitude changes produced by role-playing are mediated by intensive "biased scanning" of positive incentives, which involves two types of verbal responses: (1) fulfilling the demands of the role-playing task by recalling and inventing arguments that are capable of functioning as positive incentives for accepting a new attitude position, and (2) appraising the recalled and improvised arguments with a psychological set that fosters *open-minded cognitive exploration of their potential incentive value,* rather than a negativistic set of the type engendered by the arousal of feelings of hostility, resentment, or suspicion. Thus, for example, it would be expected that many intelligent American soldiers who were captured by the Chinese Communists during the Korean War could comply with the role-playing demands of their despised "brainwashing" captors and nevertheless remain uninfluenced: While verbalizing "good" pro-Communist arguments, the prisoners could privately label all the improvised arguments with negative epithets or could think about counterarguments that would refute the statements they were overtly verbalizing (see Lifton, 1961; Schein, 1956).

In experimental research on role-playing effects, the first of the two types of response essential for effective biased scanning can be readily assessed by examining the manifest content of the role-playing performance to see if plausible-sounding arguments were improvised, but the second type is difficult to assess because it involves private verbalizations that occur silently, along with the overt statements that are being made. Judgments of the quality of written essays, as in the present experiment, are at best an indirect measure of the second type of response, based on the assumption that a hostile or closed-minded role-player will tend to be more perfunctory in his role-playing performance and hence produce arguments of poorer quality. On this indirect measure, our ratings of the essays fail to show that the incentive variables had a significant effect on the quality of the role-playing performance. But it is quite possible, of course, that this indirect measure is too crude to detect differences in psychological sets, and that research on this problem requires much more subtle measures, such as those provided by a content analysis of detailed interviews in which each S is asked to report on his covert subjective thoughts during the role-playing performance itself.

In summary, the predictions from "incentive" theory are borne out by the main results from this experiment, which show that a gain in attitude change was produced by overt role-playing under favorable inducement conditions. Our supplementary data on the quality of the essays, however, do not provide evidence that the gain was mediated by a corresponding increase in biased scanning while Ss were improvising arguments in favor of the assigned position. Obviously, the question of how the positive inducements lead to increased attitude change remains an open question to be settled by subsequent research.

References

Brehm, J., and Cohen, A. *Explorations in cognitive dissonance.* New York: Wiley, 1962.

Festinger, L. A. *A theory of cognitive dissonance.* Stanford: Stanford University Press, 1957.

Festinger, L., and Carlsmith, J. Cognitive consequences of forced compliance. *Journal of Abnormal and Social Psychology,* 1959, *58,* 203–210.

Hovland, C., Janis, I., and Kelley, H. *Communication and persuasion.* New Haven: Yale University Press, 1953.

Janis, I. Motivational factors in the resolution of decisional conflicts. In M. R. Jones (Ed.), *Nebraska symposium on motivation: 1959.* Lincoln: University of Nebraska Press, 1959.

Janis, I., and Gilmore, J. The influence of incentive conditions on the success of role playing in modifying attitudes. *Journal of Personality and Social Psychology,* 1965, *1,* 17–27.

Janis, I., and King, B. The influence of role-playing on opinion-change. *Journal of Abnormal and Social Psychology,* 1954, *49,* 211–218.

Kelman, H. Attitude change as a function of response restriction. *Human Relations,* 1953, *6,* 185–214.

King, B., and Janis, I. Comparison of the effectiveness of improvised versus nonimprovised role playing in producing opinion changes. *Human Relations,* 1956, *9,* 177–186.

Lifton, R. *Thought reform and the psychology of totalism.* New York: W. W. Norton, 1961.

Schein, E. The Chinese indoctrination program for prisoners of war: A study of attempted "brainwashing." *Psychiatry,* 1956, *19,* 149–172.

Another controversial area in persuasion research is the relative effectiveness that a communication gains from either preceding or following an opposing viewpoint. A recent investigation of this primacy-recency problem is reported by *Corrozi and Rosnow,* who manipulated reinforcement following presentation of a two-sided argument. They cite several studies in which it has been found that either temporal proximity to a reinforcing stimulus or temporal displacement from an aversive stimulus enhances the effectiveness of a persuasive communication. Borrowing a reinforcing device described in the article by Golightly and Byrne (Chapter 10), these investigators used consonant and dissonant communications (advocating a shorter or longer school week) as positive and aversive stimuli that either preceded or followed an unrelated discussion of Picasso. They found both proactive and retroactive effects of the consonant communication on the persuasiveness of a two-sided essay about the merits of Picasso's paintings. In other words, regardless of the order in which positive or negative comments about Picasso were presented to the subjects, they reacted most favorably to those comments occurring either just before or just after a communication with which they agreed. Conversely, they reacted negatively to comments about Picasso that either preceded or followed a dissonant communication. Primacy and recency were thus seen to occur as functions of the reinforcement contingencies associated with two sides of the persuasive argument. It should be noted, in passing, that these writers use the term "negative reinforcement" inappropriately. Negative reinforcement is properly said to occur when a performance is instrumental in either avoiding or escaping from a noxious stimulus. Since no escape from the disagreeable communication was possible in this experiment, it should be viewed as an aversive stimulus, rather than as negative reinforcement.

67 Consonant and Dissonant Communications as Positive and Negative Reinforcements in Opinion Change[1]

JOHN F. CORROZI
RALPH L. ROSNOW

When both sides of an issue are presented successively, which has the advantage—the side presented first (primacy) or the side presented last (recency)? Instead of a general law of primacy (Lund, 1925), a collection of variables has been identified (Rosnow, 1966b), some of which tend to produce primacy (e.g., Janis and Feierabend, 1957; Lana, 1961, 1963a, 1963b) and others, recency (e.g., Anderson, 1959; Lana, 1961, 1963b; Miller and Campbell, 1959). One such variable is the presentation of a positive or negative reinforcer immediately before or after the usual two-sided persuasive communication (Rosnow, 1965, 1966a; Rosnow, Holz, and Levin, 1966; Rosnow and Lana, 1965; Rosnow and Russell, 1963). A fairly recurrent finding in these experiments has been that subjects' opinions tend to change in the direction of whichever arguments are closer in time to a positive reinforcement or farther from a negative reinforcement. Presumably, contiguity between a positive reinforcement and an argument serves to strengthen the tendency to respond in the direction of the argument, while negative reinforcement weakens any such tendency. Thus, primacy effects predominate if the two-sided communication follows a positive reinforcement or precedes a negative reinforcement. Recency effects predominate if the two-sided communication either precedes a positive reinforcement or follows a negative reinforcement.

In these studies, the reinforcers included such obviously pleasant or noxious events as verbal approval or disapproval, increasing grades, or surprise exams. An interesting new verbal reinforcer has recently been discovered by Golightly and Byrne (1964) in a study of discrimination learning. Statements with which their subjects strongly agreed (consonant statements) were positive reinforcers. Statements with which the subjects strongly disagreed (dissonant statements) were negative reinforcers. One purpose of the present study was to determine whether Golightly and Byrne's reinforcers would reinforce opinion. A second, related purpose was to explore the generality of the primacy-recency findings by using consonant and dissonant statements as the reinforcers which precede or follow a two-sided communication. It can then be predicted that subjects' opinions should change in the direction of whichever arguments are closer in time to a consonant statement or farther from a dissonant statement. Hence, primacy was predicted if the two-sided communication either followed a consonant communication or preceded a dissonant communication. Recency was predicted if the two-sided communication either preceded a consonant communication or followed a dissonant communication.

Method

General Procedure

Eight classes of high school juniors and seniors ($N = 152$) served as subjects in this before-after design. The design of the experiment and the predictions of primacy and recency are summarized in Table 1. Two weeks after their instructor had administered an opinion questionnaire containing items about the artist Pablo Picasso to the subjects, one of the experimenters (J.F.C.) read to each of the eight groups a two-sided communication containing positive and negative arguments about Picasso. The juxtaposition of the arguments was counterbalanced—four of the groups received the positive argument first (B_1); the other four received the negative argu-

[1] This paper is based upon a master's thesis, by the first author under the direction of the second, submitted to the faculty of the Boston University Communication Research Division. This research was supported by Grants GS-1375 from the National Science Foundation and MH-11972-01 from the National Institute of Mental Health. We thank David I. Mostofsky for his helpful criticisms of a draft of this paper. We also thank Michael Guichard, Harold M. Wilson, superintendent of instruction of the Arlington County Public Schools, Sarah G. Tanenbaum and Robert Shreve, instructors at Wakefield High School, and the other members of the thesis committee, A. George Gitter and F. Earle Barcus.

ment first (B_2). The same experimenter then read to two of the counterbalanced groups (A_1) a consonant communication on an objectively irrelevant issue. Two other groups (A_2) received the consonant communication immediately before the Picasso arguments. Of the remaining four groups, two (A_3) received a dissonant communication after the Picasso arguments, and two (A_4) received the dissonant communication before the Picasso arguments. Opinions toward Picasso were measured by the experimenter immediately thereafter.

Materials

Two-sided communication. Lana (1963a) has shown that increased controversialism of the topic produces primacy. Hence, Picasso, who is generally not perceived by students as particularly controversial (Lana[2]), was chosen as the topic of the two-sided communication. The positive and negative arguments, each about 350 words long, were constructed by Lana[3] to be perceived as equivalent in their persuasiveness.

Consonant and dissonant communications. Each of these communications was just over 200 words long. The dissonant communication advocated a longer school week (six 9-hour days), while the consonant communication took the position that the school week was already long enough. Another class of subjects ($N = 20$) from this population was found to agree strongly with the consonant communication and to disagree with the dissonant communication ($t = 9.94$, $df = 18$, $p < .05$).

Opinion questionnaires. The pretest questionnaire, administered two weeks before the communications, was represented to the students as a national high school opinion survey. The questionnaire contained eleven 5-point Likert-type items. Five of the items asked the students to evaluate Picasso; the remaining six were on other, unrelated issues. Summed responses to the Picasso items could range from a score of 5, or unfavorable, to a highly favorable 25. The posttest questionnaire consisted of just the five Picasso items contained in the pretest.

Awareness of intent. At the conclusion of the experiment, the subjects were asked to guess the purpose of the study. Of the handful who responded, not one subject drew an association between the Picasso and the school-week communications.

Results and Discussion

Table 1 lists the pretest and posttest mean scores for all groups and outlines the analytic procedure. Order effects were computed using a subtraction-difference technique, described by Hovland, Mandell, Campbell, Brock, Luchins, Cohen, McGuire, Janis, Feierabend, and Anderson (1957), where pretest scores are subtracted from their respective posttest scores, the resulting gain score for the negative-first sequence then subtracted from the gain score for the positive-first sequence. The difference-between-gain score is then tested against the null hypothesis using the t. If the final difference score is positive, primacy is indicated; if it is negative, recency. As predicted, there are clear-cut differences in Table 1 in the direction of opinion change produced by pairing contiguously the consonant or dissonant school-week communications with the two-sided Picasso communication. The results strongly support three out of four predictions concerning direction; the fourth fails to reach significance at the .05 level. Both the proactive and the retroactive effects of the consonant communication, or positive reinforcement, are in the predicted direction and are significant at the .05 level. Also, the proactive effect of the dissonant communication, or negative reinforcement, is in the predicted direction, with $p < .05$. Only the retroactive effect of the dissonant communication fails to achieve the specified level of significance.

Cochran's test, computed on the pretest scores of these eight groups, was not significant ($C = .198$, $df = 18$, $p > .05$), indicating that the subjects' original opinions are homogeneous with respect to variance. Consistent with previous findings (Rosnow, 1966a), no overall difference in the magnitude of opinion change is indicated between groups exposed to the consonant communication versus those exposed to the dissonant communication ($F = 1.04$, $df = 1/144$, $p > .25$). Also, no significant overall difference in the magnitude of opinion change can be attributed to the order of presentation of the Picasso arguments ($F = 2.76$, $df = 1/144$, $p > .05$), nor can any overall difference be attributed to the temporal placement of the reinforcements ($F = 1.15$, $df = 1/144$, $p > .25$).

These results are generally consistent with previous findings. With the exception of the insignificant retroactive effect of the negative reinforcement, opinions change significantly in the direction of whichever argument is closer in time to a consonant communication (positive reinforcement) or farther from a dissonant communication (negative reinforcement). One plausible explanation for this finding follows Golightly and Byrne (1964) and Dollard and Miller

[2] "Order Effects in Persuasive Communications," progress report to the National Institute of Mental Health, United States Public Health Service, Research Grant M-4830, 1962.

[3] See Footnote 2.

Table 1 *Research Design, Pretest and Posttest Mean Scores, and Difference Scores*

	(A_1) Consonant After		(A_2) Consonant Before		(A_3) Dissonant After		(A_4) Dissonant Before	
	(B_1) Positive First	(B_2) Negative First	(B_1) Positive First	(B_2) Negative First	(B_1) Positive First	(B_2) Negative First	(B_1) Positive First	(B_2) Negative First
Pre	18.11	16.16	17.16	17.26	17.00	17.05	17.42	15.32
Post	17.63	18.06	17.95	16.53	17.47	16.79	15.47	16.63
Gain	−.48	1.90	.79	−.73	.47	−.26	−1.95	1.31
Predicted difference	Recency		Primacy		Primacy		Recency	
Obtained difference[a]	−2.38** (Recency)		+1.52* (Primacy)		+.73 (Primacy)		−3.26*** (Recency)	

[a] One-tailed t tests used throughout.
* $p < .05$.
** $p < .025$.
*** $p < .005$.

(1950); there is a learned drive to be logical, consistent, and to interpret the environment correctly. Consonant and dissonant communications, Byrne (1962) maintained, constitute rewarding and punishing events in that they provide the recipient with social evidence of the correctness of his opinions and behavior. Contiguity between a reward and an argument strengthens the tendency to respond in the direction of the argument, while punishment weakens the tendency.

References

Anderson, N. H. Test of a model for opinion change. *Journal of Abnormal and Social Psychology,* 1959, *59,* 371–381.

Byrne, D. Response to attitude similarity-dissimilarity as a function of affiliation need. *Journal of Personality,* 1962, *30,* 164–177.

Dollard, J., and Miller, N. E. *Personality and psychotherapy.* New York: McGraw-Hill, 1950.

Golightly, C., and Byrne, D. Attitude statements as positive and negative reinforcements. *Science,* 1964, *146,* 798–799.

Hovland, C. I., Mandell, W., Campbell, E. H., Brock, T., Luchins, A. S., Cohen, A. R., McGuire, W. J., Janis, I. L., Feierabend, R. L., and Anderson, N. H. *The order of presentation in persuasion.* New Haven: Yale University Press, 1957.

Janis, I. L., and Feierabend, R. L. Effects of alternative ways of ordering pro and con arguments in persuasive communications. In C. I. Hovland, W. Mandell, E. H. Campbell, T. Brock, A. S. Luchins, A. R. Cohen, W. J. McGuire, I. L. Janis, R. L. Feierabend, N. H. Anderson, *The order of presentation in persuasion.* New Haven: Yale University Press, 1957. Pp. 115–128.

Lana, R. E. Familiarity and the order of presentation of persuasive communications. *Journal of Abnormal and Social Psychology,* 1961, *62,* 573–577.

Lana, R. E. Controversy of the topic and the order of presentation in persuasive communications. *Psychological Reports,* 1963, *12,* 163–170. (a)

Lana, R. E. Interest, media, and order effects in persuasive communications. *Journal of Psychology,* 1963, *56,* 9–13. (b)

Lund, F. H. The psychology of belief: A study of its emotional and volitional determinants. *Journal of Abnormal and Social Psychology,* 1925, *20,* 174–196.

Miller, N., and Campbell, D. T. Recency and primacy in persuasion as a function of the timing of speeches and measurements. *Journal of Abnormal and Social Psychology,* 1959, *59,* 1–9.

Rosnow, R. L. A delay-of-reinforcement effect in persuasive communication. *Journal of Social Psychology,* 1965, *67,* 39–43.

Rosnow, R. L. "Conditioning" the direction of opinion change in persuasive communication. *Journal of Social Psychology,* 1966, *69,* 291–303. (a)

Rosnow, R. L. Whatever happened to the "law of primacy"? *Journal of Communication,* 1966, *16,* 10–31. (b)

Rosnow, R. L., Holz, R. F., and Levin, J. Differential effects of complementary and competing variables in primacy-recency. *Journal of Social Psychology,* 1966, *69,* 135–147.

Rosnow, R. L., and Lana, R. E. Complementary and competing-order effects in opinion change. *Journal of Social Psychology,* 1965, *66,* 201–207.

Rosnow, R. L., and Russell, G. Spread of effect of reinforcement in persuasive communication. *Psychological Reports,* 1963, *12,* 731–735.

The Ethics of Social Change

12

Social situations have long been manipulated both practically and deliberately. Ever since Machiavelli, and perhaps before, there has been a fear of the control and the manipulation of one person's behavior for the benefit of another. With the development of a laboratory science of social psychology, where social phenomena are developed in prototype form and actually shaped and manipulated, a technology is becoming available to influence social situations rationally and self-consciously. This raises questions concerning the ethics of such manipulation.

Perhaps the ethical problems and the responsibilities that accrue from the development of an effective technology are greatest in the social sciences. Social control is the most pervasive influence on an individual, because it represents the conjoint impact of so many other persons who exert more control in concert than they do individually.

Two issues involving social control can be discussed separately. The first issue, in which the science of psychology itself can provide the best answer, concerns the characteristics of various types of control and the implications of each for the controller, the controllee, and the community. The second issue involves a political decision about how the community is to govern itself (who is to control whom and under what circumstances). The two issues are interrelated, at least ideally, because political decisions about control, as we shall see in the later articles, can benefit from a knowledge of the characteristics and by-products of various techniques for modifying human behavior. Wherever the science of psychology can describe natural practices effectively, we have a chance to observe and be aware of how we influence or control each other practically, politically, socially, and institutionally.

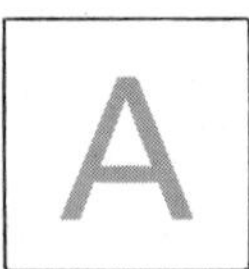

What Is Control?

A large issue in the control of behavior is the relative desirability of control by positive and aversive consequences. Frequently there is a tacit assumption that aversive control is bad and positive reinforcement is good. *Ferster* analyzes the implications of positive and negative reinforcement and attempts to spell out the conditions under which the results benefit either the controller or the controllee.

68 | *Arbitrary and Natural Reinforcement*[1]

C. B. FERSTER

It has been clear for some time that many of the ills of human behavior have come from aversive control. Behavioral scientists have studied it in the laboratory in the hope that a technical knowledge of the processes would show them how to ameliorate psychopathology. Psychologists, particularly under Skinner's (1948) influence, have speculated about a society without any aversive control. Some psychologists, experimental and otherwise, have felt so strongly about aversive control that they raised their children as much as possible by positive reinforcement alone. More recently, mostly as a result of the urgency of controlling self-destructive behavior in autistic children and because of the technical difficulties in controlling these children with positive reinforcement, the cycle has gone a full turn. Investigators, such as Lovaas et al. (1965), have turned to aversive control with stimuli such as intense electric shock, slapping, shouting, and incarceration in order to suppress self-destructive behavior, to reinforce attention, and to weaken tantrums. Other investigators and therapists have been using electric shock with adults in what is called aversion therapy.

It is difficult not to be moralistic about aversive control. The word aversive has the connotations of reject, avoid, escape, and withdraw. Most people's feelings about aversive control are that "It's better to give than to receive," which suggests something of the moral dilemma. Aversive control is obviously used widely in the normal environment because it achieves something. The reasons for its use are not hard to find. First, it changes behavior immediately. Second, if it is made severe enough, the behavior it controls will override any other performance the person might engage in. Third, the aversive stimulus itself is the motive for the behavior that is required. It is not necessary to take into account the disposition of the person who is controlled (Skinner, 1953). On the other hand, despite their immediate control aversive stimuli make us uneasy because they produce by-products such as anxiety and other general disruptions of the operant repertoire (Skinner, 1965). Aversive control leads to avoidance of the controller and general aggressiveness. Furthermore, it substitutes avoidance and escape for productive behavior. The problems that come from aversive control are not so much the behaviors that the controller intends to produce as the behaviors that occur unintentionally. The same aversive stimulus produces both.

In order to evaluate the consequences, the desirability, and the usefulness of various kinds of aversive control in human behavior two kinds of aversive stimuli, natural and arbitrary, may be described. Negative reinforcement, escape from an aversive stimulus, is very common and necessary in the natural human environment because aversive stimuli occur so widely and frequently. Anytime there is an aversive stimulus, there is potentially some performance which will terminate it. In bright sunlight we put on sunglasses, shade our eyes with our hands, turn away from the sun, or reduce the amount of light by squinting. Such aversive control obviously does not have drastic side effects, nor is it unproductive or undesirable. Youngsters quickly learn to put their fingers in their ears when there is a loud noise. Visual aversive stimuli commonly reinforce the behavior of turning the head away. Performances such as opening a window, taking off clothing, or turning on an air conditioner occur because they reduce the temperature of the air around the body. A pebble rubbing the foot inside the shoe reinforces removing it. In the presence of extreme odors we pinch our nostrils or hold our breath momentarily. The examples can be repeated at great length (Ferster and Perrot, 1968). A statement attributed to Thorndike points out that the zero point, the first level of intelligence and productive behavior, is spitting out a bitter substance that enters the mouth. These simple aversive stimuli are natural rather than arbitrary because they reinforce any behavior which reduces the aversive stimulus.

A performance reinforced by escape operates physically and directly on the aversive stimulus. For example, turning the dial of the television set blots out the commercial, or averting the gaze interrupts the light entering the eye. All of these behaviors have the same result on the aversive stimulus and they are equally effective in terminating it. The property of the aversive stimulus could be described theoretically by saying that it reinforces a class of behaviors. In most cases the aversive stimulus interacts with, and shapes, existing behavior. The particular performance that an aversive stimulus will reinforce will depend,

[1] This research was carried out with a grant from the Office of Education, Grant No. 32-20-7515-5024, Division of Handicapped Children and Youth. The paper was delivered at the 1966 Meeting of the American Association for the Advancement of Science in Washington, D.C.

From the *Psychological Record,* 1967, *17,* 341–357. Reprinted by permission.

of course, on the total repertoire the person brings to it. Bright sunlight will reinforce squinting or wearing sunglasses or a hat in the case of the person who needs to spend time outside. A person with little behavior under the control of reinforcers outdoors will simply stay out of the sun.

In contrast to the natural reinforcers there is the aversive stimulus which is applied arbitrarily by one person to control the behavior of another. Examples of this kind of arbitrary control are the child who picks up his toys because doing so terminates the parent's threat, a student who does an assignment because it avoids ridicule in class the next day, or an employee who does his job only when there is a threat of being fired.

Such arbitrary social reinforcement differs in two ways from the natural reinforcer that was just described. First, the performance that is reinforced is specified narrowly in contrast to natural reinforcers where a large class of behaviors can get rid of the natural aversive stimulus. Thus, a parent who says "Come here this minute or I'll get angry," requires one particular performance. The child cannot, for example, escape the parent altogether by leaving the room. In that case the parent will adjust the aversive stimulus until the *only* way to terminate it is to come. The usual laboratory experiment with a rat, a lever, and an electric shock illustrates this same property of arbitrary reinforcement. The electric shock can potentially reinforce lying on the back, hanging from a projection on the wall or standing between the grids on the floor. Because the experimenter needs a performance that can be recorded automatically he arranges the apparatus and procedure so that only pressing the bar can terminate the shock. He shaves the fur from the rat's back, incarcerates him in a chamber, eliminates projections from the walls and uses closely spaced grids. From the rat's point of view all that is required is that the intolerable stimulus be terminated. It is the experimenter who has an investment in lever pressing. The parent who uses aversive control to get a child to pick up his toys is establishing the same arbitrary relationship to the aversive stimulus as the experimenter has done with the rat and the electric shock. The child cannot simply escape from the parent's anger as he could from a hot fire because there is no behavior in his repertoire which has any physical relation to the aversive stimulus. The parents require a particular performance and adjust the application of the aversive stimulus until they get it.

Natural reinforcement begins with a performance already in the individual's repertoire reinforced by an event which occurs reliably in the milieux. Procedures designed to influence this kind of behavior must therefore begin with the current repertoire of the individual. Arbitrary reinforcement does not need to take the individual's current repertoire into account nearly as much as is the case with natural reinforcement.

While we sometimes apply aversive stimuli for the individual's own good, the immediate reinforcers benefit only the controller. The controller gets the behavior he wants: The child temporarily terminates an aversive stimulus which a controller such as a parent can reapply any time he wants another performance. The reinforcement is arbitrary because there is no reinforcer currently maintaining the desired behavior or behavior similar to it in the child's repertoire. With an arbitrary stimulus, the controller can coerce a particular performance, whatever the child's current repertoire. A mute child under the control of a graduate student whose course grade depends on producing speech is in such a position. Speech which is arbitrarily reinforced without reference to the child's current repertoire may disappear as soon as the acute intervention ends unless there is planned transition to a natural reinforcer. Aversive control is often said to benefit the child because the behavior that is coerced will be useful to the child later. The child does not benefit, however, in the sense of achieving a durable reinforcer which will maintain behavior without the coercive control.

Another characteristic of control by an arbitrary reinforcer is that it is designed to preempt the rest of the individual's behavior. Thus the child facing a threatening parent cannot turn to other behaviors as he could in the face of an aversive stimulus which had a fixed physical relation to his behavior. The requirement that he emit a *particular* performance will preempt all other behaviors.

The person who applies an arbitrary reinforcer intends to produce a particular form of behavior. In contrast, the motive for the natural reinforcer comes from the individual who terminates it. In a teleological vein, one might say that the natural reinforcer has no motive, and will be satisfied with any performance that terminates it. As a result the naturally occurring aversive stimulus may seldom, if ever, occur if it is aversive enough to maintain the operant behavior that avoids it. Technically the immediate and specific behavior generated by the aversive stimulus reinforces the individual in the case of natural reinforcement and the controller in the case of arbitrary reinforcement. A child may escape and avoid a hot stove for years without being burned. The hapless rat in an experiment, or the socially controlled child, however, will be re-exposed to the aversive stimulus each time the experimenter or parent wants some more behavior.

The arbitrary control of behavior, for the benefit of the controller, rather than the controllee can occur in positive as well as negative reinforcement. Consider first the properties of natural positive reinforcement. The aphorism, "You can lead a horse to water but you can't make him drink," suggests some behaviors from which to describe arbitrary and natural positive reinforcers. Water can reinforce a variety of behaviors in a water-deprived horse, such as pawing the ground, turning the faucet on the trough with its foot or searching the countryside for a stream, pond, or puddle. Each of these performances comes from the horse's existing operant repertoire.

Arbitrary reinforcement occurs when the horse isn't thirsty and a reinforcer is used to make him drink. One procedure would be to apply an electric shock which is terminated whenever he drinks. Such procedures have been carried out many times (Williams and Teitelbaum 1956), and the arbitrariness of such reinforcement has already been discussed. But we could also reinforce drinking by giving the horse food every time he drinks. It is necessary in such a procedure to restrict or incarcerate the horse so that he cannot roam the countryside looking for places to graze. From the point of view of the horse's repertoire, there are already many behaviors reinforced by food that have a higher probability than drinking water. Such restriction would have to be carried out by aversive control in order to prevent or suppress the positively-reinforced eating behaviors already in the horse's repertoire. The crux of the matter is that the horse's drinking is reinforcing to the horse only because the experimenter has arbitrary control of him. One might properly ask why one would want to make a horse drink which is not thirsty. It would be much simpler to wait a period of time, and the horse will surely drink one way or another since such behavior is always a durable part of any horse's repertoire.

This distinction between arbitrary and natural positive reinforcement becomes practically important when we consider building behavior in children in the natural environment and particularly therapeutically (Ferster, 1958, 1961, 1966, 1967). The following is an example of the arbitrary application of reinforcement by a therapist: "If you put on your coat, I'll give you a cooky." Such an episode begins with a child who has no disposition to put on his coat and has a disposition to eat cookies. The therapist is reinforced when the child puts on his coat but not necessarily when the child eats cookies. Such behavior benefits the therapist and will cease as soon as he stops giving the cookies. The child's natural environment has never reinforced putting on a coat with cookies and is not likely to do so in the future. The same performance could be reinforced naturally, however, if the coat served to prevent the child from being cold outside.

Even a small part of the repertoire may be reinforced naturally. The child may stand still and extend his arms when the therapist puts the coat on the child on a cold day before going to the playground. In this situation the child is already emitting a performance, extending his arms, which is negatively reinforced (at the end of a chain of performances) by avoiding cold air outside. Under these conditions the therapist may gradually assist the child less, paced with the child's ability to complete the task of dressing. For example, at one stage the therapist might hold the last sleeve in position until the child pushed his arm through. The completed repertoire will be natural in the sense that it will be durably maintained by its effect on the child's comfort long after the therapist has gone (Ferster and Simons, 1966).

There are many opportunities for the therapist to interact with performances which exist in the child's repertoire because they have a natural and stable effect on the child's environment. These situations are illustrated by phrases such as, 'If you want to leave the room, you need to turn the knob," as opposed to "You can have the cooky if you put the puzzle together." In the first case, the child already has engaged in the behavior of leaving the room reinforced by the new location he goes to. The therapist can successively approximate new behaviors, such as turning the knob, speaking to someone, or getting a key, by minor prompts and supplementary supports which then can be faded away. Such behavior is for the child's benefit rather than that of the therapist in the sense that the therapist has brought the child into better contact with a reinforcer that is already maintaining the child's behavior. The distinction is the same one that is suggested by Skinner's discussion of the mand and the tact (Skinner, 1957). New enlargements of the child's repertoire such as turning a door knob will, of course, make it possible for the child to come under the control of new reinforcers not currently maintaining his behavior. Opening doors is a repertoire which can lead to reinforcers other than those originally supporting the behavior.

Many clinicians implicitly understand the distinction between arbitrary and natural reinforcement (Ferster, 1967; 1968). The following statement by Jeanne Simons, Director of Linwood Children's Center, expresses the connotations of natural reinforcement.

> And that's why we walk behind the child. He feels your protection when you walk behind. If you give him a chance to go any direction, he may be wrong when he goes this way or that. Just follow him. If it's a dead end, pick him up gently and bring him to the main route. But never think that you know the answer, because you are dealing with an individual who may

want to go very different routes which for him may be better. That's why I feel more comfortable behind the children so I can see where they are going.

Walking behind the child denotes a broad statement of the principle of operant reinforcement. The repertoire may be partially ineffective, however, and these parts will decrease by extinction as the therapist supports, prompts, and otherwise encourages those behaviors which are successful. By beginning with the initial behavior and reinforcers that the child brings to the therapeutic environment, we preserve the unique contribution of his own repertoire, and we avoid decisions about his life which are too arbitrary.

In summary, the same problems arise with positive reinforcement as with aversive control in evaluating its properties and usefulness in the control of behavior in the normal environment. The undesirable by-products of aversive control are well known, but equally serious are the results of its arbitrary application. Natural reinforcers, on the other hand, have the advantage that they persist without the intervention of the parent and therapist, and they do not require collateral aversive stimuli and incarceration to be effective.

References

FERSTER, C. B. Reinforcement and punishment in the control of human behavior by social agencies. *Psychiatric Research Reports,* December 1958, 101–118.

FERSTER, C. B. Positive reinforcement and behavioral deficits of autistic children. *Child Development,* 1961, *32*(3), 437–456.

FERSTER, C. B. The repertoire of the autistic child in relation to principles of reinforcement. In L. A. Gottschalk and A. Auerback (Eds.), *Methods of research in psychotherapy.* New York: Appleton-Century-Crofts, 1966.

FERSTER, C. B. Transition from animal laboratory to the clinic. *Psychological Record,* 1967, *17*(2), 76–79.

FERSTER, C. B. Operant reinforcement of infantile autism. In S. Lesse, *An evaluation of the results of psychotherapies.* Springfield, Ill.: Charles C Thomas, 1968.

FERSTER, C. B., and PERROTT, M. C. *Behavior principles.* New York: Appleton-Century-Crofts, 1968.

FERSTER, C. B., and SIMONS, J. Behavior therapy with children. *Psychological Record,* 1966, *16*(1), 65–71.

LOVAAS, I., FREITAG, G., GOLD, V., and KASSORLA, I. Experimental studies in childhood schizophrenia: Analysis of self-destructive behavior. *Journal of Experimental Child Psychology,* 1965, *2*, 67–84.

SKINNER, B. F. *Walden two.* New York: Macmillan, 1948.

SKINNER, B. F. *Science and human behavior.* New York: Macmillan, 1953.

SKINNER, B. F. *Verbal behavior.* New York: Appleton-Century-Crofts, 1957.

SKINNER, B. F. Why teachers fail. *Saturday Review,* Oct. 16, 1965, *80.*

WILLIAMS, D. B., and TEITELBAUM, P. Control of drinking behavior by means of an operant- conditioning technique. *Science,* 1956, *124,* 1294–1296.

One of the most important consequences of our scientific understanding of human behavior in modern psychology has been an awareness of the dangers and unfortunate by-products of the aversive control of human conduct. In the next article, *Skinner,* in a recorded conversation, enumerates some of the disadvantages of controlling behavior by reinforcing it with the removal of an aversive stimulus. He suggests some alternative techniques of control which are of more benefit to the controller, the controllee, and the community.

69 | *Aversive Versus Positive Control of Behavior*

RICHARD I. EVANS
(Interview with B. F. Skinner)

EVANS: Dr. Skinner, earlier you referred to yourself as a determinist. With the shifting away from the Freudian model of biological determinism to a more environmental-social-cultural determinism in contemporary psychology, there seems to be a parallel, increasing concern with the notion of self-responsibility. This might partially be a reaction to the effects of such environmental-social-cultural theories on society. The theories themselves become a rationalization or excuse for an individual's misbehavior. For example, juvenile delinquents, as satirized in the Broadway musical *West Side Story,* in the "Officer Krupke Song," were singing, "We're not responsible for our acts, social conditions are." I wonder where you stand in relation to this issue?

SKINNER: I'm not arguing for the organism's self-responsibility. But the distinction you make is really a shift from aversive control to positive reinforcement, and it's a very important issue. For example, if you try to control alcoholism by criticizing and shaming the drunkard, he may conceivably learn to avoid criticism by controlling himself. But if you say, "Wait a minute, here. This is really a medical problem. You have a disease," he may use this as an excuse to avoid punitive action. The alternative to punishing people who behave badly is to build a world in which people are naturally good. Personal responsibility is something which even people who believe in punitive control don't understand, even though they may admire those who behave well under adverse conditions. The point is clearly made by my colleague, David McClelland, in a paper called "Psychoanalysis and Religious Mysticism" (1964). He points out that Freud is very close to the Protestant Reformation as well as to the Hasidic mystical tradition of the Jews. He makes the point that both Freud and the Christian-Jewish mystic are departing from orthodoxy in the sense of strict disciplinary control and are turning toward inner sources of control. The early Christians and Jews, in the Kumran community and the monasteries, were submitting themselves to external authority in order to control themselves. In the Dead Sea Scrolls, obedience was the thing; as it was for the Benedictines and other monastic orders. You put yourself under a punishing authority and are then responsible for your actions in the sense that if you do not behave properly you will be justly punished. That's all the word "responsible" means; it has no meaning in a society which does not control through aversive techniques. In the Hasidic movement and with Freud, it is not that inner sources of control have been substituted for the external, authoritative, orthodox sources, but that there has been a shift from negative reinforcement to positive reinforcement. People do what they want to do rather than what they have to do. The same goals are achieved—they do the same things. It's not internal control but a different kind of external control.

The notion of personal responsibility just isn't relevant. The control is still there. When you turn the delinquent over to himself, as some psychologists and psychiatrists feel you can do, you will be successful only if society has in some way implanted the kinds of control which are essential. This is a point on which I argue with Carl Rogers, who claims that somehow or other you are going to find within the client himself the controlling forces that will solve his problem. His methods work with clients who have emerged from a tradition, such as the Judeo-Christian, which gives them reasons for behaving well, but if a client suddenly announces, "Ah, yes! I see it now. I should murder my boss!" you don't just let him walk out of the office. You don't tell him that he has really found the solution to his problem. Every solution comes from some source of control. If his problem was generated by overly strict aversive control, your aim is to release him from that, but you can't therefore turn him over to nothing. You don't turn him over to absolute freedom.

EVANS: Your emphasis on positive reinforcement, then, might be said to be reflecting an already existing historical-cultural trend away from aversive control toward positive control.

SKINNER: Yes. I'm really a little embarrassed to say this, because I don't believe in arguing from history. However, I do think it is interesting to watch what is going on, even though I don't like to make predictions on historical evidences. Civilization has moved from an aversive control toward a positive approach. There are only a few places in the world today where slavery is still practiced, where labor is coerced by the whip. We have substituted the payment of wages for physical punishment, and are even concerned with finding other reinforcers. We should like to have a man work productively for the sheer love of it, and we reflect back on the old craft system as an example. You hear claims occasionally that we've got to start whipping our school boys and girls again, but this simply reminds us that until very recently, education was openly aversive. Egyptians, Greeks, and Romans all whipped their boys, and, in fact, the Latin expression for study means to hold out the hand to be whipped. In England, the cane is still used, but there is a movement away from punishment, and an effort to find positive reasons for studying. The same is true in religion. There is less and less emphasis on hell-fire and the threat of damnation; people are to be good for positive reasons, for the love of God or their fellowmen. There is a parallel trend in politics and in government. In a famous case in the thirties the Agricultural Act provided that farmers be paid for not planting acreage, instead of making it illegal to plant. This was an effort to avoid a coercive threat. It was an important trend, and supported because people generally don't like to be punished. And on a more intimate level, we prefer to have people get along well with each other because their outgoing, positive behavior is richly reinforcing rather than because they are afraid of being criticized or punished for misbehaving. I'm not a historical determinist to the point at which I would predict that this trend is going to continue, but I hope it does. A punitive society is not supported by the people under it, whereas a society which is full of good things is likely to be strong.

EVANS: I know, Dr. Skinner, that your experimental work led you to make distinctions among the conceptions of *punishment, negative reinforcement,* and *aversive control.* Could you discuss these distinctions?

SKINNER: You can distinguish between punishment, which is making an aversive event contingent upon a response, and negative reinforcement, in which the elimination or removal of an aversive stimulus, conditioned or unconditioned, is reinforcing. Aversive control is a way of generating behavior. When you say you punish a child to make him work, you are misusing the word "punish." You are arranging conditions which he can escape from by working. When you punish a child to keep him from misbehaving, however, you are trying to suppress behavior. In my earlier experiments punishment did not suppress behavior as it had been supposed to do. Punishment may only be reducing a current tendency to respond. As soon as punishment is withdrawn, the behavior bounces back. This isn't always the case, because extremely severe punishment may knock behavior out for good, at least so far as we are able to determine. But what is surprising is that if you make common punishing events contingent on behavior, the behavior will recover after the punishment ceases, and the organism will continue to behave, even though it has been rather severely punished. I object to aversive control in general because of its by-products. All sorts of emotions are generated which have negative side effects. If you make a student study to escape punishment, then he will soon escape in other ways; he'll play hookey, be a truant, or become a dropout. Or he may counterattack. Vandalism against school property is easily explained just by looking at the techniques schools use to control their students. Another common reaction of students is a kind of inactivity—an apathy or stubborn do-nothingness. These are the inevitable by-products of aversive stimuli. Positive reinforcement does not generate comparable by-products, and that's why it's better. If we knew as much about negative reinforcement as we do about positive, I suspect we would find that it can be rather effective in shaping behavior, but at the moment it isn't very effective, and the negative by-products are still in evidence, so I am opposed to it.

EVANS: But aversive control still seems to be the order of the day in our entire culture. We see it in laws, regulations, rules, salary schedules, and even in the grading system we use in our schools. Supposing we would like to shift to a more positively controlled system. Is there any way that we could gradually shift from our present system to a system based more on positive reinforcement?

SKINNER: There are always transitional problems when you shift from one framework to another, and usually they are quite troublesome. To use your earlier example, the delinquent simply pleads that he is a crazy, mixed-up kid and should be forgiven, that it isn't his fault. If you are going to control delinquency simply by punishment, then you've got to stick to that and call the delinquent guilty. He has been irresponsible, he is at fault, and he must be punished. To attempt to deal with the situation any other way will mean a transitional period in which your control is likely to be bad. It is at this point that the delinquent will choose your new formulation as an easy way to escape punishment. You can't blame him for taking advantage of the changing situation. That's predictable human behavior.

EVANS: What about *extinction* in dealing with undesirable behavior?

SKINNER: Well, extinction is another way of getting rid of undesirable behavior. But in order for it to be effective, you must be sure that no reinforcing consequences are contingent on the behavior you want to get rid of. Generally, it isn't very effective. It takes a long time, and you have to put up with the behavior while you are getting rid of it. I would prefer to use a method which reinforces incompatible behavior. Very interesting work has been done recently in teaching discrimination without errors; it involves both avoiding the reinforcement of wrong responses and using stimuli for right responses as reinforcers. The research has promise in the direction you have indicated here. The area has scarcely been developed, because we've only begun to look for alternatives to punishment. Punishment is the easy way—if you're strong enough. If the teacher is bigger than his student, he can resort to punishment and get away with it.

EVANS: Any discussion of systems of control in society, of course, raises questions of what systems of control actually operate in communist societies. For example, how about the Soviet Union?

SKINNER: I'm not too impressed by what I've seen in the Soviet Union; and theoretically, I think they are wrong. I don't think they even subscribe to their own theory. Marx's principle, "to each according to his need," is, of course, scriptural; it is not St. Karl; it's St. Augustine. But the principle misses the boat because the important thing is what a man does at the moment he receives what he needs. That's where reinforcement comes in. Anyone can sympathize with a person who is hungry and, out of simple compassion, feed him. That's a good thing, I'm all for it. I'm not for starving people in order to make them productive. In Victorian England, it was supposed that you would have to have a population of nearly starved workers in order to maintain production in the factories of the time. And it may have been necessary then, because work was very aversive. But I think the Russian principle also has been abandoned. Khrushchev reportedly told the then Senator Humphrey that the "crazy Chinese" still believed you should give to each according to his need. Yet Khrushchev promised the Russian people that by 1980 food, housing, clothing would be free. If he actually meant free, that these things are to be given away and not made contingent on productive labor, then there will be no reason for people to work. I once argued this with a Russian economist whom I met at a reception in England. I said, "If this happens, why will a man work?" He took a very smug stance, and said, "Ah, they will work for the common good." But as Karl Marx himself knew, there is a great gap between working at a given moment and participation in the common good at a later date. The Russians need some sort of incentive system. The Russian worker in general is not as productive as the American worker, and it can't be explained just on the basis of a dearth of capital equipment in Russia.

EVANS: All of the properties of this incentive system would not necessarily be positively reinforcing, would they? There would likely also be some aversive elements in the system, as I understand your meaning here, wouldn't there?

SKINNER: Oh, yes. Many people, and textbooks as well, cite the weekly wage as an example of a scheduled positive reinforcement, but actually that's quite wrong. If you reinforce a man only at five o'clock on Friday afternoon, he will work only, say, from five minutes before five to five o'clock. The reason he works on Mondays is that if he doesn't he'll be fired; he will be unable to collect his money on Friday afternoon. A schedule of payment established on an hourly, daily, or weekly basis must involve some kind of supervision in order to be effective. There must be a boss around who has the power to fire a worker and thereby cut him off from the standard of living established by that periodic pay. It is basically an aversive system. People don't actually feel strengthened by a weekly wage as a reinforcer; they work because if they don't they will be cut off from a supply of reinforcers. It's an unhealthy system. There's another schedule I've studied in some detail, the fixed-ratio schedule of reinforcement. It's seen in operation in the piece-rate system, where the worker is paid in terms of the amount of work he does. This does not require supervision, and on this type of schedule, an organism will indeed start work long before reinforcement because he must start if he is to reach the point of being reinforced. Actually, that schedule is so powerful that most labor unions oppose it; it can burn a man up—exhaust him. The home industry in nineteenth-century England operated on that basis. The housewife put the kiddies to bed, then got out a machine and knitted up a few socks, for which she got paid a penny a dozen, or something like that. It was a horrible system, but it commanded productive work. There's no doubt about that.

Incentive systems are a mixture of the two schedules.[1] There is enough of the periodic pay to provide a satisfactory base so that the ratio-type schedule doesn't completely take over. A salesman who is partly on a salary and partly on commission is an example of the way these systems can be combined. The salary he earns takes the edge off the commission basis, so he can live a sensible life without forcing himself. He doesn't have to have a supervisor traveling along with him, because the commission is on a ratio schedule, and that will keep him going. A proper mixture of salary and commission yields productive work which is also free of supervision, yet without the excessive effects of a radio schedule in a piecework system. These are just examples of the application to economics of behavioral processes studied in the laboratory. What we do in the laboratory, of course, is extremely technical, and often complex, but it points to systems that would generate almost any level of activity on the part of a worker or student—anyone, for that matter, who is being reinforced by what he is doing.

EVANS: As you reflect further on the differences in the systems operating in the United States and the Soviet Union, do you see problems emerging for the Soviets when the incentives for productive work are withdrawn and no positive reinforcements are introduced that go beyond a formalized theoretical base?

SKINNER: I think the problem is already there. The Russians are already charging their educators with the responsibility of imparting the attitudes needed to keep people working productively. And that isn't going to work. To keep people working

[1] To review for the reader to what Skinner is referring: There are two broad schedules of reinforcement that have been used as a means of increasing the probability that certain behavior will occur. One is called a *ratio* schedule, the other is called an *interval* schedule. When reinforcements are introduced on a *ratio* schedule, a certain number of responses must occur before the organism is reinforced (similar to piecework for a worker). An *interval* schedule is introduced according to the clock or calendar—say every so many minutes in an experiment, but for a worker it could be his weekly paycheck.

imaginatively, actively, and in a sustained fashion for something as abstract as a verbalized reinforcer called the "common good," or the feeling that one is engaging in socially useful behavior, is a terrific engineering job. The Soviets do not presently have such an engineered system, and while ours is not perfect, we're at least better off. Our wage systems are defective in that they breed various unwanted reactions on the part of workers. Few people enjoy working on a modern production line, but if the hours can be cut down far enough and the wages raised high enough, they can at least enjoy the rest of their lives. Much more could be done to make what they do on the job more interesting. Piping music into a factory is by no means enough. Good working conditions that include social effects which give the individual some sense of achievement can be made to pay off in a rather artificial, but healthier way. These are all possibilities, and should be exploited. A crude example is the so-called variable ratio schedule, which is at the heart of all gambling devices. We might try giving workers lottery tickets based on production, in addition to their ordinary wages, with a drawing at the end of the week. People enjoy wasting money and time and energy on gambling if it pays off at least occasionally, so why not incorporate similar schedules into industrial systems?

EVANS: A sort of "gambling model" of reinforcement of the worker in industry.

SKINNER: There is nothing wrong with the schedule. All scientific work pays off on a variable ratio schedule. So do hunting, fishing, exploring, prospecting, and so on. You never can tell when you are going to be reinforced, but reinforcements do keep turning up. The dedicated scientist is exactly like a pathological gambler. He's been hooked by a system, but in a way which is profitable for everyone. The scientist is fascinated by what he does, just as the gambler is, but nobody is taking his shirt. He's getting something out of it, and so is society.

EVANS: Gambling seems to have a unique sort of fascination for most people. It's interesting to observe in Las Vegas how really powerful the intermittentvariable reinforcement schedule apparently operating in "games of chance" is for most people.

SKINNER: Yes. I've seen people playing three or four machines at one time, going right down the line keeping them all whirring. Industry would give anything to command sustained effort like that. Actually, those machines could be changed so that they would clean out the pockets of the patrons even faster. I could design a better gambling machine—better from the point of view of the establishment but I won't.

EVANS: Moving to another area, Freud identified a group of defense mechanisms to attempt to describe certain kinds of behavior employed by an individual to avoid, at least psychologically, the consequences of aversive, ego-threatening situations. You have examined the Freudian defense mechanisms, have you not? Can they also be regarded as examples of aversive control?

SKINNER: Yes, I have analyzed the Freudian mechanisms (1954), and in a sense, I attribute them all to aversive control. They represent ways of avoiding-undesirable consequences of one sort or another, and when analyzed in that light, they suggest means of correction. If, instead of building up the behavior you want in people, you punish the behavior you don't want, the individual must discover ways which do indeed avoid the punishing consequences. But these may not be effective ways; they may be called neurotic. Society might better build effective behavior. When you simply punish the slothful student for his sloth, the ignorant student for his ignorance, and the willful student for his willfulness, you leave it to the student to figure out ways of avoiding punishment. What he does is largely a matter of accident. On the other hand, you can reinforce his behavior so that he becomes energetic and far from slothful; you can program instruction to lead him out of his ignorance; you can induce him to behave according to the dictates of society instead of his own selfish interests. You have solved the problems of sloth, ignorance, and willfulness by constructing desirable behaviors. Positive shaping of behavior is much the more successful way.

EVANS: Isn't this type of positive shaping of response and environmental manipulation being systematically applied in psychotherapy? Of course, some have challenged this method by saying that it ignores the "private world" of the patient and reduces his interaction with the therapist and his environment to such a mechanical, superficial level that the deep, underlying "psychodynamics" of his problem are ignored. How do you feel about this sort of criticism?

SKINNER: I don't think you really lose out on anything. A psychotic patient is psychotic because of his behavior. You don't institutionalize a person because of his feelings. You may say that behavior is a result of his feelings, but the feelings must be the result of something, too. When you look farther, you find environmental factors. I do not rule out the possibility of genuine internal illness, but illness in that sense is not the rich experience which I am accused of leaving out. I see nothing demeaning, nothing undignified or ignoble, about building a world in which a psychotic person can lead a decent life. True, it may be a simplified world. Many psychotics are certainly sick or damaged organisms, and they can never successfully return to an ordinary environment. But under the control of simplified environments, their lives can then be happier and possibly more productive.

EVANS: What you're suggesting would apply not only to psychotherapy but also to the patient within an institutional situation. There has been some work done (Ayllon, 1963) attempting to bring the mentally ill within the hospital setting under various reinforcement schedules which will bring them to a point where they can function more effectively and assume greater self-responsibility. Do you feel such efforts are going to prove increasingly fruitful?

SKINNER: I'm sure they're on the right track.

EVANS: How could these efforts be made most effective?

SKINNER: There are two possibilities: One is to eliminate the poor contingencies which now prevail in those institutions—where, for example, it is the troublemaker who is reinforced by getting the attention of the hospital attendants. The alternative is to be much more explicit about it and build a world which is admittedly contrived. It will not be a natural environment; but these are not natural cases. You can contrive a situation in which such people will live reasonably effective lives from day to day with a minimum of care. When you have to keep people clean and orderly against their own contributing negligence, it is expensive, and everyone suffers. There's not a great deal of money available for the care of psychotics. If you reorganize their environment so that their behavior is more effective without the constant intervention of attendants, you can give them a better life with the facilities available. To my way of thinking, this is *increasing* their dignity and nobility. It's true that they're being controlled in a rather artificial way, but if the life they then lead is reasonably adequate, I regard that as a success.

EVANS: Similar methods are being applied to the mentally retarded. Do you feel the same way about this area of application?

SKINNER: Yes. Several of my colleagues and I have experimented with institutionalized retardates whose I.Q.'s ranged around 50 (whatever that may mean). They respond well to a simplified environment, and I am sure that institutions which care for them could be reorganized along the same lines. At the present time, retardates tend to be controlled through aversive techniques, even though the attendants may be full of goodwill. No one really benefits from that. I believe that the institutionalized retardate, just below the level needed to operate in the world at large, can be placed in an environment in which he will not only live reasonably happily all day long, but will also be productive. These people are capable of performing certain kinds of work, and actually of making a living. They can enjoy happier circumstances which they actually pay for by their efforts.

EVANS: Aren't you suggesting that some of the existing conceptions of mental retardation underestimate the potential for training the retardate actually possesses?

SKINNER: No doubt about that at all. This is true of all organisms. I know one psychologist who tried to work with pigeons who couldn't teach them anything. In the last twenty years, pigeons have done things no pigeon had ever done before. It isn't that the pigeons have been improved; the contingencies under which they live have been improved. A retardate doesn't measure up to the normal environment and can't get along within it, but he is capable of perfectly acceptable behavior in an environment which has been designed for him.

EVANS: There is another broad area which it would be interesting to hear your reaction to, Dr. Skinner, and that is your concept of the role of psychology in the interpretation of literature and in creative writing. So far this field seems to have been dominated by Freudian theory. I wonder if you feel that some training in experimental analysis of behavior would be of help to the creative writer?

SKINNER: I used to be interested in Freudian interpretations of the themes of literature, as well as the themes of history and biography. I find myself much less inclined to take analyses seriously any more, because they fall into stereotyped patterns and I get awfully tired of them. But you have raised two questions. Can a writer make use of our knowledge of verbal behavior to improve his product or to maximize his productivity? I am sure that the answer is "yes." The other question is whether it is possible to design writing in such a way that the reader will almost certainly read it, and will be influenced by what he reads. I think the answer to that question is also "yes." I take special steps to maximize my verbal output. This does not mean maximizing quantity; it means arranging conditions under which I am most likely to write effectively. I catch my verbal behavior on the wing, as it were, and get it down as soon as it occurs. Then I rework in later when time permits. But these are technical details which are not appropriate here. On the side of the reader—reinforcing passages can be scheduled to keep him reading.

EVANS: This is true also for the electronic communications media, is it not? In fact, it would seem that a good deal of advertising on television and radio is the outgrowth of a hopefully effectively scheduled array of reinforcers.

SKINNER: I only hope what has been done so far is not the best that can be done, because on the whole it's pretty dreary stuff. I could probably write better copy, but I am no more inclined to help advertisers than gamblers.

EVANS: Fears concerning this whole notion of the possibility of controlling the environment because it could pervade an entire culture were brought out in the controversy which followed the publication of your highly successful novel, *Walden Two.* Such a "planned utopia" seemed to be particularly distressing to the humanist. As you conceived the culture you wrote about in *Walden Two,* did you seriously believe such a society would actually come into being?

SKINNER: I wrote the book quite seriously. It is not a dystopia. I thought such a community was possible at the time I wrote the book, and I think so now. It should be possible for a group of well-meaning people to get together and organize their lives, cutting down some of the things they normally consume to eliminate some of the aversive labors otherwise required; to organize their social environment so that they make more contacts of a satisfactory nature; to organize a school system which educates their children effectively for the life they are going to lead; to organize an economic system so that work can at least be done under pleasant circumstances; and so on. But when I described such a society, reaction was quite violent. *Life* magazine called *Walden Two* a triumph of mortmain, or the dead hand, such as had not been envisaged since the days of Sparta. Joseph Wood Krutch (1964) not only devoted half a book to attacking it, he has returned to the attack on many occasions. I've often asked myself what's eating these people? Apparently the main difficulty is that my good life was planned by someone. If Joseph Wood Krutch were one day to climb up on a mesa in his beloved New Mexico, and come across a small civilization living the life described in *Walden Two,* he would come down out of the hills saying, "What fools we are! Here is the perfect life." But if someone told him that an old Indian named Frazier[2] had designed that life, it would spoil it all for him. The fact that a way of life is not the product of a series of accidents in cultural evolution but has been designed suggests that someone is in the position of designer and, therefore, in the position of a threatening despot. But there are kinds of guarantees against despotism within any system; if there aren't, then we are without hope in any way of life.

EVANS: Allow me to play devil's advocate for a moment. Isn't it possible that such fears of despotism connected with a planned society have their referents in recent history? Attempts to plan a society could be found, of course, in Nazi Germany, the Soviet Union, and China. According to its planners, each system was designed to hopefully allow a climate of creative productivity so that each individual would operate at his most comfortable and productive level. These goals would appear to be in accord with the philosophical concept of the "good life." Yet the results of such planning in these countries, while it may be thought to be oriented toward the "good life," actually seemed to have evolved into a despotic system. How do we guarantee that the type of planning you propose will not ultimately also produce a despotic system?

SKINNER: This is the old question of value judgments. What values are we to use in judging one society good and another bad? You first question the techniques. If you govern by coercion, as the Nazis did, waking people up in the middle of the night and dragging them off to jail, you can control for a period of time, but you are controlling frightened people. Moreover, you do not encourage support from the outside. Eventually the method fails. I believe that the Russians are trying to avoid that kind of control; they've had a long history of it, and seem now to be trying to use positive reinforcement, though they are not organizing their contingencies properly.

I don't know what's going on in China today, since we're not allowed to know much. But I suspect that the Chinese are a lot closer to Karl Marx than the Russians. The Chinese probably have to fall back on coercive control from time to time, and I'm sure that they have not discovered the contingencies which make positive reinforcement successful. The primary product is successful control, but the by-product may be that those controlled are working at less than their maximum capacity. If you control through superstition and ignorance, as has been the case in India, the control may be profound (a maharaja and his descendants may prevail for centuries) but it is the control of ignorant people, and that doesn't make for a strong state. In the long run you have to consider the survival of the group, and the despot who controls through techniques which weaken the group eventually weakens himself. I don't know whether a real leader will ever realize, as Frazier did, that his power depends entirely on the strength of the people. Frazier is not currently ruling at all. He has no control. People don't know who he is. And when he asks the young architects to come around to talk with his friends, they go off swimming. True, he did put the whole thing in motion, but he didn't do that for his own aggrandizement; if he had done it for that reason, he would have failed. He has successfully suppressed himself as a leader; that was a deliberate point in the book, and I feel it is very important.

2 The character in *Walden Two* who guides the development of the utopian community.

EVANS: Cultural anthropological studies have shown that most societies do operate out of systems of aversive control. Might there not be some, however, such as the Pueblo Indians, who operate out of a less aversive system than ours, which might supply valuable data on the kind of society to which you refer in *Walden Two*?

SKINNER: I don't believe nature ever performs an experiment the right way. You might find a group in New Mexico or the South Seas where there seems to be very little competition, but you cannot argue that their happiness stems from that, because there will be a great many other things peculiar to the culture. You can't prove anything with examples. I should be very much surprised if a culture based on positive reinforcement were to come about by accident, because too many things favor aversive control. Aversive techniques are immediate, and they always work provided one person is stronger than another. The bully dominates the coward. The powerful man rules, especially when he can organize henchmen to help him dominate. It is easy to account for such control, because the effects are immediate. The results of positive reinforcement are often deferred, and so control by this means is not as effective. It's the same in education; the teacher wants the student to be quiet and study, so she threatens and gets results. But once the student is released from that kind of pressure, he'll never study again. If he can be induced to study for other reasons, using reinforcing consequences which will persist in his life, the results will be more lasting. But that requires a much better understanding of human behavior.

EVANS: On the other hand, leadership in preliterate societies seems to be based on physical dominance.

SKINNER: Yes, and then followed by trickery. The first hero is the power man, the Beowulf. Then comes the tricky hero, the Brer Rabbit, who puts it over on Brer Wolf and Brer Bear by violating the code of the group. Most cultures seem to have a cheating hero at some stage. Eventually someone gains control for the good of the controllee, and that is the genesis of a powerful group. It isn't the ruler who is powerful; it is the unit as a whole. Powerful but careless rulers lack the support of a powerful group.

EVANS: Leadership by dominance is a phenomenon which shows up even in the subhuman orders, as studies demonstrating the pecking order in chickens have shown. So even this can be viewed as essentially a system of aversive control.

SKINNER: It is a natural thing.

EVANS: Are you saying, then, that this aversive control, or control by dominance, is a more primitive, generic method, and that societies have evolved out of this root into what we have today?

SKINNER: I don't know whether the human organism is innately endowed so that he flies into a rage when someone harms him, but he certainly shows a strong tendency to do that. Our way of life encourages it because you often get what you want when you fly into a rage. People who annoy you then leave you alone. I suspect that it is an acquired response, however, because we are much more likely to get mad at people than at things. If you walk down a street and your way is blocked by several hippies who refuse to move, you may react with resentment and anger and say something to them if you dare. You may not attack them then and there, but you may suggest passing a law to keep people from blocking the sidewalk. But if you go down a street and find that a tree has fallen across it, you walk around the tree and feel no tendency to aggressively attack. This suggests that we have acquired our angers because they have paid off. Getting angry at a tree is not often reinforced. If we can build a world in which rage doesn't pay off, it will be a world in which people don't fly into a rage at the slightest annoyance.

EVANS: Is it possible that at least one effect of some of our theological teachings tends to reinforce the notion of aversive control?

SKINNER: Religions seem to move toward a positive kind of control through love and goodwill, but they certainly begin with jealous and punitive gods. I think the change in religion has been as great as in government and economics.

EVANS: The notion of aversive control seems to be so much taken for granted that there is seldom any question about it.

SKINNER: Practically all forms of governments are based on it. When you try something else, peculiar things happen. An interesting experiment was once done in New Haven. Instead of giving people tickets when they went through stop signs, someone stood around taking the numbers of those who stopped. As I remember it, they sent postcards saying, "You were observed to come to a dead stop at such and such an intersection on such and such a date. Congratulations." Something like that might increase the number of dead stops, but naturally it will not control the real lawbreaker. The procedure is so far out, though, that people laugh when they hear about it. It just doesn't seem appropriate for a government to operate through positive reinforcement.

EVANS: As you speak of shaping human resources, this brings to mind disturbing possibilities which result from so-called brainwashing American soldiers by the Chinese, such as described by Schein (1956) in the Korean war. You developed a methodology to shape behavior which appears to be incredibly effective. How can we deal with the problem of how it's going to be used? It is certainly available to anyone who chooses to use it, so how can it be controlled?

SKINNER: There is a real danger here. From what I've heard of the Chinese prison-camp methods, they don't seem to have been very original. I doubt that there was anything done in China which was not known to Torquemada in the Spanish Inquisition. The same techniques were used for the same purposes. But it is conceivable that ways of influencing human behavior can be worked out which will not breed revolt, and that is the crucial danger. When people are being pushed around, controlled by methods which are obvious to them, they know who and what is controlling them, and when things become too aversive, they turn against the controller.

EVANS: You've argued that such aversive controls never had any sustained value anyway.

SKINNER: When you know what is being done to you, you know where to turn in order to escape. But some kinds of drugs and some kinds of positive reinforcement can be used without identifying the controller. Even though you are inclined to revolt, you don't know whom to revolt against. You do revolt against positive reinforcement, of course, if it gets you into trouble. A hobby may become so engaging that you lose interest in other things and risk destroying your career. You may then revolt against the hobby. But that is possible because you can identify what is controlling you. But it is conceivable that techniques of control will be developed which cannot be discovered. The word "brainwashing" is dangerous. I don't believe, however, that there's any great danger at the present time.

EVANS: The principles which you outlined so carefully in your *Science and Human Behavior* (1953) could become quite effective if, say, a hostile government were to gain control and proceed to shape the development of children, putting such techniques totally into use. Could this not lead to a rather dangerous situation for the world?

SKINNER: There's no doubt about if, but what are you going to do? To impose a moratorium on science would be worst of all. It does not solve the problem to say we must not increase our knowledge or publish what we already know because it might fall into the hands of despots. The best defense I can see is to make all behavioral processes as familiar as possible. Let everyone know what is possible, what can be used against them.

EVANS: It seems that the same danger inherent in the technology of nuclear weapons may be potentially inherent in the science of behavior.

SKINNER: I think a science of behavior is just as dangerous as the atom bomb. It has the potential of being horribly misused. We must devote ourselves to a better governmental design which will have some control over all destructive instruments.

EVANS: An interesting parallel to this discussion is shown in Goebbels' diary (1948) as he outlined the entire formula of communications control in Nazi Germany. Many of the techniques he describes reflect the principles of reinforcement that you have written about.

SKINNER: Oh, yes. The Nazis made good use of the social sciences even though they had driven out most of the good people. It was "good" from their point of view, of course, dangerous from ours.

References

AYLLON, T. Intensive treatment of psychotic behavior by stimulus satiation and food reinforcement. *Behaviour Research and Therapy*, 1963, *1*, 53–61.

GOEBBELS, J. *The Goebbels' diaries, 1942–1943* (translated by L. P. Lochner). Garden City, N.Y.: Doubleday, 1948.

KRUTCH, J. W. *The measure of man*. New York: Bobbs-Merrill, 1964.

MCCLELLAND, D. Psychoanalysis and religious mysticism. In *The roots of consciousness*. New York: D. Van Nostrand, 1964.

SCHEIN, E. H. The Chinese indoctrination program of prisoners of war. *Psychiatry*, 1956, *19*, 149–172.

SKINNER, B. F. *Science and human behavior*. New York: Macmillan, 1953.

SKINNER, B. F. *Science and human behavior*. New York: Macmillan, 1953.

SKINNER, B. F. Critique of psychoanalytic concepts and theories. *Scientific Monthly*, 1954, *797*, 300–305.

Psychotherapy, a social practice where the patient places himself under the control of a therapist, raises ethical problems in their most acute form. *Kanfer* acknowledges a functional relationship between therapist and patient in the sense that in their interaction each reinforces the other's behavior: the reactivity of the therapist influences the patient's behavior, and the changes in the patient's behavior reinforce the therapist's techniques of control. While he acknowledges the therapist's control over the patient's behavior, however, Kanfer reasserts the importance of the patient's social milieu, including the significant persons in this life, as the major factor which determines his life's goals. Kanfer's argument is very closely related to that raised in the previous article about natural and arbitrary reinforcers. If the reinforcers that the therapist is ultimately concerned with are those in the patient's own life, then his effective control over the patient is limited. He can only help the patient to come under different and perhaps more effective control of factors already shaping his behavior. The issue, although phrased in different language, is the same one posed by Carl Rogers about nondirective therapy. Rogers states that the therapist relies upon the client's existing capacity to deal constructively with his life situation. Thus, Kanfer, like Rogers, uses the patient's currently existing repertoire as the starting point for therapy. The issue of values and goals with this concept of therapy is not so critical, because the therapist focuses on those dispositions inherent in the patient's current repertoire and functional community.

70 | *Issues and Ethics in Behavior Manipulation*[1]

FREDERICK H. KANFER

Whenever a science is ready to apply its principles or methods to the control of man's social and physical environment, public attention demands that the consequences of such application be carefully examined. This scrutiny often results in argumentative debates and emotional alignment of the public vis-a-vis the science, its contents and its practitioners. The merciless beam of the public spotlight has by no means been confined to psychology. In our own time chemistry, physics and biology have repeatedly provided discoveries which the public viewed and discussed with alarm. Public concern usually declined gradually as scientific contributions were absorbed into the social fabric. Nevertheless, the vigor of recent public reactions to progress in the study and control of human behavior has taken our academically-minded science by surprise. Perhaps the sudden widespread concern with test makers, public opinion swayers, and adjustment manipulators simply indicates that psychology finally may have something to offer which has applicability in everyday life. The hope for eventual development of the psychology of behavioral control also raises the problem of the ethics of manipulating the behavior of another person. The most surprising aspect of the psychologist's dilemma posed by this problem is its recency. After all, the manipulation of behavior reportedly first took place when Eve whetted Adam's appetite in the Garden of Eden. For centuries the issues of morality and the control of one human being over another either have been kept separated or, in fact, combined in such absurd fashion that the most cruel methods of control were perpetrated under the guise of morality. The slaughter during the crusades, the elimination of witchcraft, the conquest of the American Indian, the "liberation" of Europe by the Nazis represent a few choice historical examples of human misbehavior and the use of the ultimate in behavior control through physical force and extermination. By comparison, the minor infraction committed currently when a psychotherapist subtly alters a neurotic patient's value system or his social behavior patterns seems rather mild. Nevertheless, numerous recent popular articles and books reflect the increasing public concern with the use of psychological methods in education, in industry, in the treatment of the mentally ill, and in politics.

The purpose of this paper is to discuss several issues concerning use of psychological principles in the manipulation of human behavior. These issues may arise in the context of psychology practiced in the clinic, in industry, by the military, or by governments. This paper will focus on behavior control by psychotherapy. The issues concern: (1) the methods of control, (2) the domain of controlled behavior, and (3) the selection of ends for which control is exercised.

[1] An earlier version of this paper was presented at a symposium of the Indiana Psychological Association in Indianapolis, April 1960. The revised paper was written in conjunction with research supported by Research grant MH 06922-03 from the National Institute of Mental Health, United States Public Health Service.

From *Psychological Reports*, 1965, *16*, 187–196. Reprinted by permission.

Control by Reward Versus Punishment

With regard to the "psychology of behavior control" (Krasner, 1962a) in the clinic, the current sensitivity to the ethical issues stems largely from an increased proficiency in the control of behavior, and especially from a fear of one special kind of manipulation.[2] In the past, efforts toward improving control over adult behavior have mainly been directed at finding better methods of aversive control, e.g., by threat, coercion, or physical force. Currently, there is a tendency toward increasing use of control by positive reinforcement in all areas of life. This shift to promises, rewards, and seductions rather than coercion represents, in our opinion, the pith of public concern. In his discussion of methods used by controlling agencies, Skinner (1953) suggests that government, law, and religion mainly use practices of threat of punishment, withdrawal of positive reinforcers, or presentation of negative reinforcers to achieve obedience. Further, with use of these methods by social agencies the usual "effect of group control is in conflict with a strong primarily reinforced behavior of the individual" (Skinner, 1953, p. 327). In contrast, economic control, education, and psychotherapy rely more heavily on positive reinforcement. Recently, control by positive reinforcement has been used extensively in programs of "ideological totalism" (Lifton, 1961). In practice, such control is heightened when used only after achievement of complete control over the individual's environment and thought processes by force. As in laboratory animals, positive reinforcment is most effective following severe deprivation. If such deprivations can be created in human groups, success in behavior control should be markedly enhanced for the possessor of the positive reinforcers. The deliberate application of methods reserved earlier mostly for education, work achievement, child rearing and therapy, in politics and government represents a major innovation. Coupled with extension from control over individuals to control over groups, this advance in control techniques raises serious public concern. The shift in methods of control is illustrated in the history of psychotherapy by the progress from straitjackets, padded cells, and beatings to therapeutic communities, insight therapy, and counterconditioning.

It is interesting to speculate why control by positive reinforcement might be more dangerous than control by coercion. Manipulation by aversive control creates its own hazards. The person under aversive control usually knows it. He suffers pain, experiences humiliation, anger, or other emotional discomfort. It is also likely that aversive control inevitably breeds attempts at counter-control. Even in the young child the first response to being slapped is to try to slap back. Aversive control thus motivates behavior aimed at reducing such control by annoying, teasing, or destroying the controller. Further, aversive control is difficult to maintain by a small group. To use force effectively you have to be bigger, stronger, or more numerous than your adversary. Thus aversive control by an individual over a large group, or by a small minority, is doomed to failure in the long run. Finally, as Skinner (1953) has indicated, aversive control affects only public behavior. It is of limited use in "thought control" because a person can escape some aversive consequences by thinking silently or by nonconforming behavior in his private experiences.

In contrast, manipulation by positive control produces none of these disturbing by-products. By definition these methods use reinforcing stimuli which have the inherent potential for increasing or maintaining behaviors which procure these stimuli. People respond in blind faith to reward, to promises, and to reassurances. Large-scale use of these methods, however, has not concerned people because the age-old deceptions of the Pied Piper have been assumed to be sufficiently transparent to allow most adults to recognize them as false promises and to resist temptation by persuasion. Recently, Browning's Pied Piper of Hamlin has become more sophisticated. He has put on the disguise of a gray flannel suit, of a human relationship expert, a psychotherapist, or a friendly interrogator in a prison camp. His pipe has turned into other instruments promising such sweet things as affection and happiness to a juvenile delinquent, money-back guaranteed satisfaction with soaps and cereals, or a political paradise for the masses, all without pain, coercion, or physical violence. This increased professionalism and sophistication in the application of psychological principles has caused uneasiness to the public because the methods have lost some of their transparency and amateurish quality. Although there is contradictory experimental evidence on the question of behavioral modification without awareness (Eriksen, 1962; Kanfer and Marston, 1961), these studies also clearly indicate that Ss cannot verbalize all aspects of the controlling stimuli which affect their behavior.

Certainly, the increase in psychological sophistication has also made it easier for the controller to disguise his own motives in order to mislead Ss of his controlling influence. In addition, he can manipulate conditions which would make positive reinforcement more effective. Frank (1961) makes this point

[2] While skeptics can point to evidence of current ignorance of even the most common determinants of individual behavior, few will doubt that rapid progress has been made in the last decade. We assume here that modification of individual behavior is feasible, though all the necessary controlling variables are not yet known.

in discussing the methods of thought reform: "the essence of the relationship is that the persuader invests great effort to bring about changes in the sufferer's bodily state or attitudes that he regards as beneficial . . . (and the setting) . . . occurs in the context of hope and potential support from the persuader and the group" (p. 95). Since our democratic principles also uphold the right of consent of the governed, any use of control resulting in a change of behavior without S's awareness of the methods of influence and the intent of his controllers would be ethically objectionable to our society. Even though these emphases placed upon self-control, self-government, and self-determination are accepted by our culture and its scientist members, a deterministic behavioral psychology cannot disavow its implication that behavior is controlled by an organism's previous history and its environment, regardless of its ability to describe verbally these controlling variables. Regardless of ethic or social interest, the fiction of the complete Rational Man as the captain of his own destiny is a naive to behavioristic psychology as it was to Freudian psychoanalysis (although for different reasons).

In psychotherapy, social pressures or other devices attempting to manipulate the patient's behavior by coercion are rarely used as a primary method of control. Therapeutic operations are more likely to stress positive goals, to reduce tensions, to reinforce and strengthen new behaviors. The therapist is, of course, at an additional disadvantage in the use of aversive controls. When the therapist acts as a noxious stimulus the patient can counter by "resistance," by failing to keep his appointments, or by leaving the field altogether. Patients under strong aversive control by parental pressure or by court order are notoriously poor risks for psychotherapy.

Control of Private Experiences

The inevitability of mutual influence in a clinical relationship is well documented by recent research and some of its implications have been discussed by Krasner (1962a).

What are some of the features then which make the psychotherapeutic interaction or other similar relationships especially suited for the manipulation or control of behavior?

One factor is the distress and discomfort of the patient. The social role of the patient has been described by Parsons (Parsons and Fox, 1958). In our society the sick person can claim certain privileges. It is assumed that he is not responsible for his incapacity, and his state of sickness exempts him from his normal social obligations. In turn, it is understood that he will attempt to get well and that he has an obligation to seek help and cooperate with others who treat him. As Parsons states, the latter implies a dependency of the sick person on the healer. The act of coming for help signifies the patient's realization that he cannot cope with the problem and that he wishes another person to take responsibility for treating it. This dependency status should tend to increase the effectiveness of the therapist's reinforcing operations (cf. research on the role of dependency, prestige, and other therapist-patient variables in verbal conditioning; Greenspoon, 1962, Krasner, 1962b).

A second feature concerns the *content* of the interactions. Most psychologists agree that the specific content of the patient's verbalizations in psychotherapy is far less important than was believed by earlier theorists. One common element in all therapeutic interactions is the therapist's insistence that the patient talk about those private experiences, fears, attitudes, and beliefs which are usually not shared with other people. Recent reviews by William Sargant (1957), Jerome Frank (1961) and Robert Lifton (1961) of methods of persuasion, thought reform, and therapy all suggest that the most successful methods of behavior manipulation, including magic, religion, and political coercion, share the requirement that the person publicly expose at least some of his privately held beliefs and attitudes. This accessibility to personal and private behavior, in turn, makes the person more vulnerable to control. The more behavior is exposed to the controlling agent the easier it is to set up conditions which modify behavior. Lifton (1961) points out that the admissions of guilt over minimal crimes against the state in Chinese "brainwashing" camps and universities provide the opportunity for the controller to reinforce such self-accusing behavior, to promise relief from guilt by self-punishing procedures and generally to weaken existing behavior and introduce new responses.

Privacy, the inaccessibility of much personal behavior in a democratic society, probably represents the bulwark of democracy because it allows for variability, and for divergence of attitudes and beliefs. What is jealously guarded as a right to privacy in everyday life is, in fact, surrendered in the psychotherapeutic hour. The consequences of this making accessible of the patient's private experiences have been discussed elsewhere (Kanfer, 1961). The potentials for controlling important behavioral sequences, usually not subject to control by direct social reinforcement, increase very much the extent of the therapist's influence.

Metavalues and Personal Values

Clinicians are beginning to accept the thesis that the therapist's value system tends to affect the direction of the patient's change in treatment (Rosenthal, 1955; Schrier, 1953). Among the many problems raised by this recognition are the methods of handling valued material (e.g., Ellis, 1962; Meehl, 1959; Segal, 1959) and the ethical implications of the intrusion of personal values into psychotherapy (Williamson, 1958; Weisskopf-Joelson, 1953). Existential analysis (Weisskopf-Joelson, 1958) assumes that the purpose of treatment is the realization of creative and attitudinal values, and this school frankly admits its value-orientation.

Although the term "value" is difficult to define, two separate aspects relating to the problem of control in psychotherapy are worthy of mention.

There are clear-cut rules for many behaviors which are common to practically all members of a given culture. These rules are usually also accepted by the therapist and his client. We will call these *metavalues* (cultural values). In addition, there is a variety of situations in which several alternate behaviors and goal hierarchies are equally tolerated by society but which differ in the degree to which they lead to satisfaction in the individual. These alternatives are determined primarily by the individual's past experience. We shall call these alternatives *personal values*. Complications arise both in the patient's value system and in the psychotherapy relationship because of the inconsistencies between metavalues and personal values. Interpretation of the cultural metavalues further varies as a function of membership in a subgroup such as a socio-economic, religious, or geographic affiliation. The outcome of therapy should provide a wider choice of alternative behaviors for the patient with the only restriction that the new behaviors must also be compatible with the metavalues of the patient's cultural environment. The problem lies mainly in producing those changes which lead to socially acceptable behavior even while they result in sweeping changes in the life pattern of the patient. For example, therapists generally do not disagree whether to manipulate behavior which may avert a suicide, but they *do* disagree whether a client's vocational or marital choice should be modified. In complete absence of standards for such personal and private modes of behavior the therapist's judgments are based mainly on his theoretical orientation, on his own experiences and on his own personal values. These therapist experiences then become the standards for selecting the goals for a particular patient in psychotherapy.[3]

In most cases the neurotic patient can be of little help in deciding what personal values need changing and what range of alternatives would be tolerated both by him and by his environment. When a patient *is* able to do this, the therapist's job does not involve the problem of values. The patient might indicate that he wishes to improve his study habits or seek technical help in making a vocational choice. In these cases technical skills by the psychologist may be applied directly to a problem with an outcome defined clearly by the client himself. Unfortunately, therapists sometimes become suspicious even in these cases and the desirability of the patient's stated goal is often questioned by therapists from the viewpoint of their own personal value systems. Endowed with a tradition of depth-probing, many a therapist is tempted to substitute his own goal for that of the patient. Instead of rendering technical assistance in a circumscribed area, the therapist may then attempt to change the patient's total pattern of living.

Rules for Control

The most heated arguments are generated by the question, "Who establishes the legitimacy of means and ends in behavioral control?" The writer does not presume to have a solution to this question, but wishes to present a few thoughts designed to stimulate further debate.

The APA attempted to indicate the limitations of appropriate means and ends for psychological practice in its early code of ethics (1953). Principle 1.12–1 (p. 7) reads in part: "the psychologist's ultimate allegiance is to society, and his professional behavior should demonstrate awareness of his social responsibilities. The welfare of the profession and of the individual psychologist are clearly subordinate to the welfare of the public." Further, Principle 1.13–1 (p. 10): "The psychologist should express in his professional behavior a firm commitment to those values which lie at the foundation of a democratic society, such as freedom of speech, freedom of research, and respect for the integrity of the individual." While these statements arouse the unqualified support of all good psychologists; they do not help to resolve the conflict inherent in the problem of treating neurotic patients. On the one hand, as citizens in a democratic society, psychologists believe that every person has the right to make his own free choice about his way of life. On the other hand, as professionals they also recognize that people who are in difficulties should be helped and choices must often be made for them. The clinical psychologist is an expert in assessing and modifying human behavior by virtue of his training. Regardless of the limitations of psychological theories and methods, psychologists constitute a profession (some say the only profession) which offers extensive training in

[3] If all mental health workers were to share a single set of values, their influence would carry with it the same dangers as any system of total control. A requirement of strict conformity to the mores and values set up by the therapist's model of behavior is also tantamount to the complete subservience imposed by totalistic control systems.

behavior theory and in methods used to assist people with psychological problems. Therefore, the psychologist is better prepared to apply his knowledge than the layman.[4] However, as noted above, there is a difference between competence in bringing about behavioral changes and in judging the desirability of the behavior and the value system to be substituted. The clinician cannot accept sole responsibility for judging the adequacy of the individual's value system, nor can he become the ultimate interpreter of cultural metavalues to the patient by psychotherapy or education. In clinical practice, the patient, his social milieu and other significant persons in his life must all be considered in selecting appropriate goals for therapy.

Nor can psychology be held responsible for the application of its principles and methods by social agencies or industry in the fields of government, economics, or education. Decisions concerning the legitimacy of means and ends in use of behavioral control methods are no more the responsibility of the psychologist than is the question whether to use atomic weapons in a war in the area of competence of the physicist, or the decision to adopt sterilization procedures with some humans in the domain of the biologist. In the absence of any specific mandate from the social community through its legal, political, religious, or social agencies psychologists will continue to use methods of control which are sometimes not acceptable to the public and use these for purposes about which there is some debate.

There has already been some indication that psychological knowledge is gradually becoming incorporated into the legal system, providing some standards of behavior which are more consistent with our knowledge of man than many current laws. There is, however, a considerable lag between mores and their incorporation into the legal structure of a society. During this lag professional groups will have to provide leadership in working out rules which describe the goals for which individual human behavior may be manipulated, and the restrictions upon methods under which this purpose is to be accomplished.

When the psychologist leaves his immediate work setting, his conduct falls under the rules by which other social groups operate. A social scientist who publicly gives opinions about the implications of behavior control techniques for international politics, education, or consumer behavior must expect the same treatment as other public figures who champion controversial issues. It is probably this change in the accustomed reaction from student or patient audiences which has made psychologists so reluctant to participate in public debate and to provide information and guidance to social groups. An additional problem, of course, lies in the thin line of distinction between fact and opinion, between researcher and reformer.

From these considerations it seems that several specific contributions can be made by psychologists to further public recognition of the social implications of recent advances in psychology.

(1) In their role as scientists, continuing research on behavioral control methods and on factors limiting their effects to special circumstances should provide clearer understanding of the extent of the problem in practical situations. Research findings already exist which tend to suggest that total behavioral control requires a totally controlled environment; that verbal (and attitudinal) behavior can be influenced by a variety of variables toward maximal or minimal change; and that self-control training can modify the effect of incentives, thereby reducing greatly the utility of many conditioning procedures. Knowledge of these factors should permit a better estimate of the actual threat inherent in practical methods to which objections are currently raised. If recently described methods turn out to be no more effective than previous controlling devices, or if easy countermeasures are available, no further concern or action would be warranted.

(2) With no special prerogatives to dictate to society the rules by which its members should be educated, controlled, or changed, psychologists as educated citizens can make a contribution as resource persons to established social agencies. These activities demand of the consultant that he explicitly distinguish between facts, interpretation of facts, and his personal opinion.

(3) Our discussion suggests that continued public awareness of the growing effectiveness of psychological techniques may present the best safeguards against their misapplication. Ultimately, the products of any science become public property and only the informed public can wisely regulate their use.

(4) If psychologists have a service to perform in society's effort to evaluate itself, it is the scientific analysis of current psychological practices, embedded in our social matrix. Among those are many which appear to have relevance to the control of *Individual* behavior, i.e., practices in education, in law-enforcement, in treatment of emotional adjustment, in consumer persuasion, and industrial personnel procedures. Contributions to each of these fields lie not only in suggestions for changes but also in a thorough analysis of the present practices and their consequences.

[4] We recognize that personality variables as yet unexplored may be important determinants of therapist effectiveness. But no scientifically grounded profession can fail to assume that additional didactic training is a necessary, if not sufficient, condition for practice.

References

ELLIS, A. *Reason and emotion in psychotherapy.* New York: Lyle Stuart, 1962.

ERIKSEN, C. W. (Ed.) *Behavior and awareness.* Durham: Duke University Press, 1962.

FRANK, J. D. *Persuasion and healing: A comparative study of psychotherapy.* Baltimore: Johns Hopkins Press, 1961.

GREENSPOON, J. Verbal conditioning and clinical psychology. In A. J. Bachrach (Ed.), *Experimental foundations of clinical psychology.* New York: Basic Books, 1962. Pp. 510–553.

KANFER, F. H. Comments on learning in psychotherapy. *Psychological Reports,* 1961, *9,* 681–699.

KANFER, F. H., and MARSTON, A. R. Verbal conditioning, ambiguity and psychotherapy. *Psychological Reports,* 1961, *9,* 461–475.

KRASNER, L. Behavior control and social responsibility. *American Psychologist,* 1962, *17,* 199–204. (a)

KRASNER, L. The therapist as a social reinforcement machine. In H. Strupp and L. Luborsky (Eds.), *Research in psychotherapy.* Washington: American Psychological Association, 1962. Pp. 61–95. (b)

LIFTON, R. J. *Thought reform and the psychology of totalism.* New York: W. W. Norton, 1961.

MEEHL, P. E. Some technical and axiological problems in the therapeutic handling of religious and valuational material. *Journal of Counseling Psychology,* 1959, *6,* 255–259.

PARSONS, T., and FOX, R. Illness, therapy and the modern urban family. In E. G. Jaco (Ed.), *Patients, physicians and illness.* Glencoe: Free Press, 1958. Pp. 234–245.

ROSENTHAL, D. Changes in some moral values following psychotherapy. *Journal of Consulting Psychology,* 1955, *19,* 431–436.

SARGANT, W. *Battle for the mind, a physiology of conversion and brainwashing.* New York: Doubleday, 1957.

SCHRIER, H. The significance of identification in therapy. *American Journal of Orthopsychiatry,* 1953, *23,* 585–604.

SEGAL, S. J. The role of the counselor's religious values in counseling. *Journal of Counseling Psychology,* 1959, *6,* 270–274.

SKINNER, B. F. *Science and human behavior.* New York: Macmillan, 1953.

WEISSKOPF-JOELSON, E. Some suggestions concerning *Weltanschauung* and psychotherapy. *Journal of Abnormal and Social Psychology,* 1953, *48,* 601–604.

WEISSKOPF-JOELSON, E. Logotherapy and existential analysis. *Acta Psychotherapeutica et Psychosomatica Supplement,* 1958, *6,* 193–204.

WILLIAMSON, E. G. Value orientation in counseling. *Personnel and Guidance Journal,* 1958, *36,* 520–528.

B Who Shall Control?

Beginning about the end of World War II, there has been an increasing call by governmental agencies for psychologists to help devise practical solutions to pressing national problems. Perhaps the trend began at the time of World War I, when psychologists carried out mass intelligence testing as a procedure for selecting draftees. World War II saw a rise in human factors and engineering research designed to adapt machines to man, and the trend has continued into systems analysis and group dynamics research. The 1960's saw a peak in the involvement of social and behavioral scientists—as well as physical scientists—in a wide range of governmental affairs. This has raised questions about how appropriate it is for scientists to participate in decisions which are political or have strong political implications.

The first article in this section, by sociologist Daniel Patrick *Moynihan,* was written during the Kennedy administration while the author was a governmental official concerned with the design and implementation of the poverty program. He discusses the question: what shall be the role of social and behavioral scientists in the practical solution of community problems? In this chapter from a book which grew out of his experiences as a government official in the poverty program, Moynihan raises the issue of the proper role for social scientists in government policy. He takes as a case history the Community Action Programs (CAP), which, as he documents in this excerpt, were strongly influenced by social scientists. In many of these programs social scientists were actually involved in leading and implementing community and political changes. He proposes that behavioral research is a scientific enterprise which is never complete. Even if complete, it would not automatically lend itself to effective political application, for which a different set of skills is needed. He asserts that the proper role of the social scientist is to evaluate and measure the results obtained by existing political programs, so that government officials can make informed decisions. The article documents the assertion that the application of knowledge to government programs is essentially a political task and that social scientists, therefore, have no role in it.

71 | *Social Science and Social Policy*

DANIEL P. MOYNIHAN

The essential problem with community action was that the one term concealed at least four quite distinct meanings: organizing the power structure, as in the Ford Foundation programs of Paul Ylvisaker; expanding the power structure, as in the delinquency program of Cloward and Ohlin; confronting the power structure, as in the Industrial Areas Foundation program of Saul Alinsky; and finally, assisting the power structure, as in the Peace Corps of Sargent Shriver. The task of government, in this case of the President's advisors, was first to discern these four different meanings, to make sure they were understood by those who had to make decisions about them, and to keep all concerned alert to the dangers of not keeping the distinctions clearly enough in mind. Which is not to say that policy had to choose between the various approaches: government no less than life is suffused with ambiguities and internal contradictions. But to be surmounted they must be perceived. *And there were warnings.* At a conference on Community Development held in San Juan in December 1964, while there was still time, the British social scientist Peter Marris outlined the contradictions between three of these views of community action. He proposed not to exclude any. He proposed that there be established in each community two organizations: one, close to city hall, for the purpose of studying and analyzing the local social structure, another for organizing the poor to bring their own strength to the bargaining table. It was abundant good sense, but ignored.

Just possibly one reason is that the key decisions in the White House and the Executive Office of the President were made by lawyers and economists. None was especially familiar with the social science theory on which the various positions were based and, if an impression may be permitted, few were temperamentally attuned to the frame of mind of the reformers. Very possibly, a matter of professional style is involved here. William C. Mitchell has noted that "The political sociologist tends to view a political system as a place of *struggle* for power or influence, while the economist tends to see it as an essentially *cooperative* division of labor within which various forms and degrees of competition may take place for the various roles and rewards that constitute the system." Order and efficiency are the passions of lawyers and economists, and properly so. It may be that the presence is needed in the Executive Office Building of persons trained to other disciplines who can more readily give credence to the thought that there are those who with even greater passion seek disorder and destruction.

But this risks the tendentious: it was not social science competence that was missing in the conception and management of this program; it was intellect. By and large the political actors come off best. Their sensibilities quickly alerted them to the probability that the community action activists would cause more trouble than could be contained. Unfortunately, there was no creative political response forthcoming once this had actually begun to occur.

This is the essential fact: *The government did not know what it was doing.* It had a theory. Or rather, a set of theories. Nothing more. The U.S. Government at this time was no more in possession of confident knowledge as to how to prevent delinquency, cure anomie, or overcome that midmorning sense of powerlessness, than it was the possessor of a dependable formula for motivating Vietnamese villagers to fight Communism. At any time from 1961 to 1964 an afternoon of library research would have established that the Cloward-Ohlin thesis of opportunity structure, though eminently respectable, was nonetheless rather a minority position, with the bulk of delinquency theory pointed in quite a different direction. Nor would it have been necessary to have spent an afternoon to ascertain this not unimportant fact. Ohlin would have been pleased to make it explicit in the course of half an hour's conversation. Two practical considerations would have emerged from such a revelation. First, that most theorists in the field, because of their emphasis on early family socialization, would be much less optimistic concerning rapid social change than were Cloward and Ohlin and their supporters. Much the same would be said of the Ford Foundation theory of institutional gymnastics: nothing seems to move that rapidly, at least in the view of most students of organizational behavior. Second, the divergence of the various theories was such that what would serve to cure in the one case would exacerbate in the other. A *big* bet was being made. No responsible persons had any business acting as if it were a sure thing. Why then, it will be asked, did the social scientists involved in these events not insist on the limits of their knowledge and methodology. The answer would seem to lie in part in the essentially dual nature of the American social scientist. He is an objective "seeker after truth." But he is also very likely to be a passionate partisan of social justice and social change to bring it about. Herman Kahn has described the United States as "a white, Anglo-Saxon, Protestant, middle class, Christian-Fundamentalist country run by a coalition of minorities, which these terms do not describe." By and large, social scientists would seem to have much more in common with those minorities than otherwise. Indeed increasingly they are not only personally drawn from them, in an ethnic and cultural sense, but make up a minority in their own right. During the 1960's, in particular, they have had quite extraordinary access to power. And they have used this access in considerable measure to promote social change in directions *they* deem necessary and desirable.

The reaction among many of the more activist social scientists (obviously this risks labelling a vast number of persons from a smallish number of incidents) was not to be appalled by disorder, *but almost to welcome it.* How grand to live in interesting times! This began in earnest with the Negro riot in Watts in 1965, which was promptly declared not to have been a riot at all, but rather a revolt, an uprising, a manifesto, any term that suggested that the masses were on the move. For that love affair is still unrequited. Earlier, Midge Decter observed that the whole MFY enterprise reeked of the notion of the proletariat. This was especially to be seen in MFY's insistence that the "real" leaders of the people would not be the ostensible ones, that behind the institutional facade of political party committeemen, locality "mayors," vice lords, and parish priests, there was to be found an echelon of uncorrupted men who, given opportunity, would assume leadership and . . . what? Change the world.

The presumption of superior empathy with the problems of the outcast is surely a characteristic, and a failing, of this liberal mindset. Thus, in an otherwise helpful abstract on the "maximum feasible participation" clause, Lillian Rubin writes that many of those involved in drafting the legislation seemed not to have understood its full meaning.

> A lifetime spent in an atmosphere dominated by racism and the casework emphasis of modern rehabilitation philosophy infects even the most sophisticated and sympathetic. It is difficult indeed to fully penetrate the stereotype—to envision and comprehend a poor man grasping abstract concepts of participation, a Negro asserting his manhood.

In illustration she cites a communication from James N. Adler, a young lawyer who worked with the Shriver task force.

> I had never really conceived [he writes] that it (participation) would mean control by the poor of the community action represented on the community action organization but that organization itself. . . . I expected that the poor would be such representation would be something in the order of 15 to 25% of the board. . . . *Moreover, I don't think it ever occurred to me, or to many others, that the representatives of the poor must necessarily be poor themselves.* [Her italics.]

One might think this a candid and helpful statement, coming, as it happens from an unusually attractive and productive young political executive. But it was cited by Miss Rubin as a failure of imagination In contrast with whom? Is a female graduate student in sociology at the University of California, Berkeley, better able to grasp the meaning of "a Negro asserting his manhood"?

All this might have been innocent enough save that as the 1960's passed, signs increased that the various forms of public disorder either sanctioned, induced, or led by middle-class liberal-radicals had begun to acquire an, ominous even sinister cast in the mind of the public at large. At the necessary risk of oversimplification, if may be said that crime in the streets as a political issue began to assume the role that Communists in government had played in the 1940's and early 1950's. The parallels were striking: on the one hand an elite-proletarian axis, in which the proletarians played rather a passive role, or at least a largely non-ideological one, despite the interpretations to be read in the *Nation* or wherever. In between were the mass of fundamentalist citizens increasingly concerned, puzzled, and alarmed. The élite were in power; the fundamentalist *mass* out of power, save in institutions such as the Congress, the influence of which was largely negative. In particular, the élite controlled the major national institutions, such as the State Department in one era and the Department of Justice in the other, contrasted with the "mass" custody of such popular institutions as the police.

In both eras a distinctive posture of altogether too many members of the intellectual-academic world was to reject the legitimacy of the issue either of subversion or violence on grounds that those who raised it either were not intelligent enough to comprehend fully any complex issue or else had something other in mind than their putative concern for the public safety. The plain fact is that in both instances the intellectual group had acquired an *interest* in the political turmoil of the moment and came very near to misusing its position to advance that interest. In the first period the intellectual-academic community seemed filled with persons who, in Kristol's description, "prefer to regard Whittaker Chambers and Elizabeth Bently as pathological liars, and who believe that to plead the Fifth Amendment is the first refuge of a scholar and a gentleman. In the second period the apologetics for violence were not less curious. The community action ideology became in ways more, not less, extreme in the face of evident failures. *Complete* community control, usually meaning black control, of *all* community-affecting institutions, became the demand of the more militant whites. On the surface a reasonable enough position, in reality this took the form of denying the legitimacy of those institutions of electoral representation that had developed over the years—indeed, the centuries and which nominally *did* provide community control. Of a sudden the city councilman was not enough, the state assemblyman not enough, the Congressman not enough, the mayor and the governor and the President but tools of the power structure. Plebiscitory democracy, the people-in-council, became the seeming nonnegotiable demand of many. The institutions of representative government, imperfect as they may be, have the singular virtue of defining who speaks for the community in certain set circumstances. Thus the elected (black) representatives of the Harlem community had several times ratified the construction by Columbia University of a gymnasium in Morningside Park. But the black students of the University decided that the assemblymen and senators, councilmen and borough presidents did not speak for the community, and that *they* did. This quickly enough becomes government, as one observer has noted, by a process of private nullification, which has never been especially good news for democracy. It would be absurd to blame the community action programs of the war on poverty for this *reductio ad absurdum*, but the legitimation of something called "community control," in opposition to the established system of electoral representation, the assumption that established systems were somehow not meeting the needs of the people, was certainly much encouraged by the community action movement. It is altogether natural that more conservative citizens became alarmed.

The blunt reality is that sponsors of community action programs who expected to adopt the conflict strategy of Saul D. Alinsky and at the same time expected to be the recipients of large sums of public money, looked for, to paraphrase Jefferson, "what never was, and never will be." Alinsky emerges from the 1960's a man of enhanced stature. His influence on the formulation of the antipoverty program and its predecessors was not great. Indeed it was negligible, in that a primary motive of these efforts was to *give* things to the poor that they did not have. Alinsky's law, laid down in *Reveille for Radicals*, which appeared in 1946, was that in the process of social change there is no such thing as give, only take.

The failure of the social scientists, the foundation executives, the government officials lay in not accepting—not insisting upon—the theoretical nature of their proposition. As a matter for speculation, even for experiment, various forms of government-sponsored community action had much to commend themselves. The problems of community were properly a matter of concern at this time. But to proceed as if that which only *might* be so, in fact was so, was to misuse social science.

What then is to be said of the role of social science in social policy? Not, that is, of social scientists: a teeming and irrepressible group, they will be on hand proffering proposals for universal improvement doubtless for all time to come. And no bad thing. But this they do in their capacity as citizens, as interested, sentient beings. But is there something called social science, a body of knowledge, a methodology that men of quite disparate politics and temperaments will nonetheless agree upon, that can contribute to the formulation of public policy? I will propose that the answer is a limited but emphatic Yes.

I have sought to argue, by illustration, that social science is at its weakest, at its worst, when it offers theories of individual or collective behavior which raise the possibility, by controlling certain inputs, of bringing about mass behavioral change. No such knowledge now exists. Evidence is fragmented, contradictory, incomplete. Enough snake oil has been sold in this Republic to warrant the expectation that public officials will begin reading labels.

This hardly precludes experimentation. On the contrary, as techniques of evaluation evolve, outright laboratory-type investigations of social issues are likely to become more frequent, and certainly more useful. In 1967, for example, the Office of Economic Opportunity entered a $4 million contract with the Institute for Research on Poverty of the University of Wisconsin to carry out an experimental study of the effects of a negative income tax on one thousand low-income, intact, urban families in New Jersey, to extend over a period of fifty months. A generation ago such an undertaking would have seemed strange, if not outrageous. But the OEO announcement was accepted without apparent comment, perhaps especially owing to the professional reputations of the social scientists who would be engaged on the project. Quietly a new style in social innovation is emerging.

Very much as the national government began compiling economic statistics that were to make economic planning feasible years before such planning became politically acceptable, the Federal establishment has for some time been expanding the collection of the raw social data to which Meyer proposes the new methodologies be directed. The Bureau of the Census, one of the truly noble institutions of the Federal government, has quietly been transforming its decennial survey into a continuous measurement process. Much room remains for improvement. (In 1960, some 10 per cent of the nonwhite population was misseed, with proportions twice that and more among young adult males.) But there are not as many mysteries left as to *how* to conduct an adequate census, and with more support the Bureau will be able to do just that. The truth of John Kenneth Galbraith's observation remains: statisticians are key actors in the process of social change, for it is often only when it becomes possible to measure a problem that it also becomes possible to arouse any political interest in solving it. For all its attenuated mandate, the provision of the Employment Act of 1946 committing the American national government "to promote maximum employment, production, and purchasing power" brought about the years of analysis that in turn led to the singularly successful political economy of the 1960's. With more foresight, might not a commitment to "maximum feasible participation" lead to a similar process of measurement and feedback? Something very like this has been proposed by Bertram M. Gross who was associated with the establishment of the Council of Economic Advisors, as was provided by the Employment Act. Responding to these initiatives, Senator Walter Mondale of Minnesota in 1967 introduced legislation, the Full Opportunity and Social Accounting Act of 1957, providing for the establishment of a Council of Social Advisors who would perform for the President, and the nation generally, the counterpart of the economists' role. Others have proposed that a social scientist be substituted for one of the three economists on the present council. The concept of a social report of the President, to parallel the economic report, has been widely discussed, and a group under the leadership of Daniel Bell began work on a prototype. In 1966 Raymond A. Bauer and a group at the American Academy of Arts and Sciences published a group of papers under the heading *Social Indicators* which marked the beginning of systematic inquiry into the issue.

The potential of these proposals is easily underestimated, as are the dangers implicit in some of the present trends in social measurement. The demands of rational resource allocation, so compelling on so many grounds, have already led to an extensive development of "social measurement" techniques in the executive branches of American government, especially the Federal government. This veery largely is what the renowned, if somewhat over-touted Program Planning Budgeting System (PPBS) represents, a system largely developed in the Defense establishment and under Johnson colonized throughout the Federal establishment. Should this trend continue, and it will, the result will be a considerable exacerbation of a situation already to be observed, namely, a pronounced and growing imbalance between the "knowledge" as to what works and what does not, what is needed and what is not, available to the executive branch of government, as against the legislature. In hearings before the Subcommittee on Executive Reorganization of the U.S. Senate Committee on Government Operations in December 1966, I had occasion to comment on this development in terms that seem relevant here:

> There is nothing sinister about this state of affairs. Serious evaluation research is only just approaching the state of a developed, as against an experimental, technique. Inevitably it has been sponsored in the first instance by executive departments. However, precisely because the findings of such research are not

neutral, it would be dangerous to permit this imbalance to persist. Too often, the executive is exposed to the temptation to release only those findings that suit its purposes; there is no one to keep them honest. Similarly, universities and other private groups which often undertake such research on contract are in some measure subject to constant, if subtle, pressure to produce "positive" findings. The simple fact is that a new source of knowledge is coming into being; while it is as yet an imperfect technique, it is likely to improve; and if it comes to be accepted as a standard element in public discourse, it is likely to raise considerably the level of that discourse. This source of knowledge should not remain an executive monopoly.

What is to be done? I would offer a simple analogy. In the time this nation was founded, the principal form in which knowledge was recorded and preserved was in printed books, and accordingly in 1800 Congress established the Library of Congress as a source of information. Over the next century, techniques of accounting and budgeting developed very rapidly, and in 1921 Congress established the General Accounting Office to keep track of federal expenditures. I would like to suggest that Congress should now establish an Office of Legislative Evaluation in the GAO which would have the task of systematically reviewing the program evaluations and "PPBS" judgments made by executive departments. This office would be staffed by professional social scientists. On occasion they would undertake on their own to assess a Federal program, just as on occasion the GAO does an audit of its own; but in general their task would be to "evaluate the evaluators" and in this way both maintain and improve the quality of the regular ongoing work of the executive departments in this field, and also routinely make these findings available to the Congress. It should not be expected that their findings will be dramatic or that they will put an end to argument—just the contrary is likely to occur. But the long-run effect could be immensely useful, if only because Congress would have some clearer idea than it now has as to what it is doing.

Some will feel that the very existence and distribution of knowledge of this kind is a threat to continued experiment and innovation. I disagree. I would argue, for example, that the General Accounting Office has in its 45 years of activity raised the level of financial honesty in the programs of the Federal government to the point that it is no longer even a remote obstacle to federal legislation. Federal money may get wasted, but it rarely gets stolen. The American people know this, and I am persuaded that it profoundly affects their willingness to pay taxes for the support of federal programs. I believe further that if we began to be as careful and as open about assessing the results of social programs as we are in ensuring the personal honesty of those involved with running them, we might begin to see a more enduring willingness to keep trying—as well, perhaps, as a welcome reluctance by cabinet officers to "oversell" their program to begin with.

> We have set ourselves goals that are, in some ways, unique in history: not only to abolish poverty and ignorance, but also to become the first genuinely multi-racial and, we hope, in the end non-racial democracy the world has seen. I believe that in moving toward these goals, and in seeking to change the present reality, an unflinching insistence on fact will be a major asset.

And there is an issue beyond objectivity. The "movement of the social system into self-consciousness" has been accompanied by increasingly sophisticated efforts to shape and direct that system. Increasingly social scientists are recruited for such attempts; increasingly they themselves initiate them. There arises then a range of questions of ethical behavior that correspond to the canons of professional practice with respect to individual clients. Social workers have developed, and in some cases borrowed from other professions, a quite extensive set of rules governing and protecting professional conduct. They can for example, purchase insurance for suits against malpractice. *But what is malpractice with respect to a community?* At what point are risks taken that are not justified? In what way is it to be determined whether advice was incompetent or treatment negligent? Difficult, perhaps unavailing questions. But questions withal. A generation ago Reinhold Niebuhr forewarned us that the major difficulty of our time would be that of imposing ethical standards on the behavior of large organizations, an effort suddenly imposed on society after three millenia of slowly developing standards of personal conduct. Rather the same challenge faces those who would "engineer" social change. The problem goes beyond individual measures of professional competence to the question of the very possibility of such competence. Looking back, it is clear, for example, that the community action programs of the war on poverty lent themselves to a rise in internal domestic tensions only in part because of their intrinsic qualities, and far more because of a rise of upper middle class white disaffection with the direction of American society occurring in conjunction with an even more powerful surge of the civil rights movement associated with an inevitable, and in ways much overdue rise of militant black assertiveness. Had these developments been foreseen it may well be that wisdom in government would have dictated another course for the anti-poverty program, there having developed on its own an altogether sufficient potential for community activism. Prescriptions for arousing the "silent" students and inert mass as of the Eisenhower era may only have exacerbated the tendencies of the period of the Students for a Democratic Society and the Black Panthers. But who was to know this would be the case? Exactly. It was not possible to know: it *is* not possible. Wisdom surely bespeaks moderation in projections of the future, and restraint in its promises for it.

This is, of course, first of all a challenge for those who practice the most demanding calling of all, that of government itself. For them, Edmund Burke's conception of successive generations as possessing their society's laws and customs of governance in the form of an entailed estate, given them for lifetime use, with the condition that it be passed on at least not diminished and hopefully enhanced, seems especially relevant now in the United States. The 1960's, which began with such splendid promise of a new and higher unity for the nation, are ending in an atmosphere of disunity and distrust of the most ominous quality. For it is not the old and weak and excluded who have been ill used, or think themselves such. Rather it is the vibrant, established, *coming* young people of the nation who in large numbers have learned to distrust their government, and in many ways to loathe their society. They are not yet in power. *They will be.* When that day comes, however moderated their views may have become, their understanding of their country will have been shaped by the traumas of the 1960's. Not least of these shocks has been the debacle of the community action programs of the war on poverty: the soaring rhetoric, the minimum performance; the feigned constancy, the private betrayal; in the end, to their understanding, the sell-out. All this will be part of a past that has already shaped the future. It will then be asked, by some at least, how well the men who held office in that near to heartbreaking decade exercised their brief authority.

Social scientists in the universities, like their counterparts in the physical and biological sciences, frequently depend upon external funding agencies—both private and governmental—for research support. Equipment, travel, secretaries, research assistants, and computer time all require sums of money that universities are not always able to provide. The federal government, with its vast financial resources, has been a principle source of such support, through both contractual arrangements with the investigator and outright grants-in-aid. Indeed, the practice of "grantsmanship" by aspiring university researchers has not gone without criticism. McGrath and Altman (1966) suggest that ". . . like the drive for publication, the drive for funds and the accompanying status, power, and opportunity may also become functionally autonomous, with the original intent of using the new dollars for important and dedicated research gradually receding into the background."*

We may hope that the behavior of most researchers, even those supported by government grants, is rarely controlled by such base incentives. In truth, large-scale studies on socially important issues can rarely be undertaken with the meager facilities afforded by the average college or university. Only with the monetary assistance of granting agencies can foreign area studies, for example, be conducted. In the past few years, however, the federal government has suddenly become wary of sponsoring social science research to be conducted in other countries. The Defense Department, in particular, has been ordered to cut back drastically its support not only of foreign area research but of research that is not directly relevant to the military's mission. This development, which many social scientists believe to be short-sighted and ill-advised, was instigated in large measure by the "fallout" from *Project Camelot,* an ill-fated social science venture funded by the Departments of State and Defense with the cooperation of scholars in several Latin American countries.

In a more detailed analysis of this incident, *Horowitz* quotes from a document circulated by the Special Operations Research Office in 1964:

> Project Camelot is a study whose objective is to determine the feasibility of developing a general social systems model which would make it possible to

* J. E. McGrath and I. Altman, *Small Group Research.* New York: Holt, Rinehart and Winston, 1966, p. 83.

> predict and influence politically significant aspects of social change in the developing nations of the world. Somewhat more specifically, its objectives are, *first,* to devise procedures for assessing the potential for internal war within national societies; *second,* to identify with increased degrees of confidence those actions which a government might take to relieve conditions which are assessed as giving rise to a potential for internal war; and *finally,* to assess the feasibility of prescribing the characteristics of a system for obtaining and using the essential information needed for doing the above two things. The project is conceived as a three- to four-year effort to be funded at around one and one-half million dollars annually. It is supported by the Army and the Department of Defense, and will be conducted with the cooperation of other agencies of the government. A large amount of primary data collection in the field is planned as well as the extensive utilization of already available data on social, economic and political functions. At this writing, it seems probable that the geographic orientation of the research will be toward Latin American countries. Present plans call for a field office in that region.*

As a footnote to this general statement of the aims of Camelot, it should be noted that a spokesman for SORO claimed the project to be ". . . an objective, nonnormative study concerned with *what is* or *might be* and *not* with what *ought to be.*"** Beyond his review and commentary of the controversy surrounding Project Camelot, Horowitz makes a fervent plea for the autonomy of scientists who, he argues, should be free to pursue their objectives without government censorship, even though government funds may be involved.

* I. L. Horowitz (Ed.), *The Rise and Fall of Project Camelot.* Cambridge Mass.: M.I.T. Press, 1967.

** T. R. Vallance, Project Camelot: An interim postlude. In I. L. Horowitz (Ed.), *The Rise and Fall of Project Camelot.* Cambridge, Mass.: M.I.T. Press, 1967, p. 204.

72 | *The Life and Death of Project Camelot*

IRVING LOUIS HOROWITZ

In June of this year [1965]—in the midst of the crisis over the Dominican Republic—the United States Ambassador to Chile sent an urgent and angry cable to the State Department. Ambassador Ralph Dungan was confronted with a growing outburst of anti-Americanism from Chilean newspapers and intellectuals. Further, left-wing members of the Chilean Senate had accused the United States of espionage.

The anti-American attacks that agitated Dungan had no direct connection with sending U.S. troops to Santo Domingo. Their target was a mysterious and cloudy American research program called Project Camelot.

Dungan wanted to know from the State Department what Project Camelot was all about. Further, whatever Camelot was, he wanted it stopped because it was fast becoming a *cause célèbre* in Chile (as it soon would throughout capitals of Latin America and in Washington) and Dungan had not been told anything about it—even though it was sponsored by the U.S. Army and involved the tinderbox subjects of counter-revolution and counter-insurgency in Latin America.

Within a few weeks Project Camelot created repercussions from Capitol Hill to the White House. Senator J. William Fulbright, chairman of the Foreign Relations Committee, registered his personal concern about such projects as Camelot because of their "reactionary, backward-looking policy opposed to change. Implicit in Camelot, as in the concept of 'counter-insurgency,' is an assumption that revolutionary movements are dangerous to the interests of the United States and that the United States must be prepared to assist, if not actually to participate in, measures to repress them."

By mid-June the State Department and Defense Department—which had created and funded Camelot—were in open contention over the project and the jurisdiction each department should have over certain foreign policy operations.

On July 8, Project Camelot was killed by Defense Secretary Robert McNamara's office which has a veto power over the military budget. The decision had been made under the President's direction.

On that same day, the director of Camelot's parent body, the Special Operations Research Organization, told a Congressional committee that the research project on revolution and counter-insurgency had taken its name from King Arthur's mythical domain because "It connotes the right sort of things—development of a stable society with peace and justice for all." Whatever Camelot's outcome, there should be no mistaking the deep sincerity behind this appeal for an applied social science pertinent to current policy.

However, Camelot left a horizon of disarray in its wake: an open dispute between State and Defense; fuel for the anti-American fires in Latin America; a cut in U.S. Army research appropriations. In addition, serious and perhaps ominous implications for social science research, bordering on censorship, have been raised by the heated reaction of the executive branch of government.

Global Counter-Insurgency

What was Project Camelot? Basically, it was a project for measuring and forecasting the causes of revolutions and insurgency in underdeveloped areas of the world. It also aimed to find ways of eliminating the causes, or coping with the revolutions and insurgencies. Camelot was sponsored by the U.S. Army on a four- to six-million dollar contract, spaced out over three to four years, with the Special Operations Research Organization (SORO). This agency is nominally under the aegis of American University in Washington, D.C., and does a variety of research for the Army. This includes making analytical surveys of foreign areas; keeping up-to-date information on the military, political, and social complexes of those areas; and maintaining a "rapid response" file for getting immediate information, upon Army request, on any situation deemed militarily important.

Latin America was the first area chosen for concentrated study, but countries on Camelot's four-year list included some in Asia, Africa, and Europe. In a working paper issued on December 5, 1964, at the request of the Office of the Chief of Research and Development, Department of the Army, it was recommended that "comparative historical studies" be made in these countries:

> Latin America: Argentina, Bolivia, Brazil, Colombia, Cuba, Dominican Republic, El Salvador, Guatemala, Mexico, Paraguay, Peru, Venezuela.
> Middle East: Egypt, Iran, Turkey.
> Far East: Korea, Indonesia, Malaysia, Thailand.
> Others: France, Greece, Nigeria.

"Survey research and other field studies" were recommended for Bolivia, Colombia, Ecuador, Paraguay, Peru, Venezuela, Iran, Thailand. Preliminary consideration was also being given to a study of the separatist movement in French Canada. It, too, had a code name: Project Revolt.

In a recruiting letter sent to selected scholars all over the world at the end of 1964, Project Camelot's aims were defined as a study to "make it possible to predict and influence politically significant aspects of social change in the developing nations of the world." This would include devising procedures for "assessing the potential for internal war within national societies" and "identify(ing) with increased degrees of confidence, those actions which a government might take to relieve conditions which are assessed as giving rise to a potential for internal war." The letter further stated:

> The U.S. Army has an important mission in the positive and constructive aspects of nation-building in less developed countries as well as a responsibility to assist friendly governments in dealing with active insurgency problems.

Such activities by the U.S. Army were described as "insurgency prophylaxis" rather than the "sometimes misleading label of counter-insurgency."

Project Camelot was conceived in late 1963 by a group of high-ranking Army officers connected with the Army Research Office of the Department of Defense. They were concerned about new types of warfare springing up around the world. Revolutions in Cuba and Yemen and insurgency movements in Vietnam and the Congo were a far cry from the battles of World War II and also different from the envisioned—and planned for—apocalypse of nuclear war. For the first time in modern warfare, military establishments were not in a position to use the immense arsenals at their disposal—but were, in stead, compelled by force of a geopolitical stalemate to increasingly engage in primitive forms of armed combat. The questions of moment for the Army were: Why can't the "hardware" be used? And what alternatives can social science "software" provide?

A well-known Latin American area specialist, Rex Hopper, was chosen as director of Project Camelot. Hopper was a professor of sociology and chairman of the department at Brooklyn College. He had been to Latin America many times over a thirty-year span on research projects and lecture tours, including some under government sponsorship. He was highly recommended for the position by his professional associates in Washington and elsewhere. Hopper had a long-standing interest in problems of revolution and saw in this multi-million dollar contract the possible realization of a life-long scientific ambition.

The Chilean Debacle

How did this social science research project create a foreign policy furore? And, at another level, how did such high intentions result in so disastrous an outcome?

The answers involve a network spreading from a professor of anthropology at the University of Pittsburgh, to a professor of sociology at the University of Oslo, and yet a third professor of sociology at the University of Chile in Santiago, Chile. The "showdown" took place in Chile, first within the confines of the university, next on the floor of the Chilean Senate, then in the popular press of Santiago, and finally, behind U.S. embassy walls.

It was ironic that Chile was the scene of wild newspaper tales of spying and academic outrage at scholars being recruited for "spying missions." For the working papers of Project Camelot stipulated as a criterion for study that a country "should show promise of high pay-offs in terms of the kinds of data required." Chile did not meet these requirements—it is not on the preliminary list of nations specified as prospects.

How then did Chile become involved in Project Camelot's affairs? The answer requires consideration of the position of Hugo G. Nutini, assistant professor of anthropology at Pittsburgh, citizen of the United States and former citizen of Chile. His presence in Santiago as a self-identified Camelot representative triggered the climactic chain of events.

Nutini, who inquired about an appointment in Camelot's beginning stages, never was given a regular Camelot appointment. Because he was planning a trip to Chile in April of this year—on other academic business—he was asked to prepare a report concerning possibilities of cooperation from Chilean scholars. In general, it was the kind of survey which has mild results and a modest honorarium attached to it (Nutini was offered $750). But Nutini had an obviously different notion of his role. Despite the limitations and precautions which Rex Hopper placed on his trip, especially Hopper's insistence on its informal nature, Nutini managed to convey the impression of being an official of Project Camelot with the authority to make proposals to prospective Chilean participants. Here was an opportunity to link the country of his birth with the country of his choice.

At about the same time, Johan Galtung, a Norwegian sociologist famous for his research on conflict and conflict resolution in underdeveloped areas, especially in Latin America, entered the picture. Galtung, who was in Chile at the time and associated with the Latin American Faculty of Social Science (FLACSO), received an invitation to participate in a Camelot planning conference scheduled for Washington, D.C., in August 1965. The fee to social scientists attending the conference would be $2,000 for four weeks. Galtung turned down the invitation. He gave several reasons. He could not accept the role of the U.S. Army as a sponsoring agent in a study of counter-insurgency. He could not accept the notion of the Army as an agency of national development; he saw the Army as managing conflict and even promoting conflict. Finally, he could not accept the asymmetry of the project—he found it difficult to understand why there would be studies of counter-insurgency in Latin America, but no studies of "counter-intervention" (conditions under which Latin American nations might intervene in the affairs of the United States). Galtung was also deeply concerned about the possibility of European scholars being frozen out of Latin American studies by an inundation of sociologists from the United States. Furthermore, he expressed fears that the scale of Camelot honoraria would completely destroy the social science labor market in Latin America.

Galtung had spoken to others in Oslo, Santiago, and throughout Latin America about the project, and he had shown the memorandum of December 1964 to many of his colleagues.

Soon after Nutini arrived in Santiago, he had a conference with Vice-Chancellor Alvaro Bunster of the University of Chile to discuss the character of Project Camelot. Their second meeting, arranged by the vice-chancellor, was also attended by Professor Eduardo Fuenzalida, a sociologist. After a half-hour of exposition by Nutini, Fuenzalida asked him point-blank to specify the ultimate aims of the project, its sponsors, and its military implications. Before Nutini could reply, Professor Fuenzalida, apparently with some drama, pulled a copy of the December 4 circular letter from his briefcase and read a prepared Spanish translation. Simultaneously, the authorities at FLACSO turned over the matter to their associates in the Chilean Senate and in the left-wing Chilean press.

In Washington, under the political pressures of State Department officials and Congressional reaction, Project Camelot was halted in midstream, or more precisely, before it ever really got under way. When the ambassador's communication reached Washington, there was already considerable official ferment about Project Camelot. Senators Fulbright, Morse, and McCarthy soon asked for hearings by the Senate Foreign Relations Committee. Only an agreement between Secretary of Defense McNamara and Secretary of State Rusk to settle their differences on future overseas research projects forestalled Senate action. But in the House of Representatives, a hearing was conducted by the Foreign Affairs Committee on July 8. The SORO director, Theodore Vallance, was questioned by committee members on the worth of Camelot and the matter of military intrusion into foreign policy areas.

That morning even before Vallance was sworn in as a witness—and without his knowledge—the Defense Department issued a terse announcement terminating Project Camelot. President Johnson had decided the issue in favor of the State Department. In a memo to Secretary Rusk on August 5 the President stipulated that "no government sponsorship of foreign area research should be undertaken which in the judgment of the Secretary of State would adversely affect United States foreign relations."

The State Department has recently established machinery to screen and judge all federally-financed research projects overseas. The policy and research consequences of the Presidential directive will be discussed later.

What effect will the cancellation of Camelot have on the continuing rivalry between Defense and State Departments for primacy in foreign policy? How will government sponsorship of future social science research be affected? And was Project Camelot a scholarly protective cover for U.S. Army planning—or a legitimate research operation on a valid research subject independent of sponsorship?

Let us begin with a collective self-portrait of Camelot as the social scientists who directed the project perceived it. There seems to be general consensus on seven points.

First, the men who went to work for Camelot felt the need for a large-scale, "big picture" project in social science. They wanted to create a sociology of contemporary relevance which would not suffer from the parochial narrowness of vision to which their own professional backgrounds had generally conditioned them. Most of the men viewed Camelot as a bona fide opportunity to do fundamental research with relatively unlimited funds at their disposal. (No social science project ever before had up to $6,000,000 available.) Under such optimal conditions, these scholars tended not to look a gift horse in the mouth. As one of them put it, there was no desire to inquire too deeply as to the source of the funds or the ultimate purpose of the project.

Second, most social scientists affiliated with Camelot felt that there was actually more freedom to do fundamental research under military sponsorship than at a university or college. One man noted that during the 1950's there was far more freedom to do fundamental research in the RAND Corporation (an Air Force research organization) than on any campus in America. Indeed, once the protective covering of RAND was adopted, it was almost viewed as a society of Platonist elites or "knowers" permitted to search for truth on behalf of the powerful. In a neoplatonic definition of their situation, the Camelot men hoped that their ideas would be taken seriously by the wielders of power (although, conversely, they were convinced that the armed forces would not accept their preliminary recommendations).

Third, many of the Camelot associates felt distinctly uncomfortable with military sponsorship, especially given the present United States military posture. But their reaction to this discomfort was that "the Army has to be educated." This view was sometimes cast in Freudian terms: the Army's bent toward violence ought to be sublimated. Underlying this theme was the notion of the armed forces as an agency for potential social good—the discipline and the order embodied by an army could be channeled into the process of economic and social development in the United States as well as in Latin America.

Fourth, there was a profound conviction in the perfectibility of mankind; particularly in the possibility of the military establishment performing a major role in the general process of growth. They sought to correct the intellectual paternalism and parochialism under which Pentagon generals, State Department diplomats, and Defense Department planners seemed to operate.

Fifth, a major long-range purpose of Camelot, at least for some of its policy-makers, was to prevent another revolutionary holocaust on a grand scale, such as occurred in Cuba. At the very least, there was a shared belief that *Pax Americana* was severely threatened and its future could be bolstered.

Sixth, none of them viewed their role on the project as spying for the United States government, or for anyone else.

Seventh, the men on Project Camelot felt that they made heavy sacrifices for social science. Their personal and professional risks were much higher than those taken by university academics. Government work, while well-compensated, remains professionally marginal. It can be terminated abruptly (as indeed was the case) and its project directors are subject to a public scrutiny not customary behind the walls of ivy.

In the main, there was perhaps a keener desire on the part of the directing members of Camelot not to "sell out" than there is among social scientists with regular academic appointments. This concern with the ethics of social science research seemed to be due largely to daily confrontation of the problems of betrayal, treason, secrecy, and abuse of data, in a critical situation. In contrast, even though a university position may be created by federally-sponsored research, the connection with policy matters is often too remote to cause any *crise de conscience*.

The Insiders Report

Were the men on Camelot critical of any aspects of the project?

Some had doubts from the outset about the character of the work they would be doing, and about the conditions under which it would be done. It was pointed out, for example, that the U.S. Army tends to exercise a far more stringent intellectual control of research findings than does the U.S. Air Force. As evidence for this, it was stated that SORO generally had fewer "free-wheeling" aspects to its research designs than did RAND (the Air Force-supported research organization). One critic inside SORO went so far as to say that he knew of no SORO research which had a "playful" or unregimented quality, such as one finds at RAND (where for example, computers are used to plan invasions but also to play chess). One staff member said that "the self-conscious seriousness gets to you after a while." "It was all grim stuff," said another.

Another line of criticism was that pressures on the "reformers" (as the men engaged in Camelot research spoke of themselves) to come up with ideas were much stronger than the pressures on the military to actually bring off any policy changes recommended. The social scientists were expected to be social reformers, while the military adjutants were expected to be conservative. It was further felt that the relationship between sponsors and researchers was not one of equals, but rather one of superordinate military needs and subordinate academic roles. On the other hand, some officials were impressed by the disinterestedness of the military, and thought that far from exercising undue influence, the Army personnel were loath to offer opinions.

Another objection was that if one had to work on policy matters—if research is to have international ramifications—it might better be conducted under conventional State Department sponsorship. "After all," one man said, "they are at least nominally committed to civilian political norms." In other words, there was a considerable reluctance to believe that the Defense Department, despite its superior organization, greater financial affluence, and executive influence, would actually improve upon State Department styles of work, or accept recommendations at variance with Pentagon policies.

There seemed to be few, if any, expressions of disrespect for the intrinsic merit of the work contemplated by Camelot, or of disdain for policy-oriented work in general. The scholars engaged in the Camelot effort used two distinct vocabularies. The various Camelot documents reveal a military vocabulary provided with an array of military justifications, often followed (within the same document) by a social science vocabulary offering social science justifications and rationalizations. The dilemma in the Camelot literature, from the preliminary report issued in August 1964 until the more advanced document issued in April 1965, is the same: an incomplete amalgamation of the military and sociological vocabularies. (At an early date the project had the code name SPEARPOINT.)

Policy Conflicts over Camelot

The directors of SORO are concerned that the cancellation of Camelot might mean the end of SORO as well as a wholesale slash of research funds. For while over $1,000,000 was allotted to Camelot each year, the annual budget of SORO, its parent organization, is a good deal less. Although no such action has taken place SORO's future is being examined. For example, the Senate and House Appropriations Committee blocked a move by the Army to transfer unused Camelot funds to SORO.

However, the end of Project Camelot does not necessarily imply the end of the Special Operations Research Office, nor does it imply an end to research designs which are similar in character to Project Camelot. In fact, the termination of the contract does not even imply an intellectual change of heart on the part of the originating sponsors or key figures of the project.

One of the characteristics of Project Camelot was the number of antagonistic forces it set in motion on grounds of strategy and timing rather than from what may be called considerations of scientific principles:

1. The State Department grounded its opposition to Camelot on the basis of the ultimate authority it has in the area of foreign affairs. There is no published report showing serious criticism of the projected research itself.

2. Congressional opposition seemed to be generated by a concern not to rock any foreign alliances, especially in Latin America. Again, there was no statement about the project's scientific or intellectual grounds.

3. A third group of skeptics, academic social scientists, generally thought that Project Camelot, and studies of the processes of revolution and war in

general, were better left in the control of major university centers, and in this way, kept free of direct military supervision.

4. The Army, creator of the project, did nothing to contradict McNamara's order cancelling Project Camelot. Army influentials did not only feel that they had to execute the Defense Department's orders, but they are traditionally dubious of the value of "software" research to support "hardware" systems.

Let us take a closer look at each of these groups which voiced opposition to Project Camelot. A number of issues did not so much hinge upon, as swim about, Project Camelot. In particular, the "jurisdictional" dispute between Defense and State loomed largest.

State vs. Defense. In substance, the debate between the Defense Department and the State Department is not unlike that between electricians and bricklayers in the construction of a new apartment house. What union is responsible for which processes? Less generously, the issue is: who controls what? At the policy level, Camelot was a tool tossed about in a larger power struggle which has been going on in government circles since the end of World War II, when the Defense Department emerged as a competitor for honors as the most powerful bureau of the administrative branch of government.

In some sense, the divisions between Defense and State are outcomes of the rise of ambiguous conflicts such as Korea and Vietnam, in contrast to the more precise and diplomatically controlled "classical" world wars. What are the lines dividing political policy from military posture? Who is the most important representative of the United States abroad: the ambassador or the military attaché in charge of the military mission? When soldiers from foreign lands are sent to the United States for political orientation, should such orientation be within the province of the State Department or of the Defense Department? When under-cover activities are conducted, should the direction of such activities belong to military or political authorities? Each of these is a strategic question with little pragmatic or historic precedent. Each of these was entwined in the Project Camelot explosion.

It should be plain therefore that the State Department was not simply responding to the recommendations of Chilean left-wingers in urging the cancellation of Camelot. It merely employed the Chilean hostility to "interventionist" projects as an opportunity to redefine the balance of forces and power with the Defense Department. What is clear from this resistance to such projects is not so much a defense of the sovereignty of the nations where ambassadors are stationed, as it is a contention that conventional political channels are sufficient to yield the information desired or deemed necessary.

Congress. In the main, congressional reaction seems to be that Project Camelot was bad because it rocked the diplomatic boat in a sensitive area. Underlying most congressional criticisms is the plain fact that most congressmen are more sympathetic to State Department control of foreign affairs than they are to Defense Department control. In other words, despite military sponsored world junkets, National Guard and State Guard pressures from the home State, and military training in the backgrounds of many congressmen, the sentiment for political rather than military control is greater. In addition, there is a mounting suspicion in Congress of varying kinds of behavioral science research stemming from hearings into such matters as wire tapping, uses of lie detectors, and truth-in-packaging.

Social Scientists. One reason for the violent response Project Camelot, especially among Latin American scholars, is its sponsorship by the Department of Defense. The fact is that Latin Americans have become quite accustomed to State Department involvements in the internal affairs of various nations. The Defense Department is a newcomer, a dangerous one, inside the Latin American orbit. The train of thought connected to its activities is in terms of international warfare, spying missions, military manipulations, etc. The State Department, for its part, is often a consultative party to shifts in government, and has played an enormous part in either fending off or bringing about *coups d'état.* This State Department role has by now been accepted and even taken for granted. Not so the Defense Department's role. But it is interesting to conjecture on how matter-of-factly Camelot might have been accepted if it had State Department sponsorship.

Social scientists in the United States have, for the most part, been publicly silent on the matter of Camelot. The reasons for this are not hard to find. First, many "giants of the field" are involved in government contract work in one capacity or another. And few souls are in a position to tamper with the gods. Second, most information on Project Camelot has thus far been of a newspaper variety; and professional men are not in a habit of criticizing colleagues on the basis of such information. Third, many social scientists doubtless see nothing wrong or immoral in the Project Camelot designs. And they are therefore more likely to be either confused or angered at the Latin American response than at the directors of Project Camelot. (At the time of the blowup, Camelot people spoke about the "Chilean mess" rather than the "Camelot mess.")

The directors of Project Camelot did not "classify" research materials, so that there would be no stigma of secrecy. And they also tried to hire, and even hired away from academic positions, people well known and respected for their independence of mind. The difficulty is that even though the stigma of secrecy was formally erased, it remained in the attitudes of many of the employees and would-be employees of Project Camelot. They unfortunately thought in terms of secrecy, clearance, missions, and the rest of the professional nonsense that so powerfully afflicts the Washington scientific as well as political ambience.

Further, it is apparent that Project Camelot had much greater difficulty hiring a full-time staff of high professional competence than in getting part-time, summertime, weekend, and sundry assistance. Few established figures in academic life were willing to surrender the advantages of their positions for the risks of the project.

One of the cloudiest aspects to Project Camelot is the role of American University. Its actual supervision of the contract appears to have begun and ended with the 25 per cent overhead on those parts of the contract that a university receives on most federal grants. Thus, while there can be no question as to the "concern and disappointment" of President Hurst R. Anderson of the American University over the demise of Project Camelot, the reasons for this regret do not seem to extend beyond the formal and the financial. No official at American University appears to have been willing to make any statement of responsibility, support, chagrin, opposition, or anything else related to the project. The issues are indeed momentous, and must be faced by all universities at which government sponsored research is conducted: the amount of control a university has over contract work; the role of university officials in the distribution of funds from grants; the relationships that ought to be established once a grant is issued. There is also a major question concerning project directors: are they members of the faculty, and if so, do they have necessary teaching responsibilities and opportunities for tenure as do other faculty members.

The difficulty with American University is that it seems to be remarkably unlike other universities in its permissiveness. The Special Operations Research Office received neither guidance nor support from university officials. From the outset, there seems to have been a "gentleman's agreement" not to inquire or interfere in Project Camelot, but simply to serve as some sort of camouflage. If American University were genuinely autonomous it might have been able to lend highly supportive aid to Project Camelot during the crisis months. As it is, American University maintained an official silence which preserved it from more congressional or executive criticism. This points up some serious flaws in its administrative and financial policies.

The relationship of Camelot to SORO represented a similarly muddled organizational picture. The director of Project Camelot was nominally autonomous and in charge of an organization surpassing in size and importance the overall SORO operation. Yet at the critical point the organizational blueprint served to protect SORO and sacrifice what nominally was its limb. That Camelot happened to be a vital organ may have hurt, especially when Congress blocked the transfer of unused Camelot funds to SORO.

Military. Military reaction to the cancellation of Camelot varied. It should be borne in mind that expenditures on Camelot were minimal in the Army's overall budget and most military leaders are skeptical, to begin with, about the worth of social science research. So there was no open protest about the demise of Camelot. Those officers who have a positive attitude toward social science materials, or are themselves trained in the social sciences, were dismayed. Some had hoped to find "software" alternatives to the "hardware systems" approach applied by the Secretary of Defense to every military-political contingency. These officers saw the attack on Camelot as a double attack—on their roles as officers and on their professional standards. But the Army was so clearly treading in new waters that it could scarcely jeopardize the entire structure of military research to preserve one project. This very inability or impotence to preserve Camelot—a situation threatening to other governmental contracts with social scientists—no doubt impressed many armed forces officers.

The claim is made by the Camelot staff (and various military aides) that the critics of the project played into the hands of those sections of the military predisposed to veto any social science recommendations. Then why did the military offer such a huge support to a social science project to begin with? Because $6,000,000 is actually a trifling sum for the Army in an age of multi-billion-dollar military establishment. The amount is significantly more important for the social sciences, where such contract awards remain relatively scarce. Thus, there were differing perspectives of the importance of Camelot: an Army view which considered the contract as one of several forms of "software" investment; a social science perception of Project Camelot as the equivalent of the Manhattan Project.

Was Project Camelot Workable?

While most public opposition to Project Camelot focused on its strategy and timing, a considerable amount of private opposition centered on more basic, though theoretical, questions: was Camelot scientifically feasible and ethically correct? No public document or statement contested the possibility that, given the successful completion of the data gathering, Camelot could have, indeed,established basic criteria for measuring the level and potential for internal war in a given nation. Thus, by never challenging the feasibility of the work, the political critics of Project Camelot were providing back-handed compliments to the efficacy of the project.

But much more than political considerations are involved. It is clear that some of the most critical problems presented by Project Camelot are scientific. Although for an extensive analysis of Camelot, the reader would, in fairness, have to be familiar with all of its documents, salient general criticisms can be made without a full reading.

The research design of Camelot was from the outset plagued by ambiguities. It was never quite settled whether the purpose was to study counter-insurgency possibilities, or the revolutionary process. Similarly, it was difficult to determine whether it was to be a study of comparative social structures, a set of case studies of single nations "in depth," or a study of social structure with particular emphasis on the military. In addition, there was a lack of treatment of what indicators were to be used, and whether a given social system in Nation A could be as stable in Nation B.

In one Camelot document there is a general critique of social science for failing to deal with social conflict and social control. While this in itself is admirable, the tenor and context of Camelot's documents make it plain that a "stable society" is considered the norm no less than the desired outcome. The "breakdown of social order" is spoken of accusatively. Stabilizing agencies in developing areas are presumed to be absent. There is no critique of U.S. Army policy in developing areas because the Army is presumed to be a stabilizing agency. The research formulations always assume the legitimacy of Army tasks—"if the U.S. Army is to perform effectively its parts in the U.S. mission of counter-insurgency, it must recognize that insurgency represents a breakdown of social order. . . ." But such a proposition has never been doubted—by Army officials or anyone else. The issue is whether such breakdowns are in the nature of the existing system or a product of conspiratorial movements.

The use of hygienic language disguises the anti-revolutionary assumptions under a cloud of powder puff declarations. For example, studies of Paraguay are recommended "because trends in this situation (the Stroessner regime) may also render it 'unique' when analyzed in terms of the transition from 'dictatorship' to political stability." But to speak about changes from dictatorship to stability is an obvious ruse. In this case, it is a tactic to disguise the fact that Paraguay is one of the most vicious, undemocratic (and like most dictatorships, stable) societies in the Western Hemisphere.

These typify the sort of hygienic sociological premises that do not have scientific purposes. They illustrate the confusion of commitments with Project Camelot. Indeed the very absence of emotive words such as revolutionary masses, communism, socialism, and capitalism only serves to intensify the discomfort one must feel on examination of the documents—since the abstract vocabulary disguises, rather than resolves, the problems of international revolution. To have used clearly political rather than military language would not "justify" governmental support. Furthermore, shabby assumptions of academic conventionalism replaced innovative orientations. By adopting a systems approach, the problematic, open-ended aspects of the study of revolutions were largely omitted; and the design of the study became an oppressive curb on the study of the problems inspected.

This points up a critical implication for Camelot (as well as other projects). The importance of the subject being researched does not *per se* determine the importance of the project. A sociology of large-scale relevance and reference is all to the good. It is important that scholars be willing to risk something of their shaky reputations in helping resolve major world social problems. But it is no less urgent that in the process of addressing major problems, the autonomous character of the social science disciplines—their own criteria of worthwhile scholarship—should not be abandoned. Project Camelot lost sight of this "autonomous" social science character.

It never seemed to occur to its personnel to inquire into the desirability for successful revolution. This is just as solid a line of inquiry as the one stressed—the conditions under which revolutionary movements will be able to overthrow a government. Furthermore, they seem not to have thought about inquiring into the role of the United States in these countries. This points up the lack of symmetry. The problem should have been phrased to include the study of "us" as well as "them." It is not possible to make a decent analysis of a situation unless one takes into account the role of all the different people and groups involved in it; and there was no room in the design for such contingency analysis.

In discussing the policy impact on a social science research project, we should not overlook the difference between "contract" work and "grants." Project Camelot commenced with the U.S. Army; that is to say, it was initiated for a practical purpose determined by the client. This differs markedly from the typical academic grant in that its sponsorship had "built-in" ends. The scholar usually *seeks* a grant; in this case the donor, the Army, promoted its own aims. In some measure, the hostility for Project Camelot may be an unconscious reflection of this distinction—a dim feeling that there was something "non-academic," and certainly not disinterested, about Project Camelot, irrespective of the quality of the scholars associated with it.

The Ethics of Policy Research

The issue of "scientific rights" versus "social myths" is perennial. Some maintain that the scientist ought not penetrate beyond legally or morally sanctioned limits and others argue that such limits cannot exist for science. In treading on the sensitive issue of national sovereignty, Project Camelot reflects the generalized dilemma. In deference to intelligent researchers, in recognition of them as scholars, they should have been invited by Camelot to air their misgivings and qualms about government (and especially Army sponsored) research—to declare their moral conscience. Instead, they were mistakenly approached as skillful, useful potential employees of a higher body, subject to an authority higher than their scientific calling.

What is central is not the political motives of the sponsor. For social scientists were not being enlisted in an intelligence system for "spying" purposes. But given their professional standing, their great sense of intellectual honor and pride, they could not be "employed" without proper deference for their stature. Professional authority should have prevailed from beginning to end with complete command of the right to thrash out the moral and political dilemmas as researchers saw them. The Army, however respectful and protective of free expression, was "hiring help" and not openly and honestly submitting a problem to the higher professional and scientific authority of social science.

The propriety of the Army to define and delimit all questions, which Camelot should have had a right to examine, was never placed in doubt. This is a tragic precedent; it reflects the arrogance of a consumer of intellectual merchandise. And this relationship of inequality corrupted the lines of authority, and profoundly limited the autonomy of the social scientists involved. It became clear that the social scientist savant was not so much functioning as an applied social scientist as he was supplying information to a powerful client.

The question of who sponsors research is not nearly so decisive as the question of ultimate use of such information. The sponsorship of a project, whether by the United States Army or by the Boy Scouts of America, is by itself neither good nor bad. Sponsorship is good or bad only insofar as the intended outcomes can be predetermined and the parameters of those intended outcomes tailored to the sponsor's expectations. Those social scientists critical of the project never really denied its freedom and independence, but questioned instead the purpose and character of its intended results.

It would be a gross oversimplification, if not an outright error, to assume that the theoretical problems of Project Camelot derive from any reactionary character of the project designers. The director went far and wide to select a group of men for the advisory board, the core planning group, the summer study group, and the various conference groupings, who in fact were more liberal in their orientations than any random sampling of the sociological profession would likely turn up.

However, in nearly every page of the various working papers, there are assertions which clearly derive from American military policy objectives rather than scientific method. The steady assumption that internal warfare is damaging disregards the possibility that a government may not be in a position to take actions either to relieve or to improve mass conditions, or that such actions as are contemplated may be more concerned with reducing conflict than with improving conditions. The added statements above the United States Army and its "important mission in the positive and constructive aspects of nation building . . ." assumes the reality of such a function in an utterly unquestioning and unconvincing form. The first rule of the scientific game is not to make assumptions about friends and enemies in such a way as to promote the use of different criteria for the former and the latter.

The story of Project Camelot was not a confrontation of good versus evil. Obviously, not all men behaved with equal fidelity or with equal civility. Some men were weaker than others, some more callous, and some more stupid. But all of this is extrinsic to the heart of the problem of Camelot: what are and are not the legitimate functions of a scientist?

In conclusion, two important points must be kept clearly in mind and clearly apart. First, Project Camelot was intellectually, and from my own perspective, ideologically unsound. However, and more significantly, Camelot was not cancelled because of its faulty intellectual approaches. Instead, its cancellation came as an act of government censorship, and an expression of the contempt for social science so prevalent among those who need it most. Thus, it was political expedience, rather than its lack of scientific merit, that led to the demise of Camelot because it threatened to rock State Department relations with Latin America.

Second, giving the State Department the right to screen and approve government-funded social science research projects on other countries, as the President has ordered, is a supreme act of censorship. Among the agencies that grant funds for such research are the National Institute of Mental Health, the National Science Foundation, the National Aeronautics and Space Agency, and the Office of Education. Why should the State Department have veto power over the scientific pursuits of men and projects funded by these and other agencies in order to satisfy the policy needs—or policy failures—of the moment? President Johnson's directive is a gross violation of the autonomous nature of science.

We must be careful not to allow social science projects with which we may vociferously disagree on political and ideological grounds to be decimated or dismantled by government fiat. Across the ideological divide is a common social science understanding that the contemporary expression of reason in politics today is applied social science, and that the cancellation of Camelot, however pleasing it may be on political grounds to advocates of a civilian solution to Latin American affairs, represents a decisive setback for social science research.

This final article by *Skinner* deals with the issues of control and attempts to distinguish the technical use of the term as a functional relation between the behavior of the individual and the environment from the pejorative sense of Machiavellian control when one person uses another to his own advantage. Skinner argues that all behavior is controlled in the sense that it is functionally related to the environment. He asserts that by gaining the necessary information about our own behavior and its relation to our culture, we can effectively improve our lives and thus avoid "Machiavellian" control.

73 | *The Control of Human Behavior*

B. F. SKINNER

We are seldom willing to admit that we are engaged in controlling the behavior of other people. The commonest techniques of control use force or the threat of force and are objectionable to the controllee and have come to be censured by society. But the condoned techniques of education, persuasion, and moral discourse differ only in the behavioral processes through which they operate and in the minimizing of certain side effects. They are still devices through which one man controls the behavior of another in some measure. Cajolery, seduction, incitement, and the various forms of what biographers call "influence" suggest other techniques.

Familiar rules of thumb in controlling men are embedded in folk wisdom and in many great works of literature. This prescientific technology is rapidly being extended by the scientific study of human behavior (there are those who refuse to admit even the possibility of such a science, but I am speaking here to those who are not only aware of the science but share a deep concern for its consequences). In civilized countries, the more powerful controlling techniques have eventually been contained by a sort of ethical counter-control, which prevents exploitation by those in a position to use them. There is a real danger, however, that the rapid development of new techniques will outstrip appropriate measures of counter-control, with devastating results.

We can see how counter-control originates in the case of force or the threat of force. In primitive literature, the hero is often the man who can whip everyone else in the group in open combat. He controls with the techniques of the bully. The relevant processes have been analyzed in the scientific study of behavior under the headings of avoidance and escape. We see these techniques exemplified today in the government of conquered peoples, in despotic governments of all sorts, by religious agencies which lean heavily on the threat of punishment, by many parents in the control of their children, and by most

From *Transactions of The New York Academy of Sciences,* Series II, Vol. 17, No. 7, pp. 547–551.

teachers. The technique is psychologically and biologically harmful to the controllee and, for this reason, has generated counter-control. The weak are, at least, more numerous, and we now generally hold it to be "wrong" to control through the use of force or the threat of force(although an impartial observer might not come to this conclusion). Formalized governmental and religious precepts support this containment of the techniques of the bully. The result is called peace—a condition in which men are not permitted to use force in controlling each other.

A later type of popular hero is the cheat, who outwits the strong man by misrepresentation and deceit (in a technical analysis, the relevant processes would be classified under the extinction of conditioned reflexes). But the cheat, eventually, is almost as objectionable as the bully, and ethical control accordingly arises. It is held to be "wrong" to lie, cheat, or cry "Wolf" for one's amusement.

There are techniques which may be as effective as these but may not lead so directly to counter-control. These techniques are becoming more powerful as their processes are better understood. A few examples follow.

1. *Emotional conditioning.* Aldous Huxley, in *Brave New World,* describes a perfectly plausible process through which certain inferior types of citizens are permanently dissuaded from wasting time on books and the beauties of nature. Babies are allowed to crawl toward books and flowers but receive electric shocks just as they touch them. The example appears to be borrowed, not from the science of conditioned reflexes, but from certain forms of moral education in which, for example, a child is spanked for taking an interest in parts of his own body. The same principle is used to generate strong reactions of rage and aggression toward the enemy in preparing servicemen for combat. It is the basis of advertising which shows a product being used by or otherwise associated with pretty girls or admired public figures. The controllee is not likely to revolt against such control, and he may carry the resulting prejudices contentedly to his grave.

2. *Motivational control.* Crude instances, such as the starving of a whole people so that food may be used to reinforce those who begin to support the government, bring their own eventual containment, but the exploitation of prevailing deprivations may be more subtle and possibly equally effective. The deliberate design of art and literature (as in the movies and "comics") to appeal to people with sadistic tendencies is easily detected, but the subtle design of an automobile so that riding in it is in some measure a sexual experience is not so easily spotted. Neither practice may meet any objection from the people so controlled.

3. *Positive reinforcement.* Wages, bribes, and tips suggest a classical pattern in which we generate behavior in others through reinforcement or reward. Better ways of using reinforcement in shaping up new behavior and in maintaining the condition called interest, or enthusiasm, have been recently discovered. The reinforcing effect of personal attention and affection is coming to be better understood, especially by clinical psychologists. Lord Chesterfield and Dale Carnegie have recommended the use of feigned attention in influencing people.

4. *Drugs.* We are entering the age of the chemical control of human behavior. Drugs have been used for this purpose ever since the first man was deliberately made drunk. But better drugs are now available, not only for allaying anxiety but for other purposes of control. Our government would probably not hesitate to use a drug which, taken by servicemen before combat, would eliminate all signs of fear, thus depriving the individual of the protective reflexes which man has acquired through a long process of evolution. In the not-too-distant future, the motivational and emotional conditions of normal daily life will probably be maintained in any desired state through the use of drugs.

5. *Knowledge of the individual.* Techniques of control can be effective only when certain facts about the controllee are known. Gathering information through eavesdropping, employing spies and informers, opening mail, and wiretapping has, from time to time, come under ethical counter-control, though the present state of this in our culture is uncertain. Meanwhile, new techniques have been developed. Something like the projective tests of clinical psychology, combined with the technique of the political trial balloon, might make it possible to discover information about an individual or a whole people, not only without the knowledge of the controllee but with respect to matters of which the controllee himself has no clear understanding.

The doctrine that there is an absolute moral law applicable to all conditions of human life discourages the analysis of controlling practices and obscures our understanding of the need for counter-control. The methods by which men alter the behavior of other men change, and changing ethical measures are required. A technique need not be immediately objectionable to the controllee to engender counter-control. The gambler, for instance, is possibly the last person to ask for legal or moral restrictions on gambling enterprises. The alcoholic does not usually advocate the control of alcoholic beverages. Few workers object to being paid, even for kinds of work or according to pay schedules which society proscribes. It is the rare man who objects to the tyranny of the beautiful woman. In all these cases, society appeals to long-term consequences to justify measures of counter-control. Unfortunately, such consequences do not supply any hard-and-fast rule. We must continue to experiment in cultural design, as nature has already experimented, testing the consequences as we go. We may deal with cultural practices as a whole, as in "utopian" thinking, or piecemeal by changing one counter-controlling technique at a time. Eventually, the practices which make for the greatest biological and psychological strength of the group will presumably survive, as will the group which adopts them. Survival is not a criterion which we are free to accept or reject, but it is nevertheless, the one according to which our current decisions will eventually be tested. It is less clear-cut than some absolute criterion of right and wrong, but it is more reassuring in its recognition of the changing needs of society.

Such an experimental attitude is sometimes criticized by those who want to defend some principle appropriate to an earlier stage of our cultural history. An example is the recent book by Joseph Wood Krutch, *The Measure of Man,* which is in considerable part an attack on my utopian novel, *Walden Two.* While arguing that the notion of behavioral engineering is ultimately faulty, because man is in some sense free and hence may escape control, Krutch admits that human freedom is under attack and that, if science is not checked, freedom may vanish altogether. Krutch argues that unless we put a stop to the machinations of scientists, "we may never really be able to think again." By freedom, Krutch seems to mean merely a lack of order. The virtues of the prescientific era were the virtues of accident. The great crime of the founder of Walden Two, according to Krutch, was the destruction of the possibility of the happy chance—even such as that which gave rise to the founder himself, before "men's thoughts were controlled with precision." On the same grounds, we might object to the synthetic fibre industry for circumventing the accidental evolutionary processes which produced cotton and wool. If we can arrange better conditions of human life and growth, why should we wait for the happy accident, even if past accidents have brought us to this very point of power?

Krutch's answer is essentially a mystical one: some vague power or faculty has permitted man to transcend his chaotic environment, and this cannot continue to function in less chaotic circumstances. But the existence of such powers or faculties grows more doubtful as man's actual achievements come to be analyzed. Nothing will be lost if science is applied to education or moral discourse. A better way of teaching a child to spell words meets the objection that he is not taught something called "spelling," just as better moral and ethical training meets the objection that the child no longer "has" to be good. In the past, it was natural that some special honor should accrue to the individual who rises above his faulty intellectual and ethical training and is wise and good in spite of it. Men have been at times almost entirely occupied in deciding what is right, intellectually and morally. A world in which education is so successful that one is naturally right in both these senses is criticized because it provides for no heroism in transcending an inadequate environment. One might as well criticize fireproof buildings because the world is thus deprived of brave firemen.

It is easy to object to the control of human behavior by applying the slogans of democracy. But the democratic revolution in government and religion was directed against a certain type of control only. Men were freed from autocratic rulers employing techniques based upon force or the threat of force. It does not follow that men were thus freed of all control, and it is precisely the other forms of control which we must now learn to contain and to which the pattern of the democratic revolution is inappropriate. The democratic concept of "freedom" is no longer effective in international politics because it has lost its point. All major governments profess to be governing *for* the people, and no government will bear close scrutiny of its actual practices. A new conception of the function and practice of government is needed in dealing with the counter-control of techniques against which there is no revolt.

Mr. Krutch is justifiably concerned lest a new type of despotism arise which utilizes the more effective techniques of control provided by the science of human behavior. But his suggestion that we deny the possibility of such a science, or that we abandon it, would deprive us of important help in building adequate safeguards against its misuse. Science poses problems, but it also suggests solutions. In contending that the founder of Walden Two could as easily have been a monster, instead of the fairly benevolent figure he seems to be, Krutch misses the point that, in the long run, the strength of any government depends upon the strength of the governed. Under present conditions of competition, it is unlikely that a government can survive which does not govern in the best interests of everyone.

Unless there is some unseen virtue in ignorance, our growing understanding of human behavior will make it all the more feasible to design a world adequate to the needs of men. But we cannot gain this advantage if we are to waste time defending outworn conceptions of human nature, conceptions which have long since served their original purpose of justifying special philosophies of government. A rejection of science at this time, in a desperate attempt to preserve a loved but inaccurate conception of man, would represent an unworthy retreat in man's continuing effort to build a better world.